Social
Issues
Primary
Sources
Collection

Environmental Issues

Essential Primary Sources

Social Issues Primary Sources Collection

Environmental Issues

Essential Primary Sources

K. Lee Lerner and **Brenda Wilmoth Lerner,** Editors

THOMSON
™
GALE

Detroit • New York • San Francisco • New Haven, Conn. • Waterville, Maine • London • Munich

THOMSON
GALE

Environmental Issues: Essential Primary Sources

K. Lee Lerner and Brenda Wilmoth Lerner, Editors

Project Editor
Lemma Shomali

Editorial
Kathleen J. Edgar, Madeline Harris, Melissa Hill, Debra M. Kirby, Kristine Krapp, Michael D. Lesniak, Paul Lewon, Elizabeth Manar, Charles B. Montney, Heather Price, Mike Weaver

Permissions
Sue Rudolph, Timothy Sisler, Andrew Specht

Imaging and Multimedia
Lezlie Light, Michael Logusz, Christine O'Bryan, Denay Wilding

Product Design
Pamela A. Galbreath

Composition and Electronic Capture
Evi Seoud

Manufacturing
Rita Wimberley

Product Manager
Carol Nagel

LIBRARY OF CONGRESS CATALOGING-IN-PUBLICATION DATA

Environmental issues : essential primary sources / K. Lee Lerner and Brenda Wilmoth Lerner, editors.
    p. cm. – (Social issues primary sources collection)
Includes bibliographical references and index.
    ISBN 1-4144-0625-8 (alk. paper)
    1. Environmental sciences–Sources. 2. Human ecology–Sources. I. Lerner, K. Lee. II. Lerner, Brenda Wilmoth. III. Series.

GE105.E5825 2006
363.7–dc22   2006000857

This title is also available as an e-book.
ISBN 1-4144-06266
Contact your Thomson Gale sales representative for ordering information.

Printed in the United States of America
10 9 8 7 6 5 4 3 2

Table of Contents

1 ROOTS OF ENVIRONMENTAL AND ECOLOGICAL THOUGHT

2 THE PHYSICAL EARTH

4   EXPLORATION

5   ENVIRONMENTAL LEGISLATION

6 ENERGY USE AND PERILS

Advisors and Contributors

While compiling this volume, the editors relied upon the expertise and contributions of the following scholars, journalists, and researchers who served as advisors and/or contributors for *Environmental issues: Essential Primary Sources*:

Steven Archambault (Ph.D. Candidate)
University of New Mexico
Albuquerque, New Mexico

William Arthur Atkins, M.S.
Normal, Illinois

Julie Berwald, Ph.D.
Geologist (Ocean Sciences)
Austin, Texas

Bryan Davies, J.D.
Ontario, Canada

Sandra Galeotti, M.S.
S. Paulo, Brazil

Larry Gilman, Ph.D.
Sharon, Vermont

Amit Gupta, Ph.D.
Ahmedabad, India

William Haneberg, Ph.D.
Geologist
Portland, Oregon

Neil Heims
Writer and Journalist
Paris, France

Brian D. Hoyle, Ph.D.
Microbiologist
Nova Scotia, Canada

Alexandr Ioffe, Ph.D.
Russian Academy of Sciences
Moscow, Russia

S. Layman, M.A.
Abingdon, MD

Agnieszka Lichanska, Ph.D.
Department of Microbiology
& Parasitology
University of Queensland. Brisbane,
Australia

Adrienne Wilmoth Lerner (J.D. Candidate)
University of Tennessee College of Law
Knoxville, Tennessee

Iuri Drumond Louro, MD, PhD.
Professor Adjunto - Genética Humana e Molecular;
Departamento de Ciências Biológicas; CCHN -
UFES; Av Marechal Campos.
Vitó RIA, Brazil

Mark Phillips, Ph.D.
Abilene Christian University
Abilene, Texas

Yavor Shopov, Ph.D
Professor of Geology & Geophysics
University of Sofia, Bulgaria

Nephele Tempest
Los Angeles, California

Shelley Ann Wake
Journalist
Wishart, Queensland, Australia

Melanie Barton Zoltán, M.S.
Amherst, Massachusetts

Environmental Issues: Essential Primary Sources is the product of a global, multi-lingual group of scholars, researchers, and writers. Despite it's span of writers and researchers, however, the book suffered delays and disruptions related to Hurricanes Ivan and Katrina while the editors worked and covered environmental and health related stories along the U.S. Gulf Coast. In the aftermath, the sure and steady efforts of the primary copyeditor Ms. Kate Kretschmann helped piece together fragments of texts and sources scattered in both physical and cyberspace. Ms. Kretschmann's efforts added significant accuracy and readability to the text and her positive approach to problem solving was greatly appreciated. The editors also wish to commend Ms. Adrienne Wilmoth Lerner and Ms. Alicia Maria Cafferty for their skill and tireless research.

The editors gratefully acknowledge and extend thanks to Mr. Peter Gareffa, Ms. Carol Nagel, and Ms. Debra Kirby at Thomson Gale for their faith in the project and for their sound content advice. Profound thanks go to the Thomson Gale copyright research staff, especially Timothy Sisler, for their patience, good advice, and skilled research into sometimes vexing copyright issues. The editors also wish to acknowledge the contributions of the Thomson Gale Imaging Team, especially Denay Wilding, for their help in securing archival images. Lastly the editors offer profound thanks to Project Manager Lemma Shomali who showed patience and steady skill in managing both content and tight deadlines. Ms. Shomali's keen eyes and sound knowledge of science greatly enhanced the quality, accuracy, and readability of the text.

Acknowledgements

Copyrighted Excerpts in *Environmental Issues: Essential Primary Sources* were reproduced from the following periodicals:

The Economist (US), v. 375, April 23, 2005. © 2005 The Economist Newspaper Ltd. All rights reserved. Reprinted with permission. Further reproduction prohibited. www.economist.com—*The Heritage Foundation*, August 22, 2002. © 2002 *The Heritage Foundation*. Reproduced by permission of the publisher.—*Houston Chronicle*, October 23, 2005. Reproduced by permission of The Associated Press.—*Inter Press Service News Agency*, August 9, 2005. © 2005 IPS-Inter Press Service. All rights reserved. Reproduced by permission.—*Nature*, v. 389, September 18, 1997. © 1997 Nature Publishing Group. Reproduced by permission.—*The New York Times*, November 18, 1948; July 22, 1962; April 15, 1964; April 21, 1970; November 7, 1985; December 22, 2001; October 8, 2004; April 29, 2005. © 1948, 1962, 1964, 1970, 1985, 2001, 2004, 2005 by The New York Times Company. All reproduced by permission.—*The Philadelphia Inquirer*, March 26, 2004. © 2004, *The Philadelphia Inquirer*. Reproduced by permission.—*Planetary and Space Science*, v. 48, 2000. © 2000 Elsevier Science Ltd. All rights reserved. Reproduced with permission from Elsevier.—*Population Reference Bureau*, October, 2004. Copyright 2005, *Population Reference Bureau*. All rights reserved. Reproduced by permission.—*Regulation*, v. 19, 1996. © 1996 Cato Institute. All rights reserved. Reproduced by permission.—*San Francisco Chronicle*, December 17, 2004. Copyright 2004 *San Francisco Chronicle*. Republished with permission of *San Francisco Chronicle*, conveyed through Copyright Clearance Center, Inc.—Sarasota Herald Tribune, March 1, 2004. Copyright 2004 Sarasota Herald-Tribune. Reproduced by permission.—*Science*, v. 162, December 13, 1968; v. 170, November 27, 1970; v. 222, December 9, 1983; v. 297, July 5, 2002. Copyright 1968, 1970, 1983, 2002 by AAAS. All reproduced by permission.—*Science Magazine*, v. 155, March 10, 1967. Copyright 1967 AAAS. Excerpted with permission. http://www.sciencemag.org—Time, v. 90, August 18, 1967; v. 133, April 10, 1989; v. 137, July 1, 1991; v. 166, October 3, 2005. © 1967, 1989, 1991, 2005 Time, Inc. All rights reserved. All reproduced by permission.—*The Wall Street Journal*, January 17, 2005. All rights reserved worldwide. Reprinted with permission of *The Wall Street Journal*, conveyed through Copyright Clearance Center, Inc., and Dow Jones & Company, Inc.—*The Washington Post/Times Herald*, July 22, 1962 for "Ocean Oil Slick is Shroud for Birds" by Irston R. Barnes. Reproduced by permission of the literary estate of the author.—*World Watch*, v. 6, July-August, 1993. © *World Watch*, www.worldwatch.org. Reproduced by permission.

Copyrighted Excerpts in *Environmental Issues: Essential Primary Sources* were reproduced from the following books:

Ballard, Robert. From *The Eternal Darkness: A Personal History of Deep-Sea Exploration*. Princeton University Press, 2000. © 2000 by Princeton University Press. Reproduced by permission of Princeton University Press and the author.—Byrd, Richard E. From "The Greenland Expedition of 1925," in *To the Pole: The Diary and Notebook of Richard E. Byrd, 1925-1927*. Edited by Raimund E. Goerler. Ohio State University Press, 1998. © 1998 by the Ohio State University Press. All rights reserved.

Reproduced by permission.—Chetham, Deirdre. From *Before the Deluge: The Vanishing World of the Yangtze's Three Gorges*. Palgrave Macmillan, 2002. © Deirdre Chetham, 2002. All rights reserved. Reproduced with permission of Palgrave Macmillan.—Cousteau, Jacques-Yves, with James Dugan. From *The Living Sea*. Nick Lyons Books/ Harper & Row, 1963. © 1963 by Harper & Row, Publishers, Inc., renewed 1991. All rights reserved. Reprinted by permission of HarperCollins Publishers.—Fossey, Dian. From *Gorillas in the Mist*. Houghton Mifflin, 2000. © 1983 by Dian Fossey. All rights reserved. Reproduced by permission of Houghton Mifflin Company and Russell & Volkening as agents for the author.—Gelbspan, Ross. From *Boiling Point*. © 2004 by Ross Gelbspan. Reprinted by permission of Basic Books, a member of Perseus Books, L. L. C.—Goodman, Percival and Paul. From *Communitas: Means of Livelihood and Ways of Life*. Columbia University Press, 1989. Reproduced by permission.—Leopold, Aldo. From "Wilderness as a Form of Land Use," in *The River of the Mother of God and Other Essays by Aldo Leopold*. Edited by Susan L. Flader and J. Baird Callicott. The University of Wisconsin Press, 1991. © 1991 by the Board of Regents of the University of Wisconsin System. Reproduced by permission.—Lovelock, James E. From *Gaia: A new look at life on Earth*. Oxford University Press, 2000. © J. E. Lovelock 1979, 1987, 1995, 2000. All rights reserved. Reproduced by permission of Oxford University Press.—McPhee, John. From *Coming into the Country*. © 1977 by John McPhee. Reprinted by permission of Farrar, Straus and Giroux, LLC.—McPhee, John. From *Encounters with the Archdruid*. © 1971, renewed 1999 by John McPhee. Reprinted by permission of Farrar, Straus McPhee, John. From *The Control of Nature*. © 1989 by John McPhee. Reprinted by permission of Farrar, Straus and Giroux, LLC.—Reisner, Marc P. From *Cadillac Desert: The American West and Its Disappearing Water*, revised and updated. Viking Penguin Inc., 1986. © 1986, 1993 by Marc P. Reisner. Used by permission of Viking Penguin, a division of Penguin Group (USA) Inc.—Staudenmaier, Peter. From *Ecofascism: Lessons from the German Experience*. AK Press, 1995. Copyright 1995 Janet Biehl and Peter Staudenmaier. Reproduced by permission.— Steinbeck, John. From *The Log from the Sea of Cortez*. Penguin Books, 1995. Copyright 1941, 1951 by John Steinbeck and Edward F. Ricketts. Copyright renewed © 1969, by John Steinbeck and Edward Ricketts, Jr. Used by permission of Viking Penguin, a division of Penguin Group (USA) Inc.

Photographs and Illustrations appearing in Environmental Issues: Essential Primary Sources were received from the following sources:

Agricultural workers inspect large diversion screens for salmon, ca. 1992, photograph. © Natalie Fobes/Corbis.—Anti-nuclear activist from Robin Wood environmental group gives victory sign, March 28, 2001. Photo by Sean Gallup/Newsmaker.—Anti-nuclear activists confront police while occupying railroad tracks leading to the Gorleben nuclear waste storage facility, March 27, 2001. Photo by Sean Gallup/Newsmakers/Getty Images.—Appleseed, Johnny, nursing a tree, woodcut. © Bettmann/ Corbis.—Area deforested by soybean farmers, Novo Progreso, Para, Brazil, September 2004, photograph by Alberto Cesar. AP Images.—Aspen, Colorado, in the Rocky Mountains, June, 1949, photograph. AP Images.—Audubon, John James, print. AP Images.— Banner attached to crane at the site of the new Terminal 5, October 6, 2003, Heathrow International Airport, London. Photo by David Dyson/Getty Images.—Barges burn in the Atchafalaya River near Simmesport, Louisiana, 2000, photograph. AP Images.—Bison digs under the snow to graze inside Yellowstone National Park, Montana, photograph. AP Images.—Boyd Lake, photograph by David Azlubowski. AP Images.—Bridge to Fengdu, China, photograph. © Bob Sacha/Corbis.—Bush, George W., speaks in the East Garden of the White House, September 13, 2003, photograph. © William Philpott/Reuters/Corbis.—California Quarter, photograph by Rich Pedroncelli. AP Images.—Cars line up in two directions at a gas station in New York City, photograph by Mary Lederhandler. AP Images.— Carson, Rachel, photograph. AP Images.—Carver, George Washington, photograph. © Bettmann/ Corbis.—Castro, Fidel, center, shown with other heads of state in a group photo, from top left, Arnold Ruutel; Bernard Dowiyogo from Nauru; Prince Rainier III of Monaco; and Patricio Aylwin from Chile, bottom right; Rio de Janeiro, Brazil, Saturday, June 13, 1992, photograph by Ricardo Mazalan. AP Images.—Central Maine Power Company's hydroelectric plant, Lewiston, Maine, December 11, 1997, photograph by Robert Bukaty. AP Images.—Children of Timothy Schroeder in the front yard of their home, located over the Love Canal in Niagara Falls, New York, August 4, 1978, photograph. AP Images.— Chimneys smoking in eastern German city of Ilmenau, February 12, 1997, photograph by Jens Meyer. AP Images.—Civilian Conservation Corps (CCC) camp recruits line up for their noon-day meal at Fort Slocum, N.Y., April 9, 1933, photograph. AP Images.—Civilian Conservation Corps members form the letters of their organization, Tamworth, New Hampshire, January 17, 1934. Photo by New York Times Co./Getty Images.—Clemens, Samuel, photograph. AP Images.—Cloud of top soil parched by drought, picked up by winds and moving down a road near Boise City, Oklahoma, 1935, photograph. AP Images.—Clown faced man pokes his head out of a pseudo porthole, February 12, 2006, photograph. Jean Ayissi/AFP/Getty Images.—Construction atop Hoover Dam, Lake Mead, 1934, Boulder City, Nevada, photograph by Benjamin D. Glaha. © Corbis.—Cousteau, Jacques-Yves, his wife, Simone, and their pet dachshund, aboard his oceanographic research vessel, the Calypso, August 30, 1959, photograph. AP Images.—Cousteau, Jean-Michel, views 82 tons of marine debris collected by National Oceanic and Atmospheric Administrations Debris team, Pearl and Hermes Atoll, July 31, 2003, photograph by Tom Ordway. AP Images.—Crop-duster releases pesticide onto a crop field, October 1, 2000, photograph. © Ron Sanford/Corbis.—Cumberland mountain area scarred by strip mining, 1967. Photo by Bob Gomel/Getty Images.—Del Norte Coast Redwoods State Park, California, ca. 2001, photograph. © Darrell Gulin/Corbis.—Drake, Edwin L., shown in the right foreground with the first productive oil well, Titusville, Pennsylvania, late 19th century, photograph. © Bettmann/Corbis.—Dust storm over Beijing, China, March, 2002, photograph. Image provided by GeoEye and NASA SeaWiFs Project.—Eisenhower, Dwight D., at the United Nations General Assembly, New York, Dec. 8, 1953, photograph. AP Images.—Elementary students plant a Green Mountain Maple in recognition of Arbor Day, Lincoln, Nebraska, April 25, 2003, photograph by Bill Wolf. AP Images.—Environmental Action Group button, USA, circa 1970. Photo by Blank Archives/Getty Images.—Exxon Valdez sits at anchor in Alaska's Prince William Sound, April 12, 1989, photograph by John Gaps. AP Images.—Firefighters battle a grassfire in Toay on the western Argentine pampas, January 2, 2001, photograph. AP Images.—Fires raging across Indonesia, September 22, 1997. Photo by Space Frontiers/Hulton Archive/Getty Images.—First split ozone hole on record (r) in 2002 and the ozone hole over Antarctica (holes in blue and magenta) on the same day in 2001 (l), photograph. © NASA/epa/Corbis.—Forestry worker Holger Fischer starts to cut down a larch tree in a conifer forest, eastern Germany, December 4, 2000, photograph by Sven Daestner. AP Images.—French soldiers engage Egyptian forces in Port Said during the Suez Crisis, ca. November, 1956, photograph. © Hulton-Deutsch Collection/Corbis.—Gaslamp District in downtown San Diego, July 12, 2001, photograph by Lenny Ignelzi. AP Images.—Gauge reading zero at the Superfund clean up site of a Wyckoff Inc. wood treatment facility, Bainbridge Island, Washington, September 9, 2004, photograph by Ted S. Warren. AP Images.—Giant Sequoia, photograph by Kevork Dejansezian. AP Images.—Greeley, Horace, photograph, 1868. AP Images.—Greenland ice cap, August 17, 2005, photograph by John McConnico. AP Images.—Greenpeace activists on the roof of Ford Headquarters near Oslo, Norway, August 14, 2004, photograph. Greenpeace/AFP/Getty Images.—Greenpeace protest banner in the Porto de Moz area, Brazil. Photo by Tom Stoddart/Getty Images.—Half Dome, Yosemite National Park, Yosemite, California, October 10, 1997, photograph by Ben Margot. AP Images.—"Harper's New Monthly Magazine," 1871, about Johnny Appleseed with illustration.—Hayes, Dennis, April 22, 1970, photograph. AP Images.—Hill, Julia "Butterfly," atop a 200 ft. redwood tree, Humboldt County, California, 1998. Photo by Gerard Burkhart/Getty Images.—Hill, Octavia, engraving, 1892. Photo by Rischgitz/Getty Images.—Honda Civic GX natural gas powered vehicle, 1997, photograph. AP Images.—Illegal wildlife product display at a market, Tachileik, Myanmar, November 25, 2003, photograph by David Longstreath. AP Images.—Indian schoolgirl, Nivedita, takes part in a protest urging people to drink natural healthy beverages, August 14, 2003, Bangalore, India, photograph. Indranil Mukherjee/AFP/Getty Images.—Italian environmentalist wearing a teargas mask marches in front of Romes Chigi government office, February 15, 2005, photograph by Sandro Pace. AP Images.—Ivory-billed woodpecker, painting. AP Images.—Jogger makes his way around a puddle along a trail on the edge of downtown Houston, Texas, photograph by Pat Sullivan. AP Images.—"Lead helps to guard your health," article and illustration from National Geographic about effects of lead on health.—Liberian tanker the Torrey Canyon stuck fast on Seven Stones Rocks, March 20, 1967, photograph. AP Images.—Lines form at a gas station in Phoenix, Arizona, August 20, 2003, photograph by Matt York. AP Images.—Los Angeles skyline shrouded by smog, 1956. Photo by American Stock/Getty.—Louisiana Purchase Treaty, facsimile. AP Images.—Lower Chesapeake Bay from space, ca. June 5-14, 1991, photograph. © 1996 Corbis; Original image courtesy of NASA/Corbis.—Lower Yellowstone Falls, Yellowstone National Park, Wyoming, photograph. © Royalty-Free/Corbis.—Maathai, Wangari, 2004, photograph. © Wendy Stone/Corbis.—Main sewer of the boulevard Sebastopol and angle of Rivolis street in Paris,

France, ca. 1900. Photo by ND/Roger Viollet/Getty Images.—Malayan sun bear, photograph by Rumpenhorst. AP Images.—Map of some of the area covered by the Lewis and Clark expedition (1804-1806) drawn by expedition member Robert Frazer (Frazier), 1807. Photo by MPI/Getty Images.—McCauley, Eric, June 8, 1999, photograph by Dan Loh. AP Images.—McDuffie, Bruce, (front center) and his students stand in their lab, holding fish, New York, 1971. Photo by Art Rickerby/Time Life Pictures/Getty Images.—McPhee, John, Princeton, N. J., April 12, 1999, photograph by Charles Rex Arbogast. AP Images.—Medical waste, photograph. © A. Inden/zefa/Corbis.—Men wait outside the Army Building on Whitehall St., New York, April 12, 1934. Photo by New York Times Co./Getty Images.—Mercado, Fernando, walks away from a stack of weeds he set on fire, May 4, 1998, photograph by Anita Baca. AP Images.—Miller, Stanley, Dr., working in laboratory, photograph. © Bettmann/Corbis.—Miner burning off mercury with gas torch to separate out gold particles, Rondonia, Brazil, December 1, 1993. Photo by H. John Maier Jr./Image Works/Time Life Pictures/Getty Images.—Monroe, James, and Robert R. Livingston (standing at left), finish negotiating the Louisiana Purchase with France's Minister Talleyrand (seated at right), lunette shaped print printed by Oxford-Print, Boston. © Bettmann/Corbis.—Mother and baby western lowland gorillas, Pittsburgh, Pennsylvania, September 25, 1997, photograph by Gene J. Puskar. AP Images.—Mountains during a landslide on the Neelum river, Kashmir, November 2, 2005, photograph. © Mian Khursheed/Reuters/Corbis.—"Mt. Williamson, Sierra Nevada, from Manzanar, California, 1945," photograph by Ansel Adams. © Ansel Adams Publishing Rights Trust/Corbis.—Muir, John, 1902, photograph. © Corbis.—NASA high-resolution scanning electron microscope image of an unusual tube-like structural form, found in the meteorite ALH84001. AP Images.—News cartoon, left, documenting President Theodore Roosevelt's bear-hunting trip, shown at the Hermione Museum, Tallulah, Louisiana, photograph. AP Images.—Nixon, Richard, January 1, 1970, photograph. AP Images.—Oil-covered rocks from Exxon Valdez oil spill, photograph. © Karen Kasmauski/Corbis.—Older woman with arthritis lying near bags of uranium ore with her daughter kneeling at her head, Boulder, Montana, June 1, 1952. Photo by Carl Iwasaki/Time Life Pictures/Getty Images.—Pachauri, Rajendra K., photograph by Natacha Pisarenko. AP Images.—Pacific Ocean, photograph by TOPEX/Poseidon, NASA JPL.—"Pack Train, Sierra Club High Trip, Sierra Nevada, California,

c.1934," photograph by Ansel Adams. © Ansel Adams Publishing Rights Trust/Corbis.—Palmer, A. Mitchell, March 1, 1924, photograph. AP Images.—Photographer stands on an outcropping of rocks called Glacier Point, 1902, photograph. © Corbis.—Pioneer village rising to defend itself against Indians, photograph. © Bettmann/Corbis.—Plate tectonics, map. © 2003 KRT. Dean Hollingswort, The Dallas Morning News.—Pleasure boats tied to buoys float over a coral reef at John Pennekamp Coral Reef State Park, Florida, photograph. © Kevin Fleming/Corbis.—Polar bear with a WWF collar (World Wildlife Fund). Photo by Business Wire via Getty Images.—Posters advertising alternative energy sources at the Habitat Exposition, Vancouver, Canada, June, 1976, photograph. © Paul Almasy/Corbis.—Rakata, the former crater of the original Krakatau is seen from the new volcano, Anak Krakatau, West Java, Indonesia, April 10, 2004, photograph by Suzanne Plunkett. AP Images.—Rio Azul landfill, San Jose, Costa Rica, June 27, 2000, photograph by Ken Gilbert. AP Images.—Roads leading to gas drilling rigs on top of the Roan Plateau, July 27, 2005, photograph by Ed Andrieski. AP Images.—Roosevelt, Theodore, standing at Glacier Point, Yosemite National Park, California, May 17, 1903, photograph by Underwood and Underwood. © Corbis.—"Roseate Spoonbill," hand-colored engraving by Robert Havell, Jr., after John James Audubon. © Bettmann/Corbis.—Rotting hulks of barges and river boats on the Romanian side of the Danube River, Giurgiu, Romania, October 21, 1992. Photo by Chris Niedenthal/Time Life Pictures/Getty Images.—San Andreas Fault bisecting the Carrizo Plain, San Luis Obispo County, ca. 1995, photograph. © Tom Bean/Corbis.—Sign warns against eating fish and crab from the Hylebos Waterway, Tacoma, Washington, ca. 1970s-1990s, photograph. © Joel W. Rogers/Corbis.—Simpson Tacoma Kraft Pulp Mill spews air pollution, Tacoma, Washington, photograph. © Joel W. Rogers/Corbis.—Smoke stack of the Doe Run lead plant, Herculaneum, Missouri, February 13, 2002, photograph. AP Images.—Sounds of Earth, a gold-plated copper record being mounted on Voyager 2 spacecraft at Kennedy Space Center, August 4, 1977. Time Life Pictures/NASA/Time Life Pictures/Getty Images.—South Pole ceremonial marker flanked by flags, December 1997, photograph by Eric Baker. AP Images.—Students wearing hazmat suits protest pesticides in the environment by taking part in a butoh walk, photograph. AP Images.—Surfers against Sewage members hold a "toilet protest," 2001, Brighton Beach, United Kingdom. Photo by Sion Touhig/Getty Images.—Swans nesting in Wicken Fen, Cambridgeshire, United Kingdom,

2000, photograph. © Nik Wheeler/Corbis.—Taj Mahal facade carving detail with chips, Agra, India, 1995. Photo by Robert Nickelsberg/Time Life Pictures/Getty Images.—Saint George, a 240 foot cargo vessel, about to be sunk off the coast of Club Viva Dominicus Resort in Bayahibe, Dominican Republic, June 13, 1999. AP Images.—Thin woman carrying a bundle followed by a child, photograph. © Hulton-Deutsch Collection/Corbis.—Three Gorges Dam, Yichang, China, May 24, 2003, photograph. AP Images.—Three Mile Island nuclear power plant, Middletown, Pennsylvania, USA, January 21, 1996, photograph by Tim Shaffer. AP Images.—Total Ozone Mapping Spectrometer (TOMS) Earth Probe for the month of October 1999, graphic. AP Images.— Trans-Alaska pipeline, photograph by Al Grillo. AP Images.—Trinity River flows south past the Dallas skyline, December 10, 1997, photograph by Ron Heflin. AP Images.—Tugboats guide Queen Mary into 51st Street pier in New York City, 1936. © The Mariners Museum/Corbis.—Two Medicine Lake, Glacier National Park, Missouri, photograph by Philip Gendreau. © Bettmann/Corbis.—U. N. Framework Convention on Climate Change participant joins in with a dance at a demonstration, New Delhi, India, October 28, 2002, photograph by Gurinder Osan. AP Images.—Ukraine Green Party activists, two wearing protective suits and gas masks, protest in Kiev, December 13, 2005, photograph. Sergei Supinsky/AFP/Getty Images.—Voyager I nears Saturn, photograph. AP Images.—Walden Pond, Concord, Massachusetts, photograph. © Bettmann/ Corbis.—Wordsworth, William, portrait. © Bettmann/Corbis.—Wreckage at the World Trade Center, New York, NY, September 16, 2001. Photo by Gene Shaw/Timepix/Time Life Pictures/Getty Images.—Yosemite National Park Assistant Superintendent Chip Jenkins points to an architect's view of a new bridge with a viewer's platform over Yosemite Creek in front of Yosemite Falls, May 20, 2002, photograph by Paul Sakuma. AP Images.

Copyrighted Excerpts in *Environmental Issues: Essential Primary Sources* were reproduced from the following websites and other sources:

American Petroleum Institute, January 1, 2003. Reproduced by permission.— BBC Online, May 16, 2005. © BBC MMV. Reproduced by permission of BBC News at *www.bbcnews.co.uk.*—British Antarctic Survey, March 13, 2002. Reproduced by permission of the British Antarctic Survey/Natural Environment Council (NERC).—Clingendael International Programme (CIEP), 2004. Reproduced by permission.—"Dust Bowl Ballads," words and music by Woody Guthrie. TRO © 1964. Renewed 1997 by Ludlow Music, Inc., New York, NY. Used by permission.—Kaplan, George H. From "The Seasons of the Earth's Orbit," *http://aausno.navy.mil.* US Naval Observatory, 2005. Reproduced by permission.— "Kyoto Protocol to the United Nations Framework Convention on Climate Change," United Nations, December 11, 1997. Reproduced by permission.— Maathai, Wangari Muta, "Nobel Lecture," The Nobel Foundation, December 10, 2004. © The Nobel Foundation 2004. Reproduced by permission.— "Treaty Banning Nuclear Weapon Tests in the Atmosphere," United Nations, 1963. © 1963 United Nations. Reproduced by permission.—"United Nations Framework Convention on Climate Change," United Nations, May 9, 1992. Reproduced by permission.—"WMO Statement on the Status of the Global Climate in 2004: Global Temperature in 2004 Fourth Warmest," United Nations, December 15, 2004. © 2004 United Nations. Reproduced by permission.— World Summit Papers of the Heinrich Böll Foundation, 2001. © by Roldan Muradian and Joan Martinez-Alier and the Heinrich Böll Foundation. All rights reserved. Reproduced by permission.

About the Set

Essential Primary Source titles are part of a ten-volume set of books in the Social Issues Primary Sources Collection designed to provide primary source documents on leading social issues of the nineteenth, twentieth, and twenty-first centuries. International in scope, each volume is devoted to one topic and will contain approximately 150 to 175 documents that will include and discuss speeches, legislation, magazine and newspaper articles, memoirs, letters, interviews, novels, essays, songs, and works of art essential to understanding the complexity of the topic.

Each entry will include standard subheads: key facts about the author; an introduction placing the piece in context; the full or excerpted document; a discussion of the significance of the document and related event; and a listing of further resources (books, periodicals, Web sites, and audio and visual media).

Each volume will contain a topic-specific introduction, topic-specific chronology of major events, an index especially prepared to coordinate with the volume topic, and approximately 150 images.

Volumes are intended to be sold individually or as a set.

THE ESSENTIAL PRIMARY SOURCE SERIES

- *Terrorism: Essential Primary Sources*
- *Medicine, Health, and Bioethics: Essential Primary Sources*
- *Environmental Issues: Essential Primary Sources*
- *Crime and Punishment: Essential Primary Sources*
- *Gender Issues and Sexuality: Essential Primary Sources*
- *Human and Civil Rights: Essential Primary Sources*
- *Government, Politics, and Protest: Essential Primary Sources*
- *Social Policy: Essential Primary Sources*
- *Immigration and Multiculturalism: Essential Primary Sources*
- *Family in Society: Essential Primary Sources*

Introduction

The development of environmental consciousness is a milestone in human thought and civilization, as revolutionary as the picture of Earth taken from space on the cover. Environmental issues concern everyone. Environmental problems are the problems of all humankind, and as the astronomer Carl Sagan (1934–1996) forewarned, "there is no hint that help will come from elsewhere to save us from ourselves. It is up to us."

Only over the last two centuries has this environmental awareness resolved into to a limited understanding of the complexities of environmental science and issues. To reflect this diversity and urgency, the primary sources contained in *Environmental Issues: Essential Primary Sources* offer insights into both the origins of environmental consciousness and the sometimes contentious arguments, assertions, and tactics related to modern issues. Whether illustrating short-term concerns about wildlife rescue following an oil spill to articulating concerns related to the ongoing global debate over an effective response to greenhouse gas emissions, environmental issues offer challenges to individuals, communities, nations, and international organizations.

Environmental Issues: Essential Primary Sources attempts to present sources and commentary that are readable, interesting, and that instruct, challenge, and excite a range of student and reader interests. The sources in this book were also specifically chosen to reflect the diversity of environmental issues facing present and future generations. As with other volumes in this series, the primary intention is not to blind the reader with glints from all facets of an issue or topic, but rather to stimulate and provoke critical thinking about a variety of issues. By taking a historical perspective, *Environmental Issues: Essential Primary Sources* attempts to provide insight into subtle shifts of science and rhetoric, and to provide a foundation for investigation into topics increasingly important in scientific, social, and political discourse.

The primary sources contained in this volume were also selected to reflect the breadth of individuals and organizations concerned with environmental issues. These individuals and organizations, from local action groups to international conservation organizations, generally reflect a confluence of scientific, environmental, social, and humanitarian concern. They also reflect a growing trend to "act locally, but think globally." Such global concerns are rarely hubris. Actions to improve a local water supply or to educate communities concerning the need to conserve water, for example, can be both locally and globally important. A significant part of humanity, especially in developing countries, still lives in areas where usable water supplies are scarce. While the lack of a well with potable water can become a prime concern for a individual village, it also reflects a pixel of a global problem. With regard to water resources, the World Health Organization asserts that more than one billion people remain without access to sufficient supplies of clean water, and approximately one third of all people on Earth still lack proper sanitation facilities or the means to treat or dispose of wastewater. More than three million people still die each year from diseases related to or caused by contaminated water. Given such facts, it is often impossible, and in some cases dangerous, to attempt to draw too fine a line between "local" and "global" issues.

The link between science and environmental issues is tightly forged. Scientists from many disciplines, from geologists to molecular bacteriologists, often orient their research toward questions related to the environment. Accordingly, although not a science textbook, the editors of *Environmental Issues: Essential Primary Sources* have attempted to include articles designed to provide an understanding of the science underpinning many of the most important and current environmental issues.

Despite increasing efforts and advances in scientific understanding, environmental degradation and destruction continue. In some cases, the scientific issues are essentially known and settled; it is only the will to do what is needed or to debate the merits and costs of varying solutions that remains. In those cases, environmental issues are not questions of science, but tests of social ethics and political will. What happens in one part of the world often has a measurable impact on remote regions. Such understanding, now frequently and graphically illustrated by sweeping pictures from space, document a global intimacy and interdependence that transcends artificially drawn political boundaries as easily as clouds float over varying landscapes.

Accordingly, *Environmental Issues: Essential Primary Sources* draws on experts and resources from around the globe. Such pan-global perspective regarding environmental issues is increasingly vital. Political boundaries and differences pose real threats to both civilization and the environment, especially regarding potential use of nuclear, biological, and chemical weapons. In such a world, it is critical that citizens of all nations, and of all political persuasions voice concerns as to the long-term environmental impacts use of such weapons may bring, whether used by terrorists, or rationed as a form of strategic defense.

**K. Lee Lerner & Brenda Wilmoth Lerner,
editors**
*Siracusa, Sicily
April, 2006*

About the Entry

The primary source is the centerpiece and main focus of each entry in *Environmental Issues: Essential Primary Sources*. In keeping with the philosophy that much of the benefit from using primary sources derives from the reader's own process of inquiry, the contextual material surrounding each entry provides access and ease of use, as well as giving the reader a springboard for delving into the primary source. Rubrics identify each section and enable the reader to navigate entries with ease.

ENTRY STRUCTURE

- Primary Source/Entry Title, Subtitle, Primary Source Type
- Key Facts—essential information about the primary source, including creator, date, source citation, and notes about the creator.
- Introduction—historical background and contributing factors for the primary source.
- Primary Source—in text, text facsimile, or image format; full or excerpted.
- Significance—importance and impact of the primary source related events.
- Further Resources—books, periodicals, websites, and audio and visual material.

NAVIGATING AN ENTRY

Entry elements are numbered and reproduced here, with an explanation of the data contained in these elements explained immediately thereafter according to the corresponding numeral.

Primary Source/Entry Title, Subtitle (if used), Primary Source Type

[1] *Coming into the Country*
[2] **Subtitle**

[3] **Book excerpt**

[1] **Primary Source/Entry Title:** The entry title is usually the primary source title. In some cases where long titles must be shortened, or more generalized topic titles are needed for clarity primary source titles are generally depicted as subtitles. Entry titles appear as catchwords at the top outer margin of each page.

[2] **Subtitle:** Some entries contain subtitles.

[3] **Primary Source Type:** The type of primary source is listed just below the title. When assigning source types, great weight was given to how the author of the primary source categorized the source.

Key Facts

[4] **By:** John McPhee

[5] **Date:** 1976

[6] **Source:** McPhee, John. *Coming into the Country.* New York: Farrar, Straus, and Giroux, 1976.

[7] **About the Author:** American author John McPhee has written more than twenty nonfiction books, many of them notable contributions about humans and their interaction with the environment, since 1965. A native of Princeton, New Jersey, he attended both Princeton University and Cambridge University before embarking on a career in journalism with *Time* magazine. He

has been a staff writer with *The New Yorker* since 1965. Two of his books, *Encounters with the Archdruid* and *The Curve of Binding Energy*, were nominated for National Book Awards. McPhee received the Award in Literature from the American Academy of Arts and Letters in 1977 and received a Pulitzer Prize in 1999 for *Annals of the Former World*, his collected writings about geologists and their work. Highly regarded among professional geologists for his portrayal of their science, McPhee has also been honored by the Geological Society of America, the American Institute of Professional Geologists, the American Association of Petroleum Geologists, and the Association of Earth Science Editors.

[4]   **Author, Artist, or Organization:** The name of the author, artist, or organization responsible for the creation of the primary source begins the Key Facts section.

[5]   **Date of Origin:** The date of origin of the primary source appears in this field, and may differ from the date of publication in the source citation below it; for example, speeches are often delivered before they are published.

[6]   **Source Citation:** The source citation is a full bibliographic citation, giving original publication data as well as reprint and/or online availability.

[7]   **About the Author:** A brief bio of the author or originator of the primary source gives birth and death dates and a quick overview of the person's work. This rubric has been customized in some cases. If the primary source written document, the term "author" appears; however, if the primary source is a work of art, the term "artist" is used, showing the person's direct relationship to the primary source. For primary sources created by a group, "organization" may have been used instead of "author." Other terms may also be used to describe the creator or originator of the primary source. If an author is anonymous or unknown, a brief "About the Publication" sketch may appear.

Introduction Essay

[8]   **INTRODUCTION**

Coming into the Country, published in 1976, is a narrative about Alaska during the pivotal years of the early to mid-1970s. It was a time of both economic expansion and controversy about the future of the remote and sparsely populated Alaska. Statehood had been granted barely a decade earlier, but much of the land in Alaska remained under federal control and was being evaluated for preservation as national parks, wilderness areas, and wildlife refuges. The Alaska Native Claims Settlement Act of 1971 had formally settled long-standing disputes about the property rights of Native Americans, giving one-ninth of Alaska's land and nearly one billion dollars in cash to twelve regional Native American corporations. The trans-Alaskan pipeline was being built and there was discussion about the possibility of moving the state capital from the small and difficult-to-reach city of Juneau to the bustling commercial center of Anchorage. Pipeline construction and oil exploration brought high-paying jobs, business opportunities, and the homogeneity of virtually every other American city to Anchorage. There were fears that construction of the pipeline would lead to an oil spill and environmental ruin in pristine Prince William Sound. Some saw it as an opportunity to prosper, while others saw the end of Alaska as they knew it.

The title of *Coming into the Country* alludes to Alaskans who refer to the remote bush as "the country." When one arrives in the bush for the first time, he or she is said to have come into the country. *Coming into the Country* consists of three sections, each of which McPhee refers to as a book. The first book describes a river trip above the Arctic Circle with a group of state and federal scientists evaluating land that would eventually become the Gates of the Arctic National Park. The third book, also titled "Coming into the Country," recounts life in the remote bush town of Eagle, Alaska. The second book, titled "What They Were Hunting For" describes a life in urban Alaska during the campaign to move the state capital to Anchorage.

[8]   **Introduction:** The introduction is a brief essay on the contributing factors and historical context of the primary source. Intended to promote understanding and equip the reader with essential facts to understand the context of the primary source.

To maintain ease of reference to the primary source, spellings of names and places are used in accord with their use in the primary source. According names and places may have different spellings in different articles. Whenever possible, alternative spellings are provided to provide clarity.

PRIMARY SOURCE

[9]   **Primary Source**

There are those who would say that tens of thousands of barrels of oil erupting from a break in the Trans-Alaska Pipeline would be the lesser accident if, at more or less the same time, a fresh Anchorage were to spill into the bush. While the dream of the capital city plays on in the mind, Anchorage stands real. It is the central hive of human Alaska, and in manner and structure it represents, for all to see, the Alaskan dynamic and the

Alaskan aesthetic. It is a tangible expression of certain Alaskan's regard for Alaska—their one true city, the exemplar of the predilections of the people in creating improvements over the land.

As may befit a region where both short and long travel is generally by air, nearly every street in Anchorage seems to be the road to the airport. Dense groves of plastic stand on either side—flashing, whirling, flaky. HOOSIER BUDDY'S MOBILE HOMES. WINNEBAGO SALES & SERVICE. DISCOUNT LIQUORS OPEN SUNDAY. GOLD RUSH AUTO SALES. PROMPT ACTION LOCKSMITHS. ALASKA REFRIGERATION & AIR CONDITION. DENALI FUEL...

"Are the liquor stores really open Sundays?"

"Everything in Anchorage is open that pays."

Almost all Americans would recognize Anchorage, because Anchorage is that part of any city where the city has burst its seams and extruded Colonel Sanders.

"You can taste the greed in the air."

BELUGA ASPHALT.

Anchorage is sometimes excused in the name of pioneering. Build now, civilize later. But Anchorage is not a frontier town. It is virtually unrelated to its environment. It has come in on the wind, an American spore. A large cookie cutter brought down on El Paso could lift something like Anchorage into the air. Anchorage is the northern rim of Trenton, the center of Oxnard, the ocean-blind precincts of Daytona Beach. It is condensed, instant Albuquerque.

PANCHO'S VILLA, MEXICAN FOOD. BULL SHED, STEAK HOUSE AND SONIC LOUNGE. SHAKEY'S DRIVE-IN PIZZA. EAT ME SUBMARINES.

Anchorage has developed a high-rise city core, with glass-box offices for the oil companies and tall Miamian hotels. Zonelessly lurching outward, it has made of its suburbs a carnival of cinder block, all with a speculative mania so rife that sellers' small homesites—of modest lots scarcely large enough for small homesites—of modest lots scarcely large enough for houses—retain subsurface rights. In vacant lots, queen-post trusses lie waiting for new buildings to jump up beneath them. Roads are rubbled, ponded with chuckholes. Big trucks, graders, loaders, make the prevailing noise, the dancing fumes, the frenetic beat of the town. Huge rubber tires are strewn about like quoits, ever ready for the big machines that move hills of earth and gravel into inconvenient lakes, which become new ground.

FOR LEASE. WILL BUILD TO SUIT.

Anchorage coins millionaires in speculative real estate. Some are young. The median age in Anchorage is under twenty-four. Every three or four years, something like half the population turns over. And with thirty days of residence, you can vote as an Alaskan.

POLAR REALTY. IDLE WHEELS TRAILER PARK. MOTEL MUSH INN.

Anchorage has a thin history. Something of a precursor of the modern pipeline camps, it began in 1914 as a collection of tents pitched to shelter workers building the Alaska Railroad. For decades, it was a wooden-sidewalked, gravel-streeted town. Then, remarkably early, as cities go, it developed an urban slum, and both homes and commerce began to abandon its core. The exodus was so rapid that the central business district never wholly consolidated, and downtown Anchorage is even more miscellaneous than outlying parts of the city. There is, for example, a huge J.C. Penney department store filling several blocks in the heart of town, with an interior mall of boutiques and restaurants and a certain degree of chic. A couple of weedy vacant lots separate this complex from five log cabins. Downtown Anchorage from a distance displays an upreaching skyline that implies great pressure for land. Down below, among the high buildings, are houses, huts, vegetable gardens, and bungalows with tidy front lawns. Anchorage burst out itself and left these incongruities in the center, and for me they are the most appealing sights in Anchorage. Up against a downtown office building I have seen cordwood stacked for winter.

In its headlong, violent expansion, Anchorage had considerable, but not unlimited, space to fill. To an extent unusual among cities, Anchorage has certain absolute boundaries, and in that sense its growth has been a confined explosion. To the north, a pair of military bases establish, in effect, a Roman wall. To the west and south, fjordlike arms of the Pacific—Knik Arm, Turnagain Arm—frame the city. Behind Anchorage, east, stand the Chugach Mountains, stunning against the morning and in the evening light— Mount Magnificent, Mount Gordon Lyon, Temptation Peak, Tanaina Peak, Wolverine Peak, the Suicide Peaks. Development has gone to some extent upward there. Houses are pushpinned to the mountainsides—a Los Angelized setting, particularly at night, above the starry lights of town. But the mountains are essentially a full stop to Anchorage, and Anchorage has nowhere else to go.

Within this frame of mountains, ocean, and military boundaries are about fifty thousand acres (roughly the amount of land sought by the Capital Site Selection

Committee), and the whole of it is known as the Anchorage Bowl. The ground itself consists of silt, alluvium, eolian sands, glacial debris-material easy to rearrange. The surface was once lumpy with small knolls. As people and their businesses began filling the bowl, they went first to the knolls, because the knolls were wooded and well drained. They cut down the trees, truncated the hills, and bestudded them with buildings. They strung utility lines like baling wire from knoll to knoll. The new subdivisions within the bowl were thus hither and yon, random, punctuated with bogs. Anchorage grew like mold.

WOLVERINE ALUMINUM SIDING. ALASKA FOUR-WHEEL DRIVE. JACK BENNY'S RADIO-DISPATCHED CESSPOOL PUMPING.

Low ground is gradually being filled. The bowl has about a hundred and eighty thousand people now, or almost half of human Alaska. There are some in town—notably, Robert Atwood, of the *Times*—who would like to see Anchorage grow to seven hundred thousand. Atwood is a big, friendly, old-football-tackle sort of man, with whitening hair and gold-rimmed glasses. Forty years on the inside, this impatient advocate of the commercial potentialities of Alaska is said to be one of the two wealthiest people in the state, the other being his brother-in-law. "Idealists here in town see a need for a park in every housing development," Atwood told me one day. "They want to bury utility lines, reserve green belts, build bicycle paths. With these things, the bowl could only contain three hundred and fifty thousand. They're making it very difficult for man, these people. They favor animals, trees, water, flowers. Who ever makes a plan for man? Who ever *will* make a plan for man? That is what *I* wonder. I am known among conservationists as a bad guy."

In Anchorage, if you threw a pebble into a crowd, chances are you would not hit a conservationist, an ecophile, a wilderness preserver. In small ghettos, they are there—living in a situation lined with irony. They are in Alaska—many of them working for the federal government—because Alaska is everything wild it has ever been said to be. Alaska runs off the edge of the imagination, with its tracklessness, its beyond-the-ridge-line surprises, its hundreds of millions of acres of wilderness—this so-called "last frontier," which is certainly all of that, yet for the most part is not a frontier at all but immemorial landscape in an all but unapproached state. Within such vastness, Anchorage is a mere pustule, a dot, a minim-a walled city, wild as Yonkers, with the wildlife riding in a hundred and ninety-three thousand

trucks and cars. Yet the city—where people are, where offices are—is perforce the home address of wilderness planners, of wildlife biologists, of Brooks Range guides.

The first few days I spent in Alaska were spent in Anchorage, and I remember the increasing sense of entrapment we felt (my wife was with me), knowing that nothing less than a sixth of the entire United States, and almost all of it wilderness, was out there beyond seeing, while immediate needs and chores to do were keeping us penned in this portable Passaic. Finally, we couldn't take it any longer, and we cancelled appointments and rented a car and revved it up for an attempted breakout from town. A float plane—at a hundred and ten dollars an hour—would have been the best means, but, like most of the inmates of Anchorage, we could not afford it. For a great many residents, Anchorage is about all they ever see of Alaska, day after day after year. There are only two escape routes—a road north, a road south—and these are encumbered with traffic and, for some miles anyway, lined with detritus from Anchorage. We went south, that first time, and eventually east, along a fjord that would improve Norway. Then the road turned south again, into the mountains of Kenai—great tundra balds that reminded me of Scotland and my wife of parts of Switzerland, where she had lived. She added that she thought these mountains looked better than the ones in Europe. Sockeyes, as red as cardinals, were spawning in clear, shallow streams, and we ate our cheese and chocolate in a high meadow over a torrential river of green and white water. We looked up to the ridges for Dall sheep, and felt, for the moment, about as free. Anchorage shrank into perspective. It might be a sorry town, but it has the greatest out-of-town any town has ever had.

BIG RED'S FLYING SERVICE. BELUGA STEAM & ELECTRIC THAWING. DON'T GO TO JAIL LET FRED GO YOUR BAIL.

There is a street in Anchorage—a green-lights, red-lights, busy street—that is used by automobiles and airplanes. I remember an airplane in someone's driveway—next door to the house where I was staying. The neighbor started up its engine one night toward eleven o'clock, and for twenty minutes he ran it flat out while his two sons, leaning hard into the stabilizers, strained to hold back the plane. In Alaska, you do what you feel like doing, or so goes an Alaskan creed.

There is, in Anchorage, a somewhat Sutton Place. It is an enclave, actually, with several roads, off the western end of Northern Lights Boulevard, which is a principal Anchorage thoroughfare, a neon borealis. Walter Hickel lives in the enclave, on Loussac Drive, which winds between curbs and lawns, neatly trimmed, laid out, and landscaped, under white birches and balsam poplars. Hickel's is a heavy, substantial home, its style American Dentist. The neighbors' houses are equally expensive and much the same. The whole neighborhood seems to be struggling to remember Scarsdale. But not to find Alaska.

I had breakfast one morning in Anchorage with a man who had come to Alaska from The Trust for Public Land, an organization whose goal is to buy potential parkland in urban areas and hold it until the government, whose legislative machinery is often too slow for the land market, can get up the funds for the purpose. In overbuilt urban settings—from Watts to Newark and back to Oakland-The Trust for Public Land will acquire whatever it can, even buildings under demolition, in order to create small parks and gardens that might relieve the compressed masses. And now The Trust for Public Land had felt the need to come to Anchorage—to the principal city of Alaska—to help hold a pond or a patch of green for the people in the future to have and see.

Books were selling in Anchorage, once when I was there, for forty-seven cents a pound.

There are those who would say that the only proper place for a new capital of Alaska—if there has to be a new one—is Anchorage, because anyone who has built a city like Anchorage should not be permitted to build one anywhere else.

At Anchorage International Airport, there is a large aerial photograph of Anchorage formed by pasting together a set of pictures that were made without what cartographers call ground control. This great aerial map is one of the first things to confront visitors from everywhere in the world, and in bold letters it is titled "ANCHORAGE, ALASKA. UNCONTROLLED MOSAIC."

[9] Primary Source: The majority of primary sources are reproduced as plain text. The primary source may appear excerpted or in full, and may appear as text, text facsimile (photographic reproduction of the original text), image, or graphic display (such as a table, chart, or graph).

The font and leading of the primary sources are distinct from that of the context—to provide a visual clue to the change, as well as to facilitate ease of reading. As needed, the original formatting of the text is preserved in order to more accurately represent the original (screenplays, for example). In order to respect the integrity of the primary sources, content some readers may consider sensitive (for example, the use

of slang, ethnic or racial slurs, etc.) is retained when deemed to be integral to understanding the source and the context of its creation.

Primary source images (whether photographs, text facsimiles, or graphic displays) are bordered with a distinctive double rule. Most images have brief captions.

The term "narrative break" appears where there is a significant amount of elided (omitted) material with the text provided (for example, excerpts from a work's first and fifth chapters, selections from a journal article abstract and summary, or dialogue from two acts of a play).

Significance Essay
[10] SIGNIFICANCE

Coming into the Country paints a detailed and insightful picture of America's last frontier during a time of unprecedented change, presenting an unbiased journalistic account of a state struggling with its identity and future.

Some Alaskans look to Anchorage as a vision of what the state can be and others look at it as a sad example of what the state has become. Mcphee's portrayal reflects the universal dilemma facing Alaska and virtually every other city struggling to reconcile economic growth with environmental quality. In that regard, Alaska is no different than anywhere else. McPhee's description of the sprawling and disorganized urban growth of Anchorage, a small city by broader standards but Alaska's center of commerce, would apply just as well to anywhere in the lower forty-eight states. He describes Anchorage as an "instant Albuquerque" indistinguishable from Oxnard, El Paso, or Trenton. Yet, even thirty years after the book was published, Anchorage still harbors remnants of its rough and tumble frontier past. McPhee writes of firewood stacked alongside modern office buildings and log cabins next to a J.C. Penney store. He points out that, ironically, wildlife biologists, mountain guides, and others drawn to the vast and wild frontier more often than not end up living in Anchorage because, simply enough, that is where the jobs are. McPhee describes the sentiment of a civic booster who believes that environmental idealists favor trees and animals at the expense of humans. His concern was that bicycle paths and parks take up space that will limit the ability of Anchorage to grow to its full potential.

[10] Significance: The significance discusses the importance and impact of the primary source and the event it describes.

Further Resources

[11] Books

Borneman, Walter R.. *Alaska: Saga of a Bold Land.* New York: HarperCollins, 2003.

Web sites

Alyeska Pipeline Service Company. <http://www.alyeska-pipe.com> (accessed January 27, 2006).

National Park Service. "Gates of the Arctic National Park and Preserve." <http://www.nps.gov/gaar> (accessed January 27, 2006).

State of Alaska. "Alaska!" <http://www.state.ak.us> (accessed January 27, 2006).

University of Alaska. "Alaska Native Claims Settlement Act Resources." <http://www.ankn.uaf.edu/NPE/ancsa.html> (accessed January 27, 2006).

U.S. Geological Survey. "Alaska Science Center." <http://alaska.usgs.gov> (accessed January 27, 2006).

[11] Further Resources: A brief list of resources categorized as Books, Periodicals, Web sites, and Audio and Visual Media provides a stepping stone to further study.

SECONDARY SOURCE CITATION FORMATS (HOW TO CITE ARTICLES AND SOURCES)

Alternative forms of citations exist and examples of how to cite articles from this book are provided below:

APA Style

Books:

Kübler-Ross, Elisabeth. (1969) *On Death and Dying.*New York: Macmillan. Excerpted in K. Lee Lerner and Brenda Wilmoth Lerner, eds. (2006) *Medicine, Health, and Bioethics: Essential Primary Sources*, Farmington Hills, Mich.: Thomson Gale.

Periodicals:

Venter, J. Craig, et al. (2001, February 16). "The Sequence of the Human Genome." *Science*, vol. 291, no. 5507, pp. 1304–51. Excerpted in K. Lee Lerner and Brenda Wilmoth Lerner, eds. (2006) *Medicine, Health, and Bioethics: Essential Primary Sources*, Farmington Hills, Mich.: Thomson Gale.

Web sites:

Johns Hopkins Hospital and Health System. "Patient Rights and Responsibilities." Retrieved January 14, 2006 from http://www.hopkinsmedicine.org/patients/JHH/patient_rights.html. Excerpted in K. Lee Lerner and Brenda Wilmoth Lerner, eds. (2006) *Medicine, Health, and Bioethics: Essential Primary Sources*, Farmington Hills, Mich.: Thomson Gale.

Chicago Style

Books:

Kübler-Ross, Elisabeth. *On Death and Dying.* New York: Macmillan, 1969. Excerpted in K. Lee Lerner and Brenda Wilmoth Lerner, eds. *Medicine, Health, and Bioethics: Essential Primary Sources*, Farmington Hills, Mich.: Thomson Gale, 2006.

Periodicals:

Venter, J. Craig, et al. "The Sequence of the Human Genome." *Science* (2001): 291, 5507, 1304–1351. Excerpted in K. Lee Lerner and Brenda Wilmoth Lerner, eds. *Medicine, Health, and Bioethics: Essential Primary Sources*, Farmington Hills, Mich.: Thomson Gale, 2006.

Web sites:

Johns Hopkins Hospital and Health System. "Patient Rights and Responsibilities." <http://www.hopkinsmedicine.org/patients/JHH/patient_rights.html.> (accessed January 14, 2006). Excerpted in K. Lee Lerner and Brenda Wilmoth Lerner, eds. *Medicine, Health, and Bioethics: Essential Primary Sources*, Farmington Hills, Mich.: Thomson Gale, 2006.

MLA Style

Books:

Kübler-Ross, Elisabeth. *On Death and Dying*, New York: Macmillan, 1969. Excerpted in K. Lee Lerner and Brenda Wilmoth Lerner, eds. *Medicine, Health, and Bioethics: Essential Primary Sources*, Farmington Hills, Mich.: Thomson Gale, 2006.

Periodicals:

Venter, J. Craig, et al. "The Sequence of the Human Genome." *Science*, 291 (16 February 2001): 5507, 1304–51. Excerpted in K. Lee Lerner and Brenda Wilmoth Lerner, eds. *Terrorism: Essential Primary Sources*, Farmington Hills, Mich.: Thomson Gale, 2006.

Web sites:

"Patient's Rights and Responsibilities." Johns Hopkins Hospital and Health System. 14 January 2006. <http://www.hopkinsmedicine.org/patients/JHH/patient_rights.html.> Excerpted in K. Lee Lerner and Brenda Wilmoth Lerner, eds. *Terrorism: Essential Primary Sources*, Farmington Hills, Mich.: Thomson Gale, 2006.

Turabian Style (Natural and Social Sciences)

Books:

Kübler-Ross, Elisabeth. *On Death and Dying*, (New York: Macmillan, 1969). Excerpted in K. Lee Lerner and Brenda Wilmoth Lerner, eds. *Medicine, Health, and Bioethics: Essential Primary Sources*, (Farmington Hills, Mich.: Thomson Gale, 2006).

Periodicals:

Venter, J. Craig, et al. "The Sequence of the Human Genome." *Science*, 291 (16 February 2001): 5507, 1304–1351. Excerpted in K. Lee Lerner and Brenda Wilmoth Lerner, eds. *Medicine, Health, and Bioethics: Essential Primary Sources*, (Farmington Hills, Mich.: Thomson Gale, 2006).

Web sites:

Johns Hopkins Hospital and Health System. "Patient's Rights and Responsibilities." available from http://www.hopkinsmedicine.org/patients/JHH/patient_rights.

html; accessed 14 January 2006. Excerpted in K. Lee Lerner and Brenda Wilmoth Lerner, eds. *Medicine, Health, and Bioethics: Essential Primary Sources,* (Farmington Hills, Mich.: Thomson Gale, 2006).

Using Primary Sources

The definition of what constitutes a primary source is often the subject of scholarly debate and interpretation. Although primary sources come from a wide spectrum of resources, they are united by the fact that they individually provide insight into the historical *milieu* (context and environment) during which they were produced. Primary sources include materials such as newspaper articles, press dispatches, autobiographies, essays, letters, diaries, speeches, song lyrics, posters, works of art—and in the twenty-first century, web logs—that offer direct, first-hand insight or witness to events of their day.

Categories of primary sources include:

- Documents containing firsthand accounts of historic events by witnesses and participants. This category includes diary or journal entries, letters, email, newspaper articles, interviews, memoirs, and testimony in legal proceedings.
- Documents or works representing the official views of both government leaders and leaders of terrorist organizations. These include primary sources such as policy statements, speeches, interviews, press releases, government reports, and legislation.
- Works of art, including (but certainly not limited to) photographs, poems, and songs, including advertisements and reviews of those works that help establish an understanding of the cultural milieu (the cultural environment with regard to attitudes and perceptions of events).
- Secondary sources. In some cases, secondary sources or tertiary sources may be treated as primary sources. For example, the article "Implementation of the Program" discusses the evolution of the Red

Cross blood donation program across a time span of more than twenty years, from World War II (1938–1945) through the Vietnam War in 1964. The primary source includes recollections of communications exchanged between the U.S. Army and the Red Cross about the need for obtaining large quantities of human blood plasma for use in treating injured soldiers. Ordinarily, an historical retrospective such as this excerpt, published two decades after the initial event, might not be considered a primary source. The fact that the retrospective was written by the Army General responsible for the Army blood program during World War II, a participant in the initial effort, makes it an illuminating primary source.

ANALYSIS OF PRIMARY SOURCES

The material collected in this volume is not intended to provide a comprehensive overview of a topic or event. Rather, the primary sources are intended to generate interest and lay a foundation for further inquiry and study.

In order to properly analyze a primary source, readers should remain skeptical and develop probing questions about the source. As in reading a chemistry or algebra textbook, historical documents require readers to analyze them carefully and extract specific information. However, readers must also read "beyond the text" to garner larger clues about the social impact of the primary source.

In addition to providing information about their topics, primary sources may also supply a wealth of insight into their creator's viewpoint. For example, when reading a news article about an outbreak of disease, consider whether the reporter's words also indicate something about his or her origin, bias (an irrational disposition in favor of someone or something), prejudices (an irrational disposition against someone or something), or intended audience.

Students should remember that primary sources often contain information later proven to be false, or contain viewpoints and terms unacceptable to future generations. It is important to view the primary source within the historical and social context existing at its creation. If for example, a newspaper article is written within hours or days of an event, later developments may reveal some assertions in the original article as false or misleading.

TEST NEW CONCLUSIONS AND IDEAS

Whatever opinion or working hypothesis the reader forms, it is critical that they then test that hypothesis against other facts and sources related to the incident. For example, it might be wrong to conclude that factual mistakes are deliberate unless evidence can be produced of a pattern and practice of such mistakes with an intent to promote a false idea.

The difference between sound reasoning and preposterous conspiracy theories (or the birth of urban legends) lies in the willingness to test new ideas against other sources, rather than rest on one piece of evidence such as a single primary source that may contain errors. Sound reasoning requires that arguments and assertions guard against argument fallacies that utilize the following:

- false dilemmas (only two choices are given when in fact there are three or more options)
- arguments from ignorance (*argumentum ad ignorantiam*; because something is not known to be true, it is assumed to be false)

- possibilist fallacies (a favorite among conspiracy theorists who attempt to demonstrate that a factual statement is true or false by establishing the possibility of its truth or falsity. An argument where "it could be" is usually followed by an unearned "therefore, it is.")
- slippery slope arguments or fallacies (a series of increasingly dramatic consequences is drawn from an initial fact or idea)
- begging the question (the truth of the conclusion is assumed by the premises)
- straw man arguments (the arguer mischaracterizes an argument or theory and then attacks the merits of their own false representations)
- appeals to pity or force (the argument attempts to persuade people to agree by sympathy or force)
- prejudicial language (values or moral goodness good and bad are attached to certain arguments or facts)
- personal attacks (*ad hominem*; an attack on a person's character or circumstances)
- anecdotal or testimonial evidence (stories that are unsupported by impartial or unreproducable data)
- *post hoc* (after the fact) fallacies (because one thing follows another, it is held to cause the other)
- the fallacy of the appeal to authority (the argument rests upon the credentials of a person, not the evidence)

Despite the fact that some primary sources can contain false information or lead readers to false conclusions based on the "facts" presented, they remain an invaluable resource regarding past events. Primary sources allow readers and researchers to come as close as possible to understanding the perceptions and context of events and, thus, to more fully appreciate how and why misconceptions occur.

Chronology

1802: John Dalton introduces modern atomic theory into the science of chemistry.

1815: William Smith publishes first geological map of UK.

1830: Charles Lyell publishes *Principles of Geology* and argues Earth is a least millions of years old.

1830: World population is approximately one billion.

1831: Charles Robert Darwin begins his historic voyage on the H.M.S. *Beagle* (1831–1836). His observations during the voyage lead to his theory of evolution by means of natural selection.

1840: Louis Agassiz publishes his *Etudes sur les glaciers*. He also discovers glacial feature in Scotland away from an ice covered area and advances the theory of glaciation.

1842: Charles Robert Darwin wrote out an abstract of his theory of evolution, but he did not plan to have this theory published until after his death.

1849: U.S. Department of the Interior established.

1850: Rudolph Julius Emanuel Clausius publishes a paper which contains what becomes known as the second law of thermodynamics, stating that, "heat cannot, of itself, pass from a colder to a hotter body."

1851: Armand Hippolyte Fizeau measures the speed of light as it flows with a stream of water and as it goes against the stream. He finds that the velocity of light is higher in the former.

1851: Jean Bernard Léon Foucault conducts his spectacular series of experiments associated with the pendulum. He swings a heavy iron ball from a wire more than 200 feet long and demonstrates that the swinging pendulum maintains its plane while the Earth slowly twists under it. The crowd of spectators who witness this demonstration come to realize that they are watching the Earth rotate under the pendulum—experimental proof of a moving Earth.

1851: William Thomson, later known as Lord Kelvin, publishes *On the Dynamical Theory of Heat* in which he explores Carnot's work and deduces that all energy tends to rundown and dissipate itself as heat. This is another form of the second law of thermodynamics and is advanced further by Clausius at about the same time. Kelvin's work is considered the first nineteenth-century treatise on thermodynamics.

1852: Abraham Gesner prepares the first kerosene from petroleum. He obtains the liquid kerosene by the dry distillation of asphalt rock, treats it further, and calls the product kerosene after the Greek word *keros*, meaning oil.

1852: Alexander William Williamson publishes his study which shows for the first time that catalytic action clearly involves and is explained by the formation of an intermediate compound.

1853: Hans Peter Jorgen Julius Thomsen works out a method of manufacturing sodium carbonate from the mineral cryolite. This mineral will soon become important to the production of aluminum.

1853: William John Macquorn Rankine introduces into physics the concept of potential energy, also called the energy of position.

1854: George Airy obtains estimate of Earth mass from calculations based upon observations of underground gravity.

1854: Gregor Mendel begins studying thirty-four different strains of peas. He selects 22 kinds for further experiments. From 1856 to 1863, Mendel grew and tested over 28,000 plants and analyzed seven pairs of traits.

1854: Henry David Thoreau publishes *Walden*.

1855: Charles-Adolphe Wurtz develops a method of synthesizing long-chain hydrocarbons by reactions between alkyl halides and metallic sodium. This method is called the Wurtz reaction.

1856: Neanderthal fossil identified.

1857: Louis Pasteur demonstrated that lactic acid fermentation is caused by a living organism. Between 1857 and 1880, he performed a series of experiments that refuted the doctrine of spontaneous generation. He also introduced vaccines for fowl cholera, anthrax, and rabies, based on attenuated strains of viruses and bacteria.

1858: Charles Darwin and Alfred Russell Wallace agree to a joint presentation of their theory of evolution by natural selection.

1860: Cesium is the first element discovered using the newly developed spectroscope. Robert Wilhelm Bunsen and Gustav Robert Kirchhoff name their new element cesium after its "sky blue" color in the spectrum.

1860: Stanislao Cannizzaro publishes the forgotten ideas of Amedeo Avogadro—about the distinction between molecules and atoms—in an attempt to bring some order and agreement on determining atomic weights.

1861: Alexander Mikhailovich Butlerov introduces the term "chemical structure" to mean that the chemical nature of a molecule is determined not only by the number and type of atoms but also by their arrangement.

1861: Friedrich August Kekulé von Stadonitz publishes the first volume of *Lehrbuch der organischen Chemie*, in which he is the first to define organic chemistry as the study of carbon compounds.

1861: William Thomson, later known as Lord Kelvin, publishes his *Physical Considerations Regarding the Possible Age of the Sun's Heat* which contains the theme of the *heat death* of the Universe. This is offered in light of the principle of dissipation of energy stated in 1851.

1862: Anders Angstrom observed hydrogen in the sun.

1863: Ferdinand Reich and his assistant Hieronymus Theodor Richter examine zinc ore spectroscopically and discover the new, indigo-colored element iridium. It is used in the next century in the making of transistors.

1863: William Huggins aserts that stellar spectra indicate that stars are made of same elements found on Earth.

1864: George Perkins Marsh publishes *Man and Nature*.

1864: Yosemite in California becomes the first state park in the United States.

1865: Alexander Parkes produces celluloid, the first synthetic plastic material. After working since the 1850s with nitrocellulose, alcohol, camphor, and castor oil, he obtains a material that can be molded under pressure while still warm.

1866: August Adolph Eduard Eberhard Kundt invents a method by which he can make accurate measurements of the speed of sound in the air. He uses a *Kundt's tube* whose inside is dusted with fine powder which is then disturbed by traveling sound waves.

1869: Dimitri Ivanovich Mendeleev and Julius Lothar Meyer independently put forth the Periodic Table of Elements, which arranges the elements in order of atomic weights.

1869: Ernst Haeckel coins the term "ecology" to describe "the body of knowledge concerning the economy of nature."

1871: Charles Robert Darwin publishes *The Descent of Man, and Selection in Relation to Sex*. This work introduces the concept of sexual selection and expands his theory of evolution to include humans.

1872: Ferdinand Julius Cohn publishes the first of four papers entitled "Research on Bacteria," which establishes the foundation of bacteriology as a distinct field. He systematically divided bacteria into genera and species.

1872: Yellowstone in Wyoming becomes the first national park.

1873: James Clerk Maxwell publishes *Treatise on Electricity and Magnetism* in which he identifies light as an electromagnetic phenomenon. This landmark work brings together the three main fields of physics—electricity, magnetism, and light.

1873: Johannes Van der Waals offers an equation for the gas laws which contains terms relating to the volumes of the molecules themselves and the attractive forces between them. It becomes known as the Van der Waals equation.

1873: Walther Flemming discovers chromosomes, observes mitosis, and suggests the modern interpretation of nuclear division.

1875: American Forestry Association is founded to encourage wise forest management.

1876: Henry Augustus Rowland establishes for the first time that a moving electric charge or current is accompanied by electrically charged matter in motion and produces a magnetic field.

1879: U.S. Geological Survey established.

1880: Carl Oswald Viktor Engler begins his studies on petroleum. He is the first to state that it is organic in origin.

1882: Robert Koch discovers the tubercle bacillus and enunciates "Koch's postulates," which define the classic method of preserving, documenting, and studying bacteria.

1883: Ernst Mach publishes his *Die Mechanik in ihrer Entwickelung historisch-kritisch dargestellt*, in which he offers a radical philosophy of science that calls into question the reality of such Newtonian ideas as space, time, and motion. His work influences Einstein and prepares the way for relativity.

1883: Frank Wigglesworth Clarke is appointed chief chemist to the U.S. Geological Survey. In this position, he begins an extensive program of rock analysis and is one of the founders of geochemistry.

1883: Johann Gustav Kjeldahl devises a method for the analysis of the nitrogen content of organic material.

1886: Paul-Louis-Toussint Héroult and Charles Martin Hall independently invent an electrochemical process for extracting aluminum from its ore. This process makes aluminum cheaper and forms the basis of the huge aluminum industry.

1887: Herman Frasch patents a method for removing sulfur compounds from oil. Once the foul sulfur smell is removed through the use of metallic compounds, petroleum becomes a marketable product.

1890: Yosemite becomes a national park.

1892: Adirondack Park established by New York State Constitution, which mandated that the region remain forever wild.

1892: Henry S. Salt publishes *Animal Rights Considered in Relation to Social Progress*, a landmark work on animal rights and welfare.

1892: John Muir founds the Sierra Club to preserve the Sierra Nevada mountain chain.

1893: Augusto Righi demonstrates that Hertz (radio) waves differ from light only in wavelength and not because of any essential difference in their nature. This helps to establish the existence of the electromagnetic spectrum.

1893: Ferdinand-Frédéric-Henri Moissan produces artificial diamonds in his electric furnace.

1894: Guglielmo Marconi uses Hertz's method of producing radio waves and builds a receiver to detect them. He succeeds in sending his first radio waves 30 feet to ring a bell. The next year, his improved system can send a signal 1.5 miles.

1894: John William Strutt Rayleigh and William Ramsay succeed in isolating a new gas in the atmosphere that is denser than nitrogen and combines with no other element. They name it "argon," which is Greek for inert. It is the first of a series of rare gases with unusual properties whose existence had not been predicted.

1895: Pierre Curie studies the effect of heat on magnetism and shows that there is a critical temperature point above which magnetic properties will disappear. This comes to be called the Curie point.

1895: Wilhem Conrad Röntgen submits his first paper documenting his discovery of x-rays. This discovery leads to such a stream of ground-breaking discoveries in physics that it has been called the beginning of the second scientific revolution.

1895: William Ramsay discovers helium in a mineral named cleveite. It had been speculated earlier that helium existed only in the Sun, but Ramsay proves it also exists on Earth. It is discovered independently this year by Swedish chemist and geologist Per Theodore Cleve (1840–1905).

1896: Antoine Henri Becquerel studies fluorescent materials to see if they emit the newly-discovered x-rays and discovers instead that uranium produces natural radiation that is eventually called "radioactivity" in 1898 by Marie Skłodowska Curie.

1897: Joseph John Thomson discovers the electron.

1898: Marie Sklodowska Curie discovers thorium, which she proves is radioactive.

1898: Rivers and Harbors Act established in an effort to control pollution of navigable waters.

1899: Ernest Rutherford discovers that radioactive substances give off different kinds of rays. He names the positively charged ones alpha rays and the negative ones beta rays.

1900–1949

1900: Carl Correns, Hugo de Vries, and Erich von Tschermak independently rediscover Mendel's laws of inheritance. Their publications mark the beginning of modern genetics. Using several plant species, de Vries and Correns perform breeding experiments that paralleled Mendel's earlier studies and independently arrive at similar interpretations of their results. Therefore, upon reading Mendel's publication, they immediately recognized its significance. William Bateson describes the importance of Mendel's contribution in an address to the Royal Society of London.

1900: Friedrich Ernst Dorn analyzes the gas given off by (radioactive) radium and discovers the inert gas he names radon. This is the first clear demonstration that the process of giving off radiation transmutes one element into another during the radioactive decay process.

1900: Lacey Act regulating interstate shipment of wild animals in the United States is passed.

1900: Paul Ulrich Villard discovers what are later called gamma rays. While studying the recently discovered radiation from uranium, he finds that in addition to the alpha rays and beta rays, there are other rays, unaffected by magnets, that are similar to x-rays, but shorter and more penetrating.

1901: Antoine Henri Becquerel studies the rays emitted by the natural substance uranium and concludes that the only place they could be coming from is within the atoms of uranium. This marks the first clear understanding of the atom as something more than a featureless sphere.

1901: Guglielmo Marconi successfully sends radio signal from England to Newfoundland.

1902: Discovery of Tyrannosaurus Rex fossil.

1902: Oliver Heaviside and Arthur Edwin Kennelly independently and almost simultaneously make the first prediction of the existence of the ionosphere, an electrically conductive layer in the upper atmosphere that reflects radio waves. They theorize correctly that wireless telegraphy works over long distances because a conducting layer of atmosphere exists that allows radio waves to follow the Earth's curvature instead of traveling off into space.

1902: U.S. Bureau of Reclamation established.

1903: Antoine Henri Becquerel shares the Nobel Prize in physics with the husband-and-wife team of Marie Skłodowska Curie and Pierre Curie. Becquerel wins for his discovery of natural or spontaneous radioactivity, and the Curies win for their later research on this new phenomenon.

1903: Ernest Rutherford and Frederick Soddy explain radioactivity by their theory of atomic disintegration. They discover that uranium breaks down and forms a new series of substances as it gives off radiation.

1903: William Ramsay and Frederick Soddy discover that helium is continually produced by naturally radioactive substances.

1904: Ernest Rutherford postulates age of Earth by radioactvity dating.

1904: William Ramsay receives the Nobel Prize in Chemistry for the discovery of the inert gaseous elements in air, and for his determination of their place in the periodic system.

1905: Albert Einstein publishes *Special theory of relativity*.

1905: Albert Einstein uses Planck's theory to develop a quantum theory of light which explains the photoelectric effect.

1905: National Audubon Society formed.

1907: Georges Urbain discovers the last of the stable rare earth elements, and names it lutetium after the Latin name of Paris.

1907: Pierre Weiss offers his theory explaining the phenomenon of ferromagnetism.

1908: Alfred Wegener proposes the theory of continental drift.

1908: Chlorination is used extensively in U.S. water treatment plants for the first time.

1908: Ernest Rutherford and Hans Wilhelm Geiger develop an electrical alpha-particle counter. Over the next few years, Geiger continues to improve this device which becomes known as the Geiger counter.

1908: Ernest Rutherford is awarded the Nobel Prize in Chemistry for his investigations into disintegration of the elements and the chemistry of radioactive substances.

1908: Tunguska event occurs when a comet or asteroid that enters the atmosphere, causing major damage to a forested region in Siberia.

1911: Arthur Holmes publishes the first geological time scale with dates based on radioactive measurements.

1911: Ernst Rutherford discovers that atoms are made up of a positive nucleus surrounded by electrons. This modern concept of the atom replaces the notion of featureless, indivisible spheres that dominated atomistic thinking for 23 centuries.

1911: Victor Hess identifies high altitude radiation from space.

1912: Friedrich Karl Rudolf Bergius discovers how to treat coal and oil with hydrogen to produce gasoline.

1913: Charles Fabry first demonstrates the presence of ozone in the upper atmosphere. It is found later that ozone functions as a screen, preventing much of the Sun's ultraviolet radiation from reaching Earth's surface.

1913: Construction of Hetch-Hetchy Valley Dam approved to provide water to San Francisco; however, the dam also floods areas of Yosemite National Park.

1913: Niels Henrik David Bohr proposes the first dynamic model of the atom. It is seen as a very dense nucleus surrounded by electrons rotating in orbitals (defined energy levels).

1914: Ernest Rutherford discovers a positively charged particle he calls a proton.

1914: Martha, the last passenger pigeon, dies in the Cincinnati Zoo.

1915: Albert Einstein completes four years of work on his theory of gravitation, or what becomes known as the general theory of relativity.

1915: Richard Martin Willstätter is awarded the Nobel Prize in Chemistry for his research on plant pigments, especially chlorophyll.

1916: U.S. National Park Service established.

1918: Save-the-Redwoods League founded.

1918: U.S. and Canada sign treaty restricting the hunting of migratory birds.

1919: Arthur Eddington recorded data on the Sun's gravitational deflection of starlight during a solar eclipse, confirming Einstein's general theory of relativity.

1920: Ernest Rutherford names the positively charged part of the atom's nucleus a "proton."

1920: Mineral Leasing Act enacted to regulate mining on federal land.

1922: Izaak Walton League founded.

1924: Gila National Forest in New Mexico is designated the first wilderness area.

1927: Hermann Joseph Muller induced artificial mutations in fruit flies by exposing them to x-rays.

1928: George Gamow develops the quantum theory of radioactivity which is the first theory to successfully explain the behavior of radioactive elements, some of which decay in seconds and others after thousands of years.

1929: Walther Wilhelm Georg Franz Bothe invents *coincidence counting* by using two Geiger counters to detect the vertical direction of cosmic rays. This allows the measurement of extremely short time intervals, and he uses this technique to demonstrate that the laws of conservation and momentum are also valid for subatomic particles.

1933: Dust Bowl conditions due to extended drought in United States exacerbate depression era economic and environmental woes.

1932: James Chadwick proves the existence of the neutral particle of the atom's nucleus, called the neutron. It proves to be by far the most useful particle for initiating nuclear reactions.

1932: Karl Jansky makes first attempts at radio astronomy.

1932: Lev Davidovich Landau proposes the existence of neutron stars.

1932: Ruska builds first electron microscope.

1932: Thomas H. Morgan receives the Nobel Prize in Medicine or Physiology for his development of the theory of the gene. He was the first geneticist to receive a Nobel Prize.

1933: Tennessee Valley Authority created to assess impact of hydropower on the environment.

1934: Arnold O. Beckman invents the pH meter, which uses electricity to accurately measure a solution's acidity or alkalinity.

1934: Frédéric Joliot-Curie and IrèneJoliot-Curie discover what they call *artificial radioactivity*. They bombard aluminum to produce a radioactive form of phosphorus. They soon learn that radioactivity is not confined only to heavy elements like uranium, but that any element can become radioactive if the proper isotope is prepared. For producing the first artificial radioactive element they win the Nobel Prize in chemistry the next year.

1934: Taylor Grazing Act enacted to regulate grazing on federal land.

1935: U.S. Soil Conservation Service established to study and curb soil erosion.

1935: Wilderness Society founded by Aldo Leopold.

1936: Carl David Anderson discovers the*muon*. While studying cosmic radiation, he observes the track of a particle that is more massive than an electron but only a quarter as massive as a proton. He initially calls this new particle, which has a lifetime of only a few millionths of a second, a mesotron, but it later becomes known as a muon to distinguish it from Yukawa's meson.

1936: National Wildlife Federation established.

1937: Emilio Segre and Carlo Perrier bombard molybdenum with deuterons and neutrons to produce element 43, technetium. This is the first element to be prepared artificially.

1939: Leo Szilard and Walter Henry Zinn confirm that fission reactions (nuclear chain reactions) can be self-sustaining using uranium.

1939: Linus Carl Pauling publishes *The Nature of the Chemical Bond*, a classic work that becomes one of the most influential chemical texts of the twentieth century.

1939: Lise Meitner and Otto Robert Frisch suggest the theory that uranium breaks into smaller atoms when bombarded. Meitner offers the term *fission* for this process.

1939: Niels Hendrik David Bohr proposes a liquid-drop model of the atomic nucleus and offers his theory of the mechanism of fission. His prediction that it is the uranium-235 isotope that undergoes fission is proved correct when work on an atomic bomb begins in the U.S.

1942: Grote Reber constructs radio map of the sky.

1942: Enrico Fermi heads a Manhattan Project team at the University of Chicago that produces the first controlled chain reaction in an atomic pile of uranium and graphite. With this first self-sustaining chain reaction, the atomic age begins.

1943: Alaska Highway completed, linking lower United States and Alaska.

1943: First operational nuclear reactor is activated at the Oak Ridge National Laboratory in Oak Ridge, Tennessee.

1943: J. Robert Oppenheimer is placed in charge of United States atomic bomb production at Los Alamos, New Mexico. He supervises the work of 4,500 scientists and oversees the successful design construction and explosion of the bomb.

1944: Norman Borlaug begins his work on high-yielding crop varieties.

1944: Otto Hahn receives the Nobel Prize in Chemistry for his discovery of nuclear fission.

1945: First atomic bomb is detonated by the U.S. near Almagordo, New Mexico. The experimental bomb generates an explosive power equivalent to 15–20 thousand tons of TNT.

1945: Joshua Lederberg and Edward L. Tatum demonstrate genetic recombination in bacteria.

1945: U.S. destroys the Japanese city of Hiroshima with a nuclear fission bomb based on uranium-235 on August 6. Three days later, a plutonium-based bomb destroys the city of Nagasaki. This is the first use of nuclear power as a weapon.

1946: Atomic Energy Commission established to study the applications of nuclear power. It was later dissolved in 1975, and its responsibilities were transferred to the Nuclear Regulatory Commission and Energy Research and Development Administration.

1946: George Gamow proposes the Big Bang hypothesis.

1946: U.S. Bureau of Land Management created.

1947: A U.S. aircraft travels faster than the speed of sound.

1947: Defenders of Wildlife founded, superseding Defenders of Furbearers and the Anti-Steel-Trap League, to protect wild animals and their habitat.

1947: First carbon-14 dating.

1948: George Gamow and others assert theory of nucleosynthesis is consistent with the big bang theory.

1949: Aldo Leopold publishes *A Sand County Almanac*, in which he sets guidelines for the conservation movement and introduces the concept of a land ethic.

1950–1999

1950: Jan Oort offers explanation of origin of comets.

1952: First thermo-nuclear device is exploded successfully by the U.S. at Eniwetok Atoll in the South Pacific. This hydrogen-fusion bomb (H bomb) is the first such bomb to work by nuclear fusion.

1952: First use of isotopes in medicine.

1952: Oregon becomes first state to adopt a significant program to control air pollution.

1953: James D. Watson and Francis H. C. Crick publish two landmark papers in the journal *Nature*: "Molecular structure of nucleic acids: a structure for deoxyribose nucleic acid" and "Genetical implications of the structure of deoxyribonucleic acid." Watson and Crick propose a double helical model for DNA and call attention to the genetic implications of their model.

1953: Stanley Miller produces amino acids from inorganic compounds similar to those in primitive atmosphere with electrical sparks that simulate lightning.

1954: Humane Society founded in United States.

1954: Linus Carl Pauling receives the Nobel Prize in Chemistry for his research into the nature of the chemical bond and its applications to the elucidation of the structure of complex substances.

1955: First synthetic diamonds are produces in the General Electric Laboratories.

1956: Construction of Echo Park Dam on the Colorado River is aborted, due in large part to the efforts of environmentalists.

1957: Francis Crick proposed that during protein formation each amino acid was carried to the template by an adapter molecule containing nucleotides and that the adapter was the part that actually fits on the RNA template. Later research demonstrated the existence of transfer RNA.

1957: Soviet Union launches Earth's first artificial satellite, Sputnik, into earth orbit.

1958: Martin Ryle argues evidence for evolution of distant cosmological radio sources.

1958: George W. Beadle, Edward L. Tatum, and Joshua Lederberg were awarded the Nobel Prize in Medicine or Physiology. Beadle and Tatum were honored for the work in *Neurospora* that led to the one gene-one enzyme theory. Lederberg was honored for discoveries concerning genetic recombination and the organization of the genetic material of bacteria.

1958: National Aeronautics and Space Administration (NASA) established .

1959: Soviet Space program sends space probe to impact Moon.

1959: St. Lawrence Seaway is completed, linking the Atlantic Ocean to the Great Lakes.

1961: Agent Orange is sprayed in Southeast Asia, exposing nearly 3 million American servicemen to dioxin, a probable carcinogen.

1961: Edward Lorenz advances chaos theory and offers possible implications on atmospheric dynamics and weather.

1961: Murray Gell-Mann and YuvalNe'Eman independently introduce a new way to classify heavy subatomic particles. Gell-Mann names it the *eightfold* way, and this system accomplishes for elementary particles what the periodic table did for the elements.

1961: Soviet Union launches first cosmonaut, Yuri Gagarin, into Earth orbit.

1962: James D. Watson, Francis Crick, and Maurice Wilkins are awarded the Nobel Prize in Medicine or Physiology for their work in elucidating the structure of DNA.

1962: *Silent Spring* published by Rachel Carson to document the effects of pesticides on the environment.

1963: First Clean Air Act passed in the United States.

1963: Fred Vine and Drummond Matthews offer important proof of plate tectonics by discovering that oceanic crust rock layers show equidistant bands of magnetic orientation centered on the site of sea floor spreading.

1963: Nuclear Test Ban Treaty signed by the United States and the Soviet Union to stop atmospheric testing of nuclear weapons.

1964: Wilderness Act passed, which protects wild areas in the United States.

1965: Arno Allan Penzias and Robert Woodrow Wilson detect cosmic background radiation.

1965: Water Quality Act passed, establishing federal water quality standards.

1966: Eighty people die in New York City due to pollution-related causes.

1966: Marshall Nirenberg and Har Gobind Khorana lead teams that decipher the genetic code. All of the sixty-four possible triplet combinations of the four bases (the codons) and their associated amino acids are determined and described.

1967: American Cetacean Society founded to protect whales, dolphins, porpoises, and other cetaceans.

1967: Environmental Defense Fund established to save the osprey from DDT.

1967: Supertanker Torrey Canyon spills oil off the coast of England.

1968: Wild and Scenic Rivers Act and National Trails System Act passed to protect scenic areas from development.

1969: Apollo 11 mission to the Moon. U.S. astronauts Neil Armstrong and Buzz Aldran become first humans to walk on the moon.

1969: Greenpeace founded.

1969: Max Delbrück, Alfred D. Hershey, and Salvador E. Luria awarded the Nobel Prize in Medicine or Physiology for their discoveries concerning the replication mechanism and the genetic structure of viruses.

1970: Environmental Protection Agency (EPA) created.

1970: First Earth Day celebrated on April 22.

1970: National Environmental Policy Act passed, requiring environmental impact statements for projects funded or regulated by federal government.

1971: Consultative Group on International Agricultural Research (CGIAR) founded to improve food production in developing countries.

1972: Clean Water Act passed.

1972: Coastal Zone Management Act and Marine Protection, Research, and Sanctuaries Act passed.

1972: Discovery of 2 million year old humanlike fossil, *Homo habilis*, in Africa.

1972: *Limits to Growth* published by the Club of Rome, calling for population control.

1972: Oregon becomes first state to enact bottle-recycling law.

1972: Paul Berg and Herbert Boyer produce the first recombinant DNA molecules. Recombinant technology emerges as one of the most powerful techniques of molecular biology.

1972: UN Conference on the Human Environment held in Stockholm to address environmental issues on a global level.

1972: Use of DDT is phased out in the United States.

1973: Arab members of the Organization of Petroleum Exporting Countries (OPEC) institute an embargo preventing shipments of oil to the United States.

1973: Convention on International Trade in Endangered Species of Wild Fauna and Flora (CITES) signed to prevent the international trade of endangered or threatened animals and plants.

1973: Cousteau Society founded by Jacques-Yves Cousteau and his son to educate the public and conduct research on marine-related issues.

1973: E. F. Schumacher publishes *Small Is Beautiful*, which advocates simplicity, self-reliance, and living in harmony with nature.

1973: Endangered Species Act passed.

1974: Safe Drinking Water Act passed, requiring EPA to set quality standards for the nations drinking water.

1975: Atlantic salmon is found in the Connecticut River after a 100-year absence.

1975: Scientists at an international meeting in Asilomar, California, call for the adoption of guidelines regulating recombinant DNA experimentation.

1975: Edward Abbey publishes *The Monkey Wrench Gang* which advocates radical and controversial methods for protecting the environment, including "ecotage."

1976: Land Institute founded by Wes and Dana Jackson to encourage more natural and organic agricultural practices.

1976: Poisonous gas containing 2,4,5-TCP and dioxin is released from a factory in Seveso, Italy, causing massive animal and plant death. Although no human life was lost, a sharp increase in deformed births was reported.

1976: Resource Conservation and Recovery Act passed, giving EPA authority to regulate municipal solid and hazardous waste.

1976: U.S. Viking spacecraft lands and conducts experiments on Mars.

1977: Robotic submarine "Alvin" explored mid-oceanic ridge and discovered chemosynthetic life.

1977: Voyager spacecraft launched containing golden record recording of Earth sounds.

1978: Oil tanker *Amoco Cadiz* runs aground, spilling 220,000 tons of oil.

1978: Residents of Love Canal, New York, are evacuated after Lois Gibbs discovers that the community was once the site of a chemical waste dump.

1979: Three Mile Island Nuclear Reactor almost undergoes nuclear melt-down when the cooling water systems fail. Since this accident no new nuclear power plants have been built in the United States.

1980: Alaska National Interest Lands Conservation Act enacted, setting aside millions of acres of land as wilderness.

1980: Comprehensive Environmental Response, Compensation, and Liability Act (Superfund) enacted to clean up abandoned toxic waste sites.

1980: Earth First! founded by Dave Foreman, with the slogan "No compromise in the defense of Mother Earth."

1980: *Global 2000 Report* published, documenting trends in population growth, natural resource depletion, and the environment.

1980: Mount St. Helens explodes.

1980: Thomas Lovejoy proposes the idea of debt-for-nature swap that helps developing countries alleviate national debt by implementing policies to protect the environment.

1984: Emission of poisonous methyl isocyanate vapor, a chemical by-product of agricultural insecticide production, from the Union Carbide plant kills more than 2800 people in Bhopal, India.

1984: Ozone hole over Antarctica discovered.

1985: Rainforest Action Network founded.

1986: Chernobyl Nuclear Power Station undergoes nuclear core melt-down, spreading radioactive material over vast parts of the Soviet Union and northern Europe.

1986: Evacuation of Times Beach, Missouri, due to high levels of dioxin.

1987: *Ecodefense: A Field Guide to Monkeywrenching* published by Dave Foreman, in which he describes spiking trees and other "environmental sabotage" techniques.

1987: Montreal Protocol on Substances that Deplete the Ozone Layer signed by 24 nations, declaring their promise to decrease production of chlorofluorocarbons (CFCs).

1987: *Our Common Future* (The Brundtland Report) is published.

1987: World population reaches five billion.

1987: Yucca Mountain designated the first permanent repository for radioactive waste by the U.S. Department of Energy.

1988: Global ReLeaf program inaugurated with the motto "Plant a tree, cool the globe" to address the problem of global warming.

1988: Ocean Dumping Ban Act established.

1988: The Human Genome Organization (HUGO) is established by scientists in order to coordinate international efforts to sequence the human genome. The Human Genome Project officially adopts the goal of determining the entire sequence of DNA comprising the human chromosomes.

1989: Oil tanker *Exxon Valdez* runs aground in Prince William Sound, Alaska, spilling 11 million gallons of oil.

1990: Clean Air Act amended to control emissions of sulfur dioxide and nitrogen oxides.

1990: Hubble Space Telescope launched.

1990: Oil Pollution Act signed, setting liability and penalty system for oil spills as well as a trust fund for clean up efforts.

1991: Andrew A. Griffith, American chemist, uses an atomic force microscope to obtain extraordinarily detailed images of the electrochemical reactions involved in corrosion.

1991: K-T event impact crater identified near the Yucatan Peninsula.

1991: Mount Pinatubo in Philippines erupts, shooting sulfur dioxide 25 miles into the atmosphere.

1991: Over 4,000 people die from cholera in Latin American epidemic.

1991: Persian Gulf War begins. During the war, Saddam Hussein burns oil fields.

1991: Train containing the pesticide *meta sodium* falls off the tracks near Dunsmuir, California, releasing chemicals into the Sacramento River. Plant and aquatic life for forty-three miles downriver die as a result.

1992: Captive-bred California condors and black-footed ferrets reintroduced into the wild.

1992: Mexico City suffers general shut down as a result of incapacitating air pollution.

1992: UN Earth Summit held in Rio de Janeiro, Brazil.

1992: UN calls for an end to global drift net fishing by the end of 1992.

1993: Oil tanker runs aground in the Shetland Islands, Scotland, spilling its oil into the sea.

1993: Eight people from Biosphere 2 emerge after living for two years in a self-sustaining, glass dome.

1993: Forest Summit convened in Portland, Oregon, by President Bill Clinton, who met with loggers and environmentalists concerned with the survival of the northern spotted owl.

1993: George Washington University researchers clone human embryos and nurtured them in a Petri dish for several days. The project provokes protests from ethicists, politicians and critics of genetic engineering.

1993: Norway resumes hunting of minke whales in defiance of a ban on commercial whaling instituted by the International Whaling Commission.

1994: Astronomers observed comet Shoemaker-Levy 9 (S-L 9) colliding with Jupiter.

1994: Researchers at Fermilab discover the top quark. Scientists believe that this discovery may provide clues about the genesis of matter.

1995: Ken-Sara Wiwa is executed in Nigeria for protesting and speaking out about oil industry practices in the country.

1995: Michel Mayor and Didier Queloz identify first extra-solar planet, a Jupiter-like planet orbiting an ordinary star.

1995: Paul Crutzen, Mario Molina, and R. Sherwood Rowland receive the Nobel Prize in Chemistry for their work in atmospheric chemistry, particularly concerning the formation and decomposition of ozone.

1997: Forest fires worldwide burn a total of five million hectares of forest.

1997: Julia "Butterfly" Hill climbs a 180 ft (55 m) redwood tree in California to protest the logging of the surrounding forest as well as to protect the tree. Hill removed herself from the tree in 1999 after she negotiated a deal to save the tree and an additional three acres of the forest.

1997: Kyoto Protocol mandates a reduction of reported 1990 emissions levels by 6–8 percent by 2008.

1997: Microscopic analysis of Murchison meteorite led some scientists to argue evidence of ancient life on Mars.

1997: Monserrat volcano erupts.

1998: Ian Wilmut announced the birth of Polly, a transgenic lamb containing human genes.

1998: Two research teams succeeded in growing embryonic stem cells.

1999: Scientists announce the complete sequencing of the DNA making up human chromosome 22. The first complete human chromosome sequence is published in December 1999.

1999: World population reaches six billion.

1999: World Trade Organization (WTO) conference in Seattle, Washington, marked by heavy protests, highlighting WTO's weak environmental policies.

2000–

2000: During his presidency, Bill Clinton appropriated a total of 58 million acres of wilderness as conservation land—the largest amount of land to be set aside for conservation by any other president to date.

2000: Russian nuclear submarine the Kursk sinks off the coast of Minsk, Russia. Despite concerns, no nuclear waste escapes.

2000: West Nile virus discovered in the eastern United States.

2000: On June 26, 2000, leaders of the public genome project and Celera announce the completion of a working draft of the entire human genome sequence. Ari Patrinos of the DOE helps mediate disputes between the two groups so that a fairly amicable joint announcement could be presented at the White House in Washington, DC.

2000: The National Cancer Institute (NCI) estimates that 3,000 lung cancer deaths, and as many as 40,000 cardiac deaths per year among adult non-smokers in the United States can be attributed to passive smoke or environmental tobacco smoke (ETS).

2001: In February 2001, the complete draft sequence of the human genome was published. The public sequence data was published in the British journal *Nature* and the sequence obtained by Celera was published in the American journal *Science*.

2001: The U.S. fails to ratify the Kyoto Protocol.

2001: The World Trade Center towers in New York collapse after being struck by two commercial airplanes commandeered by terrorists. A third airplane is crashed into the Pentagon building just outside Washington, D.C., causing loss of life and major damage to the building.

2002: EPA adopts California emissions standards for off-road recreation vehicles to be implemented by 2004.

2002: EPA announces its Strategic Plan for Homeland Security to support the National Strategy for Homeland Security enacted after the September 11, 2001 terrorist attacks in the United States.

2002: President George W. Bush introduces the Clear Sky Initiative.

2002: President George W. Bush signs Bill approving the using of Yucca Mountain as a nuclear waste storage site.

2002: Satellites capture images of icebergs more than ten times the size of Manhattan Island breaking off the Antarctic ice shelf.

2002: Traces of biological and chemical weapon agents are found in Uzbekistan on a military base used by U.S. troops fighting in Afghanistan. Early analysis dates and attributes the source of the contamination to former Soviet Union biological and chemical weapons programs that utilized the base.

2002: Severe Acute Respiratory Syndrome (SARS) virus is found in patients in China, Hong Kong, and other Asian countries. The newly discovered corona virus is not identified until early 2003. The spread of the virus reaches epidemic proportions in Asia and expands to the rest of the world.

2002: UN Earth Summit held in Johannesburg, South Africa.

2003: Three Gorges Dam in China begins filling.

2003: U.S. invades Iraq and finds chemical, biological, and nuclear weapons programs but no actual weapons.

2003: Energy bill introduced in Congress includes ethanol use mandates.

2003: Electric power failure causes blackout from New York to Ontario.

2003: EPA rejects petition to regulate emissions from vehicles, EPS claims lack of authority under the Clean Air Act.

2004: Russia ratifies Kyoto treating, putting it into effect worldwide even without United States ratification.

2004: Kenyan environmentalist and human rights activist Wangari Maathai wins the Nobel Peace Prize.

2004: On December 26, the most powerful earthquake in more than 40 years occurred underwater off the Indonesian island of Sumatra. The tsunami produced a disaster of unprecedented proportion in the modern era. Less than two weeks after the tsunami impact, the International Red Cross put the death toll at over 150,000 lives and most experts expected that number to continue to climb. Many experts claim this will be the costliest, longest, and most difficult recovery period ever endured as a result of a natural disaster.

2005: Kyoto Protocol officially goes into force Feb. 16, 2005.

2005: H5N1 virus, responsible for avian flu, moves from Asia to Europe. The World Health Organization attempts to coordinate multinational disaster and containment plans. Some nations begin to stockpile antiviral drugs.

2005: Hurricane Katrina slams into the U.S. Gulf Coast, causing levee breaks and massive flooding of New Orleans. Damage is extensive across the coasts of Louisiana, Mississippi and Alabama. Federal Emergency Management Agency (FEMA) is wdiely criticized for a lack of coordination in relief efforts. Three other major hurricanes make landfall in the U.S. within a two year period stressing relief and medical supply efforts. Long term health studies begin of populations in devastated areas.

2005: A massive 7.6-magnitude earthquake leaves more than 3 million homeless and without food and basic medical supplies in the Kashmir mountains between India and Pakistan. 80,000 people die.

Roots of Environmental and Ecological Thought

Ancient religions usually connected human life with natural annual cycles of crop planting and harvesting, weather, the moon and sun, and animal fertility. Some early religious texts contain directives to preserve the sources of fertility. One such provision, for example, states that eggs and young birds may be harvested from birds' nests in the wild. However, the mother must be left untouched, presumably to produce more eggs and young. There are even warnings against overdevelopment.

Early tribes and civilizations maintained a religion-centered sense of connection to the earth and responsibility for its well being. They believed it was wise to pay close attention to the natural processes around them. Continuous attention to plants and animals produced an intimate awareness of the natural world, which yielded thousands of herbal remedies and helped establish the basic varieties of domesticated plants and animals existing today.

In the 1700s, the science of biology exploded with new discoveries. Swedish botanist Carl Linnaeus (1707–1778) developed a vast classification system for living things, still in use today. The European imperial powers launched investigative voyages throughout the world to look for resources to exploit. Many of these vessels carried a biologist on board. Human knowledge of the living world became systematic; at the same time it expanded beyond the local and traditional forms of knowledge that had always existed. Scientific knowledge about life on Earth became detailed enough to allow a sense of how the web of life interacts.

British naturalist Charles Darwin (1809–1882) furthered this sense of life as an interconnected web in the mid-1800s, especially with his book *On the Origin of Species* (1859). He argued that interactions with other living things are among the most important factors shaping the course of natural selection. Western thinkers were quickly learning to see living communities as self-interacting, self-shaping, and self-sustaining—the essence of "ecological" thought. The word "ecology" itself was coined c. 1870 by German biologist and Darwin supporter Ernst Haeckel (1834–1919).

However, there is more to environmental thought than just an awareness of nature. There is fear of the harm that human beings can do to it. The Industrial Revolution, by wreaking immense violence on the landscape, showed that human beings were not only part of the natural world, but a threat to it. In the early 1800s, British poet William Blake (1757–1827) spoke of the "dark Satanic Mills" belching air and water pollution in Great Britain. In 1859, American author Henry David Thoreau (1817–1862) wrote *Walden*. Comparing nature to a vast book, he expressed his grief at finding it mutilated. With fellow American author Ralph Waldo Emerson (1803–1882), Thoreau planted nature-awareness deeply at the heart of American thought.

This section presents writings that helped form the roots of modern environmental and ecological thought—ideas that continue to nurture many branches of social activism and philosophical viewpoints on social issues related to environmental use and abuse.

The Pioneers

Book excerpt

By: James Fenimore Cooper

Date: 1823

Source: Cooper, James Fenimore. *The Pioneers*. New York: G.P. Putnum and Sons, 1823.

About the Author: James Fenimore Cooper (1789–1851) was an American writer and pioneer novelist. He was born in Burlington, New Jersey, on September 15, 1789, to Judge William and Elizabeth Cooper. Their forefathers had immigrated to America in 1679, where Judge Cooper inherited and established large tracts of land in New York and Pennsylvania. Beginning in childhood, Cooper had a liking for pranks and freedom. He and his brothers spent their childhood in the dense woods of upstate New York. The wilderness of the surroundings greatly appealed to him. It was in the Hudson River and central New York region that Cooper came to be in touch with the native Indians. These profound experiences formed an essential foundation for many of his writings in his later life. For two years he studied at Yale, but was expelled from the college as the result of a series of pranks. He then began life as a seaman and first set sail on a ship called *Sterling* bound for Cowes, United Kingdom. His experiences on stormy North Atlantic voyages and his brief commission in the Navy form the background for many of the seafaring novels he wrote years later. Cooper began his writing career in New York, starting with *The Spy* (1821). He wrote nearly fifty other novels and books such as *The Prairie* (1827), *Notions of the Americans* (1828), *A Letter to his Countrymen* (1834), *American Democrat* (1838), *Last of the Mohicans* (1826), *The Pathfinder* (1840), and *The Deerslayer* (1841).

INTRODUCTION

Though Cooper never intended to become a writer, it was the death of his father and a series of other deaths in the family (that of his brothers and sister) that accidentally brought out his writing skills. He inherited a small tract of land and money after his father's death. In 1811, he married Susan Delancy and settled as a gentleman farmer. For nearly ten years, he moved to various locations and ultimately was left devoid of any finances. It was at this time that his wife encouraged him to write and thus his professional literary career was born.

Pioneer villagers defend themselves against Indians, a frequent episode in James Cooper's *Leatherstocking* tales. © BETTMANN/ CORBIS

While studying Cooper, it is useful to understand that his family descended from the Quakers, also called the Society of Friends in Great Britain. The Quakers perceived Christ as the inner light and believed in the reformation of the Church by conducting silent prayer. They did away completely with many customary rituals of the Catholic Church and considered priests and middlemen as barriers between God and humanity. This led to discrimination against them in England and some regions in the United States. The strict principles of the Quakers and their teachings of nonviolence find their way into *The Pioneers*.

Written in 1823, *The Pioneers* is the first book in a five-part series called the *Leatherstocking Novels*. It draws heavily on Cooper's personal experiences from his childhood days and spiritual upbringing. There are many characters in this novel. The prominent ones are Judge Marmaduke Temple, the wealthy emigrant; Elizabeth Temple, his daughter; Natty Bumppo, the ideal native; Mohegan, the great warrior; and Billy Kirby, the wasteful wood chopper.

The themes of the book revolve around American culture, the portrayal and philosophy of American independence, the perception of the whites by native Americans, the wasteful and improper ways of the settlers. Feelings about nature and civilization, advocating conservation and living within means, exhibiting restraint and self-discipline, maintaining public and personal order, and controlling chaos internally and in society are also evident throughout.

▮ PRIMARY SOURCE

. . . Marmaduke had been wandering about the grove, making observations on his favorite trees, and the wasteful manner in which the wood-chopper conducted his manufacture.

"It grieves me to witness the extravagance that pervades this country," said the Judge, "where the settlers trifle with the blessings they might enjoy, with the prodigality of successful adventurers. You are not exempt from the censure yourself, Kirby, for you make dreadful wounds in these trees where a small incision would effect the same object. I earnestly beg you will remember that they are the growth of centuries, and when once gone none living will see their loss remedied."

"Why, I don't know, Judge," returned the man he addressed: "it seems to me, if there's a plenty of anything in this mountaynious country, it's the trees. If there's any sin in chopping them, I've a pretty heavy account to settle, for I've chopped over the best half of a thousand acres with my own hands, counting both Varmount and York States; and I hope to live to finish the hull, before I lay up my axe. Chopping comes quite natural to me, and I wish no other employment; but Jared Ransom said that he thought the sugar was likely to be source this season, seeing that so many folks was coming into the settlement, and so I concluded to take the 'bush' on sheares for this one spring. What's the best news, Judge, consarning ashes? do pots hold so that a man can live by them still? I s'pose they will, if they keep on fighting across the water."

"Thou reasonest with judgment, William," returned Marmaduke. "So long as the old world is to be convulsed with wars, so long will the harvest of America continue."

"Well, it's an ill wind, Judge, that blows nobody any good. I'm sure the country is in a thriving way; and though I know you calkilate greatly on the trees, setting as much store by them as some men would by their children, yet to my eyes they are a sore sight any time, unless I'm priv-

ileged to work my will on them; in which case I can't say but they are more to my liking. I have heard the settlers from the old countries say that their rich men keep great oaks and elms, that would make a barrel of pots to the tree, standing round their doors and humsteds and scattered over their farms, just to look at. Now, I call no country much improved that is pretty well covered with trees. Stumps are a different thing, for they don't shade the land; and, besides, if you dig them, they make a fence that will turn anything bigger than a hog, being grand for breachy cattle."

"Opinions on such subjects vary much in different countries," said Marmaduke; "but it is not as ornaments that I value the noble trees of this country; it is for their usefulness We are stripping the forests, as if a single year would replace what we destroy. But the hour approaches when the laws will take notice of not only the woods, but the game they contain also."

With this consoling reflection, Marmaduke remounted, and the equestrians passed the sugar-camp, on their way to the promised landscape of Richard. The wood-chopper was left alone, in the bosom of the forest, to pursue his labors.

▮▮

SIGNIFICANCE

The Pioneers holds a singular place in American literary history. The book instantly established Cooper as a groundbreaking author. For this matter, though *The Pioneers* was not the first American novel, it was the "pioneer" American novel in many ways.

Until this time, there was a dearth of contemporary American literature. *The Pioneers* found its way directly to the wider U.S. audience, and Cooper bypassed critics with much popular acclaim. Simultaneously, the book belongs to a period that is known for many revolutionary issues and events in U.S. history. Readers, consequently, were able to identify with the characters in the book and relate it to their own experiences and aspirations about their newly adopted nation.

Experts maintain that *The Pioneers* can essentially be classified as a historic romance. It is historic as it describes a significant point in history when the Americans fought off the British colonialists to win the American Revolution. The book reflects the debate in the mind of the pioneer settlers, after the war, about the nature of their government—whether the new country would be a democracy or a republic.

The book revolves around the mindset of its various characters and the conflict of their thoughts with the surrounding environs and wilderness. To put it in simpler terms, the settlers mentioned in the book had issues of land ownership. They wanted to colonize lands that were inhabited by native Indians. At the time, the country also had abundant resources in terms of wild land and forests. The settlers in the book were also faced with the conflict of clearing forests and setting up colonies. In the book, Cooper termed this as "wastefulness" on the part of the settlers.

This is where the significance of the book lies. The issues and conflicts mentioned above were widely prevalent in the country at the time. The settlers engaged themselves in activities such as logging of woods, mass clearing of lands for settlement and farming, and killing of wildlife such as bison and pheasant, as well as other fauna that were considered sacred by native inhabitants, for pleasure and sport.

The book cautioned that excessive utilization of resources would destroy the natural landscape with which the United States had been bestowed. In the twenty-first century, the United States and most countries around the world face various conservation and sustainability issues like power, energy, decreasing domestic oil and gas production, renewable energy, and the growing consumption of natural resources such as paper, metals, and minerals. Natural resources all over the world, including those in the United States, are being used up at a high rate to fuel development and commercialism.

FURTHER RESOURCES

Web sites

Canada, Mark. "James Fenimore Cooper, 1789–1851." *University of North Carolina at Pembroke*. <http://www.uncp.edu/home/canada/work/allam/17841865/lit/cooper/index.htm> (accessed March 15, 2006).

Evans, Sarah, Abby Fifer, and Jenn Reynolds. "James Fenimore Cooper: A Literary Pioneer." *American Studies at the University of Virginia*. <http://xroads.virginia.edu/~ug02/COOPER/toc.html> (accessed March 15, 2006).

"James Fenimore Cooper." *JamesFenimoreCooper.com*. <http://www.jamesfenimorecooper.com> (accessed March 15, 2006).

"James Fenimore Cooper." *The Literature Network*. <http://www.online-literature.com/cooperj> (accessed March 15, 2006).

"James Fenimore Cooper." *Mohican Press*. <http://www.mohicanpress.com/mo08002.html> (accessed March 15, 2006).

"James Fenimore Cooper: The Last of the Mohicans." *University of Wisconsin*. <http://www.uwm.edu/Library/special/exhibits/clastext/clspg134.htm> (accessed March 15, 2006).

Birds of America

Book excerpt

By: John James Audubon

Date: 1842

Source: Audubon, John James. *Birds of America*. Philadelphia: J.B. Chevalier, 1840. Online at <http://www.audubon.org/bird/BoA/introduction.html> (accessed on March 10, 2006).

About the Author: Born in Haiti and raised in France, American ornithologist and naturalist John James Audubon (1785–1851) showed a great inclination for drawing as a boy, and was sent by his father to study with the French Neoclassical painter, Jacques-Louis David (1748–1825). Audubon left France in 1803, at the age of eighteen, in order to avoid serving in Napoleon's army and settled near Philadelphia, Pennsylvania. There he hunted and cultivated his interests in drawing and birds. Traveling through North America, Audubon studied birds closely as they moved about in their natural environments. His monumental study of the birds of America was published in four volumes in Edinburgh and London between 1827 and 1838, and became popular throughout Europe and America. *Birds of America* contained 1,065 paintings of individual birds. After publishing the prints, Audubon worked with the Scottish ornithologist William MacGillivray writing *Ornithological Biographies*—life histories of the birds he had painted.

INTRODUCTION

In Audubon's paintings, birds are dramatically posed and brilliantly colored. More than rendering anatomically precise and authentic reproductions, which he did, Audubon attempted to represent birds as they were in nature, in action, conveying their nervous dynamic in a still picture. The birds were not painted against a blank background but in their environment, interacting with each other. Audubon's prose has the same meticulous concern for detail as his paintings, as well as the same impulse to get inside the bird, to show living birds in their natural habitat.

In the following account of the ivory-billed woodpecker, Audubon shows the variety of his interest and the great range of his skill and knowledge. He describes the woodpecker's environment as if he were painting it and as it would appear to someone inside that environment, drawing the reader to experience it

Illustration of the *Roseate Spoonbill*, engraved by Robert Havell Jr. and published in *Birds of America* by John James Audubon. © BETTMANN/CORBIS

as nearly as possible through a prose rendering. Whether he is tracing the pattern of the bird's flight; describing the mechanics of flying; watching the woodpeckers build their nest and interact with each other; describing the bird's eating habits; offering ornithological, anatomical, and environmental data; or describing the woodpecker's experience of death, Audubon's command of his subject reveals the intensity and closeness of his own observation.

His painting and his prose both reveal that Audubon was not a detached observer of nature. He physically ventured into out-of-the-way places to see birds and imaginatively traveled into the realm of the bird itself. His greatest power was the power of minute observation; his greatest skill, the ability to convey it through images and words.

■ PRIMARY SOURCE

... I wish, kind reader, it were in my power to present to your mind's eye the favourite resort of the Ivory-billed Woodpecker. Would that I could describe the extent of those deep morasses, overshadowed by millions of gigantic dark cypresses, spreading their sturdy moss-covered branches, as if to admonish intruding man to pause and reflect on the many difficulties which he must encounter, should he persist in venturing farther into their almost inaccessible recesses, extending for miles before him, where he should be interrupted by huge projecting branches, here and there the massy trunk of a fallen and decaying tree, and thousands of creeping and twining plants of numberless species! Would that I could represent to you the dangerous nature of the ground, its oozing,

spongy, and miry disposition, although covered with a beautiful but treacherous carpeting, composed of the richest mosses, flags, and water-lilies, no sooner receiving the pressure of the foot than it yields and endangers the very life of the adventurer, whilst here and there, as he approaches an opening, that proves merely a lake of black muddy water, his ear is assailed by the dismal croaking of innumerable frogs, the hissing of serpents, or the bellowing of alligators! Would that I could give you an idea of the sultry pestiferous atmosphere that nearly suffocates the intruder during the meridian heat of our dogdays, in those gloomy and horrible swamps! But the attempt to picture these scenes would be vain. . . .

The flight of this bird is graceful in the extreme, although seldom prolonged to more than a few hundred yards at a time, unless when it has to cross a large river, which it does in deep undulations, opening its wings at first to their full extent, and nearly closing them to renew the propelling impulse. The transit from one tree to another, even should the distance be as much as a hundred yards, is performed by a single sweep, and the bird appears as if merely swinging itself from the top of the one tree to that of the other, forming an elegantly curved line. At this moment all the beauty of the plumage is exhibited, and strikes the beholder with pleasure. It never utters any sound whilst on wing, unless during the love-season; but at all other times, no sooner has this bird alighted than its remarkable voice is heard, at almost every leap which it makes, whilst ascending against the upper parts of the trunk of a tree, or its highest branches. Its notes are clear, loud, and yet rather plaintive. They are heard at a considerable distance, perhaps half a mile, and resemble the false high note of a clarionet. They are usually repeated three times in succession, and may be represented by the monosyllable pait, pait, pait. These are heard so frequently as to induce me to say that the bird spends few minutes of the day without uttering them, and this circumstance leads to its destruction, which is aimed at, not because (as is supposed by some) this species is a destroyer of trees, but more because it is a beautiful bird, and its rich scalp attached to the upper mandible forms an ornament for the war-dress of most of our Indians, or for the shot-pouch of our squatters and hunters. . .

The Ivory-billed Woodpecker nestles earlier in spring than any other species of its tribe. I have observed it boring a hole for that purpose in the beginning of March. The hole is, I believe, always made in the trunk of a live tree, generally an ash or a hagberry, and is at a great height. The birds pay great regard to the particular situation of the tree, and the inclination of its trunk; first, because they prefer retirement, and again, because they are anxious to secure the aperture against the access of water during beating rains. . . .

Both birds [male and female] work most assiduously at this excavation, one waiting outside to encourage the other, whilst it is engaged in digging, and when the latter is fatigued, taking its place. I have approached trees whilst these Woodpeckers were thus busily employed in forming their nest, and by resting my head against the bark, could easily distinguish every blow given by the bird. I observed that in two instances, when the Woodpeckers saw me thus at the foot of the tree in which they were digging their nest, they abandoned it for ever. For the first brood there are generally six eggs. They are deposited on a few chips at the bottom of the hole, and are of a pure white colour. The young are seen creeping out of the hole about a fortnight before they venture to fly to any other tree. . . .

The food of this species consists principally of beetles, larvae, and large grubs. No sooner, however, are the grapes of our forests ripe than they are eaten by the Ivory-billed Woodpecker with great avidity. I have seen this bird hang by its claws to the vines, in the position so often assumed by a Titmouse, and, reaching downwards, help itself to a bunch of grapes with much apparent pleasure. . . .

The Ivory-bill is never seen attacking the corn, or the fruit of the orchards, although it is sometimes observed working upon and chipping off the bark from the belted trees of the newly-cleared plantations. It seldom comes near the ground, but prefers at all times the tops of the tallest trees. Should it, however, discover the half-standing broken shaft of a large dead and rotten tree, it attacks it in such a manner as nearly to demolish it in the course of a few days. . . . The strength of this Woodpecker is such, that I have seen it detach pieces of bark seven or eight inches in length at a single blow of its powerful bill, and by beginning at the top branch of a dead tree, tear off the bark, to an extent of twenty or thirty feet, in the course of a few hours, leaping downwards with its body in an upward position, tossing its head to the right and left, or leaning it against the bark to ascertain the precise spot where the grubs were concealed, and immediately after renewing its blows with fresh vigour, all the while sounding its loud notes, as if highly delighted. . . .

When wounded and brought to the ground, the Ivory-bill immediately makes for the nearest tree, and ascends it with great rapidity and perseverance, until it reaches the top branches, when it squats and hides, generally with great effect. Whilst ascending, it moves spirally round the tree, utters its loud pait, pait, pait, at almost every hop, but becomes silent the moment it reaches a place where it conceives itself secure. They sometimes cling to the bark with their claws so firmly, as to remain cramped to the spot for several hours after death. When taken by the hand, which is rather a hazardous undertaking, they strike with great violence, and inflict very severe wounds with their bill as well as claws, which are extremely sharp and

John James Audubon, author of *Birds of America.* AP IMAGES

strong. On such occasions, this bird utters a mournful and very piteous cry.

SIGNIFICANCE

In his study, his painting, and his biographies of the birds of America, Audubon created more than a decorative, descriptive catalogue of birds. He rendered a map of the natural environment of America, of its forests, marshes, and swamps; of its dark, nearly unapproachable regions; of its insects and its trees, and of its birds. His work served as a bridge for the human species to cross in order to enter a new and unexplored territory, one that was more than a land mass, but a living environment that people were endeavoring to appropriate, to become part of, and to make theirs. Audubon showed the contours and the nature of this world. As much as the great territorial explorers who revealed both the vastness and the wonders of the North American continent, Audubon, through his exploration and his art, revealed the diversity and the particularities of the continent's natural environment. He also simply made a record of the continent's environmental wealth, not only regarding its birds, but their habitats as well.

Audubon's inventory and the wonders it presented inspired a preservationist consciousness in Americans, one that was expressed concretely through the formation of the Audubon Society for the Protection of Birds in 1886 by American naturalist George Bird Grinnell (1849–1938). Grinnell's group, which he soon disbanded because its membership became too large for him to handle, was the beginning of the National Audubon Society, founded in 1905. From its beginning as a society of bird lovers dedicated to safeguarding birds, the Audubon Society has grown into a citizen's organization devoted to environmental protection and conservation as well as bird-watching and education.

FURTHER RESOURCES

Books

John James Audubon in the West: The Last Expedition, Mammals of North America, edited by Sarah E. Boehme. New York: Harry N. Abrams/Buffalo Bill Historical Center, 2000.

Rhodes, Richard. *Audubon: The Making of an American*. New York: Alfred A. Knopf, 2004.

Souder, William. *Under a Wild Sky: John James Audubon and the Making of the Birds of America*. New York: North Point Press, 2004.

Steiner, Bill. *Audubon Art Prints: A Collector's Guide to Every Edition*. Columbia, SC: University of South Carolina Press, 2003.

Web sites

Audubon society. <http://www.audubon.org> (accessed November 14, 2005).

Walden

Book excerpt

By: Henry David Thoreau

Date: 1854

Source: Thoreau, Henry David. *Walden*. Boston: Houghton, Mifflin and Company, 1854.

About the Author: American essayist, poet, naturalist, outdoorsman, and social philosopher, Henry David Thoreau (1817–1862) was educated at Harvard in Cambridge, Massachusetts. There, he came under the influence of the New England Transcendentalists, who believed in the essential spiritual unity of man and nature, that there was one common soul shared by all creation. His reading of Ralph Waldo Emerson's *Nature* particularly shaped Thoreau's thought. A man of proud self-sufficiency and dedicated to the sanctity of the individual conscience, Thoreau felt compelled by his own beliefs to live a life close to nature and in conformity to his own principles rather than to follow convention. Thus, in the spring of 1845, when he wanted to write a book about his adventures during an 1839 canoe trip on the Concord and Merrimac rivers, he built a cabin in the woods near Walden Pond and lived in semi-seclusion for two years. He recorded all the aspects of his environment, his own sensations and his responses to the Walden woods. From his experience and observation, he drew a credo for a life, which he thought of as deliberate, simple, and in accord with nature and the promptings of individual conscience. Thoreau left Walden in 1847 but continued to explore the natural environment, particularly the Maine woods, and to think, write, and lecture about the relationship between mankind and nature.

INTRODUCTION

While Thoreau's dedication to a self-reliant exile reflected a temperament inclined to that kind of life, it was also in large part a conscious act of rebellion intended to be highly visible. In addition to *Walden*, Thoreau also wrote *Civil Disobedience* in 1849, an essay about his refusal to pay a poll tax. He was solitary in a very public way, and his withdrawal into the woods around Walden Pond was not only an experiment in simple and deliberate living—a kind of early version of Teddy Roosevelt's "strenuous life" or an attempt to commune with Emerson's world soul—but an exercise in political economy and social morality. It was designed to serve as a criticism of and an alternative to the way of life practiced by his contemporaries.

Thoreau argues that the quality of our relationship to our environment provides a more reliable indication of the quality of our economic situation than either the kind of technology we employ or the goods we consume. Consequently, he asserts, people may be "richer" living in an apparently primitive culture with fewer goods than in an advanced industrial culture.

Using the railroad as an example, Thoreau illustrates how the beauty and excitement of technology can coexist with and within natural phenomena. He then argues that technology can be faulted when people undercut the economy and rhythm of the natural environment by using technology for bad

The view from Henry D. Thoreau's cottage home in the woods, Walden Pond. © BETTMANN/CORBIS

social, political, and economic ends, essentially betraying their own nature and diminishing the natural environment.

PRIMARY SOURCE

In the savage state every family owns a shelter as good as the best, and sufficient for its coarser and simpler wants; but I think that I speak within bounds when I say that, though the birds of the air have their nests, and the foxes their holes, and the savages their wigwams, in modern civilized society not more than one half the families own a shelter. In the large towns and cities, where civilization especially prevails, the number of those who own a shelter is a very small fraction of the whole. The rest pay an annual tax for this outside garment of all, become indispensable summer and winter, which would buy a village of Indian wigwams, but now helps to keep them poor as long as they live. I do not mean to insist here on the disadvantage of hiring compared with owning, but it is evident that the savage owns his shelter because it costs so little, while the civilized man hires his commonly because he cannot afford to own it; nor can he, in the long run, any better afford to hire. But, answers one, by merely paying this tax, the poor civilized man secures an abode which is a palace compared with the savage's. An annual rent of from twenty-five to a hundred dollars (these are the country rates) entitles him to the benefit of the improvements of centuries, spacious apartments, clean paint and paper, Rumford fire-place, back plastering, Venetian blinds, copper pump, spring lock, a commodious cellar, and many other things. But how happens it that he who is said to enjoy these things is so commonly a *poor* civilized man, while the savage, who has them not, is rich as a savage? If it is asserted that civilization is a real advance in the condition of man,—and I think that it is, though only the wise improve their advantages,—it must be shown that it has produced better dwellings without making them more costly; and the cost of a thing is the amount of what I will call life which is required to be exchanged for it, immediately or in the long run. An average house in this neighborhood costs perhaps eight hundred dollars, and to lay up this sum will take from ten to fifteen years of the laborer's life, even if he is not encumbered with a family,—estimating the pecuniary value of every man's labor at one dollar a day, for if some receive more, others receive less;—so that he must have spent more than half his life commonly before his wigwam will be earned. If we suppose him to pay a rent instead, this is but a doubtful choice of evils. Would the savage have been wise to exchange his wigwam for a palace on these terms?...

The Fitchburg Railroad touches the pond about a hundred rods south of where I dwell....

The whistle of the locomotive penetrates my woods summer and winter, sounding like the scream of a hawk sailing over some farmer's yard, informing me that many restless city merchants are arriving within the circle of the town, or adventurous country traders from the other side....Here come your groceries, country; your rations, countrymen!...And here's your pay for them! screams the countryman's whistle; timber like long battering-rams going twenty miles an hour against the city's walls, and chairs enough to seat all the weary and heavy laden that dwell within them....All the Indian huckleberry hills are stripped, all the cranberry meadows are raked into the city. Up comes the cotton, down goes the woven cloth; up comes the silk, down goes the woollen; up come the books, but down goes the wit that writes them.

When I meet the engine with its train of cars moving off with planetary motion,...with its steam cloud like a banner streaming behind in golden and silver wreaths, like many a downy cloud which I have seen, high in the heavens, unfolding its masses to the light,—as if this traveling demigod, this cloud-compeller, would ere long take the sunset sky for the livery of his train; when I hear the iron horse make the hills echo with his snort like thunder, shaking the earth with his feet, and breathing fire and smoke from his nostrils,...it seems as if the earth had got a race now worthy to inhabit it. If all were as it seems, and men made the elements their servants for noble ends! If the cloud that hangs over the engine were the perspiration of heroic deeds, or as beneficent as that which floats over the farmer's fields, then the elements and Nature herself would cheerfully accompany men on their errands and be their escort.

I watch the passage of the morning cars with the same feeling that I do the rising of the sun, which is hardly more regular. Their train of clouds stretching far behind and rising higher and higher, going to heaven while the cars are going to Boston, conceals the sun for a minute and casts my distant field into the shade, a celestial train beside which the petty train of cars which hugs the earth is but the barb of the spear. The stabler of the iron horse was up early this winter morning by the light of the stars amid the mountains, to fodder and harness his steed. Fire, too, was awakened thus early to put the vital

Replica of Henry D. Thoreau's cabin at Walden Pond, in Concord, Massachusetts. AP IMAGES

heat in him and get him off. If the enterprise were as innocent as it is early!

SIGNIFICANCE

Walden was one of the most influential essays written in nineteenth-century America. Regarded as a practical utopian tract and as a guide to meaningful living, it has stood and continues to stand as a touchstone for a way of thinking which values the authority of the individual against the State, the morality of self-reliance, and the primacy of nature. In *Walden*, nature is presented as the proper guide for how mankind should live and as the model for how society should be designed, organized, and run. In contact with nature, Thoreau asserts, people experience themselves authentically and can find the strength to act on principle rather than by conforming to social rules or traditions that may actually be in violation of those principles. Thoreau chronicled the operation of principle in action in his other classic work, *Civil Disobedience*, in which he writes of his refusal to pay a poll tax in Massachusetts and consequently spends a night in jail. (An aunt paid the tax and he was released in the morning.)

In his works, Thoreau gave voice to beliefs which have found resonance in the American character throughout American culture, the spiritual power of nature, the belief in the importance of individual self-assertion against what is regarded as unjust, and faith in the individual's capacity to govern and sustain him or herself as long as he or she is unfettered by governments and unhindered in access to resources. *Walden* has become a primary text for environmentalists and an inspirational source for people disaffected from the established routines or values of organized societies. Along with *Civil Disobedience*, it has provided inspiration for world figures, too, like the Indian liberator Mohandas Gandhi and the American civil rights leader, Martin Luther King, Jr. It is often cited for the sanction it has given to the idea Thoreau advanced of marching to the music of "a different drummer."

FURTHER RESOURCES

Books

Cafaro, Philip. *Thoreau's Living Ethics: Walden and the Pursuit of Virtue.* Athens, Ga.: University of Georgia Press, 2004.

McGrath, James G. "Ten Ways of Seeing Landscapes in *Walden* and Beyond." In *Thoreau's Sense of Place: Essays in American Environmental Writing.* Iowa City, Iowa: University of Iowa Press, 2000.

Periodicals

Botkin, Daniel B. "The Depth of Walden Pond: Thoreau as a Guide to Solving Twenty-First Century Environmental Problems." *The Concord Saunterer* 9 (2001): 5–14.

Cafaro, Philip. "Thoreau's Environmental Ethics in *Walden*." *The Concord Saunterer* 10 (2002): 17–63.

Neufeldt, Leonard, and Mark A. Smith. "Going to Walden Woods: *Walden*, Walden, and American Pastoralism." *Arizona Quarterly* 55, 2 (Summer 1999): 57–86.

Nickel, John. "The Publication of Nature: *Walden* and the Struggle of Authorship." *The Concord Saunterer* 8 (2000): 49–63.

Prud'Homme, Richard. "*Walden*'s Economy of Living." *Raritan* 20, 3 (Winter 2001): 107–131.

Web sites

"Henry David Thoreau." *American Transcendentalism Web.* <http://www.vcu.edu/engweb/transcendentalism/authors/thoreau> (accessed March 10, 2006).

"The Big Trees of California"

Journal article

By: Anonymous

Date: June 5, 1858

Source: "The Big Trees of California." *Harper's Weekly* (June 5, 1858): 357.

About the Author: This article was published without a byline, and was written by a staff writer for the *Harper's Weekly*, an American journal of literature, politics, culture, and the arts.

INTRODUCTION

A staff writer with *Harper's Weekly* magazine wrote on June 5, 1858, about the discovery in 1850 of a group of gigantic trees known as the "Big Trees of Calaveras County." Believed not to exist at these huge sizes anywhere else in the world, these ninety-two trees (at that time scientifically classified as *Washingtonia gigantea*) were located in an isolated valley of about 160 mountainous acres (65 hectares) approximately 240 miles (386 kilometers) east of San Francisco, California. The tree called the "Mother of the Forest," with a circumference of 90 feet (27 meters) and a height of about 300 feet (91 meters), appeared as an artist's 1852 drawing within the original 1858 article with the caption "The 'Big Tree' in Calaveras County, California." The largest of the trees (which had already fallen to the ground), called the "Father of the Forest," measured 112 feet (34 meters) in circumference at its base, 42 feet (13 meters) in circumference at a distance of 300 feet (91 meters) from the base, and was estimated to have stood at a height of at least 450 feet (137 meters). The Big Trees became widely popular with the public after businessman George Gale and his partners employed lumbermen to strip the bark off of the Mother of the Forest tree in order to feature it in a sideshow attraction shown around the world.

■ PRIMARY SOURCE

THE BIG TREE IN CALAVERAS COUNTY, CALIFORNIA

Among the many remarkable natural curiosities of the land of gold, not the least is that solitary group of gigantic pines known as the "Big Trees of Calaveras County." Many of our readers will remember the sections of bark taken from one of the group, which were exhibited some years ago in our principal cities, and which excited the wonder of all beholders, and the doubts of many, who could not persuade themselves that so monstrous a mass could ever have grown upon a single tree.

The group in Calaveras County are solitary specimens of their race. There are no others of their kind or size on the known globe. It is a singular fact that the group, consisting of ninety-two trees, is contained in a valley only one hundred and sixty acres in extent. Beyond the limits of this little amphitheatre the pines and cedars of the country shrink into the Lilliputian dimensions of the common New England pine—say a hundred and fifty feet, or thereabout. They are situated in Calaveras County, about two hundred and forty miles from San Francisco, but may be reached with a couple of days of railroad and stagecoach traveling.

A few hunters, in 1850, were pushing their way into the then unexplored forest, when one of them, who was in advance, broke into this space, and the giants were then first seen by white men. Their colossal proportions, and the impressive silence of the surrounding woods, created a feeling of awe among the hunters; and after walking around the great trunks, and gazing reverentially up at their grand proportions, they returned to the nearest settlements and gave an account of what they had seen. Their statements, however, were considered fabulous until confirmed by actual measurement. The trees have been appropriately named the *Washingtonia Gigantea,* though some of the sapient savans of San Francisco have endeavored to have the *Washingtonia* changed to *Wellingtonia,* because some English botanist, availing himself of the discovery by American frontiersmen, hastened to appropriate the name for his countryman. The basin or valley in which they stand is very damp, and retains here and there pools of water. Some of the largest trees extend their roots directly into the stagnant water, or into the brooks. Arriving at "Murphy's Diggings" by one of the daily lines of stages, either from Sacramento or Stockton, or by the Sonora coach, you are within fifteen miles of the celebrated grove; and from here it is a pretty horseback ride to the "Mammoth Tree Hotel." This has been erected within a year or two, to accommodate the many visitors; for the "big trees" have now become objects of general interest.

Adjoining the hotel, with which it is connected by a floor, stands the stump of the "Big Tree," which was cut down three years since. It measures ninety-six feet in circumference. Its surface is smooth, and offers ample space for thirty-two persons to dance, showing seventy-five feet of circumference of solid timber. Theatrical performances were given upon it by the Chapman family and Robinson family in May, 1855. This monster was cut down by boring with long and powerful augers, and sawing the spaces between—an achievement of Vandalism as ingenious as the Chinese refinement in cruelty of pulling out the nails of criminals with pincers. It required the labor of five men twenty-five days to effect its fall, the tree standing so near perpendicular that the aid of wedges and a battering ram was necessary to complete the desecration. But even then the immense mass resisted all efforts to overthrow it, until in the dead of a tempestuous night it began to groan and sway in the storm like an expiring giant, and it succumbed at last to the elements, which alone could complete from above what the human ants had commenced below. Its fall was like the shock of an earthquake, and was heard fifteen miles away—at "Murphy's Diggings." There fell in this great trunk some thousands of cords of wood,

and it buried itself twelve feet deep in the mire that bordered the little creek near by. Not far from where it struck stand two colossal members of this family, called the "Guardsmen:" the mud splashed nearly a hundred feet high upon their trunks. As it lay on the ground, it measured three hundred and two feet clear of the stump and broken top-work. Large trees had been snapped asunder like pipe-stems, and the woods around were splintered and crushed to the earth. On its leveled surface are now situated the bar-room and two bowling alleys of the hotel, the latter running parallel a distance of eighty-one feet.

One of the most interesting of the group is that called the "Mother of the Forest," . . . It is now the loftiest of the grove, rising to the height of three hundred and twenty-seven feet, straight and beautifully proportioned, and at this moment the largest living tree in the world. It is ninety feet in circumference. Into this trunk could be cut an apartment as large as a common-sized parlor, and as high as the architect chose to make it, without endangering the tree or injuring its outward appearance. . . .

But the dimensions of the whole group pale before these of the prostrate giant known as the Father of the Forest. This monster has long since bowed his head in the dust; but how stupendous in his ruin! The tree measures one hundred and twelve feet in circumference at the base, and forty-two feet in circumference at a distance of three hundred feet from the roots, at which point it was broken short off in its fall. The upper portion, beyond this break, is greatly decayed; but, judging from the average taper of the others, this tree must have towered to the prodigious height of at least four hundred and fifty feet! A chamber or burned cavity extends through the trunk two hundred feet, broad and high enough for a person to ride on horseback through; and a pond deep enough to float a common river steam-boat stands in this great excavation during the rainy reason. Walking on the trunk, and looking from its uprooted base, the mind can scarce conceive its astonishing dimensions. Language fails to give an adequate idea of it. It was, when standing, a pillar of timber that overtopped all other trees on the globe. "To read simply of a tree four hundred and fifty feet high," observes the *Country Gentleman,* "We are struck with large figures; but we can hardly appreciate the height without some comparison. Such one as this would stretch across a field of twenty-seven rods wide. If standing in the Niagara chasm at Suspension Bridge, it would tower two hundred feet above the top of the bridge; if placed in Broadway, New York, at the head of Wall Street, it would overtop Trinity steeple one hundred and sixty feet; and would be two hundred and thirty feet higher than Bunker Hill Monument, Charlestown; or two hundred and seventy feet above Washington Monument, Baltimore. If cut up for fuel, it would make at least three thousand cords, or as much as would be yielded by sixty acres of good woodland. If sawed into two-inch boards, it would yield about three million feet, and furnish enough three-inch plank for thirty miles of plank road. This will do for the product of one little seed, less in size than a grain of wheat.''

These trees are not the California redwood, as has been affirmed of them. They are a species of cedar peculiar to the western slopes of the Sierra Nevada. The growth, bark, and leaf are different from those of any other tree. Botanists class them, and probably correctly, among the Taxodiums. Foreigners will doubtless continue to rechristen them after this or that European celebrity. All who write or speak of them should avoid being thus led, and perpetuate the glorious name given them shortly after their discovery—the *Washingtonia Gigantea.*

SIGNIFICANCE

Although Gale and his partners initially killed some of the Big Trees of California with the intent to monetarily profit from their discovery, they ultimately helped to protect these trees and the overall natural

wonders of the Sierra Nevada mountain range in California. When Gale took his Big Tree sideshow (or Mother of the Forest exhibition) on his worldwide tour with a reassembled bark section of the downed tree, it was sometimes met with skepticism. People often did not believe that authentic bark could grow two feet thick and that the tree had lived to be over 2,500 years old (as indicated by the tree's ring structure).

More importantly, most people were angry with Gale that such a grand and statuesque tree was cut down for a publicity stunt. At the time, editors of the Boston, Massachusetts-based *Gleason's Pictorial* said, "To our mind, it seems a cruel idea, a perfect desecration, to cut down such a splendid tree...what in the world could have possessed any mortal to embark in such a speculation with this mountain of wood?"

Many famous newspapermen and authors of that time such as Horace Greeley, James Russell Lowell, George Catlin, John Wesley Powell, and John Burroughs spearheaded the cause of preserving such natural wonders. Articles from New York to California described the wonders in the Yosemite area and

Sun filters through a canopy of redwood trees at the Del Norte Coast Redwood State Park in California, 2001. Redwood trees are among the largest trees to exist in nature. © DARRELL GULIN/CORBIS

suggested that such a natural beauty should be protected from human development. In March 1864, President Lincoln signed a bill to protect the Yosemite Valley and later, on May 17, 1864, the U.S. Congress transferred two federal plots of land in Mariposa County to California.

Interest grew in the following years as journalists suggested state protection of other natural beauties such as Niagara Falls and the Adirondack Mountains, and federal protection of Yellowstone Park in the Western territories. Then, on March 1, 1872, President Ulysses S. Grant designated by law that over two million federally owned acres—which would be called Yellowstone National Park—in northwestern Wyoming and parts of Montana and Idaho would be set aside specifically for public recreation. This action, which was in essence begun over the cutting down of the Big Trees of California, set about a series of global initiatives for the preservation of natural resources and public lands.

During the 1890s, three more national parks were created: Yosemite National Park (1890) in the Sierra Nevada range in California; Sequoia National Park (1890) in California; and Mount Rainier National Park (1899) in the Cascade Range of Washington State. By 1916, the U.S. Congress had created the National Park Service (NPS), a bureau of the Department of the Interior authorized to manage the growing number of national parks and preserves throughout the United States. Although Gale never had any plans to preserve the Big Trees of California, his actions and the publicity for which he received, including the *Harper's Weekly* article, helped to initiate actions to protect many distinguished trees and other valued natural resources across the United States and around the world.

Part of the area comprising the Big Trees of California became a California state park in 1931 in order to preserve the northern grove of the giant sequoia (redwood) trees. Calaveras Big Trees State Park contains the California Big Tree, or *Sequoia gigantean*, rather than the distinct species called the Coast Redwood tree, or *Sequoia sempervirens*. Both trees have pink or red roots and are gigantic in size, but are distinct in bark, foliage, habitat, and reproduction. Today, the park has grown to include the primitive southern grove of Big Trees, consisting of about 6,500 forested acres (2,630 hectares) of mixed conifer trees.

FURTHER RESOURCES
Web sites

Calaveras Big Trees State Park, California State Parks. "Calaveras Big Trees SP." <http://www.parks.ca.gov/ default.asp?page_id=551> (accessed November 25, 2005).

Environmental History Timeline, Radford University. "The Mother of the Forest." <http://www.radford.edu/ ~wkovarik/envhist/mother.html> (accessed November 25, 2005).

The Manufacturer and Builder, Cornell Making of America, Cornell University Library. "The Big Trees of California." <http://cdl.library.cornell.edu/cgi-bin/moa/moa-cgi? notisid=ABS1821-0023&byte=58615142> (accessed November 25, 2005).

Yosemite National Park. "The Giant Sequoia." <http://www. yosemite.ca.us/history/handbook_of_yosemite_national_ park/sequoia.html> (accessed November 25, 2005).

An Overland Journey from New York to San Francisco in the Summer of 1859

Book excerpt

By: Horace Greeley

Date: 1860

Source: Greeley, Horace. *An Overland Journey from New York to San Francisco in the Summer of 1859.* New York: C.M. Saxton, Barker & Co., 1860.

About the Author: American journalist and politician Horace Greeley (1811–1872) founded the *New York Tribune* in 1841 and served as its editor for the next thirty years. He made the *Tribune* one of the most influential journals of his time. It set new standards for newspaper reporting and was the platform from which Greeley advocated his progressive views as a campaigner against alcohol and tobacco consumption and for women's rights, workers' associations, and a transcontinental railroad. In 1859, Greeley traveled through the west by stagecoach, publishing accounts of his travels in the *New York Tribune*. The purpose of the trip was partially to sketch in writing the character of the western regions and the people who lived there, both the indigenous population and the settlers. It was also designed to generate enthusiasm for building a railroad, which would make a journey like the one he undertook far less arduous and more commonplace.

Author Horace Greeley, 1868. AP IMAGES

INTRODUCTION

Greeley's enthusiasm for building a transcontinental railroad was not motivated by a desire to explore or open up the west. The west had been opened and was being settled. His overland journey was in part a piece of investigative, on-site reporting and, in part, an early example of advocacy journalism. As he traveled across North America, Greeley sent dispatches back to New York to be printed in the *Tribune*. These articles, which became *An Overland Journey*, detailed what the country was like and how settlers lived. Thus he provided both a map of the natural environment, and an early sociological study. Greeley used the stories to suggest that because of the dissipation and slothfulness he kept encountering, there was a need for the railroad. He also argued that the land was fit to profit diligent and industrious men and women who devoted themselves to making a livelihood in the west.

The railroad, as Greeley saw it, would bring civilization and civility to regions that had been opened to settlement but not domesticated. He looked for "social, moral, and intellectual blessings" from a railroad. The railroad, Greeley argued, would facilitate communication through the swift exchange of letters

and the delivery of the implements of civilization, books, and journals to the west. Just as important was the need to increase the number of "intelligent, capable, virtuous women" out west, for he believed in their stabilizing and uplifting influence. The railroad, too, would allow men to establish families or bring west the families they'd left in the east when they set off to seek their fortunes.

Besides offering reasons for building a railroad in *An Overland Journey*, Greeley offered practical financial and engineering advice, arguing that it was not a daunting enterprise but could be accomplished.

■ PRIMARY SOURCE

... The social, moral, and intellectual blessings of a Pacific railroad can hardly be glanced at within the limits of an article. Suffice it for the present that I merely suggest them.

1. Our mails are now carried to and from California by steamships, via Panama, in twenty to thirty days, starting once a fortnight. The average time of transit from writers throughout the Atlantic states to their correspondents on the Pacific exceeds thirty days. With a Pacific railroad, this would be reduced to ten; for the letters written in Illinois or Michigan would reach their destinations in the mining counties of California quicker than letters sent from New York or Philadelphia would reach San Francisco. With a daily mail by railroad from each of our Atlantic cities to and from California, it is hardly possible that the amount of both letters and printed matter transmitted, and consequently of postage, should not be speedily quadrupled.

2. The first need of California to-day is a large influx of intelligent, capable, virtuous women. With a railroad to the Pacific, avoiding the miseries and perils of six thousand miles of ocean transportation, and making the transit a pleasant and interesting overland journey of ten days, at a reduced cost, the migration of this class would be immensely accelerated and increased. With wages for all kinds of women's work at least thrice as high on the Pacific as in this quarter, and with larger opportunities for honorable and fit settlement in life, I cannot doubt that tens of thousands would annually cross the Plains, to the signal benefit of California and of the whole country, as well as the improvement of their own fortunes and the profit of the railroad.

3. Thousands now staying in California, expecting to "go home" so soon as they shall have somewhat improved their circumstances, would send or come

for their families and settle on the Pacific for life, if a railroad were opened. Tens of thousands who have been to California and come back, unwilling either to live away from their families or to expose them to the present hardships of migration thither, would return with all they have, prepared to spend their remaining days in the land of gold, if there were a Pacific railroad.

4. Education is the vital want of California, second to its need of true women. School-books, and all the material of education, are now scarce and dear there. Almost all books sell there twice as high as here, and many of the best are scarcely attainable at any rate. With the Pacific railroad, all this would be changed for the better. The proportion of schoolhouses to grogshops would rapidly increase. All the elements of moral and religious melioration would be multiplied. Tens of thousands of our best citizens would visit the Pacific coast, receiving novel ideas and impressions, to their own profit and that of the people thus visited. Civilization, intelligence, refinement, on both sides of the mountain—still more, in the Great Basin inclosed by them—would receive a new and immense impulse, and the Union would acquire a greater accession of strength, power, endurance, and true glory, than it would from the acquisition of the whole continent down to Cape Horn.

The only points of view in which a railroad from the Missouri to the Pacific remains to be considered are those of its practicability, cost, location, and the ways and means. Let us look at them:

I. As to practicability, there is no room for hesitation or doubt. The Massachusetts Western, the Erie, the Pennsylvania, and the Baltimore and Ohio, have each encountered difficulties as formidable as any to be overcome by a Pacific railroad this side of the Sierra Nevada. Were the railroad simply to follow the principal emigrant trail up the Platte and down the Snake and Columbia to Oregon, or south-westwardly from the South Pass to the foot of the Sierra, it would encounter no serious obstacle...

But let that government simply resolve that the Pacific road shall be built—let Congress enact that sealed proposals for its construction shall be invited, and that whichever responsible company or corporation shall offer adequate security for that construction, to be completed within ten years, on the lowest terms, shall have public aid, provided the amount required do not exceed fifty millions of dollars, and the work will be done, certainly for fifty millions' bonus, probably for much less. The government on its part should concede to the company a mile in width, according to the section lines, of the public lands on either side of the road as built, with the right to take timber, stone and earth from any public lands without charge; and should

require of said company that it carry a daily through-mail each way at the price paid other roads for conveying mails on first-class routes; and should moreover stipulate for the conveyance at all times of troops, arms, munitions, provisions, etc., for the public service, at the lowest rates, with a right to the exclusive possession and use of the road whenever a national exigency shall seem to require it. The government should leave the choice of route entirely to the company, only stipulating that it shall connect the navigable waters of the Mississippi with those of the Pacific Ocean, and that it shall be constructed wholly through our own territory....

By adopting this plan, the rivalries of routes will be made to work for, instead of working against, the construction of the road. Strenuous efforts will be made by the friends of each to put themselves in position to bid low enough to secure the location; and the lowest rate at which the work can safely be undertaken will unquestionably be bid. The road will be the property of the company constructing it, subject only to the rights of use, stipulated and paid for by the government. And, even were it to cost the latter a bonus of fully fifty millions, I feel certain that every farthing of that large sum will have been reimbursed to the treasury within five years after the completion of the work in the proceeds of land sales, in increased postages, and in duties on goods imported, sold, and consumed because of this railroad—not to speak of the annual saving of millions in the cost of transporting and supplying troops.

Men and brethen! Let us resolve to have a railroad to the Pacific—to have it soon. It will add more to the strength and wealth of our country than would the acquisition of a dozen Cubas. It will prove a bond of union not easily broken, and a new spring to our national industry, prosperity and wealth. It will call new manufactures into existence, and increase the demand for the products of those already existing. It will open new vistas to national and to individual aspiration, and crush out filibusterism by giving a new and wholesome direction to the public mind. My long, fatiguing journey was undertaken in the hope that I might do something toward the early construction of the Pacific Railroad; and I trust that it has not been made wholly in vain.

SIGNIFICANCE

Greeley was a visionary and a pioneer in the field of communications, whether through words or through transportation. He believed in the importance of industrial technology for the development of a productive, democratic society in a world where vast amounts of territory—administered by one central authority, the United States—would nevertheless constitute a democracy and not an empire, as they had throughout past history. He was not an environmentalist in the common understanding of the word. His goal was not to preserve nature but to establish the conditions that would help people lead civilized lives through the force of their own democratic authority. Although he favored cities and industry, he was not an adherent of the industrial revolution as it prevailed in the nineteenth century. He associated human injustice with monopolistic capitalism and called for workers' associations and economic justice. He was a progressive Puritan, wishing to see religion, family, and morality prevail where there was wilderness and wildness. In many respects, his vision of a unified continent was an early version of globalism.

FURTHER RESOURCES

Books

Cross, Coy F. *Go West, Young Man!: Horace Greeley's Vision For America*. Albuquerque, NM: University of New Mexico Press, 1995.

Web sites

Horace Greeley. <http://www.tulane.edu/~latner/Greeley.html> (accessed November 14, 2005).

The Yosemite Web. "An Overland Journey from New York to San Francisco in the Summer of 1859, by Horace Greeley (1860)." <http://www.yosemite.ca.us/history/greeley/> (accessed November 14, 2005).

Man and Nature:

Or, Physical Geography as Modified by Human Action

Book excerpt

By: George Perkins Marsh

Date: 1864

Source: Marsh, George Perkins. *Man and Nature: Or, Physical Geography as Modified by Human Action*. New York: Scribners, 1864.

About the Author: American scholar, linguist, environmentalist, and diplomat, George Perkins Marsh (1801–1882) was the embodiment of a nineteenth-century renaissance man. He was born to a wealthy and politically prominent family in Woodstock, Vermont, and developed his sense of nature and love for it while exploring the Vermont forests. He was educated at Dartmouth College and was a teacher, lawyer, farmer, and businessman. He ran lumber and woolen mills, but he was unsuccessful in business. He was proficient in twenty languages, participated in designing the Washington Monument, and was a founder of the Smithsonian Institute. He was the U.S. Ambassador to Turkey and, for the last twenty years of his life, to Italy. He wrote books on philology and on the virtues of camels. At his suggestion, the U.S. Congress initiated a program to introduce camels to the Texas environment, but it did not succeed, principally because the project was neglected when the U.S. Civil War began. Marsh's most significant contribution, however, was writing *Man and Nature*. Its major thesis is that the environment is shaped by mankind, that mankind's influence on the environment is predominantly destructive, and that, historically, the destruction of the environment leads to the collapse of civilizations.

INTRODUCTION

Marsh describes nature as a harmonizing force in which an ecological balance has been slowly formed. Integrating an evolutionary view of nature with the traditional theological view, Marsh believed that through eons, nature has been "proportioning and balancing...combinations of inorganic matter and organic life." By this process, Marsh wrote, nature was preparing a habitable environment for the human species. By misusing the natural world, imposing their will upon it without regard to the way nature itself is arranged and functions, and exploiting nature rather than using and enjoying it with awareness, people destroy the natural environment, its balance, and its systems. Humans will not, Marsh argued, find it a suitable environment in which to live for very long.

Marsh recognizes that the other inhabitants of Earth are also destructive. Animals kill other animals. But he argues they do not destroy the environment in doing so and that, in fact, when animals kill each other, there are "compensations." They are ensuring the balance of nature. Marsh also recognizes that there are parts of nature that are not easily adaptable to human use, and he recognizes that human art is necessary sometimes to "combat" nature and to transform and elevate it. However, Marsh sees mankind as "reckless" in its approach to nature and in the way it "disturbs" nature.

■ PRIMARY SOURCE

Man has too long forgotten that the earth was given to him for usufruct alone, not for consumption, still less for profligate waste. Nature has provided against the absolute destruction of any of her elementary matter, the raw material of her works; the thunderbolt and the tornado, the most convulsive throes of even the volcano and the earthquake, being only phenomena of decomposition and recomposition. But she has left it within the power of man irreparably to derange the combinations of inorganic matter and of organic life, which through the night of æons she had been proportioning and balancing, to prepare the earth for his habitation, when, in the fullness of time, his Creator should call him forth to enter into its possession.

Apart from the hostile influence of man, the organic and the inorganic world are…bound together by such mutual relations and adaptations as secure, if not the absolute permanence and equilibrium of both, a long continuance of the established conditions of each at any given time and place, or at least, a very slow and gradual succession of changes in those conditions. But man is everywhere a disturbing agent. Wherever he plants his foot, the harmonies of nature are turned to discords. The proportions and accommodations which insured the stability of existing arrangements are overthrown. Indigenous vegetable and animal species are extirpated, and supplanted by others of foreign origin, spontaneous production is forbidden or restricted, and the face of the earth is either laid bare or covered with a new and reluctant growth of vegetable forms, and with alien tribes of animal life. These intentional changes and substitutions constitute, indeed, great revolutions; but vast as is their magnitude and importance, they are, as we shall see, insignificant in comparison with the contingent and unsought results which have flowed from them.

The fact that, of all organic beings, man alone is to be regarded as essentially a destructive power, and that he wields energies to resist which, nature—that nature whom all material life and all inorganic substance obey—is wholly impotent, tends to prove that, though living in physical nature, he is not of her, that he is of more exalted parentage, and belongs to a higher order of existence than those born of her womb and submissive to her dictates.

There are, indeed, brute destroyers, beasts and birds and insects of prey—all animal life feeds upon, and, of course, destroys other life—but this destruction is balanced by compensations. It is, in fact, the very means by which the existence of one tribe of animals or of vegetables is secured against being smothered by the encroachments of another; and the reproductive powers of species, which serve as the food of others, are always proportioned to the demand they are destined to supply. Man pursues his victims with reckless destructiveness; and, while the sacrifice of life by the lower animals is limited by the cravings of appetite, he unsparingly persecutes, even to extirpation, thousands of organic forms which he cannot consume.

The earth was not, in its natural condition, completely adapted to the use of man, but only to the sustenance of wild animals and wild vegetation. These live, multiply their kind in just proportion, and attain their perfect measure of strength and beauty, without producing or requiring any change in the natural arrangements of surface, or in each other's spontaneous tendencies, except such mutual repression of excessive increase as may prevent the extirpation of one species by the encroachments of another. In short, without man, lower animal and spontaneous vegetable life would have been constant in type, distribution, and proportion, and the physical geography of the earth would have remained undisturbed for indefinite periods, and been subject to revolution only from possible, unknown cosmical causes, or from geological action.

But man, the domestic animals that serve him, the field and garden plants the products of which supply him with food and clothing, cannot subsist and rise to the full development of their higher properties, unless brute and unconscious nature be effectually combated, and, in a great degree, vanquished by human art. Hence, a certain measure of transformation of terrestrial surface, of suppression of natural, and stimulation of artificially modified productivity becomes necessary. This measure man has unfortunately exceeded. He has felled the forests whose network of fibrous roots bound the mould to the rocky skeleton of the earth; but had he allowed here and there a belt of woodland to reproduce itself by spontaneous propagation, most of the mischiefs which his reckless destruction of the natural protection of the soil has occasioned would have been averted. He has broken up the mountain reservoirs, the percolation of whose waters through unseen channels supplied the fountains that refreshed his cattle and fertilized his fields; but he has neglected to maintain the cisterns and the canals of irrigation which a wise antiquity had constructed to neutralize the consequences of its own imprudence. While he has torn the thin glebe which confined the light earth of extensive plains, and has destroyed the fringe of semi-aquatic plants which skirted the coast and checked the drifting of the sea sand, he has failed to prevent the spreading of the dunes by clothing them with artificially propagated vegetation. He has ruthlessly warred on all the tribes of animated nature whose spoil he could convert to his own uses, and he has not protected the birds which prey on the insects most destructive to his own harvests.

Purely untutored humanity, it is true, interferes comparatively little with the arrangements of nature, and the destructive agency of man becomes more and more energetic and unsparing as he advances in civilization, until the impoverishment, with which his exhaustion of the natural resources of the soil is threatening him, at last awakens him to the necessity of preserving what is left, if not of restoring what has been wantonly wasted. The wandering savage grows no cultivated vegetable, fells no forest, and extirpates no useful plant, no noxious weed. If his skill in the chase enables him to entrap numbers of the animals on which he feeds, he compensates this loss by destroying also the lion, the tiger, the wolf, the otter, the seal, and the eagle, thus indirectly protecting the feebler quadrupeds and fish and fowls, which would otherwise become the booty of beasts and birds of prey. But with stationary life, or rather with the pastoral state, man at once commences an almost indiscriminate warfare upon all the forms of animal and vegetable existence around him, and as he advances in civilization, he gradually eradicates or transforms every spontaneous product of the soil he occupies.

Deforestation, as seen In Novo Progreso, Para, Brazil, in only one type of extreme damage man has inflicted on nature and the environment. AP IMAGES

SIGNIFICANCE

Marsh's voice is both a warning and a voice of moderation. It is also particularly American. It is the voice of a man who saw firsthand that a seemingly inexhaustible wealth of nature lay limitlessly before his countrymen for their use and saw, too, how they were despoiling and destroying that wealth as mankind had characteristically done throughout the ages to its own great disadvantage.

In *Man and Nature*, Marsh balanced a commitment to the authority of nature and to the intelligence and powers of mankind. He introduced the idea that people must be stewards of nature and must recognize that nature has a harmony of its own that it is disastrous to defy and, by defying, destroy. Marsh recognizes that human beings cannot live—and ought not to live—like brutes in nature and that we are not, like the rest of nature, entirely of nature. He accepts that, by our essence, human beings are a higher force able to transform and elevate other aspects of nature. Marsh himself sees some components of mankind's ability to transform as "lower" aspects, like producing crops through cultivation, domesticating animals, and engineering geography itself. But this power and authority, Marsh argued, gives people the responsibility of stewardship. It is essential that we know nature, understand its processes and work with nature as we transform it, rather than recklessly endangering ourselves by abusing it. With the advances that have been made in the magnitude and depth of destruction humans have invented—nuclear weaponry, for example, not only kills people but destroys the environment—Marsh's warnings and sense of responsible moderation have become increasingly important.

FURTHER RESOURCES

Books

Curtis, Jane, Will Curtis, and Frank Liebermann. *The World of George Perkins Marsh*. Woodstock, VT: Countryman Press, 1982.

Lowenthal, David. *George Perkins Marsh, Prophet of Conservation*. Seattle: University of Washington Press, 2000.

Web sites

"George Perkins Marsh: Renaissance Vermonter." *The George Perkins Marsh Institute*. <http://www.clarku.edu/departments/marsh/about/> (accessed March 15, 2006).

The White-Thorn Blossom

Letter

By: John Ruskin

Date: May 1, 1871

Source: Fors Clavigera, May 1, 1871.

About the Author: English writer, art and social critic, and Professor of Fine Arts at Oxford from 1867 to 1879, John Ruskin (1819–1900) was raised by a strict puritanical mother and a well-to-do sherry merchant father. He began to establish himself as, perhaps, the major art critic of the nineteenth century with the 1843 publication of the first volume of *Modern Painters*. Reacting against the ugliness, poverty, and environmental degradation associated with the industrial revolution in England, Ruskin spoke for an aesthetic of beauty, light, and vision. In 1851, he published "The Stones of Venice," an architectural study that grew out of his visits to that city. In "The Nature of Gothic," he constructed a critique of the nature of work in Venice, imagining how that city was built, which strongly contrasted with what he saw as the authoritarian, devitalized, and regimented nature of work in industrial England. In the 1860s, he began writing a series of pieces about political economy and work aimed at English workers. His political writing was marked by the same concern for beauty and appreciation for the natural environment and the integrity of the spirit which defined his art and architectural criticism.

INTRODUCTION

The writer in Victorian England, whether a writer of fiction or non-fiction, was often considered to be the shaper of morality and consciousness, an inspiring, even heroic figure who was supposed to serve as a guide and teacher. Consequently, writers often had the power to shape society itself and the course of history.

Examples abound, from the political philosophy of John Stuart Mill to the social criticism of Charles Dickens; from the moral psychology of George Eliot to the radical critique of the industrial revolution by Karl Marx; and from the ferocious sermons of Thomas Carlyle to the patient lectures of Matthew Arnold. None assumed more ceremoniously the mantle of wise man, teacher, and moral guide than Ruskin. After being appointed Slade Professor of Art at Oxford, he began to write a series of letters addressed to the working men of England. "The White-Thorn Blossom" is one of those letters. In it, Ruskin explores what he sees as the destruction of nature and the environment because of the abandonment of the ideals of beauty and majesty.

Ruskin argues that the debasement of the human spirit is a byproduct of the values and enterprises of the industrial revolution, and he offers an alternative vision—based on an appreciation of nature—of how society ought to be organized and how people ought to think and behave.

PRIMARY SOURCE

There was a rocky valley between Buxton and Bakewell, once upon a time, divine as the Vale of Tempe; you might have seen the Gods there morning and evening—Apollo and all the sweet Muses of the Light—walking in fair procession on the lawns of it, and to and fro among the pinnacles of its crags. You cared neither for Gods nor grass, but for cash (which you did not know the way to get); you thought you could get it by what the *Times* calls "Railroad Enterprise." You Enterprised a Railroad through the valley—you blasted its rocks away, heaped thousands of tons of shale into its lovely stream. The valley is gone, and the Gods with it; and now, every fool in Buxton can be at Bakewell in half an hour, and every fool in Bakewell at Buxton; which you think a lucrative process of exchange—you Fools Everywhere.

To talk at a distance, when you have nothing to say, though you were ever so near; to go fast from this place to that, with nothing to do either at one or the other: these are powers certainly. Much more, power of increased Production, if you, indeed, had got it, would be something to boast of. But are you so entirely sure that you *have* got it—that the mortal disease of plenty, and afflictive affluence of good things, are all you have to dread?...

There are three Material things, not only useful, but essential to Life. No one "knows how to live" till he has got them.

These are, Pure Air, Water, and Earth.

There are three Immaterial things, not only useful, but essential to Life. No one knows how to live till he has got them also.

These are, Admiration, Hope, and Love.

Admiration—the power of discerning and taking delight in what is beautiful in visible Form, and lovely in human Character; and, necessarily, striving to produce what is beautiful in form, and to become what is lovely in character.

Hope—the recognition, by true Foresight, of better things to be reached hereafter, whether by ourselves or others; necessarily issuing in the straightforward and undisappointable effort to advance, according to our proper power, the gaining of them.

Love—both of family and neighbour, faithful, and satisfied.

These are the six chiefly useful things to be got by Political Economy, when it *has* become a science. I will briefly tell you what modern Political Economy—the great "savoir mourir"—is doing with them.

The first three, I said, are Pure Air, Water, and Earth.

Heaven gives you the main elements of these. You can destroy them at your pleasure, or increase, almost without limit, the available quantities of them.

You can vitiate the air by your manner of life, and of death, to any extent. You might easily vitiate it so as to bring such a pestilence on the globe as would end all of you. You, or your fellows, German and French, are at present vitiating it to the best of your power in every direction;—chiefly at this moment with corpses, and animal and vegetable ruin in war: changing men, horses, and garden-stuff into noxious gas. But everywhere, and all day long, you are vitiating it with foul chemical exhalations; and the horrible nests, which you call towns, are little more than laboratories for the distillation into leaven of venomous smokes and smells, mixed with effluvia from decaying animal matter, and infectious miasmata from purulent disease.

On the other hand, your power of purifying the air, by dealing properly and swiftly with all substances in corruption; by absolutely forbidding noxious manufactures; and by planting in all soils the trees which cleanse and invigorate earth and atmosphere,—is literally infinite. You might make every breath of air you draw, food.

Secondly, your power over the rain and river-waters of the earth is infinite. You can bring rain where you will, by planting wisely and tending carefully;—drought where you will, by ravage of woods and neglect of the soil. You might have the rivers of England as pure as the crystal of the rock;—beautiful in falls, in lakes, in living pools;—so full of fish that you might take them out with your hands instead of nets. Or you may do always as you have done now, turn every river of England into a common sewer, so that you cannot so much as baptize an English baby but with filth, unless you hold its face out in the rain; and even *that* falls dirty.

Then for the third, Earth, meant to be nourishing for you, and blossoming. You have learned, about it, that there is no such thing as a flower; and as far as your scientific hands and scientific brains, inventive of explosive and deathful, instead of blossoming and life-giving, Dust, can contrive, you have turned the Mother-Earth, Demeter, into the Avenger-Earth, Tisiphone—with the voice of your brother's blood crying out of it, in one wild harmony round all its murderous sphere.

SIGNIFICANCE

By his eloquent writings dedicated to preserving the beauty of the natural environment, and through his linking of a reverence for nature with individual spiritual well-being and a socially healthy society, Ruskin offered important rationales for defending the natural environment to social reformers who followed him and inspiration to those who wished to experiment in making utopian communities.

The young Mahatma (Mohandas) Gandhi's (1869–1948) philosophy was strongly shaped by reading Ruskin, and Ruskin's younger contemporary, William Morris (1834–1896). Morris, an English painter, weaver, designer, printer, furniture maker, and writer, founded his entire aesthetic and social philosophy on Ruskin's ideals of beauty and simple, non-industrial craftsmanship, in both his crafts work and in his utopian novel, *News from Nowhere*, a vision of an England run according to Ruskinian precepts.

At the end of the nineteenth and the beginning of the twentieth centuries in the United States, several towns named Ruskin and designed to follow his principles, were created in Florida, Tennessee, and Georgia.

In the 1870s, Ruskin himself actively campaigned for his ideas. In 1876, he undertook to keep railroads from being built in the Lake District of England, and in the early 1870s he founded an organization he called the Guild of St. George. Through his writing, he recruited "Companions of St. George," who undertook to live on land that had been degraded by industrial neglect and abuse, and to transform that land into gardens through non-industrial, communal labor. In practical terms, the Guild must be judged a failure, but it succeeded in helping to keep Ruskin's vision alive. The Guild still survives, as does a Ruskin Trust, which maintains a museum of Ruskiniana in Conniston, where he lived in England's Lake District and where he is buried.

FURTHER RESOURCES

Books

Brundage, W. Fitzhugh. *A Socialist Utopia in the New South: The Ruskin Colonies in Tennessee and Georgia, 1894–1901.* Urbana, IL: University of Illinois Press, 1996.

Lang, Michael H. *Designing Utopia: John Ruskin's Urban Vision for Britain and America.* Montréal and New York: Black Rose Books, 1999.

Web sites

The Victorian Web. "John Ruskin." <http://www.victorian web.org/authors/ruskin/ruskinov.html> (accessed November 25, 2005).

"Johnny Appleseed:

A Pioneer Hero"

Magazine article

By: W. D. Haley

Date: November 1871

Source: Haley, W. D. "Johnny Appleseed: A Pioneer Hero." *Harper's New Monthly Magazine* (November 1871).

About the Author: Little is known about author W. D. Haley. *Harper's* is an American journal of literature, politics, culture, and the arts. It is one of the oldest American magazines in existence, and has been published continually since 1850.

INTRODUCTION

While few Americans would recognize the name of John Chapman, many know him by his popular nickname: "Johnny Appleseed." Chapman was born in Massachusetts in 1774. Little is known about his early life, however in 1791 he began traveling through Pennsylvania, Ohio, Indiana, and Illinois planting trees, including thousands of apple trees.

Chapman's usual practice was to find a suitable piece of land, clear it, and plant an orchard. Then, over the course of two to three years he would return to tend the orchard until the trees were ready to be sold. By locating his orchards in the path of advancing settlements, Chapman ensured himself a steady supply of ready buyers for his apple saplings, which he sold for about six cents apiece. Estimates place his total plantings at approximately 1,200 acres (486 hectares) of orchards.

The story of Johnny Appleseed is difficult to reconstruct accurately, as time has blurred the distinction between fact and legend. Chapman was apparently a bit eccentric. His clothing consisted of a coffee sack with armholes cut in it for a shirt and bare feet. The most famous images of Chapman portray him with dark shoulder-length hair and a tin kettle for a cap, though this final item may be more legend than fact. By 1806 he had been given his new nickname, and his fame began to spread.

Chapman appeared to be part agronomist, part naturalist, and part philosopher. He was a popular guest in frontier homes, welcomed not just for his gifts of apple seeds, but also for his ready wit and his tall tales. He never married, and often wove spiritual messages into his entertaining stories. In 1871,

Harper's journal entry on Johnny Appleseed. HARPER'S MONTHLY MAGAZINE, 1871. VOLUME XLIII.

Harper's New Monthly Magazine published an extensive account of his real and imaginary adventures.

PRIMARY SOURCE

The "far West" is rapidly becoming only a traditional designation: railroads have destroyed the romance of frontier life, or have surrounded it with so many appliances of civilization that the pioneer character is rapidly becoming mythical. The men and women who obtain their groceries and dry-foods from New York by rail in a few hours have nothing in common with those who, fifty years ago, "packed" salt a hundred miles to make their mush palatable, and could only exchange corn and wheat for molasses and calico by making long and perilous voyages in flat-boats down the Ohio and Mississippi rivers to New Orleans. Two generations of frontier lives have accumulated stores of narrative which, like the small but beautiful tributaries of great rivers, are forgotten in the broad sweep of the larger current of history. The march of Titans sometimes tramples out the memory of smaller but more useful lives, and sensational glare often eclipses more modest but purer lights. This has been the case in the popular demand for the dime novel dilutions of Fenimore Cooper's romances of border life, which have preserved the records of Indians rapine and atrocity as the only memorials of pioneer history. But the early days of Western settlement witnessed sublimer heroisms than those of human torture, and nobler victories than those of the tomahawk and scalping-knife.

Among the heroes of endurance that was voluntary, and of action that was creative and not sanguinary, there was one man whose name, seldom mentioned now save by some of the few surviving pioneers, deserves to be perpetuated.

The first reliable trace of our modest hero finds him in the Territory of Ohio, in 1801, with a horse-load of apple seeds, which he planted in various places on and about the borders of Licking Creek, the first orchard thus originated by him being on the farm of Isaac Stadden, in what is now known as Licking County, in the State of Ohio. During the five succeeding years, although he was undoubtedly following the same strange occupation, we have no authentic account of his movements until we reach a pleasant spring day in 1806, when a pioneer settler in Jefferson County, Ohio, noticed a peculiar craft, with a remarkable occupant and a curious cargo, slowly dropping down with the current of the Ohio River. It was "Johnny Appleseed," by which name Jonathan Chapman was afterward known in every log cabin from the Ohio River to the Northern Lakes, and westward to the prairies of what is now the State of Indiana. With two canoes lashed together he was transporting a load of apple seeds to the Western frontier, for the purpose of creating orchards on the farthest verge of white settlements. With his canoes he passed down the Ohio to Marietta, where he entered the Muskingum, ascending the stream of that river until he reached the mouth of the Walbonding, or White Woman Creek, and still onward, up the Mohican, into the Black Fork, to the head of navigation, in the region now known as Ashland and Richland counties, on the line of the Pittsburg and Fort Wayne Railroad, in Ohio. A long and toilsome voyage it was, as a glance at the map will show, and must havex occupied a great deal of time, as the lonely traveler stopped at every inviting spot to plant the seeds and make his infant nurseries. These are the first well-authenticated facts in the history of Jonathan Chapman, whose birth, there is good reason for believing, occurred in Boston, Massachusetts, in 1775.

SIGNIFICANCE

Johnny Appleseed spent forty-nine years wandering the American frontier alone. While tales of a shaggy man scattering seeds wildly about are more fiction than fact, the impact of Johnny Appleseed is undeniable. By spreading apple trees across the frontier, he helped ease the lives of pioneers, and his efforts were responsible for some of the large orchards dotting the Midwest today. More than a century after his death, some of the trees he planted are still bearing fruit.

Like most legends, the man behind the story was probably less exciting than the tall tales about him, but Johnny Appleseed played a unique role in American frontier life. In 1966, the U.S. Postal Service issued a commemorative stamp honoring Johnny Appleseed and his accomplishments.

While historians are not certain what he looked like, this popular woodcut from the 1870s shows Johnny Appleseed with his apple trees. © BETTMANN/CORBIS

FURTHER RESOURCES

Books

Hodges, Margaret. *The True Tale of Johnny Appleseed.* New York: Holiday House, 1999.

Johnny Appleseed: A Voice in the Wilderness, edited by William Ellery Jones. New York: Chrysalis Books, 2000.

Price, Robert. *Johnny Appleseed: Man and Myth.* New York: Peter Smith Publishing, Inc., 1954.

Web sites

The Johnny Appleseed Festival. <http://www.johnnyapple seedfest.com> (accessed January 26, 2006).

Urbana University. "Johnny Appleseed Society." <http://www.urbana.edu/appleseed.htm> (January 26, 2006).

"The Wonders of Yellowstone"

Journal article

By: Nathaniel Pitt Langford

Date: May, 1871

Source: Langford, Nathaniel P. "The Wonders of Yellowstone." *Scribner's Monthly* 2 (May 1871): 10.

About the Author: Nathaniel Pitt Langford (1832–1911) was born, raised, and educated in the state of New York. He was a stonemason before traveling west to the general vicinity of what is now known as the state of Montana. Langford conducted numerous governmental expeditions into the Rocky Mountains during the last half of the nineteenth century. Known as "National Park" Langford because of his advocacy to preserve public lands, he was a leading member of an 1870 expedition (along with Henry Washburn and Gustavus Doane) that explored the Yellowstone area. This pioneering endeavor helped to popularize the beauty of the park. Two years later, their effort helped to pass a bill signed by President Ulysses S. Grant that created Yellowstone National Park. Thereafter, Langford became the first superintendent of Yellowstone National Park, holding the position for five years.

INTRODUCTION

Langford wrote a story called "The Wonders of the Yellowstone" based on his 1870 experiences with the Washburn-Langford-Doane Expedition of the Yellowstone area. Later that same year, *Scribner's Monthly* magazine acquired Langford's story and published it in May 1871. Considered the first credible account of the Yellowstone area, Langford's article intrigued readers with stunning tales of fascinating geological features such as high-shooting geysers, majestic waterfalls, awesome mountain peaks, spectacular canyons, and dangerously boiling streams. Encouraged by heightened interest in the region from the Easterners who read his writings, Langford publicized the area as a site that should be reserved as a recreational area. He actively promoted the development of a railroad track by the Northern Pacific Railroad (along with hotels and other buildings) along the proposed Yellowstone route. Through the efforts of Langford and others, Yellowstone National Park became the first national park in the United States.

■ PRIMARY SOURCE

I had indulged, for several years, a great curiosity to see the wonders of the upper valley of the Yellowstone. The stories told by trappers and mountaineers of the natural phenomena of that region were so strange and marvelous that, as long ago as 1866, I first contemplated the possibility of organizing an expedition for the express purpose of exploring it. During the past year, meeting with several gentlemen who expressed like curiosity, we determined to make the journey in the months of August and September. . . .

From the summit of a commanding range, which separated the waters of Antelope and Tower Creeks, we descended through a picturesque gorge, leading our horses to a small stream flowing into the Yellowstone. Four miles of travel, a great part of it down the precipitous slopes of the mountain, brought us to the banks of Tower Creek, and within the volcanic region, where the wonders were supposed to commence. On the right of the trail our attention was first attracted by a small hot sulphur spring, a little below the boiling point in temperature. Leaving the spring we ascended a high ridge, from which the most noticeable feature, in a landscape of great extent and beauty, was Column Rock, stretching for two miles along the eastern bank of the Yellowstone. At the distance from which we saw it, we could compare it in appearance to nothing but a section of the Giant's Causeway. It was composed of successive pillars of basalt overlying and underlying a thick stratum of cement and gravel resembling pudding-stone. In both rows, the pillars, standing in close proximity, were each about thirty feet high and from three to five feet in diameter. This interesting object, more from the novelty of its formation and its beautiful surroundings of mountain and river scenery than anything grand or impressive in its appearance, excited our attention, until the gathering shades of evening reminded us of the necessity of selecting a suitable camp. We descended the declivity to the banks of Tower Creek, and camped on a rocky terrace one mile distant from, and four hundred feet above the Yellowstone....

Our journey the next day still continued through a country until then untraveled. Owing to the high lateral mountain spurs, the numerous ravines, and the interminable patches of fallen timber, we made very slow progress; but when the hour for camping arrived we were greatly surprised to find ourselves descending the mountain along the banks of a beautiful stream in the immediate vicinity of the Great Falls of the Yellowstone. This stream, which we called Cascade Creek, is very rapid. Just before its union with the river it passes through a gloomy gorge, of abrupt descent, which on either side is filled with continuous masses of obsidian that have been worn by the water into many fantastic shapes and cavernous recesses. This we named "The Devil's Den." Near the foot of the gorge the creek breaks from fearful rapids into a cascade of great beauty. The first fall of five feet is immediately succeeded by another of fifteen, into a pool as clear as amber, nestled beneath overarching rocks. Here it lingers as if half reluctant to continue its course, and then gracefully emerges from the grotto, and, veiling the rocks down an abrupt descent of eight-four feet, passes rapidly on to the Yellowstone. It received the name of "Crystal."

The Great Falls are at the head of one of the most remarkable cañons in the world—a gorge through volcanic rocks fifty miles long, and varying from one thousand to nearly five thousand feet in depth. In its descent through this wonderful chasm the river falls almost three thousand feet. At one point, where the passage has been worn through a mountain range, our hunters assured us it was more than a vertical mile in depth, and the river, broken into rapids and cascades, appeared no wider than a ribbon. The brain reels as we gaze into this profound and solemn solitude. We shrink from the dizzy verge appalled, glad to feel the solid earth under our feet, and venture no more, except with forms extended, and faces barely protruding over the edge of the precipice. The stillness is horrible. Down, down, down, we see the river attenuated to a thread, tossing its miniature waves, and dashing, with puny strength, the massive walls which imprison it. All access to its margin is denied, and the dark gray rocks hold it in dismal shadow. Even the voice of its waters in their convulsive agony cannot be heard. Uncheered by plant or shrub, obstructed with massive boulders and by hutting points, it rushes madly on its solitary course, deeper and deeper into the bowels of the rocky firmament. The solemn grandeur of the scene surpasses description. It must be seen to be felt. The sense of danger with which it impresses you is harrowing in the extreme. You feel the absence of sound, the oppression of absolute silence. If you could only hear that gurgling river, if you could see a living tree in the depth beneath you, if a bird would fly past, if the wind would move any object in the awful chasm, to break for a moment the solemn silence that reigns there, it would relieve that tension of the nerves which the scene has excited, and you would rise from your prostrate condition and thank God that he had permitted you to gaze, unharmed, upon this majestic display of natural architecture. As it is, sympathizing in spirit with the deep gloom of the scene, you crawl from the dreadful verge, scared lest the firm rock give way beneath and precipitate you into the horrid gulf....

We spent the next day in examining the wonders surrounding us. At the base of adjacent foothills we found three springs of boiling mud, the largest of which, forty feet in diameter, encircled by an elevated rim of solid tufa, resembles an immense caldron. The seething, bubbling contents, covered with steam, are five feet below the rim. The disgusting appearance of this spring is scarcely atoned for by the wonder with which it fills the beholder. The other two springs, much smaller, but presenting the same general features, are located near a large sulphur spring of milder temperature, but too hot for bathing. On the brow of an adjacent hillock, amid the green pines, heated vapor issues in scorching jets from several craters and fissures. Passing over the hill, we struck a small stream of perfectly transparent water flowing from a cavern, the roof of which tapers back to the water, which is boiling furiously, at a distance of twenty feet from the mouth, and is ejected through it in uniform jets of great force. The sides and entrance of the cavern are covered with soft green sediment, which renders the rock on which it is deposited as soft and pliable as putty.

About two hundred yards from this cave is a most singular phenomenon, which we called the Muddy Geyser. It presents a funnel-shaped orifice, in the midst of a basin one hundred and fifty feet in diameter, with sloping sides of clay and sand. The crater or orifice, at the surface, is thirty by fifty feet in diameter. It tapers quite uniformly to the depth of about thirty feet, where the water may be seen, when the geyser is in repose, presenting a surface of six or seven feet in breadth. The flow of this geyser is regular every six hours. The water rises gradually, commencing to boil when about half way to the surface, and occasionally breaking forth in great violence. When the crater is filled, it is expelled from it in a splashing, scattered mass, ten or fifteen feet in thickness, to the height of forty feet. The water is of a dark lead color, and deposits the substance it holds in solution in the form of miniature stalagmites upon the sides and top of the crater. . . .

SIGNIFICANCE

The idea of the Yellowstone area becoming a national park was considered in the United States during the period of 1865 to 1869. However, such talk did not become serious until after the Washburn Expedition of 1870. The explorers involved with the expedition brought back scientific data and material objects of the beautiful features within Yellowstone. More importantly, however, the expedition brought back Langford, who kept a very detailed diary of his experiences on the trip. He wrote about his experiences in *Scribner's Monthly*, lectured on the Yellowstone area throughout the United States, and lobbied in the U.S. Congress for legislation to create the country's first national park in the Yellowstone area. It was Langford—above anybody else—who brought the subject of a national park at Yellowstone up for national consideration.

Such vivid descriptions helped others to visualize the wonders of Yellowstone. In particular, his account helped convince Ferdinand V. Hayden to take action to make Yellowstone a national park. At this time, Hayden managed the U. S. Geological Survey of the Western Territories. While attending a lecture at Lincoln Hall in Washington, D.C., he heard Langford speak on the "Recent Explorations on the Yellowstone." After hearing the lecture, Hayden convinced the U.S. Congress (with the help of his political ally James G. Blaine, the Speaker of the House) to authorize a government expeditionary survey of the Yellowstone area for the summer of 1871.

The Hayden Expedition, as it was named, became the most extensive and costly expedition into the remote Yellowstone area that had been attempted so far. Hayden himself led a group of distinguished natural resource scientists, along with painters, photographers, and a group of military men. The Hayden Expedition produced additional scientific evidence and first-time photographic evidence concerning the beautiful natural resources within Yellowstone. Artwork by Thomas Moran and photographs by William Henry Jackson helped to show the American public and members of the U.S. Congress that efforts should be taken to preserve the area in its natural state.

On December 18, 1871, Senator Samuel C. Pomeroy of Kansas introduced Senate Bill 392 and William Clagett, the congressional delegate from the Montana Territory, introduced House Bill 764—both

Lower Yellowstone Falls. © ROYALTY-FREE/CORBIS

bills proposing that Yellowstone become a national park. At that time, Langford and Hayden, both employed by the railroads, visited members of Congress in their efforts to gain approval of the bills. The House passed its bill on February 27, 1872 and the Senate passed its bill on January 30, 1872. Then, on March 1, 1872, President Ulysses S. Grant signed the Yellowstone National Park Act to create Yellowstone National Park, a scenic area in the northern Rocky Mountains consisting of 2,219,791 acres (898,317 hectares) of wilderness.

With ideas to preserve nature, promote tourism, and various other ecological and economic reasons, Congress followed the success of Yellowstone with the establishment in the 1890s and early 1900s of the national parks of Sequoia, Yosemite, Mount Rainier, Crater Lake, and Glacier. Without the means to manage the newly created national parks, the National Park Service was created in 1916 as a part of the Department of the Interior. Most importantly, the writing of Langford about the "Wonders of Yellowstone" helped to establish the country's national park system, thus preserving millions of acres of public lands and saving untold numbers of scenic, historic, and recreational locations throughout the United States.

FURTHER RESOURCES

Books

Meyer, Judith L. *The Spirit of Yellowstone: The Cultural Evolution of a National Park.* Lanham, Md.: Rowman and Littlefield, 1996.

Web sites

Barry Mackintosh, National Park Service. "The National Park Service: A Brief History." <http://www.cr.nps.gov/history/hisnps/NPSHistory/npshisto.htm> (accessed November 22, 2005).

Eleanor Jones Harvey, Dallas Museum of Art, Dallas, Texas. "Thomas Moran and the Spirit of Place." <http://www.tfaoi.com/aa/2aa/2aa543.htm> (accessed November 22, 2005).

National Park Service. "Yellowstone National Park: Its Exploration and Establishment." <http://www.cr.nps.gov/history/online_books/haines1/ieet.htm> (accessed November 22, 2005).

The University of Virginia. "The Grand Canyon of the Yellowstone." <http://xroads.virginia.edu/~MA96/RAILROAD/ystone.html> (accessed November 22, 2005).

Wyoming Tales and Trails. "Washburn and Hayden Expeditions." <http://www.wyomingtalesandtrails.com/photos2.html> (accessed November 22, 2005).

Samuel Langhorne Clemens, better known as Mark Twain, in an undated photo. AP IMAGES

Roughing It

Book excerpt

By: Mark Twain (aka Samuel Clemens)

Date: 1872

Source: Twain, Mark. *Roughing It.* Hartford: American Publishing Company, 1872.

About the Author: "By the mark, twain," was the call of the river boatmen on the Mississippi during the nineteenth century, as they warned their pilots that the boat hull was close to the river bed. Samuel Langhorne Clemens took the name Mark Twain as the name by which he would be known as a writer, in part as a homage to his own love of boats and the great river, and as a symbol of his unique talent as a storyteller. Born in Missouri in 1835, Twain accompanied his brother Orion Clemens as his unofficial personal secretary when Orion won the position of Secretary of the Nevada Territory in 1861. At the time of Twain's travels with his brother, Nevada was gripped by silver mining fever, and the arduous overland journey to the West by the Clemens brothers is chronicled in *Roughing It*, which Twain wrote in 1872. Twain's prose style, a distillation of gentle ironies, observational humor, slapstick, satire and irreverence, is quintessentially American. The boundary between fact and a great story was sometimes only winked at by Twain, who loved the telling of a good tale irrespective of its truth or fiction—*Roughing It* may be characterized as a work that is essentially a true story. Later, Twain penned and published the works which generated him significant international acclaim beginning in the late 1870s, including the classics *Tom Sawyer, Huckleberry Finn, A Connecticut Yankee in King Arthur's Court,* and *Innocents Abroad,* as well as a number of short stories. He died in Connecticut in 1910.

INTRODUCTION

The inscription to *Roughing It* commences with the words, "To Calvin H. Higbie, Of California, an Honest Man, a Genial Comrade, and a Steadfast Friend. This Book is inscribed by the author, In Memory of the Curious Time When we Two were Millionaires for Ten Days." The irony and the wordsmithing of the introduction are common threads found in the work as a whole.

America in 1861 was a vastly different place than the United States of today. The War between the States had been recently declared, and the ability of the Union to survive intact was uncertain. The West, meaning anywhere on the continent west of the Mississippi River, remained to a large degree unsettled, and everyday life was a significant struggle for most inhabitants there. The land stretching from the Mississippi to the Pacific Ocean was subject to little real political structure or immediate control. These American territories had been gradually opened to white settlement in the face of increasing tensions with the native tribes, who were commonly displaced in the face of pioneer advances. The trans-continental railway and its power to truly make accessible the West remained a few years away, and travel to the western reaches of the country and the Pacific was still an uncomfortable and risk-filled adventure.

PRIMARY SOURCE

ROUGHING IT

CHAPTER XVIII At eight in the morning we reached the remnant and ruin of what had been the important military station of "Camp Floyd," some forty-five or fifty miles from Salt Lake City. At four P.M. we had doubled our distance and were ninety or a hundred miles from Salt Lake. And now we entered upon one of that species of deserts whose concentrated hideousness shames the diffused and diluted horrors of Sahara—an "alkali" desert. For sixty-eight miles there was but one break in it. I do not remember that this was really a break; indeed it seems to me that it was nothing but a watering depot in the midst of the stretch of sixty-eight miles. If my memory serves me, there was no well or spring at this place, but the water was hauled there by mule and ox teams from the further side of the desert. There was a stage station there. It was forty-five miles from the beginning of the desert, and twenty-three from the end of it.

We plowed and dragged and groped along, the whole live-long night, and at the end of this uncomfortable twelve hours we finished the forty-five-mile part of the desert and got to the stage station where the imported water was. The sun was just rising. It was easy enough to cross a desert in the night while we were asleep; and it was pleasant to reflect, in the morning, that we in actual person had encountered an absolute desert and could always speak knowingly of deserts in presence of the ignorant thenceforward. And it was pleasant also to reflect that this was not an obscure, back country desert, but a very celebrated one, the metropolis itself, as you may say. All this was very well and very comfortable and satisfactory—but now we were to cross a desert in daylight. This was fine—novel—romantic—dramatically adventurous—this, indeed, was worth living for, worth traveling for! We would write home all about it.

This enthusiasm, this stern thirst for adventure, wilted under the sultry August sun and did not last above one hour. One poor little hour—and then we were ashamed that we had "gushed" so. The poetry was all in the anticipation—there is none in the reality. Imagine a vast, waveless ocean stricken dead and turned to ashes; imagine this solemn waste tufted with ash-dusted sage-bushes; imagine the lifeless silence and solitude that belong to such a place; imagine a coach, creeping like a bug through the midst of this shoreless level, and sending up tumbled volumes of dust as if it were a bug that went by steam; imagine this aching monotony of toiling and plowing kept up hour after hour, and the shore still as far away as ever, apparently; imagine team, driver, coach and passengers so deeply coated with ashes that they are all one colorless color; imagine ash-drifts roosting above moustaches and eyebrows like snow accumulations on boughs and bushes. This is the reality of it.

The sun beats down with dead, blistering, relentless malignity; the perspiration is welling from every pore in man and beast, but scarcely a sign of it finds its way to the surface—it is absorbed before it gets there; there is not the faintest breath of air stirring; there is not a merciful shred of cloud in all the brilliant firmament; there is not a living creature visible in any direction whither one searches the blank level that stretches its monotonous miles on every hand; there is not a sound—not a sigh—not a whisper—not a buzz, or a whir of wings, or distant pipe of bird—not even a sob from the lost souls that doubtless people that dead air. And so the occasional sneezing of the resting mules, and the champing of the bits, grate harshly on the grim stillness, not dissipating the spell but accenting it and making one feel more lonesome and forsaken than before.

The mules, under violent swearing, coaxing and whip-cracking, would make at stated intervals a ''spurt,'' and drag the coach a hundred or may be two hundred yards, stirring up a billowy cloud of dust that rolled back, enveloping the vehicle to the wheel-tops or higher, and making it seem afloat in a fog. Then a rest followed, with the usual sneezing and bit-champing. Then another ''spurt'' of a hundred yards and another rest at the end of it. All day long we kept this up, without water for the mules and without ever changing the team. At least we kept it up ten hours, which, I take it, is a day, and a pretty honest one, in an alkali desert. It was from four in the morning till two in the afternoon. And it was so hot! and so close! and our water canteens went dry in the middle of the day and we got so thirsty! It was so stupid and tiresome and dull! and the tedious hours did lag and drag and limp along with such a cruel deliberation! It was so trying to give one's watch a good long undisturbed spell and then take it out and find that it had been fooling away the time and not trying to get ahead any! The alkali dust cut through our lips, it persecuted our eyes, it ate through the delicate membranes and made our noses bleed and kept them bleeding—and truly and seriously the romance all faded far away and disappeared, and left the desert trip nothing but a harsh reality—a thirsty, sweltering, longing, hateful reality!

Two miles and a quarter an hour for ten hours—that was what we accomplished. It was hard to bring the comprehension away down to such a snail-pace as that, when we had been used to making eight and ten miles an hour. When we reached the station on the farther verge of the desert, we were glad, for the first time, that the dictionary was along, because we never could have found language to tell how glad we were, in any sort of dictionary but an unabridged one with pictures in it. But there could not have been found in a whole library of dictionaries language sufficient to tell how tired those mules were after their twenty-three mile pull. To try to give the reader an idea of how thirsty they were, would be to ''gild refined gold or paint the lily.''

Somehow, now that it is there, the quotation does not seem to fit—but no matter, let it stay, anyhow. I think it is a graceful and attractive thing, and therefore have tried time and time again to work it in where it would fit, but could not succeed. These efforts have kept my mind distracted and ill at ease, and made my narrative seem broken and disjointed, in places. Under these circumstances it seems to me best to leave it in, as above, since this will afford at least a temporary respite from the wear and tear of trying to ''lead up'' to this really apt and beautiful quotation.

SIGNIFICANCE

Twain's description of the travails of a Utah desert crossing by mule cart in 1861 is a compelling account of how long and difficult distances were traveled overland in the pre transcontinental rail era. The discomforts of the trek are neatly contrasted with the joy that the travelers experienced in their eventual safe arrival at the desert's edge.

The passage set out above is significant on a number of levels, both historical and current. Twain's descriptions of the Utah desert as a "vast, waveless ocean," with the alkali dust cutting his lips and persecuting his eyes, tell of an experience that would have been almost fanciful to a nineteenth-century reader, as being so far beyond the range of the then-common American extent of travel experience. Few American citizens at that time would have ventured across their own state, let alone the entire country. Twain's account is both factual and provocative.

From a historical perspective, Twain captures both the physical discomfort of the journey and the feeling of being at Nature's mercy as the trek across the desert is made. This passage stands as a stark reminder of how brute animal and human force powered transportation in the mid-nineteenth century, when a combination of geography and the elements created no alternative but to cross such a place.

FURTHER RESOURCES
Books
The Complete Short Stories of Mark Twain, edited by Charles Neider. New York: Doubleday and Company, 1957.

Web sites
mtwain.com. <The Complete Works of Mark Twain." <http://www.mtwain.com> (accessed February 12, 2006).

Railton, Stephen. University of Virginia. "Mark Twain in His Times." <http://etext.lib.virginia.edu/railton/index2.html> (accessed February 12, 2006).

The Conservation of Natural Resources in the United States

''The Principles of Conservation''

Book excerpt

By: Charles Richard Van Hise

Date: 1879

Source: Van Hise, Charles Richard. *The Conservation of Natural Resources in the United States.* New York: Macmillan, 1910.

About the Author: American geologist, educator, and conservationist, Charles Richard Van Hise (1857–1918) was dedicated throughout his career to preserving and creating environmental resources as well as guaranteeing their accessibility and benefits in a democratic way to the entire body of the citizenry. As president of the University of Wisconsin from 1903 until his death, Van Hise, convinced that the boundaries of the campus ought to extend beyond the campus to the entire state, built a network of university educational and conservation services in Wisconsin. His network—called "The Wisconsin Idea"—became a model for university extension programs throughout the United States. He served as an advisor on matters of conservation to President Theodore Roosevelt, who, from 1903 until he left office in 1909, created 42 million acres (about 17 million hectares) of national forests, fifty-three national wildlife refuges, and eighteen areas of natural and national interest including the Grand Canyon. During this time, Van Hise also acted as chairman of the Wisconsin State Conservation Commission. His book, *The Conservation of Natural Resources in the United States* was the first American textbook written about America's natural resources and advocating conservation. Characteristically, its scope is wide. Van Hise includes discussions of public health, work and occupational issues, natural resources conservation, and agricultural techniques.

INTRODUCTION

The presidency of Roosevelt (1901–1909) marked a period of redefinition for the role of the Federal government in American life. Called the Progressive Era, the years surrounding Roosevelt's administration saw a great strengthening of the Federal government, which began to play a significant role in the regulation of many aspects of American life. This activism was the result of what many saw as a crisis that had developed from the growth of industrial activity. The aspects of this crisis were brought to public attention daily by a number of investigative writers in fiction and journalism. President Roosevelt called them "muckrakers" because of the way they dug up "dirt." Among them were Ida Tarbell, Lincoln Steffens, Jacob Riis, and Upton Sinclair. They wrote about corruption in industry as in the case of Standard Oil or the Chicago meat packers, in municipal politics, and in slum dwelling. While the muckrakers exposed industrial perils, naturalists and conservationists like John Muir (a founder of the Sierra Club) and Van Hise were describing the natural world and its glories, waging a battle to protect it from the ravages of industrial production and consumption.

■ PRIMARY SOURCE

PART V
CONSERVATION AND MANKIND

The Principles of Conservation The principles of conservation are different as applied to the different resources.

Coal, peat, oil, and gas are limited in amount. Their process of manufacture is so slow as to be negligible. When extracted from the earth, they must be used, if not at once, within a short time, and when so used are gone forever. Therefore the principles of conservation applicable to them are as follows:—

Conservation of coal, oil, and gas.

In reference to coal, reduce the waste in mining and in use. The waste in mining, now 50 per cent, should be reduced to 25 or 10 per cent; beehive ovens should be abolished; the smoking chimney should be condemned as a nuisance; the gas engine should be substituted for the steam engine. So far as practicable, substitutes should be used for coal; and of these that of developing power by water instead of coal is the most important. Even if all possible economics and substitutes are introduced, the most sanguine cannot hope that the supply of fuels will be sufficient to meet the needs of the people for more than a small fraction of the time we look forward to as the life of this nation. In reference to oil, so far as practicable it should be saved for the higher uses; these are for light and lubricant; only those oils not adapted to these purposes should be used for fuel. Exportation of oil should be prohibited. New wells should be opened up only as fast as necessary to meet the needs under the above principles. In reference to natural gas, the great and pressing necessity is to stop its appalling waste by enacting and enforcing proper legislation. This ideal fuel should be used with the severest economy in order to prolong its life, which will be brief at best.

The metals, like coal, are absolutely limited in amount. Their quantity cannot be added to by any effort of man; but unlike coal, when extracted from the earth and reduced to metallic form, they may be used again and again. The principles applicable to the metals are as follows:—

Conservation of the metals.

First, reduce to a minimum the waste in mining and extracting. At the present time, for certain of the metals these wastes are extraordinarily high, especially for lead and zinc. In many cases by proper practice these losses may be reduced to one half or even one third their present amounts. Second, the metals should not be used for purposes such as destroy them by a single use, as is the case with lead and zinc when made into paint. Third, the metals should not be used in such a way as rapidly to deteriorate, as is the case when iron without a protective covering is exposed to the weather....

Use water fully.

With water, the principles of conservation are different from those of coal and the metals. Each year, a vast quantity of water, through the power of the sun, is taken from the sea and added to the land supply. A roughly equivalent amount flows from the land to the sea. The water is over in circulation, passing from the ocean to the land and from the land to the sea. The problem of the conservation of the moving water is therefore its complete utilization– and that for domestic purposes, for water power, for navigation, and for irrigation. Its use for one of these purposes does not exclude its use for others. Thus, water which is used for domestic purposes may be used for irrigation; indeed this use is most advisable for such water, because of its fertilizing contents. Water used for power may be used for domestic purposes, for navigation, or for irrigation. Water used for navigation may be later used for domestic purposes, for water power, or for irrigation. Water used for irrigation is in part evaporated, but in part goes back to the stream and may be again used for other purposes.

Renew forests as fast as used.

The forests are unlike fuels and minerals in that they may be renewed, but slowly. To renew a forest takes from 50 to 100 years, and for some classes of forests an even longer time. The principle of conservation in reference to the forests is that we may use them, but not more freely than they can be renewed. This is the measure of their wisest consumption. To the present time we have been using the forests much more rapidly than they have been produced. In order to secure this balance we must reduce fire losses; we must reduce the great waste; so far as possible we must utilize by-products; we must substitute cement and stone and brick for wood. Finally, we must increase the growth of the forests....

Reduce erosion to rate of soil making.

The principles of soil conservation are somewhat like those of the forests. The soils may be renewed by the processes of nature, but very slowly; indeed probably at a rate not to exceed one inch in from 500 to 1000 years. The first principle of conservation of the soils is not to allow erosion to occur more rapidly than it is manufactured. The second principle is not to deplete the soil in those elements limited in amount which are necessary for plant food,–nitrogen, potassium, and phosphorus, and

especially phosphorus, for the latter is the element which is very scanty in the soil, and the supplies of which are extremely limited. Phosphorus is the crucial element in soil productivity. The conservation of the soil is the greatest of all the problems of conservation; because upon its products we depend for food and clothing, the basal necessities of man.

Conservation is not a simple subject which can be treated with reference to a single resource, independently of the others; it is an interlocking one. The conservation of one resource is related to that of another....

The Purpose of Conservation What is the purpose of conservation? It is for man. Its purpose is to keep the resources of the world in sufficient abundance so that man may have a happy, fruitful life, free from suffering—a relatively easy physical existence.

Subsistence the main problem of men.

The chief efforts of animal life, and it may be said of plant life also, to the present time, have been directed toward securing subsistence. It makes no difference which animal in a wild state we select,–it may be the swallow flying in the air by day, or the bat by night; it may be the lion in the jungle,–the paramount problem is subsistence. The same is true of man to the present moment. The great problem which confronts more than nine tenths of the human race to-day is that securing food. This does not apply simply to densely populated countries, such as India and China; it applies to the larger number of people in the United States and Europe. It is the aim of conservation to reduce the intensity of struggle for existence, to make the situation more favorable, to reduce mere subsistence to a subordinate place, and thus give an opportunity for development to a higher intellectual and spiritual level.

SIGNIFICANCE

A practical man of ideas, Van Hise played a significant role in redirecting the way the American people thought about the rights of industry over the resources of nature, as well as the responsibilities of government to define and regulate industrial activity and to serve as steward and guardian of natural resources and wildlife areas. His textbook, "The Conservation of Natural Resources in the United States," served as a survey of America's natural resources and promoted an attitude of responsible use with regard to them. The book not only inventoried resources within a social context but also wrote of people as a part of the natural environment needing to be conserved. Van Hise was concerned with issues we would now call "sustainability issues," "quality of life issues," and "workplace issues." He was the first to advise Americans to think of the needs of generations far in the future and also among the first to advocate preventative medical treatment by his advocacy of vaccination.

Van Hise's work extended beyond his lifetime through the programs he established, like the seed farm at the University of Wisconsin. In 1940, scientists working there developed a seed potato of a strength and quality resistant to draught and disease. In 1990, scientists at the university seed farm developed the Snowden potato, which is ideal for the manufacture of potato chips. The importance of creating something like the Snowden potato has significance beyond the obvious biogenetic one. Van Hise was dedicated to insuring that the people of Wisconsin profit economically as well as benefit environmentally from the resources of the Lake Superior region. The example of the Snowden shows how work of the scientists at the University of Wisconsin seed farm fostered the economic growth and health of the region.

FURTHER RESOURCES
Web sites

Extension New and Ideas. "For the Record." <http://www.uwex.edu/ni/documents/0201ni.pdf> (accessed November 14, 2005).

University Communications, News@UW-Madison. "A Century-old Legacy: Influence of Van Hise Lives on Through Wisconsin Idea." <http://www.news.wisc.edu/8502.html> (accessed November 14, 2005).

Wisconsin Conservation Hall of Fame. "Charles Van Hise." <http://www.wchf.org/bio/VanHise.html> (accessed November 14, 2005).

An Address by J. Sterling Morton on Arbor Day 1885

Speech

By: J. Sterling Morton

Date: April 22, 1885

Source: Morton, J. Sterling. "An Address by J. Sterling Morton on Arbor Day 1885." Nebraska City, NE: 1885.

About the Author: Public official, newspaper editor, and naturalist Julius Sterling Morton (1832–1902),

commonly called J. Sterling Morton, is known as the Father of Arbor Day after founding the first tree-planting holiday in Nebraska. Born in Adams, New York, Morton eventually settled in the Nebraska Territory, where he founded and edited the *Nebraska City News*. During his career, Morton served in the Nebraska Territorial legislature from 1855 to 1856 and from 1857 to 1858. He was the U.S. Secretary of Agriculture from 1893 to 1897 under President Grover Cleveland. Morton also served as president of the Nebraska State Agricultural Board and a charter member, in 1869, of the Nebraska State Horticultural Society.

INTRODUCTION

In 1854, Morton and his wife, Caroline, arrived from Detroit, Michigan, to the wide-open prairie of the Nebraska Territory. After enjoying nature for so many years, especially its trees, shrubs, and flowers, and finding themselves living on an almost treeless plain, the couple quickly planted a variety of trees and plants at their new home in Nebraska City, which they called Arbor Lodge.

As a journalist, Morton soon became the editor of Nebraska's first newspaper, the *Nebraska City News*. Due to his interest in agriculture, Morton regularly authored nature and environmental articles and editorials. He especially saw the need for planting trees and shrubs on the windy Nebraska plains to be used as materials to break the wind, prevent soil loss, consume as fuels, use as building materials, absorb moisture in the normally dry soil, and shade people and animals from the hot sun. In his community position as newspaper editor, Morton also encouraged various organizations and groups to join him in promoting the planting of trees. As people saw his dedication to his job and his strong environmental principles, he was offered the position of Secretary of the Nebraska Territory. This prominent political position allowed him to further his environmental opinion on the importance of planting trees in Nebraska.

On January 4, 1872, while at a meeting of the State Board of Agriculture, Morton proposed a tree-planting day to be called "Arbor Day." (About five years earlier, on March 1, 1867, the territory of Nebraska had become the thirty-seventh state of the United States.) The state government approved his idea and the first holiday was set for April 10, 1872. Publicity for the event was circulated throughout the state, with prizes offered to the counties and individuals that planted the most trees on that day. In fact, it is estimated that in one day, the people of Nebraska planted over one million trees.

Nebraskans celebrate Arbor Day on April 25, 2003, as Governor Mike Johanns, left, helps elementary students from a local school plant a Green Mountain Maple Tree. AP IMAGES

Two years later, on March 12, 1874, the citizens of Nebraska again observed Arbor Day on April 19, 1874. Then, in 1885, Arbor Day was named a legal holiday by the Nebraska state legislature. That same year, the date April 22, which was Morton's birthday, was selected as the day for its permanent observance. It is recorded that the first sixteen years of the Arbor Day observance in Nebraska resulted in approximately thirty-five million trees being planted throughout the state. Largely because of Morton's urgings to plant trees in Nebraska, the state was known as the Tree Planters State from the years 1895 to 1945.

■ PRIMARY SOURCE

**AN ADDRESS BY J. STERLING MORTON ON
ARBOR DAY 1885**

THE UNITY OF NATURE

Animal nature is engaged in a constant effort to tear down and destroy vegetable life, for it is upon the vegetable

that the animal, in all its forms, founds and has its being. Take mankind. It is a fact that every physical individualism was not long since animate in growing fields of grain, in gardens of succulent and nutritious roots, and in orchards of brilliant and delicious fruits. So dependent is man life on plant life, that the intermission of a single year of plant growth would turn from life into death every animal organism on the globe. And, on the other hand, the wealth, beauty and luxuriance of harvest fields, orchard fruits, and forest glades are rehabilitated animal life that has gone to decay, baptized into new form and glorified by the light of the sun — the sun light and sun power which plants, leaves, flowers, trees catch and invisibly imprison in the cells of their growth until these are freed and liberated for new uses. The oil which lightens the darkness of the night and the coal which warms our winters derive their qualities from the light which some sort of plant sometime in the misty past during its period of animate growth took captive by absorption from the sun, and, in this marvelous unity of nature, before these plants were either parts of the sea weed fields, or of earth borne trees they were particles of some kind of animal existence. If the doom of decay and death had not been written for animals then life would not have been decreed for flowers and foliage, forests and orchards. The generations of flesh pass away; and plants and trees, by root and leaf, take the substance of the dead forms into their being rebuilding again the vegetable kingdom whence they were ravaged for the sustenance of animals. In this earthly round of being ages come and go, as shadows and sorrows come and go over each individual human life.

The animal kingdom of today was the vegetable kingdom of an age that has been; and the physical man — all the animals — will be the plants, flowers, fruits and forests of the years yet to be. So proceed the cycles of transmutation — inevitable as death, and wonderful and the mystery involved in eternity: change unceasing, but loss never, for frugal nature permits no waste, and, though her forms disintegrate and disappear, substance, mental and material, lives forever, defying decay with the smile of conscious and ineffable immortality.

DUTY OF MAN TO HIS SUCCESSORS

Each generation of humanity takes the earth as trustees to hold until the court of Death dissolves the relation, and turns the property over to successors in trust. To each generation the trust involves the duty of, at least, permitting no deterioration in the great estate of the family of man during the continuance of the temporary trust. Comprehending thus the dependence of animal life upon contemporaneous plant life, it must be conceded that we ought to bequeath to posterity as many forests and orchards as we have exhausted and consumed. One statistician, from date that seems reliable, declares that the fifty-five millions of Americans consume daily for their varied uses 25,000 acres of forest. Basing the calculation on this estimate, on Nebraska's "Arbor Day" in 1886—one year hence—their will be 8,750,000 acres less of forest lands than there are to day—a statement which may well startle into beneficent activity a class of men who otherwise would declare "Arbor Day" a sentimental and useless holiday, and deride its statutory legislation. Hitherto the prominent fact in this land, in connection with wood, has been denudation, and no planting to repair the waste—a denudation portending evil to our people by floods and droughts, infertility and barrenness of soil, and even the extinction of entire communities. Mr. Geo. W. Hotchkiss, secretary of the Chicago Lumberman's Exchange, declares that, during the six years ending January 1st 1885, the receipt of lumber at Chicago alone amounted to 10,728,941,322 feet, and of shingles 5,235,509. The lumber would cover with a floor one inch thick, 246,301 acres of land, or more than all the plowed fields in the fertile and thrifty county of Otoe, and at 1 1/2 cents per foot, would be worth $160,934,120, while the shingles at $2 per thousand, have a value of $10,471,531, and, allowing 10 shingles to a square foot, they would enroof more than 12,000 acres of land. Such figures as these suggest the importance of humane converted action, as a matter of human necessity, for the conservation of woodlands and forests. They teach the imperative necessity of tree planting.

BEAUTY A NEED IN LIFE

The argument here suggested is enough to enforce the necessity of tree planting; but, greater than the dollar value as affecting man in his higher being, is the beautiful in nature. To preserve beauty on the earth, beauty herself beseeches us to plant trees, and renew dead landscapes with the shadow and light of plant life flitting through the pendant limbs, the willowy boughs and the waving foliage of sturdy, yet graceful woods. Our ancestors planted orchards to fruit for us, and homes to give us shelter; and, though it is a commendatory ambition, it is also no more than a desire to pay a just debt, when a man is inspired with the ambition thus also to endeavor to make the world lovely because he has been a dweller on it, during the brief space we call life, and which lies between the cradle and the grave.

In some European countries a tree is planted when a child is born; in others a few acres are devoted to trees—the heritage of the infant when it becomes of age. So the beautiful and the useful are combined; and so, on the lines thus indicated, the tree planter of today "arbor-phones" his good wishes, his name, character and tastes to generations centuries beyond his time.

PRESIDENT HARRISON AMONG NEBRASKA TREES

Years ago General Harrison, afterwards president of the United States, planted catalpa trees on his farm at North Bend, Ohio. After the lapse of years that farm came into the hands of Dr. John A. Warder, the distinguished botanist, and ardent advocate of arboriculture. Dr. Warder sent seeds from these trees to Governor Furnas, of Nebraska, which were planted in the rich alluvial of his Evergreen home in Nemaha county. The seed became trees; and, on his fiftieth birthday—three years ago today—the speaker set out fifty of the Harrison catalpas at Arbor Lodge, which trees will convey to his posterity a story of home culture—a perpetual and perfect poem singing to them of hearts and heads that hold the highest human happiness to find its expression in the embellishment and conservation of permanent and delightful homes, and uniting the names of those who have labored for tree culture, not only in Nebraska, but in the fertile state of Ohio.

PLACE FOR ALL

We are yet in the early days of forestry in Nebraska and the youngest here is not too late to join the "argonauts" in the pursuit of those golden fleeces of autumn-dyed foliage that shall clothe the grand forests with which Nebraska is yet to be crowned. In no system of religion can a ceremonial be found that so incarnates faith as the act of tree planting. We place the roots of the infant tree in their bed of mould with serene and confident certainty that the sun and earth will nourish, warm and quicken the sapling into the forest giant. Our's is an act of devotion to nature and the Supreme law; it is faith expressed in a deed; and it is a deed which conveys health, happiness and consolation to generations not our own. A monk of the seventeenth century described the place we hope for beyond the grave as substantial and no shadow—a world beautiful in grass, flowers, fruits, forests, rivers, lakes and oceans, and hills and valleys, sensible to sight and to touch; and, in picturing the heaven we long for, man's brain has always drawn largely for its imagery from man's vegetable co-tenants of the globe. This being man's concept of human happiness, let us endeavor then by our words on "Arbor Day"—and all other opportune occasions—to so embellish the world with plant life, trees, flowers and foliage, as to make our earth homes approximate to those which the prophets, poets and seers of all ages have portrayed as the Home in Heaven.

SIGNIFICANCE

After Morton founded Arbor Day in Nebraska, his environmental message quickly spread around the world. Today, Arbor Day, which is commonly celebrated on the last Friday in April, is held throughout all fifty states of the United States. Throughout the world, tree planting holidays and festivities trace their roots back to Morton's Arbor Day creation in the late nineteenth century in Nebraska. Although often called by various names, the purpose of these celebrations is to acknowledge the importance of trees to all living things on Earth. A few synonymous names for Arbor Day celebrated around the world include: Arbor Week in Australia and Canada, Greening Week in Japan, New Year's Day of the Trees in Israel, Tree-Loving Week in Korea, National Festival of Tree Planting in India, Student's Afforestation Day in Iceland, and Tree Holiday and Tree Festival in various countries of the world.

The establishment of Arbor Day has had a significant impact on the landscape and environment of Nebraska and countless other areas throughout the world. Whenever tree-planting celebrations are held at various towns and cities on Earth, they all promote the importance of trees, the Earth's oldest living organisms and a critical indicator for the health of the world's environment. Within the United States, for example, it is estimated that each U.S. citizen uses over 2,000 pounds (900 kilograms) of wood each year—the equivalent of a tree with a length of 100 feet (30.5 meters) and a diameter of 18 inches (45.7 centimeters). During that same year period, about 1.5 billion trees are planted by people throughout the United States, replacing those that they used.

Trees are tremendously significant to people and their environments worldwide due to the fact that they:

- Provide a renewable source of fuel, shelter, and food
- Reduce heating and cooling costs by providing shade to help moderate the interior temperatures of buildings
- Provide protection from winds through clustering
- Expel oxygen into the atmosphere through photosynthesis to allow humans and animals to breathe
- Absorb airborne pollutants such as carbon dioxide to improve air quality, which otherwise would harm human health
- Provide over 5,000 known products (or ingredients in products) such as asphalt, adhesives, chewing gum, cork, crayons, dyes, mouthwashes, paper, pencils, perfumes, shatterproof glass, soaps and shampoos, sunscreen lotions, tires, and toothpaste

- Provide homes, food, protection, and nests for wildlife
- Reduce levels of noises by providing natural barriers
- Return nutrients back into the soil from rotting woods and leaves
- Provide beautiful places to live, play, and work.

Trees directly benefit the economic, environmental and social health of people around the world. Due to the efforts of Morton in establishing a special day of tree-planting in Nebraska and ultimately throughout the country and the world, the overall integrity of the environment and the world's natural resources have improved. The future of the world's forests and tree-shaded streets, parks, homes, and businesses depends on each person's respect for the importance that trees give to mankind. Morton and his Arbor Day idea remind people each year about that importance for a healthy and prosperous future.

FURTHER RESOURCES
Books

Olson, James C. *J. Sterling Morton: Pioneer Statesman, Founder of Arbor Day*. Lincoln, NE: University of Nebraska Press, 1942.

Pakenham, Thomas. *Remarkable Trees of the World*. London: Weidenfeld and Nicolson, 2002.

Web sites

"The Home Page of the National Arbor Day Foundation." *National Arbor Day Foundation*. <http://www.arborday.org> (accessed March 8, 2006).

"Nebraska City: Arbor Day's Hometown." *Southwest Nebraska News*, April 14, 2005. <http://www.swnebr.net/newspaper/cgi-bin/articles/articlearchiver.pl?157270> (accessed March 8, 2006).

Schmitt, Beverly. "Arbor Day." *Love to Learn Place.com*. <http://www.lovetolearnplace.com/SpecialDays/Arbor/index.html> (accessed March 8, 2006).

Octavia Hill (1838–1912) founds English National Trust

Photograph

By: Augustin Rischgitz

Date: 1892

Source: Rischgitz, Augustin. "Octavia Hill (1838–1912) founds English National Trust." Getty Images, 1892.

About the Photographer: A collection of Augustin Rischgitz's photography is located in the Hulton Archive at Getty Images. Getty is one of the leading global providers of visual content materials to such communications groups as advertisers, broadcasters, designers, magazines, new media organizations, newspapers, and producers.

INTRODUCTION

Social reformer and housing renovation activist Octavia Hill (1838–1912) was influenced to improve living conditions of the English urban poor by her family upbringing and her belief in Christian Socialism (a movement dedicated to theological thoughts and Christian service within politics). Hill began working in London in 1852 at the Ladies' Guild, where she taught poor school children how to make toys. In this position, Hill saw firsthand the dreadful conditions in which these children lived. In 1856, Hill became a secretary at the Working Men's College and, along with her sisters, started a school in a poor section of the city several years later. While at these two jobs, Hill realized the need to reduce the housing problems of the very poor. Often financed by art critic John Ruskin (1819–1900), Hill frequently purchased small blocks of rundown properties in order to make sure the apartments were suitable to live in and to help the poor living within them.

Later, with additional financial backing, Hill built two housing developments in London. Upon the success of these two projects, Hill built many more housing developments, most with funding from wealthy individuals. At the zenith of her work, she was managing around 6,000 dwellings—always insisting that each building provide simple lodging with outside access to open space and requiring that her tenants promptly pay their rent and maintain clean properties.

Hill became a crusading pioneer when she started in 1864 a movement for housing reform and improvement for the poor. Building upon the success of her housing activities, Hill expanded her reach when she began to protect open spaces for the enjoyment of the public. She became a leader in the English open-space movement in the middle part of the nineteenth century—becoming a member of committees and commissions that dealt with housing, and aggressively promoting her ideals. Due to her successful reputation in reforming housing projects, Hill was often appointed to manage housing property for other organizations.

Hill dedicated her life to social causes, constantly supervising the careful construction and proper management of buildings and the use and preservation of parks and open spaces. Her successful management methods for housing projects were used in England, Ireland, on the continent of Europe, and in the United States. Hill also was involved in charitable activities such as the Charity Organization Society and the Kyrle Society.

One of Hill's most noteworthy accomplishments was as one of the three founders in 1895 of the National Trust for Places of Historic Interest or Natural Beauty, now commonly shortened to the National Trust or NT.

Twenty years earlier, in 1875, Hill visited the Commons Preservation Society where she met Robert Hunter (1844–1913). They realized that they had similar beliefs in improving living conditions for the poor and preserving open spaces. Worried about negative impacts to the environment and degradations of society in general, Hill and Hunter, along with Hardwicke Rawnsley (1851–1920), began to discuss what could be done to protect threatened land and historic buildings throughout England.

In the early part of 1884, Robert Hunter sent off a letter in which he proposed establishing a land company with a purpose of protecting open spaces for the public interest. Hill wrote back, suggesting The Commons and Gardens Trust as the name for the company. Hunter supposedly penciled in at the top of the letter the two words: National Trust.

The nongovernmental, nonprofit National Trust was founded at the London home (Grosvenor House) of the Duke of Westminster on January 12, 1895. The first acquisitions by the National Trust were of the 4.5 acres (1.8 hectares) of Dinas Oleu in 1895, a part of the Welsh cliffs overlooking Cardigan Bay, and the Clergy House in 1896, a fourteenth-century timber-framed house located at Alfriston in East Sussex.

■ PRIMARY SOURCE

OCTAVIA HILL (1838–1912) FOUNDS ENGLISH NATIONAL TRUST
See primary source image.

PRIMARY SOURCE

Octavia Hill (1838–1912) founds English National Trust.
Octavia Hill worked with art critic John Ruskin to improve housing conditions for the poor and co-founded the National Trust for Places of Historic Interest or Natural Beauty. PHOTO BY RISCHGITZ/ GETTY IMAGES

SIGNIFICANCE

Many social and environmental problems occurred in England during the Industrial Revolution that began in the late eighteenth century. By the middle of the nineteenth century, three major problems had already appeared: the destruction of areas of natural beauty by encroaching urban development; the deterioration of living conditions in large cities due to massive numbers of people moving from rural areas looking for jobs; and the development of previously undeveloped land in urban areas and surrounding rural areas to alleviate food shortages and the lack of housing facilities.

With the inspiration and tireless work of Hill, along with others with whom she worked throughout her life, the people of England today possess many historic buildings, open spaces, and areas of natural beauty that would have undoubtedly succumbed to the urbanization of England through the almost uncontrolled technological progress of the Industrial Revolution. The significant work of Hill in the area of housing reform also became a model for improving private housing construction and management projects, along with influencing the way that the English government made major reforms in housing, conservation, and urban development.

When Hill died in 1912, the amount of property acquired by the National Trust had exceeded the modest expectations of its three founders. Due to the success of Hill at creating and developing the National Trust and her other important endeavors at conserving natural resources, reforming urban housing, and curing society's ills, many conservationists in the United States and other countries based their own actions on the management methods used by Hill.

Because of the early work of Hill and other founding members of the National Trust, the organization, today, not only preserves properties of historic interest and natural beauty, but is also granted by parliamentary procedure the ability to declare land inalienable; that is, incapable of being sold, mortgaged, or purchased against the wishes of the Trust. Such power by the National Trust gives most of its properties a protection in perpetuity so their future protection is secure. In effect, the National Trust acts as the guardian of Great Britain—preserving its history, conserving its natural resources, and providing for the benefit of its people.

Over one hundred years after the National Trust was first established by Hill, Robert Hunter, and Hardwicke Rawnsley, it protects over 600,000 acres (242,820 hectares) of countryside in England, Northern Ireland, and Wales; nearly 600 miles (965 kilometers) of coastline; and over 200 historic buildings and gardens. Other countries have established similar national trusts.

Because Hill worried about the detrimental effects on society due to uncontrolled industrialization from England's businesses, the National Trust today is able to emphasize the importance of history, valuing historic places not just for their own sake but for the opportunities they provide in supporting education, promoting health and well-being, stimulating creativity and innovation, and involving people and communities. The National Trust has become one of the largest environmental preservation organizations in the world and the largest private society in England devoted to heritage preservation. As the country's

Wicken Fen, located in Cambridgshire, was purchased by the National Trust (NT) in 1899. Today it remains one of the few wild fens in the UK, due to the preservation groundwork laid by the NT and continuing efforts. © NIK WHEELER/CORBIS

largest private landowner, the National Trust protects gardens, villages and hamlets, farms and woodlands, islands, archaeological remains and antiquities, nature reserves, fens, moorlands, windmills and watermills, nature reserves, and important objects of England's industrial past.

FURTHER RESOURCES

Books

Newby, Howard, ed. *The National Trust: The Next Hundred Years*. London: National Trust, 1995.

Web sites

Fitzgerald, Penelope. "Earth Mother: Octavia Hill, Queen of Open Spaces." *New York Times Magazine*, 1999. <http://www.nytimes.com/library/magazine/millennium/m1/fitzgerald.html> (accessed March 10, 2006).

The National Trust. <http://www.nationaltrust.org.uk/main> (accessed March 10, 2006).

The Octavia Hill Birthplace Museum. <http://www. octavia hillmuseum.org> (accessed March 10, 2006).

Our National Parks

Book excerpt

By: John Muir

Date: 1901

Source: Muir, John. *Our National Parks*. Boston: Houghton-Mifflin, 1901.

About the Author: Naturalist John Muir (1838–1914) was a Scottish-born wilderness explorer, best known for his adventures in the glaciers of Alaska and California's Sierra Nevada. Muir feared that the United States as he had witnessed it would gradually become overdeveloped, and he wrote extensively about the importance of protecting the natural landscape and wildlife of the country. His work was instrumental in the creation of the national parks, including Yellowstone, Yosemite, Mount Rainier, and Grand Canyon National Park, and his writing inspired many of the conservation programs enacted by President Theodore Roosevelt, including the first National Monuments by Presidential Proclamation. Muir also co-founded the Sierra Club in 1892, providing a formal organization for environmental activists to continue working for the preservation of the nation's mountain ranges.

INTRODUCTION

Our National Parks is a collection of essays by Muir, originally written for the Atlantic Monthly. Muir wrote about the beauty and grandeur of the nation's forests and mountain ranges, hoping to encourage people to visit these areas and to realize the importance of maintaining a portion of the country in its original, natural state.

◼ PRIMARY SOURCE

Of the four national parks of the West, the Yellowstone is far the largest. It is a big, wholesome wilderness on the broad summit of the Rocky Mountains, favored with abundance of rain and snow,—a place of fountains where the greatest of the American rivers take their rise. The central portion is a densely forested and comparatively level volcanic plateau with an average elevation of about eight thousand feet above the sea, surrounded by an imposing host of mountains belonging to the subordinate Gallatin, Wind River, Teton, Absaroka, and snowy ranges. Unnumbered lakes shine in it, united by a famous band of streams that rush up out of hot lava beds, or fall from the frosty peaks in channels rocky and bare, mossy and bosky, to the main rivers, singing cheerily on through every difficulty, cunningly dividing and finding their way east and went to the two far-off seas.

Glacier meadows and beaver meadows are outspread with charming effect along the banks of the streams, parklike expanses in the woods, and innumerable small gardens in rocky recesses of the mountains, some of them containing more petals than leaves, while the whole wilderness is enlivened with happy animals.

Beside the treasures common to most mountain regions that are wild and blessed with a kind climate, the park is full of exciting wonders. The wildest geysers in the world, in bright, triumphant bands, are dancing and singing in it amid thousands of boiling springs, beautiful and awful, their basins arrayed in gorgeous colors like gigantic flowers; and hot paint-pots, mud springs, mud volcanoes, mush and broth caldrons whose contents are of every color and consistency, plash and heave and roar in bewildering abundance. In the adjacent mountains, beneath the living trees the edges of petrified forests are exposed to

view, like specimens on the shelves of a museum, standing on ledges tier above tier where they grew, solemnly silent in rigid crystalline beauty after swaying in the winds thousands of centuries ago, opening marvelous views back into the years and climates and life of the past. Here, too, are hills of sparkling crystals, hills of sulphur, hills of glass, hills of cinders and ashes, mountains of every style of architecture, icy or forested, mountains covered with honey-bloom sweet as Hymettus, mountains boiled soft like potatoes and colored like a sunset sky. A 'that and a' that, and twice as muckle's a' that, Nature has on show in the Yellowstone Park. Therefore it is called Wonderland, and thousands of tourists and travelers stream into it every summer, and wander about in it enchanted.

Fortunately, almost as soon as it was discovered it was dedicated and set apart for the benefit of the people, a piece of legislation that shines benignly amid the common dust-and-ashes history of the public domain, for which the world must thank Professor Hayden above all others; for he led the first scientific exploring party into it, described it, and with admirable enthusiasm urged Congress to preserve it. As delineated in the year 1872, the park, contained about 3344 square miles. On March 30, 1891 it was to all intents and purposes enlarged by the Yellowstone National Park Timber Reserve, and in December, 1897, by the Teton Forest Reserve; thus nearly doubling its original area, and extending the southern boundary far enough to take in the sublime Teton range and the famous pasturelands of the big Rocky Mountain game animals. The withdrawal of this large tract from the public domain did not harm to any one; for its height, 6000 to over 13,000 feet above the sea, and its thick mantle of volcanic rocks, prevent its ever being available for agriculture or mining, while on the other hand its geographical position, reviving climate, and wonderful scenery combine to make it a grand health, pleasure, and study resort,—a gathering-place for travelers from all the world.

The national parks are not only withdrawn from sale and entry like the forest reservations, but are efficiently managed and guarded by small troops of United States cavalry, directed by the Secretary of the Interior. Under this care the forests are flourishing, protected from both axe and fire; and so, of course, are the shaggy beds of underbrush and the herbaceous vegetation. The so-called curiosities, also, are preserved, and the furred and feathered tribes, many of which, in danger of extinction a short time ago, are now increasing in numbers,—a refreshing thing to see amid the blind, ruthless destruction that is going on in the adjacent regions. In pleasing contrast to the noisy, ever changing management, or mismanagement, of blundering, plundering, money-making vote-sellers who receive their places from boss politicians as purchased goods, the soldiers do their duty so quietly that the traveler is scarce aware of their presence.

This is the coolest and highest of the parks. Frosts occur every month of the year. Nevertheless, the tenderest tourist finds it warm enough in summer. The air is electric and full of ozone, healing, reviving, exhilarating, kept pure by frost and fire, while the scenery is wild enough to awaken the dead. It is a glorious place to grow in and rest in; camping on the shores of the lakes, in the warm openings of the woods golden with sunflowers, on the banks of the streams, by the snowy waterfalls, beside the exciting wonders or away from them in the scallops of the mountain walls sheltered from every wind, on smooth silky lawns enameled with gentians, up in the fountain hollows of the ancient glaciers between the peaks, where cool pools and brooks and gardens of precious plants charmingly embowered are never wanting, and good rough rocks with every variety of cliff and scaur are invitingly near for outlooks and exercise.

From these lovely dens you may make excursions whenever you like into the middle of the park, where the geysers and hot springs are reeking and spouting in their beautiful basins, displaying an exuberance of color and strange motion and energy admirably calculated to surprise and frighten, charm and shake up the least sensitive out of apathy into newness of life.

However orderly your excursions or aimless, again and again amid the calmest, stillest scenery you will be brought to a standstill hushed and awe-stricken before phenomena wholly new to you. Boiling springs and huge deep pools of purest green and azure water, thousands of them, are plashing and heaving in these high, cool mountains as if a fierce furnace fire were burning beneath each one of them; and a hundred geysers, white torrents of boiling water and steam, like inverted waterfalls, are ever and anon rushing up out of the hot, black underworld. Some of these ponderous geyser columns are as large as sequoias,—five to sixty feel in diameter, one hundred and fifty to three hundred feet high,—and are sustained at this great height with tremendous energy for a few minutes, or perhaps nearly an hour, standing rigid and erect, hissing, throbbing, booming, as if thunderstorms were raging beneath their roots, their sides roughened or fluted like the furrowed boles of trees, their tops dissolving in feathery branches, while the irised spray, like misty bloom is at times blown aside, revealing the massive shafts shining against a background of pine-covered hills. Some of them lean more or less, as if storm-bent, and instead of being round are flat or fan-shaped, issuing from irregular slits in silex pavements with radiate structure, the sunbeams sifting through them in ravishing splendor. Some are broad and round-headed like oaks; others are low and bunchy, branching near the ground like bushes; and a few are hollow in the centre like big daisies or water-lilies. No frost cools them, snow never covers them nor lodges in their branches; winter and summer they welcome alike; all of them, of whatever form or size, faithfully rising and sinking in fairy rhythmic dance night and day, in all sorts of weather, at varying periods of minutes, hours, or weeks, growing up rapidly, uncontrollable as fate, tossing their pearly branches in the wind, bursting into bloom and vanishing like the frailest flowers,—plants of which Nature raises hundreds or thousands of crops a year with no apparent exhaustion of the fiery soil.

The so-called geyser basins, in which this rare sort of vegetation is growing, are mostly open valleys on the central plateau that were eroded by glaciers after the greater volcanic fires had ceased to burn. Looking down over the forests as you approach them from the surrounding heights, you see a multitude of white columns, broad, reeking masses, and irregular jets and puffs of misty vapor ascending from the bottom of the valley, or entangled like smoke among the neighboring trees, suggesting the factories of some busy town or the camp-fires of an army. These mark the position of each mush-pot, paint-pot, hot spring, and geyser, or gusher, as the Icelandic words mean. And when you saunter into the midst of them over the bright sinter pavements, and see how pure and white and pearly gray they are in the shade of the mountains, and how radiant in the sunshine, you are fairly enchanted. So numerous they are and varied, Nature seems to have gathered them from all the world as specimens of her rarest fountains, to show in one place what she can do. Over four thousand hot springs have been counted in the park, and a hundred geysers; how many more there are nobody knows.

These valleys at the heads of the great rivers may be regarded as laboratories and kitchens, in which, amid a thousand retorts and pots, we may see Nature at work as chemist or cook, cunningly compounding an infinite variety of mineral messes; cooking whole mountains; boiling and steaming flinty rocks to smooth paste and mush,—yellow, brown, red, pink, lavender, gray, and creamy white,—making the most beautiful mud in the world; and distilling the most ethereal essences. Many of these pots and caldrons have been boiling thousands of years. Pots of sulphurous mush, stringy and lumpy, and pots of broth as black as ink, are tossed and stirred with constant care, and thin transparent essences, too pure and fine to be called water, are kept simmering gently in beautiful sinter cups and bowls that grow ever more beautiful the longer they are used. In some of the spring basins, the waters, though still warm, are perfectly calm, and shine blandly in a sod of overleaning grass and flowers, as if they were thoroughly cooked at last, and set aside to settle and cool. Others are wildly boiling over as if running to waste, thousands of tons of the precious liquids being thrown into the air to fall in scalding floods on the clean coral floor of the establishment, keeping onlookers at a distance. Instead of holding limpid pale green or azure water, other pots and craters are filled with scalding mud, which is tossed up from three or four feet to thirty feet, in sticky, rank-smelling masses, with gasping, belching, thudding sounds, plastering the branches of neighboring trees; every flask, retort, hot spring, and geyser has something special in it, no two being the same in temperature, color, or composition.

In these natural laboratories one needs stout faith to feel at ease. The ground sounds hollow underfoot, and the awful subterranean thunder shakes one's mind as the ground is shaken, especially at night in the pale moon-light, or when the sky is overcast with storm-clouds. In the solemn gloom, the geysers, dimly visible, look like monstrous dancing ghosts, and their wild songs and the earthquake thunder replying to the storms overhead seem doubly terrible, as if divine government were at an end. But the trembling hills keep their places. The sky clears, the rosy dawn is reassuring, and up comes the sun like a god, pouring his faithful beams across the mountains and forest, lighting each peak and tree and ghastly geyser alike, and shining into the eyes of the reeking springs, clothing them with rainbow light, and dissolving the seeming chaos of darkness into varied forms of harmony. The ordinary work of the world goes on. Gladly we see the flies dancing in the sun-beams, birds feeding their young, squirrels gathering nuts, and hear the blessed ouzel singing confidingly in the shallows of the river,—most faithful evangel, calming every fear, reducing everything to love. . . .

Author and naturalist John Muir sits in appreciation of nature, 1902. © CORBIS

SIGNIFICANCE

Muir firmly believed that at the end of the nineteenth century and the start of the twentieth, the United States was in danger of losing every last acre of its natural beauty and landscape to the ravages of industry. He saw forests being leveled for fuel, rivers polluted by factory runoff, and people becoming overly civilized in the sense that they were losing touch with nature through exposure to cities and the mechanics of the modern world. Having traveled extensively throughout the western part of the nation, where much of the unspoiled land remained, he began writing about these vast regions and encouraging people to visit them in order to appreciate their beauty for themselves. He claimed that wandering through the wilderness was beneficial to the health, calming to the nerves, and that the desire to protect these lands would come naturally to anyone who saw

them. Muir's intent was to stand as an advocate for the land, to gain the support of the nation, and thereby attract the attention of the lawmakers who could find ways to cease the endless development of the land that was destroying it.

Yellowstone National Park was the first area of the country to be set aside and protected. The region was discovered in the latter half of the nineteenth century and declared park land by Congress in 1872, with the idea that people would be able to use it for recreational purposes. Muir's writings directed people to take advantage of this natural resource by praising the wonder and variety of the landscape and the sights to be seen. He cited the wildlife that lived in the park, as well as a range of terrain, including meadows, valleys, mountains, petrified forests, geysers, and hot springs. He spoke of the area as if it were nature's own experiment, with each varied part of the park a different result. Muir also compared the sights in Yellowstone to those found all over the world, particularly in exotic countries. By mentioning that geysers were also located in such far flung places as New Zealand, Iceland, and Japan, he showed people that it was not necessary to travel to foreign lands to view such impressive natural wonders. He was careful to calm the fears of many travelers who imagined or had heard reports of the dangers in visiting the parks, assuring them that they were primarily either exaggerations of true dangers, such as the bears that lived in the forest, or pure imagination. His encouragement and vivid descriptions kept the park in the public eye, increasing the number of visitors, and also drew the attention of the government, eventually leading to the enactment of the National Park Service in 1916, which protected not only Yellowstone, but the other parks that had been designated, unifying them as a single entity designed to benefit the citizens of the United States. It also created the post of a director to oversee the properties and their management, thereby ensuring that large tracts of land would remain untouched by industrial progress, and unspoiled in the years to come.

FURTHER RESOURCES

Web sites

John Muir Project. <http://www.johnmuirproject.org> (accessed January 17, 2006).

John Muir Trust. <http://www.jmt.org> (accessed January 17, 2006).

National Park Service. "John Muir National Historic Site." <http://www.nps.gov/jomu> (accessed January 17, 2006).

Sierra Club. "John Muir Exhibit". <http://www.sierraclub.org/john_muir_exhibit/frameindex.html> (accessed January 17, 2006).

Drawing the Line in Mississippi

Cartoon in the *Washington Post* leads to President Theodore Roosevelt's Teddy Bear

Photograph

By: Clifford K. Berryman

Date: November 16, 1902

Source: AP Images

About the Artist: Clifford "Cliff" Berryman (1869–1949) grew up watching his father draw caricatures in order to entertain his eleven children. Inheriting his father's drawing talent—and without ever taking an art class in school—Berryman's career in cartooning spanned over thirty years, culminating as chief cartoonist for the *Washington Evening Star*. In 1902 Berryman was employed as a political cartoonist for the *Washington Post*, where he drew the famous cartoon "Drawing The Line In Mississippi," which directly lead to the creation of Teddy Bear stuffed animal toys in honor of a conservation action performed by President Theodore Roosevelt. This particular cartoon is now housed at Harvard University, who loaned it to the Hermione Museum in Tallulah, Louisiana, where the primary source photograph was taken. Later, in 1944, Berryman was awarded the Pulitzer Prize in cartooning for the cartoon "But Where Is The Boat Going," which showed President Franklin D. Roosevelt as the captain of a rowboat named "Manpower Mobilization." Besides appearing in newspapers across the country, Berryman's cartoons have been displayed at many famous locations including the U.S. Library of Congress.

INTRODUCTION

Already known as a sportsman, but also as a man very concerned with preserving the country's natural resources, Roosevelt, the twenty-sixth president of the United States, traveled to Smede's Plantation in Mississippi in November 1902. He supposedly went there to decide a dispute about a wilderness boundary between the states of Mississippi and Louisiana but in all likelihood he traveled there to hunt black bears.

Legend has declared that aides to the president tied a small bear cub to a tree and that Roosevelt refused to shoot the defenseless animal. Other information tends to show that the hunting party had been unsuccessfully tracking a full-sized black bear for most of the day and later, after most of the troop including Roosevelt left for a meal, a hunting guide had found the bear mauling his hunting dogs. In order to save his valuable dogs, the man clubbed the bear unconscious with his rifle. When the president was called, the guide had the animal tied around the neck by a rope that was secured to a tree. He asked the president if he would shoot the bear, which Roosevelt refused to do. As his actions proved, Roosevelt abided by a code that distained the unsportsmanlike killing of defenseless animals.

Whatever happened that day, Berryman drew a cartoon based on the description of the story told by the reporters who were covering the trip. An article about Roosevelt's hunting trip appeared in the

Washington Post on Sunday, November 16, 1902, and the next day Berryman's cartoon appeared as a front-page feature. Berryman depicted the disgruntled Roosevelt in his hunting outfit with his right hand firmly holding his gun to the ground and his left hand parallel to the ground with palm held outward in a forceful stance opposing the killing of the large, angry bear. The caption stated "Drawing The Line In Mississippi," which at the time was seen by many political experts to represent Roosevelt's criticisms of intentional killings (mostly by lynching) of southern blacks by white supremacist groups. Others saw the cartoon as a way to publicize Roosevelt's real purpose for traveling to Mississippi: to hunt bears. Still others saw the president as a person who stood solidly on his honest principles. Whatever the reason, President Roosevelt's popularity increased dramatically because of the attention given to the cartoon.

Publishers across the country decided to highlight the cartoon over the next six years. As the cartoon was distributed, the tone of the cartoon was altered along with the story of Roosevelt's hunting trip. The large, fierce bear that was tied to a tree was replaced with a small, helpless-looking bear cub being held with a rope by a hunter. In whichever way the public saw the cartoon drawn by Berryman, most public opinion saw Roosevelt as simply protecting wildlife. Today, the original 1902 drawing is nearly forgotten, while the 1906 redrawn version, which was more widely distributed, is the more recognized cartoon of the two.

Although there is some disagreement as to when the teddy bear was first created, most historians believe that a Brooklyn candy store owner by the name of Morris Michtom saw the cartoon and was inspired by Roosevelt to make a pattern of a small toy bear, which his wife Rose then sewed together. The toy was placed in his store window on top of chocolates, along with a copy of the cartoon and a handwritten sign stating "Teddy's Bear." The toy bears became so popular that Michtom eventually closed the candy store and founded the Ideal Novelty and Toy Company.

PRIMARY SOURCE

DRAWING THE LINE IN MISSISSIPPI

See primary source image.

PRIMARY SOURCE

Drawing the Line in Mississippi This cartoon, drawn by Clifford Berryman, and photographed by Bill Haber, orginally appeared in The *Washington Post*. There is speculation that the idea of the "teddy bear" was inspired by this drawing. AP IMAGES

SIGNIFICANCE

The creation of the teddy bear was just one way of many that Roosevelt was seen as a naturalist, conservationist, and sportsman, with a strong conviction in preserving such natural resources as minerals, forests, and waters. By the time Roosevelt became president, over three-quarters of the nation's original forests had been cut down, much of the southern and eastern farmlands were tragically overused, and the western states were continually in an arid climatic state. Roosevelt sided with the growing number of conservationists who wanted the land returned to its natural state.

As president of the United States, Roosevelt incorporated the conservation of public lands as a major issue of his administration. After returning from his bear hunt in Mississippi, President Roosevelt proceeded to protect hundreds of millions of acres of public lands from uncontrolled development by private land developers. He promoted the acquisition and management of public lands and their resources by the federal government. In fact, Roosevelt saw the country's landscape as part of its overall character, a source of wealth and importance, and a necessary way to strengthen and maintain American democracy, along with the country's economic stability and well being.

Roosevelt was also of critical importance in passing the Newlands Act of 1902, which permitted the federal government the right to implement water management and reclamation efforts (such as the Roosevelt Dam irrigation project) and assist farmers and ranchers in the arid western states; and later helped to establish the U.S. Bureau of Reclamation. These large-scale federal efforts transformed the environment and economy of the United States. According to the National Geographic Society, one of Roosevelt's most significant efforts was the preservation of about 230 million acres of U.S. land, including 150 national forests, fifty-one federal bird reservations, twenty-four reclamation projects, eighteen national monuments, five national parks, and four national game preserves.

During his presidency, Roosevelt wrote: "It is entirely in our power as a nation to preserve large tracts of wilderness...as playgrounds for rich and poor alike, and to preserve the game...But this end can only be achieved by wise laws and by a resolute enforcement of the laws. Lack of such legislation and administration will result in harm to all of us, but most of all harm to the nature lover who does not possess vast wealth."

FURTHER RESOURCES

Books

Cadenhead, Ivie Edward. *Theodore Roosevelt: The Paradox of Progressivism*. Woodbury, NY: Barron's Educational Series, 1974.

Gibbs, Brian. *Teddy Bear Century*. Lanham, MD: Taylor Trade, 2003.

Jefers, Harry Paul. *Roosevelt The Explorer: T.R.'s Amazing Adventures as a Naturalist, Conservationist, and Explorer*. Lanham, MD: Taylor Trade, 2003.

Morris, Edmund. *The Rise of Theodore Roosevelt*. New York: Modern Library, 2001.

———. *Theodore Rex*. New York: Random House, 2001.

Roosevelt, Theodore. "Wilderness Reserves: The Yellowstone Park." In *Outdoor Pastimes of an American Hunter*. New York: Charles Scribner's Sons, 1916.

Wilson, Robert Lawrence. *Theodore Roosevelt: Outdoorsman*. New York: Winchester Press, 1971.

Web sites

"Conservationist: Life of Theodore Roosevelt." *Theodore Roosevelt Association*. <http://www.theodoreroosevelt. org/life/conservation.htm> (accessed March 1, 2006).

"The Story of the Teddy Bear." *The Bear Museum, Petersfield*. <http://www.bearmuseum.co.uk/history1.htm> (accessed March 1, 2006).

"The Theodore Roosevelt Administration: Theodore Roosevelt and Conservation." *U-S-History.com*. <http://www.u-s-history.com/pages/h937.html> (accessed March 1, 2006).

Nature

Essay

By: Ralph Waldo Emerson

Date: 1836

Source: Ralph Waldo Emerson. "Nature." Boston: James Munroe and Company, 1836.

About the Author: American author, poet, lecturer, and philosopher, Ralph Waldo Emerson (1803–1882), educated at Harvard and Harvard Divinity School, was an ordained Christian Minister. Early in his career, however, as pastor of Boston's Second Church, he resigned his ministry because of doctrinal doubts. His misgivings about formal Christianity, however, did not shake his spirituality or religious faith. Neither did the many tragic deaths of loved ones he sustained throughout his life—although they darkened his spirit—including the death of his first wife, Ellen Tucker, in 1832, and of his young son, Waldo, in 1842. Emerson maintained a belief in the unity of man and nature and espoused a doctrine of optimism, self-reliance, mysticism, and the immanence of a God whose presence could be seen and felt in all nature. Along with such figures as Bronson Alcott (1799–1888) and Margaret Fuller (1810–1850), Emerson was a central figure in the New England Transcendentalist Movement of the 1830s and 1840s and the founder of its magazine, *The Dial*. The defining principle of Transcendentalism, which is also at the heart of Emerson's thought, is that the world itself has a soul and that the world's soul is identical with each individual person's soul.

INTRODUCTION

Emerson wrote "Nature" following a trip to Europe he made after his wife's death from tuberculosis. In England, he met the great poet of nature, William Wordsworth, and toured the Lake District with him. He spoke with the political philosopher John Stuart Mill, and developed a close friendship with Thomas Carlyle, a highly influential Scottish writer who brought together, in his powerful and highly-charged prose, a German Romantic sense of the force of nature and a stiff-backed morality of individual responsibility.

Growing out of these encounters and Emerson's own misgivings about traditional Christianity, as well as his own experiences of solitude and communion, "Nature" is a moral and inspirational essay devoted to shaping its reader's attitude towards nature. Emerson wants to elicit more than a sense of reverence for nature, although he begins with the assumption that beholding the natural world will provoke reverence. More significantly to him is the doctrine of oneness or the interdependence of the person and nature. As Emerson experiences the process of beholding nature, he comes to understand that, not only is nature responsible for what he experiences, but he is responsible for what nature expresses. With great subtlety, Emerson attempts to affect the way mankind sees and experiences nature in order to influence the way people define themselves and act in relation to nature—as the industrial tools to reconfigure nature become more sophisticated and more widely available.

■ PRIMARY SOURCE

The stars awaken a certain reverence, because though always present, they are inaccessible; but all natural objects make a kindred impression, when the mind is open to their influence. Nature never wears a mean appearance. Neither does the wisest man extort her secret, and lose his curiosity by finding out all her perfection. Nature never became a toy to a wise spirit. The flowers, the animals, the mountains, reflected the wisdom of his best hour, as much as they had delighted the simplicity of his childhood. When we speak of nature in this manner, we have a distinct but most poetical sense in the mind. We mean the integrity of impression made by manifold natural objects. It is this which distinguishes the stick of timber of the wood-cutter, from the tree of the poet. The charming landscape which I saw this morning, is indubitably made up of some twenty or thirty farms. Miller owns this field, Locke that, and Manning the woodland beyond. But none of them owns the landscape. There is a property in the horizon which no man has but he whose eye can integrate all the parts, that is, the poet. This is the best part of these men's farms, yet to this their warranty-deeds give no title. To speak truly, few adult persons can see nature. Most persons do not see the sun. At least they have a very superficial seeing. The sun illuminates only the eye of the man, but shines into the eye and the heart of the child. The lover of nature is he whose inward and outward senses are still truly adjusted to each other; who has retained the spirit of infancy even into the era of manhood. His intercourse with heaven and earth, becomes part of his daily food. In the presence of nature, a wild delight runs through the man, in spite of real sorrows. Nature says—he is my creature, and maugre [in spite of] all his impertinent griefs, he shall be glad with me. Not the sun or the summer alone, but every hour and season yields its tribute of delight; for every hour and change corresponds to and authorizes a different state of the mind, from breathless noon to grimmest midnight...

The greatest delight which the fields and woods minister, is the suggestion of an occult relation between man and the vegetable. I am not alone and unacknowledged. They nod to me, and I to them. The waving of the boughs in the storm, is new to me and old. It takes me by surprise, and yet is not unknown. Its effect is like that of a higher thought or a better emotion coming over me, when I deemed I was thinking justly or doing right.

Yet it is certain that the power to produce this delight, does not reside in nature, but in man, or in a harmony of both. It is necessary to use these pleasures with great temperance. For, nature is not always tricked in holiday attire, but the same scene which yesterday breathed perfume and glittered as for the frolic of the nymphs, is overspread with melancholy today. Nature always wears the colors of the spirit.

...Nature, in its ministry to man, is not only the material, but is also the process and the result. All the parts incessantly work into each other's hands for the profit of man. The wind sows the seed; the sun evaporates the sea; the wind blows the vapor to the field; the ice, on the other side of the planet, condenses rain on this; the rain feeds the plant; the plant feeds the animal; and thus the endless circulations of the divine charity nourish man. The useful arts are reproductions or new combinations by the wit of man, of the same natural benefactors. He no longer waits for favoring gales, but by means of steam, he realizes the fable of Aeolus's bag, and carries the two and thirty winds in the boiler of his boat. To diminish friction, he paves the road with iron bars, and, mounting a coach with a ship-load of men, animals, and merchandise behind him, he darts through the country, from town to town, like an eagle or a swallow through the air. By the aggregate of these aids, how is the face of the world changed, from the era of Noah to that of Napoleon! The private poor man hath cities, ships, canals, bridges, built for him. He goes to the post-office, and the human race run on his errands; to the book-shop, and the human race read and write of all that happens, for him; to the court-house, and nations repair his wrongs. He sets his house upon the road, and the human race go forth every morning, and shovel out the snow, and cut a path for him.

...The simple perception of natural forms is a delight. The influence of the forms and actions in nature is...needful to man...To the body and mind which have been cramped by noxious work or company, nature is medicinal and restores their tone. The tradesman, the attorney comes out of the din and craft of the street, and sees the sky and the woods, and is a man again. In their eternal calm, he finds himself. The health of the eye seems to demand a horizon. We are never tired, so long as we can see far enough...

The world proceeds from the same spirit as the body of man. It is a remoter and inferior incarnation of God, a projection of God in the unconscious. But it differs from the body in one important respect. It is not, like that, now subjected to the human will. Its serene order is inviolable by us. It is, therefore, to us, the present expositor of the divine mind. It is a fixed point whereby we may measure our departure. As we degenerate, the contrast between us and our house is more evident. We are as much strangers in nature, as we are aliens from God. We do not understand the notes of birds. The fox and the deer run away from us; the bear and tiger rend us. We do not know the uses of more than a few plants, as corn and the apple, the potato and the vine. Is not the landscape, every glimpse of which hath a grandeur, a face of him? Yet this may show us what discord is between man and nature, for you cannot freely admire a noble landscape, if laborers are digging in the field hard by. . . .

SIGNIFICANCE

That an essay like "Nature" should be written in the early years of the American Republic seems essential as well as inevitable, for it lays a philosophical groundwork for the idea of democracy. Each person's perception of the natural world, Emerson asserts, has its own validity and authority; each person is endowed, moreover, with the same power of perception as every other person if he or she will only choose to use it; and each person can participate in the experience of nature which Emerson sees as the primary spiritual exercise of mankind and as a primary way of seeing God and of knowing God's attributes.

In addition, nature provides a justification for exploration, which is the other pillar upon which America is founded. Historians and philosophers often characterize Americans as a people traditionally drawn to nature, who seek divinity in it, and find in it a limitless prospect. Nature is an extension of humanity.

Emerson, however, also uses the essay to issue a warning. Nature is given its full existence by human perception of it. But nature must be the force and guide that shapes the quality of human perception. If humans are to be true to themselves and to nature, they must interact with the natural environment with a sense of awe and respect. In "The Winter's Tale,"

Shakespeare states this idea with paradoxical irony: there "is an art/ Which doth mend Nature, change it rather; but/ The art itself is Nature." Emerson, in "Nature," states the idea with representative American pragmatism: "You cannot freely admire a noble landscape, if laborers are digging in the field hard by." Regard for nature and self-regard are one.

Emerson's influence was great and telling in its subtlety, for he set a group of ideas flowing through American culture. His ideas influenced the thought of such advocates and protectors of nature as Henry David Thoreau (1817–1862), author of *Walden*, and Walt Whitman (1819–1892), visionary poet of a democratic America in which nature and industry combine in a way that ennobles both. Emerson's work also had directly practical results. He was an important influence on the naturalist and educator John Muir (1838–1914), who explored the glaciers of Yosemite and became one of the founders of the Sierra Club, which remains today an important voice for environmental preservation and conservation.

FURTHER RESOURCES
Books

The Emerson Dilemma: Essays on Emerson and Social Reform, edited by Gregory T. Garvey. Athens, Ga: University of Georgia Press, 2001.

Geldard, Richard G. *God in Concord: Ralph Waldo Emerson's Awakening to the Infinite*. Burdett, N.Y.: Larson Publications, 1999.

Wilson, Eric. "The Electric Field of Nature." In *Emerson's Sublime Science*. New York: St. Martin's Press, 1999.

Worley, Sam McGuire. *Emerson, Thoreau, and the Role of the Cultural Critic*. Albany, N.Y.: SUNY Press, 2001.

Web sites

American Transcendentalism Web. <http://www.vcu.edu/engweb/transcendentalism/criticism/naturecrit.html> (accessed November 22, 2005).

Ralph Waldo Emerson Biography.<http://www.rwe.org/pages/biography.htm> (accessed November 22, 2005).

A Book Lover's Holiday in the Open

Book excerpt

By: Theodore Roosevelt

Date: 1916

Source: Roosevelt, Theodore. *A Book Lover's Holiday in the Open.* New York: Scribner's, 1916.

About the Author: Theodore Roosevelt (1858–1919), the twenty-sixth President of the United States and a winner of the Nobel Peace Prize, was known for his advancement of conservation and other progressive causes. He was born to a wealthy New York family and entered politics after studying at Harvard University and dropping out of the Columbia University law school, serving as a state assemblyman in New York. His wife and mother both died on the same day in 1884, after which he temporarily abandoned his political career and purchased a range in the Dakota Territory. During that time he also became an avid big game hunter and advocate of vigorous outdoor living. Two years later he returned to New York, married again, and returned to the political arena. Roosevelt served on the federal Civil Service Commission, was appointed assistant secretary of Navy by William McKinley, and led a volunteer cavalry regiment known as the Rough Riders in the Spanish-American War. He was elected governor of New York in 1898 and was nominated as the Republican vice-presidential candidate in 1900. He succeeded William McKinley as president after McKinley was assassinated in 1901 and was elected to a full four-year term in 1904. Roosevelt believed that it was the responsibility of government to actively balance competing economic interests. He was also a strong proponent of arbitration and mediation to settle international differences, and was awarded the Nobel Peace Prize for efforts to settle the ongoing war between Russia and Japan. Dissatisfied with the state of politics, Roosevelt left the Republican Party to form the progressive Bull Moose Party and ran again for the presidency in 1912. He survived an assassination attempt during the campaign but lost the election to Woodrow Wilson.

INTRODUCTION

Roosevelt was a leader in the early twentieth century conservation movement, which sought to reverse the prevailing philosophy that natural resources existed in order to be exploited with minimal government intervention. He actively supported the Newlands Reclamation Act that established the precursor to the U.S. Bureau of Reclamation in 1902, established the U.S. Forest Service in 1905, and signed the Antiquities Act of 1906 (subsequently using his authority under the act to declare the Grand Canyon and other areas national monuments).

Conservationists of Roosevelt's day supported controlled and planned exploitation, not strict preservation,

Former President Theodore Roosevelt stands in appreciation of nature and wilderness at Glacier Point in Yosemite. © CORBIS

of natural resources. Their pragmatic philosophy of multiple, but rational, use of public lands for their forests, minerals, and water differs from the objectives of the modern conservation movement, which places a heavier emphasis on preservation with little or no exploitation.

In many respects, the conservation movement was closely related to progressivism, which advocated the use of scientific knowledge to identify and solve social and economic problems. Early conservation movement accomplishments included the establishment of a national park, the world's first, in the Yellowstone region of Wyoming and Montana in 1872 and passage of the Forest Reserve Act of 1891. John Wesley Powell, the second director of the U.S. Geological Survey, advocated small-scale agrarian development of semi-arid western lands on the basis of his scientific observations. Another conservation movement leader, Gifford Pinchot, was appointed by Roosevelt to head the newly created U.S. Forest Service within the Department of Agriculture.

Wildlife preserves were a conservation movement response to widespread over-hunting and decimation of wild game populations during the nineteenth century. As president, Roosevelt established fifty-one bird reserves and four wild game preserves in addition to eighteen national monuments, five national parks, and 150 national forests. His progressive and conservationist philosophy is evident in the opening paragraphs of the following excerpt, which is a description of his visit to an early twentieth century game preserve in Quebec, Canada. In addition to describing in detail the preserve and his day-to-day activities, Roosevelt discusses the establishment of game preserves and discusses factors such as the role of predators and disease in wildlife populations.

PRIMARY SOURCE

In 1915 I spent a little over a fortnight on a private game reserve in the province of Quebec. I had expected to enjoy the great northern woods, and the sight of beaver, moose, and caribou; but I had not expected any hunting experience worth mentioning. Nevertheless, toward the end of my trip, there befell me one of the most curious and interesting adventures with big game that have ever befallen me during the forty years since I first began to know the life of the wilderness.

In both Canada and the United States the theory and indeed the practise of preserving wild life on protected areas of land have made astonishing headway since the closing years of the nineteenth century. These protected areas, some of very large size, come in two classes. First, there are those which are public property, where the protection is given by the State. Secondly, there are those where the ownership and the protection are private.

By far the most important, of course, are the public preserves. These by their very existence afford a certain measure of the extent to which democratic government can justify itself. If in a given community unchecked popular rule means unlimited waste and destruction of the natural resources—soil, fertility, water-power, forests, game, wild-life generally—which by right belong as much to subsequent generations as to the present generation, then it is sure proof that the present generation is not yet really fit for self-control, that it is not yet really fit to exercise the high and responsible privilege of a rule which shall be both by the people and for the people. The term "for the people" must always include the people unborn as well as the people now alive, or the democratic ideal is not realized. The only way to secure the chance for hunting, for the enjoyment of vigorous field-sports, to the average man of small means, is to secure such enforced game laws as will prevent anybody and everybody from killing game to a point which means its diminution and therefore ultimate extinction. Only in this way will the average man be able to secure for himself and his children the opportunity of occasionally spending his yearly holiday in that school of hardihood and self-reliance—the chase. New Brunswick, Maine, and Vermont during the last generation have waked up to this fact. Moose and deer in New Brunswick and Maine, deer in Vermont, are so much more plentiful than they were a

generation ago that young men of sufficient address and skill can at small cost spend a holiday in the woods, or on the edge of the rough backwoods farm land, and be reasonably sure of a moose or a deer. To all three commonwealths the game is now a real asset because each moose or deer alive in the woods brings in, from the outside, men who spend among the inhabitants much more than the money value of the dead animal; and to the lover of nature the presence of these embodiments of the wild vigor of life adds immensely to the vast majesty of the forests.

In Canada there are many great national reserves; and much—by no means all—of the wilderness wherein shooting is allowed, is intelligently and faithfully protected, so that the game does not diminish. In the summer of 1915 we caught a glimpse of one of these great reserves, that including the wonderful mountains on the line of the Canadian Pacific, from Banff to Lake Louise, and for many leagues around them. The naked or snow-clad peaks, the lakes, the glaciers, the evergreen forest shrouding the mountainsides and valleys, the clear brooks, the wealth of wild flowers, make up a landscape as lovely as it is varied. Here the game—bighorn and white goat-antelope, moose, wapiti, and black-tail deer and white-tail deer—flourish unmolested. The flora and fauna are boreal, but boreal in the sense that the Rocky Mountains are boreal as far south as Arizona; the crimson paint-brush that colors the hillsides, the water-ousel in the rapid torrents—these and most of the trees and flowers and birds suggest those of the mountains which are riven asunder by the profound gorges of the Colorado rather than those which dwell among the lower and more rounded Eastern hill-masses from which the springs find their way into the rivers that flow down to the North Atlantic. Around these and similar great nurseries of game, the hunting is still good in places; although there has been a mistaken lenity shown in permitting the Indians to butcher mountain-sheep and deer to the point of local extermination, and although, as is probably inevitable in all new communities, the game laws are enforced chiefly at the expense of visiting sportsmen, rather than at the expense of the real enemies of the game, the professional meat and hide hunters who slaughter for the profit.

In Eastern Canada, as in the Eastern United States, there has been far less chance than in the West to create huge governmental game reserves. But there has been a positive increase of the big game during the last two or three decades. This is partly due to the creation and enforcement of wise game laws—although here also it must be admitted that in some of the Provinces, as in some of the States, the alien sportsman is judged with Rhadamanthine severity, while the home offenders, and even the home Indians, are but little interfered with. It would be well if in this matter other communities copied the excellent example of Maine and New Brunswick. In addition to the game laws, a large part is played in Canadian game preservation by the hunting and fishing clubs. These clubs have policed, and now police many thousands of square miles of wooded wilderness, worthless for agriculture; and in consequence of this policing the wild creatures of the wilderness have thriven, and in some cases have multiplied to an extraordinary degree, on these club lands.

In September, 1915, I visited the Tourilli Club, as the guest of an old friend, Doctor Alexander Lambert, a companion of previous hunting trips in the Louisiana canebrakes, in the Rockies, on the plains bordering the Red River of the south, and among the Bad Lands through which the Little Missouri flows. The Tourilli Club is an association of Canadian and American sportsmen and lovers of the wilderness. The land, leased from the government by the club, lies northwest of the attractive Old World city of Quebec—the most distinctive city north of the Mexican border, now that the creole element in New Orleans has been almost swamped. The club holds about two hundred and fifty square miles along the main branches and the small tributaries of the Saint Anne River, just north of the line that separates the last bleak farming land from the forest. It is a hilly, almost mountainous region, studded with numerous lakes, threaded by rapid, brawling brooks, and covered with an unbroken forest growth of spruce, balsam, birch and maple....

SIGNIFICANCE

Roosevelt's essay, "A Curious Experience," presents a detailed picture of an early twentieth century game preserve. Much of the essay describes details of day-to-day camp life on the preserve, but Roosevelt also discusses the importance of public game preserves within the context of the conservation movement with which he was so closely associated.

FURTHER RESOURCES
Books

Dalton, Kathleen. *Theodore Roosevelt: A Strenuous Life*. New York: Knopf, 2002.

Morris, Edmund. *The Rise of Theodore Roosevelt*. New York: Modern Library, 2001.

———. *Theodore Rex*. New York: Modern Library, 2002.

Web sites

"Theodore Roosevelt: Icon of the American Century." *National Portrait Gallery*. <http://www.npg.si.edu/exh/roosevelt> (accessed March 15, 2006).

"About Theodore Roosevelt." *Theodore Roosevelt Association*. <http://www.theodoreroosevelt.org> (accessed March 15, 2006).

Mt. Williamson, The Sierra Nevada, from Manzanar, California

Photograph

By: Ansel Adams

Date: 1945

Source: Adams, Ansel. *Mt. Williamson, The Sierra Nevada, from Manzanar, California*, 1945.

About the Photographer: American photographer Ansel Adams (1902–1984) is best known for his dramatic black-and-white photographs of the American West, particularly the Sierra Nevada and Yosemite Valley. A native of San Francisco, Adams lived through the great earthquake of 1906 but was permanently scarred by a broken nose suffered when he fell during an aftershock. The teenaged Adams fared poorly in traditional schools and completed his education with the help of private tutors. He began a lifelong association with the Yosemite Valley during a family trip in 1916, and three years later became an active member of the Sierra Club. Adams trained as a concert pianist but, motivated in large part by mountain trips, developed a passion for photography and in 1930 decided to pursue it as a career. One of his early books, the limited edition volume *Sierra Nevada: The John Muir Trail*, was assembled during the 1930s and is considered to have been instrumental in the creation of Kings Canyon National Park. Adams also worked as a commercial photographer and spent time in New York City. He wrote three seminal books on photographic technique that remain highly respected among modern photographers: *The Camera*, *The Negative*, and *The Print*. Adams was elected a Fellow of the American Academy of Arts and Sciences in 1968 and received the Presidential Medal of Freedom in 1980.

INTRODUCTION

Adams' photograph of Mt. Williamson typifies his use of dramatic lighting, shadows, shapes, and texture to capture the essence of Western American landscapes. The photographs are remarkably sharp and vivid because he often used a large format camera with 8-by-10-inch (20-by-25-centimeter) sheets, rather than rolls, of film for most of his photographs. Photographs lose sharpness as they are optically enlarged. By using large format cameras and film, however, Adams was able to produce prints that required little or no enlargement. A typical 35mm film negative, in

Ansel Adams captures a pack train on the Sierra Club High Trip to the Sierra Nevada in California, 1934. © ANSEL ADAMS PUBLISHING RIGHTS TRUST/CORBIS

contrast, must be enlarged by a factor of sixty before it reaches the size the 8-by-10-inch negatives that Adams used for many of his landscape photographs. Large format cameras are also large and heavy, requiring a sturdy tripod that eliminates camera movement and produces sharper images.

Adams mastered the technical aspects of photography and carefully calculated the exposure necessary to produce an image that he visualized before the photograph was taken. He invented the Zone System, a widely used method of assessing the tonal variation of a scene and using that information to select the combination of shutter speed, lens aperture, and film type necessary to create the desired image. Because each sheet of large format film contains only one photograph, as opposed to a roll of film that can contain many photographs taken under different light, large format photographers such as Adams' can develop each sheet separately and adjust process to produce the best possible images.

Adams' commitment to sharp and compelling photographs is also reflected by his role as a co-founder of Group f/64, a group of photographers who disdained the soft-focus impressionistic photography that was popular during the early part of the twentieth century. Other members of Group f/64 included notable photographers Edward Weston and Imogene Cunningham. The name f/64 is in reference to the smallest lens aperture available on their cameras, which produced the greatest depth of field (portion of the photograph that is in focus).

PRIMARY SOURCE

MT. WILLIAMSON, THE SIERRA NEVADA, FROM MANZANAR, CALIFORNIA

See primary source image.

PRIMARY SOURCE

Mt. Williamson, The Sierra Nevada, from Manzanar, California. *Mt. Williamson, The Sierra Nevada, from Manzanar, California,* by Ansel Adams. © ANSEL ADAMS PUBLISHING RIGHTS TRUST/CORBIS

SIGNIFICANCE

This photograph of Mt. Williamson is one of many that could have been selected to typify Adams's approach to landscape photography. It clearly conveys his mastery of light and details of the photographic process, his straightforward approach to photography, and his love for the American landscape. Unlike some of his other photographs, however, this well-known Mt. Williamson photograph has additional historical significance because of the location from which it was taken. Working for the U.S. Department of the Interior during World War II, Adams produced series of photographs documenting daily life of Japanese-Americans imprisoned at the Manzanar Relocation Center in California. Adams later donated the collection to the Library of Congress, writing that those held at the center had suffered a great injustice and that he hoped the photographs could "...be put to good use." Some of the photographs from his Manzanar collection show the same subject, Mt. Williamson, as it was seen by the prisoners.

FURTHER RESOURCES
Books

Adams, Ansel. *Ansel Adams: An Autobiography.* New York: Bulfinch Press, 1985.

———. *The Camera.* New York: Bulfinch Press, 1995.

———. *The Negative.* New York: Bulfinch Press, 1995.

———. *The Print.* New York: Bulfinch Press, 1995.

Web sites

Adams, Ansel. "Ansel Adams & the Sierra Club: Ansel Adams Photo Gallery." *Sierra Club.* <http://www.sierraclub.org/ansel_adams/gallery> (accessed February 28, 2006).

Library of Congress. "Suffering Under a Great Injustice: Ansel Adams's Photographs of Japanese-American Internment at Manzanar." *The Library of Congress.* <http://memory.loc.gov/ammem/aamhtml/aamhome.html> (accessed February 28, 2006).

The Green Belt

Communitas

Essay

By: Paul and Percival Goodman

Date: 1947; revised 1960

Source: Goodman, Paul, and Percival Goodman. "The Green Belt." *Communitas.* New York: Vintage Books, 1960.

About the Author: American poet, novelist, essayist, playwright, social critic, psychologist, lecturer, and political activist Paul Goodman (1911–1972) revealed in all his work a fundamental interest in the interaction between people and their environments. Boundaries, he asserted, were not only barriers but areas of contact. His interest in city planning pervades his fiction in novels like *The Empire City* and *Making Do* as well as in his sociological works like *Growing Up Absurd* and in essays like "Banning Cars from Manhattan." His brother Percival Goodman (1904–1989), an architect, professor of architecture at Colombia University, painter, and sculptor, dropped out of school after the fourth grade and went to work at his uncle's architectural firm. In his early twenties he studied architecture at the Beaux Arts in Paris and began a career as an architect and a college professor. Besides *Communitas,* he also wrote "The Decay of American Cities— Alternative Habitation for Man: A Plan for Planning" in 1966 and "The Double E," about the relationship of energy and ecology in 1977.

INTRODUCTION

In *Communitas* Paul and Percival Goodman assert that, fundamentally, the quality of our lives depends on the environment in which we live and on how that environment interacts with us and causes us to behave. Since they see the environment as so great a determinant, they postulate that our living environment cannot be one which evolves by itself without human intervention, but that it is necessarily planned, if not explicitly, by one interest group or another—or the forces they unleash. Thus *Communitas* is a handbook offering several ways of thinking about designing habitable environments and offers several generic models.

In the excerpt below, the Goodmans outline a history of design plans beginning in the nineteenth century, which attempted to cope with the challenges imposed by the industrial revolution upon the way people lived and worked. The Goodmans pay particular attention to the tension between nature and industry. They outline the way a number of city planners attempted to keep the virtues of the green world, while at the same time designing habitats in a world run by machinery and staffed by the people whose job it was to operate that machinery and whose lives and living conditions were largely defined by the way that machinery determined.

PRIMARY SOURCE

The original impulse to Garden City planning was the reaction against the ugly technology and depressed humanity of the old English factory areas. On the one hand, the factory poured forth its smoke, blighted the countryside with its refuse, and sucked in labor at an early age. On the other, the homes were crowded among the chimneys as identical hives of labor power, and the people were parts of the machine, losing their dignity and sense of beauty. Some moralists, like [nineteenth-century English art and social critic John] Ruskin, [nineteenth-century English poet, painter, printer, designer, and utopian thinker, William] Morris, and [nineteenth-century Irish playwright and critic, Oscar] Wilde reacted so violently against the causes that they were willing to scrap both the technology and the profit system; they laid their emphasis on the beauty of domestic and social life, making for the most part a selection of pre-industrial values. Ruskin praised the handsome architecture of the Middle Ages, said things should not be made of iron, and campaigned for handsome tea canisters. Morris designed furniture and textiles, improved typography, and dreamed of society without coercive law. Wilde (inspired also by [nineteenth-century literary critic, Walter] Pater) tried to do something about clothing and politics and embarked on the so-called "esthetic adventure." What is significant is the effort to combine large-scale social protest with a new attitude toward small things.

Less radically, Ebenezer Howard, the pioneer of the Garden City, thought of the alternative of quarantining the technology, but preserving both the profit system and the copiousness of mass products: he protected the homes and the non-technical culture behind a belt of green. This idea caught on and has been continually influential ever since. In all Garden City planning one can detect the purpose of safeguard, of defense; but by the same token, this is the school that has made valuable studies of minimum living standards, optimum density, right orientation for sunlight, space for playgrounds, [and] the correct designing of primary schools.

Plans which in principle quarantine the technology start with the consumption products of industry and plan for the amenity and convenience of domestic life. Then, however, by a reflex of their definition of what is intolerable and substandard, in domestic life, they plan for the convenience and amenity also of working conditions, and so they meet up with the stream of the labor movement.

With the coming of the automobiles there was a second impulse to Garden City planning. To the original ugliness of coal was added the chaos of traffic congestion and traffic hazard. But there was offered also the opportunity to get away faster and farther. The result has been that, whereas for Howard the protected homes were near the factories and planned in conjunction with them, the entities that are now called Garden Cities are physically isolated from their industry and planned quite independently. We have the interesting phenomena of commutation, highway culture, suburbanism, and exurbanism.

The chief property of these plans, then, is the setting-up of a protective green belt, and the chief difference among the plans depends on how complex a unity of life is provided off the main roads leading to the industrial or business center.

We are now entering a stage of reflex also to this second impulse of suburbanism: not to flee from the center but to open it out, relieve its congestion, and bring the green belt into the city itself. This, considered on a grand scale, is the proposal of the *Ville Radieuse* [the radiant city] of [twentieth-century Swiss architect] Le Corbusier. Considered more piecemeal, it employs the principle of enclosed traffic-free blocks and the revival of neighborhoods, as proposed by disciples of Le Corbusier, like Paul Wiener, or housers like Henry Wright.

From Suburbs to Garden Cities From the countryside, the scattered people crowd into cities and overcrowd them. There then begins a contrary motion.

Consider first the existing suburbs. These are unorganized settlements springing up on the main highway and parallel railway to the city. They take advantage of the cheaper land far from the center to build chiefly one-family houses with private yards. The productive and cultural activity of the adults and even adolescents is centered in the metropolis; it is only the children who belong strictly to the suburb as such. The principal civic services—paving, light, water—are directed by the city; and the land is surveyed according to the prevailing city plan, probably in a grid. The highway to the city is the largest street and contains the shops.

Spaced throughout the grid are likely to be small developments of private real-estate men, attempting a more picturesque arrangement of the plots. But on the whole the pressure for profit is such that the plots become minimal and the endless rows of little boxes, or of larger boxes with picture windows, are pretty near the landscape of [the fourteenth century Italian poet] Dante's first volume. [The Inferno, or Hell, is the first volume of Dante's Divine Comedy.]

Such development is originally unplanned. It is best described in the phrase of [American architect, naturalist, and creator of the Appalachian Trail, Benton] Mackaye as "urban backflow." The effect of it is, within a short time, to reach out toward the next small or large town and to create a still greater and more planless metropolitan area. This is the amoeboid spreading that [late nineteenth-century, early twentieth-century Scottish biologist, sociologist, and town planner] Patrick Geddes called conurbation.

Culturally, the suburb is too city-bound to have any definite character, but certain tendencies are fairly apparent—caused partly by the physical facts and partly, no doubt, by the kind of persons who choose to be suburbanites. Families are isolated from the more diverse contacts of city culture, and they are atomized internally by the more frequent absence of the wage earner. On the other hand, there is a growth of neighborly contacts. Surburbanites are known as petty bourgeois in status and prejudice, and they have the petty bourgeois virtue of making a small private effort, with its responsibilities. There is increased dependency on the timetable and an organization of daily life probably tighter than in the city, but there is also the increased dignity of puttering in one's own house and maybe garden. . . .

When this suburban backflow is subjected to conscious planning, however, a definite character promptly emerges. Accepting such a tendency as desirable, the city makes political and economic decisions to facilitate it by opening fast highways or rapid-transit systems from the center to the outskirts. An example is the way the New York region has been developed. The effect is to create blighted areas in the depopulated center, to accelerate conurbation at the periphery and rapidly depress the older suburbs, choking their traffic and destroying their green; but also to open out much further distances (an hour away on the new highways) where there is more space and more pretentious housing. This is quite strictly a middle-class development; for the highways draw heavily on the social wealth of everybody for the benefit of those who are better off, since the poor can afford neither the houses nor the automobiles.

SIGNIFICANCE

Communitas was re-issued in 1960, at a time when the United States was entering a period of non-ideological but pragmatically American utopian thinking, especially among young people in high school and college. They had grown up in a society of comfortable affluence but felt the lack of something to give life a particular meaning, which the popular culture of entertainment, consumption, and even work failed to offer. Paul Goodman seemed to address that emptiness directly in his writing and to offer a suitably convincing explanation of it. He argued, like one of his models (the English romantic poet of nature William Wordsworth), that people were cut off from the fundamental natural experiences of meaningful and animally satisfying work and that we live like strangers in our environment. In response, Goodman proposed that—by human inventiveness—entrenched social arrangements and institutions could be revised and made to accord more with basic human needs and offer greater human satisfaction. He extended this sort of analysis to schooling, work, sexual relations, psychology, and, in *Communitas*, with Percival Goodman, to community planning. Underpinning all of his writing is the idea that the human environment is always a planned environment and, consequently, that environmental planning is a democratic task for all of a country's citizens rather than the special responsibility of experts.

Many small groups undertook to be their own planners. A group of parents in Harlem, New York, banded together and with Percival Goodman, designed and built a new school to replace the rat-infested P.S. 119. However, because of the very nature of the Goodman brothers' ideas, the proposals that the Goodmans set forth in *Communitas* have not gained mainstream acceptance. Often, if one of their ideas is introduced, it is only partially implemented. Banning cars from Manhattan and other large cities, for example, has been introduced on special occasions or in limited areas in many cities, but never seriously, and sometimes with poor results. As of 2005 in Paris, for example, many streets are closed to automobile traffic

on weekends. The result is even greater congestion on the roads where cars are allowed.

FURTHER RESOURCES
Books

Giral, A., and K. J. Elman. *Percival Goodman: Architect-Planner-Teacher- Painter*. New York: Princeton Architectural Press, 2001.

Web sites

The Communitas Group Ltd.. <http://www.communitas.ca> (accessed March 4, 2006).

Reiner, Thomas A. "Utopias and City Planning: Finding Strength in One Another." *Utopian Ideas.net*. <http://www.utopianideas.net/1st_edition/Reiner.htm> (accessed March 4, 2006).

"'Silent Spring' is Now Noisy Summer"

Newspaper article

By: John M. Lee

Date: July 22, 1962

Source: Lee, John M. " 'Silent Spring' is Now Noisy Summer." *New York Times* (July 22, 1962).

About the Author: John M. Lee was a staff writer for the *New York Times* at the time that he wrote " 'Silent Spring' is Now Noisy Summer."

INTRODUCTION

Rachel Carson's book *Silent Spring* was the first meticulously referenced, book-length attack by a scientist on the practices of an entire industry, in this case the pesticide industry. *Silent Spring* provoked a response that was also the first of its kind, as partly described in the 1962 article " 'Silent Spring' is Now Noisy Summer" by John M. Lee. A many-fronted public-relations counterattack on Carson was mounted by corporations displeased by her book.

Carson knew that her book would come under fire. At her request the book's publisher, Houghton Mifflin, had lawyers review the manuscript line by line before publication. The book was also reviewed in detail by the *New Yorker* magazine, in which it first appeared as a serial. Carson insisted that Houghton Mifflin buy libel insurance and that her book contract specify a limit on her personal monetary liability.

Forty years after the publication of Rachel Carson's controversial book, students complete a butoh walk to protest use of pesticides in the environment, September 27, 2002. AP IMAGES

The full extent of the industry response was not known at the time that Lee wrote his article. Besides the criticisms quoted there (published before the book version of *Silent Spring* appeared), the chemical and pesticide industry took a number of specific actions against Carson. A group of chemical companies, including DuPont, Monsanto, Shell, Dow Chemical, W.R. Grace, and the members of the Manufacturing Chemists Association, hired public relations experts to question Carson's credibility and even, on occasion, her sanity. The National Agricultural Chemicals Association spent over a quarter of a million dollars to oppose the book through ads, press conferences, and other public-relations methods. Velsicol Chemical Company, a pesticides manufacturer, threatened to sue Houghton Mifflin for libel. Velsicol also threatened *Audubon* magazine with a lawsuit if it published excerpts from *Silent Spring*, warning that printing "a muckraking article containing unwarranted assertions about Velsicol pesticides [might] jeopardize [the] financial security" of persons employed by the magazine and that of their families. One chemical company threatened to sue the *New Yorker* if the magazine ran the final installment of Carson's book. The editor responded, "Everything in those articles has been checked and is true. Go ahead and sue." In the end, however, no libel lawsuits were actually brought against Carson or anyone else involved in the publication of her book.

'SILENT SPRING' IS NOW NOISY SUMMER

Pesticides Industry Up In Arms Over a New Book Rachel Carson Stirs Conflict—Producers Are Crying 'Foul' The $300,000,000 pesticides industry has been highly irritated by a quiet woman author whose previous works on science have been praised for the beauty and precision of the writing.

The author is Rachel Carson, whose "The Sea Around Us" and "The Edge of the Sea" were best sellers in 1951 and 1955. Miss Carson, trained as a marine biologist, wrote gracefully of sea and shore life.

In her latest work, however, Miss Carson is not so gentle. More pointed than poetic, she argues that the widespread use of pesticides is dangerously tilting the so-called balance of nature. Pesticides poison not only pests, she says, but also humans, wildlife, the soil, food and water.

The men who make the pesticides are crying foul. "Crass commercialism or idealistic flag waving," scoffs one industrial toxicologist. "We are aghast," says another. "Our members are raising hell," reports a trade association.

Some agricultural chemicals concerns have set their scientists to analyzing Miss Carson's work, line by line. Other companies are preparing briefs defending the use of their products. Meetings have been held in Washington and New York. Statements are being drafted and counter-attacks plotted.

A drowsy midsummer has suddenly been enlivened by the greatest uproar in the pesticides industry since the cranberry scare of 1959.

Miss Carson's new book is entitled "Silent Spring." The title is derived from an idealized situation in which Miss Carson envisions an imaginary town where chemical pollution has silenced "the voices of spring."

The book is to be published in October by the Houghton Mifflin Company and has been chosen as an October selection of the Book-of-the-Month Club. About half the book appeared as a series of three articles in The New Yorker magazine last month.

A random sampling of opinion among trade associations and chemical companies last week found the Carson articles receiving prominent attention.

Many industry spokesmen preface their remarks with a tribute to Miss Carson's writing talents, and most say that they can find little error of fact.

What they do criticize, however, are the extensions and implications that she gives to isolated case histories of the detrimental effects of certain pesticides used or misused in certain instances.

The industry feels that she has presented a one-sided case and has chosen to ignore the enormous benefits in increased food production and decreased incidence of disease that have accrued from the development and use of modern pesticides.

The pesticides industry is annoyed also at the implications that the industry itself has not been alert and concerned in its recognition of the problems that accompany pesticide use.

Last week, Miss Carson was said to be on "an extended vacation" for the summer and not available for comment on the industry's rebuttal. Her agent, Marie Rodell, said she had heard nothing directly from chemical manufacturers concerning the book.

Houghton Mifflin referred all questions to Miss Rodell. The New Yorker said it had received many letters expressing great interest in the articles and "only one or two took strong objection."

In an interview, E. M. Adams, assistant director of the biochemistry research laboratory of the Dow Chemical Company, said he would be among the first to acknowledge that there were problems in the use or misuse of pesticides.

"I think Miss Carson has indulged in hindsight," he said. "In many cases we have to learn from experience and often it is difficult to exercise the proper foresight."

Emphasizing that he spoke as a private toxicologist, Mr. Adams said that in some procedures, such as large-scale spraying, the possible benefits had to be balanced against the possible ills.

He referred to the extensive testing programs and Federal regulations prevalent in the pesticides industry and said, "What we have done, we have not done carelessly or without consideration. The industry is not made up of money grubbers."

Tom K. Smith, vice president and general manager of agricultural chemicals for the Monsanto Chemical Company, said that "had the articles been written with necessary attention to the available scientific data on the subject, it could have served a valuable purpose-helping alert the public at large to the importance of proper use of pesticide chemicals."

However, he said, the articles suggested that Government officials and private and industrial scientists were either not as well informed on pesticide problems as Miss Carson, not professionally competent to evaluate possible hazards or else remiss in their obligations to society.

P. Rothberg, president of the Montrose Chemical Corporation of California, said in a statement that Miss Carson wrote not "as a scientist but rather as a fanatic defender of the cult of the balance of nature." He said the greatest upsetters of that balance, as far as man was concerned, were modern medicines and sanitation.

Montrose, an affiliate of the Stauffer Chemical Company, is the nation's largest producer of DDT, one of the pesticides that Miss Carson discusses at length. She also discusses the effect of malathion, parathion, dieldrin, aldrin and endrin.

"It is ironic to think," Miss Carson states at one point, "that man may determine his own fixture by something so seemingly trivial as his choice of insect spray." She acknowledges, however, that the effects may not show up in new generations for decades or centuries.

The Department of Agriculture reported that it had received many letters expressing "horror and amazement" at the department's support of the use of potentially deadly pesticides.

The industry had a favorite analogy to use in rebuttal. It conceded that pesticides could be dangerous. The ideal was to use them all safely and effectively.

The public debate over pesticides is just beginning and the industry is preparing for a long siege. The book reviews and publicity attendant upon the book's publication this fall will surely fan the controversy.

SIGNIFICANCE

Since *Silent Spring*, a number of books have appeared accusing industry of malfeasance or harm. The response of companies and industrial trade groups to these books has often followed the *Silent Spring* pattern, although with increasing sophistication over time. It should be noted that describing these tactics does not imply a blanket judgment on the factual correctness of the accusations made against industry: any public relations tactic may be used to defend either a valid position or an invalid position. The scientific accuracy of particular charges against the chemical, nuclear, pharmaceutical, pesticide, genetic engineering, food, and other industries must be decided on factual grounds on a case-by-case basis.

Industry responses to criticism such as Carson's take several basic forms. First, there are straightforward press releases stating that the criticism is inaccurate, biased, based on ignorance and fear, and so forth. Media interviews with company executives or representatives may be arranged.

Following are threats of legal action for libel. Lawsuits have been repeatedly threatened against authors of industry-critical books and their publishers. For example, Monsanto threatened Vital Health, the planned publisher of Marc Lappé and Britt Bailey's book *Against the Grain: Biotechnology and the Corporate Takeover of Your Food* (1998), with legal action if the book were published; Vital Health dropped the book. It was later published by Common Courage Press. An important class of legal challenges to industry-critical speech invokes not traditional libel law but "food disparagement laws." These are laws passed by thirteen U.S. states in the 1990s that make it a criminal offense to publicly criticize perishable food products. The most famous food-disparagement lawsuit was brought by a beef feedlot operator and Cactus Feeders, the world's largest cattle feed supplier, against media personality Oprah Winfrey in 1996. Winfrey was sued for saying on her television show that what she had just heard about mad cow disease (bovine spongiform encephalopathy) "stopped me cold from eating another burger." Winfrey won the case, but on a technicality, not on Constitutional free-speech grounds: the judge ruled that beef was not a "perishable agricultural product" and so the law did not apply. Winfrey spent approximately $1 million defending herself against the lawsuit, did not recover costs, and ceased to speak out about the topic, even refusing to give out videotapes of the controversial episode to the press after her legal victory. Constitutional lawyers refer to such a silencing of criticism, even when no criminal penalties are levied, as a "chilling effect."

Finally, there is the conduct of public relations using "third-party organizations" or "front groups." The Center for Media and Democracy defines a front group as "an organization that purports to represent one agenda while in reality it serves some other party or interest whose sponsorship is hidden or rarely mentioned." The purpose of a front group is to provide increased credibility for claims that might be perceived as biased if the actual source were known. Front groups organized and paid for by industries such as those criticized in *Silent Spring* include the Advancement of Sound Science Coalition (chemical industry) and the Center for Consumer Freedom (tobacco companies and agribusiness). Industry-funded groups that carry out public relations may also, without qualifying as front groups because they do not conceal their origins, adopt friendly-sounding titles modeled on the names of environmental-activist groups: for example, the Global Climate Coalition is an oil and coal industry group that disputes the reality of global climate change and the American Crop Protection Association was once the National Agricultural Chemicals Association.

In some countries, corporate or government attacks on environmentalist critics may be physical. In Brazil, over 800 rural activists working against rainforest destruction have been killed over the last thirty years. The killers are not government agents but gunmen hired by logging companies to squelch protest. In 1985, commandos of the French secret service bombed an unarmed Greenpeace vessel, the *Rainbow Warrior*, as it lay at dock in Auckland harbor in New Zealand. The Greenpeace ship was scheduled to sail to a part of the Pacific where France was carrying out nuclear weapons tests and protest there. Greenpeace activist Fernando Pereira was killed in the bombing; two of the team that carried out the attack were convicted in New Zealand courts.

FURTHER RESOURCES

Periodicals

Helvarg, David. "Poison Pens: When Science Fails, Try Public Relations." *Sierra* 82, 1 (January/February 1997). <http://www.mindfully.org/Pesticide/Our-Stolen-Future-Defense.htm> (accessed February 25, 2006).

Orlando, Laura. "Industry Attacks on Dissent: From Rachel Carson to Oprah." *Dollars & Sense* 240 (March/April 2002). <http://www.dollarsandsense.org/archives/2002/0302orlando.html> (accessed February 25, 2006).

Web sites

Center for Media and Democracy. "Front Groups." <http://www.sourcewatch.org/index.php?title=Front_group#Examples> (accessed February 25, 2006).

Rachel Carson Dies of Cancer

'Silent Spring' Author Was 56

Obituary excerpt

By: Jonathan N. Leonard

Date: April 15, 1964

Source: "Rachel Carson Dies of Cancer; 'Silent Spring' Author Was 56.". *The New York Times*, April 15, 1964.

About the Author: Along with frequent contributions to the *New York Times*, Jonathan N. Leonard is the author of several books on the sciences and arts, including *Planets*, co-authored by Carl Sagan, *Alchemy*, and *Latin American Cooking*.

INTRODUCTION

American biologist and author Rachel Louise Carson (1907–1964), known for her best-selling books *Silent Spring* and *The Sea Around Us*, was a seminal figure in the environmental movement during the 1950s and early 1960s. Born in Springdale, Pennsylvania, she was the youngest of three children. Carson wanted to become a writer and studied English at the Pennsylvania College for Women (now known as Chatham College), but eventually became interested in biology and switched her major. She graduated with honors in 1929 and went on to earn a Master of Arts in zoology from The Johns Hopkins University in 1932. After teaching biology at Johns Hopkins and the University of Maryland, Carson began to work part-time for the U.S. Bureau of Fisheries (now known as the U.S. Fish and Wildlife Service) and eventually became one of the first full-time female employees in the agency.

Although her job title at the Bureau of Fisheries was aquatic biologist, Carson functioned as a technical writer and supplemented her salary by publishing short pieces. The article "Undersea", published in 1937 by *Atlantic Monthly*, led to a book contract with Simon & Schuster. Her first book, *Under the Sea Wind* was published shortly before the Japanese attack on Pearl Harbor in 1941 and was not a commercial success. During World War II, one of Carson's duties included the promotion of fish as an alternative to meat, which was scarce during the war. In 1949, Carson was promoted to editor-in-chief of the renamed Fish and Wildlife Service.

Carson's second book, *The Sea Around Us*, was first published in parts. The first chapter appeared in the *Yale Review* and won a Westinghouse award for science

writing. Other portions were subsequently published in the *New Yorker*, *Nature*, and *Reader's Digest*. The complete *The Sea Around Us* was published in 1951 by Oxford University Press. It became a Book of the Month Club selection and remained on the *New York Times* best-seller list for a year and a half.

The commercial success of *The Sea Around Us* led to the re-release of *Under the Sea Wind*, which also became a best seller, and garnered her awards that included the Gold Medal of the New York Zoological Society, the John Burroughs Medal for excellence in natural history writing, and the National Book Award. Established as a best-selling natural history author, Carson left her government job to become an independent writer. She built a cottage along the Maine coast and wrote *The Edge of the Sea*, a personal account of life along the shore and her third commercially successful book. *Silent Spring*, an indictment of overzealous pesticide use and its effects on the environment, was published in 1962 and quickly became a controversial and enduring contribution to the environmental literature.

■ PRIMARY SOURCE

RACHEL CARSON DIES OF CANCER;

***Silent Spring* Author Was 56** Rachel Carson, the biologist and writer on nature and science, whose book "Silent Spring" touched off a major controversy on the effects of pesticides, died yesterday in her home in Silver Spring, Md. She was 56 years old.

Her death was reported in New York by Marie Rodell, her literary agent. Miss Rodell said that Miss Carson had had cancer "for some years," and that she had been aware of her illness.

With the publication of "Silent Spring" in 1962, Rachel Louise Carson, the essence of gentle scholarship, set off a nationally publicized struggle between the proponents and opponents of the widespread use of poisonous chemicals to kill insects. Miss Carson was an opponent.

Some of miss Carson's critics, admiringly and some not so admiringly, compared her to Carrie Nation, the hatchet-wielding temperance advocate.

This comparison was rejected quietly by Miss Carson, who in her very mild but firm manner refused to accept the identification of an emotional crusader.

Miss Carson's position, as a biologist, was simply that she was a natural scientist in search of truth and that the indiscriminate use of poisonous chemical sprays called for public awareness of what was going on.

She emphasized that she was not opposed to the use of poisonous chemical sprays—only their "indiscriminate use," and, at a time when their potential was not truly known.

Quoting Jean Rostand, the French writer and biologist, she said: "The obligation to endure gives us the right to know."

On April 3, 1963, the Columbia Broadcasting System's television series *C.B.S. Reports* presented the program *The Silent Spring of Rachel Carson.* In it, Miss Carson said: "It is the public that is being asked to assume the risks that the insect controllers calculate. The public must decide whether it wishes to continue on the present road, and it can do so only when in full possession of the facts. We still talk in terms of conquest. We still haven't become mature enough to think of ourselves as only a tiny part of a vast and incredible universe. Man's attitude toward nature is today critically important simply because we have now acquired a fateful power to alter and destroy nature."

"But man is a part of nature, and his war against nature is inevitably a war against himself. The rains have become an instrument to bring down from the atmosphere the deadly products of atomic explosions. Water, which is probably our most important natural resource, is now used and re-used with incredible recklessness."

"Now, I truly believe, that we in this generation, must come to terms with nature, and I think we're challenged as mankind has never been challenged before to prove our maturity and our mastery, not of nature, but of ourselves."

3 Earlier Works Miss Carson, thanks to her remarkable knack for taking dull scientific facts and translating them into poetical and lyrical prose that enchanted the lay public, had a substantial public image before she rocked the American public and much of the world with *Silent Spring.* This was established by three books, *Under the Sea Wind, The Sea Around Us,* and *The Edge of the Sea. The Sea Around Us* moved quickly into the national best-seller lists, where it remained for 86 weeks, 39 of them in first place. By 1962, it had been published in 30 languages.

"Silent Spring" four-and-a-half years in preparation and published in September of 1962, hit the affluent chemical industry and the general public with the devastating effect of a Biblical plague of locusts. The title came from an apocalyptic opening chapter, which pictured how an entire area could be destroyed by indiscriminate spraying.

Legislative bodies ranging from New England town meetings to the Congress joined in the discussion. President Kennedy, asked about the pesticide problem during a press conference, announced that Federal agencies were taking a closer look at the problem because of the public's concern.

The essence of the debate was: Are pesticides publicly dangerous or aren't they?

They Should Be Called Biocide Miss Carson's position had been summarized this way:

"Chemicals are the sinister and little-recognized partners of radiation in changing the very nature of the world— the very nature of life."

"Since the mid-nineteen forties, over 200 basic chemicals have been created for use in killing insects, weeds, rodents and other organisms described in the modern vernacular as pests, and they are sold under several thousand different brand names.

"The sprays, dusts and aerosols are now applied almost universally to farms, gardens, forests and homes—non-selective chemicals that have the power to kill every insect, the good and the bad, to still the song of birds and the leaping of fish in the streams—to coat the leaves with a deadly film and to linger on in soil—all this, though the intended target may be only a few weeds or insects.

"Can anyone believe it is possible to lay down such a barrage of poison on the surface of the earth without making it unfit for all life? They should not be called 'insecticides' but 'biocides.' "

The chemical industry was quick to dispute this.

Dr. Robert White-Stevens, a spokesman for the industry, said:

"The major claims of Miss Rachel Carson's book, *Silent Spring,* are gross distortions of the actual facts, completely unsupported by scientific, experimental evidence, and general practical experience in the field. Her suggestion that pesticides are in fact biocides destroying all life is obviously absurd in the light of the fact that without selective biologicals these compounds would be completely useless.

"The real threat, then, to the survival of man is not chemical but biological, in the shape of hordes of insects that can denude our forests, sweep over our crop lands, ravage our food supply and leave in their wake a train of destitution and hunger, conveying to an undernourished population the major diseases scourges of mankind."

The Monsanto company, one of the nation's largest chemical concerns, used parody as a weapon in the counterattack against Miss Carson. Without mentioning her book, the company adopted her poetic style in an article labeled "The Desolate Year," which began: "Quietly, then, the desolate year began. . ." and wove its own apocalyptic word picture—but one that showed insects stripping the countryside and winning.

As the chemical industry continued to make her a target for criticism, Miss Carson remained calm.

"We must have insect control," she reiterated. "I do not favor turning nature over to insects. I favor the sparing, selective and intelligent use of chemicals. It is the indiscriminate, blanket spraying that I oppose."

Actually, chemical pest control has been practiced to some extent for centuries. However it was not until 1942 that DDT, a synthetic compound, was introduced in the wake of experiments that included those with poison gas. Its long-term poisonous potency was augmented by its ability to kill some insects upon contact and without being ingested. This opened a new era in pest control and led to the development of additional new synthetic poisons far more effective even than DDT.

As the pesticide controversy grew into a national quarrel, support was quick in going to the side of Miss Carson.

Supreme Court Justice William O. Douglas, an ardent naturalist, declared, "We need a Bill of Rights against the 20th century poisoners of the human race."

Earlier, an editorial in *The New York Times* had said:

"If her series [then running in part in *The New Yorker* publication of the book] helps arouse public concern to immunize Government agencies against the blandishments of the hucksters and enforces adequate controls, the author will be as deserving of the Noble Prize as was the inventor of DDT."

Presidential Report In May 1963, after a long study, President Kennedy's Science Advisory committee, issued its pesticide report.

It stressed that pesticides must be used to maintain the quality of the nation's food and health, but it warned against their indiscriminate use. It called for more research into potential health hazards in the interim, urged more judicious care in the use of pesticides in homes and in the field.

The committee chairman, Dr. Jerome B. Wiesner, said the uncontrolled use of poisonous chemicals, including pesticides, was "potentially a much greater hazard" than radioactive fallout.

Miss Carson appeared before the Senate Committee on Commerce, which was hearing testimony on the Chemical Pesticides Coordination Act, and a bill that would require labels to tell how to avert damage to fish and wildlife.

"I suggest," she said, "that the report by the President's Science Advisors has created a climate in which creation of a Pesticide Commission within the Executive Department might be considered."

One of the sparks that caused Miss Carson to undertake the task of writing the book (whose documentation alone fills a list of 55 pages of sources) was a letter she had received from old friends, Stuart and Olga Huckins. It told of the destruction that aerial spraying had caused to their two-acre private sanctuary at Powder Point in Duxbury, Mass.

Miss Carson, convinced that she must write about the situation and particularly about the effects of spraying on ecological factors, found an interested listener in Paul Brooks, editor in chief of the Houghton-Mifflin Company, the Boston publishing house that had brought out *The Edge of the Sea*.

As to her own writing habits, Miss Carson once wrote for 20th Century Authors: "I write slowly, often in longhand, had with frequent revision. Being sensitive to interruption, I writer most freely at night.

"As a writer, my interest is divided between the presentation of facts and the interpretation of their significance, with emphasis, I think toward the latter."

"Silent Spring" became a best seller even before its publication date because its release date was broken. It also became a best seller in England after its publication there in March, 1963.

One of Miss Carson's greatest fans, according to her agent, Marie Rodell, was her mother. Miss Rodell recalled that the mother, who died of pneumonia and a heart ailment in 1960, had sat in the family car in 1952 writing letters while Miss Carson and Miss Rodell explored the sea's edge near Boothbay Harbor. To passers-by the mother would say, pointing, "That's my daughter, Rachel Carson. She wrote *The Sea Around Us*."

People remembered Miss Carson for her shyness and reserve as well as for her writing and scholarship. And so when she received a telephone call after the publication of "The Sea Around Us," asking her to speak in the Astor Hotel at a luncheon, she asked Miss Rodell what she should do.

The agent counseled her to concentrate on writing. Miss Carson nodded in agreement, went to the phone, and shortly came back and said somewhat helplessly: "I said I'd do it."

There were 1,500 persons at the luncheon, Miss Carson was "scared to death," but she plunged into the talk and acquitted herself. As part of her program she played a recording of the sounds of underseas, including the clicking of shrimp and the squeeks of dolphins and whales. With the ice broken as a public speaker, Miss Carson continued with others sporadically.

Did Research by Herself Miss Carson had some preliminary help in researching "Silent Spring" but soon found that she could go faster by doing the work herself because she could skim past so much that she already knew.

Miss Carson had few materialistic leanings. When she found "The Sea Around Us" was a great financial success, her first extravagance was the purchase of a very fine binocular- microscope, which she had always wanted. Her second luxury was the summer cottage on the Maine coast.

Her agent said that Miss Carson's work was her hobby but that she was very fond of her flower garden at Silver Spring, Md., where she also loved to watch the birds that came to visit.

Miss Carson had two favorite birds, a member of the thrush family called the veery, and the tern, a small, black-capped gull-like bird with swallow like forked tails.

She once told an interviewer that she was enchanted by the "hunting, mystical call" of the veery, which is found in moist woods and bottomlands from Newfoundland to southern Manitoba, and in mountains to northern Georgia.

In manner, Miss Carson was a small, solemn-looking woman with the steady forthright gaze of a type that is sometimes common to thoughtful children who prefer to listen rather than to talk She was politely friendly but reserved and was not given to quick smiles or to encouraging conversation even with her fans.

The most recent flare-up in the continuing pesticide controversy occurred early this month when the Public Health Service announced that the periodic huge-scale deaths of fish on the lower Mississippi River had been traced over the last four years to toxic ingredients in three kinds of pesticides. Some persons believed that the pesticides drained into the river form neighboring farm lands.

A hearing by the Agriculture Department of the Public Health Service's charges ended a week ago with a spokesman for one of the pesticide manufacturers saying that any judgment should be delayed until more information was obtained....

Rachel Carson testifies before a Senate Government Operations Subcommittee, Washington D.C., June 4, 1963, just one year after the release of *Silent Spring* caused an uproar regarding the use of pesticides in the environment. AP IMAGES

SIGNIFICANCE

Sections of *Silent Spring* were read into the *Congressional Record* and afterward, President John F. Kennedy (1917–1963) appointed a panel review pesticide regulations. Carson was criticized by the pesticide industry even though she never advocated the complete abandonment of pesticide use. Instead, she argued against indiscriminate pesticide use without consideration of its ecological consequences.

One of the practical consequences of *Silent Spring* was a significant reduction in the use of the pesticide dichlorodiphenyltrichloroethane, better known as DDT. Developed during the 1940s, DDT was used to fight malaria and other insect-borne diseases and was considered by many to be a so-called miracle pesticide. During three decades of use, approximately 675,000 tons of DDT were applied in the United

States. DDT, however, is an environmentally persistent chlorinated hydrocarbon that accumulates in the food chain and has significant environmental consequences that offset its benefits in the control of disease. Largely as a result of *Silent Spring*, DDT was banned by the United States in 1972 and is currently illegal in many other countries. It is, however, still used for disease control in some countries.

Rachel Carson died of breast cancer in 1964, only two years after the publication of *Silent Spring*. She was posthumously awarded the Presidential Medal of Freedom in 1980.

FURTHER RESOURCES
Books
Carson, Rachel. *Silent Spring*. New York: Mariner Books, 2002 (40th Anniversary Edition).

Web sites
Environmental Working Group. "Toxics in our Environment."<http://www.ewg.org/issues/siteindex/issues. php?issueid=5026> (accessed February10, 2006).

World Wildlife Fund (WWF). "Keeping Toxic Chemicals Away from Wildlife and Your Family." <http://www. worldwildlife.org/consumer/rtc.cfm> (accessed February 10 2006).

"The Historical Roots of our Ecological Crisis"

Journal article

By: Lynn Townsend White, Jr.

Date: March 10, 1967

Source: White, Lynn Townsend, Jr. "The Historical Roots of our Ecological Crisis." *Science* 155 (10 March 1967): 1203–1207.

About the Author: Lynn Townsend White, Jr. (1907–1987) was the first American historian to accurately examine the role of technological discovery in the Middle Ages. Although best known for his ideas on the causes of modern environmental problems, within the academic community White was regarded first and foremost as a pioneer in the field of medieval technology. After receiving his Ph.D. from Harvard in 1938, he taught briefly at Princeton and Stanford Universities until becoming president of Mills College in 1943. In 1958, he left Mills and until his retirement in 1974, served as a Professor of History at the University of California at Los Angeles, where he published *Medieval Technology and Social Change* (1962) and *Medieval Technology and Religion: Collected Essays* (1978). White continued to write and engage in intellectual debate until his death in 1987.

INTRODUCTION

White's article "The Historical Roots of our Ecological Crisis," published in *Science* magazine in 1967, argued that mass destruction of nature by humankind is an unintended consequence of religious viewpoints of nature. In particular, the viewpoints related to Christian theology as they were frequently applied, or misapplied, toward dealing with the natural world. A conversation with English naturalist Aldous Huxley is the article's starting point. Huxley recalls that a delightful valley that he visited as a child was now overgrown with brush because the rabbits that kept the growth under control were dying of a disease introduced by farmers to reduce the rabbits' destruction of crops.

White claimed that "all forms of life modify their contexts," and that changes can be either benign or malignant to the environment. Modifications triggered by men, however, are in general accompanied with tragic consequences in the ecological equilibrium. In 1967, White warned that "our present combustion of fossil fuels threatens to change the chemistry of the globe's atmosphere as a whole, with consequences which we are only beginning to guess."

Although the terms Scientific and Industrial Revolutions are used to describe specific turning points in European history, White points out that the actual genesis of these revolutions can be traced to earlier points in time. With regard to the Industrial Revolution, White argued that it began around 1000 A.D. when humans began "to apply water power to industrial processes other than milling grain." This led to the use of wind power in the twelfth century along with other labor-saving devices, and subsequently, automation (such as the invention of the mechanical clock in the fourteenth century). The technological superiority of the European countries empowered them to conquer countries around the world.

◼ PRIMARY SOURCE

A conversation with Aldous Huxley not infrequently put one at the receiving end of an unforgettable monologue. About a year before his lamented death he was discoursing on a favorite topic: Man's unnatural treatment of nature and its sad results. To illustrate his point he told how, during the previous summer, he had returned to a little valley in England where he had spent many happy months as a child. Once it had been composed of delightful grassy glades; now it was becoming overgrown with unsightly brush because the rabbits that formerly kept such growth under control had largely succumbed to a disease, myxomatosis, that was deliberately introduced by the local farmers to reduce the rabbits' destruction of crops.

...All forms of life modify their contexts.... Ever since man became a numerous species he has affected his environment notably. The hypothesis that his fire-drive method of hunting created the world's great grasslands and helped to exterminate the monster mammals of the Pleistocene from much of the globe is plausible, if not proved.... Quite unintentionally, changes in human ways often affect nonhuman nature....

People, then, have often been a dynamic element in their own environment, but in the present state of historical scholarship we usually do not know exactly when, where, or with what effects man-induced changes came. As we enter the last third of the twentieth century, however, concern for the problem of ecologic backlash is mounting feverishly. Natural science, conceived as the effort to understand the nature of things, had flourished in several eras and among several peoples. Similarly there had been an age-old accumulation of technological skills, sometimes growing rapidly, sometimes slowly. But it was not until about four generations ago that Western Europe and North America arranged a marriage between science and technology, a union of the theoretical and the empirical approaches to our natural environment....

Almost at once, the new situation forced the crystallization of the novel concept of ecology; indeed, the word ecology first appeared in the English language in 1873. Today, less than a century later, the impact of our race upon the environment has so increased in force that it has changed in essence. When the first cannons were fired, in the early fourteenth century, they affected ecology by sending workers scrambling to the forests and mountains for more potash, sulphur, iron ore, and charcoal, with some resulting erosion and deforestation.... By 1285, London had a smog problem arising from the burning of soft coal, but our present combustion of fossil fuels threatens to change the chemistry of the globe's atmosphere as a whole, with consequences which we are only beginning to guess. With the population explosion, the carcinoma of planless urbanism, the now geological deposits of sewage and garbage, surely no creature other than man has ever managed to foul its nest in such short order.

...Our ecologic crisis is the product of an emerging, entirely novel, democratic culture. The issue is whether a democratized world can survive its own implications. Presumably we cannot unless we rethink our axioms.

The Western Traditions of Technology and Science One thing is so certain that it seems stupid to verbalize it: both modern technology and modern science are distinctively Occidental. Our technology has absorbed elements from all over the world, notably from China; yet everywhere today, whether in Japan or in Nigeria, successful technology is Western.... Today, around the globe, all significant science is Western in style and method, whatever the pigmentation or language of the scientists.

A second pair of facts is less well recognized because they result from quite recent historical scholarship. The leadership of the West, both in technology and in science, is far older than the so-called Scientific Revolution of the 17th century or the so-called Industrial Revolution of the 18th century. By A.D. 1000 at the latest— and perhaps, feebly, as much as 200 years earlier— the West began to apply water power to industrial processes other than milling grain. This was followed in the late twelfth century by the harnessing of wind power. From simple beginnings, but with remarkable consistency of style, the West rapidly expanded its skills in the development of power machinery, labor-saving devices, and automation....

By the end of the fifteenth century, the technological superiority of Europe was such that its small, mutually hostile nations could spill out over all the rest of the world, conquering, looting, and colonizing. The symbol of this technological superiority is the fact that Portugal, one of the weakest states of the Occident, was able to become, and to remain for a century, mistress of the East Indies. And we must remember that the technology of Vasco da Gama and Albuquerque was built by pure empiricism, drawing remarkably little support or inspiration from science....

Medieval View of Man and Nature ... In the days of the scratch-plow, fields were distributed generally in units capable of supporting a single family. Subsistence farming was the presupposition. But no peasant owned eight oxen: to use the new and more efficient plow, peasants pooled their oxen to form large plow-teams, originally receiving (it would appear) plowed strips in proportion to their contribution. Thus, distribution of land was based no longer on the needs of a family but, rather, on the capacity of a power machine to till the earth. Man's relation to the soil was profoundly changed. Formerly man had been part of nature; now he was the exploiter of nature....

What did Christianity tell people about their relations with the environment?

While many of the world's mythologies provide stories of creation, Greco-Roman mythology was singularly incoherent in this respect.... In sharp contrast, Christianity inherited from Judaism not only a concept of time as non-repetitive and linear a striking story of creation. By gradual stages a loving and all- powerful God had created light and darkness, the heavenly bodies, the earth and all its plants, animals, birds, and fishes.... Man named all the animals, thus establishing his dominance over them. God planned all of this explicitly for man's benefit and rule: no item in the physical creation had any purpose save to serve man's purposes....

Especially in its Western form, Christianity is the most anthropocentric religion the world has seen.... Christianity, in absolute contrast to ancient paganism and Asia's religions (except, perhaps, Zoroastrianism), not only established a dualism of man and nature but also insisted that it is God's will that man exploit nature for his proper ends....

An Alternative Christian View ... I personally doubt that disastrous ecological backlash can be avoided simply by applying to our problems more science and more technology. Our science and technology have grown out of Christian attitudes toward man's relation to nature, which are almost universally held not only by Christians and neo-Christians but also by those who fondly regard themselves as post-Christians. Despite Copernicus, all the cosmos rotates around our little globe. Despite Darwin, we are not, in our hearts, part of the natural process. We are superior to nature, contemptuous of it, willing to use it for our slightest whim. . . .

What we do about ecology depends on our ideas of the man-nature relationship. More science and more technology are not going to get us out of the present ecologic crisis until we find a new religion, or rethink our old one. . . .

Possibly we should ponder the greatest radical in Christian history since Christ: Saint Francis of Assisi. The prime miracle of Saint Francis is the fact that he did not end at the stake, as many of his left-wing followers did. . . . The key to an understanding of Francis is his belief in the virtue of humility—not merely for the individual but for man as a species. Francis tried to depose man from his monarchy over creation and set up a democracy of all God's creatures. With him the ant is no longer simply a homily for the lazy, flames a sign of the thrust of the soul toward union with God; now they are Brother Ant and Sister Fire, praising the Creator in their own ways as Brother Man does in his. . . .

The greatest spiritual revolutionary in Western history, Saint Francis, proposed what he thought was an alternative Christian view of nature and man's relation to it; he tried to substitute the idea of the equality of all creatures, including man, for the idea of man's limitless rule of creation. He failed. Both our present science and our present technology are so tinctured with orthodox Christian arrogance toward nature that no solution for our ecologic crisis can be expected from them alone. Since the roots of our trouble are so largely religious, the remedy must also be essentially religious, whether we call it that or not. We must rethink and refeel our nature and destiny. The profoundly religious, but heretical, sense of the primitive Franciscans for the spiritual autonomy of all parts of nature may point a direction. I propose Francis as a patron saint for ecologists.

SIGNIFICANCE

The impact of White's writings on the community of environmentalists, philosophers of technology, and religious scholars concerned with environmental issues was immediate and long-lasting. In the twenty years following the publication of "The Historical Roots of Our Ecological Crisis," over 200 books and articles used White's ideas as a focal point. His ideas penetrated the popular press, appearing in *TIME*, *Horizon*, and the *New York Times*, among others.

"The Historical Roots of Our Ecological Crisis" was one of the most significant interpretations of history to come out of medieval studies in the second half of the twentieth century. Connecting the culture of medieval Christianity to the emergence of what White called an "exploitative" attitude toward nature in the Western world throughout the Middle Ages, White's ideas set off a wide debate about the role of religion in creating and supporting the developed world's increasingly successful control of the natural world through technology. The explosiveness of this debate, which still reverberates, was touched off by a confluence of factors: urgency in the late 1960s and 1970s over the newly discovered environmental crisis, White's ability to reach an audience beyond that of professional Historians, and the perception among some that White's thoughts constituted an attack on Christianity that needed to be answered before additional injury was done to the value of traditionally held religious beliefs.

White argued that the destruction of paganism by Christianity was a tremendous psychic revolution in human history. As a result, Europe received a number of key axioms that would shape the European worldview to the present day: faith in progress; the concept of time as linear (rather than cyclical according to the seasons); the creation of the world to serve the needs of humanity as set out in the Genesis account; and the creation of humanity in God's image and God (and man) as "other" than nature. Furthermore, paganism had stressed the sacredness of the created order ("In antiquity every tree, every spring, every stream, every hill had its own "guardian spirit"), yet by destroying this Christianity allowed nature to be exploited. In other religions this essential relationship between humanity and the Earth has the ability to be preserved (Hindu pantheism, as an example). However, according to White it has been the Christian account of the creation of the world *ex nihilo* ("out of nothing"), and apart from God, which has allowed this to be particularly difficult in Western European cultures.

White noted that the human capacity to wreak damage and destruction upon the environment grows out of Western technological and scientific advances made since the Medieval period. These advances have occurred in a social context informed by the Judeo-Christian tradition. White focuses his analysis on Western Christianity, understood as both Protestantism and Roman Catholicism together. He asserts that this Western Christianity is "the most anthropocentric religion the world has seen." This overt anthropocentrism gives humans permission to exploit nature in a mood of indifference to the integrity of natural objects. White argued that within Christian theology, "nature has no reason for existence save to serve (humans)." Thus, for White, Christian arrogance towards nature "bears a huge burden of guilt" for the contemporary environmental crisis.

To counteract "our ecological crisis" White is straightforward: "we shall continue to have a worsening ecological crisis until we reject the axiom that nature has no reason for existence save to serve man". He also sets that as Saint Francis of Assisi did, we need to develop another way of seeing nonhuman nature. All of living organisms must to be seen as in the same "hierarchical" level of human beings. According to Saint Francis "the ant is no longer simply a homily for the lazy, flames a sign of the thrust of the soul toward union with God; now they are Brother Ant and Sister Fire, praising the Creator in their own ways as Brother Man does in his". In addition, because of Saint Francis' ecotheologian values, White suggests Francis as a patron saint of ecologists.

The debate is still strong, as several Web pages are maintained to support or crush White's ideas. White's powerful and innovative reading of history, which has formed a generation of scholarship, remains a hallmark for current and future discussion.

FURTHER RESOURCES
Books

Wackernagel, Mathis. *Our Ecological Footprint: Reducing Human Impact on the Earth*. Philadelphia, PA: New Society Publishers, 1996.

White, Lynn Townsend. *Medieval Religion and Technology: Collected Essays*. Berkeley: University of California Press, 1978.

White, Lynn Townsend. *Medieval Technology and Social Change*. Oxford: Clarendon Press, 1962.

Periodicals

Elspeth, W. "Lynn White, Ecotheology, and History." Environmental Ethics 15 (1993): 151–169.

Kelly, H.A. "Lynn White's Legacy." *Viva Vox* 1 (2002/2003): 1–11.

Web sites

Center for Medieval and Renaissance History. <http://www.humnet.ucla.edu/humnet/cmrs/default.html>(accessed March 8, 2006).

Society for the History of Technology. <http://shot.press.jhu.edu/Publications/Publications_Main_Page.htm> (accessed March 8, 2006).

Audio and Visual Media

The Soul of Science. Video. Hawkhill Associates, Inc., 2002.

"The Tragedy of the Commons"

Journal article

By: Garrett James Hardin

Date: December 3, 1968

Source: Hardin, Garrett James. "The Tragedy of the Commons." *Science* 162 (December 3, 1968): 1243–1248.

About the Author: American ecologist and microbiologist Dr. Garrett James Hardin (1915–2003) received his Bachelor of Science degree in zoology at the University of Chicago in 1936, and his Doctor of Philosophy degree in microbiology at Stanford University (California) in 1941. At the time *The Tragedy of the Commons* article was written, Hardin was a professor of human ecology at the University of California, Santa Barbara. This essay, for which he is well known in the scientific community, was based on a presidential address presented on June 25, 1968, before the meeting of the Pacific Division of the American Association for the Advancement of Science at Utah State University. Hardin published over 350 articles and twenty-seven books, including "The Immigration Dilemma: Avoiding the Tragedy of the Commons" (1995), "Stalking the Wild Taboo" (1996), and "The Ostrich Factor: Our Population Myopia" (1999). He was awarded the 1997 Constantine Panunzio Distinguished Emeriti Award by the University of California system. Hardin was also a founding member of Planned Parenthood and a strong advocate of population control.

INTRODUCTION

Hardin's paper, entitled "The Tragedy of the Commons: The Population Problem has no Technical Solution; It Requires a Fundamental Extension in Morality," was published in *Science* magazine in December 1968. The essay is broadly identified throughout the scientific community as a fundamental statement concerning such diverse subjects as ecology, economics, environmental science, conservation, political science, and population theory.

In his essay, Hardin introduced a hypothetical Commons, or open pasture, for all individuals to use. Animals were grazed by each individual on this common ground. Motivated by their own personal aspirations, each individual added to his flock in order to increase personal wealth. Each additional animal degraded the Commons by a small amount compared to the individual's gain in wealth. However, when *all* individuals comprising the group added animals to their flocks in order to gain wealth, the Commons, according to Hardin, would eventually be destroyed, thus the concept of "the tragedy of the commons." Hardin reasoned that, if left unchecked, the uncontrolled addition of animals—by well-intentioned though self-interested individuals—to a finite space would ultimately destroy the Commons.

■ PRIMARY SOURCE

THE TRAGEDY OF THE COMMONS

The population problem has no technical solution; it requires a fundamental extension in morality. At the end of a thoughtful article on the future of nuclear war, [J.B.] Wiesner and [H.F.] York concluded that: "Both sides in the arms race are...confronted by the dilemma of steadily increasing military power and steadily decreasing national security. *It is our considered professional judgment that this dilemma has no technical solution.* If the great powers continue to look for solutions in the area of science and technology only, the result will be to worsen the situation."

I would like to focus your attention not on the subject of the article (national security in a nuclear world) but on the kind of conclusion they reached, namely that there is no technical solution to the problem. An implicit and almost universal assumption of discussions published in professional and semipopular scientific journals is that the problem under discussion has a technical solution. A technical solution may be defined as one that requires a change only in the techniques of the natural sciences, demanding little or nothing in the way of change in human values or ideas of morality.

In our day (though not in earlier times) technical solutions are always welcome. Because of previous failures in prophecy, it takes courage to assert that a desired technical solution is not possible. Wiesner and York exhibited this courage; publishing in a science journal, they insisted that the solution to the problem was not to be found in the natural sciences. They cautiously qualified their statement with the phrase, "It is our considered professional judgment...." Whether they were right or not is not the concern of the present article. Rather, the concern here is with the important concept of a class of human problems which can be called "no technical solution problems," and more specifically, with the identification and discussion of one of these.

It is easy to show that the class is not a null class. Recall the game of tick-tack-toe. Consider the problem, "How can I win the game of tick-tack-toe?" It is well known that I cannot, if I assume (in keeping with the conventions of game theory) that my opponent understands the game perfectly. Put another way, there is no "technical solution" to the problem. I can win only by giving a radical meaning to the word "win." I can hit my opponent over the head; or I can drug him; or I can falsify the records. Every way in which I "win" involves, in some sense, an abandonment of the game, as we intuitively understand it. (I can also, of course, openly abandon the game—refuse to play it. This is what most adults do.)

The class of "No technical solution problems" has members. My thesis is that the "population problem," as conventionally conceived, is a member of this class. How it is conventionally conceived needs some comment. It is fair to say that most people who anguish over the population problem are trying to find a way to avoid the evils of overpopulation without relinquishing any of the privileges they now enjoy. They think that farming the seas or developing new strains of wheat will solve the problem—technologically. I try to show here that the solution they seek cannot be found. The population problem cannot be solved in a technical way, any more than can the problem of winning the game of tick-tack-toe....

Tragedy of Freedom in a Commons The rebuttal to the invisible hand in population control is to be found in a scenario first sketched in a little-known Pamphlet in 1833 by a mathematical amateur named William Forster Lloyd (1794–1852). We may well call it "the tragedy of the commons," using the word "tragedy" as the philosopher Whitehead used it: "The essence of dramatic tragedy is not unhappiness. It resides in the solemnity of the remorseless working of things." He then goes on to say, "This inevitableness of destiny can only be illustrated in terms of human life by incidents which in fact involve unhappiness. For it is only by them that the futility of escape can be made evident in the drama."

The tragedy of the commons develops in this way. Picture a pasture open to all. It is to be expected that each herdsman will try to keep as many cattle as possible on the commons. Such an arrangement may work reasonably satisfactorily for centuries because tribal wars, poaching, and disease keep the numbers of both man and beast well below the carrying capacity of the land. Finally, however, comes the day of reckoning, that is, the day when the long-desired goal of social stability becomes a reality. At this point, the inherent logic of the commons remorselessly generates tragedy.

As a rational being, each herdsman seeks to maximize his gain. Explicitly or implicitly, more or less consciously, he asks, "What is the utility *to me* of adding one more animal to my herd?" This utility has one negative and one positive component.

1) The positive component is a function of the increment of one animal. Since the herdsman receives all the proceeds from the sale of the additional animal, the positive utility is nearly + 1.

2) The negative component is a function of the additional overgrazing created by one more animal. Since, however, the effects of overgrazing are shared by all the herdsmen, the negative utility for any particular decisionmaking herdsman is only a fraction of - 1.

Adding together the component partial utilities, the rational herdsman concludes that the only sensible course for him to pursue is to add another animal to his herd. And another, and another. . . . But this is the conclusion reached by each and every rational herdsman sharing a commons. Therein is the tragedy. Each man is locked into a system that compels him to increase his herd without limit—in a world that is limited. Ruin is the destination toward which all men rush, each pursuing his own best interest in a society that believes in the freedom of the commons. Freedom in a commons brings ruin to all.

Some would say that this is a platitude. Would that it were! In a sense, it was learned thousands of years ago, but natural selection favors the forces of psychological denial. The individual benefits as an individual from his ability to deny the truth even though society as a whole, of which he is a part, suffers. Education can counteract the natural tendency to do the wrong thing, but the inexorable succession of generations requires that the basis for this knowledge be constantly refreshed.

A simple incident that occurred a few years ago in Leominster, Massachusetts shows how perishable the knowledge is. During the Christmas shopping season the parking meters downtown were covered with plastic bags that bore tags reading: "Do not open until after Christmas. Free parking courtesy of the mayor and city council." In other words, facing the prospect of an increased demand for already scarce space, the city fathers reinstituted the system of the commons. (Cynically, we suspect that they gained more votes than they lost by this retrogressive act.)

In an approximate way, the logic of the commons has been understood for a long time, perhaps since the discovery of agriculture or the invention of private property in real estate. But it is understood mostly only in special cases which are not sufficiently generalized. Even at this late date, cattlemen leasing national land on the Western ranges demonstrate no more than an ambivalent understanding, in constantly pressuring federal authorities to increase the head count to the point where overgrazing produces erosion and weed-dominance. Likewise, the oceans of the world continue to suffer from the survival of the philosophy of the commons. Maritime nations still respond automatically to the shibboleth of the "freedom of the seas." Professing to believe in the "inexhaustible resources of the oceans," they bring species after species of fish and whales closer to extinction. . . .

Recognition of Necessity Perhaps the simplest summary of this analysis of man's population problems is this: the commons, if justifiable at all, is justifiable only under conditions of low-population density. As the human population has increased, the commons has had to be abandoned in one aspect after another.

First we abandoned the commons in food gathering, enclosing farm land and restricting pastures and hunting and fishing areas. These restrictions are still not complete throughout the world.

Somewhat later we saw that the commons as a place for waste disposal would also have to be abandoned. Restrictions on the disposal of domestic sewage are widely accepted in the Western world; we are still struggling to close the commons to pollution by automobiles, factories, insecticide sprayers, fertilizing operations, and atomic energy installations.

In a still more embryonic state is our recognition of the evils of the commons in matters of pleasure. There is almost no restriction on the propagation of sound waves in the public medium. The shopping public is assaulted with mindless music, without its consent. Our government has paid out billions of dollars to create a supersonic transport which would disturb 50,000 people for every one person whisked from coast to coast 3 hours faster. Advertisers muddy the airwaves of radio and television and pollute the view of travelers. We are a long way from outlawing the commons in matters of pleasure. Is this because our Puritan inheritance makes us view pleasure as something of a sin, and pain (that is, the pollution of advertising) as the sign of virtue?

Every new enclosure of the commons involves the infringement of somebody's personal liberty. Infringements made in the distant past are accepted because no contemporary complains of a loss. It is the newly proposed infringements that we vigorously oppose; cries of "rights" and "freedom" fill the air. But what does "freedom" mean? When men mutually agreed to pass laws against robbing, mankind became more free, not less so. Individuals locked into the logic of the commons are free only to bring on universal ruin; once they see the necessity of mutual coercion, they become free to pursue other goals. I believe it was Hegel who said, "Freedom is the recognition of necessity."

The most important aspect of necessity that we must now recognize, is the necessity of abandoning the commons in breeding. No technical solution can rescue us from the misery of overpopulation. Freedom to breed will bring ruin to all. At the moment, to avoid hard decisions many of us are tempted to propagandize for conscience and responsible parenthood. The temptation must be resisted, because an appeal to independently acting consciences selects for the disappearance of all conscience in the long run, and an increase in anxiety in the short.

The only way we can preserve and nurture other and more precious freedoms is by relinquishing the freedom to breed, and that very soon. "Freedom is the recognition of necessity"—and it is the role of education to reveal to all the necessity of abandoning the freedom to breed. Only so, can we put an end to this aspect of the tragedy of the commons.

SIGNIFICANCE

The central thesis with regard to Hardin's essay was to describe to readers a simple thought experiment. Included within it, Hardin showed the terrible consequences from promoting incorrect moral theories with respect to permitting a growing population to steadily increase the exploitation of its ecosystem. Hardin claimed that Western moral thinking was flawed and would eventually lead to the downfall of its society in the form of destruction of its ecosystems such as waters, lands, animals, and natural resources.

Hardin believed that *a priori* ethics—that is, beliefs based on principles centered only on individual entities (such as humans, families, organizations, cities, and countries) and a system of equal justice for all such entities—always led to excess material consumption and unregulated population growth. Such faulty ethics, which are currently practiced in Western society, would inevitability cause the breakdown of the ecosystems that supported the entire society.

Alternatively, Hardin proposed replacing the *a priori* ethics system with the *system-sensitive* ethics system in order to prevent ecological disaster. Such an ethics system, according to Hardin, promoted the ability to preserve the ecosystem through promoting the health of the environment over the behavior of users of that environment. Hardin believed that any ethics or moral belief system that did not place success of the environment above the success of the individual would eventually end in tragedy for the environment and all individuals using that environment.

Hardin demonstrated within his essay how generally accepted and rational behavior within individuals would eventually lead to the downfall of the group if the system was centered around self-interested individual behavior. Hardin stated that individuals have been taught over generations that equal justice and universal human rights are essential rights for all people, along with the essential rights for such benefits as education, employment, food, home, safety, and health. Concurrently, individuals also believed that the environment must be protected. However, since human rights were deemed essential by individuals and viewed as more important than environmental protection, in order to provide these human rights to more and more people in the United States, the infrastructure of cities and towns has been constantly expanding. Because of this expansion, there has been a continual need to produce more drinking water, educational facilities, consumer goods, food, health care, sanitation, and other such perceived necessities. As human needs expand, the need for more luxury goods and services also add to the expansion.

Hardin concluded that the unending expansion of human rights is only possible in a world with infinite resources because only in this scenario is there never a conflict between individual, environmental, and societal needs. However, on a closed and finite environment, such as that on Earth, conflict of these three needs will result as constant human expansion that eventually destroys the finite environment of the Earth.

Hardin's essay and his significant ideas continue to serve as a useful basis for understanding how the human race, not as a group, but as individuals, has degraded the environment. Hardin also stated within his essay his views on how to reverse that degradation. Although Hardin uses a simple analogy of a common pasture land used by all individuals of a group, he immediately recognized that such a thought experiment could be widely applied to many environmental problems that existed at the time he wrote the article. Such environmental disasters—which are as prevalent in the early years of the twenty-first century as they were when Hardin wrote his essay—are just waiting to happen, according to Hardin. Such environmental disasters include acid rain; deforestation; desertification; emissions of greenhouse gases; excessive fishing of the oceans; global climate changes, high rates of species extinction; ocean dumping of wastes; overgrazing on public lands; and pollution of air, water, and other resources.

Hardin identified a major problem in the world: Self-interested individual behavior that maximizes personal short-term gain will—even though rational on the surface—if left uncontrolled (without the implementation of an effective plan of resource management) will result in long-term harm or even destruction to the environment, the group, and the individual.

Due in great measure to Hardin's essay, researchers have begun to compare public goods and common goods (or common-pool resources, CPRs). A public good is anything that is not consumed (so available to everyone), such as a weather forecast provided by a government to farmers. A CPR is anything that is consumed (which is only available to those who consume it), such as land for farming and water for irrigation. Thus, in response to the need to control individual behavior with respect to these common goods, managing bodies (such as governments) have begun to control such resources through the use of laws and regulations for the benefit of the group, but not necessarily for the benefit of each individual within the group.

Although a long time in coming, governments have begun to manage finite environments in order to maintain a healthy ecosystem. As a result, the individual is not allowed to infinitely expand his enterprise in order to maximize profits. As Hardin argued, governments use various forms of pressure to bring about cooperation within individuals. In other words, governments control the use of resources through laws, regulations, and other forms of principles. Although such a system does not assure the avoidance of ecological disasters, when managed properly, such measures help to reduce the possibility of such disasters.

The idea of the supreme importance of the individual is difficult to stop, but Hardin has helped to change thinking with respect to what is best for the overall health of life on Earth: that of a healthy environment over the behavior of the individual. His writings, especially his essay on the "Tragedy of the Commons," are seen as important steps to the fledgling field of ecological economics, a discipline that combines the study of ecology with the study of economics.

FURTHER RESOURCES

Periodicals

Smil, Vaclav. "Garrett James Hardin (Dallas 1915—Santa Barbara 2003)." *American Scientist*, 92, no. 3 (January–February 2004): 8. Available at *American Scientist Online*, <http://www.americanscientist.org/template/AssetDetail/assetid/29864/page/1;jsessionid=aaaco0tQIRFs3J> (accessed March 10, 2006).

Web sites

Elliott, Herschel. "An Abstract of 'A General Statement of Hardin's Tragedy of the Commons.'" *Dieoff.org*, February 26, 1997. <http://dieoff.org/page121.htm> (accessed March 10, 2006).

The Garrett Hardin Society. <http://www.garretthardinsociety.org> (accessed March 10, 2006).

Hardin, Garrett. "Ethical Implications of Carrying Capacity." *Dieoff.org*, 1977. <http://dieoff.org/page96.htm> (accessed March 10, 2006).

———. "Living Within Limits and Limits on Living: Garrett Hardin on Ecology, Economy, and Ethics." Interview with Frank Meile. *Stalking the Wild Taboo*. (Originally published in *Skeptic* 4, no. 2 (1996): 42-46. <http://www.lrainc.com/swtaboo/stalkers/fm_hardn.html> (accessed March 10, 2006).

———. "The Tragedy of the Commons." *The Library of Economics and Liberty: The Concise Encyclopedia of Economics*. <http://www.econlib.org/library/Enc/TragedyoftheCommons.html> (accessed March 10, 2006).

Partridge, Ernest. "Garrett Hardin, 1915–2003—A Tribute: The Renowned Biologist and Author of 'Tragedy of the Commons' is Dead at 88." *The Online Gadfly*. <http://gadfly.igc.org/eds/envt/hardin.htm> (accessed March 10, 2006).

"American Institutions and Ecological Ideals"

Journal article

By: Leo Marx

Date: November 27, 1970

Source: Marx, Leo. "American Institutions and Ecological Ideals." *Science* 170 (November 27, 1970): 945–952.

About the Author: Leo Marx (1919–) received his Bachelor of Science degree in history and literature in 1941 and his Doctor of Philosophy degree in the history of American civilization in 1950, both from Harvard University. From there, Marx taught at the University of Minnesota (1950–1958) and Amherst College in Massachusetts (1958–1977). At the time of his writing "American Institutions and Ecological Ideals" in 1970, Marx was a professor of English and American studies at Amherst College. The article was based on a talk presented on December 29, 1969, at the Boston, Massachusetts meeting of the American Association for the Advancement of Science. As of 2002, Marx was a senior lecturer and a William R. Kenan professor of American Cultural History Emeritus in the Program in Science, Technology, and Society at Massachusetts Institute of Technology. Marx's work has focused on the relationship between technology and culture in the United States over the last two centuries. His books include *The Machine in the Garden: Technology and the Pastoral Ideal in America*; *Earth, Air, Fire, Water: Humanistic Studies of the Environment*; and *Does Technology Drive History?: The Dilemma of Technological Determinism*.

INTRODUCTION

Marx's "American Institutions and Ecological Ideals" appeared in the November 27, 1970 issue of *Science* magazine. In this article, Marx made the claim that American literature has, over the years, provided the only consistent outlet for what he called the "literary-ecological perspective"; that is, literature written from an ecological point of view. Within the article, Marx stated that American writers have been a consistent source for ecology-based writings. Early American writers such as James Fenimore Cooper (1789–1851), Ralph Waldo Emerson (1803–1882), Nathaniel Hawthorne (1894–1864), Herman Melville (1819–1891), Henry David Thoreau (1817–1862), and Walt Whitman (1819–1892) have used the term "environment" to parallel what each particular writer, in his own unique way, predicted would happen to mankind and society in general. In their writings, Marx stated, each writer "measured the quality of American life against something like an ecological ideal."

On the other hand, Marx claimed that in the past, the scientific community did not publicly state their concerns for the worsening of the environment as effectively as the literary community. Even during the 1960s, when interest in ecology and the environment became popular with the public and the mass media, the scientific community did not state its opinions in response to the vocal ecologists and alarmist environmentalists. Recently, according to Marx, the scientific community has shifted toward the views of the literary community, opinions that point to declining environmental conditions brought about by humankind's expansionary, materialistic lifestyle.

The central concept discussed by Marx is "the maintenance of a healthy life-enhancing interaction between man and the environment." Marx stated that in order to accomplish this goal, all organisms must accept responsibility for maintaining, at least, minimum standards for a healthy ecological system in order to avoid elimination from that system. Unfortunately, according to Marx, humankind's expansionary lifestyle is degrading the environment and, along with it, the future of humankind. His viewpoint is now becoming

more accepted both in the scientific and literary communities.

Seeing this degradation, Marx asks the question: "Can mankind reverse the deterioration of the physical world, especially given the dominant state of the nation's critical organizations and institutions along with the expanded role of technology overall in society?"

PRIMARY SOURCE

AMERICAN INSTITUTIONS AND ECOLOGICAL IDEALS

Scientific and literary views of our expansionary life-style are converging. Anyone familiar with the work of the classic American writers (I am thinking of men like Cooper, Emerson, Thoreau, Melville, Whitman, and Mark Twain) is likely to have developed an interest in what we recently have learned to cal1 ecology. One of the first things we associate with each of the writers just named is a distinctive, vividly particularized setting (or landscape) inseparable from the writer's conception of man. Partly because of the special geographic and political circumstances of American experience, and partly because they were influenced by the romantic vision of man's relations with nature, al1 of the writers mentioned possessed a heightened sense of place. Yet words like *place, landscape,* or *setting* scarcely can do justice to the significance these writers imparted to external nature in their work. They took for granted a thorough and delicate interpenetration of consciousness and environment. In fact it now seems evident that these gifted writers had begun, more than a century ago, to measure the quality of American life against something like an ecological ideal.

The ideal I have in mind, quite simply, is the maintenance of a healthy life-enhancing interaction between man and the environment. This is layman's language for the proposition that every organism, in order to avoid extinction or expulsion from its ecosystem, must conform to certain minimal requirements of that system. What makes the concept of the ecosystem difficult to grasp, admittedly, is the fact that the boundaries between systems are always somewhat indistinct, and our technology is making them less distinct all the time. Since an ecosystem includes not only all living organisms (plants and animals) but also the inorganic (physical and chemical) components of the environment, it has become extremely difficult, in the thermonuclear age, to verify even the relatively limited autonomy of local or regional systems. If a decision taken in Moscow or Washington can effect a catastrophic change in the chemical composition of the entire biosphere, then the idea of a San Francisco, or Bay Area, or California, or even North American ecosystem loses much of its clarity and force. Similar difficulties arise when we contemplate the global rate of human population growth. All this is only to say that, on ecological grounds, the case for world government is beyond argument. Meanwhile, we have no choice but to use the nation-states as political instruments for coping with the rapid deterioration of the physical world we inhabit.

The chief question before us, then, is this: What are the prospects, given the character of America's dominant institutions, for the fulfil1ment of this ecological ideal? But first, what is the significance of the current "environmental crusade?" Why should we be skeptical about its efficacy? How shall we account for the curious response of the scientific community? To answer these questions I will attempt to characterize certain of our key institutions from an ecological perspective. I want to suggest the striking convergence of scientific and the literary criticism of our national life-style. In conclusion I will suggest a few responses to the ecological crisis indicated by that scientific-literary critique. . . .

A PROPOSAL AND SOME CONCLUSIONS

Assuming that this sketch of America's dominant institutions as seen from a pastoral-ecological vantage is not grossly inaccurate, what inferences can we draw from it? What bearing does it have upon our current effort to cope with the deterioration of the environment? What special significance does it have for concerned scientists and technologists? I shall draw several conclusions, beginning with a specific recommendation for action by the American Association for the Advancement of Science.

First, then, let me propose that the Association establish a panel of the best qualified scientists, representing as many as possible of the disciplines involved, to serve as a national review board for ecological information. This board would take the responsibility for locating and defining the crucial problems (presumably it would recruit special task forces for specific assignments) and make public recommendations whenever feasible. To be sure, some scientists will be doing a similar job for the government, but, if an informed electorate is to evaluate the government's program, it must have an independent source of knowledge. One probable objection is that scientists often disagree, and feel reluctant to disagree in public. But is this a healthy condition for a democracy? Perhaps the time has come to lift the dangerous veil of omniscience from the world of science and technology. If the experts cannot agree, let them issue minority reports. If our survival is at stake, we should be allowed to know what the problems and the choices are. The point here is not that we laymen look to scientists for *the* answer, or that we expect them to save us. But we do ask for their active involvement in solving problems about which they are the best-informed

citizens. Not only should such a topflight panel of scientists be set up on a national basis, but—perhaps more important—similar committees should be set up to help make the best scientific judgment available to the citizens of every state, city, and local community.

But there will also be those who object on the ground that an organization as august as the American Association for the Advancement of Science must not be drawn into politics. The answer, of course, is that American scientists and technologists are now and have always been involved in politics. A profession whose members place their services at the disposal of the government, the military, and the private corporations can hardly claim immunity now. Scientific and technological knowledge unavoidably is used for political purposes. But it also is a national resource. The real question in a democratic society, therefore, is whether that knowledge can be made as available to ordinary voters as it is to those, like the Department of Defense or General Electric, who can most easily buy it. If scientists are worried about becoming partisans, then their best defense is to speak with their own disinterested public voice. To allow the burden of alerting and educating the people to fall upon a few volunteers is a scandal. Scientists, as represented by their professional organizations, have a responsibility to make sure that their skills are used to fulfill as well as to violate the ecological ideal. And who knows? If things get bad enough, the scientific community may take steps to discourage its members from serving the violators.

There is another, perhaps more compelling, reason why scientists and technologists, as an organized professional group, must become more actively involved. It was scientists, after all, who first sounded the alarm. What action we take as a society and *how quickly we take it* depend in large measure upon the credibility of the alarmists. Who is to say, if organized science does not, which alarms we should take seriously? What group has anything like the competence of scientists and technologists to evaluate the evidence? Or, to put it negatively, what group can do more, by mere complacency and inaction, to insure an inadequate response to the environmental crisis? It is a well-known fact that Americans hold the scientific profession in the highest esteem. So long as most scientists go about their business as usual, so long as they seem unperturbed by the urgent appeals of their own colleagues, it is likely that most laymen, including our political representatives, will remain skeptical.

The arguments for the more active involvement of the scientific community in public debate illustrate the all encompassing and essentially political character of the environmental crisis. If the literary-ecological perspective affords an accurate view, we must eventually take into account the deep-seated, institutional causes of our distress. No cosmetic program, no clean-up-the-landscape activity, no degree of protection for the wilderness, no antipollution laws can be more than the merest beginning. Of course such measures are worthwhile, but in undertaking them we should acknowledge their superficiality. The devastation of the environment is at bottom a result of the kind of society we have built and the kind of people we are. It follows, therefore, that environmentalists should join forces, wherever common aims can be found, with other groups concerned to change basic institutions. To arrest the deterioration of the environment it will be necessary to control many of the same forces which have prevented us from ending the war in Indochina or giving justice to black Americans. In other words, it will be necessary for ecologists to determine where the destructive power of our society lies and how to cope with it. Knowledge of that kind, needless to say, is political. But then it seems obvious, on reflection, that the study of human ecology will be incomplete until it incorporates a sophisticated mode of political analysis.

Meanwhile, it would be folly, given the character of American institutions, to discount the urgency of our situation either on the ground that technology will provide the solutions or on the ground that countermeasures are proposed. We cannot rely on technology because the essential problem is not technological. It inheres in all of the ways in which this dynamic society generates and uses its power. It calls into question the controlling purposes of all the major institutions which actually determine the nation's impact upon the environment: the great business corporations, the military establishment, the universities, the scientific and technological elites, and the exhilarating expansionary ethos by which we all live. Throughout our brief history, a passion for personal and collective aggrandizement has been the American way. One can only guess at the extent to which forebodings of ecological doom have contributed to the revulsion that so many intelligent young people feel these days for the idea of "success" as a kind of limitless ingestion. In any case, most of the talk about the environmental crisis that' turns on the word pollution, as if we face a cosmic-scale problem of sanitation, is grossly misleading. What confronts us is an extreme imbalance between society's hunger—the rapidly growing sum of human wants—and the limited capacities of the earth.

SIGNIFICANCE

Marx stated that there exists a distinct difference between the application of the words *conservation* and *ecology*. Conservation is used to represent the work of people such as naturalists, property owners, and sportspersons who are basically interested in caring

for environments due to their own individual interests. As Marx stated, "In the view of many conservationists nature is a world that exists apart from, and for the benefit of, mankind."

On the other hand, Marx said that ecology is an idea that involves a much more complicated relationship between humankind and the environment, even between the interactions of all living organisms and their environments—all under a predetermined plan of making efficient use of resources under the direction of qualified scientists and technicians. Marx believed that conservationists are practical and well-trained technicians who always sound positive with respect to making efficient use of resources and solving humanity's environmental problems, while ecologists are radical sounding persons who have negative feelings with respect to the final outcome of the environment.

Marx stated his view that over the history of the United States the "seemingly unlimited natural resources and the relative absence of cultural or institutional restrains made possible what surely has been the fastest-developing, most mobile, most relentlessly innovative society in world history." Marx furthered his stance when he said the viewpoint of the average U.S. citizen was (and is today) that "the aggressive, man-centered attitude toward the environment fostered by Judeo-Christian thought: everything in nature, living or inorganic, exists to serve man." In addition, the U.S. system has ultimately supported industrial capitalism, which maintains the viewpoint: "limits to the environment are meant to be broken."

Marx declared, for example: "Who looks after the prime agricultural lands turned over to urban expansion: Why do not scientists, technicians, and engineers speak up to counter the wastefulness of this business climate. From there downward, American society—from state, city, village neighborhood and group, family, and child—are all striving to grow as fast as possible. When resources were believed to be inexhaustible—the ability to grow as fast as one was able—was seen as a good quality. But, today, with the knowledge that resources are not inexhaustible, people are ingrained with the energies to expand, grow, and multiply. And, with everyone expanding, scientists, technicians, and engineers are doing the same thing—but are not heeding the signs that they were trained to recognize."

Marx suggested that the literary and scientific views of America's environment have been recently converging. The literary view may be expressed with inspiring words and expressive poetry and the scientific view may be expressed with facts and figures, but the meaning is the same: that the self-exaggerating way of life caused by commercialism, materialism, and other monetary-based ideas has been put to use to unconsciously but, nevertheless, effectively degrade the environment, which will ultimately destroy humankind.

Within his essay, Marx proposed that the American Association for the Advancement of Science create a panel of the best qualified scientists of all the various disciplines in order to define the primary environmental problems confronting the United States, and then to make public recommendations based on their conclusions. Marx continued to say that during this process it is important to (1) actively involve all U.S. scientists, (2) make unbiased, rational investigations into the country's problems, especially without biases caused by associations with the various powerful education, military, private, and public organizations in the country, and (3) make positive improvements in the environment based on scientific conclusions. Marx concluded by stating that use of technology is not the problem, but the main problem lies within the ways that society has developed within the United States.

FURTHER RESOURCES

Books

Marx, Leo. *Does Technology Drive History?: The Dilemma of Technological Determinism.* Cambridge, Mass: MIT Press, 1994.

————. *Earth, Air, Fire, Water: Humanistic Studies of the Environment.* Amherst, Mass: University of Massachusetts Press, 1999.

————. *The Machine in the Garden: Technology and the Pastoral Ideal in America.* London and New York: Oxford University Press, 1967.

Web sites

Albert H. Teich, Science and Policy Programs, American Association for the Advancement of Science. "Leo Marx: Chapter 1. Does Improved Technology Mean Progress?" <http://www.alteich.com/links/marx.htm> (accessed November 14, 2005).

Coming into the Country

Book excerpt

By: John McPhee

Date: 1976

Source: McPhee, John. *Coming into the Country.* New York: Farrar, Straus and Giroux, 1976.

About the Author: American author John McPhee (1931–) has written more than twenty nonfiction books, many of them notable contributions about humans and their interaction with the environment, since 1965. A native of Princeton, New Jersey, he attended both Princeton University and Cambridge University before embarking on a career in journalism with *Time* magazine. He has been a staff writer with *The New Yorker* since 1965. Two of his books, *Encounters with the Archdruid* and *The Curve of Binding Energy*, were nominated for National Book Awards. McPhee received the Award in Literature from the American Academy of Arts and Letters in 1977 and received a Pulitzer Prize in 1999 for *Annals of the Former World*, his collected writings about geologists and their work. Highly regarded among professional geologists for his portrayal of their science, McPhee has also been honored by the Geological Society of America, the American Institute of Professional Geologists, the American Association of Petroleum Geologists, and the Association of Earth Science Editors.

INTRODUCTION

Coming into the Country, published in 1976, is a narrative about Alaska during the pivotal years of the early to mid-1970s. It was a time of both economic expansion and controversy about the future of the remote and sparsely populated Alaska. Statehood had been granted barely a decade earlier, but much of the land in Alaska remained under federal control and was being evaluated for preservation as national parks, wilderness areas, and wildlife refuges. The Alaska Native Claims Settlement Act of 1971 had formally settled long-standing disputes about the property rights of Native Americans, giving one-ninth of Alaska's land and nearly one billion dollars in cash to twelve regional Native American corporations. The trans-Alaskan pipeline was being built and there was discussion about the possibility of moving the state capital from the small and difficult-to-reach city of Juneau to the bustling commercial center of Anchorage. Pipeline construction and oil exploration brought high-paying jobs, business opportunities, and the homogeneity of virtually every other American city to Anchorage. There were fears that construction of the pipeline would lead to an oil spill and environmental ruin in pristine Prince William Sound. Some saw it as an opportunity to prosper, while others saw the end of Alaska as they knew it.

The title of *Coming into the Country* alludes to Alaskans who refer to the remote bush as "the

Author John McPhee, during an interview with the Associated Press, April 12, 1999. AP IMAGES

country." When one arrives in the bush for the first time, he or she is said to have come into the country. *Coming into the Country* consists of three sections, each of which McPhee refers to as a book. The first book describes a river trip above the Arctic Circle with a group of state and federal scientists evaluating land that would eventually become the Gates of the Arctic National Park. The third book, also titled "Coming into the Country," recounts life in the remote bush town of Eagle, Alaska. The second book, titled "What They Were Hunting For" describes a life in urban Alaska during the campaign to move the state capital to Anchorage.

PRIMARY SOURCE

There are those who would say that tens of thousands of barrels of oil erupting from a break in the Trans-Alaska Pipeline would be the lesser accident if, at more or less the same time, a fresh Anchorage were to spill into the bush. While the dream of the capital city plays on in the mind, Anchorage stands real. It is the central hive of human Alaska, and in manner and structure it represents, for all to see, the Alaskan dynamic and the Alaskan aesthetic. It is a tangible expression of certain Alaskan's regard for Alaska—their one true city, the exemplar of the predilections of the people in creating improvements over the land.

As may befit a region where both short and long travel is generally by air, nearly every street in Anchorage seems to be the road to the airport. Dense groves of plastic stand on either side—flashing, whirling, flaky. HOOSIER BUDDY'S MOBILE HOMES. WINNEBAGO SALES & SERVICE. DISCOUNT LIQUORS OPEN SUNDAY. GOLD RUSH AUTO SALES. PROMPT ACTION LOCKSMITHS. ALASKA REFRIGERATION & AIR CONDITION. DENALI FUEL. . .

"Are the liquor stores really open Sundays?"

"Everything in Anchorage is open that pays."

Almost all Americans would recognize Anchorage, because Anchorage is that part of any city where the city has burst its seams and extruded Colonel Sanders.

"You can taste the greed in the air."

BELUGA ASPHALT.

Anchorage is sometimes excused in the name of pioneering. Build now, civilize later. But Anchorage is not a frontier town. It is virtually unrelated to its environment. It has come in on the wind, an American spore. A large cookie cutter brought down on El Paso could lift something like Anchorage into the air. Anchorage is the northern rim of Trenton, the center of Oxnard, the ocean-blind precincts of Daytona Beach. It is condensed, instant Albuquerque.

PANCHO'S VILLA, MEXICAN FOOD. BULL SHED, STEAK HOUSE AND SONIC LOUNGE. SHAKEY'S DRIVE-IN PIZZA. EAT ME SUBMARINES.

Anchorage has developed a high-rise city core, with glass-box offices for the oil companies and tall Miamian hotels. Zonelessly lurching outward, it has made of its suburbs a carnival of cinder block, all with a speculative mania so rife that sellers' small homesites—of modest lots scarcely large enough for small homesites—of modest lots scarcely large enough for houses—retain subsurface rights. In vacant lots, queen-post trusses lie waiting for new buildings to jump up beneath them. Roads are rubbled, ponded with chuckholes. Big trucks, graders, loaders, make the prevailing noise, the dancing fumes, the frenetic beat of the town. Huge rubber tires are strewn about like quoits, ever ready for the big machines that move hills of earth and gravel into inconvenient lakes, which become new ground.

FOR LEASE. WILL BUILD TO SUIT.

Anchorage coins millionaires in speculative real estate. Some are young. The median age in Anchorage is under twenty-four. Every three or four years, something like half the population turns over. And with thirty days of residence, you can vote as an Alaskan.

POLAR REALTY. IDLE WHEELS TRAILER PARK. MOTEL MUSH INN.

Anchorage has a thin history. Something of a precursor of the modern pipeline camps, it began in 1914 as a collection of tents pitched to shelter workers building the Alaska Railroad. For decades, it was a wooden-side-walked, gravel-streeted town. Then, remarkably early, as cities go, it developed an urban slum, and both homes and commerce began to abandon its core. The exodus was so rapid that the central business district never wholly consolidated, and downtown Anchorage is even more miscellaneous than outlying parts of the city. There is, for example, a huge J.C. Penney department store filling several blocks in the heart of town, with an interior mall of boutiques and restaurants and a certain degree of chic. A couple of weedy vacant lots separate this complex from five log cabins. Downtown Anchorage from a distance displays an upreaching skyline that implies great pressure for land. Down below, among the high buildings, are houses, huts, vegetable gardens, and bungalows with tidy front lawns. Anchorage burst out itself and left these incongruities in the center, and for me they are the most appealing sights in Anchorage. Up against a downtown office building I have seen cordwood stacked for winter.

In its headlong, violent expansion, Anchorage had considerable, but not unlimited, space to fill. To an extent unusual among cities, Anchorage has certain absolute boundaries, and in that sense its growth has been a confined explosion. To the north, a pair of military bases establish, in effect, a Roman wall. To the west and south, fjordlike arms of the Pacific—Knik Arm, Turnagain Arm—frame the city. Behind Anchorage, east, stand the Chugach Mountains, stunning against the morning and in the evening light—Mount Magnificent, Mount Gordon Lyon, Temptation Peak, Tanaina Peak, Wolverine Peak, the Suicide Peaks. Development has gone to some extent upward there. Houses are pushpinned to the mountainsides—a Los Angelized setting, particularly at night, above the starry lights of town. But the mountains are essentially a full stop to Anchorage, and Anchorage has nowhere else to go.

Within this frame of mountains, ocean, and military boundaries are about fifty thousand acres (roughly the amount of land sought by the Capital Site Selection Committee), and the whole of it is known as the Anchorage Bowl. The ground itself consists of silt, alluvium, eolian sands, glacial debris-material easy to rearrange. The surface was once lumpy with small knolls. As people and their businesses began filling the bowl, they went first to the knolls, because the knolls were wooded and well drained. They cut down the trees, truncated the hills, and bestudded them with buildings. They strung utility lines like baling wire from knoll to knoll. The new subdivisions within the bowl were thus hither and yon, random, punctuated with bogs. Anchorage grew like mold.

WOLVERINE ALUMINUM SIDING. ALASKA FOUR-WHEEL DRIVE. JACK BENNY'S RADIO-DISPATCHED CESSPOOL PUMPING.

Low ground is gradually being filled. The bowl has about a hundred and eighty thousand people now, or almost half of human Alaska. There are some in town—notably, Robert Atwood, of the *Times*—who would like to see Anchorage grow to seven hundred thousand. Atwood is a big, friendly, old-football-tackle sort of man, with whitening hair and gold-rimmed glasses. Forty years on the inside, this impatient advocate of the commercial potentialities of Alaska is said to be one of the two wealthiest people in the state, the other being his brother-in-law. "Idealists here in town see a need for a park in every housing development," Atwood told me one day. "They want to bury utility lines, reserve green belts, build bicycle paths. With these things, the bowl could only contain three hundred and fifty thousand. They're making it very difficult for man, these people. They favor animals, trees, water, flowers. Who ever makes a plan for man? Who ever *will* make a plan for man? That is what *I* wonder. I am known among conservationists as a bad guy."

In Anchorage, if you threw a pebble into a crowd, chances are you would not hit a conservationist, an eco-phile, a wilderness preserver. In small ghettos, they are there—living in a situation lined with irony. They are in Alaska—many of them working for the federal government—because Alaska is everything wild it has ever been said to be. Alaska runs off the edge of the imagination, with its tracklessness, its beyond-the-ridge-line surprises, its hundreds of millions of acres of wilderness—this so-called "last frontier," which is certainly all of that, yet for the most part is not a frontier at all but immemorial landscape in an all but unapproached state. Within such vastness, Anchorage is a mere pustule, a dot, a minim-a walled city, wild as Yonkers, with the wildlife riding in a hundred and ninety-three thousand trucks and cars. Yet the city—where people are, where offices are—is perforce the home address of wilderness planners, of wildlife biologists, of Brooks Range guides.

The first few days I spent in Alaska were spent in Anchorage, and I remember the increasing sense of entrapment we felt (my wife was with me), knowing that nothing less than a sixth of the entire United States, and almost all of it wilderness, was out there beyond seeing, while immediate needs and chores to do were keeping us penned in this portable Passaic. Finally, we couldn't take it any longer, and we cancelled appointments and rented a car and revved it up for an attempted breakout from town. A float plane—at a hundred and ten dollars an hour—would have been the best means, but, like most of the inmates of Anchorage, we could not afford it. For a great many residents, Anchorage is about all they ever see of Alaska, day after day after year. There are only two escape routes—a road north, a road south—and these are encumbered with traffic and, for some miles anyway, lined with detritus from Anchorage. We went south, that first time, and eventually east, along a fjord that would improve Norway. Then the road turned south again, into the mountains of Kenai— great tundra balds that reminded me of Scotland and my wife of parts of Switzerland, where she had lived. She added that she thought these mountains looked better than the ones in Europe. Sockeyes, as red as cardinals, were spawning in clear, shallow streams, and we ate our cheese and chocolate in a high meadow over a torrential river of green and white water. We looked up to the ridges for Dall sheep, and felt, for the moment, about as free. Anchorage shrank into perspective. It might be a sorry town, but it has the greatest out-of-town any town has ever had.

BIG RED'S FLYING SERVICE. BELUGA STEAM & ELECTRIC THAWING. DON'T GO TO JAIL LET FRED GO YOUR BAIL.

There is a street in Anchorage—a green-lights, red-lights, busy street—that is used by automobiles and airplanes. I remember an airplane in someone's driveway—next door to the house where I was staying. The neighbor started up its engine one night toward eleven o'clock, and for twenty minutes he ran it flat out while his two sons, leaning hard into the stabilizers, strained to hold back the plane. In Alaska, you do what you feel like doing, or so goes an Alaskan creed.

There is, in Anchorage, a somewhat Sutton Place. It is an enclave, actually, with several roads, off the western end of Northern Lights Boulevard, which is a principal Anchorage thoroughfare, a neon borealis. Walter Hickel lives in the enclave, on Loussac Drive, which winds between curbs and lawns, neatly trimmed, laid out, and landscaped, under white birches and balsam poplars. Hickel's is a heavy, substantial home, its style American Dentist. The neighbors' houses are equally expensive and much the same. The whole neighborhood seems to be struggling to remember Scarsdale. But not to find Alaska.

I had breakfast one morning in Anchorage with a man who had come to Alaska from The Trust for Public Land, an organization whose goal is to buy potential parkland in urban areas and hold it until the government, whose legislative machinery is often too slow for the land market, can get up the funds for the purpose. In overbuilt urban settings—from Watts to Newark and back to Oakland-The Trust for Public Land will acquire whatever it can, even

buildings under demolition, in order to create small parks and gardens that might relieve the compressed masses. And now The Trust for Public Land had felt the need to come to Anchorage—to the principal city of Alaska—to help hold a pond or a patch of green for the people in the future to have and see.

Books were selling in Anchorage, once when I was there, for forty-seven cents a pound.

There are those who would say that the only proper place for a new capital of Alaska—if there has to be a new one—is Anchorage, because anyone who has built a city like Anchorage should not be permitted to build one anywhere else.

At Anchorage International Airport, there is a large aerial photograph of Anchorage formed by pasting together a set of pictures that were made without what cartographers call ground control. This great aerial map is one of the first things to confront visitors from everywhere in the world, and in bold letters it is titled "ANCHORAGE, ALASKA. UNCONTROLLED MOSAIC."

SIGNIFICANCE

Coming into the Country paints a detailed and insightful picture of America's last frontier during a time of unprecedented change, presenting an unbiased journalistic account of a state struggling with its identity and future.

Some Alaskans look to Anchorage as a vision of what the state can be and others look at it as a sad example of what the state has become. Mcphee's portrayal reflects the universal dilemma facing Alaska and virtually every other city struggling to reconcile economic growth with environmental quality. In that regard, Alaska is no different than anywhere else. McPhee's description of the sprawling and disorganized urban growth of Anchorage, a small city by broader standards but Alaska's center of commerce, would apply just as well to anywhere in the lower forty-eight states. He describes Anchorage as an "instant Albuquerque" indistinguishable from Oxnard, El Paso, or Trenton. Yet, even thirty years after the book was published, Anchorage still harbors remnants of its rough and tumble frontier past. McPhee writes of firewood stacked alongside modern office buildings and log cabins next to a J.C. Penney store. He points out that, ironically, wildlife biologists, mountain guides, and others drawn to the vast and wild frontier more often than not end up living in Anchorage because, simply enough, that is where the jobs are. McPhee describes the sentiment of a civic booster who believes that environmental idealists favor trees and animals at the expense of humans. His concern was that bicycle paths and parks take up space that will limit the ability of Anchorage to grow to its full potential.

FURTHER RESOURCES

Books

Borneman, Walter R.. *Alaska: Saga of a Bold Land*. New York: HarperCollins, 2003.

Web sites

Alyeska Pipeline Service Company. <http://www.alyeska-pipe. com> (accessed January 27, 2006).

National Park Service. "Gates of the Arctic National Park and Preserve." <http://www.nps.gov/gaar> (accessed January 27, 2006).

State of Alaska. "Alaska!" <http://www.state.ak.us> (accessed January 27, 2006).

University of Alaska. "Alaska Native Claims Settlement Act Resources." <http://www.ankn.uaf.edu/NPE/ancsa.html> (accessed January 27, 2006).

U.S. Geological Survey. "Alaska Science Center." <http:// alaska.usgs.gov> (accessed January 27, 2006).

Dian Fossey observed gorillas similar to this mother and baby western lowland gorilla during her time in Zaire, Uganda, and Rwanda. AP IMAGES

Gorillas in the Mist

"In the Mountain Meadow of Carl Akeley and George Schaller"

Book excerpt

By: Dian Fossey

Date: 1983

Source: Fossey, Dian. "In the Mountain Meadow of Carl Akeley and George Schaller." In *Gorillas in the Mist*. New York: Houghton Mifflin, 1983.

About the Author: Dian Fossey (1932–1985) was an American zoologist who spent much of her career living and working among the mountain gorillas of central Africa. Fossey, living a solitary lifestyle for many years at her Karisoke Research Center in the Virunga Mountains of Rwanda, reached a vast understanding of the species by observing the gorillas' habits and gradually gaining their social acceptance. Fossey was also responsible for drawing attention to uncontrolled poaching in that region, especially through the publication of *Gorillas in the Mist*, a popularized account of her studies. She was found murdered at her camp by an unknown attacker in 1985.

INTRODUCTION

Prior to the 1970s, gorillas were widely perceived as aggressive, dangerous creatures. Despite this reputation, Fossey, an occupational therapist in Louisville, Kentucky, deeply longed to observe these creatures in their natural setting. In 1963, she realized her dream during a seven-week safari to Zaire. During that trip, she became convinced that the gorilla was actually a peaceful, family-oriented creature.

Three years later, Fossey raised funds to return to Zaire, where she was arrested. She escaped and traveled to Uganda, then on to Rwanda where she continued her efforts. Fossey's work was characterized by her ability to become integrated into the gorilla community. By imitating the behaviors of the other gorillas, she was able to exist among them and observe their complex social structure. In 1970 she returned to England to earn her doctorate, focusing her dissertation on her work with gorillas.

The remaining years of Fossey's life were spent living among the gorillas of Africa and teaching at Cornell University. Her 1983 book *Gorillas in the Mist* played a pivotal role in efforts to reduce gorilla poaching in Africa.

PRIMARY SOURCE

I spent many years longing to go to Africa, because of what that continent offered in its wilderness and great diversity of free-living animals. Finally I realized that dreams seldom materialize on their own. To avoid further procrastination I committed myself to a three-year bank debt in order to finance a seven-week safari throughout those parts of Africa that most appealed to me. After months spent planning my itinerary, most of which was far off the normal tourist routes, I hired a driver, by mail, from a Nairobi safari company and flew to the land of my dreams in September 1963.

Two of the main goals of my first African trip were to visit the mountain gorillas of Mt. Mikeno in the Congo and to meet Louis and Mary Leaky at Olduvai Gorge in Tanzania. Both wishes came true. How vividly I can still recal Dr. Leakey's sparkling interest in hearing that I was on my way to visit briefly the gorillas at Kabara in the Congolese sector of the Virunga Mountains, where George Schaller had worked a few years previously. Dr. Leakey spoke to me most enthusiastically about Jane Goodall's excellent field work with the chimpanzees at the Gombe Stream Research Centre in Tanzania, then only in its third year, and he stressed the importance of long-term field studies with the great apes. I believe it was at this time the seed was planted in my head, even if unconsciously, that I would someday return to Africa to study the gorillas of the mountains.

Dr. Leakey gave me permission to walk around some newly excavated sites at Olduvai, one of which contained a recent discovered giraffe fossil. As I ran down a steep slope, my exulatation at being free under African skies was abruptly shattered, along with my right ankle, when I fell into a dig containing the new find. As the ankle cracked, the sdden pain induced me to vomit unceremoniously all over the treasured fossil. As if this wasn't humiliating enough, I had to be ignominiously hauled out of the gorge, piggyback style, by disgusted members of the Leakeys' staff. Mary Leakey then very kindly served me cool lemon squash while we watched the swelling ankle turn from various shades of blue to black. Both she and my driver felt that the intended climb into the Virungas to search for gorillas would have to be forfeited. Neither of them realized that the accident only strengthened my determination to get to the gorillas I had come to meet in Africa.

Two weeks after leaving the Leakeys and aided by a walking stick carved by a sympathetic African encountered along the road, I, the hired driver, and a dozen porters carrying the basics of camping gear and food began the arduous five-hour climb to the remote Kabara meadow. Kabara lies at 10,200 feet immediately adjacent to the 14,553-foot Mt. Mikeno in the Parc des Virungas in Zaire, formerly known as the Democratic Republic of the Congo. Some three years before my visit of 1963, Kabara had been the study site of George B. Schaller. An eminent American scientist, he was the first person to conduct a reliable field study of the mouttain gorillas, amassing 458 hours of observation within that area. The Kabara meadow also contained the grave of Carl Akeley, an American naturalist who had been responsible for urging the Belgian government to create the Albert National Park for the protection of mountain gorillas and their 400,000-year-old volcanic habitat.

In 1890 the moutains had been the object of a twenty-year dispute between Belgium (representing the present Zairoise portion), Germany (the Rowanda area), and Britain (the Uganda side). It was only in 1910 that the boundaries were finally settled. By 1925 some 190 square miles were set aside and the park was established. Carl Akeley had convinced King Albert of Belgium to expand the protected area so that by 1929 most of the Virunga chain was included. It was then called the Albert National Park. In 1967 the Zairoise named their section the Parc National des Virungas and the Rowandese called theirs the Parc National des Volcans. In Uganda the Virunga gorilla habitat was designated the Kigezi Gorilla Sanctuary in 1930. Akeley died when revisiting Kabara in 1926 and was buried on the meadow's edge in accordance with his wishes. He had considered Kabara one of the loveliest and most tranquil spots in the world.

On my first visit to Kabara in 1963 I was fortunate in meeting Joan and Alan Root, photographers from Kenya who were camped at the meadow while working on a photographic documentary of the mountain gorillas. Both Joan and Alan kindly overlooked the intrusion of a some-what hobbly and inquisitive American tourist into their secluded mountain workshop and allowed me to accompany them on some of their extraordinary contacts with the relatively unhabituated gorillas of Kabara. It was only because of their generosity, coupled with the skill of Sanwekwe, a Congolese park guard and tracker, that I was able to contact and photograph the animals during that brief visit. Sanwekwe had worked as a boy tracking gorilla for Carl Akeley; as a man he worked for George Schaller. Nearly twenty years later, he became my friend and skilled tracker.

I shall never forget my first encounter with gorillas. Sound preceded sight. Odor preceded sound in the form of an overwhelming musky-barnyard, humanlike scent. The air was suddenly rent by a high-pitched series of screams followed by the rhythmic rondo of sharp *pok-pok* chest-beats from a great silverback male obscured behind what seemed an impenetrable wall of vegetation. Joan and Alan Root, some ten yards ahead on the forest trail, motioned me to remain still. The three of us froze until the echoes of the screams and chest-beats faded. Only then did we slowly creep forward under the cover of dense shrubbery to about fifty feet from the group. Peeking through the vegetation, we could distinguish an equally curious phalanx of black, leather-countenanced, furry-headed primates peering back at us. Their bright eyes darted nervously from under heavy brows as though trying to identify us as familiar friends or possible foes. Immediately I was struck by the physical magnificence of the huge jet-black bodies blended against the green palette wash of the thick forest foliage.

Most of the females had fled with their infants to the rear of the group, leaving the silverback leader and some younger males in the foreground, standing tense with compressed lips. Occasionally the dominant male would rise to chestbeat in an attempt to intimidate us. The sound reverberated throughout the forest and evoked similar displays, though of lesser magnitude, from gorillas clustered around him. Slowly, Alan set up his movie camera and proceeded to film. The openness of his motions and the sound of the camera piqued curiosity from other group members, who then treed to see us more clearly. As if competing for attention, some animals went through a series of actions that included yawning, symbolic-feeding, branch-breaking, or chestbeating. After each display, the gorillas would look at us quizzically as if trying to determine the effect of their show. It was their individuality combined with the shyness of their behavior that remained the most captivating impression of this first encounter with the greatest of the great apes. I left Kabara with reluctance but with never a doubt that I would, somehow, return to learn more about the gorillas of the misted mountains.

My reunion with Kabara, Sanwekwe, and the gorillas came about as a direct result of a visit by Dr. Leakey to Louisville, Kentucky, where I was continuing my work as an occupational therapist in order to pay off the huge bank loan amassed for the first safari. Vaguely remembering me as the clumsy tourist of three years earlier, Dr. Leakey's attention was drawn to some photographs and articles I had published about gorillas since my return from Africa. After a brief interview, he suggested that I become the "gorilla girl" he had been seeking to conduct a long-term field study. Our conversation ended with his assertion that it was mandatory I should have my appendix removed before venturing into the remote wilderness of the gorillas' high altitude habitat in central Africa. I would have agreed

to almost anything at that point and promptly made plans for an appendectomy.

Some six weeks later on returning home from the hospital sans appendix, I found a letter from Dr. Leakey. It began, "Actually there really isn't any dire need for you to have your appendix removed. That is only my way of testing applicants' determination!" This was my first introduction to Dr. Leakey's unique sense of humor.

Eight more months passed before Dr. Leakey was able to obtain funds to launch the study. During the interim I finished paying for my 1963 safari while virtually memorizing George Schaller's two superlative books about his 1959—60 field studies with the mountain gorillas, as well as a "Teach Yourself Swahili" grammar book. Quitting my job as an occupational therapist and saying goodbye to the children who had been my patients for eleven years was difficult, as were the farewells to Kentucky friends and my three dogs. The dogs seemed to sense that this was going to be a permanent separation. I can still recall them—Mitzi, Shep, and Brownie—running after my overladen car as I drove away from my Kentucky home to head for California to say farewell to my parents. There was no way that I could explain to dogs, friends, or parents my compelling need to return to Africa to launch a long-term study of the gorillas. Some may call it destiny and others may call it dismaying. I call the sudden turn of events in my life fortuitous.

SIGNIFICANCE

Fossey appeared to be an unlikely activist. Quiet and somewhat self-conscious, she once remarked that she preferred the company of gorillas to people. But her actions betrayed a deep inner determination. During her first visit to Africa, she broke her ankle. To the surprise of her hosts, she refused to shorten her trip, and completed the journey despite her injuries. She went on to spend the remainder of her life working for the preservation of gorillas and their homes.

In 1978, Fossey founded the Dian Fossey Gorilla Fund International (DFGFI), an organization dedicated to the conservation of gorillas and their habitats in Africa. The organization works to stop poaching, monitor gorilla activities, and educate and support local communities. Fossey's book "Gorillas in the Mist" was published in 1983. The story was made into a motion picture starring Sigourney Weaver in 1986. Fossey was killed by unknown persons in Rwanda in December, 1985. A Rwandan court convicted American wildlife researcher Wayne McGuire of the killing in absentia, however McGuire remains free and has denied any involvement in the killing.

FURTHER RESOURCES

Books

Bedoyere, Camilla de la. *No One Loved Gorillas More: Dian Fossey: Letters from the Mist*. New York: National Geographic, 2005.

Hayes, Harold. *The Dark Romance of Dian Fossey* . New York: Simon & Schuster, 1990.

Montgomery, Sy. *Walking with the Great Apes: Jane Goodall, Dian Fossey, Birute Galdikas*. New York: Houghton Mifflin, 1991.

Periodicals

Clark, Mike. "Gorilla Movies Bad Enough to Make Kong Run for the Hills." *USA Today* (January 3, 2006).

MacKenzie, Debora. "Great Apes Face Ebola Oblivion." *New Scientist* 188, 2524 (2005): 8.

Web sites

"Mission of DFGFI." *Dian Fossey Gorilla Fund International*. <http://www.gorillafund.org/003_dfgfi_frmset.html> (accessed March 8, 2006).

"About the International Gorilla Conservation Programme." *International Gorilla Conservation Programme*. <http://www.mountaingorillas.org/about_igcp/about_igcp.htm> (accessed March 8, 2006).

Fascist Ecology

The "Green Wing" of the Nazi Party and its Historical Antecedents

Essay

By: Peter Staudenmaier

Date: 1995

Source: Staudenmaier, Peter. "Fascist Ecology: The 'Green Wing' of the Nazi Party and its Historical Antecedents". In *Ecofascism: Lessons from the German Experience*, edited by Janet Biehl and Peter Staudenmaier. San Francisco and Edinburgh: AK Press, 1995.

About the Author: American social ecologist, writer, and activist, Peter Staudenmaier is on the faculty of the Institute for Social Ecology, an educational organization dedicated to studying the interrelation of environmental, economic, social, and political issues. It is based in Plainfield, Vermont. Staudenmaier lives in Madison, Wisconsin, and works at a collectively run co-op bookstore. He is also involved with a network of housing cooperatives providing democratically controlled, resident-owned housing. Internationally, Staudenmaier works with grassroots development organizations in Nicaragua and with the German Greens, a radical left ecological group.

INTRODUCTION

The following is an excerpt from Staudenmaier's essay on the apparently pro-environmental policies of the German Nazi Party during the 1930s and 1940s. It is an attempt by a democratic leftist, an obvious opponent of Nazism, to understand how environmental ideas and policies generally accepted as humane and benevolent—much like many of the ideas and policies of twenty-first-century environmentalists and champions of nature—could coexist with and be a part of a philosophy devoted to military conquests and racial genocide.

In his analysis, Staudenmaier traces how nationalism, love of nature, and anti-rationalist romanticism converged historically in German thought to the detriment of ideas about human dignity and freedom. He examines how the breakdown of traditional communities and community functions—caused by the industrial revolution—spurred a back-to-the-land "folk" movement that preached a mystical connection between the German people and the land.

Those who shaped this movement, Staudenmaier explains, spread the doctrine of the existence of a bond between "blood" and "soil." Rather than analyzing the social, industrial and economic conditions, Staudenmaier argues, adherents of the "folk" movement blamed the problems arising from industrial production and national unification on a traditional object of hatred, "the Jews." They accused Jews of being rootless, because they lived in cities, and therefore out of touch with the soil; of being cosmopolitan; and of spreading "modern" beliefs rather than honoring tradition. The disseminators of anti-Jewish propaganda neglected to take into account that European Jews did not live on the land because they were forbidden to own land in Europe and were frequently driven out of one country or another. Not only were Jews said to be guilty socially, moreover, but inherently—because their blood, it was argued, was not "German blood." The Nazis continued to spread both these arguments, based on a bogus environmentalism, to justify the extermination of the Jews.

PRIMARY SOURCE

Germany is not only the birthplace of the science of ecology and the site of Green politics' rise to prominence, it has also been home to a peculiar synthesis of naturalism and nationalism forged under the influence of the Romantic tradition's anti-Enlightenment irrationalism.... *On the Care and Conservation of Forests*, written at the dawn of industrialization in Central Europe, rails against short-sighted exploitation of woodlands and soil, condemning deforestation and its economic causes. At times [Ernst Moritz Ardnt] wrote in terms strikingly similar to those of contemporary biocentrism: "When one sees nature in a necessary connectedness and interrelationship, then all things are equally important—shrub, worm, plant, human, stone, nothing first or last, but all one single unity."

Arndt's environmentalism, however, was inextricably bound up with virulently xenophobic nationalism. His eloquent and prescient appeals for ecological sensitivity were couched always in terms of the well-being of the *German* soil and the *German* people, and his repeated lunatic polemics against miscegenation, demands for teutonic racial purity, and epithets against the French, Slavs, and Jews marked every aspect of his thought. At the very outset of the nineteenth century the deadly connection between love of land and militant racist nationalism was firmly set in place....

These latter two fixations matured in the second half of the nineteenth century in the context of the *völkisch* movement, a powerful cultural disposition and social tendency which united ethnocentric populism with nature mysticism.... In the face of the very real dislocations brought on by the triumph of industrial capitalism and national unification, *völkisch* thinkers preached a return to the land, to the simplicity and wholeness of a life attuned to nature's purity.... [The *völkisch* movement] pointedly refused to locate the sources of alienation, rootlessness and environmental destruction in social structures, laying the blame instead to rationalism, cosmopolitanism, and urban civilization. The stand-in for all of these was the age-old object of peasant hatred and middle-class resentment: the Jews....

"The unity of blood and soil must be restored," proclaimed Richard Walther Darré in 1930. This infamous phrase denoted a quasi-mystical connection between "blood" (the race or *Volk*) and "soil" (the land and the natural environment) specific to Germanic peoples and absent, for example, among Celts and Slavs. For the enthusiasts of *Blut und Boden*, the Jews especially were a rootless, wandering people, incapable of any true relationship with the land. German blood, in other words, engendered an exclusive claim to the sacred German soil. While the term "blood and soil" had been circulating in *völkisch* circles since at least the Wilhelmine era, it was Darré who first popularized it as a slogan and then enshrined it as a guiding principle of Nazi thought. Harking back to Arndt and Riehl, he envisioned a thoroughgoing ruralization of Germany and Europe, predicated on a revitalized yeoman peasantry, in order to ensure racial health and ecological sustainability.

Darré was one of the party's chief "race theorists" and was also instrumental in galvanizing peasant support for the Nazis during the critical period of the early 1930s. From 1933 until 1942, he held the posts of Reich Peasant Leader and Minister of Agriculture. This was no minor fiefdom; the agriculture ministry had the fourth largest budget of all the myriad Nazi ministries even well into the war. From this position Darré was able to lend vital support to various ecologically oriented initiatives. He played an essential part in unifying the nebulous proto-environmentalist tendencies in National Socialism.

It was Darré who gave the ill-defined anti-civilization, anti-liberal, anti-modern, and latent anti-urban sentiments of the Nazi elite a foundation in the agrarian mystique. And it seems as if Darré had an immense influence on the ideology of National Socialism, as if he was able to articulate significantly more clearly than before the values system of an agrarian society contained in Nazi ideology and—above all—to legitimate this agrarian model and give Nazi policy a goal that was clearly oriented toward a far-reaching re-agrarianization.

This goal was not only quite consonant with imperialist expansion in the name of *Lebensraum*, it was in fact one of its primary justifications, even motivations. In language replete with the biologistic metaphors of organicism, Darré declared: "The concept of Blood and Soil gives us the moral right to take back as much land in the East as is necessary to establish a harmony between the body of our *Volk* and the geopolitical space."

Aside from providing green camouflage for the colonization of Eastern Europe, Darré worked to install environmentally sensitive principles as the very basis of the Third Reich's agricultural policy. Even in its most productivist phases, these precepts remained emblematic of Nazi doctrine. When the "Battle for Production" (a scheme to boost the productivity of the agricultural sector) was proclaimed at the second Reich Farmers Congress in 1934, the very first point in the program read "Keep the soil healthy!" But Darré's most important innovation was the introduction on a large scale of organic farming methods, significantly labeled "lebensgesetzliche Landbauweise," or farming according to the laws of life. The term points up yet again the natural order ideology which underlies so much reactionary ecological thought....

The campaign to institutionalize organic farming encompassed tens of thousands of smallholdings and estates across Germany. It met with considerable resistance from other members of the Nazi hierarchy, above all Backe and Göring. But Darré, with the help of Hess and others, was able to sustain the policy until his forced resignation in 1942 (an event which had little to do with his environmentalist leanings). And these efforts in no sense represented merely Darré's personal predilections; as the standard history of German agricultural policy points out, Hitler and Himmler "were in complete sympathy with these ideas." Still, it was largely Darré's influence in the Nazi apparatus which yielded, in practice, a level of government support for ecologically sound farming methods and land use planning unmatched by any state before or since.

For these reasons Darré has sometimes been regarded as a forerunner of the contemporary Green movement. His biographer [Anna Bramwell], in fact, once referred to him as the "father of the Greens." Her book *Blood and Soil*, undoubtedly the best single source on Darré in either German or English, consistently downplays the virulently fascist elements in his thinking, portraying him instead as a misguided agrarian radical. This grave error in judgement indicates the powerfully disorienting pull of an "ecological" aura. Darré's published writings alone, dating back to the early 1920s, are enough to indict him as a rabidly racist and jingoist ideologue particularly prone to a vulgar and hateful antisemitism (he spoke of Jews, revealingly, as "weeds"). His decade-long tenure as a loyal servant and, moreover, architect of the Nazi state demonstrates his dedication to Hitler's deranged cause. One account even claims that it was Darré who convinced Hitler and Himmler of the necessity of exterminating the Jews and Slavs. The ecological aspects of his thought cannot, in sum, be separated from their thoroughly Nazi framework. Far from embodying the "redeeming" facets of National Socialism, Darré represents the baleful specter of ecofascism in power.

Trees such as the larch were felled and used to form a Nazi swastika encompassing 360 square meters of land in 1938. The color-changing larches could be see in the autumn season by airplanes overhead. AP IMAGES

SIGNIFICANCE

The Nazi Blood and Soil movement is not just a historical curiosity. Searching the internet will quickly reveal a number of contemporary Green Nazi groups, overtly extolling both Nazism and environmentalism. Scanning the newspapers will also inevitably bring news of genocide and ethnic conflict occurring daily somewhere on the globe. Perhaps most troubling intellectually about the Blood and Soil movement is that many people who are dedicated to environmentalism and to a humane, democratic, peaceful, and equalitarian social philosophy will recognize in Nazi environmental policies sentiments seemingly in harmony with their own. This is disturbing in itself and additionally so because opponents of environmentalism sometimes cite Nazi antecedents in arguing against environmentalism.

Staudenmaier's essay is important, then, not just as an analysis of a historical phenomenon, but because thinking about the Nazi Blood and Soil movement

brings together a number of complicated issues— even though racism and genocide, in themselves, are not complicated issues—which affect us in the ongoing present. Many environmental issues, like the importance for a group of people to have a sense of spiritual connection to actual land or to each other, or the conflict between science and alternative practices, or the conflict between thought and emotion, or between rationalism and mysticism, or between physical and intellectual labor, or between nature and culture, are at stake.

In his attempt to deal with the problem of "ecofascism," Staudenmaier advocates maintaining an analytic disposition, that is, an approach that examines a belief, a program, or a philosophy by taking it apart in order to scrutinize the conditions which created it, the nature of its various elements, and the ends those elements point to. This is a method for approaching, rather than for resolving, perplexing problems. Underlying this approach is an understanding that there are no "final solutions" but, rather, ongoing efforts to effect the best possible results given the complexity of nature, the environment, and mankind.

Perhaps the best lesson that can be derived from the Nazi Blood and Soil movement is that we must approach any idea, no matter how seductive it appears, with intellectual caution and rigor, guarding against the kind of mystical emotionalism and reckless enthusiasm that blind us to each person's humanity. A bit of wisdom from the mid-twentieth century French writer Albert Camus may be worth remembering: the obligation to value human life itself transcends any set of ideas or ideals.

FURTHER RESOURCES

Web sites

DeGregori, Thomas R. "Environmentalism, Animal Rights Activism, and Eco-Nazism." *American Council on Science and Health*, April 1, 2001. <http://www.acsh.org/healthissues/newsID.604/healthissue_detail.asp> (accessed March 1, 2006).

"Fascist Ecology," *Institute for Social Ecology; Popular Education for a Free Society*. <http://www.social-ecology.org/article.php?story=20031202115218246> (accessed March 1, 2006).

"Introduction to National Socialism." *Libertarian National Socialist Green Party*. <http://www.nazi.org/nazi/policy/introduction/> (accessed March 1, 2006).

Sakai, J. "The Green Nazi," review of Dr. Anna Bramwell's *Blood and Soil, The Biography of Nazi Reichsminister R. Walter Darre*. <http://www.geocities.com/Area51/Omega/5844/greennazi.html> (accessed March 1, 2006).

Julia "Butterfly" Hill Stands In A 200-Foot Tall Old-Growth Redwood Tree

Photograph

By: Gerard Burkhart

Date: 1998

Source: Getty Images

About the Photographer: Gerard Burkhart is a freelance photographer based in Los Angeles, California. His photographs have appeared in numerous publications worldwide, and have been featured as part of three Pulitzer Prize-winning collaborations.

INTRODUCTION

American environmental activist Julia "Butterfly" Hill (1974—) brought attention to the danger that wholesale, profit-driven, clear-cutting of forests by lumber companies presents to the preservation of old-growth rain forests and individual trees—as well as to the environment and the ecosystem as a whole—when she climbed up a thousand-year-old California Coast Redwood tree in the Headlands Forest on December 10, 1997. Hill remained living in the tree, which she named Luna, for two years. She came down from the tree on December 18, 1999 after she reached an agreement with the Pacific Lumber Maxxon Corporation not to fell that tree or to do any logging in a 200 foot radius buffer zone around the tree.

When she first climbed the tree, Hill did not intend to stay for two years. She had been one of many members of the environmental group Earth First! involved in an action, which included sitting in trees, aimed at halting the Pacific Lumber Maxxon Corporation from felling old-growth redwoods. Not only was the clear-cutting destroying ancient trees; it was creating deadly mudslides after the trees were felled.

Hill extended her stay in the tree day by day. As she remained in the tree and attracted worldwide media attention, she became resolute not to descend until she actually accomplished her goal of saving the tree. She lived on a platform, six feet by eight feet, which members of Earth First! had built in the tree. There was another, slightly smaller platform nearby where she kept provisions supplied by her support group on the ground. The platform was covered with a tarp. Her perch was quite precarious, but it did not faze her. She scrambled about 180 feet off the ground easily, usually barefoot because it afforded her a better grip. Her improvised habitat was subject to strong winds and rains. The Pacific Lumber Company made living conditions worse, sending helicopters to hover above the tree, deafeningly loud and causing a commotion of winds that trembled the platform. At night, they set bright lights shining into the tree and broadcast blaring noise, hoping to drive Hill down from the tree by depriving her of sleep. Nevertheless, Hill endured and finally prevailed.

■ PRIMARY SOURCE

JULIA "BUTTERFLY" HILL STANDS IN A 200-FOOT TALL OLD-GROWTH REDWOOD TREE
See primary source image.

PRIMARY SOURCE

Julia "Butterfly" Hill Stands In A 200-Foot Tall Old-Growth Redwood Tree. Julia "Butterfly" Hill stands in A 200-foot tall old-growth redwood tree in Humboldt County, California, in 1998. Hill spent 738 days living in the redwood tree in the Headwaters Forest to protest old-growth redwood logging by the Maxxam Corporation. PHOTO BY GERARD BURKHART/GETTY IMAGES

SIGNIFICANCE

The agreement Hill reached with the lumber company—to preserve the tree and form a buffer zone—was a compromise. Hill and her supporters paid $50,000 to the company. The company then donated the money to California's Humboldt University to be used for environmental research. Some members of Earth First! objected to such a settlement. Hill, though uncompromising in her action, believed in being flexible when dealing with adversaries, and saw her tree-sit as a clear victory that had generated enormous publicity.

Since coming down from the tree, Hill has continued her activism, creating a group called *Circle of Life* to continue raising consciousness around environmental issues and by continuing to engage in direct, non-violent action.

Hill represents a familiar, democratic, and necessary figure in American culture, a dedicated individual who pits herself with only the resources of determination and the presence of her own body against a huge, powerful, and seemingly monolithic system and demands a change in the way things are done and the way people think. Her tree-sitting is significant in and of itself as an action against a predatory lumber company in defense of a natural environment and an important ecosystem. Through her act, Hill demonstrated that common people, following their own light, can have the capacity to act effectively. It is a lesson not limited to adherents of one particular ideology or political position but can be applied across a spectrum of beliefs. Hill's tree-sitting reflects not only a particular set of goals, but an attitude toward being a citizen in a democracy. Moreover, despite her dedication to the cause she championed, Hill represents a vision of reconciliation that accepts the humanity of every person even while engaged in a struggle against particular people, values, or policies.

FURTHER RESOURCES

Books

Beach, Patrick. *A Good Forest For Dying: The Tragic Death Of A Young Man On The Front Lines Of The Environmental Wars*. New York: Doubleday, 2003.

Hill, Julia Butterfly. *The Legacy Of Luna: The Story Of A Tree, A Woman, And The Struggle To Save The Redwoods*. New York: Harper San Francisco, 2000.

Web sites

Circle of Life. <http://www.circleoflife.org> (accessed March 14, 2006).

"Julia Butterfly Hill." *The Ecology Hall of Fame*. <http://www.ecotopia.org/ehof/hill/> (accessed March 14, 2006).

Wilson, Nicholas. "Dancing in the Treetop." *MONITOR*. <http://www.monitor.net/monitor/9807a/butterfly-profile.html> (accessed March 14, 2006).

Gaia: A new look at life on Earth

Book excerpt

By: James E. Lovelock

Date: 1979

Source: Lovelock, James E. *Gaia: A new look at life on Earth*. New York: Oxford University Press, 2000.

About the Author: British scientist James Lovelock (1919–) has earned academic degrees in chemistry, medicine, and biophysics. Since 1982, he has been affiliated with the Marine Biological Association at Plymouth, England. He has authored more than two hundred scientific papers in the fields of medicine, biology, instrument science, and geophysiology, and has filed more than fifty patents. His most successful patent was for the electron capture detector, which was used to identify the presence of pesticides in the 1950s. This information was used in Rachel Carson's book *Silent Spring*, which galvanized public awareness of the environment in the late twentieth century. Lovelock is the author of four books on the Gaia hypothesis.

INTRODUCTION

Lovelock developed the Gaia hypothesis in the 1960s in collaboration with microbiologist Lynn Margulis. Lovelock was asked by NASA scientists at the Jet Propulsion Laboratories to design instruments that would search for life on Mars. As he thought about the problem he realized that any life on Mars would leave a chemical signature in the atmosphere. The Earth's atmosphere contains methane and oxygen, which are chemically reactive. The reason that they both exist in the atmosphere is because they are cycled through living organisms. In contrast, Lovelock showed that the atmosphere of Mars consisted of mostly carbon dioxide and some oxygen. Chemically, the atmosphere was completely non-reactive, and therefore life could not exist on Mars.

This realization led Lovelock to consider how the living and non-living components of Earth interacted to produce a planet that is in equilibrium over long periods of time. Along with biologist Lynn Margulis, Lovelock recognized that a variety of feedback loops between the living and non-living elements of Earth regulate the environment. The ideas resulted in the Gaia hypothesis, which was summarized in the book *Gaia: A New Look at Life on Earth* in 1979. The fundamental basis of the Gaia hypothesis is that the Earth functions like a single organism. Just as an organism controls its internal systems for its own benefit, so too does the Earth sustain itself in a condition of homeostasis. This means that the Earth regulates the atmosphere, the lithosphere (the Earth) and the hydrosphere (the oceans, rivers, and water vapor) in a way that optimizes conditions for itself. The name Gaia was used in recognition of the ancient Greek goddess, Gaia, who represents the sum of the living and non-living components of Earth.

According to Lovelock, Gaia's homeostatic system depends on the behavior of living elements of the planet. He points to three areas in which the biotic elements of the planet stabilize the environment: the temperature of the Earth, the salinity of the oceans, and the chemical composition of atmosphere. Lovelock argues that the Sun's energy has increased by 25 percent since Earth was formed; yet Earth's surface temperature has remained constant. He also proposes that the chemical composition of the atmosphere should be unstable, however it is generally constant and could only remain this way because of the contribution of living organisms. Finally Lovelock shows that the salinity of the ocean is constant and demonstrates that living organisms are involved in controlling the ocean's salinity. Lovelock describes how feedback loops in all of these systems stabilize and optimize the environment for the planet.

Introductory As I write, two Viking spacecraft are circling our fellow planet Mars, awaiting landfall instructions from the Earth. Their mission is to search for life, or evidence of life, now or long ago. This book also is about a search for life and the quest for Gaia is an attempt to find the largest living creature on Earth. Our journey may reveal no more than the almost infinite variety of living forms which have proliferated over the Earth's surface under the transparent case of the air and which constitute the biosphere. But if Gaia does exist, then we may find ourselves and all other living things to be parts and partners of a vast being who in her entirety has the power to maintain our planet as a fit and comfortable habitat for life.

The quest for Gaia began more than fifteen years ago, when NASA (the National Aeronautics and Space Administration of the USA) first made plans to look for life on Mars. It is therefore right and proper that this book should open with a tribute to the fantastic Martian voyage of those two mechanical Norsemen.

In the early nineteen-sixties I often visited the Jet Propulsion Laboratories of the California Institute of Technology in Pasadena, as consultant to a team, later to be led by that most able of space biologists Norman Horowitz, whose main objective was to devise ways and means of detecting life on Mars and other planets. Although my particular brief was to advise on some comparatively simple problems of instrument design, as one whose childhood was illuminated by the writings of Jules Verne and Olaf Stapledon I was delighted to have the chance of discussing at first hand the plans for investigating Mars.

At that time, the planning of experiments was mostly based on the assumption that evidence for life on Mars would be much the same as for life on Earth. Thus one proposed series of experiments involved dispatching what was, in effect, an automated microbiological laboratory to sample the Martian soil and judge its suitability to support bacteria, fungi, or other microorganisms. Additional soil experiments were designed to test for chemicals whose presence would indicate life at work: proteins, amino acids, and particularly optically active substances with the capacity that organic matter has to twist a beam of polarized light in a counter-clockwise direction.

After a year or so, and perhaps because I was not directly involved, the euphoria arising from my association with this enthralling problem began to subside, and I found myself asking some rather down-to-earth questions, such as, 'How can we be sure that the Martian way of life, if any, will reveal itself to tests based on Earth's life style?' To say nothing of more difficult questions, such as, 'What is life, and how should it be recognized?'

Some of my still sanguine colleagues at the Jet Propulsion Laboratories mistook my growing skepticism for cynical disillusion and quite properly asked, 'Well, what would you do instead?' At that time I could only reply vaguely, 'I'd look for an entropy reduction, since this must be a general characteristic of all forms of life.' Understandably, this reply was taken to be at the best unpractical and at worst plain obfuscation, for few physical concepts can have caused as much confusion and misunderstanding as has that of entropy.

It is almost a synonym for disorder and yet, as a measure of the rate of dissipation of a system's thermal energy, it can be precisely expressed in mathematical terms. It has been the bane of generations of students and is direfully associated in many minds with decline and decay, since its expression in the Second Law of Thermodynamics (indicating that all energy will eventually dissipate into heat universally distributed and will no longer be available for the performance of useful work) implies the predestined and inevitable run-down and death of the Universe. . . .

The design of a universal life-detection experiment based on entropy reduction seemed at this time to be a somewhat unpromising exercise. However, assuming that life on any planet would be bound to use the fluid media—oceans, atmosphere, or both—as conveyor-belts for raw materials and waste products, it occurred to me that some of the activity associated with concentrated entropy reduction within a living system might spill over into the conveyor-belt regions and alter their composition. The atmosphere of a life-bearing planet would thus become recognizably different from that of a dead planet.

Mars has no oceans. If life had established itself there, it would have had to make use of the atmosphere or stagnate. Mars therefore seemed a suitable planet for a life-detection exercise based on chemical analysis of the atmosphere. Moreover, this could be carried out regardless of the choice of landing site. Most life-detection experiments are effective only within a suitable target area. Even on Earth, local search techniques would be unlikely to yield much positive evidence of life if the landfall occurred on the Antarctic ice sheet or the Sahara desert or in the middle of a salt lake.

While I was thinking on these lines, Dian Hitchcock visited the Jet Propulsion Laboratories. Her task was to compare and evaluate the logic and information-potential of the many suggestions for detecting life on Mars. The notion of life detection by atmospheric analysis appealed to her, and we began developing the idea together. Using our own planet as a model, we examined the extent to which simple knowledge of the chemical composition of the Earth's atmosphere, when coupled with such readily accessible information as the degree of solar radiation and the presence of oceans as well as land masses on the Earth's surface, could provide evidence for life.

Our results convinced us that the only feasible explanation of the Earth's highly improbable atmosphere was that it was being manipulated on a day-to-day basis from the surface, and that the manipulator was life itself. The significant decrease in entropy—or, as a chemist would put it, the persistent state of disequilibrium among the atmospheric gases—was on its own clear proof of life's activity. Take, for example, the simultaneous presence of methane and oxygen in our atmosphere. In sunlight, these two gases react chemically to give carbon dioxide and water vapour. The rate of this reaction is such that to sustain the amount of methane always present in the air, at least 500 million tons of this gas must be introduced into the atmosphere yearly. In addition, there must be some means of replacing the oxygen used up in oxidizing methane and this requires a production of at least twice as much oxygen as methane. The quantities of both of these gases required to keep the Earth's extraordinary atmospheric mixture constant was improbable on a biological basis by at least 100 orders of magnitude.

Here, in one comparatively simple test, was convincing evidence for life on Earth, evidence moreover which could be picked up by an infra-red telescope sited as far away as Mars.

SIGNIFICANCE

The initial reaction to the Gaia hypothesis by the scientific community was highly critical. They claimed it was teleological, which means that it provides a conscious purpose for an observation with a scientific explanation. In addition, critics claimed that it was impossible to experimentally test the Gaia hypothesis. Finally, scientists reject the idea that Gaia is a living organism because the planet is not able to reproduce, a characteristic considered basic to life.

Lovelock argued against the claim that the Gaia hypothesis was teleological. He stated that he never attributed purpose or consciousness to the feedback mechanisms that regulate the planet. In 1983, Lovelock developed a mathematical model called Daisyworld that demonstrated how feedback loops could occur without any intent. In the model, both black and white daisies inhabit a planet. Light daisies reflect light, cooling the planet, and dark daisies absorb light, warming the planet. The daisies' growth depends on the temperature of the planet. When the model is run and the sun is allowed to change its temperature, the populations of the two kinds of daisies respond in a way that keeps the temperature optimal for their growth. Although the species in Daisyworld live by rules that only concern their own survival, self-regulation of the planet is an emergent property of the system.

In 1988, the American Geophysical Union organized an entire conference to discuss the Gaia hypothesis. The compelling arguments of the Daisyworld model defeated much of the early criticisms of the Gaia hypothesis. At the conference, physicist and philosopher James Kirchner expanded the Gaia hypothesis to encompass a variety of different theories. For example, Strong Gaia Theory, also called Optimizing Gaia Theory, claims that the living parts of the environment actively control the physical environment to optimize conditions for itself. On the other hand, Influential Gaia Theory gives much less influence to the biota. It states that living components influence only certain aspects of the environment, like the temperature and the atmosphere.

Although it was received critically, the Gaia hypothesis has won over most of its initial detractors and become a fundamental part of ecological science. The field of geophysiology spun out of the Gaia hypothesis, which compares the systems of the planet to those of an individual organism, with the rivers and oceans acting as veins and arteries and the atmosphere acting as a lung. Most ecologists now recognize the planet as a super ecosystem and agree that studying global ecology is key to understanding the impacts of humans on the planet.

FURTHER RESOURCES
Books

Lovelock, J.E. *The Ages of Gaia: A Biography of Our Living Earth.* New York: W.W. Norton & Company, 1988.

———. *Healing Gaia.* New York: Harmony Books, 1991.

———. *Homage to Gaia: The Life of an Independent Scientist* New York: Oxford University Press, 2001.

Margulis, L., and D. Sagan. *Slanted Truths: Essays on Gaia, Evolution and Symbiosis.* New York: Copernicus Books, 1997.

Scientists Debate Gaia: The Next Century, edited by Stephen H. Schneider, et al. Cambridge, Mass: MIT Press, 2004.

Periodicals

Lovelock, J.E. "A Numerical Model for Biodiversity." *Philosophical Transactions of the Royal Society of London, Series B* 338 (1992) 383–391.

The Physical Earth

The physical Earth refers to all of the features of Earth except those that are living. Often the physical Earth is subdivided into three spheres: the geosphere, the hydrosphere, and the atmosphere. The geosphere includes all of the mineral components of the planet, such as soil, rock, sand, and clay. The hydrosphere refers to all water on the planet, including liquid water (both fresh and saline), water vapor, and ice. The atmosphere is the gaseous material that surrounds the planet.

The physical Earth also refers to the climatological characteristics of the planet. This includes temperature and weather patterns. Because the Earth is a sphere, heat is concentrated near the equator and is more diffuse near the poles. The average temperature varies greatly with latitude (i.e., the distance from the equator).

Precipitation patterns on Earth are also greatly influenced by latitude. Equatorial heating evaporates water, which rises into the atmosphere. There, the air cools and water vapors condense bringing rains to tropical regions. At about 86 °F (30 °C), warm dry air subsides from the atmosphere, driving the trade winds and creating large swaths of desert regions.

The climate is not a predictable feature, but rather an extremely dynamic process. Seasonal variations in the tilt of Earth as well as Earth's position with respect to the sun contribute to variability in climate. Altitude is another controlling factor. Finally, the atmosphere plays a key role, acting as a thermal insulator and as a heat valve for the planet.

The various components of the physical Earth are often referred to as natural resources by ecologists and environmental scientists. To survive, all organisms depend on the geosphere, the hydrosphere, and the atmosphere. The climate is also of great importance to ecosystems. Since the mid-1900s, the human population of the planet has exploded, making human beings the dominant species on the planet. People's activities place heavy demands on the physical resources of Earth. This strains the natural resources of the planet. Mining and urban development have changed the physical landscape. Pollutants have clogged waterways. The burning of fossil fuels has polluted the atmosphere. Evidence continues to accumulate that increased carbon dioxide in the air has contributed to a rise in global temperatures.

The ecological effects of damaging the physical Earth can be severe. For example, in the 1930s in the American Southwest, domesticated animals were allowed to graze heavily in desert areas. This, in combination with an unusually long drought, converted the physical environment into a dust bowl—a vast wasteland. Dust storms became ubiquitous. The dust bowl was a great economic disaster, displacing hundreds of thousands of farmers. Native species were unable to recolonize the land for several decades.

In the early 2000s in Alaska, photographs document that glaciers are shrinking, most likely due to increased annual average temperatures. This chapter explores the events that contributed to the dust bowl and the shrinking glaciers in the Arctic, as well as other ecological threats to the physical Earth.

"Piecing Continents Together"

Magazine article

By: Anonymous

Date: August 18, 1967

Source: "Piecing Continents Together." *Time* 90 (August 18, 1967).

About the Author: This article was published without a byline, and was written by staff writers for *Time*, a widely circulated U.S. weekly news magazine.

INTRODUCTION

The theory of continental drift explains that the continents are constantly changing position relative to one another. Continental drift is part of a larger theory known as plate tectonics, which describes the processes that result in many of the major geological features on Earth.

Geologists Alfred Wegener and Frank Taylor first proposed the theory of continental drift in 1912. They believed that all of the continents had been joined together in a massive super continent called Pangaea approximately 200 million years ago. They suggested that pieces of Pangaea slowly broke apart and moved into the positions that the continents occupy today.

Wegener and Taylor used several different lines of evidence to support the idea of continental drift. The first involves the simple observation that the modern continents can be assembled so that they fit together like pieces of a puzzle. This idea was actually first mentioned by Sir Francis Bacon more than 300 years earlier. He noticed that the bulge of Africa can fit into a notch in the North American continent and that the bulge in South America where Brazil is located fits in a notch in the continent of Africa.

Wegener also noticed that identical fossil species are found on South America and on Africa. He reasoned that it would be very difficult for many of these plant and animal species to have traveled the great distance across the ocean and that the species must have existed on the same continent at one point in time. In addition, Wegener reasoned that the coal deposits on Antarctica represented fossil plants that must have grown when the continent was located in a more tropical latitude. Finally, Wegener pointed out that the locations of large grooves, called striations, in rocks made by glaciers in South America and Africa are best explained if one assumes that the Atlantic Ocean did not separate the continents.

PRIMARY SOURCE

Were all continents once snuggled together in a mammoth land mass surrounded by a single shimmering sea? Did the continents begin to drift apart some 200 million years ago? Some scientists believe so, and many recent findings support them. This month still more compelling evidence of continental drift was reported by U.S. and Brazilian geologists. Their principal finding was that two highly distinctive adjacent geological areas on the Atlantic coast of Africa match perfectly with a pair of rock regions located along Brazil's northeast coast.

Doubting & Digging. "Actually, we set out to disprove the theory when we started," said M.I.T. Geology Professor Patrick M. Hurley, 55, adding that "Harvard and M.I.T. have been hotbeds of geological conservatism for years." Hurley and his colleagues became interested in the theory at a 1964 scientific meeting in London. There, Cambridge Geophysicist Sir Edward Bullard disclosed that a computer study of shorelines on both sides of the Atlantic—at a depth of 500 fathoms, to allow for coastal idiosyncrasies—showed that they would still match if they were set side by side. "The results were rather amazing," said Hurley. "The study went right down the whole Atlantic and fitted together everything, including Greenland and all the other islands with less than one degree error in the fit."

Still leery of the theory, Hurley returned to the U.S. and organized a joint group of U.S. and Brazilian scientists to compare radioactively dated rock samples from two African regions with others from South American areas.

The African regions are divided neatly by a boundary running northeast through Ghana, Togo, Dahomey, Upper Volta, Niger, Mali, and into Algeria. To the east of the boundary lies the Pan-African region, dated as 550 million years old. West of it is the 2-billion-year-old Eburnean area. According to Bullard, if the South American bulge had once fitted under the bulge of Africa, the continuance of the delineation between the two rock regions would be found running southwest through Brazil from a point near the city of Sao Luis 2,070 miles north of Rio.

"There's never really a eureka moment on any of these projects," said Hurley, "but when I began to plot these samples, the correlation was astounding. They all fitted exactly." In addition to the identical ages of the regions, Hurley, his M.I.T. associates and their collaborators at the University of Sao Paulo found the boundary line between the 550-million- and 2-billion-year-old areas in northeast Brazil exactly where they had predicted it would be.

The discovery provides important support for the continental-drift theory. Among other recent evidence is the finding that the ocean floor is patterned with belts of rock magnetized in opposite directions. Recent studies indicate that the earth's magnetic field has reversed at least nine times in the past 3,600,000 years. Thus the belts provide a dependable time map that shows the effects of the reversing magnetic fields of the earth as the ocean floor expanded. This study also shows that the ocean floor is spreading at about the rate of two centimeters a year-which would just about account for the present distance between the continents if they began drifting apart, as estimated, 200 million years ago.

"To us, this evidence is quite conclusive," says Hurley. "It's very difficult to argue against it. It looks as though opposition to the continental-drift theory is dying."

SIGNIFICANCE

Lines of evidence supporting the theory of continental drift continued to accumulate throughout the 1960s and 1970s. The magnetic field striping found around mid-ocean ridges suggested that the ridges are actually weak parts of the ocean floor. Eventually these places were recognized as an edge of a tectonic plate. New crust is continually added to the plate along the mid-ocean ridges as magma rises from deep in the Earth to the ocean floor. This explains the observation that rocks are always youngest closest to mid-ocean ridges.

Princeton University geologist Harry H. Hess suggested that if new crust forms along mid-ocean ridges, it must be shrinking in other places. In the 1960s, the field of seismology was developed. Seismologists measure the location and energy of earthquakes. Extensive seismographic surveys indicated that earthquakes are found in zones that are generally adjacent to deep undersea canyons called trenches. These trenches are found along the edges of the Pacific Ocean.

In particular, the Atlantic Ocean is continually growing, moving the Americas farther from Europe and Africa; while the Pacific is shrinking, moving North and South America towards Australia and Asia. These ideas helped crystallize the theory of plate tectonics, which states that massive irregular slabs of the Earth's crust float on magma beneath the Earth's surface and slowly move over time. Collisions of plates result in mountain ranges. Regions where plates slip past each other, like trenches, produce dynamic geologic activity, such as earthquakes.

This image of the San Andreas Fault in California shows a difference in terrain where it bisects the Carrizo Plain. This is likley caused by fault's lateral movement over time, 1995. © TOM BEAN/CORBIS

In the 1970s, NASA developed satellites that were able to measure the precise location of points on Earth. In particular, the Global Positioning System or GPS has been very instrumental in determining movement along the faults between different tectonic plates. These measurements, which are made over the course of several years, compare well with estimated movement rates of tectonic plates made over millions of years.

The significance of the theories of continental drift and plate tectonics are vast. Understanding the relative motion of the Earth's crust provides an explanation for the presence of many geologic features such as mountain ranges, volcanoes, ocean trenches, and mid-ocean ridges. It also explains why certain regions are much more prone to earthquakes and geothermal activity than other regions. Plate tectonics also leads to an understanding of where natural resources such as fossil fuels and ore deposits are likely to be found. Finally, the theory unites a variety of scientific disciplines in the understanding that the Earth functions as a dynamic planet.

FURTHER RESOURCES

Web sites

National Aeronautics and Space Administration. "On the Move: Continental Drift and Plate Tectonics." <http://kids.earth.nasa.gov/archive/pangaea> (accessed January 6, 2006).

Pangaea.org. "The Meteorologist Who Started a Revolution." <http://pangaea.org/wegener.htm> (accessed January 6, 2006).

United States Geological Survey. "This Dynamic Earth: The Story of Plate Tectonics." <http://pubs.usgs.gov/publications/text/dynamic.html> (accessed January 6, 2006).

"A Mountain"

Book excerpt

By: John McPhee

Date: 1988

Source: McPhee, John. "A Mountain." *Encounters with the Archdruid.* New York: Farrar, Straus and Giroux, 1971.

About the Author: American author John McPhee (1931–) has written more than twenty nonfiction books, many of them notable contributions about humans and their interaction with the environment, since 1965. A native of Princeton, New Jersey, he attended both Princeton University and Cambridge University before embarking on a career in journalism with *Time* magazine. Two of his books, *Encounters with the Archdruid* and *The Curve of Binding Energy*, were nominated for National Book Awards. McPhee received the Award in Literature from the American Academy of Arts and Letters in 1977 and received a Pulitzer Prize in 1999 for *Annals of the Former World*, his collected writings about geologists and their work.

INTRODUCTION

Encounters with the Archdruid consists of chapters describing three trips that author John McPhee took with former Sierra Club executive director David

Brower (1912–2000), perhaps the leading conservationist of his time, and men who he described as Brower's natural enemies: mining geologist Charles Park (1903–1990), land developer Charles Fraser (1929–2002), and dam builder Floyd Dominy (1909–). Each of the trips was to a location chosen to provoke discussion on salient environmental issues. Reference to the "archdruid" was drawn from a comment by Hilton Head Island developer Fraser, who considered all conservationists to be modern-day druids who were, in his opinion, followers of a religion that worships trees and sacrifices people. Brower, as an outspoken conservationist, was implied to be the archdruid.

In his book, McPhee gives an account of a backpacking trip into the Glacier Peak Wilderness of northern Washington with Brower, Park, and two medical students. A company had filed a mining claim before federal declaration of the wilderness area, which would have allowed it to take ownership of the land and operate a copper mine in the midst of an otherwise undeveloped area renowned for its scenic beauty. The dialogue between Brower and Park revolves around the competing needs to preserve wild areas and provide the metals, fuels, and other resources needed to maintain a comfortable and prosperous lifestyle.

PRIMARY SOURCE

. . . Most of the pass was covered with snow, but there were some patches of bare ground, and these were blue, green, red, yellow, and white with wild flowers. The air felt and smelled like the first warm, thaw-bringing day in spring in Vermont, and, despite the calendar, spring was now the season at that altitude in the North Cascades, and summer and fall would come and go in the few weeks remaining before the first big snow of September. Brower had dropped his pack and was sitting on a small knoll among the flowers. Park and I and Brigham and Snow dropped our own packs, and felt the sudden coolness of air reaching the sweat lines where the packs had been—and the inebriate lightness that comes, after a long climb, when the backpack is suddenly gone. The ground Brower was sitting on was ten or fifteen feet higher than the ground on which we stood, and as we went up to join him our eyes at last moved above the ridgeline, and for the first time we could see beyond it. What we saw made us all stop.

One of the medical students said, "Wow!"

I said slowly, the words just involuntarily falling out, "My God, look at that."

Across the deep gulf of air, and nearly a mile higher than the ground on which we stood, eleven miles away by line of sight, was Glacier Peak—palpable, immediate, immense. In the direction we were looking, we could see perhaps two hundred square miles of land, and the big mountain dominated that scene in the way that the Jungfrau dominates the Bernese Alps. Glacier Peak had originally been a great symmetrical cone, and that was still its basic shape, but it had been monumentally scarred, from within and without. It once exploded. Pieces of it landed in what is now Idaho, and other pieces landed in what is now Oregon. The ice sheet mauled it. Rivers from its own glaciers cut grooves in it. But it had remained, in silhouette, a classic mountain, its lines sweeping up beyond its high shoulder—called Disappointment Peak—and converging acutely at the summit. The entire upper third of the mountain was white. And below the snow and ice, black-green virgin forest continued all the way down to the curving valley of the Suiattle River, a drop of eight thousand feet from the peak. Spread around the summit like huge, improbable petals were nine glaciers—the Cool Glacier, the Scimitar Glacier, the Dusty Glacier, the Chocolate Glacier—and from each of these a white line of water ran down through the timer and into the Suiattle. To our right, on the near side of the valley, another mountain—Plummer Mountain—rose up about two-thirds as high, and above its timberline its snowless faces of rock were, in the sunlight, as red as rust. Around and beyond Glacier Peak, the summits of other mountains, random and receding, led the eye away to the rough horizon and back to Glacier Peak.

Brower said, without emphasis, "That is what is known in my trade as a scenic climax."

Near the southern base of Plummer Mountain and in the deep valley between Plummer Mountain and Glacier Peak—that is, in the central foreground of the view that we were looking at from Cloudy Pass—was the lode of copper that Kennecott would mine, and to do so the company would make an open pit at least two thousand four hundred feet from rim to rim.

Park said, "A hole in the ground will not materially hurt this scenery."

Brower stood up. "None of the experts on scenic resources will agree with you," he said. "This is one of the few remaining great wildernesses in the lower forty-eight. Copper is not a transcendent value here."

"Without copper, we'd be in a pretty sorry situation."

"If that deposit didn't exist, we'd get by without it."

"I would prefer the mountain as it is, but the copper is there."

"If we're down to where we have to take copper from places this beautiful, we're down pretty far."

"Minerals are where you find them. The quantities are finite. It's criminal to waste minerals when the standard of

living of your people depends upon them. A mine cannot move. It is fixed by nature. So it has to take precedence over any other use. If there were a copper deposit in Yellowstone Park, I'd recommend mining it. Proper use of minerals is essential. You have to go get them where they are. Our standard of living is based on this."

"For a fifty-year cycle, yes. But for the long term, no. We have to drop our standard of living, so that people a thousand years from now can have any standard of living at all."

A breeze coming off the nearby acres of snow felt cool but not chilling in the sunshine, and rumpled the white hair of the two men.

"I am not for penalizing people today for the sake of future generations," Park said.

"I really am," said Brower. "That's where we differ."

"Yes, that's where we disagree. In 1910, the Brazilian government said they were going to preserve the iron ore in Minas Gerais, because the earth would run short of it in the future. People—thousands and thousands of people in Minas Gerais—were actually starving, and they were living over one of the richest ore deposits in the world, a fifteen-billion ton reserve. They're mining it now, and people there are prospering. But in the past it was poor consolation to people who were going hungry to say that in the future it was gong to be better. You have to use these things when you have them. You have to know where they are, and use them. People, in the future, will go for the copper here," Brower said.

"The kids who are in Congress in the future should make that decision, and if it's theirs to make I don't think they'll go for the copper here," Brower said.

"Sure they will. They'll have to, if people are going to expect to have telephones, electric lights, airplanes, television sets, radios, central heating, air-conditioning, automobiles. And you *know* people will want these things. I didn't invent them. I just know where the copper is."

Brower swung his pack up onto his back. "Pretend the copper deposit down there doesn't exist," he said. "Then what would you do? What are you going to do when it's gone?"

"You're trying to make everything wilderness," Park said.

"No, I'm not. I'm trying to keep at least two per cent of the terrain as wilderness."

"Two per cent is a lot."

"Two per cent is under pavement."

"Basically, our difference is that I feel we can't stop all this–we must direct it. You feel we must stop it."

"I feel we should go back, recycle, do things over again and do better, even if it costs more. We mine things and don't use them again. We coat the surface of the Earth—with beer cans and chemicals, asphalt and old television sets."

"We *are* recycling copper, but we don't have enough."

"When we knock buildings down, we don't take the copper out. Every building that comes down could be a copper mine. But we don't take the copper out. We go after fresh metal. We destroy that mountain."

"How can you ruin a mountain like Glacier Peak?" Park lifted his pick toward the mountain. "You *can't* ruin it," he went on, waving the pick. "Look at the Swiss mountains. Who could ruin *them?* A mine would not hurt this country—not with proper housekeeping."

Brower started on down the trail. We retrieved our packs and caught up with him. About five hundred feet below us and a mile ahead was another pass, Suiattle Pass, and to reach it we had to go down into a big ravine and up the other side. There were long silences, measured by the sound of boots on the trail. From time to time, the pick rang out against a rock.

Brower said, "Would America have to go without much to leave its finest wilderness unspoiled?"

We traversed a couple of switchbacks and approached the bottom of the ravine. Then Park said, "Where they are more easily accessible, deposits have been found and are being—or have been—mined."

We had seen such a mine near Lake Chelan, in the eastern part of the mountains. The Howe Sound Mining Company established an underground copper mine there in 1938, built a village and called it Holden. The Holden mine was abandoned in 1957. We had hiked past its remains on our way to the wilderness area. Against a backdrop of snowy peaks, two flat-topped hills of earth detritus broke the landscape. One was the dump where all the rock had been put that was removed before the miners reached the ore body. The other consisted of tailings-crushed rock that had been through the Holden mill and had yielded copper. What remained of the mill itself was a macabre skeleton of bent, twisted, rusted beams. Wooden buildings and sheds were rotting and gradually collapsing. The area was bestrewn with huge flakes of corrugated iron, rusted rails, rusted ore carts, old barrels. Although there was no way for an automobile to get to Holden except by barge up Lake Chelan and then on a dirt road to the village, we saw there a high pile of gutted and rusted automobiles, which themselves had originally been rock in the earth and, in the end, in Holden, were crumbling slowly back into the ground.

Park hit a ledge with the pick. We were moving up the other side of the ravine now. The going was steep, and the pace slowed. Brower said, "We saw that at Holden."

I counted twenty-two steps watching the backs of Brower's legs, above the red tops of gray socks. He was moving slower than I would have. I was close behind him. His legs, blue-veined, seemed less pink than they had the day before. They were sturdy but not athletically shapely. Brower used to put food caches in various places in the High Sierra and go from one to another for weeks at a time. He weighed two hundred and twelve pounds now, and he must have wished he were one-eighty.

Park said, "Holden is the sort of place that gave mining a bad name. This has been happening in the West for the past hundred years, but it doesn't have to happen. Poor housekeeping is poor housekeeping wherever you find it. I don't care if it's a mine or a kitchen. Traditionally, when mining companies finished in a place they just walked off. Responsible groups are not going to do that anymore. They're not going to leave trash; they're not going to deface the countryside. Think of that junk! If I had enough money, I'd come up here and clean it up."

I thought how neat Park's house, his lawn, and his gardens are—his roses, his lemon trees, his two hundred varieties of cactus. The name of the street he lives on is Arcadia Place. Park is a member of the Cactus and Succulent Society of America. He hit a fallen tree with the hammer end.

"It's one god-awful mess," Brower said.

"That old mill could be cleaned up," Park said. "Grass could be planted on the dump and the tailings."

Suiattle Pass was now less than a quarter mile ahead of us. I thought of Brower, as a child, on his first trip to the Sierra Nevada. His father drove him there from Berkeley in a 1916 Maxwell. On the western slopes, they saw both the aftermath and the actual operations of hydraulic mining for gold. Men with hoses eight inches in diameter directed water with such force against the hillsides that large parts of the hills themselves fell away as slurry.

"Holden was abandoned in 1957, and no plants of any kind have caught on the dump and the talings," Brower said.

"Holden, in its twenty years of metal production, brought out of the earth ten million tons of rock—enough to make a hundred thousand tons of copper, enough to wire Kansas City."

Park said, "You could put a little fertilizer on-something to get it started."

When we reached the pass, we stood for a moment and looked again at Glacier Peak and, far below us, the curving white line of the Suiattle. Park said, "When you create a mine, there are two things you can't avoid: a hole in the ground and a dump for waste rock. Those are two things you can't avoid."

Brower said, "Except by not doing it at all."

SIGNIFICANCE

The controversy that motivated the Glacier Peak Wilderness trip was rooted in the American Mining Law of 1872, which has stood without major modification for more than a century. The law recognizes that rich mineral deposits are extremely rare and assumes that the production of so-called hard rock minerals such as copper, gold, and molybdenum is in the public and national interest. Coal, petroleum, and commodities such as gypsum and gravel do not fall under the Mining Law of 1872. Companies or individuals who discover a mineral deposit on public land in the United States are allowed to file claims under the law and, if subsequent exploration and analysis shows that the deposit can be mined at a profit by a prudent person, patent the claim in much the same way that an inventor patents an original idea. Once the claim is patented, the land can be purchased from the government for a few dollars per acre.

Opponents of the law object to the fact that a private company can take permanent ownership of public land for a price well below its market value. Once ownership is transferred, moreover, no royalties on mineral production must be paid to the public treasury and the land does not even have to be used for mining. In contrast, coal, petroleum, and so-called industrial minerals such as potash are leased. Companies must pay royalties on their production and never take ownership of the land being mined. Proponents of the law argue that mineral production in necessary to maintain a healthy and comfortable standard of living, that hard rock mineral deposits are so rare that they must be given special consideration, and that companies would not spend millions of dollars to explore for and mine mineral deposits without the possibility of substantial economic returns on their risk.

Encounters with the Archdruid is significant for at least two reasons. First, the book provides a readable and insightful account of thinking during the late 1960s, when the environmental movement was just beginning to take an important place in the public conscience. The first Earth Day was held in 1970, while *Encounters with the Archdruid* was being written. Recycling was a novel concept, ecology was a word just beginning to be heard in everyday conversation, and concerns about energy supplies arising from the Arab oil embargo of 1973 were unimaginable to most people. Decades of ensuing discourse about issues such as petroleum exploration in pristine wildlife refuges and mining on public lands in the western United States have been framed using the same vocabulary that McPhee documented in his essays. Second, McPhee writes as a disinterested journalist whose neutral voice does not unduly influence the conversations he is reporting. Both Brower and Park (as well as Dominy and Fraser in other parts of the book) are presented as articulate and thoughtful proponents of diametrically opposed philosophies, neither one being solely a villain or a hero.

FURTHER RESOURCES

Books

Brower, David, and Steve Chapple. *Let the Mountains Talk, Let the Rivers Run: A Call to Those Who Would Save the Earth*. New York: Harper Collins, 1995.

Park, Charles F. *Affluence in Jeopardy*. San Francisco: Freeman, Cooper, and Co., 1968.

Web sites

U.S. Geological Survey. "Sustainability and Societal Needs." <http://minerals.usgs.gov/sustain.html> (accessed February 12, 2006).

Sulfur plumes off Namibia

Photograph

By: United States National Aeronautics and Space Agency (NASA)

Date: April 24, 2002

Source: "Sulfur plumes off Namibia." NASA, November 27, 1981.

About the Organization: The image of sulfur plumes rising up from the bottom of the ocean floor to produce swirls in the waters off the coast of Namibia in southern Africa was created by the Moderate Resolution Imaging Spectroradiometer (MODIS) on the Terra satellite launched by the United States' space agency NASA.

INTRODUCTION

Ocean color is the term used to describe the quantity of light of different wavelengths that reflects off of the surface of the ocean. Various components in the ocean absorb and scatter light differently at different wavelengths. For example, phytoplankton, the microscopic plants that live in the ocean, strongly absorb blue and red light. This means that when there is a lot of phytoplankton in the water, a great deal of green light is scattered out of the ocean. The ocean color is therefore greener and the amount of light measured by a light sensor that detects green wavelengths is greater. In contrast, many types of sands and soils absorb blue light very strongly, making the ocean color more red. Other compounds such as sulfur produce dramatic color swirls and currents. Such sulfur plumes or swirls result from the breakdown of plant matter by anaerobic bacteria (bacteria that do not require oxygen).

Beginning in the 1950s, oceanographers developed instruments to measure ocean color from ships. These instruments, called spectroradiometers, detect the magnitude of light in specific parts of the visible light spectrum. In addition, scientists on ships could sample the seawater and measure the absorption and scattering properties of the various components of seawater. These measurements allowed them to develop mathematical models to predict the concentrations of phytoplankton, terriginous runoff, and other materials in the ocean from measurements of ocean color.

In the 1970s, oceanographers began collaborating with NASA scientists to develop satellites that could measure ocean color from space. The first of these satellites was the Coastal Zone Color Scanner (CZCS). It was launched in 1978 as a test of concept and was only planned to remain functional for one year. Against expectations, ocean color data was collected from CZCS for eight years, until 1986.

Given the successes of CZCS, space agencies from around the world developed satellite-based ocean color sensors. As of March 2005, ten ocean color satellites are functional. MODIS (Moderate Resolution Imaging Spectroradiometer) and SeaWiFS (Sea-viewing Wide Field of View Sensor) are both operated by the United States. Other countries that have successfully launched ocean color satellites include China (COCTS), Japan (OCTS and OCI), Argentina (MMRS), the European Union (MERIS), India (OCM), Korea (OSMI), and France (PARASOL). At least six more ocean color sensors are scheduled for launch by 2009.

PRIMARY SOURCE

SULFUR PLUMES OFF NAMIBIA
See primary source image.

PRIMARY SOURCE

Sulfur plumes off Namibia. The Moderate Resolution Imaging Spectroradiometer (MODIS) shown is adapted from the color photograph. The sulfur plumes are depicted (here in black and white) as light shaded swirls off the coast of Namibia. NASA

SIGNIFICANCE

The most impressive feature of the space imaging is the high level of spatial complexity. The currents, which are strongly affected by topography of the seafloor, have highly dynamic behaviors. The eddies, rings, and vortices that result from the motion of the currents appear as circular, swirling, and ring-like features in images.

Such imaging has major advantages over shipboard measurements in terms of understanding the complexity of the ocean. Whereas a ship can only measure one point in time and space, satellites can scan large swaths of the ocean instantaneously. The point-by-point measurements can easily mask dynamic changes and complex spatial structure. For example, scientists on a ship could make many samples in a region with a large amount of phytoplankton or sulfur and never know that water with low concentrations of phytoplankton or sulfur occur only a few miles away.

The effects of temporal features have also been studied using information collected from ocean measurement satellites. For example, monsoons have an enormous impact on the growth of phytoplankton in the Arabian Sea. These heavy rains, which impact the region between July and December, result in extremely high concentrations of phytoplankton, as can be seen from satellites. This contrasts with the non-monsoon part of the year, when ocean color images show that the Arabian Sea has very low concentrations of phytoplankton. Ocean color images have also been important in identifying the effects of longer-period global features, like El Niño/La Niña.

Satellite measurements of the ocean have increased oceanographers' understanding of the ocean in other ways as well. Changes in the temperature of the water are often correlated with phytoplankton growth or other submarine growth. This is quite common in upwellings, places where deep, cool water rises to the surface. Ocean color sensors have been used throughout the oceans to identify locations of upwellings and to verify the effects of such upwellings. Ocean color measurements, are for example, used to identify harmful algal blooms, also called red tides, which can result in large fish kills. It can be used to monitor the impacts of pollution and oil spills, the magnitude of dust storms, and even the foraging patterns of sea turtles.

FURTHER RESOURCES

Web sites

International Ocean-Colour Coordinating Group. <http://www.ioccg.org> (accessed November 22, 2005).

NASA. "Ocean Color." <http://disc.gsfc.nasa.gov/oceancolor/scifocus/scifocus.shtml> (accessed November 22, 2005).

NASA. "Ocean Color Web." <http://oceancolor.gsfc.nasa.gov> (accessed November 22, 2005).

Four False Color Views of Ocean Surface Height of the Pacific Ocean

El Niño and La Niña

Photograph

By: National Aeronautics and Space Administration (NASA)

Date: 1997

Source: NASA. "Four False Color Views of Ocean Surface Height of the Pacific Ocean." 1997.

About the Organization: TOPEX/Poseidon is part of NASA's Mission to Planet Earth, a long-term research program to study the Earth as a global system, with particular emphasis on gathering data about how oceans influence global climate. The Jet Propulsion Laboratory manages the U.S. portion of the TOPEX/Poseidon mission for NASA.

INTRODUCTION

El Niño and La Niña refer to an irregular cycle of shifting climactic conditions in the tropical Pacific Ocean. El Niño and La Niña affect the dynamics of both the ocean and the atmosphere throughout the planet.

In the 1880s, South American fisherman gave the name El Niño, which means little boy in Spanish, to the climactic condition. They noticed the oceanic changes associated with El Niño around Christmas celebrations centered on a Christ-child figure. La Niña, or little girl, is a name given in opposition to El Niño. The alternating climactic conditions have also been called El Niño/Southern Oscillation or ENSO by oceanographers.

In normal conditions, the Trade Winds blow from east to west across the tropical Pacific Ocean. Friction between the winds and the ocean effectively pulls water toward the western side of the Pacific. The sea surface is about 1.6 feet (0.5 m) higher near Indonesia than it is near South America. As the Trade Winds pull water away from the eastern side of the Pacific, cool water from deep in the ocean rises to the surface in a process called upwelling. The upwelled water is cold and rich in nutrients. Microscopic ocean plants called phytoplankton flourish in this water. In turn, fish and other predators graze on the phytoplankton. As a result, the Eastern Pacific Ocean along the coast of Peru has extremely diverse ecosystems and rich fisheries.

As the warm Trade Winds pull the ocean water to the west, they heat it. A lot of evaporation occurs in the warmed water on the western side of the Pacific Ocean. This results in heavy rains near Indonesia and relatively dry conditions near Peru. La Niña conditions occur when the Trade Winds intensify across the Tropical Pacific. This leads to very strong upwelling near South America and very cold ocean waters along the coast of Peru extending westward toward the center of the Pacific Ocean. Under La Niña conditions, the weather near Indonesia and Australia tends to be extremely wet, and very dry conditions persist in the western part of South America.

When El Niño conditions arise, the Trade Winds relax. Less water is pulled from the east side of the Pacific toward the west. Upwelling of cold, nutrient-rich water decreases, leading to oceanic conditions that do not favor phytoplankton growth. Lacking adequate food supply, the fish and other predators decline in number. With the decrease in the strength of the Trade Winds, warm water from the western side of the Pacific flows eastward. This shifts the site of evaporation towards the east. Rainfall follows evaporation, so El Niño conditions bring heavy rains to the coast of Peru and result in droughts and fires in Indonesia and Australia.

El Niño conditions occur irregularly every four to seven years. Understanding the processes that control El Niño required the collaboration of atmospheric scientists and oceanographers. In the first part of the twentieth century, atmospheric scientists noticed an oscillation in the atmospheric pressure in the eastern and western Pacific Ocean. In most cases pressure was low in the west and high in the east. However, in some years the pressure differential seemed to abate and these years were associated with lighter than normal monsoons in eastern parts of Asia.

In the 1950s, atmospheric scientist Jacob Bjerknes proposed that the pattern of oscillating atmospheric pressure might be linked to the ocean. This idea was explored in the 1970s as oceanographers began to make systematic measurements of sea surface height and temperatures. Eventually, in the 1980s, David Halpern of NOAA pieced together the first array of moored sensors across the Pacific Ocean to continually measure ocean temperatures and to relay the information to researchers via satellite. In addition, oceanographic and atmospheric scientists began collaborating to build coupled models of the atmosphere and the ocean in order to develop the ability to predict the onset of El Niño. Wind and ocean temperature measurements as well as NASA ocean surface height measurements are used to make predictions about changes to El Niño and La Niña patterns and severity.

The image presented shows NASA and other agencies monitoring of ocean surface height. The data was obtained from NASA's TOPEX/Poseidon satellite and transmitted as false color images (presented here in gray scale). The shaded areas represent various ocean heights correlated to heat intensity.

SIGNIFICANCE

Although the exact impacts of El Niño and La Niña are still under study, the data suggests strong correlations between these phenomena and changes to weather and atmospheric patterns. For example, the results of the 1982–1983 El Niño were serious. Australia experienced extreme wildfires and drought. Africa also suffered from a severe drought. On the other hand, Peru and Ecuador were subjected to extremely heavy rains, resulting in flooding and mudslides. Estimates held the El Niño responsible for the loss of 2,100 lives and $13 billion in damage worldwide.

Following the 1982–1983 El Niño, scientists recognized the importance of accurately predicting El Niño. An international effort resulted in the Tropical Ocean-Global Atmosphere (TOGA) program, which deployed moored and satellite-tracked ocean temperature sensors in the Pacific Ocean. TOGA was replaced by the Tropical Ocean-Atmosphere (TAO) array of moored sensors in 1995, which has set of bands of moored ocean temperature sensors throughout the Pacific Ocean.

In 1986, using coupled ocean and atmospheric computer models along with the data collected from TOGA and from ocean viewing satellites, scientists predicted an El Niño event. The El Niño arrived as predicted and lasted until 1988.

In 1997, models predicted an El Niño. Although as severe as that of 1982, a variety of preparations occurred throughout the world. Farmers in Brazil planted drought resistant crops while Californians improved flood systems and acquired additional flood insurance. People living in the Galápagos Islands improved roads and water systems.

Currently, the Pacific Ocean is under constant monitoring for signs of El Niño. Predictions are constantly updated and given the sophistication of their coupled atmospheric and ocean models. Along with the high-quality data from satellites and moored sensors, scientists feel fairly certain that they can predict and El Niño more than a year before the actual conditions occur.

PRIMARY SOURCE

SURFACE HEIGHT OF THE PACIFIC OCEAN
See primary source image.

FURTHER RESOURCES
Books

Philander, S. George. *Our Affair with El Niño: How We Transformed an Enchanting Peruvian Current into a Global Climate Hazard.* Princeton, N.J.: Princeton University Press, 2004.

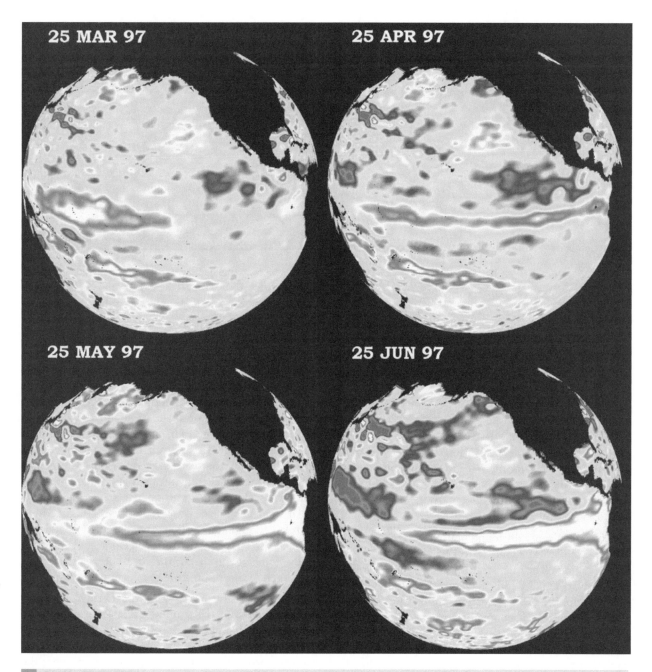

PRIMARY SOURCE

Surface Height of the Pacific Ocean. Four views of the surface height of the Pacific Ocean in 1997, shown here in gray scale with the white areas showing increased heat storage characteristic of the El Niño phenomenon. TOPEX/POSEIDON, NASA JPL

Web sites

"El Niño and La Niña: Tracing the Dance of Ocean and Atmosphere." *National Academy of Sciences.* <http://www7. nationalacademies.org/opus/elnino.html> (accessed March 15, 2006).

"El Niño Theme Page." *National Oceanic & Atmospheric Administration (NOAA), U.S. Department of Commerce.* <http://www.pmel.noaa.gov/tao/elnino/nino-home. html> (accessed March 15, 2006).

"Low Ozone Level Found Above Antarctica"

Newspaper article

By: Walter Sullivan

Date: November 7, 1985

Source: Sullivan, Walter. "Low Ozone Level Found Above Antarctica." *New York Times* (November 7, 1985).

About the Author: Walter Sullivan was a prolific science writer and editor at The *New York Times*. He also wrote several popular science books, including *We Are Not Alone: The Continuing Search for Extraterrestrial Intelligence* and *Black Holes: Edge of Space, Edge of Time.* In 1978 he won an award for distinguished public service from the National Science Foundation. The American Geophysical Union dedicated an award for excellence in scientific journalism in his name.

INTRODUCTION

The ozone hole is a large area over the continent of Antarctica where concentrations of the gas ozone in the stratosphere typically fall in the Antarctic spring between August and November of each year. Concentrations are usually about 70 percent of those found during the rest of the year.

Ozone is generally found both in the troposphere, which extends 5 to 9 miles (8 to 14.5 kilometers) above sea level, and in the stratosphere, which extends between 10 and 31 miles (17 and 50 kilometers) in altitude. In the troposphere, ozone is considered a pollutant because it contributes to the formation of smog. In the stratosphere, ozone occurs naturally and acts as an important protective shield against harmful radiation from the sun. Stratospheric ozone absorbs much of the ultraviolet energy at wavelengths between 240 and 320 nanometers that impinge on the Earth. This ultraviolet radiation is responsible for sunburn, skin cancer, damage to vegetation, and higher rates of genetic mutation in many invertebrate animals.

Ozone is formed in the stratosphere by the energy of sunlight. Oxygen molecules are generally found as two oxygen atoms joined together, symbolized O_2. When ultraviolet energy from the sun strikes an oxygen molecule, it can dissociate the two atoms of oxygen, O. The oxygen atoms are extremely reactive and quickly join with a third molecule of oxygen to form O_3, which is ozone.

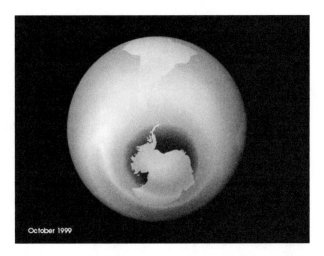

This image, generated from the Total Ozone Mapping Spectrometer (TOMS) shows the area over the Antartic where the ozone levels has been significantly depleted, October 1999. AP IMAGES

Ozone can be destroyed naturally when an atom of oxygen joins with ozone to form O_4. The O_4 molecule then splits to form two molecules of oxygen, O_2. However, this reaction occurs too slowly to account for the concentrations of ozone that are actually found in the stratosphere. Research has shown that other gases have the ability to destroy ozone as well. In particular, manmade chemicals that contain chlorine, known as chlorofluorocarbons or CFCs, are particularly effective at destroying ozone. CFCs are used in refrigeration and cooling systems, aerosols and solvents. Also, gases containing bromine and nitrogen oxides are involved in the breakdown of ozone. Nitrogen oxides result from the burning of fossil fuels.

Between 1955 and 1978, the average monthly measurements of the ozone in the stratosphere over Antarctica in October were between about 275 and 350 Dobson Units (DU). In the late 1970s the concentrations of ozone began to sharply decline. In 1985, the average measurement of ozone in the month of October had decreased to around 170 DU.

PRIMARY SOURCE

LOW OZONE LEVEL FOUND ABOVE ANTARCTICA

Satellite observations have confirmed a progressive deterioration in the earth's protective ozone layer above Antarctica, according to scientists who analyzed data recently sent back from space.

Each October, the data show a "hole" appears in the ozone layer there, scientists say, and each year the layer in that area becomes less able to shield the earth from damaging solar ultraviolet rays.

Since 1974 scientists have been predicting a gradual depletion of stratospheric ozone as a result of increased pollution of the atmosphere. The new data have persuaded some researchers that the ozone loss is proceeding much faster than expected.

Link to Skin Cancer It has been predicted that a significant depletion of the ozone layer would substantially increase the rate of skin cancer worldwide. Even under normal conditions, however, the ozone layer is subject to wide variations, and whether the recent depletion is part of a long-term trend is difficult to establish.

Several substances introduced into the atmosphere as pollutants are suspected of contributing to the depletion, chief among them fluorocarbons, such as the Freon used for refrigeration, and methane, nitrous oxide, and a variety of bromine compounds.

The satellite measurements indicating a rapid decrease over Antarctica have been made by two devices riding the Nimbus-7 satellite, which was launched in 1978. Dr. Donald F. Heath of the Goddard Space Flight Center in Greenbelt, Md., who for several years has been monitoring the recordings, said yesterday a quick look at last month's data indicated that the decline is continuing.

In his view, however, the reason for it remains uncertain. It was first blamed on sulfur compounds and other particles ejected into the stratosphere by the 1982 eruption of El Chichon in Mexico.

Scientists Backs Theory This explanation was also advanced by H. U. Dutsch of the Federal Institute of Technology in Zurich, Switzerland, based on ozone measurements at Arosa in the Swiss Alps.

The measurements there, as at numerous other ground stations, are based on recording two wavelengths of sunlight. Ozone absorbs sunlight at one of the wavelengths, so the relative strength of the two wavelengths is an indication of how much of the gas is in the atmosphere. The 1983 average was the lowest in 60 years. If that was entirely caused by material from El Chichon, Dr. Rowland said in a recent interview, the level should now be returning to normal, but it is not.

According to Dr. Heath, however, there are other possible explanations. The decrease could be linked to the sunspot cycle, which is now near a minimum. According to a study by NASA scientists, the chemical reactions that produce stratospheric ozone are stimulated by a form of ultraviolet radiation that becomes weak when sunspots are fewest.

Unusual Conditions Noted Nor is it clear, Dr. Heath said, whether the Antarctic readings manifest a local change in atmospheric circulation, rather than a global depletion. The condition of the winter atmosphere over Antarctica is not matched anywhere else. The atmosphere, immersed in the polar night, remains highly stable and becomes extremely cold. Then, when spring comes to the Southern Hemisphere about October, it is suddenly bathed in sunlight and, it is hypothesized, ozone depletion runs at full speed.

According to the report observations at Halley Bay in Antarctica, "Comparable effects should not be expected in the Northern Hemisphere where the winter polar stratospheric vortex is less cold and less stable." The report, published earlier this year in Nature, was by J. C. Farman, B. G. Gardiner and J. D. Shanklin.

That fluorocarbons are responsible for the newly observed depletion of the ozone layer has been proposed by scientists of the British Antarctic Survey, based on observations conducted since 1957 at Halley Bay, and by Dr. F. Sherwood Rowland of the University of California at Irvine. It was Dr. Rowland, Dr. Mario J. Molina and Dr. Harold Johnston who in 1974 first warned of such a danger.

In 1980 a committee of the National Academy of Sciences concluded that the projected ozone depletion, through increased ultraviolet radiation, could increase skin cancer, curtail crop production and destroy the larvae of some marine organisms. A 16 percent ozone reduction, it said, would probably produce each year "thousands" of additional cases of melanoma—the most lethal skin cancer.

Effect of Ban In 1977 a ban was imposed on fluorocarbons as spray-can propellants, but it became evident that the ozone varies in response to a variety of interacting natural and human influences. By 1984 an academy report estimated ozone reduction, due to fluorocarbons, at only 2 percent to 4 percent.

An annual 20 percent increase in the atmospheric content of bromine compounds that also endanger the ozone layer has been reported by a group from the Max Planck Institute for Aeronomy in Lindau, West Germany. Their instruments were lifted 15 miles above southern France by balloon in the fall of 1982, 1983 and 1984. Production of such compounds, including those used in fire extinguishers, appears to be increasing rapidly.

The original warning by Dr. Rowland and Dr. Molina concerned the chlorine that would be released when fluorocarbons are exposed to ultraviolet rays in the stratosphere. While those synthetic compounds are normally very stable, when exposed to ultraviolet light they break down and one of their constituents is chlorine, which can remove ozone from the atmosphere. The molecules of ozone gas are formed of three oxygen atoms, whereas oxygen gas contains only two of them. When chlorine reacts with an ozone molecule, breaking it up, the chlorine remains intact, ready to attack another one.

SIGNIFICANCE

Since the 1980s, a significant amount of scientific research has been devoted to understanding the formation of the ozone hole. Scientists discovered that the ozone hole is the result of particular conditions, which coalesce to cause a severe depletion in the concentration of ozone over Antarctica in the winter. First, a polar vortex, or circular weather pattern, forms over the continent in the winter. This isolates the air in the stratosphere from interacting with the stratosphere in the rest of the planet. Second, the temperatures inside the vortex become extremely cold. This allows for the formation of special clouds of water and nitric acid ice crystals known as Polar Stratospheric Clouds, or PSCs. The PSCs act as a substrate on which chemical reactions can occur. In particular, inactive chlorine and bromine compounds are converted to forms which are much more reactive. Finally, when the sun returns to Antarctica in the spring, it initiates a series of reactions that rapidly destroys ozone. During these cycles the chlorine compounds are not destroyed and can react again and again with ozone. This process continues until the vortex warms up and eventually dissipates. The size and timing of the ozone hole varies each year because it is dependent on the size and duration of the polar vortex.

Many of the compounds responsible for the conditions that result in the ozone hole are industrial products. In particular, CFCs, halons, carbon tetrachloride, methyl chloroform and methyl bromide all play important roles in the destruction of ozone and are classified as class I ozone-depleting substances.

A global agreement to limit the production of class I substances was part of the Montreal Protocol of 1987. In this agreement, the signatory Parties proposed to cut the production of CFCs in half by 2000. Given the large amount of public attention focused on the ozone hole and the interest placed on the situation by environmental groups, the Parties met again in 1992 in Copenhagen. At this meeting, they proposed an accelerated phase-out of class I substances. Under the revised schedule, all class I substances except methyl bromide were completely phased out by 1995 and production and consumption of methyl bromide ceased as of 2005. The United States agreed to the accelerated schedule and it was enforced under the Clean Air Act.

Subsequent to the agreement on class I ozone-depleting substances, hydrochlorofluorocarbons (HCFCs), which were used to replace CFCs in industrial uses, were found to have ozone-reducing potential. The production and consumption of these substances will be phased out by 2030.

FURTHER RESOURCES

Web sites

NASA. "Stratospheric Ozone Depletion." <http://www. nas. nasa.gov/About/Education/Ozone/ozone.html> (accessed January 6, 2006).

The Ozone Hole. <http://www.theozonehole.com> (accessed January 6, 2006).

United States Environmental Protection Agency. "The Antarctic Ozone Hole." <http://www.epa.gov/ozone/science/hole/index.html> (accessed January 6, 2006).

University of Cambridge Centre for Atmospheric Science. "The Ozone Hole Tour." <http://www.atm.ch.cam.ac.uk/tour/index.html> (accessed January 6, 2006).

"A Semidesert with a Desert Heart"

Book excerpt

By: Marc Reisner

Date: 1986

Source: Reisner, Marc. "A Semidesert with a Desert Heart." *Cadillac Desert.* New York: Viking Penguin, 1986.

About the Author: American author Marc Reisner (1948–2000) wrote three notable books about water and natural resources. The most widely known is *Cadillac Desert*, a critical account of the policy, politics, financing, and engineering behind large-scale government water supply projects in the American West. Reisner was born in Minneapolis and earned a degree in political science from Earlham College. He worked for several environmental policy organizations before receiving an Alicia Patterson Journalism Fellowship to support the work that would eventually become *Cadillac Desert*. Reisner was active in conservation and habitat protection activities with several organizations and served as a Distinguished Visiting Professor at the

University of California at Davis. He received a Pew Foundation fellowship to work on Pacific salmon issues but was unable to complete the project before his death.

INTRODUCTION

The introduction to *Cadillac Desert* begins with an account of the barren Western landscape as seen through the window of an airliner on a cross-country flight. Reisner describes the vast and largely inhospitable landscape as a prelude to his critical history of efforts to create a desert civilization by way of water projects heavily dependent upon government subsidies and political maneuvering.

The six hundred pages of *Cadillac Desert* include accounts of the ethically questionable techniques used to obtain long-term water supplies for Los Angeles, engineering triumphs such as the Depression-era construction (under budget and ahead of schedule) of the Hoover Dam, tragic failures of the St. Francis and Teton dams, the contentious Colorado River Compact, and agribusiness subsidies. An entire chapter is devoted to Floyd Dominy, a former commissioner of the U.S. Bureau of Reclamation, who became a lightning rod for critics of federal water policy and was also featured prominently in John McPhee's *Encounters with the Archdruid*.

Reisner's history of western water development is set against the early advice of John Wesley Powell (1834–1902), a one-armed American Civil War veteran and the second director of the U.S. Geological Survey, who is best known for leading the first river expedition through the Grand Canyon. Based on his observation of western drylands and the hardships suffered by mid-nineteenth century homesteaders, Powell realized that water would always be a limiting factor west of the one-hundredth meridian. This was a significant departure from the prevailing opinions of expansionists, railroads, and land promoters who vigorously maintained that water would quite literally follow the plow. Once the land had been settled and cultivated, rain would come as if by divine providence. Powell suggested smaller settlements than many people envisioned, and emphasized self-reliance, water conservation, and highly localized irrigation works as the keys to successful settlement of the West. Just a few months before Powell's death in 1902, Congress created the U.S. Bureau of Reclamation and put into motion a multi-billion dollar program of heavily subsidized and monumental engineering works intended to reclaim the arid West.

Drought and sun exposure make it possible to see the bottom of Boyd Lake in Colorado, August 3, 2002. The recession in water levels threatens the fishing industry, and the state's effort to protect rare fish. AP IMAGES

■ PRIMARY SOURCE

A SEMIDESERT WITH A DESERT HEART

One late November night in 1980, I was flying over the state of Utah on my way back to California. I had an aisle seat, and since I believe that anyone who flies in an airplane and doesn't spend most of his time looking out the window wastes his money, I walked back to the rear door of the airplane and stood for a long time at the door's tiny aperture, squinting out at Utah.

Two days earlier, a fierce early blizzard had gone through the Rocky Mountain states. In its wake, the air was pellucid. The frozen fire of a winter's moon poured cold light on the desert below. Six inches away from the tip of my nose the temperature was, according to the pilot, minus sixty-five, and seven miles below it was four above zero. But here we were, two hundred highly inventive creatures safe and comfortable inside a fat winged-cylinder racing toward the Great Basin of North America, dozing, drinking, chattering, oblivious to the frigid emptiness outside.

Emptiness. There was nothing down there on the earth—no towns, no light, no signs of civilization at all. Barren mountains rose duskily from the desert floor; isolated mesas and buttes broke the wind-haunted distance. You couldn't see much in the moonlight, but obviously there were no forests, no pastures, no lakes, no rivers; there was no fruited plain. I counted the minutes between clusters of lights. Six, eight, nine, eleven—going nine miles a minute, that was a lot of uninhabited distance in a crowded century, a lot of emptiness amid a civilization whose success was achieved on the pretension that natural obstacles do not exist.

Then the landscape heaved upward. We were crossing a high, thin cordillera of mountains, their tops already covered with snow. The Wasatch Range. As suddenly as the mountains appeared, they fell away, and the vast gridiron of lights appeared out of nowhere. It was clustered thickly under the aircraft and trailed off toward the south, erupting in ganglionic clots that winked and shimmered in the night. Salt Lake City, Orem, Draper, Provo: we were over most of the population of Utah.

That thin avenue of civilization pressed against the Wasatches, intimidated by a fierce desert on three sides, was a poignant sight. More startling than its existence was the fact that it had been there only 134 years, since Brigham Young led his band of social outcasts to the old bed of a drying desert sea and proclaimed, "This is the place!" *This* was the place? Someone in that first group must have felt that Young had become unhinged by two thousand horribly arduous miles. Nonetheless, within hours of ending their ordeal, the Mormons were digging shovels into the earth beside the streams draining the Wasatch Range, leading canals into the surrounding desert which they would convert to fields that would nourish them. Without realizing it, they were laying the foundation of the most ambitious desert civilization the world has seen. In the New World, Indians had dabbled with irrigation, and the Spanish had improved their techniques, but the Mormons attacked the desert full-bore, flooded it, subverted its dreadful indifference—moralized it—until they had made a Mesopotamia in America between the valleys of the Green River and the middle Snake. Fifty-six years after the first earth was turned beside City Creek, the Mormons had six million acres under full or partial irrigation in several states. In that year—1902—the United States government launched its own irrigation program, based on Mormon experience, guided by Mormon laws, run largely by Mormons. The agency responsible for it, the U.S. Bureau of Reclamation, would build the highest

and largest dams in the world on rivers few believed could be controlled—the Colorado, the Sacramento, the Columbia, the lower Snake—and run aqueducts for hundreds of miles across deserts and over mountains and through the Continental Divide in order to irrigate more millions of acres and provide water and power to a population equal to that of Italy. Thanks to irrigation, thanks to the Bureau—an agency few people know—states such as California, Arizona, and Idaho became populous and wealthy; millions settled in regions where nature, left alone, would have countenanced thousands at best; great valleys and hemispherical basins metamorphosed from desert blond to semitropic green.

On the other hand, what has it all amounted to?

Stare for a while at a LANDSAT photograph of the West, and you will see the answer: not all that much. Most of the West is still untrammeled, unirrigated, depopulate in the extreme. Modern Utah, where large-scale irrigation has been going on longer than anywhere else, has 3 percent of its land area under cultivation. California has twelve hundred major dams, the two biggest irrigation projects on earth, and more irrigated acreage than any other state, but its irrigated acreage is not much larger than Vermont. Except for the population centers of the Pacific Coast and the occasional desert metropolis—El Paso, Albuquerque, Tucson, Denver—you can drive a thousand miles in the West and encounter fewer towns than you would crossing New Hampshire. Westerners call what they have established out here a civilization, but it would be more accurate to call it a beachhead. And if history is any guide, the odds that we can sustain it would have to be regarded as low. Only one desert civilization, out of dozens that grew up in antiquity, has survived uninterrupted into modern times. And Egypt's approach to irrigation was fundamentally different from all the rest.

If you begin at the Pacific rim and move inland, you will find large cities, many towns, and prosperous-looking farms until you cross the Sierra Nevada and the Cascades, which block the seasonal weather fronts moving in from the Pacific and wringing out their moisture in snows and drenching rains. On the east side of the Sierra-Cascade crest, moisture drops immediately—from as much as 150 inches of precipitation on the western slope to as little as four inches on the eastern—and it doesn't increase much, except at higher elevations, until you have crossed the hundredth meridian, which bisects the Dakotas and Nebraska and Kansas down to Abilene, Texas, and divides the country into its two most significant halves—the one receiving at least twenty inches of precipitation a year, the other generally receiving less. Any place with less than twenty inches of rainfall is hostile terrain to a farmer depending solely on the sky, and a place that receives seven inches or less—as Phoenix, El Paso, and Reno do—is arguably no place to inhabit at all. Everything depends on the manipulation of water, on capturing it behind dams, storing it, and rerouting it in concrete rivers over distances of hundreds of miles. Were it not for a century and a half of messianic effort toward that end, the West as we know it would not exist.

The word "messianic" is not used casually. Confronted by the desert, the first thing Americans want to do is change it. People say that they "love" the desert, but few of them love it enough to live there. I mean in the real desert, not in a make-believe city like Phoenix with exotic palms and golf-course lawns and a five-hundred-foot fountain and an artificial surf. Most people "love" the desert by driving through it in air-conditioned cars, "experiencing" its grandeur. That may be some kind of experience, but it is living in a fools' paradise. To *really* experience the desert you have to march right into its white bowl of sky and shape-contorting heat with your mind on your canteen as if it were your last gallon of gas and you were being chased by a carload of escaped murderers. You have to imagine what it would be like to drink blood from a lizard or, in the grip of dementia, claw bare-handed through sand and rock for the vestigial moisture beneath a dry wash.

Trees, because of their moisture requirements, are our physiological counterparts in the kingdom of plants. Throughout most of the West they begin to appear high up on mountainsides, usually at five or six thousand feet, or else they huddle like cows along occasional streambeds. Higher up in the rain falls, but the soil is miserable, the weather is extreme, and human efforts are under siege. Lower down, in the valleys and on the plains, the weather, the soil, and the terrain are more welcoming, but it is almost invariably too dry. A drought lasting three weeks can terrorize an eastern farmer; a drought of five months is, to a California farmer, a normal state of affairs. (The lettuce farmers of the Imperial Valley don't even *like* rain; it is so hot in the summer it wilts the leaves.) The Napa Valley of California receives as much Godwater—a term for rain in the arid West—as Illinois, but almost all of it falls from November to March; a weather front between May and September rates as much press attention as a meteor shower. In Nevada you see rainclouds, formed by orographic updrafts over the mountains, almost every day. But rainclouds in the desert seldom mean rain, because the heat reflected off the earth and the ravenous dryness can vaporize a shower in midair, leaving the blackest-looking cumulonimbus trailing a few pathetic ribbons of moisture that disappear before reaching the ground. And if rain does manage to fall to earth, there is nothing to hold it, so it races off in evanescent brown torrents, evaporating, running to nowhere.

One does not really conquer a place like this. One inhabits it like an occupying army and makes, at best, an uneasy truce with it. New England was completely forested in 1620 and nearly deforested 150 years later; Arkansas saw nine million acres of marsh and swamp forest converted to farms. Through such Promethean effort, the eastern half of the continent was radically made over, for better or worse. The West never can be. The only way to make the region over is to irrigate it. But there is too little water to begin with, and water in rivers is phenomenally expensive to move. And even if you succeeded in moving every drop, it wouldn't make much of a difference. John Wesley Powell, the first person who clearly understood this, figured that if you evenly distributed all the surface water flowing between the Columbia River and the Gulf of Mexico, you would *still* have a desert almost indistinguishable from the one that is there today. Powell failed to appreciate the vast amount of water sitting in underground aquifers, a legacy of the Ice Ages and their glacial met, but even this water, which has turned the western plains and large portions of California and Arizona green, will be mostly gone within a hundred years— a resource squandered as quickly as oil.

At first, no one listened to Powell when he said the overwhelming portion of the West could never be transformed. People figured that when the region was settled, rainfall would magically increase, that it would "follow the plow." In the late 1800s, such theories amounted to Biblical dogma. When they proved catastrophically wrong, Powell's irrigation ideas were finally embraced and pursued with near fanaticism, until the most gigantic dams were being built on the most minuscule foundations of economic rationality and need. Greening the desert became a kind of Christian ideal. In May of 1957, a very distinguished Texas historian, Walter Prescott Webb, wrote an article for *Harper's* entitled "The American West, Perpetual Mirage," in which he called the West "a semidesert with a desert heart" and said it had too dark a soul to be truly converted. The greatest national folly we could commit, Webb argued, would be to exhaust the treasury trying to make over the West in the image of Illinois—a folly which, by then, had taken on the appearance of national policy. The editors of *Harper's* were soon up to their knees in a flood of vitriolic mail from westerners condemning Webb as an infidel, a heretic, a doomsayer.

Desert, semidesert, call it what you will. The point is that despite heroic efforts and many billions of dollars, all we have managed to do in the arid West is turn a Missouri-size section green—and that conversion has been wrought mainly with nonrenewable groundwater. But a goal of many westerners and of their federal archangels, the Bureau of Reclamation and Corps of Engineers, has long been to double, triple, quadruple the amount of desert that has been civilized and armed, and now these same people say that the future of a hungry world depends on it, even if it means importing water from as far away as Alaska. What they seem not to understand is how difficult it will be just to hang on to the beachhead they have made. Such a surfeit of ambition stems, of course, from the remarkable record of success we have had in reclaiming the American desert. But the same could have been said about any number of desert civilizations throughout history—Assyria, Carthage, Mesopotamia; the Inca, the Aztec, the Hohokam—before they collapsed.

And it may not even have been drought that did them in. It may have been salt. . . .

SIGNIFICANCE

Although it has been criticized as revisionist history, *Cadillac Desert* continues to stand as a landmark description of highly ambitious, largely unchecked, and economically debatable water development projects and the federal bureaucracy that grew up around them. Reisner points out that a century of intensive effort has managed to irrigate, at great cost, an amount of land roughly equivalent to the size of Missouri. Part of the cost of reclamation has been paid with dollars. The remainder has been paid with lost natural resources such as Glen Canyon (now flooded by a reservoir named in honor of John Wesley Powell), depleted salmon runs, and aquifers that they have permanently lost their ability to yield water. Some lives have been lost and others have no doubt been saved. The benefits have included jobs, inexpensive electricity, desert oases such as Phoenix and Las Vegas, and a multi-billion dollar agricultural business. Reisner's contribution in *Cadillac Desert* was to bring the debate to the forefront.

FURTHER RESOURCES

Books

Powell, John Wesley. *The Exploration of the Colorado River and Its Canyons.* New York: Penguin, 1987 (originally published in 1875).

Worster, Donald. *A River Running West: The Life of John Wesley Powell.* Oxford, U.K.: Oxford University Press, 2000.

Periodicals

Pisani, D.J. "Federal Reclamation and the American West in the Twentieth Century." *Agricultural History* 77 (Summer 2003): 391–419.

Web sites

National Public Radio. "The Vision of John Wesley Powell." <http://www.npr.org/programs/atc/features/2003/aug/water/part1.html> (accessed February 12, 2006).

"At Last, the Smoking Gun?"

Magazine article

By: Leon Jaroff

Date: July 1, 1991

Source: Leon Jaroff, "At Last, the Smoking Gun?" *Time.* 137 (July 1, 1991): 26.

About the Author: Since 1951, Leon Jaroff has been an editor, writer and contributor to both *Time* and *LIFE* magazines. In 1980 Jaroff became the founding editor of *DISCOVER* magazine. His writing has earned a variety of awards from both scientific and medical associations.

INTRODUCTION

The KT boundary is an actual boundary between layers of rock that refers to the end of the period of Earth's history when dinosaurs dominated the planet and the beginning of the rise of mammals. Geologists find rocks containing dinosaur fossils below the KT boundary. In the rock layers above the KT boundary, scientists find rocks containing fossils of mammals and other more modern animals and plants. The change in the types of fossils found above and below the KT boundary is very abrupt and very dramatic.

The term KT refers to two periods in geologic history, which are separated by the boundary. The older period is the Cretaceous, which is part of the Mesozoic Era and extended between 135 million years ago and 65 million years ago. (In German, Cretaceous begins with the letter K, which is the origin of the K in KT boundary). The geologic era following the Mesozoic is the Cenozoic, which extends between 65 million years ago and today. The first part of the Cenozoic is the Tertiary, which spanned the time between 65 million years ago and 1.75 million years ago. The T in KT refers to the Tertiary period.

Evidence of the KT boundary was first discovered by French naturalist George Cuvier, who was studying rock layers in the early part of the nineteenth century in the Paris basin. He found that the types of fossils found below the layer were extremely different from those found above it. In particular, Cuvier and other scientists who followed his work found that the boundary represented a period of mass extinctions of many different species. This led Cuvier to propose the idea that catastrophic events play an important role in the Earth's history. Cuvier's idea was not extremely popular in the scientific community, giving way to the theory of gradualism that stated that geologic change occurs very slowly.

In 1980, Luis and Walter Alvarez analyzed the chemistry of the gray layer of clay that comprises the KT boundary. They found extremely high concentrations of iridium in the layer. Iridium is rare on Earth but common in extra-terrestrial rocks. The Alvarezes proposed that the iridium indicated that a giant meteor hit the Earth 65 million years ago, vaporized and spread iridium-laden dust throughout the atmosphere. When it settled, it became the KT boundary.

The Alvarezes' idea was met with intense criticism from the scientific community. However, in 1991, as reported in the article below, the Alvarezes found the impact crater from a massive meteor that dated to 65 million years ago in the Yucatan Penninsula in Mexico.

PRIMARY SOURCE

AT LAST, THE SMOKING GUN?

If a comet did in the dinosaurs, where is the giant crater left by its impact? The answer may lie on the coast of the Yucatan Peninsula.

Hurtling through the atmosphere at nearly 70 km per sec. (150,000 m.p.h.), the giant comet struck with catastrophic force, punching a hole some 40 km (25 miles) deep through the earth's crust and into the mantle. The violence of the collision 65 million years ago completely vaporized the 8-km-wide (5 miles) comet and blasted out a tremendous crater. Huge rocks, hurled high into the + air, rained down for hundreds of kilometers. A great fireball rose above the atmosphere, carrying with it vast amounts of pulverized debris.

These finer particles remained suspended, drifting into a globe-enveloping shroud that blocked sunlight for months before blanketing the earth in a layer of dust. In the cold and dark, photosynthesis ceased, plants and animals died, and entire species, including the dinosaurs, perished.

This startling scenario, proposed in 1980 by the late Nobel laureate Luis Alvarez and his son Walter, ignited a scientific debate that still rages today. Opponents of the theory, notably paleontologists, blame the Great Extinction on climatic changes possibly brought on by volcanic activity. If the Alvarezes were correct, they ask, where is the smoking gun? Where is the crater?

Some 130 terrestrial impact craters had been identified, but none of them near the age of 65 million years was large enough to qualify as the Crater. Yet if a comet or asteroid massive enough to cause the extinction had struck the earth, it would have left a crater hundreds of kilometers wide. Some traces would still exist, despite the intervening millenniums of erosion, sedimentation and tectonic-plate movement.

Now, after a decade-long search, the attention of geologists is riveted on a circular basin some 180 km (112 miles) in diameter. It lies buried under 1,100 m (3,600 ft.) of limestone, centered beneath the town of Chicxulub, on the northern tip of Mexico's Yucatan Peninsula, and extending out under the Gulf of Mexico. The nature of the basin, its location and a preliminary estimate of its age suggest that it is the Crater, the one gouged into the earth by the comet or asteroid that killed the dinosaurs.

In the search for the Crater, the first clues were sifted out of clumps of gray clay. At dozens of sites around the world, that clay has been found in a thin boundary layer between the rock of the Tertiary period and the formations of the late Cretaceous period, which ended 65 million years ago. In the Cretaceous rock lie the fossil remains of giant dinosaurs and a profusion of other species. But in the Tertiary formations, just above the clay, no trace exists of the dinosaurs or many of the other Cretaceous species.

The Alvarezes analyzed this clay in the late 1970s and showed it had a far higher content of the rare element iridium than ordinarily found in the earth's crust. It was this discovery that led Luis Alvarez to his momentous insight. Comets and asteroids have high iridium content, he reasoned, and the clay layer could have been formed by the worldwide fallout of the material vaporized when an errant asteroid or, as most scientists now suspect, a giant comet smacked into the earth.

As the quest for the telltale crater intensified in the middle 1980s, William Boynton, a professor of planetary science, and graduate student Alan Hildebrand, both of the University of Arizona, wondered if the boundary clay might also help reveal the site of the impact. Measuring the content of rare earth elements in samples of the clay, they determined that it contained both the basaltic rock found in the ocean floor and a lesser amount of continental rock. Their conclusion: the comet had hit on the edge of an ocean basin.

So great an impact in water must have produced monstrous seismic waves, perhaps as great as 5 km (3 miles) high, that raced across the waters, tearing up the bottom sediments and sweeping rocky debris inland. Searching through scientific literature, they uncovered reports of chaotic mixes of large rocks at the 65-million-year boundary level in Texas, Mexico, Cuba and northern South America, but none anywhere else. This suggests, says Hildebrand, "that the comet hit somewhere between North and South America."

Scientists also reasoned that the thickest layers of ejecta—rocks that fell back to earth after the impact—would be found closer to the Crater. Investigating one suspected ejecta layer in Haiti early in 1990, Hildebrand and another Arizona colleague, David Kring, found tektites, teardrop-shape pieces of glass formed when molten rock is splashed high into the atmosphere and solidifies on its way back down. To the Arizona scientists, the tektites suggested that the impact had occurred no more than 1,000 km (622 miles) away.

A few months later, Hildebrand learned of a report made a dozen years earlier by Glen Penfield, a geophysicist who had surveyed the Yucatan Peninsula for Pemex, the Mexican national oil company. Studying both magnetic and gravity measurements, Penfield and his Pemex supervisor, Antonio Camargo, had discerned a huge circular basin buried under the peninsula and suspected it might be an impact crater. Their report was largely ignored.

Seeking out Penfield, Hildebrand teamed up with him in a search for samples of material brought up in old oil-drilling operations in the vicinity of the basin. Analyzing a few core samples, Kring discovered compelling evidence that the basin is an impact crater. Most convincing are crystals of quartz with striations that could only have been caused by powerful shock waves stemming from a great impact, as opposed to, say, from volcanic action. Finally, the dating of nearby fossil evidence has narrowed the crater's age to within 5 million years of the Great Extinction.

Unexpected confirmation of the crater site has come from a team of scientists led by Charles Duller at NASA's Ames Research Center. While examining satellite photographs of the Yucatan in the mid-1980s, the NASA scientists were intrigued by a strange semicircle of sinkhole lakes on the northern tip of the peninsula. The Chicxulub discovery could provide an explanation. Reporting in Nature magazine, the NASA team proposes that the lake pattern developed as the buried crater rim gradually collapsed, producing depressions in the overlying limestone that were filled in by groundwater.

As the evidence mounts, more researchers are convinced that the Chicxulub crater marks the impact point of the killer comet. Says Boynton: "This is nearly as close to a certainty as one can get in science." Some scientists disagree. David Archibald, a biologist at San Diego State University, believes the extinctions took place more gradually and in a complex pattern. "There is zero evidence that dinosaurs became extinct virtually overnight."

This week, at an astronomy conference in Flagstaff, Ariz., scientists will add an intriguing twist to the Alvarez scenario. Their interpretation is based on new evidence that the Cretaceous-clay boundary actually consists of two parts: a thin layer overlying a more substantial one. To Eugene Shoemaker, of the U.S. Geological Survey and a

co-author of the report, two layers indicate not one but two impacts.

As Shoemaker and his colleagues see it, a giant comet broke apart as it whipped around the sun. Over time, chunks of the comet separated but remained strung out in the same orbit. Then 65 million years ago, as the earth passed through the comet's orbit, it collided with the largest chunk, causing the Great Extinction. Perhaps only a year or two later, as the earth again entered the trail of cometary debris, it met a second, smaller chunk. Where did the second impact occur? This time no search is necessary. Shoemaker points to a well-known crater, 35 km (22 miles) across, that lies partly buried near Manson, Iowa. Its age, established by radioactive dating: 65 million years. Shoemaker believes the new findings will help persuade more scientists to "get off the fence" and side with the Alvarez theory. "Chicxulub is the smoking cannon," he says, "and Manson is the smoking pistol."

SIGNIFICANCE

Since the time of the article, scientists from around the world have measured high concentrations in iridium in a clay band from about eighteen locations throughout the world. In all cases the band dates from around 65 million years ago. In places closer to the Yucatan, like Central America, the band is approximately 1.2 inches (3 centimeters) thick. In Europe the band is only about 0.4 inches (1 centimeter) thick. The band is unique in geological studies of the Earth because it was laid down at exactly the same time throughout the world. This evidence gives additional support to the theory that the massive meteor that caused the crater in Chicxulub produced dust that surrounded the entire Earth.

After finding the impact crater in Chicxulub, most of the scientific community accepted the existence of a major meteor impact 65 million years ago, however controversy still remains as to the effect that the impact had on life on Earth. Not all scientists believe that the collision with the meteor was responsible for the mass extinctions at the KT boundary. An alternative theory involves the Deccan Traps, which are a series of volcanoes in the west central part of India. About 68 to 66 million years ago, these volcanoes underwent a period of massive eruption. They released enormous quantities of sulfur dioxide, which is toxic to air-breathing vertebrates, and carbon dioxide, which would have increased the temperature of the planet. Some paleontologists believe that these events could have led to the extinction of land-dwelling animals, or at least have had a major impact on them.

The mass extinctions of the KT boundary had a significant impact on life on Earth. Given the physical events that would have occurred in the wake of the meteor's collision with Earth, paleontologists have made predictions about the type of animals that would have been able to survive the environmental damage. These predictions suggest that the animals that persisted through the KT boundary were probably small creatures that could burrow underground during the heat wave that followed the meteor collision. In addition, these animals would have to be able to survive on insects, rather than plants, for extended periods of time. Such animals were primarily the small mammals that lived at the same time as the dinosaurs. Because approximately 75 percent of all animals and plants went extinct at the time of the collision, those that did survive the events were able to take advantage of environmental niches that had been previously occupied by other species. As a result, the mammals that survived the KT boundary underwent an enormous diversification, producing the wide variety of land-dwelling mammals, including humans, that inhabit the Earth today. In addition to the mammals that persisted following the meteor collision, some of the of the smaller dinosaurs probably also survived. Their descendents are represented by the modern birds.

FURTHER RESOURCES
Web sites

BBC Radio. "In Our Time: The KT Boundary." <http://www.bbc.co.uk/radio4/history/inourtime/inourtime_20050623.shtml> (accessed January 6, 2006).

NASA/UA Space Imagery Center. "Chicxulub Impact Event." <http://www.lpl.arizona.edu/SIC/impact_cratering/Chicxulub/Chicx_title.html> (accessed January 6, 2006).

Smithsonian National Museum of Natural History. "A Blast from the Past!" <http://www.nmnh.si.edu/paleo/blast/index.html> (accessed January 6, 2006).

Fires Raging Across Indonesia

Photograph

By: Anonymous

Date: September 22, 1997

Source: Getty Images

About the Photographer: This photograph was taken from the NOAA-14 satellite, a meteorological satellite launched for the National Oceanic and Atmospheric Administration on Dec. 12, 1994.

INTRODUCTION

This picture, taken by the U.S. National Oceanic and Atmospheric Association weather satellite NOAA-14 on September 22, 1997, combines infrared and visible-light images of the island of Borneo to show smoke from the large forest fires burning in the Indonesian part of the island at the time. (A computer has been used to draw in coastlines: the well-defined diagonal linenear the center of the image is the northwest coast of Borneo, the large gray area is smoke spreading in a northwesterly direction, the white areas are high clouds, and the darker areas are unclouded ocean.) Borneo is divided between the nations of Indonesia, Malaysia, and Brunei. The fires shown here are burning in the southeastern part of the island, the Indonesian province of Kalimantan.

In 1997 and 1998, some of the largest forest fires in history burned in Southeast Asia, most dramatically on Borneo, but also on other islands in the region. Over 12 million acres burned, with manifold consequences. Some were immediate and some long-term. Smoky haze spread over thousands of square miles of sea and land. Airports hundreds of miles away from the fires were closed because of low visibility. The Air Pollution Index exceeded 800 in the Malaysia city of Kuching (breathing air this polluted for one day is the equivalent of smoking fifty to eighty cigarettes). Record levels of air pollution were also recorded in Singapore, parts of Malaysia, and elsewhere. Schools were closed, hundreds of thousands of people were hospitalized with respiratory problems, habitat was greatly reduced for a number of endangered species (including orangutans), and regional economic losses were estimated at over $9.3 billion. A 5 percent increase in global greenhouse-gas emissions for 1997 was predicted from damage caused by the first three months of fires alone, and it was estimated that in six months the fires would release more CO_2 than is released in a year by all of western Europe's cars and fossil-fuel power stations. Large peat bogs were ignited that were capable of burning underground for years, inextinguishable even by monsoon rains. The world's largest conservation organization, the World Wildlife Federation, termed the fires a "planetary disaster."

Large fires also burned in Brazil and elsewhere in the tropics in 1997 and 1998; overall, more square miles of tropical forest burned in 1997 than in any other year on record, even 1982–1983, when 9.1 million acres of forest burned on Borneo. Large fires burned again in Indonesia in 2005, especially on Borneo and Sumatra, causing another air pollution crisis.

PRIMARY SOURCE

FIRES RAGING ACROSS INDONESIA
   See primary source image.

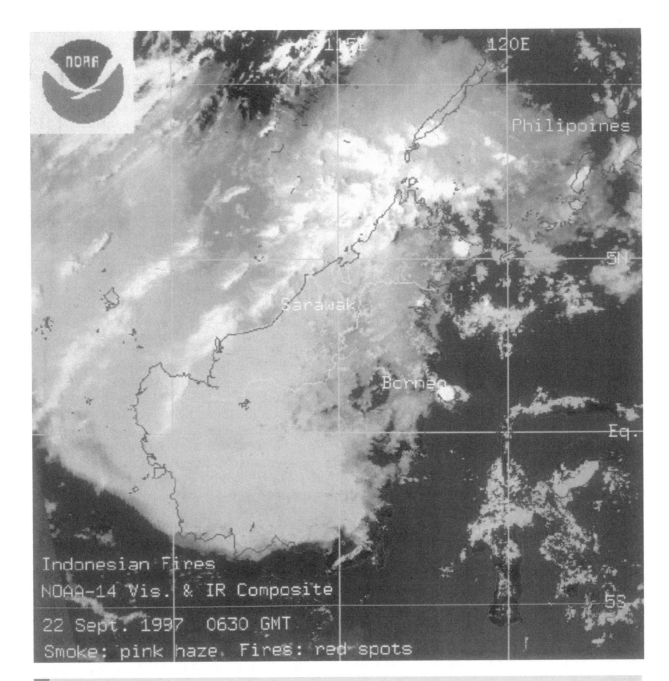

PRIMARY SOURCE

Fires Raging Across Indonesia. An image from the NOAA-14 satellite showing the fires raging across Indonesia, September 22, 1997. The darker spots show the location of the fire or the ocean, while the lighter areas represent smoke and haze. PHOTO BY SPACE FRONTIERS/HULTON ARCHIVE/GETTY IMAGES

SIGNIFICANCE

The Southeast Asian fires of 1997 and 1998 contributed to the rapid disappearance of tropical rainforests around the world, which has many causes. About seventy-five million acres of rainforest are lost each year to logging (both legal and illegal), slash-and-burn or "shifting" agriculture, conversion of forest to permanent agriculture such as palm oil plantations and soybean farms, urban development, road building, forest fires, and other threats.

Most tropical forest fires, including those depicted in this photo, are not truly natural disasters, although the 1997–1998 fires were enhanced and prolonged by drought. Such massive fires are traceable to population pressure, farming practices, ill-judged government policy, and industrial greed.

The biggest single cause of such fires is destructive logging. In their natural state, tropical forests are moist and do not usually burn easily, even in dry years, but careless logging practices change the character of the forest so that it is more vulnerable to fire. Removal of many trees lets in more light, scatters dead branches and other forestry debris on the ground, and encourages the growth of weedy pioneer species. Tropical forests are also cleared to make way for large oil palm plantations, whose product is processed to yield an oil high in vitamin K and saturated fat. Palm oil is widely used for cooking in Africa and Asia and is found in approximately 10 percent of all groceries sold in the supermarkets of industrialized countries, including lipsticks, detergents, some breads, chocolate, and many other products. Large plantations of oil-palm trees are far more vulnerable to fire than are the tropical forests that are cleared to create them. Much of the cleared land is covered with peat, which dries out when the covering forest is removed: the ground itself becomes fuel. Satellite photos showed that about 80 percent of the 1997–1998 fires in Indonesia burned in oil-palm plantations and timber concessions. Fires are also used as a weapon in land ownership disputes between large landowners and local people.

Smaller-scale land users have also started many fires in Kalimantan, where the Indonesian government has been encouraging tens of thousands of people from other islands to relocate for several decades. The new settlers often clear land with fire because it is easier than cutting, though the resulting farms are not sustainable and must be abandoned after a few years for freshly cleared land. This is "slash-and-burn" agriculture. One agricultural project, sponsored by the Indonesian government, involved the drainage of 2.5 million acres of peat bog in 1996–1997, which were then burnt to clear the peat. The stated purpose was to grow rice, but cleared peat bogs are not well-suited to rice-growing and the project (like similar projects in the past) has been largely a failure.

Massive forest fires are one result of the effort to rapidly exploit the lush but fragile forests of the tropics for profit or food without regard to the inherent limitations of these ecosystems.

FURTHER RESOURCES

Periodicals

Dell, Andrei. "Jakarta Apologizes for Raging Fires. Angry Southeast Asia Is Trapped Under an Umbrella of Pollution.> International Herald Tribune (September 17, 1997).

Mydans, Seth. "Southeast Asia Chokes on Indonesia's Forest Fires." New York Times (September 25, 1997): pg 1.

Web sites

Mongabay.com. "The Asian Forest Fires of 1997–1998." <http://rainforests.mongabay.com/08indo_fires.htm> (accessed February 9, 2006).

National Geographic News December 3, 2001. "Study Links Logging with Severity of Forest Fires." <http://news.nationalgeographic.com/news/2001/12/1203_loggingfires.html> (accessed February 9, 2006).

"The Torino Impact Hazard Scale"

Journal article

By: Richard P. Binzel

Date: 2000

Source: Binzel, Richard P. "The Torino Impact Hazard Scale." *Planetary and Space Science* 48 (2000): 297–303.

About the Author: Richard P. Binzel is a professor, chair of the program in planetary science, and Margaret MacVicar Faculty Fellow in the Department of Earth, Atmospheric, and Planetary Sciences at the Massachusetts Institute of Technology (MIT) in Cambridge, Massachusetts. His research interests include the collision of asteroids as well as the physical and surface features of the Pluto-Charon system. He earned a bachelor's degree in physics from Macalester College and a doctorate in astronomy from the University of Texas. Binzel, who published his first scientific paper at age fifteen, is a Fellow of the American Association for the Advancement of Science, the past winner of a Presidential Young Investigator Award, and recipient of the Harold C. Urey Prize from the American Astronomical Society. The International Astronomy Union has named asteroid 2873 after Binzel in recognition of his contributions to science.

INTRODUCTION

The Torino scale was devised to convey the likely severity of a collision between Earth and an asteroid or comet, known generically as a near-Earth object or NEO, in its vicinity. Although the Torino scale is often compared to the Beaufort scale used to classify wind speed or the Richter scale used to quantify earthquake magnitude, it has several differences that arise from the nature of NEO impact hazards. The scale takes its name from a 1999 scientific conference held in Torino (also known as Turin), Italy, at which it was adopted by astronomers. A modified version was released in 2005.

Used to measure wind speed, particularly at sea and in coastal areas, the Beaufort scale was created by British Admiral Sir Francis Beaufort (1774–1857). It consists of twelve so-called forces that are defined by wind speed at a height of 3.3 feet (10 meters) above the surface. Force 0 represents calm whereas Force 12, the highest level, represents hurricane-strength winds. The Beaufort scale also includes qualitative descriptors, for example "smoke rises vertically," "whole trees in motion," and "slight structural damage occurs." The Richter scale, invented by American seismologist Charles Richter (1900–1985) and his lesser-known colleague Beno Gutenberg (1889–1960), standardizes the size of earthquakes based on the maximum heights of waves on a seismogram measured by a particular kind of seismograph located 62 miles (100 kilometers) from the earthquake epicenter. Each unit on the Richter scale corresponds to a tenfold change in the height of the waves and a thirty-two-fold change in the amount of energy released. An earthquake has only one magnitude regardless of the location at which it is felt. Another scale, the Modified Mercalli Intensity Scale, is used to quantify the severity of earthquakes as a function of location. In general, maps of Mercalli earthquake intensity form a bull's eye pattern around the earthquake epicenter with intensity decreasing with distance from the epicenter. The Mercalli scale is based entirely upon qualitative descriptors (for example, "felt indoors" or "heavy furniture moved") that allow earthquake intensity to be quantified based on the observations of non-scientists. Seismologists have also developed wholly quantitative measures of earthquake intensity that can be calculated from seismograms. All three of these scales—Beaufort, Richter, and Mercalli— measure the size or intensity of an event that has occurred, and none include any consideration of the likelihood of occurrence.

The Torino scale differs from the Beaufort, Richter, and Mercalli scales because it considers the size, likelihood, and time until a potential future event. Its values range from 0, indicating that the likelihood of a collision is zero or infinitesimally small and that the size of the object is small, to 10, indicating that a collision is virtually certain and that its impacts will be catastrophic. It can be broadly subdivided into five classes: white (indicating no hazard and corresponding to level 0), green (indicating normal hazard and corresponding to level 1), yellow (indicating a hazard that merits further attention of astronomers and corresponding to levels 2–3), orange (indicating a threatening situation and corresponding to levels 5–7), and red (indicating certain collision and corresponding to levels 8–10). Torino scale levels can be changed, in general to lower levels, as astronomers learn more about the trajectories and sizes of newly discovered near Earth objects. Torino scale 10 events typically occur on average only once every 100,000 years and correspond to global catastrophes that have the potential to end civilization as we know it. The Chicxulub impact near the Yucatan Peninsula, which led to the extinction of dinosaurs and marks the boundary between the Cretaceous and Tertiary Periods (often referred to as the KT boundary, where K is an abbreviation for Cretaceous used to avoid confusion with the older Cambrian Period) was a Torino scale 10 event. The inclusion of time to likely collision is another unique feature of the Torino scale. While it is impossible to predict with any accuracy the time until a severe storm or an earthquake, once a near-Earth object is discovered astronomers can calculate the time to potential impact very accurately. A collision that is likely to occur within a century, for example, would be rated higher than one that is not anticipated to occur for several hundred years because less time is available to plan for the collision.

The likelihood of collision depends not only on the number and true paths of near-Earth objects, but also upon errors in human observations and calculations. When a near-Earth object is discovered, little is known about its path through space and it is virtually impossible to determine whether it poses a hazard to Earth. As astronomical observations continue over time, however, its path becomes more accurately known and the likelihood of collision can be refined (and generally lowered).

The highest Torino scale ranking yet assigned to a near-Earth object has been 4, for asteroid 2004 MN4 (also known as 99942 Apophis). This asteroid, which is inferred to be approximately 1,300 feet (400 meters) in diameter, will pass within 22,600 miles (36,370 kilometers) of Earth on April 13, 2029. Within a week of the Torino scale 4 rating in 2004, a review of existing data led to the conclusion that the asteroid will not strike Earth. Its current Torino scale rating is 1.

THE TORINO IMPACT HAZARD SCALE
Abstract

Newly discovered asteroids and comets have inherent uncertainties in their orbit determinations owing to the natural limits of positional measurement precision and the finite lengths of orbital arcs over which determinations are made. For some objects making predictable future close approaches to the Earth, orbital uncertainties may be such that a collision with the Earth cannot be ruled out. Careful and responsible communication between astronomers and the public is required for reporting these predictions and a 0–10 point hazard scale, reported inseparably with the date of close encounter, is recommended as a simple and efficient tool for this purpose. The goal of this scale, endorsed as the Torino Impact Hazard Scale, is to place into context the level of public concern that is warranted for any close encounter event within the next century. Concomitant reporting of the close encounter date further conveys the sense of urgency that is warranted. The Torino Scale value for a close approach event is based upon both collision probability and the estimated kinetic energy (collision consequence), where the scale value can change as probability and energy estimates are refined by further data. On the scale, Category 1 corresponds to collision probabilities that are comparable to the current annual chance for any given size impactor. Categories 8–10 correspond to certain (probability > 99%) collisions having increasingly dire consequences. While close approaches falling Category 0 may be no cause for noteworthy public concern, there remains a professional responsibility to further refine orbital parameters for such objects and a figure of merit is suggested for evaluating such objects. Because impact predictions represent a multi-dimensional problem, there is no unique or perfect translation into a one-dimensional system such as the Torino Scale. These limitations are discussed. © 2000 Elsevier Science Ltd. All rights reseved.

1. Introduction

With the advent of expanded surveys for the discovery of asteroids and comets in the vicinity of the Earth, (collectively known as near-Earth objects or NEOs), there are increasing numbers of predictable close approaches to the Earth. Because orbit determinations are limited by finite precision in positional measurements and finite lengths of measured orbital arcs, there are natural uncertainties associated with close approach predictions. When an NEO is recognized to have a future close approach to Earth and has an orbital position uncertainty that intersects the known location of the Earth on a specific date, a collision probability can be calculated. (In general, the larger the orbital uncertainty, characterized as an "error ellipse," the lower the probability of a collision). While astronomers have a responsibility for publicly communicating the dates and circumstances of these close approach events, which typically have very low collision probabilities, this responsibility poses a risk communication challenge. The challenge arises because collisions of asteroids and comets with the Earth represent a topic so provocative and so prone to sensationalism that great care must be taken to assess and publicly communicate the realistic hazard (or non hazard) posed by such events. At the heart of this risk communication challenge resides the fact that low probability/high consequence events are by their very nature not within the realm of common human experience. Risk communication about asteroid and comet encounters is further different from other natural hazard predictions in that typically it is possible to specify with precision the date of the potential hazard, even if it is decades into the future.

The risk communication challenge posed by asteroid and comet close encounters was recognized by attendees of the "International Monitoring Programs for Asteroid and Comet Threat" (IMPACT) workshop held in Torino, Italy on 1–4 June, 1999. This paper reports the outcome of a proposal presented by the author for a simple hazard scale system designed to meet this challenge. The resulting system, now known as the Torino Impact Hazard Scale (named in recognition of the workshop's endorsement and the historical asteroid science contributions of the Torino Observatory), was discussed and debated and endorsed by the workshop sponsors, select science journalists, and was approved for public release by officials of the International Astronomical Union. The genesis of the Torino Scale can be traced to a proposal (Binzel, 1997) made at the 1995 United Nations International Conference on Near-Earth Objects.

2. Development of the Torino Scale

It is desirable that any system for risk communication should: (a) communicate the time window or exact date of the potential hazard; (b) provide a context for understanding the full range of the potential hazard; (c) have a rigorous basis in scientific calculation; and (d) be understandable at many different levels. Reporting the date of the close encounter satisfies the first requirement. A one-dimensional scale such as the 0–10 system adopted here, satisfies the other three requirements. Thus, responsible risk communication of asteroid and comet close encounters *requires* the inseparable reporting of both the encounter date and its hazard scale value. The 0–10 Torino Scale has qualities similar to other systems that are familiar to the public, such as the Richter scale for earthquakes and the Beaufort scale for wind velocities. By utilizing a one-dimensional scale bounded between 0 and 10, where 0 is "good" and 10 is "bad," the reporting of a single number provides, at a very basic level, some immediate sense of context for the hazard even if thee is no deep understanding of the construction of the scale. The combined reporting of the date of the encounter provides the most simple method for assessing the time interval until the event and hence the relative urgency.

Assessing the close approach of an NEO is a multi-dimensional problem, and as such, it is a problem that cannot be translated uniquely or perfectly into a one-dimensional scale. Beyond the encounter date, which is always reported as a coupled parameter, the multiple dimensions to be considered for translation include: the impact probability of the object, the kinetic energy of the object, the potential consequences should an impact occur, the time horizon for forecasting all potential impacts, and conveyance as to whether the specific threat posed is significantly higher or lower than that posed by the multitude of similar-sized objects that remain undiscovered. Although the one-dimensional 0–10 Torino Scale is inescapably a non-unique translation of these multi-dimensional aspects, when combined with the encounter date it does represent a carefully considered and endorsed system for clear and efficient risk communication about asteroid and comet close encounters. . . .

3. Application and understanding of the Torino Scale

For an object making a close approach to Earth on a specified and reported date, assigning a corresponding Torino Scale value requires two numbers as input. The first is the best available number for the object's collision probability on the date of encounter. The second is the best available calculation (or estimate) for the object's kinetic energy. (Kinetic energy is proportional to mass times the square of velocity. The velocity is accurately calculable from the orbit, while the mass must be estimated from direct physical measurements.) The input numbers for collision probability and kinetic energy pinpoint a location within a labeled region, thereby yielding the Torino Scale value. The Torino Scale value is always reported as an integer. For solutions that place an object at a boundary between categories, or whose error bars substantially overlap more than one boundary, then a range (such as "1 to 2") may be reported. Solutions that place an object in the Category 0 region immediately below 3 and/or

8, might be referred to as a "possible 3" or "possible 8" if there is sufficient uncertainty in the kinetic energy that those ultimate categorizations are not reasonably ruled out. For an object that makes multiple close approaches over a set of dates, a Torino Scale value should be determined for each approach and reported with each date. It may be convenient to summarize the overall hazard posed by such an object by the greatest Torino Scale value within the set. The time window for the application of the Torino Scale is for close encounter events occurring one century into the future.

There are several essential aspects to the application and understanding of the Torino Scale. Primary among these is to understand that the Torino Scale is a *predictive* system whose application requires the specification of a close encounter date and that this system is based on observational measurements that accumulate and improve over time. Because the input parameters of collision probability and kinetic energy are calculated from observational data, the Torino Scale value can (and will) change as significant new data are obtained. In contrast, the precision of orbital mechanics will seldom result in substantial refinements in the date of any individual close approach event after the initial determination. Change in an object's Torino Scale value is inevitable since the ultimate outcome for any close approach event is binary: either it will hit the Earth or it won't. The challenge for astronomers is to obtain sufficient information on any object to place it securely within Category 0 or to conclusively determine that the object falls within the "certain collision" range (Categories 8–10). Fortunately, the odds tremendously favor the ultimate placement of objects within Category 0. Understanding and conveying the intrinsic variability that is inherent within a predictive scale is essential to mitigate the perception that scientists previously "got the answer wrong" when additional data allow revised Torino Scale value to be reported for a given encounter.

Finally, it must be strongly re-emphasized that the reporting of just a single Torino Scale value cannot convey, does not convey, and is not intended to convey, all of the information that is necessary for clear and responsible public communication regarding a future close encounter event. Most specifically and most importantly, the encounter date(s) always must be specified concomitantly so that an appropriate sense of urgency can be conveyed. In addition to this inseparable pairing of the Torino Scale value and the date, responsible public communication should also include: the name of the object, its estimated size, and the calculated collision probability value for each close encounter date.

For the unfortunate case of an event on a specified date that is a "certain collision," then a single Torino Scale value (such as 8–10) is wholly recognized as being grossly insufficient for communicating the consequences to a concerned public or for providing a basis for formulating a response by local, national, or international governmental agencies. Many additional parameters come into play for evaluating the urgency and likely consequences of a certain collision. These include: the impact date (and hence the time remaining), the exact location and nature of the impact site, details regarding the expected consequences of impact blast damage or tsunami effects, the exact nature of the colliding body, impact angle, season, etc. All of these details can only be addressed through extensive advisories based on the best available collision models and expert analyses. ''Certain collisions'' that fall just below 1 MT in estimated energy, and hence within Category 0, will also require substantial public advisories to address the level of concern that is merited, where these may be communicated as borderline ''possible 8'' or ''unlikely 8'' cases that have minimal likelihood of significant local damage.

4. Multi-level communication of the Torino Scale

A fundamental goal in the development of a risk communication tool such as the Torino Scale is to establish a system that can convey information at a variety of different levels, and in particular, provide information and context beyond the simple 0–10 scale value. To accomplish this goal, a color-coded text graphic for the Torino Scale, was developed as the primary ''public release'' product. Within this graphic, each scale value has a color code progressing from white to green to yellow to orange to red that attempts to further convey a context for the level of concern merited by a close encounter on a specified date. A subjective statement for the level of concern that is intended to be conveyed by each color appears as text along the left side. These levels range from (white) ''Events Having No Likely Consequences'' to (green) ''Events Meriting Careful Monitoring'' to (yellow) ''Events Meriting Concern'' to (orange) ''Threatening Events'' to (red) ''Certain Collisions.''

A still higher level of communication is provided by a text block for each scale value that provides a few sentences of qualitative explanation. Category 0 explains that the object is too small or the chance of a collision is too low to merit any practical concern. Category 1 attempts to convey the sense of a relatively normal close approach event that is sufficient to merit careful monitoring and refinement of the orbit, but not sufficient to merit any particular public concern. Category 2 also attempts to convey the sense of a ''normal'' close approach event, but one that merits some increased measure of concern relative to Category 1. For Categories 3–7, each explanation includes an indication of what the level of consequence would be in the case that the specified close encounter event becomes a certain collision. This indication is necessary

because the compression of the multi-dimensional problem into a one-dimensional scale results in objects (having constant kinetic energy but evolving probabilities) not necessarily progressing uniformly upward or downward in scale value. Within the red zone that describes ''Certain Collisions'' (Categories 8–10) the qualitative terms for collision consequences escalate from ''destruction'' to ''devastation'' to ''catastrophe'' following the kinetic energy transitions described by Chapman and Morrison (1994). The explanations for these highest categories also attempt to convey information on how often such events are likely to occur, thereby providing an additional sense of context for the overall problem of impact hazards.

The same color-coding developed for the public release text graphic is also applied to the hazard space plot that defines the Torino Scale values. This resulting color-coded plot similarly conveys context of the problem at multiple levels by adding a text description for each color code and labeling the potential consequences associated with each kinetic energy range. This color-coded plot has also been developed as a ''public release'' product, intended to be interpretable by the scientifically interested laymen.

5. Public versus professional use of the Torino Scale

It is important to emphasize that the primary purpose for the development and dissemination of the Torino Scale is to provide a tool for *public* communication and assessment for asteroid and comet impact hazard predictions in the next century. Professional astronomers can use much more sophisticated metrics that assess the need for follow-up observations and orbital refinements for objects that fall within Category 0 but with collision probabilities that are not mathematically zero.

6. Conclusion

The establishment of the Torino Scale as a tool and common lexicon for public communication and assessment of NEO close encounter predictions helps to fulfill the responsibility of astronomers to provide clear and consistent public information on celestial impact hazards. When coupled with a close encounter date that conveys the relative urgency, the single most important aspect of the Torino Scale is that it provides an immediate sense of context for the potential hazard of the encounter by reporting a value on a 10 point scale. Additional color coding and descriptive wording allow a higher level understanding of the context for any scale value. The Torino Scale has natural limitations that arise from it being a one-dimensional translation of a multi-dimensional problem. Therefore responsible public communication that announces the dates of close encounter events that represent serious potential threats, requires significantly more hazard context information than just a Torino Scale value. Similarly, astronomers have a responsibility to monitor and refine orbits for all objects that can make future close approaches. Professional interest and professional communication toward this task is by no means intended to be limited by the establishment of the Torino Scale. . . .

SIGNIFICANCE

Although the Torino scale has not seen wide use, and has not established itself in the vernacular as solidly as the Beaufort or Richter scales, it establishes a rational framework for the analysis of and response to events that are rare but potentially catastrophic. Its potential utility lies in its ability to convey complicated and sometimes subtle information about the likelihood of future events in a simple format understandable to politicians, policy makers, and other non-scientists. Because the scale deals with future, rather than past or present, events, Torino scale ratings can be modified as additional information about newly discovered near-Earth objects becomes available.

FURTHER RESOURCES

Books

Peebles, Curtis. *Asteroids: A History*. Washington, DC: Smithsonian Books, 2001.

Web sites

National Aeronautics and Space Administration. "Near Earth Object Program." <http://neo.jpl.nasa.gov/torino_scale.html> (accessed January 27, 2006).

National Aeronautics and Space Administration. "Near Earth Object Program, Radar Observations Refine the Future Motion of Asteroid 2004 MN4." <http://neo.jpl.nasa.gov/news/news149.html> (accessed January 27, 2006).

Space.com. "Measuring Asteroid Threats." <http://www.space.com/scienceastronomy/astronomy/torino_scale.html> (accessed January 27, 2006).

Climate Change Impacts on the United States

The Potential Consequences of Climate Variability and Change

Report

By: National Assessment Synthesis Team, U.S. Global Change Research Program

Date: June 12, 2000

Source: National Assessment Synthesis Team. "Climate Change Impacts on the United States: The Potential Consequences of Climate Variability and Change." U.S. Global Change Research Program. June 12, 2000.

About the Organization: The National Assessment Synthesis Team was chartered by the Federal Advisory Committee Act. The Team was composed of thirteen members from academic institutions, environmental agencies and industry. All of the members had extensive experience in environmental science and/or environmental policy. The committee was co-chaired by Jerry M. Melillo and Anthony C. Janetos. Melillo was research scientist at The Ecosystems Center of the Marine Biological Laboratory in Woods Hole, Massachusetts where his research focused on global change in the context of forest ecosystems. Janetos was a Senior Vice President for an independent policy research institute, the World Resources Institute. His scientific research involved assessment of land-use change using remote sensing.

INTRODUCTION

Climate change refers to the effects of introducing gases into the Earth's atmosphere that have the ability to hold heat, much as a greenhouse holds warmth within its glass walls. These gases are referred to as greenhouse gases, and they enter the atmosphere when fossil fuels are burned and via some industrial and manufacturing processes. The key greenhouse gases are carbon dioxide, methane, nitrous oxide, hydrofluorocarbons, perfluorocarbons, and sulphur hexafluoride. These gases have accumulated in the atmosphere since the Industrial Revolution, increasing the average temperature of the Earth. Global temperature increases have complex effects on various aspects of the environment and the economy of the United States, some of which are difficult to predict.

In order to try to understand the effects of climate change in the United States, Congress passed The Global Change Research Act of 1990. The Act established the United States Global Change Research Program (USGCRP), which was responsible for coordinating research into the causes and effects of global climate change. The Act also requires an assessment that integrates and evaluates the major findings of the Program. The report is required to discuss the effects of climate change on several aspects of life in the United States, including agriculture, energy, land and water resources, human health, transportation, biological diversity, and social systems. The report is also required to review expected trends in global climate change and its effects during the next twenty-five to one hundred years. The Act mandates updated scientific assessments at least every four years.

In November 2000 the National Assessment Synthesis team submitted its first two reports to Congress: a National Assessment Overview and a National Assessment Foundation Report. The 154-page Overview summarized the collective research and analysis of environmental scientists and policy makers regarding the effects and impacts of climate change on the United States. An excerpt of the report summarizing the National Assessment Synthesis Team's major conclusions regarding climate change in the United States is included.

The longer National Assessment Foundation Report, comprising more than six hundred pages, includes the scientific information and research used to draw conclusions and to develop the trends described in the Overview. Much of the work included in the Overview and the Foundation Report is the result of extensive workshops with scientists, policy makers and the general public throughout the United States. The project divided the issues associated with climate change into five sectors: agriculture, forests, water, human health, and coastal and marine resources. Furthermore, twenty different regions within the United States were identified for assessment.

■ PRIMARY SOURCE

Long-term observations confirm that our climate is now changing at a rapid rate. Over the 20th century, the average annual US temperature has risen by almost 1 °F (0.6 °C) and precipitation has increased nationally by 5 to 10%, mostly due to increases in heavy downpours. These trends are most apparent over the past few decades. The science indicates that the warming in the 21st century will be significantly larger than in the 20th century. Scenarios examined in this Assessment, which assume no major interventions to reduce continued growth of world greenhouse gas emissions, indicate that temperatures in the US will rise by about 5–9 °F (3–5 °C) on average in the next 100 years, which is more than the projected global increase. This rise is very likely to be associated with more extreme precipitation and faster evaporation of water, leading to greater frequency of both very wet and very dry conditions.

This Assessment reveals a number of national-level impacts of climate variability and change including impacts to natural ecosystems and water resources. Natural ecosystems appear to be the most vulnerable to the harmful effects of climate change, as there is often little that can be done to help them adapt to the projected speed and amount of change. Some ecosystems that are already constrained by climate, such as alpine meadows in the Rocky Mountains, are likely to face extreme stress, and disappear entirely in some places. It is likely that other more widespread ecosystems will also be vulnerable to climate change. One of the climate scenarios used in this Assessment suggests the potential for the forests of the Southeast to break up into a mosaic of forests, savannas, and grasslands. Climate scenarios suggest likely changes in the species composition of the Northeast forests, including the loss of sugar maples. Major alterations to natural ecosystems due to climate change could possibly have negative consequences for our economy, which depends in part on the sustained bounty of our nation's lands, waters, and native plant and animal communities.

A unique contribution of this first US Assessment is that it combines national-scale analysis with an examination of the potential impacts of climate change on different regions of the US. For example, sea-level rise will very likely cause further loss of coastal wetlands (ecosystems that provide vital nurseries and habitats for many fish species) and put coastal communities at greater risk of storm surges, especially in the Southeast. Reduction in snowpack will very likely alter the timing and amount of water supplies, potentially exacerbating water shortages and conflicts, particularly throughout the western US. The melting of glaciers in the high-elevation West and in Alaska represents the loss or diminishment of unique national treasures of the American landscape. Large increases in the heat index (which combines temperature and humidity) and increases in the frequency of heat waves are very likely.

These changes will, at minimum, increase discomfort, particularly in cities. It is very probable that continued thawing of permafrost and melting of sea ice in Alaska will further damage forests, buildings, roads, and coastlines, and harm subsistence livelihoods. In various parts of the nation, cold-weather recreation such as skiing will very likely be reduced, and air conditioning usage will very likely increase.

Highly managed ecosystems appear more robust, and some potential benefits have been identified. Crop and forest productivity is likely to increase in some areas for the next few decades due to increased carbon dioxide in the atmosphere and an extended growing season. It is possible that some US food exports could increase, depending on impacts in other food-growing regions around the world. It is also possible that a rise in crop production in fertile areas could cause prices to fall, benefiting consumers. Other benefits that are possible include extended seasons for construction and warm weather recreation, reduced heating requirements, and reduced cold-weather mortality.

Climate variability and change will interact with other environmental stresses and socioeconomic changes. Air and water pollution, habitat fragmentation, wetland loss, coastal erosion, and reductions in fisheries are likely to be compounded by climate-related stresses. An aging populace nationally, and rapidly growing populations in cities, coastal areas, and across the South and West are social factors that interact with and alter sensitivity to climate variability and change.

There are also very likely to be unanticipated impacts of climate change during the next century. Such "surprises" may stem from unforeseen changes in the physical climate system, such as major alterations in ocean circulation, cloud distribution, or storms; and unpredicted biological consequences of these physical climate changes, such as massive dislocations of species or pest outbreaks. In addition, unexpected social or economic change, including major shifts in wealth, technology, or political priorities, could affect our ability to respond to climate change.

Greenhouse gas emissions lower than those assumed in this Assessment would result in reduced impacts. The signatory nations of the Framework Convention on Climate Change are negotiating the path they will ultimately take. Even with such reductions, however, the planet and the nation are certain to experience more than a century of climate change, due to the long lifetimes of greenhouse gases already in the atmosphere and the momentum of the climate system. Adapting to a changed climate is consequently a necessary component of our response strategy.

Adaptation measures can, in many cases, reduce the magnitude of harmful impacts, or take advantage of beneficial impacts. For example, in agriculture, many farmers will probably be able to alter cropping and management practices. Roads, bridges, buildings, and other long-lived infrastructure can be designed taking projected climate change into account. Adaptations, however, can involve trade-offs, and do involve costs. For example, the benefits of building sea walls to prevent sea-level rise from disrupting human coastal communities will need to be weighed against the economic and ecological costs of seawall construction. The ecological costs could be high as seawalls prevent the inland shifting of coastal wetlands in response to sea-level rise, resulting in the loss of vital fish and bird habitat and other wetland functions, such as protecting shorelines from damage due to storm surges. Protecting against any increased risk of water-borne and insect-borne diseases will require diligent maintenance of our public health system. Many adaptations, notably those that seek to reduce other environmental stresses such as pollution and habitat fragmentation, will have beneficial effects beyond those related to climate change.

Vulnerability in the US is linked to the fates of other nations, and we cannot evaluate national consequences due to climate variability and change without also considering the consequences of changes elsewhere in the world. The US is linked to other nations in many ways, and both our vulnerabilities and our potential responses will likely depend in part on impacts and responses in other nations. For example, conflicts or mass migrations resulting from resource limits, health, and environmental stresses in more vulnerable nations could possibly pose challenges for global security and US policy. Effects of climate variability and change on US agriculture will depend critically on changes in agricultural productivity elsewhere, which can shift international patterns of food supply and demand. Climate-induced changes in water resources available for power generation, transportation, cities, and agriculture are likely to raise potentially delicate diplomatic issues with both Canada and Mexico.

This Assessment has identified many remaining uncertainties that limit our ability to fully understand the spectrum of potential consequences of climate change for our nation. To address these uncertainties, additional research is needed to improve understanding of ecological and social processes that are sensitive to climate, application of climate scenarios and reconstructions of past climates to impacts studies, and assessment strategies and methods. Results from these research efforts will inform future assessments that will continue the process of building our understanding of humanity's impacts on climate, and climate's impacts on us.

SIGNIFICANCE

The USGCRP Assessment reports were considered extremely successful by government agencies, non-governmental agencies and academic institutions. The general consensus was that the reports provided a much-needed and well-researched assessment of the impacts of global change in the United States. In addition, a major achievement of the Assessment reports was the development of an evaluation process that linked a broad spectrum of people concerned about the effects of climate change. The types of stakeholders involved in developing the Assessment included state, local, tribal, and Federal governments, businesses, labor associations, academics, non-profit organizations, and the public. By bringing together such a wide cross-section of stakeholders, the Assessment created an important dialog concerning the impacts of climate change. This dialog helped to focus scientific research to integrate the needs of these stakeholders by providing important information to policy makers, civil planners, managers, and the public.

The Assessment resulted in a set of major conclusions. It reports that the impacts of climate change will significantly affect Americans, however these effects depend on the location, time period and geographic scale considered. Some places will experience larger impacts than other places. The effects of global change should not be considered in an isolated manner, but rather in the context of multiple-stresses. Urban areas emerged as a major concern because most Americans live in cities and because climate change will tend to amplify stresses that already exist in urban areas such as water and air pollution. The effects of increased drought and changes in snowpack, along with other issues related to water quality, were also major concerns associated with global climate change. The Assessment identified vulnerabilities related to human health, which will likely increase with climate change. Finally, the Assessment concluded that many ecosystems will be negatively impacted because of climate change. However, the report did suggest that in the near-term, agriculture and forests should benefit from the increased concentration of carbon dioxide in the atmosphere. One of the greatest impacts of global change is the potential for effects that cannot be predicted because of the complexity of the Earth's systems.

The release of the USGCRP reports was timed so that the conclusions could be incorporated into the Third Assessment Report of the Intergovernmental Panel on Climate Change (IPCC), which is a document on the status of global change produced by the United Nations Environmental Programme and the World Meteorological Organization. The IPCC Report was able to incorporate significant detail regarding impacts of climate change in North America because of the input of the USGCRP Assessment reports.

In 2002, President George W. Bush created a new, cabinet-level program called the Climate Change Science Program (CCSP), which oversees the USGCRP. The CCSP took over the responsibility for producing the global change research plan every four years as required by the Global Change Research Act of 1990. In 2003, the CCSP assembled a conference to set their strategy for developing the research plan. They created a set of twenty-one topics, called Synthesis and Assessment Products, that would satisfy the Act's requirements. The CCSP was unable to meet their deadline of November 2004 for submission of these Synthesis and Assessment Products. In July 2005, the CCSP scheduled the release of these products between 2006 and 2008.

Rajendra K. Pachauri, chairman of the Intergovernmental Panal on Climate Change, at the 10th International Convention on Climate Change, Buenos Aires, December 14, 2004. AP IMAGES

One of the major reasons given by the CCSP for its failure to fulfill the requirements of the Global Change Research Act of 1990 is that the scope of delivering a comprehensive and accurate assessment on the impacts of climate change in the United States is extremely complex and broad in scope. This acknowledged difficulty emphasizes the great value of the USGCRP reports, which incorporated a diverse range of scientific and policy data and drew careful and significant conclusions based on the acquired information.

FURTHER RESOURCES

Web sites

Government Accountability Office. "Letter Concerning Climate Change Assessment: Administration Did Not Meet Reporting Deadline." <http://www.gao.gov/new.items/d05338r.pdf> (accessed January 6, 2006).

U.S. Climate Change Science Program. <http://www.climate-science.gov> (accessed January 6, 2006).

U.S. Global Change Research Program. "National Assessment of the Potential Consequences of Climate Variability and Change." <http://www.usgcrp.gov/usgcrp/nacc/default.htm> (accessed January 6, 2006).

"The New View of Natural Climate Variation"

Journal article

By: David E. Wojick

Date: January 2003

Source: Wojick, David L. "The New View of Natural Climate Variation." American Petroleum Institute, January 2003.

About the Author: David E. Wojick received his Bachelor of Science degree in civil engineering from Carnegie-Mellon University in 1964 and his Doctor of Philosophy degree from the University of Pittsburgh in 1974, where he studied mathematical logic and conceptual analysis. His doctoral thesis involved the analysis of scientific and technological breakthroughs. Wojick was a water resources engineer for the Civil Works program of the Army Corps of Engineers from 1965 to 1970; a faculty member of Carnegie-Mellon University from 1970 to 1976; and the head of the independent consulting and research group Adams & Wojick Associates from 1981 to 1999. He is also the founder and president of ClimateChangeDebate.org; a science journalist who covers climate change topics for *Electricity Daily*; and a consultant to the energy industry. His professional expertise includes issue analysis, strategic planning, and technology forecasting, especially with regard to climate science.

INTRODUCTION

The article "The New View of Natural Climate Variation: Fundamental Climate Science Issues Raised in Six Major National Academy of Science Studies" is the result of a study conducted by environmental consultant Dr. Wojick. In the article, he focused on the important uncertainties in the area of worldwide climate changes. The study was prompted by an announcement of the President George W. Bush administration that a critical review of the U.S. Global Change Research Program would be soon performed. Central to the scientific review performed by Wojick was the resolution of various major uncertainties with respect to world climate variations. The article was the basis for Wojick's presentation to the Climate Change Task Force, which met on January 14, 2003.

PRIMARY SOURCE

Six different National Academy of Science [NAS] reports since 1998 have identified very fundamental questions that have to be faced when making a credible assessment of climate change—and our current ability to understand and project possible change in the future. In many instances new scientific research is beginning to address some of these key issues, but just beginning.

When viewed in their entirety, these NAS reports go to the very core of the question of "uncertainty" in climate modeling. Traditionally, "uncertainty" has been interpreted as an "error bar"—for a given increase in Greenhouse Gas (GHG) emissions, what is the range of likely and/or potential increases in global temperature?

The issues in the NAS reports and recent research are far more fundamental and clash with an underlying premise of much climate modeling over the past decade—that climate over the past century and a half has been effectively constant and any changes are primarily because of man's activity. As stated by the National Academy of Sciences: "The evidence of natural variations in the climate system—which was once assumed to be relatively stable—clearly reveals that climate has changed, is changing, and will continue to do so with or without anthropogenic influences." (*Dec-Cen Variability*, Summary.)

If climate has been as volatile on decade to century or longer scales as is now become apparent, due to multiple mechanisms, then the following deep questions arise:

- Do we have an accurate understanding of past climate changes?
- Do we know what has caused past changes in climate?
- Do we know why climate is changing today?
- Do we know how to model these mechanisms?
- Can we separate the impact of these new factors from the potential influence of greenhouse gas emissions or other potential anthropogenic impacts?

What is so important is that this understanding—of what we do not understand—is a recent development.

The difference our newfound lack of understanding makes is also simple. In a naturally changing climate rather than a stable climate, it is far more difficult to tell if and how human activities have had a discernible influence on climate, or how human activities may influence the future. Since we do not yet know why climate changes, we do not yet know why it has changed in the last century, or even how it has changed. We also cannot yet say how it is likely to change in the future.

The conclusion is obvious. We must now direct our climate change research effort to confront our newly found lack of understanding. A decade of research has taught us what we don't know.

It has taught us important questions. Now we must seek the answers. This report has a single goal. That goal is to catalog key uncertainties in a naturally varying climate system—uncertainties that range from observation to explanation to modeling—that have been clearly documented in at least six major studies by the U.S. National Academy of Sciences. These studies were:

- *Abrupt Climate Change: Inevitable Surprises* (2001);
- *Climate Change Science: An Analysis of Some Key Questions* (2001);
- *Decade-to-Century-Scale Climate Variability and Change: A Science Strategy* (1998);
- *Global Environmental Change: Research Pathways for the Next Decade* (1999);
- *Issues in the Integration of Research and Operational Satellite Systems for Climate Research: Part I. Science and Design* (2000);
- *Research: Part I. Science and Design* (2000); and
- *The Atmospheric Sciences: Entering the Twenty-First Century* (1998).

The descriptions of these key uncertainties have been scattered within these reports, numbering thousands of pages, and thus are not clearly or widely recognized.

So, in keeping with the rest of this report, we here present a set of quotes from these major NAS studies that clearly state what we have just said—we do not know the extent of climate change in the past, we do not know why climate changes, and we must focus our research on this issue. Only then can we integrate the potential role of past increases in GHG emissions into recent climate history, and only then can we begin to assess the outlook for future climate.

"Climate research on decade to century ("dec-cen") timescales is relatively new. Only recently have we obtained sufficient high-resolution paleoclimate records, and acquired faster computers and improved models allowing long-term simulations, to examine past change on these timescales. This research has led to genuinely novel insights, most notably that the past assumption of a relatively stable climate state on dec-cen timescales since the last glaciation is no longer a viable tenet. The paleorecords reveal considerable variability occurring over all timescales, while modeling and theoretical studies indicate modes of internal and coupled variability driving variations over dec-cen timescales as well." (*Pathways*, p. 129.)

"Thus, dec-cen climate research is only at the beginning of its learning curve, with dramatic findings appearing at an impressive rate. In this area even the most fundamental scientific issues are evolving rapidly. Adaptability to new directions and opportunities is therefore imperative to advance understanding of climate variability and change on these timescales." (*Pathways*, p. 129.)

"To date, we do not have a comprehensive inventory of global patterns, nor do we understand their mechanisms, couplings, longevity, or full implications for climate predictions." (*Pathways*, p. 140.)

"The new paradigm of an abruptly changing climatic system has been well established by research over the last decade, but this new thinking is little known and scarcely appreciated in the wider community of natural and social scientists and policymakers." (*Abrupt Climate Change*, p. 1.)

"The climate change and variability that we experience will be a commingling of the ever changing natural climate state with any anthropogenic change. While we are ultimately interested in understanding and predicting how climate will change, regardless of the cause, an ability to differentiate anthropogenic change from natural variability is fundamental to help guide policy decisions, treaty negotiations, and adaptation versus mitigation strategies. Without a clear understanding of how climate has changed naturally in the past, and the mechanisms involved, our ability to interpret any future change will be significantly confounded and our ability to predict future change severely curtailed." (*Dec-Cen Variability*, Preface.)

"Large gaps in our knowledge of interannual and decade-to-century natural variability hinder our ability to provide credible predictive skill or to distinguish the role of human activities from natural variability. Narrowing these uncertainties and applying our understanding define the mission of climate and climate change research and education for the twenty-first century." (*Atmospheric Sciences*, p. 278.)

"For example, is the accelerated warming the result of natural variability caused by an unusually persistent coincidence of the NAO [North Atlantic Oscillation] and PNA [Pacific-North American teleconnection], or the result of the modification of natural modes (patterns) by anthropogenic changes in radiative forcing that alter the phasing, or some combination of both of these? Likewise, there appears to have been a distinct change in the character (frequency and severity) of El Niño and La Niña events during this period of accelerated warming. Is this a consequence of the influence of anthropogenic change on the dominant natural modes of climate variability, or is it a natural, low-frequency (dec-cen) modulation of a high-frequency (interannual) mode?" (*Dec-Cen Variability*, Summary.)

"The characteristic scales of climate variability demand long time series in order to determine the critical processes as well as to separate natural variability from anthropogenic influences. Unlike weather forecasting, the interval between stimulus and response can be years to centuries. With a high level of background variability, subtle changes in Earth's climate system can be difficult to detect." (*Integration of Research and Satellites*, p. 8.)

"A satisfactory demonstration of secular trends in the Earth's climate system...requires analysis at the forefront of science and statistical analysis. Model predictions have been available for decades, but a clear demonstration of their validity, a demonstration that will convince a reasoned critic on cross examination, is not yet available. This is not in itself either a statement of failure or a significant surprise. Rather, it is a measure of the intellectual depth of the problem and the need for carefully orchestrated, long term observations." (*Pathways*, p. 522.)

"Climate variability and change on decade to century timescales involves all of the elements of the U.S. Global Change Research Program: natural and anthropogenic variability and change; past, present, and future observational networks and databases; modeling requirements; and physical, chemical, biological, and social sciences, with considerable attention to the human dimensions of climate change." (*Pathways*, pp. 129–130.)

"Recommendation 1: Research priorities and resource allocations must be reassessed, with the objective of tying available resources directly to the major unanswered Scientific Questions identified in this report. The USGCRP's research strategy should be centered on sharply defined and effectively executed programs and should recognize the essential need for focused observations, both space-based and in situ, to test scientific hypotheses and document change." (*Pathways*, p. 521.)

"Recommendation 2: Following on Recommendation 1, the national strategy of the USGCRP for Earth observations must be restructured and must be driven by the key unanswered Scientific Questions." (*Pathways*, p. 523.)

Natural climate variability is a key element in the "major unanswered Scientific Questions" referred to above and is the topic of this report. Taken together, they present a new view of climate change, a view dominated by natural variation, in ways we do not yet understand. The implications of this new view of natural variability and the NAS studies is clear and stated succinctly in *Climate Change Science: An Analysis of Some Key Questions*:

"Predictions of global climate change will require major advances in understanding and modeling..." (*Climate Change Science*, p 23.)

SIGNIFICANCE

Wojick based his paper on six different National Academy of Science (NAS) reports that were published between 1998 and 2003. Within these NAS reports,

fundamental questions were identified whose solutions were seen by Wojick as key information needed before valid scientific assessments could be made of global climate changes in the past, present, and future. Within his article, Wojick systematically described the greatest climate science uncertainties faced by humanity. The following questions are seen by Wojick as the major uncertainties:

- What is the state of the Earth, present and past?
- How much and when has the Earth warmed?
- Why does climate change?
- How does climate work?
- Can we predict climate?
- How uncertain are we?

Wojick went on to state in his report some of the principle variations that naturally causes changes in worldwide climate. These principle variations include:

- Aerosol forcing mechanisms (methods that increase the types and amounts of microscopic airborne particles)
- Biospheric (which is the layer of air, soil, and water that is capable of supporting life)
- Cryogenic (materials at very low temperatures such as ice sheets, along with conditions involving land-ice layers)
- Direct and indirect solar energy (such as the effects of solar winds on the Earth's magnetic field)
- Hydrologic cycle (the various movements of water above and below the Earth's surface, including its storage, runoff, and changes within permafrost)
- Internal oscillations of the Earth such as PDO (Pacific Decadal Oscillation), NAO (North Atlantic Oscillation), AO (Artic Oscillation), ENSO (El Niño/Southern Oscillation), and Milankovitch Cycles (variations in the Earth's orbit)
- Ocean (such as water circulation and, especially, deepwater formations)
- Surface versus satellite temperature (such as vertical distribution of temperature in the atmosphere and how its behavior changes over time).

Based on these NAS reports and recent research performed in the field of climate science, Wojick disagreed with the currently accepted belief that the natural climate of the Earth is basically constant and the climate changes seen over the past hundred years are due only to human activities (or what is scientifically called "anthropogenic influences"). In fact, Wojick claimed that the (perceived) warming of the Earth by human-produced greenhouse gas emissions has had no more effect on world climate changes than the natural variations of the Earth. Further, he stated that although scientists have increased their overall scientific knowledge of climate change on Earth, the increase in that knowledge has been offset by a decrease in the amount of certainty with respect to mankind's contribution to such changes.

From the *Decade-to-Century-Scale Climate Variability and Change: A Science Strategy* report, Wojick quotes: "The evidence of natural variations in the climate system—which was once assumed to be relatively stable—clearly reveals that climate has changed, is changing, and will continue to do so with or without anthropogenic [human] influences."

If what Wojick reported is correct, and further scientific studies verify his statements, it is believed by many climatologists that it will be much more difficult to differentiate between natural climate variations and artificial climate variations caused by human activities. Wojick concluded in his report: " we do not know the extent of climate change in the past, we do not know why climate changes, and we must focus our research on this issue. Only then can we integrate the potential role of past increases in GHG emissions into recent climate history, and only then can we begin to assess the outlook for future climate."

FURTHER RESOURCES

Web sites

ClimateChangeDebate.org. <http://climatechangedebate.org> (accessed November 26, 2005).

Cooler Heads Coalition, GlobalWarming.org. "Climate Variation is the Norm, Not the Exception." <http://www.global warming.org/article.php?uid=204> (accessed November 26, 2005).

The Dartmouth Review. "TDR Interview: Dr. David Wojick." <http://www.dartreview.com/archives/2001/04/23/tdr_interview_dr_david_wojick.php> (accessed November 26, 2005).

President's Council on Sustainable Development. "Climate Change Task Force." <http://clinton4.nara.gov/PCSD/tforce/cctf> (accessed November 26, 2005).

Dust Cloud over Japan

Photograph

By: NASA Sea-viewing Wide Field-of-view Sensor

Date: March 25, 2002

Source: "Dust Cloud over Japan." *SeaWiFS Project*. NASA Goddard Space Flight Center, 2002.

About the Organization: NASA's Sea-viewing Wide Field-of-view Sensor (SeaWiFS) is an optical instrument mounted on the OrbView-2 satellite. Launched on August 1, 1997, the major purpose of the instrument was to detect changes in the color of the oceans. From this information, the concentration and type of phytoplankton in the Earth's oceans can be determined and the role of oceanic photosynthesis in the global carbon cycle can be understood. Because SeaWiFS is an optical instrument, it also detects particulate material, such as dust and sand, in the atmosphere. SeaWiFS provides global coverage of the Earth every forty-eight hours.

INTRODUCTION

Dust and sand storms occur when strong winds lift particles into the air. Usually these storms occur coincident with a cold front that brings dynamic weather into a region. Sand storms and dust storms occur in arid or semi-arid places, as well as in places that have experienced sustained droughts or are undergoing desertification. Major sand and dust storms commonly form in central Asia, over the Sahara desert, and in the Middle East; smaller storms form over the North American prairies and the Australian deserts.

In 2004, scientists estimated that the annual transport of dust and minerals into the atmosphere is three trillion tons per year. The Sahara Desert contributes about one third of this total. Dust storms transport sediments and minerals great distances from their source. For example, dust from the central Asian deserts can reach North America, more than 3,000 miles (5,000 kilometers) away. Dust from the Sahara is swept toward Europe and even toward the eastern coast of North America.

Sand storms often appear as giant walls of sand that move horizontally with frightening speed. Sand particles are on average 0.006 to 0.01 inches (0.15 to 0.3 millimeters) in diameter, while dust particles are typically smaller. Sand storms can reach heights of about 50 feet (15 meters) with wind speeds approaching ten miles per hour (16 kilometers per hour). Dust storms form when small particles of dust are lifted up into the air by chilled downdrafts near cold fronts. These downdrafts hit the ground at speeds as fast as 50 miles per hour (80 kilometers per hour), sweeping dust to great heights. Dust storms average 3,000 to 6,000 feet (914 to 1829 meters) in height, but some may have dust suspended as high as 40,000 feet (12,192 meters) above the ground.

The satellite image below shows a large plume of dust that was swept into the air to move and cover the region of the Pacific near Japan. The dust storm appears slightly grayer than the bright white water vapor clouds in the image. The dust storm flows eastward off the continent past Japan and over the Pacific Ocean.

PRIMARY SOURCE

DUST CLOUD OVER JAPAN
See primary source image.

PRIMARY SOURCE

Dust Cloud over Japan. Nasa Sea-viewing Wide Field-of-view Sensor (SeaWiFS) photographs substantial amounts of airborne dust (shaded pixels) over eastern Asia and the Pacific during a March 2002 storm. IMAGE PROVIDED BY GEOEYE AND NASA SEAWIFS PROJECT

SIGNIFICANCE

Dust and sand storms affect the fundamental physics of the planet. They impact temperatures in the atmosphere by absorbing and scattering light energy from the Sun. Dust in the atmosphere also acts as nuclei for the formation of water droplets in clouds. Dust that is deposited in oceans serves as an important source of minerals that phytoplankton require in order to grow. When phytoplankton grow, they use carbon dioxide, removing a major greenhouse gas from the atmosphere. Therefore, dust storms can have an influence on global warming.

Sand and dust storms also have an impact on the geology of Earth. They transport more sediment than any other geological process. Dust storms are an indicator of soil erosion and desertification. The storms also raise social issues and questions about land use. The storms increase in frequency when land is disturbed by overgrazing and clearing of land for agriculture.

There is some evidence that sand and dust storms have been increasing in frequency during the last few decades. In the 1950s the Korean Meteorological Administration reported that sand storms affected the country fewer than fifteen days per year. In 2002 the number grew to more than twenty-five days per year. Some scientists also observe or argue that warmer winters are related to an increase in sand and dust storms.

Scientists have also found that the sand and dust storms are combining with pollutants in the atmosphere, like soot and vehicle exhaust, to cause health and environmental problems. The World Health Organization blames sand and dust storms in Asia for half a million premature deaths per year. Prior to sweeping out to the Pacific, the dust storm pictured in the image above raised dust levels in Seoul to twice that considered dangerous to human health. Dust from the Sahara desert that is transported across the Atlantic Ocean by storms has been found to contain harmful microorganisms. In particular, the fungi *Aspergilus sydowii*, which was transported by dust storms from Africa, is blamed for the death of sea fans throughout the Caribbean Coral reefs.

Sand and dust storms have economic impacts as well. During severe storms, businesses and schools are closed. Transportation suffers during low visibility periods affecting the movement of airplanes, trucks, and trains. Sand and dust storms also have a negative impact on agriculture, severely damaging crops and livestock.

In response to the threats posed by dust and sand storms, international agencies have pooled their resources to study the development and impacts of those storms. In 2004, the United Nations Environmental Programme and, in 2005, the World Meteorological Organization launched research projects for improving the understanding of the mechanisms that cause sand and dust storms. The programs seek to develop forecasting models so that early warning systems for the occurrence and intensity of sand and dust storms may be used to make health and policy decisions in areas affected by storms. In addition, the programs will monitor the global incidence of storms and develop databases so that the information can be shared among nations.

FURTHER RESOURCES

Web sites

"Dust Storms, Sand Storms and Related NOAA Activities in the Middle East." *NOAA Magazine*, April 7, 2003. <http://www.magazine.noaa.gov/stories/mag86.htm> (accessed March 17, 2006).

Goudie, A.S., N. Lancaster, R.E. Vance, et al. "Dust Transport: Geoindicator." *International Union of Geological Sciences*, revised March 2004. <http://www.lgt.lt/geoin/doc.php?did=cl_dustra> (accessed March 17, 2006).

Kirby, Alex. "Asia's Dust Storm Misery Mounts." *BBC News*, march 31, 2004. <http://news.bbc.co.uk/1/hi/sci/tech/3585223.stm> (accessed March 17, 2006).

Wind Erosion Research Unit (WERU), United States Department of Agriculture, Agriculture Research Service in cooperation with Kansas State University. <http://www.weru.ksu.edu/new_weru/index.html> (accessed March 17, 2006).

"Report of the Seventh Session of the Science Steering Committee for the WWRP (October 19-23, 2004)." *World Meteorological Organization: World Weather Research Programme*, 2005. <http://www.wmo.ch/web/arep/wwrp/PUBLI/WWRP_8.pdf> (accessed March 17, 2006).

Holes in Ozone Layer of Earth

Photograph

By: National Aeronautics and Space Administration (NASA)

Date: September 30, 2002

Source: Corbis

About the Organization: The National Aeronautics and Space Administration, or NASA, is the agency of the U.S. government responsible for exploration of space and the atmosphere immediately around Earth.

INTRODUCTION

The depletion of the ozone layer of Earth's atmosphere refers to the development of a hole in the stratosphere over the south pole of the planet. This hole has been caused by mankind's steady usage of chemicals known as chlorofluorocarbons (CFCs), which pollute the air and have eaten through this protective layer. The purpose of the ozone is to block out the more dangerous rays of the sun, specifically ultraviolet (UV) rays, that would be harmful to life on the planet. UV rays first affect smaller life forms—one-celled organisms, such as plankton—but this creates a domino effect by eliminating the bottom level of the food chain and thereby creating a food shortage for the larger creatures that survive on the one-celled animals. This shortage continues to work its way up, eventually affecting humans. In addition, the thinning of the ozone overall and the gradual filtering of UV rays into the atmosphere affects the average temperature on the planet, the way sun reacts on unprotected skin, and many other aspects of the planet's ecology.

■ PRIMARY SOURCE

HOLES IN OZONE LAYER OF EARTH
See primary source image.

■

SIGNIFICANCE

CFCs were initially put into use because, while they had chemical and physical properties that allowed them multiple uses, they were far less toxic to human beings than many of the other chemicals put to similar purposes. As a result, they became primary

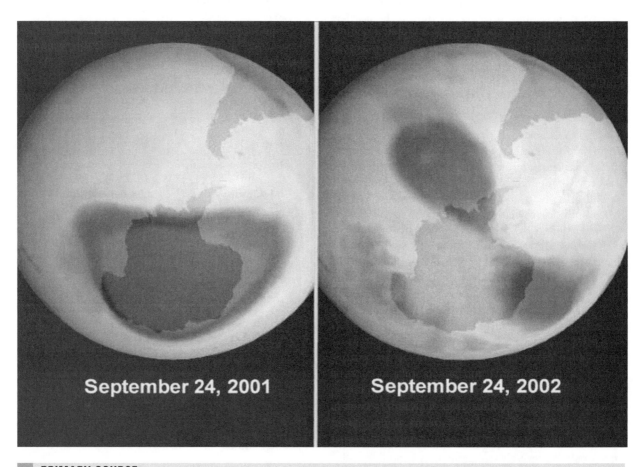

September 24, 2001   September 24, 2002

■ PRIMARY SOURCE

Holes in Ozone Layer of Earth. These two images compare the first split ozone hole on record (right, 2002) and the Antarctic ozone hole at the same time (left, 2001). The hole in each is the dark shaded portion, which only seems smaller in 2002 due to high Antarctic winter temperatures. © NASA/EPA/CORBIS

components of refrigerators and air conditioners as part of the cooling systems, and were used as a propellant for products in aerosol cans. However, in the early 1970s, Dr. Sherwood Rowland and Dr. Mario Molina, both physical chemists, discovered that CFCs were likely to break down within the ozone layer into reactive chlorine atoms, damaging the stratosphere. Although there were attempts to reduce the production of CFCs through the gradual phasing out of aerosol packaging for products, appliances that used CFCs were being marketed at an increased rate around the world. It was not until a large hole was discovered in the ozone over Antarctica that the problem was given the serious attention that it warranted.

Dr. Rowland and Dr. Molina, along with Dr. Paul Crutzen, were awarded the Nobel Prize for Chemistry in 1995 for their work at the University of California at Irvine in illuminating the dangers of CFCs to the ozone layer and the potential ramifications of that ongoing damage. The project was initiated by Dr. Rowland and Dr. Molina as part of a research contract with the Atomic Energy Commission, and began with an interest in how the expenditure of a new chemical compound into the air could potentially alter the atmosphere. Although the chemical had been proven extraordinarily stable, Rowland and Molina believed that was not sufficient reason to assume it was not harmful. They first presented their findings in 1974 at an American Chemical Society meeting, where they detailed not only the environmental ramifications of their research, but the need to enact specific public policies that would serve to combat the threat to the atmosphere. Their discoveries led to the development of an international treaty designed to end the production of CFCs, and to public policies that focus on preserving the quality of the planet's air and water quality, along with the forests and other natural resources.

Difficulties arose when it became clear that, although the science behind Rowland and Molina's findings was sound, there was no apparent evidence that CFCs were in fact damaging the ozone layer. Only in the early 1980s did the problem become visibly apparent. Joe Farman, a member of the British Antarctica survey who had been taking ozone measurements over Halley Bay for more than two decades, discovered that the levels of ozone were suddenly lower during the spring when the light first began to reappear after the long winter. The initial reaction was that the instruments were incorrect, particularly as NASA readings of the ozone over the entire planet had not indicated the problem. However, NASA returned to reexamine the area over Halley Bay and discovered that Farman's findings were indeed accurate. In fact, the ozone had depleted significantly, not just over Halley Bay, but all of Antarctica. Using the Total Ozone Mapping Spectrometer by satellite, color coding clearly delineated the hole that CFCs had created in the ozone layer.

By the mid-1980s, regular studies were in place to record the effects of CFCs on the atmosphere and to try and determine how it would be possible to reverse the damage. Products with CFCs began to be replaced with more ecologically safe technology, and a plan was developed that indicated the decades required in order to return the atmosphere to its pre-1975 ozone quality. The Environmental Protection Agency and other regulating committees joined to ensure that the restoration of the ozone would become a global initiative, and nearly 200 countries ratified the Montreal Protocol on Substances that Deplete the Ozone Layer, an international treaty written in 1987, which served as the basis for the Clean Air Act.

FURTHER RESOURCES

Web sites

"Press Release: The 1995 Nobel Prize in Chemistry." *Nobel Prize.org*, October 11, 1995. <http://nobelprize.org/chemistry/laureates/1995/press.html> (accessed March 5, 2006).

Rowland, F. Sherwood, and Mario J. Molina. "The CFC-Ozone Puzzle: Environmental Science in the Global Arena." *NCSE Online*, December 7, 2000. <http://ncseonline.org/NCSEconference/2000conference/Chafee/ChafeeMemorialLecture2000.pdf> (accessed March 5, 2006).

"Stratospheric Ozone Depletion." *National Aeronautics and Space Administration (NASA)*. <http://www.nas.nasa.gov/About/Education/Ozone> (accessed March 5, 2006).

"What Has EPA Done About Ozone Depletion?" *U.S. Environmental Protection Agency*. <http://www.epa.gov/ozone/geninfo/actions.html> (accessed March 5, 2006).

Earth Story

Photograph

By: Dean Hollingsworth

Date: 2003

Source: Hollingsworth, Dean. "New Scientist, Earth Story." The Dallas Morning News.

Tectonic forces are pushing up a new volcano, Anak Krakatau (foreground), off the coast of West Java, Indonesia. The "Child of Krakatau," broke the surface of water at the center of its mother volcano, Krakatau, in 1930. AP IMAGES

About the Photographer: Dean Hollingsworth is a graphics and news designer for the *Dallas Morning News*, a Texas-based newspaper with a daily circulation of over 100,000.

INTRODUCTION

Plate tectonics refers to the movement of rigid plates constituting Earth's lithosphere, and is the unifying theory of modern geoscience. There are a dozen major plates, all but one associated with continents, and several minor plates. The only major plate not associated with a continent is the Pacific Plate. The word "tectonics" is derived from a Greek root meaning "one who builds," and is sometimes used in reference to architecture (for example, architectonics). Used in a geological sense, however, tectonics refers to the architecture or construction of Earth's crust and lithosphere.

The earth's crust is defined in terms of the chemical composition of its rocks. It overlays the mantle, the boundary between the two being marked by an abrupt change in the speed of seismic waves known as the

Mohorovicic discontinuity (often referred to simply as the Moho). The lithosphere, in contrast, is defined in terms of its brittle response to applied stresses and lies above the ductile—meaning soft but not liquid—asthenosphere. Although the term "plate tectonics" is often used synonymously with continental drift, geoscientists have largely abandoned use of the latter term. When the term "continental drift" is used, it refers to the movement of continents without regard to the underlying mechanism.

Geoscientists explain earthquakes, volcanoes, and the origin of most mountain belts in terms of interactions between adjacent plates. The earthquake-prone San Andreas fault, for example, is the boundary between the North American and Pacific plates. Volcanic eruptions and great earthquakes of the circum-Pacific Ring of Fire occur as the Pacific and Nazca plates are forced beneath adjacent plates and melted. The Himalaya, Earth's tallest mountain range, is being formed as the Indian plate pushes northward against the southern edge of the Eurasian plate.

The origin of tectonic features, such as mountain ranges and continental-scale sedimentary basins, and events such as earthquakes and volcanic eruptions have long been of interest to geoscientists. One of the major gaps in geoscientific knowledge before the discovery of plate tectonics was the absence of a mechanism that could explain geologic observations. Processes such as the shrinking of a gradually cooling Earth were proposed to explain some features of mountain belts, for example the buckling of layered sedimentary rocks into folds. Before the elucidation of plate tectonics, however, prevailing theories could account for only a limited number of observations and were generally unsatisfactory.

The idea that continents move is not new. Sir Francis Bacon (1561–1626), Galileo (1564–1642), and Benjamin Franklin (1706–1790) all noted the curious similarity between the east coast of South America and the western coast of Africa. Franklin, in particular, suggested that Earth's crust floated on a liquid core. During the early years of the twentieth century, German meteorologist Alfred Wegener (1880–1930) used the occurrence of identical fossils on continents separated by oceans as the basis for his hypothesis of continental drift. Geologists had long explained the distribution of fossils by postulating the existence of land bridges between the continents. Wegener, however, used the ages and distributions of the fossils to infer that the currently existing continents had once been part of a single supercontinent named Pangaea, which had broken apart into smaller continents about 200 million years ago.

Wegener was ridiculed by the scientific establishment and froze to death on a meteorological expedition to Greenland more than thirty years before his hypothesis was substantiated. Some of the most important data that led to the acceptance of moving continents was collected by American geologist Harry Hess (1906–1969), who towed a depth sounder behind a transport ship he commanded during World War II. Hess later published a paper in which he suggested that Earth's oceans are underlain by rocks that are pushed apart by magma welling up along the mid-ocean ridges, a process known as seafloor spreading. His idea was substantiated when British geologists Drummond Matthews (1931–1997) and Frederick Vine (1939–) discovered that ocean floors were composed of rock with alternating magnetic polarity. The theory of plate tectonics also proposed that oceanic crust is consumed when it is subducted beneath the edge of an adjacent plate, explaining curious patterns of earthquake occurrence along the edges of continents observed by seismologists Hugo Benioff and Kiyoo Wadati. In large part, the discoveries that led to widespread acceptance of plate tectonics were made possible by the development of instruments such as sensitive magnetometers and the global deployment of seismographs in the decades after World War II.

By 1970, a preponderance of scientific evidence led to the almost universal acceptance of plate tectonics. Technological advances such as global positioning system (GPS) receivers with millimeter accuracy and seismic tomography have since allowed geoscientists to measure plate movements and produce images of plate edges disintegrating as they are subducted.

PRIMARY SOURCE

MAP OF TECTONIC PLATES
See primary source image.

SIGNIFICANCE

Plate tectonics is the unifying theory of modern geoscience, and is used to explain phenomena such as earthquakes, volcanic eruptions, and the origin of mountain ranges. It also serves as a theoretical framework for natural resource exploration, helping to locate petroleum reservoirs and mineral deposits. Although some of the ideas that led to the discovery of plate tectonics date back as far as the seventeenth century, most scholars now recognize Alfred Wegener's early twentieth-century work as the foundation for subsequent studies that solidified the theory during the second half of the twentieth century.

FURTHER RESOURCES
Books
McPhee, John. *Annals of the Former World.* New York: Farrar, Straus and Giroux, 2000.

Oreskes, Naomi. *Plate Tectonics: An Insider's History of the Modern Theory of the Earth.* Cambridge, MA: Westview Press, 2003.

Web sites
Sample, Sharon. "On the Move Continental Drift and Plate Tectonics." *National Aeronautics and Space Administration (NASA).* <http://kids.earth.nasa.gov/archive/pangaea> (accessed March 8, 2006).

Kious, W. Jacquelyne, and Robert I. Tilling. "This Dynamic Earth: the Story of Plate Tectonics." *U.S. Geological Survey,* February 1996. <http://pubs.usgs.gov/gip/dynamic/dynamic.html> (accessed March 8, 2006).

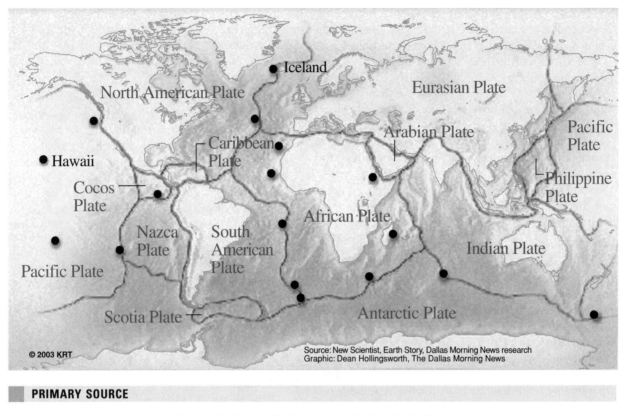

Iceland

North American Plate

Eurasian Plate

Hawaii

Caribbean Plate

Arabian Plate

Pacific Plate

Cocos Plate

Philippine Plate

Nazca Plate

South American Plate

African Plate

Indian Plate

Pacific Plate

Scotia Plate

Antarctic Plate

© 2003 KRT

Source: New Scientist, Earth Story, Dallas Morning News research
Graphic: Dean Hollingsworth, The Dallas Morning News

PRIMARY SOURCE

Map of Tectonic Plates. Map showing the distribution of rigid plates constituting Earth's lithosphere.

Water Resources of the United States

U.S. Geological Survey

Report

By: United States Geological Survey

Date: March 2004

Source: Hutson, Susan S., et al., U.S. Geological Survey. "Estimated Use of Water in the United States in 2000," USGS Circular 1268, originally released March 2004 (revised April 2004, May 2004, and February 2005) <http://pubs.usgs.gov/circ/2004/circ1268/index.html> (accessed March 17, 2006).

About the Organization: The United States Geological Survey (USGS), a part of the U.S. Department of the Interior, monitors, collects, analyzes, and provides technical and scientific information about the condition, issues, and problems of the country's natural resources (such as water, minerals, and energy) in

order to enhance and protect the quality of life in the United States.

INTRODUCTION

The USGS provides information about water resources within the United States through its Water Resources Discipline (WRD). Through a workforce of about 4,300 people located in all fifty states, the WRD uses its skilled personnel and comprehensive amount of materials to provide water resource information to local and state organizations in order to: (1) minimize loss of life and property damage as a result of water-related natural hazards such as droughts, floods, and earthquakes; (2) manage surface and ground water resources for agricultural, commercial, domestic, ecological, industrial, and recreational uses; (3) protect and improve water resources for aquatic environments, human health, and overall environmental quality; and (4) contribute to physical and economic development of the country's resources. Within its Web pages, the USGS titles each page as "Water Resources of the United States" in order to emphasize its major efforts for U.S. citizens and organizations along the lines of water resources.

PRIMARY SOURCE

Estimates of water use in the United States indicate that about 408 billion gallons per day (one thousand million gallons per day, abbreviated Bgal/d) were withdrawn for all uses during 2000. This total has varied less than 3 percent since 1985 as withdrawals have stabilized for the two largest uses-thermoelectric power and irrigation. Fresh ground-water withdrawals (83.3 Bgal/d) during 2000 were 14 percent more than during 1985. Fresh surface-water withdrawals for 2000 were 262 Bgal/d, varying less than 2 percent since 1985.

About 195 Bgal/d, or 48 percent of all freshwater and saline-water withdrawals for 2000, were used for thermo-electric power. Most of this water was derived from sur-face water and used for once-through cooling at power plants. About 52 percent of fresh surface-water with-drawals and about 96 percent of saline-water withdrawals were for thermoelectric-power use. Withdrawals for ther-moelectric power have been relatively stable since 1985.

Irrigation remained the largest use of freshwater in the United States and totaled 137 Bgal/d for 2000. Since 1950, irrigation has accounted for about 65 percent of total water withdrawals, excluding those for thermoelectric power. Historically, more surface water than ground water has been used for irrigation. However, the percentage of total irrigation withdrawals from ground water has contin-ued to increase, from 23 percent in 1950 to 42 percent in 2000. Total irrigation withdrawals were 2 percent more for 2000 than for 1995, because of a 16-percent increase in ground-water withdrawals and a small decrease in surface-water withdrawals. Irrigated acreage more than doubled between 1950 and 1980, then remained constant before increasing nearly 7 percent between 1995 and 2000. The number of acres irrigated with sprinkler and microirrigation systems has continued to increase and now comprises more than one-half the total irrigated acreage.

Public-supply withdrawals were more than 43 Bgal/d for 2000. Public-supply withdrawals during 1950 were 14 Bgal/d. During 2000, about 85 percent of the population in the United States obtained drinking water from public suppliers, compared to 62 percent during 1950. Surface water provided 63 percent of the total during 2000, whereas surface water provided 74 percent during 1950.

Self-supplied industrial withdrawals totaled nearly 20 Bgal/d in 2000, or 12 percent less than in 1995. Compared to 1985, industrial self-supplied withdrawals declined by 24 percent. Estimates of industrial water use in the United States were largest during the years from 1965 to 1980, but during 2000, estimates were at the lowest level since reporting began in 1950. Combined withdrawals for self-supplied domestic, livestock, aquaculture, and mining were less than 13 Bgal/d for 2000, and represented about 3 percent of total withdrawals.

California, Texas, and Florida accounted for one-fourth of all water withdrawals for 2000. States with the largest surface-water withdrawals were California, which had large withdrawals for irrigation and thermoelectric power, and Texas, which had large withdrawals for thermoelectric power. States with the largest ground-water withdrawals were California, Texas, and Nebraska, all of which had large withdrawals for irrigation.

SIGNIFICANCE

The work of the scientists, technicians, and sup-port staff of the USGS with respect to the country's water resources is very important for dealing with the long-term health and quality of life of the country's citizens and their overall economic strength. The water resources of the United States—including its ground water, streams, rivers, lakes, aquifers, and res-ervoirs—provide drinking water, transport products, support industries, and provide recreational opportu-nities, along with many other purposes to each and every person in the United States. Because of these complex and varied purposes, the proper management of these water resources is a critical job for local, county, state, and federal levels of government.

As a result, employees of the WRD, under the guidance of the USGS, manage the national water program, called the National Research Program, and state and regional water programs. These state and regional programs include: the National Streamflow Information Program, the Cooperative Water Program, the State Water Resources Research Institute Program, the Toxic Substances Hydrology (Toxics) Program, the National Water Quality Assessment Program, the Ground Water Resources Program, the Hydrologic Research and Development Program, and the Hydrologic Networks and Analysis Program. Personnel within the WRD also work with subprograms within the above programs and within international programs.

One USGS/WRD program of particular impor-tance is the Cooperative Water Program (CWP). The CWP provides basic scientific information that mana-gers of water resources need in order to provide the optimum water services for their particular region of the country. With its continuing cooperative partner-ships involving about 1,400 non-federal agencies (which consist of county, state, tribal, municipal, and other agencies, who are called Cooperators), as of 2003, the CWP maintains reliable and consistent procedures and quality-assurance agreements in conducting its national projects. Together, the CWP and Cooperators plan the scientific work that is necessary in order to meet all stated objectives and goals for both parties.

Consequently, the CWP has broad interest and widespread use among Cooperators due to its quick and reliable response to emerging issues, along with its technical expertise, long-standing performance record of providing high-quality measurements and assessments, and its serious commitment to providing public access to the data it has collected over the years.

Because the CWP is a non-regulatory scientific agency, disputing parties involved in complaints and arguments over jurisdictions, regulations, or other problems will generally acknowledge its data and analysis as accurate and valid due to its nonpartisan nature. In order not to repeat work already in existence, the CWP obtains information from both government and non-government organizations before proceeding with projects. It specifically lists activities and programs that it has exempted itself from performing, realizing that others are already providing valid services in such areas.

The CWP supports and encourages the collection of basic hydrologic data, along with the continuing research studies of specific water-based problems. As a result, activities of the CWP contribute significantly to emerging water-resource issues across the country. Examples of such issues include improved understanding of the association between land-use changes and the physical habitat of surface waters; the changing behavior of freshwater-saltwater interactions in ground-water environments along the Atlantic and Pacific coasts; and the specific role of the sciences in managing and maintaining ground-water resources.

The information that is collected by the CWP is gathered into the National Water Information System (NWIS), which now includes data from about 1.5 million sites in all U.S. states, the District of Columbia, and Puerto Rico, including water levels from over one million wells, stream-flow data from over 21,000 sites, and chemical data from about 338,000 sites involving ground water, lakes, rivers, springs, and streams.

As shown here in this discussion, the WRD is a valuable agency for coordinating the water resources in the United States. With the expertise and experience of its scientists and technicians, and the backing of the USGS and the Department of the Interior, the WRD is a critical partner in the country's actions and laws to maintain and improve the ways and means that all

individuals and groups within the United States use water for their personal and business activities. In actuality, water is a national resource that must be accurately coordinated and regulated at the national level for proper maintenance and use at local, municipal, state, and regional levels.

FURTHER RESOURCES

Web sites

Taggart, Bruce E. "Cooperative Water Program—A Partnership in the Nation's Water-Resources Program." *U.S. Geological Survey*, July 8, 2004. <http://water.usgs.gov/pubs/fs/2004/3068> (accessed March 17, 2006).

U.S. Department of Agriculture: National Agricultural Library. "Water Quality Information Center: Databases." *U.S. Department of Agriculture: National Agricultural Library*. <http://www.nal.usda.gov/wqic/dbases.html> (accessed March 17, 2006).

U.S. Environmental Protection Agency. "Water." *U.S. Environmental Protection Agency*. <http://www.epa.gov/ebtpages/water.html> (accessed March 17, 2006).

———. "Wetlands, Oceans, and Watersheds." *U.S. Environmental Protection Agency*. <http://www.epa.gov/owow> (accessed March 17, 2006).

U.S. Geological Survey. "National Research Program Home Page." *U.S. Geological Survey*. <http://water.usgs.gov/nrp> (accessed March 17, 2006).

———. "Water Resources of the United States: Water Resources Mission." *U.S. Geological Survey*. <http://water.usgs.gov/mission.html> (accessed March 17, 2006).

———. "Water Resources of the United States: Water Resources Programs." *U.S. Geological Survey*. <http://water.usgs.gov/programs.html> (accessed March 17, 2006).

———. "Water Supply and Demand." *U.S. Geological Survey*. <http://www.usgs.gov/science/science.php?term=1311> (accessed March 17, 2006).

WMO Statement on the Status of the Global Climate in 2004

Global Temperature in 2004 Fourth Warmest

Report

By: World Meteorological Organization (WMO)

Date: 2004

Source: "WMO Statement on the Status of the Global Climate in 2004: Global Temperature in 2004 Fourth Warmest." World Meteorological Organization, 2004.

About the Organization: Established in 1950, the World Meteorological Organization (WMO) became part of the United Nations in 1951. Its membership includes representatives from 187 countries and territories. Its purpose is to study and make recommendations on the state of the atmosphere, oceans, and climate.

INTRODUCTION

The idea that human activities can change the natural climate is not new. As far back as the early 1800s, Americans noticed that cutting down forests in a particular area seemed to lead to higher amounts of precipitation. In 1896, a Swedish scientist published the earliest known description of the "greenhouse effect," a theory describing how carbon dioxide released into the atmosphere might raise the planet's temperature. The theory initially garnered little interest.

Through the early and mid-twentieth century, scientists were able to do little more than speculate about the impact of human activities on the atmosphere. At some points during this period, scientists warned that dust and smog particles in the atmosphere were likely to lead to global cooling; at other times the predictions described an impending rise in global temperatures.

Not until the latter twentieth century did a consensus emerge among many climatologists that the actual trend was in fact upward, and the climate did actually appear to be warming. One major factor in this coalescence of opinion was the emergence of powerful computer models which could more accurately examine the available data and model the intricacies of atmospheric flow and change.

While consensus exists on the fact that the earth is warmer now than it was a century ago, disagreement continues about the causes of the change. Advocates of global warming theory note that temperatures have run consistently above average for the past twenty years. Further, eight of the ten hottest years on record have occurred since 1995, and global warming proponents argue that these numbers are a direct result of human activities.

Critics of global warming theories generally don't dispute the higher average temperatures, arguing instead that human activities are not the cause. These critics note that from the fourteenth to nineteenth centuries Europe was cold enough for festivals to be

A student tries to keep cool in the intense heat by shielding his head from the sun's rays in Philadelphia, June 8, 1999. Studies show that 1999 was one of the hottest years in the last decade. AP IMAGES

held on the frozen Thames river, suggesting that the world climate warmed noticeably prior to the twentieth century. They also observe that in any varying process such as temperature, some values will always lie above the average and some will lie below it, suggesting that the current warming is simply an above-average period.

While debate continues about the causes of rising world temperatures, agencies such as the United Nations continue to monitor climate change and report their findings, urging action to control the release of greenhouse gases which are believed to worsen the problem.

PRIMARY SOURCE

WMO STATEMENT ON THE STATUS OF THE GLOBAL CLIMATE IN 2004:

GENEVA, 15 December (WMO)—The global mean surface temperature in 2004 is expected to be +0.44 °C above the 1961–1990 annual average (14 °C), according to the records maintained by Members of the World Meteorological Organization (WMO). This value of 0.44 °C places 2004 as the fourth warmest year in the temperature record since 1861 just behind 2003 (+0.49 °C). However, 1998 remains the warmest year, when surface temperatures averaged +0.54 °C above the same 30-year mean. The last 10 years (1995–2004), with the exception of 1996, are among the warmest 10 years on record.

Calculated separately for both hemispheres, surface temperatures in 2004 for the northern hemisphere (+0.60 °C) are likely to be the fourth warmest and, for the southern hemisphere (+0.27 °C), the fifth warmest in the instrumental record from 1861 to the present.

Globally, the land-surface air temperature anomaly for October 2004 was the warmest on record for a month of October. The blended land and sea-surface temperature (SST) value for the Arctic (north of 70 °N) in July and the land-surface air temperature value for Africa south of the Equator in July were the warmest on record for July. Significant positive annual regional temperature anomalies, notably across much of the land masses of central Asia, China, Alaska and western parts of the United States, as well as across major portions of the North Atlantic Ocean, contributed to the high global mean surface temperature ranking.

Over the 20th century, the global surface temperature increased by more than 0.6 °C. The rate of change for the period since 1976 is roughly three times that for the past 100 years as a whole. In the northern hemisphere, the 1990s were the warmest decade with an average of 0.38 °C. The surface temperatures averaged over the recent five years (2000–2004) were, however, much higher (0.58 °C).

STRONG REGIONAL TEMPERATURE DIFFERENCES

During June and July, heatwaves with near-record temperatures affected southern Spain, Portugal, and Romania, with maximum temperatures reaching 40 °C. In Japan, extreme hot conditions persisted during the summer with record-breaking maximum temperatures. An exceptional heatwave affected much of eastern Australia during February, as maximum temperatures soared to 45 °C in many areas. The spatial and temporal extent of the heatwave was greater than that of any other February heatwave on record. A prolonged severe heatwave across northern parts of India during the last week of March caused more than 100 fatalities.

In July, abnormally cold conditions in the high-altitude areas of the Andes in southern Peru reportedly killed 92 people. Cold weather since late December 2003 was blamed for as many as 600 deaths across South Asia. During January 2004, maximum and minimum temperatures were below normal by 6–10 °C across northern India and Bangladesh.

PROLONGED DROUGHT IN SOME REGIONS

Drought conditions continued to affect parts of eastern South Africa, Mozambique, Lesotho and Swaziland in early 2004. However, enhanced precipitation in the last half of the rainy season provided some benefit to crops in southern Africa. The March–May rainy season was shorter and drier than normal across parts of the Greater Horn of Africa, resulting in a continuation of multi-season drought in this region. Isolated regions in the southern sector and portions of Uganda experienced driest conditions on record since 1961. In Kenya, a premature end to the 2004 long rains exacerbated the drought resulting from several years of poor rainfall in many areas. Food production in Kenya was projected at approximately 40% below normal. In spite of abundant rainfall in 2004, multi-year drought conditions also continued in Somalia, threatening agriculture and food security in the region. In Eritrea, which was struggling from nearly four years of drought, poor rains during the March–May rains exacerbated drinking-water shortages.

In India, the 2004 seasonal rainfall during the summer (south-west) monsoon season (June—September) over the country as a whole was 13% below normal with 18% of the country experiencing moderate drought conditions. In Pakistan, poor rains in July and August aggravated the long-term drought conditions, which had prevailed since the boreal spring. In Afghanistan, drought conditions that had plagued the country for the past four years continued in 2004 due to poor precipitation in the March—April season. In southern China, dry conditions persisted from August to October, resulting in the worst drought there in the last 54 years.

Long-term hydrological drought continued to affect much of southern and eastern Australia, as a result of rainfall deficits experienced since the major drought event of 2002/2003. Moderate-to-severe drought conditions continued in some areas of the western United States for the fifth year in a row. Some relief was experienced during September and October, though long-term drought remains entrenched across much of the region. Due to above-normal summer temperatures and dry conditions, a record area was burned by wildfires in Alaska.

ABUNDANT RAINFALL AND FLOODING IN MANY OTHER REGIONS

Precipitation in 2004 was above average for the globe and 2004 was the wettest year since 2000. Wetter-than-average conditions prevailed in the southern and eastern United States, eastern Europe and parts of western Asia, Bangladesh, Japan and coastal Brazil.

The Asian summer monsoon during June—September brought heavy rain and flooding to parts of northern India, Nepal and Bangladesh, leaving millions stranded. Throughout India, Nepal and Bangladesh, some 1,800 deaths were blamed on flooding brought by heavy monsoon rains. Flooding in north-east India (the states of Assam and Bihar in particular) and Bangladesh was the worst in over a decade. In eastern and southern China, heavy rains during June and July produced severe flooding and landslides that affected more than 100 million people and were blamed for more than 1,000 deaths nationwide. Heavy monsoon rainfall during July and August produced flooding along several rivers in north-eastern and central Thailand. A significant low-pressure system brought record-breaking snowfalls in the Republic of Korea on 5 March, resulting in damage to agriculture worth more than US$ 500 million. In October, two typhoons and active frontal systems brought record-breaking heavy rainfall to Japan. Tokyo received a total amount of 780 mm precipitation in October, which is the largest monthly amount on record since 1876.

Mudslides and floods due to heavy rains across areas of Brazil during January and early February left tens of thousands of people homeless and resulted in 161 deaths. In January, Peru and Bolivia also experienced hailstorms, heavy rainfall and flooding, which killed at least 50 people.

In Haiti, torrential rainfall due to the passage of Hurricane Jeanne produced disastrous flooding that claimed some 3,000 lives. This disaster came in the wake of flooding and landslides that affected Haiti and the Dominican Republic in late May 2004, in which more than 2,000 people were killed and several thousand others were affected.

In the second half of November and beginning of December, three tropical storms and a tropical depression passed over southern and central parts of the Philippines, drenching the islands with several days of torrential rainfall and triggering catastrophic flash floods and landslides, which killed, according to reports, more than 1,100 people.

Heavy rains from mid-January to March in areas of Angola produced flooding along the river system, which flows into neighbouring Zambia, Botswana and Namibia. Extensive flooding along the Zambezi River, the worst flooding since 1958, threatened more than 20,000 people in north-eastern Namibia and caused extensive damage to crops.

In Australia, parts of Tasmania, Queensland and New South Wales received unusually heavy rainfall in mid-January, which produced flooding and damage. Parts of the Northern Territory received the wettest rainy season on record. A series of strong storms during February produced heavy rainfall and damaging floods in southern parts of New Zealand's North Island. . . .

SIGNIFICANCE

This 2004 WMO report provided an extensive portrait of weather activity around the globe. The report noted not only higher average temperatures worldwide, but wide variations in rainfall, with some regions experiencing flooding and others plagued with drought. The WMO report from 2005 echoed similar themes, with higher-than-average temperatures resulting in the second warmest year on record. 2005 also brought a record number of Atlantic hurricanes, which some scientists claim are due to higher ocean temperatures brought on by global warming.

FURTHER RESOURCES

Books

Burroughs, William J. *Climate Change: A Multidisciplinary Approach.* Cambridge, U.K.: Cambridge University Press, 2001.

Bailey, Ronald, ed. *Global Warming and Other Eco Mythos: How the Environmental Movement Uses False Science to Scare Us to Death.* New York: Prima Lifestyles, 2002.

Web sites

Weart, Spencer. "The Discovery of Global Warming." *American Institute of Physics.* <http://www.aip.org/history/climate/summary.htm> (accessed March 13, 2006).

"Global Warming—Climate: Uncertainties." *U.S. Environmental Protection Agency.* <http://yosemite.epa.gov/oar/globalwarming.nsf/content/climateuncertainties.html> (accessed March 13, 2006).

"About WMO." *World Meteorological Organization.* <http://www.wmo.ch/index-en.html> (accessed March 13, 2006).

"Shrinking Glaciers Evidence of Global Warming:

Differences Seen by Looking at Photos From 100 Years Ago"

Newspaper article

By: David Perlman

Date: December 17, 2004

Source: Perlman, David. "Shrinking Glaciers Evidence of Global Warming: Differences Seen by Looking at Photos From 100 Years Ago." *San Francisco Chronicle* (December 17, 2004).

About the Author: David Perlman reports on all areas of science for the *San Francisco Chronicle*, where he has been the science editor since 1960. Perlman attended Columbia University, where he edited the college newspaper. He also served as a foreign correspondent in Europe after World War II. Perlman has served as the president of the National Association of Science Writers and received the Sustained Achievement Award in Science Journalism from the American Geophysical Union in 1997.

INTRODUCTION

Global warming refers to an increase in temperature throughout the Earth's atmosphere. The term is usually used in connection with an accumulation of certain gases in the atmosphere. These gases, which result from the combustion of fossil fuels, are able to hold heat, much as a greenhouse collects heat within its glass walls. Global warming is of particular interest in the polar regions, where ice, some of which is in the form of glaciers, covers a substantial part of the land. Glaciers act as sensitive indicators of temperature change.

Scientists know that temperature variability is a fundamental part of the Earth's climate. About one thousand years ago during a warming period known as the Medieval Warm, glaciers retreated greatly. Greenland, which is covered in ice today, was able to support an agricultural economy. The global temperature then cooled during the Little Ice Age, approximately four hundred years ago. Glaciers expanded in all of the temperate regions of the world. Following the Little Ice Age, a warming period began and continues through the present.

One of the most significant features of the current warming period is that temperatures are rising more quickly during the last fifty years than they have during the prior 250 years. A variety of reports have also shown that glaciers are melting more quickly than they have in any of the past 250 years. However, some of the information in the reports has been contradictory and temperature information is poor prior to about 1800. In addition, measurements of the size of glaciers was difficult before technological advances like satellite remote sensing.

Two geophysicists, Bruce Molnia and Ken Tape, collected thousands of photographs taken between thirty and 110 years ago in Alaska. They then returned to the same locations where the photos were taken and took pictures of the same scenes. Visual comparisons between the photographs showed that glaciers had retreated greatly and that the landscape had become much more vegetated. Both of these results indicate that, at the very least, a regional increase in temperature is having significant effects on the landscape and further suggests that more global temperature change is affecting the polar regions.

■ PRIMARY SOURCE

Glaciers throughout Alaska are shrinking more and more rapidly, and scientists comparing old photos taken up to a century ago with digital images made during climbing expeditions today say the pictures provide the most dramatic evidence yet that global warming is real.

And it's not only the glaciers reflecting the climate change. Everywhere on the treeless tundra north of the jagged slopes of Alaska's Brooks Range, explosive bursts of vegetation—willows, alders, birch and many shrubs—are thriving where permafrost once kept the tundra surface frozen in winter.

Two geophysicists and a government geologist who spend much of their working lives exploring changes in the Arctic displayed dozens of photographs from the thousands in their files Thursday at the annual meeting of the American Geophysical Union in San Francisco.

"You don't need science to prove the point," said Matt Nolan of the University of Alaska in Fairbanks. "This evidence is visual, and it's real.

"All the glaciers in the Arctic National Wildlife Refuge are retreating from their most extended positions thousands of years ago, and the only scientific explanation for their retreat is a change in climate. There's no doubt at all, and the loss of glacial volume is accelerating."

Bruce Molnia, a geologist with the U.S. Geological Survey, has gathered more than 200 glacier photos taken from the 1890s to the late 1970s and has visited more than 1,000 Alaskan glaciers in the past four years to photograph them from precisely the same locations and pointing in the same directions as the older ones.

Where masses of ice were once surging down wide mountain passes into the sea, or were hanging from high and perilously steep faces, the surfaces in Molnia's images now stand bare. What remains from many of the retreating glaciers are stretches of open water or broad, snow-free layers of sediment.

"And as the glaciers disappear," Molnia said, "you get the amazing appearance of vegetation."

As certain as the scientists are that global warming is responsible for Alaska's changing landscape, they hesitated to blame it all on the increasing levels of greenhouse gases from industry that have marked the past century and have resulted in the 1997 Kyoto Protocol, now ratified by 126 nations but which the Bush administration has rejected.

"The rapid melting of the glaciers, the increasing vegetation in the high Arctic and the invasions of insects where insects were once unknown are all happening," Molnia said, "and I would not question that a significant component of the change is due to the heat-trapping greenhouse effect—certainly a human-caused issue—but I wouldn't say it's all caused by global industries.''

The increasing pace of change is clear in the glaciers he has explored, Molnia said. Many photos he has recovered from the 1890s, the 1940s and the 1970s show how fast the glaciers have been retreating; in a few cases, however, where warming temperatures have increased precipitation at higher altitudes, some glaciers actually advanced, he said.

Geophysicist Ken Tape, of the University of Washington, has been exploring the Brooks Range in the far north of Alaska as well as the wide stretches of treeless tundra between the mountains and the Beaufort Sea along the state's north coast.

The growth of shrubs across the tundra has increased by 40 percent in less than 60 years, Tape said, ''and that perturbation is certainly due to the changing climate.''

SIGNIFICANCE

Molnia and Tape's work received considerable interest from the scientific community and generated a continuing dialog on the effects of global warming on the landscape and glaciers in the polar region of the northern hemisphere.

Tape, along with colleagues Matthew Sturm and Charles Racine, found that the types of vegetation that were found in increased abundance in Alaska were alder, birch, and willow. All three of these species grow more quickly in warmer environments. Because the locations where the comparative photographs were taken are remote and free from human interference, the researchers believe that the reason that the changes to the landscape are occurring is because of a warming climate.

By 2005, Molnia surveyed approximately two thousand of the largest glaciers in every part of Alaska that contained glacier ice. He found that at least 95 percent of the glaciers were retreating, thinning or stagnating. Glacier National Park in Montana contained approximately fifty glaciers in the mid 1800s. In 2005, only twenty remain and all of them are decreasing in size. Similar losses of glaciers have been documented in North Dakota, Wyoming, Colorado, Oregon, and Idaho, indicating that the warming climate has a significant impact on the landscape of the northern polar region.

Molnia found a dependence on the rate of retreat on altitude. Those glaciers at higher altitudes were not melting as rapidly. In fact, there is evidence that the additional melting of glaciers at low altitudes is feeding precipitation at higher altitudes. As a result some of the higher-altitude glaciers are actually increasing in size.

Molnia expects that a similar trend will continue throughout the next fifty years. In particular, glaciers at altitudes lower than 8,000 feet will continue to shrink or disappear and those at higher altitudes will not change significantly.

The melting of glaciers increases the amount of freshwater in the regions where glaciers are found. This can cause localized flooding, the effects of which have been observed. In Italy, a glacial lake was preemptively drained to decrease the risk of flooding. In Peru, overflowing glacial lakes have resulted in flooding and deaths.

The impact of the current rate of glacial melt on sea level is not enormous. However, if all of the temperate glaciers were to melt, the result would be a sea level rise of about nine inches. Global warming has a second impact on sea level rise. As water warms, it expands, causing an additional rise in sea level. Such a sea-level rise would affect low-lying regions of the world like Bangladesh, the Netherlands and South Florida, as well as island nations such as the Marshall Islands. In particular, storm surge could be extremely damaging to property in these areas given a rise in sea level.

FURTHER RESOURCES
Periodicals

Sturm, Matthew, Charles Racine, and Kenneth Tape. "Climate Change: Increasing Shrub Abundance in the Arctic." *Nature* 411 (May 31, 2001): 546–547.

Web sites

Alaska Science Forum. "Melting Alaska Makes the Front Page." <http://www.gi.alaska.edu/ScienceForum/ASF17/1731.html> (accessed January 6, 2006).

PBS's Journey to Planet Earth. "The State of the Planet: Global Warming." <http://www.pbs.org/journeyto-planetearth/stateoftheplanet/index_globwarming.html> (accessed January 6, 2006).

SeaGrant: Alaska Arctic Science Journeys. "Alaska Getting Shrubbier." <http://www.uaf.edu/seagrant/NewsMedia/01ASJ/06.01.01shrubs.html> (accessed January 6, 2006).

The Seasons and the Earth's Orbit

Essay

By: George H. Kaplan

Date: 2005

Source: Kaplan, George H. "The Seasons and the Earth's Orbit." Astronomical Applications Department, U.S. Naval Observatory. <http://aa.usno.navy.mil> (accessed December 14, 2005).

About the Author: Dr. George H. Kaplan is an astronomer at the U.S. Naval Observatory (USNO) in Washington, D.C., a position he has held since 1971. While at the USNO, Kaplan has worked on various projects within the Nautical Almanac Office, the Astrometry Department, and the office of the Scientific Director related to positional astronomy such as Earth rotation measurements, planetary orbit computations, VLBI (very long baseline interferometry) and connected-element radio interferometry, astrometry of the satellites of the planet Jupiter, optical interferometry, lunar occultations, the mathematics of celestial navigation, and the design of computer almanacs. Kaplan also acts as chief of the Science Support Division of the Astronomical Applications Department.

INTRODUCTION

While working for the U.S. Naval Observatory, George Kaplan described the Earth's orbit and its seasons with respect to their relationship to Milankovitch cycles. Kaplan provided in his paper an explanation of the major principles involved with the theory of Milankovitch cycles, which were developed by Milutin Milankovitch, a Serbian astronomer, geophysicist, and mathematician.

Milankovitch (1879–1958) worked throughout his professional career on his mathematical theory of climate change that dealt with the latitudinal and seasonal variations of radiation directed towards the Earth from the Sun. While working at the University of Belgrade, he developed a significant theory—now known as the Milankovitch theory, or the astronomical theory of climate change—which was based on orbital variations of the Earth and its association with Earth's past climatic variation (for a 600,000-year period prior to 1800). He is well known within the scientific community for carefully calculating the magnitude of Earth's precession, eccentricity, and obliquity. Milankovitch wrote his first book in 1920 based on his astronomical theory that highlighted the effects caused by the ice ages. Over twenty years later, in 1941, he published a more detailed version of his mathematical theory, which was later translated into the English language in 1969 under the title "Canon of Insolation of the Ice-Age Problem" and reprinted again in 1998.

Milankovitch cycles, which are incorporated within the Milankovitch Theory, are defined as three periodic variations—precession, eccentricity, and obliquity—in Earth's orientation with respect to the Sun.

Precessional motion is the counterclockwise, near-circular wobble (or motion caused by the change in the direction of the Earth's axis of rotation) that produces a cycle of about 21,000 years. The motion of eccentricity (or ellipticity) is the variation in shape, over about 100,000 years, in the Earth's orbit around the sun, which varies from a near circular orbit to a more elliptically shaped orbit. Obliquity (or nutation) is the variation of the Earth's axial tilt in a period of about 41,000 years, with respect to the plane for which it orbits the sun. These three variations are believed to produce significant cyclical changes in Earth's climate with a period of about 100,000 years.

PRIMARY SOURCE

We have all been taught that the seasons are caused by the tilt of the Earth's axis of rotation—the 23.4° offset of the axis from a direction perpendicular to the Earth's orbital plane. The direction of the rotational axis stays nearly fixed in space, even as the Earth revolves around the Sun once each year. As a result, when the Earth is at a certain place in its orbit, the northern hemisphere is tilted toward the Sun and experiences summer. Six months later, when the Earth is on the opposite side of the Sun, the northern hemisphere is tilted away from the Sun and experiences winter. The seasons are, of course, reversed for the southern hemisphere.

The solstices mark the two dates during the year on which the Earth's position in its orbit is such that its axis is most directly tilted either toward or away from the Sun. These are the dates when the days are longest for the hemisphere tilted toward the Sun (where it is summer) and shortest for the opposite hemisphere (where it is winter).

However, there is a complication. The Earth's orbit is very close to being a perfect circle, but not quite. It is somewhat elliptical, which means that the distance between the Earth and the Sun varies over the course of the year. This effect is too weak to *cause* the seasons, but it might have some influence over their severity. The remainder of this page explains this possibility.

The Earth reaches perihelion—the point in its orbit closest to the Sun—in early January, only about two weeks after the December solstice. Thus winter begins in the northern hemisphere at about the time that the Earth is nearest the Sun. Is this important? Is there a reason why the times of solstice and perihelion are so close? It turns out that the proximity of the two dates is a coincidence of the particular century we live in. The date of perihelion does not remain fixed, but, over very long periods of time, slowly regresses (moves later) within the year. There is some evidence that this long-term change in the date of perihelion influences the Earth's climate.

We can measure the length of the year in several different ways. The length of the year from equinox to equinox (equivalently, solstice to solstice) is called the *tropical year*, and its length is the basis for our Gregorian (civil) calendar. Basically, the tropical year is the year of a complete cycle of seasons, so it is natural that we use it for ordinary purposes. But we can also measure the length of the year from perihelion to perihelion, which is called the *anomalistic year*. On average, the anomalistic year is about 25 minutes longer than the tropical year, so the date of perihelion slowly shifts over time, regressing by about 1 full day every 58 years. The date of perihelion thus moves completely through the tropical year in about 21,000 years.

It is important to note that we are talking about long-term trends here. There are small year-to-year variations in the dates and times of solstice and perihelion due to our leap-year cycle and the effect of the Moon on the motion of the Earth....

Most of the difference in the average lengths of the two kinds of year is due to the very slight change in the direction of the Earth's rotation axis in space from one year to another. We usually think of the Earth's axis as being fixed in direction—after all, it always seems to point toward Polaris, the North Star. But the direction is not quite constant: the axis does move, at a rate of a little more than a half-degree per century. So Polaris has not always been, and will not always be, the pole star. For example, when the pyramids were built, around 2500 BCE, the pole was near the star Thuban (Alpha Draconis). This gradual change in the direction of the Earth's axis, called *precession*, is caused by gravitational torques exerted by the Moon and Sun on the spinning, slightly oblate Earth.

Because the direction of the Earth's axis determines when the seasons will occur, precession will cause a particular season (for example, northern hemisphere winter) to occur at a slightly different place in the Earth's orbit from year to year. At the same time, the orbit itself is subject to small changes, called perturbations. The Earth's orbit is an ellipse, and there is a slow change in its orientation, which gradually shifts the point of perihelion in space. The two effects—the precession of the axis and the change in the orbit's orientation—work together to shift the seasons with respect to perihelion. Thus, since we use a calendar year that is aligned to the occurrence of the seasons, the date of perihelion gradually regresses through the year. It takes 21,000 years to make a complete cycle of dates.

We would not expect the 21,000-year cycle to be very important climatologically because the Earth's orbit is almost circular—the distance to the Sun at perihelion is only about 3 percent less than its distance at aphelion. That is, whether perihelion occurs in January or July, it seems unlikely that our seasons would be much affected. At least, that is the case now; but the eccentricity of the Earth's orbit (how elliptical it is) also changes over very long periods of time, from almost zero (circular orbit) to about three times its current value. The eccentricity of the orbit varies periodically with a time scale of about 100,000 years. So, it would be reasonable to suppose that if the 21,000-year perihelion shift cycle were to have any effect on climate at all, it would only be during the more widely spaced epochs when the orbital eccentricity was relatively large. That is, climatologically, the 100,000-year cycle of eccentricity should *modulate* the 21,000-year cycle of perihelion.

In fact, Mars has an orbit much more eccentric than the Earth's, and its perihelion cycle (which has a period of 51,000 years) does apparently have a significant effect on climate and prevailing wind direction there.

There is another important cycle that has the potential to affect the Earth's climate; it is a 41,000-year variation in *obliquity*, the tilt of the Earth's axis with respect to a direction perpendicular to its orbital plane. This variation is different from precession—the two motions are at right angles to each other—and astronomically is a much smaller effect. The obliquity varies by only a few degrees back and forth, and the current value of 23.4° is near the middle of the range. However, climatologically, the obliquity variation has the potential to have a fairly direct effect on seasonal extremes. After all, it is the obliquity that causes our seasons in the first place—if the Earth's axis were perpendicular to its orbital plane, there would be no seasons at all.

The astronomical cycles described above are called *Milankovitch cycles* after Milutin Milankovitch, a Serbian scientist who provided a detailed theory of their potential influence over climate in the 1920s. Milankovitch's work was an attempt at explaining the ice ages, and it built upon previous astronomical theories of climate variation postulated by Joseph Adhemar and James Croll in the 19th century. Although the Milankovitch theory is well-grounded astronomically, it remains controversial. The theory predicts different effects at different latitudes, and thus its use as a predictor of global (or at least hemispheric) climate change is not unambiguous. The exact mechanisms by which the relatively modest variations in the Earth's orbit and axis direction might result in such large effects as the ice ages are not well established. The theory's popularity has tended to vary depending on the type of long-term climatological data that has been available and the method used to establish a time scale for the data.

The 21,000-year perihelion cycle and the 41,000-year obliquity cycle do in fact appear to be present in the climatological record. But the dominant climate cycle that is seen has a period of about 100,000 years. Although this coincides with the period of change in the eccentricity of the Earth's orbit, the theory outlined above does not predict that we should see this period directly—the effect of eccentricity should appear only as a modulation of the 21,000-year perihelion cycle. The mechanism by which the Earth's orbital eccentricity could affect the climate in such a direct and important way is not known, although recent evidence (published in 2000) indicates that atmospheric carbon dioxide may play a leading role in amplifying the orbital effect. However, some researchers still have doubts about the association between the 100,000-year climate cycle and orbital variations. Thus, many questions remain about long-term climate variations and their relationship, if any, to astronomical causes. . . .

SIGNIFICANCE

The significance of the three dominant Milankovitch cycles follows from their possible influence on climate changes over an extended cycle of time of about 100,000 years. As reported by Kaplan, Milankovitch based his studies on the hypothesis that the present Ice Age, which occurred during the Pleistocene Epoch that lasted from about 1.6 million years to about 10,000 years ago, was caused mainly by cyclical changes in the Earth's orbit about the sun. Mutual variations in the Earth's precession, eccentricity, and obliquity, as proposed by Milankovitch, created seasonal changes in the amount and angle of radiation coming from the sun to the Earth. When periods of increased or decreased solar radiation occurred, they directly influenced the Earth's seasons, thus impacting its global climate. In particular, Milankovitch charged that these major variations in the motion of the Earth impacted the advance and retreat of Earth's glaciers during the ice ages.

In the future, Kaplan stated that the theory of the Milankovitch cycles will predict climatic changes due to the variation in the Earth's orbit that occur over thousands of years. However, Kaplan also explained that the climate system of the Earth may also take thousands of years to respond to those orbital variations.

In 1976, a study published in the journal *Science* reported that evidence within sediment cores retrieved from the bottom of the ocean supported Milankovitch's theory. A record of temperature changes taken from the sediment cores found that major variations in climate going back 450,000 years were closely related with changes in precession, eccentricity, and obliquity of the Earth's orbit. The study concluded that the Ice Age occurred during a period when Earth was going through different stages of orbital variation. However, other studies performed since 1976 do not directly support the contentions of Milankovitch.

The Milankovitch theory has proven its merit with respect to its results of the major astronomical cycles of the Earth's orbit—those of precession, eccentricity, and obliquity. However, its conclusions with respect to the three cycles shaping Earth's global, or at least hemispheric, climate variations remain controversial within the scientific community. The correlation between the slight orbital variations, proposed by Milankovitch, which drastically affect Earth's past climate, is still not completely verified by scientists.

Milankovitch cycles have frequently explained climatic change over the last tens of thousands of years, and recently they have explained climate shifts over periods of 1,000 to 15,000 years. Generally, the 21,000 precession cycle and the 41,000 obliquity cycle appear to be present in past records of climate, but the dominant 100,000 eccentricity cycle is less obvious within related records.

Researchers still doubt the general validity of the Milankovitch theory with respect to predicting changes of Earth's climate. It is uncertain whether or not Milankovitch cycles will be proven in the future to explain long-term climate changes found on the Earth. Whatever the result, the cycles have nothing to do with, and are unable to account for, climate changes made by the industrial and related activities of humans. As a result, if in the future Milankovitch cycles are scientifically proven to affect natural changes to climate, then it may be easier to prove the amount that climate is affected by artificially generated emissions from human activities such as greenhouse gases.

FURTHER RESOURCES
Books

Imbrie, John, and Katherine Palmer Imbrie. *Ice Ages: Solving the Mystery*. Cambridge, MA.: Harvard University Press, 1986.

Lutgens, Frederick K., and Edward J. Tarbuck. *The Atmosphere: An Introduction to Meteorology*. Englewood Cliffs, NJ: Prentice Hall, 1995.

Web sites

Earth Observatory Library, National Aeronautics and Space Administration. "On the Shoulders of Giants: Milutin Milankovitch (1879–1958)." <http://earthobservatory.nasa.gov/Library/Giants/Milankovitch/milankovitch.html> (accessed November 26, 2005).

"Global Warming: The Culprit?

Evidence mounts that human activity is helping fuel these monster hurricanes"

Magazine article

By: Jeffery Kluger

Date: October 3, 2005

Source: Kluger, Jeffery. "Global Warming: The Culprit? Evidence mounts that human activity is helping fuel these monster hurricanes." *Time* 166, no. 14 (October 3, 2005): 42.

About the Author: Jeffery Kluger is a senior writer for *Time* magazine, having started with the publication in 1996 as a contributor. Following the cover story on global warming, Kluger and two other writers were given the Whitman Bassow Award from the Overseas Press Club of America for best reporting on international environmental issues. Kluger has also written for *Discover, New York Times Business World, Family Circle*, and *Science Digest* magazines.

INTRODUCTION

There was a record number of tropical storms and hurricanes during the 2005 Atlantic hurricane season. This included one of the most damaging hurricanes of all time, Hurricane Katrina, which displaced thousands of people and caused billions of dollars of damage to the city of New Orleans. Scientists are questioning whether the intense hurricane season is just a randomly occurring phenomenon, or whether it is a sign that global climate change is beginning to take hold.

The Atlantic hurricane season runs from June 1st until the end of November. Twenty-one names are set aside for the potential hurricanes in a given season. The names are generated from lists originally created by the US National Hurricane Center, and are now managed by the World Meteorological Organization. If there are more than twenty-one tropical storms or hurricanes in a year, Greeks letters are assigned to the storms in alphabetical order. 2005 is the first year when there were enough storms to require the use of Greek letters.

Scientists claim there is evidence that hurricanes have increased in intensity over the last thirty to thirty-five years, concluding that there has been a decrease in category one and two storms, and an increase in the proportion of category three, four, and five storms. Category five is the highest ranking a hurricane can be given, based on the Saffir-Simpson scale, with this ranking given to a storm with winds greater than 155 miles per hour, and storm surge that exceeds eighteen feet. It is believed that warmer sea-surface temperatures cause the increase in hurricane intensity. Scientists say increases in wind speeds and rainfall associated with the storms are evidence of an intensification of the natural global hydrological cycle. The cycle begins with heat provided by the sun. As the sea and atmosphere warm, the water begins to evaporate, absorbing the heat energy. The evaporated moisture then makes its way to the the upper atmosphere, where it comes in contact with much cooler temperatures. Once it begins to cool, the evaporated moisture releases the stored energy, and condenses. Global warming has increased the surface temperature of the ocean, providing added fuel to growing storms and hurricanes, making them more intense.

Despite the records set in 2005, some scientists say there is little evidence of an increasing trend in the annual number of storms. They argue that such a trend would require a more consistent increase in the number of storms over several years, or decades. There are arguments that climate change has little to do with the intensity of storms in the Atlantic. Some argue that Hurricane Katrina gained intensity over a patch of deep warm water in the Gulf of Mexico, which was not representative of an overall change in temperature of the sea. This is supported by saying that global warming only impacts the surface waters, something that hurricanes likely displace. If only the surface is warm, hurricanes would decrease in intensity by coming in contact with cool deeper waters. These scientists suggest Katrina found deeper warm water by chance.

■ PRIMARY SOURCE

If 2005 goes down as the worst hurricane season on record in the North Atlantic, it will join 2004 as one of the most violent ever. And these two seasons are part of a trend of increasingly powerful and deadly hurricanes that has been playing out for more than ten years. Says climatologist Judy Curry, chair of the School of Earth and Atmospheric Sciences at the Georgia Institute of Technology: "The so-called once-in-a-lifetime storm isn't even once in a season anymore."

Head-snapping changes in the weather like this inevitably raise the question, Is global warming to blame? For years, environmentalists have warned that one of the first and most reliable signs of a climatological crash would be an upsurge in the most violent hurricanes, the kind that thrive in a suddenly warmer world. Scientists are quick to point out that changes in the weather and climate change are two different things. But now, after watching two Gulf Coast hurricanes reach Category 5 in the space of four weeks, even skeptical scientists are starting to wonder whether something serious might be going on.

"There is no doubt that climate is changing and humans are partly responsible," says Kevin Trenberth, head of the climate-analysis section at the National Center for Atmospheric Research (NCAR) in Boulder, Colo. "The odds have changed in favor of more intense storms and heavier rainfalls." Says NCAR meteorologist Greg Holland; "These are not small changes. We're talking about a very large change."

But do scientists really know for sure? Can man-made greenhouse gases really be blamed for the intensity of storms like Rita and Katrina? Or are there, as other experts insist, too many additional variables to say one way or the other?

That global warming ought to, in theory, exacerbate the problem of hurricanes is an easy conclusion to reach. Few scientists doubt that carbon dioxide and other greenhouse gases raise the temperature of Earth's atmosphere. Warmer air can easily translate into warmer oceans—and warm oceans are the jet fuel that drives the hurricane's turbine. When Katrina hit at the end of August, the Gulf of Mexico was a veritable hurricane refueling station, with water up to 5°F higher than normal. Rita too drew its killer strength from the gulf, making its way past southern Florida as a Category 1 storm, then exploding into a Category 5 as it moved westward. "The Gulf is really warm this year, and it's just cooking those tropical storms," says Curry.

Local hot spots like this are not the same as global climate change, but they do appear to be part of a larger trend. Since 1970, mean ocean surface temperatures worldwide have risen about 1°F. Those numbers have moved in lockstep with global air temperatures, which have also inched up a degree. The warmest year ever recorded was 1998, with 2002, 2003 and 2004 close behind it.

So that ought to mean a lot more hurricanes, right? Actually, no—which is one of the reasons it's so hard to pin these trends down. The past ten stormy years in the North Atlantic were preceded by many very quiet ones—all occurring at the same time that global temperatures were marching upward. Worldwide, there's a sort of equilibrium. When the number of storms in the North Atlantic increases, there is usually a corresponding fall in the number of storms in, say, the North Pacific. Over the course of a year, the variations tend to cancel one another out. "Globally," says atmospheric scientist Kerry Emanuel of the Massachusetts Institute of Technology, "we do not see any increase at all in the frequency of hurricanes."

But frequency is not the same as intensity, and two recent studies demonstrate that difference. Two weeks ago, a team of scientists that included Curry and Holland published a study in the journal Science that surveyed global hurricane frequency and intensity over the past thirty-five years. On the whole, they found, the number of Category 1, 2 and 3 storms has fallen slightly, while the number of Categories 4 and 5 storms—the most powerful ones—has climbed dramatically. In the 1970s, there were and average of ten Category 4 and 5 hurricanes a year worldwide. Since 1990, the annual number has nearly doubled, to 18. Overall, the big storms have grown from just 20% of the global total to 35%. "We have sustained increase [in hurricane intensity] over 30 years all over the globe," says Holland.

Emanuel came at the same question differently but got the same results. In a study published in the journal Nature last month, he surveyed roughly 4,800 hurricanes in the North Atlantic and North Pacific over the past 56 years. While he too found no increase in the total number of hurricanes, he found that their power—measured by wind speed and duration—had jumped 50% since the mid–1970s. "The storms are getting stronger," Emanuel says, "and they're lasting longer."

Several factors help feed the trend. For example, when ocean temperatures rise, so does the amount of water vapor in the air. A moister atmosphere helps fuel storms by giving them more to spit out in the form of rain and by helping drive the convection that gives them their lethal spin. Warm oceans produce higher levels of vapor than cool oceans—at a rate of about 1.3% more per decade since 1988, according to one study—and nothing gets that process going better than greenhouse-heated air. "Water vapor increases the rainfall intensity," says Trenberth. "During Katrina, rainfall exceeded twelve inches near New Orleans."

It's not just warmer water on the surface that's powering the hurricanes; deeper warm water is too—at least in the Gulf of Mexico. Extending from the surface to a depth of two thousand feet or more is something scientists call the Loop Current, a U-shaped stream of warm water that flows from the Yucatan Straits to the Florida Straits and sometimes reaches as far north as the Mississippi River delta. Hurricanes that pass over the Loop typically get an energy boost, but the extra kick is brief, since they usually cross it and move on. But Rita and Katrina surfed it across the Gulf, picking up an even more powerful head of steam before slamming into the coastal sates. Even if those unlucky beelines had been entirely random, the general trend toward warmer Gulf water may well have made the Loop even deadlier than usual.

"We don't know the temperature within the Loop Current," says Nan Walker, director of Louisiana State University's Earth Scan Laboratory. "It's possible that below the surface, it's warmer than normal. This needs to be investigated."

Other greenhouse-related variables may also be fueling the storms. Temperature-boosting carbon dioxide, for example, does not linger in the atmosphere forever. Some of it precipitates out in rain, settling partly on the oceans and sinking at least temporarily out of sight. But the violent frothing of the water caused by a hurricane can release some of that entrained CO_2, sending it back into the sky, where it resumes its role in the warming cycle. During Hurricane Felix in 1995, measurements taken in one area the storm struck showed local CO_2 levels spiking one hundred-fold.

So, are hurricanes actually speeding the effects of global warming and thus spawning even more violet storms? That's a matter of some dispute. While many scientists agree that this outgassing process goes on, not everyone agrees that it makes much of a difference. "The amount of CO_2 given off is fairly insignificant in terms of the total CO_2 in the atmosphere," says atmospheric scientist Chris Bretherton of the University of Washington in Seattle. "I am fairly confident in saying that there is no direct feedback from hurricanes."

Thus scientific uncertainty enters the debate—a debate already intensified by the political passions that surround any discussion of global warming. The fact is, there is plenty of room for doubt on both sides of the argument. Chris Landsea, a science and operations officer at the National Hurricane Center in Miami, is one of many experts who believe that global warming may be boosting the power of hurricanes—but only a bit, perhaps 1% to 5%. A one hundred-mile-per-hour wind today would be a 105-mile-per-hour wind in a century," he says. "That is pretty tiny in comparison with the swings between hurricane cycles."

Skeptics are also troubled by what they see as a not inconsiderable bias in how hurricane researchers collect their data. Since most hurricanes spend the majority of their lives at sea—some never making land at all—it's impossible to measure rainfall precisely and therefore difficult to measure the true intensity of a storm.

What's more, historical studies of hurricanes like Emanuel's rely on measurements taken both before and during the era of satellites. Size up your storms in radically divergent ways, and you're likely to get radically divergent results. Even after satellites came into wide—adding a significant measure of reliability to the data collected— the quality of the machines and the meteorologists who relied on them was often uneven. "The satellite technology available from 1970 to 1989 was not up to the job,"

says William Gray of Colorado State University. "And many people in non—U.S. areas were not trained well enough to determine the very fine difference between, say, the 130-m.p.h. wind speed of a Category 4 and, below that, a Category 3."

There's also some question as to whether there's a subtler, less scientific bias going on, one driven not by the raw power of the storms but by where they do their damage. Hurricanes that claw up empty coasts don't generate the same headlines as those that strike the places we like to live—and increasingly we like to live near the shore. The coastal population in the U.S. jumped 28% between 1980 and 2003. In Florida alone, the increase was a staggering 75%. Even the most objective scientist can be swayed when whole cities are being demolished by a hurricane.

"The storm activity this year is no necessarily higher than in previous high-activity years. It's just where they are going," says meteorologist Stan Goldenberg of the National Oceanic and Atmospheric Administration in Key Biscayne, Florida. "If you've got a guy shooting a machine gun but he's not shooting toward your neighborhood, it doesn't bother you."

Even correcting for our tendency to pay more attention to what is happening in our backyard, however, the global census of storms and the general measurement of their increasing power don't lie. And what those measurements tell scientists is that this already serious problem could grow a great deal worse—and do so very fast.

Some scientists are studying not just climate change but the even more alarming phenomenon of abrupt climate change. Complex systems like the atmosphere are known to move from one steady state to another with only very brief transitions in between. (Think of water, which when put over a flame becomes hotter and hotter until suddenly it turns into steam.) Ice cores taken from Greenland in the 1990s by geoscientist Richard Alley of Pennsylvania State University show that the last ice age came to an end not in the slow creep of geological time but in the quick pop of real time, with the entire planet abruptly warming in just three years.

SIGNIFICANCE

There is evidence that natural, cyclic occurrences of weather related systems, such as the El Niño Southern Oscillation in the Pacific Ocean, can impact hurricane intensity. It has been documented that during El Niño years, when there are warmer waters in the Eastern Pacific, hurricanes in the Atlantic are less frequent. Scientists create models to monitor the interaction between the Earth's complex climate systems as they respond to global warming. Continued work on designing models that incorporate new knowledge on the understanding of climate systems are necessary to further understand how climate change impacts such things as hurricane intensity. As satellite imagery and other mapping techniques improve, the accuracy of climate change modeling is likely to improve. The variables in the models can then be augmented with actual data to improve the predictions the models provide.

The growing interest in the frequency and intensity of hurricanes is also driven by socio-economic concerns. Hurricanes have damaged billions of dollars worth of property in recent years. Some people say that it is these high monetary impacts that are driving the argument that hurricanes have increased in strength. More people live in coastal areas than ever before, increasing the odds that a hurricane making landfall will destroy homes and businesses in its path. Prior to such population densities on the coast, hurricanes were damaging forests and other uninhabited lands. Experts also say that such development has removed natural barriers, decreasing the natural hurricane buffers that forests and swamps provide.

FURTHER RESOURCES

Books

Houghton, John. *Global Warming: The Complete Briefing*. Cambridge, UK; New York: Cambridge University Press, 2004.

Michaels, Patricia. *Meltdown: The Predictable Distortion of Global Warming by Scientists, Politicians, and the Media*. Washington, D.C.: Cato Institute, 2004.

Periodicals

McDonald, R.E., D.G. Bleaken, D.R. Cresswell, V.D. Pope, and C.A. Senior. "Tropical storms: Representation and Diagnosis in Climate Models and the Impacts of Climate Change." *Climate Dynamics* 25, no. 1 (July 2005): 19-36. Available online at <http://www.springer-link.com/openurl.asp?genre=article&issn=0930-7575&volume=25&issue=1&spage=19> (accessed March 17, 2006).

Moreira, Naila. "The Wind and the Fury: Has climate Change Made Hurricanes Fiercer, or Are Such Claims Hot Air?" *Science News* 168, no. 12 (September 17, 2005): 12. Available online at <http://www.sciencenews. org/articles/20050917/bob8.asp> (accessed March 17, 2006).

Websites

"Global Warming and Hurricanes: Computer Model Simulations." *National Oceanic and Atmospheric Administration Geophysical Fluid Dynamics Laboratory*, August 2001. <http://www.gfdl.noaa.gov/~kd/One Pagers/OnePageF01.pdf> (accessed March 17, 2006).

"Interaction with El Niño: How Hurricane Frequency May Be Affected." *WW 2010: University of Illinois*. <http://ww2010.atmos.uiuc.edu/(Gh)/guides/mtr/hurr/enso.rxml> (accessed March 17, 2006).

The Biosphere

The biosphere refers to all living organisms on Earth and all organic matter that has not decomposed. Russian scientist Vladimir Vernadsky (1863–1945) first proposed the term in the 1920s to designate the diverse collection of plants, animals, fungi, and micro-organisms that inhabit Earth. The term usually includes the idea that individual members of the biosphere are interdependent.

The term biosphere is often used with a set of ecological and geophysical terms that describe relationships among various features of the planet. The atmosphere refers to the gaseous material surrounding Earth. The biosphere interacts with the atmosphere mainly through the processes of respiration and photosynthesis. The hydrosphere describes all forms of water on Earth: liquid water, water vapor, and ice. Interactions between the biosphere and the hydrosphere are numerous, as all life requires water. The geosphere includes all of Earth's mineral deposits, including rock, soil, sand, and clay. Plants are heavily dependent on the geosphere as a source of nutrients. In turn, herbivores and carnivores attain the minerals they require from plants. The geosphere is also the primary substrate for terrestrial life.

The extent of the biosphere is difficult to determine because living organisms have been found in almost every portion of Earth. Scientists have documented birds that have flown at heights reaching 36,000 feet (nearly 11,000 meters). Deep-sea fish have been found in ocean trenches as deep as 29,500 feet (nearly 9,000 meters) below sea level. Bacteria have been discovered living in frozen ice in both the Arctic and Antarctic.

The biosphere is usually subdivided into biomes, which contain similar species of plants and animals.

These biomes are characterized by the amount of precipitation they receive and the range of temperatures they experience. For example, the tropical rain forest receives some 98 inches (250 centimeters) of annual rainfall; its average temperature ranges between 68 and 86 °F (20 and 30 °C). However, the tundra receives some 19.5 inches (50 centimeters) of yearly precipitation, with temperatures averaging between 5 ° and 23 °F (−15° and −5 °C). Other typical terrestrial biomes include temperate forests, savannah, woodlands and grasslands, taiga, temperate rain forests, and desert. Aquatic biomes include estuaries and wetlands, marine shorelines, the open ocean, the deep ocean, lakes, and rivers.

The organisms living in the various biomes are each well adapted to the specific environmental conditions that exist in their unique habitats. All living things can tolerate some change in their environment. However, some organisms can survive in a wide range of environmental conditions, while others have very specific requirements. Changes to the environments can alter the conditions to which the organisms have adapted.

Humans have greatly impacted environmental conditions throughout the biosphere. Humans, Earth's most dominant species, have disturbed the majority of Earth's ecosystems. Humans have altered the species composition of ecosystems and changed the physical processes of the geosphere. Although every biome has been affected by human activities, the biomes most threatened include temperate forests, rain forests, grasslands, and wetlands. This chapter documents important issues involving the biosphere and biomes.

A Naturalist in Nicaragua

Book excerpt

By: Thomas Belt

Date: 1873

Source: Belt, Thomas. *A Naturalist in Nicaragua.* London: J. M. Dent & Sons, 1874.

About the Author: Thomas Belt (1832–1878) was a British geologist and naturalist who studied gold deposits in Australia and Nova Scotia throughout the 1850s and 1860s. His work in the mines of Nicaragua led to the writing and publication of his book, *A Naturalist in Nicaragua.*

INTRODUCTION

In the decades that followed Charles Darwin's well-chronicled trip throughout portions of South America and the publication of his book *The Origin of Species* in 1859, exploration of the continent's land and potential resources yielded a wide range of information about minerals, animal life, precious metals, fuels, and plant-based medicinal remedies. As professional and amateur geologists, biologists, geographers, and chemists explored the Amazon basin, the Andes Mountains, Patagonia, and the Brazilian rainforest, these scientists detailed their observations and discoveries in journal articles, books, and popular magazines. Understanding the natural world had become not only the province of specialists, but also a pastime for the wealthy and the educated middle class. A strong demand for published accounts of natural science developed in Europe and the United States; throughout the 1870s and 1880s, various science societies and publications, *National Geographic* among them, formed in response to this demand.

Belt, a British geologist by trade, had worked in Australia, North America, and Europe before going to Nicaragua in 1866. In 1867 he published a memoir-observation on mines in Wales in *Geological Magazine;*

A farmer employs the "slash and burn" technique on his plot of land in Managua, Nicaragua, May 3, 1998. Though the burning is necessary to prepare for planting, smoke from the fires contributes to low visability. AP IMAGES

the article was well-received and encouraged him to continue writing about his observations and analysis of natural phenomena.

Belt chronicled his four years in Nicaragua with a richly detailed account of the lands, animals, insects, plant life, and geology of the region in which he lived and worked. Belt painstakingly described the activities of ant colonies near his quarters, speculating that the ants used a particular leaf to cultivate a certain type of fungus, an observation borne out by later scientists. This relationship between the ants and bull's-horn acacia led to the naming of a portion of the plant "Beltian Bodies," in honor of Thomas Belt. Belt's theory about the symbiotic relationship between the ants and the acacia was controversial in its time.

In other sections, Belt describes the patterns of rivers, giving modern explorers a baseline from which to calculate change in the region over time. Charles Darwin praised Belt's book, and his observation of the effect of glaciers on South America generated debate and scholarly interest.

In addition to noting the conditions of the natural environment in Central and South America, Belt also wrote about the actions of the inhabitants. From discussions on "slash and burn" agriculture to descriptions of workers in the gold mines he directed, Belt created a book that encapsulated Nicaragua—and much of South America—in a frozen snapshot of the late 1860s. In keeping a "naturalist's journal," Belt's meticulous attention to detail gave fellow scientists, both professional and amateur, a blueprint of the sections of the continent he explored.

PRIMARY SOURCE

. . . Having determined to go up the [Colorado] river in this boat, we took provisions with us for the voyage, and one of the negroes agreed to act as cook. Having arranged everything, and breakfasted with my kind friends, Mr. and Mrs. Hollenbeck, I bade them adieu, and settled myself into the small space in the canoe that I expected to occupy for six days. Captain Anderson took the helm, the "Caribs" dipped their paddles into the water, and away we glided into a narrow channel amongst long grass and rushes that almost touched us on either side. Grey town, with its neat white houses, and feathery palms, and large-leaved bread-fruit trees, was soon shut from our view, and our boatmen plying their paddles with the greatest dexterity and force, made the canoe shoot along through the still water. Soon we emerged into a wider channel where a stronger stream was running, and then we coasted along close to the shore to avoid the strength of the current. The banks at first were

low and marshy and intersected by numerous channels; the principal tree was a long, coarse-leaved palm, and there were great beds of wild cane and grass, amongst which we occasionally saw curious green lizards, with leaf-like expansions (like those on the leaf-insects), assimilating them in appearance to the vegetation amongst which they sought their prey. As we proceeded up the river, the banks gradually became higher and drier, and we passed some small plantations of bananas and plantains made in clearings in the forest, which now consisted of a great variety of dicotyledonous trees with many tall, graceful palms; the undergrowth being ferns, small palms, Melastomae, Heliconiae, etc. The houses at the plantations were mostly miserable thatched huts with scarcely any furniture, the owners passing their time swinging in dirty hammocks, and occasionally taking down a canoe-load of plantains to Greytown for sale. It is one of the rarest sights to see any of these squatters at work. Their plantain patch and occasionally some fish from the river suffice to keep them alive and indolent.

At seven o'clock we reached the Colorado branch, which carries off the greater part of the waters of the San Juan to the sea. This is about twenty miles above Greytown, but only eighteen by the Colorado to the sea, and is near the head of the delta, as I have already mentioned. The main body of water formerly flowed down past Greytown, and kept the harbour there open, but a few years ago, during a heavy flood, the river greatly enlarged and deepened the entrance to the Colorado Channel, and since then year by year the Greytown harbour has been silting up. Now (I am writing in 1873) there is twelve feet of water on the bar at the Colorado in the height of the dry season, whilst at Greytown the outlet of the river is sometimes closed altogether. The merchants at Greytown have entertained the project of dredging out the channel again, but now that the river has found a nearer way to the sea by the Colorado this would be a herculean task, and it would cost much less money to move the whole town to the Colorado, where by dredging the bar a fine harbour might easily be made, but unfortunately the Colorado is in Costa Rica, the Greytown branch in Nicaragua, and there are constant bickerings between the two states respecting the outlet of this fine river, which make any well-considered scheme for the improvement of it impracticable at present. A sensible solution of the difficulty would be a federation of the two small republics. The heads of the political parties in the two countries see, however, in this a danger to their petty ambitions, and will not risk the step, and so the boundary question remains an open one, threatening at any moment to plunge the two countries into an impoverishing war.

If the Colorado were not to be interfered with by man, it would, in the course of ages, carry down great quantities of mud, sand, and trunks of trees, and gradually form sandbanks at its mouth, pushing out the delta further and further at this point, until it was greatly in advance of the rest of the coast; the river would then break through again by some nearer channel, and the Colorado would be silted up as the Lower San Juan is being at present. The numerous half filled-up channels and long lagoons throughout the delta show the various courses the river has at different times taken.

Our boatmen paddled on until nine o'clock, when we anchored in the middle of the stream, which was here about one hundred yards wide. Distant as we were from the shore, we were not too far for the mosquitoes, which came off in myriads to the banquet upon our blood. Sleep for me was impossible, and to add to the discomfort, the rain came down in torrents. We had an old tarpaulin with us, but it was full of holes, and let in the water in little streams, so that I was soon soaked to the skin. Altogether, with the streaming wet and the mosquitoes, it was one of the most uncomfortable nights I have ever passed.

The waning moon was sufficiently high at four o'clock to allow us to bring the long dreary night to an end, and to commence paddling up the river again. As the day broke the rain ceased, the mists cleared away, our spirits revived, and we forgot our discomforts of the night in admiration of the beauties of the river. The banks were hidden by a curtain of creeping and twining plants, many of which bore beautiful flowers, and the green was further varied here and there by the white stems of the cecropia trees. Now and then we passed more open spots, affording glimpses into the forest, where grew, in the dark shade, slender-stemmed palms and beautiful tree-ferns, contrasting with the great leaves of the Heliconiae. At seven we breakfasted on a sand-bank, and got our clothes and blankets dried. There were numerous tracks of alligators, but it was too early to look for their eggs in the sand; a month later, in March, when the river falls, they are found in abundance, and eaten by the canoe-men. At noon we reached the point where the Seripiqui, a river coming down from the interior of Costa Rica, joins the San Juan about thirty miles above Greytown. The Seripiqui is navigable by canoes for about twenty miles from this point, and then commences a rough mountain mule-track to San Jose, the capital of Costa Rica. We paddled on all the afternoon with little change in the river. At eight we anchored for the night, and although it rained heavily again, I was better prepared for it, and, coiling myself up under an umbrella beneath the tarpaulin, managed to sleep a little.

We started again before daylight, and at ten stopped at a small clearing for breakfast. I strolled back a little way into the gloomy forest, but it was not easy to get along on account of the undergrowth and numerous climbing plants that bound it together. I saw one of the large olive-green and brown mot-mots (*Momotus martii*), sitting upon a branch of a tree, moving its long curious tail from side to side, until it

was nearly at right angles to its body. I afterwards saw other species in the forests and savannahs of Chontales. They all have several characters in common, linked together in a series of gradations. One of these features is a spot of black feathers on the breast. In some species this is edged with blue, in others, as in the one mentioned above, these black feathers form only a small black spot nearly hidden amongst the rust-coloured feathers of the breast. Characters such as these, very conspicuous in some species, shading off in others through various gradations to insignificance, if not extinction, are known by naturalists to occur in numerous genera; and so far they have only been explained on the supposition of the descent of the different species from a common progenitor.

As I returned to the boat, I crossed a column of the army or foraging ants, many of them dragging along the legs and mangled bodies of insects that they had captured in their foray. I afterwards often encountered these ants in the forests and it may be convenient to place together all the facts I learnt respecting them.

The Ecitons, or foraging ants, are very numerous throughout Central America. Whilst the leaf-cutting ants are entirely vegetable feeders, the foraging ants are hunters, and live solely on insects or other prey; and it is a curious analogy that, like the hunting races of mankind, they have to change their hunting-grounds when one is exhausted, and move on to another. In Nicaragua they are generally called "Army Ants." One of the smaller species (*Eciton predator*) used occasionally to visit our house, swarm over the floors and walls, searching every cranny, and driving out the cockroaches and spiders, many of which were caught, pulled or bitten to pieces, and carried off. The individuals of this species are of various sizes; the smallest measuring one and a quarter lines, and the largest three lines, or a quarter of an inch.

I saw many large armies of this, or a closely allied species, in the forest. My attention was generally first called to them by the twittering of some small birds, belonging to several different species, that follow the ants in the woods. On approaching to ascertain the cause of this disturbance, a dense body of the ants, three or four yards wide, and so numerous as to blacken the ground, would be seen moving rapidly in one direction, examining every cranny, and underneath every fallen leaf. On the flanks, and in advance of the main body, smaller columns would be pushed out. These smaller columns would generally first flush the cockroaches, grasshoppers, and spiders. The pursued insects would rapidly make off, but many, in their confusion and terror, would bound right into the midst of the main body of ants. A grasshopper, finding itself in the midst of its enemies, would give vigorous leaps, with perhaps two or three of the ants clinging to its legs. Then it would stop a moment to rest, and that moment would be fatal, for the tiny foes would swarm over the prey, and after a few more ineffectual struggles it would succumb to its fate, and soon be bitten to pieces and carried off to the rear. The greatest catch of the ants was, however, when they got amongst some fallen brushwood. The cockroaches, spiders, and other insects, instead of running right away, would ascend the fallen branches and remain there, whilst the host of ants were occupying all the ground below. By and by up would come some of the ants, following every branch, and driving before them their prey to the ends of the small twigs, when nothing remained for them but to leap, and they would alight in the very throng of their foes, with the result of being certainly caught and pulled to pieces. Many of the spiders would escape by hanging suspended by a thread of silk from the branches, safe from the foes that swarmed both above and below. . . .

SIGNIFICANCE

Belt's descriptions of the natives in this passage contrast with his observations of plant life. Describing the villagers as "indolent," and the political leaders in Costa Rica and Nicaragua as having "petty ambitions" over their territorial pursuit regarding the Colorado River, Belt injects a judgmental tone that is not present as he records nature observations. His judgments, however, are related to the impact that people have on the environment. Political officials engaged in a border dispute may harm the river, or most certainly interfere with its natural progress and movement. Belt notes this as well, with great care and detail, speculating the path the river might take were it not touched by man.

The theory posited by Belt in the book concerning ants and bull's-horn acacia was not proven until the 1960s, when Daniel Janzen found that there was a mutualistic/symbiotic relationship between the two. Throughout Belt's career he put forth a controversial theory on glacier activity not only in South America, but across the globe. In *The Naturalist in Nicaragua* he used certain geological observations as evidence of glacial epochs having occurred in Nicaragua. Belt broadened those observations to develop the idea that continental glaciation may have led to the extinction of various Pleistocene plant and animal life, including early man.

Based on this research, Belt examined phenomena such as protective coloration in tropical plants. He maintained a correspondence with Charles Darwin and was well known among naturalists and scientists for his work in mining and his theory on glacier activity. Over time, Belt's theories have proven true, and his book has become not only an importance piece of

natural history, but also a baseline from which modern researchers can measure change in the Central American environment.

FURTHER RESOURCES

Books

Roberts, J. Timmons, and Nikki D. Thanos. *Trouble in Paradise: Globalization and Environmental Crises in Latin America*. New York: Routledge Press, 2003.

Soluri, John. "Altered Landscapes and Transformed Livelihoods: Banana Companies, Panama Disease, and Rural Communities on the North Coast of Honduras, 1880–1950." In *Interactions Between Agroecosystems and Rural Communities*, edited by Cornelia Butler-Flora. Boca Raton, Fla.: CRC Press, 2000

Web sites

"Environment in Latin America." *LANIC.* <http://lanic. utexas.edu/la/region/environment> (accessed March 13, 2006).

The Sewers of Paris, Purification Service

Photograph

By: Roger Viollet

Date: January 1, 1900

Source: Getty Images

About the Photographer: This photograph was taken in 1900 in the sewers of Paris, which were world-famous for their extent and modernity. Today, tourists can take tours of the sewers.

INTRODUCTION

This image gives some idea of the extent and complexity of the famous sewers of Paris, *les egouts* (pronounced lay-ZAY-goo), constructed mostly during the mid– to late–nineteenth century. Far more than a system of pipes through which waste could drain, the sewers of Paris were constructed as underground tunnels conveying runoff and sewage, fresh-water pipes, electrical and telephone cabling, and raised walkways for workers. In the 1890s, there were even boat trips through parts of the sewer system, attended by well-dressed ladies and gentlemen.

As with all European cities, the sewage system of Paris was originally no system at all. Human waste was collected in pots and thrown out of windows to drain down the middle of the street. Actually, chamber-pots were a relatively high standard: even the nobility sometimes relieved themselves indoors. In 1589, the court of England was served with the following notice: "Let no one, whoever he may be, before, at, or after meals, Early or late, foul the staircases, corridors, or closets with Urine or other filth." Disease, especially cholera, was the frequent result of such practices. Conditions were somewhat better in rural areas, where people were less crowded and could relieve themselves anywhere in the landscape.

The first underground sewer in Paris was built in 1370, a simple drain that conveyed sewage to the river. More such drains were built over the next several centuries, but most dwellings voided their waste into cesspits, which drained into the soil. In the early 1800s, under Napoleon, a massive rebuilding of the underground sewers was performed. However, the isolation of drinking water from sewage remained poor, and the city was struck with severe cholera epidemics in the 1830s that killed thousands. Improved sewers were constructed starting in the 1840s—high-ceilinged, wide, walkway-flanked tunnels such as that shown in the photograph. The goal was a sewer under every major street, which was finally attained in the 1930s. Sewage was not treated before discharge until much more recently. Human health in the city was greatly improved, but the Seine River ran as a vast open sewer until sewage treatment, which removes sludge and at least some bacteria from water before discharging it, was instituted starting in the 1960s and 70s.

■ PRIMARY SOURCE

THE SEWERS OF PARIS, PURIFICATION SERVICE
See primary source image.

■ PRIMARY SOURCE

The Sewers of Paris, Purification Service. This image, taken sometime in the 1900s, shows the size, complexity, and cleanliness of the sewers of Paris, actually a network of service tunnels. Note that telephone cables share the space with piping. PHOTO BY ND/ROGER VIOLLET/GETTY IMAGES

SIGNIFICANCE

Sewage has been a threat to human health and life ever since human communities have gathered. In ancient times, some cultures were aware that human waste should be separated from drinking water or that it was possible to make the environment more pleasant by covering or washing away human waste. The Biblical book of Deuteronomy (chapter twenty-three, verse thirteen) contains instructions for soldiers to bury their own waste. The Roman Empire had an extensive system of engineered water supply and sewage systems. With the fall of the Empire, sanitation became chaotic; many deaths resulted during the following centuries. The relationship of disease to microorganisms was not understood until the late 1600s.

Even after the development of efficient sewage *removal* systems, the development of sewage *treatment* systems was still far off. The former assure that waste is transported out of communities and into rivers, lakes, or oceans, but when human populations begin to number in the tens and hundreds of millions, this is inadequate to preserve the environment. Today, sewage treatment continues to slowly improve, for the most part, throughout the industrialized world, and sewage-related disease is rare.

For much of the world, however, the story is different. In 2000, according to the World Health Organization (an arm of the United Nations), about 1.1 billion people (a sixth of the world's population) had no access to safe water and 2.4 billion had no access to "excreta disposal facilities" (waste disposal). The consequences are severe, including approximately 4 billion cases of diarrhea every year, causing 2.2 million deaths, mostly among children below the age of five. This amounts to fifteen percent of all deaths in that age group in developing countries. Waterborne intestinal worms infect about a tenth of the developing world's population, and 200 million people are infected with schistosomiasis, a flatworm infection; 20 million are severely debilitated by schistosomiasis. Well-designed water supply and sewage disposal can reduce schistosomiasis infection rates by about eighty percent.

FURTHER RESOURCES

Web sites

"Global Water Supply and Sanitation Assessment 2000 Report." *World Health Organization (United Nations).* <http://www.who.int/docstore/water_sanitation_health/Globassessment/GlobalTOC.htm> (accessed March 10, 2006).

Pitt, Rob. "Historical Review of Wet Weather Flow Management and Designs for the Future." *University of*

Alabama, October 2005. <http://rpitt.eng.ua.edu/Class/StormWaterManagement/M0%20intro%20Internet%20material/Module%200%20Introduction%20historical%20review%20and%20the%20future.pdf> (accessed March 10, 2006).

Our Vanishing Wildlife

Book Excerpt

By: William Temple Hornaday

Date: 1913

Source: Hornaday, William Temple. *Our Vanishing Wildlife*. New York: New York Zoological Society, 1913.

About the Author: Born to William Temple Hornaday Sr. and Martha Hornaday on December 1, 1854 in Hedricks County, near Plainfield, Indiana, William Temple Hornaday (1854–1937) was a prominent naturalist and conservationist of his time in the United States. Hornaday was a keen nature enthusiast and wildlife lover since his youth. After graduating from Iowa State University, he became actively involved with the conservation movement (1850–1924) in the United States. As a professional, he was known to be a multi-faceted personality and was associated with several societies, zoos, and conservation associations in the United States. He was instrumental in many conservation efforts to save endangered species in the United States, such as the American bison, the fur seal, the prong-horned antelope, and the now-extinct passenger pigeon. He also served in a range of reputable organizations such as the National Science Establishment in New York, the United States National Museum, The Washington National Zoo, The Bronx Zoo in New York, and the American Bison Society. Hornaday wrote nearly thirty books on nature and wildlife such as *The Birds of America*, *The Quadrupeds of America*, and *Explorations and Adventures in Equatorial Africa*. He also received many honors during his lifetime and even after his death. President Theodore Roosevelt (1858–1919) named the Hornaday range in 1908 in his honor. In 1930, he was elected to the National Wildlife Federation Conservation Hall of Fame.

INTRODUCTION

The United States has been gifted with immense natural beauty, varied species of wildlife, flora and fauna, pristine rivers, streams, lakes, and scenic land-scape. Before the colonization of the United States in the sixteenth century, its natural beauty and wildlife was virtually unharmed and untouched. The vast frontiers were tribal lands, and the various tribes in essence sustained themselves from whatever the land provided. They were known to have lived in harmony with nature and the environment.

The first settlers began arriving by the early 1600s. This was followed by waves of migrant population from Britain and Europe. The plentiful lands, abundant wild-life, and the wild frontiers beckoned too many settlers at that time. Subsequently, outings for game became popular means of leisure and an easy source of food. Settlers would often kill birds and wild animals for commercial trade of fur and leather, and at times even for pleasure. Over the next two centuries or so, millions of varied species of birds such as robins, quails, grouse, pigeons and wildlife like bison, deer, goat, seals, and many others are thought to have been killed.

Our Vanishing Wildlife was written at the height of the conservation movement in 1913. In this book, Hornaday describes the abundance of American wild-life in the late nineteenth century and early twentieth century, and depicts the extermination of wildlife that had become a matter of routine in the United States.

▮ PRIMARY SOURCE

OUR VANISHING WILDLIFE

PART I. EXTERMINATION

CHAPTER 1

THE FORMER ABUNDANCE OF WILDLIFE … "Abundance" is the word with which to describe the original animal life that stocked our country, and all North America, only a short half-century ago. Throughout every state, on every shore-line, in all the millions of fresh water lakes, ponds and rivers, on every mountain range, in every forest, *and even on every desert*, the wild flocks and herds held sway. It was impossible to go beyond the settled haunts of civilized man and escape them.

It was a full century after the complete settlement of New England and the Virginia colonies that the wonderful big-game fauna of the great plains and Rocky Mountains was really discovered; but the bison millions, the antelope millions, the mule deer, the mountain sheep and mountain goat were there, all the time. In the early days, the millions of pinnated grouse and quail of the central states attracted no serious attention from the American people-at-large; but they lived and flourished just the same, far down in the seventies, when the greedy market gunners system-atically slaughtered them, and barreled them up for "the market," while the foolish farmers calmly permitted them to do it.

We obtain the best of our history of the former abundance of North American wild life first from the pages of Audubon and Wilson; next, from the records left by such pioneers as Lewis and Clark, and last from the testimony of living men. To all this we can, many of us, add observations of our own.

To me the most striking fact that stands forth in the story of American wild life one hundred years ago is the wide extent and thoroughness of its distribution. Wide as our country is, and marvelous as it is in the diversity of its climates, its soils, its topography, its flora, its riches and its poverty. Nature gave to each square mile and to each acre a generous quota of wild creatures, according to its ability to maintain living things. No pioneer ever pushed so far, or into regions so difficult or so remote, that he did not find awaiting him a host of birds and beasts. Sometimes the pioneer was not a good hunter; usually he was a stupid fisherman; but the "game" was there, nevertheless. The time was when every farm had its quota.

The part that the wild life of America played in the settlement and development of this continent was so far-reaching in extent, and so enormous in potential value, that it fairly staggers the imagination. From the landing of the Pilgrims down to the present hour the wild game has been the mainstay and the resource against starvation of the pathfinder, the settler, the prospector, and at times even the railroad-builder. In view of what the bison millions did for the Dakotas, Montana, Wyoming, Kansas and Texas, it is only right and square that those states should now do something for the perpetual preservation of the bison species and all other big game that needs help.

For years and years, the antelope millions of the Montana and Wyoming grass-lands fed the scout and Indian-fighter, freighter, cowboy and surveyor, ranchman *and sheep-herder*, but thus far I have yet to hear of one Western state that has ever spent one penny directly for the preservation of the antelope! And to-day we are in a hand-to-hand fight in Congress, and in Montana, with the Wool-Growers Association, which maintains in Washington a keen lobbyist to keep aloft the tariff on wool, and prevent Congress from taking 15 square miles of grass lands on Snow Creek, Montana, for a National Antelope Preserve. All that the wool-growers want is the entire earth, all to themselves. Mr. McClure, the Secretary of the Association says:

"The proper place in which to preserve the big game of the West is in city parks, where it can be protected."

To the colonist of the East and pioneer of the West, the white-tailed deer was an ever present help in time of trouble. Without this omnipresent animal, and the supply of good meat that each white flag represented, the commissariat difficulties of the settlers who won the country as far westward as Indiana would have been many times greater than they were. The backwoods Pilgrim's progress was like this:

Trail, deer; cabin, deer; clearing; bear, corn, deer; hogs, deer; cattle, wheat, independence.

And yet, how many men are there to-day, out of our ninety millions of Americans and pseudo-Americans, who remember with any feeling of gratitude the part played in American history by the white-tailed deer? Very few! How many Americans are there in our land who now preserve that deer for sentimental reasons, and because his forbears were nation-builders? As a matter of fact, are there any?

On every eastern pioneer's monument, the white-tailed deer should figure; and on those of the Great West, the bison and the antelope should be cast in enduring bronze, "lest we forget!"

The game birds of America played a different part from that of the deer, antelope and bison. In the early days, shotguns were few, and shot was scarce and dear. The wild turkey and goose were the smallest birds on which a rifleman could afford to expend a bullet and a whole charge of powder. It was for this reason that the deer, bear, bison, and elk disappeared from the eastern United States while the game birds yet remained abundant. With the disappearance of the big game came the fat steer, hog and hominy, the wheat-field, fruit orchard and poultry galore.

The game birds of America, as a class and a mass, have not been swept away to ward off starvation or to rescue the perishing. Even back in the sixties and seventies, very, very few men of the North thought of killing prairie chickens, ducks and quail, snipe and woodcock, in order to keep the hunger wolf from the door. The process was too slow and uncertain; and besides, the really-poor man rarely had the gun and ammunition. Instead of attempting to live on birds, he hustled for the staple food products that the soil of his own farm could produce.

First, last and nearly all the time, the game birds of the United States as a whole, have been sacrificed on the altar of Rank Luxury, to tempt appetites that were tired of fried chicken and other farm delicacies. To-day, even the average poor man hunts birds for the joy of the outing, and the pampered epicures of the hotels and restaurants buy game birds, and eat small portions of them, solely to tempt jaded appetites. If there is such a thing as "class" legislation, it is that which permits a few sordid market-shooters to slaughter the birds of the whole people in order to sell them to a few epicures.

The game of a state belongs to the whole people of the state. The Supreme Court of the United States has so decided. (Geer vs. Connecticut.) If it is abundant, it is a valuable asset. The great value of the game birds of America lies not in their meat pounds as they lie upon the table, but in the temptation they annually put before millions of field-weary farmers and desk-weary clerks and merchants to get into their beloved hunting togs, stalk out into the lap of Nature, and say "Begone, dull Care!" . . .

THE DUTY OF THE HOUR I have now said my say in behalf of wild life. Surely the path of duty toward the remnant of wild life is plain enough. Will those who read this book pass along my message that the hour for a revolution has struck? Will the millions of men commanded by General Apathy now arouse, before it is too late to act?

Will the true sportsmen rise up, and do their duty, bravely and unselfishly?

Will the people with wealth to give away do their duty toward wild life and humanity, fairly and generously?

Will the zoologists awake, leave their tables in their stone palaces of peace, and come out to the firing-line?

Will the lawmakers heed the handwriting on the wall, and make laws that represent the full discharge of their duty toward wild life and humanity?

Will the editors beat the alarm-gong, early and late, in season and out of season, until the people awake?

On the answers to these questions hang the fate of the wild creatures of the world—their preservation or their extermination.

SIGNIFICANCE

Many wildlife species are becoming endangered or have become extinct because of the growing threat of civilization all around the world. Especially in the United States, since the days of settlement, many wildlife species have disappeared and are constantly endangered. Various species like the great auk, Pallas's cormorant, Eskimo curlew, Labrador duck, passenger pigeon, and the Carolina parakeet have become extinct in North America. Some other extinct species include the Santa Barbara song sparrow, dusky seaside sparrow, Bachman's warbler, Oahu thrush, Penasco chipmunk, giant deer mouse, Florida red wolf, Caribbean monk seal, Steller's Sea Cow, and the Eastern elk. Most of these species became endangered when the settlers started coming in to the country. This continued for over centuries for various reasons. For instance, though the American Bison was saved, the

Illegal wildlife products, such as those featured at this market table on November 25, 2003, in Tachileik, Myanmar, contribute to the vanishing species in Southeast Asia's forests. AP IMAGES

passenger pigeons (which have been extinct since the early twentieth century) were killed for the use of their feathers in the millinery industry.

Hornaday mentions in his book about the near extinction of the fur seal in the United States, which was targeted for its fur. By the nineteenth century, people had started questioning such endangerment. There were many who promoted the concept of conservation. William Hornaday's book assumes significance as it was written during this period and it addresses this very issue. During his time, Hornaday was instrumental in pushing forward regulation to prevent bird plumage (feathers of birds used for ornamental purposes) from use in the millinery industry (milliners are people who design and sell hats). Through the book and other means, he also worked hard to save the bison and the fur seal from extinction.

The subject matter of this book is relevant even today. There continues an alarming decline in wildlife numbers and extinction of several species at the hands of mankind. On the other hand, there has been growing awareness about the dangers posed to wildlife due to increased human activity and rapid urbanization of the countryside. Soon after the conservation movements of the early twentieth century, the U.S. Government formed various agencies to protect wildlife.

Agencies like the U.S. Environmental Protection Agency (EPA) and the U.S. Fish and Wildlife Service are charged with the task of wildlife conservation and protection in the United States. The U.S. EPA also runs the endangered species protection program for this purpose. Various federal as well as state legislations also exist in the United States to preserve and protect wildlife. Some of the notable regulations and treaties are the Endangered Species Act of 1972, the Marine Mammal Protection Act of 1972, the Convention on International Trade in Endangered Species of Wild Fauna and Flora (CITES), and the Wild Bird Conservation Act 1992. Earlier conservation measures include the Lacey Act (1900), the establishment of the National Park Service (1916), and the Norbeck-Andresen Migratory-Bird Conservation Act (1929).

In addition, numerous conservation efforts are underway to protect various endangered species such as the bald eagle, the grey wolf, the Nashville crayfish, and the red-cockaded woodpecker. Many species have even made a comeback from the brink of extinction. However, conservationists feel that much still needs to be done in this area before future generations can benefit from the fruits of these efforts.

FURTHER RESOURCES
Web sites

"Some of the Major Laws Protecting Endangered Wildlife." *EarthTrust*. <http://www.earthtrust.org/wlcurric/appen2.html> (accessed March 13, 2006).

Kurpis, Lauren. "Facts About Endangered Species." *EndangeredSpecie.com*. <http://www.endangeredspecie.com/Interesting_Facts.htm> (accessed March 13, 2006).

"Documentary Chronology of Selected Events in the Development of the American Conservation Movement, 1847–1920." *Library of Congress*. <http://memory.loc.gov/ammem/amrvhtml/cnchron6.html> (accessed March 13, 2006).

"History: William Temple Hornaday: Visionary of the National Zoo." *Smithsonian National Zoological Park*. <http://nationalzoo.si.edu/AboutUs/History/hornaday.cfm> (accessed March 13, 2006).

"Endangered and Threatened Species." *U.S. Environmental Protection Agency*. <http://www.epa.gov/espp/coloring/especies.htm> (accessed March 13, 2006).

"EPA's Endangered Species Protection Program." *U.S. Environmental Protection Agency*. <http://www.epa.gov/espp/coloring/cover2.htm> (accessed March 13, 2006).

Lead Helps to Guard Your Health

Advertisement

By: Anonymous

Date: 1923

Source: National Lead Company. Published in *National Geographic*, 1923. <http://www.uwsp.edu/geo/courses/geog100/Icons&Photos/Lead11-23.jpg> (accessed January 6, 2006).

About the Organization: In the early 1920s, the Dutch Boy paint company began a series of advertisements aimed at teaching store owners how to cater to children, to build future customers, loyalty, and to appeal to parents. In this illustration, published in *National Geographic* magazine, Dutch Boy explains the alleged health benefits that lead provided for the household; the use of the Dutch Boy icon was carefully crafted by the company to connote warmth, family, and purity.

INTRODUCTION

The use of lead in the household has a history that stretches back to the Roman Empire. Common items containing lead included coins, cups, pitchers, and weapons. Used in aqueducts that transported water to cities, face powders for rouge and other forms of makeup, and ground into paint, lead was ubiquitous; it was even used as a wine preservative. The word "plumbing" is derived from the Roman word for lead, *plumbum*. This is also where the chemical symbol for lead comes from, which is Pb.

The Romans were well aware of the hazards that came from lead; they believed that moderation would limit the negative effects of lead exposure, for the substance was handy, malleable, and such a crucial part of technological development. It played a major role in the empire's downfall as well; some scholars point to lead poisoning, or "plumbism," in such key historical figures as Caesar, Caligula, and Nero.

Centuries later, as indoor plumbing became widespread in the United States, and as manufacturers put lead in paint, gasoline, and other common household and industrial goods, researchers began to note alarming rates of lead poisoning in children. Countries such as France, Great Britain, and Greece banned its use in indoor paint before 1920.

At the same time, paint companies such as Dutch Boy launched advertising campaigns that used images of children to help sell products, and encouraged store owners to engage children in discussion to help kids to choose their store and products. This mass marketing campaign to children ran at the same time that researchers found more and more conclusive evidence of lead's toxic effect on children; by the 1930s, U.S. researchers were in agreement that children's lead exposure—on toys, cribs, windowsills, and in gas fumes—was a serious public threat.

PRIMARY SOURCE

LEAD HELPS TO GUARD YOUR HEALTH
See primary source image.

SIGNIFICANCE

This carefully worded advertisement highlights Rome as a historical example of a society that used lead in its water transportation systems; the appeal to Rome in an advertisement was a careful strategy, designed to connect lead with power and innovation. This ad also targets the concept of "sanitation," a key issue as the Progressive Era highlighted scientific progress and achievement as pathways for decency and improvement. By allegedly making water more "sanitary," and paint helping to "protect" furniture

Lead helps to guard your health

YOU wouldn't live today in a house without an adequate plumbing system. For without modern plumbing, sickness might endanger your life. Lead concealed in the walls and under the floors of many modern buildings helps to give the best sanitation.

Lead pipe centuries old

Lead, therefore, is contributing to the health, comfort, and convenience of people today as it did when Rome was a center of civilization. Lead water and drainage pipes more than 1800 years old have been found in exactly the condition they were in when laid.

In some cities today the law specifies that lead pipe alone may be used to bring water from street mains into the building.

In drainage systems are lead traps made of lead pipe bent into the shape of the letter S, so that a little water will stay in the bend and prevent gases which collect in the pipe from getting out through the house.

The malleability of lead also makes it easy to change the direction of any pipe through the use of lead bends.

Joining the pipes

A plumber easily "wipes" a joint or repairs a pipe leak with lead and tin solder. Because this alloy melts at the low temperature of 558 degrees it can be applied without melting the lead pipe, which melts at 620 degrees.

Lead is also poured into the flanges of pipe-joints to make them absolutely tight. Pipe threads are painted with white-lead or red-lead to make a tight connection. Where vibration or movement of pipes may loosen a poured joint, lead wool is used; lead shredded into threads is packed into the joint in a dense, compact mass.

Rubber gaskets and ball washers containing lead prevent leaking at joints and faucets. Lead is used to beautify the modern bathroom. Red-lead and litharge, both lead oxides, are important ingredients in making the glossy white enamel covering the iron bodies of tub and basin and the glazed tile walls.

Lead in paint

While lead is invaluable in assuring comfort and proper sanitation, its best-known and most widespread use is as white-lead in paint. Such materials as wood would soon deteriorate unless protected with paint. And the paints that give the most thorough protection against the weather are based on white-lead.

The loss of invested capital through failure to protect the surface of property adequately has led property owners to paint frequently and well. As days and months go by, more and more of them are learning the wisdom of the phrase, "Save the surface and you save all." And they are using white-lead paint to prolong the lives of their houses.

Look for the Dutch Boy

NATIONAL LEAD COMPANY makes white-lead and sells it mixed with pure linseed oil, under the name and trade-mark of Dutch Boy white-lead. The figure of the Dutch Boy is reproduced on every keg and is a guarantee of exceptional purity.

Dutch Boy products also include red-lead, linseed oil, flatting oil, babbitt metals and solder.

More about lead

If you use lead, or think you might use it in any form, write to us for specific information.

NATIONAL LEAD COMPANY

New York, 111 Broadway; Boston, 131 State St.; Buffalo, 116 Oak St.; Chicago, 900 West 18th St.; Cincinnati, 659 Freeman Ave.; Cleveland, 820 West Superior Ave.; St. Louis, 722 Chestnut St.; San Francisco, 485 California St.; Pittsburgh, National Lead & Oil Co. of Pa.; 316 Fourth Ave.; Philadelphia, John T. Lewis & Bros. Co., 437 Chestnut St.

■ PRIMARY SOURCE

Lead Helps to Guard Your Health. This 1923 advertisement from the Dutch Boy paint company, published in *National Geographic* magazine, was part of a campaign designed to promote the benefits of lead in plumbing and paint. The company created the Dutch Boy icon to appeal to families, particularly women and children, as mass advertising became an important way for corporations to reach consumers. NATIONAL GEOGRAPHIC

and homes, this advertisement—and the Dutch Boy company—use sympathetic words and key phrases to target the reader's need for cleanliness and a safe home.

Researchers observed lead poisoning symptoms, such as impaired memory, impaired concentration, gastrointestinal problems, headaches, delayed intellectual development, and paleness in children throughout the late 1800s and first three decades of

the twentieth century. A famous 1914 case involving a toddler who died from ingesting lead paint chewed from the rails of a crib made headlines. Tetraethyl lead, lead added to gasoline to reduce knocking and pinging, was briefly taken out of gas in 1925, but replaced again soon after test results proved inconclusive. In 1929 the Surgeon General of the United States declared that there was no reason to ban tetraethyl lead.

By the 1930s, public health campaigns against lead began, especially when researchers published article after article detailing lead poisoning in children. Nonetheless, companies continued to make lead paint and leaded gasoline, in large part because of demand for both products, and manufacturers' reluctance to hurt profits; by 1936, 90 percent of all gas contained "ethyl."

With the evidence against lead mounting, companies such as Dutch Boy dropped lead from interior paint, but kept lead in exterior paint. Regulation of interior paint and the elimination of lead paint did not take place until 1978. Three years before, in 1975, leaded gas began to be phased out in the United States, under a carefully crafted timetable.

A 1983 report from the Environmental Protection Agency (EPA) showed that between 1976 and 1980, blood levels of lead in the average person dropped 37 percent; health care costs associated with lead dropped by $700 million, results completely unexpected by researchers. A 1994 study showed that blood levels of lead had dropped 78 percent by 1991. The United States officially outlawed lead as a gasoline additive in 1986. However, gasoline companies marketed leaded gas overseas; as western European nations slowly banned leaded gasoline throughout the 1980s, 1990s, and beyond, developing nations' demand increased as industrialization increased in those areas.

FURTHER RESOURCES

Books

Warren, Christian. *Brush with Death: A Social History of Lead Poisoning.* Baltimore: Johns Hopkins Press, 2001.

Periodicals

Markowitz, Gerald and David Rosner. "Cater to the Children: The Role of the Lead Industry in a Public Health Tragedy, 1900–1955." *American Journal of Public Health* 90, 1 (January 2000).

With a smoke stack towering over Herbulaneum, Missouri, it is no wonder that a study indicated that 28 percent of the children living there have elevated levels of lead in their blood. AP IMAGES

Web sites

Environmental Protection Agency. "Lead Poisoning: A Historical Perspective." <http://www.epa.gov/history/topics/perspect/lead.htm> (accessed January 6, 2006).

Botanist George Washington Carver in Arboretum

Photograph

By: Anonymous

Date: Undated

Source: Corbis

About the Photographer: This photograph of George Washington Carver was likely taken at an arboretum at the Tuskegee Normal and Industrial Institute in Tuskegee, Alabama, where he worked from 1896 to 1943.

INTRODUCTION

George Washington Carver was born circa 1864 as a slave on a plantation in Missouri. By the time this picture was taken, he had been a student and faculty member at Iowa State University—the first black student and the first black faculty member at that institution—and had probably been working at the Tuskegee Normal and Industrial Institute (now Tuskegee University) for some years. Carver was an artist and noted botanist, most famous today for his work on the peanut. (He did not, however, invent peanut butter, as is often alleged.)

Carver was originally owned by German immigrants. He was orphaned at the time of the Civil War and raised by his former owners as a family member after the abolition of slavery. Weakened by whooping cough, he tended not to perform heavy field work, but helped with gardening and became knowledgeable about plants. "My very soul thirsted for an education," Carver later wrote. "I literally lived in the woods. I wanted to know every strange stone, flower, insect, bird, or beast."

Carver moved between several Southern towns in order to get first a grade-school and then a high-school education. In the 1880s, he applied to several colleges. He attended Simpson College, Iowa, from which he transferred to Iowa State University. He not only graduated from Iowa State, but stayed on to get a master's degree. While studying for his master's he worked at the university's Iowa Agriculture and Home Economics Experiment Station, studying fungi (mycology) and plant diseases.

Carver moved to the Tuskegee Normal and Industrial Institute, a black college founded by Booker T. Washington (1856–1915), today Tuskegee University, in 1896. He worked there until 1943, the year of his death. It was while at the Tuskegee Institute that he did the work on peanut products for which he is particularly remembered today. He claimed to have developed some 325 uses for the peanut, over one hundred uses for the sweet potato, and many more for other crops that could be raised as an alternative to cotton. Such alternatives were needed because non-stop cultivation of cotton, the South's main crop, exhausted the soil of nitrogen, necessary for growth. The sweet potato and the peanut are among crops that restore nitrogen to the soil. Alternating cotton with these other crops could preserve land in production, but farmers needed a market for the nitrogen-restoring crops—hence Carver's determination to make those crops useful.

PRIMARY SOURCE

Botanist George Washington Carver in Arboretum. This image shows George Washington Carver, the African-American botanist and food product developer, at work in an arboretum in Tuskegee, Alabama. © BETTMANN/CORBIS

There is no doubt that Carver was a competent botanist and scientist. He also became internationally famous, eventually meeting three U.S. presidents, the prince of Sweden, and Mahatma Gandhi (1869–1948). However, some historians note that accounts of his life routinely exaggerate his accomplishments. According to Barry Mackintosh, a historian working for the National Park Service in Washington, D.C., "Carver displayed many peanut products not manufactured commercially, but virtually all were ersatz commodities more feasibly derived from other materials.... Because the great majority of products on Carver's list could be made more easily and cheaply from other substances, they were of little more than curiosity value." The peanut, for example, despite Carver's work, continued to be used mostly as a food (ground into a nut butter, or whole) or as a source of edible oil.

PRIMARY SOURCE

BOTANIST GEORGE WASHINGTON CARVER IN ARBORETUM
See primary source image.

SIGNIFICANCE

Carver was a prolific and early practitioner of the product-development aspect of what today is known as "food science"—the application of technology to all phases of food production. Carver saw the peanut, the sweet potato, soybeans, and the other crops which he used in new products not simply as food items to be harvested, cooked, and eaten whole—though he did develop scores of recipes for eating peanuts in relatively unprocessed forms—but as sources of industrial raw material. Some of the products he sought to derive from these raw materials might be edible, such as peanut oil, but many had nothing to do with food: plastic, dye, ink, and glue.

Today a number of crops are processed in just this way, including the peanut and the soybean. Whether or not Carver himself ever produced a workable ink from peanuts, for example, there is no doubt that a growing percentage of the printer's-ink market today is being captured by soy-based inks, which are non-toxic and less allergenic than petroleum-based inks. Soybeans are also used in plastic, soap, cosmetics, and biodiesel fuel, among other applications. Peanuts are used in varnish, paint, furniture polish, insecticide, nitroglycerin, soap, cosmetics, plastic, rayon, paper, glue, and more.

Complex food processing and the use of oils, sugars, and other products obtained from corn, peanuts, soybeans, and other plants make possible the contents of the modern supermarket, especially the shelves of highly processed snack foods, dessert foods, and prepared foods that constitute a large part of the typical person's diet in the United States and some other industrialized countries. This is not always a good thing: many of the highly processed foods in supermarkets contain hydrogenated vegetable oils, which have been associated with heart disease.

FURTHER RESOURCES
Periodicals

Mackintosh, Barry. "George Washington Carver and the Peanut: New Light on a Much-Loved Myth." *American Heritage*, vol. 28, No. 5, August 1977. Available at <http://www.americanheritage.com/articles/ magazine/ ah/1977/5/1977_5_66.shtml> (accessed March 8, 2006).

Web sites

"The Legacy of George Washington Carver: Inspiring Students to Become Their Best." *Iowa State University*. <http://www.lib.iastate.edu/spcl/gwc/home.html> (accessed March 8, 2006).

Stanley Miller Working in Laboratory

Photograph

By: Anonymous

Date: July 19, 1953

Source: Corbis

About the Photographer: The Bettmann/Corbis Archive is one of the largest photographic collections in the world, and originated with a single man, Otto Bettmann, who left Germany in 1935 for the United States with his original collection of photographs packed into two steamer trunks.

INTRODUCTION

In 1952–1953, a graduate student in chemistry at the University of Chicago named Stanley Miller (1930–) performed a series of historic experiments to test the notion that chemicals essential to the origin of life might arise by simple chemistry from non-living ingredients. Miller described his hypothesis as "the idea that the organic [carbon-containing] compounds that serve as the basis of life were formed [billions of years ago] when the earth had an atmosphere of methane, ammonia, water, and hydrogen instead of carbon dioxide, nitrogen, oxygen, and water," as it does today. "In order to test this hypothesis," Miller wrote in the journal *Science* in 1953, "an apparatus was built to circulate CH_4 [carbon dioxide], NH_3 [ammonia], H_2 [molecular hydrogen], and H_2O [water] past an electric discharge"—a spark. Miller's idea was that energy from the spark could cause molecules to form that would otherwise not be able to do so. Lightning would have been a natural source of such discharges on the primitive Earth.

Miller based his ideas about the Earth's early atmosphere on the work of Nobel laureate Harold Urey (1893–1981), discoverer of deuterium, who in 1950 was studying the chemistry of the early solar system. This led Urey to wonder about the origin of life. The Earth must have been sterile when it first formed at high temperature from the primitive dust cloud that became the Sun and planets; later, there was life. How did it arise? Urey, like virtually all modern scientists, sought a chemical rather than a miraculous explanation. In particular, he suggested that life may have arisen on Earth thanks to the chemistry made possible by a highly "reducing" atmosphere—a chemical environment in which substances strongly tend to separate from oxygen or bind with hydrogen (gaining an electron in so doing). The present-day atmosphere of the Earth is the opposite of reducing, "oxidizing," meaning that it encourages substances to combine with oxygen. It does so because it consists of 21 percent molecular oxygen, O_2: rusting, breathing, and burning are all examples of oxidation processes that the oxygen-rich atmosphere of Earth makes possible today. This oxygen is almost all produced by green plants using photosynthesis.

Miller, a second-year graduate student at the time, boldly contacted the world-famous Urey about testing Urey's ideas in the laboratory. Urey not only encouraged Miller to do so, but designed a series of experiments with him. All three experiments involved mixing carbon dioxide, ammonia, hydrogen, and water at various pressures and temperatures and subjecting them to electric sparks. Miller began running his experiments in the fall of 1952. After the first experiment had been running for a week, the inside of the glass container in which the mixture was being subjected to electric sparks became coated with an oily, brownish material.

Analysis of the goo produced by Miller's apparatus astonished the scientific world: it contained thirteen of the amino acids that are the "building blocks" of all

PRIMARY SOURCE

Stanley Miller Working in Laboratory This image shows Stanley Miller, a biochemist, studying the origin of life as a graduate student at the University of Chicago. Experiments designed by Miller with Nobel laureate Harold C. Urey and performed by Miller in 1952–1953 showed that simple chemistry could produce complex molecules essential to the origin of life. © BETTMANN/CORBIS

proteins, including DNA (deoxyribonucleic acid) and RNA (ribonucleic acid), the molecules that code for heredity in all terrestrial life. Miller had gone much further down the road to life than anyone would have thought possible. He had proved that extremely simple chemical processes could have produced the basic molecules of life on the Earth.

PRIMARY SOURCE

STANLEY MILLER WORKING IN LABORATORY
See primary source image.

SIGNIFICANCE

Miller's experiment, often referred to as the Miller-Urey (or Urey-Miller) experiment, shifted scientific thinking about the chemical origins of life from speculation to experiment. However, scientific thought about the origins of life has not proceeded in a straight line from Miller's work. First, simply running the Miller experiment does not produce life. For life to exist, self-replication must occur, and the chemicals in Miller's experiment are too simple to spontaneously produce a self-replicating system. Second, scientific opinion about whether the Earth's early atmosphere was in fact reducing has varied over time. Third, alternative chemical pathways for the origin of life have been proposed. One is that organic chemicals might have been lined up to form self-replicating structures by adhering to the surfaces of certain minerals (minerals have organized atomic structures comparable to the patterns in which tiles may be laid on a floor). Moreover, amino acids might have been supplied to the early Earth by meteorites rather than by terrestrial chemistry.

Nevertheless, the Miller-Urey experiment has not been rendered irrelevant. Recent geological and computational work has shown that the early Earth's environment may indeed have been favorable to the formation of the kind of "prebiotic soup" hypothesized by Urey and Miller. Experiments using atmospheric compositions different from Miller's experiment have produced similar results. Studies of living DNA designed to unravel the order in which amino acids were added by evolution to the set of twenty-one now used by all life show that the earliest life was probably based mostly on a smaller number of amino acids than produced in the Miller-Urey experiment. Regardless of whether the precise chemistry produced by Miller was that which actually gave rise to life on Earth, Miller's work had the important effect of making the chemical origin of life a topic for hard-core, quantitative research rather than handwaving. Much important work has been done in the origin-of-life field since 1953, although scientists still cannot describe exactly how life originated from simple chemicals. Scientists have shown that non-living organic molecules can self-replicate in appropriate environments, that natural selection can modify non-living organic chemicals in the laboratory, and that simpler forms of life based on RNA only, rather than on a combination of RNA and DNA such as is used by all modern life, probably preceded the "last universal ancestor" of all modern species—the microorganism from which all living things today have descended.

Miller's work has been attacked in recent years by creationists such as Jonathan Wells, author of *Icons of Evolution* (2000). The origin of life remains a scientific mystery, but since the Miller experiment the size of the mystery has shrunk considerably.

FURTHER RESOURCES
Periodicals

Bada, Jeffrey L. and Antonio Lazcano. "Prebiotic Soiup—Revisiting the Miller Experiment." *Science*, vol. 300, May 2, 2003, pp. 745–746. Available online at: <http://www.issol.org/miller/BadaLazcano2003.pdf> (accessed February 19, 2006).

Miller, Stanley L. "A Production of Amino Acids Under Possible Primitive Earth Conditions." *Science*, vol. 117, May 13, 1953, pp. 117–118. Available online at: <http://www.issol.org/miller/miller1953.pdf> (accessed February 19, 2006).

Web sites

Gishlick, Alan. *National Center for Science Education*. "Icons of Evolution? Miller-Urey Experiment." <http://www.ncseweb.org/icons/icon1millerurey.html> (accessed February 19, 2006).

World Wildlife Fund

Photograph

By: Anonymous

Date: August 12, 2004

Source: Getty Images

About the Photographer: Based in Seattle, Washington, Getty Images contains an archive of over two million photographs available for publishers of electronic and print media around the world.

INTRODUCTION

Life on Earth is interdependent. This means that the survival of the human race depends on the natural environment, and the survival of nature depends on the way humans act. For many years now, people have interfered with the balance of nature. This has led to the extinction of a large number of species of the world's wildlife, and placed many on the endangered list.

Human activity impacts the environment in a number of ways. Agricultural needs lead to deforestation, soil degeneration, and accumulation of toxic chemicals. Industrial development since the nineteenth century has led to an increase in carbon dioxide (CO_2) emissions. This resulted in an increase of global temperatures, as well as general chemical pollution of water, soil, and air. These changes, in turn, lead to alterations of climate on a local and global scale. Alterations include anomalies in weather patterns, severe droughts, abnormally high rainfalls, increased cyclone and storm activity, and recession of glaciers worldwide.

The changes occurring in the natural habitat of plants and animals threaten the wildlife. Disappearance of arctic glaciers threatens polar bears, and logging

A Malayan sun bear rests peacefully at the Frankfurt Zoo in Germany. Originally from southeast Asia, these bears are classified as an endangered species by the World Wildlife Fund. AP IMAGES

of the rainforests affects the great apes—orangutans, gorillas, and chimpanzees. In addition to the devastation of the habitat, there is also fragmentation of natural habitats due to either logging for commerce or agriculture. Such changes make it harder for the animals to migrate and reproduce. Moreover, the disappearance of one species can lead to a chain reaction where other species dependent on it may also disappear.

Another threat to wildlife is the introduction of non-native species. Foreign species may have no natural predators in a new area and can take over the habitat, pushing native species out. The best known example of this is the introduction of cane toads in Australia.

All these threats to wildlife led to the foundation of a number of various wildlife and conservation societies. These organizations mainly protected single spe-cies, such as turtles, tigers, elephants, pandas, and others. There was, however, the lack of a more global approach until the foundation of World Wildlife Fund in the mid-1900s. Since then, the organization has grown to a worldwide network of regional organizations in over one hundred countries.

The World Wildlife Fund (WWF) was founded on September 11, 1961, by Julian Huxley, Prince Bernhard of the Netherlands, Max Nicholson, Guy Mountford, and Sir Peter Scott. Its original logo, the black-and-white panda, was created by Peter Scott (1909–1989), an ornithologist, conservationist, and painter. Before co-founding the WWF, he founded the Severn Wildfowl Trust in 1948. In 1982, he founded the Wildscreen Festival, which every two years showcases films about the natural world. Peter Scott made numerous television appearances as an ornithologist, popularizing wildfowl. He was also a vice-president of the British Naturalist's Association and an award in his name was instituted after his death.

PRIMARY SOURCE

WORLD WILDLIFE FUND

See primary source image.

SIGNIFICANCE

The first WWF advertising campaign featuring a poster with a black-and-white panda appeared in 1961, and became the official poster of the newly founded organization. Hands surrounding the panda symbolized that human intervention is important in saving wildlife and that the future of wildlife is in our hands. This has extra significance as the human hand led to the destruction of many species and yet it is humans who must find the remedy. The logo of the organization remains a panda, and is fitting, as the panda is one of the most endangered species on the planet. In the years since the original poster, additional campaigns have featured plush animal manufacturers making animals with the WWF logo available for purchase in stores, with a percentage of the sales donated to the World Wildlife Fund. The goal of the WWF organization is to achieve harmony between people and nature. In order to achieve its goals, the WWF focuses on selected areas and works with local communities, governments, and businesses.

The initial focus of the WWF in the 1960s and 1970s was species conservation. It has launched programs like Project Tiger in India and Save the Rhino. The organization was funding conservation projects with small grants in the 1960s. The situation changed in 1970 after the establishment of A Nature Trust. This fund supports not only grants but also administration of the WWF.

During the 1980s, the WWF became involved with United Nations Environmental Program. This meant that the focus of the organization became wider than just wildlife protection. It now aimed at environmental protection and conservation of the natural environment in general as well. These new goals also led to a change in the name of the organization to World Wide Fund for Nature. The original name, however, was retained in North America.

Since 1990, it has become clear that effective wildlife protection is not just the protection of a single species but the protection of biodiversity. Therefore, considerable effort is now placed by WWF and other

PRIMARY SOURCE

World Wildlife Fund. Build-A-Bear Workshop announced the arrival of the Polar Bear in August 2004, one in a series of co-branded stuffed animals developed by Build-A-Bear Workshop and World Wildlife Fund. GETTY IMAGES

organizations on protecting entire biosystems such as oceans, rivers, and lakes, and to stop deforestation. Part of this action was the recognition of eco-regions. The Global 200 project identified 238 regions in the world consisting of all of the climatic regions. They include terrestrial, freshwater, and marine environments. Each eco-region is unique, contains distinct species and environmental conditions, and has an important role in sustaining global biodiversity. In contrast to reserves and national parks, the boundaries of these regions are not fixed.

A unique challenge for conservationists is presented by illegal trade in wildlife. The collaboration between the WWF and the World Conservation Union (IUCN) resulted in the establishment of a new organization—Trade Records Analysis of Fauna and Flora in Commerce (TRAFFIC)—in 1976 to monitor trade in wildlife. TRAFFIC mainly monitors priority species that are hunted for commercial purposes, such as elephants, tigers, rhinos, and marine turtles.

The future of wildlife conservation is dependent on the ability to educate people about the necessity of protecting the environment in general, maintaining biodiversity, and protecting individual species. WWF education programs address these goals: some are aimed at children through the Eco-Schools Project, while others are specific projects aimed at business, industry, agriculture, and local governments. These activities come in the form of special educational courses for the purpose of recognizing and developing management strategies that will consider environmental impact as well as risks associated with industry.

Saving wildlife is a complex process, and human involvement is very important for the success of that process. There is a necessity for improved legislation worldwide to prevent the predicted disappearance of 20 percent of the world's species in the next thirty years. This can be assisted by the involvement of as many people as possible in local and global conservation projects.

FURTHER RESOURCES

Web sites

IUCN Red List of Threatened Species. <http://www.redlist.org> (accessed March 14, 2006).

U.S. Environmental Protection Agency. <http://www.epa.gov> (accessed March 14, 2006).

WildAid <http://www.wildaid.org/eng.asp?CID=1> (accessed March 14, 2006).

Wildlife Protection Network. <http://www.wildlifeprotection. net> (accessed March 14, 2006).

The Wildlife Trusts. <http://www.wildlifetrusts.org> (accessed March 14, 2006).

The World Conservation Union. <http://www.iucn.org> (accessed March 14, 2006).

World Wildlife Fund. <http://www.worldwildlife.org> (accessed March 14, 2006).

"The Carbon Cycle and Climate Warming"

Journal article

By: Richard A. Kerr

Date: December 9, 1983

Source: Kerr, Richard A. "The Carbon Cycle and Climate Warming: Learning How Carbon Cycles through the Environment, With and Without Human Intervention, Is Crucial to Predicting the Greenhouse Effect." *Science* 222 (1983): 1107–1108.

About the Author: Richard A. Kerr has been a staff journalist with *Science* magazine since 1977. He has a Ph.D. in

chemical oceanography and reports on earth science, planetary science, and paleontology subjects.

INTRODUCTION

The greenhouse effect refers to a process in which gases in the atmosphere allow solar radiation to penetrate to the earth's surface, while also reabsorbing radiation as it attempts to exit the atmosphere. The result of the greenhouse effect is the trapping of heat in the atmosphere. In turn, this causes an increase in temperature. The increase in the earth's temperature over time is generally referred to as global warming or climate warming.

There are various greenhouse gases that have this effect. These include water vapor, methane, and chlorofluorocarbons. However, one of the most important of greenhouse gases is carbon dioxide (CO_2), for several reasons. Carbon dioxide is responsible for approximately half of the heat retained by the atmosphere and is especially important because it is the atmospheric gas that is increasing at the fastest rate. Carbon dioxide is produced mainly by the burning of fossil fuels and by deforestation, both of which have been increasing since industrialization. This has led to a continuing increase in the amount of carbon dioxide being released into the atmosphere. Finally, processes that have caused the increased levels of carbon dioxide have not stopped and are not likely to in the future. In fact, the burning of fossil fuels is expected to increase over time. This makes understanding the impact of increased carbon dioxide levels an important environmental issue.

■ PRIMARY SOURCE

The burning of fossil fuels and the resulting carbon dioxide greenhouse effect will heat Earth's atmosphere to new high temperatures. Researchers agree on that much (*Science*, 4 November, p. 491), but the current question is exactly how far and how fast the temperature will rise. A key element in predicting that rise is predicting the comings and goings of carbon and carbon dioxide in the tightly linked system of ocean, rock, air, and plant. Ecologists, oceanographers, and geochemists gathered in Knoxville at the end of October to consider just how well they understand the carbon cycle. Better than they did in the past, seemed to be the answer, but far from well enough to say how much of the carbon dioxide released in coming centuries will remain in the atmosphere to warm the climate.

From the beginning of the meeting, it was made clear that understanding the carbon cycle is not the only problem in predicting future warming. A major uncertainty is the timing and magnitude of future releases of carbon dioxide from the burning of fossil fuels. Today, 1.1 tons of carbon as carbon dioxide is released every year for every person on Earth. Americans contribute an impressive 5 tons per person per year.

Fossil fuels such as coal are available in what, for all practical purposes, are unlimited quantities, but economists cannot say just how much will be burned or how fast reserves will be consumed. The best guess of the recent National Research Council report (*Science*, 4 November, p. 491) is that yearly releases will fall somewhere between 12 billion and 55 billion tons. Thus, atmospheric carbon dioxide concentrations will inevitably increase, most likely doubling sometime late in the next century.

With this unavoidable social uncertainty in mind, carbon cycle researchers turned to how they might narrow the uncertainly in their own field, the first question being the concentration of atmospheric carbon dioxide before fossil fuel burning began to inflate it. They have no reliable, direct record of atmospheric carbon dioxide before 1958, but they would still like to know how much carbon dioxide has been added to the atmosphere and thus how far along the road the world has come toward a detectable warming.

If fossil fuel is assumed to be the only source of carbon dioxide and about half remains in the atmosphere, the preindustrial concentration should have been about 290 parts per million by volume. If that were the case, climatologists might have several decades to wait before the greenhouse warming became evident above the background of climatic noise. Or, computer models of greenhouse climate effects could be too sensitive to rising carbon dioxide. Recent estimates suggest that climate models are not that far off and climatologists may not have to wait that long.

Those estimates are based on indirect measurements that indicate lower concentrations of atmospheric carbon dioxide in the past than fossil fuel burning alone would suggest. Hans Oeschger and Bernard Stauffer of the University of Bern reported that Greenland and Antarctic ice up to 1000 years old contains air having about 270 parts per million carbon dioxide. The air was trapped as accumulating snow slowly turned to ice, sealing the air into bubbles. The fidelity of this ice record has not been established beyond a doubt, but Oeschger believes that 270 parts per million is probably within 10 parts per million of the true value.

Less direct measurements of past carbon dioxide concentrations can be made through isotopic analysis of tree rings. The low ratios of carbon-13 to carbon-12 in fossil fuels reflect the low ratio in the plant material that formed the fuels. Released to the atmosphere and incorporated into living plants, this fossil fuel carbon further lowers the isotopic ratio of modern plants. Hans Freyer of the Nuclear Research Center at Julich, West Germany, reported that a compilation of his tree ring analyses and those of others places preindustrial atmospheric carbon dioxide concentrations at about 260 parts per million. From six trees on the U.S. Pacific coast, Minze Stuiver of the University of Washington estimated a preindustrial value of 276 parts per million.

Apparently, the present 340 parts per million of carbon dioxide represents an initial value of roughly 270 parts per million plus the contribution of fossil fuel burning and some additional source. The most discussed possibility for the additional source has been the biosphere, principally through the clearing of forests and the destruction of soil organic matter through cultivation (*Science*, 20 June 1980, p. 1358). Everyone now agrees that the biosphere has been a source over the past century, but oceanographers still cannot find a way to accommodate the carbon dioxide from a recent, large additional source in the ocean, where it presumably went after release to the atmosphere.

SIGNIFICANCE

Scientists accept that increasing levels of carbon dioxide will cause an increase in global temperature. However, they are not able to easily predict the extent of the impact on the Earth's atmospheric temperature. The difficulty occurs because the level of carbon dioxide released into the atmosphere does not equal the level that remains in the atmosphere. This occurs because carbon dioxide exists as part of the carbon cycle.

The carbon cycle is a complex system that describes the forms that carbon takes. In the atmosphere, carbon exists as carbon dioxide gas. The carbon dioxide becomes part of the biosphere when organisms convert it to biological carbon via photosynthesis. Carbon dioxide becomes part of the hydrosphere when it is dissolved in ocean water. These two processes remove carbon dioxide from the atmosphere as it is being added. The question that remains unanswered is how much carbon dioxide is removed from the atmosphere. The ongoing rise in carbon dioxide levels in the atmosphere suggests that not all of the carbon dioxide added is removed by the carbon cycle. However, the balance that occurs is not known.

This creates a problem in predicting the impact of carbon dioxide greenhouse gases on global warming. This is further complicated because it is not known how much carbon dioxide will be released in the future. Kerr describes how carbon dioxide emissions are expected to increase. However, these predictions are far from being certain.

The next problem identified by Kerr is based on determining how carbon dioxide emissions since the industrial age have influenced atmospheric carbon dioxide levels. To understand this, scientists must first know what the concentration of atmospheric carbon dioxide was before it began to be inflated by industrialization. In completing this analysis, they found that the global warming that has already been observed cannot be explained only by industrialization—the carbon dioxide levels have increased more than the burning of fossil fuels accounts for.

This suggests that there is another source of atmospheric carbon dioxide. Kerr describes how this source is most likely to be the biosphere, where deforestation and cultivation both cause carbon that exists as part of the biosphere to be released into the atmosphere. At the same time, another issue complicates the matter, which is that the ocean is thought to have removed a lot of the carbon dioxide from the atmosphere. This means that the amount of carbon dioxide released since industrialization must have been even greater.

While Kerr does not provide any final answers that make it possible to understand the rise in carbon dioxide levels, he makes it clear that understanding global warming and greenhouse gases requires an understanding of the carbon cycle. Without this, scientists are not able to determine past levels of atmospheric carbon dioxide or understand how future levels will change. This shows that understanding the carbon cycle is crucial to being able to predict the impact of the burning of fossil fuels and deforestation and ultimately, understanding and predicting global warming.

FURTHER RESOURCES

Books

Drake, Frances. *Global Warming: The Science of Climate Change*. New York: Oxford University Press, 2000.

Harvey, Danny. *Global Warming: The Hard Science*. New York: Prentice Hall, 2000.

Houghton, John. *Global Warming: The Complete Briefing*. New York: Cambridge University Press, 1997.

Periodicals

Joos, F., G. Plattner, T.F. Stocker, O. Marchal, and A. Schmittner. "Global Warming and Marine Carbon Cycle Feedbacks on Future Atmospheric CO_2." *Science* 284 (1999): 464–467.

Kerr, Richard A. "It's Official: Humans Are Behind Most of Global Warming." *Science* 296 (2001): 566.

Artificial Reefs

Navigation and Navigable Waters

Legislation

By: United States Code

Date: 1984

Source: *United States Code*. Title 33. Chapter 35, Sections 2101, 2102, and 2103.

About the Author: The U.S. Code is the set of general and permanent laws that govern the United States. The House of Representatives prepares the Code, and revisions are published every six years. The Code is arranged into 50 Titles. Title 33 deals with navigation and navigable waters. Chapter 35 concerns artificial reefs.

INTRODUCTION

An artificial reef is any structure that is placed in the ocean to provide a habitat for marine organisms. Many marine fish and invertebrates hide in and hunt from holes and cracks in reefs. Reefs provide the hard surfaces that are necessary for sessile marine animals and plants that require firm substrate in order to grow. Because reefs play such a key role in the lives of so many marine organisms, reefs attract large numbers of animals and plants as well as a broad diversity of species.

In order to enhance sport fishing and recreational diving, many coastal communities have begun placing structures offshore to create artificial reefs. Artificial reefs have been made out of decommissioned ships, railroad cars, airplanes, automobiles, rubble from bridges, and a variety of structures specifically manufactured to be used as artificial reefs. In 1979, a decommissioned gas and oil rig was moved from Louisiana to a site off of Franklin County, Florida to be used as an artificial reef. This project was extremely successful.

In 1980, the Minerals Management Service (MMS) within the United States Department of the Interior established a task force to study the conversion of oil and gas rigs into artificial reefs. The task force was composed of representatives from the petroleum industry, universities, and state and federal governments. As a result of the work by this group, in 1984, the National Fishing Enhancement Act was signed into law. It includes a National Artificial Reef Plan (NARP), which provides for planning, permitting, constructing, installing, monitoring, managing, and maintaining artificial reefs.

PRIMARY SOURCE

TITLE 33 - NAVIGATION AND NAVIGABLE WATERS
CHAPTER 35 - ARTIFICIAL REEFS

Sec. 2101. Congressional statement of findings and purpose

(a) The Congress finds that—

(1) although fishery products provide an important source of protein and industrial products for United States consumption, United States fishery production annually falls far short of satisfying United States demand;

(2) overfishing and the degradation of vital fishery resource habitats have caused a reduction in the abundance and diversity of United States fishery resources;

(3) escalated energy costs have had a negative effect on the economics of United States commercial and recreational fisheries;

(4) commercial and recreational fisheries are a prominent factor in United States coastal economies and the direct and indirect returns to the United States economy from commercial and recreational fishing expenditures are threefold; and

(5) properly designed, constructed, and located artificial reefs in waters covered under this chapter can enhance the habitat and diversity of fishery resources; enhance United States recreational and commercial fishing opportunities; increase the production of fishery products in the United States; increase the energy efficiency of recreational and commercial fisheries; and contribute to the United States and coastal economies.

(b) The purpose of this chapter is to promote and facilitate responsible and effective efforts to establish artificial reefs in waters covered under this chapter.

Sec. 2102. Establishment of standards Based on the best scientific information available, artificial reefs in waters covered under this chapter shall be sited and constructed, and subsequently monitored and managed in a manner which will—

(1) enhance fishery resources to the maximum extent practicable;

(2) facilitate access and utilization by United States recreational and commercial fishermen;

(3) minimize conflicts among competing uses of waters covered under this chapter and the resources in such waters;

(4) minimize environmental risks and risks to personal health and property; and

(5) be consistent with generally accepted principles of international law and shall not create any unreasonable obstruction to navigation.

Sec. 2103. National artificial reef plan Not later than one year after November 8, 1984, the Secretary of Commerce, in consultation with the Secretary of the Interior, the Secretary of Defense, the Administrator of the Environmental Protection Agency, the Secretary of the Department in which the Coast Guard is operating, the Regional Fishery Management Councils, interested States, Interstate Fishery Commissions, and representatives of the private sector, shall develop and publish a long-term plan which will meet the purpose of this chapter and be consistent with the standards established under section 2102 of this chapter. The plan must include—

(1) geographic, hydrographic, geologic, biological, ecological, social, economic, and other criteria for siting artificial reefs;

(2) design, material, and other criteria for constructing artificial reefs;

(3) mechanisms and methodologies for monitoring the compliance of artificial reefs with the requirements of permits issued under section 2104 of this title;

(4) mechanisms and methodologies for managing the use of artificial reefs;

(5) a synopsis of existing information on artificial reefs and needs for further research on artificial reef technology and management strategies; and

(6) an evaluation of alternatives for facilitating the transfer of artificial reef construction materials to persons holding permits issued pursuant to section 2104 of this title, including, but not limited to, credits for environmental mitigation and modified tax obligations.

SIGNIFICANCE

The National Artificial Reef Plan is better known as Rigs-to-Reefs. The program has been successful in the Gulf of Mexico, and is a rare example of cooperation by environmental groups, the government, and the oil industry in which all members benefit. Between 1987 and 2000, 151 decommissioned oil and gas rigs were donated to states in the Gulf of Mexico, making the region the largest artificial reef complex in the world.

Under Rigs-to-Reefs, petroleum companies donate oil and gas structures to the state. The state develops a plan for converting the rig to a reef. After the rig is moved and set in place, the company donates half the cost it would have incurred to dispose of the structure to the state. The donated money is

Vessels such as the *Saint George* are popular choices for the making of artificial reefs. This particular one was donated by the Dominican Navy, and was used in Bayahibe, Domincan Republic in 1999. AP IMAGES

invested in environmental trust funds that are used for fisheries conservation, research, and environmental management. In the thirteen years between 1987 and 2000, nearly $20 million was donated to states from petroleum companies as a result of the Rigs-to-Reefs program. It is assumed that the companies involved saved a similar amount in the cost of disposing of the rigs. After conversion of the petroleum platform to an artificial reef, the state takes responsibility for the maintenance and management of the structure.

Through the Rigs-to-Reefs program, oil and gas platforms have become the most desirable type of artificial reef. The shape of their structure allows water to continuously circulate through its openings. Fish, crabs, and lobsters can easily swim through and around the surfaces. Both bottom-dwellers and animals that live near the ocean surface are attracted to these environments. Some research shows that fish densities near converted oil platforms are twenty to fifty times greater than in surrounding waters. Nearly 30 percent of the recreational fish catch in Louisiana and Texas occurs near oil and gas platforms. In addition, as oil and gas platforms are constructed to

withstand the ocean environment, they last longer and stay in place better than other types of artificial reefs.

While Rigs-to-Reefs has been a success in the Gulf of Mexico, as of 2000, California had not converted any oil and gas platforms into artificial reefs. Environmental groups in California have raised concerns that creating artificial reefs is in conflict with the state's policy to return the sea floor to its natural condition after decommissioning petroleum platforms. In addition, ecologists have concerns that artificial reefs may modify the habitat making fish easier to catch rather than producing more fish. Finally, California is struggling with determining how to assign responsibility for maintenance and management of and liability for artificial reefs made from petroleum rigs.

FURTHER RESOURCES
Periodicals

Reggio, V. C., Jr. "Rigs-to-Reefs: The Use of Obsolete Petroleum Structures as Artificial Reefs." *U.S. Department of the Interior, Minerals Management Service, Gulf of Mexico OCS Region, New Orleans, La.* OCS Report MMS 87–0015 (1987): 17 pp.

Stanley, D. R., and C. A. Wilson. "Seasonal and Spatial Variation in Abundance and Size Distribution of Fishes Associated with a Petroleum Platform." *Journal of Marine Science*. (1997): 202, 473–475.

Web sites

Dauterive, Les. "Rigs-to-Reefs Policy, Progress, and Perspective." *Department of the Interior, Minerals Management Service, Gulf of Mexico Outer Continental Shelf Region*, OCS Report MMS 2000–073, October 2000. <http://www.gomr.mms.gov/homepg/whatsnew/publicat/recpub/2000-073.pdf> (accessed March 1, 2006).

Higgins, Margot. "Rigs-to-Reefs Plan May Lack Storybook Ending." *Environmental News Network*, January 7, 2000. <http://archives.cnn.com/2000/NATURE/01/17/rigs.to.reefs.enn/> (accessed March 1, 2006).

U.S. Department of the Interior, Minerals Management Service. "Gulf of Mexico Region, Environmental Information: Rigs to Reefs Information." *Department of the Interior, Minerals Management Service, Gulf of Mexico Outer Continental Shelf Region*. <http://www.gomr.mms.gov/homepg/regulate/environ/rigs-to-reefs/information.html> (accessed March 1, 2006).

The Control of Nature

"Atchafalaya"

Book excerpt

By: John McPhee

Date: 1989

Source: McPhee, John. "Atchafalaya." *The Control of Nature*. New York: Farrar, Straus and Giroux, 1989.

About the Author: American author John McPhee (1931–) has written more than twenty nonfiction books, many of them notable contributions about humans and their interaction with the environment, since 1965. A native of Princeton, New Jersey, he attended both Princeton University and Cambridge University before embarking on a career in journalism with *Time* magazine. Two of his books, *Encounters with the Archdruid* and *The Curve of Binding Energy*, were nominated for National Book Awards. McPhee received the Award in Literature from the American Academy of Arts and Letters in 1977 and received a Pulitzer Prize in 1999 for *Annals of the Former World*, his collected writings about geologists and their work.

INTRODUCTION

English philosopher Francis Bacon (1561–1626) wrote, "Nature, to be commanded, must be obeyed." John McPhee's *The Control of Nature* describes and implicitly questions the struggle to control nature that, once started, cannot be abandoned without grave consequences. *The Control of Nature* consists of three separate essays. The first, titled "Atchafalaya" describes an attempt to keep the Mississippi River in a channel that it no longer wishes to occupy. The second and third essays, titled "Cooling the Lava" and "Los Angeles Against the Mountains" describe the efforts undertaken to divert a lava flow headed for a town on the Icelandic island of Heimaey and engineering solutions to the deadly debris flow in the San Gabriel Mountains of southern California.

If nature were to have its way, the Mississippi River would abandon its current channel and bypass New Orleans. Its flow would be captured by the nearby Atchafalaya River, which lies lower than the Mississippi and would have provided a more efficient path to the sea. There is nothing unusual about this, for it is the way that rivers work over centuries and millennia. The economic effects of a stream captured by the Atchafalaya, however, would be devastating. New Orleans and the string of petrochemical plants stretching upriver would lose their fresh water supply, their access to the open ocean, and their river access to the rest of the United States.

"Atchafalaya" is primarily about Old River Control, a massive dam-like diversion structure 300 miles (483 kilometers) upriver from New Orleans. Named for a river channel connecting the Mississippi and Atchafalaya Rivers, Old River Control was designed and built by the U.S. Army Corps of Engineers to ensure that the proportion of the Mississippi flowing into the Atchafalaya is maintained at its 1950 level, in effect freezing the dynamic river system in time. The proportion of flow being diverted from the Mississippi had been steadily increasing since the middle of the nineteenth century and had reached 30 percent by 1950. Without intervention, the Atchafalaya would have eventually captured the entire flow of the Mississippi and diverted it away from the cities of Baton Rouge and New Orleans.

In "Atchafalaya," McPhee also elaborates upon the precarious position of New Orleans next to a river that should not be flowing where it is. The city lies in a topographic bowl lower than the bodies of water that surround it, which are kept at bay by a complicated system of levees that require constant maintenance. He goes on to explain how the containment of floodwater to benefit commerce and reduce flood damage has starved coastal regions of sediment

In 2000, after running into a railroad bridge, barges holding 1.9 million gallons of gasoline burn freely in the Atchafalaya River. The Atchafalaya, near Simmseport, Louisiana, runs lower than the Mississippi River and flows straight into the open ocean. AP IMAGES

and decreased their ability to buffer hurricane storm surges.

■ PRIMARY SOURCE

... Something like half of New Orleans is now below sea level—as much as fifteen feet. New Orleans, surrounded by levees, is emplaced between Lake Pontchartrain and the Mississippi like a broad shallow bowl. Nowhere is New Orleans higher than the river's natural bank. Underprivileged people live in the lower elevations, and always have. The rich—by the river—occupy the highest ground. In New Orleans, income and elevation can be correlated on a literally sliding scale: the Garden District on the highest level, Stanley Kowalski in the swamp. The Garden District and its environs are locally known as uptown.

Torrential rains fall on New Orleans—enough to cause flash floods inside the municipal walls. The water has

nowhere to go. Left on its own, it would form a lake, rising inexorably from one level of the economy to the next. So it has to be pumped out. Every drop of rain that falls on New Orleans evaporates or is pumped out. Its removal lowers the water table and accelerates the city's subsidence. Where marshes have been drained to create tracts for new housing, ground will shrink, too. People buy landfill to keep up with the Joneses. In the words of Bob Fairless, of the New Orleans District engineers, "It's almost an annual spring ritual to get a load of dirt and fill in the low spots on your lawn." A child jumping up and down on such a lawn can cause the earth to move under another child, on the far side of the lawn.

Many houses are built on slabs that firmly rest on pilings. As the turf around a house gradually subsides, the slab seems to rise. Where the driveway was once flush with the floor of the carport, a bump appears. The front walk sags like a hammock. The sidewalk sags. The bump up to the carport, growing, becomes high enough to knock the front wheels out of alignment. Sakrete appears, like putty beside a windowpane, to ease the bump. The property sinks another foot. The house stays where it is, on its slab and pilings. A ramp is built to get the car into the carport. The ramp rises three feet. But the yard, before long, has subsided four. The carport becomes a porch, with hanging plants and steep wooden steps. A carport that is not firmly anchored may dangle from the side of a house like a third of a drop-leaf table. Under the house, daylight appears. You can see under the slab and out the other side. More landfill or more concrete is packed around the edges to hide the ugly scene. A gas main, broken by the settling earth, leaks below the slab. The sealed cavity fills with gas. The house blows sky high.

"The people cannot have wells, and so they take rainwater," Mark Twain observed in the eighteen-eighties. "Neither can they conveniently have cellars or graves, the town being built upon 'made' ground; so they do without both, and few of the living complain, and none of the others." The others may not complain, but they sometimes leave. New Orleans is not a place for interment. In all its major cemeteries, the clients lie aboveground. In the intramural flash floods, coffins go out of their crypts and take off down the street.

The water in New Orleans' natural aquifer is modest in amount and even less appealing than the water in the river. The city consumes the effluent of nearly half of America, and, more immediately, of the American Ruhr. None of these matters withstanding, in 1984 New Orleans took first place in the annual Drinking Water Taste Test Challenge of the American Water Works Association.

The river goes through New Orleans like an elevated highway. Jackson Square, in the French Quarter, is on high ground with respect to the rest of New Orleans, but even from the benches of Jackson Square one looks up across the levee at the hulls of passing ships. Their keels are higher than the Astro Turf in the Superdome, and if somehow the ships could turn and move at river level into the city and into the stadium they would hover above the playing field like blimps.

In the early nineteen-eighties, the U.S. Army Corps of Engineers built a new large district headquarters in New Orleans. It is a tetragon, several stories high, with expanses of sheet glass, and it is right beside the river. That, to a fare-thee-well, is putting your money where your mouth is.

Among the five hundred miles of levee deficiencies now calling for attention along the Mississippi River, the most serious happen to be in New Orleans. Among other factors, the freeboard—the amount of levee that reaches above flood levels—has to be higher in New Orleans to combat the waves of ships. Elsewhere, the deficiencies are averaging between one and two feet with respect to the computed high-water flow line, which goes on rising as runoffs continue to speed up and waters are increasingly confined. Not only is the water higher. The levees tend to

sink as well. They press down on the mucks beneath them and squirt materials out to the sides. Their crowns have to be built up. "You put five feet on and three feet sink," a Corps engineer remarked to me one day. This is especially true of the levees that frame the Atchafalaya swamp, so the Corps has given up trying to fight the subsidence there with earth movers alone, and has built concrete floodwalls along the tops of the levees, causing the largest river swamp in North America to appear to be the world's largest prison. It keeps in not only water, of course, but silt. Gradually, the swamp elevations are building up. The people of Acadiana say that the swamp would be the safest place in which to seek refuge in a major flood, because the swamp is higher than the land outside the levees.

As sediments slide down the continental slope and the river is prevented from building a proper lobe—as the delta plain subsides and is not replenished—erosion eats into the coastal marshes, and quantities of Louisiana steadily disappear. The net loss is over fifty square miles a year. In the middle of the nineteenth century, a fort was built about a thousand feet from a saltwater bay east of New Orleans. The fort is now collapsing into the bay. In a hundred years, Louisiana as a whole has decreased by a million acres. Plaquemines Parish is coming to pieces like old rotted cloth. A hundred years hence, there will in all likelihood be no Plaquemines Parish, no Terrebonne Parish. Such losses are being accelerated by access canals to the sites of oil and gas wells. After the canals are dredged, their width increases on its own, and they erode the region from the inside. A typical three-hundred-foot oil-and-gas canal will be six hundred feet wide in five years. There are in Louisiana ten thousand miles of canals. In the nineteen-fifties, after Louisiana had been made nervous by the St. Lawrence Seaway, the Corps of Engineers built the Mississippi River-Gulf Outlet, a shipping canal that saves forty miles by traversing marsh country straight from New Orleans to the Gulf. The canal is known as Mr. Go, and shipping has largely ignored it. Mr. Go, having eroded laterally for twenty-five years, is as much as three times its original width. It has devastated twenty-four thousand acres of wetlands, replacing them with open water. A mile of marsh will reduce a coastal-storm-surge wave by about one inch. Where fifty miles of marsh are gone, fifty inches of additional water will inevitably surge. The Corps has been obliged to deal with this fact by completing the ring of levees around New Orleans, thus creating New Avignon, a walled medieval city accessed by an interstate that jumps over the walls.

"The coast is sinking out of sight," Oliver Houck has said. "We've reversed Mother Nature." Hurricanes greatly advance the coastal erosion process, tearing up landscape made weak by the confinement of the river. The threat of destruction from the south is even greater than the threat from the north.

I went to see Sherwood Gagliano one day—an independent coastal geologist and regional planner who lives in Baton Rouge. "We must recognize that natural processes cannot be restored," he told me. "We can't put it back the way it was. The best we can do is try to get it back in balance, try to treat early symptoms. It's like treating cancer. You get in early, you may do something." Gagliano has urged that water be diverted to compensate for the nutrient starvation and sediment deprivation caused by the levees. In other words, open holes in the riverbank and allow water and sediment to build small deltas into disappearing parishes. "If we don't do these things, we're going to end up with a skeletal framework with levees around it—a set of peninsulas to the Gulf," he said. "We will lose virtually all of our wetlands. The cost of maintaining protected areas will be very high. There will be no buffer between them and the coast."

Professor Kazmann of L.S.U. seemed less hopeful. He said "Attempts to save the coast are pretty much spitting in the ocean."

The Corps is not about to give up the battle, or so much as imagine impending defeat. "Deltas wax and wane," remarks Fred Chatry, in the pilothouse of the Mississippi. "You have to be continuously adjusting the system in consonance with changes that occur." Southern Louisiana may be a house of cards, but, as General Sands suggested, virtually no one would be living in it were it not for the Corps. There is no going back, as Gagliano says—not without going away. And there will be no retreat without a struggle. The Army engineers did not pick this fight. When it started, they were still in France. The guide levees, spillways, and floodways that dangle and swing from Old River are here because people, against odds, willed them to be here. Or, as the historian Albert Cowdrey expresses it in the introduction to "Land's End," the Corps' official narrative of its efforts in southern Louisiana, "Society required artifice to survive in a region where nature might reasonably have asked a few more eons to finish a work of creation that was incomplete." . . .

SIGNIFICANCE

McPhee's description of New Orleans was remarkably prescient in light of the levee collapses and catastrophic flooding of New Orleans after Hurricane Katrina struck the city in 2005. Beyond that, however, all three sections of the book speak to the broader issue of the wisdom of attempting to control nature. Some would argue that a decision to battle nature on the scale of Old River Control should be couched in terms of hubris, not wisdom, because the river will ultimately win. All it will take is a lapse in maintenance or a series of events not imagined by the engineers, or perhaps something as simple as the passing of time. If the

Mississippi cannot flow through the Old River channel into the Atchafalaya, it will find somewhere else.

Viewed in retrospect and with a modern understanding of geologic processes, one might argue that New Orleans should never have been built or at least not allowed to grow into a major city. Likewise for homes in the unstable mountains surrounding Los Angeles and the unnamed Icelandic town on the erupting volcanic island of Heimaey. But, once cities have begun to grow it is not easy or even desirable to stop the process, let alone reverse it. It would be practically impossible to close down and relocate major cities susceptible to flooding, earthquakes, hurricanes and other hazards. The economic and cultural benefits of a thriving city, moreover, may outweigh the costs of possible future catastrophies. Although the control of nature may be a losing proposition in the long run, in many cases there may be no other practical choice.

FURTHER RESOURCES
Books

Reuss, Martin. *Designing the Bayous: The Control of Water in the Atchafalaya Basin, 1800–1995.* College Station, TX: Texas A&M University Press, 2004.

Web sites

Center for Land Use Interpretation. "Old River Control Structure." <http://ludb.clui.org/ex/i/LA3126> (accessed January 30, 2006).

O'Brien, Greg. *Mississippi History Now.* "Making the Mississippi Over Again: The Development of River Control in Mississippi." <http://mshistory.k12.ms.us/features/feature25/msriver.html> (accessed January 30, 2006).

U.S. Geological Survey. "Geologic Hazards Team." <http://geohazards.cr.usgs.gov> (accessed January 30, 2006).

Experimental Fish Guidance Devices

Position statement

By: National Marine Fisheries Southwest Division

Date: January 22, 1999

Source: National Marine Fisheries Southwest Division. "Experimental Fish Guidance Devices." January 22, 1999.

About the Author: The National Marine Fisheries Service (NMFS) is part of the National Oceanographic and

Atmospheric Administration (NOAA), which is supported through the Department of Commerce. The Southwest Division of NMFS is located in Long Beach, California, and is responsible for the management, conservation and protection of marine species and habitats off the coast of California. It serves as both a scientific and policy resource.

INTRODUCTION

For more than 300 years, Americans have used rivers, streams, and other waterways as a means of transport, for irrigation, and as a source of electricity and drinking water. People developed many different methods of changing the course of flowing water so that their own purposes could be served. For example, rivers are dammed to produce lakes and to generate electricity from the movement of water. Dykes are built to control flooding. Culverts are constructed to divert water and prevent erosion. Water diversions are used to move water into agricultural areas for irrigation.

The fish that live in the rivers are dependent on the flow of the river for their survival. Most species of fish that live in rivers and streams lay their eggs in one location and then migrate to another region of the river to feed. Juveniles often live in protected areas until they are large enough to forage in the open stream. Dams, dykes, culverts, and other manmade obstructions impede the ability of many fish to carry out the necessary movements that allow for their survival. In particular, many juvenile fish are killed trying to pass through water diversions.

In 2003, the U.S. Fish and Wildlife Service estimated that there were more than 2.5 million water diversions in the United States and that 75,000 of them were more than 6 feet (1.8 meters) high. As agricultural practices have changed through the years, many of these water diversions no longer serve their intended purpose and are obsolete. However, they still affect fish populations by fragmenting important habitat areas.

Surveys of fish populations toward the end of the twentieth century showed that some populations of fish native to streams and rivers in the United States had disappeared. Other species were severely depleted in number. One major cause was the impact of dams and other water diversions. Biologists studied potential methods for reducing the mortality of fish that pass through water diversions by building screening devices, which are structures that allow fish to swim around the diversions unharmed.

■ PRIMARY SOURCE

EXPERIMENTAL FISH GUIDANCE DEVICES

Introduction Numerous stocks of salmon and steelhead trout in California streams are at low levels and many stocks continue to decline. The Sacramento River winter-run chinook salmon is listed as "endangered" under the Federal Endangered Species Act. Petitions for additional listings are pending. It is essential to provide maximum protection for juveniles to halt and reverse these declines.

The injury or death of juvenile fish at water diversion intakes have long been identified as a major source of fish mortality [Spencer 1928, Hatton 1939, Hallock and Woert 1959, Hallock 1987]. Fish diverted into power turbines experience up to 40 percent mortality as well as injury, disorientation, and delay of migration [Bell, 1991], while those entrained into agricultural and municipal water diversions experience 100 percent mortality. Diversion mortality is the major cause of decline in some fish populations.

Positive barrier screens have long been tested and used to prevent or reduce the loss of fish. Recent decades have seen an increase in the use and effectiveness of these screens and bypass systems; they take advantage of carefully designed hydraulic conditions and known fish behavior. These positive systems are successful at moving juvenile salmonids past intakes with a minimum of delay, loss or injury.

The past few decades have also seen much effort in developing "startle" systems to elicit a taxis (response) by the fish with an ultimate goal of reducing entrainment. This Position Statement addresses research designed to prevent fish losses at diversions and presents a tiered process for studying, reviewing, and implementing future fish protection measures.

Juveniles at Intakes The three main causes of delay, injury, and loss of fish at water intakes are entrainment, impingement, and predation. Entrainment occurs when the fish is pulled into the diversion and passes into a canal or turbine. Impingement is where a fish comes in contact with a screen, a trashrack, or debris at the intake. This causes bruising, descaling, and other injuries. Impingement, if prolonged, repeated, or occurs at high velocities also causes direct mortality. Predation also occurs. Intakes increase predation by stressing or disorienting fish and/or by providing habitat for fish and bird predators.

A. Positive Barriers Positive barrier screen systems and criteria for their design have been developed, tested, and proved to minimize harm caused at diversions. Positive barriers do not rely on active fish behavior; they prevent physical entrainment with a physical barrier. Screens with small openings and good seals are designed to work with hydraulic conditions at the site, providing low velocities normal to the screen face and sufficient sweeping velocities to move fish past the screen. These screens are very effective at preventing entrainment [Pearce and Lee 1991]. Carefully designed bypass systems minimize fish exposure to screens and provide hydraulic conditions that return fish to the river, preventing both entrainment and impingement [Rainey 1985]. The positive screen and fish bypass systems are designed to minimize predation, and to reduce mortality, stress, and delay from the point of diversion, through the bypass facility, and back the river.

Carefully designed positive barrier screen and bypass systems have been installed and evaluated at numerous facilities [Abernethy et al 1989, 1990, Rainey, 1990, Johnson, 1988]. A variety of screen types (e.g. flat plate, chevron, drum) and screen materials (e.g. woven cloth, perforated plate, profile wire), have proved effective, taking into consideration their appropriateness for each site. Well-designed facilities consistently result in a guidance efficiency of over 95 percent [Hosey, 1990, Neitzel, 1985, 1986, 1990 a,b,c,d, Neitzel, 1991].

The main drawback to positive barrier screens is cost. At diversions of several hundred cubic feet per second or greater, the low velocity requirement and structural complexity can drive the cost for fish protection and the associated civil works over a million dollars. At the headwork, the need to clean the screen, remove trash, and provide regular maintenance (e.g. seasonal installation, replacing seals, etc.) also increase costs.

B. Behavioral Devices Due to higher costs of positive barrier screens, there has been much experimentation since 1960 to develop behavioral devices as a substitute for barrier screens [EPRI, 1986]. A behavioral device, as opposed to a positive (physical) barrier, requires a volitional taxis on the part of the fish to avoid entrainment. Early efforts were designed to either attract or repel fish. These studies focused on soliciting a behavioral response from the fish, usually noticeable agitation. Using these startle investigations to develop effective fish guidance systems has not been effective.

Experiments show that there is a large response variation between individual fish of the same size and species. Therefore, it cannot be predicted that a fish will always move toward or away from a certain stimulus. Even when such a movement is desired by a fish, it often cannot discern the source or direction of the signal and choose a safe escape route.

Many behavioral devices do not incorporate and use a controlled set of hydraulic conditions to assure fish guidance, as does the positive screen/bypass system. The devices can actually encourage fish movement that actually contrasts with the expected rheotactic response. Thus, the fish gets mixed signals about what direction to move. Another concern is repeated exposure; a fish may no longer react to a signal that initially was an attractant or repellant. In addition to the vagaries in the response of an individual fish, behavior variations are expected due to size, species, life stage, and water quality conditions.

In strong or accelerating water velocity fields, the swimming ability of a fish may prevent it from responding to a stimulus even if it attempts to do so. Other environmental cues (e.g., pursuing prey, avoiding predators, or attractive habitat) may cause a fish to ignore the signal.

A main motivation for opting to install behavioral devices is cost-savings. However, much of the cost in conventional systems is for the physical structure needed to provide proper hydraulic conditions. Paradoxically, complementing a behavioral device with its own structural requirements may lessen much of its cost advantage.

Present skepticism over behavioral devices is supported by the fact that few are currently being used in the field and those that have been installed and evaluated seldom exhibit consistent guidance efficiencies above 60 percent [Vogel, 1988, EPRI, 1986]. The louver system is an example of a behavioral device with a poor success record. In this case, even with the use of favorable hydraulics, performance is poor especially for smaller fish. Entrainment can be high, particularly when operated over a wide range of hydraulic conditions [Vogel, 1988, Cramer, 1982, Bates, 1961]. Due to their poor performance, some of these systems are already replaced by positive barriers. . . .

SIGNIFICANCE

In response to research into fish screening devices in the 1990s, which showed that the devices increased the survivorship of many fish species, Congress established the National Fish Passage Program in 1999. The goal of the program was to restore native fish populations to self-sustaining levels by allowing them to move throughout their natural habitat. At the same time, the program was sensitive to preventing the spread of introduced species by providing them with additional habitat. The program is broken up into seven regional offices, along with an administration in Washington D.C.

The National Fish Passage Program is a voluntary partnership between governmental agencies, private groups, and landowners. Costs are shared among these groups. Historically, the program has contributed approximately 27 percent of the cost for developing and installing fish screening devices, while the partners

Diversion screens, such as this one in the Washington Yakima Valley, can trap juvenile and adult salmon in unscreened irrigation canals. Workers routinely inspect these screens to save what they can. © NATALIE FOBES/CORBIS

pay for the balance. Between 2000 and 2002, the program was funded at just over $1.5 million per year.

The National Fish Passage Program employs fisheries biologists who survey rivers and streams and produce a set of recommendations for sites that will best improve habitat for the most endangered species of fish. The information collected by the scientists is assimilated in a database called the Fish Passage Decision Support System. This system incorporates information on the location of water barriers, fish habitat and movement, benefits of building fish screening devices, cost of fish screening devices, and feasibility. The system relies on a geographical information system (GIS) to map all of this information. Analyses generated by the system is used to prioritize projects that will be undertaken by the Fish Passage Program.

Within three years, the program supported 105 fish passage projects in twenty-five states. The program partnered with 166 different agencies and saw significant benefits to fish populations throughout the country. Eighteen species of fish that were either endangered or threatened were directly impacted. The natural flow of water and natural water temperatures were reestablished for populations of trout, herring, striped bass, shad, sturgeon, salmon, minnows, and darters. Over 3,750 miles of river and nearly 70,000 acres of wetlands were restored as a result of the National Fish Passage Program.

Restoring natural river flows has benefits to other members of the ecosystem as well as the fish. Birds that eat fish, such as eagles, ospreys, and kingfishers have improved habitat in which to forage for food. Larger predators like bears, otters, and mink also enjoy larger prey populations. In addition, recreational, commercial, and subsistence fishermen benefit from larger fish populations that are spread out over a wider area.

FURTHER RESOURCES
Web sites

Hartlerode, Ray, Steve Allen, and Annette Dabashinsky. "John Day Fish Passage and Screening." <http://

www.efw.bpa.gov/publications/H00005122-1.pdf>
(accessed January 6, 2006).

Kepshire, Bernie. "Oregon Department of Fish and Wildlife Fish Screening Program: Fish Screen Types and Costs." <http://www.st.nmfs.gov/st5/Salmon_Workshop/ 20_Kepshire.pdf> (accessed January 6, 2006).

Oregon Department of Fish and Wildlife. "Fish Screening." <http://www.dfw.state.or.us/ODFWhtml/InfoCntr Fish/PDFs/BKGFishScreen.pdf> (accessed January 6, 2006).

U.S. Fish and Wildlife Service. "National Fish Passage Program." <http://www.fws.gov/fisheries/FWSMA/ fishpassage> (accessed January 6, 2006).

U.S. Fish and Wildlife Service—Pacific Region. "Fish Passage/ Screening Program FRIMA." <http://www.fws.gov/ pacific/Fisheries/Fish%20Passage-Screening %20Program.htm> (accessed January 6, 2006).

"A New Paradigm"

Book excerpt

By: Robert Duane Ballard

Date: 2000

Source: Ballard, Robert D., with Will Hively. "A New Paradigm." *The Eternal Darkness: A Personal History of Deep-Sea Exploration.* Princeton: Princeton University Press, 2000.

About the Author: Robert Duane Ballard (1942–) is a marine geologist better known to the public because of his many published books on deep-sea exploration and the discovery of the wreckage of *Titanic* in 1985. He was part of the first team to dive with *Alvin*, the first manned submersible for deep-sea exploration used at Woods Hole Oceanographic Institute (WHOI). He worked as a researcher for thirty years at WHOI, where he became the head of the Deep Submergence Laboratory and holds the title of Scientist Emeritus in the WHOI Department of Applied Ocean Physics. Ballard was one of the first scientists to appreciate the advantages of deep-sea unmanned vehicles over manned ones for improving the study of oceanic abysses and other bottom-sea features. He founded and led the Jason Project, an interactive science educational program for elementary school children.

INTRODUCTION

The United States began to systematically explore the oceans in 1807, a Thomas Jefferson initiative that created the Survey of the Coast to study tidal currents, collect samples from the bottom sea-floor, and map near-shore sea-floor topography. In 1845, under the lead of Charles Henry Davis, the following goals were established for research vessels: to determine surface temperature and water temperature at different depths; to observe characteristics of the sea bottom; to determine direction and speed of currents at surface and various depths; to measure the depth of coastal seas; and to collect and study marine plant and animal life. Since then, the Gulf Stream has been regularly and repeatedly observed and charted at different seasons and throughout the year. The Gulf of Mexico began to be studied with the first sounding machine in 1874 and the resulting bathymetric map was the first accurate map of a portion of deep ocean. In 1922, echo sounder was introduced and the Vessel Guide was sent to the North of the Pacific Ocean through the Panama Canal and the coast of Mexico, comparing wireline and acoustic soundings in depths from 100 to 4,617 fathoms. In 1933, the Vessel Guide mapped a seamount that was later named Davidson Seamount, the first major feature mapped underwater. As new technologies were developed during the first three decades of the twentieth century, the sciences of Oceanography, Marine Biology, Geology and Geophysics, Marine Chemistry, and Geochemistry were gradually taking shape. However, it wasn't until after World War II that deep-sea exploration technology started to advance with great speed, ultimately leading to the three great resources of the 1960s: the Deep Tow instrument system, the multibeam sounding instruments known as Sonar Array Sounding System, and manned research submersibles.

The first U.S. Navy manned submersible was the bathyscaph *Trieste*, invented by a family of Swiss engineers, the Piccards. *Trieste* was initially used by the Navy in 1960 to take scientists to the deepest spots ever visited by humans. However, it was not well suited for research science purposes and the Navy decided to fund WHOI to design and build a new manned submersible that could better meet the needs of a small research crew. In 1964, *Alvin* was launched, a manned submersible with capacity for carrying three persons on board. With *Alvin*, a new era of deep-sea scientific exploration was inaugurated.

New imaging techniques such as low-light television cameras and fiber optics provided a new leap in deep sea exploration. The WHOI's Deep Submergence Laboratory, under the lead of Ballard, designed the diving craft *Argo*, a tethered instrument capable of sending clear images to the ship on the surface and working in 20,000-foot (6,100-meter) depths. In 1985, *Argo* was tested for mapping the debris of the submarine *Thresher*, which sunk in 1963 off Cape Cod. In the same year, *Argo* was used to find the wreckage of *Titanic* in the North Atlantic. In 1986, the prototype of a remotely operated craft, *Jason Jr.*, was developed to operate from *Argo* with fiber optic cables and transmit color images and other data to research scientists on the surface. *Jason Jr.* was first tested using *Alvin* instead of *Argo* to capture color images of the *Titanic*, nine months after *Argo's* discovery of the wreckage, while some technological challenges were being tackled at WHOI. The *Argo / Jason* craft system was finally tested in 1988 with the new and larger remotely operated *Jason* exploring the Mediterranean Sea off the coast of Sicily. The result was the discovery of the first deep-sea archeology site and the first image of a hydrothermal vent in that sea. The following decades saw the development of new tethered crafts, such as the Tethered Unmanned Work Vehicle System (TUWVS). TUWVS is equipped with heavy-lift hydraulic manipulators and carries motorized and remotely operated vehicles (ROVs) for data transfer, being therefore capable of performing a number of tasks, such as the recovery of military and civilian hardware. An example was the recovery of the F-14D Tomcat that crashed at sea near Point Loma in California in August 2005.

PRIMARY SOURCE

I have been waiting a long time for a chance to find that singular wreck. Even while pursuing my research as a geologist, and while working with other scientists to find undersea volcanoes, hot springs, and deep oases, I had dreamed of searching for the lost British luxury liner. Given the right technology, I thought, finding it should not be a matter of blind luck. Now, having tested *Argo* on *Thresher's* wreckage, I felt an irresistible urge to use it on something bigger. This had to be the right technology.

But why that particular target? My motive was in part sheer fascination—some at Woods Hole used the world "obsession"—but it was not a morbid fascination. There was a strong practical component. Finding the most famous wreck of all time—especially after others had failed—would prove the new *Argo* concept in a way that a mapping of *Thresher's* debris never could. And a spectacular success seemed important, for I fully believed that *Argo* (and its later companion craft *Jason*)

represented the next major advance in deep submergence technology.

For half a century, pioneers of deep exploration had invented clever new ways to cram humans into hollow capsules and send them plummeting into eternal darkness. Each new strategy—from Barton's bathysphere to Piccard's bathyscaph to *Alvin* and other submersibles—improved on previous methods. Now our group at Woods Hole was making a radical break with that trend: we wanted to detach the crew cabin from the diving craft—permanently. *Argo*, our tethered eyeball, represented the first part of that plan. A more advanced tethered vehicle would follow, carrying a motorized remotely operated vehicle (ROV) named *Jason* as its passenger—a robot that could sally out to explore, take pictures, and collect samples while its human "crew" remained on the surface. Detached from the actual discomfort and danger, they would still be virtually present down below, still probing the black abyss.

Once again, new technology was changing the nature of deep-sea exploration. Surely such a potent robotic combination would outperform the current generation of submersibles. Or so I believed in 1984, as my thoughts turned from *Thresher* to *Titanic*. Perhaps foolishly, I declared my confidence ahead of time. "You'll never see much in *Alvin*," I told an interviewer for the *Cape Cod Times*. Manned submersibles are doomed."

My enthusiasm for new, unmanned vehicles irritated some colleagues, especially among the *Alvin* group at Woods Hole. *Alvin* was, after all, a dear old friend. Remarks that its days were numbered seemed especially unwelcome coming from me—a marine geologist who had built his career on the ability of manned submersibles to open a new frontier, and who had originally joined the team as *Alvin's* cheerleader. Now that I was advancing a new paradigm for deep-sea exploration, the skeptical and sometimes angry responses coming from this group were understandable. Yet I could not believe any differently. By the end of the 1980s I would log more diving time inside *Alvin* than any other scientist-observer. And that experience was leading me to this conclusion: Manned submersibles, despite their many successes, have inherent problems that will always limit their efficiency. Ultimately, those limits will become intolerable.

The chief advantage and glory of manned submersibles is clearly the human intelligence on board. Allyn Vine, who championed the idea of submersibles in the 1950s, viewed this human presence—constantly sensing, probing, adjusting, and guiding—as irreplaceable. Think back a century, he urged his colleagues, to the great age of surface exploration. What would be the best scientific instrument you could take on an observing and sampling expedition—that you could, say, load aboard the *Beagle*, a British ship that traveled the world in the 1830s collecting biological specimens and copious amounts of data on habitats and climates? The best possible instrument aboard the *Beagle*? Why, Charles Darwin, of course.

Submersibles, Vine argued, could be this century's *Beagles*. Oceanographers have long been dragging nets and dredges through the deep ocean; they would eventually add remote-sensing techniques and instruments on sleds. But if a few modern Darwins actually went down to explore in submersibles, Vine insisted, the results would be incomparably richer. Whole fields of science might take off in profoundly different directions.

The truth of this argument, however, depended on a small technicality: humans must stay alive to exercise their wonderful intelligence. On the surface, most of the time, that's easy. In the deep sea, however, we are fragile trespassers. The environment we need in order to survive there—a roomful of air, constantly refreshed—must be surrounded by thick, heavy walls. The vessel that houses this fortified chamber requires extraordinary design, construction, and maintenance. None of this comes cheap. *Alvin*, for example, would cost $25 million to build today. But *Jason*—a miniature, unmanned, remote-controlled version of *Alvin* without a pressure sphere and other technology needed to keep humans alive—would cost about $5 million. In light of such enormous differences in cost, it has always been a debatable question whether human presence in a deep-diving craft is more a liability or an asset.

Consider the working space, for example. Because of technical challenges and cost, the amount of space inside a pressure sphere must be limited. Such tight quarters greatly reduce the number of instruments and the amount of documentation a scientist can have there. The small space also reduces, of course, the number of scientists—often to just one or two. From the human point of view, then, the crew space inside a submersible is cramped. But from a budgetary point of view it's bloated. Human presence requires even a "small" submersible to be relatively large and expensive, with backup systems for life support and safety. And once the diving craft gets big, its operating costs escalate as well. A typical manned vehicle weighing twenty tons requires a large, sophisticated support ship with matching crew. The much larger bathyscaphs that preceded small submersibles required even more surface support, which was one reason why small submersibles replaced them.

Now consider removing the humans. You immediately achieve another reduction in size, comparable to the reduction from bathyscaphs to submersibles—this time from "small" submersibles to even smaller, unmanned tethered eyeballs and robots. That, once gain, reduces

operating costs. At the same time, the space available to participating scientists increases. The number of researchers who can join a remotely controlled "dive" is now large: the number who can fit into the control van on the surface ship. Eventually it will be even larger: the number who can establish a virtual presence—through the Internet, say—from anywhere on the planet.

In addition to creating far more space for crew members, ROVs give each participant much more observing time. A typical dive to 12,000 feet in a manned submersible requires two and a half hours in the morning for the descent and a similar amount of time in the late afternoon for the return to the surface. Such a dive yields only three to four hours on the bottom, with one or two scientists exploring, at best, approximately one mile of terrain. This short period of time on the bottom, and the small observing area, come with a very high price tag-currently $25,000 or more per day at sea, or roughly $8,000 per hour of observing time on the bottom. ROVs, by contrast can remain underwater for weeks at a time without resurfacing at a cost per observing hour of $1,000 or less—which, when combined with the larger number of scientists who can observe, greatly increases the payoff. Equally important, ROVs can be deployed from a large number of support ships around the world with dynamic positioning capabilities. As a result, they are far more portable, working one month from a ship in the Mediterranean Sea and the next from a different ship in the north Pacific, while submersibles like *Alvin* can be operated only from a single specialized support ship, greatly limiting their range.

Finally, a more subtle notion began to shape my thinking in the late 1970s, turning me toward new technology. I realized that "manned" operations in submersibles like *Alvin* are never completely manned. That is to say, they never use the whole person. Most of the human body that's sealed inside goes along as extra baggage.

Unlike an astronaut on the moon, or Darwin on a tropical island, a scientist in a submersible cannot get out to explore. He or she cannot walk around on the bottom, feeling brittle rocks crunch underfoot or soft mud-sucking; cannot bend over to inspect a burrowing creature; cannot use feeling in the fingers to pick just-right samples like fruit in a market; cannot tweak or fine-tune instruments. All that freedom of motion, seeing, and sensing contributes in subtle ways to data gathering and discovery. But instead, an aquanaut must always remain crouched inside a tiny capsule. He or she must peer through small windows with restricted views and must fumble with a remote mechanical arm to accomplish anything outside. In other words, "manned" submersibles are in large part remotely operated—and thus unmanned. They are really a hybrid of the human intellect and mechanical, robotic extensions.

Despite these inherent limitations, a large part of the scientific community decided in the late 1970s and throughout the 1980s that sending a researcher to the bottom of the ocean was worth the expense, given the unique contribution a controlling human intelligence could make on site. That decision proved wise at the time. A steady stream of humans diving in submersibles produced some of the most important discoveries ever made by marine scientists seeking to understand the geology, geophysics, biology, and chemistry of the deep sea.

But history has often shown that just when a new paradigm begins to receive broad acceptances, its replacement is already close at hand. By the time that diving on the Midocean Ridge was becoming routine, new technology was making it possible to consider a different way for humans to explore the abyss. Vehicles that could respond immediately to a controlling human intelligence, yet be operated even more remotely, were becoming possible. With the new technology, it would make little practical difference whether the person exercising commands was situated just a few feet away from the robotic arms of a diving craft, inside a pressure sphere, or many thousands of feet away, on the surface. Manipulator commands can move back and forth through a telecommunications cable at the speed of light. In theory, a person could perform every mechanical function just as well from the surface.

There was still, however, the matter of visual inspection. Submersibles often take passengers right up to lava flows, rocky outcrops, warm springs, wreckage, and other features. Crew members stare intently while deciding what to do—make a measurement, take a sample, creep closer to some unexpected feature, or move on. In the end, my thinking about the two paradigms came down to one question: Was an observer's view of the deep-sea environment superior from inside a submersible, or could we replicate that view in a system controlled from the surface? Was it possible, in other words, to achieve the illusion of *telepresence*?

The answer has always been no—we could not replicate the view. Neither ANGUS, the Woods Hole camera sled, nor Deep-Tow, the Scripps system, achieved anything remotely resembling telepresence. ANGUS could not transmit images; it had to be hauled back to the surface and its film developed. Deep-Tow had a data link embedded in the tether, but its small capacity permitted only a slow-scan black-and-white image to be transmitted to the surface. These time-delayed, snapshot-like views, if they showed much at all, could not be used to control the sled from the surface. In theory, telepresence could make deep-sea operations far more efficient. In practice, into the 1980s, our technology was not up to the challenge.

SIGNIFICANCE

Manned deep-sea submersibles played a crucial role in the advancement of marine sciences and oceanography in a time when robotics and other technologies were still in their infancy. They took scientists to new territories never dreamed of before, allowing direct observation, selective sample collection, and measurement in the deep sea. However, they were risky, expensive, and limiting, due to both their capacity (only two or three individuals could be onboard at a time) and underwater topographic features such as narrow canyons, caves, or other features that would limit scientists' access. The advent of ROVs and new imaging technologies constituted a widening of horizons for researchers by allowing a larger number of observers to access real-time images and control the equipment from the surface. They could also see images of places and collect dwelling life-forms and other samples where only a small robot could enter. For instance, in 2004 the National Oceanic and Atmospheric Administration (NOAA) started Operation Deep Scope in the northern Gulf of Mexico. In this complex geological region, an ROV equipped with the eye-in-the-sea camera made it possible to film animals under extremely dim light and without disturbing them, a task impossible for a larger and noisier craft carrying humans inside.

The *Argo/Jason* vehicle system inaugurated a new concept in deep-sea exploration by adding new information capability, access, and mobility to prospective instruments. It also allowed the simultaneous access of a greater number of researchers to information in real time. Further technological advances has led to new generations of ROVs, capable of performing a growing number of complex operations at lower costs and with better efficiency than manned submersibles could ever do.

FURTHER RESOURCES

Books

Ballard, Robert D., and M. Hamilton. *Graveyards of the Pacific: From Pearl Harbor to Bikini Atoll.* Washington, DC: National Geographic Books, 2001.

Web sites

National Oceanic and Atmospheric Administration (NOAA). "Explorations: Operation Deep Scope: Seeing with 'New Eyes'." <http://oceanexplorer.noaa.gov/explorations/04deepscope/welcome.html> (accessed January 17, 2006).

National Oceanic and Atmospheric Administration (NOAA). "History of NOAA Ocean Exploration." <http://oceanexplorer.noaa.gov/history/early/early.html> (accessed January 17, 2006).

"From the Modern Synthesis to Lysenkoism, and Back?

Portraits Of Science"

Journal article

By: Uwe Hossfeld and Lennart Olsson

Date: July 5, 2002

Source: Hossfeld, Uwe, and Lennart Olsson. "Portraits of Science: From the Modern Synthesis to Lysenkoism, and Back?" *Science* 297 (July 5, 2002) 55–56.

About the Author: Uwe Hossfeld and Lennart Olsson are both professors at the Friedrich-Schiller-Universitat in Jena, Germany. Hossfeld is in the Department of History of Medicine, Science, and Technology. Lennart is in the Department of Systematic Zoology and Evolutionary Biology.

INTRODUCTION

During the Soviet era, the Communist party extensively controlled the manner in which scientific research was carried out. This was most notable in the biological sciences, as modern thinking and widely accepted research methods were exchanged for Lysenkoism, a non-traditional approach to genetic studies that had little backing by scientific evidence or theories. Although Lysenkoism originated in the Soviet Union, countries throughout the Soviet Bloc, including Poland, Czechoslovakia, and East Germany, implemented its practices. Scientific cooperation between the Soviet Union and China led to the appearance of Lysenkoism at three Chinese institutions in 1949.

Leaders of the Soviet Union institutionalized Lysenkoism in the 1920s, as Trofin Lysenko promised new varieties of food crops, improved harvests, and unlimited supplies of milk and meat. At the time, famine was taking hold in places like the Ukraine, and Lysenkoism was to be the answer for the Soviet collectivized and state-owned farms, which were struggling to keep up with the demands for food. Many of the promises of Lysenkoism failed to reach fruition. However, the approach remained the primary mode of agricultural and biological research in the Soviet Union until the later part of the twentieth century.

One influential scientist in East Germany was Georg Schneider. He was supported by the Communist leadership for promoting the Lysenkoism approach, as it was the same approach the Soviets were

Lysenkoism was predicted to be the solution to the Russian famine in the 1920s in Ukraine. © HULTON-DEUTSCH COLLECTION/CORBIS

using. Schneider had received his educational training in Moscow, while in exile from Germany. He claimed there were deficiencies in the Darwinian approach to biology and maintained his position even when an important book against Lysenkoism was published in East Germany.

Lysenko's ideas began following his work manipulating the germination of winter wheat plants to make them more efficient. He exposed the seeds to varying humidity and temperature levels in order to have them germinate in the spring. Although Lysenko claimed he had discovered something new, the process, called vernalization, was discovered earlier by both Russian and American researchers. Lysenko used his work to promote an idea from an earlier agronomist, Ivan Michurin, who suggested an organism's genetic structure could be changed through the controlling of external factors. Lysenko argued that the generally accepted Mendelian-based genetic knowledge was false, claiming that once a seed was manipulated to germinate in the spring, further generations of that wheat plant would germinate in the springtime automatically with a new genetic disposition. He predicted that improved varieties of seeds could be developed in two to three years, as opposed to the normal eight to ten years it took for the cross breeding of plants.

Many of Lysenko's theories had little scientific backing, with many ideas backed by unverified data from surveys distributed to farms throughout the Soviet Union. Lysenko himself is thought to have had a questionable scientific background. In 1925, Lysenko did receive an agronomy certificate at the Kiev Agricultural Institute. He pursued higher-level degrees, but had some academic deficiencies and was unable to complete a dissertation for a master's or doctoral degree. Lysenko also never took the standard scientific examinations for his field of studies.

PRIMARY SOURCE

After the end of the Second World War, German scientists wanted to separate science from ideology. They hoped for a new beginning without misanthropic political doctrines, but in East Germany [German Democratic Republic (GDR)], this hope was thwarted. There it soon became clear that the communists would decide in which direction scientific research would go, just as the national socialists had done before. This was true especially of biology and philosophy. In the 1950s and 1960s, the attitude of a scientist to the mode of thought encapsulated by the theory of evolution known as Lysenkoism and to the "the socialist achievements of the Soviet Union" was used as a measure of his or her political stance. It was within the doctrine of Lysenkoism that the self-styled developmental biologist, Georg Schneider, elaborated his career in the GDR.

The Ukrainian agronomist Trofim D. Lysenko (1898–1976) became well known in the 1930s through his research into Jarowization (the cold treatment of seed to stimulate germination), which meant grain could be sown in the spring instead of the previous fall. This made it theoretically possible to extend land use within the Soviet Union for agriculture. Building on this early success, Lysenko developed his anti-Mendelian theories over the next few decades. His idea—that acquired characters could be inherited—was totally at odds with what was known about genetics at this time. This notion was first known as "Michurin biology" [Ivan D. Michurin (1855–1935) was an early proponent of acquired inheritance, gaining his ideas from fruit-tree selection studies] and later as "creative Darwinism."

By the 1930s, Lysenko had gained Joseph Stalin's support, which helped him to become president of the Lenin Academy for Agricultural Sciences (VASKhNIL) in 1938 and director of the Department of Genetics at the USSR Academy of Science in 1940. Because of Lysenko's political power, Soviet geneticists abstained from criticizing his theories at their conferences in Moscow in 1936 and 1939. Finally, after the VASKhNIL conference in August 1948 (during times of general repression, denunciation, imprisonment, and murder), the principles of classical genetics were suppressed in the Soviet Union. Soviet genetics, which had until then been of the highest international standards and was led by researchers including S. S. Cetverikov, T. Dobzhansky, G. F. Gauze, N. V. Timofeeff-Ressovsky, and N. I. Vavilov, was given a blow from which it would take a long time to recover. Lysenko's ideas found their way into textbooks and were taught in schools and universities. There were even attempts to apply his ideas to the evolution of man (e.g., in the ideas of I. I. Prezent).

After Stalin's death in 1953, Lysenko's influence weakened for some time but regained influence under Nikita Khrushchev until the latter was over-thrown in 1964. Since the mid-1990s, Russian historians have worked intensely on the Lysenko era, but no comprehensive account yet exists in languages other than Russian. It is a fortunate peculiarity of the historical development of the GDR that Lysenkoism never gained much hold and did not do much damage. This is all the more remarkable because, in the 1950s, many school textbooks were full of Lysenko's ideas, and it was almost impossible to give lectures on classical genetics at the universities. However, Lysenkoism did become influential at Jena University. It is here that the Marxist and Lysenkoist, Georg Schneider, having returned from exile in the Soviet Union in 1945, became director of the Ernst Haeckel house (EHH) and professor of theoretical biology. Schneider's political connections with Walter Ulbricht and other important communists enabled him to become an influential figure in East German science, and he held leading positions in the Thuringian Communist Party from July 1945 until April 1946.

Schneider was born in Saarbrucken, studied in Jena between 1928 and 1931, and became a schoolteacher. As a member of the German Communist Party (KPD) he had difficulties finding a job and in 1931 emigrated to the Soviet Union. In 1936, after working as a teacher in Moscow schools for a few years, another German émigré and communist, Julius Schaxel, then doing research in developmental biology at the Institute for Experimental Morphogenesis, hired him. Schaxel and Schneider later moved to the famous Severtsov Institute for Evolutionary Morphology at the Academy of Sciences of the USSR in Moscow.

In October 1945, Schneider earned a PhD in Jena with a thesis called "The Role of the Nervous System in the

Regeneration of the Limbs in the Axolotl." The thesis apparently no longer exists but is believed to consist of work carried out in collaboration with Schaxel in Moscow. Only a few days after receiving his Ph.D. degree, Schneider started the "democracy courses" at the university in his function as secretary of the local KPD. After 9 months as a teacher in Berlin at the Karl-Marx-Parteihochschule, Schneider applied for the position as director of the EHH. Doubts were raised about his qualifications, and he was at first given a temporary post. In 1947, Schneider tried to obtain the "Habilitation," a title normally required to qualify for professorships in Germany. His Habilitation thesis received mixed, and some very negative, reviews so he withdrew his proposal. Despite this failure, Schneider became a tenured professor of theoretical biology in Jena in 1951. As with the Ph.D. thesis, there were doubts as to how much of his thesis was actually his work and how much was Schaxel's (who had died in 1943).

In his research, Schneider attempted to continue the research on ontogenetic determination in Mexican axolotls. He aimed to change hereditary characters through environmental influences by using the "Pfropfung" method in which whole organs or organ parts were joined to those of an animal of the same or a different species. From reading Schneider's papers, it would appear to have been very difficult for him to reconcile his experimental results with Lysenko's ideas. Nevertheless, in his lecture notes (EHHH archive), he interpreted results from his axolotl research as support for his Lysenkoism.

Schneider used his position as director of the EHH and Professor of theoretical biology to promote Lysenko's teaching as creative Darwinism. He acted as propagandist for an allegedly progressive, antifascist Soviet biology, which it was important to defend against a supposedly reactionary bourgeois genetics with its racist tendencies. From 1950 onward, Schneider gave a lecture series on Michurin and creative Darwinism, and he led colloquia on related topics. His book, *The Theory of Evolution: The Fundamental Problem of Modern Biology*, was published in 1950 and by 1952 was in its third edition. The book offers many examples of his rigid Lysenkoism: "The essence of the teachings of Michurin and Lysenko is that their theories and methods are no dogmas, no stiff system, but quite the opposite. They promote further developments... They represent the most advanced in today's biology... Also the teachings of Michurin and Lysenko are the further development of the natural science aspect of Marxism... Therefore let us boldly apply the theories and methods of Michurin and Lysenko!"

Schneider was also very active outside academia, giving lectures to members of organizations such as the Society for German-Soviet Friendship. He thereby promoted Lysenko's ideas and their use in agricultural practice, and he was given the highest awards for these activities. His many commitments left almost no time for scientific work. One of his initiatives in 1947 was to resurrect and act as editor of the popular science journal, *Urania*, which had been created in 1924 by Schaxel and forbidden in 1933 by the national socialists. After Stalin's death, Lysenko's doctrine lost any influence it might have held in the GDR, the scientific debate had been won by the Darwinists, and Schneider's largely unsuccessful agrobiological suggestions were no longer of any interest.

An important milestone in establishing the modern evolutionary synthesis in the Soviet Union was the book *Faktory evoljucii (Factos of Evolution)*, published in 1946 by Ivan I. Schmalhausen. Long before Theodosius Dobzhansky published an English translation in 1949, Schneider had translated the book into German in 1946 and had visited Schmalhausen's institute, but his German translation was never printed. Student witnesses later recounted how Schneider performed a ritualistic burning of the translation in the courtyard of the EHH in the winter semester of 1949–50. In 1948, Schmalhausen had been denounced as "leader of the Mendelist-Morganists" and lost his professorship at Moscow University, as well as his Academy of Science institute directorship. Apparently this denunciation made Schneider realize that Schmalhausen was "an incorrigible enemy of the progressive teachings of Lysenko," and a "formal geneticist."

Whatever he burnt in 1949–50 was not Schneider's translation of Schmalhausen. He kept it and took it with him to Moscow in 1959, when his career took a new turn as he became a diplomat in charge of cultural affairs at the embassy of the GDR. He must have returned the manuscript to the EHH, where one of us (U.H.) recently found it in the library. Apparently Schneider was sufficiently impressed by the ideas that became part of the modern evolutionary synthesis to preserve his Schmalhausen translation, but for the sake of his career prospects, publicly he was a Lysenkoist.

Many leading researchers in the GDR resisted Lysenko's pseudoscientific ideas. Research in classical genetics continued at the institutes run by the Academy of Sciences and Agriculture. At Gatersleben, Hans Stubbe played a leading role. Under his leadership, a large-scale (in terms of resources and personnel) experimental research program was conducted between 1949 and 1960 in which irrefutable, reproducible results in support of Mendelian genetics were produced. Stubbe and co-workers also showed that Lysenko and his followers often worked with contaminated material; used uncritical, lax, and careless experimental procedures; and misused the terminology of dialectic-historical materialism. Conscious manipulation of experimental results to bring them into line with expected results was also usual, as was any activity against scientific enemies.

In addition to Stubbe, Hermann Kuckuck (director of the Erwin Baur Institute for Plant Breeding in Muncheberg) was an ardent early critic of Lysenko. The publication of his *Lehrbuch der Pflanzenzuchtung* in 1949 was canceled by the publisher in the GDR because a chapter on Michurin biology was missing. However, the book was, published in West Germany 1 year later. In his lectures and papers, Kuckuck criticized the Lysenkoists for mixing science and politics, and he pointed out the scientific weaknesses of their doctrine. Kuckuck left his institute and moved to West Berlin in 1950 Hans Nachtscheim was forced to leave his position at the Humboldt University, after having resisted Lysenkoism, and moved to West Berlin; Wolfdietrich Eichler was suspended from his academic position in 1954 for the same reason.

Georg Schneider gained no scientific recognition: His work in evolutionary biology had no influence on the further development of biology in the GDR, where most biologists avoided the Lysenko doctrines and were able to separate science from ideology. On returning to Jena in 1962, Schneider resumed teaching theoretical biology until in 1970, when drunk, he drove his car into an armored vehicle belonging to the Red Army.

Example of an experiment using the Pfopfung technique. Schneider wrote: "...it can be clearly seen that this animal developed rather normally on the back of the other animal It did not eat anything itself, but received all its nutrients from the Hypoboint (the host animal)...This animal lived for more than 2.5 years."

SIGNIFICANCE

It is thought that Lysenko's ideas fit Joseph Stalin's collectivization mindset for agriculture in the Soviet Union, and this is what helped his career advance quickly, earning him high-level positions despite his questionable education. Lysenko was a full academician at the Ukrainian Academy of Sciences, the Lenin All-Union Academy of Agricultural Sciences, and the USSR Academy of Sciences. He was also the director of several breeding and genetic institutes in the Soviet Union. For over twenty-five years, Lysenko controlled the decisions made by many governmental agencies dealing with agriculture, biology, and medicine. He won many awards, including the coveted Stalin Prize, and was an eight-time recipient of the country's highest honor, the Order of Lenin.

Throughout the Soviet Union, those scientists who were against Lysenkoism were forced from their positions, persecuted, and generally silenced. In East Germany, some scientists who were resistant to the Lysenkoism approach were able to move to West Germany, where a strong voice against Lysenkoism was maintained.

Although Lysenkoism was a Soviet era approach, it is reported that similar anti-science movements were developing in the late nineteenth and twentieth centuries in the western world as well. Although these were not necessarily backed by western governments, some people were disenchanted with science, believing that it had become detached from society, and was overly mechanistic. Since the fall of Communism, there has been a strong movement of anti-science and anti-technology in Russia.

FURTHER RESOURCES

Books

Schneider, Laurence. *Biology and Revolution in Twentieth-Century China.* Lanham, MD: Rowman & Littlefield, 2003.

Soyfer, Valerie N., Leo Gruliow, and Rebecca Gruliow. *Lysenko and the Tragedy of Soviet Science.* Piscataway, NJ: Rutgers University Press, 1994.

Periodicals

Dombrowski, Paul M. "Plastic Language for Plastic Science: The Rhetoric of Comrade Lysenko." *Journal of Technical Writing and Communication* 31, no. 3 (2001): 293–333.

"Turning the Tide?"

Newspaper article

By: Mark Zaloudek

Date: October 8, 2004

Source: Zaloudek, Mark. "Turning the Tide? Scientists Hope that New Research, Reef-building Efforts and Public Support Can Help Reverse Decades of Damage to Florida's Extraordinary Coral Reefs." *Sarasota Herald Tribune*, October 8, 2004.

About the Author: Mark Zaloudek writes on a variety of topics for the *Sarasota Herald Tribune*.

INTRODUCTION

The coral reefs off of the coast of Florida are some of the most threatened in the world. The reefs are being impacted by agriculture and urban water pollution, destructive boating and fishing practices, and environmental stresses such as global warming and hurricanes. It is documented that the last thirty to forty years have been extremely devastating, as many corals have died within this time period with minimal recovery.

Corals are small polyp-shaped animals with tentacles. They look like upside-down versions of their relative, the jellyfish. However, coral polyps are stationary. Corals and jellyfish are in the phylum *Cnidaria*, as both animals have stinging cells on their tentacles, which are used to catch food particles from the water. Corals found in the tropics have an important symbiotic relationship with an algae called zooxanthellae, which lives in the tissue of the corals. In addition to giving the corals many different colors, the unicellular zooxanthellae provide food nutrients to the corals by carrying out photosynthesis. The corals provide the zooxanthellae with protection, and access to light. Because the zooxanthellae need light, tropical corals cannot grow beyond the ocean's photic zone.

The base of a coral reef is made up of a large structures of stony calcium carbonate, which is excreted by coral polyps. Calcium carbonate is made when calcium is removed from the sea water by the corals, and combined with carbon dioxide. The mounds of calcium carbonate that make up the coral reef off Florida have been building up over the last 5,000 to 6,000 years. Coral reef growth requires warm and stable water temperatures, normal oceanic salinity, clear water, low levels of phosphate and nitrogen nutrients, and moderate levels of water movement that can circulate wastes out and bring plankton and oxygen to the reef. Depending on these water conditions, the reef growth rates are one to sixteen feet every 1,000 years.

To better understand the corals, many studies have been designed to track the effect of various impacts on the reefs. Evidence links increased human impact with the health of coral reefs. Water pollution from urban areas, acid rain, boats, and other sources can bring toxins, including heavy metals, that are damaging to the reefs. Runoff from agricultural fields and sewage treatment plants are thought to increase the levels of nitrogen and phosphorous nutrients in the coastal waters. It is thought that such stresses make corals susceptible to disease.

Coral reefs also receive physical damage from tourists, divers, improper boat anchoring, and boat groundings. Overfishing and removal of important reef organisms can alter important symbiotic relationships on the reefs, making corals defenseless against

certain predators. Strong hurricanes can often have a devastating impact on reefs.

Scientists note an increase in instances of coral bleaching, which occurs when the symbiotic zooxanthellae leave the coral polyps. In addition to giving coral a white color, without the zooxanthellae the coral does not receive all of the oxygen and nutrients it requires. Prolonged bleaching causes the coral to die. Bleaching is a sign that corals are stressed. This can be from pollution, turbidity of the water, and changes in sea temperature. One probable cause for bleaching is the increase in sea water temperature as a result of global warming.

▮ PRIMARY SOURCE

Scientists hope that new research, reef-building efforts and public support can help reverse decades of damage to Florida's extraordinary coral reefs.

It's taken only 30 years to threaten coral reefs that have flourished along the Florida Keys for more than 5,000 years.

"These are the only coral reefs along the continental United States and they're in very bad shape," says coral researcher Kim Ritchie, Ph.D., a marine scientist at Sarasota's Mote Marine Laboratory.

"They're worse off, really, than any other corals in the Caribbean. And the Caribbean corals are in worse shape than the other corals around the world."

That may not trigger an alarm if you're not a scuba diver or snorkeler who has marveled at the aquarium-like splendor of Florida's living reefs, the third-largest in the world after Australia's Great Barrier Reef and the extensive reef off Belize in Central America.

But perhaps it should.

More than three million people annually visit Florida's 220-mile reef tract that stretches from Miami to the Dry Tortugas past Key West. Along the way they spend an estimated eight hundred million dollars at tourism-related businesses, boosting state revenues that support essential state services.

And if you like seafood, the waters surrounding the reef produce more than twenty million pounds of commercially harvested seafood each year.

Coral reefs have been compared to tropical rain forests because of their dense biodiversity and fragile ecosystems. Florida's reef tract is home to more than 60 reef-building corals and more than 150 species of fish.

Some shallow-water and deep-water corals can be found elsewhere along Florida's coastline, but their greatest concentration is along the state's southern tip.

Bill Causey, manager of the Florida Keys National Marine Sanctuary, calls the reef tract a "national treasure" in serious trouble.

"Some portions of the reef have died—as much as 30% in a very short time frame, while other areas have had less decline. But the end result is we've seen a major decline n the Florida Keys over the last three decades, with the greatest decline occurring in the 1990s," he said.

Environmental changes, humans share the blame.

Part of the problem is environmental changes. Fluctuating sea-surface temperatures that some scientists attribute to global warming are interfering with the beneficial algae that live on the corals and provide them with nutrients.

As a result, acres of corals that have become temporarily stressed appear "bleached." Many have died when their conditions didn't improve after as little as a month or two, Causey said.

The pounding surf from hurricanes squarely deserve the blame for other setbacks.

Pollution from septic tanks throughout the Keys and storm water carrying fertilizers and other nutrients into South Florida's coastal waters have placed the string of reefs in jeopardy.

At least seven coral diseases have been documented along the reef.

Boat groundings and other careless actions by recreational boaters, anglers, snorkelers and scuba divers, compound the problem.

Officials at the Florida Keys National Marine Sanctuary and others have closely monitored whether more than two hundred million gallons of treated industrial waste water dumped last summer and fall into the Gulf of Mexico 120 miles off Florida's west coast brought harm to the reefs as it migrated southward. The discharge was authorized by the state to reduce the risk of an environmental disaster at the abandoned Piney Point phosphate plant, south of Tampa Bay.

"The closest the discharge came to the Keys was when it came about seventy miles to the west of the Dry Tortugas. And to the south of the Keys, it was about thirty miles off shore," Causey said. Although the treated water contained phosphorus, which can produce harmful algal blooms, it was sufficiently diluted so as not to pose a threat, he said.

The reef tract can be affected by other pollutants entering the Gulf, though.

Forty percent of the U.S. land mass drains into the Gulf of Mexico, and pollutants carried from the land into rivers and streams eventually flow past the Florida Keys, Causey said.

The Fort Pierce-based Philippe Cousteau Foundation is helping advance the development of a coral bank that would maintain a genetic stock of coral species and reproduce them for transplantation back into the reefs.

The foundation, named for the late environmentalist and Emmy Award-winning filmmaker who was the son of legendary oceanographer Jacques Cousteau, is headed by Jacques Cousteau's twenty-four-year-old grandson, marine scientist Philippe Pierre Cousteau.

"There are over sixty species of Caribbean corals, and at the moment we have at least ten species we're growing," Ritchie said of Mote's coral aquaculture program. "But within months, our goals is to have many more species and, ultimately with the help of the Philippe Cousteau Foundation, the goal is to have representatives of a majority of the corals worldwide."

Essential timing?

Experts believe the next several years could be critical to the survival of the Florida reef tract.

"What we have to do is address all the problems at the same time: the pollution issues at the local level, but also the bigger issues at the regional and global levels," Causey said.

"You just don't fix things at the local level and forget what's happening on a regional and global scale because then perhaps you'll have done this for nothing. But at the same time, you can't just address this at the global level and miss things that could have made a difference locally."

SIGNIFICANCE

Coral reefs are considered one of the world's most biologically diverse ecosystems on earth, and provide many important services. The coral reef acts as an important breakwater, sheltering the Florida coastline from storms. Corals provide important habitat and breeding areas for many types of plants and animals and contribute to Florida's economy. Many tourists spend money to snorkel or SCUBA dive around the corals. Millions of dollars are generated through recreational and commercial fishing that occurs on the reefs. Small hard and soft corals, and many other organisms that grow on the reef, are sold in the aquarium industry. The National Oceanic and Atmospheric Administration estimates that coral reefs generate $4.4 billion in sales and employment.

The coral reef provides entertainment to vacationers at the Coral Reef State Park off Key Largo, Florida. To avoid damaging the reef, buoys warn boaters not to drop anchor. © KEVIN FLEMING/CORBIS

The contribution of reefs to Florida's economy, as well as general concern for the reefs, has generated support for further studies of corals, and the development of management strategies to prevent coral degradation. Work is also being carried out to regenerate reefs through aquaculture methods. Species of corals are raised in laboratories or in areas of the sea that can support their growth. Then, these corals can be placed on reefs, in hopes of bringing life back to some of the degraded areas.

FURTHER RESOURCES
Books

Daniels, Camille A. *Coral Reef Assessment: An Index Utilizing Sediment Constiuents.* Tampa, FL: University of South Florida, 2005.

Johns, Grace M. *Socioeconomic Study of Reefs in Southeast Florida: Final Report.* Hollywood, FL: Hazen and Sawyer, in association with Florida State University, National Oceanic and Atmospheric Administration, 2001.

Periodicals

Santavy, D.L., J.K. Summers, and V.D. Engle. "The Condition of Coral Reefs in South Florida (2000) Using Coral Disease and Bleaching as Indicators." *Environmental Monitoring and Assessment* 100 (2005): 129–152.

Websites

Buddemeier, Robert W., Joan A. Kleypas, and Richard B. Aronson."Coral Reefs & Global Climate Change: Potential Contributions of Climate Change to Stresses on Coral Reef Ecosystems." *Pew Center on Global Climate Change*, February 2004. <http://www.pewclimate.org/docUploads/Coral%5FReefs%2Epdf> (accessed March 17, 2006).

The National Oceanic and Atmospheric Administration's (NOAA) Coral Reef Conservation Program. <http://www.coralreef.noaa.gov/> (accessed March 17, 2006).

Southeast Florida Coral Reef Initiative (SFCRI), Florida Department of Environmental Protection. <http://www.dep.state.fl.us/coastal/programs/coral/> (accessed March 17, 2006).

United Nations Environment Programme, Coral Reef Unit. <http://corals.unep.org/> (accessed March 17, 2006).

"Pesticide Persisting Beyond Scheduled Elimination Date"

Newspaper article

By: Felicity Barringer

Date: October 8, 2004

Source: Barringer, Felicity. "Pesticide Persisting Beyond Scheduled Elimination Date." The *New York Times*. (October 8, 2004).

About the Author: Felicity Barringer is a reporter for the *New York Times* who has written numerous articles related to environmental topics and other issues of social concern.

INTRODUCTION

Methyl bromide is an important agricultural chemical used as a fumigant for treating soil, storage facilities, and fruit and vegetable plants to ensure that microorganisms do not damage valuable crops. However, there is opposition to its use, since methyl bromide is considered a strong contributor to the reduction of the earth's ozone layer, and the farm workers who apply methyl bromide are known to have health problems, including increased rates of cancer.

The Montreal Protocol, an international treaty designed to reduce degradation of the ozone layer, came into effect in 1987. Following its signing, the use of methyl bromide and other ozone-depleting chemicals such as chlorofluorocarbons (CFCs) began to drop significantly. When countries become party to the protocol, they pledge to systematically reduce the use of damaging chemicals, including methyl bromide, in accordance with the standards of the protocol. Ozone-depleting chemicals have application in industry, agriculture, and many other human activities.

Over the last few years though, the use of methyl bromide has begun to rise in many parts of the world. In 2005, the United States, one of the initial signatory countries to the Montreal Protocol, obtained international approval for a 16 percent increase in the use of methyl bromide over its 2003 levels. Some argue that this trend will reduce progress made toward lessening the damage being done to earth's protective ozone layer. Methyl bromide is considered forty times more harmful to the ozone layer than other ozone-harming gases.

The ozone layer naturally occurs in the earth's stratosphere (31 miles or 50 kilometers high), and is important for protecting the earth's surface from the sun's harmful ultra-violet (UV) radiation, which can cause skin cancer, damage vegetation, and increase global warming. Ozone molecules (chemically O_3) are made up of three oxygen atoms, and are formed naturally from the combination of UV radiation from the sun and oxygen gas (O_2). The ozone layer is naturally denser near the poles and thinner near the equator. Ironically, ozone is a major component of smog, and can be harmful to humans at the earth's surface.

Ozone-degrading chemicals released in the atmosphere interact with ozone and sunlight to break apart the O_3 molecules. Although thinning of the ozone layer occurs throughout the stratosphere, the most severe degradation happens near the South Pole, and to a lesser degree near the North Pole. Significant depletion of the ozone layer forms a hole over Antarctica annually, as ozone-depleting chemicals react with intense spring and summer sunlight.

When British scientists first took measurements of the ozone hole over Antarctica in 1985, they thought something was wrong with their equipment, as the depletion was much more significant than they had expected. Shortly after the magnitude of the ozone hole was realized, the international community enacted the Montreal Protocol. Although the ozone hole reached a record size of 10.9 million square miles

(28.3 million square kilometers) in September of 2000, progress towards slowing ozone thinning has been reported. Currently, over 180 countries have signed the Montreal Protocol.

■ PRIMARY SOURCE

Planting time is near in John Steinbeck's old haunts. A fork on the back of a tanker-tractor dips 12 inches down into the solid and emits a gaseous cocktail to kill any fungus or micro-organism that could threaten next spring's strawberries. Mexican workers, wearing antiseptic white suits but no face masks, follow close behind, tamping down the white plastic sheeting that covers the loamy fields.

They are fumigating Will Garroutte's strawberry fields with methyl bromide, a pesticide so witheringly effective it is a farmer's dream. But it is not an environmentalist's.

Methyl bromide is considered more destructive to the protective ozone layer in the stratosphere than some banned chemicals and has been linked to an increased risk of prostate cancer in farm workers.

After a decade in which the use of the fumigant decreased by more than 70 percent among developed nations, consumption of methyl bromide is poised to rise next year. That has environmentalists worried.

Under a treaty known as the Montreal Protocol, the chemical was to be banned for most uses by the end of this year. But local and international politics have allowed methyl bromide to elude elimination the way some stubborn bacteria resist antibiotics.

The United States, on behalf of strawberry growers like Mr. Garroutte in California, tomato growers in Florida and other agribusinesses, has already obtained international approval for a 16 percent increase in consumption next year over the nation's reported use in 2003. This has happened through a new process that provides for exemptions from the ban in the case of "critical uses." With approval in hand for the use of 8,942 tons of methyl bromide in 2005, compared with 7,659 tons in 2003, the government is now seeking to add 840 tons to the permissible amount in next year's total.

Like the United States, other developed countries are now seeking new exemptions from the treaty, and environmentalists fear a domino effect. Although the amount of methyl bromide currently at issue is less than 1 percent of ozone-depleting chemicals, the gas quickly attacks the ozone layer, which scientists say is now beginning to heal itself.

"The United States has been the driving force for the protocol up until now," said David Doniger, who is policy director of the Climate Center at the Natural Resources

Defense Council, and environmental group. "This is the first time the U.S. is driving in reverse."

Environmental Protection Agency officials disagree. "I don't think it's fair to say we're headed in the opposite direction," said Jeffrey R. Holmstead, the assistant administrator for air and radiation at the agency. "We are committed to completing the phase-out, but in a way that allows the temporary continued exemptions for critical uses."

The Montreal Protocol has eliminated 97 percent of ozone-depleting substances, James L. Connaughton, chairman of the White House's Council on Environmental Quality, said, adding, "The U.S. has led the way."

He added, "The fact we are now focused on a discussion that deals with one-tenth of one percent of our commitment to reduce is the signature of just how successful this effort has been." Rodger Wesson of the California Strawberry Commission in Watsonville said: "Everybody's agreed we want to have a healthy, protective ozone layer. What's the best way to accomplish that?"

The international community has, in gross terms, made significant progress in phasing out methyl bromide since 1992. That was when the chemical was added, under the Montreal Protocol, to a list of chemicals whose unabated use would thin the ozone layer and thus increase the risk of skin cancer.

The latest data from the National Oceanographic and Atmospheric Administration show that the rate at which methyl bromide is being eliminated from the atmosphere has slowed by about 50 percent in the last two years, compared with the previous four years. Stephen Montzka, a research scientist with NOAA, said that he could not determine from his data whether manmade emissions or a natural occurrence, like a bad fire season, account for the change.

This summer, after the United States' request for exemptions, other countries including Israel, New Zealand and Germany applied for the right to use more of the chemical that they had been learning to do without.

Jiri Hlavacek, The Czech Republic's representative to the Montreal Protocol meetings, is perplexed and dismayed by the sudden thirst for the chemical.

"Why is it such big countries and economically strong countries like the United States," he said, "are not able to speed up the process of seeking alternatives for these plants and for the treatment of the soil?"

Requests for 2006 exemptions, led by the United States, Italy and Spain, already exceed the amounts granted for 2005, Mr. Hlavacek said.

Mr. Garoutte, a second-generation Watsonville farmer who is 59, finds economic pressure in all directions. To keep his profit margins up, he must lease more land

each year. By law, he leaves a buffer between his fumigated fields and schools.

He believes that methyl bromide has increased his production by as much as 30 percent. "You can say whatever you want about whether methyl bromide is good or bad," he said. "But we have to be profitable."

Still, Mr. Garroutte says he understands the need for methyl bromide replacements. "The most important thing is to get alternatives on a greased track and get them here."

Mr. Wesson of the strawberry commission also expresses frustration that there are not enough new compounds to try. The federal Department of Agriculture has spent $150 million over a decade on the development of alternatives, but the only one that has taken any hold in the Watsonville area is organic farming, which has a fierce proponent in Vanessa Bogenholm. More than a decade ago, when she was working in the University of California's agricultural extension office, her original assignment was testing methyl bromide alternatives. . . .

SIGNIFICANCE

In addition to the United States, other countries who have signed the Montreal Protocol have been applying for permission to increase their methyl bromide use. There is concern that this will lead to a global increase in the use of methyl bromide and other harmful chemicals. Scientists and government leaders agree that continued adherence to Montreal Protocol, and even strengthening its mandates, is vital to ensure that the thinning of the ozone layer diminishes, and perhaps begins to recover completely.

Government and agricultural leaders in the United States say that more needs to be done to find replacements for methyl bromide. Many large-scale industrial agriculture firms claim that using methyl bromide is necessary for them to maintain their profitability and meet the demands of the consumer. Although they claim to want a healthy environment, they say there are no viable alternatives to using methyl bromide. Some argue that methyl bromide's harmful impacts on the environment can be contained with the development of application technology that traps the gas so it is unable to escape into the atmosphere.

There are other viewpoints that say the use of methyl bromide continues to be allowed because large agricultural firms are not interested in seeking alternatives to their current methods. Claims that methyl bromide is one more piece of evidence that large-scale agriculture firms operate in an unsustainable manner are mentioned. Organic farmers, and those who use more environmentally conscious agriculture approaches, claim they are able to be profitable without using harmful chemicals such as methyl bromide.

Opponents of methyl bromide use also claim that low paid agricultural workers are in immediate danger from the toxicity of the chemical, as they are paid low wages and forced to apply the chemicals. In some cases, it is reported that these workers are not given the proper protective gear for applying the chemicals.

FURTHER RESOURCES

Books

United Nations Environment Programme (UNEP) Division of Technology, Industry and Economics. *Sourcebook of Technologies for Protecting the Ozone Layer: Alternatives to Methyl Bromide.* Paris: UNEP, 2003.

Periodicals

"Fruit Pesticide Threat to the Ozone Layer." *New Scientist* 2476 (December 04, 2004).

Macilwain, Collin. "Organic: Is It the Future of Farming?" *Nature* 428 (April 22, 2004): 792–793.

Web sites

Kirby, Alex. "Arctic Ozone Damage Likely by 2020." *BBC News Online* (October 26, 2000). <http://news.bbc.co.uk/1/hi/sci/tech/990391.stm> (accessed March 10, 2006).

"Ozone Depletion." *United States Environmental Protection Agency.* <http://www.epa.gov/ozone> (accessed March 10, 2006).

"The Vienna Convention and the Montreal Protocol." *United Nations Development Programme.* <http://www.undp.org/montrealprotocol/montreal.htm> (accessed March 10, 2006).

Annual Permit Limits for Nitrogen and Phosphorus for Permits Designed to Protect Chesapeake Bay and Its Tidal Tributaries from Excess Nutrient Loading under the National Pollutant Discharge Elimination System

Memorandum

By: James A. Hanlon

Date: March 19, 2004

Source: Hanlon, James A. "Annual Permit Limits for Nitrogen and Phosphorus for Permits Designed to Protect Chesapeake Bay and Its Tidal Tributaries from Excess Nutrient Loading under the National Pollutant Discharge Elimination System." March 19, 2004. <http://www.epa.gov/npdes/pubs/memo_chesapeakebay.pdf> (accessed March 16, 2006).

About the Author: James (Jim) Hanlon was appointed as director of the U.S. Environmental Protection Agency (EPA) Office of Wastewater Management (OWM) with the Chesapeake Bay Program in April 2002. The OWM is a body that is responsible for issuing wastewater discharge permits to industries and municipalities. Prior to this, Hanlon was appointed as Director of the Municipal Construction Division in 1984. His responsibilities included managing funds and grants for construction projects. He also provided assistance to various municipalities for the construction of various wastewater infrastructure projects. In his capacity as Deputy Director of Science and Technology in the Office of Water since 1991, he was responsible for providing the scientific and technological foundation for federal water quality and various safe drinking water programs. He also served as Acting Deputy Assistant Administrator for the same office between 2001 and 2002. Hanlon holds a Bachelor of Science Degree in Civil Engineering from the University of Illinois and a Master of Business Administration from the University of Chicago.

INTRODUCTION

Dissolved nutrients like nitrogen and phosphorus are an important source of nutrition and growth. However, when these are present in excess, they pose a significant hazard to the presence of the existing biodiversity. Excessive nutrients can cause the formation and growth of harmful algae and phytoplankton (organisms that usually drift in fresh water). Their presence reduces the amount of sunlight available to aquatic plants. Decomposing algae can reduce the amount of dissolved oxygen in the water necessary for aquatic life. This can lead to disastrous consequences for any ecosystem, and also lead to its ultimate death.

The Chesapeake Bay is the largest estuary (an arm of the sea that extends inland to meet the mouth of a river) located on the eastern coast of the United States. It is encompassed by seven states that include New York, Pennsylvania, Delaware, Maryland, Virginia, West Virginia, and the District of Columbia. Connected by nine major tributaries, the bay is a complex, vast, and diverse ecosystem that supports a large variety of plant and animal life. This includes many

This aerial photo of Chesapeake Bay shows where the current of the bay meets the Atlantic Ocean at the southern tip of the Delmarva Peninsula. Significant nutrient damage to the bay could spread to other bodies of water by virtue of this connection. © 1996 CORBIS; ORIGINAL IMAGE COURTESY OF NASA/CORBIS

species of small sharks, blue crab, various exotic oysters, and a myriad of species of birds.

Since the 1990s, the ecosystem of Chesapeake Bay has been under threat of varied degrees from many forms of land, air, and water pollution. The most serious form of pollution the bay faces is that of excessive nutrient loading. In other words, there is an excessive discharge of nutritive content like phosphorus and nitrogen into the bay that can prove extremely harmful to aquatic life.

Earlier, much of the excessive nutrient was held back by wild marshes (wet soft land near water) and farmland. However, due to rapid industrialization, these areas have given way to cities and industrial zones. Industrial discharge into the bay also contains elements like nitrogen and phosphorus, leading to an overall increase in the nutrient levels in the bay ecosystem.

To tackle this problem, the Chesapeake Bay Program—a cooperative program between the U.S. Environmental Protection Agency Regions I & III, and the member states—was formed in 1983 to encompass the bay and its tributaries within their jurisdiction.

The twin goals of the Chesapeake 2000 agreement and The Clean Water Act initiated the Chesapeake Bay Program. The program involves the EPA and partner states setting nutrient discharge limits for the National Pollution Discharge Elimination System—a national-level program aimed at reducing discharge of pollutants into water resources—in the Chesapeake Bay and its tributaries.

Hanlon's memorandum was written to Jon Capacasa, Director of the Water Permits Division of EPA Region 3, and Rebecca Hammer, Director of the Chesapeake Bay Program Office. Briefly, the memo establishes annual limits for the discharge of nutrients under the National Pollution Discharge Elimination System (NPDES). It describes practical difficulties in setting daily, weekly, or monthly discharge limits for nutrients like phosphorus, nitrogen, and ammonia.

▮ PRIMARY SOURCE

ANNUAL PERMIT LIMITS FOR NITROGEN AND PHOSPHORUS FOR PERMITS DESIGNED TO PROTECT CHESAPEAKE BAY AND ITS TIDAL TRIBUTARIES FROM EXCESS NUTRIENT LOADING UNDER THE NATIONAL POLLUTANT DISCHARGE ELIMINATION SYSTEM

This memo responds to your proposal to use National Pollutant Discharge Elimination System (NPDES) permit effluent limits for nitrogen and phosphorus expressed as an annual limit in lieu of daily maximum, weekly average, or monthly average effluent limitations, for the protection of Chesapeake Bay and its tidal tributaries from excess nutrient loading. Based on the information provided by your staff and for the reasons and under the circumstances outlined herein, I concur that permit limits expressed as an annual limit are appropriate and that it is reasonable in this case to conclude that it is "impracticable" to express permit effluent limitations as daily maximum, weekly average, or monthly average effluent limitations. This memo describes the scientific and policy rationales that support this approach.

EPA Region 3 has developed recommended water quality criteria for certain parameters designed to protect water quality in Chesapeake Bay and its tidal tributaries. The main cause of water quality impairment for these parameters in the main stem of the Bay is loading of nutrients, specifically nitrogen and phosphorus, from point and nonpoint sources throughout the entire Chesapeake Bay watershed. The States are in the process of adopting revised water quality standards based on EPA Region 3's recommended water quality criteria and developing wasteload allocations for point sources discharging to the Chesapeake Bay watershed that are designed to protect water quality in Chesapeake Bay and its tidal tributaries from excess nutrient loading.

Establishing appropriate permit limits that implement nitrogen and phosphorus wasteload allocations for discharges that cause, have the reasonable potential to cause, or contribute to excursions of water quality criteria for Chesapeake Bay and its tidal tributaries is different from setting limits for other parameters such as toxic pollutants because: the exposure period of concern for nutrients loadings to Chesapeake Bay and its tidal tributaries is very long; the area of concern is far-field (as opposed to the immediate vicinity of the discharge); and the average pollutant load rather than the maximum pollutant load is of concern. Thus, developing appropriate effluent limitations requires innovative implementation procedures.

Applicablility Your proposal addresses implementation of wasteload allocations for nitrogen and phosphorus designed to achieve compliance with water quality standards of Chesapeake Bay. Your proposal and the rationale discussed in this memorandum are not intended to address wasteload allocations to meet other water quality standards in areas outside of Chesapeake Bay and its tidal tributaries. Smaller scales such as embayments and smaller tributaries than the major Eastern and Western shore rivers were not examined and therefore the rationale in this memorandum does not address and may not apply to the protection of these smaller scale situations.

This rationale also does not apply to parameters other than nitrogen and phosphorus that may exhibit an oxygen demand to waters of the Bay. Such parameters include dissolved oxygen, biochemical oxygen demand, and ammonia.

Of course, all local water quality standards apply and must be met when evaluating appropriate point source permit effluent limits. States are developing water quality standards for nutrients to be applied to local waters as stand-alone criteria. In any case where the nutrient wasteload allocations for protection of water quality in a river, tributary, or other part of Chesapeake Bay are expressed on a shorter term basis, i.e., seasonal, monthly, weekly or daily values, the permit limits that derive from and comply with the wasteload allocation expressed on such shorter term basis must be used. Shorter averaging periods might be appropriate and necessary to protect against local nutrient impacts in rivers or streams in the basin.

Additionally, it is important to note that the nutrient dynamics of the Bay may not be unique. The establishment of an annual limit with a similar finding of "impracticability" pursuant to 40 CFR 122.45(d) may be appropriate for the implementation of nutrient criteria in other watersheds when: attainment of the criteria is dependent on long-term average loadings rather than short-term maximum loadings; the circumstances match those outlined in this memo for Chesapeake Bay and its tidal

tributaries; annual limits are technically supportable with robust data and modeling as they are in the Chesapeake Bay context; and appropriate safeguards to protect all other applicable water quality standards are employed.

Why are annual loadings appropriate for wasteload allocations for nutrients for Chesapeake Bay and its tidal tributaries? The nutrient dynamics of Chesapeake Bay and its tidal tributaries are complex. Unlike toxics and many conventional pollutants that have a direct and somewhat immediate effect on the aquatic system, nutrients have no direct effect, but instead are "processed" in several discreet steps in the Bay ecosystem before they have their full effect. Each processing "step" further delays and buffers the time between the time of nutrient discharge in an effluent and the resultant nutrient effect on the receiving waterbody. Chesapeake Bay and its tidal tributaries' biological and physical processes can be viewed as "integrating" variations of nutrient load magnitude over time. The integration of nutrient loads from all sources over time ameliorates intraannual load fluctuations from individual sources, with the Bay responding to overall loads on an annual scale, while showing little response to monthly variations within an annual load.

EPA has conducted complex modeling of the effect of nutrient loading to the Bay specifically from individual point source discharges. Based on the results of the model, EPA concluded that Chesapeake Bay and its tidal tributaries in effect integrate variable point source monthly loads over time, so that as long as a particular annual total load of nitrogen and phosphorus is met, constant or variable *intraannual* load variation from individual point sources has no effect on water quality of the main bay.

Based on the model, EPA and the affected States are developing "tributary strategies" that will assign wasteload allocations expressed as annual loads for the point source dischargers to the Bay and it tributaries that achieve the water quality standards of Chesapeake Bay and its tidal tributaries.

Why is it impracticable to express limits for nutrients on a daily, weekly or monthly basis? The NPDES regulations at 40 CFR 122.45(d) require that all permit limits be expressed, unless impracticable, as both average monthly limits and maximum daily limits for all dischargers other than publicly owned treatment works (POTWs), and as average weekly limits and average monthly limits for POTWs.

The Office of Wastewater Management cautions that the steady-state statistical procedures described in EPA's *Technical Support Document for Water Quality-based Toxics Control* (TSD) are not applicable or appropriate for developing nutrient limits for the main stem of Chesapeake Bay and its tribal tributaries. Developing permit limits for nutrients affecting Chesapeake Bay and its tidal tributaries is different from setting limits for toxic pollutants because the exposure period of concern for nutrients is longer than one month, and can be up to a few years, and the average exposure rather than the maximum exposure is of concern. The statistical derivation procedure described in the TSD for acute and chronic aquatic life protection is not applicable to exposure periods more than 30 days. If the procedures described in the TSD for aquatic life protection (i.e., criteria with 1-day and 4-day averaging periods) were used for developing permit limits for nutrients (with much longer averaging periods), both the maximum daily limit or the average weekly limit (as appropriate) and average monthly limit would be less stringent than the wasteload allocation necessary to protect the criteria. Thus, even if a facility was discharging in compliance with permit limits calculated using these procedures, it would be possible to constantly exceed the wasteload allocation. Such an approach clearly is unacceptable.

The TSD in Section 5.4.4 provides guidance for establishing daily and monthly effluent limits for human health protection based on long term exposure periods. However, this approach is also not appropriate for deriving permit limits for nutrients. This is because this TSD procedure is a steady-state approach that assumes that the distribution of effluent load is constant. However, the efficiency of treatment of nutrients by biological nutrient removal is highly sensitive to ambient temperature and is not effective at lower temperatures. Thus, the effluent loading of nutrients is not constant due to seasonal temperature fluctuations in northern climates. Even a simple steady-state model for permit development such as dividing the annual limit by 12 and establishing that value as the monthly limit is therefore, not appropriate. Such a limit does not account for seasonal fluctuations in effluent loading. To establish appropriate weekly or monthly limitations, due to the effect of temperature on treatment efficiency for nutrients, the permitting authority would need to be able to predict with some accuracy the expected annual temperature over that time frame, which is virtually impossible to do given the normal temperature variability in any given week or month. Because of the effect of temperature on the treatment efficiency and the normal variation in ambient temperature over shorter time periods, it is impracticable to develop appropriate daily, weekly or monthly limits for nutrients that are protective of the wasteload allocation expressed as an annual load.

Thus, we conclude that due to the characteristics of nutrient loading and its effects on the water quality in Chesapeake Bay and its tidal tributaries and because the derivation of *appropriate* daily, weekly or monthly limits is not possible for the reasons described above, that it is therefore "impracticable" to express permit effluent limitations as daily maximum, weekly average, or monthly average effluent limitations.

Recommendations for implementing an annual limit The permit should state the method for determining compliance with the annual limit. When expressing an effluent limit as an annual value, it is recommended that the permit provide the ability to assess compliance at interim dates.

The frequency of compliance monitoring should also be specified in the permit. The Office of Wastewater Management recommends that the effluent discharge volume should be monitored continuously. Nutrient monitoring should be specified on at least a weekly basis, and the monthly mass load should be summarized based on the total flow during the month and reported as a monthly load.

SIGNIFICANCE

Pollution of water resources and important ecosystems has been a topic of great concern in the United States. Overexploitation of natural resources, coupled with land, water, and air pollution emanating from industries in ecosystems, such as the Chesapeake Bay area, have contributed to the increased threat to plant and aquatic life in these regions.

As with many other ecosystems, the Chesapeake Bay has suffered in varying degrees from pollutants from numerous sources. Although there was a considerable reduction in the nutrient discharge into the Chesapeake Bay after the implementation of the Chesapeake Bay program, experts were of the opinion that there still needed to be a further reduction in the discharge.

Consequently, since the 1990s and early 2000s, there have been talks of imposing daily or weekly nutrient discharge nutrient limits in the region. Member states issuing nutrient discharge permits need to ensure that nutrient discharge remains within acceptable limits. However, there are legitimate hindrances in determining the nutrient discharge on a maximum daily, average weekly, or monthly basis.

This memorandum, issued in 2004, enumerates various scientific and policy grounds that give basis to this approach. It sets the pace for allowing member states to issue nutrient discharge permits with the specification of annual limits for nutrient disposal into the Chesapeake estuary and its supporting components.

Hanlon argues on the basis of various scientific and technical interpretations that it is more practical to implement a permit system based around the annual limits of discharge allowed rather than a system permitting daily maximum, weekly, or monthly average discharge of nutrients into the bay.

Through the early 2000s, various companies still continue to discharge nutrients into the river, based upon the amounts allowed in the EPA issued permits. The problem of growing nutrient pollution in the bay is not completely resolved. The bay's natural capacity to repair itself is fairly limited, though evidence suggests that the bay system integrates out the nutrient overload over a duration of time.

Though the EPA has tried to keep the levels of nutrient discharge into the bay system under the limits specified, the states that encompass the bay system within their jurisdiction and various industries still discharge nutrients, albeit controlled by EPA permits. This, experts assert, could cause major environmental concerns in the long run.

FURTHER RESOURCES
Web sites

"Chesapeake Bay: Measuring Pollution Reduction." *U.S. Geological Survey.* <http://water.usgs.gov/wid/html/chesbay.html> (accessed March 16, 2006).

Chesapeake Bay Program. "Nutrient Pollution." *Chesapeakebay.net.* <http://www.chesapeakebay.net/nutr1.htm> (accessed March 16, 2006).

U.S. Environmental Protection Agency. "Decision on Petition for Rulemaking to Address Nutrient Pollution from Significant Point Sources in the Chesapeake Bay Watershed." *U.S. Environmental Protection Agency.* <http://www.epa.gov/water/cbfpetition/petition.pdf> (accessed March 16, 2006).

———. "NPDES Permitting Approach for Discharges of Nutrients in the Chesapeake Bay Watershed." *U.S. Environmental Protection Agency.* <http://72.14.203.104/search?q=cache:JQFdCYC8ITMJ:www.epa.gov/reg3wapd/npdes/pdf/CB_Permitting_Approach_12_29_04.pdf+NPDES+Permitting+Approach+for+Discharges+of+Nutrients+in+the+Chesapeake+Bay+Watershed&hl=en&gl=us&ct=clnk&cd=1&client=firefox-a> (accessed March 16, 2006).

"Deep In the Swamp, an 'Extinct' Woodpecker Lives"

Newspaper article

By: James Gorman

Date: April 29, 2005

Source: Gorman, James. "Deep In the Swamp, an 'Extinct' Woodpecker Lives." *New York Times* (April 29, 2005).

About the Author: James Gorman is editor of the "Science Times" section of the *New York Times*.

INTRODUCTION

After last having been sighted and photographed in Cuba in 1948, an ivory-billed woodpecker, believed to have become extinct, was spotted in the Cache River National Wildlife Refuge (the Big Woods) in Arkansas on February 11, 2004. Gene Sparling, who spotted the bird while kayaking on the river, eventually met up with Tim Gallagher, editor of *Living Bird* magazine, and Bobby Harrison, associate professor at Oakwood College in Huntsville, Alabama. On February 27, 2004, all three of them went kayaking on the Cache, again catching a glimpse of the ivory-billed woodpecker.

Following these two sightings, Sparling, Gallagher, and Harrison formed a larger search team, the Big Woods Conservation Partnership. On April 5, 10, and 11, three other searchers sighted an ivory-billed woodpecker in the same vicinity. On April 25, 2004, David Luneau, associate professor at the University of Arkansas at Little Rock, recorded four seconds of video footage of an ivory-billed woodpecker perched on and then alighting from the trunk of a tupelo tree. On February 14, 2005, Casey Taylor of the Cornell Lab saw an ivory-billed woodpecker in flight in the midst of a flock of crows.

Sight of the bird has encouraged greater search efforts, especially to discover if any breeding pairs of ivory-billed woodpeckers exist. Their existence would, of course, be a surer sign that the bird has come back from the brink of extinction. Since its rediscovery, only one woodpecker has been spotted at each sighting, and searchers have only covered some 16 square miles (42 square kilometers) of the 850 square miles (2,200 square kilometers) of wetlands. Whether it is the same bird or not, observers do not know. If it is the only one, then it is just as likely the last ivory-billed woodpecker as the harbinger of the ivory-billed woodpecker's return. There is cause for optimism, however, since the life span of the ivory-billed woodpecker is between fifteen and twenty years, which would indicate that the woodpecker spotted in 2004 was hatched well after the last sighting in 1948 (some sources say 1944).

The ivory-billed woodpecker is an extraordinary bird with a long, powerful, ivory-colored beak. It has a wingspan of over 30 inches (76 centimeters) when its wings are fully extended. The male's plumed, scarlet-tufted head was a valuable trophy among the tribes indigenous to the bird's habitat and to later generations of hunters, collectors, and even ornithologists.

It was partly for that reason that the bird was wiped out. The destruction of its habitat also has accounted for its disappearance.

Historically, the ivory-billed woodpecker was found in old-growth wetland forests of the southeastern United States and Cuba. It found congenial habitat from east Texas to North Carolina, from southern Illinois through Florida and south to Cuba. In the United States it lived among swampy bottomland hardwood forests, inside deep old-growth woods. It fed on insects, beetle larvae, fruits, and nuts. The beetle larvae were particularly important to the bird for the strength of its bill. The larvae (unhatched eggs) lay under the bark of recently dead trees. In order to get to the beetle larvae, the woodpeckers stripped the bark from the trunks of those trees, to which it still clung tightly, using their powerful bills. Since the European settlement of North America, however, the amount of wetland forest that served as habitat for the ivory-billed woodpecker has shrunk drastically, from 24 million acres (9.7 million hectares) to a little over 4 million acres (1.6 million hectares).

▌ PRIMARY SOURCE

The ivory-billed woodpecker, a magnificent bird long given up for extinct, has been sighted in the cypress and tupelo swamp of the Cache River National Wildlife Refuge here in Arkansas, scientists announced Thursday.

Bird experts, government agencies and conservation organizations involved kept the discovery secret for more than a year, while they worked to confirm the discovery and protect the bird's territory. Their announcement on Thursday brought rejoicing among birdwatchers, for whom the ivory bill has long been a holy grail—a creature that has been called the Lord God bird, apparently because that is what people exclaimed when they saw it.

Dr. John Fitzpatrick, director of the Cornell Lab of Ornithology, who led the effort to confirm the sightings, said at a news conference in Washington, "This is really the most spectacular creature we could imagine rediscovering."

He was joined by Interior Secretary Gale A. Norton, who announced that her agency, along with the Department of Agriculture, had proposed to spend $10 million in federal money for research, habitat protection and law enforcement efforts to protect the bird. The Nature Conservancy and other conservation groups have bought land in the region of the refuge to help preserve a larger area.

The bird was seen in thickly forested bottomland near here, the deep, wet woods immortalized by Faulkner. On Thursday, researchers were traveling by canoe down slow-flowing clay-colored bayous hoping for another sighting, and working to finish up surveys of the territory.

With its 30-inch wingspan and formidable bill, its sharp black and white coloring, and the male's carmine crest, the ivory bill was the largest of American woodpeckers, described by John James Audubon as "this great chieftain of the woodpecker tribe."

Once a dominant creature of great Southern hardwood forest, its numbers dwindled as logging increased. The woodpecker inspired one of the first conservation efforts in the nation's history, but its seeming failure turned the ivory bill into a symbol of loss. The last documented sighting was in Louisiana in 1944.

But the ivory bill lived on as a kind of ghost in rumor and in numerous possible sightings. Despite lengthy expeditions, no sighting was confirmed, until Feb. 11, 2004.

On that date Gene M. Sparling III sighted a large woodpecker with a red crest in the Cache River refuge. Tim W. Gallagher at the Cornell Lab saw the report from Mr. Sparling on a Web site where he was describing a kayak trip.

Within two weeks Mr. Gallagher and Bobby R. Harrison of Oakwood College in Huntsville, Ala., were in a canoe in the refuge, with Mr. Sparling guiding them.

Mr. Gallagher said he had expected to camp out for a week, but after one night out, on Feb. 27, he and Mr. Harrison were paddling up a bayou bounded on both sides by cypress and tupelo when they saw a very large woodpecker fly in front of their canoe.

When they wrote down their notes independently and compared them, Mr. Gallagher said, Mr. Harrison was struck by the reality of the discovery and began sobbing, repeating, "I saw an ivory bill."

Mr. Gallagher felt the same. "I couldn't speak," he said.

Once Mr. Gallagher convinced Dr. Fitzpatrick of Cornell, the effort to confirm the sightings began in earnest, and the result, published in the online version of Science, carried the names of sixteen people from seven institutions who participated in a search that turned up seven confirmed new sightings and a blurry bit of videotape.

An analysis of the video to determine the size and manner of flying of the bird, as well as the other sightings and the detailed reports of experts like Mr. Gallagher, proved convincing.

Dr. Edward O. Wilson, the Harvard ecologist and writer who has called the ivory bill the signature bird of the Southern forest, said the question now was whether there was a breeding population.

"I'm a little hopeful," he said, given that the previous confirmed sighting was sixty years ago. The birds live about fifteen years, so some breeding population had to have survived for some time.

Frank Gill, former president of the National Audubon Society, said of the news, "You get so depressed by the state of things, to suddenly have this happen in your back-yard" is wonderful, "just the thought that there are places in the world still—deep wilderness—harboring a secret like this."

One particularly bright spot, Dr. Fitzpatrick said, is that the place where the bird was seen is already protected.

The bayou where the bird was sighted is in thick swamp where even a great blue heron taking off not 20 yards away disappeared immediately.

On a paddle through the bayou led by researchers from the Cornell Lab and a representative of the Nature Conservancy, the flat, clay-colored water was broken only by the splashing of turtles and the rapid-fire paddling of a frightened wood duck chick. Birds in the distance were heard but not seen. There was no sign of an ivory bill.

As Dr. Fitzpatrick put it, the woodpecker is doing a good job of "protecting itself." He added, "It is really scarce and really wary."

Now the effort to protect the bird will continue, as will the search for other individuals.

Scott Simon, state director of the Nature Conservancy in Arkansas, said the finding was a validation of the kind of cooperative conservation on the part of private organizations and government that had thrived in Arkansas. Mr. Simon said he hoped it would promote conservation and acknowledged that ecotourism, fed by the ivory bill, could have benefits.

But for now, he said, "we would like people to give us a little bit of time."

As for the woodpeckers, there is only proof of one bird so far. If there are more, then perhaps, Dr. Gill said, "we can put Humpty Dumpty back together again."

Nobody wants to think about the alternative. If the last living ivory bill has been found, the discovery may be more bitter than sweet.

SIGNIFICANCE

Just as the disappearance of the ivory-billed wood-pecker indicated how badly the American forests and wetlands had been undervalued and destroyed, so the return of the woodpecker bespeaks the importance of the forests and wetlands and the value of the programs

Illustration of the ivory-billed woodpecker, which was thought to be extinct, but was officially sited in eastern Arkansas in the winter of 2004. AP IMAGES

already instituted to preserve them. In great measure, by reconstituting the natural environment, they have contributed to the bird's reappearance. Although the ivory-billed woodpecker was sighted in February 2004, the announcement of its rediscovery was held back for over a year in order to set in place further environmental protections for the bird. The United States Government, conservation organizations like The Nature Conservancy, and naturalist institutions like the ornithological laboratory at Cornell University began to work together to establish programs to continue to search for the ivory-billed woodpecker, to safeguard its environment, and to promote ecological balance.

The reappearance of the ivory-billed woodpecker also offers hope that the forest can be restored to its primeval conditions and is a spur to further endeavors to reclaim lands touching the Big Woods in Arkansas, where the bird was found. Such ecological restoration will not only support the ivory-billed woodpecker, but it will ensure the health of the forest rivers, create continuous stretches of forest, enrich the earth, and provide habitat for black bears, water fowl, and many other species that cannot survive without the wetlands and the woods.

FURTHER RESOURCES

Books

Hoose, Phillip. *The Race To Save the Lord God Bird*. New York: Farrar, Straus and Giroux, 2004.

Jackson, Jerome A. *In Search of the Ivory-billed Woodpecker*. Washington, D.C.: Smithsonian Books, 2004.

Periodicals

Fitzpatrick, John W., et al. "Ivory-billed Woodpecker (Campephilus principalis) Persists in Continental North America." *Science* 307, 5772 (2005).

Web sites

Cornell Lab of Ornithology. "Rediscovering the Ivory-billed Woodpecker." <http://birds.cornell.edu/ivory> (accessed November 8, 2005).

The Nature Conservancy "The Ivory-billed Woodpecker Has Returned." <http://www.nature.org/ivorybill/search> (accessed November 8, 2005).

"Ecological Land Mines"

Himalayan Land Use and Environmental Degradation

Newspaper article

By: Denis D. Gray

Date: October 23, 2005

Source: Gray, Denis D. "Ecological Land Mines." *Houston Chronicle* (October 23, 2005).

About the Author: Czech-born Denis D. Gray, the Associated Press Bangkok bureau chief, reports news from throughout Asia. His family fled Czechoslovakia after the Communist takeover in 1948, and Gray spent his youth traveling between France, Germany, South Africa, and the United States. He received a degree in history from Yale University, where he was also enrolled in the Reserve Officers Training Corps (ROTC), and subsequently entered the U.S. Army during the Vietnam War. His military assignments kindled an interest in both Asia and journalism. Upon discharge from the army, he returned to the United States and joined the Associated Press bureau in Albany, New York. A series of Associated Press

assignments took him back to Indochina, Germany, and finally the Bangkok bureau.

INTRODUCTION

The magnitude 7.6 Kashmir, Pakistan, earthquake of October 8, 2005, killed at least 79,000 people. Another 65,000 people were reported to have been injured and more than 32,000 buildings collapsed. By way of comparison, it was slightly smaller than the 1906 San Francisco earthquake (magnitude 7.8) and slightly larger than the 1992 Landers, California, earthquake (magnitude 7.3). The Kashmir earthquake produced waves only 1/100 as large and released energy only 1/1000 as great as the 1964 Alaskan earthquake (magnitude 9.2). Each increment of magnitude, for example from 7 to 8, corresponds to a tenfold increase in seismic wave height and a thirty-two-fold increase in the amount of energy released. According to statistics compiled by the U.S. Geological Survey, there are on average fourteen earthquakes of magnitude 7.0 to 7.9 and one of magnitude 8.0 to 8.9 somewhere in the world each year. Thus, the Kashmir earthquake was a large but not unprecedented event.

Most of the deaths and injuries associated with the 2005 Kashmir earthquake occurred when buildings collapsed and buried their inhabitants. There were many reports of people swept away or buried by landslides during the days immediately after the earthquake. In other cases, landslides closed roads and hindered rescue efforts in the remote and mountainous region. Gray's article assigns much of the blame for the post-earthquake landslides—as well as many other Himalayan landslides that occur in response to rainfall—to deforestation and overgrazing on steep mountainsides. Gray quotes a young schoolteacher who believed that losses would have been reduced if forests were intact. He goes on to write that commercial logging, small-scale logging by local residents, and overgrazing create erosion and landslide problems throughout the Himalayan region.

■ PRIMARY SOURCE

'ECOLOGICAL LAND MINES'

JABLA, INDIA - The earthquake didn't destroy Mohammad Shafi Mir's house and bury his mother, but what followed seconds later did—a torrent of bounding boulders that thundered down the mountainside at killer speed.

As he watched in shock from a nearby field, the quake-triggered landslide, resounding like "tank fire on a battlefield," mowed down trees as thick as 5 feet, bombarded houses and enveloped the village with a dust storm that turned day into dusk.

By the time its deadly run ended in the Jabla Nala River far below, nearly half the village's 296 buildings, including the mosque, had been shattered. Only the skeleton of Mohammad's two-story home was left standing, the inside gutted by rocks, boulders and other detritus.

Mohammad's injured mother was dug out from under the rubble and the only other person inside, his leprosy-afflicted father, miraculously survived.

"I had just invested in a new kitchen but I didn't even have a chance to enjoy a single cup of tea in it," said the 35-year-old breadwinner for 14 family members.

Jabla was not alone. Landslides tumbled across the zone of the Oct. 8 earthquake, dramatizing not only the power of one of nature's great killers, but also how humans have brought tragedy upon themselves through massive deforestation and other ecological assaults on the mighty Himalayas.

In Pakistan's quake-hit region, just 1.2 miles from Jabla, landslides swept away uncounted numbers of homes and severed roads, cutting off hundreds of communities which can still only be reached by helicopters.

Mountain slopes were shorn away, exposing gray earth and rubble that still emit great clouds of dust two weeks after the quake. Aftershocks continue to trigger new landslides, hampering efforts to clear roads for relief trucks.

"If there had been more trees we would not have lost as much," said Qayoon Shah, a young teacher, standing by the ruins of the village school. "It is our mistake."

Spawned more often by heavy rains and flash floods during the monsoons, landslides and high-speed mud flows plague the entire "roof of the world," the 1,800-mile arc of the Himalayas that runs through seven countries from Afghanistan in the west to Myanmar in the east.

In this once remote region, commercial logging, local felling and overgrazing have exposed rock and soil, making the land less compact and able to retain water, which now rushes easily down mountainsides to set off what some call "ecological land mines."

Adding to the threat are watershed mismanagement, wholesale replacements of natural forest by tree plantations, which don't absorb as much water, and greater, irregular waterflows as global warming melts Himalayan glaciers, said Nithin Sethi, of the Delhi-based Center for Science and Technology.

"The problem is immense and it's a daily one," Sethi said.

"New towns are going up in the mountains, urbanization and populations are increasing, so we are now perhaps more aware of the impact than before."

SIGNIFICANCE

This newspaper article is significant for three reasons. First, it documents some of the devastation that occurred during and shortly after a major earthquake in a remote and impoverished area. Modern science, engineering, and land use planning have effectively reduced the number of casualties expected from large earthquakes in developed countries such as the United States. Third World countries such as Pakistan, however, remain susceptible to natural disasters in which thousands, or even tens of thousands, are killed and injured. Weak building codes, government corruption, poor construction, and a lack of land use planning all contribute to the human cost of natural disasters such as floods, earthquakes, and landslides. The situation is exacerbated in areas such as Kashmir, where steep mountain topography is naturally prone to landsliding and land use planning can be ineffective because there are few areas that are not susceptible to one hazard or another.

Second, the article brings to the forefront the potential of humans to alter their landscape to a dangerous degree. It is widely held that deforestation has been responsible for increased flooding and landsliding throughout the Himalayas, because natural forests are thought to act as sponges that absorb rainfall and prevent flooding. The argument that disasters would not occur if it were not for logging, however, does not reflect the full complexity of the problem because landscapes are not as simple as sponges. Landsliding is a natural occurrence in mountainous areas and, although trees can help to stabilize thin layers of soil, they may not be effective during large earthquakes. Geologic studies have shown that large landslides involving millions of cubic meters of rock occurred before any substantial human presence. Therefore, it is impossible to assess whether deforestation caused a particular earthquake-triggered landslide without detailed investigations. Other studies have shown that deforestation does not increase the severity of very large floods emanating from the Himalayas. Dense forests may, however, decrease the severity of small to moderate floods and tree roots can help to stabilize soil up to several feet deep. Research has shown that land use practices after logging are as important as the occurrence of logging itself, and many Himalayan landslides can be attributed to roads that would exist even without logging. Tree plantations planted after logging, which are typically kept free of understory brush, do not appear to be as effective as natural forests in buffering floods. Although human activities may incrementally increase the severity of hazards such as landslides and floods, it is doubtful that they are the sole cause in steep and naturally hazardous areas such as the Himalayas.

In the aftermath of the deadly earthquake that hit Pakistan in October 2005, landslides that destroyed homes contributed to the country's environmental devastation. © MIAN KHURSHEED/REUTERS/CORBIS

Third, this article highlights the difficulty of responsible environmental journalism during a time of crisis. A local schoolteacher is quoted about her interpretation of a complicated natural system and references are made to unnamed experts. But, the relevant scientific literature is not consulted or weighed against public opinion. The result is an article that accurately describes a tragedy but inappropriately casts blame without adequate evidence.

FURTHER RESOURCES
Books

Achouri, Moujahed, et al. *Forests and Floods: Drowning in Fiction or Thriving on Facts*. Bogor, Indonesia: Center for International Forestry Research, 2005.

Periodicals

Ali, Jawad, and Tor A. Benjaminsen. "Fuelwood, Timber and Deforestation in the Himalayas." *Mountain Research and Development* 24 (2004): 312–318.

Gerrard, John, and Rita Gardner. "Relationships Between Landsliding and Land Use in the Likhu Khola Drainage Basin, Middle Hills, Nepal." *Mountain Research and Development* 22 (2002): 48–55.

Web sites

"Forestry Highlights." *Center for International Forestry Research (CIFOR)*. <http://www.cifor.cgiar.org> (accessed March 6, 2006).

Heimsath, Arjun M. "Himalayan Erosion." <http://www.india-seminar.com/2000/486/486%20heimsath.htm> (accessed March 6, 2006).

Exploration

Since the beginning of human history, people have explored their surroundings. Historians believe that early humans migrated out of Africa and into Eurasia about 60,000 years ago. They were seeking new food sources and leaving areas with unfavorable environmental conditions. Asia was likely populated 40,000 years ago, the Americas about 30,000 years ago. Evidence suggests that agriculture developed in the Middle East around 10,000 years ago. This important innovation spread throughout Europe and Asia during the next 5,000 years.

The first evidence of ocean voyages dates from 1200 BCE, when Phoenicians sailed simple ships along the Mediterranean coast to find places to sell their wares. Between c. 900 and 700 BCE, Greeks, Chinese, and Polynesians began exploring their surroundings by ship. Sailors started producing charts documenting important features along the coastline.

Ancient Greeks made steady progress exploring the globe between c. 200 and 100 BCE. Using information from camel traders and measurements of the sun's shadows, Greek astronomer Eratosthenes of Cyrene (c. 275 BCE–c. 195 BCE) calculated the circumference of Earth. Soon after, explorers learned to navigate using the stars, and cartography evolved.

During the first millennium, the Polynesians made many explorations. The Chinese launched major travels throughout Asia and the Pacific. However, the Dark Ages in Europe led to few explorations beyond those of the Vikings. The Renaissance marked the beginning of the Age of Discovery in Europe. Prince Henry (1394–1460) helped the Portuguese become a marine power, exploring much of the African coast. Italian navigator Christopher Columbus (1451–1506) explored the Americas, developing charts of the Atlantic Ocean. Ferdinand Magellan (c. 1480?–1521)) made the first trip around the world by ship.

Fueled by various motives—some noble, others greedy or religious—exploration of the Americas continued. The Dutch, Spanish, French, and British explored mainly for economic riches. Juan Ponce de Leon (1460–1521) explored the Florida coast, while fellow Spaniard Francisco Vásquez de Coronado (1510?–1554) trekked across what is now the southwestern United States. British navigator James Cook (1728–1779) traveled extensively along the Pacific Ocean. In 1804, the Lewis and Clark expedition ventured across the North American West. In some cases, the explorations were intrusive and harmful to existing native populations, cultures, and environments.

By 1900, the most accessible regions of the globe had been explored. Only the most extreme environments remained undiscovered. These places included areas high in the mountains and deep in the ocean, or amid frigid polar regions and dense rain forests. By the mid-1900s, adventurers had climbed the highest mountain, Mount Everest, and explored the North and South Poles. However, new environments continue to beckon, including the ocean depths and space.

This chapter discusses the relationships and issues that have evolved from the discovery of diverse environments. One common element related to social issues and debate is how human exploration has changed and challenged new environments. Another element is how explorers define new environments in terms that are understandable to their culture, sometimes endangering or disregarding the native populations, cultures, and environments.

The Louisiana Purchase

Treaty

By: Governments of the United States and the French Republic

Date: 1803

Source: Governments of the United States and the French Republic. *The Louisiana Purchase*. Paris: 1803.

About the Author: No specific author is credited, as multiple statesmen were involved in the drafting of the Louisiana Purchase agreement.

INTRODUCTION

At the dawn of the nineteenth century, the United States extended from the Atlantic Ocean to the Mississippi River. Even within this region, large sections of land consisted of sparsely settled territories which were not yet recognized as states. To the west of the Mississippi, a large swath of land including the port city of New Orleans was controlled by Spain. New Orleans was a critical shipping point for North American agriculture, and a treaty with Spain gave U.S. producers the right to store and ship goods from the city.

In the year 1800, Spain secretly transferred control of New Orleans to France. President Thomas Jefferson, though fundamentally opposed to large acquisitions by the government, was convinced that the French posed a threat to U.S. security. Jefferson quietly began exploring how the U.S. might buy New Orleans from the French.

In Europe, Napoleon and France were facing possible war with England, and by early 1803, conflict seemed inevitable. Forced to ration his limited resources, Napoleon concluded that his plan to rebuild French might in North America was ill-timed. In April, France offered to sell the Americans not only New Orleans, but all of the Louisiana Territory. This vast expanse, stretching Northwest from New Orleans through parts of Texas and Colorado and up to the Canadian border of Montana, would double the size of the United States.

American negotiators were caught off-guard by this offer. While prepared to pay about $2 million for New Orleans, they had never considered spending $22.5 million for such an enormous piece of property. However the price of three cents per acre, along with the added security the purchase

A facsimile of the Louisiana Purchase Treaty between the United States and the Republic of France. The Lousiana Purchase doubled the size of the United States and included an array of mountains, praries, meadows, and forests. AP IMAGE

would bring to the United States, made the offer difficult to pass up. Despite the fact that they were not officially authorized to sign such an agreement, U.S. negotiators Robert Livingstone and James Monroe recognized the importance of the offer and quickly accepted it.

■ PRIMARY SOURCE

THE LOUISIANA PURCHASE
TREATY BETWEEN THE UNITED STATES
OF AMERICA AND THE FRENCH REPUBLIC

The President of the United States of America and the First Consul of the French Republic in the name of the French People desiring to remove all Source of misunderstanding relative to objects of discussion mentioned in the Second and Fifth articles of the Convention of the 8th Vendémiaire an 9/30 September 1800 relative to the rights claimed by the United States in virtue of the Treaty concluded at Madrid the 27 of October 1795, between His Catholic Majesty & the Said United States, & willing to Strengthen the union and friendship which at the time of the Said Convention was happily reestablished between the two nations have respectively named their Plenipotentiaries to wit The President of the United States, by and with the advice and consent of the Senate of the Said States; Robert R. Livingston Minister Plenipotentiary of the United States and James Monroe Minister Plenipotentiary and Envoy extra-ordinary of the Said States near the Government of the French Republic; And the First Consul in the name of the French people, Citizen Francis Barbé Marbois Minister of the public treasury who after having respectively exchanged their full powers have agreed to the following Articles.

Article I Whereas by the Article the third of the Treaty concluded at St Ildefonso the 9th Vendémiaire an 9/1st October 1800 between the First Consul of the French Republic and his Catholic Majesty it was agreed as follows.

''His Catholic Majesty promises and engages on his part to cede to the French Republic six months after the full and entire execution of the conditions and Stipulations herein relative to his Royal Highness the Duke of Parma, the Colony or Province of Louisiana with the Same extent that it now has in the hand of Spain, & that it had when France possessed it; and Such as it Should be after the Treaties subsequently entered into between Spain and other States.''

And whereas in pursuance of the Treaty and parti-cularly of the third article the French Republic has an incon-testible title to the domain and to the possession of the said Territory—The First Consul of the French Republic desiring to give to the United States a strong proof of his friendship doth hereby cede to the United States in the name of the French Republic for ever and in full Sovereignty the said territory with all its rights and appur-tenances as fully and in the Same manner as they have been acquired by the French Republic in virtue of the above mentioned Treaty concluded with his Catholic Majesty.

Article II In the cession made by the preceeding article are included the adjacent Islands belonging to Louisiana all public lots and Squares, vacant lands and all public buildings, fortifications, barracks and other edifices which are not private property.—The Archives, papers & docu-ments relative to the domain and Sovereignty of Louisiana and its dependances will be left in the possession of the Commissaries of the United States, and copies will be afterwards given in due form to the Magistrates and Municipal officers of such of the said papers and docu-ments as may be necessary to them.

Article III The inhabitants of the ceded territory shall be incorporated in the Union of the United States and admit-ted as soon as possible according to the principles of the federal Constitution to the enjoyment of all these rights, advantages and immunities of citizens of the United States, and in the mean time they shall be maintained and protected in the free enjoyment of their liberty, prop-erty and the Religion which they profess.

Article IV There Shall be Sent by the Government of France a Commissary to Louisiana to the end that he do every act necessary as well to receive from the Officers of his Catholic Majesty the Said country and its dependances in the name of the French Republic if it has not been already done as to transmit it in the name of the French Republic to the Commissary or agent of the United States.

Article V Immediately after the ratification of the present Treaty by the President of the United States and in case that of the first Consul's shall have been previously obtained, the commissary of the French Republic shall remit all military posts of New Orleans and other parts of the ceded territory to the Commissary or Commissaries named by the President to take possession—the troops whether of France or Spain who may be there shall cease to occupy any military post from the time of taking pos-session and shall be embarked as soon as possible in the course of three months after the ratification of this treaty.

Article VI The United States promise to execute Such treaties and articles as may have been agreed between Spain and the tribes and nations of Indians until by mutual consent of the United States and the said tribes or nations other Suitable articles Shall have been agreed upon.

Article VII As it is reciprocally advantageous to the com-merce of France and the United States to encourage the communication of both nations for a limited time in the country ceded by the present treaty until general arrange-ments relative to commerce of both nations may be agreed on; it has been agreed between the contracting parties that the French Ships coming directly from France or any of her colonies loaded only with the produce and manufactures of France or her Said Colonies; and the Ships of Spain coming directly from Spain or any of her colonies loaded only with the produce or manufactures of Spain or her Colonies shall be admitted during the Space of twelve years in the Port of New-Orleans and in all other legal ports-of-entry within the ceded territory in the Same manner as the Ships of the United States coming directly from France or Spain or any of their Colonies without being Subject to any other or greater duty on merchandize or other or greater tonnage than that paid by the citizens of the United States.

During that Space of time above mentioned no other nation Shall have a right to the Same privileges in the Ports of the ceded territory—the twelve years Shall commence three months after the exchange of ratifications if it Shall take place in France or three months after it Shall have been notified at Paris to the French Government if it Shall take place in the United States; It is however well understood that the object of the above article is to favour the manufactures, Commerce, freight and navigation of France and of Spain So far as relates to the importations that the French and Spanish Shall make into the Said Ports of the United States without in any Sort affecting the regulations that the United States may make concerning the exportation of the produce and merchandize of the United States, or any right they may have to make Such regulations.

Article VIII In future and for ever after the expiration of the twelve years, the Ships of France shall be treated upon the footing of the most favoured nations in the ports above mentioned.

Article IX The particular Convention Signed this day by the respective Ministers, having for its object to provide for the payment of debts due to the Citizens of the United States by the French Republic prior to the 30th Sept. 1800 (8th Vendémiaire an 9) is approved and to have its execution in the Same manner as if it had been inserted in this present treaty, and it Shall be ratified in the same form and in the Same time So that the one Shall not be ratified distinct from the other.

Another particular Convention Signed at the Same date as the present treaty relative to a definitive rule between the contracting parties is in the like manner approved and will be ratified in the Same form, and in the Same time and jointly.

Article X The present treaty Shall be ratified in good and due form and the ratifications Shall be exchanged in the Space of Six months after the date of the Signature by the Ministers Plenipotentiary or Sooner if possible.

In faith whereof the respective Plenipotentiaries have Signed these articles in the French and English languages; declaring nevertheless that the present Treaty was originally agreed to in the French language; and have thereunto affixed their Seals.

Done at Paris the tenth day of Floreal in the eleventh year of the French Republic; and the 30th of April 1803.

SIGNIFICANCE

Not everyone in the United States supported the Louisiana Purchase, and several political factions believed the purchase was ill-advised or possibly illegal. The Federalist Party in particular believed that the purchase would alienate Great Britain and potentially lead to war with Spain over boundary disputes. Some leaders along the East Coast also worried that this new expansion might shift national influence from the coast to the interior of the continent. Despite this opposition, Jefferson proceeded with the purchase.

The treaty ceding the Louisiana Territory to the United States was ratified by the U.S. Senate in October, 1803, and France turned over control of New Orleans in December of that year. The boundaries of the purchase were left intentionally vague by France, partly to avoid conflict with Spain over which land was included, and partly because the region was largely unexplored. Disputes with Spain over the actual boundaries of the territory continued for more than a decade, and were eventually settled by treaty in 1819. In 1804, Lewis and Clark began their historic expedition to map the area included in the Louisiana Purchase.

With the proceeds of the Louisiana Purchase, Napoleon expanded his already sizeable war funds and eventually gained control over much of Europe. Today, the land purchased from France forms all or part of thirteen U.S. states.

FURTHER RESOURCES
Books

Ambrose, Stephen. *Undaunted Courage: Meriwether Lewis, Thomas Jefferson, and the Opening of the American West.* New York: Touchstone, 1996.

Cerami, Charles A. *Jefferson's Great Gamble: The Remarkable Story of Jefferson, Napoleon, and the Men Behind the Louisiana Purchase.* New York: Sourcebooks, 2003.

The Journals of Lewis and Clark, edited by Bernard DeVoto. New York: Houghton Mifflin, 1997.

Web sites

Discovering Lewis & Clark. "The Expedition." <http://www.lewis-clark.org/content/content-channel.asp?ChannelID=54> (accessed January 20, 2006).

Gateway New Orleans. "Louisiana Purchase." <http://gatewayno.com/history/LaPurchase.html> (accessed January 31, 2006).

Despite protests from other political leaders regarding the Louisiana Purchase, President Thomas Jefferson sent U.S. representitives James Monroe and Robert Livingston (left) to negotiate with France' Minister Talleyrand over the terms of the treaty that doubled the U.S. territory in size. © BETTMANN/CORBIS

National Archives and Records Administration. "Louisiana Purchase Treaty, 1803." <http://www.archives.gov/exhibits/american_originals_iv/sections/louisiana_purchase_treaty.html> (accessed January 31, 2006).

Expedition Chart

Lewis and Clark Expedition

Photograph

By: Robert Frazier

Date: 1807

Source: Photo of original map by Getty Images.

About the Artist: Robert Frazier was a thirty-one-year-old private in the United States Army when he was assigned to the Lewis and Clark expedition in 1805. He completed a map two years later to illustrate his journal that he intended to publish upon completion of the expedition. Frazier lost the journal, but the map survived and is now in the archives of the Library of Congress.

INTRODUCTION

When he took the Oath of Office in 1801, President Thomas Jefferson spoke of his desire to expand the Union, that America seek a "water Connection, linked by a low portage, that would lead to the Pacific."

For 30 years, Jefferson had dreamed of an America that would assert its dominance over the entire North American continent; in 1801, with the British, the Spanish, the French and the Russians all positioned to stake their own claims to parts of the desired land, Jefferson resolved to act. In 1802, Jefferson appointed his secretary, Meriwether Lewis, to lead an expedition to find the desired "water connection" to the Pacific; if unsuccessful in that quest, Jefferson was confident that through this expedition, the United States would cement its claim to the vast territory, said to be rich in precious silver, gold, coal and iron. Jefferson and other American leaders also held the belief that the vast open spaces of the West were fertile farm land, sufficient to accommodate the young nation's rising tide of immigrants.

Lewis secured William Clark as his assistant to both plan and to lead the project in early 1803. Together they led the expeditionary force that bore their name on a route that traversed the continent. Lewis and Clark crossed the then largely unexplored lands of what is modern day Minnesota, the Dakotas, Montana, Wyoming, Washington, and Oregon. Several maps of the region were created during and shortly after the expedition, including Private Frazier' map of showing the Lewis River, now known as the Snake River, along with the Columbia River, in present-day Idaho and Oregon.

■ PRIMARY SOURCE

EXPEDITION CHART
See primary source image.

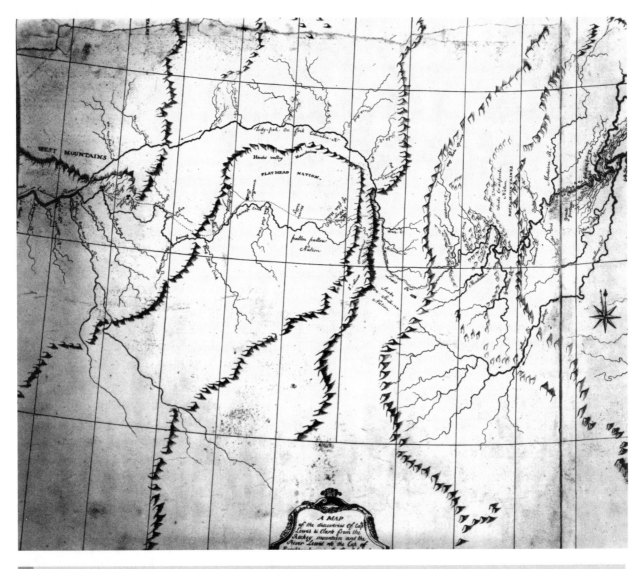

■ PRIMARY SOURCE

Expedition Chart. The Lewis and Clark expedition (1804–1806) visited the territory shown on this map, showing the Lewis (Snake) River and the Columbia River. PHOTO BY MPI/GETTY IMAGES

SIGNIFICANCE

Clark maintained detailed journals from the commencement of their trek in 1803 to their return to Washington in 1806. Part work of art, part geographical journal, and part land survey, the information set out in a 1814 expedition map became an essential reference source for subsequent explorations. The data collected by the Lewis and Clark expedition would form a part of many subsequent American maps of the West until the construction of the transcontinental rail system in the 1860s.

Lewis was made Governor of the Louisiana Territory as a reward for his services to the nation by Jefferson in 1807. He died in circumstances that were equally suggestive of murder or suicide in 1809. After the death of Lewis, Clark took responsibility for the publication of the expedition journals and maps. Clark was appointed a Superintendent of Indian Affairs by the federal government. The expedition journals and related maps were published in 1814, a lucid and detailed account of the geography, vegetation, animal life and the human inhabitants of the then virtually unknown and unexplored West. Clark died in 1838.

The maps stand today as a testament to both the ambition of President Thomas Jefferson , as well as the fortitude and the vigor of the expeditioners Lewis and Clark. Jefferson's desire to claim the western portion of the continent had been spurred in part by the publication of the journals of Alexander MacKenzie, the Scottish explorer who had chronicled his explorations across what is now western Canadian and the Rocky Mountains to the Pacific from 1787 to 1793. MacKenzie, working on behalf of British interests, was seeking a land passage to the Pacific by which England could build her Asian trade. Jefferson assumed that if America did not similarly assert its interests on a continent wide basis, the British might lay a further claim to those lands west of the Mississippi which Jefferson and others saw as crucial to the long-term interests of America. In this sense, Lewis and Clark were by equal measures explorers, geographers, and the flag bearers of Jefferson's dream of a truly continental nation.

FURTHER RESOURCES
Books

Ambrose, Stephen E. *Undaunted Courage; Meriwether Lewis, Thomas Jefferson and the Opening of the American West.* New York: Simon and Schuster, 1996.

Web sites

David Rumsey Historical Map Collection. <http://www.davidrumsey.com> (accessed February 10, 2006).

University of Virginia Library/Lewis and Clark: The Maps of Exploration. <http://www.lib.virginia.edu/small/exhibits/lewis_clark> (accessed February 10, 2006).

Discovery of the Yosemite

Book excerpt

By: Lafayette H. Bunnell

Date: 1880

Source: Bunnell, Lafayette H. *Discovery of the Yosemite and the Indian War of 1851 Which Let to That Event.* Chicago: Fleming H. Revell, 1880.

About the Author: American medical doctor Lafayette H. Bunnell was assigned to the Mariposa Battalion, which discovered Yosemite Valley during the Indian War of 1851. His party is generally understood to have been the first group of non-natives to enter the valley. Bunnell described his military experience in California in the book *Discovery of the Yosemite and the Indian War of 1851, which Led to that Event.*

INTRODUCTION

The Yosemite region is part of the Sierra Nevada Mountains in eastern California, and much of the area lies within the present-day Yosemite National Park. Although Native Americans had no doubt visited the area for centuries, it was not known among non-natives until Bunnell and his voluntary military party, the Mariposa Battalion, entered the Yosemite Valley while pursuing Native Americans in 1851.

Bunnell and his compatriots found themselves in Yosemite as a direct consequence of the California Gold Rush of 1849, which began when John Sutter discovered gold near his sawmill in the small town of Coloma, along the South Fork of the American River east of Sacramento. Although Sutter discovered gold in 1848, it was a year before the fortune seekers known as Forty-Niners descended upon the area. The total amount of gold removed during the rush is unknown, but the influx of people and capital and extraction of wealth helped California to achieve statehood. One of the people drawn to California was the Bavarian immigrant and dry goods merchant Levi Strauss (1829–1902), who manufactured sturdy denim pants reinforced with rivets. Popular among miners and

This view of the Half Dome as seen from the valley floor of Yosemite National Park is only one of the stunning views of untouched wilderness the park offers, October 20, 1997. AP IMAGES

originally known as waist overalls, his pants evolved into the American icons now known simply as Levis.

The California Gold Rush of 1849 was a consequence of geology. The high Sierra Nevada consists of granite and compositionally similar rocks formed by the slow cooling of molten magma at great depths. Individual bodies of granite known as plutons and stocks coalesced to form a composite body known to geologists as the Sierra Nevada batholith (from the Greek words *bathos*, meaning depth, and *lithos*, meaning rock). The magma was generated from tectonic plates subducted and melted along the western edge of North America. At the same time, gold-bearing marine sediments were being scraped, or accreted, from the top of the plate being subducted. Gold, which is thought to have originated around submarine hydrothermal vents, was concentrated as the sediments were buried and heated (a process known as metamorphosis), and settled as veins within the Sierra Nevada foothills. The greatest concentration of gold is known as the Mother Lode. Much of the gold removed by the Forty-Niners, however, was eroded, transported, and deposited in gravel beds along rivers draining the

foothills. These gold-bearing gravels are known as placer deposits.

The snow-free foothills of the Sierra Nevada between Sacramento and Yosemite were rich in game and nuts, and were densely inhabited by Native Americans who initially welcomed the opportunity for trade. Tensions grew as the non-native population increased, however, and led to a Native American uprising. The first attack, which occurred in late 1850, was against a trading post owned by James Savage. He was a flamboyant character that had taken several Native American wives from different tribes. Continuing battles led to the formation of the Mariposa Battalion and negotiations with the Native Americans. Six tribes signed a treaty with the United States but two, the Yosemites and the Chowchillas, refused and were pursued into the Sierra Nevada during the early months of 1851. It was during the pursuit that the Mariposa Battalion, including Bunnell, entered Yosemite Valley for the first time.

In response to rapid development of the newly discovered valley, in 1864 President Abraham Lincoln ceded it to the State of California with the intention that it be preserved for public enjoyment. This was the first time that land had been reserved as a park by a national government but, because the land was given to California, it was not the first national park. (That honor belongs to Yellowstone National Park, which was created as the world's first national park in 1872.) Yosemite was not declared a national park until 1890 and remained under joint state and federal control until 1906, when ownership reverted solely to the federal government.

A combination of glacial ice and the granitic rocks of the Sierra Nevada batholith created the scenery of the Yosemite Valley. The polished granite surfaces and sheer rock walls exemplified by Half Dome and El Capitan, which have made Yosemite a mecca for rock climbers, were created in part by glaciers moving over fractured granite. Although the glacial origin of Yosemite Valley was recognized by the American naturalist and writer John Muir (1883–1914), he was challenged by geologists who inferred the steep-sided valley to be a result of vertical movement along faults. The controversy was not settled until 1930, when a definitive U.S. Geological Survey report showed that Yosemite Valley was created by a combination of glacial and river erosion.

Yosemite Valley was the focal point for one of the early battles in the American conservation movement. Increasing water demand in San Francisco led to plans to dam equally scenic Hetch Hetchy Valley, which lies just north of Yosemite Valley and within the present-day national park. Dam construction, which would drown the valley in order to create a water storage reservoir, was strongly opposed by John Muir, the Sierra Club, and even *The New York Times* editorial page. The dam, however, was eventually constructed during the early years of the twentieth century, and its reservoir continues to supply water to San Francisco.

PRIMARY SOURCE

The date of our discovery into the Yosemite was about the 21st of March, 1851. We were afterward assured by Ten-ie-ya and others of his band, that this was the first visit ever made to this valley by white men. Ten-ie-ya said that a small party of white men once crossed the mountains at the north side, but were so guided as not to see it ....

It was to prevent the occurrence of such an event, that Ten-ie-ya had consented to go to the commissioner's camp and make peace, intending to return to his mountain home as soon as the excitement form the recent outbreak had subsided. The entrance to the Valley had ever been carefully guarded by the old chief, and the people of his band. As part of it's traditional history, it was stated: "That when Ten-ie-ya left the tribe of his mother and went to live in Ah-wah-ne, he was accompanied by a very old Ah-wah-ne-chee, who had been the great 'medicine man' of his tribe."

. . . The old "medicine man" was the counselor of the young chief. Not long before the death of this patriarch, as if endowed with prophetic wisdom, he assured Ten-ie-ya that while he retained possession of Ah-wah-ne his band would increase in numbers and become powerful. That if he befriended those who sought his protection, no other tribe would come to the valley to make war upon him, or attempt to drive him from it, and if he obeyed his counsels he would put a spell upon it that would hold it sacred for him and his people alone: none other would ever dare to make it their home. . . .

For this reason, Ten-ie-ya declared, had he so rigidly guarded his valley home, and all who sought his protection. No one ventured to enter it, except by his permission . . .

The ford was found to be rocky, but we passed over it without serious difficulty, although several repeated their morning ablutions while stumbling over the boulders.

The open ground on the north side was found free from snow. The trail led toward "El Capitan," which had from the first, been the particular object of my admiration.

At this time no distinctive names were known by which to designate the cliff, waterfalls, or any of the especial objects of interest, and the imaginations of some ran wild in search of *appropriate* ones. None had any but a limited idea of the height of this cliff, and but a few appeared conscious of the vastness of the granite wall before us; although an occasional ejaculation betrayed the feelings which the imperfect comprehension of the grand and wonderful excited. A few of us remarked upon the great length of time required to pass it, and by so doing, probably arrived at more or less correct conclusions regarding its size.

SIGNIFICANCE

Yosemite Valley and the surrounding high country, much of which has been preserved in Yosemite National Park, is recognized for its scenic beauty and geologic features. The California Gold Rush of 1849, which precipitated the discovery of Yosemite by the Mariposa Battalion and its physician, Lafayette Bunnell, was also a pivotal event in the history of both California and the United States. The influx of people and accumulation of wealth associated with the gold rush accelerated the establishment of the State of

California, which has since grown into one of the world's largest economies.

FURTHER RESOURCES

Books

Harden, Deborah. *California Geology (2nd Edition)*. Upper Saddle River, New Jersey: Prentice Hall, 2003.

Matthes, Francois E. *Geologic History of the Yosemite Valley*. Washington, DC: U.S. Government Printing Office, 1930.

Periodicals

Bunnell, Lafayette H. "The Date of Discovery of the Yosemite." *Century* (September 1890).

The Pampas and Andes

A Thousand Miles' Walk Across South America

Book excerpt

By: Nathaniel H. Bishop

Date: 1869

Source: Bishop, Nathaniel H. *The Pampas and Andes: A Thousand Miles' Walk Across South America*. Ann Arbor: University of Michigan Library, 2005.

About the Author: Nathaniel Bishop left Massachusetts at the tender age of seventeen in 1855 with a goal to travel throughout South America on foot. He had forty-five dollars to his name. Over the next two years, he traveled more than 1,000 miles (1,600 kilometers) throughout Argentina and Chile. His book discusses the landscape, the environment, and Charles Darwin's theories, and it makes keen observations about the land. Bishop later became a member of the Boston Society of Natural History, and of the New York Academy of Sciences, as well as a distinguished canoeing specialist and popular author of travel memoirs.

INTRODUCTION

The Pampas and Andes chronicles Nathaniel Bishop's two-year odyssey throughout South America. During his travels, Bishop carefully documented his observations of the actions of the natives, his personal activities, and the landscapes, plants, and animal life he encountered. Unlike many naturalist books published in this time period, Bishop's work blends observation of nature with travel memoir, focusing more on his own personal experiences than on meticulous recounting of information with the goal of expanding scientific knowledge.

In contrast to Thomas Belt's *The Naturalist in Nicaragua* or Charles Darwin's *The Origin of Species*, Bishop's goal was not to broaden scientific literature on geology, geography, biology, or natural science, but instead to tell his story of travel and to describe his personal experiences. Focusing more on native interactions, Bishop's book reads like a travelogue.

Its publication in 1869, fourteen years after the author's journeys, fed the American and European public's demand for nature-based stories; Bishop went on to publish two other travel memoirs, *The Voyage of the Paper Canoe* and *Four Months in a Sneak-Box*. *The Pampas and Andes* was a very popular book in its time, promoted as a travel memoir as well as a book for young boys; by 1883 it was in its eleventh edition.

A number of books detailing South America, such as Domingo Faustino Sarmiento's *Facundo*, Mary Peabody Mann's translation of *Life in the Argentine Republic in the Days of the Tyrants*, and Belt's *The Naturalist in Nicaragua*—all published within a few years of Bishop's work—collectively generated tremendous interest in the flora and fauna of South America. Together with *The Origin of Species*, these books provided both scientific information and literary entertainment for the upper and middle classes. In addition, Bishop's rich narrative provides a snapshot of the native groups he encountered, their beliefs and rituals, and their use of the land.

■ PRIMARY SOURCE

...Taking a south-westerly course across the desert, I travelled until three o'clock over the same dreary waste, when a deep fissure was observed in the sierra, which I entered, and soon found myself within the Flecha. Before passing this peculiar gap, a word or two regarding it may prove interesting. For many leagues along its course the sierra presents an impassable barrier to man or beast. The Flecha is a narrow passage from the desert on the east to the valley on the western side. The sides of the Flecha are of solid rock, rising perpendicularly to a great height.

The pass exhibits the action of water upon its sides, for the rock has been worn smooth in past ages, and the bed of the passage is covered with pebbles. Undoubtedly, a long time since, a strong body of water found its way through this place, and may have submerged the plain below; but whether this gap was the bed of a natural stream, or mere vent, through which the melting snow escaped during the spring mouths, cannot now be well determined. The effect that the lofty sides of the Flecha have upon independent objects is very curious. My horse seemed to dwindle to the size of a Shetland pony when I removed a few yards from him, and two muleteers, who passed through at the same time, looked like pygmies.

Half way up the precipice were holes, said to have been cut by the ancient discoverers of the country, to assist in searching for precious metals, but, proving unprofitable, had been abandoned. I continued along the valley until dusk, when the barking of dogs, and occasional glimpses of a light, guided me to one side of the valley, where a few huts constitute the hamlet of El Durazno. These huts were inhabited by muleteers, who suffered greatly from poverty. Here and there the rough soil had been levelled, so as to be susceptible of irrigation, and a few patches of clover gave a cheering aspect, when contrasted with the barren mountains behind the hamlet. An old woman invited me to enter her house, and pass the night, as it was damp outside, and the heavy clouds that hovered about us looked as if about to descend.

The hut was built of sticks and mud, and adjoining it was the kitchen. Having turned my horse adrift, I entered, and, as I reclined upon a skin couch, commenced inquiring of the hostess relative to the snow on the main Cordillera. I was unable, however, to obtain any information from that source. Our party was soon increased by the entry of several rude-looking fellows, armed with long knives. The place was so small that we reclined, packed one against the other, men, women, and children, promiscuously. The old woman commenced cooking an *asado* upon the fire; it had hardly begun to splutter and crackle, when the dog that had sat beside the fire caught up the meat in his mouth, and commenced masticating it with great *gusto*. The woman, screaming out, "*O, sus Ave Maria!*" made a clutch at the dog, but was unsuccessful in recovering the prize. One of the men caught the animal by the throat, and choked him until the meat was drawn from his mouth, when, with a hasty "*Ha, perro!*" it was returned to the fire, and cooked for the lookers-on. More men and dogs came in, and, thinking it best to retreat while it remained in my power to do so, I requested my hostess to allow me to retire. Taking a saucer of fat, in which a bit of rag was burning, she led the way into the other shanty, and assisted in spreading my saddle cloths upon a rough sofa, built of boards, which had been placed in the middle of the floor to prevent the approach of the *binchucas* that were secreted in the crevices in the walls.

These uncomfortable disturbers of night dreams are as large as the common May beetle, and are armed with a bill that of a mosquito, which is used with great effect upon the victim. Before fixing upon a person, the body of the *binchuca* is thin and flat; but after his feast is over, he is bloated and disgusting to hook upon. As this tormentor is many times larger than the mosquito, so does the

irritability caused by its leeching process exceed in like proportion that of the other pest.

When about to withdraw from the room, the woman bade me sleep with the utmost confidence, and not fear any harm. But as the conversation of the men in the kitchen had been about the *plata* that might be in my possession, I was very particular to impress her with the idea that North Americans feared nothing; and at the same time I drew a long knife from under my *poncho*, and placed it beneath the sheep-skin that was to serve for my bed. When she withdrew, I lay down; but as I had a thought of the *Binchucas* before I prepared for sleep, I carefully rolled myself in my blankets, Indian fashion, and defied them to do their worst.

Hardly had I begun to doze, when a sensation of something disagreeable, touching me, aroused me to the fact that the vile pests were coming from every quarter of the hovel. I could hear them crawling up the sides of the room and across the ceiling, when with their usual degree of impudence, one after another dropped plump upon my body. But my swathing clothes served as an armor, and they could not enter in to the feast. All the while they clung with considerable tenacity to the coarse blankets, trying to effect an entrance, but they had met their conqueror; for, after waiting until the swarming was over, and the army had fairly camped upon me, I suddenly and carefully rolled over and over upon the sofa, until the life was forced out of nearly all of them, when, satisfied that a great victory had been achieved, I dropped into a deep slumber.

When morning came, and I passed out of the hut, I found that the valley was filled with mist, and I deferred setting out until the thick clouds had scattered. About nine o'clock a breeze sprang up, which soon cleared the valley of mists, and I resumed my journey. Soon after my leaving El Durazno, the valley expanded into a plain of a desert character. The country between the mountains again became undulating and broken; at three leagues from the last hamlet, El Sequion, a collection of two or three mud houses and several ranchos, appeared.

From one of these ranchos a *China* (half Indian) woman came out, and questioned me as to my motives for traveling alone, on foot, in the desolate valley. When I spoke of crossing the Cordillera, the good creature lifted both her hands, and exclaimed in colloquial Spanish, "*Por Dios*, don't go any farther. A man from Chili stopped here the other day—his mouth and cheeks were like a soft peach with the frost!" Another woman joined us, and declared that I was too young to be so far from home, and questioned me to the effect "if my mother knew that I was out." In their inquiries, however, they exhibited a kindness that to me was very gratifying, and I felt that in case of accident upon the road, I had at least two friends near at hand.

Beyond the Sequion, the valley grew narrower, and in places was so filled with stones and detritus as to lame the old horse. The road now became a mere defile, the steep sides of the sierras towering above it to a great height, their bareness being sometimes relieved by dwarf cacti, that grew in crevices where soil had lodged; these plants were in flower, some white, others of a yellow hue.

The clouds again enveloped the mountains, and while I was groping along over the broken rock, the tinkling of a mule's bell broke the stillness, and a moment later I came upon a circle of packsaddles and mules' cargoes, lying upon the ground. A deep voice called out, "Come here, friend;" and I was soon acquainted with the capataz and muleteers of Don Fernando de Oro, a rich San Juan merchant, who had sent his troop to Uspallata to await an opportunity to cross to Chili, in advance of the troops of the other merchants. The don was daily expected by the capataz; who had been three or four days on the road already. The capataz urged me to remain with the troop until the next morning, which invitation I accepted, and tying my horse to some resinous bushes, I sat down to a sumptuous meal of boiled corn, dried beef, and pepper, while my jaded animal satisfied himself in cropping the tops of the bushes, and a kind of stunted weed that grew among the rocks. Towards dusk it rained, but my heavy blanket kept me dry. The guides huddled around the dying embers, vainly endeavoring to warm their benumbed limbs; around us the hills seemed to be shaken by the heavy thunders that reverberated along the mountain tops.

Fearing that my horse would give out, as he had lived mostly upon bushes and coarse herbage since leaving San Juan, I arose early, and, guided by the bright starlight, caught my animal, and led him up the valley. A spur of the sierra blocked up the valley, and this steep ascent had to be climbed by the poor animal, he halting every few steps to draw breath. Having reached the summit, he heaved a deep sigh, as if conscious of having finished a hard task.

A magnificent view rewarded me for the exertion of making the ascent. The rocky grandeur filled me with awe, for I was surrounded by a sublime chaos— broken hills, valleys, and barren cliffs of the sierra.

A white cloud passed over the valley, shutting me out from sight of the world below; it was no easy task to follow the rocky path beyond; sometimes it led down abrupt descents into dismal valleys, then again almost to the level of the summit of the mountain range. Along this crooked path but one mule can pass at a time, and there are places where it requires but a single unsteady movement to send the loaded animal into the abyss below. For nearly a mile the sierra on the left side was formed of red freestone, and was, in many places, as regular as a castle wall. In this lonely place the least sound would catch my ear.

The sierra that I had crossed is called the Paramilla, or "bleak place;" in the warmest day a cold wind from the snow peaks of the Andes blows drearily across it. Leaving the broken mass of rock, the path descended abruptly into a little valley, which contained a stone hut, and a corral for goats. This desolate spot was enlivened by the presence of one of the prettiest señoras that I ever met. She informed me that her husband, who was then hunting guanacos, supported himself principally by keeping goats that browsed upon the sides of the mountains. When he wished to butcher any of the guanacos, he, with the assistance of a pack of trained curs, drove them into natural rock walled corrals among the mountains, where, hemmed in, the animals were easily dispatched with the *boliadores* and knife.

Leaving the valley, I ascended to a high plain that seemed to be on a level with the summits of the neighboring range of the Cordilleras, and as the sun was about sinking below the western horizon, I perceived that this was to be my camping-place for the night. Laying the saddle upon the ground for a pillow, and carefully spreading the blankets, I lay down to rest, having first tied my horse to a stunted bush, which he vainly tried to eat.

I dropped into a restless slumber; but an hour later, a wild, desolate cry caused me to spring from my blankets, and prepare for defense. I had been told many stories of the cruelty of the puma, or American lion, and at this moment feared that one of these animals was on the plain. It was along this part of the road the guides had seen their tracks, and hunters had run them down with dogs a few miles from the plain upon which I had encamped.

Another wild cry, and the animal passed along the plain without heeding either my horse or me, to be left in peace, into a sound sleep, that continued unbroken until the rising sun gilded the snowy crests of the lofty Cordillera.

It was a beautiful scene that lay before me. Across the plain floated white clouds of mist, like airy spirits, while before me lay a narrow valley, through which the road led to Uspallata. Upon one side of the plain rose several low hills, green with coarse herbage, upon which a small herd of llamas were as if unconscious of the presence of man.

I soon was ready to start; but my old horse seemed incapable of moving. I rubbed his stiff limbs until I had worked myself into a perspiration; he was so far recovered as to be able to move slowly. I seized the lasso, and led him on as before.

The road descended to the ravine just referred to, and for an hour or so my journey led through the surrounding cliffs; but at length we again emerged upon a flat plain, covered with low bushes, and over this I led the way until afternoon, when a green spot at the foot of a high of mountains, and the hut of a farmer, caught my eye, and soon after I drew up before the last house in the Argentine Republic—the Guardo of Uspallata....

SIGNIFICANCE

After returning to the United States from his excursion throughout South America, Bishop developed a lifelong interest in canoeing and became an expert in the field. He went on to write other travel memoirs that involved the details of canoeing expedition, using the same precise, descriptive language not only to convey information about canoes and the sport, but also to deliver to the audience a rich narrative that evoked the natural world in which he traveled.

Bishop's next book, *The Voyage of the Paper Canoe* (1878), was devoted to his 2,500-mile (4,000-kilometer) canoe journey through North America, traversing the waterways from Quebec to Mexico in a canoe made of paper. Using only an 18-foot (5.5-meter) canoe and

traveling with one assistant, Bishop followed the rivers and detailed his experience. The following year he published *Four Months in a Sneak Box*, yet another travelogue recounting his 2,500-mile (4,000-kilometer) canoe adventure through the Ohio and Mississippi rivers to the Gulf of Mexico.

Bishop describes at length his experience passing through the Cumbre Pass, the best route for crossing the Andes to reach Chile from Argentina. Nearly fifty-five years after his travels, the Transandine Railway connected Buenos Aires to Santiago by train; Bishop covered the trek on foot and by mule, a dangerous trip he discusses in the book as locals describe stories of those who died trying to go through Cumbre Pass.

Bishop's publications solidified his standing as a naturalist and adventure writer. His attention to the Argentinian Pampas gives modern-day environmentalists and scientists insight into the terrain 150 years ago, and helps in the creation of environmental tracking timelines. The Pampas—like African savannahs, the Australian Outback, or the Great Plains in the United States—recover slowly from environmental

Firefighters struggle to save the Toay, on the western Argentine pampas, from a vicious grassfire, January 2, 2001. AP IMAGES

impacts, a result of rain and wind erosion as well as soil composition. Bishop's descriptions engaged the imaginations of lay readers and piqued scientific curiosity in contemporary scientists. *The Pampas and the Andes* gives current biologists, environmental engineers, and other scholars and researchers specializing in the southern cone historical insight into the terrain and the people in the areas Bishop documented.

FURTHER RESOURCES

Books

Briones, Claudia, and Jose Luis Lanata, eds. *Archaeological and Anthropological Perspectives on the Native Peoples of Pampa, Patagonia, and Tierra del Fuego to the Nineteenth Century*, Westport, Conn.: Bergin & Garvey, 2002.

Roberts, J. Timmons, and Nikki D. Thanos. *Trouble in Paradise: Globalization and Environmental Crises in Latin America*. New York: Routledge Press, 2003.

Web sites

"Environment in Latin America." *LANIC*. <http://lanic.utexas.edu/la/region/environment> (accessed March 13, 2006).

Photographers are thrilled to be able to photograph the beauty of Yosemite Falls, as seen from Glacier Point. Yosemite National Park remains untouched by industrialization, due in part to John Muir's advocacy of preservation. © CORBIS

"Yosemite Glaciers"

Newspaper article

By: John Muir

Date: December 5, 1871

Source: Muir, John. "Yosemite Glaciers." *New York Tribune*. December 5, 1871.

About the Author: Naturalist John Muir (1838–1914) was a Scottish-born wilderness explorer, best known for his adventures in the glaciers of Alaska and California's Sierra Nevada. Muir feared that the United States as he had witnessed it would gradually become overdeveloped, and he wrote extensively about the importance of protecting the natural landscape and wildlife of the country. His work was instrumental in the creation of the national parks, including Yellowstone, Yosemite, Mount Rainier, and Grand Canyon National Park, and his writing inspired many of the conservation programs enacted by President Theodore Roosevelt, including the first National Monuments by Presidential Proclamation. Muir also co-founded the Sierra Club in 1892, providing a formal organization for environmental activists to continue working for the preservation of the nation's mountain ranges.

INTRODUCTION

In the following excerpt from Muir's first published work, the author compares various aspects of the Yosemite Valley to the pages of a book. By examining those aspects, he is able to read—that is, to reconstruct—the shape and activity of the glacier itself.

Unlike the geologists of his time, who argued that the Yosemite Valley was formed by the activity of an earthquake, Muir asserted (and convincingly demonstrated) that it was carved out by the work of glaciers, mighty rivers of ice that rushed over the surface of the earth. The glacier shaped it and left sediments that became its soil, beds for its rivers, and ranges of mountains. More, however, than a first-rate geologist, in his descriptions of the valley and the glacier that formed it, Muir showed his love for nature and the processes of nature that excited his admiration and his reverence.

■ PRIMARY SOURCE

Two years ago, when picking flowers in the mountains back of Yosemite Valley, I found a book. It was blotted and storm-beaten; all of its outer pages were mealy and crumbly, the paper seemed to dissolve like the snow beneath which it had been buried; but many of the inner pages were well preserved, and though all were more or less stained and torn, whole chapters were easily readable. In this condition is the great open book of Yosemite glaciers today; its granite pages have been torn and blurred by the same storms that wasted the castaway book. The grand central chapters of the Hoffman, and Tenaya, and Nevada glaciers are stained and corroded by the frosts and rains, yet, nevertheless, they contain scarce one unreadable page; but the outer chapters of the Pohono, and the Illilouette, and the Yosemite Creek, and Ribbon, and Cascade glaciers, are all dimmed and eaten away on the bottom, though the tops of their pages have not been so long exposed, and still proclaim in splendid characters the glorious actions of their departed ice. The glacier which filled the basin of the Yosemite Creek was the fourth ice-stream that flowed to Yosemite Valley. It was about fifteen miles in length by five in breadth at the middle of the main stream, and in many places was not less than 1,000 feet in depth. It united with the central glaciers in the valley by a mouth reaching from the east side of El Capitan to Yosemite Point, east of the falls. Its western rim was rayed with short tributaries, and on the north its divide from the Tuolumne glacier was deeply grooved; but few if any of its ridges were here high enough to separate the descending ice into distinct tributaries. The main central trunk flowed nearly south, and, at a distance of about 10 miles, separated into three nearly equal branches, which were turned abruptly to the east.

Those branch basins are laid among the highest spurs of the Hoffman range and abound in small, bright lakes, set in the solid granite without the usual terminal moraine dam. The structure of those dividing spurs is exactly similar, all three appearing as if ruins of one mountain, or rather as perfect units hewn from one mountain rock during long ages of glacial activity. As their north sides are precipitous, and as they extend east and west, they were enabled to shelter and keep alive their hiding glaciers long after the death of the main trunk. Their basins are still dazzling bright, and their lakes have as yet accumulated but narrow rings of border meadow, because their feeding streams have had but little time to carry the sand of which they are made. The east bank of the main stream, all the way from the three forks to the mouth, is a continuous, regular wall, which also forms the west bank of the Indian Cañon glacier-basin. The tributaries of the west side of the main basin touched the east tributaries of the cascade, and the great Tuolumne glacier from Mount Dana, the mightiest ice-river of this whole region, flowed past on the north. The declivity of the tributaries was great, especially those which flowed from the spurs of the Hoffman on the Tuolumne divide, but the main stream was rather level, and in approaching Yosemite was compelled to make a considerable ascent back of Eagle Cliff. To the concentrated currents of the central glaciers, and to the levelness

and width of mouth of this one, we in a great measure owe the present height of the Yosemite Falls. Yosemite Creek lives the most tranquil life of all the large streams that leap into the valley, the others occupying the cañons of narrower and, consequently, of deeper glaciers, while yet far from the valley, abound in loud falls and snowy cascades, but Yosemite Creek flows straight on through smooth meadows and hollows, with only two or three gentle cascades, and now and then a row of soothing, rumbling rapids, biding its time, and hoarding up the best music and poetry of its life for the one anthem at Yosemite, as planned by the ice.

When a bird's-eye view of Yosemite Basin is obtained from any of its upper domes, it is seen to possess a great number of dense patches of black forest, planted in abrupt contact with bare gray rocks. Those forest plots mark the number and the size of all the entire and fragmentary moraines of the basin, as the latter eroding agents have not yet had sufficient time to form a soil fit for the vigorous life of large trees.

Wherever a deep-wombed tributary laid against a narrow ridge, and was also shielded from the sun by compassing rock-shadows, there we invariably find more small terminal moraines, because when such tributaries were melted off from the trunk they retired to those upper strongholds of shade, and lived and worked in full independence, and the moraines which they built are left entire because the water-collecting basins behind are too small to make streams large enough to wash them away; but in the basins of exposed tributaries there are no terminal moraines, because their glaciers died with the trunk. Medial and lateral moraines are common upon all the outside slopes, some of them nearly perfect in form, but down in the main basin there is not left one unaltered moraine of any kind, immense floods having washed down and leveled them into harder meadows for the present stream, and into sandy flower beds and fields for forests.

Such was Yosemite glacier, and such is its basin, the magnificent work of its hands. There is sublimity in the life of a glacier. Water rivers work openly, and so the rains and the gentle dews, and the great sea also grasping all the world: and even the universal ocean of breath, though invisible, yet speaks aloud in a thousand voices, and proclaims its modes of working and its power: but glaciers work apart from men, exerting their tremendous energies in silence and darkness, outspread, spirit-like, brooding above predestined rocks unknown to light, unborn, working on unwearied through unmeasured times, unhalting as the stars, until at length, their creations complete, their mountains brought forth, homes made for the meadows and the lakes, and fields for waiting forests, earnest, calm as when they came as crystals from the sky, they depart.

The great valley itself, together with all its domes and walls, was brought forth and fashioned by a grand combination of glaciers, acting in certain directions against granite of peculiar physical structure. All of the rocks and mountains and lakes and meadows of the whole upper Merced basin received their specific forms and carvings almost entirely from this same agency of ice. I have been drifting about among the rocks of this region for several years, anxious to spell out some of the mountain truths which are written here; and since the number, and magnitude, and significance of these ice-rivers began to appear, I have become anxious for more exact knowledge regarding them; with this object, supplying myself with blankets and bread, I climbed out of the Yosemite by Indian Cañon, and am now searching the upper rocks and moraines for readable glacier manuscript.

SIGNIFICANCE

Muir can be seen, by his legacy, as the vital spur and center of a movement which is responsible for preserving countless acres of North American wilderness through practical political action and by active dissemination of a gospel of nature.

Because of Muir's work, America's system of National Parks was created and the strand of belief in the sanctity of nature that runs through American thought was strengthened. In his nature writings he endowed natural phenomena with often awesome spiritual dimensions. Primarily because of his writings and his activism, Yosemite, Sequoia, Mount Rainier, Petrified Forest, and Grand Canyon National Parks were created. Not only did he venture into nature alone, but he encouraged others to encounter nature face to face. Because of Muir's work and friendship, President Theodore Roosevelt pressed the United States Congress for the Antiquities Act and the National Monuments Act in 1906, which gave the president of the United States the power to proclaim a region a national monument. Through this process, Congress created Yosemite National Park in 1906. Using the same Act in 2000, and citing John Muir, President Bill Clinton established the Giant Sequoia National Monument in the California Sequoia National Park.

Muir was not always successful in his campaigns to defend nature against modification and exploitation. In 1913, the U.S. Congress permitted the state of California, despite Muir's fierce opposition, to dam the Tuolumne River in Yosemite and flood the Hetch Hetchy Valley, a nearly exact, although smaller, replica of the Yosemite Valley to supply drinking water to San Francisco. Although the project was completed in 1923, the Sierra Club is still fighting to remove the dam and restore the valley. The Sierra Club, following

The California state quarter bears a figure of John Muir and Yosemite Valley, selected by Govenor Arnold Schwarzenegger on March 29, 2004. The artist, Garrett Burke, calls it John Muir/ Yosemite. AP IMAGES

in Muir's footsteps, continues to oppose threats to the natural environment. In 2005, the George W. Bush administration decided to permit logging inside the area President Clinton had designated the Giant Sequoia Monument, and the Sierra Club moved to oppose the decision through a court challenge.

In his books, Muir conveyed his desire to instill in others a similar devotion; he succeeded so well that even in the twenty-first century he remains highly honored. Forests have been named after him, and so have three kinds of plants. Two U.S. stamps have been issued in his honor. The California legislature has declared April 21 John Muir Day, and the California state quarter issued in 2005 bears his likeness.

Muir's work and legacy are not only honored in the United States. The John Muir Trust of Scotland also works to celebrate, explore, and protect the natural landscape and, in 1997, established the John Muir Award to encourage the continuation of his work.

FURTHER RESOURCES
Books

Ehrlich, Gretel. *John Muir: Nature's Visionary.* Washington, D.C.: National Geographic Society, 2000.

Holmes, Steven J. *The Young John Muir: An Environmental Biography.* Madison, WI: University of Wisconsin Press, 1999.

Miller, Sally M., ed. *John Muir in Historical Perspective*. New York: Peter Lang, 1999.

Web sites

The John Muir Project of Earth Island Institute. <http://www.johnmuirproject.org> (accessed March 16, 2006).

"John Muir Exhibit." *The Sierra Club*. <http://www.sierraclub.org/john_muir_exhibit> (accessed March 16, 2006).

"The Excursion"

Poem

By: William Wordsworth

Date: 1888

Source: Wordsworth, William. "The Excursion." 1888.

About the Author: English romantic poet William Wordsworth (1770–1850) expressed in his poetry a faith that the experience of the natural environment was essential for the health and wholesomeness of the human spirit. He believed nature was the source of a moral and humane disposition and of sociable behavior. He wrote about his own encounters with the natural world and its invigorating effect upon him as a man and as a poet. He also chronicled the rustic life and the troubles that country people living in England's Lake District experienced during the growth of industrial cities. Along with his friend, Samuel Taylor Coleridge (1772–1834), Wordsworth revolutionized English poetry with the publication of "Lyrical Ballads" in 1798. In their poetry, the formal language of eighteenth-century English verse is replaced by the common speech of ordinary people as distilled through the sensibilities of the poets. Wordsworth lived through the French Revolution and the Napoleonic Wars and in his youth shared the fervor for revolutionary change that marked the generation of the 1790s. He was moved not only by the call of liberty, equality, and brotherhood, but also by outrage against the degradation of nature and of human values, which he saw resulting from the onset of the Industrial Revolution.

INTRODUCTION

For Wordsworth, the outrage committed against nature was not the result of the advance of industrial knowledge or technology itself but the immorality of

William Wordsworth. © BETTMANN/CORBIS

"gain," which governed it. When Wordsworth used the word "gain," he meant the force of greed that puts the exploitation of people and nature above a respect for their living spiritual value. He was pained by the desecration of nature and humanity resulting from the way the countryside was despoiled to make factories and the ugly towns that housed people who were stripped of their humanity when they became laborers in the factories. The factories trammeled upon natural beauty, and the workers were excluded from its enjoyment and the beneficial effects that come from living in nature, working in it, and communing with it. However, Wordsworth did not call for the destruction of industry. He hoped, as can be seen in "The Excursion," rather, that people might learn to use industrial knowledge wisely, creating a well-tempered harmony between nature and industry. He hoped that men might be "strengthened, yet not dazzled, by the might" of the new dominion over nature they were acquiring. Eleven years after the optimism expressed in "Steamboats," however, Wordsworth expressed in his sonnet that he was dispirited when he saw a railroad brought into his beloved home country, England's Lake District. He now saw only "blight," "ruthless change," and a "rash assault" against nature and the dreams mankind project onto nature.

PRIMARY SOURCE

The Excursion

Meanwhile, at social Industry's command,
How quick, how vast an increase! From the germ
Of some poor hamlet, rapidly produced
Here a huge town, continuous and compact,
Hiding the face of earth for leagues—and there,
Where not a habitation stood before,
Abodes of men irregularly massed
Like trees in forests,—spread through spacious tracts,
O'er which the smoke of unremitting fires
Hangs permanent, and plentiful as wreaths
Of vapour glittering in the morning sun.
And, wheresoe'er the traveller turns his steps,
He sees the barren wilderness erased,
Or disappearing; triumph that proclaims
How much the mild Directress of the plough
Owes to alliance with these new-born arts!
—Hence is the wide sea peopled,—hence the shores
Of Britain are resorted to by ships
Freighted from every climate of the world
With the world's choicest produce: Hence that sum
Of keels that rest within her crowded ports,
Or ride at anchor in her sounds and bays;
That animating spectacle of sails
That, through her inland regions, to and fro
Pass with the respirations of the tide,
Perpetual, multitudinous! . . .

. . . I grieve, when on the darker side
Of this great change I look; and there behold
Such outrage done to nature as compels
The indignant power to justify herself;
Yea, to avenge her violated rights,
For England's bane.—When soothing darkness spreads
O'er hill and vale, "the Wanderer thus expressed
His recollections, "and the punctual stars,
While all things else are gathering to their homes,
Advance, and in the firmament of heaven
Glitter—but undisturbing, undisturbed;
As if their silent company were charged
With peaceful admonitions for the heart
Of all-beholding Man, earth's thoughtful lord;
Then, in full many a region, once like this
The assured domain of calm simplicity
And pensive quiet, an unnatural light
Prepared for never-resting Labour's eyes
Breaks from a many-windowed fabric huge;
And at the appointed hour a bell is heard—
Of harsher import than the curfew-knoll
That spake the Norman Conqueror's stern behest—
A local summons to unceasing toil!
Disgorged are now the ministers of day;
And, as they issue from the illumined pile,
A fresh band meets them, at the crowded door—
And in the courts—and where the rumbling stream,
That turns the multitude of dizzy wheels,
Glares, like a troubled spirit, in its bed

Among the rocks below. Men, maidens, youths,
Mother and little children, boys and girls,
Enter, and each the wonted task resumes
Within this temple, where is offered up
To Gain, the master idol of the realm,
Perpetual sacrifice. Even thus of old
Our ancestors, within the still domain
Of vast cathedral or conventual church,
Their vigils kept; where tapers day and night
On the dim altar burned continually,
In token that the House was evermore
Watching to God. Religious men were they;
Nor would their reason, tutored to aspire
Above this transitory world, allow
That there should pass a moment of the year,
When in their land the Almighty's service ceased.

Triumph who will in these profaner rites
Which we, a generation self-extolled,
As zealously perform! I cannot share
His proud complacency:—yet do I exult,
Casting reserve away, exult to see
An intellectual mastery exercised
O'er the blind elements; a purpose given,
A perseverance fed; almost a soul
Imparted—to brute matter. I rejoice,
Measuring the force of those gigantic powers
That, by the thinking mind, have been compelled
To serve the will of feeble-bodied Man.
For with the sense of admiration blends
The animating hope that time may come
When, strengthened, yet not dazzled, by the might
Of this dominion over nature gained,
Men of all lands shall exercise the same
In due proportion to their country's need;
Learning, though late, that all true glory rests,
All praise, all safety, and all happiness,
Upon the moral law. . . .

SIGNIFICANCE

Wordsworth stands at the head of a line of English poets, writers, and thinkers for whom nature and the appreciation of nature represent the fundamentally benevolent shaping forces of the human spirit. They see the degradation of nature as harmful to the quality of the development of humanity. This interconnection between the beauty of the natural world, the rectitude of the human spirit, and the strength of its development is what supports their environmental concerns. In his verse, Wordsworth gave this relationship voice and authority, making it a foundation of Romantic thought. It was a vision transmitted from Wordsworth to the novelist George Eliot (Marian Evans) as she expressed it in *Silas Marner*, her tale of the beneficial influences of living a simple life close to nature. It was the basis for the indignant vision of an industrialism that violates the essential relationship between people and nature that fired Charles Dickens in the writing of *Hard Times.* It is at the core of the resonant sermons of the late-Victorian John Ruskin—who met Wordsworth in 1839—when Ruskin fulminates against the Industrial Revolution's destruction of the natural world. Through Ruskin, Wordsworth influenced the sensibility of the great Indian political leader, Mohandas Gandhi (1869–1948). To many in the twenty-first century, Wordsworth's adoration of nature and reluctant acceptance of a tamed technology may seem quaint. However, it is exactly Wordsworth's understanding of the importance of nature and the limitations which ought to be imposed upon industrial technology and commercial incursions into nature that either guide or underpin a great deal of present-day environmental thinking and action.

FURTHER RESOURCES

Books

Bloom, Harold, and Neil Heims, eds. *William Wordsworth.* Philadelphia: Chelsea House Publishers, 2003.

Periodicals

Miall, David S. "The Alps Deferred: Wordsworth at the Simplon Pass." *European Romantic Review* 9 (1998): 87–102.

Web sites

The Wordsworth Trust. <http://newsite.wordsworthtrust. org.uk> (accessed March 15, 2006).

"Expedition of 1898–1902"

Book excerpt

By: Robert E. Peary

Date: 1907

Source: Peary, Robert E. "Expedition of 1898–1902." *Nearest the Pole.* New York: Doubleday, Page & Company, 1907.

About the Author: Robert E. Peary was born in Pennsylvania, but moved with his mother to southern Maine after the death of his father. He attended Bowdoin College and earned a degree in civil engineering. Peary then joined the U.S. Naval Civil Engineer Corps in 1881 and began work on an unrealized canal project in Nicaragua. The project,

however, led to his interest in exploring Greenland. In the 1890s, he took several trips to Greenland in preparation for his expeditions to the North Pole. He reached the North Pole on April 6, 1909, on his third expedition.

INTRODUCTION

Peary was born on May 6, 1856 in Cresson, Pennsylvania. After graduating from college, he worked as a town surveyor for Fryeburg, Maine. In 1881, Peary joined the U.S. Navy Civil Engineers Corps. He began work on an Inter-Oceanic Ship Canal Project in Central America and was tasked to explore the interior of Nicaragua. During this time, he was introduced to a fellow civil engineer, Matthew Henson, who would later become his assistant during his exploration of Greenland and his expeditions to the North Pole. He was also introduced to the exploration of Greenland in search for a northern passage by British explorers.

By 1886, Peary made his first expedition into Greenland and asserted that Greenland was an island and that the North Pole lay beyond Greenland, not within it. On this expedition, Peary also succeeded in reaching further inland and establishing a new northern limit. Supply shortages forced his team to return prematurely. He made several trips to explore Greenland during the 1890s and determined that the "American route" to the North Pole by way of Ellesmere Island was more viable than a route previously followed through Greenland. During these expeditions of Greenland, Peary also discovered three large pieces of meteorites. One 34-ton (31-metric-ton) meteorite was called Ahnighito and is now housed at the Hayden Planetarium in New York's American Museum of Natural History. Peary's explorations during the 1890s prepared him for his expeditions to the North Pole in several ways.

In 1897, Peary obtained a leave of absence from the U.S. Navy in order to organize and lead an expedition to the North Pole. After a year of preparation, he set out in 1898 but was forced to return in 1902 after losing three toes to frostbite. In 1905, Peary made his second attempt to reach the North Pole. This expedition began from the ship *Roosevelt*, which allowed Peary to sail further into Arctic waters, but was also unsuccessful due to supply shortages. However, he did reach the farthest point north and made it within 175 miles (282 kilometers) of the North Pole.

On March 1, 1909, Peary, accompanied by twenty-three men, 133 dogs, and nineteen sleds, set out from Ellesmere Island. Previous expeditions had led Peary to the conclusion that traveling in late winter when the ice was firmer would reap greater success. In addition, Peary planned the expedition to be completed in stages. Groups of men would advance and lay supplies and then retreat. On April 6, 1909, six men reached the North Pole: Peary, his assistant, Matthew Hensar and four Inuit—Oatah, Egingwah, Seegloo, and Ookeah.

When Peary returned to the United States, he was faced with controversy. Fellow explorer Frederick Cook claimed that he had reached the pole a year before. Cook, who once accompanied Peary on an expedition of Greenland, made his claim days prior to Peary's announcement. In 1911, a Congressional investigation discovered that two of the Inuit who accompanied Cook claimed that his photographic evidence was a fake. However, even with the official declaration of being first to reach the North Pole, controversy remained. Many questioned whether Peary could actually reach the pole in the time frame documented. Subsequent recreations of his expedition have proved that the trek was possible.

◼ PRIMARY SOURCE

. . . June 28th, a sufficient number of dogs had recovered from the effect of their work to enable me to make up two teams, and Henson was sent with these, four of the natives and a dory, to make his way to Etah and communicate with the summer ship immediately on her arrival, so that her time would not be wasted even should the *Windward* be late in getting out of the ice.

June 29th, I started with two sledges and three natives to complete my survey of Princess Marie and Buchanan bays, and make a *reconnaissance* to the westward from the head of the former. My feet, which I had been favouring since my return from Conger, were now in fair condition, only a very small place on the right one remaining unhealed. Travelling and working at night, and sleeping during the day, I advanced to Princess Marie Bay, crossed the narrow neck of Bache Peninsula, and camped on the morning of July 4th near the head of the northern arm of Buchanan Bay. Hardly was the tent set up when a bear was seen out in the bay, and we immediately went in pursuit, and in a short time had him killed. He proved to be a fine large specimen.

While after the bear, I noticed a herd of musk-oxen a few miles up the valley, and after the bear had been brought into camp and skinned, and we had snatched a few hours' sleep, we went after the musk-oxen. Eight of these were secured, including two fine bulls and two live calves, the latter following us back to camp of their own accord. The next three days were occupied in getting the

beef to camp. I then crossed to the southern arm of Buchanan Bay, securing another musk-ox. Returning to Princess Marie Bay, I camped on the morning of the 14th at the glacier, which fills the head of Sawyer Bay.

During the following six days I ascended the glacier, crossed the ice cap to its western side, and from elevations of from 4,000 to 4,700 feet, looked down upon the snow-free western side of Ellesmere Land, and out into an ice-free fiord, extending some fifty miles to the northwest. The season here was at least a month earlier than on the east side, and the general appearance of the country reminded me of the Whale Sound region of Greenland. Clear weather for part of one day enabled me to take a series of angles, then fog and rain and snow settled down upon us. Through this I steered by compass back to and down the glacier, camping on the 21st in my camp of the 15th.

The return from here to the ship was somewhat arduous, owing to the rotten condition of the one-year ice, and the deep pools and canals of water on the surface of the old floes. These presented the alternative of making endless detours or wading through water often waist deep. During seven days our clothing, tent, sleeping-gear and food were constantly saturated. The *Windward* was reached on the 28th of July.

In spite of the discomforts and hardships of this trip, incident to the lateness of the season, I felt repaid by its results. In addition to completing the notes requisite for a chart of the Princess-Marie-Buchanan-Bay region, I had been fortunate in crossing the Ellesmere Land ice-cap, and looking upon the western coast. The game secured during this trip comprised 1 polar bear, 7 musk-oxen, 3 oogsook, and 14 seals.

When I returned to the *Windward* she was round in the eastern side of Franklin Pierce Bay. A party had left two days before with dogs, sledge and boat, in an attempt to meet me and supply provisions. Three days were occupied in communicating with them and getting them and their outfit on board. The *Windward* then moved back to her winter berth at Cape D'Urville, took the dogs on board, and on the morning of Wednesday, August 2d, got under way.

During the next five days we advanced some twelve miles, when a southerly wind jammed the ice and drifted us north, abreast of the starting point. Early Tuesday morning, the 8th, we got another start, and the ice gradually slackening, we kept under way, reached open water a little south of Cape Albert, and arrived at Cape Sabine at 10 P.M.

At Cape Sabine I landed a cache and then steamed over to Etah, arriving at 5 A.M. of the 9th. Here we found mail and learned that the *Diana* returned, and I had the great pleasure of taking Secretary Bridgman, commanding the Club's Expedition, by the hand.

The year had been one of hard and continuous work for the entire party. In that time I obtained the material for an authentic map of the Buchanan-Bay-Bache-Peninsula-Princess-Marie-Bay region; crossed the Ellesmere Land ice-cap to the west side of that land, established a continuous line of caches from Cape Sabine to Fort Conger, containing some fourteen tons of supplies; rescued the original records and private papers of the Greely Expedition; fitted Fort Conger as a base for future work, and familiarized myself and party with the entire region as far north as Cape Beechey.

With the exception of the supplies at Cape D'Urville, all the provisions, together with the current supplies and dog-food (the latter an excessive item), had been transported by sledge.

Finally, discouraging as was the accident to my feet, I was satisfied, since my effort to reach the northwest coast of Greenland from Fort Conger in May, proved that the season was one of extremely unfavourable ice conditions north of Cape Beechey, and I doubt, even if the accident had not occurred, whether I should have found it advisable on reaching Cape Hecla to attempt the last stage of the journey.

My decision not to attempt to winter at Fort Conger was arrived at after careful consideration. Two things controlled this decision: First, the uncertainty of carrying dogs through the winter, and, second, the comparative facility with which the distance from Etah to Fort Conger can be covered with light sledges.

After the rendezvous with the *Diana* I went on board the latter ship, and visited all the native settlements, gathering skins and material for clothing and sledge equipment, and recruiting my dog-teams.

The *Windward* was sent walrus-hunting during my absence. The *Diana* also assisted in this work. August 25th the *Windward* sailed for home, followed on the 28th by the *Diana*, after landing me with my party, equipment, and additional supplies at Etah.

The *Diana* seemed to have gathered in and taken with her all the fine weather, leaving us a sequence of clouds, wind, fog, and snow, which continued with scarcely a break for weeks.

After her departure the work before me presented itself as follows: To protect the provisions, construct our winter quarters, then begin building sledges, and grinding walrus meat for dog pemmican for the spring campaign.

During the first month a number of walrus were killed from our boats off the mouth of the fiord; then the usual Arctic winter settled down upon us, its monotony varied only by the visits of the natives, occasional deer-hunts, and a December sledge journey to the Eskimo settlements in Whale Sound as far as Kangerdlooksoah. In this nine days'

trip some 240 miles were covered in six marches, the first and the last marches being of 60 to 70 miles. I returned to Etah just in time to escape a severe snowstorm, which stopped communication between Etah and the other Eskimo settlements completely, until I sent a party with snowshoes and a specially constructed sledge, carrying no load, and manned by double teams of dogs, to break the trail.

During my absence some of my natives had crossed to Mr. Stein's place at Sabine, and January 9th I began the season's work by starting a few sledge-loads of dog-food for Cape Sabine, for use of my teams in the spring journey. From this time on, as the open water in Smith Sound permitted, more dog-food was sent to Sabine, and as the light gradually increased some of my Eskimos were kept constantly at Sonntag Bay, some twenty miles to the South, on the lookout for walrus.

My programme for the spring work was to move three divisions of sledges north as far as Conger, the first to be in charge of Henson; while I brought up the rear with the third.

From Fort Conger I should send back a number of Eskimos; retain some at Conger; and with others proceed north via Hecla or the north point of Greenland, as circumstances might determine.

I wanted to start the first division on the 15th of February, the second a week later, and leave with the third March 1st; but a severe storm, breaking up the ice between Etah and Littleton Island, delayed the departure of the first division of seven sledges until the 19th.

The second division of six sledges started on the 26th, and March 4th I left with the rear division of nine sledges. Three marches carried us to Cape Sabine, along the curving northern edge of the north water. Here a northerly gale, with heavy drift, detained me for two days. Three more marches in a temperature of 40° F brought me to the house at Cape D'Urville. Records here informed me that the first division had been detained here a week by stormy weather, and the second division had left but two days before my arrival. I had scarcely arrived when two of Henson's Eskimos came in from Richardson Bay, where one of them had severely injured his leg by falling under a sledge. One day was spent at D'Urville drying our clothing, and on the 13th I got away on the trail of the other divisions with seven sledges, the injured man going to Sabine with the supporting party.

I hoped to reach Cape Louis Napoleon on this march, but the going was too heavy, and I was obliged to camp in Dobbin Bay, about five miles short of the cape. The next day I hoped on starting to reach Cape Fraser, but was again disappointed, a severe windstorm compelling me to halt a little south of Hayes Point, and hurriedly build snow igloos in the midst of a blinding drift. All that night and the next day, and the next night, the storm continued. An early start was made on the 16th, and in calm but very thick weather. We pushed on to Cape Fraser. Here we encountered the wind and drift full in our faces, and violent, making our progress from here to Cape Norton Shaw along the ice-foot very trying.

The going from here across Scoresby and Richardson bays was not worse than the year before; and from Cape Wilkes to Cape Lawrence the same as we had always found it. These two marches were made in clear but bitterly windy weather.

Another severe southerly gale held us prisoners at Cape Lawrence for a day. The 20th was an equally cruel day, with wind still savage in its strength, but the question of food for my dogs gave me no choice but to try to advance. At the end of four hours we were forced to burrow into a snow-bank for shelter, where we remained till the next morning.

In three more marches we reached Cape Leopold von Buch. Two more days of good weather brought us to a point a few miles north of Cape Defosse. Here we were stopped by another furious gale with drifting snow, which prisoned us for two nights and a day.

The wind was still bitter in our faces when we again got under way the morning of the 27th, the ice-foot became worse and worse up to Cape Cracroft, where we were forced down into the narrow tidal joint, at the base of the ice-foot; this path was a very narrow and tortuous one, frequently interrupted, and was extremely trying one men and sledges. Cape Lieber was reached on this march. At this camp the wind blew savagely all night, and in the morning I waited for it to moderate before attempting to cross Lady Franklin Bay. While thus waiting the returning Eskimos of the first and second divisions came in. They brought the very welcome news of the killing of 21 musk-oxen close to Conger. They also reported the wind out in the bay as less severe than at the Cape.

I immediately got under way and reached Conger just before midnight of the 28th—24 days from Etah—during six of which I was held up by storms.

The first division had arrived four days and the second two days earlier. During this journey there had been the usual annoying delays of broken sledges, and I had lost numbers of dogs.

The process of breaking in the tendons and muscles of my feet to their new relations, and the callousing of the amputation scars, in this, first serious demand upon them, had been disagreeable, but was, I believed, final and complete. I felt that I had no reason to complain.

SIGNIFICANCE

Peary's expeditions accomplished more than reaching the North Pole. Peary made detailed scientific observations of Greenland's geography, tides, and flora and fauna that prepared him for his final expedition to the Pole. Peary also discovered three meteorites, including one of the world's largest. In addition, Peary also made friends with the indigenous people and observed their techniques to endure the harsh temperatures. Previous British explorers held the indigenous peoples in lower standards, inhibiting the explorers' ability to learn from the natives. Peary's ability to learn from them allowed him to make necessary changes to equipment in order to survive the harsh weather.

FURTHER RESOURCES

Periodicals

"Robert Peary." *American Science Leaders* (January 1, 2001).

Web sites

Arlington National Cemetery. "Robert Edwin Peary: Rear Admiral, United States Navy." <http://www.arlington cemetery.net/roberted.htm> (accessed February 25, 2006).

PBS.org. "American Experience. Robert Peary: To the Top of the World." <http://www.pbs.org/wgbh/amex/ice/sfeature/peary.html> (accessed February 25, 2006).

My First Summer in the Sierra

Book excerpt

By: John Muir

Date: 1911

Source: Muir, John. *My First Summer in the Sierra.* Boston: Houghton Mifflin, 1911.

About the Author: Naturalist John Muir (1838–1914) was a Scottish-born wilderness explorer, best known for his adventures in the glaciers of Alaska and California's Sierra Nevada. Muir feared that the United States as he had witnessed it would gradually become overdeveloped, and he wrote extensively about the importance of protecting the natural landscape and wildlife of the country. His work was instrumental in the creation of the national parks, including Yellowstone, Yosemite, Mount Rainier, and Grand Canyon National Park, and his writing inspired many of the conservation programs enacted by President Theodore Roosevelt, including the first National Monuments by Presidential Proclamation. Muir also co-founded the Sierra Club in 1892, providing a formal organization for environmental activists to continue working for the preservation of the nation's mountain ranges.

INTRODUCTION

Published in 1911, only three years before his death, Muir's *My First Summer in the Sierra* recalls his first trip to the range more than forty years earlier. Muir was an amateur naturalist, and his descriptions of rocks and vegetation show a command of basic mineralogy and botany. Likewise, his description of the history of a raindrop shows an understanding of the hydrologic cycle, particularly the role of stored groundwater in the maintenance of perennial stream flow. His travelogue contains a mixture of high adventure and studious observations of the flora, fauna, and geology of the Yosemite region. He was the first to suggest that Yosemite Valley is the product of glaciation. Before Muir had arrived in California, prominent California geologist Josiah Whitney had visited Yosemite and inferred that the steep-walled valley was a graben, the geological term for a fault-bounded block of rock lowered relative to the blocks on either side. This was in part because Whitney recognized that Yosemite was unlike the well-known glaciated valleys of Europe. Several years of traveling through the Yosemite region, however, convinced Muir that the valley was carved by glaciation. The controversy was settled by a 1930 U.S. Geological Survey report that concluded Yosemite Valley owed its unique shape to a combination of glacial and river erosion of fractured rocks. Thus, although its shape is not solely the result of glaciation, glaciers played an important part in the history of Yosemite Valley.

Although Yosemite Valley was no doubt known to Native Americans for centuries, it was not entered by non-Native Americans until 1851, two years after the California gold rush began in 1849. News of its scenic beauty spread and the valley was soon the site of homes, hotels, orchards, and heavily grazed meadows. President Abraham Lincoln ceded Yosemite Valley to the State of California in 1864 so that it could be preserved in the public trust. Although it was not officially a national park (Yellowstone National Park would become the world's first national park in 1872), it was the first time that a tract of land had been reserved by a national government as a park for public enjoyment. Despite the protected status of the Yosemite Valley, heavy grazing threatened meadows around the protected area. Largely as the result of Muir's advocacy, a larger Yosemite National Park

was created in 1890 and passed completely into federal control in 1906. Muir was a co-founder of the Sierra Club, which was created to advocate the protection of Yosemite Valley from grazing interests, and served as its president until his death in 1914.

■ PRIMARY SOURCE

MY FIRST SUMMER IN THE SIERRA

Chapter 5: The Yosemite July 15. —Followed the Mono Trail up the eastern rim of the basin nearly to its summit, then turned off southward to a small shallow valley that extends to the edge of the Yosemite, which we reached about noon, and encamped. After luncheon I made haste to high ground, and from the top of the ridge on the west side of Indian Cañon gained the noblest view of the summit peaks I have ever yet enjoyed. Nearly all the upper basin of the Merced was displayed, with its sublime domes and cañons, dark upsweeping forests, and glorious array of white peaks deep in the sky, every feature glowing, radiating beauty that pours into our flesh and bones like heat rays from fire. Sunshine over all; no breath of wind to stir the brooding calm. Never before had I seen so glorious a landscape, so boundless an affluence of sublime mountain beauty. The most extravagant description I might give of this view to any one who has not seen similar landscapes with his own eyes would not so much as hint its grandeur and the spiritual glow that covered it. I shouted and gesticulated in a wild burst of ecstasy, much to the astonishment of St. Bernard Carlo, who came running up to me, manifesting in his intelligent eyes a puzzled concern that was very ludicrous, which had the effect of bringing me to my senses. A brown bear, too, it would seem, had been a spectator of the show I had made of myself, for I had gone but a few yards when I started one from a thicket of brush. He evidently considered me dangerous, for he ran away very fast, tumbling over the tops of the tangled manzanita bushes in his haste. Carlo drew back, with his ears depressed as if afraid, and kept looking me in the face, as if expecting me to pursue and shoot, for he had seen many a bear battle in his day.

Following the ridge which made a gradual descent to the south, I came at length to the brow of that massive cliff that stands between Indian Cañon and Yosemite Falls, and here the far-famed valley came suddenly into view throughout almost its whole extent. The noble walls— sculptured into endless variety of domes and gables, spires and battlements and plain mural precipices—all a tremble with the thunder tones of the falling water. The level bottom seemed to be dressed like a garden,—sunny meadows here and there, and groves of pine and oak; the river of Mercy sweeping in majesty through the midst of them and flashing back the sunbeams. The great Tissiack, or Half-Dome, rising at the upper end of the valley to a height of nearly a mile, is nobly proportioned and life-like, the most impressive of all the rocks, holding the eye in devout admiration, calling it back again and again from falls or meadows, or even the mountains beyond—marvelous cliffs, marvelous in sheer dizzy depth and sculpture, types of endurance. Thousands of years have they stood in the sky exposed to rain, snow, frost, earthquake and avalanche, yet they still wear the bloom of youth.

I rambled along the valley rim to the westward; most of it is rounded off on the very brink, so that it is not easy to find places where one may look clear down the face of the wall to the bottom. When such places were found, and I had cautiously set my feet and drawn my body erect, I could not help fearing a little that the rock might split off and let me down, and what a down—more than three thousand feet. Still my limbs did not tremble, nor did I feel the least uncertainty as to the reliance to be placed on them. My only fear was that a flake of the granite, which in some places showed joints more or less open and running parallel with the face of the cliff, might give way. After withdrawing from such places, excited with the view I had got, I would say to myself, "Now don't go out on the verge again." But in the face of Yosemite scenery cautious remonstrance is vain; under its spell one's body seems to go where it likes with a will over which we seem to have scarce any control.

After a mile or so of this memorable cliff work I approached Yosemite Creek, admiring its easy, graceful, confident gestures as it comes bravely forward in its narrow channel, singing the last of its mountain songs on its way to its fate—a few rods more over the shining granite, then down half a mile in snowy foam to another world, to be lost in the Merced, where climate, vegetation, inhabitants, all are different. Emerging from its last gorge, it glides in wide lace-like rapids down a smooth incline into a pool where it seems to rest and compose its gray, agitated waters before taking the grand plunge, then slowly slipping over the lip of the pool basin, it descends another glossy slope with rapidly accelerated speed to the brink of the tremendous cliff, and with sublime, fateful confidence springs out free in the air.

I took off my shoes and stockings and worked my way cautiously down alongside the rushing flood, keeping my feet and hands pressed firmly on the polished rock. The booming, roaring water, rushing past close to my head, was very exciting. I had expected that the sloping apron would terminate with the perpendicular wall of the valley, and that from the foot of it, where it is less steeply inclined, I should be able to lean far enough out to see the forms and behavior of the fall all the way down to the bottom. But I found that there was yet another small brow over which I

could not see, and which appeared to be too steep for mortal feet. Scanning it keenly, I discovered a narrow shelf about three inches wide on the very brink, just wide enough for a rest for one's heels. But there seemed to be no way of reaching it over so steep a brow. At length, after careful scrutiny of the surface, I found an irregular edge of a flake of the rock some distance back from the margin of the torrent. If I was to get down to the brink at all that rough edge, which might offer slight finger holds, was the only way. But the slope beside it looked dangerously smooth and steep, and the swift roaring flood beneath, overhead, and beside me was very nerve-trying. I therefore concluded not to venture farther, but did nevertheless. Tufts of artemisia were growing in clefts of the rock near by, and I filled my mouth with the bitter leaves, hoping they might help to prevent giddiness. Then, with a caution not known in ordinary circumstances, I crept down safely to the little ledge, got my heels well planted on it, then shuffled in a horizontal direction twenty or thirty feet until close to the outplunging current, which, by the time it had descended thus far, was already white. Here I obtained a perfectly free view down into the heart of the snowy, chanting throng of comet-like streamers, into which the body of the fall soon separates.

While perched on that narrow niche I was not distinctly conscious of danger. The tremendous grandeur of the fall in form and sound and motion, acting at close range, smothered the sense of fear, and in such places one's body takes keen care for safety on its own account. How long I remained down there, or how I returned, I can hardly tell. Anyhow I had a glorious time, and got back to camp about dark, enjoying triumphant exhilaration soon followed by dull weariness. Hereafter I'll try to keep from such extravagant, nerve-straining places. Yet such a day is well worth venturing for. My first view of the High Sierra, first view looking down into Yosemite, the death song of Yosemite Creek, and its flight over the vast cliff, each one of these is of itself enough for a great life-long landscape fortune—a most memorable day of days—enjoyment enough to kill if that were possible.

July 16. —My enjoyments yesterday afternoon, especially at the head of the fall, were too great for good sleep. Kept starting up last night in a nervous tremor, half awake, fancying that the foundation of the mountain we were camped on had given way and was falling into Yosemite Valley. In vain I roused myself to make a new beginning for sound sleep. The nerve strain had been too great, and again and again I dreamed I was rushing through the air above a glorious avalanche of water and rocks. One time, springing to my feet, I said, "This time it is real—all must die, and where could mountaineer find a more glorious death!"

Left camp soon after sunrise for an all day ramble eastward. Crossed the head of Indian Basin, forested with *Abies magnifica*, underbrush mostly *Ceanothus cordulatus* and manzanita, a mixture not easily trampled over or penetrated, for the *ceanothus* is thorny and grows in dense snow-pressed masses, and the manzanita has exceedingly crooked, stubborn branches. From the head of the cañon continued on past North Dome into the basin of Dome or Porcupine Creek. Here are many fine meadows imbedded in the woods, gay with *Lilium parvum* and its companions; the elevation, about eight thousand feet, seems to be best suited for it—saw specimens that were a foot or two higher than my head. Had more magnificent views of the upper mountains, and of the great South Dome, said to be the grandest rock in the world. Well it may be, since it is of such noble dimensions and sculpture. A wonderfully impressive monument, its lines exquisite in fineness, and though sublime in size, is finished like the finest work of art, and seems to be alive.

July 17. —A new camp was made today in a magnificent silver fir grove at the head of a small stream that flows into Yosemite by way of Indian Cañon. Here we intend to stay several weeks, —a fine location from which to make excursions about the great valley and its fountains. Glorious days I'll have sketching, pressing plants, studying the wonderful topography, and the wild animals, our happy fellow mortals and neighbors. But the vast mountains in the distance, shall I ever know them, shall I be allowed to enter into their midst and dwell with them?

We were pelted about noon by a short, heavy rainstorm, sublime thunder reverberating among the mountains and cañons, —some strokes near, crashing, ringing in the tense crisp air with startling keenness, while the distant peaks loomed gloriously through the cloud fringes and sheets of rain. Now the storm is past, and the fresh washed air is full of the essences of the flower gardens and groves. Winter storms in Yosemite must be glorious. May I see them!

Have got my bed made in our new camp, —plushy, sumptuous, and deliciously fragrant, most of it magnifica fir plumes, of course, with a variety of sweet flowers in the pillow. Hope to sleep to-night without tottering nerve-dreams. Watched a deer eating ceanothus leaves and twigs.

July 18. —Slept pretty well; the valley walls did not seem to fall, though I still fancied myself at the brink, alongside the white, plunging flood, especially when half asleep. Strange the danger of that adventure should be more troublesome now that I am in the bosom of the peaceful woods, a mile or more from the fall, than it was while I was on the brink of it.

Bears seem to be common here, judging by their tracks. About noon we had another rain-storm with keen startling thunder, the metallic, ringing, clashing, clanging notes gradually fading into low bass rolling and muttering in the distance. For a few minutes the rain came in a grand torrent like a waterfall, then hail; some of the hailstones an inch in diameter, hard, icy, and irregular in form, like those oftentimes seen in Wisconsin. Carlo watched them with intelligent astonishment as they came pelting and thrashing through the quivering branches of the trees. The cloud scenery sublime. Afternoon calm, sunful, and clear, with delicious freshness and fragrance from the firs and flowers and steaming ground.

July 19. —Watching the daybreak and sunrise. The pale rose and purple sky changing softly to daffodil yellow and white, sunbeams pouring through the passes between the peaks and over the Yosemite domes, making their edges burn; the silver firs in the middle ground catching the glow on their spiry tops, and our camp grove fills and thrills with the glorious light. Everything awakening alert and joyful; the birds begin to stir and innumerable insect people. Deer quietly withdraw into leafy hiding-places in the chaparral; the dew vanishes, flowers spread their petals, every pulse beats high, every life cell rejoices, the very rocks seem to thrill with life. The whole landscape glows like a human face in a glory of enthusiasm, and the blue sky, pale around the horizon, bends peacefully down over all like one vast flower.

About noon, as usual, big bossy cumuli began to grow above the forest, and the rain storm pouring from them is the most imposing I have yet seen. The silvery zigzag lightning lances are longer than usual, and the thunder gloriously impressive, keen, crashing, intensely concentrated, speaking with such tremendous energy it would seem that an entire mountain is being shattered at every stroke, but probably only a few trees are being shattered, many of which I have seen on my walks hereabouts strewing the ground. At last the clear ringing strokes are succeeded by deep low tones that grow gradually fainter as they roll afar into the recesses of the echoing mountains, where they seem to be welcomed home. Then another and another peal, or rather crashing, splintering stroke, follows in quick succession, perchance splitting some giant pine or fir from top to bottom into long rails and slivers, and scattering them to all points of the compass. Now comes the rain, with corresponding extravagant grandeur, covering the ground high and low with a sheet of flowing water, a transparent film fitted like a skin upon the rugged anatomy of the landscape, making the rocks glitter and glow, gathering in the ravines, flooding the streams, and making them shout and boom in reply to the thunder.

How interesting to trace the history of a single raindrop! It is not long, geologically speaking, as we have seen, since the first raindrops fell on the newborn leafless Sierra landscapes. How different the lot of these falling now! Happy the showers that fall on so fair a wilderness, —scarce a single drop can fail to find a beautiful spot, —on the tops of the peaks, on the shining glacier pavements, on the great smooth domes, on forests and gardens and brushy moraines, plashing, glinting, pattering, laving. Some go to the high snowy fountains to swell their well-saved stores; some into the lakes, washing the mountain windows, patting their smooth glassy levels, making dimples and bubbles and spray; some into the water-falls and cascades, as if eager to join in their dance and song and beat their foam yet finer; good luck and good work for the happy mountain raindrops, each one of them a high waterfall in itself, descending from the cliffs and hollows of the clouds to the cliffs and hollows of the rocks, out of the sky-thunder into the thunder of the falling rivers. Some, falling on meadows and bogs, creep silently out of sight to the grass roots, hiding softly as in a nest, slipping, oozing hither, thither, seeking and finding their appointed work. Some, descending through the spires of the woods, sift spray through the shining needles, whispering peace and good cheer to each one of them. Some drops with happy aim glint on the sides of crystals, —quartz, hornblende, garnet, zircon, tourmaline, feldspar, —patter on grains of gold and heavy way-worn nuggets; some, with blunt plap-plap and low bass drumming, fall on the broad leaves of veratrum, saxifrage, cypripedium. Some happy drops fall straight into the cups of flowers, kissing the lips of lilies. How far they have to go, how many cups to fill, great and small, cells too small to be seen, cups holding half a drop as well as lake basins between the hills, each replenished with equal care, every drop in all the blessed throng a silvery newborn star with lake and river, garden and grove, valley and mountain, all that the landscape holds reflected in its crystal depths, God's messenger, angel of love sent on its way with majesty and pomp and display of power that make man's greatest shows ridiculous.

Now the storm is over, the sky is clear, the last rolling thunder-wave is spent on the peaks, and where are the raindrops now—what has become of all the shining throng? In winged vapor rising some are already hastening back to the sky, some have gone into the plants, creeping through invisible doors into the round rooms of cells, some are locked in crystals of ice, some in rock crystals, some in porous moraines to keep their small springs flowing, some have gone journeying on in the rivers to join the larger raindrop of the ocean. From form to form, beauty to beauty, ever changing, never resting, all are speeding on with love's enthusiasm, singing with the stars the eternal song of creation.

SIGNIFICANCE

Although he lacked formal credentials as a scientist, Muir became the leading American conservationist

of the late nineteenth and early twentieth centuries. His adventurous travelogues and passionate writing about the natural world were published in the major magazines of his time. In all, he wrote ten books and three hundred shorter articles. Muir exerted significant influence on other leading conservation-minded figures, including President Theodore Roosevelt and Gifford Pinchot, the country's first professional forester. Unlike Roosevelt and Pinchot, who favored a utilitarian approach to conservation that allowed for controlled commercial use of forests, Muir advocated preservation of natural areas. Modern environmental policy within the United States is a mixture of the utilitarian and preservationist schools.

FURTHER RESOURCES

Books

Gretel Ehrlich. *John Muir: Nature's Visionary*. Washington, D.C.: National Geographic, 2000.

Web sites

John Muir Trust. "John Muir Information Guide." <http://www.jmt.org/award/award/johnmuir2.html> (accessed January 17, 2006).

Sierra Club. "John Muir Exhibit." <http://www.sierraclub.org/john_muir_exhibit> (accessed January 17, 2006).

Yosemite National Park. "History." <http://www.nps.gov/yose/nature/history.htm> (accessed January 17, 2006).

The Living Sea

"Drop-Off"

Book excerpt

By: Jacques-Yves Cousteau

Date: 1963

Source: Cousteau, Jacques Yves. *The Living Sea*. New York: Harper and Row, 1963.

About the Author: Jacques-Yves Cousteau (1910–1997) was one of the most famous ocean explorers of the twentieth century. He authored more than fifty books and encyclopedias about the oceans, produced numerous films and television shows featuring his adventures at sea, and founded a society for the protection of the oceans. He was a member of the United States National Academy of Sciences and was awarded the United Nations International Environmental Prize in 1977.

INTRODUCTION

Jacques Cousteau is arguably the most well-known personality associated with the ocean in the twentieth century. He was born in 1910 in Saint-André-de-Cubzac, France. His father was a lawyer and traveled extensively for work, so the family lived in various places during Cousteau's childhood. For some time, the Cousteau family lived in New York, where Jacques received much of his education. During this time Cousteau had his first underwater experiences, diving in a lake in New Hampshire. Following his secondary education, Cousteau attended the Naval Academy in Brest where he was trained as a gunnery officer.

Cousteau served in the French Navy during World War II, where he gained extensive experience at sea. Also during this time, he met Emile Gagnan, an engineer, with whom he developed the first apparatus that allowed a person to remain underwater for several hours. They called their equipment "Aqua-Lung" and it was the precursor to the Self-Contained Underwater Breathing Apparatus, or SCUBA. The development of the Aqua-Lung is the topic of Cousteau's first book *The Silent World*, which was an enormous success. It sold more than 3 million copies in English and was translated into 22 languages. Cousteau produced a film about underwater diving of the same title, which won the grand prize at the 1956 Cannes Film Festival and an Academy Award in 1957. *The Silent World* book and the film made Cousteau a celebrity, launching his career as a spokesperson for the oceans.

Excerpted below is the first chapter of *The Living Sea*, the second book written by Cousteau. Part of the book's success is Cousteau's great ability to describe the ocean ecosystem using words and phrases that engage the reader and make a world that is generally inaccessible to many, very available. *The Living Sea* describes the acquisition and construction of Cousteau's research vessel, *Calypso*, along with several of its early voyages. It also discusses the development of novel equipment used to explore the ocean at greater depth and for longer periods of time. In the excerpt, which describes one of the first underwater dives in the Red Sea, Cousteau refers to marine organisms that are not commonly known. These include madrepores, which are reef-building corals; alcyonarians, which include some corals and sea anemones; ascidians, which are soft-bodied marine organisms that colonize hard surfaces; hydrozoans, which are soft anemone-like animals; and calcareous algae, which is a type of plant that forms a hard encrusting layer. Jacks, bonitos, and silver sardinellas are all types of fish found near coral reefs. Acropora are staghorn

Captain Jacques-Yves Cousteau takes a diving break to pose with his wife Simone and their puppy aboard the *Calypso* in New York Harbor on August 30, 1959. AP IMAGES

coral, and tridacna clams are giant clams with large colored mantles found on coral reefs.

■ PRIMARY SOURCE

CHAPTER ONE: DROP-OFF

It was a hushed hour before sunrise in December 1951 in the Red Sea. Frédéric Dumas and I were about to start work on our own first full-scale underwater scientific expedition. We were inside the dangerous Far-San reefs of Saudi Arabia, aboard my new civilian research ship *Calypso*. Off in the gloom on the desert island of Abu Latt were the green tents of our field party.

The capstan swallowed the anchor chain with a cheerful rattle. From the forepeak the boatswain Jean Beltran sang out, "*L'ancre est haute et claire!*"

On the bridge my old French Navy comrade, skipper Francois Saôut, grumbled, "The weather is too good. It can only get worse."

I said, "This is not like your old Cape Horn!" However, I liked Saôut to feel that our precious new vessel was surrounded by evil—especially now that she really was. Between us and the day's diving grounds on the outer Far-San bank were ten miles of poorly charted, shallow coral heads and reefs.

I pushed both motors forward and climbed above the wheelhouse to the high observation bridge. From there *Calypso* looked small enough to snake her way through the half-concealed obstacles. In the faint light I took bearings from island features we had named Aircraft Carrier, Petite Termitière, and Scotch Cairn. Saôut swerved to avoid reefs and headed due west.

Below me in the chartroom my wife, Simone, manned the echo sounder, interpreting its pings through a headset and calling off soundings to a bearded, turbaned "Arab" on the bridge wing who relayed them to Saout and me. The "native" was an Arabic-speaking French parachute lieutenant, Jean Dupas, detached to us for the cruise.

Under my lofty perch *Calypso* was wakening. I looked down on the white bonnet of Fernand Hanen, the cook, as he brought a pot of coffee to the bridge. Below decks René Montupet, the chief engineer, started our clattering compressors, which supply air for the day's dives, with a noise that finished sleep for all. On the diving deck aft, Dumas, Beltran, and Jacques Ertaud, our amphibious cameraman, charged the triple-tank Aqua-Lungs and protected them from the impending heat with water-soaked mats.

The sun came up like a blow, implacable to the skin. I inflated my lungs in eager anticipation of the big day. The program was deep exploration of the virgin reefs of Shab Suleim on the seaward fringe of the Far-Sans. We were going to investigate to a depth of two hundred feet, take specimens of fixed animal life in various environmental layers, and document the reef with artificial-light color photography. We also hoped to determine the thickness of living coral and to outline the general topography. For years I had looked forward to helping marine science with free-diving and hand-held submarine photography.

Shab Suleim is a long narrow chain of reefs oriented northwest-southeast, with a coral rim *à fleur d'eau*, or so near the surface that the prevailing wind sweeps the sea across in a white flowering. On the northwest cape I found a blue creek wide enough to anchor *Calypso*.

We swung our flat-bottomed aluminum work launch overboard. Five of us dropped in and moved to the reef. Wearing our masks, Dumas and I stepped into knee-deep water and waddled across the coral fringe, which was gnarled and trenched and bursting with life. We swam to the drop-off line. In the blue crystal below were tier upon tier of majestic gray-and-brown sharks interweaving lazily in a slow-motion ballet.

We returned to the launch and conferred with Ertaud and Professor Pierre Drach, a stocky, rosy-cheeked specialist in fixed marine fauna and the first oceanographer to seek out the Aqua-Lung as a working tool. Dumas said,

"The shark problem can be handled by diving along the wall with our backs to it, so we have to watch only half the space around us."

Professor Drach said, "I'm here to collect specimens, not to turn round and watch sharks." He delivered a lecture on *travaux pratiques sous-marine* as though he were in a classroom at the Sorbonne instead of in a broiling pan on a desolate reef with a sea full of sharks below. He reviewed for us the main categories of madrepores, alcyonarians, ascidians and calcareous algae. I could not help thinking that his diving experience was a bit thin. Drach had been the first academician to pass our tough professional diving course at the Toulon Navy Undersea Research Group, but since then he had made few difficult descents—and only one to the two-hundred-foot level we faced today.

As the professor concluded his briefing, I said, "I believe the best technique for the dive will be for Dumas and me to act as bodyguards for Drach, to permit him maximum collecting time. Ertaud can go on his own to take pictures, and Beltran will stay in the boat, tracking our bubbles, ready for any emergency." They submerged—but I did not join them immediately. I found myself checking my equipment with a priestly solemnity. I was not exactly afraid of this dive, but I had a strong intuition that it was going to be meaningful for me. I was in an unaccustomed individualistic mood.

I went in, scarcely feeling the blood-warm water on my skin. The rest of the world passed. Down along the riotous plumage of the shelf my companions hung like marionettes, waiting for me. I joined them and we crossed the brink. Half the space below was a vertical living wall; the other half, infinity. Dumas scouted a protective rock fissure leading down, and we followed him to it. As we sank along the crack, out of nothingness appeared the nomads—powerful jacks, bonitos with intense blue scales, and silver sardinellas. They came to the wall, flirted about, and receded into the outer waters where they belonged. Big transparent jellyfish dragged along, pulsating drowsily. Those that came too near the reef were torn to pieces by fish as black as soot.

Ertaud began popping flash bulbs. Professor Drach halted to pry off animal colonies with his burglar's jimmy, made notes on a plastic tablet, and plumped his samples into the string shopping bag on his belt. He dribbled his way downward, his nose to the reef, seeing alive for the first time creatures he had known only from books or as specimens disfigured and beached in jars of formaldehyde. He was in a biotope both familiar and new to him. He was no longer with us. I felt uneasy about it and pointed him out to Dumas. We exchanged glances, confirming that we must watch him diligently.

But when I stood off from that dainty and yet majestic cliff, it was hard to be a mere bodyguard. The coral took unexpected shapes and hues. There were skulls of dwarfs and giants; tufts of ocher and magenta mingled with petrified mauve bushes and red tubiporae fabricated like honeycombs. Superb parasols of acropora spread over idling fish that were painted with electric pigments of red and gold. Through this splendid tilted forest hump-backed sea snails traveled their winding ways. In reef recesses there were enough tridacna clams to furnish fonts for the churches of Christendom. Their shells were ajar, displaying swollen mantles painted like the lips of harlots.

The reef of Shab Suleim was an intaglio structure with porches of coral, winding *couloirs*, and countless narrow cracks aswarm with beings waiting in the wings like walk-on players at the opera. When I poked my head into one of these little grottoes, anxious fish huddled together snout to snout, or molded themselves to the walls, while the spiny-rayed animals erected their dorsals in fear. The little caves were plastered with gaudy patches of ascidians, hydrozoans, and calcareous algae.

As I wandered along the reef, mixed hordes of fish vanished ahead of me, as if retreating into the reef, then reassembled behind. There were yellow-spotted groupers, gold-and-blue-striped butterfly fish, and a gay unicorn fish with a long horizontal horn protruding from its otherwise unprepossessing head. There were fish as flat as pancakes that flourished whip antennas, and mottled triggerfish with Fernandel profiles. The natives were out in their Sunday dress.

Moray eels glowered from crevices and bared their teeth to impress us. They were the concierges of the reef city, and the promenading tenants were not scared of them. My eye fell on an odd object hanging motionless in the water. It looked like a crumpled feather bonnet from the attic trunk of the Madwoman of Chaillot. The feathers were barred black-and-white. All at once the hat exploded into bristles—the stinging spines of a lion fish. I poked a finger at the venomous quills, taking care not to touch them. The fish did not flinch; it had confidence in its defenses.

I trudged on, occasionally stopping to press my mask close to the reef like a child at a candy-store window. Each square foot was a microcosm of worms, tiny hairy crabs, flowering slugs, and carousing vermin. Sixty feet down, I entered the alcyonarian kingdom—a vertical field of pliant growths shaped like celery plants, each stalk a different hue. Here and there in the hanging garden were tall coral umbrellas, funnel-shaped sponges, and gorgonian screens. Beneath the rainbow celery patch a tangle of white lines trailed ten feet out of the cliff. They were rigid and horny virgularians that looked like a slack lamp cord on a blue rug.

After all this novelty, at a depth of 130 feet came a shock of recognition—a landscape almost exactly like our customary cliffs at Cassis or Riou in the Mediterranean-the same small loggias in the dead walls, the same random splatter of ascidians and algae, and the same dusty appearance. The only things missing were the lobsters that lounge on such balconies at home and the red jeweler's coral, which oddly enough is not found in "coral seas."

Sharks had been in sight throughout the dive. As I progressed deeper, they turned faster, making me dizzy as I tried to keep them under scrutiny. There were one or two in every direction, and now they were closing in. Some swam straight toward me with vacant eyes and then withdrew. When I reached 150 feet, I glanced up. A dozen torpedo-shaped shadows were outlined against the viridescent ceiling. I looked down. Fifty feet below, pale sharks were strolling on a sand slope. I sighted my forgotten companions, naked and far from our boat, surrounded by Red Sea sharks of whose traits we knew nothing. It struck me that our situation was simply untenable.

Out of the roving pack, the biggest shark, an animal about twelve feet long, advanced with seeming deliberation toward the professor. I was thirty feet from Drach, and the shark was approaching him at ankle level. The sight of a man ogling a reef while *Carcharhinus* sniffed his legs was utterly revolting. I rushed toward them, grunting as loudly as I could through the mouthpiece but despairing of the outcome. Drach heard nothing. When I was ten feet from them, the big shark wheeled ponderously and swam away. I patted Drach's shoulder and tried to explain by signs what had happened. He looked at me severely and turned back to the reef. He did not wish to be disturbed again.

The scholar's *sang-froid* was contagious. I felt strangely reassured about everything. I sank lower, relaxed and receptive. At a depth of two hundred feet the cliff broke off into a forty-five-degree incline of gray soil. I was disappointed that the pageant was ending in this dull, lifeless bank. At second look I found the slope extended only fifty feet out to another blue horizon, another drop-off. I was on a *corniche* laden with fossils and waste that had fallen through the ages from the bustling metropolis above.

I hovered, contemplating the brink ahead. I stretched my arms and legs in space and greedily inhaled a lungful of thick, tasty air. Between the sibilants of my air regulator I heard rhythmic grating sounds and cycles of bubbles rustling overhead. Other human beings were alive nearby. Their commonplace respirations took on a cosmic significance. I was being seized by depth rapture. I knew it and I welcomed it as a challenge to whatever controls I had left.

The gray bank two hundred feet down was the boundary of reason; over the precipice lay madness. Danger became voluptuous. My temples pounded. Extending my arms like a sleepwalker, I stroked my fins and glided over the edge of beyond.

Hundreds of white walking canes stuck out of the vertiginous wall. I dropped slowly along a torment of life forms. Witches' heads stared at me. Pale gelatinous tumors grew on giant sponges ornamented with spider webs. As far down as I could see, untold populations clung along that wall. But they were denied to me. I trimmed off 240 feet down.

I heard a distant mechanical sigh—one of my companions opening his air-reserve valve. I paused. *Now I must soar out of here, pick up my friends, and obey the law of sun and air that rules my kind. Now? Why now?*

I stole another minute, clutching a white sea whip and looking down longingly. Then I knew I had an appointment with the second reef. I swore I would design, build, and operate devices that would deliver me the sunken ridges of the silent world.

SIGNIFICANCE

The Living Sea represents the beginning of Cousteau's concern for the preservation of the oceans, as well as other ecosystems throughout the world, an idea that would become a theme throughout his life. Through film and writing, Cousteau's work aboard the *Calypso* enchanted the public and exposed people to the beauty and fragility of many different, and often inaccessible, environments. He was able to demonstrate the threats that pollution and overexploitation posed through his dramatic images and descriptive prose. His writing, in which scientific concepts are explained in a compelling manner similar to storytelling, is a major part of his legacy, as it increased the public's awareness of the great beauty and diversity found in environments throughout the world.

Cousteau's success in film and writing made him a major spokesperson in the environmental movement of the late twentieth century. As such, Cousteau chose several environmental problems on which he focused his attention and the attention of the public. This often resulted in important changes to government policy. In 1960, Cousteau became concerned about the environmental effects of dumping radioactive waste in the Mediterranean Sea by the European Atomic Energy Community. He launched a publicity campaign pressuring governments to stop the practice. Eventually, dumping radioactive waste into the Mediterranean was banned.

In 1975, Cousteau took the *Calypso* on an expedition to Antarctica. He was one of the first people to ever dive below the ice that surrounds the continent. His work brought the sculptured beauty of the frozen continent into the consciousness of the world. Following this expedition, Cousteau used his platform as a filmmaker to encourage the signing of the Antarctic Treaty. The treaty establishes the entire continent of Antarctica as a natural preserve, free from exploitation for natural resources and waste disposal. It also ensures that Antarctica is used only for peaceful purposes. In a similar manner, Cousteau used his celebrity to pressure governments to protect both the Alaska wilderness and the Amazon River.

Much of Cousteau's environmental work centered around the non-profit organization, The Cousteau Society, that he established in 1974. The mission of the Society is to teach the public about threats to the environment that are caused by human activities. The membership of The Cousteau Society includes more than 300,000 members.

Cousteau received numerous environmental prizes for his work encouraging the discussion of environmental protection and increasing the awareness of human responsibility for other species on the planet. He was a member of the National Academy of Sciences in the United States and the Académie Française. Cousteau received the United Nations Environmental Prize in 1977. President Ronald Regan presented him with the National Medal of Freedom in 1995. He was an invited guest at the 1992 Earth Summit held in Rio de Janiero, Brazil.

FURTHER RESOURCES

Books

Cousteau, Jacques. *Jacques Cousteau: The Ocean World*. New York: Harry N. Abrams, 1985.

———. *The Silent World*. Washington, D.C.: National Geographic, 2004.

Web sites

The Cousteau Society. <http://www.cousteau.org/en> (accessed March 7, 2006).

"The Story of NLM Historical Collections." *National Library of Medicine, National Institutes of Health*. <http://www.nlm.nih.gov/hmd/about/collectionhistory.html> (accessed March 7, 2006).

Audio and Visual Media

Turner Home Entertainment. *Lilliput in Antarctica*. Cousteau Society, 1990.

Warner Home Video. *The Jacques Cousteau Odyssey—The Complete Series*. All 12 episodes from the 1978 season. 2005.

Voyager II's Gold Disc "Sounds of Earth"

Photograph

By: Carl Edward Sagan

Date: August 20, 1977

Source: *Voyager II's* Gold Disc "Sounds of Earth." Time Life Pictures/Getty Images, 1977.

About the Author: Carl Sagan (1934–1996) was the producer of "Sounds of Earth." An astronomer, author, and educator, Sagan made exceptional contributions to the advancement of science education, public policy/government regulation of science and the environment, planetary exploration, Earth history, and exobiology. As the David Duncan Professor of Astronomy and Space Sciences and Director of the Laboratory for Planetary Studies at Cornell University, Sagan played an important role in the *Mariner, Galileo, Viking,* and *Voyager* spacecraft missions to the neighboring planets of Earth. During his professional career, Sagan was commonly considered the best science educator of the twentieth century. He casually but effectively communicated the intricacies of science so laypersons could easily understand.

INTRODUCTION

Voyager I and *Voyager II* are the names of two 1,820-pound (825-kilogram) U.S. spacecrafts that were launched from the National Aeronautics and Space Administration (NASA) Kennedy Space Center at Cape Canaveral, Florida on September 5, 1977 and August 20, 1977, respectively. Launched from Titan 3E-Centaur expendable rockets by NASA Mission Control flight controllers, each spacecraft was originally sent to explore (under the direction of scientists at the Jet Propulsion Laboratory in Pasadena, California) the planets of Jupiter and Saturn. However, due to enhanced reprogramming of its software, both probes were endowed with greater capabilities, so that *Voyager II* was able to research the other two giant outer planets (Neptune and Uranus). Both probes were given the ability to communicate while traveling into the interstellar space beyond the solar system.

A time capsule-like message, called "Sounds of Earth," was placed aboard both spacecrafts in order to communicate to any extraterrestrial civilization that might come across the spacecraft as they travel through the solar system and out to interstellar space.

The message, which was contained within two identical 12-inch (30-centimeter) "golden records" made of a gold-plated copper, was carried onboard each spacecraft. Each record, along with a cartridge and needle, was protected in an aluminum jacket. A sample of uranium-238 was electroplated onto the cover in order to provide a reference for the extraterrestrials as to the time of manufacture (the half-life of uranium-238 is about 4.5 billion years).

The two-hour record contained many messages that described the diversity of life on Earth. The record, produced by Dr. Carl Sagan and a committee of associates, contained 115 images such as those of a seashore, Earth, tree toad, family, and chemical definition; and a variety of natural sounds such as those made by a bird, cricket, human kissing, brainwave, volcanic eruption, surf, thunder, whale-song, elephant, automobile gears, footsteps, heartbeats, and wind.

The record also included ninety-five minutes of musical selections from different societies and time periods, spoken greetings from people in fifty-five different languages representing most of the human population, and printed messages from U.S. President Jimmy Carter and United Nations Secretary-General Kurt Waldheim. The musical selections included a variety of selections such as the Bach Brandenberg Concerto Number Two, First Movement; an Australian Horn and Totem song; a Bulgarian Shepherdess Song "Izlel Delyo Hajdutin"; and Chuck Berry's "Johnny B. Goode." The spoken greetings included Akkadian (spoken in Sumer about six thousand years ago), Wu (a modern Chinese dialect), and Latin (the still-used language of ancient Rome).

PRIMARY SOURCE

VOYAGER II'S GOLD DISC "SOUNDS OF EARTH"
  See primary source image.

SIGNIFICANCE

Upon exploration of the four large outer planets, along with their multiple moons, ring systems, and magnetic fields, the two *Voyager* spacecraft have significantly expanded the scientific knowledge of the solar system, specifically the knowledge of how Earth was formed and developed over time. The twin probes found that Jupiter has complicated dynamics within its twisting, turbulent atmosphere, including auroras, lightning, and storms three times the size of Earth itself. *Voyager* also discovered three new satellites (it has four large and many small moons). It was also

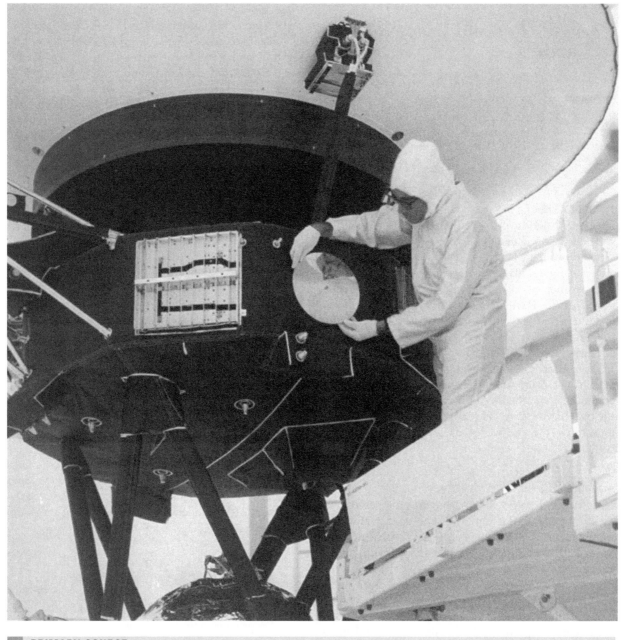

■ **PRIMARY SOURCE**

***Voyager II's* Gold Disc "Sounds of Earth"** A gold-plated copper record containing photos, greetings and images from Earth, produced by Carl Sagan, is mounted on *Voyager II* prior to the spacecraft's journey to Neptune and Uranus, August 4, 1977.
TIME LIFE PICTURES/NASA/TIME LIFE PICTURES/GETTY IMAGES

learned that Jupiter has rings around it, with one thin, dusty ring that altered how scientists viewed the origins and mechanics of planetary ring systems. It was also discovered that Io, Jupiter's innermost major moon, has nine volcanoes—with eight of them still erupting—which dramatically affect the magnetosphere of its parent planet.

With regard to Saturn, an already-known ringed planet, *Voyager* found that it is encircled with a complex series of magnificent rings that contain kinks, spokes, and braids (which also forced scientists to rewrite theories about rings). In addition, both probes discovered four regular satellites and three shepherd satellites, which were predicted to exist (but never

By 1980, *Voyager I* was within 66 million miles of Saturn. Scientists were able to determine facts about the planet from the photos *Voyager I* was able to take. AP IMAGES

seen) in order to maintain ring stability. According to *Voyager*, Saturn has giant jet streams in its atmosphere, but its weather is relatively calm when compared with Jupiter's weather. Its satellite Titan has a smoggy atmosphere, while another satellite, Mimas, contains a gigantic impact crater.

Voyager II extended its planetary voyage and visited Uranus and Neptune, where ring systems around both planets—which were barely visible from Earth observations—were detected in great detail. Surprising to scientists was Uranus' highly slanted magnetic axis, which is nearly parallel to its axis of rotation, thus giving it an unusual magnetosphere. Its satellites of Ariel and Miranda contain icy channels that showed up like a weird patchwork. *Voyager II* discovered ten new regular satellites around Uranus (it currently has fifteen regular satellites), along with one new ring.

Neptune was found by *Voyager II* to contain very active weather, complete with abundant cloud features within its atmosphere. *Voyager II* showed dynamic weather (which was contrary to theories that showed passive weather since the planet received little sunlight) with winds blowing westward (opposite to the direction of rotation) and with speeds faster than winds on any other planet. Neptune also revealed for the first time what is now called its Great Dark Spot, a storm system similar to Jupiter's Great Red Spot but different in that it is smaller in size, eastwardly traveling, and circling the planet every sixteen hours. *Voyager* also found six new satellites (now bringing the total number of moons to eight, along with Nereid and Triton). Blue in color, the probe found that Neptune is encircled with scattered, dusty rings, finding two new rings around the planet. *Voyager II* found that Neptune's magnetic axis was also slanted.

As of 2005, *Voyager I* is expected to possess sufficient fuel to maintain contact with scientists on Earth until 2040, while *Voyager II* should have enough fuel until 2034. However, the extended missions of *Voyager I* and *II* have already rewritten much of the scientific knowledge of planetary astronomy. The mission of the twin probes has helped to resolve critical questions about the origin and evolution of the planetary systems within the solar system—including the Earth and her Moon—while modifying former elementary ideas of the formation and development of the solar system. The *Voyager* mission also raised new questions that will undoubtedly be answered with future missions within the solar system. Because of its ability to analyze four planets, *Voyager* also initiated a new field in science, that of the study of comparative planetology.

As of 2005, both spacecraft are flying near the outer boundary of the solar system—at a distance of between about 5 billion and 14 billion miles (8 billion and 23 billion kilometers) beyond the Sun. The *Voyagers* should reach the boundary sometime in the first twenty-five years of the twenty-first century. *Voyager*'s last photographs of the solar system were a reverse look at the planets of the solar system, showing the emptiness that lies between the tiny planet called Earth and the gigantic expanse of the universe.

FURTHER RESOURCES

Books

Sagan, Carl. *Murmurs of Earth: The Voyager Interstellar Record*. New York: Random House, 1978.

Web sites

Jet Propulsion Laboratory, California Institute of Technology. "Planetary Voyage." <http://voyager.jpl.nasa.gov/science/planetary.html> (accessed January 17, 2006).

The Planetary Society. "Voyager." <http://www.planetary.org/explore/topics/voyager/> (accessed March 13, 2006).

University of Wisconsin, Green Bay. "The Voyager Record." <http://www.uwgb.edu/dutchs/CosmosNotes/voygrec.htm> (accessed January 17, 2006).

The Log from the Sea of Cortez

March 31

Book excerpt

By: John Steinbeck and E.F. Ricketts

Date: 1951

Source: John Steinbeck and E.F. Ricketts. *The Log from the Sea of Cortez*. New York: Penguin, 1951.

About the Author: American author John Steinbeck (1902–1968) was born in Salinas, California, and attended Stanford University for several years without taking a degree. Best known for his fictional portrayals of the down-and-out and others on the margins of society, he wrote *Of Mice and Men*, *The Grapes of Wrath*, *Cannery Row*, *Tortilla Flat*, and *East of Eden*. His nonfiction works include two travel narratives: the record of an early 1960s cross-country trip with his standard poodle, titled *Travels with Charley*, and an account of a biological collecting expedition to the Gulf of California, *Sea of Cortez*. Scorned by some Californians for his stark portrayals of the underside of their society, Steinbeck spent his later years living in New York. He was awarded a Pulitzer Prize in 1940 for *The Grapes of Wrath* and the 1962 Nobel Prize in Literature. E.F. Ricketts, a close friend of Steinbeck, was a marine biologist who earned a living by writing and selling biological specimens to schools. His book *Between Pacific Tides* was published in 1939 and remains a highly regarded reference about the intertidal biology of California's seacoast. Ricketts and his business, Pacific Biological Laboratories, figured prominently as Doc and Western Biological in Steinbeck's fictional *Cannery Row*. Although the text of *The Log from the Sea of Cortez* has been attributed solely to Steinbeck, scholarly research after its publication showed that Steinbeck wrote not from his own journal, but rather from those of Ricketts and the ship's master. Some of the more philosophical sections of the narrative, moreover, appear to have been originally written by Ricketts and incorporated into the text by Steinbeck.

INTRODUCTION

The Log from the Sea of Cortez is the daily journal of a six-week biological collecting trip to the Sea of Cortez organized by Steinbeck and American marine biologist Edward Ricketts (1897–1948). Known officially as the Gulf of California, the Sea of Cortez is an arm of the Pacific Ocean that lies between the Baja Peninsula and mainland Mexico. Steinbeck and

Ricketts chartered a fishing boat, the *Western Flyer*, and hired a small crew for their expedition to an area that to this day remains remote.

The text of *The Log from the Sea of Cortez* was originally the first part of a much longer book, *Sea of Cortez: A Leisurely Journal of Travel and Research*. The latter was a collaboration between Steinbeck and Ricketts, and included a catalogue of biological specimens collected during the trip. *Sea of Cortez* was published during the first week of December 1941, just days before Pearl Harbor was attacked and the United States was drawn into World War II, and has faded into obscurity. The narrative that constitutes *The Log from the Sea of Cortez*, however, has endured to become a classic environmental travelogue that reveals as much about human nature as it does marine biology.

The log for March 31, 1940, is typical of the daily entries in *The Log from the Sea of Cortez*. It mixes a combination of marine biology, philosophical reflections about a world on the brink of global war (the European portion of World War II was already underway), and insightful descriptions of shipboard life that ring true with any scientist or explorer who has been on an expedition.

■ PRIMARY SOURCE

MARCH 31. The tide was very poor this morning, only two and a half to three feet below the uppermost line of barnacles. We started about ten o'clock and had a little collecting under water, but soon the wind got up and so ruffled the surface that we could not see what we were doing. To a certain extent this was a good thing. Not being able to get into the low littoral, where no doubt the spectacular spiny lobsters would have distracted us, we were able to make a more detailed survey of the upper region. One fact increasingly emerged: the sulphury-green and black cucumber is the most ubiquitous shore animal of the Gulf of California, with *Heliaster,* the sun-star, a close second. These two are found nearly everywhere. In this region at San Carlos, Sally Lightfoot lives highest above the ordinary high tide, together with a few *Ligyda occidentalis*, a cockroach-like crustacean. Attached to the rocks and cliffsides, high up and fully exposed to this deadly sun, were barnacles, and limpets, so placed that they must experience only occasional immersion, although they may be often dampened by spray. Under rocks and boulders, in the next association lower down, were the mussel-like ruffled clams and the brown chitons, many cucumbers, a few *Heliasters,* and only two species of brittle-stars—another common species, *Ophiothrix spiculata*, we did not find here although we had seen it everywhere else.

In this zone verrucose anemones were growing under overhangs on the sides of rocks and in pits in the rocks. There were also a few starfish, garbanzo clams were attached to the rock undersides by the thousands together with club urchins. Farther down in a new zone was a profusion of sponges of a number of species, including a beautiful blue sponge. There were octopi here, and one species of chiton; there were many large purple urchins, although no specimens were taken, and heart-urchins in the sand and between the rocks. There were some sipunculids and a great many tunicates.

We found extremely large sponges, a yellow form (probably *Cliona*) superficially resembling the Monterey *Lissodendoryx noxiosa*, and a white one, *Steletta*, of the wicked spines. There were brilliant-orange nudibranchs, giant terebellid worms, some shell-less air-breathing (pulmonate) snails, a ribbon-worm, and a number of solitary corals. These were the common animals and the ones in which we were most interested, for while we took rarities when we came upon them in normal observation, our interest lay in the large groups and their associations—the word "association" implying a biological assemblage, all the animals in a given habitat.

It would seem that the commensal idea is a very elastic thing and can be extended to include more than host and guest; that certain kinds of animals are often found together for a number of reasons. One, because they do not eat one another; two, because these different species thrive best under identical conditions of wave-shock and bottom; three, because they take the same kinds of food, or different aspects of the same kinds of food; four, because in some cases the armor or weapons of some are protection to the others (for instance, the sharp spines of an urchin may protect a tide-pool Johnny from a larger preying fish); five, because some actual commensal partition of activities may truly occur. Thus the commensal tie may be loose or very tight and some associations may partake of a real thigmotropism.

Indeed, as one watches the little animals, definite words describing them are likely to grow hazy and less definite, and as species merges into species, the whole idea of definite independent species begins to waver, and a scale-like concept of animal variations comes to take its place. The whole taxonomic method in biology is clumsy and unwieldy, shot through with the jokes of naturalists and the egos of men who wished to have animals named after them.

Originally the descriptive method of naming was not so bad, for every observer knew Latin and Greek well and was able to make out the descriptions. Such knowledge is fairly rare now and not even requisite. How much easier if the animals bore numbers to which the names were auxiliary! Then, one knowing that the phylum Arthropoda was represented by the roman figure *VI*, the class Crustacea by a capital *B*, order by Arabic figure *13*, and genus and species by a combination of small letters, would with little training be able to place the animals in his mind much more quickly and surely than he can now with the descriptive method tugged bodily from a discarded antiquity.

As we ascended the Gulf it became more sparsely inhabited; there were fewer of the little heat-struck *rancherias*, fewer canoes of fishing Indians. Above Santa Rosalia very few trading boats travel. One would be really cut off up here. And yet here and there on the beaches we found evidences of large parties of fishermen. On one beach there were fifteen or twenty large sea-turtle shells and the charcoal of a bonfire where the meat had been cooked or smoked. In this same place we found also a small iron harpoon which had been lost, probably the most valued possession of the man who had lost it. These Indians do not seem to have firearms; probably the cost of them is beyond even crazy dreaming. We have heard that in some of the houses are the treasured weapons of other times, muskets, flintlocks, old long muzzle-loaders kept from generation to generation. And one man told us of finding a piece of Spanish armor, a breastplate, in an Indian house.

There is little change here in the Gulf. We think it would be very difficult to astonish these people. A tank or a horseman armed cap-a-pie would elicit the same response—a mild and dwindling interest. Food is hard to get, and a man lives inward, closely related to time; a cousin of the sun, at feud with storm and sickness. Our products, the mechanical toys which take up so much of our time, preoccupy and astonish us so, would be considered what they are, rather clever toys but not related to very real things. It would be interesting to try to explain to one of these Indians our tremendous projects, our great drives, the fantastic production of goods that can't be sold, the clutter of possessions which enslave whole populations with debt, the worry and neuroses that go in to the rearing and educating of neurotic children who find no place for themselves in this complicated world; the defense of the country against a frantic nation of conquerors, and the necessity for becoming frantic to do it; the spoilage and wastage and death necessary for the retention of the crazy thing; the science which labors to acquire knowledge, and the movement of people and goods contrary to the knowledge obtained. How could one make an Indian understand the medicine which labors to save a syphilitic, and the gas and bomb to kill him when he is well, the armies which build health so that death will be more active and violent. It is quite possible that to an ignorant Indian these might not be evidences of a great civilization, but rather of inconceivable nonsense.

It is not implied that this fishing Indian lives a perfect or even a very good life. A toothache may be to him a terrible thing, and a stomachache may kill him. Often he is hungry, but he does not kill himself over things which do not closely concern him.

A number of times we were asked, Why do you do this thing, this picking up and pickling of little animals? To our own people we could have said any one of a number of meaningless things, which by sanction have been accepted as meaningful. We could have said, "We wish to fill in certain gaps in the knowledge of the Gulf fauna." That would have satisfied our people, for knowledge is a sacred thing, not to be questioned or even inspected. But the Indian might say, "What good is this knowledge? Since you make a duty of it, what is its purpose?" We could have told our people the usual thing about the advancement of science, and again we would not have been questioned further. But the Indian might ask, "Is it advancing, and toward what? Or is it merely becoming complicated? You save the lives of children for a world that does not love them. It is our practice," the Indian might say, "to build a house before we move into it. We would not want a child to escape pneumonia, only to be hurt all its life." The lies we tell about our duty and our purposes, the meaningless words of science and philosophy, are walls that topple before a bewildered little "why." Finally, we learned to know why we did these things. The animals were very beautiful. Here was life from which we borrowed life and excitement. In other words, we did these things because it was pleasant to do them.

We do not wish to intimate in any way that this hypothetical Indian is a noble savage who lives in logic. His magics and his techniques and his teleologies are just as full of nonsense as ours. But when two people, coming from different social, racial, intellectual patters, meet and wish to communicate, they must do so on a logical basis. Clavigero discusses what seems to our people a filthy practice of some of the Lower California Indians. They were always hungry, always partly starved. When they had meat, which was a rare thing, they tied pieces of string to each mouthful, then ate it, pulled it up and ate it again and again, often passing it from hand to hand. Clavigero found this a disgusting practice. It is rather like the Chinese being ridiculed for eating twenty-year-old eggs who said, "your cheese is rotten milk. You like rotten milk—we like rotten eggs. We are both silly."

Costume on the *Western Flyer* has degenerated completely. Shirts were no longer worn, but the big straw hats were necessary. On board we went barefoot, clad only in hats and trunks. It was easy then to jump over the side to freshen up. Our clothes never got dry; the salt deposited in the fibers made them hygroscopic, always drawing the humidity. We washed the dishes in hot salt water, so that little crystals stuck to the plates. It seemed to us that the little salt adhering to the coffee pot made the coffee delicious. We ate fish nearly every day: bonito, dolphin, sierra, red snappers. We made thousands of big fat biscuits, hot and unhealthful. Twice a week Sparky created his magnificent spaghetti. Unbelievable amounts of coffee were consumed. One of our party made some lemon pies, but the quarreling grew bitter over them; the thievery, the suspicion of favoritism, the vulgar traits of selfishness and perfidy those pies brought out saddened all of us. And when one of us who, from being the most learned should have been the most self-controlled, took to hiding pie in his bed and munching it secretly when the lights were out, we decided there must be no more lemon pie. Character was crumbling, and the law of the fang was too close to us.

One thing had impressed us deeply on this little voyage: the great world dropped away very quickly. We lost the fear and fierceness and contagion of war and economic uncertainty. The matters of great importance we had left were not important. There must be an infective quality in these things. We had lost the virus, or it had been eaten by the anti-bodies of quiet. Our pace had slowed greatly; the hundred thousand small reactions of our daily world were reduced to very few. When the boat was moving we sat by the hour watching the pale, burned mountains slip by. A playful swordfish, jumping and spinning, absorbed us completely. There was time to observe the tremendous minutiae of the sea. When a school of fish went by, the gulls followed closely. Then the water was littered with feathers and the scum of oil. These fish were much too large for the gulls to kill and eat, but there is much more to a school of fish than the fish themselves. There is constant vomiting; there are the hurt and weak and old to cut out; the smaller prey on which the school feeds sometimes escape and die; a moving school is like a moving camp, and it leaves a camp-like debris behind it on which the gulls feed. The sloughing skins coat the surface of the water with oil.

At six P.M. we made anchorage at San Francisquito Bay. This cove-like bay is about one mile wide and points to the north. In the southern part of the bay there is a pretty little cove with a narrow entrance between two rocky points. A beach of white sand edges this cove, and on the edge of the beach there was a poor Indian house, and in front of it a blue canoe. No one came out of the house. Perhaps the inhabitants were away or sick or dead. We did not go near; indeed, we had a strong feeling of intruding, a feeling sharp enough even to prevent us from collecting on that little inner bay. The country hereabouts was stony and barren, and even the brush had thinned out. We anchored in four fathoms of water on the westerly side of the bay, then went ashore immediately and set up our tide stake at the water's edge, with a bandanna on it so we could see it from the boat. The wind was blowing and the water was painfully cold. The tide had dropped two feet below the highest line of barnacles. Three types of crabs were common here. There were many barnacles and great limpets and two species of snails, *Tegula* and a small *Purpura*. There were many large smooth brown chitons, and a few bristle-chitons. Farther down under the rocks were great anastomosing masses of a tubeworm with rusty red gills, some tunicates, *astrometis*, and the usual holothurians.

Tiny found the shell of a fine big lobster newly cleaned by isopods. The isopods and amphipods in their millions do a beautiful job. It is common to let them clean skeletons designed for study. A dead fish is placed in a jar having a cap pierced with holes just large enough to permit the entrance of the isopods. This is lowered to the bottom of a tide pool, and in a very short time the skeleton is clean of every particle of flesh, and yet is articulated and perfect.

The wind blew so and the water was so cold and ruffled that we did not stay ashore for very long. On board, we put down the baited bottom nets as usual to see what manner of creatures were crawling about there. When we pulled up one of the nets, it seemed to be very heavy. Hanging to the bottom of it on the outside was a large horned shark. He was not caught, but had gripped the bait through the net with a bulldog hold and he would not let go. We lifted him unstruggling out of the water and up onto the deck, and still he would not let go. This was at about eight o'clock in the evening. Wishing to preserve him, we did not kill him, thinking he would die quickly. His eyes were barred, rather like goat's eyes. He did not struggle at all, but lay quietly on the deck, seeming to look at us with a baleful, hating eye. The horn, by the dorsal fin, was clean and white. At long intervals his gill-slits opened and closed but he did not move. He lay there all night, not moving, only opening his gill-slits at great intervals. The next morning he was still alive, but all over his body spots of blood had appeared. By this time Sparky and Tiny were horrified by him, Fish out of water should die, and he didn't die. His eyes were wide and for some reason had not dried out, and he seemed to regard us with hatred. And still at intervals his gill-slits opened and closed. His sluggish tenacity had begun to affect all of us by this time. He was a baleful personality on the boat, a sluggish, gray length of hatred, and the blood spots on him did not make him more pleasant. At noon we put him into the formaldehyde tank, and only then did he struggle for a moment before he died. He had been out of the water for sixteen or seventeen hours, had never fought or flopped a bit. The fast and delicate fishes like the tunas and mackerels waste their lives out in a complete and sudden flurry and die quickly. But about this shark there was a frightful quality of stolid, sluggish endurance. He had come aboard because he had grimly fastened on the bait and would

not release it, and he lived because he would not release life. In some earlier time he might have been the basis for one of those horrible myths which abound in the spoken literature of the sea. He had a definite and terrible personality which bothered all of us, and, as with the sea-turtle, Tiny was shocked and sick that he did not die. This fish, and all the family of the Heterodontidae, ordinarily live in shallow, warm lagoons, and although we do not know it, the thought occurred to us that sometimes, perhaps fairly often, these fish may be left stranded by a receding tide so that they may have developed the ability to live through until the flowing tide comes back. The very sluggishness in that case would be a conservation of vital energy, whereas the beautiful and fragile tuna make one frantic rush to escape, conserving nothing and dying immediately.

Within our own species we have great variation between these two reactions. One man may beat his life away in furious assault on the barrier, where another simply waits for the tide to pick him up. Such variation is also observable among the higher vertebrates, particularly among domestic animals. It would be strange if it were not also true of the lower vertebrates, among the individualistic ones anyway. A fish, like the tuna or the sardine, which lives in a school, would be less likely to vary than this lonely horned shark, for the school would impose a discipline of speed and uniformity, and those individuals which would not or could not meet the school's requirements would be killed or lost or left behind. The overfast would be eliminated by the school as readily as the over-slow, until a standard somewhere between the fast and slow had been attained. Not intending a pun, we might note that our schools have to some extent the same tendency, A Harvard man, a Yale man, a Stanford man—that is, the ideal—is easily recognized as a tuna, and he has, by a process of elimination, survived the tests against idiocy and brilliance. Even in physical matters the standard is maintained until it is impossible, from speech, clothing, haircuts, posture, or state of mind, to tell one of these units of his school from another. In this connection it would be interesting to know whether the general collectivization of human society might not have the same effect. Factory mass production, for example, requires that every man conform to the tempo of the whole. The slow must be speeded up or eliminated, the fast slowed down. In a thoroughly collectivized state, mediocre efficiency might be very great, but only through the complete elimination of the swift, the clever, and the intelligent, as well as the incompetent. Truly collective man might in fact abandon his versatility. Among school animals there is little defense technique except headlong flight. Such species depend for survival chiefly on tremendous reproduction. The great loss of eggs and young to predators is the safety of the school, for it depends for its existence on the law of probability that out of a great many which start some will finish.

It is interesting and probably not at all important to note that when a human state is attempting collectivization, one of the first steps is a frantic call by the leaders for an increased birth rate—replacement parts in a shoddy and mediocre machine.

Our interest had been from the first in the common animals and their associations, and we had not looked for rarities. But it was becoming apparent that we were taking a number of new and unknown species. Actually, more than fifty species undescribed at the time of capture will have been taken. These will later have been examined, classified, described, and named by specialists. Some of them may not be determined for years, for it is one of the little byproducts of the war that scientific men are cut off from one another. A Danish specialist in one field is unable to correspond with his colleague in California. Thus some of these new animals may not be named for a long time. We have listed in the Appendix those already specified and indicated in so far as possible those which have not been worked on by specialists.

Dr. Rolph Bolin, ichthyologist at the Hopkins Marine Station, found in our collection what we thought to be a new species of commensal fish which lives in the anus of a cucumber, flipping in and out, possibly feeding on the feces of the host but more likely merely hiding in the anus from possible enemies. This fish later turned out to be an already named species, but, carrying on the ancient and disreputable tradition of biologists, we had hoped to call it by the euphemistic name *Proctophilus winchellii*.

There are some marine biologists whose chief interest is in the rarity, the seldom seen and unnamed animal. These are often wealthy amateurs, some of whom have been suspected of wishing to tack their names on unsuspecting and unresponsive invertebrates. The passion for immortality at the expense of a little beast must be very great. Such collectors should to a certain extent be regarded as in the same class with those philatelists who achieve a great emotional stimulation from an unusual number of perforations or a misprinted stamp. The rare animal may be of individual interest, but his is unlikely to be of much consequence in any ecological picture. The common, known, multitudinous animals, the red pelagic lobsters which litter the sea, the hermit crabs in their billions, scavengers of the tide pools, would by their removal affect the entire region in widening circles. The disappearance of plankton, although the components are microscopic, would probably in a short time eliminate every living thing in the sea and change the whole of man's life, if it did not through a seismic disturbance of balance eliminate all life on the globe. For these little animals, in their incalculable numbers, are probably the base food supply of the world. But the extinction of one of the rare animals, so avidly sought and caught and named, would probably go unnoticed in the cellular world.

Our own interest lay in relationships of animal to animal. If one observes in this relational sense, it seems apparent that species are only commas in a sentence, that each species is at once the point and the base of a pyramid, that all life is relational to the point where an Einsteinian relativity seems to emerge. And then not only the meaning but the feeling about species grows misty. One merges into another, groups melt into ecological groups until the time when what we know as life meets and enters what we think of as non-life; barnacle and rock, rock and earth, earth and tree, tree and rain and air. And the units nestle into the whole and are inseparable from it. Then one can come back to the microscopic and the tide pool and the aquarium. But the little animals are found to be changed, no longer set apart and alone. And it is a strange thing that most of the feeling we call religious, most of the mystical out-crying which is one of the most prized and used and desired reactions of our species, is really the understanding and the attempt to say that man is related to the whole thing, related inextricably to all reality, known and unknowable. This is a simple thing to say, but the profound feeling of it made a Jesus, a St. Augustine, a St. Francis, a Roger Bacon, a Charles Darwin, and an Einstein. Each of them in his own tempo and with his own voice discovered and reaffirmed with astonishment the knowledge that all things are one thing and that one thing is all things—plankton, a shimmering phosphorescence on the sea and the spinning planets and an expanding universe, all bound together by the elastic string of time. It is advisable to look from the tide pool to the stars and then back to the tide pool again.

SIGNIFICANCE

The Log from the Sea of Cortez has stood the test of time as an environmental travelogue and commentary about the madness of an advanced society consumed with superficialities and stumbling toward a global war. In the entry for March 31, Steinbeck describes in typical fashion a morning of specimen collection made difficult by an unfavorable tide, critiques the scientific practice of using Latin to classify organisms in an age when nobody speaks the language, speculates how western civilization would be viewed by the subsistence fishermen of Baja, and warns about the danger of a single lemon pie on a ship of hungry men. (Although one woman, Steinbeck's wife, was also on board, she is never mentioned and they divorced shortly after the trip.) He emphasizes that their work, like that of most scientists, is more concerned with the normal than the exotic. Like geologists who are far more interested in common minerals like quartz than gems such as diamonds, working biologists concern themselves with the organisms that constitute the bulk of an ecosystem.

As a travelogue, *The Log from the Sea of Cortez* is a classic description of an area that is now as much a tourist destination as a frontier. It is also an accurate description of the often mundane day-to-day work of scientists in the field, complete with references to their continual frustration with a balky outboard motor that Steinbeck christened the Sea Cow. The biological catalogue included in the original *Sea of Cortez* but omitted in the more popular *Log of the Sea of Cortez* was a major contribution to the marine biology literature. The philosophical aspects, for which Steinbeck was often criticized, paint an introspective picture of a world and have retained their relevance for more than half a century.

FURTHER RESOURCES
Books

Ricketts, Edward F. *Between Pacific Tides.* Stanford, Calif.: Stanford University Press, 1939.

Steinbeck, John. *Cannery Row.* New York: Viking, 1945.

Tamm, Eric Enno. *Beyond the Outer Shores: The Untold Odyssey of Ed Ricketts, the Pioneering Ecologist who Inspired John Steinbeck and Joseph Campbell.* New York: Four Walls Eight Windows, 2004.

Web sites

Anonymous. "Back to the Sea of Cortez." <http://www.seaofcortez.org> (accessed March 13, 2006).

"John Steinbeck's Pacific Grove." *93950.com.* <http://www.93950.com/steinbeck> (accessed March 13, 2006).

"Isotopic Evidence for Extraterrestrial Non-Racemic Amino Acids in the Murchison Meteorite"

Journal article

By: Michael H. Engel and Stephen A. Macko

Date: September 18, 1997

Source: Engel, Michael H. and Stephen A. Macko. "Isotopic Evidence for Extraterrestrial Non-Racemic Amino Acids in the Murchison Meteorite." *Nature* 389 (September 18, 1997): 265.

About the Author: Michael H. Engel is the Willard Miller Professor at the School of Geology and Geophysics at the University of Oklahoma in Norman, Oklahoma. His research focuses on the stable isotopes and steroisomer composition of terrestrial and extraterrestrial materials. Stephen A. Macko is a professor in the Department of Environmental Sciences, University of Virginia in Charlottesville, Virginia. His work involves using isotope analysis to study the cycling of organic matter in fossil and modern ecosystems.

INTRODUCTION

The Murchison meteorite fell onto farmland near the town of Murchison, Victoria in Australia about 60 miles (97 kilometers) north of Melbourne on September 28, 1969. Witnesses near Murchison observed the fall of the meteorite and nearly 220 pounds (100 kilograms) of fragments were collected within a short period of time.

Terrestrial bacteria are quick to colonize surfaces and cracks in meteorites after they fall to Earth. Meteorites that are found long periods of time after they have fallen to Earth are almost certainly contaminated by terrestrial organisms. The rapid collection of the Murchison meteorite fragments increased chances that its composition was pristine. In addition, because the meteorite fell to Earth during the same period as NASA's lunar missions, laboratories around the world were prepared to perform analyses on extraterrestrial rocks. The Murchison meteorite garnered much attention in the scientific community for two major reasons: its organic chemical composition and the possibility that it contained fossilized bacteria.

The Murchison meteorite is a primitive meteorite containing materials that coalesced even before the Earth's solar system formed. It contains carbon-based molecules just like the molecules found in living organisms on Earth. In particular it contains a large number of amino acids, the molecules that make up proteins in living organisms. Many of these amino acids are found on Earth, but it contains more than fifty amino acids that are extremely rare. In addition, the chirality (structure) of the amino acids in the meteorite is closer to that of amino acids that are found in organisms on Earth, which are all left-handed, than the structure predicted for amino acids produced through chemical reactions in space, which are predicted to be equally left and right-handed.

In 1997 and again in 2000, scientists revealed data showing that the Murchison meteorite contained more than just organic molecules. Microscopic photographs from freshly broken regions of the meteorite contained microfossils that looked like bacteria. Although these claims generated much discussion among the scientific community, they were met with a great deal of skepticism. Many researchers believe that the microfossils resulted from contamination of terrestrial origin.

In 2001, researchers found that the Murchison meteorite contained polyols, which are organic sugar compounds similar to glucose. Glucose is considered fundamental to metabolism on Earth. Sugars also make up parts of cell membranes and the backbone of the DNA molecule.

In the period of time since it fell to Earth, the Murchison meteorite has become one of the most well-studied meteorites in the world. It has been closely scrutinized for the differences it reveals between organic molecules and microfossils found on Earth and those of purported extraterrestrial origin.

PRIMARY SOURCE

Many amino acids contain an asymmetric centre, occurring as laevorotatory, L, or dextrorotatory, D, compounds. It is generally assumed that abiotic synthesis of amino acids on the early Earth resulted in racemic mixtures (L- and D-enantiomers in equal abundance). But the origin of life required, owing to conformational constraints, the almost exclusive selection of either L- or D-enantiomers, and the question of why living systems on the Earth consist of L-enantiomers rather than D-enantiomers is unresolved. A substantial fraction of the organic compounds on the early Earth may have been derived from comet and meteorite impacts. It has been reported previously that amino acids in the Murchison meteorite exhibit an excess of L-enantiomers, raising the possibility that a similar excess was present in the initial inventory of organic compounds on the Earth. The stable carbon isotope compositions of individual amino acids in Murchison support an extraterrestrial origin—rather than a terrestrial overprint of biological amino acids—although reservations have persisted. Here we show that individual amino-acid enantiomers from Murchison are enriched in ^{15}N relative to their terrestrial counterparts, so confirming an extraterrestrial source for an L-enantiomer excess in the Solar System that may predate the origin of life on the Earth.

SIGNIFICANCE

Research into the origins of life on Earth predicts that life probably started around one billion years after the planet was formed. Several scientists, most notably Francis Crick, who helped discover the structure of DNA, have suggested that meteorites crashing into Earth during the early part of its formation may have seeded the planet with the types of molecules required for life.

Classic experiments by Stanley Miller and Harold Urey in the early 1950s at the University of Chicago showed that organic molecules present in the primordial Earth could, under the proper conditions, result in the chemical synthesis of amino acids. However, if meteorites like the Murchison meteorite were crashing into Earth and bringing with them complements of amino acids, this might have accelerated the process.

The theory that extraterrestrial forces influenced life on Earth is called panspermia. The idea has a variety of social and scientific implications, including the possibility that if life could have been seeded extraterrestrially on Earth, such seeding could also have occurred on other planets.

One of the most debated issues around the composition of the Murchison meteorite concerns the chirality of its amino acids. Chirality refers to molecules that occur in forms that are mirror images of each other. A good example of chirality is a person's two hands. They have the same structure, but are mirror images of each other.

On Earth, all biological processes use one of the two chiral forms of amino acids, referred to as left-handed molecules or L-enantiomers. When chemists synthesize amino acids from molecules that have no chirality, the result is an equal number of right-handed and left-handed molecules, a mixture known as racemic. A meteorite formed in space is expected to have a racemic mixture of amino acids.

As stated by Engel and Macko, analyses of the chirality of the amino acids in the Muchison meteorite in 1997, as well as in 1971, 1982, and 1990, show that the composition of the meteorite is predominately left-handed. Such a finding supports the hypothesis that left-handed extraterrestrial molecules could have seeded life on Earth.

One of the major issues surrounding the findings from the Murchison meteorite involves questions of contamination. A variety of experiments were performed on the meteorite to address the question of contamination by terrestrial molecules. In one, several amino acids that are not found on Earth were studied. These were found to have a left-handed dominance just like the analysis of the studies of the full complement of amino acids. In addition, stable isotope analyses were performed on the isotopes of atoms found in

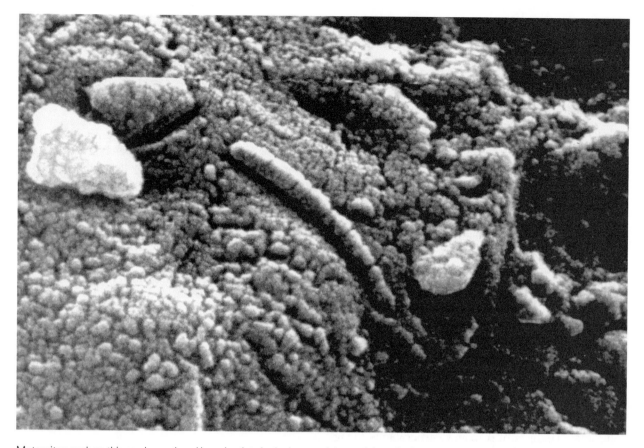

Meteorites such as this can be analyzed by scientists in the hopes of determining whether or not extraterrestrial life contributed to the development of life on Earth. AP IMAGES

the meteorite. These experiments showed that the isotopic composition of both the left-handed and right-handed molecules was identical. Although both of these studies suggest that contamination was unlikely, the question of contamination of the meteorite by terrestrial organisms is still heavily debated in the scientific community.

FURTHER RESOURCES
Periodicals

Engel, Michael H. and Stephen A. Macko. "Stable Isotope Analysis of Amino Acid Enantiomers in the Murchison Meteorite at Natural Abundance Levels." *Proceedings of the SPIE—The International Society for Optical Engineering* 3111 (1997): 82.

Hoover, Richard B. "Meteorites, Microfossils, and Exobiology." *Proceedings of the SPIE—The International Society for Optical Engineering* 3111 (1997): 115.

MacDermott, Alexandra J. "Distinguishing the Chiral Signature of Life in the Solar System and Beyond." *Proceedings of the SPIE—The International Society for Optical Engineering* 3111 (1997): 272.

Web sites

Astrobiology Magazine. "Murchison's Amino Acids: Tainted Evidence?" <http://www.astrobio.net/news/article375.html> (accessed November 14, 2005).

BookRags.com. "Murchison Meteorite." <http://www.bookrags.com/sciences/earthscience/murchison-meteorite-woes-02.html> (accessed November 14, 2005).

Cosmic Ancestry. "Fossilized Life Forms in the Murchison Meteorite." <http://www.panspermia.org/hoover.htm> (accessed November 14, 2005).

Science@NASA. "Sweet Meteorites." <http://science.nasa.gov/headlines/y2001/ast20dec_1.htm> (accessed November 14, 2005).

SPACE.com. "Fossilized Bacteria Found in Ancient Meteorite." <http://www.space.com/scienceastronomy/generalscience/murchison_metor_000221.html> (accessed November 14, 2005) .

"The Greenland Expedition of 1925"

Book excerpt

By: Richard Evelyn Byrd

Date: 1925

Source: Byrd, Richard E. "The Greenland Expedition of 1925." *To the Pole.* Columbus, OH: Ohio State University Press, 1998.

About the Author: Richard Evelyn Byrd (1888–1957) was a naval aviator and transatlantic flyer who instilled such confidence in the public with his naval record and early explorations that his admirers financed his early trips to Antarctica. Prior to his southerly trip, Byrd's explorations took him to Greenland and then over the North Pole, a trip that he documented in his diary.

INTRODUCTION

Admiral Byrd began his career in the U.S. Navy and earned his wings as an aviator in 1918. His early career was marked by his successful attempts at night-time water landings of seaplanes, experiments flying over water out of sight of land, and his contributions to the war. His high-risk flights led him to further experimentation, this time with various scientific instruments used for navigation when there were no solid land-based points of reference. In 1919, he was involved in prepping the Navy-Curtiss (NC) flying boats for their first transatlantic flights, assigned by the Navy to plan the flight navigation. But a childhood fascination with polar exploration led to his eventual involvement in flights to both the Arctic and Antarctic regions. When Byrd announced in 1926 that he, with copilot Floyd Bennett, had flown over the North Pole during a trip to Greenland, his claim was met with a certain amount of skepticism as it was the first time such a trip had been completed successfully. The primary reason behind the skepticism was that Byrd stated the entire trip took sixteen hours, and it was believed that his plane would have been incapable of making the trip in such a short amount of time.

The years 1924 and 1925 were eventful both for aerial Arctic exploration and Byrd. In 1924, President Calvin Coolidge authorized a plan according to which a U.S. Navy dirigible, the *Shenandoah*, would fly from Point Barrow in Alaska, pass over the North Pole, and then land at Spitzbergen in Norway. Scientists and veterans of polar exploration like Captain Robert Bartlett, who had accompanied Robert Peary in 1909,

lobbied for the attempt. The expedition was the project of the Navy Bureau of Aeronautics and Admiral William Moffett. Byrd, who reported to Moffett, was responsible for planning the expedition and doing the navigating. Unfortunately, in January, storms damaged the *Shenandoah*, and the expedition ended before it began.

Byrd and Bartlett, undaunted, continued to plan for an aerial expedition to the North. Because Congress seemed reluctant, they decided to raise the money from private backers, as Peary and Cook had done. Bartlett agreed to find a suitable vessel and generous donors; Byrd's job was to ask the Navy for seaplanes and help with fund-raising. Byrd went to Detroit, met with Edsel Ford, and won his promise of $15,000. John D. Rockefeller contributed a similar amount, and the expedition seemed likely to become a reality.

Byrd and Bartlett were not without competitors. In 1924, Roald Amundsen, who had reached the South Pole by dogsled in 1911, planned to fly airplanes into Greenland and the Arctic. Amundsen allied himself with Commander Lincoln Ellsworth, the son of an American millionaire, to purchase planes and begin an expedition in 1925. Byrd had originally volunteered to join Amundsen, but he was rejected.

PRIMARY SOURCE

Thursday, January 1, 1925.

I wonder what the new year holds. Strange but the first seven months in every new year interesting things seem to happen to me. Every year seems to hold something unusual. I was married in January. Got severely broken up in December. When I was a kid my trip around the world was decided in May. Entered the naval academy in May. Graduated in June. Went to Mexico in March. Left in England nearly dead with typhoid fever in June on one of the battleships. Went through Haitian and San Dominican revolutions in May–June. Went to war in April. Was assigned to aviation in June. Returned to states from war in January. Assigned to navigational preparations for first transatlantic flight in Jan. Was promised flight across Atlantic Ocean on ZR-2 in July. Escaped explosion of ZR-2 in August. Volunteered for Amundsen flight in Jan. but was ordered same month to Washington to assist Admiral Moffett in preparation for trans-Polar flight in *Shenandoah*, Got Bureau Aviation Bill through Congress in February.

I have been dreaming all winter of a trans-polar flight. I wonder if it will materialize. The President will not, I am sure, permit the *Shenandoah*, or the *Los Angeles* to make the trip. When Congress adjourns, I shall wire Bob Bartlett and try to work out some scheme with him to raise some money and somehow or other get hold of a small dirigible—one of the e-type—and try the pack [ice] and unexplored region of the Arctic. I was greatly disappointed last year when the President called off the transpolar flight of the *Shenandoah*. There is a bill up in Congress to promote me. It will mean a tremendous lot to me but there are hundreds of bills on the calendar. What chance will my bill have?

Saturday, January 3, 1925

Is the human race an accidental by-product of the cosmical processes? If God directs us, remaining silent and inscrutable to us, then he means either that he does not want us to know him or he is indifferent or he has made the knowing of him a difficult task.

Saturday, June 20, 1925

The 20th has come at last and we left Wiscassett [Maine] at 2.45 P.M. today on schedule date. As anxious as I have been to get started on the expedition, I have felt so sad at leaving my precious family that I haven't been able to mention the subject to Marie. I am doing her (apparently) a miserable mean trick in causing her to go through all the apprehensions she has felt for weeks and will for weeks to come. I feel mightily low and wicked today on account of it and the wonderful send off we got from thousands of people has meant absolutely nothing to me for nothing could matter with this terrible ache I have tried so hard to hide.

Dear little Dickie [Richard Byrd, Jr.] didn't realize what it was all about and that made me feel still more useless. Poor little fellow. He is too young to realize what an irresponsible "dad" he has. Marie as always was a wonderful sport.

With all this on my mind, I had to make a speech on the City Common to hundreds of people and also accept for the naval unit wonderful hunting knives presented to the personnel by the National Aeronautic Association of Maine.

Tuesday, July 7, 1925

Met famous Mr. Perritt and family at Hopedale [Labrador].

Wednesday, July 8, 1925

Had a very narrow escape from death a few minutes ago. [Harold E.] Gray and [Paul J.] McGee had just run a heavy copper uninsulated cable from the radio room across the gangway about the height of my head. They were trying it out with 1,000,000 volts and watching and listening to anyone passing by. I had on rubber shoes and was coming from aft behind their radio room door which was half open so that they neither heard nor saw me. My

head got six inches from that wire before I was stopped and the 1,000,000 volts would have jumped to my head had I gotten one inch nearer! Gray was white as a sheet. There's another narrow squeak. The gods of chance have been good to me. That wire will have to be well insulated.

Sunday, July 12, 1925

At last we are underway again. I am so anxious to get to Etah that every day's delay seems like a week. We had another near tragedy today. While standing on the bridge about 2 P.M. taking some sights I saw some thick smoke coming from amidships. I was there in a jiffy and found a pile of life preservers on fire. They were piled against one of the wooden wing crates near the planes. I threw one of the preservers overboard and put the fire extinguisher on the rest of them. We are already short on life preservers, so the incident is unfortunate but it could have been so much worse. Another minute and the flame would have ignited the oil and kerosene the plane is soaked in and nothing in the world could have saved this ship with 7600 gallons of gasoline around her decks.

As a result of this fire McDonald has agreed with my recommendation to put on a fire watch including the personnel of the naval unit and the doctor, [Jacob] Gayer and Kelty of the last three will volunteer, which of course they will do. When I suggested a watch, [A.C.] Neld immediately volunteered to go on watch. I have never seen such spirit as my men have. They never require orders.

Got a ticker today. Chronometer "A" 3.5 seconds fast. That is bad.

Wednesday, July 15, 1925

We should reach Disco [Island, near Greenland] tomorrow morning. McDonald told me today that MacMillan had given orders for us to wait for him at Disco. I told McDonald that the project might be a failure if we had to do that for it would probably be another two days before the *Bowdoin* would leave Hopedale and probably five or six days more getting here. Then a day or two wait here and we would get up at Etah too late to accomplish our mission. I urged McDonald in the strongest terms to ask MacMillan to let us leave Disco as soon as we got coal and water and to call his attention to the urgency of the matter. He promised to do that.

Thursday, July 16, 1925

Arrived Godhavn. Disco this morning 5:30. The local and district Danish governor came aboard early and gave us the startling information that we can get not a single ton of coal here. We haven't enough coal to get up to Etah and back here. There seems to be no coal on the Greenland coast. It looks as if the expedition is ruined but we'll get that coal somehow. The governor admits that he has coal and is mining it at the other end of the island but when winter comes he will have just enough for the eskimos here and in surrounding villages.

On top of this no one is allowed to go to the village (about 150 eskimos) because the eskimos have an epidemic of whooping cough. The governor says he is afraid we will carry the disease north and give it to the Etah eskimos. I tried to get the governor to have some laundry done for me but he said it couldn't be done. There has been no evidence what so ever of any hospitality.

Saturday, July 25, 1925

Do not the enigmas which life presents keep our interest as nothing else could. It is the inscrutableness of the sweetheart that keeps the lover happy and thrilled. There can be few bored moments if one can be alive to the contradictions which life presents. Does not there seem to be wisdom used for our good.

Sunday, July 12 1925

This is the day I had hoped to reach Etah but here we are [at Godhavn].

Monday, July 27, 1925

Got underway this morning at 4:20. Seven more precious hours lost. I wish I could see this thing as MacMillan sees it. At 9:30 the *Bowdoin* hoisted sail and stopped her engine. For an hour and a half we trailed after her making only five knots.

Tuesday July 28, 1925

7:45 a.m. Ran into flat pack ice today about 60 miles north of Upernivik. At first the flat pack ice was in cakes and far apart but gradually the cakes got larger and larger until about 5 this morning the *Peary* and *Bowdoin* were completely surrounded by an apparently unbroken field of ice. A number of the boys went over the ship's side on the ice and walked several miles from the ships seal hunting. [Bromfied?] from the *Bowdoin* shot a seal in the head (a seal floats only when shot in the head). The seal was in a lead opened up by the *Peary*. We went after her in one of the *Bowdoin* boats. The *Peary* has been under a great strain bucking ice for the past seventeen hours. She is however very staunch and powerful and has stood the strain well.

10 P.M. A lead opened up for us about 8 A.M. and we got out of the solid ice but there was continual bucking of large flat cake[s] of ice until 6 P.M.. Now the water is a dead calm and only a few ice bergs are in sight.

Wednesday, July 29, 1925

About 5 A.M. ran into fog and thick ice-caked field of pack ice. It is now 10 P.M. and the fog still envelops us. After lunch we walked a mile and a half to the northward but there was no break of any kind. It was a curious sensation to be enveloped in fog out on a flat field of ice in the middle of the summer. [Peter] Sorenson and [Floyd]

Bennett [both of the naval aviation unit] went with me. We did not pass a living thing the whole way.

After dinner walked two miles to the westward with [Albert] Francis and found an open lead that melted away in the fog. It ran northwest and southeast, the direction we want to go. I told MacMillan about it hoping that we would follow it through. He could get into it by following the lead we came here in. MacMillan says we will get underway if it clears a bit. Another precious day has been lost. We saw the track of a huge polar bear near the *Bowdoin* but no sign of [the bear] Bruno.

Our plane could probably get off this snow with skis.

The snow is quite sloshy in places and I was glad to find my eskimo boots water proof. Francis went in up to his knees. I had two close squeaks from getting a wetting.

The trouble is that we are heading for land too far to the eastward. We are bound to get into ice.

SIGNIFICANCE

In 1924, when Byrd's assigned transport flight by dirigible from Alaska to Spitzbergen was cancelled, he began looking for other ways to make a flight expedition to the Arctic. He ended up joining a National Geographic Society-sponsored trip to Greenland in 1925. The journey was the MacMillan Expedition, and with it Byrd made his first flights to Ellsmere Island and interior portions of Greenland. This was the first of his expeditions to be chronicled in a slim diary that was discovered among Byrd's papers in the late 1990s. In it, he included details of the dangers faced during the voyage, not all of which were related to the wildness of the region.

For his next trip, Byrd joined a privately-funded expedition to the Arctic in 1926. The purpose of the venture was to make a number of flights over the pack ice, including over the North Pole. At the time Byrd and his copilot claimed to have made the North Pole flight, there was controversy over whether or not they were telling the truth, based primarily on the short time frame and unfavorable wind direction during the reported journey. Byrd's diary, however, serves as an indication that they did, in fact, make the trip over the North Pole successfully.

Beyond being a record of Byrd's flights, his diary chronicles many of the experiences he had during his expeditions, and reflects the uniqueness of the regions he was one of the first people to explore. It also bears witness to the hardships of traveling through less populated parts of the world, illustrating that the explorers not only faced their own problems, but created them for others as well. On one occasion they

The view obtained by flying over Greenland encompasses glaciers, icebergs, and the Greenland ice cap. AP IMAGES

faced coal shortages that threatened their progress, while on another they found themselves shut out of an Eskimo village where there was an epidemic of the whooping cough, for fear that they would transport the disease to regions that had no experience with the ailment. Thick fog stranded the explorers on several days, preventing them from traveling due to lack of visibility. Sea-bound portions of the journey were sometimes hindered by cold northerly temperatures, when the water froze around the boat to the point where it was no longer able to break through the ice.

Byrd's early expeditions set the foundation for his later explorations to Antarctica. He worked to adapt various types of machinery to accompany him on his trips, whether for the purpose of collecting samples of the ecosystems he studied on his voyages, or simply for hauling supplies over different types of ice and terrain when he had reached his destinations. Only the onset of World War II and his return to active Naval duty as Chief of Naval Operations slowed his explorations, but he continued to promote expeditions to the polar regions, particularly Antarctica, once the war was over, up until his death in 1957. The Institute for Polar Studies was founded in 1960, to unite scientists

dedicated to polar research, and in 1985, the Institute acquired Byrd's collected papers. In 1987, they renamed the Institute the Byrd Polar Research Center.

FURTHER RESOURCES

Web sites

Browne, Malcolm W. "Byrd's-Eye View," review of *To the Pole: The Diary and Notebook of Richard E. Byrd, 1925–1927*, edited by Raimund E. Goerler. *New York Times Book Review Online*, June 7, 1998. <http://www.nytimes.com/books/first/g/goerler-pole.html?_r=2&oref=slogin&oref=slogin> (accessed March 17, 2006).

Goerler, Raimund, and Richard Cullather. "Admiral Robert E. Byrd, 1888–1957." *Byrd Polar Research Center, Ohio State University*. <http://polarmet.mps.ohio-state.edu/AboutByrd/AboutByrd.html> (accessed March 17, 2006).

"Richard Byrd's Greenland Expedition, 1925." *ArcticWebsite.com*. <http://arcticwebsite.com/Byrd1925GreDir.html> (accessed March 17, 2006).

The Science Bit... Part 3... The Larsen B Ice Shelf Disintegration

Journal entry

By: Carol Pudsey

Date: March 13, 2002

Source: Pudsey, Carol. "The Science Bit... Part 3... The Larsen B Ice Shelf Disintegration." RRS *James Clark Ross Diary*. Available online at *British Antarctic Survey* <http://www.antarctica.ac.uk/Living_and_Working/Diaries/RRS_James_Clark_Ross/antarctic2001_2002/jrupdate11_26.html> (accessed February 10, 2006).

About the Author: Carol Pudsey was the principal scientist aboard the RRS *James Clark Ross*, which was in the region of the Larsen B Ice Sheet when it began to disintegrate. She received her Ph.D. in geology in 1977. Pudsey worked with the British Antarctic survey between 1987 and 2005 where she participated in twelve geoscience research cruises, five of which she acted as principal scientist. Pudsey's research interests involve understanding the history and formation of sediments and ice cores.

INTRODUCTION

Antarctic ice shelves are horizontal sheets of ice that extend away from the land and float on top of the ocean. Ice shelves ring the entire continent, with extremely large shelves occupying the large gulfs in western portion of Antarctica. The total volume of ice in the ice shelves off of Antarctica is 173,369 cubic miles (722,635 cubic km), which accounts for 2.4 percent of the total ice on the continent. Ice shelves comprise eleven percent of the surface area of the continent.

Ice shelves form when glaciers and ice sheets moving across the land discharge into the ocean. The ice floats on top of the ocean and the shelf spreads out over the water by the force of gravity. Friction of the ice against walls, islands, and sea floor raises, retards, and stabilizes the movement of the ice flow.

The balance of ice added and ice removed controls the size of ice shelves. They increase in size when glaciers and ice sheets contribute more ice and when there is more snowfall. They decrease in size when icebergs calve off the edge into the ocean and when ice melts into the ocean below.

The Larsen Ice Shelf is a series of small shelves on the east coast of the Antarctic Peninsula in the western part of the continent from about seventy-one to sixty-four degrees South latitude. The shelf is divided into sections: the northernmost named Larson A. The much larger Larson B abuts Larson A to the south, followed by Larson C.

In the 1940s, Larson A began retreating. In January 1995, a dramatic disintegration of the ice shelf occurred, resulting in 772.2 square miles (2000 square km) of ice breaking into small icebergs during a storm. This disintegration was attributed to the climactic warming around Antarctica in the second half of the twentieth century.

Between January 31 and March 7, 2002, the Larson B ice shelf disintegrated. Within 45 days, satellites captured the dramatic breakup of 1255 square miles (3,250 square km) of ice shelf. The British research ship, *James Clark Ross*, happened to be in the area of the Larson Ice Shelf during its destruction. The principal scientist on the ship, Pudsey, recorded her observations in the ship's diary on March 13, 2002.

PRIMARY SOURCE

We had been planning to survey and core in the area of the Larsen-B ice shelf where some large icebergs have calved in recent years. Early in the cruise we heard that there had been another calving event, about 8 km of icefront amounting to 600 sq. km, between 31/1/02 and 17/2/02. In the memorable words of our colleague David Vaughan at BAS Cambridge, "*And if it's still warm and you're near the icefront keep your eyes open and note anything that goes bump in the night. There is no reason to think that it's all over for this season.*"

On March 5th we received a satellite image revealing the complete disintegration of the northern half of Larsen-B. From this and the ship's Dartcom HRPT satellite images [High Resolution Picture Transmission satellites receive digital images from National Oceanic and Atmospheric Administration environmental satellites], the mass of disintegration debris seemed to be expanding eastwards and southwards, as the Larsen-A debris was observed to do in 1995. On March 7th the ship made a considered approach in between the southern edge of the debris and a row of four very large tabular bergs extending NE of Jason Peninsula [the southern extent of the Larson B ice shelf]. These four bergs were drifting northwards towards the edge of the debris, and in the limited time available a systematic swath survey was not possible. We were able to observe and photograph the debris and take one core before escaping to the south at nightfall. The large tabular bergs which we knew to be freshly broken were an amazing sight, beautiful clean ice cliffs with a vertical or overhanging profile. The main mass of debris looked like the aftermath of a huge explosion - certainly brought home the fact that disintegration is a different process from iceberg calving. It was exciting to be there, though a little frustrating given that we couldn't see very far from the top of the ship.

SIGNIFICANCE

The breakup of the Larsen B ice shelf was the largest single ice shelf retreat documented. The surface area lost was nearly twice the size of Rhode Island. Using information gathered from the sediments below the ice shelf, it had likely been in place for at least 400 years, and was likely formed nearly 12,000 years ago during the last Ice Age. Because ice shelves float on top of the ocean, the melting of the ice shelf has no effect on the total sea level.

Although the reason for the ice shelf disintegration is still under debate, it is clear that the local climate played an important role. The local temperature around Antarctica increased 4.5 °F (2.5 °C) between the 1952 and 2002. This is five times greater than the global temperature increase.

Increases in temperature hasten the melting of the ice shelves in two major ways. First sea surface temperatures increase, which increases melting of the ice sheet from below. Second, melt ponds are formed on the surface of the ice shelves. The water from the ponds seeps into cracks in the ice. The pressure of the water is greater than the pressure of the air and the water forces the cracks through the entire thickness of the shelf. The buildup of large cracks throughout the shelf compromises its stability.

Satellite imagery of the ice shelves contributed greatly to the understanding of the Larson B break up. NASA's (National Aeronautical and Space Administration's) MODIS sensor (a satellite imager) was able to document the changes that took place on the ice shelf. Analysis of the satellite images showed that the ice shelf disintegrated in the same regions that were covered by melt ponds. In addition, the melt ponds became smaller just before the breakup, suggesting that the cracks formed by the water reached the bottom of the shelf, allowing the melt water to flow into the ocean below.

In the aftermath of the Larson B collapse, scientists measured the flow rates of glaciers that used to flow onto the ice shelf. They found that the glaciers flowed into the ocean at speeds up to 250 percent greater then when the ice shelf was in place. The ice shelf had acted like a brake. These results have major implications for the ice sheets on continent. Although the disintegration of ice shelves do not contribute to a rise in sea level because they are already floating, adding ice from land-bound glaciers into the ocean would contribute to an increased sea level.

Computer modeling combined with the satellite imagery of the shelves have resulted in a theory that links summertime temperatures to shelf instability. These efforts demonstrate that the next shelf south of Larson B is close to its stability limit. The summertime temperatures of one of the largest ice shelves, the Ross Ice Shelf, are only slightly cooler than necessary to make it stable. Scientists predict that if the warming trend in Antarctica continues, these shelves may begin to recede in future decades.

FURTHER RESOURCES

Web sites

Dykstra, Peter. *CNN.com*. "Monster iceberg breaks off Antarctic ice shelf." <http://archives.cnn.com/2002/TECH/space/05/09/iceberg.satellite/> (accessed February 10, 2006) .

Hulbe, C. L. *Natural Science*. "Recent changes to Antarctic Peninsula ice shelves: What lessons have been learned?" <http://www.naturalscience.com/ns/articles/01-06/ns_clh.html> (accessed February 10, 2006).

———. *Portland State University* "Larsen Ice Shelf 2002: Warmest summer on record leads to disintegration." <http://web.pdx.edu/%7Echulbe/science/Larsen/larsen2002.html> (accessed February 10, 2006).

Naranjo, Laura. *NASA Earth Observatory*. "Fragment of its Former Shelf." <http://earthobservatory.nasa.gov/Study/LarsenIceShelf/> (accessed February 10, 2006).

National Snow and Ice Data Center The Cryosphere. "Antarctic Glaciers Speed Up." <http://nsidc.org/news/press/20031219_speed_up.html > (accessed February 10, 206) .

Williams, Jack. *USA-Today.com*. "124-mile-long iceberg breaks off Antarctica." <http://www.usatoday.com/news/science/cold-science/2002-05-12-rossiceberg.htm> (accessed February 10, 2006) .

Environmental Legislation

The legal systems of early civilizations concerned themselves with land law, water rights, and agricultural practices. Today, these practices would be considered "environmental" affairs. Some ancient religious texts describe mandated rest periods for the land, stating that a field must be left fallow (not cropped) every seventh year.

However, one can find a comparatively lawless relationship to the environment. For the first century or more of its existence, the United States did little to govern its relationship with the environment. Buffalo were legally hunted to near-extinction. Also, essentially no legal restrictions on dumping waste into the water or air existed, except when the practice might annoy nearby neighbors rich enough to fight back. In the mid-1800s, scientific awareness of the interdependence of living systems grew rapidly along with cultural awareness of the value of unspoiled land and of the human tendency to spoil land. In 1864, *The Maine Woods* by Henry David Thoreau (1817–1862) was published posthumously. In the book, he called for the creation of "national preserves" of wild forests. That same year, the U.S. Congress gave California the Yosemite Valley to be a state park. In 1872, Congress made Yellowstone the first national park in the world. Congress began establishing other national parks in 1890.

These early environmental actions were all location-specific. They set aside spectacular parcels of land for the perpetual enjoyment of people. They did nothing to restrict pollution or to protect the environment at large. Such laws were few until the 1950s and 1960s. One of the first major U.S. environmental laws was the Air Pollution Control Act of 1955. The Wilderness Act (1964) legally defined wilderness and set aside 9.6 million acres (3.9 million hectares) of federal land as wilderness (0.38 percent of the United States). In 2006, some 106 million acres (42.9 million hectares) were being protected as wilderness, and thousands of state and federal laws governed air and water quality, the disposal of toxic substances, the destruction of wetlands, and other environmental issues.

International environmental laws (treaties) also exist. The Antarctica Treaty (1959) began as a split-the-pie agreement but was amended in the 1960s and 1970s to include environmental protection. Some notable international environmental laws include the Basel Convention against disposing toxic waste in developing nations. This law was cited by protestors blocking the scrapping of the French warship *Clémenceau* in India in 2006 and discussed in "Demonstration against Transfer of French Warship to India for Asbestos Removal." Other international environment laws include the Montreal Protocol (1987), which protects the ozone layer against harmful chemicals, and the Kyoto Protocol on Climate Change, which commits nations to reduced greenhouse-gas emissions (1997). The United States has not signed the Kyoto Protocol.

Environmental legislation generates both economic and social controversy. Such laws are often weakly defined so they do not interfere with economic interests. Plus, spotty or reluctant enforcement of environmental laws often weakens their effectiveness even more.

R. v. Medley and others

Legal decision

By: The English Reports

Date: 1834

Source: "*R. v. Medley and others*" in Carrington and Payne. *The English Reports*. London: 1834, 292.

About the Author: The reported text of the case of *R. v. Medley and others* was not authored, in the sense of being created by a writer. In 1834, the *English Reports*, the digest of legal decisions where the Medley case was first published, was the oldest continuous legal reporting service in the world. The short form "C.&P." as set out below the title of the case stands for Carrington and Payne, the editors of the English Reports between 1823 and 1841. In 1865, the *English Reports* were subsumed into a new legal reporting service known as the *Law Reports*, which became one of the world's most comprehensive legal databases, a publication maintained to this day under the authority of the Chief Justice of England. A separate legal reporting service commenced in 1936 known as the *All England Reports*, also digested the Medley case, and it is for this reason that both citations are mentioned.

INTRODUCTION

The city of London, England, in 1834, the setting for the incident that led to the landmark Medley prosecution, was the world's largest and most dynamic city. The Industrial Revolution begun in the eighteenth century had carried with it remarkable societal changes and contrasts in the English cities. The hereditary privileged English classes were now rivaled in wealth and influence by a rising and prosperous middle class of merchants and business people. The graceful building construction that had taken place in London during the English Restoration and Georgian periods was commonly situated not far from sprawling, teeming slums that housed a segment of the population whose existence was famously chronicled by Charles Dickens. There was little legal protection for those on the margins of society.

The English legal system prior to 1834 had no particular recognition of the now well-ordered concepts of corporate responsibility and citizenship, environmental protection or public welfare laws. Companies that had grown quickly in the face of the technological advances precipitated by the development of commercial steam power were accustomed to

acting in their best interests, with no regard for any perceived rights of others—"the law of the jungle" fairly represented the notion of corporate responsibility.

Further, the common law of England at the time reflected the historic notion, springing from Anglican Christian beliefs, that criminal responsibility for any act required proof that there existed an intent to commit the act in question. A lack of care on the part of a wrongdoer, as opposed to an intentional act, was not sufficient in England to establish a criminal wrong.

In 1834, the Equitable Gas Company operated a gas producing works on the shores of the River Thames in east London. As it had done on numerous occasions in the months before, defective machinery in the plant did not properly contain coal tar sludge, and a large quantity of this noxious overflow spilled into the river. A contemporaneous media report described the discharge as if it "smelt ready to knock anybody down." The sludge polluted the Thames in the vicinity of the Equitable plant to such an extent that fish were killed and local fisherman were deprived of their living for a considerable period. As a news report commented at the time, there was a public outcry, and as a result the directors and a number of employees of Equitable Gas were charged with criminal negligence in the discharge of this waste from the plant.

At trial, the directors claimed, consistent with the general understanding of the law at that time, that they did not order, participate in, or otherwise approve of the discharge of the coal tar. Therefore, they lacked the necessary criminal intent known as *mens rea* ("guilty mind"), to have committed any crime.

Medley, the Equitable Gas chairman, the deputy chairman, and two employees were convicted on the basis that so long as they conferred authority to others to actually operate the plant, they were morally responsible and in law guilty. The law of strict liability, and its companion, the public welfare prosecution, was born.

PRIMARY SOURCE

"Defendants unlawfully and injuriously conveyed great quantities of filthy, noxious, unwholesome and deleterious liquids, matters, scum and refuse into the river Thames, whereby the waters became charged and impregnated with the said liquid and became corrupted and insalubrious and unfit for the use of his Majesty's subjects . . . People who supported themselves and their families by catching and selling fish were deprived of their employment and reduced to great poverty and distress; (all) to the common nuisance and grievous injury of his Majesty's subjects, to the evil example, and against the peace.''

The trial proceeded before a High Court judge and jury on February 7, 1834. After the evidence was presented to the jury, they received their instructions on how to deal with the evidence from the trial judge, then Chief Justice Denman, who instructed the jury as follows:

''With respect to fishermen being thrown out of work, I ought to lose no time in informing you that will not of itself be ground for an indictment, as if it were sufficient every successful speculation in trade might be the subject of a prosecution... The words of the indictment convey the law upon the subject as well as any person sitting here can do. The question will be, whether there has been a noxious and deleterious ingredient conveyed into the river, whereby the water has been corrupted and rendered unfit for use; and if there has been, then whether, in the concluding words of the indictment, it was to the common nuisance of the king's subjects. If you think that this has been done, and that it was conveyed from the premises of the defendants then you will find them guilty...

The second question you will have to consider will be, which of the defendants are guilty of the nuisance... It is said that the directors were ignorant of what had been done. In my judgment that makes no difference; provided that you think that they gave authority to the plant superintendent to conduct the works they will be answerable. It seems to me both common sense and law that, if a person for their own advantage employ servants to conduct works, they must be answerable for what is done by those servants... In the present case you will say whether these particular individuals have done an act to the common nuisance of the king's subjects.''

SIGNIFICANCE

The jury found Medley, the Chairman of Equitable Gas, the deputy chairman, plant superintendent, and plant engineer guilty. The Court imposed fines on the individual defendants ranging from ten to twenty-five British pounds each (accounting for inflation, a twenty-five-pound fine is roughly equivalent to a one thousand dollar penalty today).

In *R. v. Medley and others*, Medley represented a dramatic first in the laws of England regarding the power and the legal ability of the state to prosecute careless—as opposed to intentional—wrongdoers. Medley quickly became a well-established precedent in similar prosecutions commenced both in England

as well as in various jurisdictions in the United States.

Medley's first notable application as a precedent was in the English case of *Regina v. Stephens*, where a quarry owner was successfully prosecuted for the obstruction of a public waterway with waste and excess rock mined from his quarry operations. It was established at trial that Stephens at no time personally oversaw the day-to-day operations of the quarry, but consistent with the theories advanced in Medley, he was deemed accountable. The Latin expression and civil law principle, *respondeat superior* ("let the master answer"), was applied in the Stephens case and became a short-form expression of how liability was assessed against company owners and directors in many legal decisions that followed. It was not a valid defense for companies, in essence, to lay responsibility entirely on the shoulders of those who were carrying out their directives as employers to their employees.

U.S. state courts also began to apply the principles of the Medley case, including its public welfare sentiments and the doctrine of respondeat superior. As the evolving American legal system moved from the 1860s and into the latter nineteenth century, there were decisions in a line of similar cases, including a number in the U.S. Supreme Court, that culminated in the Dotterweich decision of 1943, a case dealing with the duty of care imposed on a pharmaceutical company in the sale of rebranded drugs.

Medley is also an early example of what is now popularly called "judicial activism," the notion that a court can act in the absence of a stated law to advance the common good.

FURTHER RESOURCES
Books

"R. v. Medley and others" in *All England Reports*. London: 1824–1834, 123.

Sopinka, John, Sidney N. Lederman, and Alan W. Bryant. *The Law of Evidence*. Toronto: Butterworths, 1994.

Web sites

"CALI Lessons Subject List—Torts." *The Center for Computer-Assisted Legal Instruction*. <http://www2.cali.org/index.php?fuseaction=lessons.subjectlist&cat=TRT> (accessed March 10, 2006).

Kovarik, William. "Environmental History Timeline." <http://www.radford.edu/~wkovarik/envhist/> (accessed March 10, 2006).

"Legal Electronic Document Archive Home Page." *Harvard Law Review*. <http://leda.law.harvard.edu/leda/> (accessed March 10, 2006).

Department of the Interior Established

Legislation excerpt

By: United States Congress

Date: March 3, 1849

Source: Act of March 3, 1849, c. 108, 9 Stat. 395, creating the Department of the Interior. Excerpt in: *The Department of Everything Else: Highlights of Interior History.* "Appendix." by Robert M. Utley and Barry Mackintosh. Available online at: <http://www.cr.nps.gov/history/online_books/utley-mackintosh/interiora.htm> (accessed March 17, 2006).

About the Author: Robert James Walker (1804–1869), a Senator from Mississippi elected in 1835, was responsible for drafting the 1849 bill that eventually established the U.S. Department of the Interior.

INTRODUCTION

The idea to establish a department for domestic affairs, or the Home Department as it was often called, was first discussed during the formative years of the United States. The First Congress, which first met in 1789, considered such a department but finally agreed to merge together domestic and foreign affairs, thus forming the Department of State. The idea for a Home Department—what today is called the Interior Department—stayed a popular topic of discussion over the next fifty years, but never actually materialized during this period.

Between 1845 and 1848, the United States enlarged its physical proportions by more than 1 million square miles (2.6 million square kilometers), expanding its northern border to Canada and its southern border to Mexico. During this time, there was much heated debate at the federal government level as to the management of these new territories, along with the management of the states already a part of the Union. One particularly outspoken politician was Secretary of the Treasury Robert J. Walker, who favored a separate department responsible for domestic lands. He did not feel the responsibilities of the General Land Office—which under the Treasury was authorized to manage the public domain (or the public lands)—should really be a part of his department.

After performing a comprehensive review of the duties of the agencies under his control and other agencies throughout the federal government, Walker officially announced that the General Land Office, along with the Indian Affairs Office (in the War Department), The Patent Office (in the State Department), and the pension offices (in the War and Navy departments), had little in common with their (respective) departments. He suggested that they be moved into a new department, and went about drafting a bill to accomplish his objective. After the bill passed the U.S. House of Representatives on February 15, 1849, it was sent to the U.S. Senate. On the last day of the Thirtieth U.S. Congress, on March 3, 1849, the legislation was approved by the Senate, thus creating a cabinet agency known as the Department of the Interior (DOI).

PRIMARY SOURCE

An Act to establish the Home Department...

Be it enacted by the Senate and House of Representatives of the United States of America in Congress assembled, That, from and after the passage of this act, there shall be created a new executive department of the government of the United States, to be called the Department of the Interior; the head of which department shall be called the Secretary of the Interior, who shall be appointed by the President of the United States, by and with the advice and consent of the Senate, and who shall hold his office by the same tenure, and receive the same salary, as the Secretaries of the other executive departments, and who shall perform all the duties assigned to him by this act.

SEC. 2. *And be it further enacted,* That the Secretary of the Interior shall exercise and perform all the acts of supervision and appeal in regard to the office of Commissioner of Patents, now exercised by the Secretary of State; and the said Secretary of the Interior shall sign all requisitions for the advance or payment of money out of the treasury on estimates or accounts, subject to the same adjustment or control now exercised on similar estimates or accounts by the First or Fifth Auditor and First Comptroller of the Treasury.

SEC. 3. *And be it further enacted,* That the Secretary of the Interior shall perform all the duties in relation to the General Land Office, of supervision and appeal, now discharged by the Secretary of the Treasury; and the said Secretary of the Interior shall sign all requisitions for the advance or payment of money out the treasury, on estimates or accounts, approved or certified by the Commissioner of the General Land Office, subject to the same control now exercised by the First Comptroller of the Treasury.

SEC. 4. *And be it further enacted,* That the supervisory power now exercised by the Secretary of the Treasury over the accounts of the marshals, clerks, and other officers of all the courts of the United States, shall be exercised by the Secretary of the Interior, who shall sign all requisitions for the advance or payment of money out of the treasury, on estimates or accounts, subject to the same control now exercised on like estimates or accounts by the First Auditor and First Comptroller of the Treasury.

SEC. 5. *And be it further enacted,* That the Secretary of the Interior shall exercise the supervisory and appellate powers now exercised by the Secretary of the War Department, in relation to all the acts of the Commissioner of Indian Affairs; and shall sign all requisitions for the advance or payment of money out of the treasury, on estimates or accounts, subject to the same adjustment or control now exercised on similar estimates or accounts by the Second Auditor and Second Comptroller of the Treasury.

SEC. 6. *And be it further enacted,* That the Secretary of the Interior shall exercise the supervisory and appellate powers now exercised by the Secretaries of the War and Navy Departments, in relation to all the acts of the Commissioner of Pensions; and shall sign all requisitions for the advance or payment of money out of the treasury, on estimates or accounts, subject to the same adjustment or control now exercised on similar estimates or accounts by the Third or Fourth Auditors and Second Comptroller of the Treasury.

SEC. 7. *And be it further enacted,* That the Secretary of the Interior shall exercise all the supervisory and appellate powers now exercised by the Secretary of State, in relation to all acts of marshals and others in taking and returning the census of the United States; and shall sign all requisitions for the advance or payment of money out of the treasury, on estimates or accounts, subject to the same adjustment or control now exercised over similar estimates and accounts by the Fifth Auditor and First Comptroller of the Treasury.

SEC. 8. *And be it further enacted,* That the supervisory and appellate powers now exercised by the Secretary of the Treasury over the lead and other mines of the United States, and over the accounts of the agents thereof, shall be exercised by the Secretary of the Interior; who shall sign all requisitions for the advance or payment of money out of the treasury, on estimates or accounts, subject to the same adjustment or control now exercised on similar estimates or accounts by the Second Auditor and Second Comptroller of the Treasury. . . .

SIGNIFICANCE

When it was established, the Interior Department possessed a very wide range of responsibilities. Its two major divisions of duties were the country's internal development and the well-being of its people. It was further divided by such specific responsibilities as: the construction of the water system for the District of Columbia; supervision of the federal jail at the nation's capital; settlement of freed Haitian slaves; exploration of western territories; management of territorial governments; oversight of universities and hospitals; supervision of public parks; and general obligations toward Native Americans, patents, pensions, and public lands. Since the new Department was involved in just about everything else not under the jurisdiction of the other federal departments, the DOI became known in political cartoons and in discussions around Washington D.C. as "The Department of Everything Else."

The Department of Interior was largely created as a result of the acquisition of many western lands. It is, therefore, not surprising that the DOI, through the General Land Office, played a significant role in expanding the western frontiers of the country. In fact, the DOI helped to arrange for over 1.8 million homesteaders to obtain 160-acre (64.75-hectare) plots of free land (through the Homestead Act) and to secure over 94 million acres (38 million hectares) for the use of the railroads (through the Railroad Act). Money collected from such programs financed, among other things, various environmental and conservation activities for state universities and agricultural colleges.

Under the auspices of the DOI, Major John Wesley Powell helped to change the way that the government dealt with the country's natural resources. Powell conducted the Geographical and Geological Survey of the Rocky Mountain region in 1874, a significant exploration of some of the new western U.S. territories. At this time, the general opinion of most people was that the country's natural resources were boundless and, thus, did not need to be conserved because they would never run out. However, Powell disagreed with such opinions. Since Powell believed that the country's natural resources were not limitless, he strenuously fought to manage these resources based on proven science and technology and regulated under the authority of governments.

Powell aggressively argued for using sensible and methodical procedures in the management of the country's natural resources for the benefit of all U.S. citizens. The studies of the western states, such as the ones performed by Powell, provided much of the scientific research that, ultimately, resulted in the rational use of western lands and resources. Largely due to the DOI-funded studies of Powell and others, the popularity of the conservation movement came about in the 1900s. These scientific studies were also critical in

The Department of Interior, after debate, released their plans to restore a path to Yosemite Falls. The path, as modeled, includes a platform over the creek for public appreciation. AP IMAGES

deciding how the federal government would eventually irrigate arid regions of the west in order to create productive agricultural lands.

Today, the Interior Department manages for the federal government about 507 million acres (205 million hectares) of public land, which is about 20 percent of all the land of the United States; 700 million acres (283 million hectares) of underwater minerals; and the immersed lands of the Outer Continental Shelf. The DOI also protects most of the country's cultural and natural resources such as national parks, historic places, and recreational areas, and serves as the largest supplier and manager of water in seventeen western states. The U.S. Department of Interior—often called the custodian of natural resources—is considered the major conservation agency for the federal government.

FURTHER RESOURCES
Web sites

Utley, Robert M., and Barry Mackintosh. "The Department of Everything Else: Highlights of Interior History." *The National Park Service: Links to the Past*, 1989. <http:// www.cr.nps.gov/history/online_books/utley-mackintosh/index.htm> (accessed March 17, 2006).

"U.S. Department of the Interior Library." *United States Department of the Interior*. <http://library.doi.gov> (accessed March 17, 2006).

"History of the U.S. Department of the Interior." *U.S. Department of the Interior University*. <http://www.doiu. nbc.gov/orientation/history1.html> (accessed March 17, 2006).

Yellowstone National Park Act

Legislation

By: United States Congress

Date: March 1, 1872

Source: U.S. Congress. 17 Stat. 32. "Yellowstone National Park Act." March 1, 1872.

About the Author: The Congress of the United States was established by Article 1 of the U.S. Constitution of 1787. It is the legislative arm of the U.S. Federal Government. Although the actual text of the act creating Yellowstone National Park is legislative boilerplate, fashioned anonymously by the staff of a congressional committee, the real authors of the act may be regarded as a number of men who explored, mapped, and brought the Yellowstone area to the attention of the American people. The first expedition was undertaken by mine workers David E. Folsom, Charles W. Cook, and William Peterson in 1869. After thirty-six days in the Yellowstone region, they told of wonders that strained credibility, such as waterfalls shooting upwards (geysers). Reputable magazines refused to publish their accounts. Henry P. Langford was one of the members of the second expedition of 1870. It was led by Henry D. Washburn, surveyor-general of the Montana territory and comprised nineteen men, including several journalists. Afterwards, Langford traveled east to give public talks about Yellowstone. Ferdinand V. Hayden, head of the newly formed U.S. Geological Survey, after hearing him speak in Washington, D.C., convinced Congress to allocate $40,000 for a government scientific expedition into Yellowstone. This party included geologists, botanists, zoologists, the artist Thomas Moran, and the photographer William H. Jackson. It was the culmination of Langford's campaign to make the region a park. Hayden submitted a 500-page report to

Congress, and soon the Congress passed a bill making Yellowstone a national park preserve; President Ulysses S. Grant signed it into law. Langford, however, was not a disinterested environmentalist. An employee of the Northern Pacific Railroad, he combined environmentalism and development, marketing the park as part of a campaign to promote the railroad and encourage its use.

INTRODUCTION

The Congressional Act of 1872, making Yellowstone a National Park under the control of the United States Secretary of the Interior, is divided into two sections. The first, relying on the work of the expeditionary parties, defines the boundaries of the park and declares it federal property. The second section outlines what it means for a tract of land to be so designated and lays down a set of environmental guidelines. It put the newly created park under the "exclusive control" of the Secretary of the Interior and specified his responsibilities, first and foremost the creation of a body of rules, inside the congressional guidelines, to govern the use and determine the development of the park.

By creating Yellowstone National Park, the U.S. Congress recognized the wonders contained in that tract of land. They also recognized and accepted two responsibilities. The first was to preserve the land in its natural condition and protect its resources from alteration or despoliation. The second was to develop it in accord within the limits of the Act. These two responsibilities were not always compatible.

PRIMARY SOURCE

SECTION 1. *Be it enacted by the Senate and House of Representatives of the United States of America in Congress assembled,* That the tract of land in the Territories of Montana and Wyoming, lying near the head-waters of the Yellowstone river, and described as follows, to wit, commencing at the junction of Gardiner's river with the Yellowstone river, and running east to the meridian passing ten miles to the eastward of the most eastern point of Yellowstone lake; thence south along said meridian to the parallel of latitude passing ten miles south of the most southern point of Yellowstone lake; thence west along said parallel to the meridian passing fifteen miles west of the most western point of Madison lake; thence north along said meridian to the latitude of the junction of Yellowstone and Gardiner's rivers; thence east to the place of beginning, is hereby reserved and withdrawn from settlement, occupancy, or sale under the laws of the United States, and dedicated and set apart as a public park or pleasuring-ground for the benefit and enjoyment of the people; and all persons who shall locate or settle upon or occupy the same, or any part thereof, except as hereinafter provided, shall be considered trespassers and removed therefrom.

SECTION 2. That said public park shall be under the exclusive control of the Secretary of the Interior, whose duty it shall be, as soon as practicable, to make and publish such rules and regulations as he may deem necessary or proper for the care and management of the same. Such regulations shall provide for the preservation, from injury or spoliation, of all timber, mineral deposits, natural curiosities, or wonders within said park, and their retention in their natural condition. The Secretary may in his discretion, grant leases for building purposes for terms not exceeding ten years, of small parcels or ground, at such places in said park as shall require the erection of buildings for the accommodation of visitors; all of the proceeds of said leases, and all other revenues that may be derived from any source connected with said park, to be expended under his direction in the management of the same, and the construction of roads and bridle-paths therein. He shall provide against the wanton destruction of the fish and game found within said park, and against their capture or destruction for the purposes of merchandise or profit. He shall also cause all persons trespassing upon the same after the passage of this act to be removed therefrom, and generally shall be authorized to take all such measures as shall be necessary or proper to fully carry out the objects and purposes of this act.

SIGNIFICANCE

By creating Yellowstone National Park, the federal government became active in matters of environmental conservation and management regarding designated areas deemed in need of oversight, and took such land out of the direct control of the private sector. Not only a significant political act, establishing the park seemed to guarantee that parts of the North American continent would remain in their natural condition despite whatever alterations the advances of technology and industry might bring. However, it did not quite turn out that way. Commercialization of the Yellowstone area was inextricably joined to the cause of environmental conservation from its inception, and by the 1950s Yellowstone National Park was contributing nearly $20 million yearly to the economies of Wyoming, Montana, and Idaho and was the center of litigations in the three states over ownership of park concessions.

Creating the Yellowstone National Park allows an environment for the bison that roam the area. Continued controversy in the method of preserving the park could lead to trouble for this and other animals who call the park home. AP IMAGES

From the time of its creation as a national park, the Yellowstone area was seen as a rich source of income from tourism and as a recreational area. While private industrial development or construction that encroached upon and altered the land was forbidden by law, the government could and did award contracts for building roads, dining, lodging, and other tourist facilities such as gift shops. Yellowstone Park was promoted as a collection of must-see wonders, and by 1917, five thousand cars a year drove through it. In 1990, the pollution from snowmobiles at peak times surpassed pollution levels in Los Angeles.

Since the environmentally conscious 1970s, there has been a great deal of contention about how the Yellowstone ought to be treated. Some advocated scaling back its function as a recreation site. In 1974, fishing from Fishing Bridge was prohibited in order to protect the spawning of the native cutthroat trout. In 1976, the park was designated a Biosphere Reserve, and in 1978 a World Heritage Site. Other forces, however, have advocated exploiting Yellowstone's resources for profit. In 1996, President Bill Clinton opposed plans to mine for gold near Yellowstone,

which would have endangered the ecosystem. Throughout its history, the Yellowstone area has been not only a site of nature's marvels but a center of environmental and commercial controversies.

FURTHER RESOURCES
Books

Nabokov, Peter, and Lawrence Loendorf. *Restoring a Presence: American Indians and Yellowstone National Park.* Norman, OK: University of Oklahoma Press, 2004.

Olliff, Tom, Kristin Legg, and Beth Kaeding, eds. *Effects Of Winter Recreation on Wildlife of the Greater Yellowstone Area: A Literature Review and Assessment,* Washington, D.C.: Greater Yellowstone Winter Wildlife Working Group, 1999.

Wakefield, Sophia, and Angele Ferre. *Cleaning National Parks: Using Environmentally Preferable Janitorial Products at Yellowstone and Grand Teton National Parks.* Denver, CO: U.S. Environmental Protection Agency, Region 8 Pollution Prevention Program, 2000.

Wallace, Linda L., ed. *After The Fires: The Ecology of Change in Yellowstone National Park,* New Haven, CT: Yale University Press, 2004.

Web sites

Whittlesey, Lee, and Beth Kaeding. "Early Expeditions to Yellowstone," March 1997. <http://www.geocities.com/~dmonteit/explore_hist.html> (accessed March 16, 2006).

Johns, Joshua. "Thomas Moran and the American Landscape," April 1, 1996. <http://xroads.virginia.edu/~CAP/NATURE/cap3.html> (accessed March 16, 2006).

Gourley, Bruce, Russ Finley, and Tim Gourley. "National Park History," *Yellowstone Net.* <http://www.yellowstone.net/history.htm> (accessed March 16, 2006).

Rivers and Harbors Appropriation Act of 1899

Legislation

By: United States Congress

Date: 1899

Source: U.S. Congress. "Rivers and Harbors Appropriation Act of 1899." As Amended Through P.L. 106–580, December 29, 2000.

About the Author: The Congress of the United States was established by Article 1 of the U.S. Constitution of 1787. It is the legislative arm of the U.S. Federal Government.

INTRODUCTION

The Rivers and Harbors Appropriation Act of 1899 consolidated several existing laws and laid the groundwork for federal oversight of navigable waters within the United States.

The historical precedent for the Rivers and Harbors Appropriation Act of 1899 dates back to thirteenth century English common law. At that time, the Magna Carta required fish weirs—structures that impounded water to improve fishing conditions but impeded river travel and commerce—to be removed from rivers throughout England. The legal right to unimpeded navigation continued when the land that was to become the United States was colonized in the seventeenth century by England.

In 1824, the U.S. Supreme Court ruled that river navigation fell under the constitutionally granted authority of the U.S. Congress to regulate interstate commerce (*Gibbons v. Ogden*). Aaron Ogden operated steam-powered ferries between New Jersey and New York under an exclusive license granted to Robert Fulton and Robert Livingston by the State of New York. Thomas Gibbons was a competing businessman operating ferries between the same two states in violation of the exclusive license granted by New York. The court, in a decision written by Chief Justice John Marshall, ruled that river navigation between states constituted interstate commerce and therefore fell under the authority of Congress, not individual states such as New York.

Congress passed the first rivers and harbors act in 1888. It authorized the U.S. Army Corps of Engineers to require the owners of bridges obstructing navigation to remedy the situation at their own expense. At the time, the Corps of Engineers was the only existing government agency with the necessary engineering expertise. Engineering agencies such as the U.S. Bureau of Reclamation and the Tennessee Valley Authority were not created until the next century. The 1888 act was expanded in 1890 to give the Corps of Engineers broad authority over navigable waters, amended in 1892, and finally completely rewritten as the Rivers and Harbors Appropriation Act of 1899.

The concept of navigable waters has itself been the subject of legal controversy, but in terms of federal authority the definition of navigable is broad. It includes small streams along which only the smallest of boats can travel as well as rivers with stretches of unnavigable hazards such as rapids. A series of court decisions have also helped to better define the limits of federal authority over waterfront activities. Attorney General rulings during the first two decades of the twentieth century limited federal authority to activities that might impede navigation, but in 1933 the Supreme Court ruled that the Corps of Engineers could deny a permit for construction of a wharf along the Potomac River because it would be ugly. Because the proposed wharf would not have impeded navigation, the court decision provided a precedent for federal authority over activities not directly related to navigation. By the 1960s, the non-navigational activities over which the federal government claimed authority included those that might affect fish and wildlife, water quality, and the general public interest.

The most widely used provision of the Rivers and Harbors Appropriation Act of 1899 is likely Section 10, which requires a Corps of Engineers permit for any activity that fills or modifies any navigable water within the United States. Section 10 permits are a major requirement for almost every construction project along shorelines or riverbanks within the United States.

With the Manhattan skyline in the background, small tugboats draw the Queen Mary into its berth on the 51st Street pier in New York City, once such harbor covered by the River and Harbor Act, 1936. © THE MARINERS' MUSEUM/CORBIS

Another part of the act, Section 13, specifically forbids the discharge of any waste other than sewage into navigable waters. As such, it was the precursor of modern water quality protection laws and is sometimes referred to as the Refuse Act. Although the provisions of Section 13 cover a wide variety of activities harmful to water quality, the exemption of sewer discharge caused problems that would persist for more than a century. In 1921, for example, the government found that it had no authority to stop the discharge of oil dumped into sewers even though it posed a significant fire hazard in New York and other cities. It would also be many decades before municipalities, especially smaller cities, built adequate sewage treatment plants to reduce the discharge of human and industrial waste into navigable waters.

PRIMARY SOURCE

RIVERS AND HARBORS ACT OF 1899
SECTION 10

33 U.S.C. 403 The creation of any obstruction not affirmatively authorized by Congress, to the navigable capacity of any of the waters of the United States is prohibited; and it shall not be lawful to build or commence the building of any wharf, pier, dolphin, boom, weir, breakwater, bulkhead, jetty, or other structures in any port, roadstead, haven, harbor, canal, navigable river, or other water of the United States, outside established harbor lines, or where no harbor lines have been established, except on plans recommended by the Chief of Engineers and authorized by the Secretary of the Army; and it shall not be lawful to excavate or fill, or in any manner to alter or modify the course, location, condition, or capacity of, any port, roadstead, haven, harbor, canal, lake, harbor of refuge, or inclosure within the limits of any breakwater, or of the channel of any navigable water of the United States, unless the work has been recommended by the Chief of Engineers and authorized by the Secretary of the Army prior to beginning the same.

SIGNIFICANCE

The Rivers and Harbors Appropriation Act of 1899 is significant because it established the authority of the federal government to regulate activities along almost all waters within the United States. Although the initial motivation was the need for unimpeded movement of vessels in support of interstate commerce, the act also contained provisions that recognized the importance of water quality and eventually led to specific anti-pollution legislation during the second half of the twentieth century.

FURTHER RESOURCES

Books

Office of History, U.S. Army Corps of Engineers. *The History of the U.S. Army Corps of Engineers*. Honolulu, Hawaii: University Press of the Pacific, 2004.

Web sites

Kovarik, Bill. "Oil Pollution and the National Coast Anti-Pollution League." *The Environmental History Timeline*. <http://www.radford.edu/~wkovarik/envhist/coast.html> (accessed February 28, 2006).

Panza, Kenneth S. "Ogden vs. Gibbons (1824): Breaking the Fulton-Livingston Monopoly." *Hudson River Maritime Museum*. <http://www.ulster.net/~hrmm/steamboats/monopoly.html> (accessed February 28, 2006).

Federal Power Act of 1920, as amended

Legislation

By: United States Congress

Date: 1920

Source: U.S. Congress. Federal Power Act of 1920, Section 797. Washington, D.C.: 1920.

About the Author: The Congress of the United States was established by Article 1 of the U.S. Constitution of 1787. It is the legislative arm of the U.S. Federal Government.

INTRODUCTION

The United States has used hydroelectric power for meeting its energy demands since the late nineteenth century. Earlier, hydropower was used largely for pumping and milling corn and grain. The first hydroelectric plant in the United States generated electricity on July 24, 1880, to power sixteen Brush arc lamps used to provide theater and storefront illumination in Grand Rapids, Michigan. Subsequently, hydroelectric projects gained rapid popularity, and around 1,500 hydroelectric projects were set up in a short span, producing around one-third of the United States' energy requirements.

By the early twentieth century, the Federal Power Commission was established under the Federal Power Act of 1920. The primary task of the commission was to license and oversee the commissioning of hydroelectric power projects in the United States. It performed various other tasks such as investigating and collecting data regarding water utilization in areas marked for hydroelectric power development, cooperation with other national and regional agencies, publishing relevant information with regard to the status and development of hydroelectric projects, and other such information.

The jurisdiction of the Commission continued to expand over the coming years keeping in mind the technological development in the field of energy. Throughout the twentieth century, many hydroelectric plants were set up under the guidance and jurisdiction of the Federal Power Commission. In 1997, the U.S. Congress reorganized the Federal Power Commission and named it as the Federal Energy Regulatory Commission (FERC).

Thanks to a high number of hydroelectric projects, the United States in the early twenty-first century has high hydroelectric capacity. According to the National Hydropower Association, the total installed hydroelectric capacity in the United States stands at around 103.8 gigawatts. In 2003, facilities in the United States developed around 96,000 megawatts of hydroelectricity—equivalent to around 500 million barrels of oil.

Consequently, the United States produces nearly 10 percent of its electricity from hydropower, making it one of the largest producers of hydroelectricity in the world. Nearly half of the hydroelectric power produced worldwide is generated in the United States.

A typical hydroelectric power plant at Gulf Island on the Androscoggin River in Lewiston, Maine. Studies show that hydroelectric power plants are 90 percent efficient at producing electricity. AP IMAGES

The primary source details Section 797 of the Federal Power Act of 1920, which mentions various powers and authorities including licensing rights the commission availed under the said Act.

PRIMARY SOURCE

The Commission is authorized and empowered—

(a) Investigations and data To make investigations and to collect and record data concerning the utilization of the water resources of any region to be developed, the water-power industry and its relation to other industries and to interstate or foreign commerce, and concerning the location, capacity, development costs, and relation to markets of power sites, and whether the power from Government dams can be advantageously used by the United States for its public purposes, and what is a fair value of such power, to the extent the Commission may deem necessary or useful for the purposes of this chapter.

(b) Statements as to investment of licenses in projects; access to projects, maps, etc. To determine the actual legitimate original cost of and the net investment in a licensed project, and to aid the Commission in such determinations, each licensee shall, upon oath, within a reasonable period of time to be fixed by the Commission, after the construction of the original project or any addition thereto or betterment thereof, file with the Commission in such detail as the Commission may require, a statement in duplicate showing the actual legitimate original cost of construction of such project addition, or betterment, and of the price paid for water rights, rights-of-way, lands, or interest in lands. The licensee shall grant to the Commission or to its duly authorized agent or agents, at all reasonable times, free access to such project, addition, or betterment, and to all maps, profiles, contracts, reports of engineers, accounts, books, records, and all other papers and documents relating thereto. The statement of actual legitimate original cost of said project, and revisions thereof as determined by the Commission, shall be filed with the Secretary of the Treasury.

(c) Cooperation with executive departments; information and aid furnished Commission To cooperate with the executive departments and other agencies of State or National Governments in such investigations; and for such purpose the several departments and agencies of the National Government are authorized and directed upon the request of the Commission, to furnish such records, papers, and information in their possession as may be requested by the Commission, and temporarily to detail to the Commission such officers or experts as may be necessary in such investigations.

(d) Publication of information, etc.; reports to Congress To make public from time to time the information secured hereunder, and to provide for the publication of its reports and investigations in such form and manner as may be best adapted for public information and use. The Commission, on or before the 3d day of January of each year, shall submit to Congress for the fiscal year preceding a classified report showing the permits and licenses issued under this subchapter, and in each case the parties thereto, the terms prescribed, and the moneys received if any, or account thereof.

(e) Issue of licenses for construction, etc., of dams, conduits, reservoirs, etc. To issue licenses to citizens of the United States, or to any association of such citizens, or to any corporation organized under the laws of the United States or any State thereof, or to any State or municipality for the purpose of constructing, operating, and maintaining dams, water conduits, reservoirs, power houses, transmission lines, or other project works necessary or convenient for the development and improvement of navigation and for the development, transmission, and utilization of power across, along, from, or in any of the streams or other bodies of water over which Congress has jurisdiction under its authority to regulate commerce with foreign nations and among the several States, or upon any part of the public lands and reservations of the United States (including the Territories), or for the purpose of utilizing the surplus water or water power from any Government dam, except as herein provided: Provided, That licenses shall be issued within any reservation only after a finding by the Commission that the license will not interfere or be inconsistent with the purpose for which such reservation was created or acquired, and shall be subject to and contain such conditions as the Secretary of the department under whose supervision such reservation falls shall deem necessary for the adequate protection and utilization of such reservations: Provided further, That no license affecting the navigable capacity of any navigable waters of the United States shall be issued until the plans of the dam or other structures affecting the navigation have been approved by the Chief of Engineers and the Secretary of the Army. Whenever the contemplated improvement is, in the judgment of the Commission, desirable and justified in the public interest for the purpose of improving or developing a waterway or waterways for the use or benefit of interstate or foreign commerce, a finding to that effect shall be made by the Commission and shall become a part of the records of the Commission: Provided further, That in case the Commission shall find that any Government dam may be advantageously used by the United States for public purposes in addition to navigation, no license therefor shall be issued until two years after it shall have reported to Congress the facts and conditions relating thereto, except that this provision shall not apply to any Government dam constructed prior to June 10, 1920: And provided further, That upon the filing of any application for a license which has not been preceded by a preliminary permit under subsection (f) of this section, notice shall be given and published as required by the proviso of said subsection. In deciding whether to issue any license under this subchapter for any project, the Commission, in addition to the power and development purposes for which licenses are issued, shall give equal consideration to the purposes of energy conservation, the protection, mitigation of damage to, and enhancement of, fish and wildlife (including related spawning grounds and habitat), the protection of recreational opportunities, and the preservation of other aspects of environmental quality.

(f) Preliminary permits; notice of application To issue preliminary permits for the purpose of enabling applicants for a license hereunder to secure the data and to perform the acts required by section 802 of this title: Provided, however, That upon the filing of any application for a preliminary permit by any person, association, or corporation the Commission, before granting such application, shall at once give notice of such application in writing to any State or municipality likely to be interested in or affected by such application; and shall also publish notice of such application once each week for four weeks in a daily or weekly newspaper published in the county or counties in which the project or any part hereof or the lands affected thereby are situated.

(g) Investigation of occupancy for developing power; orders Upon its own motion to order an investigation of any occupancy of, or evidenced intention to occupy, for the purpose of developing electric power, public lands, reservations, or streams or other bodies of water over which Congress has jurisdiction under its authority to regulate commerce with foreign nations and among the several States by any person, corporation, State, or municipality and to issue such order as it may find appropriate, expedient, and in the public interest to conserve and utilize the navigation and water-power resources of the region.

SIGNIFICANCE

There is an ongoing debate in the United States about the use of fossil fuels and conventional resources for meeting its energy requirements. The United States consumes nearly 25 percent of the global oil production. Until 1970, it was able to meet its oil demands internally. However in the decades that have followed, the country has become overly dependent on external sources for oil. In 2004, it imported nearly 57 percent of its total needs. It is predicted that the United States will need to import nearly two-thirds of its oil and gas by 2025.

Various studies have proved that the excessive use of conventional oil-based technology is detrimental to the environment. The United States is one of the very few countries in the world that has not ratified the Kyoto protocol—a treaty aimed at reducing greenhouse gas emissions. There are renewed concerns that greenhouse gas emissions are a major contributor to global warming.

Subsequently, several alternative energy resourcing methods have been proposed. Among the favorites are hydroelectric power projects. Hydroelectric projects in the United States deliver around 90 percent of the energy exploitable from non-conventional resources. Experts maintain that all this can be attributed to the Federal Energy Regulatory Commission.

There are many benefits of using hydroelectric power. According to the National Hydropower Association, the use of hydropower provides a cleaner and safer alternative for generating electricity. Additionally, in 1999, the use of hydropower prevented the burning of a combined asset of nearly 121 million tons (110 metric tons) of coal, 27 million barrels of oil, and 741 billion cubic feet (21 billion cubic meters) of natural gas.

Modern hydroelectric plants are capable of operating at nearly 90 percent energy efficiency levels, meaning thereby that nearly 90 percent of the hydroenergy is converted into electricity. In contrast, the best fossil fuel plants can operate at around only 50 percent efficiency levels.

As a result, hydroelectric power projects have gained tremendous popularity. As of 2006, there are around 2,500 hydroelectric plants in operation in the United States. However, this represents only around 3 percent of the nearly seventy thousand dams being currently utilized for hydroelectric generation.

Though there are a significant number of advantages of utilizing hydropower, the procedure for licensing of hydroelectric projects takes between eight and ten years due to a complex web of legislations and court rules. This is in stark contrast to the licensing of conventional fossil-fuel-based power plants, which takes around eighteen months.

There is a growing opinion in the United States that the government and the FERC should simplify the legislation for licensing hydropower projects in view of significant benefits to the environment compared to fossil fuel resources.

FURTHER RESOURCES

Web sites

"Clean Energy: How Hydroelectric Energy Works." *Union of Concerned Scientists.* <http://www.ucsusa.org/clean_energy/renewable_energy_basics/how-hydroelectric-energy-works.html> (accessed March 8, 2006).

"An Energy Summary of the United States of America." *Carbon Sequestration Leadership Forum.* <http://www.cslforum.org/usa.htm> (accessed March 8, 2006).

"Federal Energy Regulatory Commission's Student's Corner." *Federal Energy Regulatory Commission.* <http://ferc.gov/students/index.htm> (accessed March 8, 2006).

Hodgson, Godfrey. "Oil and American Politics." *Open-Democracy* March 10, 2005. <http://www.open-democracy.net/debates/article.jsp?id=3&debateId=77&articleId=2887> (accessed March 8, 2006).

"Hydro Facts: A Clean Energy Source For Our Future." *National Hydropower Association.* <http://www.hydro.org/hydrofacts/future.asp> (accessed March 8, 2006).

"Hydro Facts: Facts You Should Know About Hydropower." *National Hydropower Association.* <http://www.hydro.org/hydrofacts/facts.asp> (accessed March 8, 2006).

"Hydropower Today." *Hydro Research Foundation.* <http://www.hydrofoundation.org/hydropower/index.html> (accessed March 8, 2006).

"Reclamation's Role in Hydropower." *U.S. Department of the Interior, Bureau of Reclamation.* <http://www.usbr.gov/power/data/role_rpt.html> (accessed March 8, 2006).

"The True History of Teapot Dome"

Magazine article

By: Thomas J. Walsh

Date: July 1924

Source: Walsh, Thomas J. "The True History of Teapot Dome." *Forum Magazine* 72 (July, 1924).

About the Author: American statesman and politician Thomas J. Walsh (1859–1933) was elected to the senate of the United States as a Democrat in 1912. As the chairman of the Senate Investigating Committee in 1922 and 1923, he headed the investigation into Teapot Dome. Walsh also chaired the Committee of Mines and the Committee of Pensions. He was a supporter of women's rights and an opponent of child labor. President Franklin Roosevelt appointed him Attorney General in 1933, but Walsh died before taking office.

INTRODUCTION

America's twenty-ninth president, Warren G. Harding, was remembered for having presided over one of the most corrupt administrations in American history. He was a principal player in the political scandal that came to be known as Teapot Dome, along with his Secretary of the Interior, Albert Fall; his Secretary of the Navy, Edward Denby; Admiral John Robison, Chief of the Navy's Bureau of Engineering and the administrator of the Naval Petroleum Reserves; and two oil tycoons, Harry F. Sinclair, head of the Mammoth Oil Corporation, and Edward L. Doheny, head of the Pan-American Petroleum and Transport Company.

In 1912, President William Howard Taft set aside government-owned land in three areas where oil had been discovered: Elk Hill, California; Buena Vista, California; and Teapot Dome, Wyoming (so called because of the shape of a large rock on the land). Taft designated these regions as reserves to be kept for use by the U.S. Navy in time of crisis. In 1920, the Congress of the United States passed legislation giving the Secretary of the Navy the authority to use these reserves as he saw fit, to conserve, develop, operate, or lease them, and to use, store, or sell the oil and gas they produced.

When Fall became Secretary of the Interior, with Harding's approval, he persuaded Denby to transfer control of Elk Hill, Buena Vista, and Teapot Dome from the Navy's jurisdiction to his at the Department of the Interior. Denby complied, and Fall proceeded to grant Sinclair and Doheny the rights to drill the land and sell the oil. In return they paid Fall more than $400,000, delivered to him in a little black bag by Doheny's son. They later characterized this transfer of funds as a no-interest loan—which Fall never repaid. From Sinclair, Fall also received six heifers, a yearling bull, two six-month-old boars, four sows, and an English thoroughbred horse.

Former Attorney General of the United States, A. Mitchell Palmer, appeared before a special Senate investigation of the Teapot Dome oil lease, March 1, 1924. AP IMAGES

The deal was intended to be secret, but the significant improvement that Fall immediately began to make in his manner of living, especially his land purchases, drew attention to him, and on April 14, 1922, a front-page story in the *Wall Street Journal* substantiated the rumors that Fall had leased Teapot Dome to Sinclair and had been paid off for doing so.

President Calvin Coolidge, who succeeded to the presidency after Harding's sudden death on August 2, 1923, appointed two special prosecutors, Atlee Pomerene (Democrat) and Owen Roberts (Republican). The Congress of the United States, guided by Thomas Walsh, subsequently began a detailed inquiry into the matter. (President Harding's well-timed and somewhat mysterious death was not connected to the Teapot Dome scandal but was, if not a natural event, thought to be the result of poisoning by his wife, who was enraged at his marital infidelity.)

Perhaps most interesting fact when reviewing accounts of Teapot Dome from the 1920s is that there is no mention of any environmental issues.

Teapot Dome was a political, not an environmental or conservationist, scandal. Never was there concern for what drilling or building storage tanks would do to the landscape and the ecology of the region, nor was any thought given to oil conservation. By all parties involved, land and oil were regarded as commodities. The issues involved bribery, influence, and power: who benefited financially from those commodities and who had the power and authority to exploit them.

PRIMARY SOURCE

THE TRUE HISTORY OF TEAPOT DOME

In the spring of 1922, rumors reached parties interested that a lease had been or was about to be made of Naval Reserve No. 3 in the state of Wyoming,—popularly known, from its local designation, as the Teapot Dome. This was one of three great areas known to contain petroleum in great quantity which had been set aside for the use of the Navy—Naval Reserves No. 1 and No. 2 in California by President Taft in 1912, and No. 3 by President Wilson in 1915. The initial steps toward the creation of these reserves—the land being public, that is, owned by the government—were taken by President [Theodore] Roosevelt, who caused to be instituted a study to ascertain the existence and location of eligible areas, as a result of which President Taft in 1909 withdrew the tracts in question from disposition under the public land laws. These areas were thus set apart with a view to keeping in the ground a great reserve of oil available at some time in the future, more or less remote, when an adequate supply for the Navy could not, by reason of the failure or depletion of the world store, or the exigencies possibly of war, be procured or could be procured only at excessive cost; in other words to ensure the Navy in any exigency the fuel necessary to its efficient operation.

From the time of the original withdrawal order, private interests had persistently endeavored to assert or secure some right to exploit these rich reserves, the effort giving rise to a struggle lasting throughout the Wilson administration. Some feeble attempt was made by parties having no claim to any of the territory to secure a lease of all or a portion of the reserves, but in the main the controversy was waged by claimants asserting rights either legal or equitable in portions of the reserves antedating the withdrawal orders, on the one hand, and the Navy Department on the other. In that struggle Secretary Lane was accused of being unduly friendly to the private claimants, Secretary Daniels being too rigidly insistent on keeping the areas intact. President Wilson apparently supported Daniels in the main in the controversy which became acute and Lane retired from the cabinet, it is said, in consequence of the differences which had thus arisen.

The reserves were created, in the first place, in pursuance of the policy of conservation, the advocates of which, a militant body, active in the Ballinger affair, generally supported the attitude of Secretary Daniels and President Wilson.

They too became keen on the report of the impending lease of Teapot Dome. Failing to get any definite or reliable information at the departments, upon diligent inquiry, Senator Kendrick of Wyoming introduced and had passed by the Senate on April 16, 1922, a resolution calling on the secretary of the interior for information as to the existence of the lease which was the subject of the rumors, in response to which a letter was transmitted by the acting secretary of the interior on April 21, disclosing that a lease of the entire Reserve No. 3 was made two weeks before to the Mammoth Oil Company organized by Harry Sinclair, a spectacular oil operator. This was followed by the adoption by the Senate on April 29, 1922, of a resolution introduced by Senator LaFollette directing the Committee on Public Lands and Surveys to investigate the entire subject of leases of the naval oil reserves and calling on the secretary of the interior for all documents and full information in relation to the same.

In the month of June following, a cartload of documents said to have been furnished in compliance with the resolution was dumped in the committee rooms, and a letter from Secretary Fall to the President in justification of the lease of the Teapot Dome and of leases of limited areas on the other reserves was by him sent to the Senate. I was importuned by Senators LaFollette and Kendrick to assume charge of the investigation, the chairman of the committee and other majority members being believed to be unsympathetic, and assented the more readily because the Federal Trade Commission had just reported that, owing to conditions prevailing in the oil fields of Wyoming and Montana, the people of my state were paying prices for gasoline in excess of those prevailing anywhere else in the Union.

SIGNIFICANCE

Teapot Dome was about greed, the misuse of power, and the problematic relationship between money and influence—the control and exploitation of oil reserves just happening to be the matter at hand— and had far greater significance as a political scandal than as an environmental offense. It destroyed many men and many careers, while it also made some men and careers. Doheny's son was murdered in the course of the events, Sinclair and Fall were jailed. Roberts, one of the special prosecutors, was appointed to the United States Supreme Court in 1930. Pomerene, the other special prosecutor, was appointed by President

Herbert Hoover to head the Reconstructionist Finance Corporation during the early years of the Depression.

On a national scale, Teapot Dome signified not only a political scandal but a test of the political machinery for combating corruption and recovering for the people what belongs to the people. In this respect, Teapot Dome showed a victory for justice and the strength of the government to right wrongs. Less important were the punishments meted out to the principals rather than the fact that the regions and resources stolen from the people were returned.

Teapot Dome itself, because of the magnitude of the scandal and because it was a scandal that reached to the highest levels of government and industry, has become a touchstone. When other stories of widespread corruption come to light, such as the Watergate scandal during the Nixon administration or the Enron scandal during the administration of George W. Bush, parallels with Teapot Dome inevitably arise.

FURTHER RESOURCES

Books

Davis, Margaret Leslie. *Dark Side of Fortune: Triumph and Scandal in the Life of Oil Tycoon Edward L. Doheny.* Berkeley, CA: University of California Press, 1998.

Stratton, David H. *Tempest over Teapot Dome: The Story of Albert B. Fall.* Norman, OK: University of Oklahoma Press, 1998.

Web sites

The Brookings Institute. "One Lesson from History: Appointment of Special Counsel and the Investigation of the Teapot Dome Scandal." <http://www.brook.edu/gs/ic/teapotdome/teapotdome.htm#TOC> (accessed November 8, 2005).

History News Network. "What Was Teapot Dome?" <http://hnn.us/articles/550.html> (accessed November 8, 2005).

Spartacus Educational. "Teapot Dome Scandal." <http://www.spartacus.schoolnet.co.uk/USAteapot.htm> (accessed November 8, 2005).

Tree-toting members of Civilian Conservation Corps

Photograph

By: Anonymous

Date: January 17, 1934

Source: Getty Images

About the Photographer: This picture was taken at the start of a tree-planting project by a New England company of the Civilian Conservation Corps, a U.S. federal employment and conservation effort established in response to the Great Depression.

INTRODUCTION

The Civilian Conservation Corps (CCC) was a civilian work program run by the U.S. Federal Government from 1933 to 1942. By 1933, the Great Depression—a period of mass unemployment unprecedented in U.S. history—had been under way for several years, and millions of Americans were desperate for work. President Franklin Delano Roosevelt (1882–1945; President 1933–1945), elected partly on the strength of promises to relieve the suffering caused by the Depression, proposed the CCC during his first month in office. Congress authorized his proposal in an emergency session called by Roosevelt on March 9, 1933.

The CCC tasked small "companies" for specific projects. The company pictured here, the 117th, was based at a camp ten miles northwest of the town of Tamworth and was formed for a reforestation project, designated project S-53, which began on May 5, 1933. About thirty-five camps (each with its own company) were built in New Hampshire alone; nationwide, CCC camps were built in every state and major U.S. territory, about 4,000 in all. Separate companies were usually formed for white men, black men, and veterans; the company numbers of these groups were distinguished by a "C" (for colored) or "V" (for veteran), as for example New Hampshire company 392-V. There were several veterans CCC companies in New Hampshire but no "colored" companies, since African Americans were rare in New England at the time. Women were not hired by the CCC. In the early years of the Corps, only veterans, experienced supervisors, and men eighteen to twenty-five years old whose fathers were on welfare were eligible to join; after 1937, eligibility was extended to all men seventeen to twenty-three years old.

The CCC company shown in the picture was about to plant trees. This was one of the main tasks of the CCC, which is estimated to have planted three billion trees; the CCC was known popularly as "Roosevelt's Tree Army." Many millions of CCC-planted trees are still growing in national forests and national parks. However, CCC enrollees performed scores of different kinds of work besides tree-planting, including trail-building, canal

PRIMARY SOURCE

Tree-toting members of the 117th Company of the New England Civilian Conservation Corps form the initials of their organization in Tamworth, NH, January 17, 1934. Members of the 117th Company of the New England Civilian Conservation Corps form the initials of their organization in Tamworth, NH. The company was just preparing to plant trees. PHOTO BY NEW YORK TIMES CO./ GETTY IMAGES

renovation, firefighting, fire-road building, fire-tower construction, soil erosion control projects, stringing of telephone lines, pond-building, and even sheep rescue (during the 1936–1937 blizzards in Utah, which stranded a million sheep in deep snow). CCC enrollees wore pseudo-military uniforms and lived in standardized camps.

PRIMARY SOURCE

TREE-TOTING MEMBERS OF THE 117TH COMPANY OF THE NEW ENGLAND CIVILIAN CONSERVATION CORPS FORM THE INITIALS OF THEIR ORGANIZATION IN TAMWORTH, NH, JANUARY 17, 1934.

See primary source image.

SIGNIFICANCE

The CCC was hugely popular with the public, even among Republicans, who were usually critical of the policies of Franklin Roosevelt, a Democratic president. Three million men were gainfully employed by the CCC during its tenure; forty thousand illiterate enrollees were taught to read and write; useful public works were performed in rural and wilderness areas across the continent. Heavier construction projects, including the building of dams, airstrips, and bridges, were performed by another Roosevelt-founded organization, the Works Progress Administration (WPA). The WPA also ran a number of cultural projects in writing, theatre, and art.

A minority of the CCC's projects, including pond-building and wilderness-access projects, would today be viewed as environmentally destructive. For example, in the 1.1-million acre Boundary Waters

Dozens of men mill outside the Army Building in New York, hoping to enroll in the CCC on April 12, 1934. PHOTO BY NEW YORK TIMES CO./GETTY IMAGES

Canoe Area Wilderness of Minnesota, docks, signs, and canoe rests built by the CCC were removed after 1964 to restore the wilderness character of the area.

By 1941, the CCC was weakening. Unemployment had greatly declined and World War II was clearly imminent. Young men would be needed for the armed services rather than tree planting. Congress finally cut off all funding for the Corps in June 1942.

Nevertheless, the CCC remained as a memory and a model, proof that an organized corps of young people could do constructive forestry and other conservation work in a politically popular program. As a result, the CCC has been emulated and revived in many forms in recent decades. In 1976, Governor Jerry Brown of California instituted the California Conservation Corps; the resemblance of its name and even its initials to the old CCC was not coincidental. Workers in the new CCC—an equal-opportunity employer, unlike the old CCC—carried out

work much like those in the old: trail-building and tree-planting. The mission statement of the California Conservation Corps reads, in part, "The CCC hires young men and women to assist governmental and nongovernmental organizations in conserving, protecting, and restoring natural resources while providing Corps-members with on-the-job training and educational opportunities. The CCC... dispatches crews within hours to respond to fires, floods, earthquakes, oil spills, agricultural pest infestations, and security threats."

As of 2006, there were 109 conservation corps for people ages sixteen to twenty-five in the United States, a mixture of state and local programs united under the auspices of the National Association of Civilian Conservation Corps. Many of the young people hired by these miscellaneous corps were ex-convicts or high-school dropouts seeking a second chance at life. Funding has been reduced for some of these organizations in recent years, including the

California Corps. Many are funded entrepreneurially, performing fee-for-service contracts for nonprofit and government agencies. The movement seeks a renewal of federal investment, but given that funding for almost all social and environmental programs has been cut drastically under the George W. Bush Administration—which, in 2006, proposed selling off National Forest lands to private investors—this seems highly unlikely.

FURTHER RESOURCES

Web sites

The National Association of Civilian Conservation Corps. <http://www.nascc.org/> (accessed February 12, 2006).

The National Association of Civilian Conservation Corps Alumni. "Roosevelt's Tree Army: A Brief History of the Civilian Conservation Corps." <http://www.cccalumni.org/history1.html> (accessed February 12, 2006).

U.S. National Park Service. John C. Paige. "The Civilian Conservation Corps and the National Park Service, 1933–1942: An Administrative History." <http://www.cr.nps.gov/history/online_books/ccc/> (accessed February 16, 2006).

A Radio Address on the Third Anniversary of C.C.C.

Works of Franklin D. Roosevelt

Speech excerpt

By: Franklin D. Roosevelt

Date: April 17, 1936

Source: Roosevelt, Franklin D. "A Radio Address on the Third Anniversary of C.C.C." April 17, 1936. Available online at *New Deal Network.* <http://www.newdeal.feri.org/speeches/1936c.htm> (accessed February 23, 2006).

About the Author: Franklin D. Roosevelt (1882–1945) was the thirty-second president of the United States. Born in 1882 in New York, he assumed the office of the President in 1932. The New Deal Program became one highlight of Roosevelt's presidential career. Roosevelt launched the program at the height of the great American Depression in the 1930s. The New Deal Program was initially popular and boosted Americans at a time when the country was deeply in

crisis. However, Roosevelt became defensive about the program toward the end of the decade, as he faced considerable criticism about some of his New Deal Programs.

INTRODUCTION

The stock market crash of 1929 left the United States deep in an economic depression. When Roosevelt became President in 1932, more than fifteen million U.S. citizens, who represented more than a quarter of the existing workforce at that time, were unemployed.

Immediately after he assumed power, Roosevelt announced a series of measures that, between 1933 and 1938, collectively came to be known as the New Deal, which were designed to restructure the ailing workforce in the United States following the vice-grip of the Depression. Two of the most well known of these measures were the Tennessee Valley Authority (TVA) and the Civilian Conservation Corps (CCC).

The economy of the Tennessee Valley was among the worst hit during the Depression. The valley suffered from a number of problems including deforestation, erosion, overuse of farmland, and a depleted rate of agricultural return. The CCC set up camp in the Tennessee Valley and, with their help, the TVA executed a variety of activities such as controlling the flooding of the Tennessee River, preventing the erosion of top soil from Tennessee Valley farms into the river, making the river more navigable to sustain the economy and the commerce of the region, teaching farmers the correct use of fertilizers, and providing cheap electricity for the residents.

The CCC employed more than one and a half million young men and war veterans in several outdoor projects such as forestry, soil conservation, flood control, civilian assistance-in-distress situations, constructing roads, building bridges, laying telephone lines, fire fighting, designating state parks, distinguishing wildlife sanctuaries, erecting observation towers, and others, all over the United States.

Roosevelt delivered the following speech on April 17, 1936—the third anniversary of the formation of the CCC. In his speech, Roosevelt thanked the many volunteers who chose to work with the Corps.

The CCC camp at Fort Slocum in New York take a break for lunch. Across the United States, similar camps were set up as part of the New Deal program initiated by U.S. President Franklin D. Roosevelt. AP IMAGES

PRIMARY SOURCE

TO THE million and a half young men and war veterans who have been or are today enrolled in the Civilian Conservation Corps camps, I extend greetings on this third anniversary of the establishment of the first C.C.C. camp. Idle through no fault of your own, you were enrolled from city and rural homes and offered an opportunity to engage in healthful, outdoor work on forest, park, and soil-conservation projects of definite practical value to all the people of the Nation. The promptness with which you seized the opportunity to engage in honest work, the willingness with which you have performed your daily tasks, and the fine spirit you have shown in winning the respect of the communities in which your camps have been located merit the admiration of the entire country. You

and the men who have guided and supervised your efforts have cause to be proud of the record the C.C.C. has made in the development of sturdy manhood and in the initiation and prosecution of a conservation program of unprecedented proportions.

I recall that on July 17, 1933, at a time when the corps was just getting into stride, I predicted that through the C.C.C. we would graduate a fine group of strong young men, trained to self-discipline and willing and proud to work. I did not misjudge the loyalty, the spirit, the industry, or the temper of American youth. Although many of you entered the camps undernourished and discouraged through inability to obtain employment as you came of working age, the hard work, regular hours, the plain, wholesome food, and the outdoor life of the C.C.C. camps brought a quick response in improved morale. As muscles hardened and you became accustomed to outdoor work you grasped the opportunity to learn by practical training on the job and through camp educational facilities. Many of you rose to responsible positions in the camps. Since the corps began, some 1,150,000 of you have been graduated, improved in health, self-disciplined, alert, and eager for the opportunity to make good in any kind of honest employment.

Our records show that the results achieved in the protection and improvement of our timbered domain, in the arrest of soil wastage, in the development of needed recreational areas, in wildlife conservation, and in flood control have been as impressive as the results achieved in the rehabilitation of youth. Through your spirit and industry it has been demonstrated that young men can be put to work in our forests, parks, and fields on projects which benefit both the Nation's youth and conservation generally.

SIGNIFICANCE

The Tennessee River flows through seven southern states, all of which suffered a hard hit during the Depression: Tennessee, Kentucky, Virginia, North Carolina, Georgia, Alabama, and Mississippi. Much of the river valley, however, is part of the state of Tennessee. The river basin covers an area of approximately 41,000 sq. miles (106,200 sq. kilometers). The CCC undertook many significant conservation efforts in the Tennessee River Valley during this time.

Under the support of the TVA, the CCC were involved with planting trees, preventing soil erosion, controlling floods, repairing canals, replenishing rivers with fish, and other assorted activities in the region. These measures are considered by many to have been greatly responsible for reviving the environmental soundness of these southern states, as well as the economy, during the Depression.

In the early 1940s, the CCC, with TVA guidance, helped create twelve hydroelectric projects that produced a significant portion of the electricity required by the manufacturing industry for the war efforts during World War II. Although the CCC was instrumental in developing various initiatives, it also faced enormous budgetary allocation problems during World War II. Though President Roosevelt desired that the CCC be a permanent agency, Congress voted to discontinue funding it by the end of June 1942. The agency was thereafter disbanded on July 1, 1942.

After the disbanding of the CCC, the TVA continued its development initiatives. In the 1950s, it concentrated on increasing the navigability of the Tennessee River. During the 1960s, it focused on

producing electricity, establishing nuclear plants for this purpose. The TVA's business of electric generation continued until the late 1990s, when it began conservation efforts once again.

Ever since its inception, the TVA has initiated various programs that limit the disposal of pollutants in the atmosphere and the Tennessee Valley system. Some of its achievements include the Clean Water Initiative of 1992. It maintains an aggressive clean-air program, under which it has significantly reduced nitrous oxide emissions and is, as of the early 2000s, proceeding to drastically cut its sulfur dioxide emissions also for its coal-fired electric plants. The TVA has also carried out water improvements, and in 2005, completed an extensive two-year-long study on its operations policy for the Tennessee River system.

FURTHER RESOURCES
Web sites

"Document Library: Civilian Conservation Corps." *New Deal Network*. <http://www.newdeal.feri.org/texts/browse.cfm?MainCatID=55> (accessed March 8, 2006).

"Document Library: Tennessee Valley Authority." *New Deal Network*. <http://www.newdeal.feri.org/texts/browse.cfm?MainCatID=91> (accessed February 20, 2006).

Gupta, Pranav, and Jonathan Lee. "Successes and failures of Roosevelt's 'New Deal' programs." <http://www.bergen.org/AAST/Projects/depression/successes.html> (accessed March 8, 2006).

"A National Initiative on American History, Civics, and Service." *Franklin D. Roosevelt Presidential Library and Museum*. <http://www.fdrlibrary.marist.edu/ourdocs.html> (accessed March 8, 2006).

Federal Insecticide, Fungicide, and Rodenticide Act

Legislation

By: United States Congress

Date: June 25, 1947

Source: U.S. Code. "Federal Insecticide, Fungicide, and Rodenticide Act (FIFRU)." Title 7, Chapter 6, Subchapter II. June 25, 1947.

About the Author: The Congress of the United States was established by Article 1 of the U.S. Constitution of

1787. It is the legislative arm of the U.S. Federal Government.

INTRODUCTION

Insecticides are used to control the destruction or infestation of crops by insects. While problematic insects can be dealt with in more environmentally friendly ways by the use of competing species or the presence of repellent plants, as two examples, the traditional approach still involves the application of chemical insecticides to agricultural fields.

Of the more than one million known insect species, approximately 10,000 are crop-eaters. Of these, some 700 cause significant losses of crops worldwide. Their control helps make more crops available to the developed and developing world.

This need spawned the use of chemicals that targeted insects. Since chemical insecticides are designed to kill living species, there is apt to be problems with their use, especially when the chemicals enter ground or surface waters. As well, the process of bioaccumulation (where one chemically laden species is a food source for another, and so on, causing the accumulation of the toxic compound in species higher up in the food chain) can result in the ingestion of considerable amounts of harmful chemicals by humans.

Humans may also be exposed to the residual application of insecticides, including other agents present in the insecticide mixture, via crop dusting, preparation of the insecticides, or accidents. Health problems can result.

Recognizing such dangers, the United States enacted pesticide control legislation as far back as 1910. Then, the intent was more to protect people from faulty products and misleading labeling. A more comprehensive safety-oriented legislation called the Federal Insecticide, Fungicide, and Rodenticide Act (FIFRA) was passed in 1947.

With the publication of *Silent Spring* by Rachel Carson in 1962, society became aware of the potential harm posed by agricultural control chemicals, in this case DDT. The legacy of DDT is an ever-present reminder of the dangers that can be posed to the ecosystem from the use of chemical control agents.

In part, this growing awareness prompted major amendments to FIFRA in 1972 and in 1996 mandated the U.S. Environmental Protection Agency to regulate the manufacture and sale of agents including insecticides and enforce compliance with agents that are banned from use. This includes inspecting facilities that use insecticides to ensure that the chemicals being used are approved for use and that the

application of the insecticides is being done in accordance with the regulations.

Within the past few decades, the use of genetic controls for insects has become a reality. This will undoubtedly be reflected in the next (as yet unplanned) amendment of the insecticide use regulations.

◾ PRIMARY SOURCE

TITLE 7—AGRICULTURE
CHAPTER 6—INSECTICIDES AND ENVIRONMENTAL PESTICIDE CONTROL
SUBCHAPTER II—ENVIRONMENTAL PESTICIDE CONTROL
Sec. 136. Definitions For purposes of this subchapter—

(a) Active ingredient

The term "active ingredient" means—

1. in the case of a pesticide other than a plant regulator, defoliant, desiccant, or nitrogen stabilizer, an ingredient whichwill prevent, destroy, repel, or mitigate any pest;
2. in the case of a plant regulator, an ingredient which, through physiological action, will accelerate or retard the rate ofgrowth or rate of maturation or otherwise alter the behavior of ornamental or crop plants or the product thereof;
3. in the case of a defoliant, an ingredient which will cause the leaves or foliage to drop from a plant;
4. in the case of a desiccant, an ingredient which will artificially accelerate the drying of plant tissue; and
5. in the case of a nitrogen stabilizer, an ingredient which will prevent or hinder the process of nitrification, denitrification, ammonia volatilization, or urease production through action affecting soil bacteria.

(b) Administrator

The term "Administrator" means the Administrator of the Environmental Protection Agency.

(c) Adulterated

The term "adulterated" applies to any pesticide if—

1. its strength or purity falls below the professed standard of quality as expressed on its labeling under which it is sold;
2. any substance has been substituted wholly or in part for the pesticide; or
3. any valuable constituent of the pesticide has been wholly or in part abstracted.

(d) Animal

The term "animal" means all vertebrate and invertebrate species, including but not limited to man and other mammals, birds, fish, and shellfish.

The idea of crop dusting plants by spraying insecticides is still a valid prodecure in many places, though the Insecticide Act aims to reduce the number, frequency, and harmfulness of such sprays. © RON SANFORD/CORBIS

(e) Certified applicator, etc.

1. Certified applicator. The term "certified applicator" means any individual who is certified under section 136i of this title as authorized to use or supervise the use of any pesticide which is classified for restricted use. Any applicator who holds or applies registered pesticides, or uses dilutions of registered pesticides-consistent with subsection (ee) of this section, only to provide a service of controlling pests without delivering any unapplied pesticide to any person so served is not deemed to be a seller or distributor of pesticides under this subchapter.

2. Private applicator. The term "private applicator" means a certified applicator who uses or supervises the use of any pesticide which is classified for restricted use for purposes of producing any agricultural commodity on property owned or rented by the applicator or the applicator's employer or (if applied without compensation other than trading of personal services between producers of agricultural commodities) on the property of another person.

3. Commercial applicator. The term "commercial applicator" means an applicator (whether or not the applicator is a private applicator with respect to some uses) who uses or supervises the use of any pesticide which is classified for restricted use for any purpose or on any property other than as provided by paragraph (2).

4. Under the direct supervision of a certified applicator. Unless otherwise prescribed by its labeling, a pesticide shall be considered to be applied under the direct supervision of a certified applicator if it is applied by a competent person acting under the instructions and control of a certified applicator who is available if and when needed, even though such certified applicator is not physically present at the time and place the pesticide is applied.

(f) Defoliant

The term "defoliant" means any substance of mixture of substances intended for causing the leaves or foliage to drop from a plant, with or without causing abscission.

(g) Desiccant

The term "desiccant" means any substance or mixture of substances intended for artificially accelerating the drying of plant tissue.

(h) Device

The term "device" means any instrument or contrivance (other than a firearm) which is intended for trapping, destroying, repelling, or mitigating any pest or any other form of plant or animal life (other than man and other than bacteria, virus, or other microorganism on or in living man or other living animals); but not including equipment used for the application of pesticides when sold separately therefrom.

(i) District court

The term "district court" means a United States district court, the District Court of Guam, the District Court of the Virgin Islands, and the highest court of American Samoa.

(j) Environment

The term "environment" includes water, air, land, and all plants and man and other animals living therein, and the interrelationships which exist among these.

(k) Fungus

The term "fungus" means any non-chlorophyll-bearing thallophyte (that is, any non-chlorophyll-bearing plant of a lower order than mosses and liverworts), as for example, rust, smut, mildew, mold, yeast, and bacteria, except those on or in living man or other animals and those on or in processed food, beverages, or pharmaceuticals.

(l) Imminent hazard

The term "imminent hazard" means a situation which exists when the continued use of a pesticide during the time required for cancellation proceeding would be likely to result in unreasonable adverse effects on the environment or will involve unreasonable hazard to the survival of a species declared endangered or threatened by the Secretary pursuant to the Endangered Species Act of 1973 [16 U.S.C. 1531 et seq.].

(m) Inert ingredient

The term "inert ingredient" means an ingredient which is not active.

(n) Ingredient statement

The term "ingredient statement" means a statement which contains—

1. the name and percentage of each active ingredient, and the total percentage of all inert ingredients, in the pesticide; and
2. if the pesticide contains arsenic in any form, a statement of the percentages of total and water soluble arsenic, calculated as elementary arsenic.

(o) Insect

The term "insect" means any of the numerous small invertebrate animals generally having the body more or less obviously segmented, for the most part belonging to the class insecta, comprising six-legged, usually winged forms, as for example, beetles, bugs, bees, flies, and to other allied classes of anthropods whose members are wingless and usually have more than six legs, as for example, spiders, mites, ticks, centipedes, and wood lice.

SIGNIFICANCE

The potential environmental damage posed by insecticides, as well as the need for economic regulation of their sale, was recognized by the federal government in the first decade of the twentieth century with the passage of the Insecticide Act of 1910. The modern-day version of the act was passed in 1947.

The 1947 version of the insecticide act and subsequent amendments have helped curb the misuse and unauthorized use of insecticides. This has benefited both those who could be exposed to the chemicals and, more broadly, the environment.

An example of the strength of the act is the 1964 amendment, which allows unsafe or ineffective pesticides (and more specifically insecticides) to be denied the registration that is required for their sale and use.

Since 1970, the administration of the use of insecticides has been under the auspices of the Environmental Protection Agency. Now, insecticides are assessed more from an environmental viewpoint than an economic viewpoint.

Without the original Insecticide Act and the subsequent modification and revisions, environmental protection would not be as stringent as it is. Furthermore, the power of the act to regulate the introduction of insecticides helps ensure that harmful chemicals will either be banned from use or have qualifications attached to their use.

FURTHER RESOURCES
Books

Ishaaya, Isaac. *Biochemical Sites of Insecticide Action and Resistance*. New York: Springer, 2001.

Pretty, Jules N. *The Pesticide Detox: Towards a More Sustainable Agriculture*. London: Earthscan Publications, 2005.

Stenersen, Jorgen. *Chemical Pesticides: Mode of Action and Toxicology*. Boca Raton, FL: CRC Press, 2004.

Web sites

"The Federal Insecticide, Fungicide, and Rodenticide Act (FIFRA)." *United States Environmental Protection Agency, Office of Enforcement, Compliance and Environmental Justice,* Fall 2002. <http://www.epa.gov/region08/compliance/fifra.html> (accessed March 8, 2006).

The Antarctic Treaty

Treaty

By: Governments of twelve nations

Date: December 1, 1959

Source: Governments of Argentina, Australia, Belgium, Chile, the French Republic, Japan, New Zealand, Norway, the Union of South Africa, The Union of Soviet Socialist Republics, the United Kingdom of Great Britain and Northern Ireland, and the United States of America. *The Antarctic Treaty.* United Nations, December 1, 1959.

About the Author: The Antarctic Treaty was composed and signed by representatives of twelve nations. The official document is currently stored in the archives of the U.S. Government.

INTRODUCTION

The first known sighting of Antarctica took place in 1820; that year two separate expeditions claimed to have been the first to actually see the last continent on earth. The following year, the first known landings were made, not by explorers, but by seal hunters working in the area.

The first significant scientific expedition to Antarctica did not occur until more than 70 years later. In 1898, the Belgian ship *Belgica* embarked with an international crew of nineteen scientists. The expedition carried out an extensive program of research, including twenty-two separate trips ashore. The trip was fraught with danger, with the ship becoming trapped in the ice pack and nearly crushed. While trapped, the ship was carried along with the ice, covering approximately 2,175 miles (3,500 kilometers) in this manner. After her crew manually cut a 246-foot (75-meter) channel through the ice, the ship was freed and returned home, bringing hundreds of biological samples and extensive meteorological data for further study.

Many other expeditions to Antarctica followed. Some were undertaken simply for the challenge they afforded. In 1911, a team of Norwegians reached the South Pole, planting their national flag and spending three days at the tip of the world. In 1914, Sir Ernest Shackleton and a crew of twenty-seven attempted an Antarctic crossing on foot. Their ship, the *Endurance*, was trapped by ice before they could reach the continent. As the shifting bergs crushed the wooden ship, Shackleton and his men found themselves marooned. They would wait more than twenty months for eventual rescue.

As the Cold War dawned in the late 1940's, the world's major powers began to look toward the South, asking what military value this harsh region might hold. Several nations established permanent bases on the continent, and in 1946, the U.S. Navy launched Operation Highjump, deploying 4700 troops along with helicopters, ships, and caterpillar tractors. The expedition surveyed large, previously unexplored sections of the continent, producing detailed maps of the region as it provided U.S. military planners with experience operating in sub-zero temperatures.

From July 1957 to December 1958, an unprecedented international cooperative effort to study the Earth and environment was launched. This event, called the International Geophysical Year (IGY) led to the discovery of the Van Allen radiation belts and seismic rifts along the ocean floors, as well as an improved understanding of cosmic rays and the earth's magnetic field. As the largest international scientific effort ever undertaken, the IGY also produced an international agreement governing the use of Antarctica. This international treaty declared the Antarctic continent a permanent non-military zone, reserved for scientific efforts only.

■ PRIMARY SOURCE

THE ANTARCTIC TREATY

The Governments of Argentina, Australia, Belgium, Chile, the French Republic, Japan, New Zealand, Norway, the Union of South Africa, The Union of Soviet Socialist Republics, the United Kingdom of Great Britain and Northern Ireland, and the United States of America,

Recognizing that it is in the interest of all mankind that Antarctica shall continue forever to be used exclusively for peaceful purposes and shall not become the scene or object of international discord;

Acknowledging the substantial contributions to scientific knowledge resulting from international cooperation in scientific investigation in Antarctica;

Convinced that the establishment of a firm foundation for the continuation and development of such cooperation on the basis of freedom of scientific investigation in Antarctica as applied during the International Geophysical Year accords with the interests of science and the progress of all mankind;

Convinced also that a treaty ensuring the use of Antarctica for peaceful purposes only and the continuance of international harmony in Antarctica will further the purposes and principles embodied in the Charter of the United Nations;

Have agreed as follows:

ARTICLE I

[Antarctica for peaceful purposes only]

1. Antarctica shall be used for peaceful purposes only. There shall be prohibited, inter alia, any measures of a military nature, such as the establishment of military bases and fortifications, the carrying out of military maneuvers, as well as the testing of any type of weapons.

2. The present Treaty shall not prevent the use of military personnel or equipment for scientific research or for any other peaceful purposes.

ARTICLE II

[freedom of scientific investigation to continue] Freedom of scientific investigation in Antarctica and cooperation toward that end, as applied during the International Geophysical Year, shall continue, subject to the provisions of the present Treaty.

ARTICLE III

[plans and results to be exchanged]

1. In order to promote international cooperation in scientific investigation in Antarctica, as provided for in Article II of the present Treaty, the Contracting Parties agree that, to the greatest extent feasible and practicable:

(a) information regarding plans for scientific programs in Antarctica shall be exchanged to permit maximum economy and efficiency of operations;
(b) scientific personnel shall be exchanged in Antarctica between expeditions and stations;
(c) scientific observations and results from Antarctica shall be exchanged and made freely available.

2. In implementing this Article, every encouragement shall be given to the establishment of cooperative working relations with those Specialized Agencies of the United Nations and other international organizations having a scientific or technical interest in Antarctica.

ARTICLE IV

[territorial claims]

1. Nothing contained in the present Treaty shall be interpreted as:

(a) a renunciation by any Contracting Party of previously asserted rights of or claims to territorial sovereignty in Antarctica;
(b) a renunciation or diminution by any Contracting Party of any basis of claim to territorial sovereignty in Antarctica which it may have whether as a result of its activities or those of its nationals in Antarctica, or otherwise;
(c) prejudicing the position of any Contracting Party as regards its recognition or nonrecognition of any other State's right of or claim or basis of claim to territorial sovereignty in Antarctica.

2. No acts or activities taking place while the present Treaty is in force shall constitute a basis for asserting, supporting or denying a claim to territorial sovereignty in Antarctica. No new claim, or enlargement of an existing claim, to territorial sovereignty shall be asserted while the present Treaty is in force.

ARTICLE V

[nuclear explosions prohibited]

1. Any nuclear explosions in Antarctica and the disposal there of radioactive waste material shall be prohibited.

2. In the event of the conclusion of international agreements concerning the use of nuclear energy, including nuclear explosions and the disposal of radioactive waste material, to which all of the Contracting Parties whose representatives are entitled to participate in the meetings provided for under Article IX are parties, the rules established under such agreements shall apply in Antarctica.

ARTICLE VI

[area covered by treaty] The provisions of the present Treaty shall apply to the area south of 60° South latitude, including all ice shelves, but nothing in the present Treaty shall prejudice or in any way affect the rights, or the exercise of the rights, of any State under international law with regard to the high seas within that area.

ARTICLE VII

[free access for observation and inspection]

1. In order to promote the objectives and ensure the observation of the provisions of the present Treaty, each Contracting Party whose representatives are entitled to participate in the meetings referred to in Article

IX of the Treaty shall have the right to designate observers to carry out any inspection provided for by the present Article. Observers shall be nationals of the Contracting Parties which designate them. The names of the observers shall be communicated to every other Contracting Party having the right to designate observers, and like notice shall be given of the termination of their appointment.

2. Each observer designated in accordance with the provisions of paragraph 1 of this Article shall have complete freedom of access at any time to any or all areas of Antarctica.

3. All areas of Antarctica, including all stations, installations and equipment within those areas, and all ships and aircraft at points of discharging or embarking cargoes or personnel in Antarctica, shall be open at all times to inspection by any observers designated in accordance with paragraph 1 of this Article.

4. Aerial observation may be carried out at any time over any or all areas of Antarctica by any of the Contracting Parties having the right to designate observers.

5. Each Contracting Party shall, at the time when the present Treaty enters into force for it, inform the other Contracting Parties, and thereafter shall give them notice in advance, of

(a) all expeditions to and within Antarctica, on the part of its ships of nationals, and all expeditions to Antarctica organized in or proceeding from its territory;

(b) all stations in Antarctica occupied by its nationals; and

(c) any military personnel or equipment intended to be introduced by it into Antarctica subject to the conditions prescribed in paragraph 2 of Article I of the present Treaty.

ARTICLE VIII

[personnel under jurisdiction of their own states

1. In order to facilitate the exercise of their functions under the present Treaty, and without prejudice to the respective positions of the Contracting Parties relating to jurisdiction over all other persons in Antarctica, observers designated under paragraph 1 of Article VII and scientific personnel exchanged under subparagraph 1(b) of Article III of the Treaty, and members of the staffs accompanying any such persons, shall be subject only to the jurisdiction of the Contracting Party of which they are nationals in respect to all acts or omissions occurring while they are in Antarctica for the purpose of exercising their functions.

2. Without prejudice to the provisions of paragraph 1 of this Article, and pending the adoption of measures in pursuance of subparagraph 1(e) of Article IX, the Contracting Parties concerned in any case of dispute with regard to the exercise of jurisdiction in Antarctica shall immediately consult together with a view to reaching a mutually acceptable solution.

ARTICLE IX

[Treaty states to meet periodically]

1. Representatives of the Contracting Parties named in the preamble to the present Treaty shall meet at the City of Canberra within two months after date of entry into force of the Treaty, and thereafter at suitable intervals and places, for the purpose of exchanging information, consulting together on matters of common interest pertaining to Antarctica, and formulating and considering, and recommending to their Governments, measures in furtherance of the principles and objectives of the Treaty including measures regarding:

(a) use of Antarctica for peaceful purposes only;

(b) facilitation of scientific research in Antarctica;

(c) facilitation of international scientific cooperation in Antarctica;

(d) facilitation of the exercise of the rights of inspection provided for in Article VII of the Treaty;

(e) questions relating to the exercise of jurisdiction in Antarctica;

(f) preservation and conservation of living resources in Antarctica. . . .

SIGNIFICANCE

The Antarctic Treaty made the Antarctic continent a politically unique region, free of national territorial claims. Further, the treaty specifically prohibited military use of the area, protecting it from some of the abuses suffered by other regions during the Cold War. However, given the unimaginably harsh conditions found near the South Pole, where temperatures often reach $-100\,°F$ ($-73\,°C$), it seems likely that nations would have largely ignored this area even without the treaty.

Today, Antarctica is home to more than a dozen research stations, some manned throughout the months-long winter night. Current scientific efforts include a project to extract an ice core from the 2.3-mile-thick (3.7-kilometer-thick) ice sheet, along with a wide range of biological and climatological experiments.

Flags of countries who signed treaties to protect the South Pole and Antartica billow in the wind, December 1997. AP IMAGES

FURTHER RESOURCES
Books

Fox, William. *Terra Antarctica: Looking into the Emptiest Continent*. San Antonio, Texas: Trinity University Press, 2005.

McGonigal, David, and Lynn Woodworth. *Antarctica: The Blue Continent*. Buffalo, New York: Firefly Books, 2003.

Smith, Roff. *Life on the Ice: No One Goes to Antarctica Alone*. New York: National Geographic Society, 2005.

Periodicals

Gedamke, Jason. "Sounds of the 'Silent World.'" *Australian Antarctic Magazine* 9 (Spring 2005): 14–15.

Seigert, Martin. "Antarctica's Lake Vostok." *American Scientist* (November-December 1999).

Web sites

Antarctic Connection. "News & Info." <http://www.antarcticconnection.com/antarctic/info-index.shtml> (accessed January 20, 2006).

Australian Antarctic Division. "Mawson Station." <http://www.aad.gov.au/default.asp?casid=6909> (accessed January 20, 2006).

Center for Astrophysical Research in Antarctica. "Virtual Tour—McMurdo Station, Antarctica." <http://astro.uchicago.edu/cara/vtour/mcmurdo> (accessed January 20, 2006).

Treaty Banning Nuclear Weapon Tests in the Atmosphere, in Outer Space and Under Water

(Limited Test Ban Treaty)

Treaty

By: Governments of the United States of America, the United Kingdom of Great Britain and Northern Ireland, and the Union of Soviet Socialist Republics

Date: August 5, 1963

Source: "Treaty Banning Nuclear Weapon Tests in the Atmosphere, in Outer Space, and Under Water (Limited Test Ban Treaty)." August 5, 1963.

Available online at <http://www.ucsusa.org/assets/documents/global_security/limited_test_ban_treaty.pdf> (accessed February 20, 2006).

About the Author: The Governments of the United States of America, the United Kingdom of Great Britain and Northern Ireland, and the Union of Soviet Socialist Republics were the original parties to the Limited Test Ban Treaty.

INTRODUCTION

World War II (1938–1941) saw the first use of the atomic bomb when the United States dropped two bombs over the Japanese cities of Hiroshima and Nagasaki. The devastation was such that even at the turn of the twenty-first century, the survivors of the atomic bombing in Japan and their descendents suffer from long-term consequences of exposure to radioactivity.

At the end of the war, the United States and other nations, including China, the Union of Soviet Socialist Republics (USSR), and Great Britain, began an era of atomic weapons testing. This involved exploding atomic bombs in the open environment. The United States conducted nearly 193 tests between 1945 and 1962 in the open atmosphere, while the USSR conducted nearly 142 such open-environment tests. Subsequently, throughout the world, there was increased concern over the frequency and nature of these tests, and many scientists and citizens feared that the world faced an unstoppable arms race that could end in the total destruction of the planet's ecosystem and its inhabitants.

At the height of the Cold War in 1962, the Cuban missile crisis accelerated the debate of a nuclear arms embargo, as U.S. naval ships blocked a convoy of Soviet ships delivering intermediate-range nuclear ballistic missiles to Cuba. The events that followed nearly brought the United States and the USSR to the brink of war.

In response to the general feeling of insecurity and the fear of total nuclear destruction of the world in a future war, the Nuclear Test Ban Treaty (NTBT) was formed on August 5, 1963, and took effect on October 10, 1963. The NTBT (also known as the Limited Test Ban Treaty) was a result of substantial arms control efforts taken by both the United States as well as the USSR. This treaty banned the testing of nuclear weapons over the ground, in air, and in water by member countries. However, the treaty did not ban nuclear testing underground.

The treaty also banned tests that could cause radioactive fallout to settle beyond the territorial limits of the country conducting the tests. Therefore, it set certain territorial limits for radioactive tests and banned countries from conducting those tests that affected regions beyond the specified territory limits. The treaty proclaimed its principal aim as the speedy end to the arms race and to stamp out incentives for nuclear weapons production and testing. The treaty also declared itself to be of unlimited duration. The ultimate aim of this treaty was to prevent nuclear testing aboveground in the future.

■ PRIMARY SOURCE

TREATY BANNING NUCLEAR WEAPON TESTS IN THE ATMOSPHERE, IN OUTER SPACE, AND UNDER WATER (LIMITED TEST BAN TREATY)

Signed at Moscow: August 5, 1963 Ratification advised by U.S. Senate: September 24, 1963 Ratified by U.S. President: October 7, 1963 U.S. ratification deposited at Washington, London, and Moscow: October 10, 1963 Proclaimed by U.S. President: October 10, 1963 Entered into force: October 10, 1963

The Governments of the United States of America, the United Kingdom of Great Britain and Northern Ireland, and the Union of Soviet Socialist Republics, hereinafter referred to as the "Original Parties,"

Proclaiming as their principal aim the speediest possible achievement of an agreement on general and complete disarmament under strict international control in accordance with the objectives of the United Nations which would put an end to the armaments race and eliminate the incentive to the production and testing of all kinds of weapons, including nuclear weapons,

Seeking to achieve the discontinuance of all test explosions of nuclear weapons for all time, determined to continue negotiations to this end, and desiring to put an end to the contamination of man's environment by radioactive substances,

Have agreed as follows:

Article I

1. Each of the Parties to this Treaty undertakes to prohibit, to prevent, and not to carry out any nuclear weapon test explosion, or any other nuclear explosion, at any place under its jurisdiction or control:

(a) in the atmosphere; beyond its limits, including outer space; or under water, including territorial waters or high seas; or

(b) in any other environment if such explosion causes radioactive debris to be present outside the territorial limits of the State under whose jurisdiction or control such explosion is conducted. It is understood in this connection that the provisions of this subparagraph are without prejudice to the conclusion of a Treaty resulting in the permanent banning of all nuclear test explosions, including all such explosions underground, the conclusion of which, as the Parties have stated in the Preamble to this Treaty, they seek to achieve.

2. Each of the Parties to this Treaty undertakes furthermore to refrain from causing, encouraging, or in any way participating in, the carrying out of any nuclear weapon test explosion, or any other nuclear explosion, anywhere which would take place in any of the environments described, or have the effect referred to, in paragraph 1 of this Article.

Article II

1. Any Party may propose amendments to this Treaty. The text of any proposed amendment shall be submitted to the Depositary Governments which shall circulate it to all Parties to this Treaty. Thereafter, if requested to do so by one-third or more of the Parties, the Depositary Governments shall convene a conference, to which they shall invite all the Parties, to consider such amendment.

2. Any amendment to this Treaty must be approved by a majority of the votes of all the Parties to this Treaty, including the votes of all of the Original Parties. The amendment shall enter into force for all Parties upon the deposit of instruments of ratification by a majority of all the Parties, including the instruments of ratification of all of the Original Parties.

Article III

1. This Treaty shall be open to all States for signature. Any State which does not sign this Treaty before its entry into force in accordance with paragraph 3 of this Article may accede to it at any time.

2. This Treaty shall be subject to ratification by signatory States. Instruments of ratification and instruments of accession shall be deposited with the Governments of the Original Parties—the United States of America, the United Kingdom of Great Britain and Northern Ireland, and the Union of Soviet Socialist Republics—which are hereby designated the Depositary Governments.

3. This Treaty shall enter into force after its ratification by all the Original Parties and the deposit of their instruments of ratification.

4. For States whose instruments of ratification or accession are deposited subsequent to the entry into force of this Treaty, it shall enter into force on the date of the deposit of their instruments of ratification or accession.

5. The Depositary Governments shall promptly inform all signatory and acceding States of the date of each signature, the date of deposit of each instrument of ratification of and accession to this Treaty, the date of its entry into force, and the date of receipt of any requests for conferences or other notices.

6. This Treaty shall be registered by the Depositary Governments pursuant to Article 102 of the Charter of the United Nations.

Article IV This Treaty shall be of unlimited duration.

Each Party shall in exercising its national sovereignty have the right to withdraw from the Treaty if it decides that extraordinary events, related to the subject matter of this Treaty, have jeopardized the supreme interests of its country. It shall give notice of such withdrawal to all other Parties to the Treaty three months in advance.

Article V This Treaty, of which the English and Russian texts are equally authentic, shall be deposited in the archives of the Depositary Governments. Duly certified copies of this Treaty shall be transmitted by the Depositary Governments to the Governments of the signatory and acceding States.

IN WITNESS WHEREOF the undersigned, duly authorized, have signed this Treaty.

DONE in triplicate at the city of Moscow the fifth day of August, one thousand nine hundred and sixty-three.

For the Government of the United States of America

DEAN RUSK

For the Government of the United Kingdom of Great Britain and Northern Ireland

SIR DOUGLAS HOME

For the Government of the Union of Soviet Socialist Republics

A. GROMYKO

SIGNIFICANCE

The Nuclear Test Ban Treaty did not stop nuclear weapons testing completely. It simply moved the testing underground. Kennedy's hope for a more comprehensive test ban treaty was not realized, and subsequently, over one thousand nuclear tests of various yields have reportedly been conducted worldwide.

The NTBT did pave the way for future similar treaties to be formed. The Nuclear Non-Proliferation Treaty (NPT) that prevents the spread of nuclear weapons and nuclear technology was ratified in 1975. Signed by more than 180 countries, it remains the most acceptable arms reduction treaty signed between countries. Other treaties include the Anti-Ballistic Missile Treaty (ABM) signed in 1972, and the strategic arms reduction treaties START-I and START-II, which pursued the reduction in the number of warheads owned by the USSR and the United States.

However, there were still serious concerns around the world about the need for a comprehensive treaty that banned nuclear testing completely. In 1991, signatory countries of the NTBT held a conference to discuss the possibility of expanding the reach of the NTBT to ban all nuclear weapon tests. Consequently, the Comprehensive Test Ban Treaty (CTBT) was formulated in September 1996 and was signed by seventy-one countries. However, as of 2006, this treaty has yet to be signed by all countries, and thus has not come into force. If this happens, it could mean an end to nuclear testing globally.

There has been continuous public apprehension since the beginning of the era of atomic testing about potential exposure to radiation. A U.S. government report released in 1997 revealed that the fallout of radioactive iodine I-131 from the Nevada nuclear tests could have spread all across the United States, yielding devastating repercussions. The Institute for Environmental Energy and Research (IEER), in a press release in February 2002, reported that fallout from worldwide open-atmospheric atomic bomb testing contributed to cancer in about 80,000 people in the United States by the year 2000.

The five nuclear weapons states—the United States, Russia (formerly the USSR), the United Kingdom, France, and the People's Republic of China—collectively possess approximately 20,000 nuclear weapons. There are estimates of at least 10,000 more warheads in possession by other countries, such as India, Pakistan, and Israel. North Korea has also claimed to possess nuclear weapons, although this claim has not been verified by evidence of nuclear testing.

FURTHER RESOURCES
Web sites

CTBTO Preparatory Commission. <http://www.ctbto.org> (accessed February 20, 2006).

GlobalIssues.org. "Nuclear Weapons." <http://www.global issues.org/Geopolitics/ArmsControl/Nuclear.asp> (accessed February 20, 2006).

Institute for Energy and Environmental Research. "About Eighty Thousand Cancers in the United States, More Than 15,000 of Them Fatal, Attributable to Fallout from Worldwide Atmospheric Nuclear Testing." <http://www.ieer.org/comments/fallout/pr0202.html> (accessed February 20, 2006).

National Center for Environmental Health. "Report on the Feasibility of a Study of the Health Consequences to the American Population from Nuclear Weapons Tests Conducted by the United States and Other Nations." <http://www.cdc.gov/nceh/radiation/fallout/falloutreport.pdf> (accessed February 20, 2006).

The Water Quality Act of 1965

Legislation

By: United States Congress

Date: October 2, 1965

Source: U.S. Congress. "The Water Quality Act of 1965." 79 Stat. 903, 70 Stat. 498. Washington, D.C.: October 2, 1965.

About the Author: The Congress of the United States was established by Article 1 of the U.S. Constitution of 1787. It is the legislative arm of the U.S. Federal Government.

INTRODUCTION

The Water Quality Act of 1965 and the amendments that became law in 1977 represent two of several initiatives by the federal government of the United States to protect and ensure the quality of surface and ground waters.

Legislative concern over water quality began in 1948, with the passage of the Water Pollution Control Act. The act was essentially an adoption of principles to be followed in the pursuit of water quality. It was the Water Quality Act of 1965 that put some legislative teeth to these principles.

The 1965 legislation directed the states to develop water quality standards. A federally directed initiative was deemed necessary since many watersheds and waterways crossed state boundaries. By the early 1970s, water quality standards had been developed and enacted by all the states. Since then, revisions have occurred to reflect changing scientific information and new testing procedures.

In 1972, the Clean Water Act legislation came into effect. The act aimed to "restore and maintain the chemical, physical, and biological integrity of the nation's waters." The act was slightly modified in 1977 by the implementation of amendments that expanded the mandate of the Environmental Protection Agency (EPA) to encompass the release of toxic compounds into sewers and surface waters. Thus, EPA had the legislative muscle to regulate runoff.

Legislation specifically directed at drinking water was tabled in 1974. The Safe Drinking Water Act required the EPA to establish standards for a variety of contaminants and requirements for the operation and upkeep of municipal drinking water treatment systems. The 1974 legislation was amended in 1986

Rivers that do not meet water quality standards, such as the Trinity River in Dallas, Texas, are among the first to be come under inspection for pollution reduction and clean up. AP IMAGES

PRIMARY SOURCE

THE WATER QUALITY ACT OF 1965

An Act To amend the Federal Water Pollution Control Act to establish a Federal Water Pollution Control Administration, to provide grants for research and development, to increase grants for construction of sewage treatment works, to require establishment of water quality criteria, and for other purposes.

Be it enacted by the Senate and House of Representatives of the United States of America in Congress assembled, That (a) (1) section 1 of the Federal Water Pollution Control Act (33 U.S.C. 466) is amended by inserting after the words "SECTION 1." a new subsection (a) as follows:

"(a) The purpose of this Act is to enhance the quality and value of our water resources and to establish a national policy for the prevention, control, and abatement of water pollution." . . .

FEDERAL WATER POLLUTION CONTROL ADMINISTRATION

SEC. 2. Effective ninety days after the date of enactment of this section there is created within the Department of Health, Education, and Welfare a Federal Water Pollution Control Administration (hereinafter in this Act referred to as the "Administration"). . . .

GRANTS FOR RESEARCH AND DEVELOPMENT

SEC. 6. (a) The Secretary is authorized to make grants to any State, municipality, or intermunicipal or interstate agency for the purpose of assisting in the development of any project which will demonstrate a new or improved method of controlling the discharge into any waters of untreated or inadequately treated sewage or other waste from sewers which carry storm water or both storm water and sewage or other wastes, and for the purpose of reports, plans, and specifications in connection therewith. The Secretary is authorized to provide for the conduct of research and demonstrations relating to new or improved methods of controlling the discharge into any waters of untreated or inadequately treated sewage or other waste from sewers which carry storm water or both storm water and sewage or other wastes, by contract with public or private agencies and institutions and with individuals without regard to sections 3648 and 3709 of the Revised Statutes, except that not to exceed 25 per centum of the total amount appropriated under authority of this section for any fiscal year may be expended under authority of this sentence during such fiscal year.

(b) Federal grants under this section shall be subject to the following limitations: (1) No grant shall be made for any project pursuant to this section unless such project shall have been approved by an appropriate State water pollution

because many contaminants identified in water had not been regulated. Since then, a list of contaminants is published every three years and is used to drive future regulatory changes.

In 1987, another series of amendments to the Clean Water Act, which were also referred to as the Water Quality Act, strengthened EPA's mandate to control runoff. Chesapeake Bay and the Great Lakes were specifically targeted by the formation of remediation and protection programs. The Great Lakes Program authorized research into the bioaccumulation of toxic pollutants in aquatic species, particularly those of commercial and recreational interest. As well, this Water Quality Act broadened the reporting of the harmful effects of "acid rain" in water courses and created a program for states to identify and control surface runoff (also known as nonpoint source pollution).

Revisions to the Clean Water Act in 1995 and 1996 were intended to provide states more latitude in determining the quality of water within their jurisdictions, and to harmonize the Safe and Clean drinking Water Acts.

control agency or agencies and by the Secretary; (2) no grant shall be made for any project in an amount exceeding 50 per centum of the estimated reasonable cost thereof as determined by the Secretary; (3) no grant shall be made for any project under this section unless the Secretary determines that such project will serve as a useful demonstration of a new or improved method of controlling the discharge into any water of untreated or inadequately treated sewage or other waste from sewers which carry storm water or both storm water and sewage or other wastes.

(c) There are hereby authorized to be appropriated for the fiscal year ending June 30, 1966, and for each of the next three succeeding fiscal years, the sum of $20,000,000 per fiscal year for the purposes of this section. Sums so appropriated shall remain available until expended. No grant or contract shall be made for any project in an amount exceeding 5 per centum of the total amount authorized by this section in any one fiscal year. . . .

(3) Standards of quality established pursuant to this subsection shall be such as to protect the public health or welfare, enhance the quality of water and serve the purposes of this Act. In establishing such standards the Secretary, the Hearing Board, or the appropriate State authority shall take into consideration their use and value for public water supplies, propagation of fish and wildlife, recreational purposes, and agricultural, industrial, and other legitimate uses. . . .

(5) The discharge of matter into such interstate waters or portions thereof, which reduces the quality of such waters below the water quality standards established under this subsection (whether the matter causing or contributing to such reduction is discharged directly into such waters or reaches such waters after discharge into tributaries of such waters), is subject to abatement in accordance with the provisions of paragraph (1) or (2) of subsection (g) of this section, except that at least 180 days before any abatement action is initiated under either paragraph (1) or (2) of subsection (g) as authorized by this subsection, the Secretary shall notify the violators of other interested parties of the violation of such standards. In any suit brought under the provision of this subsection the court shall receive in evidence a transcript of the proceedings of the conference and hearing provided for in this subsection, together with the recommendations of the conference and Hearing Board and the recommendations and standards promulgated by the Secretary, and such additional evidence, including that relating to the alleged violation of the standards, as it deems necessary t a complete review of the standards and to a determination of all other issues relating to the alleged violation. The court, giving due consideration to the practicability and to the physical and economic feasibility of complying with such standards, shall have jurisdiction to enter such judgment and orders enforcing such judgment as the public interest and the equities of the case may require.

(6) Nothing in this subsection shall (A) prevent the application of this section to any case to which subsection (a) of this section would otherwise be applicable, or (B) extend Federal jurisdiction over water not otherwise authorized by this Act.

(7) In connection with any hearings under this section no witness or any other person shall be required to divulge trade secrets or secret processes.

Public Law 89-235

Joint Resolution Authorizing and requesting the President to extend through 1966 his proclamation of a period to "See the United States," and for other purposes.

Resolved by the Senate and House of Representatives of the United States of America in Congress assembled, That the president is authorized and requested (1) to extend through 1966 the period designated pursuant to the joint resolution approved August 11, 1964 (Public Law 88-416), as a period to see the United States and its territories; (2) to encourage private industry and interested private organizations to continue their efforts to attract greater numbers of the American people to the scenic, historical, and recreational areas and facilities of the United States of America, its territories and possessions, and the Commonwealth of Puerto Rico; and (3) to issue a proclamation specially inviting citizens of other ceremonials to be celebrated in 1966 in the United States of America, its territories and possessions, and the Commonwealth of Puerto Rico.

SEC. 2. The President is authorized to publicize any proclamations issued pursuant to the first section and otherwise to encourage and promote vacation travel within the United States of America, its territories and possessions, and the Commonwealth of Puerto Rico, both by American citizens and by citizens of other countries, through such departments or agencies of the Federal Government as he deems appropriate, in cooperation with State and local agencies and private organizations.

SEC. 3. For the purpose of the extension provided for by this joint resolution, the President is authorized during the period of such extension to exercise the authority conferred by section 3 of the joint resolution approved August 11, 1964 (Public Law 88-416), and for such purpose may extend for such period the appointment of any person serving as National Chairman pursuant to such section.

Approved October 2, 1965.

SIGNIFICANCE

The Water Quality Acts have been an integral part of the evolving water quality strategy in the decades since the principles underlying safe and clean water were first proposed in the 1940s.

FURTHER RESOURCES

Books

Copeland, Claudia. *Clean Water Act: Current Issues and Guide to Books*. Hauppauge, N.Y.: Nova Science Publishers, 2003.

Ryan, Mark A. *The Clean Water Act Handbook*, 2nd ed. Washington, D.C.: American Bar Association, 2004.

Web sites

United States Environmental Protection Agency. "Water Quality Standards Program History." <http://www. epa.gov/waterscience/standards/about/history.htm> (accessed February 17, 2006).

United States v. Standard Oil

Document

By: United States Supreme Court

Date: May 23, 1966

Source: U.S. Supreme Court. *United States v. Standard Oil, 384 US 224*. May 23, 1966. <http://caselaw. lp.find law.com/scripts/getcase.pl?court=us&vol=384&invol= 224> (accessed March 16, 2006).

About the Author: Established in 1789 by the U.S. Constitution, the Supreme Court of the United States is the highest federal judicial body court in the country. The court stands as the final authority of the law in the United States and is the ultimate guardian of the U.S. Constitution. It endeavors to provide equal justice under law for the American people.

INTRODUCTION

In the early days of industrialization in the United States, all kinds of waste oil would be discharged into rivers and streams with impunity. There was a general lack of awareness about water pollution control.

Various oil companies were engaged in oil exploration in the late nineteenth century and the early twentieth century. Due to the rapid increase in the demand for petroleum as fuel, there was a massive increase in the production of oil for use as gasoline.

Issues such as short-term economic gains, and beliefs like rapid economic and technical progress shared by industrialists and the government alike,

took precedence over pollution and other environmental concerns. Discharge of waste and oil upstream became a major concern for fishing and other maritime activities downstream and in the coastal areas. Further, the use of petroleum additives also increased the risk of poisoning in rivers and other waters. Consequently, the Rivers and Harbors Act of 1899, one of the earliest environmental legislations, was enacted to prevent and make the discharge of any waste or refuse matter into rivers an unlawful act.

Standard Oil, a conglomerate trust of companies formed in 1863 by enterprising American tycoon J. D. Rockefeller, was one such entity that came under the scanner for disposing oil in river waters. Rockefeller had succeeded in monopolizing the refining and transportation segment of the oil industry in its early days in the United States.

United States v. Standard Oil Co. was a Supreme Court case (384 US 224) in which the United States was a litigant against Standard Oil of Kentucky—one of the many Standard Oil companies that marketed oil and gasoline to consumers in the states of Kentucky, Florida, Georgia, Alabama, and Mississippi. In 1966, Standard Oil of Kentucky was indicted for having released 100-octane gasoline fuel into the St. Johns River in Florida. However, the district court of Florida was of the view that commercially valuable gasoline did not constitute "refuse matter," and decided that the aviation gasoline discharged into the river did not violate the provisions of the Rivers and Harbors Act of 1899.

Subsequently, the United States approached the Federal Supreme Court, which reversed the decision and criminally indicted Standard Oil in this case. The case provides an insight into the awareness about pollution of rivers in the United States since the nineteenth century.

PRIMARY SOURCE

UNITED STATES V. STANDARD OIL CO.

APPEAL FROM THE UNITED STATES DISTRICT COURT FOR THE MIDDLE DISTRICT OF FLORIDA. Appellant was indicted for discharging gasoline into navigable waters in violation of the proscription in 13 of the Rivers and Harbors Act against discharge therein of "any refuse matter of any kind or description." The District Court dismissed the indictment on the ground that "refuse matter" does not include commercially valuable material. Held: The discharge of commercially valuable gasoline into navigable waters is encompassed by 13 of the Act. Pp. 225–230.

(a) Petroleum products, whether useable or not, when discharged into navigable waters constitute a menace to navigation and pollute rivers and harbors. P. 226.

(b) The Rivers and Harbors Act of 1899 was a consolidation of prior acts which enumerated various pollutants and impediments to navigation, drawing no distinction between valuable and valueless substances; the term "refuse matter" in the present Act is a shorthand substitute for the exhaustive list of substances found in the earlier Acts. Pp. 226-229.

(c) The word "refuse" includes all foreign substances and pollutants except, as provided in 13, those "flowing from streets and sewers and passing therefrom in a liquid state" into the watercourse. P. 230.

Reversed.

Nathan Lewin argued the cause for the United States. With him on the brief were Solicitor General Marshall, Assistant Attorney General Vinson and Beatrice Rosenberg.

Earl B. Hadlow argued the cause and filed a brief for appellee.

MR. JUSTICE DOUGLAS delivered the opinion of the Court.

The question presented for decision is whether the statutory ban on depositing "any refuse matter of any [384 U.S. 224, 225] kind or description" in a navigable water covers the discharge of commercially valuable aviation gasoline.

Section 13 of the Rivers and Harbors Act provides:

"It shall not be lawful to throw, discharge, or deposit . . . any refuse matter of any kind or description whatever other than that flowing from streets and sewers and passing therefrom in a liquid state, into any navigable water of the United States . . ." 33 U.S.C. 407 (1964 ed.).

The indictment charged appellee, Standard Oil (Kentucky), with violating 13 by allowing to be discharged into the St. Johns River "refuse matter" consisting of 100-octane aviation gasoline. Appellee moved to dismiss the indictment, and, for the purposes of the motion, the parties entered into a stipulation of fact. It states that the gasoline was commercially valuable and that it was discharged into the St. Johns only because a shut-off valve at dockside had been "accidentally" left open.

The District Court dismissed the indictment because it was of the view that the statutory phrase "refuse matter" does not include commercially valuable oil. The United States appealed directly to this Court under the Criminal

Appeals Act (18 U.S.C. 3731 (1964 ed.). We noted probable jurisdiction. 382 U.S. 807.

This case comes to us at a time in the Nation's history when there is greater concern than ever over pollution—one of the main threats to our free-flowing rivers and to our lakes as well. The crisis that we face in this respect would not, of course, warrant us in manufacturing offenses where Congress has not acted nor in stretching statutory language in a criminal field to meet strange conditions. But whatever may be said of the rule of strict construction, it cannot provide a substitute for common sense, precedent, and legislative history. We [384 U.S. 224, 226] cannot construe 13 of the Rivers and Harbors Act in a vacuum. Nor can we read it as Baron Parke would read a pleading.

The statutory words are "any refuse matter of any kind or description." We said in United States v. Republic Steel Corp., 362 U.S. 482, 491, that the history of this provision and of related legislation dealing with our free-flowing rivers "forbids a narrow, cramped reading" of 13. The District Court recognized that if this were waste oil it would be "refuse matter" within the meaning of 13 but concluded that it was not within the statute because it was "valuable" oil. That is "a narrow, cramped reading" of 13 in partial defeat of its purpose.

Oil is oil and whether useable or not by industrial standards it has the same deleterious effect on waterways. In either case, its presence in our rivers and harbors is both a menace to navigation and a pollutant. This seems to be the administrative construction of 13, the Solicitor General advising us that it is the basis of prosecution in approximately one-third of the oil pollution cases reported to the Department of Justice by the Office of the Chief of Engineers.

Section 13 codified pre-existing statutes:

An 1886 Act (24 Stat. 329) made it unlawful to empty "any ballast, stone, slate, gravel, earth, slack, rubbish, wreck, filth, slabs, edgings, sawdust, slag, or cinders, or other refuse or mill-waste of any kind into New York [384 U.S. 224, 227] Harbor"—which plainly includes valuable pre-discharge material.

An 1888 Act (25 Stat. 209) "to prevent obstructive and injurious deposits" within the Harbor of New York and adjacent waters banned the discharge of "refuse, dirt, ashes, cinders, mud, sand, dredgings, sludge, acid, or any other matter of any kind, other than that flowing from streets, sewers, and passing therefrom in a liquid state"—which also plainly includes valuable pre-discharge material. (Emphasis added.)

The 1890 Act (26 Stat. 453) made unlawful emptying into navigable waters "any ballast, stone, slate, gravel, earth, rubbish, wreck, filth, slabs, edgings, sawdust, slag, cinders, ashes, refuse, or other waste of any kind . . . which shall tend to impede or obstruct navigation." Here also valuable pre-discharge materials were included.

The 1894 Act (28 Stat. 363) prohibited deposits in harbors and rivers for which Congress had appropriated money for improvements, of "ballast, refuse, dirt, ashes, cinders, mud, sand, dredgings, sludge, acid, or any other matter of any kind other than that flowing from streets, sewers, and passing therefrom in a liquid state." (Emphasis added.) This Act also included valuable pre-discharge material.

The Acts of 1886 and 1888, then, dealt specifically with the New York Harbor; the scope of the latter was considerably broader, covering as it did the deposit of "any other matter of any kind." The Acts of 1890 and 1894 paralleled the earlier enactments pertaining to New York, applying their terms to waterways throughout the Nation.

The 1899 Act now before us was no more than an attempt to consolidate these prior Acts into one. It was indeed stated by the sponsor in the Senate to be "in accord with the statutes now in existence, only scattered . . . from the beginning of the statutes down [384 U.S. 224, 228] through to the end" (32 Cong. Rec. 2296), and reflecting merely "[v]ery slight changes to remove ambiguities." Id., p. 2297.

From an examination of these statutes, several points are clear. First, the 1894 Act and its antecedent, the 1888 Act applicable to the New York Harbor, drew on their face no distinction between valuable and valueless substances. Second, of the enumerated substances, some may well have had commercial or industrial value prior to discharge into the covered waterways. To be more specific, ashes and acids were banned whether or not they had any remaining commercial or industrial value. Third, these Acts applied not only to the enumerated substances but also to the discharge of "any other matter of any kind." Since the enumerated substances included those with a pre-discharge value, the rule of ejusdem generis does not require limiting this latter category to substances lacking a pre-discharge value. Fourth, the coverage of these Acts was not diminished by the codification of 1899. The use of the term "refuse" in the codification serves in the place of the lengthy list of enumerated substances found in the earlier Acts and the catch-all provision found in the Act of 1890. The legislative history demonstrates without contradiction that Congress intended to codify without substantive change the earlier Acts.

The philosophy of those antecedent laws seems to us to be clearly embodied in the present law. It is plain from its legislative history that the "serious injury" to our watercourses (S. Rep. No. 224, 50th Cong., 1st Sess., [384 U.S. 224, 229] p. 2) sought to be remedied was caused in part by obstacles that impeded navigation and in part by pollution—"the discharge of sawmill waste into streams"

(ibid.) and the injury of channels by "deposits of ballast, steam-boat ashes, oysters, and rubbish from passing vessels." Ibid. The list is obviously not an exhaustive list of pollutants. The words of the Act are broad and inclusive: "any refuse matter of any kind or description whatever." Only one exception is stated: "other than that flowing from streets and sewers and passing therefrom in a liquid state, into any navigable water of the United States." More comprehensive language would be difficult to select. The word "refuse" does not stand alone; the "refuse" banned is "of any kind or description whatever," apart from the one exception noted. And, for the reasons already stated, the meaning we must give the term "refuse" must reflect the present codification's statutory antecedents.

The Court of Appeals for the Second Circuit in United States v. Ballard Oil Co., 195 F.2d 369 (L. Hand, Augustus Hand, and Harrie Chase, JJ.) held that causing good oil to spill into a watercourse violated 13. The word "refuse" in that setting, said the court, "is satisfied by anything which has become waste, however useful it may earlier have been." Id., p. 371. There is nothing [384 U.S. 224, 230] more deserving of the label "refuse" than oil spilled into a river.

That seems to us to be the common sense of the matter. The word "refuse" includes all foreign substances and pollutants apart from those "flowing from streets and sewers and passing therefrom in a liquid state" into the watercourse.

That reading of 13 is in keeping with the teaching of Mr. Justice Holmes that a "river is more than an amenity, it is a treasure." New Jersey v. New York, 283 U.S. 336, 342. It reads 13 charitably as United States v. Republic Steel Corp., supra, admonished.

We pass only on the quality of the pollutant, not on the quantity of proof necessary to support a conviction nor on the question as to what scienter requirement the Act imposes, as those questions are not before us in this restricted appeal.

SIGNIFICANCE

By the early 1900s, the growth in the maritime industry and relative abundance and cheapness of oil made it the chief source of power for ships in the United States. During this period there were numerous instances of the rampant discharge of oil into rivers and sewers, especially in the industrial cities of the United States. This would result in massive amounts of waste oil traveling downstream towards the river mouths and the coast.

As discussed, the Rivers and Harbors Act of 1899 was passed for the judicious and efficient use of water resources in the United States. Also, to prevent the growing menace of dumping waste and refuse into the river, section 13 was incorporated into the act to make the activity of discharging and disposing of any kind of waste or refuse into the waters illegal.

In 1966, Standard Oil of Kentucky was indicted in proscription of section 13 of the Rivers and Harbors Act. Although the District court ruled in favor of Standard Oil, the United States appealed directly to the Federal Supreme Court against this decision under the Criminal Appeals Act. While ruling against the district court's decision, the Supreme Court opined that this case was referred at a crucial phase in the country's history, when there was significant concern over matters like environmental and waste pollution that was significantly affecting America's rivers and lakes.

According to the Supreme Court, the district court's interpretation that the gasoline oil was not waste or refuse oil and was therefore valuable was actually a narrow and cramped interpretation of section 13. This interpretation partially defeated the purpose of the act. It also became important to examine the legislative history of this act. Section 13 of the Rivers and Harbors act consolidated earlier statutes like the 1894 Act (28 Stat. 363), the 1886 Act (24 Stat. 329), and the 1888 Act (25 Stat. 209).

Upon closely examining these statutes, it became clear that they did not distinguish between valuable and valueless substances. Parallel acts of 1890 and 1994 applied them to waterways in the entire country. Though some substances might have been valuable prior to discharging them into the waterways, the court said that oil spilled into a river rightly deserved the label of "refuse" and merited the application of section 13 of the act. The acts also applied them to the disposal of "any other matter of any kind."

It became clear that earlier legislations sought to remedy the dangers like pollution posed to rivers and navigation. In another case, *United States v. Ballard Oil Co.*, 195 F.2d 369, The Court of Appeals for the Second Circuit had ruled that good oil caused to spill into a river or watercourse violated section 13.

The Supreme Court also cited another case—*New Jersey v. New York*, 283 U.S. 336, 342—wherein the presiding honorable justice had mentioned that rivers were more than amenities; they were actually a national treasure. It was held that the discharge of commercially valuable gasoline was included in section 13 of the act, and Standard Oil of Kentucky thus stood criminally prosecuted.

Following this criminal prosecution, it becomes important to examine the status of water pollution in America. The issue of pollution of rivers and streams has become more serious with each passing decade. Since the ruling, a number of various statutes were enacted to prevent this growing problem.

There was not enough legislation along with the Rivers and Harbors Act of 1899 and the Oil Pollution Act of 1924 to tackle the growing problem of oil discharge in streams and rivers. The issue of Standard Oil achieves considerable significance because until 1970, the environmental laws in the United States were considered weak.

However, since the 1970s there has been significant activity on the environmental front in the United States. A number of laws have been enacted to tackle the problem of water and environmental pollution. They include the National Environmental Policy Act (NEPA) of 1969, the Clean Air Act (CAA) of 1970, the Clean Water Act (CWA) of 1977, the Comprehensive Environmental Response, Compensation, and Liability Act (CERCLA) of 1980, the Pollution Prevention Act (PPA) of 1990, the Resource Conservation and Recovery Act (RCRA) of 1976, the Safe Drinking Water Act (SDWA) of 1974, the Superfund Amendments and Reauthorization Act (SARA) of 1986, and the Toxic Substances Control Act (TSCA) of 1976.

FURTHER RESOURCES
Web sites

Henderson, Wayne. "How about those Crowns?" *Petroleum Collectibles Monthly*, June 2001. <http://www.pcmpub lishing.com/articles/22.html> (accessed March 16, 2006).

Krantz, David, and Brad Kifferstein. "Water Pollution and Society." *Earth and Society project for Geological Sciences 265, University of Michigan* 1998. <http://www.umich.edu/~gs265/society/waterpollution.htm> (accessed March 16, 2006).

Tarbell, Ida M. "The History of Standard Oil Company." from the book *The History of The Standard Oil Company*, New York: McClure, Phillips, and Co., 1904. Available online at <http://www.history.rochester.edu/fuels/tarbell/MAIN.HTM> (accessed March 16, 2006).

Wild and Scenic Rivers Act

Legislation

By: United States Code

Date: October 2, 1968

Source: U.S. Code. "Wild and Scenic Rivers Act." Title 16, Chapter 28, Sections 1271, 1272, 1277.

About the Author: The U.S. Code is the set of general and permanent laws that govern the United States. The House of Representatives prepares the Code and revisions are published every six years. The Code is arranged into fifty Titles. Title 16 deals with Conservation. Chapter 28 describes the laws pertaining to Wild and Scenic Rivers.

INTRODUCTION

The rivers and waterways of the United States have always been used for transportation, irrigation, drinking water, and for the removal of waste. In the twentieth century, many rivers were dammed to prevent flooding and to be harnessed for hydroelectric power. Rivers were diverted or channeled to so that their flow could be controlled. Levees were built to contain flooding. Development of the rivers and their adjacent land was seen as a means to increased productivity and economic growth.

During the 1960s, there was considerable concern that the rivers and waterways of the United States were being changed in a manner that destroyed their natural character. In particular, conservationists Frank and John Craighead, who had some notoriety through their work with National Geographic, recognized the need for a national system that protected the character and natural value of rivers and waterways. They enlisted the help of Senator Frank Church of Idaho, who developed legislation with the goal of preserving some of the most unspoiled rivers in the country.

The Wild and Scenic Rivers Act was signed into the U.S. Code on October 2, 1962 by President Lyndon B. Johnson. The Act established the Wild and Scenic Rivers System that oversees the preservation of all rivers that are designated under the Act. In order to be designated, a river must be free-flowing and contain an "outstandingly remarkable" feature, such as scenery, historical value, geological features or particular fish and wildlife.

The first three sections and the seventh section of the Act are excerpted below. The first section describes the policy that provides for development along designated rivers. In order for a section of a designated river to be artificially changed, a similar section of river must be preserved in its natural form. The second section lists the original eight rivers that were designated under the Act. It also describes the three different classifications by which a river may be designated. These classifications impact how study of the river and permitting for development occurs. Section seven is a

key portion of the Act because it prevents the building of any hydroelectric plants or other water diversion projects that would impede the free-flowing nature of the river.

■ PRIMARY SOURCE

WILD AND SCENIC RIVERS ACT
P.L. 90-542, as amended

16 U.S.C. 1271–1287

AN ACT

To provide for a National Wild and Scenic Rivers System, and for other purposes.

Be it enacted by the Senate and House of Representatives of the United States of America in Congress assembled, that

(a) this Act may be cited as the "Wild and Scenic Rivers Act."

Congressional declaration of policy.

(b) It is hereby declared to be the policy of the United States that certain selected rivers of the Nation which, with their immediate environments, possess outstandingly remarkable scenic, recreational, geologic, fish and wildlife, historic, cultural, or other similar values, shall be preserved in free-flowing condition, and that they and their immediate environments shall be protected for the benefit and enjoyment of present and future generations. The Congress declares that the established national policy of dam and other construction at appropriate sections of the rivers of the United States needs to be complemented by a policy that would preserve other selected rivers or sections thereof in their free-flowing condition to protect the water quality of such rivers and to fulfill other vital national conservation purposes.

Congressional declaration of purpose.

(c) The purpose of this Act is to implement this policy by instituting a national wild and scenic rivers system, by designating the initial components of that system, and by prescribing the methods by which and standards according to which additional components may be added to the system from time to time.

Composition of system; requirements for State-administered components.

SECTION 2.

(a) The national wild and scenic rivers system shall comprise rivers (i) that are authorized for inclusion therein by Act of Congress, or (ii) that are designated as wild, scenic or recreational rivers by or pursuant to an act of the legislature of the State or States through which they flow, that are to be permanently administered as wild, scenic or recreational rivers by an agency or political subdivision of the State or States concerned, that are found by the Secretary of the Interior, upon application of the Governor of the State or the Governors of the States concerned, or a person or persons thereunto duly appointed by him or them, to meet the criteria established in this Act and such criteria supplementary thereto as he may prescribe, and that are approved by him for inclusion in the system, including, upon application of the Governor of the State concerned, the Allagash Wilderness Waterway, Maine; that segment of the Wolf River, Wisconsin, which flows through Langlade County; and that segment of the New River in North Carolina extending from its confluence with Dog Creek downstream approximately 26.5 miles to the Virginia State line. Upon receipt of an application under clause (ii) of this subsection, the Secretary shall notify the Federal Energy Regulatory Commission and publish such application in the *Federal Register*. Each river designated under clause (ii) shall be administered by the State or political subdivision thereof without expense to the United States other than for administration and management of federally owned lands. For purposes of the preceding sentence, amounts made available to any State or political subdivision under the Land and Water Conservation [Fund] Act of 1965 or any other provision of law shall not be treated as an expense to the United States. Nothing in this subsection shall be construed to provide for the transfer to, or administration by, a State or local authority of any federally owned lands which are within the boundaries of any river included within the system under clause (ii).

Classification.

(b) A wild, scenic or recreational river area eligible to be included in the system is a free-flowing stream and the related adjacent land area that possesses one or more of the values referred to in Section 1, subsection (b) of this Act. Every wild, scenic or recreational river in its free-flowing condition, or upon restoration to this condition, shall be considered eligible for inclusion in the national wild and scenic rivers system and, if included, shall be classified, designated, and administered as one of the following:

(1) *Wild river areas*—Those rivers or sections of rivers that are free of impoundments and generally inaccessible except by trail, with watersheds or shorelines essentially primitive and waters unpolluted. These represent vestiges of primitive America.

(2) *Scenic river areas*—Those rivers or sections of rivers that are free of impoundments, with shorelines or watersheds still largely primitive and shorelines largely undeveloped, but accessible in places by roads.

(3) *Recreational river areas*—Those rivers or sections of rivers that are readily accessible by road or

railroad, that may have some development along their shorelines, and that may have undergone some impoundment or diversion in the past. . . .

Restrictions on hydro and water resource development projects on designated rivers.

SECTION 7.

(a) The Federal Power Commission [FERC] shall not license the construction of any dam, water conduit, reservoir, powerhouse, transmission line, or other project works under the Federal Power Act (41 Stat. 1063), as amended (16 U.S.C. 791a et seq.), on or directly affecting any river which is designated in section 3 of this Act as a component of the national wild and scenic rivers system or which is hereafter designated for inclusion in that system, and no department or agency of the United States shall assist by loan, grant, license, or otherwise in the construction of any water resources project that would have a direct and adverse effect on the values for which such river was established, as determined by the Secretary charged with its administration. Nothing contained in the foregoing sentence, however, shall preclude licensing of, or assistance to, developments below or above a wild, scenic or recreational river area or on any stream tributary thereto which will not invade the area or unreasonably diminish the scenic, recreational, and fish and wildlife values present in the area on the date of designation of a river as a component of the national wild and scenic rivers system. No department or agency of the United States shall recommend authorization of any water resources project that would have a direct and adverse effect on the values for which such river was established, as determined by the Secretary charged with its administration, or request appropriations to begin construction of any such project, whether heretofore or hereafter authorized, without advising the Secretary of the Interior or the Secretary of Agriculture, as the case may be, in writing of its intention so to do at least sixty days in advance, and without specifically reporting to the Congress in writing at the time it makes its recommendation or request in what respect construction of such project would be in conflict with the purposes of this Act and would affect the component and the values to be protected by it under this Act. Any license heretofore or hereafter issued by the Federal Power Commission [FERC] affecting the New River of North Carolina shall continue to be effective only for that portion of the river which is not included in the national wild and scenic rivers system pursuant to section 2 of this Act and no project or undertaking so licensed shall be permitted to invade, inundate or otherwise adversely affect such river segment.

Restrictions on hydro and water resource development projects on study rivers.

(b) The Federal Power Commission [FERC] shall not license the construction of any dam, water conduit, reservoir, powerhouse, transmission line, or other project works under the Federal Power Act, as amended, on or directly affecting any river which is listed in section 5, subsection (a), of this Act, and no department or agency of the United States shall assist by loan, grant, license, or otherwise in the construction of any water resources project that would have a direct and adverse effect on the values for which such river might be designated, as determined by the Secretary responsible for its study or approval—(i) during the ten-year period following enactment of this Act [October 2, 1968] or for a three complete fiscal year period following any Act of Congress designating any river for potential addition to the national wild and scenic rivers system, whichever is later, unless, prior to the expiration of the relevant period, the Secretary of the Interior and where national forest lands are involved, the Secretary of Agriculture, on the basis of study, determine that such river should not be included in the national wild and scenic rivers system and notify the Committees on Interior and Insular Affairs of the United States Congress, in writing, including a copy of the study upon which the determination was made, at least one hundred and eighty days while Congress is in session prior to publishing notice to that effect in the *Federal Register.* Provided, That if any Act designating any river or rivers for potential addition to the national wild and scenic rivers system provides a period for the study or studies which exceeds such three complete fiscal year period the period provided for in such Act shall be substituted for the three complete fiscal year period in the provisions of this clause (i); and (ii) during such interim period from the date a report is due and the time a report is actually submitted to the Congress; and (iii) during such additional period thereafter as, in the case of any river the report for which is submitted to the President and the Congress for inclusion in the national wild and scenic rivers system, is necessary for congressional consideration thereof or, in the case of any river recommended to the Secretary of the Interior for inclusion in the national wild and scenic rivers system under section 2(a)(ii) of this Act, is necessary for the Secretary's consideration thereof, which additional period, however, shall not exceed three years in the first case and one year in the second.

Nothing contained in the foregoing sentence, however, shall preclude licensing of, or assistance to, developments below or above a potential wild, scenic or recreational river area or on any stream tributary thereto which will not invade the area or diminish the scenic, recreational, and fish and wildlife values present in the potential wild, scenic or recreational river area on the date of designation of a river for study as provided in section 5 of this Act. No department or agency of the United States shall, during the periods hereinbefore specified, recommend authorization of any water resources project on any such river or request appropriations to begin construction of any such project, whether heretofore or hereafter authorized, without advising the Secretary of the Interior and, where national forest lands are involved, the Secretary of Agriculture in writing of its intention so to do at least sixty days in advance of doing so and without specifically reporting to the Congress in writing at the time it makes its recommendation or request in what respect construction of such project would be in conflict with the purposes of this Act and would affect the component and the values to be protected by it under this Act.

(c) The Federal Power Commission [FERC] and all other Federal agencies shall, promptly upon enactment of this Act, inform the Secretary of the Interior and, where national forest lands are involved, the Secretary of Agriculture, of any proceedings, studies, or other activities within their jurisdiction which are now in progress and which affect or may affect any of the rivers specified in section 5, subsection (a), of this Act. They shall likewise inform him of any such proceedings, studies, or other activities which are hereafter commenced or resumed before they are commenced or resumed.

Grants under Land and Water Conservation Fund Act of 1965.

(d) Nothing in this section with respect to the making of a loan or grant shall apply to grants made under the Land and Water Conservation Fund Act of 1965 (78 Stat. 897; 16 U.S.C. 460l-5 et seq.).

SIGNIFICANCE

The Wild and Scenic Rivers Act is considered an important piece of environmental regulation. Since its inception, 156 rivers comprising nearly 11,000 miles (17,700 kilometers) of waterways have been designated part of the Wild and Scenic Rivers System. While this is an impressive achievement, it contrasts with the more than 600,000 miles (966,000 kilometers) of once free-flowing rivers in the U.S. that are contained by more than 60,000 dams.

About half of the rivers in the System are in the northwest part of the country. Oregon contains the most designated rivers with forty-seven, while Alaska contains the most mileage designated with 3,210 miles (5,166 kilometers). The designated rivers in Idaho are among the nation's most celebrated: the Salmon, the Snake, and the Selway. The Tuolomne River, described by John Muir, is protected under the act. The Missouri River, immortalized by Lewis and Clark in their great expedition through the West, is also designated as part of the system. To the east, Massachusetts's Concord, Sudbury, and Assebet Rivers as well as Connecticut's Farmington River have been designated part of the system. The Delaware River, which is the largest undammed river east of the Mississippi, was designated by Congress in 1978. Two rivers that flow through subtropical swamps in the South have been protected by the act: the Saline Bayou in Louisiana and the Loxahtchee River in Florida. Three rivers in the rainforests of Puerto Rico have also been added to the list of designated rivers.

Although the Wild and Scenic Rivers Act has been criticized for not doing enough to protect rivers, in those places where it has been used, it has generally been considered a valuable conservation tool. No river that has been designated by Congress has ever been removed from the system, indicating that the benefits of the act outweigh any detriments. Part of the reason that the act has been successful is because its intent is not to completely block the use of a designated river, but instead to require that the river be managed so that the fundamental character of the river is preserved. Any development on the river must respect the free flow of water and protect its natural features. The Wild and Scenic Rivers System must co-exist with development so as to create a management plan that protects natural values as well as property values.

FURTHER RESOURCES

Web sites

Congressional Research Service Report for Congress. "The Wild and Scenic Rivers Act and Federal Water Rights." <http://www.ncseonline.org/NLE/CRSreports/Public/pub-16.cfm?&CFID=7246664&CFTOKEN=65919120> (accessed January 17, 2006).

Friends of the River. "California Rivers: The National Wild and Scenic Rivers Act." <http://www.friendsoftheriver.org/CaliforniaRivers/NationalWildAndScenicRiversAct.html> (accessed January 17, 2006).

The National Wild and Scenic Rivers System. <http://www.nps.gov/rivers> (accessed January 17, 2006).

National Park Service Organic Act

Legislation

By: United States Congress

Date: August 25, 1916

Source: U.S. Congress. "The National Park Service Organic Act." Washington, DC: August 25, 1916.

About the Author: The Congress of the United States was established by Article 1 of the U.S. Constitution of 1787. It is the legislative arm of the U.S. Federal Government.

INTRODUCTION

Although Yellowstone National Park, the world's first national park, was established in 1872, it was not until 1916 that the National Park Service was established within the Department of the Interior by an act of Congress. Today the national park system consists of nearly 400 units occupying more than 83 million acres (33.6 million hectares), ranging from Yellowstone, Yosemite, and Grand Canyon National Parks, to the White House. The system consists of nineteen different kinds of units that include national parks, battlefields and battlefield parks, historical parks, monuments, memorials, parkways, lakeshores and seashores, recreation areas, and wild and scenic rivers. Since the establishment of Yellowstone National Park, more than 1,200 national parks have been created in one hundred countries.

One of the first steps towards the creation of the National Park Service occurred when the Yellowstone National Park Act of 1872 reserved more than 1 million acres (405,000 hectares) in Montana and Wyoming as a park for recreation (described as a "pleasuring ground") and the preservation of "... timber, mineral deposits, lumber, natural curiosities, or wonders." Authority for operation of the new national park was given to the Secretary of the Interior. Its remote location and expansive boundaries made it difficult to enforce regulations, so from 1886 to 1918 the U.S. Army patrolled the park. The federal government had previously ceded the Yosemite Valley to the State of California in 1864 and it became a national park under dual state and federal control in 1890. As in Yellowstone, the U.S. Army provided ranger services during the early years. Yosemite National Park was returned to the federal government in 1906. Part of the Grand Canyon was declared a national forest in 1893, a federal game preserve in 1906, and a national monument in 1908. The Grand Canyon National Park was finally established in 1919.

The National Park Service Organic Act was signed into law on August 25, 1916. By that time there were already forty national parks and monuments within the United States, all of which were folded into the newly created National Park Service. The Organic Act, however, did not affect monuments and historical sites operated by the U.S. Forest Service and the War Department (now the Department of

The National Park Service Organic Act makes it possible for today's generation to enjoy parks such as the Glacier National Park in Montana, undated photo pictured here. © BETTMANN/CORBIS

Defense). These separate entities were placed under Park Service control by an executive order issued by Franklin D. Roosevelt in 1933. Other legislation that has affected the national park system over the years has included the Wilderness Act of 1964 and the General Authorities Act of 1970. Passage of the Wilderness Act led to the inclusion of approximately 43 million acres (17.4 million hectares) of land managed by the National Park Service into the 105-million-acre (42.5-million-hectare) National Wilderness Preservation System. The General Authorities Act emphasized that all of the National Park Service units have equal standing within the national park system.

New national parks can be created only by acts of Congress. Most other kinds of National Park Service units also require congressional approval. An important exception is the creation of national monuments on land already owned by the federal government, which can be created by presidential degree under the Antiquities Act of 1906.

PRIMARY SOURCE

THE NATIONAL PARK SERVICE ORGANIC ACT

An act to establish a National Park Service, and for other purposes.
Be it enacted by the Senate and House of Representatives of the United States of America in Congress assembled, That there is hereby created in the Department of the Interior a service to be called the National Park Service, which shall be under the charge of a director, who shall be appointed by the Secretary and who shall receive a salary of $4,500 per annum. There shall also be appointed by the Secretary the following assistants and other employees at

the salaries designated: One assistant director, at $2,500 per annum, one chief clerk, at $2,000 per annum; one drafts-man, at $1,800 per annum; one messenger, at $600 per annum; and, in addition thereto, such other employees as the Secretary of the Interior shall deem necessary: Provided, That not more than $8,100 annually shall be expended for salaries of experts, assistants, and employees within the District of Columbia not herein specifically enumerated unless previously authorized by law. The service thus established shall promote and regulate the use of the Federal areas known as national parks, monuments, and reservations hereinafter specified by such means and meas-ures as conform to the fundamental purposes of the said parks, monuments, and reservations, which purpose is to conserve the scenery and the natural and historic objects and the wildlife therein and to provide for the enjoyment of the same in such manner and by such means as will leave them unimpaired for the enjoyment of future generations.

SEC. 2. That the director shall, under the direction of the Secretary of the Interior, have the supervision, man-agement, and control of the several national parks and national monuments which are now under the jurisdiction of the Department of the Interior, and of the Hot Springs Reservation in the State of Arkansas, and of such other national parks and reservations of like character as may be hereafter created by Congress: Provided, That in the supervision, management, and control of national monu-ments contiguous to national forests the Secretary of Agriculture may cooperate with said National Park Service to such extent as may be requested by the Secretary of the Interior.

SEC. 3. That the Secretary of the Interior shall make and publish such rules and regulations as he may deem necessary or proper for the use and management of the parks, monuments, and reservations under the jurisdiction of the National Park Service, and any violations of any of the rules and regulations authorized by this Act shall be punished as provided for in section fifty of the Act entitled "An Act to codify and amend the penal laws of the United States," approved March fourth, nineteen hundred and nine, as amended by section six of the Act of June twenty-fifth, nineteen hundred and ten (Thirty-sixth United States Statutes at Large, page eight hundred and fifty-seven). He may also, upon terms and conditions to be fixed by him, sell or dispose of timber in those cases where in his judgment the cutting of such timber is required in order to control the attacks of insects or diseases or other-wise conserve the scenery or the natural or historic objects in any such park, monument, or reservation. He may also provide in his discretion for the destruction of such animals and of such plant life as may be detrimental to the use of any of said parks, monuments, or reservations. He may also grant privileges, leases, and permits for the use of land for the accommodation of visitors in the various parks,

monuments, or other reservations herein provided for, but for periods not exceeding thirty years; and no natural curi-osities, wonders, or objects of interest shall be leased, rented, or granted to anyone on such terms as to interfere with free access to them by the public: Provided, however, That the Secretary of the Interior may, under such rules and regulations and on such terms as he may prescribe, grant the privilege to graze live stock within any national park, monument, or reservation herein referred to when in his judgment such use is not detrimental to the primary purpose for which such park, monument, or reservation was created, except that this provision shall not apply to the Yellowstone National Park: And provided further, That the Secretary of the Interior may grant said privileges, leases, and permits and enter into contracts relating to the same with responsible persons, firms, or corporations without advertising and without securing competitive bids: And provided further, That no contract, lease, permit, or privilege granted shall be assigned or transferred by such grantees, permittees, or licensees, without the approval of the Secretary of the Interior first obtained in writing: And provided further, That the Secretary may, in his discretion, authorize such grantees, permittees, or licensees to exe-cute mortgages and issue bonds, shares of stock, and other evidences of interest in or indebtedness upon their rights, properties, and franchises, for the purposes of installing, enlarging or improving plant and equipment and extending facilities for the accommodation of the pub-lic within such national parks and monuments.

SEC. 4. That nothing in this Act contained shall affect or modify the provisions of the Act approved February fifteenth, nineteen hundred and one, entitled "An Act relating to rights of way through certain parks, reser-vations, and other public lands."

SIGNIFICANCE

The National Park Service Organic Act is signifi-cant because it formally established an organizational structure specifically for a growing network of parks and monuments that included the world's first national park. Before passage of the act, the national park sys-tem was operated by the Department of the Interior using soldiers rather than professional park rangers to administer its lands. Since passage of the act, the national park system within the United States has grown nearly tenfold, from forty to nearly four hun-dred parks, monuments, and other units. Although the language of the Organic Act has been amended and supplemented by subsequent acts of Congress, the core idea of a nationwide system of parks with unique scenic, natural, or historical values has remained intact for nearly a century.

FURTHER RESOURCES

Books

Albright, Horace M., and Mary Albright Schenk. *Creating the National Park Service: The Missing Years*. Norman, OK.: University of Oklahoma Press, 1999.

Schullery, Paul, and Lee H. Whittlesey. *Myth and History in the Creation of Yellowstone National Park*. Lincoln, NE: University of Nebraska Press, 2003.

Sellars, Richard W. *Preserving Nature in the National Parks: A History*. New Haven, CN: Yale University Press, 1999.

Web sites

National Park Service. <http://www.nps.gov> (accessed January 17, 2006).

National Environmental Policy Act

Legislation excerpt

By: United States Congress

Date: Decemebr 1969

Source: U.S. Congress. "The National Environmental Policy Act of 1969." Washington, D.C.: 1969. Available online at <http://ceq.eh.doe.gov/nepa/regs/nepa/nepaeqia.htm> (accessed January 30, 2006).

About the Author: The Congress of the United States was established by Article 1 of the U.S. Constitution of 1787. Congress is the legislative arm of the U.S. Federal Government.

INTRODUCTION

Public law 91–190, also known as The National Environmental Policy Act of 1969, or NEPA, is a comparatively short piece of legislation that has had far-reaching effects during the decades since it took effect on January 1, 1970. The four major purposes of the act were to establish a national policy promoting harmony between humans and their environment; to decrease or eliminate damage to the environment; to promote a better understanding of the ecological systems and resources deemed important to the country; and to create the Council on Environmental Policy within the executive branch of government.

NEPA mandated that an integrated and interdisciplinary approach be used when making decisions or plans that might adversely affect the environment, that qualitative environmental values be considered along

President Richard Nixon signed in the National Environment Policy Act of 1969. AP IMAGES

with economic and technical factors when making decisions, and that proposed federal projects include a document that evaluates the environmental impact of the project. The requirement for an environmental evaluation of all federally funded projects is probably the most widely known provision of the act.

■ PRIMARY SOURCE

National Environmental Policy Act of 1969, as amended

Sec. 2.

The purposes of this Act are: To declare a national policy which will encourage productive and enjoyable harmony between man and his environment; to promote efforts which will prevent or eliminate damage to the environment and biosphere and stimulate the health and welfare of man; to enrich the understanding of the ecological systems and natural resources important to the Nation; and to establish a Council on Environmental Quality.

TITLE I

CONGRESSIONAL DECLARATION OF NATIONAL ENVIRONMENTAL POLICY

Sec. 101.

(a) The Congress, recognizing the profound impact of man's activity on the interrelations of all components of the natural environment, particularly the profound influences of population growth, high-density urbanization, industrial expansion, resource exploitation, and new and expanding technological advances and recognizing further the critical importance of restoring and maintaining environmental quality to the overall welfare and development of man, declares that it is the continuing policy of the Federal Government, in cooperation with State and local governments, and other concerned public and private organizations, to use all practicable means and measures, including financial and technical assistance, in a manner calculated to foster and promote the general welfare, to create and maintain conditions under which man and nature can exist in productive harmony, and fulfill the social, economic, and other requirements of present and future generations of Americans.

(b) In order to carry out the policy set forth in this Act, it is the continuing responsibility of the Federal Government to use all practicable means, consistent with other essential considerations of national policy, to improve and coordinate Federal plans, functions, programs, and resources to the end that the Nation may—

1. fulfill the responsibilities of each generation as trustee of the environment for succeeding generations;
2. assure for all Americans safe, healthful, productive, and aesthetically and culturally pleasing surroundings;
3. attain the widest range of beneficial uses of the environment without degradation, risk to health or safety, or other undesirable and unintended consequences;
4. preserve important historic, cultural, and natural aspects of our national heritage, and maintain, wherever possible, an environment which supports diversity, and variety of individual choice;
5. achieve a balance between population and resource use which will permit high standards of living and a wide sharing of life's amenities; and
6. enhance the quality of renewable resources and approach the maximum attainable recycling of depletable resources.

(c) The Congress recognizes that each person should enjoy a healthful environment and that each person has a responsibility to contribute to the preservation and enhancement of the environment.

Sec. 102.

The Congress authorizes and directs that, to the fullest extent possible: (1) the policies, regulations, and public laws of the United States shall be interpreted and administered in accordance with the policies set forth in this Act, and (2) all agencies of the Federal Government shall —

(A) utilize a systematic, interdisciplinary approach which will insure the integrated use of the natural and social sciences and the environmental design arts in planning and in decisionmaking which may have an impact on man's environment;

(B) identify and develop methods and procedures, in consultation with the Council on Environmental Quality established by title II of this Act, which will insure that presently unquantified environmental amenities and values may be given appropriate consideration in decisionmaking along with economic and technical considerations;

(C) include in every recommendation or report on proposals for legislation and other major Federal actions significantly affecting the quality of the human environment, a detailed statement by the responsible official on —

(i) the environmental impact of the proposed action,
(ii) any adverse environmental effects which cannot be avoided should the proposal be implemented,
(iii) alternatives to the proposed action,
(iv) the relationship between local short-term uses of man's environment and the maintenance and enhancement of long-term productivity, and
(v) any irreversible and irretrievable commitments of resources which would be involved in the proposed action should it be implemented.

Prior to making any detailed statement, the responsible Federal official shall consult with and obtain the comments of any Federal agency which has jurisdiction by law or special expertise with respect to any environmental impact involved. Copies of such statement and the comments and views of the appropriate Federal, State, and local agencies, which are authorized to develop and enforce environmental standards, shall be made available to the President, the Council on Environmental Quality and to the public as provided by section 552 of title 5, United States Code, and shall accompany the proposal through the existing agency review processes;

(D) Any detailed statement required under subparagraph (C) after January 1, 1970, for any major Federal action funded under a program of grants to States shall not be deemed to be legally insufficient solely by reason of having been prepared by a State agency or official, if:

(i) the State agency or official has statewide jurisdiction and has the responsibility for such action,
(ii) the responsible Federal official furnishes guidance and participates in such preparation,
(iii) the responsible Federal official independently evaluates such statement prior to its approval and adoption, and
(iv) after January 1, 1976, the responsible Federal official provides early notification to, and solicits the views of, any other State or any Federal land management entity of any action or any alternative thereto which may have significant

impacts upon such State or affected Federal land management entity and, if there is any disagreement on such impacts, prepares a written assessment of such impacts and views for incorporation into such detailed statement.

The procedures in this subparagraph shall not relieve the Federal official of his responsibilities for the scope, objectivity, and content of the entire statement or of any other responsibility under this Act; and further, this subparagraph does not affect the legal sufficiency of statements prepared by State agencies with less than statewide jurisdiction.

(E) study, develop, and describe appropriate alternatives to recommended courses of action in any proposal which involves unresolved conflicts concerning alternative uses of available resources;

(F) recognize the worldwide and long-range character of environmental problems and, where consistent with the foreign policy of the United States, lend appropriate support to initiatives, resolutions, and programs designed to maximize international cooperation in anticipating and preventing a decline in the quality of mankind's world environment;

(G) make available to States, counties, municipalities, institutions, and individuals, advice and information useful in restoring, maintaining, and enhancing the quality of the environment;

(H) initiate and utilize ecological information in the planning and development of resource-oriented projects; and

(I) assist the Council on Environmental Quality established by title II of this Act.

Sec. 103.

All agencies of the Federal Government shall review their present statutory authority, administrative regulations, and current policies and procedures for the purpose of determining whether there are any deficiencies or inconsistencies therein which prohibit full compliance with the purposes and provisions of this Act and shall propose to the President not later than July 1, 1971, such measures as may be necessary to bring their authority and policies into conformity with the intent, purposes, and procedures set forth in this Act.

Sec. 104.

Nothing in section 102 or 103 shall in any way affect the specific statutory obligations of any Federal agency (1) to comply with criteria or standards of environmental quality, (2) to coordinate or consult with any other Federal or State agency, or (3) to act, or refrain from acting contingent upon the recommendations or certification of any other Federal or State agency.

Sec. 105.

The policies and goals set forth in this Act are supplementary to those set forth in existing authorizations of Federal agencies.

TITLE II

COUNCIL ON ENVIRONMENTAL QUALITY

Sec. 201.

The President shall transmit to the Congress annually beginning July 1, 1970, an Environmental Quality Report (hereinafter referred to as the "report") which shall set forth (1) the status and condition of the major natural, manmade, or altered environmental classes of the Nation, including, but not limited to, the air, the aquatic, including marine, estuarine, and fresh water, and the terrestrial environment, including, but not limited to, the forest, dryland, wetland, range, urban, suburban an rural environment; (2) current and foreseeable trends in the quality, management and utilization of such environments and the effects of those trends on the social, economic, and other requirements of the Nation; (3) the adequacy of available natural resources for fulfilling human and economic requirements of the Nation in the light of expected population pressures; (4) a review of the programs and activities (including regulatory activities) of the Federal Government, the State and local governments, and non-governmental entities or individuals with particular reference to their effect on the environment and on the conservation, development and utilization of natural resources; and (5) a program for remedying the deficiencies of existing programs and activities, together with recommendations for legislation.

Sec. 202.

There is created in the Executive Office of the President a Council on Environmental Quality (hereinafter referred to as the "Council"). The Council shall be composed of three members who shall be appointed by the President to serve at his pleasure, by and with the advice and consent of the Senate. The President shall designate one of the members of the Council to serve as Chairman. Each member shall be a person who, as a result of his training, experience, and attainments, is exceptionally well qualified to analyze and interpret environmental trends and information of all kinds; to appraise programs and activities of the Federal Government in the light of the policy set forth in title I of this Act; to be conscious of and responsive to the scientific, economic, social, aesthetic, and cultural needs and interests of the Nation; and to formulate and recommend national policies to promote the improvement of the quality of the environment....

SIGNIFICANCE

NEPA provided broad guidance that has had a permanent effect on the way that environmental issues are considered when planning federally funded projects within the United States. It elevated environmental concerns to the same level as economic and engineering considerations, outlined an interdisciplinary process by which the environmental impacts of proposed federal projects must be evaluated, and created an executive branch Council on Environmental Quality to advise the president and coordinate environmental policy activity.

The required environmental evaluations of proposed projects can take one of three forms. The simplest is known as a categorical exclusion, and applies to types of activities that do not have an individual or cumulative impact on the environment. A categorical exclusion might be issued, for example, to allow private citizens to collect small amounts of fallen timber from national forests in order to heat their homes. If an activity does not qualify for a categorical exclusion, as most major projects do not, then an environmental assessment, or EA, must be undertaken and made available for public comment. If, after taking into account public comments, the environmental assessment concludes that the proposed project will have insignificant impacts, then a finding of no significant impact (also known as a FONSI) may be issued. If the environmental assessment finds that significant impacts will occur, then a more detailed environmental impact statement or EIS must be prepared.

Each environmental impact statement must describe the purpose of and need for the project, the environmental impact of a proposed project, any adverse effects that may be impossible to avoid, one or more alternatives to the proposed activity, the balance between short-term gains and long-term environmental productivity, and any permanent loss of natural resources that would occur if the proposed activity is undertaken. A list of the specialists who prepared the statement and their professional qualifications must also be included. Environmental impact statements typically include so-called no-action alternatives that weigh the effects of a proposed project against those that would occur if nothing were done. Furthermore, environmental impact statements must be prepared in consultation with other relevant scientific expertise or legal jurisdiction. For example, the U.S. Fish and Wildlife Service must be consulted if a riverfront construction project has the potential to harm fisheries. Copies of the environmental impact statement must be provided to the President, the Council on Environmental Quality, and the general public. In practice, environmental impact statements for major

projects can be hundreds or thousands of pages long. Comments from the general public on a draft environmental impact statement must also be addressed and incorporated into the final statement. Once an environmental impact statement has been finalized a circulated, a document known as the record of decision or ROD is published. It explains the justification for selection of a preferred alternative, describes the other alternatives considered and identifies an environmentally preferably alternative, and elaborates upon the measures that will be taken to reduce environmental impacts.

The Council on Environmental Quality, another product of NEPA, coordinates environmental activities among federal agencies and helps to develop federal environmental policies. The council also reviews disputes related to environmental assessments and prepares an annual report on the environment. Its chair is appointed by the President with the advice and consent of the U.S. Senate.

FURTHER RESOURCES

Books

Bass, Ronald E., Albert I. Herson, and Kenneth M. Bogdan. *The NEPA Book: A Step-By-Step Guide on How to Comply with the National Environmental Policy Act*. Point Arena, Calif.: Solano Press, 2001.

Eccleston, Charles H. *Environmental Impact Statements: A Comprehensive Guide to Project and Strategic Planning*. New York: Wiley, 2000.

Web sites

U.S. Environmental Protection Agency. "National Environmental Policy Act (NEPA)." <http://www.epa.gov/compliance/nepa> (accessed January 17, 2006).

DOI Trans-Alaska Pipeline Authorization Act

Legislation

By: United States Congress

Date: November 16, 1973

Source: U.S. Congress. "DOI Trans-Alaska Pipeline Authorization Act." November 16, 1973. <http://www.usdoj.gov/crt/cor/byagency/doi1651.htm> (accessed March 16, 2006).

The 800-mile Trans-Alaska pipeline carries oil from Prudhoe Bay to Valdez, and is considered necessary to the economy of the United States, as well as an environmental threat. AP IMAGES

About the Author: The Congress of the United States was established by Article 1 of the U.S. Constitution of 1787. It is the legislative arm of the U.S. Federal Government.

INTRODUCTION

In 1968, oil was discovered in the Prudhoe Bay area in northern Alaska. Many oil companies discussed various methods of transporting the oil, but it was decided that the most economical method was to construct a pipeline system. This would transport the oil from the icy northern slopes of Alaska to the comparatively warmer, ice-free Port of Valdez in southern Alaska. From here it would be easier to transport oil to other refineries in the United States by ships, tankers, and other means.

Subsequently, in 1970 a consortium of oil companies together formed Alyeska, a pipeline service company to construct, maintain, and service the pipeline.

The U.S. Department of the Interior issued an environmental impact statement for the Trans-Alaska Pipeline System (TAPS) project in 1972. In November 1973, the Trans-Alaska Pipeline Authorization Act that authorized this construction was signed into law by President Richard Nixon. However, the construction of the pipeline was deferred because of environmental concerns and disputes.

The DOI Trans-Alaska Pipeline Authorization Act aims to reduce American dependence on foreign sources of oil by allowing easy transportation and availability of crude oil for domestic use. The Act begins with the congressional finding and declaration that the delivery of northern Alaskan oil to the national markets was in the national interest due to growing shortages and increased American dependence on foreign oil. The construction of a pipeline would favor the transportation and availability of Alaskan oil for domestic use, and would be of immense benefit to the U.S. economy.

As mentioned above, the Act also authorizes the construction of the Trans-Alaska Pipeline System to transport crude oil from Prudhoe Bay to Valdez. In 1974, the Federal Government granted a right of way to the pipeline. Construction of the pipeline began in April 1974 and was completed in May 1977. The first oil was pumped through the system in July 1977.

PRIMARY SOURCE

SEC. 1651. CONGRESSIONAL FINDINGS AND DECLARATION
The Congress finds and declares that:

(a) The early development and delivery of oil and gas from Alaska'sNorth Slope to domestic markets is in the national interest because ofgrowing domestic shortages and increasing dependence upon insecureforeign sources.

(b) The Department of the Interior and other Federal agencies, have,over a long period of time, conducted extensive studies of the technical aspects and of the environmental, social, and economic impacts of the proposed trans-Alaska oil pipeline, including consideration of a trans-Canada pipeline.

(c) The earliest possible construction of a trans-Alaska oilpipeline from the North Slope of Alaska to Port Valdez in that Statewill make the extensive proven and potential reserves of low-sulfur oilavailable for domestic use and will best serve the national interest.

(d) A supplemental pipeline to connect the North Slope with a trans-Canada pipeline may be needed later and it should be studied now, but it should not be regarded as an alternative for a trans-Alaska pipeline that does not traverse a foreign country.

Short Title of 1990 Amendment Pub. L. 101–380, title VIII, Sec. 8001, Aug. 18, 1990, 104 Stat.564, provided that: ''This title [enacting sections 1642 and 1656 ofthis title, amending sections 1350 and 1653 of this title and section3145 of Title 16, Conservation, and enacting provisions set out as notes under this section and section 1653 of this title] may be cited as the ''Trans-Alaska Pipeline System Reform Act of 1990''

Short Title Section 201 of title II of Pub. L. 93–153 provided that: ''Thistitle [enacting this chapter] may be cited as the ''Trans-Alaska Pipeline Authorization Act''

Separability Section 411 of Pub. L. 93–153 provided that: ''If any provision ofthis Act [enacting this chapter, section 1456a of this title, andsection 3512 of Title 44, Public Printing and Documents, amendingsection 1608 of this title, sections 45, 46, 53, and 56 of Title 15,Commerce and Trade, section 185 of Title 30, Mineral Lands and Mining,section 3502 of Title 44, and section 391a of former Title 46, Shipping, and enacting provisions set out as notes under sections 1608 and 1651 of this title, section 1904 of Title 12, Banks and Banking, section 45 of Title 15, section 791a of Title 16, Conservation, and section 1221 of Title 33, Navigation and Navigable Waters] or the applicability thereof is held invalid the remainder of this Act shall not be affected thereby.''

Presidential Task Force Pub. L. 101–380, title VIII, Sec. 8103, Aug. 18, 1990, 104 Stat.567, established a Presidential Task Force on the Trans-Alaska PipelineSystem, to conduct an audit of the Trans-Alaska Pipeline System and make recommendations to the President, Congress, and the Governor of Alaska, authorized appropriations for the Task Force, and required it to transmit its final report to the President, Congress, and the Governor no later than 2 years after the date on which funding was made available.

North Slope Crude Oil; Report on Equitable Allocation Pub. L. 94–586, Sec. 18, Oct. 22, 1976, 90 Stat. 2916, directed thatthe President, within 6 months of Oct. 22, 1976, determine specialexpediting procedures necessary to insure the equitable allocation ofNorth Slope crude oil to the Northern Tier States of Washington, Oregon, Idaho, Montana, Illinois, Indiana, and Idaho to carry out the provisions of section 410 of Pub. L. 93–153 [set out below], and to report his findings to Congress, such report to include a statement demonstrating the impact that the delivery system would have on reducing the dependency of New England and the Middle Atlantic States on foreign oil imports.

Trans-Canada Pipeline; Negotiations With Canada; Feasibility Study Title III (Secs. 301–303) of Pub. L. 93–153 authorized the President to enter into negotiations with the Government of Canada to determine Canadian willingness to permit construction of pipelines or other transportation systems across its territory to bring gas and oil from Alaska's North Slope to the United States; the need for intergovernmental agreements to protect interests of any parties involved with construction, operation, and maintenance of such natural gas or oil transportation systems; terms and conditions for construction across Canadian territory; desirability of joint studies to insure environmental protection, reduce regulatory uncertainty, and insure meeting energy requirements; quantity of oil and gas for which Canada would guarantee transit; and acquisition of other energy sources so as to make unnecessary the shipment of oil from the Alaska pipeline by tanker into the Puget Sound area. The President was to report to Congress on actions taken and recommendations for further action. In addition, the Secretary of the Interior was to investigate, and to report to Congress within 2 years of Nov. 16, 1973, as to the feasibility of oil or gas pipelines from the North Slope of Alaska to connect with a pipeline through Canada that would deliver oil or gas to United States markets. Nothing in title III was to limit the authority of the Secretary or any other Federal official to grant a gas or oil pipeline right-of-way or permit, which that official was otherwise authorized by law to grant.

Exclusion of Persons From Trans-Alaska Pipeline Activities on Basis ofRace, Creed, Color, National Origin, or Sex Prohibited Section 403 of Pub. L. 93–153 provided that: "The Secretary of the Interior shall take such affirmative action as he deems necessary to assure that no person shall, on the grounds of race, creed, color, national origin, or sex, be excluded from receiving, or participating in any activity conducted under, any permit, right-of-way, public land order, or other Federal authorization granted or issued under title II[this chapter]. The Secretary of the Interior shall promulgate such rules as he deems necessary to carry out the purposes of this subsection and may enforce this subsection, and any rules promulgated under this subsection, through agency and department provisions and rules which shall be similar to those established and in effect under title VI of the Civil Rights Act of 1964 [section 2000d et seq. of Title 42, The Public Health and Welfare]."

Equitable Allocation of North Slope Crude Oil Section 410 of Pub. L. 93–153 provided that: "The Congress declares that the crude oil on the North Slope of Alaska is an important part ofthe Nation's oil resources, and that the benefits of such crude oil should be equitably shared, directly or indirectly, by all regions of the country. The President shall use any authority he may have to insure an equitable allocation of available North Slope and other crude oil resources and petroleum products among all regions and all of theseveral States."

SIGNIFICANCE

TAPS traverses a distance of nearly 800 miles (1,300 kilometers) across Alaska. It also crosses thirty-four major rivers, around 800 mountain streams, and three mountain ranges. In general, the construction of a trans-geographical pipeline such as this entails significant environmental concerns.

The construction of TAPS was a major issue during the time of its construction, due to the potential environmental impact it could have on the fragile Alaskan environment. However, the growing oil needs of the United States, and also the increasing need of reliability on domestic sources, tipped the scales in favor of building the pipeline.

Over the years, the broad view that transportation of oil by pipeline would be more economical and safe has not been true. Since the early 2000s, a number of concerns and issues like the physical condition of pipeline, the operations, and management aspects of the system have plagued TAPS.

The fragile Alaskan environment dictated that the pipeline be built above ground. Also considering that the hot crude flowing through the Alaskan environment would be a danger to the Alaskan permafrost (permanently frozen subsoil), special supporting structures were constructed to support the 48-inch (1.2-meter) diameter pipeline.

However, the physical condition of many of the structures that support the pipeline above ground is questionable. There have been reports of corrosion in the pipeline also. At some places the pipeline walls have been reduced to nearly half their original thickness.

In 1988, an 8.5-mile (13.7-kilometer) section of the pipe had to be replaced because of corrosion. Further, accidents have routinely occurred on the pipeline. These include shutdowns, spills, fires, and flow reductions. Reportedly, there was an alarming increase in the number of such incidents in 1994 and 1995. All of these have affected the environment significantly.

One such accident occurred in March 1989 at Port Valdez, the main loading point for the pipeline. Just outside Port Valdez, a transport tanker ship called the *Exxon Valdez* ran aground, spilling nearly 250,000 barrels of crude oil. A study to examine the magnitude of the disaster revealed that nearly 5,000 otters, 300 harbor seals, 200,000 birds of ninety different species, and many hundreds of other fish and animals were killed due to the oil spill. The spill also caused significant decrease in the population of a number of plant and marine species. It caused damage to a number of ecosystems and subsidiary components. Exxon eventually spent $2 billion toward cleanup operations.

In addition to the accidents, considering the age of the pipeline, many experts are seriously concerned about safety issues in the system. Environmental agencies such as the Alaska Forum for Environmental Responsibility and the Northern Alaska Environmental Center have raised doubts about the structural integrity of the pipeline. There also have been scientific reports that climate changes may affect the pipeline.

However, in 1994, the federal government renewed the right of way granted to the pipeline owners for another thirty years, until 2024. The renewal was granted without any modifications to the original plans. Factors like climate change, age of the pipeline, technological modifications needed, current concerns like TAPS performance, and the environment were not considered.

Environmental protection groups feel that the consequences of the ability or the inability of TAPS to function as planned in the years to come can make or break the case for the Alaskan environment. Should the pipe fail, it could be an enormous disaster to the Alaskan environment, and could unwind the positive environmental actions taken over the decades.

FURTHER RESOURCES

Web sites

Sorensen, Steve P., and Keith J. Meyer. "Effect of the Denali Fault Rupture on the Trans-Alaska Pipeline." *Alyeska Pipeline Service Company*. <http://www.alyeska-pipe.com/Inthenews/techpapers/2-TAPS%20Fault%20Crossing%20Denali%20EQ.pdf> (accessed March 16, 2006).

"Alaska Oil Disaster 'Imminent'." *BBC News*, July 12, 1999. <http://news.bbc.co.uk/1/hi/world/americas/391698.stm> (accessed March 16, 2006).

Northern Alaska Environmental Center. "Alaska's Arctic: Current Situation." *Northern Alaska Environmental Center*. <http://www.northern.org/artman/publish/acurrent.shtml> (accessed March 16, 2006).

———. "The Trans-Alaska Pipeline (TAPS)." *Northern Alaska Environmental Center*. <http://www.northern.org/artman/publish/taps.shtml> (accessed March 16, 2006).

EPA Establishes Hazardous Waste Enforcement and Emergency Response System

Names 60 New Sites

Press release

By: U.S. Environmental Protection Agency (EPA)

Date: July 11, 1979

Source: U.S. Environmental Protection Agency (EPA). "EPA Establishes Hazardous Waste Enforcement and Emergency Response System: Names 60 new sites." July 11, 1979. <http://www.epa.gov/history/topics/hazard/01.htm> (accessed January 6, 2006).

About the Organization: The Environmental Protection Agency (EPA) is a U.S. agency set up to protect the environment from various hazards. The EPA is an independent statutory body. Among its primary duties are to provide independent advice to the government on environmental protection legislation; put forward new environmental related proposals; and monitor the environment within the United States according to the limits set by various federal and state legislations.

INTRODUCTION

Disposal of hazardous waste has been an enormous problem in the past few decades, even for a developed nation like the United States. Hazardous wastes, especially those generated by industry, can pose significant risks to public health and can be a long-standing danger to the environment. In the 1960s, hazardous waste dumps throughout the country raised serious health concerns for the public.

Subsequently, in 1979 the Environmental Protection Agency (EPA) established the formation of a Hazardous Waste Enforcement and Emergency Response System to counter this issue. It also identified sixty various sites that were targets of hazardous waste. The system recognized and gave top priority to cleaning up hazardous waste sites. It acknowledged the danger posed by hazardous waste dumps, such as the leaching of toxic substances into ground water systems, to the public.

The EPA press release dated July 1979 reports the announcement by Deputy Administrator Barbara Blum about the introduction of a Hazardous Waste Enforcement and Emergency Response System by the EPA to tackle the growing problem of hazardous waste disposal in the United States.

Earlier pollution control norms largely succeeded in keeping pollutants out of the air and water. However, a large number of open land dumps came into existence due to lack of effective regulations to prevent dumping of solid waste on land sites.

The EPA, after establishing Hazardous Waste Enforcement, discovered numerous hazardous dumpsites, initiating federal and state action against some of those sites. They conceded that various dumpsite owners lacked information, knowledge, and the funds to correct environmental and related damages occurring due to their haphazard dumping practices.

Environmental Protection Agency Deputy Administrator Barbara Blum today named the clean-up of hazardous waste dump sites threatening public health the "highest Agency priority" and established an agency-wide Hazardous Waste Enforcement and Emergency Response System to respond to hazardous waste emergencies.

Blum also released today the names of 60 newly-discovered sites containing wastes which may be public health and environmental hazards.

"We are now aware of 151 sites across the country which may contain potentially dangerous quantities of hazardous wastes," said Blum. "We will continue to evaluate the extent of the hazards at these sites and force responsible parties to alleviate any immediate threat to the public."

EPA is currently in the process of evaluating potential hazards at 111 sites known to contain hazardous wastes. These evaluations may result in legal actions or emergency Federal actions to contain the spread of contaminants where there is an imminent hazard and existing local authority and funding is insufficient.

At the moment, Federal legal action is pending on five sites, and the States are acting against 34 sites. Forty-five dump sites named earlier this year as potentially dangerous have been cleaned up or removed from the current inventory of imminent hazards.

Blum also stressed the need for greater Federal authority and funding to act in emergencies when it becomes clear that sites containing hazardous wastes are threatening public health.

"EPA must now identify a responsible party and prove that imminent danger exists before it takes legal action, often delaying emergency cleanup," Blum said. "Responsible parties—generally site owners or operators if known—are often financially and logistically incapable of remedying hazards resulting from past careless dumping practices."

Legislation proposed by President Carter and now before Congress would give EPA authority and money to clean up such hazards in emergencies from abandoned or inactive waste sites without going to court first. The legislation, referred to as "superfund," would give EPA $1.625 billion in fees and appropriations over a four-year period for emergency cleanup of waste sites and spills. The fees would be levied on segments of the oil, petrochemical, and inorganic chemical industries.

Under the legislation, owners of abandoned or inactive hazardous waste sites would have to notify the government of the site's presence. The government could recover any cleanup costs incurred from the liable parties, if such parties could be identified.

EPA has also requested an additional $45 million and 70 positions to aid in cleanup investigations and to prepare legal casework. At the moment, the Agency has devoted some 100 people, primarily in its Regional Offices, to hazardous waste site investigation and enforcement.

To implement the system, Blum created a National Hazardous Waste Enforcement Task Force and a new unit in the Oil and Special Materials Control Division. The Enforcement Task Force, which will report directly to Blum, will coordinate Federal cleanup activity with its Regional Offices and with the States, including technical, scientific and legal support work. A status report will be kept of the number of sites containing hazardous wastes known to EPA and their cleanup status.

SIGNIFICANCE

There has been considerable development in the area of hazardous waste enforcement since the late 1970s, when EPA introduced its landmark Hazardous Waste Enforcement and Emergency Response System. A number of related federal legislations have passed since 1979 to tackle the growing problem of hazardous waste and implementation of effective enforcement against this menace.

Prior to the establishment of the Hazardous Waste Enforcement System, the Resource Conservation and Recovery Act (RCRA) was passed in 1976. Under Federal Law, the EPA was ultimately responsible for identifying and publishing a list of hazardous waste sites within eighteen months of passing of the RCRA act. It was also responsible for setting the standards of organizing, transportation, and final disposal of hazardous waste.

In a similar development, the U.S. Congress passed the Toxic Control Substance Act in 1976. Though this act gave the EPA wide powers to track more than seventy-five thousand toxic chemicals, like asbestos, entering or being produced in the United States, it was amended in 1979 with stronger provisions. The production and distribution of substances like polychlorinated biphenyl and other toxic substances were banned under the amendment.

Soon after the EPA's Hazardous Waste Enforcement System, in December 1980, the Congress passed the Comprehensive Environmental Response, Compensation and Liability Act (CERCLA). Creating a 'superfund' for the money needed to clean up hazardous wastes in open sites, this act gave the EPA wider powers to search for parties dumping hazardous waste in open sites, take measures to include them in the cleanup operations, and also make them liable for the costs incurred.

The above-mentioned acts, along with the Hazardous Waste Enforcement System, also stipulated the discontinuation of hazardous solid waste disposal in open spaces by 1983. Such stipulations brought the disposal of hazardous waste under federal and state law.

In 1984 the RCRA was revised to include the Hazardous and Solid Waste Amendment. This was done to alter the limitations posed by the act in its earlier versions. As discussed, this amendment required the phasing out of disposal of hazardous waste on open land. It also mandated tougher standards for waste disposal.

In 1992, the Congress passed the Federal Facility Compliance Act (FFCA). This act includes specific restrictions necessary for the disposal of hazardous waste. It also includes various conditions to be met for treatment of hazardous waste prior to its storage or disposal. Environmental Action groups state that most of these laws were passed after awareness about the risks of hazardous waste dumps was created by the Hazardous Waste Enforcement System and other EPA initiatives.

Since the late 1990s and early 2000s, the EPA has been actively organizing cleanup activities at various waste dumpsites. It also initiates action where dangerous chemicals may have leaked into the air, water, or the ground—for instance, leakage from underground tanks or fires at chemical or industrial plants. The EPA works out the damages caused in economical terms and costs incurred for this disposal, making the offending party pay for the damage caused.

FURTHER RESOURCES
Web sites

"Environmental Laws." *Missouri Department of Natural Resources.* <http://www.dnr.mo.gov/env/hwp/laws.htm> (accessed March 16, 2006).

U.S. Environmental Protection Agency. "Civil Enforcement." *U.S. Environmental Protection Agency.* <http://www.epa. gov/compliance/civil/econmodels> (accessed March 16, 2006).

———. "Cleaning up our Land, Water, and Air." *U.S. Environmental Protection Agency.* <http://www.epa.gov/ oswer/cleanup/basicinfo.htm> (accessed March 16, 2006).

———. "Cleaning up the Nation's Hazardous Waste Sites." *U.S. Environmental Protection Agency.* <http://www.epa. gov/superfund> (accessed March 16, 2006).

Comprehensive Environmental Response, Compensation, and Liability Act (CERCLA)

Superfund

Legislation

By: United States Code

Date: December 11, 1980

Source: U.S. Code "National Contingency Plan." Title 42, Chapter 103, Subchapter I, Section 9605(a).

About the Author: The U.S. Code is the set of general and permanent laws that govern the United States. The House of Representatives prepares the Code and revisions are published every six years. The Code is arranged into fifty Titles. Title 42 deals with Public Health and Welfare. Chapter 103 describes the laws pertaining to Superfund.

INTRODUCTION

Throughout the 1970s, chemical companies in the United States underwent a period of enormous innovation. In particular, petrochemical companies discovered a wide variety of techniques for making synthetic chemicals. In many cases, these production methods resulted in extremely toxic byproducts. At the time, regulations associated with dumping these byproducts were weak or poorly enforced, many companies simply released their wastes into oceans and rivers or buried them in the ground.

The seriousness of the problem was typified by events surrounding a toxic dump site in Niagara Falls, New York. The area known as Love Canal contained a landfill where barrels filled with toxic chemicals had been buried. Some of the chemicals leaked from the barrels and residents of the nearby community suffered health problems, including a high incidence of cancer, birth defects, and respiratory problems as a result of exposure to the toxins. Eventually, nearly one thousand families were forced to leave their homes because of damage to the environment by the toxins.

In light of the Love Canal tragedy, along with other environmental disasters stemming from the release of toxic wastes into the environment, the U.S. Congress enacted the Comprehensive Environmental Response Compensation and Liability Act—also called CERCLA—on December 11, 1980. The act created a tax on petroleum producers and chemical companies.

The money collected from the tax became known as Superfund, and was used for remediation in the case of the release of hazardous materials that pose a threat to humans or the environment. Over five years, the tax resulted in a fund of $1.6 billion dollars.

A major part of CERCLA involved the authorization of a revision of the National Contingency Plan (NCP). This plan explains the guidelines and procedures required for dealing with the release of hazardous chemicals and toxins into the environment. Part of the NCP is a list of sites that require long-term remediation. This list is known as the National Priorities List, or NPL. CERCLA also authorizes short-term responses to acute environmental risks. On October 17, 1986, CERCLA was amended by the Superfund Amendments and Reauthorization Act (SARA).

PRIMARY SOURCE

TITLE 42—THE PUBLIC HEALTH AND WELFARE
CHAPTER 103—COMPREHENSIVE ENVIRONMENTAL RESPONSE, COMPENSATION, AND LIABILITY
SUBCHAPTER I—HAZARDOUS SUBSTANCES RELEASES, LIABILITY, COMPENSATION

Sec. 9605. National contingency plan

(a) Revision and republication

Within one hundred and eighty days after December 11, 1980, the President shall, after notice and opportunity for public comments, revise and republish the national contingency plan for the removal of oil and hazardous substances, originally prepared and published pursuant to section 1321 of title 33, to reflect and effectuate the responsibilities and powers created by this chapter, in addition to those matters specified in section 1321(c)(2) of title 33. Such revision shall include a section of the plan to be known as the national hazardous substance response plan which shall establish procedures and standards for responding to releases of hazardous substances, pollutants, and contaminants, which shall include at a minimum:

(1) methods for discovering and investigating facilities at which hazardous substances have been disposed of or otherwise come to be located;

(2) methods for evaluating, including analyses of relative cost, and remedying any releases or threats of releases from facilities which pose substantial danger to the public health or the environment;

(3) methods and criteria for determining the appropriate extent of removal, remedy, and other measures authorized by this chapter;

(4) appropriate roles and responsibilities for the Federal, State, and local governments and for interstate and nongovernmental entities in effectuating the plan;

(5) provision for identification, procurement, maintenance, and storage of response equipment and supplies;

(6) a method for and assignment of responsibility for reporting the existence of such facilities which may be located on federally owned or controlled properties and any releases of hazardous substances from such facilities;

(7) means of assuring that remedial action measures are cost-effective over the period of potential exposure to the hazardous substances or contaminated materials;

(8)(A) criteria for determining priorities among releases or threatened releases throughout the United States for the purpose of taking remedial action and, to the extent practicable taking into account the potential urgency of such action, for the purpose of taking removal action. Criteria and priorities under this paragraph shall be based upon relative risk or danger to public health or welfare or the environment, in the judgment of the President, taking into account to the extent possible the population at risk, the hazard potential of the hazardous substances at such facilities, the potential for contamination of drinking water supplies, the potential for direct human contact, the potential for destruction of sensitive ecosystems, the damage to natural resources which may affect the human food chain and which is associated with any release or threatened release, the contamination or potential contamination of the ambient air which is associated with the release or threatened release, State preparedness to assume State costs and responsibilities, and other appropriate factors;

(B) based upon the criteria set forth in subparagraph (A) of this paragraph, the President shall list as part of the plan national priorities among the known releases or threatened releases throughout the United States and shall revise the list no less often than annually. Within one year after December 11, 1980, and annually thereafter, each State shall establish and submit for consideration by the President priorities for remedial action among known releases and potential releases in that State based upon the criteria setforth in subparagraph (A) of this paragraph. In assembling or revising the national list, the President shall consider any priorities established by the States. To the extent practicable, thehighest priority facilities shall be designated individually and shall be referred to as the "top priority among known response targets," and, to the extent practicable, shall include among theone hundred highest priority facilities one such facility from each State which shall be the facility designated by the State as presenting the greatest danger to public health or welfare or the environment among the known facilities in such State. A State shall be allowed to designate its highest priority facility only once. Other priority facilities or incidents may be listed singly or grouped for response priority purposes;

(9) specified roles for private organizations and entities in preparation for response and in responding to releases of hazardous substances, including identification of appropriate qualificationsand capacity therefor and including consideration of minority firms in accordance with subsection (f) of this section; and

(10) standards and testing procedures by which alternative or innovative treatment technologies can be determined to be appropriate for utilization in response actions authorized by this chapter.

The plan shall specify procedures, techniques, materials, equipment, and methods to be employed in identifying, removing, or remedying releases of hazardous substances comparable to those required under section 1321(c)(2)(F) and (G) and (j)(1) of title 33. Following publication of the revised national contingency plan, the response to and actions to minimize damage from hazardous substances releases shall, to the greatest extent possible, be in accordance with the provisions of the plan. The President may, from time to time, revise and republish the national contingency plan.

SIGNIFICANCE

One of the major accomplishments of CERCLA is providing a formal structure within which polluted sites can be cleaned up. When a site is identified as potentially hazardous, the Environmental Protection Agency (EPA) screens the area to assess its potential harm to humans and to the environment. The site is then assigned a numerical rank according to a Hazard Ranking System (HRS). If the site ranks higher than 28.5, it undergoes further study and is listed on the National Priorities List (NPL).

Three years after CERCLA was enacted, 406 toxic sites were identified and placed on the NPL. In 1987, federal facilities were added to the NPL and thirty-two were immediately listed. By 2004, the EPA had listed

The Wyckoff Inc. wood treatment facility on Bainbridge Island in Washington was treated by the EPA Superfund in 2004, where they attempted a high-tech steam-injection project to speed up the work. The gauge reading zero is a sign that the project failed. AP IMAGES

1,529 sites on the NPL, 158 of which were federal facilities.

The types of remediation that the EPA uses at Superfund sites varies depending on the type of hazard in the location. In emergency situations, the EPA removes hazardous material immediately, often incinerating the waste. In some cases, people are relocated to protect them from exposure to the toxins. In most cases, removal of the toxic material takes much longer, up to months or even years.

When a site is listed on the NPL, the EPA will try to fund the cleanup from those responsible for dumping the chemicals. These groups are known as Potentially Responsible Parties (PRPs). If these groups cannot be identified or are no longer viable entities, then the money for the cleanup comes from the Superfund trust that is generated from taxes on petrochemical companies.

By 2004, the EPA under CERCLA had completed the cleanup of more than 900 sites and removed 292 from the NPL. In order for a site to be removed from the NPL, all of the toxic chemicals are removed from the site and the area is named ready for economic, social and environmental use. In addition, 67 percent of the sites on the NPL had completed plans for remediation. The EPA had at least 800 CERCLA projects active in 2004.

Although not every clean-up project has succeeded, CERCLA can still point to a variety of significant success stories, in particular, the Love Canal area of Niagara Falls, New York, which contained 40 acres (16.2 hectares) of contaminated land. A barrier to water drainage now surrounds the area and a treatment facility for toxins controls contamination. These remediation techniques prevent the toxins from reaching the soil or drinking water. As a result of the work by the EPA, the Love Canal site was declared free from toxins in 2004. More than 200 homes and ten apartment buildings in the area have been renovated or built. Some light industry has also moved into the area.

FURTHER RESOURCES

Periodicals

Magnusun, Ed. "The Poisoning of America." *Time* 116 (September 22, 1980): 12.

Web sites

"Love Canal." *U.S. Environmental Protection Agency.* <http://www.epa.gov/history/topics/lovecanal> (accessed March 7, 2006).

"Superfund." *U.S. Environmental Protection Agency.* <http://www.epa.gov/superfund> (accessed March 7, 2006).

Crude Oil Windfall Profit Tax Act of 1980 (WPT)

Legislation

By: United States Congress

Date: April 2, 1980

Source: U.S. Congress. "Crude Oil Windfall Profit Tax Act of 1980." Washington, D.C.: 1980.

About the Author: The Congress of the United States was established by Article 1 of the U.S. Constitution of 1787. It is the legislative arm of the U.S. Federal Government.

INTRODUCTION

The Crude Oil Windfall Profit Tax Act (U.S. Public Law 96–223) was enacted in 1980 in response

to sharp oil price increases during the 1970s. Implementation was expensive and revenue was consistently below expectations, so the tax was repealed in 1988. The word "windfall" originally referred to fruit blown from trees by the wind, which could be easily collected from the ground. Its use evolved to describe any kind of economic godsend or good fortune, and the term "windfall profit" is often used in a manner that implies undeserved good fortune.

The early 1970s was a time of high inflation rates and rising consumer prices in the United States. At the time, the United States was importing about one-third of its oil supply and domestic oil exploration had decreased because it was in many cases less expensive to import oil than produce it from American oilfields. The early 1970s also marked the emergence of the Organization of Petroleum Exporting Countries (OPEC), which had been founded in 1960 to assert the rights of petroleum-producing countries in the international oil market. At the time OPEC was founded, international oil production and prices were dominated by a group of multinational companies known as the Seven Sisters (Exxon, Mobil, Chevron, Texaco, Gulf, British Petroleum, and Royal Dutch/Shell). The stated intentions of OPEC were to coordinate oil policy among its members, ensure fair and stable oil prices (and therefore revenue) for its members, provide an efficient and steady supply to oil-importing countries, and offer fair returns to oil investors. It is commonly considered to be a cartel, which is an organization that maintains prices at high levels by restricting the supply of its products. The OPEC member countries are Algeria, Indonesia, Iran, Iraq, Kuwait, Libya, Nigeria, Qatar, Saudi Arabia, the United Arab Emirates, and Venezuela. Ecuador was a member from 1973 to 1992 and Gabon was a member from 1975 to 1994. Major oil-producing countries that are not members of OPEC include the United States, Mexico, Russia, Norway, and Great Britain.

After a failed Egyptian and Syrian invasion of Israel on the Jewish holy day of Yom Kippur in October 1973, OPEC imposed a complete oil embargo on the United States and raised prices for European countries from $3.00 to $5.11 per barrel in retaliation for their support of Israel. Three months later OPEC raised the price to $11.65 per barrel. As a consequence of the international price increases and the OPEC embargo against the United States (often referred to as the Arab oil embargo in reference to the OPEC membership), gasoline prices quadrupled from 30 cents per gallon to as much as $1.20 per gallon. Gasoline was in short supply, causing long waits at gas stations. President Nixon banned Sunday gasoline sales and extended daylight savings time to stimulate energy conservation. Congress also approved construction of the Trans-Alaskan Pipeline to transport crude oil from the North Slope of Alaska to the port of Valdez, where it could be transferred to tankers bound for the lower forty-eight states.

Although oil company profits increased substantially as a result of the OPEC embargo and price increases, the overall economy fell into a recession. The Dow Jones Industrial Average, which reflects the prices of a broad range of stocks, fell from 1,051 in January of 1973 to 577 in December of 1974. A second and even larger global oil price increase occurred during the Iranian Revolution of 1979. The Crude Oil Windfall Profit Tax Act was passed as a response to increasing oil-company profits at a time when the remainder of the United States economy was struggling. The tax was complicated, with rates depending on the size of the company to which it was being applied, the type of oil, the age of the well from which the oil was produced, and the amount of oil produced by the well each day. It was also based on the difference between a 1979 base price of oil and the current market price, with annual adjustments for inflation.

The Crude Oil Windfall Profit Tax Act was repealed in 1988 because it was expensive to implement and its revenues never met expectations. Worldwide oil supplies from non-OPEC countries had increased, for example from Alaska and the North Sea (the latter controlled by Norway and Great Britain) and, although they never reached the pre-embargo prices of the early 1970s, prices began to fall sharply in 1981 and plummeted even more sharply in 1986. New technologies and higher prices also allowed increased production from newly discovered oilfields in areas such as the Gulf of Mexico. Although oil prices had fallen below the inflation-adjusted 1979 base price, oil producers and purchasers remained obligated to keep records and file tax reports. The federal government also incurred the expense of overseeing a tax program that produced no revenues.

PRIMARY SOURCE

PL 96–223 (HR 3919)

APRIL 2, 1980

An Act to impose a windfall profit tax on domestic crude oil, and for other purposes.

Be it enacted by the Senate and House of Representatives of the United States of America in Congress assembled,

SECTION 1. SHORT TITLE; AMENDMENT OF 1954 CODE; TABLE OF CONTENTS.

(a) Short Title.—This Act // 26 USC 1 // may be cited as the "Crude OIL Windfall Profit Tax Act of 1980."

"CHAPTER 45—WINDFALL PROFIT TAX ON DOMESTIC CRUDE OIL

"SEC. 4986. // 26 USC 4986. // IMPOSITION OF TAX.

"(a) Imposition of Tax.—An excise tax is hereby imposed on the windfall profit from taxable crude oil removed from the premises during each taxable period.

"(b) Tax Paid by Producer.—The tax imposed by this section shall be paid by the producer of the crude oil.

"SEC. 4987. // 26 USC 4987. // AMOUNT OF TAX.

"(a) In General.—The amount of tax imposed by section 4986 with respect to any barrel of taxable crude oil shall be the applicable percentage of the windfall profit on such barrel.

"(b) Applicable Percentage.—For purposes of subsection (a)—,

"(1) General rule for tiers 1 and 2.—The applicable percentage for tier 1 oil and tier 2 oil which is not independent producer oil is—,Tier 1: 70; Tier 2: 60.

"(2) Independent producer oil.—The applicable percentage for independent producer oil which is tier 1 oil or tier 2 oil is—,Tier 1: 50; Tier 2: 30.

"(3) Tier 3 oil.—The applicable percentage for tier 3 oil is 30 percent.

"(c) Fractional Part of Barrel.—In the case of a fraction of a barrel, the tax imposed by section 4986 shall be the same fraction of the amount of such tax imposed on the whole barrel.

"SEC. 4988. // 26 USC 4988. // WINDFALL PROFIT; REMOVAL PRICE.

"(a) General Rule.—For purposes of this chapter, the term 'windfall profit' means the excess of the removal price of the barrel of crude oil over the sum of—,

"(1) the adjusted base price of such barrel, and

"(2) the amount of the severance tax adjustment with respect to such barrel provided by section 4996(c).

"(b) Net Income Limitation on Windfall Profit.—,

"(1) In general.—The windfall profit on any barrel of crude oil shall not exceed 90 percent of the net income attributable to such barrel.

"(2) Determination of net income.—For purposes of paragraph (1), the net income attributable to a barrel shall be determined by dividing—, (A) the taxable income from the property for the taxable year attributable to taxable crude oil, by (B) the number of barrels of taxable crude oil from such property taken into account for such taxable year.

"(3) Taxable income from the property.—For purposes of paragraph (2)—, (A) In general.— Except as otherwise proviced in this paragraph, the taxable income from the property shall be determined under section 613(a).

// 26 USC 613. //

"(B) Certain deductions not allowed.—No deduction shall be allowed for—,

"(i) depletion,

"(ii) the tax imposed by section 4986,

"(iii) section 263(c)

// 26 USC 263. // costs, or

"(iv) qualified tertiary injectant expenses to which an election under subparagraph (E) applies.

"(C) Taxable income reduced by cost depletion.—Taxable income shall be reduced by the cost depletion which would have been allowable for the taxable year with respect to the property if—,

"(i) all—,

"(I) section 263(c) costs, and

"(Ii) qualified tertiary injectant expenses to which an election under subparagraph (E) applies, incurred by the taxpayer had been capitalized and taken into account in computing cost depletion, and

"(ii) cost depletion had been used by the taxpayer with respect to such property for all taxable periods.

"(D) Section 263(c) costs.—For purposes of this paragraph, the term 'section 263(c) costs' means intangible drilling and development costs incurred by the taxpayer which (by reason of an election under section 263(c)) may be deducted as expenses for purposes of this title (other than this paragraph). Such term shall not include costs incurred in drilling a nonproductive well.

"(E) Election to capitalize qualified tertiary injectant expenses.—,

"(i) In general.—Any taxpayer may elect, with respect to any property, to capitalize qualified tertiary injectant expenses for purposes of this paragraph. Any such election shall apply to all qualified tertiary injectant expenses allocable to the property for which the election is made, and may be revoked only with the consent of the Secretary. Any such election shall be made at such time and in such manner as the Secretary shall by regulations prescribe.

"(ii) Qualified tertiary injectant expenses.—The term 'qualified tertiary injectant expenses' means any expense allowable as a deduction under section 193.

"(4) Special rule for applying paragraph (3)(c) to certain transfers of proven oil or gas properties.—,

"(A) In general.—In the case of any proven oil or gas property transfer which (but for this subparagraph), would result in an increase in the amount determined under paragraph (3)(C) with respect to the transferee, paragraph (3)(C) shall be applied with respect to the transferee by taking into account only those amounts which would have been allowable with respect to the transferor under paragraph (3)(C) and those costs incurred during periods after such transfer.

"(B) Proven oil or gas property transfer.—For purposes of subparagraph (A), the term 'proven oil or gas property transfer' means any transfer (including the subleasing of a lease or the creation of a production payment which gives the transferee an economic interest in the property) after 1978 of an interest (including an interest in a partnership or trust) in any proven oil or gas property (within the meaning of section 613 A)(c)(9)(A)).

// 26 USC 613 A. // "(5) Special rule where there is production payment.—For purposes of paragraph (2), if any portion of the taxable crude oil removed from the property is applied in discharge of a production payment, the gross income from such portion shall be included in the gross income from the property of both the person holding such production payment and the person holding the interest from which such production payment was created.

"(c) Removal Price.—For purposes of this chapter—,

"(1) In general.—Except as otherwise provided in this subsection, the term 'removal price' means the amount for which the barrel is sold.

"(2) Sales between related persons.—In the case of a sale between related persons (within the meaning of section 103(b)(6)(C)),

// 26 USC 103. // The removal price shall not be less than the constructive sales price for purposes of determining gross income from the property under section 613.

// 26 USC 613. //

"(3) Oil removed from premises before sale.—If crude oil is removed from the premises before it is sold, the removal price shall be the constructive sales price for purposes of determining gross income from the property under section 613.

"(4) Refining begun on premises.—If the manufacture or conversion of crude oil into refined products begins before such oil is removed from the premises—,

"(A) such oil shall be treated as removed on the day such manufacture or conversion begins, and

"(B) the removal price shall be the constructive sales price for purposes of determining gross income from the property under section 613.

SIGNIFICANCE

The Crude Oil Windfall Profit Tax Act, was signed into law in 1980 in response to sharp oil price increases during the 1970s, as an attempt to contain oil industry profits resulting from a temporary but significant increase in global oil prices. The tax ceased to be economical and was abolished in 1988 after oil prices fell. There is continuing debate among economists about the utility of taxes on windfall profits. Some argue that windfall profits are an important part of a free market economy, because they indicate shortages to which the market will respond with increased production and, eventually, lower prices. The possibility of a similar windfall profit tax was raised when oil prices rose sharply in 2005 as the result of political instability in the Middle East and a series of hurricanes that limited United States domestic oil production from the Gulf of Mexico.

FURTHER RESOURCES

Books

Deffeyes, Kenneth F. *Hubbert's Peak: The Impending World Oil Shortage*. Princeton, N.J.: Princeton University Press, 2003.

Web sites

Thorndike, Joseph J. "Historical Perspective: The Windfall Profit Tax—Career of a Concept." *Tax History Project*, November 10, 2005. <http://www.taxhistory.org/thp/readings.nsf/0/edf8de04e58e4b14852570ba0048848b? OpenDocument> (accessed March 5, 2006).

"World Oil Market and Oil Price Chronologies: 1970–2004." *Department of Energy*, March 2005. <http://www.eia.doe.gov/emeu/cabs/chron.html> (accessed March 5, 2006).

Alaska National Interest Lands Conservation Act

Legislation

By: United States Congress

Date: December 2, 1980

Source: U.S. Congress. "Alaska National Interest Lands Conservation Act." December 2, 1980. Available online at: <http://www.r7.fws.gov/asm/anilca/title01.html#101> (accessed January 6, 2006).

About the Author: The Congress of the United States was established by Article 1 of the U.S. Constitution of 1787. It is the legislative arm of the U.S. Federal Government.

INTRODUCTION

The Alaska National Interest Land Conservation Act (ANILCA) was enacted by the Congress headed by President Jimmy Carter (born October 1, 1924), in December 1980. The act intends to protect and conserve the vast wilderness and refuge system of the state of Alaska, also traditionally known as North America's last frontier. It represents a delicate balance between conservation and development efforts in Alaska. The state of Alaska is gifted with immensely valuable scenic, natural, geographical and geological resources. It is home to many exotic and threatened species of wildlife, as well as pristine and scenic surroundings, rivers, mountains, and vast areas of wilderness. ANILCA designates to protect the natural wilderness of Alaska from commercial exploitation. It attempts to strike a balance between the preservation of vast Alaskan wealth and the development of its public lands for the ultimate good of the present and future generations.

PRIMARY SOURCE

THE ALASKA NATIONAL INTEREST LANDS CONSERVATION ACT

Purposes

SEC. 101(a) In order to preserve for the benefit, use, education and inspiration of present and future generations certain lands and waters in the State of Alaska that contain nationally significant natural, scenic, historic, archeological, geological, scientific, wilderness, cultural, recreational, and wildlife values, and units described in the following titles are hereby established.

(b) It is the intent of Congress in this Act to preserve unrivaled scenic and geological values associated with natural landscapes; to provide for the maintenance of sound populations of, and habitat for, wildlife species of inestimable value to the citizens of Alaska and the Nation, including those species dependent on vast relatively undeveloped areas; to preserve in their natural state extensive unaltered arctic tundra, boreal forest, and coastal rainforest ecosystems, to protect the resources related to subsistence needs; to protect and preserve historic and archeological sites, rivers, and lands, and to preserve wilderness resource values and related recreational opportunities including but not limited to hiking, canoeing fishing, and sport hunting, within large arctic and subarctic wildlands and on freeflowing rivers; and to maintain opportunities for scientific research and undisturbed ecosystems.

(c) It is further the intent and purpose of this Act consistent with management of fish and wildlife in accordance with recognized scientific principles and the purposes for which each conservation system unit is established, designated, or expanded by or pursuant to this Act, to provide the opportunity for rural residents engaged in a subsistence way of life to continue to do so.

(d) This Act provides sufficient protection for the national interest in the scenic, natural, cultural and environmental values on the public lands in Alaska, and at the same time provides adequate opportunity for satisfaction of the economic and social needs of the State of Alaska and its people; accordingly, the designation and disposition of the public lands in Alaska pursuant to this Act are found to represent a proper balance between the reservation of national conservation system units and those public lands necessary and appropriate for more intensive use and disposition, and thus Congress believes that the need for future legislation designating new conservation system units, new national conservation areas, or new national recreation areas, has been obviated thereby. . . .

SIGNIFICANCE

ANILCA is a significant and complex legislation because it takes the history of Alaska, native interests, and political rights into perspective. The act attains greater significance in the background of previous acts like The Treaty of Cession (1867), the Organic Act (1884), and the Statehood Act (1957).

The traditional view in the United States is that these acts deliberately avoided addressing native issues and interests in Alaska. Before 1958, the lands in Alaska were federal property. However, under the Statehood Act, Alaska was given an opportunity to select nearly 144 million acres of land to manage as a revenue base. Within eight years of its existence as a state, Alaska identified nearly 24 million acres (9.7 million hectares) for this purpose.

It soon became evident that Alaskan natives had a traditional interest in the land. A land freeze was declared to prevent more land from being identified. However, once oil was discovered in Alaska in 1968, the Alaskan Native Claims Resettlement Act was enacted in 1971 to push for a land settlement with the native Alaskans.

This act resulted in the resettlement of Native American families in Alaska. The natives were granted nearly 40 million acres (16.2 million hectares) in return, and also nearly $100 million as financial support.

Subsequently, ANILCA was enacted in 1980 to strike a balance between many conflicting interests, like the need for conservation of public lands in Alaska, traditional needs like hunting and fishing, and developmental needs as well. ANILCA also attempted to resolve some of the long-standing issues pertaining to land use by native Alaskans, use of lands for traditional activity, and classification of the region into parklands, native corporations, and wilderness areas.

The passing of the act is considered to be an enormous attempt at land conservation in the history of the United States. Soon after, nearly 100 million acres (40 million hectares) of land was brought under conservation. It also doubled the area of the country's refuge system, and increased the areas earmarked as wilderness nearly threefold.

As of the early 2000s, the balance begins to tip in favor of development and commercial exploitation, as various constituents of this act are being threatened. A number of provisions of ANILCA are under litigation. Key issues like the use of motorized transport in wilderness areas, snowmobiles, and hunting have cropped up owing to newer interpretations of various provisions in the act.

According to environmental groups, issues regarding vested interests and inappropriate access to parks, native corporations, and wilderness areas by commercial tourism operators have cropped up. The use of newer technology that bypasses some important statutory provisions, growing population, and growing interest in the Alaskan region are subverting its original spirit.

FURTHER RESOURCES
Web sites

McNabb, Steven. "Native Claims in Alaska: A Twenty-Year Review." <http://www.alaskool.org/projects/ancsa/mcnabb/s_mcnabb.htm> (accessed January 6, 2006).

National Parks Conservation Association. "The Alaska National Interest Lands Conservation Act." <http://www.npca.org/media_center/factsheets/anilca.asp> (accessed January 6, 2006).

National Public Lands News. "Public Land History." <http://www.nplnews.com/toolbox/history/publiclandhistory.htm> (accessed January 6, 2006).

U.S. Fish & Wildlife Services. "Alaska Region." <http://alaska.fws.gov> (accessed January 6, 2006).

Oil Pollution Act

Legislation

By: United States Congress

Date: 1990

Source: U.S. Congress. "Oil Pollution Act." 33 U.S.C.A. 40. II, sec. 2731-8. Washington, D.C.: 1990.

About the Author: The Congress of the United States was established by Article 1 of the United States Constitution of 1787. It is the legislative arm of the U.S. Federal Government.

INTRODUCTION

On March 24, 1989, while trying to steer clear of icebergs, the fully loaded *Exxon Valdez* (a tanker carrying oil) sailing from the port of Valdez, Alaska, hit the Bligh Reef in Prince William Sound, Alaska, at top speed. The ship spilled nearly 30 million gallons (114 million liters) of crude oil into the Gulf of Alaska.

The oil spill caused colossal damage and death to marine life. Various studies stated that more than 300,000 common murres, more than 500,000 assorted seabirds, around four hundred to a thousand ducks, up to twenty-two killer whales, around six thousand otters, four hundred loons, more than three hundred harbor seals, and large numbers of other species were immediately killed as a result of the oil spill. Entire populations of fish such as salmon and herring were immediately wiped away from that area. Since then, many surviving species suffered a population crash and those surviving are not even close to recovering.

Strong winds that blew later expanded the disaster area and nearly 1,200 miles (1,900 kilometers) of shoreline, as far as 470 miles (760 kilometers) away from the point of disaster, were affected. Considerable stretches of habitat were endangered as a result of the oil spill. Shoreline communities suffered as a result of exposure to toxic vapors. As of 2006, several workers involved in the oil spill are still suffering from respiratory and brain-related problems.

This incident had extreme implications as it was not just a major shipping accident, but it occurred in an extremely fragile and ecologically sensitive area—the Alaskan waters. The *Exxon Valdez* Oil disaster of 1989 was instrumental in the passing of the Oil Pollution Act of 1990. At the time there were no acts that actually ensured prevention of such disasters. The Oil Pollution Control Act of 1924 mentioned that it is

against the law to dump or spill oil into any coastal area, or area that boats travel through. This Act, and its later versions, was too narrow in scope and not politically enforceable in the above case, as it did not deal with oil spills due to accidents.

Over the years, several amendments and new provisions were added in the Act to broaden its scope and to strengthen it. Eventually, this Act culminated into the Water Quality Improvement Act of 1970 and two years later into the Clean Water Act of 1972. The *Exxon Valdez* spill emphasized the need for a comprehensive Oil Pollution Control act and hence proved to be the foundation stone for The Oil Pollution Act of 1990. This Act, as of 2006, is reflected as Title 33 of the U.S. Code.

The primary source is a document that lists sections 2731 to 2738 of Title 33, Chapter 40, Subchapter II of the U.S. Code. The Prince William Sound amendment mentioned in the Act directs the U.S. Secretary of Commerce to establish a Prince William Sound Oil Spill Recovery Institute through the Prince William Sound Science and Technology Institute in Cordova, Alaska. As per the guidelines mentioned in this section of the Act, the Institute is required to carry out specific procedures to deal with oil spills in the Arctic and Sub-Arctic marine environments and analyze the long-term effects of the spills on the wildlife in that area. Additionally, the Act directs the U.S. Secretary of Commerce to establish a North Pacific Marine Research Institute to be administered at the Alaska SeaLife Center by the North Pacific Research Board.

PRIMARY SOURCE

OIL POLLUTION ACT OF 1990

Section 2731. Oil Spill Recovery Institute

(a) Establishment of Institute

The Secretary of Commerce shall provide for the establishment of a Prince William Sound Oil Spill Recovery Institute (hereinafter in this section referred to as the "Institute") through the Prince William Sound Science and Technology Institute located in Cordova, Alaska.

(b) Functions

The Institute shall conduct research and carry out educational and demonstration projects designed to—

1. identify and develop the best available techniques, equipment, and materials for dealing with oil spills in the arctic and subarctic marine environment; and
2. complement Federal and State damage assessment efforts and determine, document, assess, and understand the long-range effects of Arctic or Subarctic oil

spills on the natural resources of Prince William Sound and its adjacent waters (as generally depicted on the map entitled "EXXON VALDEZ oil spill dated March 1990"), and the environment, the economy, and the lifestyle and well-being of the people who are dependent on them, except that the Institute shall not conduct studies or make recommendations on any matter which is not directly related to Arctic or Subarctic oil spills or the effects thereof....

Section 2734. Vessel traffic service system The Secretary of Transportation shall within one year afterAugust 18, 1990—

1. acquire, install, and operate such additional equipment (which may consist of radar, closed circuit television, satellite tracking systems, or other shipboard dependent surveillance), train and locate such personnel, and issue such final regulations as are necessary to increase the range of the existing VTS system in the Port of Valdez, Alaska, sufficiently to track the locations and movements of tank vessels carrying oil from the Trans-Alaska Pipeline when such vessels are transiting Prince William Sound, Alaska, and to sound an audible alarm when such tankers depart from designated navigation routes; and
2. submit to the Committee on Commerce, Science, and Transportation of the Senate and the Committee on Merchant Marine and Fisheries of the House of Representatives a report on the feasibility and desirability of instituting positive control of tank vessel movements in Prince William Sound by Coast Guard personnel using the Port of Valdez, Alaska, VTS system, as modified pursuant to paragraph (1).

Section 2735. Equipment and personnel requirements under tank vessel and facility response plans

(a) In general

In addition to the requirements for response plans for vesselsestablished by section 1321(j) of this title, a response plan for atanker loading cargo at a facility permitted under the Trans-AlaskaPipeline Authorization Act (43 U.S.C. 1651 et seq.), and a responseplan for such a facility, shall provide for—

1. prepositioned oil spill containment and removal equipmentin communities and other strategic locations within the geographic boundaries of Prince William Sound, including escort vessels with skimming capability; barges to receive recovered oil; heavy duty sea boom, pumping, transferring, and lightering equipment; and other appropriate removal equipment for the protection of the environment, including fish hatcheries;
2. the establishment of an oil spill removal organization at appropriate locations in Prince William Sound,

consisting of trained personnel in sufficient numbers to immediately remove, to the maximum extent practicable, a worst case discharge or a discharge of 200,000 barrels of oil, whichever is greater;
3. training in oil removal techniques for local residents and individuals engaged in the cultivation or production of fish or fish products in Prince William Sound;
4. practice exercises not less than 2 times per year which test the capacity of the equipment and personnel required under this paragraph; and
5. periodic testing and certification of equipment required under this paragraph, as required by the Secretary....

Section 2737. Limitation Notwithstanding any other law, tank vessels that have spilled more than 1,000,000 gallons of oil into the marine environment after March 22, 1989, are prohibited from operating on the navigable waters of Prince William Sound, Alaska.

Section 2738. North Pacific Marine Research Institute
(a) Institute established

The Secretary of Commerce shall establish a North Pacific Marine Research Institute (hereafter in this section referred to as the "Institute") to be administered at the Alaska SeaLife Center by the North Pacific Research Board.

(b) Functions

The Institute shall—

1. conduct research and carry out education and demonstration projects on or relating to the North Pacific marine ecosystem with particular emphasis on marine mammal, sea bird, fish, and shellfish populations in the Bering Sea and Gulf of Alaska including populations located in or near Kenai Fjords National Park and the Alaska Maritime National Wildlife Refuge; and
2. lease, maintain, operate, and upgrade the necessary research equipment and related facilities necessary to conductsuch research at the Alaska SeaLife Center....

(c) Availability of research

The Institute shall publish and make available to any person on request the results of all research, educational, and demonstration projects conducted by the Institute. The Institute shall provide a copy of all research, educational, and demonstration projects conducted by the Institute to the National Park Service, the United States Fish and Wildlife Service, and the National Oceanic and Atmospheric Administration.

This photo, taken in 1998, nearly ten years after the Exxon Valdez oil spill, show rocks from an island in Prince William Sound that still carry traces of oil. © KAREN KASMAUSKI/CORBIS

SIGNIFICANCE

The *Exxon Valdez* spill is considered to be the largest oil spill in American shipping history. The incident acted as a driving force to amend and strengthen the provisions of the original Oil Pollution Act of 1924. As mentioned, these provisions are now incorporated in the Oil Pollution Control Act (OPA) 1990. OPA 1990 is a federal act that defines Valdez and the surrounding areas as an exclusive economic zone. It prohibits and thereby imposes severe liability on discharge of oil into navigable waters in this area. It also establishes liabilities for resulting injuries, and also for loss of natural resources.

The Oil Spill Recovery Institute (OSRI) was established by the U.S. Congress in response to the 1989 *Exxon Valdez* oil spill. The Act identifies the Prince William Sound Science and Technology Institute (known as the PWS Science Center) situated in Cordova, Alaska, as administrator and headquarters for OSRI. The purpose of the Institute was to understand the impact of oil spills on the environment,

especially the marine ecosystem, to enhance the response ability of rescue teams, to gather information and bring general awareness, and to collaborate with other organizations and take benefit of their research and analytical knowledge.

Soon after the Institute was formed, the OSRI program was primarily funded by Congress. However, after 1996, a trust was formed for the program by the U.S. Treasury to streamline the funding procedure for the Institute. In 1995, OSRI focused on the risks and costs of oil spills as a part of its initial strategic plan for oil pollution research and development. Since 1998, OSRI has supported several projects and environmental research programs. The OSRI programs are in the fields of Applied Technology, Predictive Ecology, and Public Education and Outreach.

A section of OPA 1990 prohibits tankers that have spilled more than 1 million gallons (3.8 million liters) of oil in Prince William Sound to operate from the Port of Valdez. Subsequently, this has stopped the

Exxon Valdez from operating in the Artic ever again. The *Exxon Valdez* now operates in the Mediterranean as the *Exxon Mediterranean*.

Furthermore, Section 2738 of this Act also established the North Pacific Marine Research Institute administered by The North Pacific Research Board at the Alaska SeaLife Center. The purpose of this Institute was to undertake research, education, and demonstration projects in the Alaskan land and marine ecosystem. As of 2006, marine research projects worth $1 million are in the pipeline, all of which are funded by The North Pacific Marine Research Institute. According to government sources, the Institute will continue to play a major role in marine research off Alaska contingent on availability of new funds.

Before the *Exxon Valdez* spill there were weak legislations in regard to oil spills. The incident provided the much-needed impetus to amend the existing act and ensure stronger legislation to prevent such disastrous oil spills. The OPA of 1990, as well as the institutes that were formed as a result of this act, have carried out various initiatives to protect the Alaskan region. However, experts are still of the opinion that not much has changed in the workings of shipping and oil industry as a consequence of this oil disaster and the Act of 1990. Reportedly, the oil industry continues to pollute the marine environment around the world. Even though Exxon was severely reprimanded for the oil spill and was required to pay more than $4 billion as interest, as of 2006 it is still appealing against the ruling. More than fifteen years after the disaster, Exxon claims that the region has recovered; however, various studies suggest the recovery is merely superficial.

Environmentalists do agree that there has been a rise in the awareness of the implications of oil spills among the media and general public as a result of the Prince William Sound Amendments to the OPA Act of 1990, and the subsequent establishment of the Oil Spill Recovery Institute and the North Pacific Marine Research Institute.

FURTHER RESOURCES
Web sites

Miller, Pamela A. "*Exxon Valdez* Oil Spill: Ten Years Later." *Arctic Circle*, March 1999, <http://arcticcircle.uconn.edu/SEEJ/Alaska/miller2.htm> (accessed February 28, 2006).

Musgrave, Ruth Shippen, Judy Flynn-O'Brien, and Pam Lambert. "Oil Pollution Act of 1990." *Federal Wildlife and Related Laws Handbook*. <http://ipl.unm.edu/cwl/fedbook/oilpollu.html> (accessed February 28, 2006).

North Pacific Research Board. "North Pacific Marine Research Institute." *North Pacific Research Board*. <http://www.nprb.org/npmri/index.htm> (accessed February 28, 2006).

Oil Spill Recovery Institute. <http://www.pws-osri.org/about_osri/history.shtml> (accessed February 28, 2006).

Clean Air Act

Legislation

By: United States Code

Date: November 15, 1990

Source: U.S. Code. "Air Pollution Prevention and Control." Title 42, Chapter 85, Subchapter I, Part A, Section 7401.

About the Author: The U.S. Code is the set of general and permanent laws that govern the United States. The House of Representatives prepares the Code and revisions are published every six years. The Code is arranged into fifty titles. Title 42 deals with Public Health and Welfare. Chapter 85 describes the laws pertaining to air pollution.

INTRODUCTION

Air pollution is the collective term for any substance that poses a risk to human health or to the environment and that can be found in the air. Common types of air pollutants include particulates, smog, and harmful gases. Examples of these harmful gases include nitrogen oxides and sulfur oxides, which contribute to acid rain; ozone, which contributes to smog; carbon monoxide, which is a poison; and carbon dioxide, which contributes to global warming. Chemicals like chlorofluorocarbons (CFCs) are also considered air pollutants. CFCs reduce the amount of ozone in the stratosphere, increasing the amount of harmful ultraviolet radiation from the Sun that reaches the surface of the Earth.

In 1955 the U.S. Congress passed its first legislation in response to evidence of increased air pollution. This Air Pollution Control Act of 1955 identified air pollution as a problem and launched a public awareness and research campaign into the situation.

The first Clean Air Act was passed in 1963. It set standards for emissions of air pollutants by power plants and steel mills. Amendments to the Act were passed in 1966, 1967, and 1969. These regulations set standards for moving sources of emissions, like cars, trucks, and trains, and established research grants for improving fuel efficiency.

By 1970, Congress realized that the Clean Air Act required major revision. The Clean Air Act of 1970 established much stricter emission controls than its predecessor. It was an extremely ambitious act and industries were economically challenged to comply with its standards. This act was revised throughout the 1970s, extending deadlines and rewriting standards.

After two decades, Congress again revisited the Clean Air Act. In 1990 it underwent a major revision, strengthening standards and improving regulations. The Act contains six subchapters. The first deals with the programs and activities governed by the Act. The second sets emission standards for moving sources. The third subchapter discusses general provisions of the Act, such as impact assessment, monitoring and auditing. The fourth and sixth subchapters are concerned with acid rain and stratospheric ozone depletion. The fifth subchapter deals with permitting for large stationary sources of air pollution. The first section of the Clean Air Act, included below, lays out the purpose of the Act.

PRIMARY SOURCE

CLEAN AIR ACT

7401. Congressional findings and declaration of purpose Sec. 101. (a) The Congress finds—

1. that the predominant part of the Nation's population is located in its rapidly expanding metropolitan and other urban areas, which generally cross the boundary lines of local jurisdictions and often extend into two or more States;
2. that the growth in the amount and complexity of air pollution brought about by urbanization, industrial development, and the increasing use of motor vehicles, has resulted in mounting dangers to the public health and welfare, including injury to agricultural crops and livestock, damage to and the deterioration of property, and hazards to air and ground transportation;
3. that air pollution prevention (that is, the reduction or elimination, through any measures, of the amount of pollutants produced or created at the source) and air pollution control at its source is the primary responsibility of States and local governments; and
4. that Federal financial assistance and leadership is essential for the development of cooperative Federal,

State, regional, and local programs to prevent and control air pollution.

(b) The purposes of this title are—

1. to protect and enhance the quality of the Nation's air resources so as to promote the public health and welfare and the productive capacity of its population;
2. to initiate and accelerate a national research and development program to achieve the prevention and control of air pollution;
3. to provide technical and financial assistance to State and local governments in connection with the development and execution of their air pollution prevention and control programs; and
4. to encourage and assist the development and operation of regional air pollution prevention and control programs.

(c) Pollution prevention A primary goal of this chapter is to encourage or otherwise promote reasonable Federal, State, and local governmental actions, consistent with the provisions of this Act, for pollution prevention. [42 U.S.C. 7401]

SIGNIFICANCE

One of the most important features of the 1990 version of the Clean Air Act is that it gives states significant control over air pollution issues so that they can establish standards and deadlines for improvements locally. Although the Environmental Protection Agency (EPA) sets standards for how much air pollution can be released throughout the country, each state develops its own implementation plan, or SIP, which describes exactly how it will fulfill its obligations under the act.

The Clean Air Act also establishes a permit system for large sources of air pollution, such as factories and power plants. This system clarifies the source's requirements under the SIP and condenses the information on the amount and type of air pollution that the source releases. The source must pay a fee for the permit and the fee is used to fund air pollution control activities.

Another major impact of the 1990 Clean Air Act is that it institutes a market-based approach for cleaning up air pollution. The EPA establishes pollution allowances for different sources of air pollution. If a business produces less pollution than it is allowed, it can trade or sell its allowances to another company. On the other hand, if a company releases air pollutants in excess of its allowance, it must acquire allowances through purchase or trade. This program allows businesses to make their own decisions about how they will best solve their air pollution problems.

The impact that the Clean Air Act has had on the air quality in the United States is extremely large. The EPA has developed computer models that calculate the differences in economic conditions and human health in the United States given the policies enacted by the Clean Air Act and in the absence of those policies. If the Clean Air Act were not in place, the models predicted that by 1990, approximately 200,000 additional Americans would have died prematurely and millions would have suffered from respiratory and heart diseases. The economic benefits of the Clean Air Act during its first twenty years were estimated at approximately $22 trillion, compared to the costs of the pollution reductions during the same time period, which were $523 billion.

A 2004 report by the National Academy of Sciences confirmed the EPA's claims that the Clean Air Act has greatly improved air quality in the United States. The report shows that emissions standards for trucks and cars, as well as controls on the quality of fuel used in vehicles, have greatly reduced the pollutants released in exhaust. The concentrations of air pollutants in most urban areas of the country have also decreased greatly. In particular, the deposition of sulfur through acid rain in the Eastern United States has been greatly reduced. The report also documents the economic benefits imparted by the Clean Air Act.

FURTHER RESOURCES

Books

Committee on Air Quality Management in the United States, National Research Council. *Air Quality Management in the United States*. Washington D.C.: National Academies Press, 2004.

Periodicals

Lemonick, Michael D. "Forecast: Clearer Skies." *Time* (November 5, 1990).

Web sites

Fleming, James R., and Bethany R. Knorr "Legislation: A Look at U.S. Air Pollution Laws and Their Amendments." *American Meteorological Society*. <http:// www.ametsoc.org/sloan/cleanair> (accessed March 6, 2006).

"The Plain English Guide to the Clean Air Act." *U.S. Environmental Protection Agency*, April 1993. <http:// www.epa.gov/oar/oaqps/peg_caa/pegcaain.html> (accessed March 6, 2006).

United Nations Framework Convention on Climate Change

Treaty excerpt

By: United Nations

Date: 1992

Source: United Nations Framework Convention on Climate Change. 1992. Available online at <http:// unfccc.int/essential_background/convention/background/items/1349.php> (accessed March 16, 2006).

About the Organization: The United Nations (UN) is an organization established on October 24, 1945. The fifty-one founding countries and additional member countries are committed to the preservation of peace through international cooperation and providing collective security.

INTRODUCTION

In June 1992, the United Nations Conference on Environment and Development (UNCED) convened in Rio de Janeiro. Participants of the summit included 108 heads of state and representatives from non-governmental organizations (NGOs), intergovernmental organizations (to include international financial institutions), businesses, academia, and the media. The conference was the first summit of its kind since the 1972 United Nations Conference on the Human Environment, which asserted that a relationship existed between economic development and environmental degradation. The summit convened with the stated objective to stabilize greenhouse emissions in a time frame that is sensitive to natural climate changes, continued food production, and sustainable economic development.

The United Nations Framework Convention on Climate Change was signed by over 150 countries at the summit in 1992.

PRIMARY SOURCE

The Parties to this Convention,

Acknowledging that change in the Earth's climate and its adverse effects are a common concern of humankind, Concerned that human activities have been substantially increasing the atmospheric concentrations of greenhouse gases, that these increases enhance the natural greenhouse effect, and that this will result on average in an additional warming of the Earth's surface and atmosphere and may adversely affect natural ecosystems and humankind, Noting that the largest share of historical and current global emissions of greenhouse gases has originated in developed countries, that per capita emissions in developing countries are still relatively low and that the share of global emissions originating in developing countries will grow to meet their social and development needs,

Aware of the role and importance in terrestrial and marine ecosystems of sinks and reservoirs of greenhouse gases, Noting that there are many uncertainties in predictions of climate change, particularly with regard to the timing, magnitude and regional patterns thereof,

Acknowledging that the global nature of climate change calls for the widest possible cooperation by all countries and their participation in an effective and appropriate international response, in accordance with their common but differentiated responsibilities and respective capabilities and their social and economic conditions, Recalling the pertinent provisions of the Declaration of the United Nations Conference on the Human Environment, adopted at Stockholm on 16 June 1972,

Recalling also that States have, in accordance with the Charter of the United Nations and the principles of international law, the sovereign right to exploit their own resources pursuant to their own environmental and developmental policies, and the responsibility to ensure that activities within their jurisdiction or control do not cause damage to the environment of other States or of areas beyond the limits of national jurisdiction,

Reaffirming the principle of sovereignty of States in international cooperation to address climate change, Recognizing that States should enact effective environmental legislation, that environmental standards, management objectives and priorities should reflect the environmental and developmental context to which they apply, and that standards applied by some countries may be inappropriate and of unwarranted economic and social cost to other countries, in particular developing countries,

Recalling the provisions of General Assembly resolution 44/228 of 22 December 1989 on the United Nations Conference on Environment and Development, and resolutions 43/53 of 6 December 1988, 44/207 of 22 December 1989, 45/212 of 21 December 1990 and 46/169 of 19 December 1991 on protection of global climate for present and future generations of mankind,

Recalling also the provisions of General Assembly resolution 44/206 of 22 December 1989 on the possible adverse effects of sea-level rise on islands and coastal areas, particularly low-lying coastal areas and the pertinent provisions of General Assembly resolution 44/172 of 19

December 1989 on the implementation of the Plan of Action to Combat Desertification,

Recalling further the Vienna Convention for the Protection of the Ozone Layer, 1985, and the Montreal Protocol on Substances that Deplete the Ozone Layer, 1987, as adjusted and amended on 29 June 1990,

Noting the Ministerial Declaration of the Second World Climate Conference adopted on 7 November 1990, Conscious of the valuable analytical work being conducted by many States on climate change and of the important contributions of the World Meteorological Organization, the United Nations Environment Programme and other organs, organizations and bodies of the United Nations system, as well as other international and intergovernmental bodies, to the exchange of results of scientific research and the coordination of research,

Recognizing that steps required to understand and address climate change will be environmentally, socially and economically most effective if they are based on relevant scientific, technical and economic considerations and continually re-evaluated in the light of new findings in these areas,

Recognizing that various actions to address climate change can be justified economically in their own right and can also help in solving other environmental problems, Recognizing also the need for developed countries to take immediate action in a flexible manner on the basis of clear priorities, as a first step towards comprehensive response strategies at the global, national and, where agreed, regional levels that take into account all greenhouse gases, with due consideration of their relative contributions to the enhancement of the greenhouse effect,

Recognizing further that low-lying and other small island countries, countries with low-lying coastal, arid and semi-arid areas or areas liable to floods, drought and desertification, and developing countries with fragile mountainous ecosystems are particularly vulnerable to the adverse effects of climate change,

Recognizing the special difficulties of those countries, especially developing countries, whose economies are particularly dependent on fossil fuel production, use and exportation, as a consequence of action taken on limiting greenhouse gas emissions,

Affirming that responses to climate change should be coordinated with social and economic development in an integrated manner with a view to avoiding adverse impacts on the latter, taking into full account the legitimate priority needs of developing countries for the achievement of sustained economic growth and the eradication of poverty,

Recognizing that all countries, especially developing countries, need access to resources required to achieve sustainable social and economic development and that, in order for developing countries to progress towards that goal, their energy consumption will need to grow taking into account the possibilities for achieving greater energy efficiency and for controlling greenhouse gas emissions in general, including through the application of new technologies on terms which make such an application economically and socially beneficial,

Determined to protect the climate system for present and future generations,

Have agreed as follows:

ARTICLE 1

DEFINITIONS For the purposes of this Convention:

1. "Adverse effects of climate change" means changes in the physical environment or biota resulting from climate change which have significant deleterious effects on the composition, resilience or productivity of natural and managed ecosystems or on the operation of socio-economic systems or on human health and welfare.

2. "Climate change" means a change of climate which is attributed directly or indirectly to human activity that alters the composition of the global atmosphere and which is in addition to natural climate variability observed over comparable time periods.

3. "Climate system" means the totality of the atmosphere, hydrosphere, biosphere and geosphere and their interactions.

4. "Emissions" means the release of greenhouse gases and/or their precursors into the atmosphere over a specified area and period of time.

5. "Greenhouse gases" means those gaseous constituents of the atmosphere, both natural and anthropogenic, that absorb and re-emit infrared radiation.

6. "Regional economic integration organization" means an organization constituted by sovereign States of a given region which has competence in respect of matters governed by this Convention or its protocols and has been duly authorized, in accordance with its internal procedures, to sign, ratify, accept, approve or accede to the instruments concerned.

7. "Reservoir" means a component or components of the climate system where a greenhouse gas or a precursor of a greenhouse gas is stored.

8. "Sink" means any process, activity or mechanism which removes a greenhouse gas, an aerosol or a precursor of a greenhouse gas from the atmosphere.

9. "Source" means any process or activity which releases a greenhouse gas, an aerosol or a precursor of a greenhouse gas into the atmosphere.

ARTICLE 2

OBJECTIVE The ultimate objective of this Convention and any related legal instruments that the Conference of the Parties may adopt is to achieve, in accordance with the relevant provisions of the Convention, stabilization of greenhouse gas concentrations in the atmosphere at a level that would prevent dangerous anthropogenic interference with the climate system.

Such a level should be achieved within a time-frame sufficient to allow ecosystems to adapt naturally to climate change, to ensure that food production is not threatened and to enable economic development to proceed in a sustainable manner.

SIGNIFICANCE

Although the primary objective of UNCED surrounded climate changes as the result of greenhouse emissions, the discussion expanded to include a variety of topics such as poverty and sustainable development. As a result, six conventions emerged from the summit: The Rio Declaration, The United Nations Framework Convention of Climate Change, The United Nations Convention on Biological Diversity, The Rio Forestry Principles, The United Nations Convention to Combat Desertification, Agenda 21, and The Commission on Sustainable Development.

The document, Agenda 21, emerged from the summit as the most influential document as it promoted a paradigm shift in the concept of the environment and development. The agreement attempts to recognize a balance with a region's environmental capacity and its population's use of that environment for economic development. As a result, Agenda 21 became the blueprint for sustainable development. Sustainable development is identified as development that not only considers meeting present needs, but also meeting the needs of future generations. The document plans for the reduction of inefficient consumption in the developed countries and sustainable development in the developing nations. It calls for the participation of *major groups*, as identified by the United Nations: women, youth, indigenous peoples, NGOs, trade unions, farmers, business people, scientists, and the technical communities. Agenda 21 also called for the creation of a commission to ensure progress toward the goals reached at the summit. As a result, the Commission for Sustainable Development was created as an international body under the UN Economic and Social Council.

Other important conventions that emerged from the UNCED include the Rio Declarations and the

Activists gather and demonstrate in New Delhi, India, because of the United Nations Framework Convention on Climate Change's failure to meet goals in curbing harmful gas emissions in developing countries, October 2002. AP IMAGES

United Nations Framework Convention on Climate Change (UNFCCC). The Rio Declarations identified twenty-seven legally non-binding principles created to commit governments to responsible development and environmental protection. Designed as an *Environmental Bill of Rights*, the declaration establishes the principle of "common but differentiated responsibilities" and the "precautionary principle." The UNFCCC focused on the reduction of greenhouse emissions and led to the Kyoto Protocol in 1997.

The United Nations Convention on Biological Diversity also emerged from the Rio Summit. This agreement, signed by 154 participating countries, identified the goal of conservation of biological species, genetic resources, habitats, and ecosystems. Signatory nations pledged to create strategies for conservation and sustainable use of biological diversity within their borders. These strategies include conservation in policy-making, establishing laws to protect threatened species and systems, rehabilitation of degraded ecosystems, and educational programs. This convention led to the Cartenga Protocol on Biosafety, which expressed risks involved in cross-border trade and created a Biosafety Clearinghouse.

The Rio Forestry Principles and the United Nations Convention to Combat Desertification (UNCCD) also emerged from the UNCED. The Rio Forestry Principles are fifteen non-binding principles surrounding the sustainable use and protection of global forest resources. As a contentious aspect of the summit, the principles emerged as governments failed to start a process for a UN convention on forests. The principles recognize forests as reservoirs for water and carbon, homes to wildlife, and storehouses of biological resources. Developed nations viewed the forests as global commons. Developing nations, however, viewed the issue as a question of sovereignty over a country's resources. On the other hand, the UNCCD was mentioned in Agenda 21 and was added to the conference in 1994. It states the goals of exploring the causes of desertification and the formation of regionally adopted programs to combat desertification.

Although progress toward the goals outlined at the UNCED in Rio has been slow, the majority of participants categorized the summit as highly significant, as documented in a study entitled, "From Rio to Johannesburg: Progress and prospects." The study identifies the success of the summit in its ability to place the global environment onto the international agenda by its participants. In addition, the summit in Rio is credited with a shift in thinking toward development policies, moving the international community toward the goal of sustainable development that involves a developing nation's major groups. Years later, Rio is still celebrated, in spite of slow progress toward its goals, as a landmark in creating global awareness of the environment.

FURTHER RESOURCES

Periodicals

Najam, Adil, Janice M. Poling, Naoyuki Yamagishi, Daniel G. Straub, et al. "From Rio to Johannesburg: Progress and Prospects." Environment, September 1, 2002.

Web sites

"Outcomes of the Earth Summit 1992 Process." *Heinrich Boell Foundation.* <http://www.worldsummit2002.org/index.htm?http://www.worldsummit2002.org/guide/unced.htm> (accessed March 16, 2006).

"Earth Summit Agenda 21." *United Nations.* <http://www.un.org/esa/sustdev/documents/agenda21/index.htm> (March 16, 2006).

Framework Convention on Climate Change

Treaty

By: The United Nations

Date: May 9, 1992

Source: The United Nations. *EPA Global Warming Publications.* "Framework Convention on Climate Change." <http://yosemite.epa.gov/oar/globalwarming.nsf/content/ResourceCenterPublicationsReferenceFrameworkConventiononClimateChangeConvention.html> (accessed January 17, 2006).

About the Organization: The United Nations, or UN, is a global organization established in 1945. The purposes of the United Nations are to maintain international peace and security, to cooperate in solving international problems, and to be a center for harmonizing the actions of nations.

INTRODUCTION

Carbon dioxide is a gas that is naturally present in the atmosphere and is known to play an important role in maintaining the earth's temperature. Solar radiation enters the earth's atmosphere and heats the surface of the earth. Part of this radiation is then reflected back and leaves the atmosphere. Carbon dioxide and other greenhouse gases play their role by trapping the exiting radiation and reflecting it back toward the Earth's surface. This causes heat to be retained within the atmosphere, which causes an increase in global temperature.

Carbon dioxide is released into the atmosphere by the burning of oil, natural gas, coal, and wood products. All of these processes have increased since the industrial revolution, and so carbon dioxide has been released into the atmosphere at increasing rates.

The impact of industrialization on carbon dioxide levels and temperature was considered by the Swedish chemist Svante Arrhenius (1859–1927) in his 1908 book *Worlds in the Making*. In this book, Arrhenius asserted that the burning of coal and the use of petroleum was increasing carbon dioxide levels in the atmosphere, which would cause a global temperature increase. At this time, it was known that carbon dioxide acted as a greenhouse gas by trapping heat in the atmosphere. However, the idea that the earth's temperature would rise as a result of the increased production of carbon dioxide was new.

At the time of Arrhenius's suggestion, he did not consider that a rise in global temperature would be a problem. Instead, he suggested that it would provide benefits including warming the colder regions of the earth and making them more suitable for growing crops. He also suggested that a warmer climate would be an improvement for people of all areas.

It was not until the 1980s that serious concerns were raised about the potential negative effects of global warming. Considering Arrhenius's claims, scientists generally accept that he was correct in linking human activities producing carbon dioxide to a rise in global temperature. However, most scientists do not agree that the rise in temperature is a positive thing. In contrast, global warming has become an environmental issue raising much concern.

While it is generally accepted that global warming is a problem, the exact effects are not certain. It is assumed that global warming will impact global weather and cause an increase in sea level. It is also thought that weather patterns could become more unpredictable, with more storms, hurricanes, cyclones, floods, and droughts likely. An increase in the global temperature could negatively impact agriculture, wildlife, and forests.

Thousands of people still use coal-burning heaters, which release carbon dioxide, in the winter months in Germany, despite the need to reduce carbon dioxide in the atmosphere to combat global warming, February 12, 1997. AP IMAGES

One of the difficulties that scientists face is trying to predict how global warming will impact local regions. However, even if local effects cannot be predicted, it is still assumed that there will be significant negative effects on various regions across the globe. This has made global warming an issue of global concern.

As an organization dedicated to international affairs, the United Nations has made global warming one of its areas of concern. In 1992, the Framework Convention on Climate Change was created by the United Nations to promote the stabilization of greenhouse gas concentrations so as to prevent the dangerous effects of global warming.

PRIMARY SOURCE

ARTICLE 2

OBJECTIVE The ultimate objective of this Convention and any related legal instruments that the Conference of the Parties may adopt is to achieve, in accordance with the relevant provisions of the Convention, stabilization of greenhouse gas concentrations in the atmosphere at a level that would prevent dangerous anthropogenic

interference with the climate system. Such a level should be achieved within a time-frame sufficient to allow ecosystems to adapt naturally to climate change, to ensure that food production is not threatened and to enable economic development to proceed in a sustainable manner.

ARTICLE 3

PRINCIPLES In their actions to achieve the objective of the Convention and to implement its provisions, the Parties shall be guided, INTER ALIA, by the following:

1. The Parties should protect the climate system for the benefit of present and future generations of humankind, on the basis of equity and in accordance with Their common but differentiated responsibilities and respective capabilities. Accordingly, the developed country Parties should take the lead in combating climate change and the adverse effects thereof.
2. The specific needs and special circumstances of developing country Parties, especially those that are particularly vulnerable to the adverse effects of climate change, and of those Parties, especially developing country Parties, that would have to bear a

disproportionate or abnormal burden under the Convention, should be given full consideration.

3. The Parties should take precautionary measures to anticipate, prevent or minimize the causes of climate change and mitigate its adverse effects. Where there are threats of serious or irreversible damage, lack of full scientific certainty should not be used as a reason for postponing such measures, taking into account that policies and measures to deal with climate change should be cost-effective so as to ensure global benefits at the lowest possible cost. To achieve this, such policies and measures should take into account different socio-economic contexts, be comprehensive, cover all relevant sources, sinks and reservoirs of greenhouse gases and adaptation, and comprise all economic sectors. Efforts to address climate change may be carried out cooperatively by interested parties.

4. The Parties have a right to, and should, promote sustainable development. Policies and measures to protect the climate system against human-induced change should be appropriate for the specific conditions of each Party and should be integrated with national development programmes, taking into account that economic development is essential for adopting measures to address climate change.

5. The Parties should cooperate to promote a supportive and open international economic system that would lead to sustainable economic growth and development in all Parties, particularly developing country Parties, thus enabling them better to address the problems of climate change. Measures taken to combat climate change, including unilateral ones, should not constitute a means of arbitrary or unjustifiable discrimination or a disguised restriction on international trade.

ARTICLE 4

COMMITMENTS 1. All Parties, taking into account their common but differentiated responsibilities and their specific national and regional development priorities, objectives and circumstances, shall:

(a) Develop, periodically update, publish and make available to the Conference of the Parties, in accordance with Article 12, national inventories of anthropogenic emissions by sources and removals by sinks of all greenhouse gases not controlled by the Montreal Protocol, using comparable methodologies to be agreed upon by the Conference of the Parties;

(b) Formulate, implement, publish and regularly update national and, where appropriate, regional programmes containing measures to mitigate

climate change by addressing anthropogenic emissions by sources and removals by sinks of all greenhouse gases not controlled by the Montreal Protocol, and measures to facilitate adequate adaptation to climate change;

(c) Promote and cooperate in the development, application and diffusion, including transfer, of technologies, practices and processes that control, reduce or prevent anthropogenic emissions of greenhouse gases not controlled by the Montreal Protocol in all relevant sectors, including the energy, transport, industry, agriculture, forestry and waste management sectors;

(d) Promote sustainable management, and promote and cooperate in the conservation and enhancement, as appropriate, of sinks and reservoirs of all Greenhouse gases not controlled by the Montreal Protocol, including biomass, forests and oceans as well as other terrestrial, coastal and marine Ecosystems;

(e) Cooperate in preparing for adaptation to the impacts of climate change; develop and elaborate appropriate and integrated plans for coastal zone management, water resources and agriculture, and for the protection and rehabilitation of areas, particularly in Africa, affected by drought and desertification, as well as floods;

(f) Take climate change considerations into account, to the extent feasible, in their relevant social, economic and environmental policies and actions, and employ appropriate methods, for example impact assessments, formulated and determined nationally, with a view to minimizing adverse effects on the economy, on public health and on the quality of the environment, of projects or measures undertaken by them to mitigate or adapt to climate change;

(g) Promote and cooperate in scientific, technological, technical, socio-economic and other research, systematic observation and development of data archives related to the climate system and intended to further the understanding and to reduce or eliminate the remaining uncertainties regarding the causes, effects, magnitude and timing of climate change and the economic and social consequences of various response strategies;

(h) Promote and cooperate in the full, open and prompt exchange of relevant scientific, technological, technical, socio-economic and legal information related to the climate system and climate change, and to the economic and social consequences of various response strategies;

(i) Promote and cooperate in education, training and public awareness related to climate change and encourage the widest participation in this process, including that of non- governmental organizations; and

(j) Communicate to the Conference of the Parties information related to implementation, in accordance with Article 12.

SIGNIFICANCE

The Framework Convention on Climate Change was an international treaty created based on the United Nation's recognition that climate change is a global issue and relevant to all countries. It was also created based on recognizing that human activities would increase the concentration of greenhouse gases, especially carbon dioxide, which would then cause an increase in global temperature, assuming that global warming will have a negative impact, even if the exact impact cannot be predicted.

The United Nations recognized that the management of carbon dioxide emissions needs to be based on a global agreement. It is not suitable for every country to develop their own standards because the decisions made by one country can impact other countries. This especially applies to those countries more vulnerable to changes in temperature, including developing countries in Africa, small island countries, and countries with low-lying areas vulnerable to flooding.

Based on these recognitions, the treaty requires that all countries provide information on their carbon dioxide emissions, implement plans to manage emissions and mitigate climate change, promote and cooperate in activities related to managing climate change, and take climate change into account when developing social, economic, and environmental plans.

The framework did not specifically require countries to reduce emissions and it did not set standards for emissions. However, it was a first step toward recognizing global warming as a significant environmental issue and achieving international cooperation on the issue.

In 1997, the Framework Convention on Climate Change was amended with the addition of the Kyoto Protocol. This addition required countries to reduce their emissions of greenhouse gases and also set greenhouse gas emission limits.

FURTHER RESOURCES
Books

Arrhenius, Svante. *Worlds in the Making*. New York: Harper & Row, 1908.

Climate Change Policy: A Survey, edited by Stephen H. Schneider and Armin Rosencranz. Washington, D.C.: Island Press, 2002.

Houghton, John. *Global Warming: The Complete Briefing*. New York: Cambridge University Press, 1997.

Leggett, Jeremy. *The Carbon War: Global Warming and the End of the Oil Era*. New York: Routledge, 2001.

Periodicals

Bolin, B. "The Kyoto Negotiations on Climate Change: A Science Perspective." *Science* 279 (1998): 330–331.

Web sites

United Nations Framework Convention on Climate Change. "Kyoto Protocol to the United Nations Framework Convention on Climate Change." <http://unfccc.int/resource/docs/convkp/kpeng.html> (accessed January 17, 2006).

Kyoto Protocol

Treaty

By: United Nations Framework Convention on Climate Change

Date: December 11, 1997

Source: United Nations Framework Convention on Climate Change. "The Kyoto Protocol." December 11, 1997.

About the Organization: The United Nations Framework Convention on Climate Change includes representatives from 154 countries, including the United States. It was formed during the second Earth Summit in Rio de Janeiro, Brazil in 1992.

INTRODUCTION

The Kyoto Protocol is a system of rules, regulations, and requirements that were agreed upon by a group of countries known as the United Nations Framework Convention on Climate Change (UNFCCC). The major goal of the Protocol is to decrease the global emissions of six critical greenhouse gases to levels that are 5 percent below what they were in 1990.

The negotiations to develop an international treaty controlling greenhouse gases began in 1972, with the first Earth Summit in Stockholm, Sweden. Leaders from around the world gathered to assess the environmental conditions of the planet and decided to meet every decade for further discussions. The 1982 Earth Summit was scheduled to meet in Nairobi, Kenya, but because of the Cold War, the Summit was not successful.

The second Earth Summit took place in 1992 in Rio de Janeiro, Brazil, where world leaders convened to discuss the growing concern over greenhouse gases in the atmosphere. The result was the formation of the UNFCCC, which includes 154 industrialized countries including the United States, the countries of the European Union, Japan, Russia, Canada, New Zealand, and Australia. The UNFCCC does not include China or India. The convention concluded with a resolution to bring the emissions of greenhouse gases back to the levels that they were in 1990. This resolution was signed by the United States.

Following the second Earth Summit, the countries in the UNFCCC began meeting to flush out the details of the resolution signed in Rio de Janeiro. The first of these meetings, called Conference of Parties I or COP I, occurred in 1995 in Berlin. The meeting reiterated the Parties' commitment to the reduction of greenhouse gases and set timeframes and goals for member nations to achieve agreed-upon reductions.

COP II took place in Geneva, Switzerland. The major outcome of this meeting was a declaration confirming that scientific information provided compelling evidence that global change was occurring as a result of human activities.

The Kyoto Protocol was the result of the third meeting of the UNFCCC, or COP III, between December 1–11, 1997. The Parties agreed that the emissions goals set at the second Earth Summit were not stringent enough. They reduced the global targets by five percent with mandatory targets for all the member countries. These targets depend on each country's individual economy and future emissions projections. For example, the United States' goal is a 7 percent reduction in the emissions of greenhouse gases; Germany's is 25 percent; and Japan's is 6 percent. A key feature of the Protocol is that it establishes an emissions trading program so that countries can best decide how they will reach their goals. The Protocol also calls for additional meetings so that Parties can agree on penalties if a country fails to meet its emission targets.

The Protocol contains twenty-five articles. Articles 1 through 3 and Articles 25 and 28 are included here. Also included are Annexes A and B. Annex A identifies greenhouse gases and sources of

greenhouse gases. Annex B lists the Parties to the agreement as well as their emission commitment. The numbers are percentages compared to their 1990 emissions.

PRIMARY SOURCE

The Parties to this Protocol,

Being Parties to the United Nations Framework Convention on Climate Change, hereinafter referred to as "the Convention,"

In pursuit of the ultimate objective of the Convention as stated in its Article 2,

Recalling the provisions of the Convention,

Being guided by Article 3 of the Convention,

Pursuant to the Berlin Mandate adopted by decision 1/CP.1 of the Conference of the Parties to the Convention at its first session,

Have agreed as follows:

Article 1 For the purposes of this Protocol, the definitions contained in Article 1 of the Convention shall apply. In addition:

1. "Conference of the Parties" means the Conference of the Parties to the Convention.
2. "Convention" means the United Nations Framework Convention on Climate Change, adopted in New York on 9 May 1992.
3. "Intergovernmental Panel on Climate Change" means the Intergovernmental Panel on Climate Change established in 1988 jointly by the World Meteorological Organization and the United Nations Environment Programme.
4. "Montreal Protocol" means the Montreal Protocol on Substances that Deplete the Ozone Layer, adopted in Montreal on 16 September 1987 and as subsequently adjusted and amended.
5. "Parties present and voting" means Parties present and casting an affirmative or negative vote.
6. "Party" means, unless the context otherwise indicates, a Party to this Protocol.
7. "Party included in Annex I" means a Party included in Annex I to the Convention, as may be amended, or a Party which has made a notification under Article 4, paragraph 2(g), of the Convention.

Article 2

1. Each Party included in Annex I, in achieving its quantified emission limitation and reduction commitments under Article 3, in order to promote sustainable development, shall:

(a) Implement and/or further elaborate policies and measures in accordance with its national circumstances, such as:

(i) Enhancement of energy efficiency in relevant sectors of the national economy;

(ii) Protection and enhancement of sinks and reservoirs of greenhouse gases not controlled by the Montreal Protocol, taking into account its commitments under relevant international environmental agreements; promotion of sustainable forest management practices, afforestation and reforestation;

(iii) Promotion of sustainable forms of agriculture in light of climate change considerations;

(iv) Research on, and promotion, development and increased use of, new and renewable forms of energy, of carbon dioxide sequestration technologies and of advanced and innovative environmentally sound technologies;

(v) Progressive reduction or phasing out of market imperfections, fiscal incentives, tax and duty exemptions and subsidies in all greenhouse gas emitting sectors that run counter to the objective of the Convention and application of market instruments;

(vi) Encouragement of appropriate reforms in relevant sectors aimed at promoting policies and measures which limit or reduce emissions of greenhouse gases not controlled by the Montreal Protocol;

(vii) Measures to limit and/or reduce emissions of greenhouse gases not controlled by the Montreal Protocol in the transport sector;

(viii) Limitation and/or reduction of methane emissions through recovery and use in waste management, as well as in the production, transport and distribution of energy;

(b) Cooperate with other such Parties to enhance the individual and combined effectiveness of their policies and measures adopted under this Article, pursuant to Article 4, paragraph 2(e)(i), of the Convention. To this end, these Parties shall take steps to share their experience and exchange information on such policies and measures, including developing ways of improving their comparability, transparency and effectiveness. The Conference of the Parties serving as the meeting of the Parties to this Protocol shall, at its first session or as soon as practicable thereafter, consider ways to facilitate such cooperation, taking into account all relevant information.

2. The Parties included in Annex I shall pursue limitation or reduction of emissions of greenhouse gases not controlled by the Montreal Protocol from aviation and marine bunker fuels, working through the International Civil Aviation Organization and the International Maritime Organization, respectively.

3. The Parties included in Annex I shall strive to implement policies and measures under this Article in such a way as to minimize adverse effects, including the adverse effects of climate change, effects on international trade, and social, environmental and economic impacts on other Parties, especially developing country Parties and in particular those identified in Article 4, paragraphs 8 and 9, of the Convention, taking into account Article 3 of the Convention. The Conference of the Parties serving as the meeting of the Parties to this Protocol may take further action, as appropriate, to promote the implementation of the provisions of this paragraph.

4. The Conference of the Parties serving as the meeting of the Parties to this Protocol, if it decides that it would be beneficial to coordinate any of the policies and measures in paragraph 1(a) above, taking into account different national circumstances and potential effects, shall consider ways and means to elaborate the coordination of such policies and measures.

Article 3

1. The Parties included in Annex I shall, individually or jointly, ensure that their aggregate anthropogenic carbon dioxide equivalent emissions of the greenhouse gases listed in Annex A do not exceed their assigned amounts, calculated pursuant to their quantified emission limitation and reduction commitments inscribed in Annex B and in accordance with the provisions of this Article, with a view to reducing their overall emissions of such gases by at least 5 per cent below 1990 levels in the commitment period 2008 to 2012.

2. Each Party included in Annex I shall, by 2005, have made demonstrable progress in achieving its commitments under this Protocol.

3. The net changes in greenhouse gas emissions by sources and removals by sinks resulting from direct human-induced land-use change and forestry activities, limited to afforestation, reforestation and deforestation since 1990, measured as verifiable changes in carbon stocks in each commitment period, shall be used to meet the commitments under this Article of each Party included in Annex I. The greenhouse gas emissions by sources and removals by sinks associated with those activities shall be reported in a transparent and verifiable manner and reviewed in accordance with Articles 7 and 8. . . .

Article 25

1. This Protocol shall enter into force on the ninetieth day after the date on which not less than 55 Parties to the Convention, incorporating Parties included in Annex I which accounted in total for at least 55 per cent of the total carbon dioxide emissions for 1990 of the Parties included in Annex I, have deposited their instruments of ratification, acceptance, approval or accession.

2. For the purposes of this Article, ''the total carbon dioxide emissions for 1990 of the Parties included in Annex I'' means the amount communicated on or before the date of adoption of this Protocol by the Parties included in Annex I in their first national communications submitted in accordance with Article 12 of the Convention.

3. For each State or regional economic integration organization that ratifies, accepts or approves this Protocol or accedes thereto after the conditions set out in paragraph 1 above for entry into force have been fulfilled, this Protocol shall enter into force on the ninetieth day following the date of deposit of its instrument of ratification, acceptance, approval or accession.

4. For the purposes of this Article, any instrument deposited by a regional economic integration organization shall not be counted as additional to those deposited by States members of the organization.

Article 28 The original of this Protocol, of which the Arabic, Chinese, English, French, Russian and Spanish texts are equally authentic, shall be deposited with the Secretary-General of the United Nations. **DONE** at Kyoto this eleventh day of December one thousand nine hundred and ninety-seven.

IN WITNESS WHEREOF the undersigned, being duly authorized to that effect, have affixed their signatures to this Protocol on the dates indicated.

Annex A

Greenhouse gases

Carbon dioxide (CO_2)
Methane (CH_4)
Nitrous oxide (N_2O)
Hydrofluorocarbons (HFCs)
Perfluorocarbons (PFCs)
Sulphur hexafluoride (SF_6)

Sectors/source categories

Energy
Fuel combustion
Energy industries
Manufacturing industries and construction
Transport
Other sectors

Other
Fugitive emissions from fuels
Solid fuels
Oil and natural gas
Other
Industrial processes
Mineral products
Chemical industry
Metal production
Other production
Production of halocarbons and sulphur hexafluoride
Consumption of halocarbons and sulphur hexafluoride
Other
Solvent and other product use
Agriculture
Enteric fermentation
Manure management
Rice cultivation
Agricultural soils
Prescribed burning of savannas
Field burning of agricultural residues
Other
Waste
Solid waste disposal on land
Wastewater handling
Waste incineration
Other

Annex B

Party Quantified emission limitation orreduction commitment (percentage of base year or period)

Australia 108
Austria 92
Belgium 92
Bulgaria* 92
Canada 94
Croatia* 95
Czech Republic* 92
Denmark 92
Estonia* 92
European Community 92
Finland 92
France 92
Germany 92
Greece 92
Hungary* 94
Iceland 110
Ireland 92
Italy 92
Japan 94
Latvia* 92
Liechtenstein 92
Lithuania* 92
Luxembourg 92

Monaco 92
Netherlands 92
New Zealand 100
Norway 101
Poland* 94
Portugal 92
Romania* 92
Russian Federation* 100
Slovakia* 92
Slovenia* 92
Spain 92
Sweden 92
Switzerland 92
Ukraine* 100
United Kingdom of Great Britain and Northern
    Ireland 92
United States of America 93

*Countries that are undergoing the process of transition to a market economy.

SIGNIFICANCE

The Kyoto Protocol text was adopted unanimously at the end of the COP III meeting. However, it was opened for signatures by the various countries in March of 1998. As described in Article 25, in order for the Protocol to be enforced, it must be signed by fifty-five countries representing at least 55 percent of the global greenhouse emissions.

Following the meeting in Kyoto, the Conference of Parties met to negotiate some of the technical details of the Kyoto Protocol. Of key importance was the definition of a carbon sink, which is a natural mechanism that reduces the amount of carbon dioxide in the atmosphere. Examples of carbon sinks are forests and phytoplankton in lakes and oceans. The definition of a carbon sink has implications for the emissions trading program. Other issues involved the regulations and operating structures in the emissions trading program. Many of these details were worked out in a meeting in Marrakech and are referred to as the Marrakech Accords.

After the U.S. presidential election in 2000, George W. Bush announced that the United States was not going to ratify the Kyoto Protocol because of the economic impacts it would have on the country. Instead, he announced that the U.S. had decided to pursue alternative measures for controlling of greenhouse gas emissions. The loss of the United States called the future of the Kyoto Protocol into question, because the United States was responsible for a significant portion—thirty-six percent—of the total

On February 15, 2005, environmentalists in Italy show their pleasure at the implementation of the Kyoto Protocol by marching in front of Rome's Chigi government office. The protocol became effective February 16, 2005. AP IMAGES

greenhouse emissions in 1990. In order for the Kyoto Protocol to become enforceable all of the industrialized countries, including the entire European Union, Japan, and Russia, would have to ratify the agreement.

In 2002, COP VIII was held in New Delhi, India. The conference made clear that there was a growing concern in the international community regarding the responsibilities of developing and industrialized countries. In particular, the industrialized countries in the European Union felt that developing countries, in particular India and China, should be required to decrease their greenhouse gas emissions. On the other hand, the developing countries have called on the industrialized countries to provide aid to compensate for economic losses that would result from efforts to reduce greenhouse emissions. The fact that the United States refused to support the Kyoto Protocol exacerbated the divisions between countries.

On November 18 2004, Russia ratified the Kyoto Protocol. The sum of the emissions by signatories of the Protocol thus reached 62 percent. This surmounted the 55 percent threshold required for the Protocol to come into effect, which occurred on February 16, 2005. When the Protocol became binding, the eighty-four countries that had signed it became responsible for meeting the obligations for reducing their greenhouse gas emissions as set out in the agreement.

FURTHER RESOURCES

Web sites

Greenpeace Canada. "A Brief History of the Kyoto Protocol." <http://www.greenpeace.ca/e/campaign/climate_energy/depth/kyoto/history.php> (accessed January 17, 2006).

Mapleleafweb.com. "The Kyoto Protocol and Global Warming." <http://www.mapleleafweb.com/features/environment/Kyoto> (accessed January 17, 2006).

United Nations Framework Convention on Climate Change. <http://unfccc.int/2860.php> (accessed January 17, 2006).

U.S. Environmental Protection Agency. "Fact Sheet on the Kyoto Protocol, October 1999." <http://yosemite.epa.gov/oar/globalwarming.nsf/content/Resource CenterPublicationsKyoto_99.html> (accessed January 17, 2006).

U.S. Environmental Protection Agency. "Kyoto Protocol Introduction." <http://yosemite.epa.gov/oar/globalwarming.nsf/content/ResourceCenterPublications ReferenceKyotoProtocolIntroduction.html> (accessed January 17, 2006).

HR3515–Medical Waste Tracking Act of 1988

Legislation

By: United States Code

Date: January 25, 1988

Source: U.S. Code. "Medical Waste Tracking Act of 1988. An Amendment to the Solid Waste Disposal Act."

About the Author: The U.S. Code is the set of general and permanent laws that govern the United States. The House of Representatives prepares the Code and revisions are published every six years. The Code is arranged into fifty Titles. Title 42 deals with Public Health and Welfare. Chapter 82 describes the laws pertaining to solid waste disposal.

INTRODUCTION

Medical waste is legally defined by individual states. It most often includes solid materials that have been used in the medical treatment of humans or animals or in research directed toward the treatment of humans or animals. Medical waste can include used bandages, swabs, surgical gloves, medical instruments, needles, and lancets. It also includes discarded glassware, microbial culture dishes, microbial cultures, and anything used to transfer cultures from one medium to another. Discarded blood, body fluids, and body parts are also usually included in the definition of medical waste.

In July of 1988, medical waste was found washing up on the shores of the East Coast of the United States. Visitors to beaches along the coast of northern New Jersey, New York, Connecticut, Rhode Island, and Massachusetts found a variety of medical debris including vials, syringes, prescription drug bottles, and packages of sutures. Several dozens of vials of blood were also discovered. Some of these vials contained blood that tested positive for the hepatitis B virus and others contained blood with antibodies to the AIDS virus. More than fifty miles of beaches in New York and New Jersey were closed to swimming because of medical waste pollution.

In response to the pollution of beaches by medical waste, Congress enacted the Medical Waste Tracking Act of 1988 (MWTA) as an amendment to the Solid Waste Disposal Act. The MWTA established a two-year program that studied the disposal of medical wastes in several states on the East Coast as well as states adjacent to the Great Lakes. The program had four major goals. The first was to develop clear definitions of medical waste. The second was to develop a tracking system for medical waste from the point of origin through the final disposal point. The program also developed standardized measures for packing, labeling, and storing medical waste. Finally, it established penalties for not adhering to the medical waste tracking system.

■ PRIMARY SOURCE

Be it enacted by the Senate and House of Representatives of the United States of America in Congress assembled,

SECTION 1. SHORT TITLE.

This Act may be cited as the "Medical Waste Act of 1988".

SEC. 2. TRACKING OF MEDICAL WASTE.

(a) Amendment of Solid Waste Disposal Act.—The Solid Waste Disposal Act is amended by adding the following new subtitle at the end:

"Subtitle J—Demonstration Medical Waste Tracking Program

"SEC. 11001. SCOPE OF DEMONSTRATION PROGRAM FOR MEDICAL WASTE.

"(a) Covered States.—The States within the demonstration program established under this subtitle for tracking medical wastes shall be New York, New Jersey, Conneticut, the States contiguous to the Great Lakes and any State included in the program through the petition procedure described in subsection (c), except for any of such States in which the Governor notifies the Administrator under subsection (b) that such State shall not be covered by the program. . . .

"SEC. 11002. LISTING OF MEDICAL WASTES.

"(a) List.—Not later than 6 months after the enactment of this subtitle, the Administrator shall promulgate regulations listing the types of medical waste to be tracked under the demonstration program. Except as provided in subsection (b), such list shall include, but need not be limited to, each of the following types of solid waste:

"(1) Cultures and stocks of infectious agents and associated biologicals, including cultures from medical and pathological laboratories, cultures and stocks of infectious agents from research and industrial laboratories, wastes from the production of biologicals , dicarded live and attenuated vaccines, and culture dishes and devices used to transfer, inoculate and mix cultures.

"(2) Pathological wastes, including tissues, organs, and body parts that are removed during surgery or autopsy.

"(3) Waste human blood and products of blood, including serum, plasma, and other blood components.

"(4) Sharps that have been used in patient care or in medical, research, or industrial laboratories, including hypodermic needles, syringes, pasteur pipettes, broken glass, and scalpel blades.

"(5) Contaminated animal carcasses, body parts, and bedding of animals that were exposed to infectious agents during research, production of biologicals, or testing of pharmaceuticals.

"(6) Wastes from surgery or autopsy that were in contact with infectious agents, including soiled dressings, sponges, drapes, lavage tubes, drainage sets, underpads, and surgical gloves.

"(7) Laboratory wastes from medical, pathological, pharmaceutical, or other research, commercial, or industrial laboratories that were in contact with infectious agents, including slides and cover slips, disposable gloves, laboratory coats, and aprons.

"(8) Dialysis wastes that were in contact with the blood of patients undergoing hemodialysis, including contaminated disposable equipment and supplies such as tubing, filters, disposable sheets, towels, gloves, aprons, and laboratory coats.

"(9) Discarded medical equipment and parts that were in contact with infectious agents.

"(10) Biological waste and discarded materials contaminated with blood, excretion, excudates or secretion from human beings or animals who are isolated to protect others from communicable diseases.

"(11) Such other waste material that results from the administrationof medical care to a patient by a health care provider and is found by the Administrator to pose a threat to human health or the environment. . . .

"SEC. 11003 TRACKING OF MEDICAL WASTE.

"(a) Demonstration Program.—Not later than 6 months after the enactment of this subtitle, the Administrator shall promulgate regulations establishing a program for the tracking of the medical waste listed in section 11002 which is generated in a State subject to the demonstration program. The program shall (1) provide for the tracking of the transportation of the waste from the generator to the disposal facility, except that waste that is incinerated need not be tracked after incineration, (2) include a system for providing the generator of the waste with assurance that the waste is recieved by the disposal facility, (3) use a uniform form for tracking in each of the demonstration States, and (4) include the following requirements:

"(A) A requirement for segregation of the waste at the point of generation where practicable.

"(B) A requirement for placement of the waste in containers that will protect waste handlers and the public from exposure.

"(C) A requirement for appropriate labeling of containers of the waste.

"(b) Small Quantities.—In the program under subsection (a), the Administrator may establish an exemption for generators of small quantities of medical waste listed under section 11002, except that the Administrator may not exempt from the program and person who, or facility that, generates more 50 pounds or more of such waste in any calender month.

"(c) On-Site Incinerators.—Concurrently with the promulgation of regulations under subsection (a), the Administrator shall promulgate a recordkeeping and reporting requirement for any generator in a demonstration State of medical waste listed in section 11002 that (1) incinerates medical waste listed in section 11002 on site and (2) does not track such waste under the regulations promulgated under subsection (a). Such requirement shall require the generator to report to the Administrator on the volume and types of medical waste listed on section 11002 that the generator incinerated on site during the 6 months following the effective date of the requirements of this subsection.

"(d) Type of Medical Waste and Types of Generators.—For each of the reuirements of this section, the regulations may vary for different types of medical waste and different types of medical waste generators.

An assorment of typical medical waste. © A. INDEN/ZEFA/CORBIS

SIGNIFICANCE

The major finding of the MWTA was that medical wastes pose the greatest risk to health at the point where they are generated. The risk falls off markedly the farther in distance and time that the wastes are removed from their origin. Accordingly, the study determined that the risk posed to the general public by medical waste was exceedingly small. On the other hand, the health risk to those occupationally involved with disposing of medical waste was significant. The study recommended that the state and local governments where medical waste was generated should be responsible for regulating and tracking the disposal of medical waste.

The formal outcome of the Medical Wastes Tracking Act of 1988 was a set of recommendations called Standards for the Tracking and Management of Medical Waste. These Standards were enacted by New York, New Jersey, Connecticut, Rhode Island, and Puerto Rico between 1989 and 1991.

Although the Standards were only in place for two years, the MWTA resulted in stricter laws and regulations for the disposal of medical wastes in state and local governments. A multi-billion dollar industry developed in response to these requirements. Facilities that are properly equipped to autoclave, incinerate, microwave, chemically disinfect, or thermally inactivate medical wastes have become an important part of the medical waste disposal stream. Businesses that contract with hospitals, doctors and dentists offices, veterinarians, and research laboratories are required to obtain permits and to adhere to strict performance standards.

An investigation by the Environmental Protection Agency (EPA) found that the source of the medical waste that washed up on the beaches along the East Coast in the summer of 1988 likely did not result from improper handling of medical waste from hospitals, laboratories, or other medical facilities. Instead, the source was most likely poor management of ordinary garbage that contained medical waste generated by home health care or illegal drug use. The garbage containing syringes, blood soaked bandages, and other medical waste generated in homes was probably dumped offshore, but unusual currents are thought to have brought the waste back toward the coast, where it washed up on beaches.

FURTHER RESOURCES
Web sites
"EPA Tracking Program for Medical Waste Starts Today." Press release, March 13, 1989. *U.S. Environmental Protection Agency.* <http://www.epa.gov/history/topics/medical/01.htm> (accessed March 10, 2006).

"Medical Waste." *U.S. Environmental Protection Agency.* <http://www.epa.gov/epaoswer/other/medical/index.htm> (accessed March 10, 2006).

"Regulated Medical Waste." *New York State Department of Environmental Conservation.* <http://www.dec.state.ny.us/website/dshm/sldwaste/medwaste.htm> (accessed March 10, 2006).

Economic and Security and Recovery Act of 2001

Legislation

By: United States Congress

Date: 2001

Source: U.S. Congress. *Economic Security and Recovery Act of 2001, as amended..* Washington, DC: 2001. Available online at *Library of Congress.* <http://thomas.loc.gov/cgi-bin/cpquery/?&dbname=cp107&sid=cp107GyS4i&refer=&r_n=hr367.107&item=&sel=TOC_127897> (accessed March 10, 2006).

About the Author: The Congress of the United States was established by Article 1 of the U.S. Constitution of 1787. It is the legislative arm of the U.S. Federal Government.

INTRODUCTION

In the wake of the September 11, 2001 terrorist attacks, many Americans were deeply fearful that the U.S. economy might plunge into recession. In order to stimulate the economy, Congress introduced the Economic Security and Recovery Act of 2001. This piece of legislation, introduced exactly one month after the attacks, was intended to provide tax incentives for economic recovery. The legislation covered diverse topics including capital gains on stock sales, credits for people leaving welfare, and tariffs on imported liquor. The motivation for the act was relatively simple: facing a situation in which fear and uncertainty might lead Americans to reduce spending (which would slow the economy), the act offered a wide array of incentives and tax cuts to encourage spending.

The environmental impact of the legislation was seen as largely positive, with several aspects of the bill helping environmental causes. Among the items praised by environmentalists was an extension on tax breaks for individuals or organizations purchasing clean-fuel vehicles that burn natural gas, hydrogen, or ethanol mixtures. Whereas the credit was originally scheduled to be phased out beginning in 2001, the act postponed this phase-out for two years. Similar extensions were offered on tax credits for individuals installing clean fuel refueling equipment. Other provisions of the act extended credits for electric vehicles and for electricity produced from renewable sources.

Following several months of debate in and between the House and Senate, the bill was eventually signed into law in March, 2002 under the title "Job Creation and Worker Assistance Act of 2002." In reading the actual text of the act, it appears to be little more than a series of phrases or short sentences strung together with headings. In most cases, when the bill states to "strike" one date and insert another, it is authorizing the extension of a cutoff date or deadline. For example, the date extensions for qualified electric vehicles means that tax credits for buyers of electric cars would be offered for two additional years before expiring.

▓ PRIMARY SOURCE

SEC. 602. CREDIT FOR QUALIFIED ELECTRIC VEHICLES

(a) IN GENERAL—Section 30 is amended—

(1) in subsection (b)(2)—

(A) by striking 'December 31, 2001,' and inserting'December 31, 2003,' and

(B) in subparagraphs (A),(B), and (C), by striking'2002', '2003', and '2004', respectively, and inserting '2004', '2005', and '2006', respectively, and

(2) in subsection (e), by striking 'December 31, 2004' and inserting 'December 31, 2006'.

(b) CONFORMING AMENDMENTS—

(1) Subparagraph (C) of section 280F(a)(1) is amended by adding at the end the following new clause: '(iii) APPLICATION OF SUBPARAGRAPH.—This subparagraph shall apply to property placed in service after August 5, 1997, and before January 1, 2007.'

(2) Subsection (b) of section 971 of the Taxpayer Relief Act of 1997 <<NOTE: 26 USC 280F note.>> is amended by striking 'and before January 1, 2005.'

(c) EFFECTIVE DATE—The amendments made by this section shall apply to property placed in service after December 31, 2001.

SEC. 603. CREDIT FOR ELECTRICITY PRODUCED FROM CERTAIN RENEWABLE RESOURCES.

(a) IN GENERAL—Subparagraphs (A), (B), and (C) of section 45(c)(3) are both amended by striking '2002' and inserting '2004'.

(b) EFFECTIVE DATE—The amendments made by subsection (a) shall apply to facilities placed in service after December 31, 2001.

SEC. 606. DEDUCTION FOR CLEAN-FUEL VEHICLES AND CERTAIN REFUELING PROPERTY.

(a) IN GENERAL—Section 179A is amended—

(1) in subsection (b)(1)(B)—

(A) by striking 'December 31, 2001,' and inserting 'December 31, 2003,', and

(B) in clauses (i), (ii), and (iii), by striking '2002', '2003', and '2004', respectively, and inserting '2004', '2005', and '2006', respectively, and

(2) in subsection (f), by striking 'December 31, 2004' and inserting 'December 31, 2006'.

(b) EFFECTIVE DATE—The amendments made by subsection (a) shall apply to property placed in service after December 31, 2001.

SIGNIFICANCE

While a simple two-year extension of these energy tax incentives might not appear significant, short-term extensions are often the only way to keep such tax breaks alive, since lawmakers are often far more willing to support tax changes with a set ending date. In some cases, tax provisions remain part of U.S. law for many years, kept alive only by a series of short-term reauthorizations.

As often happens, the extensions authorized in the Economic Security Act were adequate to keep these tax breaks on the books until new extensions could be passed. On August 8, 2005, President Bush signed into law the Energy Policy Act of 2005, which included tax credits of up to $3,400 for buyers of hybrid gas-electric vehicles. The new law also provided new credits for producers of biodiesel and ethanol fuels, as well as a 30 percent tax credit for organizations installing clean-fuel refueling equipment, such as E85 fuel pumps.

FURTHER RESOURCES

Books

Bechtold, Richard L. *Alternative Fuels Guidebook: Properties, Storage, Dispensing, and Vehicle Facility Modifications.* New York: SAE International, 1997.

Tickell, Joshua, et al. *From the Fryer to the Fuel Tank: The Complete Guide to Using Vegetable Oil as an Alternative Fuel.* Tallahassee, Florida: Tickell Energy Consulting, 2000.

U.S. Government. *21st Century Ethanol and Renewable Fuels Digest.* Washington, DC: Progressive Management, 2005.

Web sites

Uncle Fed's Tax Board. "Job Creation and Worker Assistance Act of 2002." <http://www.unclefed.com/TaxHelp Archives/legislation/hr3090.html> (accessed January 26, 2006).

U.S. Department of Energy. "The Energy Policy Act of 2005." <http://www.energy.gov/taxbreaks.htm> (accessed January 26, 2006).

U.S. House of Representatives. "Technical Explanation of the 'Job Creation and Worker Assistance Act of 2002.'" <http://www.house.gov/jct/x-12-02.pdf> (accessed January 26, 2006).

Benefits and Costs of the Clean Air Act, 1970 to 1990

Government report excerpt

By: United States Environmental Protection Agency

Date: October 15, 1997

Source: U.S. Environmental Protection Agency. "Benefits and Costs of the Clean Air Act, 1970 to 1990." <http://www.epa.gov/air/sect812/812exec2.pdf> (accessed January 17, 2006).

About the Organization: The U.S. Environmental Protection Agency (EPA), established in 1970, is generally responsible for protecting the U.S. environment and preserving its integrity for future generations. Its specific aims include controlling and reducing water and air pollution, noise pollution, and pollution by pesticides, radiation, and various toxic substances.

INTRODUCTION

Air pollution is a relatively new concept, first perceived as the impact of human activity in the industrial era upon the public health. The correlation between industrial emissions of air pollutants and the increase of cases of allergy, asthma, and other respiratory disorders in a given population was initially noticed by physicians and public health researchers known as epidemiologists. Epidemiology research had shown that air pollution had a major impact on the augmented incidence of respiratory diseases among infants, small children, and elderly citizens, the most affected groups among the general population. Stationary emissions (pollutants released in the atmosphere by power plants, factories, oil refineries, and steel mills) were identified as the main sources of air pollution in the first half of the twentieth century. Examples of such air pollutants are sulfur dioxide (SO_2), carbon monoxide (CO), carbon dioxide (CO_2), nitrogen oxides (NOx), dioxins, furans, polycyclic aromatic hydrocarbons (PAHs), and suspended particulate matter. Particulate matter may be already present as solid particles, such as visible smoke from industrial smokestacks and motor vehicle exhaustion, or can be formed due to the chemical reaction of gaseous pollutants, such as nitrogen oxides and sulfur dioxide, in the atmosphere. In the first case, such emissions are known as "primary particulates," while those formed by gaseous pollutants are known as "secondary particles or particulates."

More recent studies have shown that dioxins, furans, and PAHs are carcinogenic compounds that induce DNA mutations, thus leading to cancer and fetus malformation. Well-known sources of atmospheric dioxins are timber mills, which apply chemical treatments to timber, and paper mills. PAHs and sulfur dioxides are released by oil refineries, motor vehicle emissions, paint factories, and the manufacturing of oil-derived chemical products and byproducts such as benzene and domestic and industrial solvents.

Respiratory allergies and correlated respiratory disorders are also associated with the increase of ozone gas (O_3) in the lower layer of atmosphere (known as the troposphere) due to emissions of organic compounds such as PAHs, dioxins, methane, nitrous oxides, and furans, among others. In the stratosphere, the ozone layer plays the crucial role of decreasing the incidence of ultraviolet radiation upon the Earth. However, the formation and build-up of ozone gas in the troposphere results in the man-made fog known as "smog," which besides being highly allergenic also contributes to the greenhouse effect. Therefore, the air pollution derived from human activity affects atmospheric ozone in two different ways: by abnormally increasing ozone concentrations in the troposphere and by destroying the stratospheric ozone layer. In the last case, a direct impact on public health is also reported, since a thinner stratospheric ozone layer permits higher amounts of ultraviolet radiation to reach the planet's surface, causing an increase in skin cancer and melanoma incidence among humans.

In 1955, several state and local administrations had already passed legislation to control air pollution and improve air quality when the U.S. Congress approved the first federal Air Pollution Control Act. The document recognized air pollution as a public health problem and provided research funds for the Public Health Service. However, it did not tackle air pollution control and prevention directly, recommending only that additional measures should be taken to improve air quality. This Act was amended in 1960 to provide research funds for another period of four years. The 1955 Act had its focus only on stationary sources of air pollution, not taking into consideration emissions by motor vehicle exhaust. It was only when the second amendment was approved by Congress in 1962 that funds were allocated for the research of the effects upon public health of motor vehicle exhaust emissions and its chemical compounds.

The first concrete Congressional effort to effectively control air pollution came in 1963 under the Clean Air Act, defined as "An Act to improve, strengthen, and accelerate programs for the prevention and abatement of air pollution." The 1963 Act recognized the impact of motor vehicle emissions as a deteriorating factor for air quality in urban areas and recommended the establishment of emission-control standards for both stationary sources and motor vehicles alike. The Act also allocated a $95 million fund for a three-year research effort by local, state, and federal air pollution control agencies to conduct studies and develop standardized control programs. The Clean Air Act also recommended the removal of sulfur from fuels derived from coal and oil, and the reduction of these emissions. This legislation was amended in 1965 to include standards for automobile emissions, and in 1966 to expand local air pollution control programs. A further amendment in 1967 divided the country into "Air Quality Control Regions" (AQCRs) in order to implement a program of ambient air monitoring. This 1967 amendment also adopted national standards for stationary emissions and established a schedule for State Implementation Plans (SIPs). It also recommended (and allocated federal grants) to the research and development of new control technologies to achieve the SIPs' objectives. The amendment of 1969 extended funds research on low-emission automobiles and fuels.

In 1970, the Clean Air Act of 1963 was completely revamped, yielding a new and more ambitious piece of legislation on air pollution abatement, known as the Clean Air Act of 1970. Its goals were defined as "An Act to amend the Clean Air Act to provide for a more effective program to improve the quality of the

Nation's air." Standards for motor vehicle emissions and for hazardous stationary emission were set, and a $30 million fund was designated for research of the impact of noise pollution upon public health, especially in large urban centers. In order to protect public health, the Act established the National Ambient Air Quality Standards as well as a rigorous emissions regulation, under the New Source Performance Standards. The latter was applicable to new companies entering an area. Another innovation was the provision stating that citizens were entitled to take legal action against companies, individuals, or the government if found in violation of this Act. The standards and deadlines for motor vehicles emissions control and the ambient air quality proved to be beyond the existing technology of the time, which prevented the compliance with the established timetable. Therefore, they were extended in the Amendment of 1977 and more realistic goals were set.

About a decade of pollution-control legislative silence ensued after the 1977 Amendment, as environmental issues were not a priority during the Reagan Administration. It was only in 1990 that a new amendment was approved, "An Act to amend the Clean Air Act to provide for attainment and maintenance of health protective national ambient air quality standards, and for other purposes." Federal government extended in this bill deadlines for state compliance with ambient air standards, according to the level of air pollution in each area. The motor vehicles emissions standards were also raised to new limits in these most polluted areas, with a strict timetable of emission reductions to be enforced. The issue of acid rain and its impact on agriculture and forests was also tackled by the 1990 amendment as well as the need for emission reduction of chlorofluorocarbons (CFCs), which affect the stratospheric ozone. A "Best Available Control Technology" (BACT) mandate was issued, aiming to reduce levels of toxic air pollutants, beside a recommendation for the development and use of alternative fuels and reduction of sulfur in conventional fuels, since sulfur dioxide emissions are the main cause of acid rain. The Clean Air Act Amendments of 1990 also required that the EPA conduct periodic assessments of the benefits and costs of the Clean Air Act, issuing reports to Congress based on scientifically reviewed studies. Under section 812 of the 1990 Clean Air Act, the EPA is required to design and implement each study with the cooperation of the Departments of Labor and Commerce, in addition to a panel of outside experts, and to issue periodic reports such as "Benefits and Costs of the Clean Air Act, 1970 to 1990."

PRIMARY SOURCE

AIR QUALITY

The substantial reductions in air pollutant emissions achieved by the Clean Air Act translate into significantly improved air quality throughout the U.S. For sulfur dioxide, nitrogen oxides, and carbon monoxide, the improvements in air quality under the control scenario are assumed to be proportional to the estimated reduction in emissions. This is because, for these pollutants, changes in ambient concentrations in a particular area are strongly related to changes in emissions in that area. While the differences in control and no-control scenario air quality for each of these pollutants vary from place to place because of local variability in emissions reductions, by 1990 the national average improvements in air quality for these pollutants were: 40 percent reduction in sulfur dioxide, 30 percent reduction in nitrogen oxides, and 50 percent reduction in carbon monoxide.

Ground-level ozone is formed by the chemical reaction of certain airborne pollutants in the presence of sunlight. Reductions in ground-level ozone are therefore achieved through reductions in emissions of its precursor pollutants, particularly volatile organic compounds (VOCs) and nitrogen oxides (NO_X) [2]. The differences in ambient ozone concentrations estimated under the control scenario vary significantly from one location to another, primarily because of local differences in the relative proportion of VOCs and NO_X, weather conditions, and specific precursor emissions reductions. On a national average basis, ozone concentrations in 1990 are about 15 percent lower under the control scenario. For several reasons, this overall reduction in ozone is significantly less than the 30 percent reduction in precursor NO_X and 45 percent reduction in precursor VOCs. First, significant natural (i.e., biogenic) sources of VOCs limit the level of ozone reduction achieved by reductions in man-made (i.e., anthropogenic) VOCs. Second, current knowledge of atmospheric photochemistry suggests that ozone reductions will tend to be proportionally smaller than reductions in precursor emissions. Finally, the plume model system used to estimate changes in urban ozone for this study is incapable of handling long-range transport of ozone from upwind areas and multi-day pollution events in a realistic manner.

There are many pollutants which contribute to ambient concentrations of particulate matter. The relative contributions of these individual pollutant species to ambient particulate matter concentrations vary from one region of the country to the next, and from urban areas to rural areas. The most important particle species, from a human health standpoint, may be the fine particles which can be respired deep into the lungs. While some fine particles are directly emitted by sources, the most important fine particle species are formed in the atmosphere through chemical conversion of gaseous pollutants. These species are referred to as secondary particles. The three most important secondary particles are (1) sulfates, which derive primarily from sulfur dioxide emissions; (2) nitrates, which derive primarily from nitrogen oxides emissions; and (3) organic aerosols, which can be directly emitted or can form from volatile organic compound emissions. This highlights an important and unique feature of particulate matter as an ambient pollutant: more than any other pollutant, reductions in particulate matter are actually achieved through reductions in a wide variety of air pollutants. In other words, controlling particulate matter means controlling "air pollution" in a very broad sense. In the present analysis, reductions in sulfur dioxide, nitrogen oxides, volatile organic compounds, and directly-emitted primary particles achieved by the Clean Air Act result in a national average reduction in total suspended particulate matter of about forty-five percent by 1990. For the smaller particles which are of greater concern from a health effects standpoint (i.e., PM_{10} and $PM_{2.5}$), the national average reductions were also about 45 percent.

Reductions in sulfur dioxide and nitrogen oxides also translate into reductions in formation, transport, and deposition of secondarily formed acidic compoundssuch as sulfate and nitric acid. These are the principal pollutants responsible for acid precipitation, or "acid rain." Under the control scenario, sulfur and nitrogen deposition are significantly lower by 1990 than under the no-control scenario throughout the 31 eastern states covered by EPA's Regional Acid Deposition Model (RADM). Percentage decreases in sulfur deposition range up to more than 40 percent in the upper Great Lakes and Florida-Southeast Atlantic Coast areas, primarily because the no-control scenario projects significant increases in the use of high-sulfur fuels by utilities in the upper Great Lakes and Gulf Coast states. Nitrogen deposition is also significantly lower under the control scenario, with percentage decreases reaching levels of 25 percent or higher along the Eastern Seaboard, primarily due to higher projected emissions of motor vehicle nitrogen oxides under the no-control scenario.

Finally, decreases in ambient concentrations of light-scattering pollutants, such as sulfates and nitrates, are estimated to lead to perceptible improvements in visibility throughout the eastern states and southwestern urban areas modeled for this study....

CONCLUSIONS AND FUTURE DIRECTIONS

First and foremost, these results indicate that the benefits of the Clean Air Act and associated control programs substantially exceeded costs. Even considering the large number of important uncertainties permeating each step of the analysis, it is extremely unlikely that the converse could be true.

A second important implication of this study is that a large proportion of the monetized benefits of the historical Clean Air Act derive from reducing two pollutants: lead and particulate matter. . . .

SIGNIFICANCE

The first EPA report to Congress was based on retrospective studies addressing the benefits and costs associated with the 1970 and 1977 Amendments until 1990. A second, prospective study for the period of 1990 to 2020 is in progress.

The investments in research and development of new technologies, implementation of regulations, and monitoring mechanisms and agencies were initially borne mainly by the public sector. However, in order to comply with these new regulations, private companies also invested in pollution-abatement equipments, installation, operation, and maintenance. This represented approximately a $523 billion investment during this thirty-year period. Such costs were reflected in prices of merchandise and services and were ultimately paid by the final consumers, business owners, stockholders, and taxpayers. On the other hand, emissions of toxic and hazardous substances were significantly lower by 1990. For instance, sulfur dioxide emissions were reduced by 40 percent; nitrogen oxides were 30 percent lower; carbon monoxide emissions were reduced by 50 percent; and emissions of primary particulate matter were reduced by 75 percent. Another dangerous substance, a lead compound added to gasoline, was also reduced by 1990 by 99 percent. An important point to keep in mind is that such reductions in toxic emissions were achieved during a period of economic growth and a significant population increase, which alone are known factors of increased air and environmental pollution if left uncontrolled.

The Clean Air Acts of 1970 and 1977 adopted as criteria six pollutants—sulfur dioxide, tropospheric ozone, nitrogen oxides, carbon monoxide, lead, and particulate matter—to be given prioritized emission reductions. The total monetized benefits (money saved in medical care, reduced illness leaves, etc.) between 1970 and 1990 reached the trillions of dollars. Additional benefits include the reduction of acid rain and its damaging effect on forest and crops; reduction of corrosion of historical monuments, statues, and buildings; and a positive impact on aquatic and terrestrial ecosystems, improving the quality of freshwater in open reservoirs, rivers, and lakes.

FURTHER RESOURCES

Web sites

Intergovernmental Panel on Climate Change. "IPCC/ TEAP Special Report: Safeguarding The Ozone Layer and The Global Climate System: Issues Related To Hydrofluorocarbons and Perfluorocarbons—Summary for Policymakers." *Intergovernmental Panel on Climate Change*. <http://www.ipcc.ch/press/SPM.pdf> (accessed March 17, 2006.)

Pearce, Fred. "Climate Change: Instant Expert." *New Scientist*, updated January 19, 2006. <http://www. newscientist.com/popuparticle.ns?id=in20> (accessed March 17, 2006.)

U.S. Environmental Protection Agency. "Clean Air Act: Title I—Air Pollution Prevention and Control." *U.S. Environmental Protection Agency*. <http://www.epa.gov/ air/caa/title1.html£ia> (accessed March 17, 2006.)

Testimony of Christine Todd Whitman

Before the Clean Air Subcommittee of the Committee on Environment and Public Works

Testimony

By: Christine Todd Whitman

Date: April 8, 2003

Source: Whitman, Christine Todd. Testimony of Christine Todd Whitman, Administrator United States Environmental protection Agency, Before the Clean Air Subcommittee of the Committee on Environment and Public Works United States Senate, April 8, 2003. Available online at <http://www.epa.gov/clearskies/testimony. html> (accessed January 17, 2006).

About the Author: Christine Todd Whitman was appointed Administrator of the U.S. Environmental Protection Agency under President George W. Bush; she resigned in 2003. Prior to heading the EPA, Whitman was elected the first female governor of New Jersey, serving that post from 1994 to 2000.

INTRODUCTION

The growing awareness among scientists of the impact of industrial and other human activities upon the gaseous composition and balance of atmosphere is leading the United States and other countries to promote stronger legislation to curb air pollution levels. Among the multiple effects of air pollution, the first to draw the attention of authorities was its impact upon the public health in specific communities exposed to industrial emissions of air pollutants. These effects were initially considered local or regional problems, with further implications for the environment (e.g. agriculture, wildlife, forests, freshwater sources, and climate) widely ignored or challenged. However, since the late nineteenth century, scientists created predictive models or scenarios to illustrate how the Industrial Revolution and its polluting practices would affect the climate in the future. Jean-Baptiste Fourier (1768–1830), John Tyndall (1820–1893) Svante Arrhenius (1859–1927), and T.C. Chamberlain (1843–1928) first assessed how the increased emissions of carbon dioxide (CO_2) could cause what Fourier called a "greenhouse effect," leading to global warming and unpredictable climate changes.

During the 1950s, American Scientists David Keeling and Roger Revelle raised again the issue of greenhouse gases and their possible role in global warming, with Keeling starting the first continuous monitoring-program of CO_2 levels in the atmosphere. His reports illustrated yearly increases of atmospheric carbon dioxide levels. The American Society for the Advancement of Science issued a comprehensive report on human-induced climate changes and global warming in the early 1980s, which again raised controversy among skeptical scientists and politicians, and was largely ignored by most governments. The suggestions from this and other reports for the need of governmental commitment in reducing and preventing further emissions from fossil-derived fuels (such as coal, gasoline, and diesel fuel) were seen as an economic burden that would arrest or prevent development and jeopardize employment. In 1988, climate scientists gathered in Toronto, Canada, and strongly recommended the immediate adoption of reduction measures to cut 20 percent of CO_2 emissions by 2005. In the same year, the United Nations founded the Intergovernmental Panel on Climate Change (IPCC), a permanent work-group with the mission of analyzing and periodically reporting on the subject. In the United States, the Clean Air Acts of 1970 and 1977 were the only air pollution regulatory measures until January 2002, when the Bush Administration proposed the Clear Skies and Global Climate Change Initiatives.

Earth's atmosphere is a relatively thin layer of naturally occurring gases. The troposphere is the lower strata where all exchanges between living beings (such as plants, animals, and humans), natural ecosystems (such as oceans, forests, mountain ridges, and hydrographic systems), and the atmosphere take place. Methane and CO_2 are released into the troposphere by plant respiration and organic matter decomposition, and cyclically reabsorbed by plants and the oceans, therefore maintaining planetary temperatures in a delicate and dynamic balance. Dramatic increases or decreases of large populations of ruminating animals (animals that chew the cud, such as cattle, sheep, goats, or deer), for instance, may affect the amounts of methane in the troposphere. Methane and carbon concentrations are also affected by the increase or decrease in size of forests and marshlands, along with volcanic activity.

Paleoclimatology, or the study of ancient climatic cycles, has greatly contributed to the understanding of climatic changes that have naturally occurred throughout Earth's history. Polar icecaps and old glaciers trap different concentrations of atmospheric gases over thousands of years in their many layers. Data analysis from glacial samples has shown that changes in concentrations of carbon dioxide, methane, and water vapor are directly associated with climate changes, the whether the changes result in cooling or warming the planet. The more recent increase in the greenhouse effect, however, is mainly attributed to human-related emissions of carbon dioxide, methane, nitrous oxides, perfluorocarbon compounds, and tropospheric ozone, called the "greenhouse gases". For example, industrial activity was responsible in the last one hundred years for a 30 percent increase in carbon dioxide concentrations and a 100 percent increase of methane, plus a 15 percent increase in nitrous oxides in the troposphere. In the United States, power factories, heating systems, and motor vehicles do account for approximately 98 percent of the country's carbon dioxide emissions, 24 percent of methane, and about 18 percent of nitrous oxides emissions. If no further reduction and preventive measures are adopted, estimates point to a thirty to 150 percent elevation of these concentrations in the atmosphere by the year 2100, with a major impact on climatic patterns and global temperature. Several studies have reported that the United States alone is responsible for about one-fifth of the total emissions of the planet.

In 2001, the Bush administration commissioned the EPA to present an analytical study with models designed to reduce greenhouse gas emissions while not adversely affecting economic growth and jobs. This project was named "The Clear Skies and Global Climate Change Initiatives." In 2002, the Presidential Clear Skies Act was presented to the Senate, aiming to cut emissions of the three worst air pollutants and greenhouses gases. The Clear Skies Initiative aimed to cut three toxic air pollutants by 70

Clouds of smoke, likely containing carbon dioxide and other harmful gases are emitted from the Simpson Tacoma Kraft Pulp Mill, polluting the air and surrounding environment. © JOEL W. ROGERS/CORBIS

percent: nitrogen oxides, sulfur dioxide, and mercury, therefore improving air quality and public health. The Global Climate Change initiative provided research grants and was designed to achieve an 18 percent reduction of greenhouse gases concentrations over the following ten years.

The Clear Skies Initiative had as its central goals the following: to dramatically and steadily cut power plant emissions of the three worst air pollutants mentioned earlier; to develop new tools to measure emissions and a system to credit emission reductions, under the form of incentives, for businesses that register voluntary reductions; to review progress on climate change and take new actions in 2012, if necessary; to secure the provision of yearly federal funds, during five years, for climate-change-related prevention programs; to develop a comprehensive new set of domestic and international policies to promote expanded

President Gearge W. Bush backed the Clear Skies proposal, calling on the U.S. Congress to pass the legislation into law, September 16, 2003. © WILLIAM PHILPOTT/CORBIS

FINAL REPORT TO CONGRESS ON BENEFITS AND COSTS OF THE CLEAN AIR ACT, 1970 TO 1990

Testimony of Christine Todd Whitman

Administrator

U.S. Environmental Protection Agency

Before the Clean Air Subcommittee

Of the Committee on Environment and Public Works

United States Senate

April 8, 2003

I. Introduction Thank you, Mr. Chairman and Members of the Committee for the opportunity to speak with you today about the Clear Skies Act of 2003. Based on one of the most successful programs created by the Clean Air Act, Clear Skies is a proposal to substantially reduce emissions of the three most harmful pollutants from power generation— and to do so in a way that is much faster and more efficient than under current law. As President Bush said in the State of the Union Address, Clear Skies will advance our goal of "promot[ing] energy independence for our country, while dramatically improving our environment." The Administration is committed to working with this Subcommittee and Congress to pass legislation this year. The widespread support for multi-pollutant legislation to reduce power plant emissions is a strong indicator that the time for action on this critical issue is now. Failure to enact Clear Skies this year will delay important public health and environmental benefits.

This country should be very proud of the progress we have already made in cleaning up our air. Since the Clean Air Act was first enacted in 1970, we have reduced emissions of the six primary air pollutants by 25 percent. During the same time period, the economy has grown significantly—the Gross Domestic Product increased 160%; vehicle miles traveled increased 150%; energy consumption increased 40%; and the U.S. population increased 35%.

Although we have made much progress since 1970, we still face major air quality challenges in many parts of the country. Clear Skies is the most important next step we can take to address these challenges and achieve healthy air and a clean environment for all Americans. Clear Skies would make great strides towards solving our remaining air quality problems in a way that also advances national energy security and promotes economic growth. It would reduce power plant emissions of SO_2, NOx and mercury by approximately 70 percent from today's levels and do it faster, with more certainty, and at less cost to American consumers than would current law. Last year's EPA estimates project that, over the next decade, all the

research and development of climate-related science and technology, expanded use of renewable energy, and incentives for sequestration of already emitted air pollutants; and to design a better alternative for emission reductions and prevention than that of the Kyoto Protocol (an international agreement among developed nations that limits emissions of greenhouse gases).

The Clear Skies Initiative of 2002 was further improved by the Clear Skies Act of January 28, 2003. The 2003 Act established federally enforceable limits (or caps) for all three pollutants, and presented a dynamic regulatory policy of emission caps and trading, thus providing power plants with the necessary flexibility to achieve reductions in a cost-effective manner. It also encouraged state and local governments to set their own limiting regulations for source-specific emissions to ensure that the air quality standards are achieved.

programs of the existing Clean Air Act would reduce power plant emissions of SO_2 and NOx by approximately 23 million tons. Over the same time period, Clear Skies would reduce emissions of these same pollutants by 58 million tons—a reduction of 35 million tons of pollution that will not be achieved under current law.

When fully implemented, Clear Skies would prolong thousands of lives each year, providing billions of dollars in economic benefits, save millions of dollars in health care costs, and increase by millions the number of people living in areas that meet our new, more stringent health-based national air quality standards. Clear Skies would also virtually eliminate chronic acidity in northeastern lakes, reduce nitrogen loading in coastal waters, and help restore visibility in our national parks.

The Clean Air Act has been, and continues to be, a vehicle for great progress in improving the health and welfare of the American people. The Clear Skies Act substantially expands one of the most successful Clean Air Act programs—the Acid Rain Program—and reduces the need to rely on complex and less efficient programs. The result would be significant nationwide human health and environmental benefits; certainty for industry, states and citizens; energy security; and continuing low costs to consumers.

II. Clear Skies Provides Significant Benefits The heart of Clear Skies is a proven cap-and-trade approach to emissions reductions. Mandatory caps restrict total emissions and decline over time. Clear Skies would continue the existing national cap-and-trade program for SO_2, but dramatically reduce the cap from 9 million to 3 million tons. Clear Skies would also use a national cap-and-trade program for mercury that would reduce emissions from the current level of about 48 tons to a cap of 15 tons, and would employ two regional cap-and-trade programs for NOx to reduce emissions from current levels of 5 million tons to 1.7 million tons.

. . . Although national in scope, Clear Skies recognizes and adjusts for important regional differences in both the nature of air pollution and the relative importance of emissions from power generation. The eastern half of the country needs reductions in NOx emissions to help meet the ozone and fine particle standards, which generally are not an issue in the western half of the county (with the exception of California, which does not have significant emissions from existing coal-fired power plants). The western half of the country needs NOx reductions primarily to reduce the regional haze that mars scenic vistas in our national parks and wilderness areas, and the nitrogen deposition that harms fragile forests. Recognizing these regional differences, Clear Skies would establish two trading zones for NOx emissions and prohibit trading between

the zones to ensure that the critical health-driven goals in the East are achieved.

Clear Skies also recognizes the special visability protection measures that have been developed by states participating in the Western Regional Air Partnership (WRAP). Clear Skies would essentially codify the WRAP's separate SO_2 backstop cap-and-trade program, which would come into effect only if the WRAP states did not meet their 2018 SO_2 emissions targets.

Finally, Clear Skies requires tough, technology-based new source standards on all new power generation projects and maintains special protections for national parks and wilderness areas when sources locate within 50 km of "Class I" national parks and wilderness areas.

Significant Public Health and Environmental Benefits The public health and environmental benefits of Clear Skies present compelling reasons for its immediate passage. EPA projects that, by 2010, reductions in fine particle and ozone levels under Clear Skies would result in billions of dollars in health and visibility benefits nationwide each year, including as many as 6,400 prolonged lives. Using an alternative methodology, 3,800 lives would be prolonged by 2010. Under EPA's base methodology for calculating benefits, Americans would experience significant benefits each year by 2020, including:

- 12,000 fewer premature deaths (7,000 under an alternative analysis),
- 11,900 fewer visits to hospitals and emergency rooms for cardiovascular and respiratory symptoms,
- 370,000 fewer days with asthma attacks, and
- 2 million fewer lost work days.

Using the alternative methodology, by 2020 Americans would experience 7,000 fewer premature deaths each year.

Methodologies do not exist to quantify or monetize all the benefits of Clear Skies. Still, it is clear that the benefits far exceed the costs. EPA estimates that the health benefits we can quantify under Clear Skies are worth $93 billion annually by 2020—substantially greater than the annual costs of approximately $6.5 billion. An alternative approach projects annual health benefits of $11 billion, still significantly outweighing the costs. The Agency estimates an additional $3 billion in benefits from improving visibility at select National Parks and Wilderness Areas. These estimates do not include the many additional benefits that cannot currently be monetized but are likely to be significant, such as human health benefits from reduced risk of mercury emissions, and ecological benefits from improvements in the health of our forests, lakes, and coastal waters.

Clear Skies would achieve most of these benefits by dramatically reducing fine particle pollution caused by SO_2 and NOx emissions, which is a year-round problem. Of the many air pollutants regulated by EPA, fine particle pollution is perhaps the greatest threat to public health. Hundreds of studies in the peer reviewed literature have found that these microscopic particles can reach the deepest regions of the lungs. Exposure to fine particles is associated with premature death, as well as asthma attacks, chronic bronchitis, decreased lung function, and respiratory disease. Exposure is also associated with aggravation of heart and lung disease, leading to increased hospitalizations, emergency room and doctor visits, and use of medication.

By reducing NOx emissions, Clear Skies also would reduce ozone pollution in the eastern part of the country and help keep ozone levels low in the western portion of the country. Ozone (smog) is a significant health concern, particularly for children and people with asthma and other respiratory diseases who are active outdoors in the summertime. Ozone can exacerbate respiratory symptoms, such as coughing and pain when breathing deeply, as well as transient reductions in lung function and inflammation of the lung. Ozone has also been associated with increased hospitalizations and emergency room visits for respiratory causes. Repeated exposure over time may permanently damage lung tissue.

Current estimates indicate that more than 350 counties fail to meet the health-based fine particle and ozone standards. As a result, 45% of all Americans live in counties where monitored air was unhealthy at times because of high levels of fine particles and ozone. Clear Skies, in combination with existing control programs, would dramatically reduce that number.... Throughout the West, Clear Skies would hold emissions from power plants in check, preserving clean air in high-growth areas and preventing degradation of the environment, even as population and electricity demand increase.

Clear Skies would also reduce mercury emissions from power plants. EPA is required to regulate mercury because EPA determined that mercury emissions from power plants pose an otherwise unaddressed significant risk to health and the environment, and because control options to reduce this risk are available. Mercury, a potent toxin, can cause permanent damage to the brain and nervous system, particularly in developing fetuses when ingested in sufficient quantities. People are exposed to mercury mainly through eating fish contaminated with methylmercury.

Mercury is released into the environment from many sources. Mercury emissions are a complex atmospheric pollutant transported over local, regional, national, and global geographic scales. EPA estimates that 60% of the mercury falling on the U.S. is coming from current man-made sources. Power generation remains the largest man-made source of mercury emissions in the United States. In 1999, coal-fired power plants emitted 48 tons of mercury (approximately 37% of man-made total). These sources also contribute one percent of mercury to the global pool.

Mercury that ends up in fish may originate as emissions to the air. Mercury emissions are later converted into methylmercury by bacteria. Methylmercury accumulates through the food chain: fish that eat other fish can accumulate high levels of methylmercury. EPA has determined that children born to women who may have been exposed to high levels may be at some increased risk of potential adverse health effects. Prenatal exposure to such levels of methylmercury may cause developmental delays and cognitive impairment in children. Clear Skies will require a 69% reduction of mercury emissions from power plants.

In addition to substantial human health benefits, Clear Skies would also deliver numerous environmental benefits. For example, under Clear Skies, we project that 10 million fewer pounds of nitrogen would enter the Chesapeake Bay annually by 2020, reducing potential for water quality problems such as algae blooms and fish kills. In fact, the Chesapeake Bay States, including NY, VA, MD, PA, DE, WV and DC, recently agreed to incorporate the nitrogen reductions that would result from Clear Skies legislation as part of their overall plan to reduce nutrient loadings to the Bay. Clear Skies would also accelerate the recovery process of acidic lakes, virtually eliminating chronic acidity in many Northeastern lakes. For decades fish in the Adirondacks have been decimated by acid rain, making many lakes completely incapable of supporting populations of fish such as trout and smallmouth bass. The Acid Rain Program has allowed some of these lakes and the surrounding forests to begin to recover; Clear Skies would achieve additional needed reductions. Clear Skies would also help other ecosystems suffering from the effects of acid deposition by preventing further deterioration of Southeastern streams. Finally, Clear Skies would improve visibility across the country, particularly in our treasured national parks and wilderness areas.

Clear Skies is designed to ensure that these public health and environmental benefits are achieved and maintained. By relying on mandatory caps, Clear Skies would ensure that total power plant emissions of SO_2, NOx and mercury would not increase over time. This is a distinct advantage over traditional command-and-control regulatory methods that establish source-specific emission rates but which allow total emissions to increase over time. Like the Acid Rain Program, Clear Skies would have much higher levels of accountability and transparency than most other regulatory programs. Sources would be required to continuously monitor and report all emissions, ensuring accurate and complete emissions data. If power plants emit more than allowed, financial penalties are automatically levied - without the need for an enforcement action. More importantly, every ton emitted over the allowed amount would have to be offset in the following year, ensuring no net environmental harm. This high level of environmental assurance is rare in existing programs; Clear Skies would make it a hallmark of the next generation of environmental protection.

SIGNIFICANCE

According to the 2003 testimony of EPA Administrator Christine Todd Whitman before the Senate Clean Air Subcommittee, the Clear Skies Act of 2003 will show a most significant positive effect on public health by 2010. Reductions in fine particulate matter (such as black smoke and soot) and tropospheric ozone should yield several public health benefits, such as a reduction in premature deaths by 7,000–12,000 cases per year; a 11,900-visit decrease in hospitalization and emergency rooms calls due to cardiovascular and respiratory symptoms per year; the prevention of 2 million lost work days due to air-pollution-related illnesses; and 370,000 fewer incidences of asthma attacks.

Other benefits of Clear Skies legislation should have a direct effect on the recovery of lakes and aquatic animals, due to less acid rain, which kills fish and disturbs the food chain in rivers, marshlands, and lakes. Forests are also affected by acid rain, and the resulting acidification of soils is a chief cause of the drastic reductions in maple sap extraction (from which maple syrup is made) in the last three decades. Air visibility should also improve as emissions steadily are reduced, and should therefore benefit migrating birds, wilderness areas, and national parks. New jobs and economic activities will be created as new technologies are developed, such as eco-friendly car engines and fuels, new energy sources and know-how, emission-prevention equipment, and recycling technologies.

FURTHER RESOURCES
Web sites

"Clear Skies Act of 2003—Fact Sheet." U.S. Environmental Protection Agency, February 7, 2003. <http://www.epa.gov/air/clearskies/pdfs/fsfeb27.pdf> (accessed March 7, 2006).

"Global Warming—Emissions." U.S. Environmental Protection Agency. <http://yosemite.epa.gov/oar/global warming.nsf/content/Emissions.html> (accessed January 17, 2006).

"Ice Core Extends Climate Record Back 650,000 Years." Scientific American.com, November 28, 2005. <http://www.sciam.com/print_version.cfm?articleID=00020983-B238-1384-B23883414B7F0000> (accessed March 7, 2006).

"President Bush Announces Clear Skies and Global Climate Change Initiatives." U.S. Environmental Protection Agency. <http://www.epa.gov/clearskies/pdfs/clear_skies_factsheet.pdf> (accessed January 17, 2006).

Mercury Reduction Act of 2003

Legislation

By: United States Congress

Date: February 27, 2003

Source: Library of Congress. "S.484: Omnibus Mercury Emission Reduction Act of 2003." <http://thomas.loc.gov/cgi-bin/query/z?c108:S.484> (accessed November 24, 2005).

About the Author: The Congress of the United States was established by Article 1 of the U.S. Constitution of 1787. It is the legislative arm of the U.S. Federal Government.

INTRODUCTION

Mercury is a pollutant that can be present in groundwater, ocean water, soils, and the atmosphere. Mercury was once thought to be of little concern because its release into the environment is much less than that of other metal pollutants. This changed in 1970 when fish in Lake Saint Clair between Michigan and Ontario, Canada, were found to have high levels of mercury present. The mercury levels were so high that the Canadian government banned all commercial fishing in Lake Saint Clair. In response, the U. S. Federal Water Quality Administration conducted a survey and found elevated levels of mercury in fish in other areas throughout the Unites States and Canada. This revealed that mercury pollution was a significant environmental issue.

The reason that mercury levels were significantly higher than expected is based on the form the mercury takes once it is in the environment. Mercury can enter oceans, lakes, and rivers directly. It can also enter the atmosphere, the groundwater, and soil. When first released, mercury is in an insoluble form. However, bacteria can then convert the mercury into a soluble form known as methylmercury. Fish in oceans, lakes, and rivers become contaminated by the methylmercury. This contamination involves methylmercury being deposited in the fatty tissue of the fish. Once deposited, the compound remains in the fatty tissue and is not broken down or removed. The end result is that mercury levels accumulate in fish. This explains why the mercury levels in fish were higher than expected, since even a relatively small amount of pollution becomes significant because the pollutant is persistent and accumulates. The methylmercury concentration in fish also increases toward the top of the food chain because larger fish feed on smaller fish, accumulating the contaminants from the smaller fish in the process.

The high levels of methlymercury in fish pose significant health risks. A report by the National Academy of Sciences, titled "Toxicological Effects of Methylmercury," describes how methylmercury is a neurotoxin, meaning that it interferes with the correct functioning of the nervous system. This can cause irritability, impaired coordination, muscle weakness, paralysis, and blindness. The report found that these effects can occur from single cases of high exposure to methylmercury as well as from continued exposure to low doses of mercury.

Methylmercury also interferes with the development of the nervous system of a fetus, making high mercury levels a significant risk factor for pregnant women. Unborn babies exposed to high levels of methylmercury have been born with serious defects, including mental retardation, cerebral palsy, and deafness. In cases where unborn babies were exposed to lower levels of methylmercury, children have been seen to develop poor motor skills, short attention spans, reduced language skills, and poor memory. It was also found that the effects on the child have been observed even though the mother showed no symptoms of methylmercury poisoning. This suggests that fetuses are more susceptible to the neurotoxic effects of methylmercury and are affected at lower concentrations.

PRIMARY SOURCE

108TH CONGRESS
1st Session
S. 484

To amend the Clean Air Act to establish requirements concerning the operation of fossil fuel-fired electric utility steam generating units, commercial and industrial boiler units, solid waste incineration units, medical waste incinerators, hazardous waste combustors, chlor-alkali plants, and Portland cement plants to reduce emissions of mercury to the environment, and for other purposes.

IN THE SENATE OF THE UNITED STATES
February 27, 2003

Mr. LEAHY (for himself and Ms. SNOWE) introduced the following bill; which was read twice and referred to the Committee on Environment and Public Works

A BILL

To amend the Clean Air Act to establish requirements concerning the operation of fossil fuel-fired electric utility steam generating units, commercial and industrial boiler units, solid waste incineration units, medical waste incinerators, hazardous waste combustors, chlor-alkali plants, and Portland cement plants to reduce emissions of mercury to the environment, and for other purposes.

Be it enacted by the Senate and House of Representatives of the United States of America in Congress assembled, . . .

SEC. 2. FINDINGS AND PURPOSES.

(a) FINDINGS.—Congress finds that—

(1) on the basis of available scientific and medical evidence, exposure to mercury and mercury compounds (collectively referred to in this Act as "mercury") is of concern to human health and the environment;

(2) according to the report entitled "Toxicological Effects of Methylmercury" and submitted to Congress by the National Academy of Sciences in 2000, and other scientific and medical evidence, pregnant women and their fetuses, women of childbearing age, children, and individuals who subsist primarily on fish are most at risk for mercury-related health impacts such as neurotoxicity;

(3) although exposure to mercury occurs most frequently through consumption of mercury-contaminated fish, such exposure can also occur through—

(A) ingestion of drinking water, and food sources other than fish, that are contaminated with methyl mercury;

(B) dermal uptake through soil and water; and

(C) inhalation of contaminated air;

(4) on the basis of the report entitled "Mercury Study Report to Congress" and submitted by the Environmental Protection Agency under section 112(n)(1)(B) of the Clean Air Act (42 U.S.C. 7412(n)(1)(B)), the major sources of mercury emissions in the United States are, in descending order of volume of emissions—

(A) fossil fuel-fired electric utility steam generating units;

(B) solid waste incineration units;

(C) coal- and oil-fired commercial and industrial boiler units;

(D) medical waste incinerators;

(E) hazardous waste combustors;

(F) chlor-alkali plants; and

(G) Portland cement plants;

(5)(A) the Environmental Protection Agency report described in paragraph (4), in conjunction with available scientific knowledge, supports a plausible link between mercury emissions from anthropogenic combustion and industrial sources and mercury concentrations in air, soil, water, and sediments;

(B) the Environmental Protection Agency has concluded that the geographical areas that have the highest annual rate of deposition of mercury in all forms are—

(i) the southern Great Lakes and Ohio River Valley;

(ii) the Northeast and southern New England; and

(iii) scattered areas in the South, with the most elevated deposition occurring in the Miami and Tampa areas and 2 areas in northeast Texas; and

(C) analysis conducted before the date of the Environmental Protection Agency report demonstrates that mercury is being deposited into the waters of Canada;

(6)(A) the Environmental Protection Agency report described in paragraph (4) supports a plausible link between mercury emissions from anthropogenic combustion and industrial sources and concentrations of methyl mercury in freshwater fish;

(B) in 2002, 44 States issued health advisories that warned the public about consuming mercury-tainted fish, as compared to 27 States that issued such advisories in 1993;

(C) the total number of mercury advisories nationwide increased from 899 in 1993 to 2,073 in 1999, an increase of 131 percent; and

(D) the United States and Canada have agreed on a goal of virtual elimination of mercury from the transboundary waters of the 2 countries;

(7) the presence of mercury in consumer products is of concern in light of the health consequences associated with exposure to mercury;

(8) the presence of mercury in certain batteries and fluorescent light bulbs is of special concern, particularly in light of the substantial quantities of used batteries and fluorescent light bulbs that are discarded annually in the solid waste stream and the potential for environmental and health consequences associated with land disposal, composting, or incineration of the batteries and light bulbs;

(9) a comprehensive study of the use of mercury by the Department of Defense would significantly further the goal of reducing mercury pollution;

(10) since excess stockpiled mercury, if sold domestically or internationally for commercial or industrial use, has the potential to threaten the environment and public health, there is a need for methods to retire excess mercury permanently;

(11) accurate, long-term, nationwide monitoring of atmospheric mercury deposition is essential to—

(A) determining current deposition trends;

(B) evaluating the local and regional transport of mercury emissions; and

(C) assessing the impact of emission reductions; and

(12)(A) a January 2003 report by the Centers for Disease Control and Prevention found that 1 in 12 women of childbearing age has mercury levels above the safe health threshold established by the Environmental Protection Agency; and

(B) the statistic described in subparagraph (A) means that—

(i) nearly 4,900,000 women of childbearing age have elevated levels of mercury from eating contaminated fish; and

(ii) approximately 320,000 newborns per year are at risk of neurological effects from being exposed to elevated mercury levels before birth.

(b) PURPOSES—The purposes of this Act are—

(1) to greatly reduce the quantity of mercury entering the environment by controlling air emissions of mercury from fossil fuel-fired electric utility steam generating units, coal- and oil-fired commercial and industrial boiler units, solid waste incineration units, medical waste incinerators, hazardous waste combustors, chlor-alkali plants, and Portland cement plants;

(2) to reduce the quantity of mercury entering solid waste landfills, incinerators, and composting facilities by promoting recycling or proper disposal of used batteries, fluorescent light bulbs, and other products containing mercury;

(3) to increase the understanding of the volume and sources of mercury emissions throughout North America;

(4) to promote efficient and cost-effective methods of controlling mercury emissions;

(5) to promote permanent, safe, and stable disposal of mercury recovered through coal cleaning, flue gas control systems, and other methods of mercury pollution control;

(6) to reduce the use of mercury in cases in which technologically and economically feasible alternatives are available;

(7) to educate the public concerning the collection, recycling, and proper disposal of mercury-containing products;

(8) to increase public knowledge of the sources of mercury exposure and the threat to public health, particularly the threat to the health of pregnant women and their fetuses, women of childbearing age, children, and individuals who subsist primarily on fish;

(9) to significantly decrease the threat to human health and the environment posed by mercury; and

(10) to ensure that the health of sensitive populations, whether in the United States, Canada, or Mexico, is protected, with an adequate margin of safety, against adverse health effects caused by mercury.

SIGNIFICANCE

The most concerning form of mercury is methylmercury, a soluble form that accumulates in fish and other seafood and acts as a neurotoxin. Mercury also exists elsewhere in the environment, including elemental mercury in liquid and gaseous form. One of the most important points is that although mercury can change forms, it is not biodegradable and will not be removed from the environment. This means that the only way to manage the problem of mercury pollution is to prevent it from entering the environment.

The Mercury Reduction Act of 2003 was proposed to reduce emissions of mercury to the environment. The act covers the major sources of mercury including fossil fuel-fired electric utility steam generating units, commercial and industrial boiler units, solid waste incineration units, medical waste incinerators, hazardous waste combustors, chlor-alkali plants, and Portland cement plants.

The act describes required actions relating to the use and release of mercury. This includes requirements for the reduction of mercury emissions, the monitoring of mercury emissions, the disposal of captured mercury in a suitable manner, and the separation of mercury-containing waste from other waste. The act also prohibits the sale of manufactured products containing mercury unless the manufacturer is granted an exemption.

The Mercury Reduction Act was proposed with the intention of decreasing mercury release to the environment, which would lead to a reduction of methylmercury levels in fish and seafood, therefore reducing the health risks to the population and especially to pregnant women and unborn babies. The bill was introduced in the Senate and referred to the Committee on Environment and Public Works, but was not passed and did not become law.

FURTHER RESOURCES

Books

National Research Council. *Toxicological Effects of Methylmercury*. Washington, D.C.: National Academies Press, 2000.

Periodicals

Harris, Hugh, Ingrid Pickering, and Graham George. "The Chemical Form of Mercury in Fish." *Science* 301 (2003): 1203.

Myers, Gary J., and Philip W. Davidson. "Does Methylmercury Have a Role in Causing Developmental Disabilities in Children?." *Environmental Health Perspectives* 108 (2000): 413–420.

Web sites

"Mercury Study Report to Congress." *United States Environmental Protection Agency*. <http://www.epa.gov/mercury/report.htm> (accessed March 16, 2006).

"Mercury in the Environment." *United States Geological Survey*, October 2000. <http://www.usgs.gov/themes/factsheet/146-00> (accessed March 16, 2006).

Coastal Zone Renewable Energy Act of 2003

Legislation

By: William D. Delahunt and Jim Saxton

Date: March 11, 2003

Source: U.S. Congress. "Coastal Zone Renewable Energy Act of 2003." Washington, D.C.: 2003.

About the Author: Representative William D. Delahunt has been a Democratic member of the U.S. House of Representatives since 1997. He represents the tenth district of Massachusetts. As of 2006, he is a member of the 109th Congress and proposed the aforementioned bill while serving the 108th Congress in 2003. Delahunt served in the U.S. Coast Guard Reserve and as District Attorney of the Norfolk County before serving the Massachusetts House of Representatives. He was elected to The 105th U.S. Congress in 1997, and has been elected to the succeeding U.S. Congress as well. Representative Jim Saxton is Republican member of the House of Representatives in the U.S. Congress. As of 2006, he is serving the 109th U.S.

Congress as Congressional Delegate from New Jersey. He is a member of the Armed Service Committee and the Resources Committee. He is also Vice President of the Joint Economic Committee.

INTRODUCTION

Since the latter part of the twentieth century, the use of fossil fuels and nonrenewable resources for energy needs has led to innumerable environmental problems such as pollution and climate change, in the United States and around the world. Further, the United States has a need to import oil from foreign sources, located mostly in the politically unstable parts of the world. Since September 11, 2001, when the World Trade Center was destroyed in an act of terrorism, there has been a growing introspection within the country about the source of its energy needs.

Renewable energy is energy which can be obtained from almost inexhaustible sources such as ocean tides, wind harvesting, geothermal sources, and natural sunlight. The potential of these sources is a vast unlimited source of energy for future generations. Basic technology for this purpose already exists in the United States. Since the beginning of the new millennium, various individuals and companies in the United States have expressed willingness to explore unconventional means of generating energy. It is for these reasons that experts have been advocating the use of renewable energy as a source of electricity. In the past, the U.S. Government has also thought in this direction.

The Coastal Zone Renewable Energy Act of 2003 is a bill which significantly explores this possibility. Originally tabled in the first session of the 108th Congress on March 11, 2003, it proposes to zone coastal areas for the production of energy from renewable resources. The bill also proposes the use of renewable energy sources such as wind, tidal, geo-thermal, hydropower, biomass energy, and such. Unlike fossil fuels, the availability of these resources is virtually bottomless, but the amount of energy that can be obtained from these resources is restricted to their immediate availability.

Sponsored by Democrat Representative William Delahunt and cosponsored by Republic Representative Jim Saxton, the aforementioned bill was referred for various house/subcommittee actions in March 2003. It was forwarded to the U.S. Department of Commerce in March 2003 for executive comment, which as of 2006 was being awaited.

The primary source in an excerpt from this bill. The included sections enumerate the findings, purposes, and objectives of the Act. This bill also proposes amendments to the coastal zone management act of 1972. In a formal context, the bill describes the systems and infrastructure that needs to be set up to tap the renewable energy sources in the marine environment. It describes the various agencies that would need to coordinate to enable the appropriate use of these resources for the energy needs of the country.

■ PRIMARY SOURCE

108th CONGRESS

1st Session

H. R. 1183

To promote the Sensible Development of Renewable Energy in the Waters of the Coastal Zone, and for other purposes.

IN THE HOUSE OF REPRESENTATIVES

March 11, 2003

Mr. DELAHUNT (for himself and Mr. SAXTON) introduced the following bill; which was referred to the Committee on Resources

A BILL

To promote the Sensible Development of Renewable Energy in the Waters of the Coastal Zone, and for other purposes.

Be it enacted by the Senate and House of Representatives of the United States of America in Congress assembled,

SECTION 1. SHORT TITLE. This Act may be cited as the "Coastal Zone Renewable Energy Promotion Act of 2003."

SEC. 2. FINDINGS; PURPOSES AND OBJECTIVES.

(a) FINDINGS.—The Congress finds that—

1. There is an increasing need for the production of electricity from energy facilities that use renewable resources and some of these facilities may be located in waters under the jurisdiction of the United States, including the coastal zone;
2. Energy companies have already sought to construct energy facilities in State and Federal waters that will use renewable wind energy resources;
3. Nationwide there are more than 50 proposals to construct and operate "wind farms" for producing electricity in State and Federal waters, and some of these proposals include anchoring more than five hundred wind towers to the ocean seabed within sight of land;

4. Existing Federal and State law does not provide a process to address the unique issues raised by proposals to locate energy facilities for renewable resources in the marine environment, thereby hindering or jeopardizing sensible development of these renewable energy resources; and

5. New Federal and State policies are needed to ensure the timely and sensible development of renewable energy resources that are accessible in the marine environment and to provide a mechanism to resolve the significant public trust issues involved in resource allocation and multiple uses in the marine environment.

(b) PURPOSES AND OBJECTIVES.—The purposes and objectives of this Act are to—

1. promote the sensible development of energy facilities that use renewable energy resources in the marine environment by authorizing the Secretary of Commerce to establish a licensing regime and permitting process to ensure due consideration of the public trust issues involved in resource allocation, multiple use, and impacts on the marine environment;

2. direct the Secretary of Commerce, acting through the Administrator of the National Oceanic and Atmospheric Administration (NOAA), to use NOAA's expertise about the marine environment and coastal zone to develop new Federal rules and regulations to authorize and govern the sensible development of renewable energy resources in a manner that provides for public safety, safe navigation, protection of the marine environment, prevention of waste, conservation of natural resources, access to important commercial and recreational fishing areas, the protection of correlative rights, protection of national security interests, and payments to the Federal Government for constructing and operating renewable energy facilities in waters under the jurisdiction of the United States seaward of the coastal zone; and

3. encourage coastal States to amend their coastal zone management plans to include policies and procedures that address—

   (A) issues arising from the location in the marine environment of energy facilities that utilize renewable energy sources;
   (B) conflicting and competing resource allocation and multiple use issues; and
   (C) any adverse impacts from such facilities on the marine environment, commercial and recreational fishing and other activities, the boating community and aesthetic, cultural and historic values.

TITLE I—COASTAL STATE MANAGEMENT

SEC. 101. COASTAL ZONE ENHANCEMENT OBJECTIVES. Section 309 of the Coastal Zone Management Act of 1972 (16 U.S.C. 1456b) is amended—

(1) in subsection (a) by inserting at the end the following new paragraph—

(8) The procedures and enforceable policies adopted to facilitate the location of renewable energy facilities in the marine environment, including any wind energy facility, shall, among other things—

   (A) identify priority locations for renewable energy facilities in the coastal zone;

   (B) ensure continued access to commercial and recreational fishing areas, including shellfish beds;

   (C) include an environmental review of the potential impacts on—(i) marine mammals and endangered species and their designated critical habitat; (ii) birds; (iii) the marine environment including the seabed; (iv) aesthetic, cultural and historical resource values; and (v) the cumulative impacts of multiple renewable energy facilities;

   (D) evaluate navigational and public safety concerns, including but not limited to aviation safety, and ensure continued access to important traditional recreational boating areas;

   (E) include obligations for the payment of funds necessary to pay for the decommissioning and removal of renewable energy facilities;

   (F) include an assessment of the need for the energy produced by renewable energy facilities; and

   (G) take into account national security interests.

(2) in subsection (c) by inserting at the end the following new sentence: "In making funding decisions, the Secretary shall give special consideration to those proposals for management program changes related to the implementation of the objectives identified in paragraph (a)(8) in States with pending renewable energy facility proposals."

TITLE II—FEDERAL MARINE RENEWABLE ENERGY PROGRAM

SEC. 201. LICENSE FOR THE OPERATION OF RENEWABLE ENERGY FACILITIES IN WATERS UNDER THE JURISDICTION OF THE UNITED STATES SEAWARD OF THE COASTAL ZONE. The Coastal Zone Management Act of 1972 (16 U.S.C. 1451 et seq.) is amended by adding at the end the following new section—

SEC. 314. RENEWABLE ENERGY FACILITIES.

(a) LICENSE REQUIREMENT.—No person may construct or operate a renewable energy facility in waters under the jurisdiction of the United States seaward of the coastal zone except in accordance with a license issued pursuant to this section.

(b) LETTER OF INTENT, PUBLIC NOTICE AND REQUEST FOR PROPOSALS.—

(1) Any person who seeks to apply for a license under this section shall notify the Secretary in writing of their intent to apply for a license under this section. A letter of intent shall include, at a minimum, a description of the proposed renewable energy facility, the specific location where the applicant proposes to construct the facility, the proposed timeframe for construction and operation of the facility and the names of the applicant, owners and operators of the proposed facility.

(2) Within 30 days of receipt of a letter of intent, the Secretary shall publish in the Federal Register notice containing the requirements for a license application in the area identified in the notice issued under paragraph (2), and a request for proposals from all persons who seek a license to construct and operate a renewable energy facility in the same location. The Secretary shall determine the time within which proposals must be submitted, but shall not set the submission date less than 60 days from the date notice is published in the Federal Register.

(c) PUBLIC INTEREST EVALUATION.—In evaluating applications received under this section, the Secretary shall consider the amount of energy the proposed project will produce, the economic impact to the region where the facility will be located, the environmental impacts of the proposed facility, the displacement of competing uses of the proposed site and other relevant factors to determine which proposed project best serves the public interest.

(d) LICENSE ISSUANCE PREREQUISITES.—The Secretary may only issue a license under this section after the Secretary determines that—

1. based on recommendations from the Secretary of Defense, the facility will be consistent with national security needs;
2. based on recommendations from the Corps of Engineers and the Coast Guard, the facility will not create an obstruction to navigation;
3. the application is consistent with the approved management programs of affected states;
4. construction or operation of the facility will not unduly restrict access to commercial and recreational fishing areas, including shellfish beds, and recreational boating areas;
5. the facility will not adversely affect marine mammals, threatened or endangered species, migratory birds, or designated critical habitat;
6. construction or operation of the facility will not adverselyaffect aesthetic, cultural, or historical resources

recognized or protected under Federal law or the laws of the affected coastal States;
7. after consultation with the Secretary of Transportation, that the renewable energy facility does not pose a threat to aviation safety;
8. as a result of the Environmental Impact Statement, the facility can be constructed or operated in a manner that minimizes any adverse impact on the marine environment, including the seabed and any other natural resources;
9. after consultation with the Secretary of Energy, that the electricity that will be produced by the facility is needed;
10. the location of the facility is not within the boundaries of a National Marine Sanctuary or Marine Protected Area;
11. the applicant will pay the fees required in the application; and
12. the application was determined by the Secretary under subsection (c) to best serve the public interest.

SEC. 202. PRIORITY SITE IDENTIFICATION AND EVALUATION. (a) PRIORITY SITE IDENTIFICATION AND EVALUATION.— To accelerate the sensible development of renewable energy facilities in the marine environment, the Secretary shall immediately begin to identify, list, and evaluate those locations within the marine waters under the jurisdiction of the United States seaward of the coastal zone that have the greatest potential, consistent with this Act and section 309(a)(8) of the Coastal Zone Management Act of 1972, as added by section 101 of this Act, for producing energy from renewable energy facilities. In identifying and listing these priority areas the Secretary shall consult with the Secretary of Energy, the Coast Guard, the Administrator of the Environmental Protection Agency, affected coastal states and other public and private institutions and companies with relevant expertise. In evaluating potential sites to be listed, the Secretary shall, to the maximum extent possible, consult with the Office of Energy Efficiency and Renewable Energy and the National Renewable Energy Laboratory of the Department of Energy.

SIGNIFICANCE

The excessive use of exhaustible resources such as oil, gas, and coal to meet human energy needs has led to the severe depletion of these resources worldwide. In addition to causing pollution, the use of environmentally finite resources has led to the extinction of several species worldwide, with many more species left endangered.

Experts have been debating the use of other resources for essential elements of life such as electricity. One such resource is renewable energy. In the past, several alternatives have been proposed to facilitate the use of renewable energy in lieu of conventional fossil fuels. There is a worldwide awareness that the overuse of fossil fuels has contributed to many problems—global warming being one such extremely significant and sensitive problem.

Researchers all over the world look for ways to generate energy from renewable resources that pose no harm to the earth's environment. A promising alternative for generating energy is wind power. One viable proposal is the construction of wind farms in coastal areas and in the marine environment that would allow energy to be harvested and distributed through conventional energy infrastructure. On the island of Nantucket in Massachusetts, a wind farm called Cape Wind is fast progressing toward its aim of providing electricity to most of the island. According to Tom Gray, deputy executive director of the American Wind Energy Association, as of 2005 there was a substantial upswing in the use of wind power, mainly because of high oil prices and dependence on foreign energy reserves.

Proponents of renewable energy say that although such research looks promising, and a lot of interest has been shown by various companies to set up renewable energy production facilities, as of 2006, there was still a lack of viable federal and state policy, and with it clear direction in this area.

The reason for this can be attributed to lack of government support. Government officials argue that though the use renewable energy has many advantages, fossil fuel remains the popular source of energy in the United States. They state that the level and scale of technology in the twenty-first century makes it relatively easier and economical to produce and distribute energy obtained from fossil fuels on a large scale. Though suitable renewable energy technology exists the economics of renewable energy makes it exceedingly more expensive than conventional energy.

Experts maintain that apart from weak government policy, market factors and industry self-interests such as the economics of power generation, demand for large scale utilization, and transfer of technology for larger interests affect the renewable energy sector to a great extent. Moreover, the United States was the world leader in renewable energy generation in the 1990s. However, it lost that position to Europe and Japan in subsequent years. This, experts say, can be largely attributed to the domestic inability to balance the long-and short-term interests of power generation and energy utilization.

FURTHER RESOURCES

Web sites

Cape Wind. "More Turning to Wind Power as Alternative." <http://www.capewind.org/news561.htm> (accessed February 20, 2006).

CATO Institute. "Renewable Energy: Not Cheap, Not Green" <http://www.cato.org/pubs/pas/pa-280.html> (accessed February 20, 2006).

Coastal Guide. "Energy." <http://www.coastalguide.org/trends/energy.html> (accessed February 20, 2006).

Martinot, Eric, Ryan Wiser, and Jan Hamrin. "Renewable Energy Policies and Markets in the United States." <http://www.efchina.org/documents/RE_Policies&Markets_US.pdf> (accessed February 20, 2006).

Proceedings of the 14th Biennial Coastal Zone Conference. "Coastal Wind Energy and the United States: An Overview." <http://www.csc.noaa.gov> (accessed February 20, 2006).

Marine Debris Research Prevention and Reduction Act

Legislation

By: United States Congress

Date: February 10, 2005

Source: U.S. Congress. "Marine Debris Research Prevention and Reduction Act." February 10, 2005. <http://www.govtrack.us/congress/billtext.xpd?bill=s109-362> (accessed March 16, 2006).

About the Author: The Congress of the United States was established by Article 1 of the U.S. Constitution of 1787. It is the legislative arm of the U.S. Federal Government.

INTRODUCTION

Marine debris is urban or industrial waste that has ended up polluting the oceans. Various substances, such as empty cans, plastic bottles, cigarette lighters, damaged fishing line, plastic packaging, and Styrofoam pellets are examples of marine debris.

Marine debris is first-hand evidence of humans directly meddling on land and sea. A report posted on the Web site of the U.S. Environmental Protection Agency (EPA) mentions that waste from the land contributes up to nearly 80 percent of marine debris.

Quite often, debris accumulates on the ocean floor and becomes an unwanted part of the marine ecosystem. Floating debris can travel deep into the sea. This causes immense harm to coral reefs and other fragile components of the marine ecosystem.

Marine animals like seals, sea lions, and seabirds mistake floating debris such as burst balloons, plastic packaging, and floating thermoCole pellets for food. Ingestion of this debris has caused the death of many marine animals and seabirds. This includes many endangered species as well. An EPA report mentioned that nearly 30,000 fur seals are entangled in discarded fishing nets every year. Most drown or suffocate.

The concept of stronger legislation to combat this menace has gained further ground, with the problem of marine debris in coastal areas and even the open seas assuming acute proportions. This concern has been reflected in the bill introduced by Democratic Senator Daniel Inouye.

Since the introduction of the bill, it has passed through various stages. The Senate passed the bill in July 2005, and as of late 2005 was awaiting approval from the House of Representatives. The bill proposes to seek coordination between federal agencies such as the National Oceanic and Atmospheric Administration (NOAA) and the U.S. Coast Guard for marine debris research, prevention, and reduction. It also seeks to introduce a monetary fund of around $10 million for this task.

PRIMARY SOURCE

SEC. 2. FINDINGS AND PURPOSES.

(a) FINDINGS- The Congress makes the following findings:

1. The oceans, which comprise nearly three quarters of the Earth's surface, are an important source of food and provide a wealth of other natural products that are important to the economy of the United States and the world.
2. Ocean and coastal areas are regions of remarkably high biological productivity, are of considerable importance for a variety of recreational and commercial activities, and provide a vital means of transportation.
3. Ocean and coastal resources are limited and susceptible to change as a direct and indirect result of human activities, and such changes can impact the ability of the ocean to provide the benefits upon which the Nation depends.
4. Marine debris, including plastics, derelict fishing gear, and a wide variety of other objects, has a harmful and persistent effect on marine flora and fauna and can have adverse impacts on human health.
5. Marine debris is also a hazard to navigation, putting mariners and rescuers, their vessels, and consequently the marine environment at risk, and can cause economic loss due to entanglement of vessel systems.
6. Modern plastic materials persist for decades in the marine environment and therefore pose the greatest potential for long-term damage to the marine environment.
7. Insufficient knowledge and data on the source, movement, and effects of plastics and other marine debris in marine ecosystems has hampered efforts to develop effective approaches for addressing marine debris.
8. Lack of resources, inadequate attention to this issue, and poor coordination at the Federal level has undermined the development and implementation of a Federal program to address marine debris, both domestically and internationally.

(b) PURPOSES- The purposes of this Act are—

1. to establish programs within the National Oceanic and Atmospheric Administration and the United States Coast Guard to help identify, determine sources of, assess, reduce, and prevent marine debris and its adverse impacts on the marine environment and navigation safety, in coordination with other Federal and non-Federal entities;
2. to re-establish the Inter-agency Marine Debris Coordinating Committee to ensure a coordinated government response across Federal agencies;
3. to develop a Federal information clearinghouse to enable researchers to study the sources, scale and impact of marine debris more efficiently; and
4. to take appropriate action in the international community to prevent marine debris and reduce concentrations of existing debris on a global scale.

SEC. 3. NOAA MARINE DEBRIS PREVENTION AND REMOVAL PROGRAM.

(a) ESTABLISHMENT OF PROGRAM— There is established, within the National Oceanic and Atmospheric Administration, a Marine Debris Prevention and Removal Program to reduce and prevent the occurrence and adverse impacts of marine debris on the marine environment and navigation safety.

(b) PROGRAM COMPONENTS— Through the Marine Debris Prevention and Removal Program, the Under Secretary for Oceans and Atmosphere (Under Secretary) shall carry out the following activities:

(1) MAPPING, IDENTIFICATION, IMPACT ASSESSMENT, REMOVAL, AND PREVENTION— The Under Secretary shall, in consultation with relevant Federal agencies, undertake marine debris mapping, identification, impact assessment, prevention, and removal efforts, with a focus on marine debris posing a threat to living marine resources (particularly endangered or protected species) and navigation safety, including—

(A) the establishment of a process, building on existing information sources maintained by Federal agencies such as the Environmental Protection Agency and the Coast Guard, for cataloguing and maintaining an inventory of marine debris and its impacts found in the United States navigable waters and the United States exclusive economic zone, including location, material, size, age, and origin, and impacts on habitat, living marine resources, human health, and navigation safety;

(B) measures to identify the origin, location, and projected movement of marine debris within the United States navigable waters, the United States exclusive economic zone, and the high seas, including the use of oceanographic, atmospheric, satellite, and remote sensing data; and

(C) development and implementation of strategies, methods, priorities, and a plan for preventing and removing marine debris from United States navigable waters and within the United States exclusive economic zone, including development of local or regional protocols for removal of derelict fishing gear.

(2) REDUCING AND PREVENTING LOSS OF GEAR— The Under Secretary shall improve efforts and actively seek to prevent and reduce fishing gear losses, as well as to reduce adverse impacts of such gear on living marine resources and navigation safety, including—

(A) research and development of alternatives to gear posing threats to the marine environment , and methods for marking gear used in specific fisheries to enhance the tracking, recovery, and identification of lost and discarded gear; and

(B) development of voluntary or mandatory measures to reduce the loss and discard of fishing gear, and to aid its recovery, such as incentive programs, reporting loss and recovery of gear, observer programs, toll-free reporting hotlines, computer-based notification forms, and providing adequate and free disposal receptacles at ports.

(3) OUTREACH— The Under Secretary shall undertake outreach and education of the public and other stakeholders, such as the fishing industry, fishing gear manufacturers, and other marine-dependent industries, on sources of marine debris, threats associated with marine debris and approaches to identify, determine sources of, assess, reduce, and prevent marine debris and its adverse impacts on the marine environment and navigational safety. Including outreach and education activities through public-private initiatives. The Under Secretary shall coordinate outreach and education activities under this paragraph with any outreach programs conducted under section 2204 of the Marine Plastic Pollution Research and Control Act of 1987 (33 U.S.C. 1915).

(c) Grants—

(1) IN GENERAL— The Under Secretary shall provide financial assistance, in the form of grants, through the Marine Debris Prevention and Removal Program for projects to accomplish the purposes of this Act.

(2) 50 percent matching requirement—

(A) IN GENERAL— Except as provided in subparagraph (B), Federal funds for any project under this section may not exceed 50 percent of the total cost of such project. For purposes of this subparagraph, the non-Federal share of project costs may be provided by in-kind contributions and other noncash support.

(B) WAIVER— The Under Secretary may waive all or part of the matching requirement under subparagraph (A) if the Under Secretary determines that no reasonable means are available through which applicants can meet the matching requirement and the probable benefit of such project outweighs the public interest in such matching requirement.

(3) Amounts paid and services rendered under consent—

(A) CONSENT DECREES AND ORDERS— The non-Federal share of the cost of a project carried out under this Act may include money paid pursuant to, or the value of any in-kind service performed under, an administrative order on consent or judicial consent decree that will remove or prevent marine debris.

(B) OTHER DECREES AND ORDERS— The non-Federal share of the cost of a project carried out under this Act may not include any money paid pursuant to, or the value of any in-kind service performed under, any other administrative order or court order.

(4) ELIGIBILITY— Any natural resource management authority of a State, Federal or other government authority whose activities directly or indirectly affect research or

regulation of marine debris, and any educational or non-governmental institutions with demonstrated expertise in a field related to marine debris, are eligible to submit to the Under Secretary a marine debris proposal under the grant program.

(5) GRANT CRITERIA AND GUIDELINES— Within 180 days after the date of enactment of this Act, the Under Secretary shall promulgate necessary guidelines for implementation of the grant program, including development of criteria and priorities for grants. Such priorities may include proposals that would reduce new sources of marine debris and provide additional benefits to the public, such as recycling of marine debris or use of biodegradable materials. In developing those guidelines, the Under Secretary shall consult with:—

(A) the Interagency Marine Debris Committee;
(B) regional fishery management councils established under the Magnuson-Stevens Fishery Conservation and Management Act (16 U.S.C. 1801 et seq.);
(C) State, regional, and local governmental entities with marine debris experience;
(D) marine-dependent industries; and
(E) non-governmental organizations involved in marine debris research, prevention, or removal activities.

(6) PROJECT REVIEW AND APPROVAL— The Under Secretary shall review each marine debris project proposal to determine if it meets the grant criteria and supports the goals of the Act. Not later than 120 days after receiving a project proposal under this section, the Under Secretary shall:—

(A) provide for external merit-based peer review of the proposal;
(B) after considering any written comments and recommendations based on the review, approve or disapprove the proposal; and
(C) provide written notification of that approval or disapproval to the person who submitted the proposal.

(7) PROJECT REPORTING— Each grantee under this section shall provide periodic reports as required by the Under Secretary. Each report shall include all information required by the Under Secretary for evaluating the progress and success in meeting its stated goals, and impact on the marine debris problem.

SEC. 4. COAST GUARD PROGRAM. The Commandant of the Coast Guard shall, in cooperation with the Under Secretary, undertake measures to reduce violations of MARPOL Annex V and the Act to Prevent Pollution from Ships (33 U.S.C. 1901 et seq.) with respect to the discard of plastics and other garbage from vessels. The measures shall include—

1. the development of a strategy to improve monitoring and enforcement of current laws, as well as recommendations for statutory or regulatory changes to improve compliance and for the development of any appropriate amendments to MARPOL;
2. regulations to address implementation gaps with respect to the requirement of MARPOL Annex V and section 6 of the Act to Prevent Pollution from Ships (33 U.S.C. 1905) that all United States ports and terminals maintain receptacles for disposing of plastics and other garbage, which may include measures to ensure that a sufficient quantity of such facilities exist at all such ports and terminals, requirements for logging the waste received, and for Coast Guard comparison of vessel and port log books to determine compliance;
3. regulations to close record keeping gaps, which may include requiring fishing vessels under 400 gross tons entering United States ports to maintain records subject to Coast Guard inspection on the disposal of plastics and other garbage, that, at a minimum, include the time, date, type of garbage, quantity, and location of discharge by latitude and longitude or, if discharged on land, the name of the port where such material is offloaded for disposal;
4. regulations to improve ship-board waste management, which may include expanding to smaller vessels existing requirements to maintain ship-board receptacles and maintain a ship-board waste management plan, taking into account potential economic impacts and technical feasibility;
5. the development, through outreach to commercial vessel operators and recreational boaters, of a voluntary reporting program, along with the establishment of a central reporting location, for incidents of damage to vessels caused by marine debris, as well as observed violations of existing laws and regulations relating to disposal of plastics and other marine debris; and
6. a voluntary program encouraging United States flag vessels to inform the Coast Guard of any ports in other countries that lack adequate port reception facilities for garbage.

SIGNIFICANCE

Marine debris has become a recurring problem since the late 1980s and poses a grave threat to the pristine marine environment. It is a considerable hazard to marine life and is a constant danger for marine navigation. Disasters like shipwrecks, oil tanker

The National Oceanic and Atmospheric Administration team collected eighty-two tons of marine debris at Pearl and Hermes Atoll. This is conclusive evidence that something must be done to reduce the amount of debris to preserve beaches and waterfronts. AP IMAGES

accidents, and offshore oil rig fires contribute to this problem, as does the disposal of urban garbage into oceans, dumping of waste oil by passing ships, commercial coastal and offshore entertainment, and deep-sea industrial and nuclear waste dumps.

Expanding oil and gas exploration activities into deeper seas is a serious threat to the marine environment. Over a prolonged period, accumulated debris fouls the seas and kills marine life. Marine debris is also a growing problem for fishing communities and shipping because it causes a loss in fishing harvest, a vital source of sustenance for many fishing communities. Vessels damaged by marine debris collisions can cost a shipping company a fortune to repair.

The Act aims to establish a variety of federal programs involving various federal agencies like the NOAA and the U.S. Coast Guard for marine debris research, prevention, and reduction. It will provide a $10 million annual fund for the NOAA and $5 million for the U.S. Coast Guard for the proposed activities. There is also a proposal to pursue research activities by setting up a clearinghouse for academics and research. The Act also calls for global steps to prevent further dumping of debris into the marine environment and to include punitive measures in the event of its breach.

Many marine environmental agencies like Ocean Conserve and Project Aware have lauded the introduction of this bill. It is seen by environmentalists as a step in the right direction to tackle this problem, though the impact this bill would have on the improvement of marine debris control and the general improvement on the coastal and marine environment remains to be observed.

FURTHER RESOURCES
Web sites

"The Problem with Marine Debris." *California Coastal Commission*. <http://www.coastal.ca.gov/publiced/marine debris.html> (accessed March 16, 2006).

"Marine Debris." *Pacific Whale Foundation*. <http://www. pacificwhale.org/childrens/fsdebris.html> (accessed March 16, 2006).

"Assessing and Monitoring Floatable Debris." *U.S. Environmental Protection Agency*. <http://www.epa.gov/owow/ oceans/debris/floatingdebris/toc.html> (accessed March 16, 2006).

"Marine Debris Abatement." *U.S. Environmental Protection Agency*. <http://www.epa.gov/owow/oceans/debris> (accessed March 16, 2006).

Energy Use and Perils

Energy is described as an invisible ingredient in every product. Although it is not a tangible substance, energy moves the machines that harvest, transport, and process Earth's raw materials. Energy contained in light heats and illuminates the spaces where people live and work, and it drives the tools of civilization. Energy is essential to food production, especially in modern industrialized agriculture. In a sense, energy is food. Counting pesticides, fertilizers, and transport, about 10 calories of energy from petroleum are used to supply each calorie of food energy consumed in the United States.

The amount of energy used by modern industrial society is unprecedented. Uninterrupted energy supplies are essential to a modern economy. Even a slight shortfall can cause an industrial economy to stagger. Military and political conflicts, therefore, swirl around nations rich in petroleum. As discussed in "Study on Energy Supply Security and Geopolitics," the world's largest energy consumers—the United States, Europe, Japan, and other industrialized nations—cannot supply their own oil needs. Thus, they are engaged in political and cultural tension with those nations that can, including Russia, Iraq, Saudi Arabia, Venezuela, and others.

This combination of non-negotiable need and distant supply is fundamentally unstable. But chronic political-military insecurity and war are not the only kind of harm that arises from energy addictions. Severe human and environmental costs are also associated with extracting and burning fuels.

First, Earth's fuels are extracted. Most electricity is currently produced by burning coal. Most coal is produced by strip-mining, which often involves complete destruction of the overlying landscape.

When fuel burns, air pollution results, contributing to some 50,000 to 100,000 early deaths annually in the United States. Sulfur combines with water and falls as acid rain, sickening forests and marine life. Vehicles spew even more pollution than power stations. The resulting smog envelops major cities such as Los Angeles. All fossil fuels, including clean-burning natural gas, contribute to global climate change, which endangers weather systems.

An alternative is nuclear power—a greenhouse-friendly energy source that breaks up atomic nuclei rather than combining carbon with oxygen. But nuclear power has its disadvantages, including the high cost to create it; the highly radioactive wastes it produces; the danger of a catastrophic accident, such as the 1986 Chernobyl disaster in the former Soviet Union; and the power plants' vulnerability to terrorist attacks. Renewable energy sources, also greenhouse-friendly, have their limitations too. It can be difficult using sun, wind, water, and other renewables to satisfy modern industrial energy needs.

The world's energy appetite is much larger than it needs to be, however. A large fraction of the energy demand actually consists of energy waste. For example, 70 percent of the raw heat energy produced at a typical coal-fired (or nuclear) electric plant simply goes up the chimney as waste. Energy conservation and end-use efficiency is key to any workable energy future.

The long-standing idea of cheap, endless energy is ending, threatening multiple forms of crisis. Painless solutions should not be expected.

Edwin L. Drake Strikes Oil in Titusville, Pennsylvania

Photograph

By: Anonymous

Date: 1861

Source: Corbis

About the Photographer: The black-and-white photograph accompanying this article was taken by a photographer whose identity is unknown. The photographic technique employed in the subject work is similar to that used by noted American Civil War photographer Matthew Brady between 1861 and 1865.

INTRODUCTION

Edwin L. Drake, the "Colonel" of the early Pennsylvania oil industry, did not discover oil in Titusville, Pennsylvania in August of 1859, so much as he proved a point—oil could be extracted from the ground in large, commercially viable quantities by drilling for it beneath the earth.

Drake was born in Greenville, New York in 1819, and his early career gave no indication that at age forty he would revolutionize the world petroleum industry. As a young man, Drake worked in a succession of railroading and sales jobs before becoming a minority shareholder in the newly formed Seneca Oil company of Pennsylvania in 1857.

Oil, in its crude and undistilled form, had been gathered by the native Seneca tribes in the vicinity of what was known as Oil Creek, in west central Pennsylvania, since the 1400s. The native people used the oil that they skimmed from the water surface by canoe as medicine and as a tar patch to repair their crafts. A significant trade in this oil had developed through the New York and Pennsylvania regions into the early nineteenth century, where the oil was used both as a liniment and as a lubricant for wagon wheels. The native practice of skimming oil from Oil Creek had grown by 1810 to a full-fledged small industry, with the raw product shipped to Pittsburgh for processing.

Oil was also an all-too-frequent contaminant in the salt wells of the regions; various entrepreneurs began to collect such oil. By 1850, crude distillation methods that processed only 5 gallons (19 liters) at a time were converting the crude oil to a refined substance variously marketed as "carbon oil" and "rock oil." This purer form was used primarily as lamp fuel, a cost-effective alternative to increasing rare whale oil that had been a staple lamp fuel for decades. Lamps were an essential aspect of American life, and it was clear that crude oil could play a much larger commercial role if there was a better way to obtain it.

Drake had observed throughout his life the operation of both salt wells and the artesian water wells employed in New York and Pennsylvania. He concluded that oil could be extracted from below the surface of the earth in the vicinity of Oil Creek using similar drilling methods. It is a remarkable aspect of Drake's efforts that he was not highly educated, nor had he any particular training or experience in geology or oil exploration.

In the spring of 1859, Drake assembled a crew to assist him, secured his equipment, and set to work to confirm his oil extraction theory. Using a 6-horsepower (4,500-watt) steam engine, a custom built drill, and a stationary boiler, Drake and his men began to drill into the earth at a rate of 3 feet (0.9 meter) per day. There was widespread incredulity regarding what was perceived as Drake's folly—the notion that oil could be extracted by drill seemed impossible.

Problems with seeping groundwater and quicksand impeded the progress of the drilling, as the drill hole would become flooded, causing the edge of the drilling pit to collapse. Drake hit upon an ingenious solution—a cast iron pipe which was driven 32 feet (9.8 meters) into the earth, with the drill bit inserted inside the pipe so as to be unaffected by flooding water or sand.

On August 26, 1859, Drake's crew completed their work for that day—the drill had passed 69 feet (21 meters) into the ground. When work commenced on August 27, oil was found near the top of the drilling tube, and Drake was proven right—he was then the first person to successfully drill for oil. The original Drake well is believed to have produced crude oil at a rate of between 8 to 10 barrels (320 to 400 gallons, or 1,200 to 1,500 liters) per day, and it continued in production for approximately two years.

The discovery of oil in large quantities in Pennsylvania spurred the creation of a hugely profitable industry. It is one of the ironies of nineteenth-century American capitalism that Drake never profited to any great degree from his revolutionary discovery—he had failed to patent his drilling mechanism, and he was bankrupted a few years after his oil strike at Titusville. Drake died a poor man in 1880.

PRIMARY SOURCE

Edwin L. Drake Strikes Oil in Titusville, Pennsylvania. Edwin L. Drake (right), sporting a beard and top hat, poses near the first productive oil well in the United States, located in Titusville, Pennsylvania, in 1861. © BETTMANN/CORBIS

PRIMARY SOURCE

EDWIN L. DRAKE STRIKES OIL IN TITUSVILLE, PENNSYLVANIA

See primary source image.

SIGNIFICANCE

The oil well established by Drake at Titusville in 1859 sparked a revolution, the echoes of which continue to sound across the world to this day. In the short term, western Pennsylvania became a magnet for other, more ambitious, and commercially minded men who sought to push this nascent industry forward.

By the 1880s, the commercial viability of oil exploration first proven by Edwin Drake had grown inexorably into the development of the forerunner of the modern petroleum industry. Greater quantities of oil through drilled wells led to both research into refinery techniques as well as a seeking out of other equally viable oil fields. As crude oil began to be recognized as being capable of having a multitude of useful commercial products contained within it—including gasoline—oil refining became a sophisticated, multifaceted process. It was the creation of the tremendous variety of petroleum products that was poised to alter the entire commercial structure of the world, primarily through the development of an efficient, gasoline-powered internal combustion engine. The early American petroleum industry, rooted in the sale of lamp oil and Drake's first well in Titusville, had become a world Colossus by the end of the century.

Drake's drilling techniques, revolutionary in 1859, remain the base standard for underground oil extraction today. Oil drilling has evolved from Drake's crude structure pictured here into an industry with the capability to drill many miles below the earth's surface, on land and by sea-anchored platforms—Drake's idea to drive a watertight housing into the earth in which the protected drill would operate is the essential principle at play in modern oil drilling operations.

As the Pennsylvania oil fields were the subject of an oil rush following Drake's discovery, other early oil drillers sought other fertile ground. Oil was discovered in California in Kern County in 1861, and the first great Texas oil find was identified in 1901.

It has been hypothesized by naturalists that the Drake oil well may have been a factor in saving the sperm whale from extinction. The whaling industry, based in the northeastern United States, sent its ships around the globe, seeking sperm whales to kill for their oil, which was primarily used as lamp fuel. It is believed that by the 1850s the sperm whale had been hunted close to extinction; Melville's "Moby Dick," the classic whaling saga written in 1851, is a stirring testament to the whale hunt and its utter relentlessness. Sperm oil was very expensive by the standards of Drake's time, and the availability of cheaper petroleum products with the commercialization of the oil industry helped to bring an end to commercial whaling.

FURTHER RESOURCES

Web sites

Drake Well Museum. <http://www.drakewell.org> (accessed March 8, 2006).

"Drilling Hall of Fame Directory." *Drilshop.com.* <http://www.drilshop.com/hallfame/> (accessed March 8, 2006).

"Pennsylvania State Archives." *Pennsylvania Historical and Museum Commission.* <http://www.phmc.state.pa.us/bah/dam/overview.htm?secid=31> (accessed March 8, 2006).

Hoover Dam

Photograph

By: Benjamin D. Glaha

Date: 1934

Source: Corbis

About the Photographer: Benjamin D. Glaha was an employee of the Unites States Bureau of Reclamation in the 1930s, and was assigned to document the construction of the Boulder Dam (now called Hoover Dam) by photographing all aspects of the project. He also photographed native Americans in the West, and some of these photographs reside in the United States National Anthropological Archives. Glaha's photographs were the subject of *Hoover Dam: The Photographs of Ben Glaha* by Barbara Vilander, published in 1999.

INTRODUCTION

The Colorado River originated high in the Rocky Mountains and flowed uncontrolled for about 1,400 miles (2,250 kilometers). It slowly but deliberately eroded lands for millions of years—forming such majestic landforms as the Grand Canyon—before finally emptying into the Gulf of California. The wild flow of the Colorado River was left in this natural state until mankind began to seriously populate its riverbanks and outlying regions. Farmlands were regularly flooded in spring and summer when heavy snows in the mountains melted and violently raced along its downward route. It caused massive problems for farmers as it eroded valuable topsoil, destroyed planted crops, and uprooted trees and other vegetation. In the dry months, the river would diminish or even disappear, leaving farmers with no water supply to sustain their crops and domesticated animals. People within regions of the states of Arizona, California, and Nevada, as well as the country of Mexico, were especially hurt by the Colorado River's destructive rampages.

In the early 1900s, the U.S. federal government authorized studies to evaluate the possibility of controlling the river for the benefit of its western citizens. Then, in 1928, the U.S. Congress passed the Boulder Canyon Project Act, which authorized the construction of Hoover Dam near the border of Arizona and Nevada.

The primary purposes for the construction of the Hoover Dam were to control floods of fertile, but arid agricultural land, and to provide a reliable source of water and electrical power for millions of people in its adjacent areas. With a height of 726 feet (221 meters), length of 1,244 feet (380 meters), and thickness of 660 feet (201 meters) at its base, the dam, after about six years of construction, was dedicated by President Franklin D. Roosevelt on September 30, 1935.

Hoover Dam. Construction workers on Boulder Dam in Boulder City, Nevada, 1934. Now called Hoover Dam, it is one of the world's largest dams, and functions to hold back the waters of the Colorado River between Arizona and Nevada. © CORBIS

HOOVER DAM

See primary source image.

SIGNIFICANCE

The U.S. Bureau of Reclamation used this and other photographs taken by Glaha to document the construction of the dam from start to finish. As the dam was built during the height of the Depression (1929–1941), these photographs appeared in press releases, books, advertisements, and pamphlets in order to illustrate that government money allocated to the dam was spent wisely.

When the Hoover Dam was being constructed, four primary reasons were cited by federal officials as to why the dam was being built: flood control, water conservation, domestic water supply, and power. By controlling floods and permitting a steady stream of water throughout each year, the Hoover Dam holds about two years of water flow behind its structure. Before the dam was built, the Colorado River irrigated about 660,000 acres (267,100 hectares) of land, subject to less acreage during low water months. By storing excessive waters from spring and summer runoff of melted snow, about 2.16 million acres (874,100 hectares) are now available to be irrigated. For example, the All-American Canal, with a width of 170 feet (52 meters), transports and supplies water from the Colorado River (near Yuma, Arizona) to the Imperial Valley of southern California. Many times, the amount of water is now available through the facilities of Hoover Dam; numerous new and varied crops are now able to be produced, such as cantaloupe, alfalfa, lettuce, barley, corn, small fruits, and cotton.

Due to the Hoover Dam's capacity to store water within Lake Mead, the reservoir created by the construction of Hoover Dam, billions of gallons of water are used to supply people with their daily needs for water. For example, the city of Las Vegas, Nevada, receives most of its drinking water from Lake Mead through the Southern Nevada Water Project. In addition, the original electrical power-producing capacity of the dam was about 1.803 million horsepower (1,345 megawatts). (At the end of 1992, the power capacity of the dam's generators were upgraded to about 2.681 million horsepower, or 2,000 megawatts).

The significance of the construction of the Hoover Dam is apparent from the description of the four aforementioned reasons that were declared during the construction of the dam. However, since then, there have been many negative environmental criticisms of the Hoover Dam. The environmental criticisms of the building of the Hoover Dam include disruption of ecosystems, decline of fish stocks and other animals found along the river, forced human resettlements, degradation of water quality, and introduction of diseases.

For example, fish are one of the primary creatures that were hurt by the Hoover Dam. Fish that once swam up and down its waters are now stopped from crossing the structure of the dam. In addition, changes in the flow pattern of the Colorado River increase the turbidity (the muddiness) and siltation (the actions of fine-grained sediment) of the river. Sediments such as gravel and pebbles are held back by the Hoover Dam, which because of its absence downstream causes the erosion of downstream banks. The landscape—including the ecosystem's flora and fauna—that the river flows through is also negatively affected by the damming of the river. Fluctuations in the water levels of the Colorado River, due to the dam, have also been scientifically shown to cause disruption to the habitat in and along the river.

There are many positive and negative aspects to the environmental effects that have occurred due to the construction of the Hoover Dam. Scientists are now delving into the impacts and benefits from the Hoover Dam—and other such dams constructed around the world—onto the environment and the people that use the dam for its various purposes.

FURTHER RESOURCES

Books

Mann, Elizabeth. *Hoover Dam*. New York: Mikaya Press, 2001.

Maxon, James C. *Lake Mead-Hoover Dam*. Las Vegas: KC Publications, 1980.

Stevens, Joseph Edward. *Hoover Dam: An American Adventure*. Norman, OK: University of Oklahoma Press, 1988.

Vilander, Barbara. *Hoover Dam: The Photographs of Ben Glaha*. Tempe, AZ: University of Arizona, 1999.

Web sites

"Fortune Magazine, September 1933." *Lower Colorado Region, Bureau of Reclamation, Department of the Interior*. <http://www.usbr.gov/lc/hooverdam/History/articles/fortune1933.html> (accessed March 8, 2006).

Moore, David. "The Hoover Dam: A World Renowned Concrete Monument." *RomanConcrete.com*, 1999. <http://www.romanconcrete.com/docs/hooverdam/hooverdam.htm> (accessed March 8, 2006).

Atoms for Peace

Speech

By: Dwight D. Eisenhower

Date: 1953

Source: Eisenhower, Dwight D. "Atoms for Peace." United National General Assembly, Geneva, Switzerland. December 8, 1953.

About the Author: Dwight D. Eisenhower was a decorated U.S. Army General who led the Allied Forces in North Africa during World War II and acted as Supreme Commander of forces on D-Day during the same war. He was the thirty-fourth president of the United States (1953–1961). Eisenhower delivered this speech during his tenure as president.

INTRODUCTION

The Manhattan Project, led by physicist Robert Oppenheimer throughout the early 1940s, led to the development of the atom bomb and ushered in a new age of weaponry: the Atomic Age. United States President Harry S. Truman's decision to use the atomic bomb in Japan in the cities of Hiroshima on August 6, 1945, and Nagasaki on August 9, 1945, gave the world a remarkable, yet horrifying, example of atomic energy's power when used as a weapon in wartime; more than 140,000 people died as a direct result of the two bombs.

Although many historians cite Truman's order to use the bomb as an accelerating force in ending the war in the Pacific and shortening its duration, the United States' possession of atomic power set off a worldwide debate about the proper uses of atomic energy. The

USSR raced furiously to develop its own atomic bomb, while U.S. military officials pushed for the next generation in bombing technology: the creation of a hydrogen bomb. As the USSR accomplished nuclear chain reactions in 1946, a crucial step in atom bomb development, the United States determined that 150 bombs represented an appropriate stockpile to defend itself against the USSR. In 1947, the United States had approximately fifty weapons similar to those used on Nagasaki. The arms race was in its infancy, and rapidly growing. However, in March of 1953, Soviet leader Joseph Stalin died, leaving a power vacuum in the Soviet Union and a perceived weakness in the arms race. Just five months later, however, the Soviet Union reported that it had a hydrogen bomb.

That same year, President Eisenhower sought to inform the international community of the United States' recognition of the impact atomic energy on international relations. In addition, President Eisenhower set forth a series of proposals concerning the peaceful use of fissionable material to direct this energy toward productive, non-violent ends.

▮ PRIMARY SOURCE

On July 16, 1945, the United States set off the world's first atomic explosion. Since that date in 1945, the United States of America has conducted 42 test explosions.

Atomic bombs today are more than 25 times as powerful as the weapons with which the atomic age dawned, while hydrogen weapons are in the ranges of millions of tons of TNT equivalent.

Today, the United States' stockpile of atomic weapons, which, of course, increases daily, exceeds by many times the explosive equivalent of the total of all bombs and all shells that came from every plane and every gun in every theatre of war in all of the years of World War II.

A single air group, whether afloat or land-based, can now deliver to any reachable target a destructive cargo exceeding in power all the bombs that fell on Britain in all of World War II.

In size and variety, the development of atomic weapons has been no less remarkable. The development has been such that atomic weapons have virtually achieved conventional status within our armed services. In the United States, the Army, the Navy, the Air Force, and the Marine Corps are all capable of putting this weapon to military use.

But the dread secret, and the fearful engines of atomic might, are not ours alone.

In the first place, the secret is possessed by our friends and allies, Great Britain and Canada, whose scientific genius made a tremendous contribution to our original discoveries, and the designs of atomic bombs.

The secret is also known by the Soviet Union.

The Soviet Union has informed us that, over recent years, it has devoted extensive resources to atomic weapons. During this period, the Soviet Union has exploded a series of atomic devices, including at least one involving thermo-nuclear reactions.

If at one time the United States possessed what might have been called a monopoly of atomic power, that monopoly ceased to exist several years ago. Therefore, although our earlier start has permitted us to accumulate what is today a great quantitative advantage, the atomic realities of today comprehend two facts of even greater significance.

First, the knowledge now possessed by several nations will eventually be shared by others—possibly all others.

Second, even a vast superiority in numbers of weapons, and a consequent capability of devastating retaliation, is not preventive, of itself, against the fearful material damage and toll of human lives that would be inflicted by surprise aggression.

The free world, at least dimly aware of these facts, has naturally embarked on a large program of warning and defense systems. That program will be accelerated and expanded.

But let no one think that the expenditure of vast sums for weapons and systems of defense can guarantee absolute safety for the cities and citizens of any nation. The awful arithmetic of the atomic bomb does not permit any such easy solution. Even against the most powerful defense, an aggressor in possession of the effective minimum number of atomic bombs for a surprise attack could probably place a sufficient number of his bombs on the chosen targets to cause hideous damage.

Should such an atomic attack be launched against the United States, our reactions would be swift and resolute. But for me to say that the defense capabilities of the United States are such that they could inflict terrible losses upon an aggressor—for me to say that the retaliation capabilities of the United States are so great that such an aggressor's land would be laid waste—all this, while fact, is not the true expression of the purpose and the hope of the United States.

To pause there would be to confirm the hopeless finality of a belief that two atomic colossi are doomed malevolently to eye each other indefinitely across a trembling world. To stop there would be to accept helplessly the probability of civilization destroyed—the annihilation of the irreplaceable heritage of mankind handed down to us generation from generation—and the condemnation of mankind to begin all over again the age-old struggle upward from savagery toward decency, and right, and justice.

Surely no sane member of the human race could discover victory in such desolation. Could anyone wish his name to be coupled by history with such human degradation and destruction.

Occasional pages of history do record the faces of the "Great Destroyers" but the whole book of history reveals mankind's never-ending quest for peace, and mankind's God-given capacity to build.

It is with the book of history, and not with isolated pages, that the United States will ever wish to be identified. My country wants to be constructive, not destructive. It wants agreement, not wars, among nations. It wants itself to live in freedom, and in the confidence that the people of every other nation enjoy equally the right of choosing their own way of life.

So my country's purpose is to help us move out of the dark chamber of horrors into the light, to find a way by which the minds of men, the hopes of men, the souls of men every where, can move forward toward peace and happiness and well being.

In this quest, I know that we must not lack patience.

I know that in a world divided, such as our today, salvation cannot be attained by one dramatic act.

I know that many steps will have to be taken over many months before the world can look at itself one day and truly realize that a new climate of mutually peaceful confidence is abroad in the world.

But I know, above all else, that we much start to take these steps—now.

The United States and its allies, Great Britain and France, have over the past months tried to take some of these steps. Let no one say that we shun the conference table.

On the record has long stood the request of the United States, Great Britain, and France to negotiate with the Soviet Union the problems of a divided Germany.

On that record has long stood the request of the same three nations to negotiate the problems of Korea.

Most recently, we have received from the Soviet Union what is in effect an expression of willingness to hold a Four Power meeting. Along with our allies, Great Britain and France, we were pleased to see that this note did not contain the unacceptable preconditions previously put forward.

As you already know from our joint Bermuda communiqué, the United States, Great Britain, and France have agreed promptly to meet with the Soviet Union.

The Government of the United States approaches this conference with hopeful sincerity. We will bend every effort of our minds to the single purpose of emerging from that conference with tangible results toward peace—the only true way of lessening international tension.

We never have, we never will, propose or suggest that the Soviet Union surrender what is rightfully theirs.

We will never say that the people of Russia are an enemy with whom we have no desire ever to deal or mingle in friendly and fruitful relationship.

On the contrary, we hope that this coming Conference may initiate a relationship with the Soviet Union which will eventually bring about a free inter mingling of the peoples of the east and of the west—the one sure, human way of developing the understanding required for confident and peaceful relations.

Instead of the discontent which is now settling upon Eastern Germany, occupied Austria, and countries of Eastern Europe, we seek a harmonious family of free European nations, with none a threat to the other, and least of all a threat to the peoples of Russia.

Beyond the turmoil and strife and misery of Asia, we seek peaceful opportunity for these peoples to develop their natural resources and to elevate their lives.

These are not idle works or shallow visions. Behind them lies a story of nations lately come to independence, not as a result of war, but through free grant or peaceful negotiation. There is a record, already written, of assistance gladly given by nations of the west to needy peoples, and to those suffering the temporary effects of famine, drought, and natural disaster.

These are deeds of peace. They speak more loudly than promises or protestations of peaceful intent.

But I do not wish to rest either upon the reiteration of past proposals or the restatement of past deeds. The gravity of the time is such that every new avenue of peace, no matter how dimly discernible, should be explored.

These is at least one new avenue of peace which has not yet been well explored—an avenue now laid out by the General Assembly of the United Nations.

In its resolution of November 18th, 1953 this General Assembly suggested—and I quote—"that the Disarmament Commission study the desirability of establishing a sub-committee consisting of representatives of the Powers principally involved, which should seek in private an acceptable solution . . . and report on such a solution to the General Assembly and to the Security Council not later than 1 September 1954."

The United States, heeding the suggestion of the General Assembly of the United Nations, is instantly prepared to meet privately with such other countries as may be "principally involved," to seek "an acceptable solution" to the atomic armaments race which over shadows not only the peace, but the very life, of the world.

We shall carry into these private or diplomatic talks a new conception.

The United States would seek more than the mere reduction or elimination of atomic materials for military purposes.

It is not enough to take this weapon out of the hands of the soldiers. It must be put into the hands of those who will know how to strip its military casing and adapt it to the arts of peace.

The United States knows that if the fearful trend of atomic military build up can be reversed, this greatest of destructive forces can be developed into a great boon, for the benefit of all mankind.

The United States knows that peaceful power from atomic energy is no dream of the future. That capability, already proved, is here—now—today. Who can doubt, if the entire body of the world's scientists and engineers had adequate amounts of fissionable material with which to test and develop their ideas, that this capability would rapidly be transformed into universal, efficient, and economic usage.

To hasten the day when fear of the atom will begin to disappear from the minds of people, and the governments of the East and West, there are certain steps that can be taken now.

I therefore make the following proposals:

The Governments principally involved, to the extent permitted by elementary prudence, to begin now and continue to make joint contributions from their stockpiles of normal uranium and fissionable materials to an international Atomic Energy Agency. We would expect that such an agency would be set up under the aegis of the United Nations.

The ratios of contributions, the procedures and other details would properly be within the scope of the "private conversations" I have referred to earlier.

The United states is prepared to under take these explorations in good faith. Any partner of the United States acting in the same good faith will find the United States a not unreasonable or ungenerous associate.

Undoubtedly initial and early contributions to this plan would be small in quantity. However, the proposal has the great virtue that it can be under taken without the irritations and mutual suspicions incident to any attempt to set up a completely acceptable system of world-wide inspection and control.

The Atomic Energy Agency could be made responsible for the impounding, storage, and protection of the contributed fissionable and other materials. The ingenuity of our scientists will provide special safe conditions under which such a bank of fissionable material can be made essentially immune to surprise seizure.

The more important responsibility of this Atomic Energy Agency would be to devise methods where by this fissionable material would be allocated to serve the peaceful pursuits of mankind. Experts would be mobilized to apply atomic energy to the needs of agriculture, medicine, and other peaceful activities. A special purpose would be to provide abundant electrical energy in the power-starved areas of the world. Thus the contributing powers would be dedicating some of their strength to serve the needs rather than the fears of mankind.

The United States would be more than willing—it would be proud to take up with others "principally involved" the development of plans where by such peaceful use of atomic energy would be expedited.

Of those "principally involved" the Soviet Union must, of course, be one.

I would be prepared to submit to the Congress of the United States, and with every expectation of approval, any such plan that would:

First—encourage world-wide investigation into the most effective peace time uses of fissionable material, and with the certainty that they had all the material needed for the conduct of all experiments that were appropriate;

Second—begin to diminish the potential destructive power of the world's atomic stockpiles;

Third—allow all peoples of all nations to see that, in this enlightened age, the great powers of the earth, both of the East and of the West, are interested in human aspirations first, rather than in building up the armaments of war;

Fourth—open up a new channel for peaceful discussion, and initiate at least a new approach to the many difficult problems that must be solved in both private and public conversations, if the world is to shake off the inertia imposed by fear, and is to make positive progress toward peace.

Against the dark background of the atomic bomb, the United Stats does not wish merely to present strength, but also the desire and the hope for peace.

The coming months will be fraught with fateful decisions. In this Assembly; in the capitals and military headquarters of the world; in the hearts of men every where, be they governors, or governed, may they be decisions which will lead this work out of fear and into peace.

To the making of these fateful decisions, the United States pledges before you—and therefore before the world—its determination to help solve the fearful atomic dilemma—to devote its entire heart and mind to find the way by which the miraculous inventiveness of man shall not be dedicated to his death, but consecrated to his life.

I again thank the delegates for the great honor they have done me, in inviting me to appear before them, and in listening to me so courteously. Thank you.

SIGNIFICANCE

Eisenhower's speech introduced, formally, the idea of using atomic energy as a conduit for economic development. His message to the United Nations (UN) and the world is clear: the United States alone holds the greatest stockpiles of atomic energy, and knows full well the implications of such power.

In acknowledging the role of Great Britain and Canada as possessors of atomic technology, Eisenhower implied a coalition that isolated the USSR. As the Cold War and the arms race converged, Eisenhower's declaration that the United States would come to the table for talks of stockpile reduction, and his specific mention of the various ways that the USSR had made concessions, spoke to a broader theme of controlled development of atomic technology.

His call for the creation of an International Atomic Energy Agency (IAEA), administered by the United Nations, came to fruition in 1957 with the unanimous support of all eighty-one members of the UN. The IAEA began as an organization that worked with UN member nations to monitor peaceful and secure atomic energy developments. The agency has three primary roles: verification of nuclear capability, safety monitoring, and supervision of technology transfer. In its early years, between 1958 and 1962, political ten-

U.S. President Dwight D. Eisenhower (lower right) addresses the public with his "Atoms for Peace" speech, which eventually led to the formation of the International Atomic Energy Agency. AP IMAGES

sions between the United States and the Soviet Union made IAEA's role difficult; after the Cuban Missile Crisis in 1962, however, the need for international negotiations and arms control between the two superpowers led to IAEA's increased diplomatic role.

In 1968, with the signing of the Treaty on the Non-Proliferation of Nuclear Weapons, IAEA became the primary international agency for monitoring compliance of this treaty, which limited nuclear technology development to Russia, the United States, Great Britain, France, and China. IAEA's role in helping countries develop economic uses of nuclear technology—such as nuclear power plants and irradiation of food supplies—spread over the next three decades.

Eisenhower's original goal—the creation of an international atomic energy regulatory body to help develop peaceful uses of atomic energy—resulted not only in the development and monitoring of these technologies, but also in the recognition that atomic energy as a weapon could take the world to the brink of annihilation. Between the Cuban Missile Crisis and "mutually assured destruction" (MAD), as the United States and the Soviet Union stockpiled greater numbers of weapons capable of greater destructive abilities, a political and existential crisis emerged. The IAEA's role in mediation and oversight was far greater than Eisenhower imagined, and yet his call for such an agency was prescient.

FURTHER RESOURCES

Books

Chernus, Ira. *Eisenhower's Atoms for Peace.* College Station, TX: Texas A&M University Press, 2002.

Web sites

International Atomic Energy Association. <http://www.iaea. org> (accessed March 16, 2006).

Eisenhower, Dwight D. "Atoms for Peace." *World Nuclear University.* <http://www.world-nuclear-university.org/ html/atoms_for_peace/index.htm> (accessed March 16, 2006).

1975 State of the Union Address

Arab Oil Embargo

Speech

By: Gerald R. Ford

Date: January 15, 1975

Source: Ford, Gerald R. "1975 State of the Union Address." <http://www.fordlibrarymuseum.gov/library/ speeches/750028.htm> (accessed February 23, 2006).

About the Author: Gerald R. Ford was sworn into the office of the President of the United States on August 9, 1974 after President Richard Nixon resigned. Ford served as the House Minority Leader from 1965 to 1973. He grew up in Grand Rapids, Michigan and starred on the University of Michigan football team. After completing his undergraduate studies, Ford attended Yale Law School. During World War II, he served in the U.S. Navy and earned the rank of lieutenant commander. Ford won the Republican nomination for the Presidency in 1976, but lost the election to Jimmy Carter.

INTRODUCTION

The Arab-Israeli conflict has affected international politics since the inception of the state of Israel in 1948. In the 1970s, the conflict reached global proportions as the oil-producing nations in the Arab world, operating as a cartel under the Organization of Petroleum Exporting Countries (OPEC), halted its production and supply of oil meant for the western countries. As a result, the western nations spiraled into a gas shortage. The significance of the Arab oil embargo of 1973 was more than political. The embargo forced nations to acknowledge their dependence on foreign oil, seek alternate energy resources, and enact public policies to reduce oil consumption.

At the close of World War II, the Zionist movement gained enough support for the creation of a Jewish homeland. By 1948, the Mandate for Palestine, by which the British had administered the region, was terminated by the United Nations (UN) Resolution 181. As a result, the Jewish inhabitants of the region declared their independence and the statehood of Israel. Arab nations rejected the state of Israel while western powers acknowledged the new country. After the British left the newly formed state, several Arab nations, including Egypt, Syria, Iraq, Lebanon, Jordan, and Saudi Arabia, declared war on Israel. Invasions by Egyptian, Syrian and Jordanian forces began the Israeli War of Independence. The armistice for this war, signed in 1949, partitioned additional land to Israel than originally agreed to by the United Nations resolution. By 1967, the Cold War between the United States and the Soviet Union was in full force. Many Arab countries enjoyed military and financial support from the Soviet Union, while the U.S., Britain, and France continued to support Israel. The 6-day war occurred in June of 1967 as a response to the

This New York city gas station was open on December 23, 1973, though President Nixon had suggested stations close on Sundays in an effort to alleviate oil shortages brought on by the 1973 Arab Oil Embargo. AP IMAGES

actions of Egyptian President Gamal Abdel Nasser who closed the straits of Tiran to Israeli shipping and expelled UN peacekeepers. In response, Israel launched attacks on the Egyptian air force and began an occupation of Sinai and Gaza, as well as the West Bank and Golan Heights. Tentative peace was established through UN Resolution 242. However, many Arabs, including those within the Palestinian Liberation Organization (PLO), rejected the terms of the resolution. As a result, on October 6, 1973, Egyptian and Syrian forces launched an attack on Israel during the Jewish holy day of atonement. Both the U.S. and the Soviet Union aided in supplying their respective allies with arms. In an effort to respond to the U.S. and western powers' support of Israel during this war, the oil-producing nations under the cartel of OPEC reduced their production of oil and halted their commerce with those nations—thus resulting in the Arab oil embargo of 1973.

Meanwhile, in the United States, several events and policy changes prior to the embargo led to an increased consumption of oil, which resulted in the embargo creating a deeper impact on the nation.

Policies designed to protect the environment as well as economic policies also led to and increased reliance on oil. Both the Clean Air Act and the Mine Safety Act created greater regulations that increased the cost to mine coal. As a result, the industry was unable to meet the growing demands for energy. In addition, local governments blocked the building of alternate energy resources, such as nuclear power, in campaigns known as "Not in My Back Yard." The federal government also created policies that affected the demand for oil. An oil import quota system, which was initially designed to reduce the amount of imported oil, included price controls. These price controls provided a disincentive for domestic investment in new reserves and the replacement of those depleted. The price controls also affected the production of natural gas. Before 1973, the U.S. regulated the natural gas market and kept the price artificially low by selling below market values. This reduced incentives for producers to open new fields. Consumers in regulated markets were forced to switch to oil due to a lack of supply.

Large, gas-hungry vehicles made up a sizable portion of this demand increase. In a 1974 position paper, the Environmental Protection Agency (EPA) cited that "of total increase in demand for gasoline in the past five years, two-thirds is attributable to additional automobiles being on the road. 23 percent is due to more miles being driven per car." According to the EPA, the demand for crude oil imports from Arab nations increased from 0.38 million barrels per day to 1.1 million barrels per day. This was due to the 1971–1972 overall increase by 69 percent of energy supplied by oil.

PRIMARY SOURCE

... Economic disruptions we and others are experiencing stem in part from the fact that the world price of petroleum has quadrupled in the last year. But in all honesty, we cannot put all of the blame on the oil-exporting nations. We, the United States, are not blameless. Our growing dependence upon foreign sources has been adding to our vulnerability for years and years, and we did nothing to prepare ourselves for such an event as the embargo of 1973.

During the 1960s, this country had a surplus capacity of crude oil which we were able to make available to our trading partners whenever there was a disruption of supply. This surplus capacity enabled us to influence both supplies and prices of crude oil throughout the world. Our excess capacity neutralized any effort at establishing an effective cartel, and thus the rest of the world was assured of adequate supplies of oil at reasonable prices.

By 1970, our surplus capacity had vanished, and as a consequence, the latent power of the oil cartel could emerge in full force. Europe and Japan, both heavily dependent on imported oil, now struggle to keep their economies in balance. Even the United States, our country, which is far more self-sufficient than most other industrial countries, has been put under serious pressure.

I am proposing a program which will begin to restore our country's surplus capacity in total energy. In this way, we will be able to assure ourselves reliable and adequate energy and help foster a new world energy stability for other major consuming nations.

But this Nation and, in fact, the world must face the prospect of energy difficulties between now and 1985. This program will impose burdens on all of us with the aim of reducing our consumption of energy and increasing our production. Great attention has been paid to the considerations of fairness, and I can assure you that the burdens will not fall more harshly on those less able to bear them.

I am recommending a plan to make us invulnerable to cutoffs of foreign oil. It will require sacrifices, but it—and this is most important—it will work.

I have set the following national energy goals to assure that our future is as secure and as productive as our past:

First, we must reduce oil imports by 1 million barrels per day by the end of this year and by 2 million barrels per day by the end of 1977.

Second, we must end vulnerability to economic disruption by foreign suppliers by 1985.

Third, we must develop our energy technology and resources so that the United States has the ability to supply a significant share of the energy needs of the free world by the end of this century.

To attain these objectives, we need immediate action to cut imports. Unfortunately, in the short term there are only a limited number of actions which can increase domestic supply. I will press for all of them.

I urge quick action on the necessary legislation to allow commercial production at the Elk Hills, California, Naval Petroleum Reserve. In order that we make greater use of domestic coal resources, I am submitting amendments to the Energy Supply and Environmental Coordination Act which will greatly increase the number of powerplants that can be promptly converted to coal.

Obviously, voluntary conservation continues to be essential, but tougher programs are needed—and needed now. Therefore, I am using Presidential powers to raise the fee on all imported crude oil and petroleum products. The crude oil fee level will be increased $1 per barrel on February 1, by $2 per barrel on March 1, and by $3 per barrel on April 1. I will take actions to reduce undue hardships on any geographical region. The foregoing are interim administrative actions. They will be rescinded when broader but necessary legislation is enacted.

To that end, I am requesting the Congress to act within 90 days on a more comprehensive energy tax program. It includes: excise taxes and import fees totaling $2 per barrel on product imports and on all crude oil; deregulation of new natural gas and enactment of a natural gas excise tax.

I plan to take Presidential initiative to decontrol the price of domestic crude oil on April 1. I urge the Congress to enact a windfall profits tax by that date to ensure that oil producers do not profit unduly.

The sooner Congress acts, the more effective the oil conservation program will be and the quicker the Federal revenues can be returned to our people.

I am prepared to use Presidential authority to limit imports, as necessary, to guarantee success.

I want you to know that before deciding on my energy conservation program, I considered rationing and higher gasoline taxes as alternatives. In my judgment, neither would achieve the desired results and both would produce unacceptable inequities.

A massive program must be initiated to increase energy supply to cut demand, and provide new standby emergency programs to achieve the independence we want by 1985. The largest part of increased oil production must come from new frontier areas on the Outer Continental Shelf and from the Naval Petroleum Reserve No. 4 in Alaska. It is the intent of this Administration to move ahead with exploration, leasing, and production on those frontier areas of the Outer Continental Shelf where the environmental risks are acceptable.

Use of our most abundant domestic resource—coal—is severely limited. We must strike a reasonable compromise on environmental concerns with coal. I am submitting Clean Air [Act] amendments which will allow greater coal use without sacrificing clean air goals.

I vetoed the strip mining legislation passed by the last Congress. With appropriate changes, I will sign a revised version when it comes to the White House.

I am proposing a number of actions to energize our nuclear power program. I will submit legislation to expedite nuclear leasing [licensing] and the rapid selection of sites.

In recent months, utilities have cancelled or postponed over 60 percent of planned nuclear expansion and 30 percent of planned additions to non-nuclear capacity. Financing problems for that industry are worsening. I am therefore recommending that the 1-year investment tax credit of 12 percent be extended an additional 2 years to specifically speed the construction of powerplants that do not use natural gas or oil. I am also submitting proposals for selective reform of State utility commission regulations.

To provide the critical stability for our domestic energy production in the face of world price uncertainty, I will request legislation to authorize and require tariffs, import quotas, or price floors to protect our energy prices at levels which will achieve energy independence.

Increasing energy supplies is not enough. We must take additional steps to cut long-term consumption. I therefore propose to the Congress: legislation to make thermal efficiency standards mandatory for all new buildings in the United States; a new tax credit of up to $150 for those homeowners who install insulation equipment; the establishment of an energy conservation program to help low-income families purchase insulation supplies; legislation to modify and defer automotive pollution standards for 5 years, which will enable us to improve automobile gas mileage by 40 percent by 1980.

These proposals and actions, cumulatively, can reduce our dependence on foreign energy supplies from 3 to 5 million barrels per day by 1985. To make the United States invulnerable to foreign disruption, I propose standby emergency legislation and a strategic storage program of 1 billion barrels of oil for domestic needs and 300 million barrels for national defense purposes.

I will ask for the funds needed for energy research and development activities. I have established a goal of 1 million barrels of synthetic fuels and shale oil production per day by 1985 together with an incentive program to achieve it.

I have a very deep belief in America's capabilities. Within the next 10 years, my program envisions: 200 major nuclear powerplants; 250 major new coal mines; 150 major coal-fired powerplants; 30 major new [oil] refineries; 20 major new synthetic fuel plants; the drilling of many thousands of new oil wells; the insulation of 18 million homes; and the manufacturing and the sale of millions of new automobiles, trucks, and buses that use much less fuel....

SIGNIFICANCE

The Arab oil embargo lasted only one year; however, the price of oil had nearly quadrupled. As a result, car manufacturers began to develop smaller, more energy-efficient vehicles. Standards were created for fuel efficiency as well as efficiency stickers placed on vehicles. Japanese cars were imported as they already met the standards for emissions and efficiency. In addition, Congress set a speed limit of 55 miles per hour on the highway, leading to better fuel efficiency as well as fewer fatalities. Consumers were encouraged to develop energy saving practices, such as setting their thermostats to 65° F (18° C) during the winter.

The oil shortage also created a debate on the role of government in ensuring an energy supply. Many of the price controls and regulations in place before the embargo began deterred the development or expansion of alternate forms of energy supply. Plans such as the oil import quota system and the price controls on natural gas were ended. President Nixon developed a strategic oil reserve to be used in times of duress and implemented the Department of Energy, a cabinet-level department charged with developing and implementing a national energy strategy.

FURTHER RESOURCES
Periodicals

Feldman, David Lewis. "How Far Have We Come? (Revisiting the Energy Crisis)." *Environment* (May 1, 1995).

Web sites

Energy Information Administration. "25th Anniversary of the 1973 Oil Embargo." *Energy Information Administration.* <http://www.eia.doe.gov/emeu/25opec/anniversary.html> (accessed March 2, 2006).

EPA Office of Public Affairs. "EPA's Position Paper on the Energy Crisis." *Environmental Protection Agency.* <http://www.epa.gov/history/topics/energy/01.htm> (accessed February 23, 2006).

Energy Policy Act of 1992

Legislation

By: United States Congress

Date: 1992.

Source: U.S. Congress. "Energy Policy Act of 1992." Washington, D.C.: 1992.

About the Author: The U.S. Congress is the nation's primary law-making body. In important areas such as energy conservation, Congress regularly revisits previous legislation in order to bring it up to date and to ensure that it is meeting its objectives.

INTRODUCTION

The U.S. government plays a central role in determining the amount of energy the nation uses. By raising fuel taxes, the government can potentially reduce the amount of fuel used and encourage citizens to make more efficient choices. By offering tax credits for solar or wind power, the government can encourage homeowners to install solar water heaters or wind generators.

One of the most direct ways the government influences energy usage is by establishing fuel efficiency standards for U.S. automobiles. Following the Arab oil embargo of 1973–74, Congress enacted the Corporate Average Fuel Economy (CAFE) standards for passenger cars and light trucks. These standards set a minimum average fuel efficiency level for any company selling cars in North America. If a company's "fleet" of vehicles fail to meet the required level, the Environment Protection Agency (EPA) levies a fine against the automaker.

While EPA fuel standards have improved automobile mileage significantly since 1975, progress has slowed in recent years, due largely to an increase in

sales of light trucks, which have lower mileage standards than cars. Revised rules proposed in 2005 are expected to improve light truck mileage beginning in 2008.

In 1992, Congress passed the Energy Policy Act. This act was intended to create a unified energy policy which would help make the United States less dependent on foreign sources of energy. The Act also set standards for energy production, nuclear waste disposal, and a variety of other administrative matters related to energy production and distribution.

One of the act's major initiatives encouraged efforts to make the United States less dependent on traditional fuel sources. This portion of the Act, labeled Title V, instructed the Secretary of Transportation to create standards similar to CAFE which would require set percentages of vehicles purchased by public and private fleet operators (such as city bus services) to be so-called "dual fuel" vehicles, able to run on ethanol (made from corn), bio-diesel (made partly from soy oil), natural gas, or regular gasoline. These requirements followed a gradually increasing scale as the law was phased in over several years.

PRIMARY SOURCE

TITLE V—AVAILABILITY AND USE OF REPLACEMENT FUELS, ALTERNATIVE FUELS, AND ALTERNATIVE FUELED PRIVATE VEHICLES
SEC. 501. MANDATE FOR ALTERNATIVE FUEL PROVIDERS. 42 USC 13251.

(a) In general

(1) The Secretary shall, before January 1, 1994, issue regulations requiring that of the new light duty motor vehicles acquired by a covered person described in paragraph (2), the following percentages shall be alternative fueled vehicles for the following model years:

(A) 30 percent for model year 1996.

(B) 50 percent for model year 1997.

(C) 70 percent for model year 1998.

(D) 90 percent for model year 1999 and thereafter.

(2) For purposes of this section, a person referred to in paragraph (1) is —

(A) a covered person whose principal business is producing, storing, refining, processing, transporting, distributing, importing, or selling at wholesale or retail any alternative fuel other than electricity;

(B) a non-Federal covered person whose principal business is generating, transmitting, importing, or selling at wholesale or retail electricity; or

(C) a covered person - (i) who produces, imports, or produces and importsin combination, an average of 50,000 barrels per day or more of petroleum; and(ii) a substantial portion of whose business is producing alternative fuels.

(3)

(A) In the case of a covered person described in paragraph (2) with more than one affiliate, division, or other business unit, only an affiliate, division, or business unit which is substantially engaged in the alternative fuels business (as determined by theSecretary by rule) shall be subject to this subsection.

(B) No covered person or affiliate, division, or other business unit ofsuch person whose principal business is - (i) transforming alternative fuels into a product that is not an alternative fuel; or (ii) consuming alternative fuels as a feedstock or fuel in the manufacture of a product that is not an alternative fuel, shall be subject to this subsection.

(4) The vehicles purchased pursuant to this section shall be operated solely on alternative fuels except when operating in an area where the appropriate alternative fuel is unavailable.

(5) Regulations issued under paragraph (1) shall provide for the prompt exemption by the Secretary, through a simple and reasonable process, from the requirements of paragraph (1) of any covered person, in whole or in part, if such person demonstrates to the satisfaction of the Secretary that —

(A) alternative fueled vehicles that meet the normalrequirements and practices of the principal business of thatperson are not reasonably available for acquisition; or

(B) alternative fuels that meet the normal requirementsand practices of the principal business of that person are notavailable in the area in which the vehicles are to be operated.

(b) Revisions and extensions With respect to model years 1997 and thereafter, the Secretary may —

1. revise the percentage requirements under subsection (a)(1) of this section downward, except that under no circumstances shall the percentage requirement for a model year be less than 20 percent; and

2. extend the time under subsection (a)(1) of this section for up to 2 model years.

(c) Option for electric utilities The Secretary shall, within 1 year after October 24, 1992, issue regulations requiring

that, in the case of a covered person whose principal business is generating, transmitting, importing, or selling at wholesale or retail electricity, the requirements of subsection (a)(1) of this section shall not apply until after December 31, 1997, with respect to electric motor vehicles. Any covered person described in this subsectionwhich plans to acquire electric motor vehicles to comply with the requirements of this section shall so notify the Secretary before January 1, 1996.

(d) Report to Congress The Secretary shall, before January 1, 1998, submit a report to the Congress providing detailed information on actions taken to carry out this section, and the progressmade and problems encountered thereunder.

SIGNIFICANCE

While the Energy Policy Act of 1992 had far-reaching effects in many areas, its net impact on gasoline usage was almost nonexistent. In 2001, testimony before the Senate Finance Committee, Jim Wells, the Director of Natural Resources and the Environment, noted extremely limited progress in increasing the number of alternative fuel vehicles in use. As of 2000, the number was around 1 million, or about 0.2 percent of total vehicles in service. The report cited the low price of oil, lack of alternative fuel infrastructure (such as fueling stations), and the generally high purchase price of alternative fuel vehicles.

In the years since 1992, a variety of tax incentives have been offered to encourage alternative fuel use. Many new automobiles are able to burn E85, an ethanol/gasoline mixture, without modification. However, E85 use remains low despite this capability.

FURTHER RESOURCES
Books

Lerner, Steve. *Eco-Pioneers: Practical Visionaries Solving Today's Environmental Problems.* Boston: The MIT Press, 1997.

Perrin, Noel. *Solo: Life with an Electric Car.* New York: W. W. Norton & Company, 1992.

Sperling, Daniel. *Future Drive: Electric Vehicles and Sustainable Transportation.* Washington, D.C.: Island Press, 1995.

Web sites

"Is Your Vehicle E85 Compatible? For All the Right Reasons." *National Ethanol Vehicle Coalition.* <http://www.e85fuel.com> (accessed March 8, 2006).

"Energy Policy Act (EPAct)." *U.S. Department of Energy.* <http://www.eere.energy.gov/vehiclesandfuels/epact> (accessed March 8, 2006).

Long lines form at the gas station, proving the nation's dependency on traditional fuels and vulnerability to disruptions, similar to the short-lived pipeline closure in Phoenix, AZ, on August 20, 2003. AP IMAGES

"Flex-Fuel Vehicles." *www.fueleconomy.gov*. <http://www.fueleconomy.gov/feg/flextech.shtml> (accessed March 8, 2006).

"The Dam"

Book excerpt

By: Deirdre Chetham

Date: 2002

Source: Chetham, Deirdre. "The Dam." *Before the Deluge: The Vanishing World of the Yangtze's Three Gorges*. New York: Palgrave Macmillan, 2002.

About the Author: Deirdre Chetham is the executive director of the Harvard University Asia Center and a former director of the Fairbank Center for East Asian Research, also at Harvard. She earned a baccalaureate degree in East Asian Languages and Civilizations from Harvard and did graduate work in Chinese Studies at Columbia University. She became interested in the Three Gorges area while serving as a guest lecturer on Yangtze River cruise ships during the early 1980s. Chetham subsequently spent time working for the U.S. Foreign Service in Burma, Beijing, and East Berlin before returning to Harvard in 1996.

INTRODUCTION

The Three Gorges Dam in China is the largest in the world. It stretches more than a mile across the Yangtze River and rises 600 feet (183 meters) above the valley floor. When full, the reservoir it impounds stretches 350 miles (563 kilometers) upriver and contains nearly 1.4 trillion cubic feet (39.6 billion cubic meters) of water. The Three Gorges Dam is a concrete gravity dam. Unlike curved concrete arch

The series of three narrow river gorges that give the dam its name have attracted the attention of dam builders since the early twentieth century. A dam was first proposed for the area in 1919, and plans were drawn up by Chinese, Japanese, American, and Soviet engineers over the next sixty years. The Chinese government began construction of a smaller dam, the Gezhouba Dam, in 1970. Construction and engineering problems led to a suspension of activities in 1972, and the Gezhouba Dam was not completed until 1989. The main Three Gorges Dam was approved in 1992 and construction began in 1994. The dam was completed in 2003, at which time the reservoir was partially filled and the first electricity generated. Final project completion and electricity generation at full capacity is scheduled for 2009.

Aerial view of the Three Gorges Dam, which is only partially complete, and already has water levels of 135 meters. AP IMAGES

PRIMARY SOURCE

The groundbreaking ceremony for the Three Gorges Dam was held December 14, 1994. After years of discussion and postponement, actually digging a hole in the ground for the dam meant far more than all the approvals and votes and study papers of the past forty years. During the summer and fall of 1994, thousands of peasants from Sandouping left their homes because of the Three Gorges Dam and went off to new villages and towns and factory jobs, and early in 1995, iron and steel bridges and gates, concrete walls and deep passageways began to emerge out of the gargantuan holes and dirt piles. A seventeen-mile road to Yichang, with seven miles of bridges and tunnels and a price tag of U.S. $110 million, cut through the mountains of Xiling Gorge. Yellow and red bulldozers and jeeps rumbled back and forth, still looking odd and out of place to people sailing by below. From opposite banks, the two ends of what would become the first bridge in the gorges stretched out to reach one another. At 2,950 feet, it is the longest suspension bridge in China, except for the Tsing Ma airport bridge connecting Hong Kong to Lantau Island, completed in 1997.

Three years after the groundbreaking, Chinese President Jiang Zemin and Premier Li Peng took part in the celebration to mark the damming of the river and the opening of a diversion channel that would permit river traffic to continue without interruption during construction on the riverbed. The diversion of the river, which ended the first phase of construction of the project and allowed work on the actual dam site to begin, had originally been planned for 1998, but the date was moved up so that this event and Hong Kong's return to China could take place in the same year. A local publication described the event:

"On November 8th, 1997 a slight fog filled the Xiling Gore and a warm wind blew gently. At nine o'clock,

dams such as Hoover Dam, which transfer the weight of the water to rock at the edges of the dam, gravity dams rely upon their great mass to resist the weight of the water behind them. Designed for both hydroelectric power generation and flood control, the Three Gorges will ultimately use twenty-six turbines to generate 18.2 million kilowatts of electricity, about one-ninth of China's electricity. The estimated project cost was approximately $25 billion.

Hydroelectric power is generated by using flowing water to drive turbines and generators as the water falls to a lower elevation, much like harnessing the energy of a waterfall. The advantage of a dam and reservoir is that water can be stored when the demand for electricity is low and released to generate electricity when the demand is high. One of the benefits of the Three Gorges Dam is that it will reduce the amount of coal burned to generate electricity, which causes air pollution problems in China. A second benefit is that the dam will decrease the danger of floods, which are estimated to have killed 300,000 people along the Yangtze during the twentieth century. Floodwater is stored in the reservoir and then released slowly over time. Finally, the dam will make river navigation safer and easier by creating a large lake and locks.

Premier Li Peng ordered the start of the closure at the work site near the dragon's mouth. Three signal flares sent up by the vice-general rose to the sky, and instantly trucks on the four embankments of the upper and lower coffer dams approached the dragon's mouth like powerful lions. More than 4,000 giant loading trucks poured stones into the dragons' mouth, like thunder. The dragon's mouth was narrowed to 30m, 20m, 15m, 5m. . . . The dam site had a grand, festive atmosphere. An enormous five-star red flag made up of woven blankets covered a space of 1,080 square meters and looked magnificent from the reviewing stand."

In his speech that afternoon, President Jiang Zemin emphasized the benefits of the dam and extolled China's long and successful history of combating nature.

Since the dawn of history, the Chinese nation has been engaged in the great feat of conquering, developing, and exploiting nature. The legend of the mythical bird Jingwei determined to fill the sea with pebbles, the Foolish Old Man resolved to move the mountains standing in his way, and the tale of the Great Yu who harnessed the Great Floods are just some of the examples of the Chinese people's indomitable spirit in successfully conquering nature. The scale and overall benefits of the water conservancy and hydropower project we are building today on the Three Gorges of the Yangtze River, which have no parallel in the world, will greatly promote the development of our national economy and prove to be of lasting service to present and future generations. It also embodies the great industrious and dauntless spirit of the Chinese nation and displays the daring vision of the Chinese people for new horizons and a better future in the course of their reform and opening up.

If you ask people in the gorges what they think about the dam, the most common first answer is "it will be very big!" (bao da!). If you wonder what the area will be like once the dam is finished or how life will change, responses vary but reflect the widespread belief that most people in the cities will be better off, and that many in the countryside will not. Whatever does happen, and expectations for the future tend to be vague here, everyone agrees that it will be out of their control. Though where everyone in the way of the water will go and how this happens is crucial to the dam's success or failure, many young people project a deep indifference. "We'll all be gone," says a young woman in her early twenties, sucking on a purple popsicle outside a shop in Shibao Block, "and it doesn't matter." "It will be fun when we all move" states a chambermaid from the Wushan Hotel with enthusiasm. Pressed to explain why, she giggles and says everything will be new. The opinion of a local schoolteacher traveling third class on a local ferry is that the dam will cause widespread hardship but is necessary to bring economic development. He sees

no other choice. "The people are bitterly poor and we have to do something." An assistant dockmaster in Zigui is more fatalistic and fed up. "Who knows what the dam will do in the long run, or what will become of the people. It's the cadres who make the decisions and take the money and work things out to suit themselves." The refrain from the local travel service is consistently and officially positive. Despite the tremendous cultural loss, the local offices of the China International Travel Service tout the enhanced scenery that will result when the water level is raised. A big lake will be more beautiful, and once-inaccessible spots will become easy-to-reach tourist destinations on newly created rivers.

The Three Gorges Dam will certainly be big. At the height of 607 feet, it will be about as tall as a 60-story building, and stretch 1.45 miles across the Yangtze, five times as long as the Hoover Dam. Twenty-six huge turbines will generate 18.2 million kilowatts of energy, comparable to the output of eighteen nuclear power plants and eight times greater than that of the Aswan Dam in Egypt. The reservoir's water level will rise to 574 feet, with an average increase in the water level within the gorges of about 290 feet, creating a 360-mile reservoir stretching from the dam site to Chongqing. About the length of Lake Superior, this will be the largest man-made body of water in the world, with a capacity of 11 trillion gallons. Once the Wuhan Bridge is somehow altered to allow taller ships to pass underneath it, 10,000-ton vessels will be able to sail through twin 65-foot-high five-stage locks, assisted in their passage by the highest ship elevator in the world. Construction of the dam will require over 10 billion pounds of cement, 4.24 billion pounds of rolled steel, and over 56 million cubic feet of timber. Two billion cubic feet of rock were blasted away to carve out space for the massive locks alone; 240 square miles of land will be flooded, submerging at least thirteen cities, 140 towns, 1,350 villages, 657 factories, and approximately 74,000 acres of cultivated land under about 300 feet of water. Some 1.2 million people may eventually be moved away from those towns, factories, and farms.

Although each of the Three Gorges will be affected by the new dam, as will the towns and countryside as far away as Chongqing, no place has or will suffer greater change than Xiling Gorge, the easternmost part of which will be totally destroyed. In the fifth century, Li Daoyuan, a scholar of the Northern Wei dynasty wrote,

"About fifty kilometers east of the Yellow Cow shoal is the mouth of the Xiling Gorge. Here, the landscape features high peaks and winding waterways, the flanking mountains being so high that sunshine can filter in only at midday and moonlight can come only at midnight. The precipitous cliffs tower thousands of feet and bear colorful streaks with myriad images. Ancient and tall trees abound.

Apart from the singing streams, one can hear clearly the echoing wails of monkeys inhabiting the mountains."

For 1,500 years, this remained almost unchanged, and in the space of a decade it has become unrecognizable.

The numbers of tons of earth do not begin to convey the enormity of the construction and destruction, the walls of concrete as high as skyscrapers in the midst of what will soon be remembered only from old photos. The sounds are different too. The moneys are long gone, and so are the shouts of the boatmen, for it has become too dangerous for sampans and other small craft to maneuver around the dredges and cranes, and the gurgling of the river has been drowned out by the rhythmic slam of pressure drills. On one side of the riverbank, slogans in huge red characters declare, *Yiliu guanli, yiliu zhiliang, yiliu shigong, wenming jiansbe* (Top-rate management, top-rate quality, top-rate workmanship, and civilized construction), on the other, *Kaifa sanxia, fazban changjiang!* (Open the Three Gorges, develop the Yangtze!).

Worldwide, there are now over one hundred dams with heights over one hundred meters (equal to 328 feet). Their reservoirs cover more than 230,000 square miles, and have a total water capacity of 212 billion cubic feet, equivalent to 15 percent of the annual runoff of the world's rivers. With the exception of the Zaire, the Amazon, and rivers flowing into the Arctic, all of the earth's thirty largest rivers have been dammed; these include the Ganges, Panama, Tocantis, Columbia, Zambezi, Niger, Danube, Nile, and Indus. The Three Gorges Dam will generate 50 percent more power than the Itaipu Dam in Paraguay, currently the world's largest dam. Despite a worldwide trend against building mega-dams, a consequence of the environmental damage and social problems resulting from many of the projects listed above, the Chinese government views the Three Gorges Dam as the most effective method of energy generation and flood control along the Yangtze, as well as a way to improve transportation to the interior of China and jump-start the economy in one of the country's poorest regions.

By 2009, the dam should provide 10 percent of China's total electric power supply, but most of the newly generated power will go to the eastern cities and provinces of the Yangtze River delta. Power originally designated for Chongqing will instead be sold to Guangzhou, and any deficiency in Chongqing will be made up by the Ertan Dam in southwestern Sichuan. The Three Gorges region will receive little of the electricity and, at least for the time being, has little need of it, for there has been a power glut in most of Sichuan since the mid-1990s, the result of increased production by small generating stations and the closure of many large state-run factories. Nonetheless, blackouts and brownouts are still common, mainly because of unequal distribution rather than lack of supply. Even if electricity from the Three Gorges were to become available locally, it would not necessarily be welcome. Many county officials do not want electricity from the dam, for they fear it will result in the closure of local power-generating stations, and consequently the loss of tax revenue, greater unemployment, and generally higher electricity rates.

Though some foreign calculations run up to U.S. $30 billion and higher, in early 2001 the Chinese government put the anticipated cost of the dam at 180 billion yuan (U.S. $21.74 billion), almost all of which is coming from domestic sources. This is 23.9 billion yuan (U.S. $2.89 billion) less than the 203.9 billion yuan (U.S. 24.63 billion) predicted in 1994. One hundred billion yuan, or close to 50 percent of the original estimate, is being raised directly from a .7 fen (.08 U.S. cents) per-kilowatt tax levied on electricity on all homes and businesses in developed regions of China. (Less-developed areas are charged .3 fen and the poorest counties are exempt.) Revenue from the Gezhouba Dam is providing 25 percent of the funding. A ten-year, 30 billion yuan (U.S. $3.6 billion) loan was granted by the China Development Bank, established in 1996 to fund state-owned enterprises and major infrastructure projects, including, in particular, the Three Gorges Dam. The remainder of the financing comes from export credits and corporate bonds, some of which have been purchased by U.S. financial institutions despite significant opposition and pressure from American environmental activists. In 2003, when the first turbines begin generating energy, the Three Gorges project will begin contributing to its own support and will eventually pay for about 7.5 percent of the total cost. While China had originally hoped for outside financing, the World Bank and other international financial institutions declined to provide assistance because of concerns about the environmental impact of the dam. Financial investment from the United States has been limited compared to that from Europe and Asia because of a 1996 decision by the Export-Import Bank of the United States not to offer credit guarantees (generally required by China) to American companies wishing to provide equipment or services to the Three Gorges project. Despite this, U.S. companies, either acting directly or through overseas subsidiaries, have still managed to do over U.S. $100 million worth of business related to the project, and there has been no shortage of interest from major engineering and construction companies throughout the world.

In part to simplify the administration of central government and other funds coming into the Sichuan side of the gorges, as well as to coordinate the population relocations and infrastructure development, in 1997 the city of Chongqing was elevated to the level of a municipality, like Beijing, Atianjin, and Shanghai, and enlarged to include the counties of the Three Gorges as far east as the Hubei border. Chongqing municipality, no longer a part of Sichuan province, now reports directly to the central government. Wanxian, which had administrative responsibility for most of the Three Gorges counties from 1992 to 1997, was renamed Wanzhou, or Wan district (though many people still call it Wanxian), in 1998. Also referred to as the Wanzhou Resettlement Development District *(Wanzbou Yimin Kaifa Qu)*, it includes Fengjie, Wushan, Wuxi, Yunyang, Kaixian, and Zhongxian counties, and reports to the Chongqing government.

The biggest question about the dam is whether or not it will be successful in reducing flooding in the middle reaches of the river, where most of the worst floods occur and the lives and livelihoods of hundreds of thousands of people living behind the Jingzhou Dike on the flat farmland of Hubei are threatened. Such floods happen during the summer rainy season when there is a sudden infusion of water from tributaries, usually the Han and Huai rivers near Wuhan, and the Yangtze is already rising rapidly as melting snow swells its uppermost regions. The Yangtze flows from west to east. In late spring and summer, rainfall along the river moves in the opposite direction, from east to west. Heavy rains often fall in central China, in Hubei and Sichuan, in mid-summer, coinciding with the time when the Yangtze is already at its highest. Several situations can lead to catastrophic floods: excess water entering the Yangtze from its tributaries, too much water flowing from the upper Yangtze above Chongqing into the gorges and the middle reaches of the river below, or a combination of these circumstances. While concurring that the Three Gorges Dam will have some impact on flooding by limiting the flow out of the reservoir area, and thus reducing the overall volume of water below Yichang, many experts argue that a dam in this location can only be effective in preventing disasters caused by flooding in the upper reaches. The flood of 1870, considered a ''thousand-year flood'' (a flood which is so rare that statistically it should occur only once every thousand years), is an example of what happens when there is far too much water pouring into both the upper Yangtze near Chongqing and the gorges and the middle Yangtze (from the tributaries) simultaneously. A dam located in Sandouping might have reduced the damage caused by a flood of this sort by containing the water from the upper reaches of the river in the reservoir.

The hundred-year floods of 1954 and 1998, in contrast, were the result of water pouring into the Yangtze from tributaries below Yichang. Critics claim that when the tributaries are the source of flooding, lowering the reservoir's level above the tributaries, in anticipation of the increased volume of water up-river, will not significantly improve the situation, certainly not enough to justify the building of a huge dam with so many other problems and potentially negative consequences. Supporters claim that

it will. A reservoir provides flood control by working like a sink, allowing water that enters it to be drained at a controlled rate, rather than overflowing unexpectedly. Before the rainy season, the reservoir level can be lowered, providing additional storage capacity that will prevent flooding in this region and below the dam. If, however, the increase in the water level below the dam from the tributaries in the middle reaches of the Yangtze is so great as to cause flooding, a dam above may reduce the scope the disaster, but it will not prevent it.

SIGNIFICANCE

Despite its projected benefits, the Three Gorges Dam has been a controversial project. It has flooded cities and towns along a stretch of the Yangtze River known for its scenic beauty, requiring more than one million people to be relocated. Prime farmland along the river bottom will be flooded and the remaining land above the reservoir is too steep for farming. Critics of the project also point out that the Yangtze functions as a sewer, carrying human and industrial waste downstream. Once the dam is completed, it may impound a reservoir of heavily polluted water. The Yangtze also carries a heavy load of silt, which will eventually fill the reservoir if it is not continuously removed. A final concern is that poor construction standards may create an unsafe dam that could fail catastrophically. In response to environmental and safety concerns, both the World Bank and the U.S. Export-Import Bank refused to issue loans and loan guarantees for the project.

The Three Gorges Dam is controversial in large part because it was built during a time when the wisdom of large dams in general was being called into question. Had the technology, capital, and expertise existed to build the dam when it was first proposed in 1919, it would have likely been regarded an engineering triumph. Although John Muir and others protested construction of the Hetch Hetchy Dam in Yosemite National Park during the early years of the twentieth century, there was virtually no opposition to major projects such as the Hoover Dam during the middle twentieth century. Unanticipated environmental problems after construction of the Aswan Dam in Egypt, which disrupted the beneficial flooding of the Nile River, and an increasing interest in environmental issues during the late twentieth and early twenty-first centuries have made all large dam projects controversial.

Controversies involving large dams are difficult to resolve because they typically include intangibles such as the loss of scenic areas and archeological sites. Can a

Construction of the Three Gorges Dam, although seeming necessary to China's developement, has several repercussions, including submersion of whole or partial cities along the riverbanks such as Fengdu, shown here in 2005. © BOB SACHA/CORBIS

future reduction in air pollution and lung disease be fairly weighed against the value of scenic beauty, cultural heritage, or the disruption of lives in inundated areas? Other difficulties include accurate projection of benefits such as flood control, which involve complicated calculations and many assumptions, so that they can be compared to project costs.

FURTHER RESOURCES
Web sites

British Geomorphological Research Group. "The Big Dam Debate, Case Study: Three Gorges Dam, China." <http://www.bgrg.org/pages/education/alevel/tgd> (accessed January 27, 2006.

Public Broadcasting System. "Great Wall Across the Yangtze." <http://www.pbs.org/itvs/greatwall> (accessed January 27, 2006.

WGBH Educational Foundation. "Building Big: Databank: Three Gorges Dam." <http://www.pbs.org/wgbh/buildingbig/wonder/structure/three_gorges.html> (accessed January 27, 2006.

Energy Policy Act of 2005

Sec. 1342, Sec. 30B. Establishes Tax Credits for Alternative Fuel Automobiles

Legislation

By: United States Congress

Date: 2005

Source: U.S. Congress. "Energy Policy Act of 2005." Sec. 1342, Sec. 30B. Washington, D.C.: 2005.

About the Author: The Congress of the United States was established by Article 1 of the U.S. Constitution of 1787. It is the legislative arm of the U.S. Federal Government.

INTRODUCTION

Public Law 109–58, commonly known as the Energy Policy Act of 2005, consists of an introduction

This 1997 Honda Civic GX is one of the cleanest vehicles with an internal combustion engine because it operates on natural gas rather than gasoline. This fact qualifies it as the type of car needed for fleet customers who must buy alternative fuel vehicles. AP IMAGES

and sixteen sections, known as titles, that occupy more than 1,700 pages of text and cover a broad range of energy issues during the early years of the twenty-first century. Its full title is "An Act to Ensure Jobs for Our Future with Secure, Affordable, and Reliable Energy." The act includes provisions such as incentives to increase domestic oil and gas exploration, the promotion of nuclear power and hydropower, advanced research and development, tax credits to encourage hybrid automobiles, and bureaucratic maneuvering such as the authorization of an additional Assistant Secretary of Energy.

The Energy Policy Act of 2005 is also notable for controversial items that were originally included but later removed. One of those items was a provision that would have eliminated liabilities for manufacturers of methyl tertiary butyl ether (MTBE), a chemical that increases the oxygen content of gasoline to help it burn more completely and reduce automotive emissions. MTBE in low concentrations can render groundwater undrinkable by adding an unpleasant odor and taste.

Although the Environmental Protection Agency (EPA) has not yet established a safe level for MTBE in drinking water, there is some evidence to suggest that it may be a carcinogen in high concentrations. A second controversial provision would have allowed oil exploration in a portion of the Artic National Wildlife Refuge along the northern coast of Alaska. Some estimates suggest that the area, which is near the active oilfields of Prudhoe Bay and the Alaskan North Slope, may contain significant amounts of oil and gas. Opponents of drilling, however, maintain that oil exploration and production has the potential to cause significant environmental damage to a nearly pristine and intact ecosystem.

The Congressional Budget Office (CBO) estimated that the act would increase federal spending between 2006 and 2015 by $1.6 billion. At the same time, the CBO estimated that tax revenues over the same period would fall by about $12 billion.

Title I of the act mandates energy conservation in Federal buildings, the installation of meters on Federal buildings, and increased procurement of energy-efficient products for government use, specifying a 20 percent reduction in government agency energy consumption by the year 2015. This portion of the act also authorizes energy and home weatherization assistance for low-income residents, and extends daylight savings time to begin the second Sunday in March and end the first Sunday in November.

Title II concerns renewable energy, including increased use of solar cells on federal buildings, grants to increase the use of forest products for energy generation, leasing of public lands for geothermal energy production, and the installation of fish passages in hydroelectric dams.

Titles III through V involve fossil fuels. This portion of the act authorizes an increase the national Strategic Petroleum Reserve, exempts oil and gas producers from some provisions of the Clean Water Act, authorizes expenditures to develop environmentally clean methods of coal use such as coal gasification, and streamlines the procedures for energy exploration and development on tribal lands.

Title VI is devoted to nuclear energy, including an extension of the Price-Anderson Act to provide compensation to victims of nuclear power plant accidents, subsidizes the owners of new nuclear power plants, prohibits the export of nuclear materials to countries that support terrorism, and instructs the Nuclear Regulatory Commission to evaluate the security of licensed nuclear facilities. It also extends the protection of so-called whistleblowers who report problems within the Department of Energy and the Nuclear Regulatory Commission.

Title VII pertains to automobiles and their fuels. It modifies a previous federal law to include federal agency purchasing guidelines for alternative fuel and hybrid vehicles. Perhaps more significantly with regard to the public, it revises the Corporate Average Fuel Economy (CAFE) standards that automobile manufacturers must achieve across their lines of products.

Title XII of the act pertains to electricity. It creates an independent board to improve the reliability of the electrical transmission infrastructure and promulgate standards, adopts new procedures for electric power line location, authorizes punishment of those who manipulate electricity markets (including specific provisions for the termination of contracts with the bankrupt energy company Enron), and specifies a new procedure for the relicensing of hydroelectric dams.

Title XV is also related to automobiles. It mandates the increased use of ethanol derived from agricultural products and strengthens underground fuel storage tank inspection requirements (leaking underground storage tanks have historically been a significant source of groundwater contamination). Title XV also bans the use of the fuel additive methyl tertiary-butyl ether (commonly known as MTBE) after 2014 and commissions the National Academy of Sciences to prepare a report on MTBE by 2013.

Other sections (titles) of the act include tax incentives for energy-saving activities, training programs for energy company employees, encouragement of minority students to pursue technical careers, and revision of royalty payments for offshore oil and gas leases.

PRIMARY SOURCE

SEC. 30B. ALTERNATIVE MOTOR VEHICLE CREDIT.

(a) Allowance of Credit—There shall be allowed as a credit against the tax imposed by this chapter for the taxable year an amount equal to the sum of—

(1) the new qualified fuel cell motor vehicle credit determined under subsection (b),

(2) the new advanced lean burn technology motor vehicle credit determined under subsection (c),

(3) the new qualified hybrid motor vehicle credit determined under subsection (d), and

(4) the new qualified alternative fuel motor vehicle credit determined under subsection (e).

(b) New Qualified Fuel Cell Motor Vehicle Credit—

(1) IN GENERAL—For purposes of subsection (a), the new qualified fuel cell motor vehicle credit determined under this subsection with respect to a new qualified fuel cell motor vehicle placed in service by the taxpayer during the taxable year is—

(A) $8,000 ($4,000 in the case of a vehicle placed in service after December 31, 2009), if such vehicle has a gross vehicle weight rating of not more than 8,500 pounds,

(B) $10,000, if such vehicle has a gross vehicle weight rating of more than 8,500 pounds but not more than 14,000 pounds,

(C) $20,000, if such vehicle has a gross vehicle weight rating of more than 14,000 pounds but not more than 26,000 pounds, and

(D) $40,000, if such vehicle has a gross vehicle weight rating of more than 26,000 pounds.

(2) INCREASE FOR FUEL EFFICIENCY—(A) IN GENERAL—The amount determined under paragraph (1)(A) with

respect to a new qualified fuel cell motor vehicle which is a passenger automobile or light truck shall be increased by—

    (i) $1,000, if such vehicle achieves at least 150 percent but less than 175 percent of the 2002 model year city fuel economy,

    (ii) $1,500, if such vehicle achieves at least 175 percent but less than 200 percent of the 2002 model year city fuel economy,

    (iii) $2,000, if such vehicle achieves at least 200 percent but less than 225 percent of the 2002 model year city fuel economy,

    (iv) $2,500, if such vehicle achieves at least 225 percent but less than 250 percent of the 2002 model year city fuel economy,

    (v) $3,000, if such vehicle achieves at least 250 percent but less than 275 percent of the 2002 model year city fuel economy,

    (vi) $3,500, if such vehicle achieves at least 275 percent but less than 300 percent of the 2002 model year city fuel economy, and

    (vii) $4,000, if such vehicle achieves at least 300 percent of the 2002 model year city fuel economy.

(3) NEW QUALIFIED FUEL CELL MOTOR VEHICLE—For purposes of this subsection, the term 'new qualified fuel cell motor vehicle' means motor vehicle—

    (A) which is propelled by power derived from 1 or more cells which convert chemical energy directly into electricity by combining oxygen with hydrogen fuel which is stored on board the vehicle in any form and may or may not require reformation prior to use,

    (B) which, in the case of a passenger automobile or light truck, has received on or after the date of the enactment of this section a certificate that such vehicle meets or exceeds the Bin 5 Tier II emission level established in regulations prescribed by the Administrator of the Environmental Protection Agency under section 202(i) of the Clean Air Act for that make and model year vehicle,

    (C) the original use of which commences with the taxpayer,

    (D) which is acquired for use or lease by the taxpayer and not for resale, and

    (E) which is made by a manufacturer.

New Advanced Lean Burn Technology Motor Vehicle Credit—

(1) IN GENERAL—For purposes of subsection (a), the new advanced lean burn technology motor vehicle credit determined under this subsection for the taxable year is the credit amount determined under paragraph (2) with respect to a new advanced lean burn technology motor vehicle placed in service by the taxpayer during the taxable year.

(2) CREDIT AMOUNT—

(A) FUEL ECONOMY—

(i) IN GENERAL—The credit amount determined under this paragraph shall be determined in accordance with the following table:

In the case of a vehicle which achieves a fuel economy of (expressed as a percentage of the 2002 model year city fuel economy) the credit amount is—

    At least 125 percent but less than 150 percent: $400
    At least 150 percent but less than 175 percent: $800
    At least 175 percent but less than 200 percent: $1,200
    At least 200 percent but less than 225 percent: $1,600
    At least 225 percent but less than 250 percent: $2,000
    At least 250 percent: $2,400.

(ii) 2002 MODEL YEAR CITY FUEL ECONOMY—For purposes of clause (i), the 2002 model year city fuel economy with respect to a vehicle shall be determined on a gasoline gallon equivalent basis as determined by the Administrator of the Environmental Protection Agency using the tables provided in subsection (b)(2)(B) with respect to such vehicle.

(B) CONSERVATION CREDIT—The amount determined under subparagraph (A) with respect to a new advanced lean burn technology motor vehicle shall be increased by the conservation credit amount determined in accordance with the following table:

In the case of a vehicle which achieves a lifetime fuel savings of (expressed in gallons of gasoline) the conservation credit amount is—

    At least 1,200 but less than 1,800: $250
    At least 1,800 but less than 2,400: $500
    At least 2,400 but less than 3,000: $750
    At least 3,000: $1,000.

(3) NEW ADVANCED LEAN BURN TECHNOLOGY MOTOR VEHICLE—For purposes of this subsection, the term 'new advanced lean burn technology motor vehicle' means a passenger automobile or a light truck—

(A) with an internal combustion engine which—(i) is designed to operate primarily using more air than is necessary for complete combustion of the fuel, (ii) incorporates direct injection, (iii) achieves at least 125 percent of the 2002 model year city fuel economy, (iv) for 2004 and later model vehicles, has received a certificate that such vehicle meets or exceeds—

    (I) in the case of a vehicle having a gross vehicle weight rating of 6,000 pounds or less, the Bin 5

Tier II emission standard established in regulations prescribed by the Administrator of the Environmental Protection Agency under section 202(i) of the Clean Air Act for that make and model year vehicle, and

(II) in the case of a vehicle having a gross vehicle weight rating of more than 6,000 pounds but not more than 8,500 pounds, the Bin 8 Tier II emission standard which is so established,

(B) the original use of which commences with the taxpayer,

(C) which is acquired for use or lease by the taxpayer and not for resale, and

(D) which is made by a manufacturer.

(4) LIFETIME FUEL SAVINGS—For purposes of this subsection, the term 'lifetime fuel savings' means, in the case of any new advanced lean burn technology motor vehicle, an amount equal to the excess (if any) of—

(A) 120,000 divided by the 2002 model year city fuel economy for the vehicle inertia weight class, over

(B) 120,000 divided by the city fuel economy for such vehicle.

(d) New Qualified Hybrid Motor Vehicle Credit—

(1) IN GENERAL—For purposes of subsection (a), the new qualified hybrid motor vehicle credit determined under this subsection for the taxable year is the credit amount determined under paragraph (2) with respect to a new qualified hybrid motor vehicle placed in service by the taxpayer during the taxable year.

(2) CREDIT AMOUNT—

(A) CREDIT AMOUNT FOR PASSENGER AUTOMOBILES AND LIGHT TRUCKS— In the case of a new qualified hybrid motor vehicle which is a passenger automobile or light truck and which has a gross vehicle weight rating of not more than 8,500 pounds, the amount determined under this paragraph is the sum of the amounts determined under clauses (i) and (ii).

(i) FUEL ECONOMY—The amount determined under this clause is the amount which would be determined under subsection (c)(2)(A) if such vehicle were a vehicle referred to in such subsection.

(ii) CONSERVATION CREDIT—The amount determined under this clause is the amount which would be determined under subsection (c)(2)(B) if such vehicle were a vehicle referred to in such subsection.

(B) CREDIT AMOUNT FOR OTHER MOTOR VEHICLES—

(i) IN GENERAL—In the case of any new qualified hybrid motor vehicle to which subparagraph (A) does not apply, the amount determined under this paragraph is the amount equal to the applicable percentage of the qualified incremental hybrid cost of the vehicle as certified under clause (v).

(ii) APPLICABLE PERCENTAGE—For purposes of clause (i), the applicable percentage is—(I) 20 percent if the vehicle achieves an increase in city fuel economy relative to a comparable vehicle of at least 30 percent but less than 40 percent, (II) 30 percent if the vehicle achieves such an increase of at least 40 percent but less than 50 percent, and (III) 40 percent if the vehicle achieves such an increase of at least 50 percent.

(iii) QUALIFIED INCREMENTAL HYBRID COST—For purposes of this subparagraph, the qualified incremental hybrid cost of any vehicle is equal to the amount of the excess of the manufacturer's suggested retail price for such vehicle over such price for a comparable vehicle, to the extent such amount does not exceed—(I) $7,500, if such vehicle has a gross vehicle weight rating of not more than 14,000 pounds, (II) $15,000, if such vehicle has a gross vehicle weight rating of more than 14,000 pounds but not more than 26,000 pounds, and (III) $30,000, if such vehicle has a gross vehicle weight rating of more than 26,000 pounds.

(3) NEW QUALIFIED HYBRID MOTOR VEHICLE—For purposes of this subsection—

(A) IN GENERAL—The term 'new qualified hybrid motor vehicle' means a motor vehicle—

(i) which draws propulsion energy from onboard sources of stored energy which are both— (I) an internal combustion or heat engine using consumable fuel, and (II) a rechargeable energy storage system,

(ii) which, in the case of a vehicle to which paragraph (2)(A) applies, has received a certificate of conformity under the Clean Air Act and meets or exceeds the equivalent qualifying California low emission vehicle standard under section 243(e)(2) of the Clean Air Act for that make and model year, and (I) in the case of a vehicle having a gross vehicle weight rating of 6,000 pounds or less, the Bin 5 Tier II emission standard established in regulations prescribed by the Administrator of the Environmental Protection Agency under section 202(i) of the Clean Air Act for that make and model year vehicle, and (II) in the case of a vehicle having a gross vehicle weight rating of more than 6,000 pounds but not more than 8,500 pounds, the Bin 8 Tier II emission standard which is so established,

(iii) which has a maximum available power of at least—(I) 4 percent in the case of a vehicle to which paragraph (2)(A) applies, (II) 10 percent in the case of a vehicle which has a gross vehicle weight rating of more than 8,500 pounds and not more than 14,000 pounds, and (III) 15 percent in the case of a vehicle in excess of 14,000 pounds,

(iv) which, in the case of a vehicle to which paragraph (2)(B) applies, has an internal combustion or heat engine which has received a certificate of conformity under the Clean Air Act as meeting the emission standards set in the regulations prescribed by the Administrator of the Environmental Protection Agency for 2004 through 2007 model year diesel heavy duty engines or ottocycle heavy duty engines, as applicable,

(v) the original use of which commences with the taxpayer,

(vi) which is acquired for use or lease by the taxpayer and not for resale, and

(vii) which is made by a manufacturer.

SIGNIFICANCE

The Energy Policy Act of 2005 is a wide-ranging and controversial piece of legislation that is intended to provide long-term guidance for national energy policy decisions. It contains a mixture of provisions that promote innovative technologies such as hybrid automobiles and hydrogen fuel cells as well as subsidies for those producing traditional forms of energy such as oil and nuclear power.

FURTHER RESOURCES
Web sites

Axtman, Kris. "How Much New U.S. Oil? Not a Lot." *Christian Science Monitor* (August 8, 2005). <http://www.csmonitor.com/2005/0808/p01s01-uspo.htm> (accessed March 8, 2006).

"The Energy Policy Act of 2005: What the Energy Bill Means to You." *U.S. Department of Energy*. <http://www.energy.gov/taxbreaks.htm> (accessed March 8, 2006).

"To Ensure Jobs for Our Future with Secure, Affordable, and Reliable Energy." *Library of Congress*. <http://thomas.loc.gov/cgi-bin/bdquery/z?d109:h.r.00006:> (accessed March 8, 2006).

Study on Energy Supply Security and Geopolitics

Report

By: Coby van der Linde

Date: 2004

Source: van der Linde, Coby. *Study of Energy Supply Security and Geopolitics*. The Netherlands Institute of International Relations, Clingendael International Programme (CIEP), 2004.

About the Organization: The Netherlands Institute of International Relations conducts research and provides training related to international affairs, with special attention devoted to European issues. Coby van der Linde has directed the center's Energy Program since 2001.

INTRODUCTION

In 1973, following an armed conflict between Israel and forces from Egypt and Syria (the Yom Kippur War), the Organization of Petroleum Exporting Countries (OPEC) declared an embargo against the United States and the Netherlands, cutting off shipments to these nations. OPEC also hiked the price of oil by 70 percent for Western European nations, and doubled the price again the following year. As gasoline prices in the United States quadrupled, an economic shock wave hit the West, leading to a recession which lasted well into 1974, when the embargo was eventually lifted.

Beyond the immediate discomfort and economic misery caused by the embargo, Americans and Europeans recognized for perhaps the first time that their comfortable lifestyle was dependent on a continuous supply of inexpensive energy from the Middle East. While political scientists still debate the actual impact of the 1973 oil embargo, American and European politicians clearly learned that insuring energy supplies must be a priority if economic growth is to continue.

In the years since the oil embargo, foreign policy and energy policy have become inexorably intertwined. Oil producers and oil consuming nations have formed shaky bonds in order to insure supplies. The United States and European countries have invested billions of dollars in both political and military efforts intended to insure the steady flow of oil from the Middle East to the West. Russia and the

African nations have emerged as powerful players in world energy markets.

Recent events have also reminded the European Union (EU) of its energy dependence. In early 2006, in response to an ongoing dispute over natural gas prices, Russia cut off gas supplies to Ukraine. Following the cut-off, European nations, which import one-fourth of their gas from Russia, noted an 18 percent drop in gas arriving in Hungary, Poland, Austria, and Slovakia. Analysts quickly concluded that this gas, most of it delivered through pipelines traversing Ukraine, was being siphoned off in Ukraine to meet local energy needs. Once again, outside political events had an immediate and tangible impact on European economic health.

In 2004, in response to continued growth in both the population and energy needs of Europe, the EU commissioned a study to assess the future energy supply and demands of European nations in the future. This report, assessing expected developments through the year 2020, predicted that the EU will face significant challenges in obtaining steady energy supplies. It also recommended that energy policy be fully integrated into trade, foreign, and security policy-making, given the importance of energy to the EU economy.

PRIMARY SOURCE

MAIN CONCLUSION AND POLICY RECOMMENDATIONS
7.1 Conclusion

The main result of this study on *EU Energy Supply Security and Geopolitics* is that energy must become an integral part of EU external trade and foreign and security policy-making. EU foreign and security policy and external trade policy are crucial energy policy tools to achieve future security of supply. The recommendation to include energy issues more prominently in external trade and foreign and security policy-making is based on the fact that the dependency on imported energies will increase substantially in the coming decades (COM 769 final, 2000) and that the uninterrupted flow of energy will mainly depend on the political and economic stability of the producer regions. Even though this study has focused on geopolitical issues from a predominantly energy perspective and that other important issues of external trade and foreign and security policy have not been directly analysed, the conclusion is nevertheless that energy will greatly determine foreign relations in the future.

Overall, security of energy supply is of vital interest to the member states. If security of supply is or becomes uncertain (for some or all member states) or the level of security

is asymmetric among the member states, the urge to implement national energy security policy by certain member states, to guarantee these supplies, might well become stronger. However, due to the integration and liberalisation of the EU energy markets, the scope for national policies to ensure adequate levels of security of their own has decreased significantly. To the extent that member states find it necessary to forge national security of supply policies at the level of national foreign policy-making, this strategy to deal with supply concerns will not only interfere with EU energy policies but could have negative effects on the development of EU foreign and security policies. Considering the external energy dependency of the EU and given the internal market, it may be that the EU has no other alternative but to develop a coherent energy security policy that addresses the current asymmetry in exposure among the member states.

The EU is a project that is fundamentally embedded in the multilateral post-1945 world system. Any weakening of multilateralism will strongly impact the environment in which EU enlargement and the deepening of integration can take place. In a less multilateral oriented world system, the EU can be expected to change from an economically driven project into a political-strategic driven project. This does not mean to say that a re-orientation of the EU to a political-strategic project is in conflict with a multilateral world order. However, when such a re-orientation must take place under the mounting external pressure of a less multilateral oriented geopolitical system rather than as a result of internal choices, the EU member states might find that the time frame to realise such a re-orientation does not fit the usually long process of consultations and could therefore create new complications and unpredictable contingencies. Under the circumstances, it is altogether possible, given the wide divergence in political-strategic issues among the member states and the difficulty in the EU to address the power question that the political-strategic project may not succeed. Notably absence of a common direction in political-strategic issues could jeopardise the formulation of an EU security of energy supply policy and fuel the preference for national approaches.

Due to the growing energy import dependency of other main consumer regions, such as the US, India, China and other Asian countries, energy relations will become increasingly politicised. In other consumer countries, energy security will also become a more integral part of foreign and security policymaking. Competition among consumer countries for energy supplies is likely to become more intense than in the previous two decades. The changed circumstance will necessarily have an impact on the international economic and political relations in the world.

In the past decades, the Trans-Atlantic relationship has been of great importance in EU-Middle East relations, and has left little room for an independent EU approach (for instance the 1970s Euro-Arab Dialogue). The energy interests of the US are a primary factor why the independent approach of the EU has not received much support in the US. In recent years, the fate of the Energy Charter has been similar to earlier initiatives towards energy producing countries. The current Charter is a much-diluted measure compared to the initial plan to build and to strengthen the European-CIS energy relationship. The promotion of the long term energy interests of the EU is important and can coincide with stronger relations with neighbouring countries and/or regions. For instance, North Africa, the Persian Gulf, the Caspian Sea region and Russia are neighbouring regions of the enlarged EU and are all economies that are, some more than others, important trading partners. With the east and southward shifting borders of the EU, the external trade and foreign and security policy of the EU will certainly be influenced by enlargement; in particular by the possible enlargement with Turkey, which would create direct borders with Iran and Iraq. There is clearly room for neighbouring countries or regions to integrate their markets with the EU. Consequently, the EU could, as a part of its (energy) policy-making strategy, facilitate a deeper integration of markets.

EU external trade policy and foreign and security policy will be instrumental in securing an uninterrupted supply of oil and gas by underpinning the political and economic stability in producer countries and maintaining good relations with these countries. Security of demand is of vital interest to the producer countries, which has to be acknowledged. A coherent and well co-ordinated EU approach in producer consumer relations is an important precondition to achieve an acceptable level of energy supply security.

As a consequence of the geopolitical developments in the period to 2020, the probability of events affecting the energy security of supply and the exposure of the EU (to the vulnerability of society to risks) is likely to increase. In addition to traditional energy policies, such as strategic reserves, foreign and security policy should also be seen as crucial element of the energy security toolset. The effectiveness of the policy tools depends not only on the ability to employ domestic energy assets, technical and operational factors, transportation and import facilities, investment climate and the availability of foreign oil and gas supplies, but also on the geopolitical setting in which these policies must perform. Given the dynamic developments in the international political and economic relations, a static approach to energy security does not suffice.

Energy supply security therefore requires a dynamic external trade and foreign and security policy towards North Africa, the Persian Gulf, the Caspian Sea region and Russia. Moreover, the EU policies should be focussed

on political and economic sustainability in producer regions/countries to guarantee the long term security of supply of oil and gas. For this reason, stability in North Africa and the Persian Gulf must be seen in the wider context of stability in the Middle East and in Central Eurasia. Given the current level and kind of instability in these regions, the realisation of a more stable situation will take time....

SIGNIFICANCE

While the United States is often the most visible (and militarily active) player in the international petroleum game, the EU economy is today the largest marketplace in the world. This report acknowledges that the European Union, if it wishes to achieve its goals for economic growth, must act to insure its energy future.

Because of its geographical proximity to many of the petroleum producing nations, Europe appears likely to follow the report's recommendations, potentially inviting neighboring petroleum producers to join the EU as a means of insuring continued supplies. In

Oil reserves are shown burning in the background near the Suez Canal, the main shipping route for Middle Eastern oil to reach Europe, during the Suez Crisis of 1956. Energy for Europe (and the United States) remain intertwined with the political security of many Middle Eastern and African nations. © HULTON-DEUTSCH COLLECTION/CORBIS

addition, European governments, which have historically been resistant to political involvement in the Middle East, may find themselves forced to take more aggressive steps to insure stability in the region.

FURTHER RESOURCES
Books

Electricity Trade in Europe: Review of Economic and Regulatory Challenges, edited by Janusz Bielecki and Melaku Geboye Desta. The Hague, The Netherlands: Kluwer Law International, 2004.

Huber, Peter W. and Mark Mills. *The Bottomless Well: The Twilight of Fuel, the Virtue of Waste, and Why We Will Never Run out of Energy*. New York: Basic Books, 2005.

Strategic Energy Policy: Challenges for the 21st Century, edited by Amy Jaffe. New York: Council on Foreign Relations, 2001.

Periodicals

Majstrovic, Goran. "EC: Russian Gas Dispute Shows Need for Common EU Energy Policy." *Platts News* January (2006): 1.

U.S. Department of Energy. "DOE Loans Oil from Strategic Petroleum Reserve." *DOE This Month* 27 (2004): 6.

Web sites

Energy Trends. "European Union: National Energy Policy/ Overview." <http://energytrends.pnl.gov/eu/eu004.htm> (accessed January 26, 2006).

EU-Energy. "Nuclear Power." <http://www.eu-energy.com/ Nuclear%20Power.html> (accessed January 20, 2006).

European Commission. "Energy." <http://www.eu.int/comm/ energy/index_en.html> (accessed January 26, 2006).

Environmental Disasters

Environmental disasters have a severely detrimental effect on ecosystems. These catastrophes are often short in duration, but have a lasting impact on the animals and plants that live in the affected habitat. Occasionally, environmental catastrophes change the physical environment so much that the damage to the ecosystem is irreversible. In other cases, environmental damage can be contained and the habitat rehabilitated.

Environmental disasters fall into two general categories. Some disasters are caused by natural climate or weather events. These include wild fires, landslides, floods, earthquakes, droughts, tornadoes, tsunamis, and volcanic eruptions. Although the causes of these natural environmental disasters do not involve human activities, in some cases the effects are worsened by the influence of people. For example, the environments that suffered the most damage during the Indian Ocean tsunami of 2004 were those where urban development and construction had damaged coral reefs. In places where coral reefs were healthy, the reef acted like a buffer, deflecting the power of the giant wave.

A second category of environmental disasters includes those caused by human activities. Examples of human-induced environmental disasters include oil spills, chemical spills, and nuclear incidents. In addition, wars and terrorist activities can be disastrous to ecosystems. In many cases, environmental disasters caused by humans have longer lasting effects on the environment than catastrophes brought on by natural events. For example, the enormous oil spill that occurred when the *Exxon Valdez* supertanker ran aground in Prince William Sound in 1989 continues to have major environmental repercussions. Twelve years after the oil spill, significant deposits of oil, which is toxic to many species, persisted throughout the affected area. In 2002, the population size of at least eight species of fish and mammals was still severely impacted from the oil spill.

Although environmental disasters take a terrible toll on ecosystems, they can bring increased attention to threatened habitats. In some cases, the increased oversight by governmental, intergovernmental, and non-governmental agencies results in legislation, which reduces the impact of future environmental disasters. For example, the *Exxon Valdez* oil spill led to much stronger regulation of the oil shipping industry. Also, additional funds were allocated for cleaning up oil spills, should they occur again. In the wake of the 2004 tsunami, the United Nations began organizing an Indian Ocean Tsunami warning system to alert citizens when another gigantic wave is heading to shore.

Humans have long believed that their scientific creativity could meet the challenges of natural forces. However, as Earth's resources continue to be eroded by the growing population and its demand for natural resources, it is ever more likely that environmental disasters will increase both in number and intensity. The following section explores some of the better-known environmental disasters that have occurred. It delves into the effects that these catastrophes have taken on the environment and on the human communities involved.

Debate of Senate Bill 203. 38th Congress, 1864

Mother of the Forest Cut Down

Congressional debate

By: United States Senate, 38th Congress

Date: 1864

Source: 38th Congress, *Congressional Globe* 2300–301 (17 May 1864)

About the Author: The 38th U.S. Congress met from 1863 to 1865. Convening during the Civil War, the legislation of the 38th Congress initially applied only to Union states until the war's end. The parcel of land that the 38th Congress granted to the State of California for the conservation of the Mariposa Grove of Big Trees became part of Yosemite National Park in 1906.

INTRODUCTION

On February 20, 1864, Israel Ward Raymond, a representative of the Central American Steamship Transit Company (New York), sent a letter to U.S. Senator John Conness (California), urging the preservation of Yosemite Valley and the Mariposa Grove of giant sequoias. Soon afterwards, George Catlin (1796–1872), a U.S. explorer, painter, and writer of the western territories, proposed legislation to Conness that would preserve these lands. (Catlin had advocated the preservation of lands solely for their aesthetic beauty around forty years before the U.S. Congress acted formally to set aside such lands.) In fact, many writers such as James Russell Lowell, Ralph Waldo Emerson, and Henry David Thoreau played important roles in encouraging the preservation of beautiful lands and in starting the environmental movement in the United States. Henry David Thoreau (1817–1862), in particular, played an especially critical role when he published his 1854 book *Walden*, which ultimately became an important starting point for the conservation movement of the nineteenth century and later as a significant reference book for environmentalists in the twentieth century.

On March 28, 1864, Conness introduced a bill into the U.S. Senate that, if passed, would establish two preservation areas in the state of California described as Yosemite Valley and Mariposa Big Tree Grove. In both cases, Conness expressed his opinion during his reporting to the Senate on May 17, 1864 (as stated in the *Congressional Record*), that the two tracts of

This giant Sequoia is inside the Trail of 100 Giants at the Giant Sequoia National Monument, and is among one of the largest and oldest (2000 years) in existance, thanks to preservation laws. AP IMAGES

land are "for all public purposes worthless, but which constitute, perhaps, some of the greatest wonders of the world." He went on to state, "The trees contained in that grove have no parallel, perhaps, in the world. They are subject now to damage and injury; and this bill, as I have before stated, proposes to commit them to the care of the authorities of that State for their constant preservation, that they may be exposed to public view, and that they may be used and preserved for the benefit of mankind."

Within the discussion as recorded by the *Congressional Record*, Conness referred to an incident that happened in 1852 when a giant sequoia tree—300 feet (91.4 meters) tall, 92 feet (28.0 meters) in circumference, and about 2,500 years old—was stripped of some of its bark for a carnival sideshow. The tree, called the Mother of the Forest, was located in

Calaveras Grove, an isolated valley of the Sierra Nevada mountain range that contained about 160 mountainous acres (65 hectares) and was approximately 240 miles (385 kilometers) east of San Francisco, California. Many people who saw the publicity stunt were angered that such a statuesque tree was injured for the sole purpose of monetary gain. The outrage of the Mother of the Forest incident is considered by many as the one key event that eventually led to the establishment of the U.S. national park system.

Such legislation—preservation of the big trees and the land for the benefit of all—was considered unusual by most Congressmen at the time. Even during the Senate discussion, Senator Foster from Connecticut voiced his feelings that such action was "rather a singular grant, unprecedented so far as my recollection goes." However, after serious discussion, the members of the U.S. Senate passed the bill on May 17, 1864. The members of the U.S. House of Representatives passed the measure on June 29, 1864, and, the following day, President Abraham Lincoln signed the Act of 1864 into law. Today, this legislation is commonly considered the first act to bring about conservation of wilderness areas, along with helping to establish the U.S. national park system.

PRIMARY SOURCE

Mr. Conness. I now move that the Senate proceed to the consideration of Senate bill No. 203, reported by the Senator from Vermont [Mr. Foot] this morning from the Committee on Public Lands.

There being no objection, the Senate, as in Committee of the Whole, proceeded to consider the bill (S. No. 203) authorizing a grant to the State of California of the "Yosemite valley" and of the land embracing the "Mariposa Big Tree Grove."

The first section of the bill provides that there shall be granted to the State of California the "cleft" or "gorge" in the Granite peak of the Sierra Nevada mountains, situated in the county of Mariposa and the headwaters of the Merced river, and known as the Yosemite valley, with its branches or spurs in estimated length fifteen miles, and in average width one mile back from the main edge of the precipice on each side of the valley, with the stipulation, nevertheless, that the State is to accept this grant upon the express conditions that the premises are to be held for public use, resort, and recreation, and are to be inalienable for all time; but leases, not exceeding ten years, may be granted for portions of the premises. All incomes derived from leases of privileges are to be expended in the preservation and improvement of the property, or the roads

leading thereto; the boundaries to be established at the cost of the State by the United States surveyor general of California, whose official plat, when affirmed by the Commissioner of the General Land Office, is to constitute the evidence of the *locus*, extent, and limits of the cleft or gorge. The premises are to be managed by the Governor of the State, with eight other commissioners, to be appointed by the Executive of California, and who are to receive no compensation for their services.

The second section provides that there shall likewise be granted to the State of California the tracts embracing what is known as the "Mariposa Big Tree Grove," not to exceed the area of four sections, and to be taken in legal subdivisions of one quarter section each, with the like stipulations as expressed in the first section of this act as to the State's acceptance, with like conditions as to inalienability, yet with the same lease privilege; the income to be expended in the preservation, improvement, and protection of the property; the premises to be managed by commissioners, as stipulated in the first section, and to be taken in legal subdivisions, and the official plat of the United States surveyor general, when affirmed by the Commissioner of the General Land Office, to be the evidence of the *locus* of the "Mariposa Big Tree Grove."

Mr. Conness. I will state to the Senate that this bill proposes to make a grant of certain premises located in the Sierra Nevada mountains, in the State of California, that are for all public purposes worthless, but which constitute, perhaps, some of the greatest wonders of the world. The object and purpose is to make a grant to the State, on the stipulations contained in the bill, that the property shall be inalienable forever, and preserved and improved as a place of public resort, to be taken charge of by gentlemen to be appointed by the Governor, who are to receive no compensation for their services, and who are to undertake the management and improvement of the property by making roads leading thereto and adopting such other means as may be necessary for its preservation and improvement. It includes a grant of a few sections of ground of that State is located, of which most Senators doubtless have heard. The trees contained in that grove have no parallel, perhaps, in the world. They are subject now to damage and injury; and this bill, as I have before stated, proposes to commit them to the care of the authorities of that State for their constant preservation, that they may be exposed to public view, and that they may be used and preserved for the benefit of mankind. It is a matter involving no appropriation whatever. The property is of no value to the Government. I make this explanation that the Senate may understand what the purpose is.

The bill was reported to the Senate without amendment.

Mr. Foster. I should like to ask the Senator from California whether the State of California—

The President *pro tempore*. The Chair must interrupt the Senator to call up the special order of the day, the time fixed for its consideration having arrived.

Mr. Conness. I hope it will lie over for the present.

Mr. Wilson. Let it go over informally for a few minutes.

The President *pro tempore*. That course will be taken, if there be no objection.

Mr. Foster. I should like to ask the Senator from California whether the State of California has intimated any wish that we should thus make this grant to them, and how it comes about that we propose making it.

Mr. Conness. I will state to the Senator from Connecticut and to the Senate, that they may understand it, that the application comes to use from various gentlemen in California, gentlemen of fortune, of taste, and of refinement, and the plan proposed in this bill has been suggested by them, that this property be committed to the care of the State. I submitted the plan as presented by these gentlemen to the Land Office, and the bill now before the Senate has been prepared by the Commissioner of the General Land Office, who also takes a great interest in the preservation both of the Yosemite valley and the Big Tree Grove. Such was the origin of the measure, and such are its purposes.

Mr. Foster. I did not by any means mean to intimate any opposition to the bill; but it struck me as being rather a singular grant, unprecedented so far as my recollection goes, and unless the State through her appropriate authorities signified some wish in the matter, it might be deemed by the State officious on our part to make a grant of this kind.

Mr. Conness. Ordinarily I should hope I spoke for the State of California here. I feel authorized to do so under existing circumstances. There is no parallel, and can be no parallel for this measure, for there is not, as I stated before, on earth just such a condition of things. The Mariposa Big Tree Grove is really the wonder of the world, containing those magnificent monarchs of the forest that are from thirty to forty feet in diameter.

Mr. Davis. How old?

Mr. Conness. Well, sir, they are estimated to reach an age of three thousand years. There are two such groves in the State. One is known as the Mariposa grove, the one contemplated in this bill; and the other is known as the Calaveras grove. From the Calaveras grove some sections of a fallen tree were cut during and pending the great World's Fair that was held in London some years since. One joint of the tree was sectionized and transported to that country in sections, and then set up there. The English who saw it declared it to be a Yankee invention, made from beginning to end; that is was an utter untruth that such trees grew in the country; that it could not be; and, although the section of the tree was transported there at an expense of several thousand dollars, we were not able to convince them that it was a specimen of American growth. They would not believe us. The purpose of this bill is to preserve one of these groves from devastation and injury. The necessity of taking early possession and care of these great wonders can easily be seen and understood.

Mr. Foster. I certainly did not mean to say anything which implied that the honorable Senator from California had not the most perfect and entire right to speak for his State, and I am at a loss to understand what I was so unfortunate as to say which led him to suppose that I doubted it.

The bill was ordered to be engrossed for a third reading, and was read the third time, and passed.

SIGNIFICANCE

The passage of the Act of 1864, which granted the state of California two tracts of land, did not give the U.S. federal government any responsibility for managing nor preserving any lands or objects. Responsibility was placed solely on the state of California for all duties relating to Yosemite Valley and Mariposa Big Tree Grove. After the U.S. Congress passed its legislation, the state legislature of California quickly passed the State Park Act in 1864 and, on September 28, 1864, the governor of California appointed a board of commissioners to manage the parks. However, it is unfortunate that these persons in charge of the managements and preservations did not follow through with what was promised. This lack of follow-through on the part of Californian politicians resulted in the failure to preserve these two land tracts and what is generally considered the first formal attempt at preserving land in the United States.

Soon after the California lands were set aside, it was recognized by conservationists that additional land needed to be set aside within Yosemite Valley. Then, upon the failures by California, members of the U.S. Senate asked representatives from California to honor the obligation to protect the Yosemite Valley. When the state failed in its promise, the federal government took formative action to establish the national park system. In March 1890, a bill in the U.S. House of Representatives called for land surrounding Yosemite Valley to be preserved as a national park. Both the U.S.

House and Senate easily passed the measure and the act was approved on October 1, 1890, by President Benjamin Harrison.

Ultimately, the historic significance of this legislation "the Act of 1864, for which discussion was recorded within the *Congressional Record*" is simply that land was set aside for the first time strictly for conservation purposes. Senator Conness' innovative bill was pioneering legislation that set a precedent for the conservation of public lands. Although California's attempt to preserve land was not successful, the tireless work by California Senator Conness, along with conservationists, explorers, writers, and artists, helped to identify the need to protect and conserve land and, eventually, to establish the U.S. national park system.

FURTHER RESOURCES
Books

Hampton, H. Duane. "The Genesis of an Idea." in *How the U.S. Calvary Saved Our National Parks*, Bloomington, IN: Indiana University Press, 1971. Also available online at <http://www.cr.nps.gov/history/online_books/hampton/chap1.htm> (accessed March 15, 2006).

Neuzil, Mark, and Bill Kovarik. "The Media and Social Change: 1. Mother of the Forest." in *Mass Media & Environmental Conflict: America's Green Crusades*, Thousand Oaks, CA: Sage Publications, 1996. Also available online on the *Environmental History Timeline, Radford University*, <http://www.radford.edu/~wkovarik/envhist/mother.html> (accessed March 15, 2005).

Runte, Alfred. "First Park." in *Yosemite: The Embattled Wilderness*, Lincoln, NE: University of Nebraska Press, 1990. Also available online at <http://www.cr.nps.gov/history/online_books/runte2/chap2.htm> (accessed March 15, 2006).

Web sites

Smith, David A. "Yosemite: The Cavalry Years." *California State Military Museum, California State Military Department*. <http://www.militarymuseum.org/YosemiteCavalry.html> (accessed March 15, 2006).

Dust Bowl Blues

Song

By: Woodrow Wilson Guthrie

Date: April 1940

Source: Guthrie, Woody. "Dust Bowl." Ludlow Music, 1940.

About the Author: American folk singer and guitarist Woodrow Wilson "Woody" Guthrie (1912–1967) was born in Okemah, Oklahoma. Guthrie moved onto the panhandle of Texas in 1931 after the extended illness and death of his mother left his family penniless. With the Great Depression upon the nation, Guthrie was barely able to survive in Texas. When the harrowing drought that helped bring on the Dust Bowl arrived on the Great Plains in 1935, Guthrie left for California like many other thousands of farmers and unemployed workers who were looking for a better life. Songs about the desperate predicament found among the poor and homeless quickly made him a popular personality and opinionated spokesman for those he sang about. Some of these songs include "Dust Bowl Blues," "This Land Is Your Land," and "I Ain't Got No Home." After witnessing firsthand a giant black dust storm blowing across the Texas plains, Guthrie wrote the song "So Long, It's Been Good To Know Yuh (Dusty Old Dust)."

INTRODUCTION

Beginning around the 1880s, pioneer settlers started to extensively farm the former short grasslands of the Great Plains with improper agricultural practices for such a semi-arid climatic environment. With the removal of these stable grasses, a sustained period of drought and perpetually strong and destructive wind and dust storms (often called Black Blizzards) caused severe soil erosion, removal of topsoil, and nutrient leaching in the latter half of the 1930s in many areas of eastern Colorado, western Kansas, eastern New Mexico, the Oklahoma Panhandle, and western Texas. As conditions worsened, any soil conservation measures that had been previously used were drastically cut or eliminated in order to reduce costs. In order to make more money, farmers often expanded onto poorer lands that caused even more vulnerability to loss of soil moisture, depletion of soil nutrients, wind erosion, and other environmental problems.

In 1935, the Federal Soil Conservation Service (SCS, now called the Natural Resources Conservation Service) estimated that about 100 million acres (40 million hectares) of land in the southern Great Plains were affected, with about one-third to one-half of the area severely damaged after the total removal of the native grasses.

Consequently, many environmental problems were created. Crops were damaged or destroyed by low rainfall, high temperatures, wind and dust storms,

A little ranch in Boise City, OK is subjected to one of the violent dust storms that frequently occurred in the 1930s. Dust storms such as these caused much environmental damage to the afflicted areas. AP IMAGES

and hungry swarms of insects. These problems not only caused business losses, unemployment, and other hardships to people, but also harmed wildlife and plant life. This ecologically and economically devastated area became known as the Dust Bowl. The series of storms that occurred in the 1930s in the southern Great Plains are considered one of the worst environmental disasters in history.

PRIMARY SOURCE

Dust Bowl Blues
I just blowed in and I got them dust bowl blues,
I just blowed in and I got them dust bowl blues,
I just blowed in and I'll blow back out again.

I guess you've heard about every kind of blues,
I guess you've heard about every kind of blues,
But when the dust gets high you can't even see the sky.

I've seen the dust so black that I couldn't see a thing,
I've seen the dust so black that I couldn't see a thing,
And the wind so cold boy, it nearly cut your water off.

I've seen the wind so high that it blowed my fences
    down
I've seen the wind so high that it blowed my fences
    down
Buried my tractor six feet underground.

Well, it turned my farm into a pile of sand
Yes, it turned my farm into a pile of sand
I had to hit that road with a bottle in my hand.

I spent ten years down in that old dust bowl
I spent ten years down in that old dust bowl
When you get that dust pneumonia boy, it's time to go.

I had a gal and she was young and sweet,
I had a gal and she was young and sweet,
But a dust storm buried her sixteen hundred feet.

She was a good gal long tall and stout
She was a good gal long tall and stout
I had to get a steam shovel just to dig my darlin' out.

These dusty blues are the dustiest ones I know
These dusty blues are the dustiest ones I know
Buried head over heels in the black old dust,
I had to pack up and go.
And I just blowed in, and I'll soon blow out again.

SIGNIFICANCE

With thousands of people leaving the Dust Bowl area for better living and working conditions, most of the remaining people were forced to take government aid due to the unworkable conditions of their lands and the concurrent hardships of the Great Depression. By 1935, soil conservation and rehabilitation projects of the federal and various state governments were countering the effects of the Dust Bowl with such programs as large-area grass seeding; three-year rotation plantings of wheat-sorghum (no crops); contour, lister, and chisel plowing; terracing; strip planting; and the planting of hardy plants and shelter trees. For instance, in chisel plowing the plow blade was dug deeply into the soil, which left large chunks of dirt above the surface to be used as a windbreak, which helped to slow erosion.

One especially important federal program was the Dalhart Wind Erosion Control Project (by the Soil Erosion Service of the Department of Commerce). In 1934, it made widespread loans to cattlemen to feed starving stock and to farmers to buy seeds; it also provided jobs to unemployed workers for the improvement of lands.

Another organization, the Southwest Agricultural Association, helped to create greater government control onto the proper conservation of lands throughout the southern plains. During this time, the SCS publicized soil conservation practices through its new soil conservation districts. Farmers were shown the benefits of such conservation practices as contouring and terracing. Irrigation was also promoted, as was the benefits of crop diversity. In order to help the environmental condition of the Dust Bowl, the federal government also created new reservoirs and enlarged existing reservoirs, improved farm policies, added insurance and aid programs, and removed the most sensitive agricultural lands from crop production.

Such relief and conservation programs instituted within President Franklin D. Roosevelt's New Deal were used to prevent the reoccurrence of the problem. However, various dry spells on the southern plains between the early 1950s and the late 1970s were responsible for recurrences of dust storms—indicating that such programs had not been totally successful.

The lessons learned from the Dust Bowl show the destructive power that inappropriate and untested human actions can have on environmental conditions. As farmers expanded into new lands with new agricultural ideas and equipment, the native environment was replaced with a vast farmland. As farmers made more profits with their expanding operations, they caused more and more damage to the environment. Within a few years of such actions, much of the native grasses that had firmly held the soil together were destroyed by greedy farming and ranching practices.

Such inappropriate practices went directly against the soil conservation methods used by former generations of farmers and ranchers and the collection of agricultural data by scientists (such as the evidence of cyclical drought periods in the Great Plains over the past hundreds of years). Appropriate farming practices that had been used in the moist eastern areas of the country had been unwisely continued in the dryer western plain states—much to the detriment of the soil and ultimately to the fate of its users.

Farmers seeking profits over environmental conservation led to the disastrous consequences of the Dust Bowl. The significance of the Dust Bowl showed the amount of damage and destruction that can happen to the ecological and social infrastructure of society when short-term actions are made without due consideration to the environment. However, on the other hand, the widespread damage brought on by the storms of the Dust Bowl helped to bring national attention to the necessity of soil and water conservation measures to maintain farm productivity. Today, such measures are a critical part of all farming practices throughout the United States.

FURTHER RESOURCES

Books

Isaacs, Sally Senzell. *Life in the Dust Bowl*. Chicago: Heinemann Library, 2002.

Lookingbill, Brad D. *Dust Bowl, U.S.A.: Depression America and the Ecological Imagination, 1929-1941*. Athens, OH: Ohio University Press, 2001.

Worster, Donald. *Dust Bowl: The Southern Plains in the 1930s*. Oxford, UK and New York: Oxford University Press, 2004.

Web sites

Sites, Geoff. "The Dust Bowl and Agricultural Capitalism: An Environmental Disaster to the Plains Region." *English Discourse—the e-journal*. <http://www.english discourse.org/edc.1.1sites.html> (accessed March 8, 2006).

"Surviving the Dust Bowl." *PBS Online/WGBH, 1999.* <http://www.pbs.org/wgbh/amex/dustbowl> (accessed March 8, 2006).

"Voices from the Dust Bowl." *American Folklife Center, Library of Congress.* <http://lcweb2.loc.gov/ammem/afctshtml/tshome.html> (accessed March 8, 2006).

"What is Drought: Drought in the Dust Bowl Years." *National Drought Mitigation Center.* <http://www.drought.unl.edu/whatis/dustbowl.htm> (accessed March 8, 2006).

"Welcome to the Woody Guthrie Website." *The Woody Guthrie Foundation and Archives.* <http://www.woodyguthrie.org> (accessed March 8, 2006).

Audio and Visual Media

Gazit, Chana. "Surviving the Dust Bowl." Television program in *The American Experience* series. PBS/WGBH, 1998.

Skyline of Downtown Los Angeles Shrouded and Obscured by Smog

Photograph

By: Anonymous

Date: 1956

Source: "Skyline of Downtown Los Angeles Shrouded and Obscured by Smog." Hulton Archive/Getty Images, 1956.

About the Photographer: This picture was taken on a particularly bad day for smog in 1956. The tall building at the center of the picture is the Los Angeles City Hall. The photographer is unknown.

INTRODUCTION

Los Angeles is the U.S. city most notorious for smog. The word "smog" is a combination of "smoke" and "fog" first coined in 1905 to describe chronic severe ground-level air pollution in London caused by the burning of coal. In many modern cities, smog is mostly caused by exhaust from motor vehicles, although coal can also contribute.

The first recognized episodes in Los Angeles occurred in the summer of 1943, when California had about 2.8 million registered motor vehicles that were being driven some 24 billion miles (38.6 billion kilometers) per year. During these smog attacks it was only possible to see clearly for about three blocks, and people suffered breathing problems, vomiting, and smarting eyes. Two years later, Los Angeles established its own state Bureau of Smoke Control. The state of California passed the Air Pollution Control Act in 1947. Despite these and other legislative efforts, the smog problem continued. With each passing year there were more cars in California (as in the rest of the United States). By 1950, there were 4.5 million vehicles in the state traveling a total of 44.5 billion miles (71.6 billion kilometers) per year. By 1960, there were 8 million vehicles.

The air in Los Angeles got somewhat better when California mandated standards and controls for motor vehicle emissions starting in 1959. In 1960, California mandated the first automotive emissions control technology in the world, positive crankcase ventilation. In the 1970s, California was the first U.S. state to mandate catalytic converters to reduce vehicle pollution, and in 1990 was the first state to establish standards for Cleaner Burning Fuels and Low and Zero Emission Vehicles. (Zero Emission Vehicles include electric cars, though this is something of a misnomer: an electric car is only as "low emission" as the generating plant that made the electricity to charge its batteries.)

California's efforts to improve air quality—especially in the Los Angeles metropolitan area, where about half of the population of California lives—have been partly successful. By 1990, when there were 23 million vehicles and 242 billion vehicle miles (389 billion kilometers) traveled per year, the number of Stage 1 Smog Alert days stood at forty-two, half as many as in 1985. Yet in 2001 Los Angeles once again became the U.S. city with the most high-ozone days per year, and could not meet Federal pollution standards for carbon monoxide, particulates, and ozone.

PRIMARY SOURCE

SKYLINE OF DOWNTOWN LOS ANGELES SHROUDED AND OBSCURED BY SMOG

See primary source image.

SIGNIFICANCE

Los Angeles is located in a broad valley or basin surrounded by mountains. This, plus the proximity of the ocean, encourages the formation of temperature inversions over the city. A temperature inversion is a weather condition in which warm air is layered above cool air. Usually, temperature goes down with altitude: that is, the air is warmest at the ground and cooler

PRIMARY SOURCE

Skyline of Downtown Los Angeles Shrouded and Obscured by Smog. This image shows smog hanging as a visible low-altitude haze over the city of Los Angeles, California, in 1956. Smog is a form of air pollution. Despite more than half a century of efforts to control air pollution, Los Angeles and some other cities continue to have a smog problem. PHOTO BY AMERICAN STOCK/GETTY IMAGES

higher up. Since warm air is less dense than cool air, it tries to float, convect upward through the cool air. This produces constant mixing of low-altitude air with high-altitude air. When an inversion occurs, however, cold air sits near the ground beneath a layer of warm air and has no tendency to mix with higher-altitude air. Under these conditions, air pollution produced at ground level by cars, power plants, and other sources does not rise and mix with cleaner air, but accumulates at low altitude like steam under a pot lid.

The pollutants that form smog are transformed by sunlight into even more harmful chemicals. Nitric oxide (NO) from automobile exhaust, a toxic gas, reacts with ordinary molecular oxygen in the air (O_2) to form nitrogen dioxide (NO_2, another toxic gas), which then breaks back down into nitric oxide and free oxygen (O). This free oxygen combines with O_2 to form ozone, or O_3 ($O + O_2 = O_3$). Ozone is beneficial in the stratosphere, where it blocks ultraviolet radiation from the Sun, but it is a pollutant at lower altitudes, where it is poisonous to plants and animals. As the sun shines, then, air pollution in the form of nitric oxide breeds additional air pollution in the form of ozone, and the air gets worse as the day goes on. Smog of the type seen over Los Angeles is thus sometimes called "photochemical (light-chemical) smog."

Vehicles emit other pollutants, too, particularly hydrocarbons. These also react with nitric oxide to form peroxyacetyl nitrate and other poisonous chemicals that are also part of smog.

Smog has long-term health effects and can also kill people with preexisting health problems. In 1930, in the Meuse Valley, Belgium, an inversion trapped industrial air pollution, killing sixty people and making thousands sick. In 1952, a smog inversion killed 12,000 people in London. (Estimates at the time were only 4,000 dead, and this number is still often cited; however, the British government raised its official estimate to 12,000 in 2002.) Another "Killer Fog" killed well over 1,000 people in London in 1956, the year this picture of Los Angeles was taken.

Hong Kong has particularly acute smog, fed largely by coal-burning factories and electrical power plants in nearby Guangdong Province, China.

FURTHER RESOURCES

Periodicals

Knipp, Steven. "Hong Kong Fades Under China's Smog." *Christian Science Monitor* (December 23, 2004). <http://www.csmonitor.com/2004/1223/p16s01-sten.html> (accessed March 10, 2006).

Web sites

"California's Air Quality History Key Events." *California Air Resources Board*. <http://www.arb.ca.gov/html/brochure/history.htm> (accessed March 10, 2006).

"Deadly Smog." *Public Broadcasting Service (PBS)*, January 17, 2003. <http://www.pbs.org/now/science/smog.html> (accessed March 10, 2006).

"Oil Slick is Shroud for Birds"

Newspaper article

By: Irston R. Barnes

Date: July 22, 1962

Source: Barnes, Irston R. "Oil Slick is Shroud for Birds." *The Washington Post*, July 22, 1962.

About the Author: Irston R. Barnes (1904–1988), at the time that his article appeared in the *Washington Post*, was the chairman of the board of directors of the Audubon Naturalist Society, a post he maintained from 1961 to 1968. Previous to this position, Barnes was president of the Audubon Naturalist Society (which, after 1960, was called the Audubon Society of the District of Columbia) from 1946 to 1961. He was also the president of the Potomac Valley Conservation and Recreation Council and an economic adviser to the U.S. Civil Aeronautics Board.

INTRODUCTION

In his 1962 article, Barnes wrote about the serious negative consequences to seabirds with respect to the dumping of petroleum products (such as oil) and byproducts by ships while at sea. The intentional dumping of oil while at sea is commonly done by the flushing out of oil tankers with sea water, but it can also be done by the dumping of used crankcase oil, the pumping out of oily wastes from bilges, and the careless disposing of oil products and byproducts by such sources as refineries, water recreational users, and general consumers. Illegal dumpers take the chance of being fined, imprisoned, or other such penalties in order to eliminate the cost necessary to properly dispose and decompose their waste oil. If caught dumping oil off of Canadian waters, for example, the captain and the owners of a tanker can be fined under the Canada Shipping Act a maximum of one million dollars; however the largest fine ever recorded was $125,000 and the average fine is about $21,000.

Ocean dumping of oil—which was legal in 1962 if performed beyond 50 miles (80 kilometers) of a coast—negatively affects sea birds because released oil remains floating on the surface of the water, often traveling within the 50-mile limit of coastlines, and sometimes even washing up onto shores. When sea birds come into contact with this discarded oil, even the smallest, dime-sized amount can kill a bird by breaking down its ability to waterproof and insulate itself (so that the bird dies from hypothermia, or exposure to the cold weather); removing its ability to stay buoyant (so that the bird drowns); interfering with its ability to fly (so it is unable to eat, eventually resulting in starvation); being swallowed or inhaled by the bird (which introduces toxic compounds that can damage the bird's liver, kidneys, intestines, lungs, and other body organs); or interfering with its ability to reproduce (by reducing the number of eggs, thinning the shell of eggs, allowing oil to soak into eggs and killing the embryo, or causing abnormalities in developing chicks).

PRIMARY SOURCE

IF YOU HAVE been swimming at the ocean this summer or walking along the beach, you have very likely picked up a glob of oil on your feet. It was not easily removed; it could not be washed away, and rubbing was difficult after the oil was mixed with water. If your experience matched mine, you probably had to resort to cleaning fluid to get rid of the oil.

Did you give a thought to how the oil got on the beach? The most serious and most common source is the flushing out of oil tankers with sea water. A second common source is the dumping of old crankcase oil and the pumping of oily wastes from bilges.

But careless handling of oil or wastes by pleasure craft and spillage from shore refineries are also possible sources.

WHERE DID the oil enter the sea? Not necessarily near the beach where you were "oiled." Oil floats on the water indefinitely; in one experiment, oil floated on a tank of water for 18 months.

Oil may travel far with ocean and coastal currents. In one experiment at sea in 1926–7 by the United States, a discharge of oil was traced 90 miles in 72 hours. In the Red Sea, oil has been detected 500 miles from its point of discharge.

A Bureau of Mines report in 1926 established that fuel oils, when agitated by sea water, form a thick emulsion of oil, water and air. The emulsion continues to float for months, being very viscous and having the quality of a heavy grease. This is the consistency often encountered on the beach.

OIL POLLUTION is one of the most serious, most widespread and most cruel causes of death among sea birds of all kinds. There is no more unhappy experience for those who enjoy bird watching than to come upon dead or dying oil-smeared birds lying on the beach or struggling in the water. It is too late to do anything for them; they are fated for a slow, starving death.

A bird that gets oiled tries to preen the oil off its feathers, accomplishing nothing but ingesting the oil. Sea birds heavily smeared on their wings are unable to fly. They are also unable to dive. They are as completely crippled as though they had been shot.

A bird need not be completely smeared with oil to be doomed. The sea birds depend on the insulation of their feathers to protect them from the cold and on the abundance of their feathers to enable them to swim. A small patch of oil, only an inch in diameter, is enough to kill a murre by destroying insulating air pockets in the down so that the bird dies of exposure. It does not take much oil to make it difficult for the bird to remain afloat, and many thousands are believed to drown at sea.

SOME BIRDS are particularly susceptible to oil at sea. An oil slick has the same appearance as a school of small fish coming to the surface. Gannets and murres often dive or fly directly into the oiled area.

All of the sea-going ducks are victims, the elder ducks and old squaws being particularly exposed. The little dovkies also suffer heavy mortality from oil pollution.

All of the gulls are likely to be victims, although their dispersed flocks make it unlikely that any large number will be killed at one time. A few such birds are encountered on almost any winter trip to the ocean.

THE SERIOUSNESS of oil pollution of the sea has been recognized in an international convention that forbids the dumping of oil within 50 miles of the coast of any nation adhering to the convention. Some of the important shipping nations have not yet adhered to the convention; their ships continue to dump their oil wastes anywhere.

A convention that permits dumping of oil at sea, any where, is a completely inadequate solution. Oil floating at sea moves with the winds and the currents, with no respect for 50–mile limits. And the sea-birds likewise get into oil beyond the protected zone.

The only solution is an international convention preventing the dumping of oil anywhere at sea.

SIGNIFICANCE

Over forty years after Barnes wrote the article "Ocean Oil Slick Is Shroud for Birds," the dumping of oil into the ocean is still a very serious pollution and conservation problem. In Canadian waters, one of the world's primary oil transportation routes, oil pollution is conservatively estimated to kill hundreds of thousands of seabirds every year. Both the World Wildlife Fund and the Memorial University of Newfoundland estimate that well over 300,000 seabirds are killed off the southeastern coast of Canada each year, a number greater than the number of birds killed by the much-publicized 1989 *Exxon Valdez* tanker disaster when the ship ran aground on the Bligh Reef in Prince William Sound, Alaska.

Due to articles such as the one written by Barnes in 1962, many new ways have been developed to catch illegal ocean oil dumping. Members of the Canadian government search with pollution patrol aircraft within its Exclusive Economic Zone, an area 200 nautical miles (370 kilometers) off both its eastern and western coasts. Unfortunately, this huge area makes it very expensive to patrol, and very unlikely that a polluting ship will even be seen, especially at night when aircraft cannot be used.

Among high-technology methods used to catch oil dumping violators are earth-orbiting satellites that monitor the movements of ships and detect the different types of motion in the water; specifically, those caused by oil. For instance, since September 2002, environmental groups in Canada have been working alongside the Canadian Space Agency to monitor the

A tanker carrying thousands of tons of crude oil gets stuck on Seven Stones Rocks, March 20, 1967. The oil released from the crash is estimated to kill thousands of plant and bird life inhabitating the area. AP IMAGES

Atlantic coast with the earth-observation RADARSAT satellite, as part of the program called Integrated Satellite Targeting of Polluters.

In addition, scientists within the Canadian Wildlife Service and other organizations have been able to match oil found on birds with the dumped oil once located on a particular ship. Legislation—including the Canada Shipping Act, the Fisheries Act, the Migratory Birds Convention Act, and the Canada Wildlife Act—help to control such illegal oil dumping at sea. Educational programs have been created to educate ship crews of the extensive damage done to birds and animals by ocean oil dumping.

Using such methods, it has become easier for countries to enforce ocean oil dumping laws and to catch offenders. However, such enforcement remains difficult, with the responsibility still largely resting with each tanker captain to obey local, national, and international environmental laws associated with ocean dumping.

FURTHER RESOURCES

Books

National Research Council. *Oil in the Sea III.* Washington, D.C.: National Academies Press, 2003.

Periodicals

Wells, P.G. "Oil and Seabirds—The Imperative for Preventing and Reducing the Continued Illegal Oiling of the Seas by Ships." *Marine Pollution Bulletin* 42, no. 4 (2001): 251–252.

Web sites

"How Oil Pollution Affects Birds and Other Wildlife." *Space for Species.* <http://www.spaceforspecies.ca/meeting_place/news/features/oil_pollution_effects.htm> (accessed March 10, 2006).

"What is an Oil Spill?." *Space for Species.* <http://www.spaceforspecies.ca/meeting_place/news/features/oil_pollution_oilspills.htm> (accessed March 10, 2006).

"Wildlife and Nature." *Environment Canada.* <http://www.atl.ec.gc.ca/wildlife> (accessed March 10, 2006).

"World Oil Pollution: Causes, Prevention and Clean-Up." *Oceanlink.* <http://oceanlink.island.net/oceanmatters/oil%20pollution.html> (accessed March 10, 2006).

Cumberland Mountain Area Scarred by Strip Mining

Photograph

By: Bob Gomel

Date: January 1, 1967

Source: Getty Images

About the Photographer: Bob Gomel's photographs of notable individuals were frequently featured in *Life* magazine in the 1960s. This photograph was taken at the site of a coal mine in the Cumberland region of the Appalachian Mountains in 1967.

INTRODUCTION

The Cumberland Mountains are a southeastern portion of the Appalachian Mountains in the United States. The Cumberlands include parts of Kentucky, Virginia, and Tennessee and constitute part of the Appalachian Coal Field, the largest bituminous coal deposit in the world. Coal has been mined in the Cumberlands and elsewhere in the Appalachians for over two hundred years, but until the 1940s was usually mined using subsurface or tunnel mining. After World War II (1938–1941), the large earthmoving machines necessary for strip mining became available. Strip mining increased dramatically in the 1960s and 1970s, as did organized political opposition to the practice.

Strip mining produces many more tons of coal per worker-hour than does tunnel mining and therefore is more profitable. However, it is also more destructive. In strip mining, the landscape is literally stripped away—including trees and soil—in order to access a layer of coal beneath. In the language of strip mining, a landscape overlying coal is termed "overburden." Once the overburden is removed using giant shovels that hoist up to 200 tons at a bite, the coal is trucked away to be burned, for the most part, in electricity-generating plants. Coal, most of it strip-mined, supplies about half of U.S. electricity.

In the photograph, a small piece of overburden has been left intact, showing how much of a layer has been removed. In this case the overburden layer was shallow—perhaps only ten or twenty feet—and the coal layer (the dark, lower two thirds of the mesa seen here) about two or three times as thick.

Strip mining in the Appalachian region was for many years facilitated by a legal instrument called the "broad-form deed." At the beginning of the twentieth century, coal companies began buying mineral rights from rural landowners using broad-form deeds. These contracts turned over ownership of the coal underlying the seller's land and, crucially, gave the owner of the coal the right to do *anything necessary* to get at the coal. Also, the landowner remained responsible for all property taxes. By 1930, coal companies held broad-form deed rights to over 70 percent of the land in some rural towns, as for example the village of Scotts Run, West Virginia. When strip-mining began decades later, the mining company's access rights were held to extend to complete destruction of whatever happened to be on top of the coal—trees, soil, fields, streams, houses. Land on which a coal company held a broad-form deed was thus fair game for strip mining, without further compensation or any right of refusal. In 1987, the Kentucky Supreme Court declared the broad-form deed unconstitutional.

Eventually, reclamation procedures such as soil restoration and tree-planting were mandated by laws such as West Virginia's 1967 Surface Mine Reclamation Act and the federal Surface Mining and Reclamation Act of 1977. However, such laws have often been ignored or skirted by mine operators. Reclamation is at best only partially effective in restoring ecosystems annihilated in the first stage of the strip-mining process.

PRIMARY SOURCE

CUMBERLAND MOUNTAIN AREA SCARRED BY STRIP MINING

See primary source image.

SIGNIFICANCE

Strip mining's impact on the environment is at least twofold. First, it involves the complete destruction of the area to be mined. Second, the overburden itself must be moved aside to get at the coal, a process which uses even more land and creates other problems as well. Where steep slopes are adjacent to the stripped area, this material can cascade or avalanche downslope into valleys and streams.

Water pollution is also a common environmental side effect of strip mining. The mineral iron pyrite (FeS_2) is usually part of the shale layer that is pushed aside by strip mining as tailings or waste; when exposed to weathering, this mineral yields sulfur, producing sulfuric acid. This acid turns streams a reddish color and can kill whatever is living in them.

Cumberland Mountain Area Scarred by Strip Mining. This 1967 photograph of the Cumberland Mountains region in the southeastern United States shows the remnants the strip mining process. By the early 2000s, strip mining had come to include "mountaintop removal," the destruction of entire mountains to obtain the coal beneath. PHOTO BY BOB GOMEL/GETTY IMAGES

In the mid and late 1990s, a form of strip mining known as mountaintop removal came into much wider use. Mountaintop removal allows the mining of much more deeply buried layers of coal than traditional strip mining. Despite its name, this procedure involves not only the removal of the top of a mountain, but of most of it. The coal layer in the photograph was only a few yards below the surface: in contrast, mountaintop removal allows access to coal as far as 1,000 feet below the surface. Mountaintop removal generally entails the removal of the mountain being mined, as well as the filling in of adjacent valleys with the bulk of the former mountain. The 1977 federal Surface

Mining and Reclamation Act mandates that mining companies restore stripped land so that it "closely resembles the general surface configuration of the land prior to mining", which includes restoring the land to its "approximate original contour", but according to a 1998 *Charleston Gazette* investigation "these rules are routinely skirted by dozens of huge mountaintop-removal strip mines."

FURTHER RESOURCES

Web sites

Charleston Gazette. "Mining the Mountains." <http://wvgazette. com/static/series/mining/> (accessed February 24, 2006).

Save Our Cumberland Mountains (SOCM). Home page. <http://www.socm.org/> (accessed February 24, 2006).

U.S. Environmental Protection Agency. "Mid-Atlantic Mountaintop Mining: Draft Programmatic Environmental Impact Statement." May 23, 2005. <http://www.epa. gov/region3/mtntop/eis.htm> (accessed February 24, 2006).

"The Love Canal Tragedy"

Journal article

By: Eckardt C. Beck

Date: January 1979

Source: Beck, Eckardt C. "The Love Canal Tragedy." *EPA Journal.* (January 1979).

About the Author: Eckardt Beck served as Administrator of the U. S. Environmental Protection Agency (EPA) Region II from 1977–1979. As Administrator, he was responsible for all environmental programs established under federal legislation. Prior to this assignment, he acted as the EPA's Deputy Assistant Administrator for Water Planning and Standards, where he managed the nation's industrial water pollution cleanup program. Beck's educational background involved many aspects of public health, including a master's degree in Public Administration from New York University and graduate work in Epidemiology and Public Health (Yale University) as well as in Air Pollution Administration (University of Southern California).

INTRODUCTION

A few names conjure up images of man-made environmental disasters. Bhopal is one example;

another is Love Canal. The catastrophe of Love Canal also exemplifies the dangers of unrestricted dumping of chemicals. Sadly, Love Canal is not an isolated case. Many chemical dump sites exist. However, few become subdivisions.

Love Canal took its name from William T. Love, who planned to construct a canal to connect the upper and lower Niagara Rivers, near Niagara Falls. The canal would supply power to a new city that he envisioned for the area.

Work on the canal did begin in 1894. Then, Louis Tesla's discovery that allowed electricity to be transmitted over long distances via alternating current negated the need for a nearby source of electrical power. The need for Love Canal vanished and the project was abandoned.

By the 1920s, the portion of the canal that had been built was being used by several chemical companies located in the Niagara Falls area to dispose of unwanted chemicals. Until 1953, a vast amount of chemicals was added to the canal, mainly by Hooker Chemical and Plastics Corporation. The disposal was virtually unregulated.

In the mid-1950s, the canal—which now contained some 19,000 cubic yards (14,000 square meters) of toxic waste—was covered with dirt. Then, a few years later, land in the vicinity of the landfill was bought from Hooker Chemical by the local school board, who were in need of land for a new elementary school. Hooker had long resisted selling the land. When they capitulated, they sold the land for only one dollar, and included in the sales agreement a seventeen-line caveat that explained the potential danger of building on the site.

The school board began construction of the new school several years later, directly over the top of the landfill. Construction had to be halted and the building relocated when chemical-filled pits were unearthed. Nonetheless, the school was constructed nearby, followed a few years later by construction of sewers to permit construction of housing. Those buying the land on which houses were built were not told of the existence of the landfill. However, it was not long before residents began to complain of objectionable odors and the appearance of unknown substances in their yards. Officials from the City of Niagara Falls investigated some of the complaints, but no action was taken.

By the mid-1970s, residents were becoming alarmed over the high rate of cancer and birth defects among the residents and the large number of illnesses in children attending the elementary school. The

Children play carelessly, unaware of the toxic waste that may be under their front yard, while their parents continue to voice concerns and irritation over unknowingly purchasing a house built on property overlaying the toxic Love Canal. AP IMAGES

tipping point came when a period of heavy rains and excessive snowfalls added a great deal of water to the soil, driving the toxic mixture further away from the canal site.

Attempts by a resident organization to link the illness to the canal were rebuffed by Occidental Petroleum (Hooker Chemical's parent company) and by civic and state governments. The official position was that the chemicals had been adequately contained within the canal and that the illnesses were unrelated.

The school, which was located within the former boundaries of the Hooker plant, was finally closed and demolished. The houses, however, remained standing. Because homeowners were unable to secure financial compensation, as well as being unable to sell their houses and move, many continued to live and suffer in the dwellings.

Despite this frustration, the infamy of Love Canal began to grow. In 1978, U.S. President Jimmy Carter declared a federal emergency at Love Canal. Still, even that declaration could not secure the funds necessary for relocation of the residents. However, the publicity did spur official investigations. Inspections revealed unacceptable levels of toxic chemicals such as benzene, a known human carcinogen, as well as chloroform, trichloroethene, tetrachloroethene, chlorobenzene, and chlorotoluene. Soil samples collected from sites in the housing development detected more noxious compounds including lindane, benzene and toluene. More than eighty toxic compounds were identified. Geological analyses established that underground formations had directed leachate from the canal underneath many of the houses in the subdivision.

The litany of the toxic loading of Love Canal were elevated levels of miscarriages, birth defects, and occurrences of cancer among the residents, as well as documented chromosome damage.

In response, the Carter White House evacuated all the residents, initially temporarily, and finally, as funds were secured, permanently after purchasing their homes. These were demolished. Some residents in less affected neighborhoods actually chose to remain. In the late 1990s, new development began at Love Canal, away from the contaminated site.

▌ PRIMARY SOURCE

Quite simply, Love Canal is one of the most appalling environmental tragedies in American history.

But that's not the most disturbing fact.

What is worse is that it cannot be regarded as an isolated event. It could happen again—anywhere in this country—unless we move expeditiously to prevent it.

It is a cruel irony that Love Canal was originally meant to be a dream community. That vision belonged to the man for whom the three-block tract of land on the eastern edge of Niagara Falls, New York, was named—William T. Love.

Love felt that by digging a short canal between the upper and lower Niagara Rivers, power could be generated cheaply to fuel the industry and homes of his would-be model city.

But despite considerable backing, Love's project was unable to endure the one-two punch of fluctuations in the economy and Louis Tesla's discovery of how to economically transmit electricity over great distances by means of an alternating current.

By 1910, the dream was shattered. All that was left to commemorate Love's hope was a partial ditch where construction of the canal had begun.

In the 1920s the seeds of a genuine nightmare were planted. The canal was turned into a municipal and industrial chemical dumpsite.

Landfills can of course be an environmentally acceptable method of hazardous waste disposal, assuming they are properly sited, managed, and regulated. Love Canal will always remain a perfect historical example of how not to run such an operation.

In 1953, the Hooker Chemical Company, then the owners and operators of the property, covered the canal with earth and sold it to the city for one dollar.

It was a bad buy.

In the late 1950s, about 100 homes and a school were built at the site. Perhaps it wasn't William T. Love's model city, but it was a solid, working-class community. For a while.

On the first day of August, 1978, the lead paragraph of a front-page story in the New York Times read:

NIAGARA FALLS, N.Y.—Twenty five years after the Hooker Chemical Company stopped using the Love Canal here as an industrial dump, 82 different compounds, 11 of them suspected carcinogens, have been percolating upward through the soil, their drum containers rotting and leaching their contents into the backyards and basements of 100 homes and a public school built on the banks of the canal.

In an article prepared for the February, 1978 EPA Journal, I wrote, regarding chemical dumpsites in general, that "even though some of these landfills have been closed down, they may stand like ticking time bombs." Just months later, Love Canal exploded.

The explosion was triggered by a record amount of rainfall. Shortly thereafter, the leaching began.

I visited the canal area at that time. Corroding waste-disposal drums could be seen breaking up through the grounds of backyards. Trees and gardens were turning black and dying. One entire swimming pool had been popped up from its foundation, afloat now on a small sea of chemicals. Puddles of noxious substances were pointed out to me by the residents. Some of these puddles were in their yards, some were in their basements, others yet were on the school grounds. Everywhere the air had a faint, choking smell. Children returned from play with burns on their hands and faces.

And then there were the birth defects. The New York State Health Department is continuing an investigation into a disturbingly high rate of miscarriages, along with five birth-defect cases detected thus far in the area.

I recall talking with the father of one the children with birth defects. "I heard someone from the press saying that there were only five cases of birth defects here," he told me. "When you go back to your people at EPA, please don't use the phrase 'only five cases.' People must realize that this is a tiny community. Five birth defect cases here is terrifying."

A large percentage of people in Love Canal are also being closely observed because of detected high white-blood-cell counts, a possible precursor of leukemia.

When the citizens of Love Canal were finally evacuated from their homes and their neighborhood, pregnant women and infants were deliberately among the first to be taken out.

"We knew they put chemicals into the canal and filled it over," said one woman, a long-time resident of the Canal area, "but we had no idea the chemicals would invade our homes. We're worried sick about the grandchildren and their children."

Two of this woman's four grandchildren have birth defects. The children were born and raised in the Love Canal community. A granddaughter was born deaf with a cleft palate, an extra row of teeth, and slight retardation. A grandson was born with an eye defect.

Of the chemicals which comprise the brew seeping through the ground and into homes at Love Canal, one of the most prevalent is benzene—a known human carcinogen, and one detected in high concentrations. But the residents characterize things more simply.

"I've got this slop everywhere," said another man who lives at Love Canal. His daughter also suffers from a congenital defect.

On August 7, New York Governor Hugh Carey announced to the residents of the Canal that the State Government would purchase the homes affected by chemicals.

On that same day, President Carter approved emergency financial aid for the Love Canal area (the first emergency funds ever to be approved for something other than a "natural" disaster), and the U.S. Senate approved a "sense of Congress" amendment saying that Federal aid should be forthcoming to relieve the serious environmental disaster which had occurred.

By the month's end, 98 families had already been evacuated. Another 46 had found temporary housing. Soon after, all families would be gone from the most contaminated areas—a total of 221 families have moved or agreed to be moved.

State figures show more than 200 purchase offers for homes have been made, totaling nearly $7 million.

A plan is being set in motion now to implement technical procedures designed to meet the seemingly impossible job of detoxifying the Canal area. The plan calls for a trench system to drain chemicals from the Canal. It is a difficult procedure, and we are keeping our fingers crossed that it will yield some degree of success.

I have been very pleased with the high degree of cooperation in this case among local, State, and Federal governments, and with the swiftness by which the Congress and the President have acted to make funds available.

But this is not really where the story ends.

Quite the contrary.

We suspect that there are hundreds of such chemical dumpsites across this Nation.

Unlike Love Canal, few are situated so close to human settlements. But without a doubt, many of these old dumpsites are time bombs with burning fuses—their contents slowly leaching out. And the next victim cold be a water supply, or a sensitive wetland.

The presence of various types of toxic substances in our environment has become increasingly widespread—a fact that President Carter has called "one of the grimmest discoveries of the modern era."

Chemical sales in the United States now exceed a mind-boggling $112 billion per year, with as many as 70,000 chemical substances in commerce.

Love Canal can now be added to a growing list of environmental disasters involving toxics, ranging from industrial workers stricken by nervous disorders and cancers to the discovery of toxic materials in the milk of nursing mothers....

SIGNIFICANCE

Love Canal is symbolic of the havoc that unregulated chemical disposal can cause. While much suffering and death came from Love Canal, the disaster did galvanize opposition to the unregulated environmental disposal of dangerous compounds. In the wake of Love Canal, the U.S. Congress enacted the Superfund legislation holding polluters accountable for cleanup of high-priority sites. Under the Superfund program, over 10,000 toxic dump sites have been identified across the United States. Remediation efforts are underway or planned.

FURTHER RESOURCES
Books
Bryan, Nichol. *Love Canal: Pollution Crisis (Environmental Disasters)*. New York: World Almanac Library, 2003.

Fletcher, Thomas H. *From Love Canal to Environmental Justice: The Politics of Hazardous Waste on the Canada-U.S. Border*. Orchard Park: Broadview Press, 2003.

Sherrow, Victoria. *Love Canal: Toxic Waste Tragedy (American Disasters)*. Berkeley Heights, N.J.: Enslow Publishers, 2001.

Web sites

"Despite Toxic History, Residents Return to Love Canal." *CNN.com.* <http://www.cnn.com/US/9808/07/love.canal> (accessed November 6, 2005).

"Eckardt C. Beck." *U.S. Environmental Protection Agency.* <http://www.epa.gov/history/admin/reg02/beck.htm> (accessed November 6, 2005).

"Love Canal: Public Health Time Bomb." *New York State Department of Health.* <http://www.health.state.ny.us/nysdoh/lcanal/lctimbmb.htm/> (accessed November 6, 2005).

"The Big Spill:

Bred from Complacency, the Valdez Fiasco Goes from Bad to Worse to Worst Possible"

Magazine article

By: George J. Church

Date: April 10, 1989

Source: Church, George J. "The Big Spill: Bred from Complacency, the Valdez Fiasco Goes from Bad to Worse to Worst Possible." *Time* Volume 133: Issue 15 (April 10, 1989).

About the Author: George J. Church was a journalist at *Time* magazine for twenty-five years. He produced an enormous number of cover articles and was known for his excellence in writing and reporting.

INTRODUCTION

In 1968, oil was discovered in the North Slope, in northern Alaska between the Brooks Range Mountains and the Beaufort Sea in the Arctic Ocean. In 1970, a group of oil companies established the Alyeska Pipeline Service Company, which designed and built a pipeline to transport oil from the North Slope to the port of Valdez. Known as the trans-Alaskan pipeline, it was the largest construction project ever attempted at the time. The pipeline stretches 800 miles (1,290 kilometers) and carries between one and two million barrels of oil per day over rivers, streams and permafrost.

The trans-Alaskan pipeline terminates at the port of Valdez, which is the northernmost ice-free port with access to the Pacific Ocean through Prince William Sound. This access provides a means of transporting oil relatively easily from northern Alaska to the West and Gulf coasts of the United States.

Along with the pipeline, Alyeska was responsible for oversight of shipping through Prince William Sound. Prior to the Exxon Valdez accident, oil tankers carried approximately 2 million gallons (7.6 million liters) of oil through Prince William Sound each day. Ships carrying oil had safely made more than 8,700 trips from the trans-Alaskan pipeline to the West and Gulf coasts of the United States.

The *Exxon Valdez* was an oil tanker owned by the Exxon Shipping Company. On the day of the spill, it was transporting just over 53 million gallons (200.6 million liters) of oil from the port of Valdez. Just after midnight on March 24, 1989, the *Exxon Valdez* ran aground on Bligh Reef in Prince William Sound off the coast of Alaska. Eight of the tanker's eleven oil holds ruptured, spilling about 11 million gallons (41.6 million liters) of oil into the ocean.

This event is considered one of the worst environmental disasters ever to have occurred in the United States. It happened in an ecologically rich habitat, with rugged and inaccessible coastlines. The weather, along with failures by the parties responsible for the spill, confounded the cleanup process.

The *Exxon Valdez* oil spill was extremely well publicized. Environmental groups used it as a serious example of negligence by industry. In addition, the environmental repercussions from the accident were thoroughly studied by ecologists, petroleum engineers and a wide range of government agencies.

PRIMARY SOURCE

A captain with too much alcohol in his blood turns over command of his tanker to an unqualified third mate. The mate shouts contradictory orders to the helmsman and eventually impales the vessel on a reef, causing millions of gallons of oil to gush from the mangled hull. Companies that boasted they had the equipment and manpower in place for a quick cleanup turn out to have hardly anything available and lose irreplaceable days getting into action. Then, almost predictably, the calm weather gives way to high winds that render their efforts ineffective.

By midweek Exxon, owner of the wounded tanker, admitted that the largest oil spill in U.S. history was spreading out of control; by week's end the slick covered almost 900 sq. mi. southwest of Valdez, Alaska, posing a deadly danger to the marine and bird life that teems in Prince William Sound. The story, a tale of unrelieved gloom with no heroes, resembled a Greek tragedy updated by Murphy's Law. Everything that could go wrong did; everyone involved, including the Alaska state government and the U.S. Coast Guard, made damaging errors; hubris in the form of complacency (it has never happened, so it won't) took a heavy toll; and events marched relentlessly from bad to worse toward the worst possible.

In this case, the worst possible is an unprecedented ecological disaster. Though Exxon insists it will persist in cleanup efforts for months if necessary and promises to leave the highly scenic area "the way it was before," that is close to a physical impossibility. Earlier mishaps suggest that only about 10% of the oil from such a massive spill (this one totaled at least 10.1 million gal., perhaps 12.6 million) will ever be recovered. Some of the rest evaporates. But as the lighter components escape into the air, most of the oil turns into a thick black gunk that eventually sinks to the bottom. There it is joined by oil that first coated beaches but little by little washes back into the water.

What happens next is a matter of theorizing. Nearly all previous massive spills have occurred in areas of moderate climate, where the waves, currents and winds of the open ocean dispersed them; the hemorrhage from the tanker Exxon Valdez is the first big spill to foul an enclosed body of cold water. Clifton Curtis, executive director of the Oceanic Society, predicts that the oil deposits on the bottom will act "as lethal time-release capsules," turning loose "harmful petroleum hydrocarbons for months and even years." Birds, fish and marine animals such as seals and otters that are not killed quickly by being coated with crude will still be in danger, as the bottom oil contaminates first microorganisms, then the small fish that eat them, then the larger creatures up the food chain. Fishermen in the port of Cordova (pop. 3,000) fear that their catches of salmon, herring, shrimp and crab will be ruined for years, possibly wiping out their livelihood. Says Barbara Jenson, wife of a fourth-generation fisherman: "I don't think we are going to survive this one."

. . . The supposedly impossible had happened. Since the building 15 years ago of the pipeline that carries Alaskan oil from the North Slope to Valdez for shipment by tanker to the West Coast, oil companies had been shrugging off environmentalists' forebodings of just such an occurrence. In January 1987, Alyeska Pipeline Service Co., the consortium of oil companies (including Exxon) that manages the pipeline, filed a contingency plan with the Federal Government detailing how it would handle a 200,000-bbl. spill in Prince ; William Sound. Alyeska did so only grudgingly, however, protesting, "It is highly unlikely that a spill of this magnitude would occur. Catastrophic events of this nature are further reduced because the majority of tankers calling on Port Valdez are of American registry and all of these are piloted by licensed masters or pilots."

Alyeska nonetheless boasted that it would have equipment on the scene of any major spill within five hours. When the unthinkable happened, the reality was somewhat different: the first crews and equipment did not get to the spill until ten hours after the accident. And then they could do little because booms to contain the oil and mechanical skimmers to scoop it up were pitifully insufficient. Moreover, the barge capable of receiving the skimmed oil had been damaged and could not be deployed until the next day.

What was the hang-up? In a word, says an Alyeska supervisor, "complacency." Lulled by almost twelve years of oil shipping through Valdez without a major accident, Alyeska let its old equipment run down to the point that it was taxed to the limit when it cleaned up a small spill of a mere 1,500 bbl. in January. Workers who had been hired to devote full time to combatting oil spills were replaced by people whose primary duties lay elsewhere. The state government failed to keep Alyeska up to the mark; the legislature denied its watchdog agency funds for inspecting oil terminals and was pretty much reduced to taking the oil companies' word for their preparedness. The Coast Guard too has sustained deep budget cuts and, says a friendly observer, "is held together with baling wire." Its closest concentration of cleanup ships and equipment is in the San Francisco area, more than 2,000 miles south of Valdez.

Frank Iarossi, president of Exxon Shipping Co., flew from his Houston home to Valdez and by Friday night took command of the cleanup. By then the slick was spreading and chemical dispersants could not be used because the seas were too calm for them to be effective. On Sunday winds picked up to 70 m.p.h., hindering boats from booming and skimming the oil. The winds drove the oil into a froth known as mousse; workers who tried to apply a napalm-like substance to the oil and ignite it with laser beams did not succeed.

The company compounded the damage to its image by initially misleading the press and local residents with assurances that its beach cleanups and booming operations were well under way. But on Wednesday Exxon spokesman Donald Cornett admitted that beach cleanup had not started and that one boat had just sailed around gauging the extent of the spill. Later that night he was greeted in nearby Cordova by citizens displaying signs that read, DON'T BELIEVE EVERYTHING YOU HEAR. ESPECIALLY AT ALYESKA AND EXXON PRESS CONFERENCES.

Not until Wednesday was a ragtag fleet in full operation. A team from Washington, consisting of Secretary of Transportation Samuel Skinner, Environmental Protection Agency Administrator William Reilly and Coast Guard Commandant Paul Yost, flew to Alaska at midweek and reported back to Bush that the cleanup was going well enough that there was no need for the Federal Government to take over. That seemed to be a polite

The *Exxon Valdez* oil spill contaminated the environement and habitat of thousands of animals in Prince William Sound, likely including these sea lions swimming in the southern bay of Naked Island. AP IMAGES

way of saying there was no way for the feds to speed things, so Washington might as well stay out and avoid sharing the blame for what the President called a major tragedy.

The spill happened in almost the worst place and at nearly the worst time possible. The jagged coast of Prince William Sound is dotted with innumerable coves and inlets where the spilled oil can collect and stay for months, killing young fish that spawn in the shallows. Fishermen have already written off the herring season that was to start this week. Soon waterfowl by the tens of thousands will finish their northward migrations and settle into summer nesting colonies in Prince William Sound. For them, says Ann Rothe, Alaska regional representative of the National Wildlife Federation, "it will be like returning home after somebody came in and ransacked your house, took some gunk and dumped it all over the place." She fears the sea otter population of 4,000 to 5,000 "will be totally wiped out."

In a highly unusual public apology, published as an advertisement in TIME and about 100 other magazines and newspapers, Exxon Chairman L.G. Rawl promised that his company not only will pay all direct cleanup costs but "also will meet our obligations to all those who have suffered damage from the spill." Under federal law, the company must pay the first $14 million in cleanup costs, then can tap a fund set up by the Trans-Alaska Pipeline Act for an additional $86 million.

And after that? Although the pipeline law limits a company's liability to $100 million in most cases, that lid is off if a spill and the damage that results are due to negligence. A court may find that the actions of Captain Hazelwood and Third Mate Cousins—and the failure of both Alyeska and Exxon to respond quickly to the spill—meet that test. Both the state of Alaska and the Federal Government have opened criminal investigations of the spill. "It will be a long war of experts," says James McNerney, a Houston specialist in environmental and maritime law. The battle over this spill and its consequences could prove almost as messy and unpredictable as the environmental damages.

SIGNIFICANCE

Following the accident, the National Transportation Safety Board conducted an investigation into the causes. They found five events contributed to the grounding of the ship. First, the third mate, Cousins, did not maneuver the ship properly, probably because he was tired. Second, the ship's captain, Hazelwood, did not provide an appropriate navigation watch. In his criminal trial, Hazelwood was found not guilty of operating a vessel while intoxicated, but guilty of negligent discharge of oil. Third, the Exxon Shipping Company was negligent in its supervision of Hazelwood and his crew. Fourth, the U.S. Coast Guard failed to adequately monitor the shipping traffic. Finally, the ship should have had more effective pilot and escort service.

Nearly 11 million gallons (41.6 million liters) of oil were spilled by the *Exxon Valdez*. The spill stretched 460 miles (740 kilometers) and affected 1,300 miles (2,100 kilometers) of shoreline. It is estimated that 250,000 seabirds, 2,800 sea otters and 300 harbor seals were killed by the oil spill. In addition, 250 bald eagles and at least 22 orcas were killed. Billions of salmon and herring eggs were also destroyed.

One of the surprising results from studies of the area affected by the oil spill was the persistence of oil in the environment. Twelve years after the accident, surveys of beaches found significant amounts of oil below the surface in areas affected by the oil spills. This oil has toxic effects that spread throughout the food web and have hindered the recovery of the ecosystem. Six bird species, along with the Pacific herring and the harbor seal, were listed as "not recovering" in 2002. Other species, however, like the bald eagle, the pink salmon, and the sockeye salmon, recovered to population levels similar to those prior to the oil spill.

Following the disaster, a variety of mechanisms were put in place to prevent similar scenarios from ever occurring again. In 1970, the Oil Pollution Act was passed, which strengthened regulations on the structure of oil tanker hulls. By 2015, all ships carrying oil through Prince William Sound will be required to have a double hull. In addition, the Act calls for improved communications between ship captains and traffic centers. In Prince William Sound, all tankers are tracked by satellite and escorted by pilot ships.

Contingency planning for oil spills has also greatly improved. Skimming systems, containment booms and stockpiles of dispersants are all immediately available in the case of an emergency. In addition, the staff and vehicles for applying the remediation measures are all in place. Drills and training programs are regularly scheduled in Prince William Sound to maintain preparedness for oil spills.

FURTHER RESOURCES

Web sites

"*Exxon Valdez* Oil Spill Research." *Alaska Fisheries Science Center*. <http://www.afsc.noaa.gov/abl/OilSpill/oilspill.htm> (accessed March 8, 2006).

The Exxon Valdez Oil Spill Trustee Council. <http://www.evostc.state.ak.us> (accessed March 8, 2006).

"Exxon Valdez." *U.S. Environmental Protection Agency*. <http://www.epa.gov/oilspill/exxon.htm> (accessed March 8, 2006).

Mercury Residues and Poisoning

Photograph

By: H. John Maier, Jr.

Date: 1993

Source: Time Life Pictures/Getty Images

About the Photographer: John Maier, Jr. is an artist and photographer who regularly contributes photographs to travel publications, especially from South American locations, and also specializes in nature photography. This photograph was taken in Brazil in the early 1990s.

INTRODUCTION

Mercury is used in many industrial processes and is a highly potent toxin that can cause blindness, insanity, and death. One mercury thermometer contains enough mercury to render a typical drinking-water reservoir unusable. One aspect of the mercury problem is its entry into the environment. Another concern involves the entry of mercury into the human body as a pollutant, often through contaminated fish.

Fine particles of gold are found in the sediments of a number of rivers in South America. These low concentrations of gold are often extracted by informal gold mining, gold extraction by individuals or small groups rather than by industrial-size operations. Sediments are pumped from river bottoms or hosed from riverbanks, and separated by settling speed. The heaviest sediments are combined with mercury, which causes gold particles to agglutinate or come together into larger particles, an amalgam. Other elements amalgamate with the mercury. The amalgam is strained out using cloth, often an old T-shirt, with unamalgamated mercury flowing through the cloth

mining activities were eating mercury in river fish, consuming at least six to ten times the international average amount of mercury. In Brazil, about ninety tons of gold are mined every year, releasing about 130 tons of mercury into rivers. Similar practices occur in French Guiana.

PRIMARY SOURCE

MERCURY RESIDUES AND POISONING

See primary source image.

Mercury Residues and Poisoning. An image from 1993 showing a Brazilian worker separating gold from ore using mercury. He inhales mercury fumes as he works and waste mercury ends up in the soil and water. Over a decade later, much gold extraction in South America is still performed by this highly polluting method. PHOTO BY H. JOHN MAIER JR./IMAGE WORKS/IMAGE WORKS/TIME LIFE PICTURES/GETTY IMAGES

SIGNIFICANCE

Mercury is a global pollutant because it is a byproduct of many processes and has been used to make many products. Thousands—perhaps millions—of tons of mercury have been used in thousands of products and industrial processes, including battery manufacture, gold mining, paint, batteries, thermometers, sphygmomanometers, flat-screen computer monitors, thermostats, fluorescent light bulbs, and many other devices. Although mercury has been eliminated from some products—for example, many thermometers and blood-pressure devices are now electronic or use liquids other than mercury—virtually all of the mercury used by industrial society has simply gone into nearby waterways, the air, or the trash (and continues to do so). Morever, burning coal, the primary source of electricity in the United States and around the world, releases mercury into the air, which is transported to the soil and water by downwind rainfall.

Mercury, like other toxic metals such as lead, is a permanent pollutant. It never breaks down or disappears, but remains active in the food chain as long as it is in contact with living things. Eventually it may become sequestered under sediments, and so be rendered harmless unless disturbed again. Uptake of mercury into organisms is concentrated progressively up the food chain; predatory fish such as tuna and swordfish are particularly efficient mercury concentrators and can biomagnify environmental mercury levels by a factor of up to 100,000. Mercury poisoning from eating fish first drew global attention in the 1950s, when contaminated fish caused often-fatal poisoning of many Japanese fishermen and their families.

In 1970, a chemistry professor at State University of New York at Binghamton, Bruce McDuffie, responding to suggestions from his wife and a student, took a random can of tuna fish off the shelf of his home pantry and analyzed it for mercury. He found mercury

into a container for re-use. The strained amalgam is then heated with a torch, as shown in the photograph. Mercury evaporates at a lower temperature than gold and the other elements in the amalgam, so heating leaves impure gold, which can be sold. These processes release mercury as a vapor and as scattered waste in the surrounding soil. A suitable industrial gold-refining process could capture the mercury vapor for re-use and so release little mercury to the environment, but this is not the norm in South American mining practice.

Miners inhaling mercury vapor incur health risks. A 2001 study by French toxicologists found that American Indians living many miles away from gold

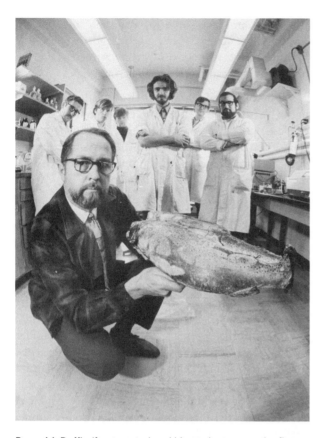

Bruce McDuffie (front center) and his students were the first to discover that deep-sea tuna and swordfish can contain levels of mercury too high for human consumption. PHOTO BY ART RICKERBY/ TIME LIFE PICTURES/GETTY IMAGES

at 0.75 parts per million, 150 percent of the maximum level allowed by the U.S. Food and Drug Administration (FDA). Mercury contamination of fresh-water fish was already known, but mercury in ocean fish had not been found before.

The tuna-mercury story made national headlines. In response, the FDA analyzed 12 million cans of tuna and found many with high mercury. It also found excessive mercury in some other ocean fish. In 1971 the FDA announced that the contaminated tuna had been removed from grocery shelves. Little tuna was tested for decades following. However, a 2005 an investigation by the *Chicago Tribune* found that "canned tuna still contains mercury—sometimes in amounts as high as those found by [McDuffie]."

The U.S. government has long advised pregnant women and children to limit their albacore intake (albacore is a white-meat tuna species) and to eat "light tuna" instead on the grounds that "light tuna"

consists of skipjack, a smaller tuna species with lower mercury. However, tens of millions of cans of "light tuna" sold in the United States are actually yellowfin tuna, which has been found to contain just as much mercury on average as albacore. Moreover, as is often the case with regulations governing pollutants, mercury standards for tuna have been set by government officials after receiving private input from the industry being regulated, which opposes strict standards because they would decrease sales: the *Chicago Tribune* found FDA records showing that "industry leaders met privately with FDA officials five times in late 2000 when the agency was crafting its mercury warning."

The FDA then issued a warning for children and pregnant women to avoid shark, swordfish, king mackerel, and tilefish—making no mention of tuna. The FDA explained that Americans did not eat enough tuna to merit a warning; however, its own data state that tuna is the number one seafood consumed in the U.S.

Coal-fired electric generation causes 41 percent of U.S. industrial mercury pollution, about 41 tons per year. About 6,500 tons of mercury vapor are circulating the world's atmosphere at any one time, half from volcanoes and other natural sources and half from human activity. Fish and shellfish, both freshwater and salt, concentrate mercury and deliver it to carnivores higher up the food chain, including people. An study sponsored by the environmental group Greenpeace found in 2004 that the EPA limit of 1 microgram of mercury per gram of human hair (an easy way of sampling human mercury burden) is exceeded in 21 percent of U.S. women of childbearing age tested.

FURTHER RESOURCES
Web sites

Biller, Dan. "Informal Gold Mining and Mercury Pollution in Brazil." World Bank. Policy Research Working Paper 11304. May, 1994. Available at <www-wds. worldbank.org/.../WDSP/IB/1994/05/01/000009265_ 3970625091321/Rendered/PDF/multi_page.pdf> (accessed Feb. 22, 2006).

"Food for Thought: A dietary cost of our appetite for gold." Science News. May 12, 2001. Available at <http:// www.sciencenews.org/articles/20010512/food.asp> (accessed February 22, 2006).

Roe, Sam and Hawthorne, Michael. "How safe is tuna?Federal regulators and the tuna industry fail to warn consumers about the true health hazards of an American favorite." Chicago Tribune. Dec. 13, 2005. Available at <http://www.chicagotribune.com/news/ nationworld/chi-0512130114dec13,1,2843261.story?

page=2&coll=chi-newsnationworld-hed> (accessed February 22, 2006).

Smith, Hal. "The Plowboy Interview: Bruce McDuffie." Mother Earth News. No. 9, May, 1971. Available at <http://www.motherearthnews.com/library/1971_May_June/The_Plowboy_Interview_R_Buckminster_Fuller> [sic] (accessed Feb. 22, 2006).

"Study Finds Airborne Mercury Pollution." Santa Cruz Sentinel. Dec. 20, 2002. Available at <http://www.santacruzsentinel.com/archive/2002/December/20/local/stories/05local.htm> (accessed February 22, 2006).

Taj Mahal Facade Carving Detail with Chips

Effects of Regional Industry Pollution

Photograph

By: Robert Nickelsberg

Date: September 30, 1995

Source: Nickelsberg, Robert. "Taj Mahal Facade Carving Detail with Chips, Effects of Regional Industry Pollution." Getty Images, 1995.

About the Photographer: Robert Nickelsberg is a nomadic photojournalist based in New York. He is best known for his work as a veteran war photographer for *Time* magazine.

INTRODUCTION

The Taj Mahal, located in northern India, was built between 1631 and 1653 by the Mughal Emperor Shah Jahanas as tomb for his wife. It is considered one of the great architectural treasures of the world. Some three million tourists visit the Taj Mahal each year. Unfortunately, it is also surrounded by pollution sources, including vehicular traffic, private electrical generators (which are run to compensate for frequent grid blackouts), brick kilns, glass-making units, and iron foundries. Air pollution emitted by these industries are slowly destroying the monument, whose primary building material is white marble. Marble, like limestone, consists mostly of calcite (calcium carbonate, CO_3), which is readily broken down by acids.

The Taj Mahal, like all buildings and monuments built from limestone and marble, is vulnerable to acid rain—precipitation in which sulfur dioxide and nitrogen oxides from burning fossil fuels have been dis-

solved to produce sulfuric acid and nitric acid. Although the acidity of any given raindrop is too low to inflict visible damage on a structure such as the Taj Mahal, over decades the damage accumulates.

Finely detailed carvings, such as the flowers shown in the photograph, are the first features to be damaged or destroyed. Even inside the building, where rain cannot reach, airborne sulfur dioxide can settle directly onto the stone, reacting with humidity to form a fungus-like crust called "marble cancer."

The government of India began monitoring atmospheric sulfur dioxide levels at the Taj Mahal in 1981. In 1984, an environmental lawyer, Mahesh Chandra Mehta, filed suit with the Indian Supreme Court demanding that the government force polluters in the Taj Mahal's vicinity to stop. The case was decided in Mehta's favor in 1996, when the Court ordered 292 coal-based industries inside a 4,000 square mile (10,400 square kilometer) area containing the Taj Mahal and several other historic monuments, the "Taj Trapezium Zone," to either switch to natural gas (a low-polluting fossil fuel) or to relocate outside the zone. However, manufacturers and labor unions in the zone resisted the relocation policy. Many simply took no action at all. Although the government is funding the construction of new gas pipelines to industrial areas in the Trapezium, there is a natural gas shortage in India and both employers and workers at foundries and other facilities in the Zone are fearful of shutdown or relocation. In 1999, the Supreme Court ordered the closure of 160 factories in the area, including fifty-three iron foundries, that had not yet reduced their emissions.

However, many such industries remain in operation in the protected zone and pollution at the shrine has not improved. In early 2005, the Central Pollution Control Board of the Indian government told the Supreme Court of India that air pollution at the Taj Mahal was worsening, stating that "There is a gross violation of sensitive area ambient air quality norms with respect to both suspended particulate matters and respiratory particulate matters."

PRIMARY SOURCE

TAJ MAHAL FACADE CARVING DETAIL WITH CHIPS, EFFECTS OF REGIONAL INDUSTRY POLLUTION

See primary source image.

PRIMARY SOURCE

Taj Mahal Facade Carving Detail with Chips, Effects of Regional Industry Pollution. Decades of air pollution has been causing the marble of which the Taj Mahal is constructed to break down. PHOTO BY ROBERT NICKELSBERG/TIME LIFE PICTURES/GETTY IMAGES

SIGNIFICANCE

The kind of air pollution that afflicts the Taj Mahal is commonplace worldwide. In the United States, acid rain falls over much of the Northeast. Two thirds of the acid in U.S. rain is caused by coal-fired electric plants and one third by other industries and by road traffic. Marble and limestone monuments, statues, and buildings in India, Europe, and the U.S. (including Washington, D.C.) are being broken down by decades of sulfur and nitrogen compounds in the air, whether mixed with rain or deposited directly.

Air pollution is a threat not only to monuments and buildings but to human health and to ecosystems. Air pollution causes an estimated 50,000–100,000 premature deaths annually in the United States alone (24,000 of them due to emissions from coal-fired electric plants, as of 2004) and far more worldwide, while severe damage to forests, lakes, and rivers from acid rain has been documented in the U.S., Europe, China, and elsewhere.

Even while continuing to burn fossil fuels, measures can be taken to reduce these effects. For example, sulfur can be removed from coal-plant emissions by "scrubbers," which force the sulfur-dioxide-bearing smoke from burning coal to react with a limestone-water mixture rather than venting it to the atmosphere. Electrostatic precipitators can pull smoke particles out of the flue gas before it is vented. Such technologies have reducing pollution from a few modern coal plants by 80–90 percent, not counting the greenhouse gas carbon dioxide. Europe has been particularly successful in reducing acid rain in recent decades, while the United States has seen moderate reduction in acid rain due to Clean Air Act (first passed in 1966, amended and renewed in 1970, 1977, and 1990).

However, the struggle over industrial activity in the Taj Trapezium Zone illustrates the role of economics in the air pollution problem. It is often cheaper to pollute than to not pollute, at least from the polluter's point of the view. (The polluter does not have to pay the medical bills of people sickened downwind or for other damages caused by pollutants: such costs are said to be "externalized" by the polluter.) Scrubbers, electrostatic precipitators, conversion to natural gas, and other antipollution measures all cost more money than simply allowing raw smoke to go up a chimney. Industry has usually taken antipollution measures only when they generate a profit or are required by law. In the early 2000s, U.S. coal burners were supported by the administration of President George W. Bush in their efforts to loosen Federal legal restrictions on sulfur dioxide and other emissions. The Environmental Protection Agency (EPA), overseen by appointees of the Administration, was given the task of trying to weaken the provisions of the Clean Air Act. In 2005, at the request of a coalition of environmental groups, the U.S. Court of Appeals for the D.C. Circuit struck down new (2002) EPA rules that would have allowed increased pollution from fuel-burning industries. The court agreed that the new rules would violate the Clean Air Act.

FURTHER RESOURCES

Periodicals

"Air Pollution Around India's Taj Mahal Growing: Environment Watchdog." *Agence France Press* (English) (February 23, 2005).

"Pollutants Lay Siege to Taj Mahal." *Hindustan Times* (March 8, 2005).

Web sites

Rajalakshmi, R. K. *United Nations Educational, Scientific, and Cultural Organization (UNESCO).* "Toxins and the Taj." <http://www.unesco.org/courier/2000_07/uk/signe.htm> (accessed February 17, 2006).

U.S. Environmental Protection Agency. "Acid Rain." <http://www.epa.gov/acidrain/index.html> (accessed February 17, 2006).

Wreckage at the Site of the World Trade Center

Photograph

By: Gene Shaw

Date: September 16, 2001

Source: Time Life Pictures/Getty Images

About the Photographer: This picture was taken by Gene Shaw on September 16, 2001, at the site of the World Trade Center collapse, New York City. The buildings collapsed just five days earlier after being struck by jetliners piloted by hijackers; debris cleanup lasted months.

INTRODUCTION

The World Trade Center was a pair of identical 110-story towers along with a separate forty-seven-building, Seven World Trade Center, built in 1966–1973. All three buildings burned and collapsed catastrophically on September 11, 2001 after each of the two towers was struck by a hijacked commercial jetliner. At least 2,726 people were killed and seven thousand injured. The resulting rubble pile weighed approximately 1.2 million tons, and a cloud of smoke obscured lower Manhattan Island for days.

Thousands of police officers, firefighters, medical services personnel, transport workers, ironworkers, construction workers, and other rescue personnel converged on the scene at once, scouring the rubble for survivors. A few of these workers are visible in the photograph.

Fires burned at the site until at least Dec. 19, 2001, and the complex job of cleanup would last until May 30, 2002. There was concern at the time about the health affects of the smoke and dust cloud on the workers and on the residents of Manhattan and nearby areas, but the U.S. Environmental Protection Agency (EPA) quickly issued assurances that the air was safe. Workers returned to work on the New York Stock Exchange on Wall Street on Sep. 17, walking through a visible haze of dust and smoke past police officers wearing filtering masks. The EPA has been intensely criticized—and taken to court—for its misleading air-safety assurances after September 11. In 2006, a class-action lawsuit on behalf of residents, students, and workers in Brooklyn and lower Manhattan was proceeding in Federal court against the EPA and former EPA chief Christine Todd Whitman, claiming that they issued false information about the air quality in the aftermath of the World Trade Center attack, and seeking damages and reimbursement.

 PRIMARY SOURCE

WRECKAGE AT THE SITE OF THE WORLD TRADE CENTER DISASTER

See primary source image.

SIGNIFICANCE

When the towers collapsed, almost everything in them but their steel structural supports was converted

Wreckage at the Site of the World Trade Center Disaster. The World Trade Center contained many tons of lead, asbestos, and other toxic materials, some of which was liberated into the surrounding environment when the building collapsed catastrophically. Although the U.S. Environmental Protection Agency hastened to assure the public that the air was safe to breathe in the vicinity soon after the disaster, many cleanup workers and area residents have since suffered health problems. PHOTO BY GENE SHAW/TIMEPIX/TIME LIFE PICTURES/GETTY IMAGES

to fine dust: concrete, carpeting, paint, glass, plastics, insulation, tens of thousands of personal computers containing mercury and lead, and so forth. All these substances are toxic, whether burned or pulverized. Moreover, according to a widely cited 2004 Sierra Club report on the disaster, "The towers housed a Secret Service shooting range that kept millions of rounds of lead ammunition on site and a U.S. Customs lab that stored thousands of pounds of arsenic, lead, mercury, and chromium." All these materials were converted into dust in a few seconds when the tower collapsed, and an unknown amount dispersed at once as a large dust cloud. Potentially toxic dust and smoked blanketed the area of the World Trade Center complex and traveled downwind. Fires continued to burn in the rubble for three months at temperatures up to 1,800°F (982°C), releasing more toxins.

The EPA issued repeated reassurances in the days immediately following the attack that the air in the vicinity of the World Trade Center site was safe. These reassurances were widely questioned at the time. The EPA's own Inspector General reported in August, 2003 that "EPA's basic overriding message [in the days following September 11] was that the public did not need to be concerned about airborne contaminants caused by the [World Trade Center] collapse," yet "it did not have sufficient data and analyses to make such a blanket statement." The reassurances were issued, according to the Inspector General, in response to pressure from the White House.

The health consequences of the EPA's assurances will be difficult to measure precisely. If the EPA had issued warnings, many more people could have avoided the area or used breath masks and other precautions.

A study of the U.S. Centers for Disease Control released in 2004, which focused only on persons involved in the rescue and recovery response to the disaster, not on residents, estimated that in the aftermath of the disaster some forty thousand workers and volunteers "potentially were exposed to numerous psychological stressors, environmental toxins, and other physical hazards." The report stated that "a substantial portion" of participants in its study of workers exposed to hazards during rescue and recovery operations "experienced new-onset or worsened preexisting lower and upper respiratory symptoms, with frequent persistence of symptoms for months after their WTC (World Trade Center) response work stopped." Longer-term results of exposure to the many toxic substances in WTC dust and smoke will take many years to measure.

Whitman, former Republican governor of New Jersey, was head of the EPA at the time of the 9/11 attacks. In 2006, the U.S. District Judge, hearing the class-action lawsuit being brought against her and the EPA because of the potentially misleading assurances issued after 9/11, refused to grant Whitman immunity to prosecution. The judge stated: "No reasonable person would have thought that telling thousands of people it was safe to return to lower Manhattan, while knowing that such return could pose long-term health risks and other dire consequences, was conduct sanctioned by our laws."

FURTHER RESOURCES
Web sites

Environmental Protection Agency. "EPA's Response to the World Trade Center Collapse: Challenges, Successes, and Areas for Improvement. Report No. 2003-P-00012." August 22, 2003. <http://www.epa.gov/oig/reports/2003/WTC_report_20030821.pdf > (accessed February 17, 2006).

Sierra Club. "Pollution and Deception at Ground Zero." September 10, 2004. <http://www.infoimagination.org/ps/kerry/docs/GroundZero.pdf> (accessed February 17, 2006).

The Amazonian Rainforest under Siege from Illegal Loggers

Photograph

By: Tom Stoddart

Date: November 2003

Source: Getty Images

About the Photographer: This picture was taken from the air in November, 2003 over the state of Pará, Brazil, showing devastation wrought by illegal logging. The banner at the center was erected by Greenpeace protestors trying to draw global attention to the problem.

INTRODUCTION

Greenpeace is an international, nongovernmental, environmental organization that is most famous for its attention-getting protests against the killing of whales, global warming, and rainforest logging. This banner was erected by Greenpeace campaigners in the Porto de Moz region of the Pará state of Brazil, the hardest-hit part of the Amazon rainforest. Pará's rainforests have lost an area equal to that of Austria, Holland, Portugal, and Switzerland combined—mostly to illegal logging. The Greenpeace activists reached the area by sailing up river waters in one of Greenpeace's four major ships, the *Arctic Sunrise*, a fifty-meter seagoing motor yacht with a rounded (keelless) bottom suitable for both Arctic ice navigation and river work.

Greenpeace was founded by a handful of environmentalists in Vancouver, Canada, in 1970 in order to sail to Amchitka, Alaska, to protest U.S. underground nuclear testing there. Greenpeace became an international organization in 1979. It began studying illegal logging in the Brazilian Amazon in 1992. It began working directly with communities in the Porto de Moz area in 2000, seeking the creation of an "extractive reserve"—no commercial logging region—called the Verde Para Sempre ("Green Forever") Extractive Reserve. A victory for the campaign pictured here was achieved in 2004, when the Brazilian President, Luis Inacio Lula da Silva, signed decrees establishing two extractive reserves, Verde Para Sempre and Riozinho do Anfrisio. The two reserves protect over two million hectares (20,000 square kilometers, 7,700 square miles) of rainforest. In the protected area, native peoples will receive collective or group rights to land and natural resources (timber, fish, etc.); they will be allowed to harvest the rainforest through "traditional economic activities" but commercial clear-cutting will be illegal. In early 2006, President Lula decreed a 6.4 million hectare (640,000 square kilometer, 247,000 square mile) conservation in the Amazon.

Despite the impressive size of the preserves, they cover a fraction of the area that continues to be destroyed throughout the Amazon by illegal logging. In 2003–2006 an area of Amazon rainforest equal in

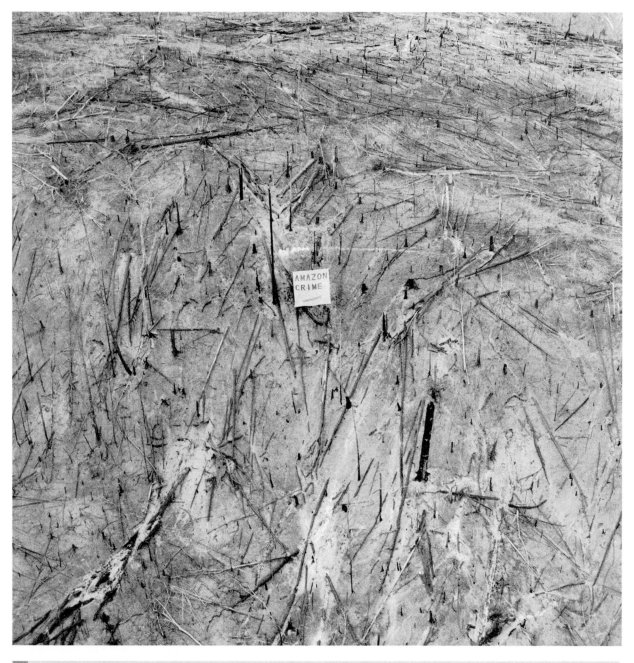

PRIMARY SOURCE

The Amazonian Rainforest under Siege from Illegal Loggers. An aerial photograph taken in November, 2003 as part of the effort of the environmental organization Greenpeace to impede illegal destruction of rainforests in the Amazon region of Brazil. The picture was taken in the state of Pará, which is the largest timber exporting region in the Amazon. PHOTO BY TOM STODDART/GETTY IMAGES

size to the 6.4 million hectare conservation area decreed in 2006 was destroyed.

Greenpeace and local activists risk their lives—and sometimes lose them—by being active in the Amazon. In Pará, gunmen can be hired to assassinate almost anyone for a small fee; almost eight hundred rural activists have been have been assassinated in the region over the last three decades. Slavery is also prevalent in Pará state; according to a commission of the Catholic Church in Brazil, 25,000 people in Pará are working in slavery or semi-slavery.

THE AMAZONIAN RAINFOREST UNDER SIEGE FROM ILLEGAL LOGGERS

See primary source image.

SIGNIFICANCE

Rainforests, which contain the great majority of the world's plant, animal, fresh-water fish, and insect species and are important in shaping global weather patterns, are disappearing rapidly. Wood from tropical forests is sold for construction throughout the world, and soya and other crops grown on the cleared land are harvested for export. The Amazon rainforest contains about 40 percent of all tropical rainforest remaining in the world and hosts approximately sixty thousand species of plant, one thousand species of bird, two thousand species of fish, three hundred species of mammal, and some twenty million people (including about 180,000 indigenous people). The Amazon basin covers one twentieth of the land area of the Earth.

Illegal logging is the greatest enemy of the rainforest: in 2004 alone, the Amazon lost an area about equal to that of Belgium. Forestry work is often performed by slaves, workers who are lured into the forest with promises of high-paying work only to find themselves in bondage— they may be killed if they try to escape. Land ownership law is confused in the Amazon—Greenpeace characterizes the area as a "legal quagmire"—making it easier for loggers to seize land using a combination of quasi-legal or fictitious claims and brute force (gunmen).

Much as with the international trade in cocaine and heroin, illegal lumber production in the developing world (and attendant local violence) are driven largely by demand in the developed world, especially Europe and the United States. The United States and Europe are primary markets for wood illegally stripped from Pará; the United States is the largest buyer of timber and timber products from the Amazon, buying almost three times as much as the second largest buyer, China. In Europe, the UK is the largest importer of illegal tropical timber. Almost 60 percent of all UK tropical timber imports come from illegal logging in Africa, Indonesia, and the Amazon.

In 2003, Greenpeace launched a campaign in the UK to stop the importation of illegal tropical timber. Greenpeace has also blocked the unloading of tropical timber in Italy and protested the use of illegal tropic wood to build offices for the European Union. Although President George W. Bush announced the "President's Initiative Against Illegal Logging" in 2003, and U.S. officials have held or turned back some shipments of illegal mahogany, the United States has in practice been far more intent on prosecuting Greenpeace than illegal loggers. In 2002, when Greenpeace activists boarded a ship carrying over ten million dollars of illegal Brazilian mahogany to the United States, the U.S. Justice Department charged the entire organization under an extremely obscure 1872 law (last applied in 1890) against "sailormongering." ("Sailormongering" is the practice of using prostitutes to entice sailors away from their posts when a ship is in port.) The case was decided in favor of Greenpeace by a Federal judge who ruled that "the indictment is a rare—and maybe unprecedented—prosecution of an advocacy group" for free speech conduct.

Certification programs have been developed so that buyers can be assured that the lumber they are purchasing has been legally harvested. Such lumber may be more expensive than illegally harvested lumber.

FURTHER RESOURCES

Web sites

Greenpeace. "Amazon."<http://www.greenpeace.org/international/campaigns/forests/amazon> (accessed Feb. 17, 2006).

Greenpeace. "State of Conflict: An Investigation into the Landgrabbers, Loggers and Lawless Frontiers in Pará State, Amazon." 2003. <http://www.greenpeace.org/international/press/reports/state-of-conflict> (accessed Feb. 9, 2006).

Romaguer, Boris. Food and Agriculture Organization of the United Nations. "Barriers to and Opportunities for Sustainable Forestry in the Amazon." No date. <http://www.fao.org/docrep/article/wfc/xii/0429-b1.htm> (accessed Feb. 17, 2006).

"Memories Still Linger 25 Years After Three Mile Island Accident"

Newspaper article

By: Dawn Fallik

Date: March 26, 2004

Source: Fallik, Dawn. "Memories Still Linger 25 Years After Three Mile Island Accident." The *Philadelphia Inquirer* (March 26, 2004).

About the Author: Dawn Fallik covers the science and medicine beat for the *Philadelphia Inquirer*. She has won many state and national awards for her investigative reporting, breaking news stories, and column writing. Prior to the *Inquirer*, she had been with the *St. Louis Post-Dispatch*, The Associated Press, and the (Troy, N.Y.) *Record*. Her graduate degree is from the University of Missouri, where she became a database specialist and co-directed the National Institute of Computer-Assisted Reporting.

INTRODUCTION

The United States came close to experiencing a nuclear catastrophe on March 28, 1979, at the Three Mile Island nuclear power plant in Harrisburg, Pennsylvania. A partial nuclear meltdown of the plant's Unit 2 reactor released radiation into the atmosphere, and left a lingering skepticism about the use of nuclear energy among the U.S. public.

Operators of the reactor knew they were in trouble when red lights began flashing and warning sirens sounded in the control room shortly after 4 A.M. on the night of the accident. Due to inadequate levels of coolant, the nuclear core had begun a massive meltdown and released 10 million Curies of radioactivity into the environment. Equipment problems led to worker miscalculations of how much coolant was in the core. Although the meltdown was critical, experts say there was not a steam explosion which would have caused massive amounts of radioactivity to breach the containment structures and be released into the atmosphere. Such an explosion would likely have led to many casualties.

The reactor was cooled off by the evening of March 28, but in the days that followed, new concerns arose. A hydrogen bubble had formed in the dome of the pressurizing vessel that contains the core. If the bubble had burned or exploded, the core would have been further destabilized. By April 1, after the evacuation of residents within 5 miles (8 kilometers) of the plant, authorities gained control of the situation. Unit 2 was eventually secured and permanently shut down.

Many Harrisburg residents and former employees remember the days following the incident. However, the public was not given much information as to exactly what had happened, and what the magnitude of the accident was. At the time, the Lieutenant Governor of Pennsylvania claimed everything was under control and there was no safety or health dangers from Three Mile Island. It took several weeks for community leaders and the media to sift through conflicting reports provided by the plant's management and the government to get a grasp on the seriousness of

the situation. Even twenty-five years after the accident, controversy remains over how much radiation was released, and what the long-term health effects were.

Some current and former residents say friends and family have died from cancer, which they claim is from fallout from Three Mile Island. Official reports from the Nuclear Regulatory Committee (NRC) say there were no injuries or deaths of plant workers or nearby community workers that resulted from the accident. Government officials also say there was not enough radiation released to impact the long-term health of nearby residents.

The Three Mile Island accident occurred as Congressional hearings were being held about the safety and risks of U.S. nuclear plants. The Union of Concerned Scientists (UCS) had recommended that sixteen different nuclear plants, including Three Mile Island, be closed for repairs to improve safety. At the time, the nuclear industry claimed that nuclear plant accidents were highly unlikely. However, just nine days before the Three Mile incident, the Executive Director of UCS, Daniel Ford, stated to the congressional Subcommittee on Energy and the Environment that he felt the safety risks at the plants were too high and needed to be closely addressed. Ford made his statements based on observations of low performance and near accidents that had already occurred at many plants.

▇ PRIMARY SOURCE

MEMORIES STILL LINGER 25 YEARS AFTER THREE MILE ISLAND ACCIDENT.

Tom Richards retired from his job at Three Mile Island 10 years ago, but the nuclear power plant remains ever-present, shadowing his moves on the Sunset Golf Course, where he works as a groundskeeper.

Some day when the still-operating Unit 1 is closed and the complex razed, maybe people will stop asking about what happened in Middletown, Pa., during the early morning of March 28, 1979.

"It'll be just like Pearl Harbor—they won't know what happened at Three Mile Island and where it happened," he said.

Yet those memories still linger. Twenty-five years after the accident, America's closest brush with nuclear disaster looms large for the plant's neighbors and former workers, even as they focus on the future, not the past.

There is plenty to remember for people such as Richards and three other men—a former Middletown resident, the mayor, and a retired radiation inspector.

Aerial view of the the Three Mile Island nuclear plant in Pennsylvania, where a nuclear accident that happened in 1979 is stil a topic of controversy for people in close proximity to the plant. AP IMAGES

Richards, who worked at Unit 1 for more than 25 years, believes nuclear fuel is the energy of the future.

''I was surprised at how bad it was, but I was younger then and thought nothing could happen to me,'' he said.

Robert Reid, who was mayor of Middletown during the crisis and took the office again in 2002, said he feels safe again beneath the steam of Unit 1. Yet a Geiger counter remains in his office, sputtering sporadically.

John Garnish, whose home directly across from the plant became ground zero for reporters, left for Florida, more toward the sun than away from TMI. He harbors bitterness toward the reporters he feels abused his hospitality. And he worries about friends and family lost to cancer—fallout, he believes, from a still-contentious nuclear disaster.

''No one wrote about all the dead birds that I found, or how people would get a metallic taste in their mouths,'' he said. ''The press were just a bunch of liars who wanted to use the telephone.''

And Thomas Gerusky, former head of the Pennsylvania Bureau of Radiation Protection, who went on to help clean up some of the nation's most contaminated nuclear sites, wonders if there should be a future for nuclear fuel.

''I've got mixed emotions. Even working for the Department of Energy, it's hard to figure out whether we need nuclear plants or not,'' he said.

Disaster Reminders Nestled among small islands, which once held fishing shacks, Three Mile Island appears small and weary today, dressed in faded '70s blue and beige.

For 25 years, only two of the hourglass cooling towers have waved the signature white steam flags. The other two stand empty, gray skeletal reminders of the nation's most dangerous nuclear disaster.

It began at 4 a.m. on March 28, 1979, with a simple malfunction in a valve that drained water from the Unit 2 reactor. That led to a release of radiation—how much remains a matter of contention—a potentially explosive hydrogen bubble and the meltdown of five feet of the radioactive core.

Five days later, the nightmare ended with a visit from President Jimmy Carter, touring the plant in white plastic booties. Since then, the plant, which is about 10 miles from Harrisburg, Pa., has been emptied of radioactive material, at a cost of a billion dollars and 10 years. A spokesman for TMI's new owner, First Energy Corp., refused requests to tour the plant, saying "there is nothing there to look at."

The Way Things Were Richards worked at Crawford Station, a coal plant, before going to TMI. He would return home with "a nose full of coal dust." When he started at the nuclear plant, he was relieved to get away from the dirt and the dust. He was working the 11-P.M.-to-7-A.M. shift at Unit 1 when he heard there were problems across the way. He went home and went to bed, and two hours later his wife woke him up, wondering what had happened.

After the accident, Richards remained at TMI, working as a mechanical supervisor. Although Unit 1 was shut down for a year, there was plenty of work to be done upgrading safety measures and cleaning Unit 2. Several years after the accident, he went in to check the bolts on the Unit 2 reactor head and received a quarter-year's worth of radiation in less than an hour—he says he does not remember how much.

"I didn't worry about the radiation. I couldn't see it or feel it or smell it," he said. "But then again, I'm still a smoker, too."

John Garnish never believed that what he could not see could not hurt him. He used to live on Meadow Lane, and his window view was one of plumes and reactors. During the accident, reporters camped out on his lawn in droves, offering $25 to make a phone call, offering to send copies of stories that never appeared. Although he thought the accident was "overblown," Garnish said the plant had been bad news since it opened.

"They had contaminated the area long before the accident," he said. "They would do releases of gas—everyone would get a metallic taste in their mouths." Garnish left for Florida in 1983, returned in 1988, and then left for good two years later.

"It was more the small-town feel that we couldn't get used to again. You could predict what everybody was going to do," he said.

When he left, he took a dosimeter, which registers radiation, that had been put on the tree in his front yard. He said he did not remember what it registered anymore.

"Our next-door neighbor died of liver cancer. The man down the street died of brain cancer. My sister, she had breast cancer," Garnish said. "It's just a farce that they're not reporting it."

When Garnish left Middletown, Reid was the mayor of the Dauphin County town. He is the mayor once again, having served from 1978 to 1994, and returning in 2002. The elementary school here bears Reid's name, and he substitute-teaches there from time to time.

Reid said that it took 10 years after TMI for Middletown to feel "close to normal" again and that it is always on his citizens' minds. Every year at the high school, the football coach shows a documentary about the accident, and Reid talks afterward.

There have been changes, and they have been for the better.

"They know to be truthful to the people they're neighbors with," Reid says of the current TMI management. "If a siren goes off, I get a call. If a fish jumps out of the water onto the island, I get a call." . . .

SIGNIFICANCE

The NRC says that the Three Mile Island incident led to significant changes to nuclear power plant operations, including emergency response planning, nuclear reactor operator training, operational design, and radiation protection. NRC says they also strengthened regulatory oversight, forcing the nuclear power industry to enhance its own safety measures. The industry created its own regulatory body, the Institute of Nuclear Power Operations (INPO), and the Nuclear Energy Institute, to serve as a unified voice of the industry. Their goal is to operate with a common approach, and to communicate as a body with government agencies, including the NRC.

The Union of Concerned Scientists (UCS) was commissioned by the Governor of Pennsylvania to carry out studies concerning nuclear safety shortly after the accident occurred in 1979. Since then, the UCS has maintained its role as a voice advocating for strong nuclear regulation, often at odds with the nuclear power industry. UCS claims to be a representative of public interest in debates over the safety of nuclear energy.

It is thought by some people that the Three Mile Island accident, and the larger 1986 Chernobyl nuclear disaster in the present day Ukraine, created a public fear of nuclear energy that has been difficult to change.

Proponents of nuclear energy say the public is not knowledgeable enough about the benefits of modern day technology, and claim today's nuclear technology is a safe alternative to the burning of fossil fuels. In addition to safety, there are public concerns over the nuclear waste produced by nuclear plants, as well as access to nuclear material by terrorists.

Regardless of public fears, nuclear energy use is increasing globally, currently producing 16 percent of the world's electricity. The United States is the largest nuclear energy producer, currently receiving 20 percent of its electricity from nuclear sources.

FURTHER RESOURCES

Periodicals

Fain, P. "Remembering the Meltdown." *Nucleus: The Magazine of the Union of Concerned Scientists* 21, 2 (1999).

Ford, Daniel. "The Hole in the Reactor." *New York Times* (April 13, 2002).

Rennie, Gabriele. "Nuclear Energy To Go: A Self-contained, Portable Reactor." *Science and Technology Review* (July–August 2004). <http://www.llnl.gov/str/JulAug04/pdfs/07_04.3.pdf> (accessed March 10, 2006).

Websites

"Fact Sheet on the Accident at Three Mile Island." *United States Nuclear Regulatory Commission*. <http://www.nrc.gov/reading-rm/doc-collections/fact-sheets/3mile-isle.html> (accessed March 10, 2006).

"Three Mile Island: 1979. Nuclear Issues Briefing Paper 48." *Uranium Information Center*, March 2001. <http://www.uic.com.au/nip48.htm> (accessed March 10, 2006).

Wave's Environmental Toll:

Indian Ocean Tsunami

Newspaper article

By: Eric Bellman and Timothy Mapes

Date: January 17, 2005

Source: Bellman, Eric and Timothy Mapes. "Wave's Environmental Toll: Salt Water, Oil Poison a Lake And Threaten Rice Harvest; Rainforests Are Safe—For Now." *Wall Street Journal* January 17, 2005.

About the Author: Eric Bellman and Timothy Mapes are staff reporters for the *Wall Street Journal*. Bellman reported the story from Lake Hikkaduwa, Sri Lanka, and Mapes reported from Banda Aceh, Indonesia.

INTRODUCTION

On December 26, 2004, a massive earthquake on the seafloor near Sumatra produced one of the largest ever-recorded tsunamis in the Indian Ocean. The earthquake and its aftershocks set off a series of massive waves that affected at least twelve countries in Southeast Asia. The hardest hit included Sri Lanka, Indonesia, India, and Thailand. The human toll from the event was enormous; it is estimated that at least 275,000 lost their lives in the disaster and that millions of people were displaced from their homes and villages, many of which were completely destroyed.

The impact of the wave and the subsequent flooding associated with the tsunami imposed significant material damage as well. The area of destruction varied from the high tide line to a kilometer inland from the shore. The destruction was unusual because places where the waves demolished everything were near to places that were remained undamaged.

The United Nations mobilized several rapid environmental impact studies in the wake of the tsunami. The major environmental concern was disposal of the enormous amount of debris that was generated from the destroyed buildings and other man-made structures as well as household items, automobiles, and trees that had been washed away by the waves. In addition, the massive forces of the waves redistributed tons of sand, clogging estuaries and rivers and destroying sanitations systems. The movement of sand also changed the contours of the coastlines in several places. Finally, saltwater intrusion into regions that are usually freshwater posed environmental risk to agriculture and contaminated sources of drinking water.

In the immediate wake of the disaster, environmental scientists were concerned about the health of the fragile coastal ecosystems. These include coral reefs and mangroves. Coral reefs are made up of small animals that produce rock-like colonies in shallow tropical waters. The reefs that form from the coral structures are home to a large diversity of fish, invertebrate and plant species. Mangroves are tropical trees that grow on the ocean's edge. Their root systems form intricate complexes that are home to many juvenile marine animals. In addition, mangroves play an important role in preventing coastal erosion.

PRIMARY SOURCE

Asia's killer tsunami was just a slow-moving, one-foot wave by the time it reached Tyrone Weerasooriya's lakeside hotel on the southwest coast of Sri Lanka. But he is still struggling to understand the effects.

The hundreds of heron, cormorant and Siberian ducks that usually crowd Lake Hikkaduwa are gone, as are the four-foot-long monitor lizards that used to swim around Mr. Weerasooriya's nature resort. Fruit trees near the lake are dying. Rice has stopped growing in fields close to shore. Even the weather seems different: Clear blue skies, the norm this time of year, have turned into muggy days with fierce evening thunderstorms.

"It all changed the day of the tsunami," says Mr. Weerasooriya, who built the eight-room Nature Resort Hotel four years ago to introduce people to the lake's rich ecosystem. "Something is wrong."

Environmental experts aren't surprised. It is too early to say whether the effects are temporary or permanent, localized or widespread, but after coastal dwellers across South and Southeast Asia finally come to grips with the loss of loved ones and property, some also will have to deal with lasting environmental damage.

"It wasn't just a wave. It was a wave of debris, cars, et cetera, and wherever the water slowed down or was trapped it deposited that sediment," says Daniel Renault, a senior officer for the United Nations Food and Agriculture Organization, who is based in Rome. "That will completely change [some] agricultural ecosystems."

Governments in affected countries are already trying to figure out precisely how the salt water, debris and destruction have altered their coastal ecosystems. India's Ministry of Environment and Forests is investigating how the tsunami changed the subcontinent's coastline and how much it has polluted the groundwater. Thailand and Indonesia are setting up environmental crisis centers.

The U.N. Environment Program, based in Geneva, is helping coordinate efforts across the region. It has pledged $1 million to kick off international environmental investigations and created a task force to study satellite photos and collect water and soil samples.

Damage surveys have just begun, but early reports suggest that some 40,000 hectares of rice land in Indonesia's Aceh province and 800 hectares of farm land in Thailand were damaged, says the FAO's Mr. Renault. (A hectare is 2.47 acres.) He says the damage in Sri Lanka seems to be concentrated around rivers and lagoons, like Lake Hikkaduwa, where salt water and pollution have been trapped.

Many parts of Asia are regularly hit by floods from monsoon rains or cyclones, but this disaster is different. Ecological experts say there are no records of environmental effects of previous tsunamis of this size. "We are trying to get information from people all over the world" to gauge the potential effects of the tsunami, says Mr. Renault. "We are facing something that has not been previously monitored."

In some areas, tons of salt water that rushed inland as far as three kilometers, or 1.86 miles, could permanently pollute the soil and the groundwater, poisoning plants and animals, experts say. Debris from thousands of wrecked buildings, as well as gasoline and oil from hundreds of cars, trucks and boats overturned by the waves, may also be contaminants. The giant waves moved mountains of sand, soil, rocks and coral, radically changing offshore habitats along the Indian Ocean's eastern rim.

"The waste and different kinds of debris are an issue, salinity is a matter [that affects] water resources, and industrial sites and waste depots need to be looked at" to insure there haven't been dangerous leaks, says Pasi Rinne, chairman of the UNEP task force.

Sri Lankans living on Lake Hikkaduwa's shores are trying to cope with the ecological breakdown and the impact on their livelihoods. K.G. Chandrikapadmini's village was barely touched by the tsunami. But the next morning, she was awakened by thumping noises on the roof of her simple home. The 30-year-old breadfruit trees in front of her house were dropping their spiny, green fruit—which her family depends on for their income—three months too early. "This has never happened before," she says pointing to hundreds of fallen fruit around her property.

Plantain, papaya and mango trees also are dying along the affected coast, unable to tolerate the salt water that flowed into lakes and rivers. G.K. Janaka, who farms a yellowing rice field near the lake, says he doesn't expect his land to yield a decent harvest for years. "Maybe we can find a seed that can survive in salty soil," he says hopefully.

Even mangrove forests, which should have no trouble with a little extra salt water, are struggling. The leaves of the mangroves that surround Mr. Weerasooriya's hotel are turning yellow and falling off. He thinks they have been affected by the film of gasoline and oil that still floats in the water more than two weeks after the disaster. "If they die, this will be a desert," says Mr. Weerasooriya, who has planted more than 400 mangrove trees around the lake. "The tourists come to see them, the birds nest in them, and the shrimp and crabs lay their eggs in them."

On the island of Sumatra, lush rainforests, home to endangered species including orangutans, wild elephants and the rare Sumatran tiger, as well as to coveted tropical hardwoods, suffered little damage in the tsunami. But the forests may not emerge unscathed when Indonesia begins rebuilding devastated Aceh province at the island's northern tip.

Two decades of heavy international demand for timber have kept the rainforests under pressure. Two of the largest pulp and paper plants in the world are on Sumatra, and hundreds of smaller sawmills, often operating without formal government approval, line the island's roads.

When the rebuilding effort is under way, the government and aid agencies will need to build at least 300,000 new homes for those displaced by the tsunami, according to WWF Indonesia, a local affiliate of the global environmental group. That will mean massive demand for wood.

"There's quite a strong likelihood that any tree left standing is going to get grabbed," says Moray McLeish, who manages a project in Indonesia run by the Nature Conservancy, which aims to curb illegal logging. He says 70% to 85% of all the timber cut down in Indonesia is harvested by people operating without government permits. "The danger is that people will go after the timber in the national parks," Mr. McLeish says. "Those are pretty much the only sources left in Sumatra."

Sand and debris, not the giant waves, scraped fragile young coral off reefs on Sri Lanka's coast. Near Hikkaduwa, reefs that usually attract hundreds of tourists this time of year are covered with sand, silt, sunken fishing boats and debris. Much, if not all, of the coral can come back, experts say. But as people rebuild the island's infrastructure, demand for lime—which in Sri Lanka is made by burning coral in kilns—will surge.

Thailand's reefs also suffered, especially around the tourist islet of Phi Phi, near Phuket, a site popular with divers. As much as 50% of the coral on two key reefs there has been degraded, according to the U.N. Development Programme, in Bangkok. Divers report finding deck chairs, suitcases, smashed television sets and other items that were swept out of hotels and onto the coral. A kitchen sink was found resting on a reef.

Environmentalists are pressing local officials to make some areas off-limits to divers for three years or more. "We have to come very quickly, or we might lose what we have saved," says Suwit Khunkitti, Thailand's Minister for Natural Resources and Environment.

Optimists say nature is resilient enough to bounce back quickly, and a few heavy rains may be enough to wash the salt and pollution out of the soil and water. Still, the hardest hit areas could take years to recover. "The natural systems will take some time to regenerate," says Manel Jayamanna, director general of Sri Lanka's Central Environmental Authority in Colombo. "All we can do is remove debris and not put further debris in the environment."

While he waits for nature to bounce back, Mr. Weerasooriya has developed his own theories about what is happening to his lake.

He figures birds have moved further inland because gasoline in the water has killed the bugs they like to eat. He even thinks he knows where the scavenger monitor lizards went.

"They went to the other side with the bodies," he says, pointing toward the ocean.

SIGNIFICANCE

The *Wall Street Journal* article cited above is typical of reports in the wake of the 2005 Indian Ocean Tsunami. Most environmental experts expected that the environmental toll of the event would be devastating. In fact, studies following the event show that the environmental damage caused by the tsunami was severe but uneven. The major environmental result from the event is that the places that were already suffering from environmental damage were the places most affected by the tsunami. On the other hand, places that had healthy coastal ecosystems sustained substantially less human and environmental damage.

Healthy coastal ecosystems such as mangroves, coral reefs, and vegetated sand dunes acted as buffers to the tsunami, protecting both structures as well as human life. For example, in the Yala and Bundala National parks in Sri Lanka, where sand dunes were completely vegetated, the tsunami had almost no environmental impact. Conversely, in places where the coral reefs had been mined, damage by the waves was most destructive.

Environmental predictions concerning the affects of saltwater intrusion on areas where freshwater usually occurs were generally correct. Some of the major problems following the event involved saltwater contamination of agricultural areas, freshwater wells, and septic systems. The United Nations Environmental Program estimated that 62,000 freshwater wells in Sri Lanka were contaminated by marine water.

As expected, debris was also a major environmental problem, but it was much more severe in places where environmental conditions were already threatened. Both inert debris and toxic debris were mixed together in the wake of the tsunami. Some harmful debris was burned, in particular debris containing asbestos, a known carcinogen. Somalia, which had a coastline that was already heavily polluted with toxic materials, was heavily impacted by the tsunami. Because the country suffered from civil war for years, the government was unable to properly dispose of nuclear and chemical wastes, which were simply deposited along the coast. The waves stirred up a collection of hazardous substances that caused human health concerns in the region.

FURTHER RESOURCES

Web sites

Benfield Hazard Research Center. "The Indian Ocean Tsunami and Its Implications." <http://www.benfieldhrc.org/tsunamis/indian_ocean_tsunami/indian_ocean_tsunami.htm> (accessed October 3, 2005).

Joint UNEP/OCHA Environment Unit. "Indian Ocean Tsunami Disaster of December 2004." <http://www.benfieldhrc.org/disaster_studies/rea/indonesia_REA_tsunami_aceh.pdf > (accessed February 2005).

United Nations Atlas of the Oceans. "Impact of Tsunami on Ecosystems." <http://www.oceansatlas.org/servlet/CDSServlet?status=ND03MTY4NyY2PWVuJjMzPSSomMzc9a29z> (accessed October 3, 2005).

United Nations Environmental Programme. "After the Tsunami: Rapid Environmental Assessment." <http://www.unep.org/tsunami/tsunami_rpt.asp> (accessed October 24, 2005).

United Nations Office for the Coordination of Human Affairs. "Draft Field Report:Rapid Environmental Impact Assessment—Sri Lanka Tsunami." <http://www.benfieldhrc.org/disaster_studies/rea/SFieldReportSri_Lanka.pdf > (accessed February 1, 2005).

In Harm's Way: Hurricanes, Population Trends and Environmental Change

Research paper

By: Roger-Mark De Souza

Date: October 2004

Source: De Souza, Roger-Mark. "In Harm's Way: Hurricanes, Population Trends and Environmental Change." October 2004. <http://www.prb.org/Template.cfm?Section=PRB&template=/Content-Management/ContentDisplay.cfm&ContentID=11713> (accessed January 6, 2006).

About the Author: Roger-Mark De Souza is Technical Director at the Population Reference Bureau (PRB) in Washington, D.C. He holds a Master of Arts degree from the George Washington University and a postgraduate degree in International Relations from the University of West Indies. At the PRB, De Sousa conducts research on a wide range of development policy issues. He also provides technical support on health, environment, development, and related issues to countries in the Caribbean region.

INTRODUCTION

Hurricanes are a constant natural threat in the United States and the Caribbean regions. Between 1991 and 1999, nearly fourteen hurricanes struck coastal areas in the United States. Five of these were major. In fact, the United States is hit by a category four or stronger hurricane around once every six years. In 2005, Hurricane Katrina completely devastated the city of New Orleans. More than a million people were displaced as a direct consequence of this disaster.

Besides being huge environmental hazards, hurricanes cause great economical damage to regions they hit. Human population becomes vulnerable in more than one way to such environmental disasters. Hurricanes leave entire populations susceptible to several economic and social consequences.

Population trends in hurricane-affected regions also keep changing. Since the late twentieth century, coastal regions affected by hurricanes have seen a marked increase in population. The ability of populations to rebuild themselves after tropical storms significantly depends upon the regional or the national economy. Often, smaller island nations find themselves economically handicapped to rebuild hurricane-damaged regions.

Factors such as an increase in migration from rural to urban areas also influence a region's ability to recover from the economic impact of hurricanes. Hurricane activity has also been increasing over the years. Less-understood factors such as climate change and an increase in greenhouse gases tend to contribute to increased hurricane activity.

Before rural-to-urban migration became a trend, and later a social economical need, natural disasters like hurricanes were a lesser threat to human population and economy.

De Souza's paper describes growing population trends and the threats faced in relation to the increased risk from hurricanes caused by global climate change. Factors like population and urbanization of previously uninhabited lands have increased the severity of economic damages faced in the aftermath of hurricanes. This trend is more visible in the case of island countries in the Caribbean that are primarily dependent on tourism for their sustenance.

Dictated by economic needs, the last few decades have seen an increasing trend in the urbanization of these areas. Hurricanes affect both affluent and poor populations from developed and developing countries. In the United States, a significant number of people keep migrating to warm coastal areas such as Florida and California. Federal studies have revealed that less affluent people generally tend to stay in marginally developed areas such as coastlines, riverbanks, and low-lying areas. People residing or living in these areas can be more vulnerable to natural disasters. The economic void created in the aftermath of such disasters creates a myriad of problems for administrators and governments alike.

■ **PRIMARY SOURCE**

IN HARM'S WAY: HURRICANES, POPULATION TRENDS AND ENVIRONMENTAL CHANGE

In September 2004, four devastating hurricanes and tropical storms killed more than 1,500 Haitians, destroyed roughly 90 percent of Grenada, and wreaked billions of dollars of damage on the southern United States.

But such calamities from extreme weather are hardly an accident of nature. Instead, these tragedies highlight when and how environmental hazards combine with socioeconomic conditions—particularly population and environmental trends—to magnify the threat of disaster for tens of millions of people in both the developed and the developing world.

The Factors That Increase Vulnerability to Hurricanes Hurricanes and tropical storms have always been one of the primary causes of natural disasters in the Caribbean and the coastal southern United States. But the economic impact of hurricanes in these areas is growing far more severe.

The insurance industry in the United States has paid out more than $39 billion since 2000 to cover hurricanes and other natural disasters—a figure more than half the total of all catastrophic event payments made by the industry in the preceding 30 years.

This rise in insurance costs reflects not just greater hurricane activity, but people's increased vulnerability to those storms due to three factors: population pressures, the effects of poverty and affluence, and other environmental changes that exacerbate a hurricane's strength and effects.

Vulnerable Locations and Population Pressures To some extent, human vulnerability to natural disaster is a geographical misfortune. For example, because of their fragile environments and economies, islands are highly vulnerable to devastating hydrometeorological and geological disasters. According to the United Nations Conference on Trade and Development, 13 of the 25 countries that suffered the greatest number of natural disasters during the 1970s and 1980s were small island states.

But accelerating numbers of people are choosing to live in areas that are at increasing risk for natural devastation. For example, approximately 13 million Floridians now live in coastal counties, up from 200,000 a century ago. And more people live in South Florida's Dade and Broward counties now than lived in the entire southeastern United States in 1930.

Aggressive coastal development, especially the building of homes and businesses in these fragile areas, is also increasing human vulnerability to natural disasters.

A 2000 study commissioned by the Federal Emergency Management Agency found that Americans have built more than 350,000 structures within 500 feet of U.S. coasts. The study also warned that coastal erosion could claim one in four of those buildings within the next 60 years.

Caribbean countries are equally vulnerable to tropical storms. Major population centers, agricultural areas, ports, and centers of industrial and commercial activity are mostly located in the coastal zone. And tourism—a mainstay of many Caribbean economies—is also largely concentrated in coastal areas.

The vulnerability of these urban coasts is exacerbated by population growth. While fertility rates have fallen nearly everywhere in the developing world, population in the Caribbean will continue to grow as large numbers of young people move into their reproductive years.

On average, roughly one-third of people in the Caribbean are under age 15. (Haiti has the most youthful population in the region, with 43 percent of its population under age 15.) This population growth is particularly acute among the poor, who have traditionally had the least capacity to exercise their reproductive preferences.

Rural-to-urban migration and increasing urbanization has also aggravated the impact of natural disasters among developing countries in the Caribbean. Indeed, the Caribbean is the most urbanized island region in the world, with an urban population that grew an average of 1.58 percent annually from 1995 to 2000. Several islands—such as the Bahamas, Cuba, Dominica, Puerto Rico, and Trinidad and Tobago—are already predominantly urban.

The trend towards urbanization provides additional pressures on the environment and increases vulnerability to natural hazards, particularly among the poor. The urban poor tend to live in informal settlements, and their housing is often inadequately constructed.

Large urban areas such as Kingston in Jamaica and San Juan in Puerto Rico tend to be more hazardous locations than sparsely populated rural areas because of their population size and the potential scale of damage. In these urban areas, impervious surfaces such as roads and buildings generate more runoff than forested land. And fixed drainage channels may be unable to contain runoff from intense rains.

Poverty and Affluence Poverty is a central component of vulnerability to tropical storms: Developing countries contain 90 percent of the victims from natural disasters and bear 75 percent of their economic damages.

The World Bank estimates that 80 percent of the poor in Latin America, 60 percent of the poor in Asia, and 50 percent of the poor in Africa live on marginal lands characterized by poor productivity and high vulnerability to natural degradation and natural disasters.

Where the poor live in the developing world contributes enormously to their vulnerability to tropical storms and their aftermath. These people often have no choice but to occupy the least-valued plots of land in disaster-prone areas such as riverbanks, unstable hillsides, deforested lands, or fragile water-catchment areas.

These patterns predetermine not only the poor's susceptibility to natural disasters, but also their capacity to cope with their aftermath. Poorer families may be forced into increased debt in order to rebuild their homes, replace assets, and meet basic needs until they are able to recommence income-generating activities.

More affluent societies and individuals also have put themselves at increased risk for natural disasters such as hurricanes, although they have more resources with which to brace for and handle the aftermath of such events.

As noted above, disaster-prone areas of the United States are being settled by people with higher-than-average incomes—often to find jobs, to be near to recreation possibilities, or to build secondary homes. In some cases, economic incentives for responsible land use have been curtailed by legislated insurance rates and federal aid programs that effectively subsidize development in hazard-prone areas.

Environmental Changes Environmental degradation also increases vulnerability to tropical storms. Serious coral bleaching and mangrove loss, for example, make coastlines more susceptible to flooding. Similarly, deforestation contributes to droughts, flash floods, and landslides. For example, rains from Tropical Storm Jeanne pounded land in Haiti that had been cleared for charcoal production, ultimately leading to the death of more than 1,000 people. By contrast, greater land cover buffered the coastline of the Dominican Republic (which shares the island of Hispabola with Haiti) against widespread flooding from Jeanne as well as subsequent landslides—resulting in significantly less deaths.

Global warming could also contribute to a rise in the number and the intensity of hurricanes that will hit the Caribbean and the southern United States, although scientists are still debating the precise impact of such warming.

Recent research suggests that, by 2080, seas warmed by rising atmospheric concentrations of heat-trapping greenhouse gases could cause a typical hurricane to intensify about an extra half-step on the five-step scale of destructive power. Rainfall up to 60 miles from the storm's core would also be nearly 20 percent more intense.

Moving Out of Harm's Way Reducing vulnerability to hurricanes in the Caribbean and the southern United States must include an understanding of how population trends and environmental changes interact with geographic predisposition to natural hazards, policy choices, and economic drivers of change.

The upcoming World Conference on Disaster Reduction (WCDR) in Japan (in January 2005) will be an opportunity for world leaders to recognize these important linkages. In preparation for the conference, the International Strategy for Disaster Reduction (ISDR) Secretariat and the United Nations Development Program have developed five focus areas for understanding, guiding and monitoring disaster risk reduction at all levels. These areas are: governance, risk identification, knowledge management, risk-management applications, and preparedness and emergency management.

SIGNIFICANCE

Population trends worldwide are significant indicators of economic hardships faced, especially in times of distress and disaster. Growing population trends in areas that face natural disaster mean increased consequential economical risk from natural disasters. Factors like climate change can compound the risks faced by populations migrating to or residing in these regions.

According to environmental groups, the growing population trend in hurricane probable zones is a matter of great concern. A World Bank study noted that nearly 90 percent of the world's poor stay in marginalized areas that can become the most affected zones in event of natural disasters like hurricanes. Another study by the same organization showed that an immense amount of funds could be saved if governments invest appropriate sums in planning for disaster preparation and alleviation.

In his paper, De Souza examines how populations of countries in the Caribbean region and the United States are being increasingly exposed to hurricanes brought about by environmental change. He argues that hurricanes not only affect people in the developing world, but populations in the developed world as well. He further discusses that smaller island countries can be more susceptible to damage caused by hurricanes. The devastation caused thereby is not entirely an environmental accident, but can be linked to the socioeconomic factors affecting the populations of that region.

Furthermore, the economical damage caused by hurricanes is far greater than the geographical damage they cause. He notes it has cost the insurance industry more than $39 billion since 2000 to cover hurricane damage in the United States.

De Souza states that although it is not possible to completely escape the disastrous aftermath of hurricanes, it is possible to mitigate the harm they can cause. Changing population trends need not necessarily mean more economic damage and harm if hurricane affected nations include prudent safety and rehabilitation measures in every disaster plan.

For this purpose, De Souza outlines a number of recommendations in his paper. These include understanding deforestation and global warming, encouraging reforestation, implementing measures that reduce harmful emissions, developing conventional disaster plans that include contingency measures, and allocating surplus funds in the wake of hurricanes.

Amongst other measures, De Souza states that long-term resettlement plans should be drawn up for people living in commonly hurricane-affected areas, so that future hurricanes do not cause massive economic damage. These steps could go a long way in identifying the need for assistance in the right areas where, for example, aid from crucial areas like foreign governments and agencies could be channeled and integrated with regional and local funding plans. As natural hazards can pose a serious hindrance to sustainable development, this aspect should be considered by various governments in all areas of economic planning.

FURTHER RESOURCES

Web sites

Benson, Charlotte. "The Cost of Disasters." *Benfield Hazard Research Centre*. <http://www.benfieldhrc.org/activities/misc_papers/DEVRISK/BENSON.HTM> (accessed March 17, 2006).

Jarrell, Jerry D., Max Mayfield, Edward N. Rappaport, and Christopher W. Landsea. "The Deadliest, Costliest, and Most Intense United States Hurricanes from 1900 to 2000." *Atlantic Oceanographic and Meteorological Laboratory*, updated October 2001. <http://www.aoml.noaa.gov/hrd/Landsea/deadly> (accessed March 17, 2006).

Lynas, Mark. "Warning in the Winds." *MarkLynas.org*, September 19, 2004. <http://www.marklynas.org/wind/document/23.html> (accessed March 17, 2006).

Conservation and Activism

Since the mid-1900s, the roots of environmental consciousness have flowered into calls for conservation. This has spurred broad activism in the environment and the use of environmental resources.

Conservation and activism often unite in rallies, Earth Day celebrations, protests, and position papers calling for sustainable development. However, environmental activists are not always united. They may differ on matters such as the benefits vs. costs of nuclear energy; which alternative energy sources provide the greatest potential relief from pollution caused by the use of fossil fuels (e.g., petroleum, coal, natural gas); how to best mitigate the environmental impacts of large hydroelectric dams; etc.

Nuclear power, for example, remains in a gray zone. In some ways, it is cleaner for the environment, yet has the potential to poison Earth for generations. It has been a significant part of electricity production in some countries for many years. France, for example, obtains 78 percent of its electricity from nuclear power. However, the use of nuclear power remains a lightening rod for fractious debate and passionate protest.

Especially since the fall of the Soviet Union in 1991, the world has begun to grasp the full extent of environmental destruction and degradation that occurred behind the former Iron Curtain. Debate has emerged about the use of former Soviet republics and other developing nations as "dumping grounds" for the dirty work of environmental remediation (e.g., as sites for dumping toxins and wastes or removing asbestos).

Economic development of the world's remaining wild areas may also prove threatening to humans. As humans increasingly encroach on previously remote habitats, communicable diseases (especially zoonotic diseases) may not remain isolated. Some epidemiologists suggest that the AIDS and Ebola viruses might have entered the human population because of human encroachment on formerly remote environmental habitats.

This chapter provides a glimpse into the hundreds of causes and issues that stir debate worldwide. Among the most passionate and far-reaching is the debate over climate change. Few would disagree that climate data recorded during the last 100 years show Earth is warming at an extremely fast rate—a rate that some scientists claim is unprecedented. Observations gathered since the early 1900s indicate that the average land surface temperature has increased by 0.8 to 1.0 °F (0.45 to 0.6 °C). Scientific data also show that atmospheric concentrations of carbon dioxide, methane, nitrous oxide, and human-made chemicals called halocarbons are increasing as a result of emissions associated with human activities. In 2001, the United Nations Intergovernmental Panel on Climate Change (IPCC) asserted that human activity was responsible for much of the recent climate change resulting in global warming.

The question for scientists, critical to the social and political debates, is which of the many climate models will best predict future global temperatures and to what extent are temperatures rising due to increased concentrations of atmospheric gases related to human activity. Activists will continue to debate how to best present studies and issues related to climate change and how to challenge and change current pollution policies.

"An Anti-Smoke Rally"

Newspaper article

By: Anonymous

Date: November 18, 1948

Source: "An Anti-smoke Rally." *New York Times* 26, 3 (November 18, 1948).

About the Author: This article was published without a byline, and was written by a staff writer for the *New York Times*, a daily newspaper with a circulation of over one million readers worldwide.

INTRODUCTION

A staff editorial writer for the *New York Times* reported to its readers on November 18, 1948 that "An Anti-smoke Rally" would be held that same day. The tone of the editorial implied that all interested readers should show members of the city administration that they are concerned about the air pollution problem enveloping the city by attending the rally. The writer expressed the feeling that such readers no doubt would want "to see more effective city action against the smoke and soot nuisance" that was troubling the city. According to the author, members of the Outdoor Cleanliness Association and Citizens Union Committee on Air Pollution along with representatives of the city council and the health department and other prominent citizens would be some of the people attending the rally at the Hunter College Playhouse. In this editorial report, the *New York Times* writer explained that this "is a critical time in the movement to control air pollution, because legislation reorganizing the City Government's machinery to abate the nuisance is now being written and rewritten."

PRIMARY SOURCE

We remind all our readers who want to see more effective city action against the smoke and soot nuisance that a rally at which they may express their interest will be held at 5 o'clock this afternoon at the Hunter College Playhouse, on Sixth-eighth Street between Park and Lexington Avenues. This meeting, to which the public is invited without fee or obligation, is being held under the sponsorship of the Outdoor Cleanliness Association, whose president is Mrs. C. Frank Reavis. Robert W. Dowling will be chairman of the meeting, and those participating will include Joseph T. Sharley, vice chairman of the City Council; John J. Ryan

of the Health Department; Arthur C. Stern, chairman of the Citizens Union Committee on Air Pollution; Col. Leopold Philipp, who has been active in the campaign for voluntary agreement in business and industry to reduce pollution; Dr. Foster Kennedy, Brig. Gen. Ralph G. DeVoe and, expressing the women's point of view, Nanete Fabray, the actress, and Fannie Hurst, the novelist.

This is a critical time in the movement to control air pollution, because legislation reorganizing the City Government's machinery to abate the nuisance is now being written and rewritten. We urge housewives and others to take this opportunity to become better informed on the problem and, by their presence at the rally, demonstrate to the City Administration their determination to keep fighting until effective action is taken.

SIGNIFICANCE

American women took a major role in social reform beginning in the late nineteenth century. These women, who traditionally stayed at home and generally refrained from actively participating in social causes, started to become very concerned with pollution brought on by the Industrial Revolution that had begun in the United States early that same century. They joined civic organizations in order to protest the terrible conditions that existed in many urban industrialized areas most affected by the mostly unregulated capitalism that was sweeping the country.

In New York City—the major area in the United States where polluting factories had been established—women were especially active in trying to resolve the problems that had resulted from changes brought about by hundreds of thousands of people leaving rural areas for the newly created manufacturing jobs in the city. These problems that faced the citizens of New York City included the often-times unethical enforcement of the rules, regulations, and conditions that companies arbitrarily forced upon its workers such as dangerous working conditions, long hours, and poor pay. In addition to the direct hazards and hardships levied against the workers of these companies, there were the indirect problems such as air, water, and soil pollution that were inflicted by the polluting companies upon the general populace surrounding such sites.

Women belonging to many New York women's clubs and civic improvement groups contributed greatly to the activist causes of conservation and environmental protection within the city. Members of these reform groups, commonly called progressive reformers, tried to counter the powerful corporate leaders who were often controlling high-ranking members, as well as the rank-and-file, of the city, state, and, in some instances, federal governments. By 1940, air pollution—one of many major types of pollution existing in the city—was still a serious problem in New York City, even with the earlier protests against the condition of the air during the first forty years of the twentieth century.

In 1948, the editors of the *New York Times* promoted an anti–smoke rally when an article on the editorial page stated that: "… housewives and others [should] take this opportunity to become better informed on the problem and, by their presence at the rally, demonstrate to the City Administration their determination to keep fighting until effective action is taken."

Still, by 1966, after two more decades of activist protests and reform, a New York City mayoral task force concluded that individuals and organizations within the city were putting more poisons into the air on an equivalent volume basis than any other major U.S. city. Although cleaning up air pollution took many decades, the federal Clean Air Act of 1970, along with specific actions by the New York City Council helped city governmental and corporate leaders start reducing the pollution levels in the 1970s for major airborne contaminants and pollutants in the atmosphere.

Within New York City, such newspaper articles as "An Anti-smoke Rally" helped to identify pollution problems, suggest solutions to environmental problems within the city, and rally public support against the effects of pollution. As a result of these editorials that regularly appeared in major newspapers in New York City and the early environmental protests against unregulated manufacturing facilities, new federal environmental groups were created, such as the U.S. Environmental Protection Agency, established in December 1970.

That same year, on April 22, 1970, millions of U.S. citizens from all over the country participated in the first Earth Day celebrations. The day before Earth Day and about 21 years, 5 months after the November 18, 1948 editorial on the New York City anti-smoke rally, the *New York Times* gave front-page coverage of the major environmental event including a list of scheduled events throughout the city. Such newspaper articles—those of the past, the present, and no doubt into the future—help to identify environmental problems in New York City and are a primary way to institute improvements with regard to the quality of life in large metropolitan cities and throughout the United States.

FURTHER RESOURCES

Books

Cohn, Morris M. *The Pollution Fighters: A History of Environmental Engineering in New York State*. Albany, N.Y.: New York State Department of Health, 1973.

Hoy, Suellen M. "Municipal Housekeeping: The Role of Women in Improving Urban Sanitation Practices." In *Pollution and Reform in American Cities 1870-1930*, edited by Martin V. Melosi. Austin: University of Texas Press, 1980.

Web sites

Dublin, Thomas, and Kathryn Kish Sklar. "Women and Social Movements in the United States, 1600-2000." *Women and Social Movements* <http://womhist.binghamton.edu/projectmap.htm> (accessed March 1, 2006).

Goldstein, Eric. "Environment: Internet Resources for What You Need to Know on NYC Environment." *GothamGazette.com*, April 2002. <http://www.gothamgazette.com/environment/apr.02.shtml#five> (accessed March 1, 2006).

Kovarik, Bill. "Ellen Swallow Richards and the Progressive Women's Reform Movement." *Environmental History Timeline*. <http://www.radford.edu/~wkovarik/envhist/richards.html> (accessed March 1, 2006).

Radon Health Mines

With Daughter Watching, Woman Lying by Bags of Uranium Ore, Used to Increase Radon Gas in the Mines

Photograph

By: Carl Iwasaki

Date: June 1, 1952

Source: Time Life Pictures/Getty Images.

About the Photographer: This photograph was taken in the Free Enterprise Mine, a "radon health mine" in Boulder, Montana, in 1952.

INTRODUCTION

This image shows an elderly woman suffering from an unspecific chronic health disorder who sought relief in a "radon health mine" in Boulder, Montana in 1952. There are four radon health mines in Montana. The first, the Free Enterprise Mine, opened to the public in 1952, the year this picture was taken. All were still open for business as of early 2006. Many of the customers are Amish or Mennonite, religious groups who tend to shun technical medical treatments in favor of "natural" remedies. Three of the four health mines in Montana, including that shown here, were originally working uranium mines.

In the radon health mines, treatment consists of staying in the mine for some various lengths of time to be exposed to the radium that is given off by uranium in the rocks. (The bagged uranium seen in the picture does not necessarily raise the radon concentration in the space significantly.) Radon concentrations in air are usually measured in units of picocuries per liter of air (pC/L), where a curie is a unit of radioactivity and a picocurie is a billionth of a curie. The United States Environmental Protection Agency (E.P.A.) suggests an upper limit of 4 pC/L in homes and considers higher concentrations dangerous; radon concentrations in the Montana health mines range from 233 to 1,296 pC/L. Levels as high as 1,600 pC/L have been measured.

Radon therapy is also available at in a number of mines, tunnels, steam baths, and spas in Europe.

▋ PRIMARY SOURCE

WITH DAUGHTER WATCHING, WOMAN LYING BY BAGS OF URANIUM ORE, USED TO INCREASE RADON GAS IN THE MINES.

See primary source image.

▋▋

SIGNIFICANCE

The radon health mines recall the earliest phase of the modern relationship to radiation—enthusiasm. In the 1890s and early years of the twentieth century, x rays and radium were fresh discoveries. Both were widely hailed as health-giving. Numerous products containing radium—now known to be highly carcinogenic—were sold over the counter. Sir William Ramsay, winner of the Nobel Prize for physics, said in 1904 that with radium "the philosopher's stone had been discovered, and it is not beyond the bounds of possibility that it may lead to that other goal of the philosophers of the Dark Age—the *elixir vitae*," a potion conferring eternal life. After public horror at the painful deaths suffered by girls working in clock factories who licked radium paint off paintbrushes used to mark glow-in-the-dark clock dials, public fear of radiation began to grow, and eventually became commonplace. However, a belief that low-level radiation may have curative powers persists and has lately acquired some scientific allies.

Radium, itself a breakdown product of uranium, decays into radon, which is also radioactive and so eventually decays as well. Radiation is given off at each stage of decay. Radon is produced continuously by rocks containing uranium, such as those in the radium health mines of Montana or (at lower concentrations) the granite bedrocks of New England. Radon

▋ PRIMARY SOURCE

With Daughter Watching, Woman Lying by Bags of Uranium Ore, Used to Increase Radon Gas in the Mines. This picture was taken in the Free Enterprise Mine, a "radon health mine" that opened in Boulder, Montana, in 1952. The elderly woman is seeking relief from a chronic health disorder by breathing the high concentrations of radon gas in the mine. PHOTO BY CARL IWASAKI/TIME LIFE PICTURES/GETTY IMAGES.

is a heavy radioactive gaseous element, atomic number 83, with twenty known isotopes.

Radon can seep from the ground into enclosed spaces such as homes, presenting a lung cancer hazard; the EPA estimates that radon is the second most common cause of lung cancer in the United States after cigarette smoking. Radon has long been known as a health hazard to uranium miners, but it was not until 1984 that scientists were aware of the home-environment radon pollution problem. An engineer named Stanley Watras was working at the Limerick, Pennsylvania nuclear power station that year, which he was helping to bring online, when flashing and wailing alarms went off. He was found to be heavily contaminated with radiation. The radiation was eventually traced not to the nuclear power plant where he worked, but to his home, where radon was measured at 2,500 pC/L.

Radon is present in millions of U.S. homes. It is particularly prevalent in New England, as the area's geology features different forms of granite that emit radon. According to the EPA, homes in New England are four times likelier to have elevated radon levels than homes elsewhere. A variety of commercial home radon test kits are available, and their use is recommended by the EPA. Radon, if present, can usually abated by improved ventilation of a home's basement.

There is actually a real scientific debate over whether extremely low amounts of radiation can promote health, an effect termed "hormesis." Hormetic effects are not unusual in nature; there are many substances that may be beneficial (or at least are relatively harmless) at small doses, but toxic at high doses (e.g., alcohol). There is mixed evidence for the existence of a radiation hormesis effect. In 2005, the U.S. National Academy of Sciences, after exhaustive review of the scientific literature, announced in its seventh report on the biological effects of ionizing radiation, BEIR VII, that the most appropriate model for the health effects of low levels of ionizing radiation is "LNT"—linear, no threshold. According to this model, halving the amount of radiation to which a creature is exposed halves the amount of harm done, right down to zero. The hormesis model, according to which there is some level below which radiation does not less harm but positive good, was thus rejected by the Academy. BEIR VII also rejected the threshold model, which proposes that there is some level of radiation exposure (a threshold) below which there is no harm.

FURTHER RESOURCES

Periodicals

Calabresi, Edward J., and Baldwin, Linda A. "Toxicology Rethinks Its Central Belief." *Nature* 421 (February 13, 2003).

Web sites

Environmental Protection Agency. "A Physician's Guide - Radon: The Health Threat with a Simple Solution." September 1993. <http://www.epa.gov/radon/pubs/physic.html> (accessed February 25, 2006).

Environmental Protection Agency. "Radionuclides (including Radon, Radium and Uranium): Hazard Summary." April 1992; Revised January 2000. <http://www.epa.gov/ttn/atw/hlthef/radionuc.html> (accessed February 25, 2006).

National Academy of Sciences. "Health Risks from Exposure to Low Levels of Ionizing Radiation: BEIR [Biological Effects of Ionizing Radiation] VII." 2005. Available online at <http://fermat.nap.edu/catalog/11340.html> (accessed February 25, 2006).

RoadsideAmerica.com. "Radon Health Mines." 1996. <http://www.roadsideamerica.com/attract/MTBASradon.html> (accessed February 25, 2006).

Environmental Action Group

Photograph

By: Anonymous

Date: 1970

Source: Getty Images

About the Photographer: This photograph shows a symbol combining graphic elements symbolizing environmentalism, the American Flag, and the activist group Environmental Action. The photographer is unknown.

INTRODUCTION

Environmental Action, founded in 1970 shortly after the first Earth Day, was one of the earliest (though never one of the largest) environmental organizations to come out of the social and political ferment of the 1960s. The quasi-American flag symbol pictured here, not invented by Environmental Action but adopted by it and other groups, including Greenpeace, is known as the "ecology flag." In this design, green—the symbolic color of environmentalism, as in the "Green" political parties of Europe and the United States—has replaced the red and blue of the U.S. flag, and a design resembling the Greek letter theta has replaced the conventional field of stars. The theta-like symbol is actually a combination of the letters "o" and "e," for "organism" and "environment." (Ecology is the study of the relations between organisms, their environment, and other organisms.) The symbol was invented by a cartoonist, Ron Cobb (who later worked as a conceptual designer for the films *Star Wars*, 1977, and *Alien*, 1979) and was first published in the Los Angeles Free Press in 1969. It was first used in an ecology-flag design in the April 21, 1970 issue of *Look* magazine.

Environmental Action was eventually disbanded, though it reformed in the early 2000s. The version of the group that flourished in the early 1970s is perhaps most often cited today not by environmentalists but by right-wing anti-environmentalists, who point to it as an early advocate of "ecoterrorism." The ground for this

PRIMARY SOURCE

Environmental Action Group. This button showing an "ecology flag" was distributed by the group Environmental Action circa 1970. It combines an appeal to patriotism (the American flag motif) with advocacy of an Earth-connected, ecology-oriented values system.
PHOTO BY BLANK ARCHIVES/GETTY IMAGES

charge is the book *Ecotage!* (1972), which offered suggestions for ecological sabotage (ecotage) techniques such as plugging pipes emitting pollutants, destroying billboards, and pulling up survey stakes placed for construction projects. The suggestions were submitted by members of the general public in response to a nationwide contest run by Environmental Action.

Although ecotage is illegal, virtually all ecotage is vandalism, not terrorism, because it is not designed to terrorize—that is, to make human beings fear for their personal safety. Environmentalists damaging property—and only a small minority have ever done so—have in almost all cases sought to do so in ways that are politically pointed but non-dangerous. A rare exception is tree-spiking (which was not advocated in *Ecotage!*), the practice of driving metal spikes into trees to damage chainsaws when the trees are later cut down.

Tree-spiking deters logging by posing a direct danger to loggers. While tree-spiking can be construed as a small-scale form of terrorism, it is notable that illegal pollution of the environment by corporations is never termed "ecoterrorism" by those who condemn tree-spiking, even though such actions are also illegal and threaten the lives of many more people than even the most extreme forms of ecotage, including arson and tree-spiking—air pollution alone kills 50,000–100,000 people every year in the United States.

PRIMARY SOURCE

ENVIRONMENTAL ACTION GROUP
   See primary source image.

SIGNIFICANCE

In the 1960s and 1970s, a mass movement arose—the "environmental" movement—that was supported by people who believed that human activities, including development, mining, forestry, agriculture, fuel extraction and burning, and garbage creation were destroying the ecology of the planet and its ability to sustain life. The environmental movement has continued to be a significant force in public affairs, spreading from Western industrial nations to much of the world. The general purpose of environmental groups such as Environmental Action is to advocate for ways of living and doing business that do not exhaust the Earth's resources, cause species of plants and animals to become extinct, or otherwise befoul or damage the planet.

Almost every movement or group—political, religious, or other—invents or appropriates visual symbols to focus its sense of purpose and identity, and the environmental movement is no exception. Since the environmental movement tends (though not exclusively) to be associated with progressive or left-leaning politics, which have historically been accused of being "un-American" or unpatriotic, it has repeatedly merged the most powerful symbol of U.S. national identity, the flag, with its own symbology so as to suggest that patriotism is compatible with its own agenda. The goal is to counter a negative perception. The ecology flag is one of these symbols. The peace or antiwar movement has also designed hybrid peace-flag symbols, and for the same reasons. Hybrid symbols such as the ecology flag reveal political and cultural tensions inside American society over the question of ultimate loyalty or identity.

The ecology symbol, unlike the peace symbol, has not achieved universal recognition in popular culture, and remains relatively uncommon.

FURTHER RESOURCES

Web sites

Environmental Action. <http://www.environmental-action.org/index.html> (accessed February 17, 2006).

University of San Diego. "Environmentalism 1960–1986." <http://history.acusd.edu/gen/nature/environ5.html> (accessed February 17, 2006).

"Nation Set to Observe Earth Day"

Newspaper article

By: Gladwin Hill

Date: April 21, 1970

Source: Hill, Gladwin. "Nation Set to Observe Earth Day." *New York Times* (April 21, 1970): pg. 36.

About the Author: Gladwin Hill wrote for the *New York Times* for forty-four years and was bureau chief of the Los Angeles office for twenty-three years. He also wrote *Dancing Bear: An Inside Look at California Politics* and *Madman in a Lifeboat: Issues of the Environmental Crisis.*

INTRODUCTION

The first Earth Day was initiated by Democratic Senator Gaylord Nelson of Wisconsin. His interest in the environment began in 1962, when he observed evidence of environmental degradation around him. He found that his constituents were concerned with environmental problems and yet the issues were not included in the public or political dialogue. At Nelson's urging, President Kennedy went on a five-day "conservation tour" through eleven states in September of 1963 to raise concern about issues related to environmental well-being. Nonetheless, lawmakers were hesitant to give the ideas much notice.

Over the next six years, Nelson's concern with the environment evolved into the idea for Earth Day. After observing the grassroots momentum generated by "teach-ins" protesting against the United States' involvement in the Vietnam Conflict, Nelson proposed a similar demonstration in support of a healthy, sustainable environment. He announced his idea at a conference in Seattle in September of 1969.

Efforts to organize Earth Day were initially headquartered out of Nelson's Senate office, however, the public response to the event was massive and quickly overwhelmed the staff. Eventually, Nelson enlisted a young graduate of Stanford University, Denis Hayes, as coordinator of the first Earth Day. Much of the organizational work involved grassroots initiatives by volunteers such as writing letters to schools and universities and contacting local community groups informing them about the event.

The first Earth Day was held on April 22, 1970. Approximately 20 million people from thousands of schools and communities joined in the events. Demonstrators marched in parades and organized rallies to show their support for a clean, healthy environment. Other events included nature walks,

Dennis Hayes coordinates Earth Day activities from the Washington D.C. office on April 22, 1970. AP IMAGES

workshops, lectures and school assemblies focusing on environmental issues.

PRIMARY SOURCE

NATION SET TO OBSERVE EARTH DAY

Thousands of colleges, schools and communities across the country were getting ready yesterday for an unprecedented event: tomorrow's Earth Day—an interlude of national contemplation of problems and man's deteriorating environment.

Scores of marches and demonstrations are scheduled, along with mock funerals of "polluting" objects from automobiles to toilets. Countless lectures, workshops, nature walks and other observances are also planned.

Formally endorsed by officials ranging from the United Nations Secretary General, U Thant, to governors, mayors and school superintendents, the event promised to pre-empt the attention of a large part of the nation from customary pursuits.

Although the national Administration's posture toward Earth Day formalities has been one of calculated or involuntary detachment, organizers of the event see it as not only a massive alert to public awareness but also as the dawn of a new era of "ecological politics."

'To Make Life Better' "Earth Day is a commitment to make life better, not just bigger and faster, to provide real rather than rhetorical solutions," says the organizers' main manifesto.

"It is a day to re-examine the ethnic of individual progress at mankind's expense—a day to challenge the corporate and governmental leaders who promise change, but who short-change the necessary programs . . . April 22 seeks a future worth living."

Superficially, the observances will focus on the various "pollutions"—air, water, solid waste, chemicals, noise. But running deeper are currents of thought ranging from ending the Vietnam war to dispelling racial friction and underprivilege and achieving a "no-growth society" keyed to quality rather than quantity.

The "teach-in," as it was originally called, was suggested by Senator Gaylord Nelson, Democrat of Wisconsin, soon after last November's national demonstrations protesting the United States's Vietnam involvement. It was thought that if public sentiment could be galvanized on a negative theme, it could be mobilized even more forcefully toward the positive goal of improved environment.

$125,000 Spent Since January a largely volunteer force of young people, working out of a small, shabby office in Washington, has been conducting a national campaign by mail, telephone, advertisements and personal visits to stimulate local participation.

About $125,000 has been spent on the effort, with the money coming from conservation organizations, a few wealthy donors and many small contributors.

Today the headquarters reported that its mail had been running 2,000 to 3,000 letters a day, and that specific contracts over the past months indicated that at least 2,000 college, 10,000 grammar and high schools, and citizen groups in 2,000 communities would participate.

Senator Nelson and Representative Paul N. McCloskey Jr., Republican of California, have been honorary co-chairmen of the campaign. Its national coordinator is Denis Hayes, a 24-year-old Stanford graduate from Camas, Wash.

Assailed as Diversion The campaign has been widely derided by campus radicals and black militants as a "white middle-class diversion" of public attention from the issues of Vietnam and racial equality.

To this, Earth Day organizers' answer has been that a satisfactory environment encompasses peace, civil rights and an end to poverty, but that no such causes will have meaning if the globe's physical deterioration is not arrested.

By ironic coincidence, the Washington headquarters of the past year's Vietnam protest demonstrations announced Sunday that it was closing up shop. It cited the Administration's commitment to the withdrawal of troops.

The theme of a physically imperiled globe has received extensive support among scientists, some of whom insist that the present rate of ecological deterioration—such as contamination of the atmosphere with combustion products and poisoning of the seas with chemicals—could result in an uninhabitable world within a generation or two.

Drive to Continue Many schools and colleges have Earth Day programs extending through this week and beyond, and the officials of Environmental Action, Inc., the national organization, have already decided to keep it in existence as a national coordinating agency.

"We feel that the most important achievement of April 22d already has happened," said Stephen Cotton, one of the principal organizers. "That is the organization of groups and the establishment of a solid base in communities. Most of them say they're going beyond the 22d, and we're going to be working with them."

At least several dozen members of Congress and a number of Federal officials will be participating in Earth Day activities all over the country, although there is little or no formal Federal involvement.

Teach-in leaders, wary of such involvements lest it appear that the movement has been "captured" by the Nixon Administration, said they had turned down a White House invitation in recent weeks for a discussion session because "we didn't feel there was a great deal to chat about."

SIGNIFICANCE

One of the major impacts of the first Earth Day was that it brought together diverse groups of people who all shared an interest in the environment. This collaboration of people from across the social spectrum eventually formed the basis for the environmental movement, which was highly visible during the last quarter of the twentieth century.

The second major accomplishment of Earth Day was that it demonstrated that the public wanted government to address environmental issues. In the wake of the first Earth Day, President Nixon established United States Environmental Protection Agency (EPA). The U.S. EPA is the government agency mandated with protecting the environment and public health. Congress also passed three key acts in response to the Earth Day movement: the Clean Air Act, the Clean Water Act and the Endangered Species Act. These three acts served as the administrative foundation of the environmental movement for more than three decades.

In 1990, Earth Day coordinators, with the leadership of Denis Hayes, expanded the events to include 200 million people in 141 countries. The visibility of Earth Day issues on the global level was an important signal to the organizers of the Earth Summit in Rio de Janiero in 1992.

In 1995, President Bill Clinton awarded Gaylord Nelson with the Presidential Medal of Freedom in recognition of his efforts to inform the government and the American public about environmental issues.

The overriding theme of the 2000 Earth Day was the development and use of clean energy in response to global warming. Actor Leonardo DiCaprio was chosen as the spokesperson for the event. Participants in 184 countries were involved and at least 5,000 different environmental groups planned activities. In Gabon, Africa members of different villages formed a drum chain to signal their support of a sustainable environment. Other supporters gathered on the Mall in Washington D.C. demonstrating for clean, renewable forms of energy.

In the decades since the first Earth Day, the environment received much attention and discussion, both publicly and politically. A variety of changes greatly improved the quality of the environment. For example, the air quality is much higher throughout most of the United States. The loss of wetlands habitat has been greatly slowed and some wetland restoration has occurred. Several species, including the bald eagle, were taken off the endangered species list. Americans began to recycle products rather then simply throw them away. Hybrid cars, which are much more fuel-efficient and have cleaner exhaust, started being produced by large car manufacturers.

Although less widely recognized, a grassroots coalition based in northern California headed by John McConnell celebrates an alternative Earth Day on the spring solstice. The group successfully lobbied the United Nations to support Earth Day. In 1970, U Thant, Secretary General of the United Nations, signed a proclamation to observe Earth Day on March 21 each year.

FURTHER RESOURCES

Web sites

"Earth Day Home." *U.S. Environmental Protection Agency.* <http://www.epa.gov/earthday/index.htm> (accessed March 8, 2006).

"History of Earth Day." *Earth Day Network.* <http://www.earthday.net/resources/2005materials/history.aspx> (accessed March 8, 2006).

Nelson, Gaylord. "All About Earth Day." *The Wilderness Society.* <http://earthday.wilderness.org/history> (accessed March 8, 2006).

"Portal for U.S. Events and Information." *EarthDay.gov.* <http://www.earthday.gov> (accessed March 8, 2006).

"Welcome to Earth Day 2006 Online." *Envirolink.* <http://earthday.envirolink.org> (accessed March 8, 2006).

"Wilderness as a Form of Land Use"

Book excerpt

By: Aldo Leopold

Date: 1991

Source: Leopold, Aldo. "Wilderness as a Form of Land Use." *The River of the Mother of God: And Other Essays by Aldo Leopold.* Madison: The University of Wisconsin Press, 1991.

About the Author: American biologist Aldo Leopold (1887–1948) was a prolific author known for his advocacy of formally established wilderness areas and ethical land use. Born in Burlington, Iowa, he studied science at Yale before embarking on a career with the U.S. Forest Service in 1909. His initial assignments were in New Mexico and Arizona, but in 1924 he was transferred to an administrative post at the Forest Products Laboratory in Wisconsin. Unhappy with the emphasis on commercial products that prevailed at the laboratory, he resigned in 1928 to become a consultant and lecturer. His seminal textbook *Game Management* was published in 1931 and is still in print as a classic reference. Leopold was also a hunter, which was not as unusual among early twentieth-century conservationists as it would be today. Many of his essays revolve around hunting, and some of his Depression-era consulting work was funded by the firearms industry. In 1933 Leopold accepted an appointment in the Agricultural Economics Department at the University of Wisconsin, and later became the

founding chairman of the Department of Wildlife Management at the same university. As the result of his efforts, the 500,000 acre (202,000 hectares) Gila Wilderness in southwestern New Mexico was set aside in 1924 by the Forest Service. An adjacent 200,000 acres (81,000 hectares) was declared the Aldo Leopold Wilderness in 1980. Leopold died of a heart attack in 1948 while helping a neighbor to fight a brush fire. His most widely read work, *A Sand County Almanac,* was published posthumously in 1949 and became an environmental classic.

INTRODUCTION

"Wilderness as a Form of Land Use" was published in 1925, the year after Aldo Leopold was transferred from Albuquerque, New Mexico to a U.S. Forest Service research laboratory in Madison, Wisconsin. It was also the year after the U.S. Forest Service, as a result of Leopold's lobbying, declared the Gila Wilderness in southwestern New Mexico to be the first federal wilderness preserve.

Leopold's interest in wilderness as a resource was kindled by his experience as a forest ranger in New Mexico and Arizona, and stoked by a well-known meeting with fellow U.S. Forest Service employee Arthur Carhart in 1919. Carhart was a landscape architect who had recently recommended to his superiors that a Colorado lakefront slated for development be left in a wild state. His recommendation was accepted in 1920. Leopold had previously written about wilderness in the sense that it need not be incompatible with development, but his meeting with Carhart appears to have been a pivotal event that led Leopold to decide that wilderness has its own intrinsic value and is a valid form of land use. Other, more basic, experiences also shaped his ideas about wilderness. Leopold poignantly recalled the fire in the eyes of a dying mother wolf killed by his party.

PRIMARY SOURCE

WILDERNESS AS A FORM OF LAND USE

From the earliest times, one of the principal criteria of civilization has been the ability to conquer the wilderness and convert it to economic use. To deny the validity of this criterion would be to deny history. But because the conquest of wilderness has produced beneficial reactions on social, political, and economic development, we have set up, more or less unconsciously, the converse assumption that the ultimate social, political, and economic development will be produced by conquering the wilderness entirely—that is, by eliminating it from our environment.

My purpose is to challenge the validity of such an assumption and to show how it is inconsistent with certain cultural ideas which we regard as most distinctly American. . . .

What Is a Wilderness Area? The term wilderness, as here used, means a wild, roadless area where those who are so inclined may enjoy primitive modes of travel and subsistence, such as exploration trips by pack-train or canoe.

The first idea is that wilderness is a resource, not only in the physical sense of the raw materials it contains, but also in the sense of a distinctive environment, which may, if rightly used, yield certain social values. Such a conception ought not to be difficult, because we have lately learned to think of other forms of land use in the same way. We no longer think of a municipal golf links, for instance, as merely soil and grass.

The second idea is that the value of wilderness varies enormously with location. As with other resources, it is impossible to dissociate value from location. There are wilderness areas in Siberia which are probably very similar in character to parts of our Lake states, but their value to us is negligible, compared with what the value of a similar area in the Lake states would be, just as the value of a golf links would be negligible if located so as to be out of reach of golfers.

The third idea is that wilderness, in the sense of an environment as distinguished from a quantity of physical materials, lies somewhere between the class of non-reproducible resources like minerals, and the reproducible resources like forests. It does not disappear proportionately to use, as minerals do, because we can conceive of a wild area which, if properly administered, could be traveled indefinitely and still be as good as ever. On the other hand, wilderness certainly cannot be built at will, like a city park or a tennis court. If we should tear down improvements already made in order to build a wilderness, not only would the cost be prohibitive, but the result would probably be highly dissatisfying. Neither can a wilderness be grown like timber, because it is something more than trees. The practical point is that if we want wilderness, we must foresee our want and preserve the proper areas against the encroachment of inimical uses.

Fourth, wilderness exists in all degrees, from the little accidental wild spot at the head of a ravine in a Corn Belt woodlot to vast expanses of virgin country—

Where nameless men by nameless rivers wander
And in strange valleys die strange deaths alone.

What degree of wilderness, then, are we discussing? The answer is *all degrees*. Wilderness is a relative condition. As a form of land use it cannot be a rigid entity of unchanging content, exclusive of all other forms. On the contrary, it must be a flexible thing, accommodating itself to other forms and blending with them in that highly localized give-and-take scheme of land-planning which employs the criterion of "highest use." By skillfully adjusting one use to another, the land planner builds a balanced whole without undue sacrifice of any function, and thus attains a maximum net utility of land. . . .

Lastly, to round out our definitions, let us exclude from practical consideration any degree of wilderness so absolute as to forbid reasonable protection. It would be idle to discuss wilderness areas if they are to be left subject to destruction by forest fires, or wide open to abuse. Experience has demonstrated, however, that a very modest and unobtrusive framework of trails, telephone line and lookout stations, will suffice for protective purposes. Such improvements do not destroy the wild flavor of the area, and are necessary if it is to be kept in usable condition.

Wilderness Areas in a Balanced Land System What kind of case, then, can be made for wilderness as a form of land use?

To preserve any land in a wild condition is, of course, a reversal of economic tendency, but that fact alone should not condemn the proposal. A study of the history of land utilization shows that good use is largely a matter of good balance—of wise adjustment between opposing tendencies. The modern movements toward diversified crops and live stock on the farm, conservation of eroding soils, forestry, range management, game management, public parks—all these are attempts to balance opposing tendencies that have swung out of counterpoise. . . .

Now after three centuries of overabundance, and before we have even realized that we are dealing with a non-reproducible resource, we have come to the end of our pioneer environment and are about to push its remnants into the Pacific. For three centuries that environment has determined the character of our development; it may, in fact, be said that, coupled with the character of our racial stocks, it is the very stuff America is made of. Shall we now exterminate this thing that made us American? . . .

What the Wilderness Has Contributed to American Culture
. . . There is little question that many of the attributes most distinctive of America and Americans are the impress of the wilderness and the life that accompanied it. If we have any such thing as an American culture (and I think we have), its distinguishing marks are a certain vigorous individualism combined with ability to organize, a certain intellectual curiosity bent to practical ends, a lack of subservience to stiff social forms, and an intolerance of drones, all of which are the distinctive characteristics of successful pioneers. These, if anything, are the indigenous part of our Americanism, the qualities that set it apart as a new rather than an imitative contribution to civilization. Many observers see these qualities not only bred into our

people, but built into our institutions. Is it not a bit beside the point for us to be so solicitous about preserving those institutions without giving so much as a thought to preserving the environment which produced them and which may now be one of our effective means of keeping them alive?

Wilderness Locations ... In selecting areas for retention as wilderness, the vital factor of location must be more decisively recognized. A few areas in the national forests of Idaho or Montana are better than none, but, after all, they will be of limited usefulness to the citizen of Chicago or New Orleans who has a great desire but a small purse and a short vacation. Wild areas in the poor lands of the Ozarks and the Lake states would be within his reach. For the great urban populations concentrated on the Atlantic seaboards, wild areas in both ends of the Appalachians would be especially valuable....

Generally speaking, it is not timber, and certainly not agriculture, which is causing the decimation of wilderness areas, but rather the desire to attract tourists. The accumulated momentum of the good-roads movement constitutes a mighty force, which, skillfully manipulated by every little mountain village possessed of a chamber of commerce and a desire to become a metropolis, is bringing about the extension of motor roads into every remaining bit of wild country, whether or not there is economic justification for the extension.

Our remaining wild lands are wild because they are poor. But this poverty does not deter the booster from building expensive roads through them as bait for motor tourists.

I am not without admiration for this spirit of enterprise in backwoods villages, nor am I attempting a censorious pose toward the subsidization of their ambitions from the public treasuries; nor yet am I asserting that the resulting roads are devoid of any economic utility. I do maintain, (1) that such extensions of our road systems into the wilderness are seldom yielding a return sufficient to amortize the public investment; (2) that even where they do yield such a return, their construction is not necessarily in the public interest, any more than obtaining an economic return from the last vacant lot in a parkless city would be in the public interest. On the contrary, the public interest demands the careful planning of a system of wilderness areas and the permanent reversal of the ordinary economic process within their borders. ...

Practical Aspects of Establishing Wilderness Areas Public wilderness playgrounds differ from all other public areas in that both their establishment and maintenance would entail very low costs. The wilderness is the one kind of public land that requires no improvements. To be sure, a simple system of fire protection and administrative patrol would be required, but the cost would not exceed two or three cents per acre per year. Even that would not usually be a new cost, since the greater part of the needed areas are already under administration in the rougher parts of the national forests and parks. The action needed is the permanent differentiation of a suitable system of wild areas within our national park and forest system. ...

The retention of certain wild areas in both national forests and national parks will introduce a healthy variety into the wilderness idea itself, the forest areas serving as public hunting grounds, the park areas as public wildlife sanctuaries, and both kinds as public playgrounds in which the wilderness environments and modes of travel may be preserved and enjoyed.

The Cultural Value of Wilderness Are these things worth preserving? This is the vital question. I cannot give an unbiased answer. I can only picture the day that is almost upon us when canoe travel will consist in paddling in the noisy wake of a motor launch and portaging through the back yard of a summer cottage. When that day comes, canoe travel will be dead, and dead, too, will be a part of our Americanism. Joliet and LaSalle will be words in a book, Champlain will be a blue spot on a map, and canoes will be merely things of wood and canvas, with a connotation of white duck pants and bathing "beauties." ...

There is a strong movement in this country to preserve the distinctive democracy of our field sports by preserving free hunting and fishing, as distinguished from the European condition of commercialized hunting and fishing privileges. Public shooting grounds and organized cooperative relations between sportsmen and landowners are the means proposed for keeping these sports within reach of the American of moderate means. Free hunting and fishing is a most worthy objective, but it deals with only one of the two distinctive characteristics of American sport. The other characteristic is that our test of skill is primarily the act of living in the open, and only secondarily the act of killing game. It is to preserve this primary characteristic that public wilderness playgrounds are necessary.

Herbert Hoover aptly says that there is no point in increasing the average American's leisure by perfecting the organization of industry, if the expansion of industry is allowed to destroy the recreational resources on which leisure may be beneficially employed. Surely the wilderness is one of the most valuable of these resources, and surely the building of unproductive roads in the wrong places at public expense is one of the least valuable of industries. If we are unable to steer the Juggernaut of our own prosperity, then surely there is an impotence in our vaunted Americanism that augurs ill for our future. The self-directed evolution of rational beings does not apply to us until we become collectively, as well as individually, rational and self-directing. ...

The vanguard of American thought on the use of land has already recognized all this, in theory. Are we too poor in spirit, in pocket, or in idle acres to recognize it likewise in fact?

SIGNIFICANCE

Although other pioneering American conservationists ranging from John Muir (1838–1914) to Theodore Roosevelt (1858–1919) recognized the importance of wild areas, it was Leopold who was best known for articulating the idea that wilderness is a valid and important form of land use. He had previously written on the subject, but "Wilderness as a Form of Land Use" was Leopold's first fully developed public statement of the concept.

Leopold was a pragmatic advocate of wilderness preservation. He explained that, just as a golf course is more than grass and sand, wilderness has a social value that extends beyond the trees and minerals that it might produce. Wilderness in proximity to populated areas, Leopold suggested, is even more socially valuable than inaccessible wilderness. Using language that would likely be shunned by modern wilderness advocates, he described wilderness areas as playgrounds and ascribed recreation to be one of their primary values. Beyond that, though, Leopold realized the deeper cultural significance of the American wilderness. Without wilderness and the opportunity to travel through it, he argued that icons such as Jim Bridger and Kit Carson would be reduced to little more than names in history books.

Leopold's vision of American wilderness, while revolutionary in its day, was also a moderate idea. He wrote in "Wilderness as a Form of Land Use" that absolutes are generally not beneficial. He thought it sound for cities to be built and trees to be felled, but not for all the land to be developed and logged. This moderation may have sprung from his early encounter with the dying wolf, before which he believed that if fewer wolves meant more deer, a world without wolves would be a hunter's paradise. The extension of this thinking is that while it was good to carve a civilization out of the wilderness, it is not desirable to completely eliminate wilderness.

Aerial view of Roan Plateau, where gas drilling rigs have been set up for energy development. Aldo Leopold targeted wilderness areas such as these to be reserved for recreation, July 27, 2005. AP IMAGES

FURTHER RESOURCES

Books

Leopold, Aldo. *Game Management*. Madison, Wisc: University of Wisconsin Press, 1986.

———. *A Sand County Almanac and Sketches Here and There*. Oxford, England: Oxford University Press, 1987.

Meine, Curt. *Aldo Leopold: His Life and Work*. Madison, Wisc.: University of Wisconsin Press, 1991.

Web sites

U.S. Forest Service. "Aldo Leopold Wilderness Research Institute." <http://leopold.wilderness.net> (accessed January 17, 2006).

U.S. Forest Service. "Arthur Carhart National Wilderness Training Center." <http://carhart.wilderness.net> (accessed January 17, 2006).

Environmental Damage in Post-Soviet Eastern Europe

Photograph

By: Chris Niedenthal

Date: March 21, 1992

Source: Time Life Pictures/Getty Images

About the Photographer: This photograph was taken on the Romanian shore of the Danube River in the town Giurgiu, which contains Romania's largest shipyard. Air pollution and abuse of the river are rife here, as along much of the Danube's course through Eastern Europe.

INTRODUCTION

The photograph gives a glimpse of some of the disastrous conditions that industry has created along the shores of the Danube River. The Danube, which begins in Germany, flows eastward, and empties into the Black Sea, is the second longest river in Europe. Its drainage basin includes much of Eastern Europe; parts of Albania, Bosnia and Herzegovina, Bulgaria, Germany, Italy, the Czech Republic, Moldova, Poland, Switzerland, Ukraine, and Yugoslavia; most of Austria, Croatia, Romania, Slovenia, and Slovakia; and all of Hungary.

Until the breakup of the Soviet Union (Union of Soviet Socialist Republics, or USSR) in 1991, control of the Danube's basin was divided between deeply hostile military-political blocks, namely the North Atlantic Treaty Alliance (NATO, led by the United States) and the USSR; cooperation for environmental quality was a low priority for both powers. Today, several of the individual states flanking the Danube, such as Romania and Bulgaria, are still preoccupied by national feuds. Although most of the Danube states joined in the early 1990s to establish an integrated program for the control of water quality throughout the Danube's basin, severe pollution and other problems persist along the river. Particularly troubled are the parts of the river running through states that were part of the USSR until 1991.

Overuse and pollution feed the Danube with raw sewage, agricultural chemicals, factory waste, and bilge oil flushed by shipping. Mining and manufacturing are the biggest polluters: in 2000, for example, a tailings lagoon at a Hungarian mine ruptured, spilling hundreds of thousands of cubic meters of water heavily laced with cyanide and heavy metals into the Tisza river, a tributary of the Danube. Hundreds of tons of dead fish had to be removed from the river using power equipment. Because of water pollution, the Danube's fishing industry is essentially dead. The NATO bombing of Yugoslavia in 1999 clogged the Danube with rubble from destroyed bridges and released chemical spills from bombed factories near the river. Rivers are among the most vulnerable of all ecological systems, second perhaps only to landlocked lakes like the Aral Sea (completely destroyed by Soviet-era civil engineering projects that have starved the great lake of water): both rivers and lakes eventually receive all toxins that are added to water in their watershed, no matter how distant.

■ PRIMARY SOURCE

ENVIRONMENTAL DAMAGE IN POST-SOVIET EASTERN EUROPE

See primary source image.

SIGNIFICANCE

The Soviet Union controlled Russia, most of Eastern Europe, and much of Central Asia from 1922 to 1991. Officially socialist, the USSR considered economic development and military power top priorities: protection of the environment was a secondary concern at best. In fact, Soviet ideology proclaimed that socialism (as practiced by the USSR) was inherently better for the environment than western-style capitalism, so any complaints about the environment could only reflect disloyalty. Without even the slight

PRIMARY SOURCE

Environmental Damage in Post-Soviet Eastern Europe. This photograph shows discarded ships and ship parts lying on the Romanian shore of the Danube River in the town Giurgiu. Air and water pollution are rife here, as along much of the Danube's course through Eastern Europe. PHOTO BY CHRIS NIEDENTHAL/TIME LIFE PICTURES/GETTY IMAGES

restraints applied by citizen activism in democratic Western countries, Soviet military and industrial activities severely damaged the environment. Chemical and radioactive wastes were carelessly dumped or stored; rivers were diverted without regard to the consequences; air pollution went unchecked. When the power structure of the USSR began to weaken in the late 1980s, popular dissatisfaction with the environmental damage caused by the existing regime was one of the factors helping to bring about its final breakup. Politicians agitating for secession from the USSR cited its neglect of the environment as one reason for becoming nationally independent.

Unfortunately, little changed regarding environmental protection after 1991. Economic "reform" in former countries of the Soviet Union has tended strongly toward an extreme free-market ideology that affirms the power of unrestrained profit-making to produce the maximum good—including environmental good—for the maximum number. As one Russian citizen put it shortly after the breakup of the USSR, "We have traded great god Marx for great god Market." Unregulated industry tends to treat the environment as external to calculations of cost and benefit, except insofar as it can supply raw material or act as a sump for waste. In the absence of appropriate legal feedbacks, treating or minimizing waste, whether polluted water or flue gasses or any other type, is always an accounting loss for the polluting enterprise (at least in the short term). In practice, therefore, the breakup of the Soviet Union has not resulted in striking improvements in pollution.

FURTHER RESOURCES
Web sites

"Environmental degradation in Eastern Europe, Caucasus and Central Asia: past roots, present transition and future hopes." Department of Environmental Sciences and Policy, Central European University, Budapest, Hungary. <http://www.ceu.hu/envsci/aleg/research/EnvDegradationEastEurope090903.pdf> (accessed February 17, 2006).

"The Environmental Program for the Danube River." October 2002. <http://www.transboundarywaters.orst.edu/projects/casestudies/danube.html> (accessed February 17, 2006).

"An African Success Story"

Journal article

By: Nancy Chege

Date: July 1993

Source: Chege, Nancy. "An African Success Story." *The Worldwatch Institute* 6, no. 4 (July 1993).

About the Author: Nancy Chege was a staff member for the Worldwatch Institute, which carries out interdisciplinary research on global economic, social, and environmental issues. The work of Worldwatch is focused on the concepts of environmental sustainability and social justice, and how these concepts can become reality in society.

INTRODUCTION

The Machakos region of Kenya is southeast of the capital Nairobi, in the south central part of the country, and has been inhabited by the Akamba people for the past four hundred years. The Akamba are anthropologically classified as Bantu, and may have moved to the area from coastal regions, or from farther south in Tanzania, near Mount Kilimajaro. The early Akamba were said to be hunters, but settled into farming due to the fertile Machakos soil and the relatively higher precipitation received there. As population grew in the area, particularly in the times of European colonization, land degradation began to become a problem, and the area's food production steadily decreased.

Overgrazing, deforestation, and the intensification of agriculture are all causes of land degradation, which can be observed when soil loses nutrients and organic matter, becomes salinated, has higher levels of acidity, or undergoes desertification. Often, land is further compromised by erosion from wind and rain, which can rapidly carry soil particles away. Although soil erosion can happen easily on many agricultural soil types, it is more severe on steep slopes, which are not covered by vegetation. Many agricultural development specialists work toward improving land quality through soil conservation, by reducing erosion and maintaining fertility. Terrace farming is one way in which the speed of water can be reduced, helping it to seep into soils.

Scientists estimate that 15 percent of vegetated soils, as much as 5 billion acres (2 billion hectares) of land, were degraded during the second half of the twentieth century. Some suggest that 740 million acres (300 million hectares) of land have been degraded to the point that they will be unable to recover their original biological function. The majority of degraded land is found in the developing countries of Latin America, Asia, and Africa, and has resulted in lower productivity and smaller agricultural harvests. Officials at the International Food and Policy Research Institute (IFPRI) and other agriculture development experts say that the degradation of land and other aspects of the environment is exasperated by poverty, population pressure, and poor government policies. Over 700 million of the world's population has health problems associated with malnutrition, due to inadequate supplies of nutritious food. Lack of food is often linked to poor land use practices, and the decreasing availability of fertile lands. The Green Revolution, launched in the 1940s by the Rockefeller Foundation, was successful in raising capacity and agriculture production in Latin America and Asia. However, Africa has made little or no progress in improving the food security of its inhabitants. In addition to degraded soil on farmlands, war, drought, and lack of farming inputs such as fertilizer make it difficult to adequately feed African populations.

■ PRIMARY SOURCE

In the Machakos district of south-eastern Kenya, bananas, coffee, and maize grow thick on terraces that climb the sloping land like many staircases. Standing in cool, green contrast to the parched, scrub vegetation that spreads beyond the horizon, and across much of Kenya, the terraces of Machakos make the region more than just an aesthetic exception; it is an economic one too. With approximately 70 percent of its arable land terraced, the region has produced on of Africa's best records of soil and water conservation, and its growth in agricultural output has even outpaced its high population growth rate of 3 percent.

A look at the fields in Machakos gives the impression that the area has always been productive and well managed. But that is not the case. At the beginning of the century, colonial British farmers established large coffee and sisal plantations that attracted migrant laborers from surround villages. As the number of people and livestock in the area grew, so did the pressures on the land, and the consequences of the migrant influx began to take their toll. By the early 1930s, Machakos was overgrazed, denuded, and in trouble. Agricultural productivity was plummeting and soil was eroding at rates as high as 13 tons per acre annually.

In response, the colonial government in Nairobi imposed a mandatory reconditioning program that forced villagers to reduce their herds of livestock, fence off extremely degraded land and allow "natural healing," and construct terraces for growing crops. At first, little progress was made because the farmers despised and resisted the coercive program. During the mid-1940s, the reconditioning activities gained momentum when a local leader, Chief Mutinda, imposed a fine of two bulls on any farmer who cultivated un-terraced land.

But solid conservation efforts in Machakos languished when men left home to fight the colonial forces during Kenya's struggle for independence from British rule in the 1950s, and during the turbulent resettlement period of the 1960s.

Once life returned to normal, the people of Machakos, the Akamba, were eager to reverse the deteriorating condition of their land. In 1974, Kenya's Ministry of Agriculture established the National Soil and Water Conservation Project, with support from the Swedish International Development Agency. The Soil and Water officials worked closely with the Akamba, treating them as partners and successfully persuading them to restart the construction of terraces. The Swedish agency offered additional incentives by creating a farmers' training program, providing tools and establishing tree nurseries.

Terraces are ingeniously simple but hard to build. A farmer begins by digging a trench perpendicular to the fall line, then throws the soil up the slope to form a solid ridge, hence the Akamba name "fanya juu," which translates "do upwards." The terraces even out as shifting soils build up behind the ridge. Rain water seeps into the soil rather than running down the slope, making better use of the region's sparse precipitation. To stabilize the soil and prevent the ridges from collapsing, farmers plant grass on top of the ridges. The grass then provides fodder for livestock.

In building their terraces, the Akamba rediscovered an ancient technology that has enabled subsistence farmers to make poor land productive in scattered locations from the Philippines to the Andes. A 1988 study by Eva Holmgren and Gunilla Johansson of the Swedish University of Agricultural Sciences found that corn and bean yields were 33 percent and 16 percent higher, respectively, on terraced versus unterraced land. In addition, the terraces have helped to reduce the siltation of waterways, which extends the lifetime of reservoirs in the area.

Machakos farmers are taking other steps to increase the productivity and health of their land. They have begun using manure in place of more expensive chemical fertilizer because it both enriches the soil and helps hold it in place. Recognizing that the health of their livestock is more important than the quantity, they are thinning their herds of livestock, making prudent decisions to graze only the few that their land can support. As the supply of grazing land shrinks through conversion to crops, or through retirement from overgrazing, the need to thin herds becomes even more pressing.

Without the help of heavy machinery, it would take one farmer approximately two years to construct terraces on a five-acre plot. But Machakos is densely populated, and there are plenty of helping hands. The Akamba have organized into self-help groups known as "mwethya." Unified by the common vision of increased food security and a higher standard of living, the mwethya work on each other's fields on a rotating basis. When first formed in the 1920s, they consisted of men and women who belonged to the same clan, and performed services ranging from helping families recover from disasters to building houses and pitching in with farming tasks. During the years of political turmoil, the groups disintegrated—and did not reassemble until after 1963, when Kenya received its independence from the British government.

In recent years, the composition of the mwethya has changed as village men have left for the cities in search of jobs. Today, a typical group is composed of 25 to 70 women who reside in the same neighborhood. In most groups, the only qualification for membership is a willingness to participate in communal work. The groups have played a central role in combating the forces of land degradation, and are currently the most active of the local institutions. The project's success—primarily fueled by the enthusiasm and commitment of women—is exemplary of an economic potential among women that often remains ignored and unrecognized throughout the world.

The conservation project has not been without its drawbacks. Overgrazing is still prevalent, and stricter measures are required to curb the problem. And although the Akamba have made great strides in conserving their soil and water, erosion rates are still relatively high during the harvesting and plowing months, when terrace construction and maintenance do not receive adequate attention.

But despite the low rainfall, the fragile soils, and the growing human and livestock populations that have left so much of Sub-Saharan Africa impoverished, the Akamba women have successfully managed to transform their scrubby and denuded homeland into an agriculturally productive area. The residents of Machakos district have set a significant example for Africa. They have made their accomplishments without the importation of complex and costly technologies, succeeding instead with simple tools, local resources, and their own communal labor.

SIGNIFICANCE

Development studies have shown that when there are high levels of poverty in a rural area, land is often degraded quickly as residents strive to meet daily needs, using resources in a manner that maximizes short-term benefits. However, this shortsightedness often increases poverty in the long-term as the resources are diminished with degradation of land. Developing national governments, as well as international development agencies, are tasked with the difficult job of helping the poor meet their daily needs and plan for longer-term sustainability.

The Akamba people have been able to improve agriculture productivity by implementing innovative farming techniques suitable for their unique landscape and climate. Ideally, agricultural specialists survey an area to find what techniques may work best given the characteristics and topography of a particular region. In addition to terracing, no-till agriculture, a method that minimizes disturbance to soil, has been used to successfully maintain soil quality in some locations. Regardless of the technology, when implementing new farming techniques, community participation is vital for success, something realized in the Akamba experience.

Despite the success of the Akamba, poverty remains a limitation to the Machakos region. Primarily, the Akamba people rely on the capital provided by members of the community in order to carry out their conservation programs. This limits the improvements that can be made, as the farmers cannot typically afford useful equipment such as water tanks, or animals to plow terraces. It is sometimes difficult to find the resources to improve roads, which better enable farmers to connect with markets. The majority of farmers are without electricity, and the availability of off-farm jobs, which bring in money to the area, are not always available. Drought has also been an obstacle for the region.

FURTHER RESOURCES

Periodicals

Scherr, Sara J., and Satya Yadav. "Land Degradation in the Developing World: Issues and Policy Options For 2020." *International Food Policy Research Institute* 44 (June 1997).

Web sites

"Agricultural Case Studies." *Bill Moyers Reports: Earth on Edge*. <http://www.pbs.org/earthonedge/ecosystems/agricultural2.html> (accessed March 17, 2006).

"Land Degradation and Desertification." *United States Department of Agriculture, Natural Resources Conservation Service*. <http://soils.usda.gov/use/worldsoils/landdeg> (accessed March 17, 2006).

United Nations Development Programme, United Nations Environment Programme, World Bank, and World Resources Institute. "Agroecosystems: Regaining the High Ground: Reviving the Hillsides of Machakos." Excerpt in *World Resources 2000-2001: People and Ecosystems: The Fraying Web of Life*, 2000. <http://pdf.wri.org/wr2000_agroecosystems_machakos.pdf> (accessed March 17, 2006).

"Rent-Seeking Behind the Green Curtain"

Journal article

By: Jonathan H. Adler

Date: 1996

Source: Adler, Jonathan H. "Rent-Seeking Behind the Green Curtain." *Regulation: The CATO Review of Business and Government* 19, 4 (1996).

About the Author: Jonathan H. Adler is an associate professor teaching free-market environmental law and Associate Director of the Center for Business Law and Regulation at the Case Western Reserve University School of Law. Formerly a director of environmental studies at the Competitive Enterprise Institute, Adler is a contributing editor to the *National Review* and hosts his own free-market-oriented Web site.

INTRODUCTION

In the years since the first Earth Day was held in 1970, environmentalism and environmental activism have rapidly become big businesses. Environmental activist groups such as Earth First and Greenpeace raise millions of dollars each year to support environmental causes, and many of these dollars have funded legislative initiatives at both the state and federal levels. Environmentally friendly politicians have passed numerous acts intended to clean up environmental mistakes of the past and prevent their recurrence in the future. These acts, including the Wilderness Act, the Clean Air Act, the Clean Water Act, and the Superfund Act, have cost taxpayers billions of dollars and have had an enormous impact on the lives and livelihoods of Americans.

The Superfund, for example, currently costs about $1.5 billion per year to run, and is expected to consume a total of more than $16 billion by 2009. While this total amount appears reasonable, given the difficulty involved in cleaning up toxic waste sites, estimates place the administrative and support expenses of Superfund efforts at 18–25 percent of the project's total costs, raising questions about how efficiently the resources are being used.

Environmental activist groups have generally portrayed themselves as morally superior to lawmakers who pander to political contributors and seek political gain. Many environmental debates have been framed as pitting the small, idealistic forces of environmentalism against the money-hungry, heartless polluters of industry. While this portrayal of underfunded environmentalists might have been true in the past, today's environmental movement is a politically connected, well-funded machine.

In this article, the author explores two questions. First, he asks whether environmentalists have become just another political constituency jockeying for power and influence in Washington. Second, he suggests that in many cases, the center stage pieces of legislation passed by the movement have not only failed to accomplish their stated goals, but may have actually worsened the situations they were intended to repair.

▌ PRIMARY SOURCE

RENT-SEEKING BEHIND THE GREEN CURTAIN

On August 4, 1992, vice-presidential candidate Senator Al Gore appeared in Orange County, California, to attack the incumbent President's regulatory record. In a speech at an Evergreen Company used-oil treatment facility, Gore attacked President George Bush for making it "impossible [for] companies like this one to survive." Because of the Bush administration's inaction, Gore charged that "A lot of jobs were lost."

Senator Gore was not calling for "reinventing" regulation or reducing the paperwork burden. He was not attacking President Bush for presiding over too much regulation, but too little. Gore's complaint was that the Bush administration hurt companies that rely on federal regulations to turn profit by failing to promulgate *more* regulatory standards.

In particular, Gore attacked the administration's failure to define used motor oil as a hazardous waste under the Resource Conservation and Recovery Act (RCRA). Such regulation would have increased the cost of oil changes for consumers and discouraged the recovery and recycling of used oil; however, it would have

guaranteed additional business for the Evergreen Company and for members of the Hazardous Waste Treatment Council (HWTC). This policy proposal had as much to do with promoting narrow economic interests as with protecting environmental concerns.

Green Politics is Still Politics Most Americans recognize that politics has a lot to do with the pursuit of power, privilege, and special interests; however, there is a generel presumption that environmental polotics is somehow different. We take for granted that environmental laws are what they seem; that the legislators who enact those laws and the bureaucrats who implement them are earnestly struggling to protect public interests; and, that these laws wil be enforced in a fair and sensible manner. All too often, however, environmental regulations are designed to serve narrow political and economic interests, not the public interest.

The details of environmental policies have major economic consequences. America spends well over 2 percent of the gross domestic product on pollution control, and the figure is rising. As the cost of environmental regulation increases, so does the value of potential potential comparative advantages in the marketplace. Seeking regulatory policies that will carve out niche markets or obstruct competition becomes an increasingly profitable investment. One should not be surprised that economic interests lobby, litigate, and make alliances with "public interest" organizations to ensure favorable treatment for their own interests and to utilize environmental regulations to transfer wealth.

Attempts "to gain a competitive advantage through manipulation of the regulatory process [are] occurring with increasing frequency," notes former Environmental Protection Agency Deputy Administrator A. James Barnes. Examples are everywhere:

- The Business Council for a Sustainable Energy Future, a coalition of gas, wind, solar, and geo-thermal power producers and related firms, is lobbying for deep cuts in greenhouse gas emissions.
- The Environmental Technology Council, a successor to the Hazardous Waste Treatment Council (HWTC), wants to ensure that various wastes, such as fluorescent bulbs, are covered by hazardous-waste regulations.
- The Alliance for Responsible Thermal Treatment (ARTT), an HWTC spinoff of incinerator operators, wants to prevent the burning of hazardous waste in cement kilns, and thereby eliminate its members' toughest competitors.
- Major utilities recently lobbied to require the sale of electric vehicles in California and the northeastern United States and have sought policies that would

- subsidize the purchase of electric cars at the rate-payers' expense.
- Ethanol producers attempted to secure a portion of the lucrative oxygenate market for federally mandated reformulated gasoline.
- A primary purpose of the Conservation Reserve Program is to increase farm commodity prices by taking acreage out of production, though the program does little to control agricultural runoff.

The list can go on and on, for painting special interest policies green makes them easier to enact, irrespective of whether they further environmental protection. In this sense, environmental politics is as polluted as the rest.

SIGNIFICANCE

Like most other political causes, the environmental movement brings together a complex mixture of personalities, motivations, and intentions. While indicting the entire movement for the mistakes of some members would be senseless, Adler's work makes an important point, especially given that environmental expenditures now consume more than 2 percent of the nation's Gross National Product. For this reason alone, serious attention should be paid to how funds are being spent, and whether they are producing the desired benefits.

FURTHER RESOURCES

Books

Barnett, Harold. *Toxic Debts and the Superfund Dilemma*. Chapel Hill, N.C.: University of North Carolina Press, 1994.

Kubasek, Nancy K. and Gary Silverman. *Environmental Law*, 5th ed. Upper Saddle River, N.J.: Prentice-Hall, 2000.

Novello, David P. and Robert Martineau, eds. *The Clean Air Act Handbook*, 2nd ed. New York: American Bar Association, 2005.

Periodicals

Olson, Dan. "Waste is a Terrible Thing to Waste." *Minnesota Environment* 5, 3 (2005): 1–4.

Ribaudo, Marc. "New Clean Water Act Regulations Create Imperative for Livestock Producers." *Amber Waves* 1, 1 (February 2003): 30–37.

Web sites

Ichniowski, Tom. "Study Pegs Superfund's Cost at $14–16 Billion Through 2009." *Engineering News-Record*, July 12, 2001. <http://www.construction.com/NewsCenter/Headlines/ENR/20010712d.asp> (accessed February 28, 2006).

Killam, Gayle, Paul Koberstein, and Gabriella Stocks. "Understanding the Clean Water Act Online Course."

River Network. <http://www.cleanwateract.org> (accessed February 28, 2006).

U.S. Environmental Protection Agency. "The Plain English Guide to the Clean Air Act." *U.S. Environmental Protection Agency Web site*, April 1993. <http://www.epa.gov/oar/oaqps/peg_caa/pegcaain.html> (accessed February 28, 2006).

The Water Sourcebooks: K–12.

Book excerpt

By: United States Environmental Protection Agency

Date: 2000

Source: U.S. Environmental Protection Agency. *The Water Sourcebooks: K–12*. Washington, DC: 2000.

About the Organization: The U.S. Environmental Protection Agency (EPA), established in 1970, is generally responsible for protecting the U.S. environment and preserving its integrity for future generations. Its specific aims include controlling and reducing water and air pollution, noise pollution, and pollution by pesticides, radiation, and various toxic substances. The EPA Office of Ground Water and Drinking Water, within the Office of Water, is generally responsible for working with many environmental partners in order to protect the public health by ensuring a safe supply of drinking water and by protecting groundwater.

INTRODUCTION

The Water Sourcebook Series is a project of the Office of Ground Water and Drinking Water (OGWDW). Developed in 2000, the Water Sourcebook Series is the result of a partnership among the EPA Region Four (based in Atlanta, Georgia), the Alabama Department of Environmental Regulation, and Legacy, Inc.

Water Sourcebooks: K–12 is an environmental education program that contains over three hundred activities for schoolchildren from kindergarten to twelfth grade—with the reoccurring environmental message, "Use What You Need and Don't Pollute." The activities are divided into four major groups: kindergarten to second grade (K–2), third grade to fifth grade (3–5), sixth grade to eighth grade (6–8), and ninth grade to twelfth grade (9–12). Each group is divided into five chapters: Introduction to Water,

Drinking Water and Wastewater Treatment, Surface Water Resources, Ground Water Resources, and Wetlands and Coastal Waters.

The Water Sourcebook program describes the water management cycle and its effect on all parts of the environment. The curriculum involves science and mathematics, along with subject areas in the social studies, language arts, reading, and other educational areas. The activities involved with the program vary from fact sheets, reference materials, hands-on investigations, and a glossary of terms. Each activity is organized by objectives, materials needed, background information, advance preparation, procedures, and resources.

An example of one of the activities of the Water Sourcebook Series is called *Thirstin's Water Cycle Adventure*, which visually describes the cycle of water: falling moisture (in such forms as rain and snow) onto the surface of the Earth (while Thirstin looks on from underneath his umbrella), its submergence into groundwater within bedrock, its eventual use in providing drinking water from wells and as part of water bodies (such as lakes and rivers), and its evaporation due to the sun back into the sky where it returns to clouds to repeat its perpetual cycle.

■ PRIMARY SOURCE

WATER SOURCEBOOKS: K–12

INTRODUCTION The value of clean, safe water for individuals, communities, businesses, and industries can't be measured. Every living thing depends on water. The economy requires it. Water issues should be everyone's concern, but most people take water quality and availability for granted. After all, clean, safe water is available to most Americans every time they turn on the tap. Water issues do not become a concern until there is a crisis such as a drought or wastewater treatment plant failure. Educating citizens who must make critical water resource decisions in the midst of a crisis rarely results in positive change. Developing awareness, knowledge, and skills for sound water use decisions is very important to young people, for they will soon be making water resource management decisions. Properly equipping them to do so is essential to protect water resources.

WATER SOURCEBOOK PROGRAM The Water Sourcebook educational program is directed specifically toward the in-school population. The program consists of supplemental activity guides targeting kindergarten through high school. Water Sourcebooks are available for primary (K–2), elementary (3–5), middle (6–8), and secondary (9–12) levels. Materials developed in the program are compatible with existing curriculum standards established by State Boards of Education throughout the United States as well as national standards in science, social studies and geography. Concepts included in these standards are taught by using water quality information as the content.

The Water Sourcebooks include five chapters—Introduction, Drinking Water and Wastewater Treatment, Groundwater, Surface Water, and Wetlands.

DEVELOPMENT The Water Sourcebooks are developed in three stages. First, classroom teachers are selected to write the activities with assistance of education specialists. Teams of teachers are given the task of developing and writing the activities for each of the five instructional chapters. The second step involves testing activities in the classroom and technical reviews by water experts. From the evaluations provided by the testing teachers and technical reviewers, revisions are made. Finally, editing, and illustrations are complete and the Water Sourcebook is published.

ACTIVITY DESIGN All of the activities include "hands-on" components and are designed to blend with existing curricula in the areas of general sciences, language arts, math, social studies, art, and in some cases, reading or other areas. Each activity details (1) objectives, (2) subjects(s), (3) time, (4) materials, (5) background information, (6) advance preparation, (7) procedure (including activity, follow-up, and extension), and (8) resources. Fact sheets and a glossary section are included at the end of the guide to help equip teachers to deal with concepts and words used in the text which may be unfamiliar.

■

SIGNIFICANCE

Environmental education—as provided by the EPA Water Sourcebooks—at the grade-school through high-school levels increases student awareness and knowledge of environmental issues and challenges. As a result, children and young adults are provided various sources to better understand how their individual actions affect the environment and how large groups, such as corporations and countries, also affect the environment. As students develop critical skills in problem solving and decision making, as provided by the numerous sources of the EPA, they will be able to better judge and decide various sides of issues based on facts and common sense—often without advocating a particular viewpoint or taking a specific course of action.

With the use of the Water Sourcebook Series, members of the Office of Environmental Education (within the EPA) can better coordinate the quality and quantity of environmental education in the formal educational system throughout the United States. In fact, the Office of Environmental Education, because of its placement within the EPA, has access to a wide variety of programs that help to inform and educate students throughout the United States.

On the Internet site of the Office of Environmental Education, students are able to access such information as basic facts, nearby EPA environmental education offices ("Where You Live"), various activities ("You Can Do"), grant and fellowship programs, and President's environmental youth awards, along with information on educator training, advisory groups, partnerships, resources, a calendar of events, and glossary terms. Among the student projects created by the EPA—also available on the Internet— is the Environmental Kids Club, the EPA Student Center, and the High School Environmental Center.

Through such EPA programs as the Water Sourcebook Series, students from kindergarten to high school gain a better understanding about how their individual actions will affect the environment. Such understanding is very significant for maintaining and improving environments from the local community level to the global environment of the Earth.

FURTHER RESOURCES

Books

Basile, Carole, Cameron White, and Stacey Robinson. *Awareness to Citizenship: Environmental Literacy for the Elementary Child*. Lanham, MD: University Press of America, 2000.

Educating for a Culture of Social and Ecological Peace, edited by Anita L. Wenden. Albany, NY: State University of New York Press, 2004.

Environmental Education: A Resource Handbook, edited by Joe E. Heimlich. Bloomington, IN: Phi Delta Kappa Educational Foundation, 2002.

Suzuki, David T. *Eco-fun: Great Projects, Experiments, and Games for a Greener Earth*. Vancouver and New York: Greystone Books, 2001.

Teaching Green: The Middle Years, Hands-on Learning in Grades 6–8, edited by Tim Grant and Gail Littlejohn. Gabriola, BC: New Society Publishers, 2004.

Web sites

Environmental Protection Agency. "Environmental Kids Club." <http://www.epa.gov/kids> (accessed November 26, 2005).

Environmental Protection Agency. "EPA Student Center." <http://www.epa.gov/students> (accessed November 26, 2005).

Environmental Protection Agency. "Welcome to the Water Sourcebooks." <http://www.epa.gov/safewater/kids/wsb> (accessed November 26, 2005).

Sewage Protestors Hold a "Toilet Protest"

Photograph

By: Sion Touhig

Date: August 7, 2001

Source: Getty Images

About the Photographer: This photograph was taken in Brighton, England, on August 7, 2001, during a protest by the group Surfers Against Sewage demonstrating against the discharge of untreated sewage into English coastal waters.

INTRODUCTION

Surfers Against Sewage (SAS) is an environmental organization based in Brighton, England, that opposes the discharge of raw sewage into ocean waters. On August 7, 2001, the group staged a "sitting protest" against the fact that all sewage from the seaside resort city of Brighton, population 275,000, is pumped directly into the ocean without treatment. Twenty toilets were lined up on the sand and occupied by twenty protestors. One member of the group, Vicky Garner, said: "Whilst some may be questioning our sanity, we are simply creating an image that reflects reality in Brighton! ...We thought we'd cut out the middle man, save Southern Water [the local water utility] the time and money and take our loos to the water's edge!" The surfers were joined on the beach by local Member of Parliament Des Turner, who spoke to the press about the legal and environmental need to treat Brighton's sewage before dumping it into the ocean.

Soon after its founding in 1990, SAS was dressing up in wet suits and gas masks and handing out fliers. In 1991, the group launched a ten foot inflatable "turd" bearing the name of the group, a pointed visual joke that drew media attention. SAS performed other stunts as well, including lobbying the British House of Commons in full regalia: wet suits, surfboards, and gas masks.

SAS, which started from a small group of fifty or so Brighton surfers angry at bumping into feces in the water, matured into a serious player in the drafting of water-quality standards. By 1999, SAS was contributing to the drafting of a World Health Organization protocol on recreational water quality. (The World Health Organization is a United Nations body.)

Progress toward full treatment of Britain's sewage has been slow and not entirely steady, but there have been advancements. In 1990, only 30 percent of bathing waters along designated swimming beaches in England and Wales met the European Union's strict guidelines for water cleanliness; by 2004, according to the British government, eighty percent did so, and ninty-nine percent met the EU's less-strict "mandatory" quality standards. Nevertheless, SAS still has plenty of work to do. The group argues that unseasonal rainfall due to climate change may increasingly cause unplanned sewage runoff. In August 2004, a delegation of male SAS surfers dressed in wet suits, high heels, wigs, and makeup—carrying surfboards, of course—protested outside the Department of the Environment office in London. They were calling attention to the discharge of pharmaceuticals and other bio-active ("gender-bending") substances into the rivers, lakes, and seas of the United Kingdom. Their official statement said, "Recreational water users, such as surfers, are now becoming increasingly concerned over the long-term effects a cocktail of chemicals, hormones and antibiotics may be having on their bodies when marine and freshwater wildlife are already showing such alarming changes."

PRIMARY SOURCE

SURFERS AGAINST SEWAGE HOLD A "TOILET PROTEST"
See primary source image.

PRIMARY SOURCE

Surfers Against Sewage Hold a "Toilet Protest." Members of the environmental group Surfers Against Sewage sit on the toilets at the seaside resort city of Brighton, U.K., 2001, intending to dramatize their complaint that Brighton is dumping untreated sewage into the sea. PHOTO BY SION TOUHIG/GETTY IMAGES

SIGNIFICANCE

Like the environmental group Greenpeace, SAS uses humor to draw attention to facts that are not funny. Untreated sewage contains not only human waste but everything else that goes down any domestic or industrial drain: bleach, soaps, paints, solvents, heavy metals, and more. In 1997, a British study found that surfers were three times more likely than the general public to contract hepatatis A, presumably from exposure to contaminated water.

SAS has strongly advocated "full treatment" of sewage, as opposed to partial treatment followed by ocean dumping of effluent through long pipes that would supposedly not allow the material to wash back to shore. Full treatment involves bacterial digestion of waste, separation of solids, filtering, and (often) the use of ultraviolet light to kill microorganisms before the effluent is finally discharged. SAS also opposes dumping sludge solids produced by sewage treatment into the sea.

Since all human communities produce sewage, pollution of water by sewage is a global problem. Off the coast of California, would-be surfers often have the choice of ignoring beach closure signs or exposing themselves to sewage spills from the United States or Mexico or runoff from city streets. Short-term consequences of exposure to contaminated water include vomiting, diarrhea, and hepatitis A. In November 2004, also in the United States, the Surfrider Foundation brought a lawsuit against President George W. Bush, the Environmental Protection Agency, and other government entities for supporting the use of injection wells for the disposal of sewage in Florida. According to the Surfrider Foundation, studies show that instead of being filtered by underground rock the sewage simply squirts back up into the sea, contaminating some six hundred miles of coastal waters. In Bali, an island in the Indonesian archipelago that depends on tourism for 90 percent of its economy, raw sewage often contaminates some rivers and beaches, threatening not only aquatic life but the island's economic base. Money and the environment are at odds in this case, as usual: treating sewage is always more costly in dollars than simply dumping it into the nearest body of water.

FURTHER RESOURCES

Periodicals

Martin, Hugo. "Stay out of the water? No way." *Los Angeles Times*, (January 30, 2006): p. 1.

Web sites

Surfers Against Sewage. <http://www.sas.org.uk/index.asp> (accessed March 10, 2006).

Globalization and Poverty: An Ecological Perspective

Book excerpt

By: Roldan Muradian and Joan Martinez-Alier

Date: 2001

Source: Muradian, Roldan, and Joan Martinez-Alier. *Globalization and Poverty: An Ecological Perspective.* Heinrich Böll Foundation, 2001.

About the Author: Roldan Muradian is a Venezuelan biologist. He holds an M.S. in Ecological Economics, has been a research fellow at the Universite de Versailles (2000–2002), and as of 2006 was a Ph.D. candidate at the Universitat Autonoma de Barcelona. His main area of research involves the relationship between trade and the environment. Joan Martinez-Alier is a professor at the Universitat Autonoma de Barcelona. He is a founding member of the International Society for Ecological Economics, a member of the Scientific Committee of the European Environment Agency, and a member of the Green Academy of the Heinrich Böll Foundation. He is the author of *Ecological Economics: Energy, Environment and Society* (with Kalus Schluepmann); *Varieties of Environmentalism: Essays North and South* (with Ramachandra Guha); and *The Environmentalism of the Poor: A Study of Ecological Conflicts and Valuation.*

INTRODUCTION

Since the 1950s, the world has experienced an unparalleled movement of currency, capital, trade, and human resources between countries. This flow across borders, called globalization, has fueled debates regarding development and economic theory, largely due to its impact on workers and the environment in low-income countries. Supporters of globalization believe that this free flow of trade and currency has facilitated the expansion of economic growth and opportunities globally. Dissenters in the globalization debate assert that globalization has promoted unfair labor practices and environmentally detrimental policies in low-income countries, as well as an increase in the income gap between high-income and low-income nation-states. In the globalization discourse, low-income and developing nations are referred to as the South due to their geographic location south of the equator and include areas in Latin America, Africa, and Asia. Likewise, developed countries are referred to as countries in the North. This difference in globalization experiences in the North and South embodies the globalization debate.

What is globalization? Globalization implies a global economy where goods and services move across borders without difficulty. This movement across borders includes investments, capital, labor, and technology. Globalization also includes the advances in technology that allow the flow of knowledge, investment, and trade. The emergence of globalization reflects an increased integration of global economies in the form of advanced world trade and vibrant international financial markets. Although globalization suggests a movement toward a one-world economy, national interests and sovereignty continue to play a role in international transactions. Supporters of globalization assert that globalization has also facilitated the spreading of knowledge and democracy, which facilitates a stronger, more widely employed workforce and therefore a peaceful future. At the helm of the globalization movement are multi-national corporations (MNCs) and trans-national corporations (TNCs). Dissenters in the globalization debate suggest that these corporations are the cause of a decline in standards in developing countries. The dissenters assert that the integration of global markets has allowed MNCs and TNCs to pressure low-income countries in the South to relax environmental regulations and labor standards or risk losing jobs and international investment.

Globalization in the form of movement of trade, labor, and capital is not a phenomenon that is exclusive to the latter half of the twentieth century. At the end of the nineteenth century, the world also experienced a similar flow of resources and information, particularly from 1870 to 1913. The flow of information was facilitated by the telegraph, which sped communications, and the flow of human resources and trade was facilitated by the railroad and steamship, which made transportation cheaper and faster than before. During this period, immigration relocated waves of people in unprecedented numbers. However, the Great Depression, followed by periods of economic isolation and war, brought this wave of globalization to a halt.

At the close of World War II, the members of the international community met in Bretton Woods, New Hampshire to create a global financial system. The system that emerged included the International Monetary Fund (IMF) and the World Bank. The IMF was created with the purpose of creating policies that would reestablish the economies of the world that had been destroyed by war and by poor economic policies in the 1930s. Members of the IMF were voluntary donor nations and lent money to member states

Poverty is evident in San Jose, Costa Rica, where this man is sifting through the Rio Azul lanfill for items of worth to sell or recycle, June 27, 2000. AP IMAGES

and others who agreed to undertake economic policy changes. On the other hand, the World Bank was established to undertake programs that would eradicate poverty throughout the globe. The World Bank membership consisted of developing and developed nations and is a source for funding development projects globally.

As a result of the increased cooperation and integration, global exports rose from 12 percent in 1965 to 22 percent in 2000. Although detractors of globalization have submitted that policies and treaties of cooperation create unemployment, employment has actually been affected by the reallocation of jobs from one industry to another. However, countries with higher trade levels have higher employment than those countries with low trade levels. Likewise, Southern countries whose trade levels are low continue to maintain high unemployment.

The increased flow created by globalization has created an unprecedented openness by countries. As a result, the international community, in the form of inter-governmental organizations like the United Nations and Bretton Woods organizations, as well as non-governmental organizations, has placed pressure on Southern countries to adopt high environmental standards and fair labor practices. Northern countries assert that the creation of an international fair labor stand, to include the freedom of association, the freedom to organize and bargain collectively, the freedom from forced labor, child labor and job discrimination, is needed to affect the quality of life in the South. Many countries in the South reject the imposition of regulated environmental and labor standards in order to remain competitive. Those who support the implementation in international fair labor standards and environmental regulations believe that the lack of such standards and regulations propels the low-income countries of the South toward lower wages and declining environments.

PRIMARY SOURCE

GLOBALIZATION AND POVERTY: AN ECOLOGICAL PERSPECTIVE

1. Introduction Does increasing integration into the world economy represent an engine for development, no matter how countries choose to achieve this integration? How will the economic and environmental costs and benefits of globalization be allocated internationally? Which policies are suitable for correcting global income inequality? This paper examines these questions from a political ecology perspective. Our analysis is very broad in scope, and several matters are covered (not always in complete depth). We revisit the structuralist paradigm of development, taking environmental issues into consideration and providing relevant empirical data. In addition, we introduce a general framework for addressing distributional issues within North-South economic and environmental relations. The paper begins by discussing the vision of Bretton Woods institutions on the subject of international economic integration. Subsequent sections (2–5) argue that the Bretton Woods approach can be contested if one takes into consideration both income inequalities as well as the peripheralization of the environmental burdens of global-level material consumption. Section 6 discusses the environmental and developmental consequences of policies that expand natural resource exports as a means for achieving increased integration into the world economy. The case of Latin America is discussed in some detail in Section 7. Section 8 focuses on the role of transnational corporations and financial flows in the distribution of profits in a context of economic liberalization. The paper concludes with alternative policy suggestions that maintain the goal of

preventing increased income inequality and environmental burden displacement as consequences of globalization.

2. Bretton Woods Optimism, Southern Pessimism? At least until September 2001, it appears that the Western world has entered the 21st century with a sense of optimism. Several facts support this optimistic sense of prosperity and are largely related to the economic and technological performance of the industrialized world in recent decades. During this period, affluent countries have witnessed almost relentless economic growth. New inventions and discoveries, such as the Internet and the human genome, have paved the way to a "new economy." Capitalism has consolidated its position as the leading economic system, and gross world product has grown rapidly since 1986, a fact which is explained by increasing global trade liberalization and capital migration. Moreover, since the Second World War, there have been no violent conflicts between former enemies in Europe and Asia, and authoritarian governments seem impossible in the capitalist core of the world. Furthermore, environmental issues, which three decades ago constituted the main point of criticism to the idea of limitless growth, are nowadays viewed as fully compatible with market-based economic expansion. Economic growth is seen as the best cure for the environmental consequences of economic growth. Based on empirical evidence, most economists perceive trade and global economic integration as engines of growth (Edwards, 1993). Therefore, globalization and free trade policies are compatible with sustainable patterns of development (Bommer and Schulze, 1999). Even if export expansion entails the increasing exploitation of natural resources, mainstream thought views export promotion as desirable because it allows both (1) the use of resources that would remain idle in the absence of trade and (2) the establishment and enlargement of backward and forward links between primary and other sectors of the economy. These processes are believed to induce higher rates of aggregate income growth and a progressive shift toward economic activity based on manufacturing and the provision of services (Xu, 2000). Classic examples of this kind of development based on natural resource exports include Australia, Scandinavia, and Canada, as the "staple" theory of growth proclaimed long ago.

The market is generally viewed as the most appropriate arena for resolving environmental externalities that arise precisely due to "market failures." Thus eco-efficiency can be reached through economic growth and market liberalization. Furthermore, material scarcity is no longer perceived as a threat to the global economy. First, the material and energy intensity of economic output has decreased in industrialized nations due to technological innovation. Second, sufficient mineral reserves have been identified, at least for the next century (Hodges,

1995). Third, technological improvements in recent decades, which have enabled the development of substitutes for relatively scarce minerals, warrant the optimistic idea that mineral constraints on production can be overcome for an indefinite period (Mikesell, 1994).

Neoclassical theory predicts that rates of return to capital diminish as it becomes more abundant relative to labor. Since capital in developing countries is in scarce supply, its rates of return should exceed that in industrial countries. Thus, in the absence of barriers, capital will migrate from rich to poor regions in search of higher rates of return, raising growth rates in developing countries and closing the income gap between the developing and industrialized worlds (UNCTAD, 1999a). Therefore most of the benefits of globalization will be located in developing countries because a convergence of income at a global level is expected (Park and Brat, 1995). A reduction of income inequality within poor countries is also expected due to an expanded supply of workers possessing basic skills (Williamson, 1997). This optimistic vision of future global economic and environmental performance, which has been labeled the "Bretton Woods paradigm" (Therien, 1999), is shared by many politicians (in the North and South), mainstream economists, and international institutions such as the World Bank, the WTO, and the IMF. This vision has also determined the tone of globally influential documents on the economy-environment relationship, such as the Brundtland report (Doyle, 1998).

Nonetheless, this optimistic vision is challenged by several remarkable facts. First, the gap in per capita income between the world's poorest and wealthiest populations, and between developed and developing geographic regions, has increased continuously since the 1970s (UNDP, 1997; WRI, 1999). Second, most developing countries are experiencing economic decline, stagnation, or slower growth than industrialized nations (Broad and Landi, 1996). Income inequality is increasing not only at the global level; it is also increasing within many developing nations and, surprisingly, even within industrialized countries such as the United Kingdom and the United States (Atkinson, 1999). Third, violent conflicts, famines, and autocratic governments are still common in the Third World. Fourth, while forested areas are generally expanding within developed countries, the rates of species extinction and deforestation are considerably high in poor regions of the world. Fifth, the AIDS epidemic has assumed dramatic and unpredicted dimensions in Africa, partly as a consequence of property rights on medical products in developed countries. Finally, international aid is decreasing, and recurrent economic crises have occurred in the semi-periphery of the world economy, affecting "emerging" countries such as Mexico, Argentina, Brazil, Turkey, Indonesia, Korea, Malaysia, Philippines, Thailand, and Ecuador.

Most of these economic problems are viewed by the optimistic mainstream as the result of misguided economic policies implemented in the past, such as import substitution and inward-oriented development strategies. Hence the "Washington consensus"—adjustment reforms promoting market liberalization and increasing integration into the world economy—is proposed as the best path available to developing countries (Baer and Maloney, 1997). The generalized application of this strategy, it is believed, will generate a new world order of widespread prosperity. . . .

SIGNIFICANCE

An IMF study in 2000 found that per capita income globally rose during the twentieth century. However, the study revealed disparity among countries. This disparity identified that income distribution had become more unequal among countries than at the beginning of the century. The quality of life in developing countries revealed the abject poverty and poor living conditions of those in the South. In addition, the study found that the spread of AIDS demonstrated a need for policies to alleviate poverty in the South. The IMF study asserts that developing countries in the South should be assisted by developed nations through policies of financial and technical assistance, as well as debt relief. According to the study, these policies promote trade, encourage the flow of private capital into Southern countries, and provide debt relief.

FURTHER RESOURCES
Periodicals
Ross, Robert. "From North-North to South-South." *Foreign Affairs* (September 2002).

Taylor, Timothy. "The Truth About Globalization." *Public Interest* (April 2002).

Web sites
International Monetary Fund. "Globalization: Threat or Opportunity." <http://www.imf.org/external/np/exr/ib/2000/041200.htm> (accessed January 30, 2006).

Antinuclear Activists Confront Police

Photograph

By: Sean Gallup

Date: January 1, 1956

Source: Hulton Archive/Getty Images

About the Photographer: This picture was taken by Sean Gallup near Lueneberg, Germany, on March 27, 2001, during a peaceful phase of the confrontation between police and protestors trying to stop a rail shipment of nuclear waste to the Gorleben nuclear waste storage facility.

INTRODUCTION

The fuel on which most nuclear power plants run consists of metal tubes filled with an alloy uranium. When this alloy has changed its elemental composition too much to continue functioning in a reactor, the spent rods are removed. In Germany, which has nineteen nuclear power plants, the spent rods are shipped to La Hague in France and to Sellafield in the U.K. for "reprocessing," that is, for the extraction of uranium from the rods. The uranium can then be made into fresh fuel rods. The highly radioactive waste left over from the reprocessing is melted into a glassy slag which is sealed inside steel canisters. These canisters are then bundled inside large containers called "castors," an acronym from "CAsk for Storage and Transport Of Radioactive material." Each castor contains twenty-eight canisters holding a total of about twenty thousand pounds of nuclear waste.

Protests against the transport of nuclear-waste castors through Germany have been frequent. Such large protests occurred in 1997-98 that the German government imposed a ban on waste transport on safety grounds. This caused reprocessed waste to accumulate in France until, under pressure from the French, the German Chancellor lifted the ban in 2001. The renewal of shipments triggered large protests. In this photograph, protestors occupy railroad tracks at Lueneberg, Germany. Here they managed to stop the first of the resumed waste shipments, a train carrying six of the white-painted castors (not visible in the photograph). The protestors, who chanted slogans and sang hymns and folk songs, were eventually cleared by the police, who arrested about two hundred. One man—illustrating the vulnerability of such shipments to terrorist attack—jumped from a low bridge onto the top of a passing castor, forcing another brief stoppage of the train.

Further protests met the train further north. On March 28, the day after the picture was taken, a few protestors fired flares: police used water cannon, plastic shields, and billy clubs against protestors. About ten thousand people tried to stop the train; some twenty

thousand police were on hand to assure passage of the castors. Although the very great majority of the protestors were nonviolent, a few violent militants clashed with police in the streets of the small town of Gorleben, resulting in injuries and arrests. The shipment was completed on March 29, 2001.

 PRIMARY SOURCE

ANTI-NUCLEAR ACTIVISTS CONFRONT POLICE WHILE OCCUPYING THE RAILROAD TRACKS LEADING TO THE GORLEBEN NUCLEAR WASTE STORAGE FACILITY, MARCH 27, 2001, NEAR LUENEBERG IN NORTHERN GERMANY.
See primary source image.

PRIMARY SOURCE

Anti-nuclear activists confront police while occupying the railroad tracks leading to the Gorleben nuclear waste storage facility, March 27, 2001, near Lueneberg in northern Germany. Anti-nuclear activists from the environmental group Robin Hood encase their arms in concrete tubes in the railway tracks leading to the Gorleben nuclear wasted storage facility in an effort to stop a shipment on March 28, 2001. PHOTO BY SEAN GALLUP/NEWSMAKERS

SIGNIFICANCE

Although German antinuclear protestors have never managed to turn back a castor shipment, their actions have had profound consequences for German politics and possibly for the global energy picture as well.

The anti-shipment protests in 1997 and 1998 were among the largest ever. Some twenty thousand German protestors sought to block the progress of the waste through the country, usually by sitting down on roads or rail lines. The largest security operation in post-World War II Germany, involving some thirty thousand police, was mounted to clear the way for the waste shipments. Over one hundred and fifty demonstrators and twenty police officers were injured, about five hundred demonstrators were arrested, and German newspapers reported the cost of the transport effort at one hundred million dollars. Shipments were halted because of safety concerns. Some observers have attributed the gains of the Greens and Social Democrats in the September, 1998 German elections to the political furor over the protests. The Greens and Social Democrats formed a coalition government that in 2000 committed Germany to shutting down of all of

its nuclear power plants in about twenty years. The German government's massive commitment of money and resources to wind and solar power as alternatives to nuclear energy has helped reshape the global renewable-energy market, lowering prices for wind and solar worldwide. By 2006, about 40 percent of the world's installed wind-generation capacity was in Germany, with rapid growth continuing. There is a possibility that with changing political power balances in Germany, the 2000 commitment to phase out nuclear power may be canceled. No German nuclear power plant has, as of 2006, been shut down as a result of the phaseout commitment.

Protests against nuclear materials shipments have continued since 2001. Protestors have blocked the shipment of spent nuclear fuel from Germany to France, as well as the shipment of waste slag from France to Germany. In 2004, a protestor was killed in France when the train he was attempting to block ran over his legs.

The fact that castor transports are happening at all is, in a sense, a result of antinuclear protest: in the 1970s the West German government planned to

Approximately 1400 activists congregate on the railway tracks leading to the Gorleben nuclear waste storage facility in Germany on March 27, 2001, to attempt to stop the Castor shipment coming from France. PHOTO BY SEAN GALLUP/NEWSMAKERS

build a nuclear reprocessing facility of its own, but mass protests forced cancellation of that plan. Shipments of nuclear material to and from reprocessing facilities in the U.K. and France were one result. The United States does not do any reprocessing of spent fuel from commercial reactors, but is accumulating it unprocessed in some 125 temporary surface facilities in thirty-nine states pending possible disposal in the highly controversial deep-burial site at Yucca Mountain, Nevada. German's storage facility at Gorleben is also temporary, with possible long-term burial to occur under a nearby salt dome (a type of underground geological formation).

FURTHER RESOURCES

Periodicals

Reuters. "Police Clash with Nuclear Protestors in Germany." *Toronto Star* March 28, 2001.

Web sites

"German Waste Transport." *Nuclear Information and Resource Service.* <http://www.nirs.org/mononline/germanwastetransport.htm> (accessed February 16, 2006).

"Where Now for Atomic Waste?" Deutsche Welle (English), November 12, 2002. <http://www.dw-world.de/dw/article/0,,673725,00.html> (accessed February 16, 2006).

"And Now, a New York Version of Star Wars"

Newspaper article

By: James C. McKinley Jr.

Date: December 22, 2001

Source: McKinley, James C. "And Now, a New York Version of Star Wars." The *New York Times* (December 22, 2001).

About the Author: James McKinley covers legislation and other political and social concern topics for the *New York Times*.

INTRODUCTION

There are a growing number of environmentalists, astronomers, and advocacy groups who claim that poorly planned city lighting unnecessarily brightens up the night sky, leading to such unwanted things as urban glow, energy waste, and the disturbance of plant and animal species. Government bodies have listened to these claims, as hundreds of cities, towns, and regions across North America, Europe, and Asia have passed laws and ordinances to limit the amount of light pollution urban areas emanate into the night sky. The United Nations and other international bodies have been involved in discussions on light pollution and its impacts, and how it can be limited.

During the 1970s and 1980s, the first nighttime pictures of the earth were produced by the U.S. Air Force's Defense Meteorological Satellite. These pictures were able to show the worldwide geographical distribution of light sources, but due to the high saturation of light flux, the satellite detectors did not produce quantifiable measurements of light emittance. This changed with technological advancements in 1998, enabling regular data collection and monitoring of global light production. Using satellite measurements of the upward flux of light, scientists are now able to map nighttime light while taking into account such things as the scattering of light by aerosols, the curvature of the Earth, natural sky brightness, and the differences in the Earth's altitude. Western Europe, the East and West coasts of the United States, and East Asia emit some of the highest levels of nighttime light.

Unlike indoor lighting, which usually leads to only a small percentage of escaped light, outdoor lighting is said to be very inefficient, with over fifty percent going directly up into the sky. Depending on the angle of the outdoor light, it is claimed that light is polluting when it goes where it is not wanted, and when it creates visual hazards. Many laws designed to decrease light pollution are often aimed at decreasing glare and improving visibility for drivers.

PRIMARY SOURCE

AND NOW, A NEW YORK VERSION OF STAR WARS

Seldom in this capital of compromises can a fight over a bill be called a battle between darkness and light, but that describes the struggle over a bill passed this year that was intended to let more New Yorkers see the stars.

The forces of light, led by Mayor Rudolph W. Giuliani and other mayors across the state, are trying to stop the legislation, which would foster more darkness for stargazers, who want unobstructed night skies.

The bill passed both houses of the Legislature in June with little fanfare or debate. The measure would require the state and local governments to gradually replace streetlights and other outdoor lights with ones that focus light downward rather than spraying it out to the heavens. It would also make it illegal to erect lights that bother neighbors and would direct the state to designate darkness preserves where outdoor lighting would be restricted.

But Gov. George E. Pataki, who prides himself on his environmental record, has not been keen on the bill, in part because it would cost the state millions of dollars to carry out, his aides said. For six months, he has kept the legislation at bay by threatening to veto it if it is sent to him in its current form.

"I appreciate the goal of the bill. In fact my brother is an astronomer, so I mean he's got to be in favor if it," the governor said this week during a radio interview. "And I remember going with him many a time and looking out in a telescope and trying to find the darkest part of the sky.

"In concept," he said, "the idea of taking measures to make our energy use lower when it's unnecessary and to help neighbors from being blinded in the middle of the night is something that I would like to support." But, he added, he did not know whether he would sign the bill, because he had not read all the provisions.

The sponsors, Senator Michael A.L. Balboni and Assemblyman Alexander B. Grannis, have proposed amendment after amendment in an effort to satisfy the governor's concerns, so far without success.

Mayor Giuliani and others have argued that the measure would not only cost hundreds of millions dollars for new lights but would also jeopardize the safety of urban residents, since cities could no longer light up high-crime areas as they see fit, without the state's approval.

But astronomers, environmentalists and groups like the International Dark-Sky Association argue that the dome of glaring light over cities and towns from mercury-vapor bulbs and other security lights is a form of pollution. They argue that the current lighting systems keep people from seeing the stars, disrupt the rhythms of wildlife and waste millions of dollars on light projected upward.

"The city could save money in the long run," said Susan Harder, a retired art dealer from East Hampton who is a member of the International Dark-Sky Association. "There is a horrible financial waste."

If Mr. Pataki were to sign the bill, New York would become the seventh state in the nation to enact a light-pollution law intended to allow people to see the stars better. In addition, hundred of municipalities in North America, including San Diego, Tucson and Calgary, Alberta, have converted to the downward focused lights.

"This is a major bill," said Assemblyman Grannis, a Democrat from Manhattan. "This is what noise pollution was a decade ago."

David L. Crawford, a retired astronomer who heads the International Dark-Sky Association, based in Arizona,

said recent studies suggest about 70 percent of the people in the United States cannot see the Milky Way because of light pollution.

"That part of the environment is disappearing and disappearing fast," he said. "If the children aren't in touch with the sky, it's really criminal. The only place they get to see these things is in an artificial environment, a planetarium."

But Mr. Giuliani and other city managers are less worried about children learning the constellations than they are about deterring crime. They are also concerned about the cost of installing new fixtures and what the new lights might do to street lighting systems based on older lights.

In a letter to Mr. Pataki, Mr. Giuliani said replacing the city's 180,000 streetlights with fixtures that focus downward, known as full cut-off lights, would create patches of dark on the roadways.

The city would have to double the number of streetlights, Mr. Giuliani wrote, to keep the lighting even, at a cost he estimated at $700 million. That sum would not include the cost of changing 130,000 other floodlights in parks, playgrounds, overpasses and above signs, he said.

The mayor also made it plain he did not want the state meddling in the city's decisions about lighting aimed at stopping crime. The law would require a city to apply to the state for a waiver to install security lights.

"In terms of public safety it is extremely unwise for a state statute to dictate the appropriate lighting standards to a municipality," Mr. Giuliani wrote.

Edward C. Farrell, the executive director of the New York State Conference of Mayors, said many city managers are bristling at the notion that local police officers will have to enforce the bill's "light trespass" provisions, which prohibit putting up lights that disturb a neighbor's sleep or privacy.

"At a time when local public safety resources are being stretched to the limit because of concerns about terrorism," Mr. Farrell said, "becoming the light police would be a very low priority."

Legislative aides say Governor Pataki is also worried the definition of "light trespassing" might be too broad. He also is troubled that the bill treats outdoor lighting solely as an environmental issue, ignoring its role in reducing crime or attracting tourism. Times Square's lights, for instance, might run afoul of the bill's provisions, aides said.

"We are still working with the sponsors to remedy some of the concerns," said Suzanne Morris, a spokeswoman for the governor. "It's too soon to say what's going to happen."

Senator Balboni, a Long Island Republican who sponsored the bill in the Senate, said he still hopes to reach a compromise with the governor. He said many of the governor's and mayors' worries about the cost of new lights were shortsighted. "Most of these places would save money," he said.

Many environmental groups, meanwhile, have been pushing hard to get the bill signed. About a third of the outdoor lighting in the United States is pointed skyward, a federal study has shown. The dark-sky association estimates the country now spends about $4.5 billion a year on what it considers wasted light, the equivalent of 30 million barrels of oil. It is unclear how much energy could be saved in New York.

"This is the only bill passed by the New York State Legislature this year that will actually lead to a reduction in energy," said Jeff Jones, a spokesman for Environmental Advocates. "We think the bill is great, and could be signed as it is."

SIGNIFICANCE

Environmentalists have documented the effects of artificial light on many different living creatures. Newly hatched sea turtles are often disoriented due to lighting on beaches and in some cases the glow of light from cities. As a result, these turtles have become more vulnerable to predators when they are unable to reach the ocean in a timely manner. Birds migrating at night are known to mistake city lights for stars, which they use as a directional guide. Scientists say the flowering cycles of plants can be disrupted by the presence of artificial light, reacting as though days are longer. Mammals, amphibians, fishes, and invertebrates have also shown disrupted cycles due to unnatural nighttime light.

It is possible to determine and map those areas of the Earth where it is dark enough for people to see the stars. Undeveloped places in Africa and many other rural regions provide the most ideal setting for stargazing. Nighttime light makes it difficult to see stars in urban areas. Astronomers say that light pollution creates tremendous difficulties in carrying out important observations and studies. Astronomers and amateur stargazers alike say that regaining the ability to see stars and other celestial bodies from within urban areas is a motivation to reduce light pollution. The

Lights like those that line the Gaslamp district in downtown San Diego are exactly the kind of light pollution that astronomers are afraid will obscure star and galaxy observation. AP IMAGES

American Astronomical Society suggests that government should keep development projects out of the vicinity of observational telescopes.

Light pollution legislation is often passed with the goal of making lighting more efficient, typically by mandating the use of cut-off fixtures which direct light to the ground. These fixtures utilize bulbs requiring as little as 10 percent of the energy that traditional bulbs need to light the same area, providing an additional cost savings. Japan's Environment agency estimated that nighttime light energy savings could be as high as 18 percent if lighting were limited to lighting needs. With lower energy needs, advocates claim that efficient light reduces carbon dioxide emissions and other air pollutants. Opponents of light pollution legislation say the costs of converting lights to cutoff fixtures, installing filters, reflectors, and other devices to improve efficiency is not worth the benefit. There are also claims that controlling the way streets are lit could compromise safety, because light pollution laws may limit how bright street lights may shine.

FURTHER RESOURCES

Periodicals

Longcore, Travis, and Catherine Rich.. "Ecological Light Pollution." *Frontiers in Ecology and the Environment* 2, 4 (May 2004): 191–198.

Web sites

Cinzano, P. "The Night Sky in the World." *Light Pollution Science and Technology Institute (Istituto di Scienza e Tecnologia dell'Inquinamento Luminoso).* <http://www.lightpollution.it/dmsp/index.html> (accessed March 7, 2006).

International Dark-Sky Association. <http://www.darksky.org> (accessed March 7, 2006).

Sullivan, W.T. *The Special IAU/COSPAR/UN Environmental Symposium: Preserving the Astronomical Sky (IAU Symposium 196)*, July 1999. <http://www.jb.man.ac.uk/iaucom50/s196rep.html> (accessed March 7, 2006).

Vision Statement for the World Summit on Sustainable Development

Vision statement

By: Paula J. Dobriansky

Date: May 23, 2002

Source: U.S. Department of State, Office of the Spokesman. "Vision Statement for the World Summit on Sustainable Development." May 23, 2002. <http://www.state.gov/r/pa/prs/ps/2002/10442.htm> (accessed February 19, 2006).

About the Author: As the Under Secretary of State for Global Affairs, Paula J. Dobriansky is in charge of coordinating the United States's foreign relations in regard to a number of issues, including: democracy, human rights, and labor on a global level; the environment, oceans, and science; the control of narcotics and law enforcement; population, refugees, migration to the United States; and women's issues.

INTRODUCTION

The purpose of the U.S. Department of State is to attempt to provide the citizens of the United States, and the world at large, with a safer, more democratic environment, and with an atmosphere that encourages prosperity through globalization, diplomacy, and national defense policies. As a part of an overall initiative, their goal is to help ensure that basic human needs are met around the world, including sufficient food, clean water for drinking and hygiene, the availability of energy, a safe and maintainable living environment, and health services. This includes the department's participation in global summits designed to provide a forum for representatives from various nations to discuss the state of the world and ways in which they can cooperate to improve conditions in less fortunate or less developed regions. The Vision Statement for the World Summit on Sustainable Development was released as a precursor to the World Summit held in Johannesburg, South Africa, from August 26 to September 4, 2002, as an outline of U.S. expectations for the event.

■ PRIMARY SOURCE

Media Note
Office of the Spokesman
Washington, DC
May 23, 2002

VISION STATEMENT FOR THE WORLD SUMMIT ON SUSTAINABLE DEVELOPMENT

In a speech today, Under Secretary of State for Global Affairs Paula Dobriansky identified U.S. objectives for the World Summit on Sustainable Development. The United States intends to work in partnership with governments, the private sector and NGOs to achieve sustainable development initiatives to reduce the number of people living without safe drinking water; enhance access to clean energy, reduce hunger and increase agricultural productivity; ensure universal access to basic education; stem AIDS and reduce TB and malaria; and manage and conserve forests and oceans.

As the United States Delegation heads to the preparatory conference in Indonesia, it offers to the international community the U.S. vision for how we can work together to build prosperity. Following is the text released today by Under Secretary Dobriansky that sets out that vision.

Vision Statement

World Summit on Sustainable Development

Working Together to Build Property

We believe sustainable development begins at home and is supported by effective domestic policies, and international partnerships. Self-governing people prepared to participate in an open world marketplace are the very foundation of sustainable development. President Bush has emphasized that the hopes of all people, no matter where they live, lie in greater political and economic freedom, the rule of law, and good governance. These fundamental principles will generate and harness the human and financial resources needed to promote economic growth, a vibrant civil society, and environmental protection. Democracy and respect for human rights empower people to take charge of their own destinies. We pledge strong support for efforts to promote peace, security, and stability, and to enhance democracy, respect for human rights, open and transparent governance, and the rule of law.

We endorse and continue to support national efforts to improve transparency and domestic governance, and to fight against corruption because we share, together with our partners, a strong commitment to the reality that only open, law-based societies that foster private investment, enterprise and entrepreneurship can unleash our human potential to build lasting and widely-shared prosperity. We also believe investment in basic health, education, and the environment is vital to advance social development and give every person, especially children, a chance at sharing in the benefits of economic growth.

We recognize poverty remains a global problem of huge proportions that demands our action. Following the successful outcomes of the Doha Trade Ministerial, the Monterrey Conference on Financing for Development and the World Food Summit, the World Summit on Sustainable Development can take practical measures to enhance human productivity, reduce poverty and foster economic growth and opportunity together with environmental quality. We can strive together for freer and more open societies, thriving economies, healthy environments, and help developing countries integrate fully into the global

economy to reap the benefits from international trade, investment, and cooperative partnerships.

We will work effectively to address the challenges of sustainable development in partnership with governments, the private sector, NGOs, and other elements of civil society. We invite developed and developing nations alike to join us to:

- *Open our economies and societies to growth;*
- *Provide freedom, security, and hope for present and future generations;*
- *Provide all our people with the opportunity for healthy and productive lives;*
- *Serve as good stewards of our natural resources and our environment.*

To this end, we will work to advance through concrete actions the following goals:

- Reduce the number of people living without safe drinking water and provide integrated, watershed approaches to manage water and land resources;
- Enhance access to and adoption, where appropriate, of clean energy, including renewables, from village to metropolis;
- Stem the global pandemic of AIDS, and drastically reduce tuberculosis and malaria;
- Ensure universal access to basic education, and eliminate gender disparities;
- Reduce hunger and increase sustainable agricultural productivity in the developing world without further degradation of forests and fragile lands; and
- Manage and conserve our forests and the vital resources of our oceans.

In partnership, we will work to unite governments, the private sector and civil society to strengthen democratic institutions of governance, open markets, and to mobilize and use all development resources more effectively. These resources include domestic savings, trade and investment, traditional aid and private philanthropy, capacity building programs, and efforts to promote the spread of environmentally sensitive industrial, agricultural, educational and scientific technologies. Our shared commitment will be to provide all people with the opportunities to lead healthy, productive, and fulfilling lives.

SIGNIFICANCE

Prior to the start of the World Summit on Sustainable Development in 2002, the United States Department of State outlined their agenda for the meeting, which was designed to promote self-sufficiency and a rise from poverty in underdeveloped nations, while preserving natural resources that have been

Leaders gathered from around the globe on June 13, 1992, to participate in the Earth Summit in Rio de Jinero, including (from top left) Arnold Ruutel (Estonia), Bernard Dowiyogo (Nauru), Prince Rainier III (Monaco), Patricio Aylwin (Chile), and Fidel Castro (Cuba) in the center. AP IMAGES

steadily depleted due to pollution and industry, including the Earth's forests, bodies of water, and atmosphere. The meeting was intended to be a follow up to the Earth Summit that was held in Brazil in 1992, where a plan had been initiated to improve the quality of life on a global scale, and to further the participating governments' unified efforts to help promote prosperity in disadvantaged parts of the world. This global development is considered sustainable only if it meets the needs of the current population without jeopardizing the needs of future generations. Resources must not be used to the point of extinction, and progress must not endanger the future of the planet and its inhabitants. One of the more prosperous nations involved in the Summit, the United States provided a strong framework of ideas to be included during the meetings and panels that took place over the ten days in Johannesburg.

As outlined by Dobriansky, the focus of the Summit was divided into a number of areas, including

the need for sufficient food, drinkable water, reliable sources of energy, medical care, basic education, equal treatment regardless of gender, and the preservation of the world's natural resources. The plan included the stance that people must be able to work toward self-improvement in order to best benefit from assistance from outside sources. From there, the governments participating in the Summit would be able to move forward to encourage open societies and increased economic growth by opening themselves to free trade and providing educational programs designed to foster democratic behavior and improved understanding of the global economy. These specific goals contributed to the formation of the Type 2 partnership initiatives at the Summit, which consisted of organization between governments, non-governmental organizations, and businesses to achieve specific, quantitative improvements regarding certain of these pre-determined needs. These initiatives were also intended to encourage the success of the earlier Type 1 initiatives, which were based on government-negotiated goals. Emphasis was placed on making significant progress toward the elimination of poverty by 2015, with attention paid to availability of food and clean water, sanitation, and education regarding proper hygiene, and the aim to reduce the number of people living without these basic human conditions by half.

Healthcare and the need to concentrate on slowing or eliminating the spread of serious disease through impoverished parts of the world received equally high emphasis. In addition to the global spread of AIDS, the prevalence of tuberculosis in less developed nations caused concern, and both underlined the need not only for medical supplies and treatment, but education regarding the transmission of these illnesses that have either been contained or slowed in more prosperous countries. The South Pacific region was targeted as particularly in need of sufficient health care in the years immediately following the Summit.

In an effort to not only improve the lives of the current global population but to ensure that the planet's resources will continue to sustain future generations, Under Secretary Dobriansky concluded her agenda for the Summit by mentioning the need to preserve both the forests and the oceans as a vital part of the planet's natural balance. She called for the cooperation of governments around the globe in using those resources more wisely and with an eye toward preservation. This translated into the ongoing agreement at the Summit that governments needed to work together in order to prevent illegal logging and the destruction of the forests, as well as the allocation of funding to help promote the diversity of the ecosystems around the world. The depletion of the planet's resources and the subsequent alteration of the atmosphere and weather patterns served as a reminder that, without the maintenance of the planet, all other initiatives to improve the quality of life among the population would prove pointless.

FURTHER RESOURCES

Web sites

Earth Summit 2002.org. <http://www.earthsummit2002.org> (accessed February 23, 2006).

"Johannesburg Summit 2002" *Johannesburg Summit.org*, 2002. <http://www.johannesburgsummit.org> (accessed February 23, 2006).

"World Summit on Sustainable Development." *UN.org*, 2002. <http://www.un.org/events/wssd> (accessed February 23, 2006).

U.S. Department of State. <http://www.state.gov/> (accessed February 19, 2006).

Warming Up to the Truth: The Real Story About Climate Change

Speech

By: Sallie Baliunas

Date: June 19, 2002

Source: Baliunas, Sallie. "Warming Up to the Truth: The Real Story About Climate Change." Heritage Lecture #758, June 19, 2002. <http://www.heritage.org/Press/Events/2002archive.cfm> (accessed March 17, 2006.)

About the Author: Sallie Baliunas received her Master of Arts degree in 1975 and her Doctor of Philosophy degree in 1980, both in astrophysics from Harvard University. Among some of her professional interests are solar variability, climate change, visible and ultraviolet spectroscopy of stars, adaptive optics, astronomical physics, and magnetohydrodynamics of the Sun and other similar stars. Baliunas is an astrophysicist and senior scientist at the George Marshall Institute, along with chairing its Science Advisory Board. She is also a visiting professor at Brigham Young University; adjunct professor at Tennessee State University; and enviro-sci host for TechCentralStation.com, along with maintaining an academic appointment at the Harvard-Smithsonian Center for Astrophysics. Baliunas has been awarded the Newton Lacey Pierce Prize by the American Astronomical Society and the Bok Prize from Harvard University. Baliunas has also been a contributing editor to the World Climate Report (a publication of the Western Fuels Association); advisory board member of the UK Scientific Alliance; expert at the Competitive Enterprise Institute; global warming and ozone layer expert for the National Center of Public Policy Research; Robert Wesson Endowment Fund Fellow at the Hoover Institution; and technical consultant for the television series, "Gene Roddenberry's Earth: Final Conflict." She has written over 200 scientific research articles and such publications for the George C. Marshall Institute as "The Ozone Crisis," "Are Human Activities Causing Global Warming?," and "Ozone and Global Warming, Are the Problems Real?"

INTRODUCTION

Baliunas is one of a small group of scientists who oppose proposed actions such as the Kyoto Protocol to

Large puddles from excessive rainfall make it difficult for this jogger's routine. Heavier rainfall and higher temperatures in coastal cities like Houston could occur if global warming continues. AP IMAGES

reduce the combustion of fossil fuels (such as oil, coal, and natural gas) and the resulting emissions of greenhouse gases (such as carbon dioxide). These human-made activities, which occurred predominately during most of the twentieth century and now continue into the twenty-first century, have been blamed for the rapid warming of the Earth's atmosphere along with its oceans and landmasses.

Baliunas agrees with the overwhelming scientific evidence that the amount of carbon dioxide in the atmosphere has been increasing during this period of about one hundred years. However, she stated within her speech "Warming Up to the Truth: The Real Story About Climate Change" that scientific evidence collected in the latter part of the twentieth century does not support the idea of drastically reducing greenhouse gases in order to prevent (presumed)

massive declines within the global environment. Instead, Baliunas claimed that changes in the energy output of the sun are the natural and prime cause of the noticeable warming of the planet. As a result, she is a strong opponent of the generally accepted scientific connection between recent temperature increases in the global climate and the increase of the concentration of carbon dioxide in the atmosphere.

■ PRIMARY SOURCE

The scientific facts on which everyone agrees are that, as a result of using coal, oil, and natural gas, the carbon dioxide content of the air is increasing. The air's concentration of other human-produced greenhouse gases, like methane, has also increased. These greenhouse gases absorb infrared radiation from the sun, and they retain some of that energy close to earth.

All computer simulations of climate change say that, based on how we understand climate to work, the low layer of air for 1 to 5 miles up (the low troposphere), where the radiation is trapped, should warm. That low layer of air warming should, in turn, warm the surface.

Scientific facts gathered in the past ten years do not support the notion of catastrophic human-made warming as a basis for drastic carbon dioxide emission cuts. . . .

Now for the science. There are two important records that we'll look at. I just told you how we think climate operates in the presence of increasing carbon dioxide and greenhouse gases in the air from human activities. The layer of air 1 to 5 miles up retains energy and that layer, in turn, heats the surface of the earth. The human-made greenhouse warming component must warm both layers of air, with computer simulations indicating the low troposphere would warm more quickly and to a greater amount than the surface. . . .

To see if the twentieth century surface warming is from human activity or not, we begin looking in detail at the surface record. In the twentieth century, three trends are easily identified. From 1900 to 1940, the surface warms strongly. From 1940 to about the late 1970s, a slight cooling trend is seen. Then from the late 1970s to the present, warming occurs. Briefly, the surface records show early twentieth century warming, mid-twentieth century cooling, and late twentieth century warming.

Most of the increase in the air's concentration of greenhouse gases from human activities—over eighty percent—occurred after the 1940s. That means that the strong early twentieth century warming must be largely, if not entirely, natural.

The mid-twentieth century cooling can't be a warming response owing to the air's added greenhouse gases. The only portion of this record that could be largely human-made is that of the past few decades. The slope of that trend calculated over the past few decades is about one-tenth of a degree Centigrade per decade.

Now, most all the computer models agree that the human-made warming would be almost linear in fashion. So over a century the extrapolated warming trend expected from continued use of fossil fuels would amount to about 1 degree Centigrade per century. That's what the surface temperature says would be the upper limit. . . .

NASA launched satellites starting in 1979 to measure this layer of air. The satellites look down and record these measurements daily. I've plotted the monthly averages. There are lots of jigs and jags in the data, and they are real. . . .

I asked the computer to naively draw a linear trend through the data recorded by satellites. This linear trend probably has a bias, an upward bias because of that strong 1997-1998 El Niño warm pulse. Nonetheless, the fitted trend is: positive four-hundredths of a degree Centigrade per decade.

Now, this is the layer of air sensitive to the human-made warming effect, and the layer that must warm at least as much as the surface according to the computer simulations. Yet, the projected warming from human activities can't be found in the low troposphere in any great degree. The four-hundredths of a degree Centigrade might be entirely due to this El Niño bias. If the small warming trend in the low troposphere were assumed to be entirely human-caused, the trend is much smaller than forecast by any model. Extrapolated over a century, the observed trend indicates a human-made warming trend no greater than four-tenths of a degree Centigrade.

In contrast, the computer models say this very key layer of air must be warming from human activities. The predictions are that the air must be warming at a rate of approximately a quarter of a degree Centigrade per decade.

Comparing what the computer models say should be happening with the actual satellite observations shows a mismatch of around a factor of six. That is, this layer of air just is not warming the way the computer simulations say it should. There should have been a half a degree Centigrade per decade warming in this layer of air over the period of satellite observations. The human-made warming trend isn't there. . . .

In other words, the satellite data and the balloon data both say that the records reflect the actual change in this layer of air. Again, as with the satellite record, one can recognize short-term natural variations—El Niño, La Niña,

volcanic eruptions—but one does not see the decades-long human-caused warming trend projected by climate models. . . .

And also known from computer simulations is that the human-made warming trend is supposed to grow steadily over decades. So, a shift all at once in 1976–1977 is ruled out by those two reasons. One, it's not what the models project; and two, we see this event before the build-up of human-made greenhouse gases, and it is therefore natural.

The satellite data and the balloon data agree when both records coexist, from 1979 to the present. The balloon record reaches back four decades. Neither record sees a meaningful human-made warming trend.

Now, just remember this one thing from this talk, if nothing else: That layer of air cannot be bypassed; that layer of air must warm if computer model projections are accurate in detailing the human-made warming trend from the air's increased greenhouse gases. But that layer of air is not warming. Thus the human-made effect must be quite small.

Additionally, the recent warming trend in the surface record must not owe to the human-made effect. The surface temperature is warming for some other reason, likely natural influences. The argument here, from NASA and NOAA data, is that this layer of air from 1 to 5 miles in altitude is not warming the way computer simulations say it must warm in the presence of human activity. Therefore, the human-made effect is small. The surface data must be warming from natural effects, because the human-made warming trend must appear both in the low troposphere and at the surface. All models are in agreement on that.

Now, if the surface data are warming for a natural reason, what might that be? Our research team studies changes in the energy output of the sun and its influence on life and the environment of earth. . . .

Over the past half-century, the sun has become very active, and the sun is more active than it has been for four hundred years. Therefore, the sun is likely at its brightest in four hundred years.

Also noteworthy is a feature called the Maunder Minimum. In the seventeenth century, the observations of sunspots show extraordinarily low levels of magnetism on the sun, with little or no eleven-year cycle. That phase of low solar activity has not been encountered in modern times (although radiocarbon records indicate that a Maunder-minimum episode occurs for a century every several centuries). The seventeenth-century Maunder Minimum corresponds with the coldest century of the last millennium. . . .

The ups and downs of each record match fairly well. The coincident changes in the sun's changing energy output and temperature records on earth tend to argue that the sun has driven a major portion of the twentieth century temperature change. For example, a strong warming in the late nineteenth century, continuing in the early twentieth century, up to the 1940s, seems to follow the sun's energy output changes fairly well.

The mid-twentieth century cooling, and some of the latter twentieth century warming, also seem matched to changes in the sun.

To review: The surface warming that should be occurring from human-made actions, which is predicted to be accompanied by low troposphere warming, cannot be found in modern records from balloon and satellite platforms.

Thus, the recent surface warming trend may owe largely to changes in the sun's energy output. . . .

In summary, little evidence supports the idea of catastrophic human-made global warming effects. Undertaking a Kyoto-type program would produce little abatement of the forecast risk, while the cost of such a program would divert resources and attention from major environmental, health, and welfare challenges. . . .

The latest scientific results are good news: The human influence on global climate change is small and will be slow to develop. The conclusion comes from the lack of meaningful warming trends of the low layer of air, in contradiction to the computer simulations that project a strong human effect should already be present. Those results present an opportunity to improve climate theory, computer simulations of climate, and obtain crucial measurements.

The economic consequences of not relying on science but instead on the anti-scientific Precautionary Principle, are considerable, and are not so speculative. The economic impact of significantly cutting fossil fuel use will be hard-felt, and they will be devastating to those on fixed incomes, those in developing countries, and those on the margins of the economy.

For the next several decades, fossil fuel use is key to improving the human condition. Freed from their geologic repositories, fossil fuels have been used for many economic, health, and environmental benefits. But the environmental catastrophes that have been forecast from their use have yet to be demonstrated by their critics.

SIGNIFICANCE

In her paper, Baliunas stated there is no solid evidence that the Earth's global climate is excessively warming due to the emission of greenhouse gases by human activities. Instead, she claimed that changes in temperatures on Earth are just part of a naturally occurring cycle that warms and cools the Earth over hundreds or even thousands of years. In addition, Baliunas claimed that whatever climate changes have been artificially generated by human activities, they are not large enough to recommend or require large and expensive reductions in greenhouse gas emissions. Such reduction measures, Baliunas believes, would put unreasonable economic pressures on the United States and other industrialized countries who would most likely first implement such reductions.

Baliunas based her conclusions on the air temperature at the lowest level of the troposphere—the most dense layer of the atmosphere where most of the weather occurs—which extends from about 1 to 5 miles (1.6 to 8 kilometers) from the surface of the Earth. Based on computer simulations, Baliunas stated that the low troposphere would warm first, directly resulting in a warmer surface on the Earth—although less quickly and to a smaller degree.

Comparing theoretical computer models of what *should* be happening to the global climate based on the emissions of greenhouse gases to actual measurements from NASA (National Aeronautics and Space Administration) satellites and NOAA (National Oceanic and Atmospheric Administration) weather balloons, Baliunas found agreement between the NASA and NOAA measurements: short-term natural variations were present but long-term variations (in the range of decades) caused by human activities were not present. These two measurements conflicted with what was predicted by computer models.

Baliunas concluded the warming in global climate that has occurred in the last one hundred years or so is predominately due to changes in the sun's energy output. If Baliunas is correct in this statement, then any reductions in greenhouse gas emissions will have little impact on the rise in global temperatures. For instance, the implementation of the Kyoto Protocol, a 1997 international accord that sets limits on greenhouse gas emissions, would slightly but insignificantly lower the temperature (warming) trend around the globe. However, if implemented, the Kyoto Protocol would cost an enormous amount of money. Baliunas stated that a Yale University study predicted Kyoto-type costs would cause a loss of about $2.7 trillion in gross domestic product in the United States over a ten-year period.

In conclusion, Baliunas believes that actions to reduce the threat of global warming based on reductions of greenhouse gases will not significantly improve global climatic conditions, but will, instead, only inflict tremendous expenses to countries that implement such actions.

FURTHER RESOURCES

Books

Labohm, Hans H.J. *Man-made Global Warming: Unravelling a Dogma.* Brentwood, UK: Multi-Science Publishing, 2004.

Willis, Henry. *Earth's Future Climate.* Coral Springs, FL: Llumina Press, 2003.

Web sites

Nesmith, Jeff. "Foes of Global Warming Theory Have Energy Ties." *Cox News Service*, June 2, 2003. <http://seattlepi.nwsource.com/national/124642_warming02.html> (accessed March 17, 2006).

"Separating Climate Fact From Fiction: Testimony of March 13, 2002, by Dr. Sallie Baliunas provided to the Senate Committee on Environment and Public Works, chaired by Sen. James M. Jeffords." *Science and Environmental Policy Project.* <http://www.sepp.org/NewSEPP/Testimony-baliunas.htm> (accessed March 17, 2006).

Koski, Olivia. "Sallie Baliunas, the Global Warming Debate, and Think Tank Scholarship." *Occasions Online, Program for Writing and Rhetoric, University of Colorado, Boulder.* <http://www.colorado.edu/pwr/occasions/salliebaliunas.htm> (accessed November 8, 2005).

Protesters at Site of New Terminal 5, Heathrow

Photograph

By: David Dyson

Date: October 6, 2003

Source: Getty Images

About the Photographer: This picture was taken by David Dyson near Heathrow Airport in London. Protestors were dramatizing their objection to the massive planned expansion of the airport.

INTRODUCTION

A number of environmental and local activist groups have opposed the planned expansion of Heathrow Airport in London—the world's busiest airport. The ten-year expansion plan would cost $12.77 billion and involve the construction of a third runway and a fifth terminal building. The owner of Heathrow, BAA (British Airports Authority), has published plans for the demolition of some seven hundred homes in order to make room for the new construction, and

according to the British Department of Transport, noise pollution from the expansion will affection an additional 26,000 people (up from 307,000).

The proposed Terminal five is far larger than the existing four terminals; the planned expansion would approximately double the size of Heathrow. The number of flights would increase by about 40 percent and the number of passengers handled annually from about sixty million a year to over eighty million a year. Advocates of expansion say that it is necessary to "develop Heathrow in a way that allows it to retain its premier position" as the primary "hub" airport of western Europe, a status also sought by airports in Amsterdam and Paris.

Heathrow was built on farmland just outside London in 1947. Opponents argue that the airport expansion breaks a 1980 promise by BAA that Terminal four would be the last expansion, contradicts the Government's own planning inspector's 2001 statement that a third runway would create "such severe and widespread impacts on the environment as to be totally unacceptable," and would increase air pollution from road traffic to the airport and from increased air traffic. They also point out that some proposed expansions, such as of the airport at Stansted, England, will destroy nearby green spaces. In the case of Stansted, the proposal would result in the total or partial clearing of six areas of "ancient" woods, i.e., forest that has been continuously wooded for at least four hundred years. Only 2 percent of Britain is covered by ancient woodland.

PRIMARY SOURCE

PROTESTORS ATTACH A BANNER TO THE ARM OF A CRANE AT THE SITE OF THE NEW TERMINAL 5, HEATHROW AIRPORT

See primary source image.

SIGNIFICANCE

Airport expansion, and opposition to it, is occurring not only at Heathrow but at a number of airports in the UK and Europe. Proposed expansions at Gatwick and Manchester airports in England, at Belfast airport in Northern Ireland (UK), and at Edinburgh airport in Scotland are all being opposed. In the United States as of 2005, eighteen of the country's thirty-one large "hub" airports intended to build new runways. Air traffic is expanding globally.

Jet aircrafts burn high-grade kerosene, a liquid fossil fuel, and are highly polluting. U.S. airlines burn

PRIMARY SOURCE

Protestors Attach a Banner to the Arm of a Crane at the Site of the New Terminal 5, Heathrow Airport. Protestors dramatize their opposition to the planned $12.77 billion, ten-year expansion of Heathrow Airport, London. They believe that expanding the airport would be economically unnecessary, increase noise and pollution, and destroy seven hundred homes. PHOTO BY DAVID DYSON/GETTY IMAGES

about twenty billion gallons of fuel a year. Boston's Logan airport, a typical large U.S. airport, is one of the largest polluters in Massachusetts and is forecasted by the state to be the largest polluter by 2010. An eight hundred-mile hop by a Boeing 737 (a typical European flight) produces twenty seven tons of the greenhouse gas carbon dioxide (CO_2) as well as nitrogen oxides, sulfur dioxide, and volatile organic compounds. Even the water produced by jet aircraft, which crystallizes into jet vapor trails (contrails) at high altitude, is a pollutant: the large number of contrails formed by global jet traffic, and of the cirrus clouds whose formation is triggered by them, are believed to contribute to global climate change. As of 2005, commercial air travel was contributing about 3.5 percent of global greenhouse-gas emissions, as opposed to 25 percent from electric generating stations (mostly coal), but

commercial air traffic was growing steadily and its contribution to greenhouse emissions was forecast to rise to 15 percent by about 2016.

The problem may be slightly lessened by more efficient airplanes. Jet aircraft of modern design burn significantly less than those of the 1960s, when jumbo jets for civilian travel first became commonplace—the aircraft industry claims that new aircraft are 70 percent more efficient than 60s-vintage craft. The European-built Airbus A380, the world's largest airliner, holds up to eight hundred passengers and burns thirteen percent less fuel than the Boeing 747, which holds only 524 passengers. Assuming no empty seats, an A380 would thus use only 0.57 times as much fuel as a 747 per passenger mile. Switching entirely to A380s while doubling the number of passenger-miles would lead to only a 1.14 times increase in fuel consumption.

However, these are oversimplified calculations. Most aircraft will not be Airbus A380s but will continue to be older aircraft, for reasons of cost. Also, calculations of the contribution of air travel to greenhouse gases already take into account the likely increased average efficiency of the aircraft fleet. Improved air-traffic control can also save fuel: aircraft that idle on the ground or circle waiting to land consume tremendous quantities of fuel without providing any service.

Low-pollution alternatives to air travel include vacationing closer to home, teleconferencing for business travelers, and rail travel.

FURTHER RESOURCES

Periodicals

"Anger at Heathrow Expansion Plans." *BBC News*. June 20, 2005. Available online at: <http://news.bbc.co.uk/1/hi/england/london/4613957.stm> (accessed February 18, 2006).

Bonné, Jon. "Crowded Skies Impact Air Quality: Jet Emissions Get Scant Focus in U.S., but Issue on U.N. Agenda for Climate Talks.> *MSNBC News*. July 16, 2005. Available online at: <http://www.msnbc.com/news/595039.asp?cp1=1> (accessed February 18, 2006).

"Gatwick Runway Protest Launched.> *BBC News*. May 30, 2005. Available online at: <http://news.bbc.co.uk/1/hi/england/southern_counties/4593733.stm> (accessed February 18, 2006).

Symonds, Tom. "Airlines Sport Their Green Colours.> *BBC News*. June 20, 2005. Available online at: <http://news.bbc.co.uk/1/hi/uk/4111310.stm> (accessed February 18, 2006).

Web sites

Friends of the Earth [an anti-expansion group]. December 3, 2001. "London Heathrow Airport." <http://www.foe.co.uk/campaigns/transport/case_studies/heathrow.html> (accessed February 9, 2006).

Future Heathrow [a pro-expansion group]. <http://www.futureheathrow.org/> (accessed February 17, 2006).

Indian Schoolgirl Urges People to Drink Natural Beverages

Photograph

By: Indranil Mukherjee

Date: August 14, 2003

Source: AFP/Getty Images

About the Photographer: This photograph was taken by Indian photographer Indranil Mukherjee on August 14, 2003, in the Indian city of Bangalore.

INTRODUCTION

In February 2003, the Indian nongovernmental organization Centre for Science and Environment (CSE) released data that shocked India. "Your bottled water," they announced, "is contaminated by pesticides." (Pesticides are chemicals used to kill insects, often on crops; they can accumulate in fatty tissues and cause developmental problems in children and other health effects.) The CSE analyzed seventeen brands of packaged drinking water sold in India and found that they contained a "deadly cocktail" of pesticides. The four chemicals most often found by the CSE analysis were lindane, DDT, malathion, and chlorpyrifos. On average, the bottled water analyzed contained 36.4 times the allowed levels of total pesticide. (The "allowed level" referenced by the CSE was the European Economic Commission Directive 80/778/EEC maximum residue limit for total pesticides, 0.0005 milligrams per liter.) One brand, Aquaplus, had 104 times the allowed level.

In August 2003, the CSE released a second report showing that high pesticide residues had also been found in soft drinks as well as bottled water. Twelve soft-drink brands sold in and around the city of Delhi were analyzed. Coca-Cola bottled in India was found to have forty-five times the allowed limit on total pesticides; Pepsi bottled in India, thirty-seven times. Coca-Cola and Pepsi bottled in the United States, in contrast, were found to have no detectable level of pesticides at all.

Anger was widespread in India, although the country has one of the world's lowest rates of soft-drink consumption—about eight beverages per person per year, versus about eight hundred per person per year in the United States.

In India, CSE's tests showed that the pesticides were coming from the groundwater being used to manufacture the beverages. In the case of bottled water, the contaminated groundwater is simply pumped, bottled, and sold: in the case of soft drinks, the groundwater is carbonated (made fizzy by the addition of carbon dioxide) and mixed with syrup supplied by a centralized manufacturer before being bottled. The ultimate source of the pesticides in the groundwater was agriculture.

PRIMARY SOURCE

Indian Schoolgirl Nivedita, eight, Urges People to Drink Natural Beverages Instead of Drinks Contaminated by Pesticides. This image typifies widespread outrage in India over the discovery, in 2003, that bottled water and soft drinks sold in that country contain high levels of toxic pesticides (unlike similar beverages sold in the United States and Europe). INDRANIL MUKHERGEE/AFP/ GETTY IMAGES

A Joint Parliamentary Committee (official body convened by the Indian government) confirmed the CSE's findings on February 5, 2004. It pointed out that unlike other aspects of the food industry, the soft drink industry in India was ungoverned by government-mandated purity standards. PepsiCo Inc. argued that it could not be held responsible for product purity at bottling plants owned by franchisees, that is, by local companies that contracted with PepsiCo for the right to bottle its sodas. The Joint Parliamentary Committee, however, rejected this argument as invalid, stating that although franchisees were responsible for product purity, so was the franchiser—in this case, PepsiCo. In December 2004 the Supreme Court of India ruled that Pepsi and Coca–Cola would have to display warning labels stating that their products might contain pesticides.

PRIMARY SOURCE

INDIAN SCHOOLGIRL URGES PEOPLE TO DRINK NATURAL BEVERAGES.
See primary source image.

SIGNIFICANCE

The appearance of pesticides in Indian bottled water and soda is entangled with several larger problems. First, many pesticides that have long been banned in the United States and Europe were only banned relatively recently in India, or are still not banned, or may be legally banned but are used anyway. Greenpeace India has demanded that the Indian government ban all pesticides from Indian agriculture, beginning with those that are already banned in other countries.

Second, multinational corporations are widely perceived in India as valuing the lives of Indians and people living in other developing countries less than those of people living in the developed world, especially the United States and Europe. Many Indian writers and protestors explicitly linked the new pesticide scandal to the 1984 disaster in Bhopal, India, where chemicals escaping from a chemical plant owned by Union Carbide, a U.S. company, killed at least 18,000 people. Compensation to Bhopal survivors was only about $500 per person, far less than typically would have been awarded to American victims of a similar accident. (As of 2004, much of this money, paid by Union Carbide to the Indian Government, had still not reached the victims.)

The Coca-Cola Company is widely opposed in India not only for the high levels of pesticides in its products but for lowering groundwater levels in the vicinity of its bottling plants in the province of Kerala. Coca-Cola has stated that it is harvesting rainwater to alleviate this problem: the director of the CSE, Sunita Narain, said in early 2006 that Coke was, in fact, harvesting less than 10 percent of the water it was using, and that its claims of significant water harvesting were therefore erroneous.

Third, Indian agriculture has been shifting toward cash-crop monocultures of introduced hybrid and genetically modified crop varieties supported by cash-intensive inputs of fertilizer and pesticide. Pesticide use has increased, some of it ending up in groundwater. Pressed by drought and debt, thousands of Indian farmers have committed suicide in recent years—many by symbolically drinking raw pesticides, a painful death.

According to CSE, as of January 2006, there had still been no change in the levels of pesticides in drinks in India. Over a dozen U.S. universities had by that date terminated their contracts with Coca-Cola in protest of the continued draw-down of water tables by Coca-Cola bottling plants in India and the presence of pesticides in soda.

FURTHER RESOURCES
Web sites

"Community Commemorates Thousand Day Anniversary of Vigil Against Coca-Cola in Kerala." *India Resource Center*, January 13, 2005. <http://www.indiaresource.org/press/2005/plachimadablockjan.html> (accessed Feb. 16, 2006).

Ashish, Kumar Sen. *The Tribune India, online edition*, May 1, 2004. "Coke's water-harvesting claims 'fraudulent.'" <http://www.tribuneindia.com/2006/20060111/edit.htm#7> (accessed Feb. 16, 2006).

Mather, H. B., Sapna Johnson, and Avinash Kumar. "Analysis of Pesticide Residues in Soft Drinks." *Centre for Science and Environment*, August 5, 2003. <http://www.cseindia.org/html/cola-indepth/softdrinks_report.pdf> (accessed Feb. 16, 2006).

Boiling Point

How Politicians, Big Oil and Coal, Journalists and Activists Are Fueling the Climate Crisis—And What We Can Do to Avert Disaster

Book excerpt

By: Ross Gelbspan

Date: 2004

Source: Gelbspan, Ross. *Boiling Point: How Politicians, Big Oil and Coal, Journalists and Activists Are Fueling the Climate Crisis—And What We Can Do to Avert Disaster.* New York: Basic Books, 2004.

About the Author: Ross Gelbspan is a retired journalist who worked at the *Philadelphia Bulletin*, the *Washington Post*, the *Village Voice*, and the *Boston Globe* over his thirty-one-year career. As the Special Projects Editor of the *Boston Globe*, he edited and directed a series of articles on job discrimination against African-Americans in the Boston area by corporations, unions, colleges and universities, newspapers, and state and city civil services. The series won the 1984 Pulitzer Prize. His cover article on climate change, published in the December 1995 issue of *Harper's Magazine*, yielded a National Magazine Award. Gelbspan has published books on global climate warming, including *The Heat Is On: The High Stakes Battle Over Earth's Threatened Climate* and *Boiling Point: How Politicians, Big Oil and Coal, Journalists and Activists are Fueling the Climate Crisis—and What We Can Do to Avert Disaster.* He is also the author of several book chapters and articles on global warming and climate change, published in newspapers throughout the USA. Gelbspan also taught at the Columbia University School of Journalism.

INTRODUCTION

The significance of human impact on the increase of greenhouse effect and global warming that is inducing climate changes everywhere is a controversial issue, involving environmental movements, concerned scientists, oil and coal companies, and political interests.

Strong financial interests form a formidable barrier against measures to cut down carbon dioxide emissions and other greenhouse gases. A systematic denial by skeptic scientists siding with such big oil and coal interests dismisses the significant human role on the greenhouse effect and climate change. A main strategy of fossil-fuel lobbyists has been to convince both the public and their policy makers that the climate changes observed in recent decades are part of a natural cycle, with little, if any, contribution from industrial emissions. Furthermore, the lack of coordination among the several environmental movements and non-governmental organizations, according to Ross Gelbspan, has prevented activists from effectively galvanizing the public opinion around the issue, since a common environmental agenda is not developed by these groups to counteract the heavyweight interest groups lobbying in Washington.

The greenhouse effect is in fact a natural phenomenon, thanks to which multi-cellular life forms evolved and thrived on Earth. Indeed, life itself was the major contributor to the optimum greenhouse effect and its atmospheric gaseous composition, as well as median global temperatures of the last 400 million years, which favored biological evolution and species diversification. Cyanobacteria and other primordial photosynthetic organisms living in water and, later, primeval plants growing on marshlands and land, gradually increased the level of oxygen in the atmosphere. 3.5 billion years ago, the atmospheric oxygen level was nearly 0 percent, as opposed to the 20 percent it was approximately 400 million years ago. Other atmospheric gases, such as methane, nitrogen, and carbon dioxide were also regulated through the ages by the natural process of respiratory exchange of living beings, such as plants in forests, animal populations, microrganic activity in soils and waters, organic matter decomposition, etc. Such interdependence and interchange between life and atmospheric balance and gaseous composition shows a self-regulatory activity, oscillating in a dynamic balance, which is expressed in alternate cycles of warmer and colder climatic periods. For instance, plant respiration and organic matter decomposition are natural sources of carbon dioxide and methane, released in the atmosphere in amounts ten times higher than human-related emissions. However, forests, soil bacteria, and microrganic life forms in oceans and waters also act like natural sinks, by reabsorbing methane and carbon dioxide.

The rapid expansion of human population of the last 250 years, associated with increased deforestation, burning of coal and wood, and augmented emissions of water vapor—in addition to the Industrial Revolution practices and fossil fuel burning of the nineteenth and twentieth centuries—have elevated atmospheric carbon dioxide concentration to 31 percent since 1750. Industrial activity also released (and keeps releasing) into the atmosphere millions of tons of black smoke soot, sulfur dioxides, dioxins, furans, mercury, lead alkaloids, and other toxic compounds that altered the composition of troposphere (the lower atmospheric layer), increasing tropospheric ozone formation with its typical "smog." Such emissions increased the greenhouse effect and caused sulfuric acid formation precipitation to soils, lakes, and rivers under the form of acid rains. On the other hand, the increased concentrations of carbon monoxide in the atmospheric upper layers, known as stratosphere, are literally destroying the ozone shield that protects the surface of Earth from direct exposure to cosmic ultraviolet radiation. The dramatic increase in human population of the last 250 years and the rapid deforestation of large areas in both hemispheres cannot be ruled out as important factors in global warming and climate change. Human-derived emissions and contamination of the environment presently exceeds the capacity of the natural forces involved in the environmental self-regulation during the last 400 million years.

Throughout the last millions of years, climate has undergone sudden oscillations, which led to alternating periods of intense cold weather, known as Glacial Ages, and more tempered ones, the Interglacial Ages. The study of the climate history of the last 400,000 years enabled paleoclimatologists to understand that small changes, when persistent for a long enough period, may result in radical climate changes. The atmospheric composition of each of these ages is well recorded today, because ice in glaciers and polar ice caps trap air inside their structure. By perforating and drilling mile-long cylinders of ice and analyzing each layer, investigators can measure the gaseous composition and the proportion among gases associated with each climatic period, as well as the progressive changes occurred in the years preceding a major climate shift. Based on the gathered data, computer scenarios were developed to assess the recent human impact on climate and global temperature. Greenhouses gases emitted by humans have already altered the capacity of thermal radiation release from Earth to the space. The planet is absorbing more heat from solar radiation than releasing it, because such gases absorb and retain thermal energy, preventing its escape and dispersion, thus returning to the Earth's surface. In other words, Earth is getting warmer, and the temperature of ocean surface is gradually increasing, which causes, for instance, more hurricanes and tropical storms in certain regions, and longer and more intense draughts in other regions.

Since the end of the nineteenth century, the median global temperature has increased 1.3 °F (0.75 °C). Estimates are that it will further increase between 0.7 °–1.2 °F (0.4 °–0.7 °C) in the next fifty years, because of the existing levels of greenhouse gases. In the Arctic region (Greenland, Alaska, and Siberia), global warming is already evident as the progressive melting and shrinking of glaciers has been annually registered for the last thirty years. As the median global temperature rises, permafrost—the underground frozen soil of Arctic lands such as those of Siberia, Alaska, and northern parts of Canada—is also thawing and releasing in the process huge amounts of methane into the atmosphere, thus aggravating the greenhouse effect. Bush plants are invading areas in the northeastern parts of Alaska that until 1949 were covered only by Arctic tundra, due to the decrease of 30–40 percent of the Alaskan glaciers. U.S. Geological Survey researchers recorded in 1986 a temperature increase in the Alaskan soil of 3.6–7.2 °F (2–4 °C) since 1949. As these and other regions where huge quantities of frozen fresh water are gradually melting into the seas, the salinity of the surrounding oceans is being modified and its surface waters are becoming less dense. Ocean temperatures are also rising, a direct impact on climate that will ultimately raise sea levels over the next decades. Since most of the human populations around the globe are concentrated along coastal lines, even a slight sea level elevation can result in the flooding of entire coastal cities and villages and the displacement of millions of people. Another consequence of increased sea temperatures are stronger and more frequent hurricanes, tropical storms and floods, with their heavy toll upon human lives and the economy of entire regions.

Although concerned scientists and environmental groups have warned for decades on the need of global measures to revert the destructive policy of unchecked economic growth by destroying the environment, they have received little credit until recently. In 1989, the United Nations finally created a permanent agency for the research and monitoring of global warming and climate change, aiming the development of global policies to curb the human impact. The agency was named Intergovernmental Panel on Climate Change (IPCC). The 1990 IPCC's first report acknowledged the human impact on global warming in the last one hundred years and strongly recommended governmental

actions to reduce emissions of greenhouse gases by state members around the globe. This report also provided the UN with arguments to start an annual debate among its nation members, known as Climate Change Conventions (CCCs). During the CCC of 1992, held in the city of Rio de Janeiro, Brazil, 154 countries signed a letter of intention to reduce emissions in industrialized countries back to the existing levels of 1990 by the year 2000. The United States, however, declined to sign the Rio document of 1992 and the CCC Berlin Mandate of 1995. The American Government agreed for the first time, in 1996, to support the IPCC against opposing scientists and to legally adopt emissions reduction targets. However, the U.S. did not ratify the 1997 Kyoto Protocol, targeting to reduce emissions until 2010. Further discussions of the Kyoto Protocol in 1998 and 2000 failed to reach a consensus, scheduling a new discussion in 2001, when the new Bush Administration quit the U.S. participation. In 2002 the European Union members, Japan, and hundreds of other countries finally ratified the Kyoto Protocol, although its full legal force still depends on the ratification by those industrialized nations responsible for 55 percent of global emissions. This occurred in 2005, when Albania ratified the protocol.

As an American alternative to the Kyoto Protocol, the Bush Administration has commissioned the U.S. Environmental Protection Agency (EPA) to develop a different strategy for cutting down greenhouse gases emissions without causing a negative impact in the U.S. economy. EPA developed two simultaneous approaches to the issue, presented in 2002 by President Bush as "The Clear Skies Act" and "The Global Climate Change Initiative." The Clear Skies Act aims to cut by 2010 73 percent of sulfur dioxide emissions, 67 percent of nitrogen oxides, and 69 percent of mercury emissions, the three gases considered the worst pollutants for public health. The Global Climate Change Initiative consists of a strategy to reduce greenhouse gases emissions by 18 percent over the next decade and also allocates research funds for climate change studies. In 2003, the Clear Skies Act established federally enforceable limits of the three above-mentioned gases and also a flexible regulatory policy to reduce such emissions by power generation plants and other industrial activities. Nevertheless, these Acts did not tackle the emissions of carbon dioxide in an effective way, whose tropospheric levels were 280 parts per million (ppm) before the industrial era and now represent 370 ppm and rising.

PRIMARY SOURCE

... Finally, the environmental establishment insists on casting the climate crisis as an environmental problem. But climate change is no longer the exclusive franchise of the environmental movement. Any successful movement must include horizontal alliances with groups involved in international relief and development, campaign finance reform, public health, corporate accountability, labor, human rights, and environmental justice. The real dimensions of climate change directly affect the agendas of a wide spectrum of activist organizations.

Regrettably, the environmental movement has proven it cannot accomplish large-scale change by itself. Despite occasional spasms of cooperation, the major environmental groups have been unwilling to join together around a unified climate agenda, pool resources, and mobilize a united campaign on the climate. Even as the major funders of climate and energy-oriented groups hold summit meetings in search of a common vision, they shy away from the most obvious of imperatives: using their combined influence and outreach to focus attention—and demand action—on the climate crisis. As the major national groups insist on promoting exclusive agendas and protecting carefully defined turf (in the process, squandering both talent and donor dollars on internecine fighting), the climate movement is spinning its wheels. ...

Take the critical issue of climate stabilization—the level at which the world agrees to cap the buildup of carbon concentrations in the atmosphere. The major national environmental groups focusing on climate—groups like the Natural Resources Defense Council, the Union of Concerned Scientists and the World Wildlife Federation—have agreed to accept what they see as a politically feasible target of 450 parts per million of carbon dioxide. ...

While the 450 goal may be politically realistic, it would likely be environmentally catastrophic. With carbon levels having risen by only 90 parts per million (from their pre-industrial level of 280 ppm to more than 370 ppm today), glaciers are now melting into puddles, sea levels are rising, violent weather is increasing and the timing of the seasons has changed—all from a $1°F$ rise in the last century. Carbon concentrations of 450 ppm will most likely result in a deeply fractured and chaotic world ...

The major, national environmental groups, moreover, are trapped in a "Beltway" mentality that measures progress in small, incremental victories. They are operating in a Washington environment that is at best indifferent and at worst actively antagonistic. And too often these organizations are at the mercy of fickle funders whose agendas range from protecting wetlands to keeping disposable diapers out of landfills. ...

The fossil fuel lobby has hijacked America's energy and climate policies. An appropriate response would seem to require a coalition of corporate and financial institutions of equivalent force and influence to counteract the carbon industry's stranglehold on Congress and the White House. ...

The vast majority of climate groups shun confrontation and work instead to get people to reduce their personal energy footprints. That can certainly help spread awareness of the issue. ...

... By persuading concerned citizens to cut back on their personal energy use, these groups are promoting the implicit message that climate change can be solved by individual resolve. It cannot.

The implicit message behind this approach is one of blaming the victim: People are made to feel guilty if they own a gas guzzler or live in a poorly insulated home. In fact, people should be outraged that the government does not require automakers to sell cars that run on clean fuels, that building codes do not reduce heating and cooling energy requirements by 70 percent and that government energy policies do not mandate decentralized, home-based or regional sources of clean electricity.

What many groups offer their followers instead is the consolation of personal sense of righteousness that comes from living one's life a bit more frugally. That feeling of righteousness, coincidentally, is largely reserved for wealthier people who can afford to exercise some control over their housing and transportation expenditures. Many poorer people—who cannot afford to trade in their 1990 gas guzzlers for a shiny new Toyota Prius—are deprived by their circumstances of the chance to enjoy the same sense of righteousness, illusory though it may be. ...

The tragedy underlying the failure of the environmental community lies in the fact that so many talented, dedicated and underpaid people are putting their lives on the line—in ways that will make little difference to the climate crisis. They are outspoken in their despair about what is happening to the planet. They are candid about their acceptance of a self-defeating political realism that requires relentless accommodation. What is missing from virtually all these groups is an expression of the rage they all feel.

When small, unimposing woman refused to yeild her bus seat to a white man in Montgomery, Alabama, it led to more than some sympathetic shoulder shrugging. It led to a few brave African American students demanding service at a white-only diner. And that, in turn, led to a movement that refused to be stifled until it had achieved full voting rights, equal job opportunities, and a full and complete measure of political representation—with or without the approval of the majority of the country.

The United States, similarly, did not withdraw from Vietnam because a few individuals moved to Canada or Sweden to avoid military service—or because the leaders of the antiwar movement negotiated a reduction of the bombing runs over North Vietnam. The United States left Vietnam because of a succession of massive demonstrations and dramatic episodes of civil disobedience that the press could not ignore. Ultimately, the United States withdrew from that war because of a sustained uprising of popular will that ultimately forced one president of the United States to drop his plans for reelection and pressured his successor to scramble until he had achieved something he could call "peace with honor."

These comparisons to the climate movement may be seen as too harsh until one considers the most fundamental fact about the climate crisis.

Activists compromise. Nature does not.

SIGNIFICANCE

In spite of the recent endeavors by the United Nations through those countries committed to the Kyoto Protocol, and despite the United States recent initiatives, such measures presently in process of implementation will hardly suffice to deter and revert the climatic changes already in course as a consequence of emissions of the last hundred years. Present and past emissions such as carbon dioxide, methane, tropospheric ozone, nitrous oxide, and perfluorocarbon compounds are climate forcing agents, which elevate the ocean median temperature as a result of the greenhouse effect. Another impact of ocean heating is being already felt upon the warm ocean current (derived from the Gulf Stream) that provides Western Europe with warming winds, which add between $9°-18°F$ ($5°-10°C$) to European median temperatures. The Gulf Stream carries warm tropical waters to the North Atlantic Ocean, and near $40°N$. Latitude, it divides itself into two currents. One of these two daughter-currents progresses around the Western coast of Europe and heads to the European side of Greenland while the other heads to the Canadian side of Greenland. From there they sink to the ocean floor and return southward, because the water coming from the south contains more salt (higher density) than the seawater around Arctic glaciers. The United Kingdom National Oceanography Centre (NOC) in Southampton has reported, in 2004, a 30 percent decrease in the current flow from the Gulf Stream waters entering the European current. Further analysis by the NOC team, by adding data previously collected by the National Oceanic and Atmospheric Administration (NOAA), has shown that most of such

slow-down has occurred between 1992 and 1998. The NOC study found that the sinking water site on the European side of Greenland is not fully functional, thus sending South only 50 percent of deep water. The recent extra increase of fresh water is making the Arctic waters even less dense, altering the salinity of the incoming current. Whether such extra fresh water originates from rapidly Arctic melting glaciers or from increased flow of Siberian rivers into the sea (or both) is still in dispute. Nevertheless, the recent density decrease on surface seawaters does prevent the warm current to sink completely and therefore slows down the current flow coming from the South. If such current flow is further slowed, temperatures may drop between $9°-18°F$ ($5°-10°C$) in Western Europe, plunging the region into a new Little Ice Age, similar to that predominating in Europe between the thirteenth and the mid-nineteenth centuries.

Since some greenhouse gases take long periods to be dissipated from the atmosphere, the levels already present may continue to promote median temperature elevation for at least fifty more years. For instance, carbon monoxide takes more than one hundred years to dissipate, whereas perfluorocarbon compounds take more than one thousand years, and nitrous oxide takes one hundred years. Oceans are slow absorbers of heat but are also slow energy releasers, which suggests that the present atmospheric gaseous composition not only will continue to promote the heating process but also implies another one-hundred-year period for oceans to return to their previous energy balance.

Gelbspan alerts that the U.S. recent governmental provisions to deal with climate change are shy measures and may turn out to be ineffective if major national environmental groups continue to promote their individual agendas instead of jointly prioritizing the climate change issues that ultimately affect their own particular areas of interest. Stronger environmental activism and aggressive educational campaigns to improve public awareness about the human impact on climate change are essential and urgent measures to put real pressure on politicians in the United States and around the world to actually act to prevent further emissions and to prioritize the funding of existing and new green technologies, including those necessary to reabsorp the greenhouse gases already emitted.

FURTHER RESOURCES
Books

Gelbspan, Ross. *The Heat Is On: The Climate Crisis, the Cover-Up, the Prescription*. New York: Perseus Books Group, 1998.

Thomas, Lewis. *The Fragile Species*. New York: Macmillan Publishing Co., 1993.

Weart, Spencer. "Rapid Climate Change." In *The Discovery of Global Warming*. Boston: Harvard University Press, 2003.

Williams, Michael A. *Deforesting the Earth: From Prehistory to Global Crisis*. Chicago: University of Chicago Press, 2003.

Periodicals

Serreze, M., et al. "Observational Evidence of Recent Change in the Northern High-latitude Environment." *Climatic Change* 46 (2000): 159–207.

Vellinga, M., and R.A. Wood. "Global Climatic Impacts of a Collapse of the Atlantic Thermoline Circulation." *Climatic Change* 54, 3 (2002): 251–267.

Web sites

"Climate of 2004 Annual Review." *The National Oceanic and Atmospheric Administration*, January 13, 2005. <http://www.ncdc.noaa.gov/oa/climate/research/2004/ann/global.html> (accessed March 2, 2006).

Gelbspan, Ross. "Katrina's Real Name." *Boston.com*, August 30, 2005. <http://www.boston.com/news/globe/editorial_opinion/oped/articles/2005/08/30/katrinas_real_name?mode=PF> (accessed March 2, 2006).

Pearce, Fred. "Failing Ocean Current Raises Fears of Mini Ice Age." *The NewScientist.com*, November 30, 2005. <http://www.newscientist.com/article.ns?id=dn8398> (accessed March 2, 2006).

"Working Group I: The Science of Climate Change (Summary for Policy Makers)." *Intergovernmental Panel on Climate Change*. <http://www.ipcc-wg2.org/index.html> (accessed March 2, 2006).

Wangari Maathai-Nobel Lecture

Speech

By: Wangari Maathai

Date: December 10, 2004

Source: Maathai, Wangari. Nobel Lecture. Delivered before members of the Nobel Foundation on December 10, 2004, Oslo, Norway. Available online at <http://nobelprize.org/peace/laureates/2004/maathai-lecture-text.html> (Accessed March 10, 2006).

About the Author: Wangari Muta Maathai, chairman of the department of veterinarian anatomy at the University of Nairobi, is a biologist, environmentalist, and human rights activist.

INTRODUCTION

Wangari Maathai was awarded the Nobel Peace Prize in 2004, in recognition of her work with the Green Belt Movement, a group that organizes disadvantaged women in Africa to plant trees in order to preserve the environment and improve women' quality of life.

While working for the National Council of Women of Kenya in 1976, Maathai came up with the idea to replenish part of the local landscape with trees planted by impoverished women with few opportunities for employment and social advancement. The grass-roots movement quickly blossomed into the organization known as the Green Belt Movement.

In 2002, Maathai was elected to Kenya's parliament, and was later appointed Kenya's Assistant Minister for Environment and Natural Resources.

In awarding the 2004 Nobel Peace Prize to Maathai, the foundation specifically commended Maathai "for her contribution to sustainable

Wangari Maathai, Nobel Peace Prize winner in 2004, and founder of the Green Belt movement, which encouraged the planting of trees in Africa to improve the quality of life and the environement.
© WENDY STONE/CORBIS

development, democracy and peace." In a press release announcing the prize, the foundation asserted that Maathai had "taken a holistic approach to sustainable development that embraces democracy, human rights and women's rights in particular. She thinks globally and acts locally."

■ PRIMARY SOURCE

Your Majesties

Your Royal Highnesses

Honourable Members of the Norwegian Nobel Committee

Excellencies

Ladies and Gentlemen

I stand before you and the world humbled by this recognition and uplifted by the honour of being the 2004 Nobel Peace Laureate.

As the first African woman to receive this prize, I accept it on behalf of the people of Kenya and Africa, and indeed the world. I am especially mindful of women and the girl child. I hope it will encourage them to raise their voices and take more space for leadership. I know the honor also gives a deep sense of pride to our men, both old and young. As a mother, I appreciate the inspiration this brings to the youth and urge them to use it to pursue their dreams.

Although this prize comes to me, it acknowledges the work of countless individuals and groups across the globe. . . . To all who feel represented by this prize I say use it to advance your mission and meet the high expectations the world will place on us.

This honour is also for my family, friends, partners and supporters throughout the world. . . . Because of this support, I am here today to accept this great honour.

I am immensely privileged to join my fellow African Peace laureates, Presidents Nelson Mandela and F.W. de Klerk, Archbishop Desmond Tutu, the late Chief Albert Luthuli, the late Anwar el-Sadat and the UN Secretary General, Kofi Annan.

. . . I have always believed that solutions to most of our problems must come from us.

In this year's prize, the Norwegian Nobel Committee has placed the critical issue of environment and its linkage to democracy and peace before the world. For their visionary action, I am profoundly grateful. . . .

. . . As I was growing up, I witnessed forests being cleared and replaced by commercial plantations, which destroyed local biodiversity and the capacity of the forests to conserve water.

Excellencies, ladies and gentlemen,

In 1977, when we started the Green Belt Movement, I was partly responding to needs identified by rural women, namely lack of firewood, clean drinking water, balanced diets, shelter and income.

Throughout Africa, women are the primary caretakers, holding significant responsibility for tilling the land and feeding their families. As a result, they are often the first to become aware of environmental damage as resources become scarce and incapable of sustaining their families.

The women we worked with recounted that unlike in the past, they were unable to meet their basic needs. . . .

Tree planting became a natural choice to address some of the initial basic needs identified by women. Also, tree planting is simple, attainable and guarantees quick, successful results within a reasonable amount time. . . .

So, together, we have planted over 30 million trees that provide fuel, food, shelter, and income to support their children's education and household needs. The activity also creates employment and improves soils and watersheds . . . This work continues.

Initially, the work was difficult because historically our people have been persuaded to believe that because they are poor, they lack not only capital, but also knowledge and skills to address their challenges. Instead they are conditioned to believe that solutions to their problems must come from "outside." . . .

In order to assist communities to understand these linkages, we developed a citizen education program, during which people identify their problems, the causes and possible solutions. They then make connections between their own personal actions and the problems they witness in the environment and in society. . . .

On the environment front, they are exposed to many human activities that are devastating to the environment and societies. These include widespread destruction of ecosystems, especially through deforestation, climatic instability, and contamination in the soils and waters that all contribute to excruciating poverty.

In the process, the participants discover that they must be part of the solutions. . . . They come to recognize that they are the primary custodians and beneficiaries of the environment that sustains them.

Entire communities also come to understand that while it is necessary to hold their governments accountable, it is equally important that in their own relationships with each other, they exemplify the leadership values they wish to see in their own leaders, namely justice, integrity and trust.

Although initially the Green Belt Movement's tree planting activities did not address issues of democracy and peace, it soon became clear that responsible governance of the environment was impossible without democratic space.

Therefore, the tree became a symbol for the democratic struggle in Kenya. . . .

In time, the tree also became a symbol for peace and conflict resolution, especially during ethnic conflicts in Kenya when the Green Belt Movement used peace trees to reconcile disputing communities. . . . Using trees as a symbol of peace is in keeping with a widespread African tradition. For example, the elders of the Kikuyu carried a staff from the thigi tree that, when placed between two disputing sides, caused them to stop fighting and seek reconciliation. . . .

Such practices are part of an extensive cultural heritage, which contributes both to the conservation of habitats and to cultures of peace. With the destruction of these cultures and the introduction of new values, local biodiversity is no longer valued or protected and as a result, it is quickly degraded and disappears. For this reason, The Green Belt Movement explores the concept of cultural biodiversity, especially with respect to indigenous seeds and medicinal plants. . . .

It is 30 years since we started this work. . . . Today we are faced with a challenge that calls for a shift in our thinking, so that humanity stops threatening its life-support system. We are called to assist the Earth to heal her wounds and in the process heal our own—indeed, to embrace the whole creation in all its diversity, beauty and wonder. This will happen if we see the need to revive our sense of belonging to a larger family of life, with which we have shared our evolutionary process.

In the course of history, there comes a time when humanity is called to shift to a new level of consciousness, to reach a higher moral ground. A time when we have to shed our fear and give hope to each other.

That time is now.

The Norwegian Nobel Committee has challenged the world to broaden the understanding of peace: there can be no peace without equitable development; and there can be no development without sustainable management of the environment in a democratic and peaceful space. This shift is an idea whose time has come.

. . . Those of us who have been privileged to receive education, skills, and experiences and even power must be role models for the next generation of leadership. . . .

Culture plays a central role in the political, economic and social life of communities. Indeed, culture may be the missing link in the development of Africa. . . .

Africans, especially, should re-discover positive aspects of their culture. In accepting them, they would give themselves a sense of belonging, identity and self-confidence.

Ladies and Gentlemen,

There is also need to galvanize civil society and grassroots movements to catalyze change. I call upon governments to recognize the role of these social movements in building a critical mass of responsible citizens, who help maintain checks and balances in society. On their part, civil society should embrace not only their rights but also their responsibilities.

Further, industry and global institutions must appreciate that ensuring economic justice, equity and ecological integrity are of greater value than profits at any cost. The extreme global inequities and prevailing consumption patterns continue at the expense of the environment and peaceful co-existence. The choice is ours.

I would like to call on young people to commit themselves to activities that contribute toward achieving their long-term dreams. They have the energy and creativity to shape a sustainable future. To the young people I say, you are a gift to your communities and indeed the world. You are our hope and our future.

The holistic approach to development, as exemplified by the Green Belt Movement, could be embraced and replicated in more parts of Africa and beyond. It is for this reason that I have established the Wangari Maathai Foundation to ensure the continuation and expansion of these activities. Although a lot has been achieved, much remains to be done.

Excellencies, ladies and gentlemen,

As I conclude I reflect on my childhood experience when I would visit a stream next to our home to fetch water for my mother. I would drink water straight from the stream. Playing among the arrowroot leaves I tried in vain to pick up the strands of frogs' eggs, believing they were beads. But every time I put my little fingers under them they would break. Later, I saw thousands of tadpoles: black, energetic and wriggling through the clear water against the background of the brown earth. This is the world I inherited from my parents.

Today, over 50 years later, the stream has dried up, women walk long distances for water, which is not always clean, and children will never know what they have lost. The challenge is to restore the home of the tadpoles and give back to our children a world of beauty and wonder.

Thank you very much.

SIGNIFICANCE

In recent decades, the Nobel Foundation has broadened its definition of peace when considering the Nobel Peace Prize to include how benefits to the environment and human rights can help the world's chances for attaining a lasting peace.

The award of the Nobel Peace Prize to Maathai also helped to focus international attention on the concept of sustainable development and how a range of actions from local to international can foster such development. Sustainable development practices are also argued to reduce risk of environmental disaster. The ISDR Secretariat of the U.N. International Strategy for Disaster Reduction defines sustainable development as, "Development that meets the needs of the present without compromising the ability of future generations to meet their own needs. It contains within it two key concepts: the concept of 'needs', in particular the essential needs of the world's poor, to which overriding priority should be given; and the idea of limitations imposed by the state of technology and social organization on the environment's ability to meet present and the future needs. (Brundtland Commission, 1987)."

Advocates of sustainable development practice argue that ecosystem protection is part of an overall concept of sustainable development that integrates political systems, cultures, economic viability, and environmental protection.

FURTHER RESOURCES

Books

Lappé, F.M. *Hopes Edge: The Next Diet for a Small Planet.* New York: Jeremy P. Tarcher/Putnam, 2002.

Maathai, W. *The Canopy of Hope: My Life Campaigning for Africa, Women, and the Environment.* New York: Lantern Books, 2002.

———. *The Green Belt Movement: Sharing the Approach and the Experience.* New and Expanded Edition. New York: Lantern Books, 2004.

Web sites

The Green Belt Movement. <http://www.greenbeltmovement.org> (accessed March 15, 2006).

"15 arrested in Land Rover protest"

Newspaper article

By: Anonymous

Date: May 16, 2005

Source: British Broadcasting Corporation. "15 arrested in Land Rover protest." May 16, 2005.

<http://news.bbc.co.uk/2/hi/business/4550593.stm> (accessed March 8, 2006).

About the Author: This article was published without a byline, and was written by a staff writer for the British Broadcasting Corporation (BBC). The BBC is Britain's public media broadcaster, and has evolved since its founding into a widely recognized global news resource.

INTRODUCTION

Climate change is considered among the greatest threats faced by the planet today, one that is compounded by increased presence of greenhouse gases in the atmosphere.

The developed world is a significant contributor of greenhouse gases into the environment. One of the chief contributors of greenhouse gases is vehicular emissions. There is a trend to manufacture low-emission vehicles, which pose a lesser risk to the environment, and controversy brews about the fuel consumption capacity of Sport Utility Vehicles (SUVs), a class of automobiles designed for non-urban use.

The environmental action group Greenpeace has held demonstrations since the beginning of 2000 against American vehicle giant Ford Motor Company. Ford is the parent company of Land Rover, the British manufacturer of Range Rover SUVs, which Greenpeace claims are posing a serious threat to the environment.

Greenpeace is a non-political environmental watchdog with a presence in many countries worldwide. Its members use mass awareness tactics to bring pressure on governments on various environmental issues and hotspots around the globe. One such issue is the high levels of vehicle emissions.

In May 2005, thirty-five members of Greenpeace evaded security at Land Rover's United Kingdom plant at Solihull and chained themselves to the chassis of unfinished vehicles as part of their protest against the manufacturer.

The article "15 arrested in Land Rover Action" is a BBC news report covering the demonstration. Greenpeace publicly stated that this event was to protest against excessive emissions from the Range Rover. This action by Greenpeace triggered a heated environmental argument—while Greenpeace maintained that excessively high emissions from the vehicles were polluting the environment, Ford argued that the production of Land Rover in the United Kingdom was constituted of around 70 percent of Ford's exports from the country—something that contributed greatly to the region's economy.

15 ARRESTED IN LAND ROVER PROTEST

A protest that disrupted production at a Land Rover factory in the West Midlands has ended with the arrest of 15 Greenpeace activists. Some 30 members of the environmental action group breached security at the plant in Solihull on Monday morning.

Greenpeace said that the action was in protest at what it claims are the "climate-wrecking" emissions from Range Rovers, Land Rover's premium model.

Land Rover said only a "small part" of the plant had been affected

The protest came to an end at 1500 GMT after campaigners who had handcuffed themselves to unfinished vehicles on an assembly line at the factory were cut free by police.

West Midlands police said on Monday evening that they were questioning 15 people in relation to the incident.

A number of senior Greenpeace members are understood to have been among those arrested.

"We have arrested some men and women on suspicion of aggravated trespass," a police spokesman told the Press Association.

Environmental argument "The action taken by Greenpeace ... is both regrettable and damaging—Land Rover is a leading British business and exports over 70% of it's production, and contributes significantly to the country's wealth creation," a company spokesman said.

He said Land Rover, which is owned by US giant Ford, employed 11,000 staff and supported another 50,000 jobs in the supply chain.

According to a Greenpeace statement, its members "used safety shut-down buttons to cut off power to the assembly line" before chaining themselves to the production line at 0600 GMT on Monday.

Greenpeace said that although "climate change is the greatest threat the planet is facing" Land Rover "continues to make gas-guzzling vehicles, most of which will tackle nothing steeper than a speed bump".

Misleading "Making cars like this for urban use is crazy when 150,000 people are dying every year from climate change," said Greenpeace's Ben Stewart.

Range Rover do less miles to the gallon than the model T Ford.

However, Land Rover said it took its responsibilities to the environment "very seriously".

"We find many of the claims made by Greenpeace both misleading and inaccurate," the Land Rover spokesman said.

He said most of the factory was "generally running as normal", with one production line affected.

The Transport and General Workers' Union (T&G) criticised Greenpeace's action at the Land Rover plant, describing it as "insensitive and potentially dangerous".

"They [Greenpeace] ought to think through the consequences of hitting production at a difficult time for the industry and for the people of the West Midlands, who only recently have seen the closures at Jaguar's Browns Lane plant and mass redundancies at MG Rover," said T&G regional secretary Gerard Coyne.

■

SIGNIFICANCE

SUVs are four-wheel-drive vehicles that have become popular in across the world, due to their non-urban appeal and rugged comfortable looks. The Range Rover (Land Rover's premium model), marketed by Ford, is one of the most popular SUVs in the United States and United Kingdom.

Since the early 2000s, SUVs have come under the scanner not just for their climate-wrecking emissions but also for their high gas consumption. According to CNN, the Range Rover SUVs recorded a mileage of 12 miles per gallon (20 liters per 100 kilometers) in the city, and 15 miles to the gallon (16 liters per 100 kilometers) on the highway. This is less fuel-efficient than even the Model T Ford, which Henry Ford originally built in the early 1900s. Some reports note that the Toyota Prius, an electric hybrid family car, does more than 55 miles per gallon (4 liters per 100 kilometers) in urban areas.

According to Greenpeace, instead of producing more fuel-efficient cars and helping the United States reduce its dependence on oil, Ford is continuing its production of fuel-inefficient models. The Deputy Administrator of the U.S. Environmental Protection Agency (EPA) noted that, although America is home to less that five percent of the world's population, it consumes around twenty six percent of the world's energy. Greenpeace is of the opinion that manufacturers like Ford are increasing the dependence of the United States on foreign oil as well. Higher oil consumption can give rise to serious environmental issues in the long run.

Members of Greenpeace argue that federal regulations in the United States such as the Corporate Average Fuel Economy (CAFE) have not helped either. CAFE regulations allow for 27 miles per gallon

Greenpeace activists rally against the Ford decision to crush 400 Norwegian ''Think'' cars at Ford Headquarters near Oslo, Norway on August 24, 2004. The electric cars are meant to be much more environmentally friendly than the gas-guzzling SUVs. GREENPEACE/AFP/GETTY IMAGES

(9 liters per 100 kilometers) for passenger cars. However, for SUVs this limit is set to only 12 miles per gallon—allowing them to consume more fuel. The reason for this is that SUVs are classified as light trucks and not passenger cars. Greenpeace states that SUVs are used mainly as family cars in the United States and Britain. Also, Ford has marketed the Range Rover to an urban audience, making it more of a city car rather than a light truck.

Subsequently, since the early 2000s, Greenpeace has demonstrated against Ford. A Greenpeace news release stated that in April 2003, Ford broke its promise of trying to improve the efficiency of its SUV fleet despite having acknowledged in July 2000 that the fuel efficiency of the SUVs it produced was poor.

Also, in August 2004, instead of promoting cleaner transport, Ford planned to send its entire range of electric cars to be crushed to scrap. Under pressure from Greenpeace and other environmental action groups, this decision was ultimately reversed.

Greenpeace further alleged that on behalf of the vehicle manufacturing lobby in the United States and Britain, Ford had pressured various governments on national and regional levels to prevent various legislative changes like cutting vehicular emissions, giving informed choice to citizens to assist their buying decisions, and opposing measures to introduce more fuel-efficient and non-fuel-dependent transportation in the United States. These events achieve greater significance given that the United States and Australia are the only countries in the world not to have signed the Kyoto Protocol, an agreement that obliges countries to conform to gas emission norms.

Greenpeace and other environmental action groups maintain that by cutting down on vehicle emissions and limiting the use of SUVs, Americans can also contribute to the reduction in vehicular emissions that pose a significant threat to the environment. The group states that the incident mentioned in the news article was part of their campaign to create awareness for this issue.

Since the incident, the issue of vehicular fuel consumption has reached the limelight. Various agencies maintain fuel efficiency guides for vehicles on their Web sites to educate vehicle owners about fuel efficiency. Environmental action groups continue to demonstrate against cars they deem to be dangerous to the environment.

FURTHER RESOURCES
Web sites

"The Case Against Land Rover." *Greenpeace.org.uk*. <http://www.greenpeace.org.uk/climate/climatecriminals/landrover/case.cfm> (accessed March 8, 2006).

"Environmental Double Standards for Sport Utility Vehicles." *SUV.org*. <http://www.suv.org/environ.html> (accessed March 8, 2006).

"Fuel Efficient Vehicles Outnumbered by Gas Guzzlers in U.S. Showrooms." *CNN.com*, October 2, 2000. <http://archives.cnn.com/2000/US/10/02/epa.mileage.ap> (accessed March 8, 2006).

"Land Rover." *Greenpeace.org.uk*. <http://www.greenpeace.org.uk/climate/climatecriminals/landrover/index.cfm> (accessed March 8, 2006).

"Rescuing Environmentalism"

Environment and Economics

Newspaper article

By: Anonymous

Date: April 21, 2005

Source: "Rescuing Environmentalism." *Economist (US)*. 375, no. 8423 (April 21, 2005): 11. Available online at <http://www.economist.com/opinion/displayStory.cfm?story_id=3888006>

About the Author: This article was written by a staff writer. The *Economist* does not usually attach an author to articles it publishes.

INTRODUCTION

The effectiveness of the environmental movement to influence government policy, public opinion, and the decisions made in the business world is being questioned by environmentalists themselves. There is fear that the methods used to protect the environment and create a green society are outdated. The latest thinking suggests the environmental movement needs to fully embrace the use of economic incentives and market-based approaches to be successful in tackling environmental challenges, and sparking public interest to get involved.

Market-based approaches provide economic incentives for companies, government, and individuals to prevent and reduce their polluting ways and find alternatives to degrading the environment. The traditional approach requires protecting the environment by creating laws that mandate pollution abatement. By including economic incentives, it is hoped that firms will be encouraged to implement pollution prevention strategies that consider the value of important ecosystem services.

There are many parts of the world where natural environmental services are considered to have a large economic impact. One example is in the operation of the Panama Canal, which requires 52 million gallons of freshwater for each of the forty-five ships that cross daily between the Pacific and Atlantic Oceans. With deforestation of the surrounding Panama Canal watershed, there is clear evidence that this water supply is diminishing. The disappearance of the trees has also removed a natural filtration system, accelerating the rate at which sediment reaches and clogs the canal. These problems raise the cost of operating the canal, and threaten to limit its operation. Many of the large companies that ship their goods through the Panama Canal have insurance policies to offset the enormous costs of shipping goods all the way around South America, which would be the alternative if the Canal was not operational. Reforesting is occurring in the area because of the clear economic incentives for both insurance companies and the government of Panama, as well as the local communities who rely on wood from the forests.

The carbon dioxide (CO_2) trading markets that have taken off in Europe, as well as sulfur dioxide trading schemes in the United States, use economic incentives to reduce pollution. The CO_2 markets allow companies and individuals to buy the legal right to emit CO_2, typically in units of metric tons. The number of permits available equate to the total limit of CO_2 emissions set by a particular country's government. The market price of these permits fluctuates, depending on the demand from buyers. A company may realize money can be saved by reducing CO_2 emissions instead of paying for one of the permits. Proponents say this reduces pollution that is easy to control and provides the proper incentives for companies to develop innovative ways to reduce pollution that is more difficult to eliminate.

■ PRIMARY SOURCE

Market forces could prove the environment's best friend—if only greens could learn to love them.

"The environmental movement's foundational concepts, its method for framing legislative proposals, and its very institutions are outmoded. Today environmentalism is just another special interest." Those damning words come not from any industry lobby or right-wing think-tank. They are drawn from "The Death of Environmentalism," an influential essay published recently by two greens with impeccable credentials. They claim that environmental groups are politically adrift and dreadfully out of touch.

They are right. In America, greens have suffered a string of defeats on high-profile issues. They are losing the battle to prevent oil drilling in Alaska's wild lands, and have failed to spark the public's imagination over global warming. Even the stridently ungreen George Bush has failed to galvanize the environmental movement. The solution, argue may elders of the sect, is to step back from day-to-day politics and policies and "energise" ordinary punters with talk of global-warming calamities and a radical "vision of the future commensurate with the magnitude of the crisis."

Europe's green groups, while politically stronger, are also starting to lose their way intellectually. Consider, for example, their invocation of the woolly "precautionary principle" to demonize any complex technology (net–generation nuclear plants, say, or genetically modified crops) that they do not like the look of. A more sensible green analysis of nuclear power would weight its (very high) economic costs and (fairly low) safety risks against the important benefit of generating electricity with no greenhouse-gas emissions.

Small victories and bigger defeats The coming into force of the UN's Kyoto protocol on climate change might seem a victory for Europe's greens, but it actually masks a larger failure. The most promising aspect of the treaty—its innovative use of market-based instruments such as carbon-emissions trading—was resisted tooth and nail by Europe's greens.

With courageous exceptions, American green groups also remain deeply suspicious of market forces.

If environmental groups continue to reject pragmatic solutions and instead drift toward Utopian (or dystopian) visions of the future, they will lose the battle of ideas. And that would be a pity, for the world would benefit from having a thoughtful green movement. It would also be ironic, because far-reaching advances are already under way in the management of the world's natural resources—changes that add up to a different kind of green revolution. This could yet save the greens (as well as doing the planet a world of good).

"Mandate, regulate, litigate." That has been the green mantra. And it explains the world's top-down command-and-control approach to environmental policymaking. Slowly, this is changing. Yesterday's failed hopes, today's heavy costs and tomorrow's demanding ambitions have been driving public policy quietly towards market-based approaches. One example lies in the assignment of property rights over "commons," such as fisheries, that are abused because they belong at once to everyone and no one. Where tradable fishing quotas have been issued, the result has been a drop in over-fishing. Emissions trading is also taking off. America led the way with its sulphur-dioxide trading scheme, and today the EU is pioneering carbon-dioxide trading with the (albeit still controversial) goal of slowing down climate change.

These, however, are obvious targets. What is really intriguing are efforts to value ignored "ecological services," both basic ones such as water filtration and flood prevention, and luxuries such as preserving wildlife. At the same time, advances in environmental science are making those valuation studies more accurate. Market mechanisms can be employed to achieve these goals at the lowest cost. Today, countries from Panama to Papua New Guinea are investigating ways to price nature in this way (see article).

Rachel Carson meets Adam Smith If this new green revolution is to succeed, however, three things must happen. The most important is that prices must be set correctly. The best way to do this is through liquid markets, as in the case of emissions trading. Here, politics merely sets the goal. How that goal is achieved is up to the traders.

A proper price, however, requires proper information. So the second goal must be to provide it. The tendency to regard the environment as a "free good" must be tempered with an understanding of what it does for humanity and how. Thanks to the recent Millennium Ecosystem Assessment and the World Bank's annual "Little Green Data Book" (released this week), that is happening. More work is needed, but thanks to technologies such as satellite observation, computing and the internet, green accounting is getting cheaper and easier.

Which leads naturally to the third goal, the embrace of cost-benefit analysis. At this, greens roll their eyes, complaining that it reduces nature to dollars and cents. In one sense, they are right. Some thing in nature are irreplaceable—literally priceless. Even so, it is essential to consider trade-offs when analyzing almost all green problems. The marginal cost of removing the last five% of a given pollutant is often far higher than removing the first five% or even 50%: for public policy to ignore such facts would be inexcusable.

If governments invest seriously in green data acquisition and co-ordination, they will no longer be flying blind. And by advocating data-based, analytically rigorous policies rather than pious appeals to "save the planet," the green movement could overcome the skepticism of the ordinary voter. It might even move from the fringes of politics to the middle ground where most voters reside.

Whether the big environmental groups join or not, the next green revolution is already under way. Rachel Carson, the crusading journalist who inspired greens in the 1950s and 60s, is joining hands with Adam Smith, the hero of free-marketeers. The world may yet leapfrog from the dark ages of clumsy, costly, command-and-control regulations to an enlightened age of informed, innovative, incentive-based greenery.

SIGNIFICANCE

Market-based approaches also call for further economic valuation of ecosystem services such as water filtration by wetlands, hurricane buffering by coastal forests, and biodiversity in coral reefs. The valuation approach translates the beneficial services of nature into dollar amounts. Valuation quantifies the costs to governments, businesses, and people, if the ecosystems are disturbed or damaged in a way that affects the services they provide. These quantifications provide information useful for policy makers and business leaders who may recognize the economic sense in protecting the environment.

Advances in environmental science are making valuation studies more accurate and useful. There is a need for further observation of ecosystems, something that has become easier with the use of satellite technology. In order for society to stop regarding the environment as a free good, it is thought that there needs to be a realization of the benefits the environment provides to society.

The valuation of ecosystem services is one of the key components of The Millennium Ecosystem Assessment (MA), an international effort to provide ecological impact data to the general public,

government, and business leaders. The MA evolved from the assessment needs of several international treaties, including the Convention on Biological Diversity and Ramsar Convention on Wetlands. It is a unique synthesis of scientific literature, datasets, and scientific models, including knowledge from the private sector, practitioners, local communities, and indigenous people. According to the World Bank, this source of ecological data is a key step in carrying out accurate environmental valuation studies.

Some environmentalists have voiced concern that the intrinsic value of nature is not fully captured when doing a cost benefit analysis of ecological services. Proponents who have accepted the mixing of economics and environmental protection suggest that a monetary approach will convince more people to make the effort to protect nature.

FURTHER RESOURCES
Books

Anderson, Terry L., and Donald R. Leal. *Free Market Environmentalism.* San Francisco: Palgrave Macmillan, 2001.

Goodstein, Eban S. *Economics and the Environment.* Hoboken, NJ: Wiley, 2004.

Periodicals

Norberg-Hodge, Helena. "Localize, Localize, Localize: Alternative to Globalization." *The Ecologist,* June 2001.

Web sites

Anderson, Terry R. "Free Market Environmentalism Explained." Interview by Candice Jackson Mayhugh. *Hoover Digest* 1998, no. 2. (Reprinted from the *Stanford Review*, October 21, 1997, from an article entitled "New Hoover Fellow Terry Anderson Explains Free Market Environmentalism.") <http://www.hooverdigest.org/982/anderson_t.html> (accessed March 17, 2006).

"FAQs about Free Market Environmentalism." *The Thoreau Institute.* <http://www.ti.org/faqs.html> (accessed March 17, 2006).

"Laws Don't Work if They're Only on Paper"

Newspaper article

By: Raúl Pierri

Date: August 9, 2005

Source: Pierri, Raúl. "Laws Don't Work if They're Only on Paper." *Inter Press Service News Agency* (August 9, 2005).

About the Author: Raúl Pierri is a reporter with the Inter Press Service News Agency, covering Latin American issues and publishing his work in both Spanish and English.

INTRODUCTION

Latin-American economic development surged from the 1930s through the 1970s with intensive industrialization. Using programs such as "import substitution industrialization," which involved having Latin-American countries produce the same products they normally imported, the economies of Argentina, Chile, Mexico, Brazil, and other Latin-American countries grew at record rates. Substituting imports for domestic products helped to boost the economy, created jobs, stimulated foreign investment, and created home industries that allowed for improvements in infrastructure. As domestic factories created products and jobs, the governments invested capital into these enterprises while placing high tariffs on imported goods, protecting native production.

While countries throughout Latin America urbanized and industrialized at different rates and times, the continent on the whole entered international markets, with finished goods competing with those produced by developed nations. Between import substitution and production for export to North America and Europe, industrialization in larger Latin-American countries changed the demographics of Latin America but also permanently altered the continent's physical landscape.

As environmental problems such as air pollution, water pollution, waste storage, public health issues, deforestation, and erosion began to plague Latin-American countries, national and international attention started to spotlight these problems. While groups such as Greenpeace traditionally focused on the natural environment, especially rainforests, marine life, and farmland nutrient depletion, over time a second aspect of the environment—the urban environment—came into play when discussing Latin-American environmental crises. International conventions such as the Montreal Protocol (1987), the United Nations (U.N.) Framework Convention on Climate Change (1992), the Biodiversity Convention (1992), the World Summit on Sustainable Development (2002), and the ongoing Kyoto Protocol question worked toward finding government-corporate solutions to environmental degradation in Latin America, while preserving economic development.

Existing laws in Latin America and international agreements, if followed, would contain much of the environmental damage sustained, but convincing countries to follow their own laws and abiding by international treaties has been an ongoing source of frustration for national and international non-governmental organizations, political activists, and leaders.

■ PRIMARY SOURCE

The governments of Latin America and the Caribbean will not be able to curb the growing environmental destruction in the region unless they enforce the laws and international conventions they have adopted, fight poverty, and put a stop to the interference of big corporations in their public polices.

MONTEVIDEO, Aug 9 (IPS)—This was the consensus reached by 35 experts from 10 countries in the region who have gathered for seven days in Montevideo to draw up the agenda for issues to be addressed in the next Global Environment Outlook (GEO), a periodic, comprehensive environmental report organised by the United Nations Environment Programme (UNEP).

The GEO reports are produced through a participatory and consultative approach with input from the international, regional and national levels. Three have been published so far, in 1997, 1999, and 2002, and the next is scheduled for completion in 2007.

In an interview with IPS, Ricardo Sánchez, the director of the UNEP Regional Office for Latin America and the Caribbean, commented that the region's governments "demonstrate a certain political will for protecting the environment. They have laws, they have ministries and parliamentary commissions, but there hasn't been enough progress in making environmental policies a crosscutting issue."

The result, he said, is that "countries undertake a great many projects aimed at development that focus solely on economic growth, without taking environmental impact into account. There needs to be a greater will on the part of governments to include the environmental aspect in all sectors, in order to genuinely pursue a strategy of sustainable development," he stressed.

"It should be made clear that the most important thing is not growth at any cost, but rather growth in terms of quality, growth in those aspects that have a greater impact on people's quality of life, in balance with the ecosystems," he added.

The GEO reports are drawn up in coordination with governments, civil society and academia. They do not simply provide a diagnosis of the state of the environment, but also put forward proposals for action through public policies, Eduardo Gudynas, director of the Latin American Centre for Social Ecology (CLAES), told IPS.

CLAES, based in Uruguay, is one of the GEO collaborative centres that participate in coordinating the input for the report from the Latin American and Caribbean region.

At the Forum of Environment Ministers of Latin America and the Caribbean, held in Panama in 2003, the participants resolved to follow the recommendations put forward in the GEO reports.

The experts who are meeting in Montevideo until Wednesday have compiled a list of "grave" environmental problems facing the region: deforestation, soil degradation, water and air pollution, inadequate disposal of urban solid waste, and the situation of thousands of peoples living without access to basic public services like drinking water and sanitation.

However, one of the greatest concerns expressed at the meeting was the failure of governments to comply with their own environmental regulations, reported Edgar Gutiérrez Ezpeleta, director of the University of Costa Rica Development Observatory.

"The countries make commitments on a global level through conventions, but at the national level, they neither fulfill them nor ensure that they are fulfilled. I would say that Latin America has sufficient regulations for making proper use of natural resources in an efficient manner, but they are not applied," Gutiérrez Ezpeleta remarked to IPS.

He also stressed the danger posed by the growing interference of multinational corporations in the public policies of Latin America and the Caribbean.

"Companies negotiate with a small number of people in Latin American countries, almost always with the economy minister and the president. There is a process whereby national democracies are being transformed into what have been called 'delegatory democracies,' in the sense that only one or two people in the government take part in negotiations and adopt major decisions," he said.

"The corporations like this, because they only have to deal with one or two people. They don't have to talk with the congress or with eight different ministers," he added.

Gutiérrez Ezpeleta maintained that when governments "put financial needs before the well-being of the population, the country starts heading downhill."

"Getting caught up in the wild race to achieve economic growth or attract investment and boost exports is turning our countries into what they were during the colonial era—mere exporters of natural resources. This is neither sustainable nor just," he said.

The experts agreed that the next GEO report on Latin America and the Caribbean should highlight the importance of including the environmental component in trade and regional integration initiatives.

"There is a major challenge facing Latin America. This is a region with natural wealth unlike any other area in the world. However, it is not used in accordance with local needs, but rather the needs created by consumption in the countries of the North. This poses an enormous challenge, because while it is true that this demand brings in financial resources, it also represents a formidable potential for environmental degradation," said Gutiérrez Ezpeleta.

"This shows us that we should be seeking a new kind of integration. Not just trade-related integration, but rather integration that includes aspects like cooperation, mutual understanding and ethics, that can promote our relations with other parts of the world on the basis of trade that is more just, more equitable and mutually beneficial," he added.

The experts gathered in Montevideo also emphasised the need for governments to address environmental issues from an integrated perspective, while stepping up efforts to combat poverty.

"Environmental matters are not only environmental, because they are also linked to social, economic and institutional issues, just as economic matters are no longer simply economic, because they are connected to social and environmental questions. Everything is interconnected," stressed Gutiérrez Ezpeleta.

"And if this interconnection isn't grasped, we are going to continue fostering partial visions and short-term strategies that lead to what we have observed in Latin America: an accelerated process of environmental degradation," he concluded.

SIGNIFICANCE

Non-governmental organizations such as CorpWatch, Greenpeace, and the Center for Media and Democracy echo the United Nations Environment Programme's concern regarding the interference of multinational corporations in Latin America's environmental policy setting and adherence. These advocacy and watchdog groups point to multinational corporations such as Shell, British Petroleum, and Dole and the role each plays in creating conditions that promote economic development at the expense of the environment.

While multinational organizations claim that voluntary regulation is the key to sustainable growth in Latin America, some of the most egregious environmental problems, such as soil erosion, solid waste storage and overflow, poor water quality, urban air pollution, and deforestation require large-scale regulation and management that require a governmental approach. In response to criticism levied at multinational corporations, in 1995 the World Business Council for Sustainable Development (WBCSD), a lobbying group of over 180 multinational corporations, formed to set voluntary policy, and to set forth corporate goals and ideas about the coexistence of economic development and sustainable business practices. The WBCSD has come under sharp criticism by groups such as Greenpeace, as well as Latin American presidents such as Hugo Chavez of Venezuela, for acting as public relations machines for multinational corporations, putting a veneer of environmental and social concern over policy promotion that aids corporate profits.

The WBCSD and similar organizations such as the International Chamber of Commerce point to projects such as Public-Private Partnerships for the Urban Environment, a cooperative program between the U.N., academia, corporations, and WBCSD, as a success story in which partnerships across the board help to promote positive change in Latin America.

Some governments in Latin America, however, are setting policies that include environmental sustainability in their economic development plans. Argentina has worked with genetically engineered crops to increase yield and decrease deforestation. Chile has worked in recent years to reduce the environmental damage caused by mining. Most government leaders also recognize the fact that environmental degradation and economic development are intertwined with extreme poverty and the ravages of rapid urbanization; without addressing these systemic issues, sustainable development will be difficult, if not impossible.

One of the greatest stumbling blocks in asking Latin-American countries to adhere to their own laws and those set forth by international treaties and conferences comes from the non-compliance of large developed nations such as the United States. As Latin American economies shifted from import substitution industrialization to high levels of export production, the need to remain competitive on an international scale intensified. One common thread in international discussions revolves around the balance between remaining competitive with developed nations—who have already experienced the early problems of rapid industrialization—and the need to address environmental consequences of development. While sustainable growth is important, it is viewed as a luxury by many leaders as Latin America struggles to maintain economic stability.

FURTHER RESOURCES

Books

Franco, Patrice. *The Puzzle of Latin American Development.* Lanham, Md.: Rowman & Littlefield Publishers, 2003.

Martin, Juan and Jose Antonio Ocampo. *Globalization and Development: A Latin American and Caribbean Perspective.* Stanford, Calif.: Stanford University Press, 2003.

Web sites

USAID. "Latin America and the Caribbean: Environment." <http://www.usaid.gov/locations/latin_america_caribbean/environment> (accessed January 13, 2006).

The World Bank. "Market Based Instruments for Environmental Policymaking in Latin America and the Caribbean: Lessons from Eleven Countries." <http://www.worldbank.org/nipr/work_paper/huber/huber2.pdf> (accessed January 13, 2006).

Chernobyl Disaster Spurs Ecological Movements in Eastern Europe

Photograph

By: Sergei Supinsky

Date: December 13, 2005

Source: Getty Images

About the Photographer: Sergei Supinsky is a photojournalist who works primarily for the AFP news agency, a contributary to Getty Images. His work covers much of Eastern Europe and Russia, with an emphasis on military photos.

INTRODUCTION

The nuclear power accident at Chernobyl, Ukraine, formerly part of the USSR, occurred between April 25th and 26th, 1986, and was documented as the worst incident of its kind in the world to date. The accident was a result of a failure to observe various safety procedures during the testing of one of the plant's four nuclear reactors. A chain reaction went out of control, leading to explosions and a fireball that forced the lid off of the reactor. More than thirty people died immediately, and an estimated 2,500 ultimately. 135,000 people were forced to evacuate from the area because of high radiation levels within a 20-mile (32-kilometer) radius. Following the accident, the region suffered from numerous consequences, including increased

PRIMARY SOURCE

Young Activists of Ukraine's Green Party. Activists garbed in suits and masks rally at the protest against storing foreign nuclear waste in Chernobyl, Ukraine. SERGEI SUPINSKY/AFP/GETTY IMAGES

levels of cancer, particularly thyroid cancer; psychological repercussions, such as anxiety, depression, and other stress-induced mental disorders; a severe fall in income for the area due to numerous evacuations and the limiting of industry and agriculture; a decline in the birth rate; and a 12.8 billion dollar cost to the Soviet economy. The longer-reaching effects of the event included an increased awareness of the dangers inherent in nuclear power, and a strong activist movement in Eastern Europe to mitigate these dangers through increased security measures and limited use of nuclear energy, as well as conservation efforts to help restore and protect those areas of ecosystems most effected by the Chernobyl accident.

PRIMARY SOURCE

YOUNG ACTIVISTS OF UKRAINE'S GREEN PARTY
   See primary source image.

SIGNIFICANCE

In the years following the nuclear reactor accident at Chernobyl, a number of agencies and groups worked to study and counteract the long-term effects of the incident, as well as to help prevent future occurrences. The International Atomic Energy Agency (IAEA) regarded the accident as a turning point in their efforts to improve safety conditions at nuclear power plants, and spent more than a decade examining the various causes of the Chernobyl explosions, regarding both the condition of the reactor itself and the human error that led to the loss of control during the testing procedure. As a result, the Early Notification and Assistance Conventions were adopted, followed by the Convention on Nuclear Safety. These documents governed not only safety guidelines for nuclear power plants, but for those nations that housed nuclear weapons. Countries with nuclear reactors, particularly Russia and those in Eastern and Central Europe, paid particular attention to any structural weaknesses in their plants and to improving the safety of their reactor designs.

Beyond the attention the Chernobyl accident brought to nuclear safety, there was renewed concern regarding the affect of nuclear energy usage on the environment, particularly as pertained to those parts of Eastern Europe that experienced fallout from the accident itself. Belarus and Ukraine were most seriously affected by the incident, with radioactive contamination eliminating large portions of those countries' farming communities. In order to counteract the results of the radiation, the IAEA arranged for rapeseed plants to be planted over large areas of farmland. The plant absorbs radionuclides out of the soil, but while the radiation affects the plant's stalks and seed coats, the seeds themselves remain toxin-free, enabling them to be harvested for use in products such as cooking oil and cattle feed, and thereby allowing the land to be used to help restore the region's economy. Other areas were likewise affected to lesser extents, depending on their proximity to Chernobyl, with much of the northern hemisphere ultimately experiencing some consequences. Grazing livestock, such as sheep, cattle, and reindeer, were found to have radioactive caesium in their systems, and were therefore introduced to a chemical additive in their feed, known as Prussian Blue, which helped slow the absorption of the radioactive material into their tissue and reduced the potential for contamination levels in meat and milk products.

At the political level, the question as to whether nuclear power is safe has caused numerous debates, and ecology-minded groups such as the Green Party have pressed for more planet-friendly solutions to energy and waste concerns. When President Viktor Yushchenko suggested that the Ukraine might take advantage of the already damaged area of Chernobyl by offering to store other nations' radioactive waste in that region for a fee, the Green Party immediately protested, pointing out that it would be tantamount to turning their country into a nuclear dumping ground, hardly respectful to the citizens or the land. The Green Party has continued to honor the dead and mark the anniversaries of the Chernobyl accident, traditionally though annual efforts to cleanse chemical waste sites around Ukraine. The United Nations, likewise, provided workers and funds as emergency support, starting soon after the accident and continuing in an effort to help both the immediate and outlying areas return to normal, with a particular focus on teaching the inhabitants how to protect themselves from lingering radiation and contamination of animals and agriculture.

FURTHER RESOURCES

Books

Mould, R.F. *Chernobyl Record: The Definitive History of the Chernobyl Catastrophe*. New York: Taylor and Francis, 2000.

Web sites

"Green Party Slams Idea to Store Foreign Nuclear Waste in Ukraine," *Interfax*, December 10, 2005. <http://www.interfax.com/> (accessed February 24, 2006; article no longer available).

International Atomic Energy Agency. "Chernobyl: Clarifying Consequences." *International Atomic Energy Agency*, April 16, 2004. <http://www.iaea.org/NewsCenter/News/2004/consequences.html> (accessed February 24, 2006).

"The United Nations and Chernobyl." *The United Nations Office for the Coordination of Humanitarian Affairs*. <http://www.un.org/ha/chernobyl> (accessed February 24, 2006).

Visscher, Ross. "Chernobyl Nuclear Disaster." <http://www.chernobyl.co.uk> (accessed February 24, 2006).

How to Conserve Water and Use It Effectively

Government Web site

By: United States Environmental Protection Agency

Date: 2006

Source: *U.S. Environmental Protection Agency*. "How to Conserve Water and Use It Effectively." <http://www.epa.gov/ow/you/chap3.html> (accessed January 17, 2006).

About the Organization: The U.S. Environmental Protection Agency (EPA) is a federal agency that was established by the U.S. Congress in 1970. The EPA develops and enforces environmental regulations; performs research; funds state and local environmental partnerships and programs; promotes environmental education; and publishes information and guidelines for the public.

INTRODUCTION

The EPA—whose assignment is to regulate and reduce air, water, noise pollution, and pollutions concerning pesticides, radiation, and various other toxic materials—offers a number of water-related Internet sites in order to increase public awareness with the issues and problems relating to water quality throughout the United States. One such EPA site that emphasizes water concerns is called "Cleaner Water Through Conservation." By providing important conservation information about water, the EPA encourages involvement in water quality issues by individuals, conservation and environmental groups, and other interested parties. An especially important chapter within the site is called "How to Conserve Water and Use It Effectively," which outlines practices for industrial and commercial users, specifically discussing a number of conservation and water use efficiency practices—from both an engineering and behavioral standpoint—available within that sector.

PRIMARY SOURCE

HOW TO CONSERVE WATER AND USE IT EFFECTIVELY

Practices for Industrial/Commercial Users Industrial/commercial users can apply a number of conservation and water use efficiency practices. Some of these practices can also be applied by users in the other water use categories.

Engineering Practices

Water Reuse and Recycling Water reuse is the use of wastewater or reclaimed water from one application such as municipal wastewater treatment for another application such as landscape watering. The reused water must be used for a beneficial purpose and in accordance with applicable rules (such as local ordinances governing water reuse). Some potential applications for the reuse of wastewater or reclaimed water include other industrial uses, landscape irrigation, agricultural irrigation, aesthetic uses such as fountains, and fire protection (USEPA, 1992). Factors that should be considered in an industrial water reuse program include (Brown and Caldwell, 1990):

- Identification of water reuse opportunities
- Determination of the minimum water quality needed for the given use
- Identification of wastewater sources that satisfy the water quality requirements
- Determination of how the water can be transported to the new use

The reuse of wastewater or reclaimed water is beneficial because it reduces the demands on available surface and ground waters (Strauss, 1991). Perhaps the greatest benefit of establishing water reuse programs is their contribution in delaying or eliminating the need to expand potable water supply and treatment facilities (USEPA, 1992). Water recycling is the reuse of water for the same application for which it was originally used. Recycled water might require treatment before it can be used again.

Factors that should be considered in a water recycling program include (Brown and Caldwell, 1990):

- Identification of water reuse opportunities
- Evaluation of the minimum water quality needed for a particular use
- Evaluation of water quality degradation resulting from the use
- Determination of the treatment steps, if any, that might be required to prepare the water for recycling

Cooling Water Recirculation The use of water for cooling in industrial applications represents one of the largest water uses in the United States. Water is typically used to cool heat-generating equipment or to condense gases in a thermodynamic cycle. The most water-intensive cooling method used in industrial applications is once-through cooling, in which water contacts and lowers the temperature of a heat source and then is discharged.

Recycling water with a recirculating cooling system can greatly reduce water use by using the same water to perform several cooling operations. The water savings are sufficiently substantial to result in overall cost savings to the industry. Three cooling water conservation approaches that can be used to reduce water use are evaporative cooling, ozonation, and air heat exchange (Brown and Caldwell, 1990).

In industrial/commercial evaporative cooling systems, water loses heat when a portion of it is evaporated. Water is lost from evaporative cooling towers as the result of evaporation, drift, and blowdown. (Blowdown is a process in which some of the poor-quality recirculating water is discharged from the tower in order to reduce the total dissolved solids.) Water savings associated with the use of evaporative cooling towers can be increased by reducing blowdown or water discharges from cooling towers.

The use of ozone to treat cooling water (ozonation) can result in a five-fold reduction in blowdown when compared to traditional chemical treatments and should be considered as an option for increasing water savings in a cooling tower (Brown and Caldwell, 1990).

Air heat exchange works on the same principle as a car's radiator. In an air heat exchanger, a fan blows air past finned tubes carrying the recirculating cooling water. Air heat exchangers involve no water loss, but they can be relatively expensive when compared with cooling towers (Brown and Caldwell, 1990).

The Pacific Power and Light Company's Wyodak Generating Station in Wyoming decided to use dry cooling to eliminate water losses from cooling-water blowdown, evaporation, and drift. The station was equipped with the first air-cooled condenser in the western hemisphere. Steam from the turbine is distributed through overhead pipes to finned carbon steel tubes. These are grouped in rectangular bundles and installed in A-frame modules above 69 circulating fans. The fans force some 45 million cubic feet per minute (ft3/min) of air through 8 million square feet of finned-tube surface, condensing the steam (Strauss, 1991).

The payback comes from the water savings. Compared to about 4,000 gallons per minute (gal/min) of makeup (replacement water) for equivalent evaporative cooling, the technique reduces the station's water requirement to about 300 gal/min (Strauss, 1991).

Rinsing Another common use of water by industry is the application of deionized water for removing contaminants from products and equipment. Deionized water contains no ions (such as salts), which tend to corrode or deposit onto metals. Historically, industries have used deionized water excessively to provide maximum assurance against contaminated products. The use of deionized water can be reduced without affecting production quality by eliminating some plenum flushes (a rinsing procedure that discharges deionized water from the rim of a flowing bath to remove contaminants from the sides and bottom of the bath), converting from a continuous-flow to an intermittent-flow system, and improving control of the use of deionized water (Brown and Caldwell, 1990).

Deionized water can be recycled after its first use, but the treatment for recycling can include many of the processes required to produce deionized water from municipal water. The reuse of once-used deionized water for a different application should also be considered by industry, where applicable, because deionized water is often more pure after its initial use than municipal water (Brown and Caldwell, 1990).

Landscape Irrigation Another way that industrial/commercial facilities can reduce water use is through the implementation of efficient landscape irrigation practices. There are several general ways that water can be more efficiently used for landscape irrigation, including the design of landscapes for low maintenance and low water requirements (refer to the previous section on xeriscape landscaping), the use of water-efficient irrigation equipment such as drip systems or deep root systems, the proper maintenance of irrigation equipment to ensure that it is working properly, the distribution of irrigation equipment to make sure that water is dispensed evenly over areas where it is needed, and the scheduling of irrigation to ensure maximum water use (Brown and Caldwell, 1990). For additional information on efficient water use for irrigation, refer to the practices for residential users and agricultural users in this chapter.

Behavioral Practices Behavioral practices involve modifying water use habits to achieve more efficient use of water, thus reducing overall water consumption by an industrial/commercial facility. Changes in behavior can save water without modifying the existing equipment at a facility.

Monitoring the amount of water used by an industrial/commercial facility can provide baseline information on quantities of overall company water use, the seasonal and hourly patterns of water use, and the quantities and quality of water use in individual processes. Baseline information on water use can be used to set company goals and to develop specific water use efficiency measures. Monitoring can make employees more aware of water use rates and makes it easier to measure the results of conservation efforts. The use of meters on individual pieces of water-using equipment can provide direct information on the efficiency of water use. Records of meter readings can be used to identify changes in water use rates and possible problems in a system (Brown and Caldwell, 1990).

Many of the practices described in the section for residential users can also be applied by commercial users. These include low-flow fixtures, water-efficient landscaping, and water reuse and recycling (e.g., using recycled wash water for pre-rinse).

SIGNIFICANCE

Scientists working for the EPA are very concerned with improving water quality throughout the United States. Although water quality has improved in most regions of the country since 1970 (the year that the EPA was created), there are always problems associated with maintaining a safe supply of water for humans, along with other living animals and plants. When the quality of water becomes degraded in a particular area, the cause is often diffuse, or non-point source (NPS), pollution. NPS pollution is the type of pollution that results when no specific source of pollution is identified from widespread activities. Examples of non-point pollution include urban run-off of substances such as grease, oil, and road salt and agricultural run-off of materials such as fertilizers and pesticides. Other NPS examples include acid rain (such as toxic airborne particles), changes in the natural flow of water in streams and rivers (such as dams), and failures of disposal systems (such as septic systems).

When such NPS water pollution happens, hydrological EPA scientists have proven that the application of a water conservation program along with a pollutant source reduction program is a good way to control pollution. An example of a pollutant source reduction program includes the use of an appropriate system of pesticide and nutrient management.

Along with the use of such pollutant source reduction programs, the quality of water can be further enhanced by the conservation of water. When conservation programs are instituted, the quantity of water is increased—which directly leads to an improvement in the quality of the water. Reductions in the use of water lead to such improvements as the renewal of dried-up wetlands, minimization of agricultural runoff, and the general renovations of environmental habitats.

As of the beginning of 2005, over forty U.S. states use some program based on water conservation and more than 80 percent of U.S. water utility customers use some type of water conservation measure such as water restriction/water pressure reduction plans, zoning ordinances, and pricing policies based on usage or other means. One such resource program provided by the EPA is "A Guide to Cleaner Water Through Conserving Water," which provides information to protect water quality. Such topics included within the program are effects from excessive water use from non-point source pollution, overall trends in water usage, and examples of various environmental programs.

Of particular interest to this discussion is the section on various technical conservation methods that help to reduce water use and, as a result, protect the quality of water in the United States. In this section, EPA writers have described many different water-use practices based on updates in plumbing, fixtures, and operating procedures, along with ways that are scientifically proven to more efficiently use water. Part of this discussion involves how agricultural, industrial, residential, and system operator users are able to conserve water.

Since many U.S. citizens work in industrial and commercial areas, it is of particular interest to note the various ways that company officials can conserve water. Water provided for industrial use includes such purposes as cooling, diluting, fabricating, processing, transporting, and processing a product, along with including water into the production of a product and using water as a sanitary device within an industrial facility.

Information provided by the EPA with regard to ways to conserve water in the industrial/commercial sector of the U.S. economy is important to the overall health of water in the country. In 2000, the U.S. Geological Survey (USGS) estimated that the use of water for industries in the United States totaled about 19.7 billion gallons (74.6 billion liters) each working day. This amount was about 11 percent more than in 1995. Surface water was used for about 82 percent of those industrial uses while ground water was used for the other 18 percent. In nearly both cases (92 percent for surface water and 99 percent for ground water), fresh water was used most often.

The states of Louisiana, Indiana, and Texas together used 38 percent of all water for industrial purposes. Louisiana consumed the most industrial water of any state, primarily for its chemical and paper industries. Other U.S. states with high consumption of industrial water are Michigan, Ohio, Pennsylvania, West Virginia, Tennessee, Alabama, Georgia, and Washington.

It is important, for many reasons, that the EPA continue to supply information related to the efficient use of water through conservational means to residential, industrial, and agricultural consumers. The EPA possesses the expertise and knowledge to deal with the problems and issues that occur from a small town to a particular section of the country and beyond the physical boundaries of the United States. With such valuable information provided by the EPA, consumers are better equipped to deal with pollution and better informed on the wise use of water.

FURTHER RESOURCES
Books

Environmentalism and the Technologies of Tomorrow: Shaping the Next Industrial Revolution, edited by Robert Olson and David Reieski. Washington, D.C.: Island Press, 2005.

Pearce, Fred. *Keepers of the Spring: Reclaiming Our Water in an Age of Globalization*. Washington, D.C.: Island Press, 2004.

Web sites

Pollution Prevention Pays: North Carolina Department of Environment and Natural Resources. "Industry-specific Pollution Prevention Techniques." <http://wrrc.p2pays.org/industry/indsector.htm> (accessed January 17, 2006).

Troeh, Frederick R., J. Arthur Hobbs, and Roy L. Donahue. *Soil and Water Conservation: For Productivity and Environmental Protection*, fourth ed. Upper Saddle River, N.J.: Pearson Education/Prentice Hall, 2004.

United Nations Educational, Scientific and Cultural Organization. "World Water Assessment Programme." <http://www.unesco.org/water/wwap/facts_figures/water_industry.shtml> (accessed January 17, 2006).

U.S. Environmental Protection Agency. <http://www.epa.gov> (accessed January 17, 2006).

——— "Cleaner Water Through Conservation." <http://www.epa.gov/ow/you/intro.html> (accessed January 17, 2006).

Demonstrations against Transfer of French Warship to India for Asbestos Removal

Photograph

By: Jean Ayissi

Date: February 12, 2006

Source: Getty Images

About the Photographer: Jean Ayissi is a journalist for the AFP news agency. This photo was taken during a demonstration in Paris on February 12, 2006.

INTRODUCTION

The *Clémenceau* is a French aircraft carrier that was launched in 1957. It was decommissioned in 1997 and parked at the port of Toulon for asbestos removal. According to the French government, approximately 115 tons (104 metric tons) of asbestos were removed from the ship. However, the environmental group Greenpeace claims that Technopure, the company removing the asbestos, left over 500 tons (454 metric tons) of asbestos on board—at least 80 percent of the original amount. Asbestos, a potent carcinogen, has been banned in recent years in twenty-six countries, including France.

In 2005, the French government made arrangements to have the *Clémenceau* towed to India under military escort for disposal. The journey began in December. However, protestors from Greenpeace and other environmental groups objected to the transfer, arguing that it constituted a shipment of toxic waste (asbestos) to a vulnerable Third World nation. They contended that such a shipment would be illegal under the international treaty known as the Basel Convention. Greenpeace protestors boarded the ship in the Mediterranean on January 12, 2006, and climbed its mast to hang a banner reading "Asbestos carrier stay out of India." The French phrase on the protestor's sign in the photo, *porte amiante*, means "asbestos carrier," a pun on the fact that the *Clémenceau* is an aircraft carrier (*porte-avion*).

PRIMARY SOURCE

MAN DRESSED AS CLOWN DEMONSTRATES AGAINST TRANSFER OF FRENCH WARSHIP TO INDIA FOR ASBESTOS REMOVAL

See primary source image.

SIGNIFICANCE

The *Clémenceau* was sent to India to undergo "shipbreaking." Shipbreaking is the process of breaking a ship to pieces to recover its steel, a valuable commodity (about 95 percent of a modern ship is steel by weight). About six hundred to seven hundred large seagoing ships meet this fate every year, sixty percent of them in India. Most seagoing vessels are ready to be scrapped after about 25–30 years at sea; vessels that are kept at sea too long can literally fall apart, endangering their crews and spilling pollution. Since the 1970s, most shipbreaking has moved from European dockyards to beaches on the shores of Bangladesh, China, India, Pakistan, and Turkey. Low-paid workers with no protection against toxic materials take the ships to pieces and dump any toxins into the local environment. Toxins can include asbestos and oil.

Large ships are not the only form of unsavory waste to be exported by industrialized countries to poorer countries. The United States has exported incinerator ash to Haiti, and it is estimated that from 1997 to 2007 the United States alone will generate 500 million obsolete computers. These will contain 6.32 billion pounds (2.87 billion kilograms) of plastics, 1.58 billion pounds (717 million kilograms) of lead, 3 million pounds (1.36 million kilograms) of cadmium, 1.9 million pounds (862,000 kilograms) of chromium, and 632,000 pounds (287,000 kilograms) of mercury. It is illegal in the U.S. for large corporations and other institutions to dump computers in many landfills (though many millions of units from individual owners will in fact end up in U.S. landfills), so many look abroad for disposal. Millions of obsolete computers are sent to China, where barehanded laborers earning $1.50 a day break them to pieces in open fields and pour acid on circuit parts to extract tiny amounts of silver and gold. They also burn wiring to remove the plastic insulation so that the copper can be resold. These processes are intensely polluting for both the air and water: one river in the area of a waste site was found to contain 190 times as much pollution as allowed by World Health Organization guidelines (a U.N. body).

PRIMARY SOURCE

Man Dressed as Clown Demonstrates against Transfer of French Warship to India for Asbestos Removal. This photograph shows a playful protest with a serious purpose—stoppage of the transfer of a decommissioned French aircraft carrier to India for "shipbreaking" or final disposal. The ship, according to the Indian government and European environmentalists, still contained hundreds of tons of asbestos. JEAN AYISSI/AFP/GETTY IMAGES

The economic logic behind these transfers (and similar ones) is not hard to discern: environmental standards are more lax in poorer countries because the people there are desperate for employment. This reasoning was laid out in an extraordinary 1991 memo signed by Larry Summers (1954–), then chief economist of the World Bank. The memo asked, "shouldn't the World Bank be encouraging MORE migration of the dirty industries to the [less developed countries]?" and went on to say that "the demand for a clean environment for aesthetic and health reasons is likely to have very high income elasticity"—that is, the poorer you are, the more ugliness and disease you can be forced to put up with. "I think," the document went on to say, "the economic logic behind dumping a load of toxic waste in the lowest wage country is impeccable and we should face up to that." Summers later became Deputy Secretary of the Treasury Department under President Bill Clinton and was president of Harvard

University from 2001 to 2006. He maintained that the memo was meant as a "sardonic counterpoint," not seriously: in any case, it describes the reasoning operative in actual waste transfer to poor countries.

The transfer of toxic waste to developing countries was banned by the treaty known as the Basel Convention, which entered into force in May of 1992 (but has been far from universally honored). One hundred and sixty-six nations have signed the treaty: Afghanistan, Haiti, and the United States have signed but not ratified the treaty. Those protesting the transfer of the *Clémenceau* to India argued that the transfer was illegal under the Basel Convention.

On February 15, 2006, French President Chirac announced that the *Clémenceau* would be towed back to France. In an disturbing footnote, the Indian Supreme Court banned all protests and discussion in the (Indian) media about the fate of the *Clémenceau*, asserting that any discussion of the issue whatever—"pro or against or a middle line"—constituted a challenge to the Court's right to decide the fate of the ship.

FURTHER RESOURCES

Periodicals

"Much Toxic Computer Waste Lands in Third World." *USA Today* (February 25, 2002). <http://www.usatoday.com/tech/news/2002/02/25/computer-waste.htm> (accessed February 24, 2006).

"U.S. Waste is Third World Hazard." *Associated Press* (September 25, 2002).

Web sites

Puckett, Jim, et al. "Exporting Harm: The High-Tech Trashing of Asia." *Basel Action Network and Silicon Valley Toxics Coalition*, February 25, 2002. <http://www.svtc.org/cleancc/pubs/technotrash.pdf> (accessed February 24, 2006).

Secretariat of the Basel Convention: United Nations Environment Programme. <http://www.basel.int> (accessed February 24, 2006).

Vallette, Jim. "Larry Summers' War Against the Earth." *Counterpunch.* <http://www.counterpunch.org/summers.html> (accessed Feb. 24, 2006).

Sources Consulted

BOOKS AND WEB SITES

Achouri, Moujahed, et al. *Forests and Floods: Drowning in Fiction or Thriving on Facts*. Bogor, Indonesia: Center for International Forestry Research, 2005.

Adams, Ansel. *Ansel Adams: An Autobiography*. New York: Bulfinch Press, 1985.

Adler, Jonathan H. "Rent-Seeking Behind the Green Curtain." *Regulation: The CATO Review of Business and Government* 19, 4 (1996).

Albright, Horace M., and Mary Albright Schenk. *Creating the National Park Service: The Missing Years*. Norman, OK.: University of Oklahoma Press, 1999.

Ali, Jawad, and Tor A. Benjaminsen. "Fuelwood, Timber and Deforestation in the Himalayas." *Mountain Research and Development* 24 (2004): 312–318.

Ambrose, Stephen E. *Undaunted Courage; Meriwether Lewis, Thomas Jefferson and the Opening of the American West*. New York: Simon and Schuster, 1996.

American Association for the Advancement of Science (AAAS). "American Association for the Advancement of Science (AAAS)." <http://www.aaas.org> (accessed April 7, 2006).

American Folklife Center, Library of Congress "Voices from the Dust Bowl." <http://lcweb2.loc.gov/ammem/afctshtml/tshome.html> (accessed March 8, 2006).

American Institute of Physics (AIP). <http://www.aip.org/aip/> (accessed April 7, 2006).

Anderson, Terry L., and Donald R. Leal. *Free Market Environmentalism*. San Francisco: Palgrave Macmillan, 2001.

Annual Review of Public Health. <http://arjournals.annualreviews.org/loi/publhealth> (accessed April 7, 2006).

Arlington National Cemetery. "Robert Edwin Peary: Rear Admiral, United States Navy." <http://www.arlingtoncemetery.net/roberted.htm> (accessed February 25, 2006).

Arrhenius, Svante. *Worlds in the Making*. New York: Harper & Row, 1908.

Audubon Society. <http://www.audubon.org> (accessed November 14, 2005).

Bailey, Ronald, ed. *Global Warming and Other Eco Mythos: How the Environmental Movement Uses False Science to Scare Us to Death*. New York: Prima Lifestyles, 2002.

Ballard, Robert D., and M. Hamilton. *Graveyards of the Pacific: From Pearl Harbor to Bikini Atoll*. Washington, DC: National Geographic Books, 2001.

Barnett, Harold. *Toxic Debts and the Superfund Dilemma*. Chapel Hill, N.C.: University of North Carolina Press, 1994.

Basile, Carole, Cameron White, and Stacey Robinson. *Awareness to Citizenship: Environmental Literacy for the Elementary Child*. Lanham, MD: University Press of America, 2000.

Bass, Ronald E., Albert I. Herson, and Kenneth M. Bogdan. *The NEPA Book: A Step-By-Step Guide on How to Comply with the National Environmental Policy Act*. Point Arena, Calif.: Solano Press, 2001.

Beach, Patrick. *A Good Forest For Dying: The Tragic Death Of A Young Man On The Front Lines Of The Environmental Wars*. New York: Doubleday, 2003.

Bechtold, Richard L. *Alternative Fuels Guidebook: Properties, Storage, Dispensing, and Vehicle Facility Modifications*. New York: SAE International, 1997.

Bedoyere, Camilla de la. *No One Loved Gorillas More: Dian Fossey: Letters from the Mist*. New York: National Geographic, 2005.

Bielecki, Janusz and Melaku Geboye Desta, eds. *Electricity Trade in Europe: Review of Economic and Regulatory*

Challenges. The Hague, The Netherlands: Kluwer Law International, 2004.

Biller, Dan. "Informal Gold Mining and Mercury Pollution in Brazil." *World Bank*. Policy Research Working Paper 11304. May, 1994. Available at <www wds.worldbank.org/WDSP/IB/1994/05/01/000009265_3970625091321/Rendered/PDF/multi_page.pdf.>

Bloom, Harold, and Neil Heims, eds. *William Wordsworth*. Philadelphia: Chelsea House Publishers, 2003.

Boehme, Sarah E., ed. *John James Audubon in the West: The Last Expedition, Mammals of North America*. New York: Harry N. Abrams/Buffalo Bill Historical Center, 2000.

Bolin, B. "The Kyoto Negotiations on Climate Change: A Science Perspective." *Science* 279 (1998): 330–331.

Borneman, Walter R. *Alaska: Saga of a Bold Land*. New York: HarperCollins, 2003.

Botkin, Daniel B. "The Depth of Walden Pond: Thoreau as a Guide to Solving Twenty-First Century Environmental Problems." *The Concord Saunterer* 9 (2001): 5–14.

Briones, Claudia, and Jose Luis Lanata, eds. *Archaeological and Anthropological Perspectives on the Native Peoples of Pampa, Patagonia, and Tierra del Fuego to the Nineteenth Century*. Westport, Conn.: Bergin & Garvey, 2002.

British Library. "British Library Images Online." <http://www.imagesonline.bl.uk/britishlibrary/> (accessed April 7, 2006).

British Medical Journal. "British Medical Journal." <http://bmj.bmjjournals.com> (accessed April 7, 2006).

Brower, David, and Steve Chapple. *Let the Mountains Talk, Let the Rivers Run: A Call to Those Who Would Save the Earth*. New York: Harper Collins, 1995.

Brundage, W. Fitzhugh. *A Socialist Utopia in the New South: The Ruskin Colonies in Tennessee and Georgia, 1894–1901*. Urbana, IL: University of Illinois Press, 1996.

Bryan, Nichol. *Love Canal: Pollution Crisis (Environmental Disasters)*. New York: World Almanac Library, 2003.

Bunnell, Lafayette H. *Discovery of the Yosemite and the Indian War of 1851 Which Let to That Event*. Chicago: Fleming H. Revell, 1880.

Burroughs, William J. *Climate Change: A Multidisciplinary Approach*. Cambridge, U.K.: Cambridge University Press, 2001.

Cadenhead, Ivie Edward. *Theodore Roosevelt: The Paradox of Progressivism*. Woodbury, NY: Barron's Educational Series, 1974.

Cafaro, Philip. "Thoreau's Environmental Ethics in *Walden*." *The Concord Saunterer* 10 (2002): 17–63.

Cafaro, Philip. *Thoreau's Living Ethics: Walden and the Pursuit of Virtue*. Athens, Ga.: University of Georgia Press, 2004.

Cambridge University. "Cambridge University, Institute of Public Health." <http://www.iph.cam.ac.uk> (accessed April 7, 2006).

Carson, Rachel. *Silent Spring*. New York: Mariner Books, 2002 (40th Anniversary Edition).

CDC (Centers for Disease Control and Prevention). "CDCSite Index A-Z." <http://www.cdc.gov/az.do> (accessed April 7, 2006).

Cerami, Charles A. *Jefferson's Great Gamble: The Remarkable Story of Jefferson, Napoleon, and the Men Behind the Louisiana Purchase*. New York: Sourcebooks, 2003.

Chernus, Ira. *Eisenhower's Atoms for Peace*. College Station, TX: Texas A&M University Press, 2002.

Clark, Mike. "Gorilla Movies Bad Enough to Make Kong Run for the Hills." *USA Today* (January 3, 2006).

ClinicalTrials.gov. "Information on Clinical Trials and Human Research Studies: Search." <http://clinicaltrials.gov/ct/action/GetStudy> (accessed April 7, 2006).

Cohn, Morris M. *The Pollution Fighters: A History of Environmental Engineering in New York State*. Albany, NY: New York State Department of Health, 1973.

Committee on Air Quality Management in the United States, National Research Council. *Air Quality Management in the United States*. Washington DC: National Academies Press, 2004.

Copeland, Claudia. *Clean Water Act: Current Issues and Guide to Books*. Hauppauge, NY: Nova Science Publishers, 2003.

Cousteau, Jacques. *Jacques Cousteau: The Ocean World*. New York: Harry N. Abrams, 1985.

Cross, Coy F. *Go West, Young Man!: Horace Greeley's Vision For America*. Albuquerque, NM: University of New Mexico Press, 1995.

Curtis, Jane, Will Curtis, and Frank Liebermann. *The World of George Perkins Marsh*. Woodstock, VT: Countryman Press, 1982.

Dalton, Kathleen. *Theodore Roosevelt: A Strenuous Life*. New York: Knopf, 2002.

Daniels, Camille A. *Coral Reef Assessment: An Index Utilizing Sediment Constiuents*. Tampa, FL: University of South Florida, 2005.

Davis, Margaret Leslie. *Dark Side of Fortune: Triumph and Scandal in the Life of Oil Tycoon Edward L. Doheny*. Berkeley, CA: University of California Press, 1998.

Deffeyes, Kenneth F. *Hubbert's Peak: The Impending World Oil Shortage*. Princeton, NJ: Princeton University Press, 2003.

Devoto, Bernard, ed. *The Journals of Lewis and Clark*. New York: Houghton Mifflin, 1997.

Dombrowski, Paul M. "Plastic Language for Plastic Science: The Rhetoric of Comrade Lysenko." *Journal of*

Technical Writing and Communication 31, no. 3 (2001): 293–333.

Drake, Frances. *Global Warming: The Science of Climate Change*. New York: Oxford University Press, 2000.

Earth Observatory Library, National Aeronautics and Space Administration. "On the Shoulders of Giants: Milutin Milankovitch (1879–1958)." <http://earthobservatory. nasa.gov/Library/Giants/Milankovitch/ milankovitch.html> (accessed November 26, 2005).

Earth Summit 2002.org. <http://www.earthsummit2002.org> (accessed February 23, 2006).

EarthDay.gov "Portal for U.S. Events and Information." <http://www.earthday.gov> (accessed March 8, 2006).

EarthTrust "Some of the Major Laws Protecting Endangered Wildlife." <http://www.earthtrust.org/wlcurric/appen2. html> (accessed March 13, 2006).

Eccleston, Charles H. *Environmental Impact Statements: A Comprehensive Guide to Project and Strategic Planning*. New York: Wiley, 2000.

Ehrlich, Gretel. *John Muir: Nature's Visionary*. Washington, DC: National Geographic Society, 2000.

Elspeth, W. "Lynn White, Ecotheology, and History." *Environmental Ethics* 15 (1993): 151–169.

Engel, Michael H. and Stephen A. Macko. "Stable Isotope Analysis of Amino Acid Enantiomers in the Murchison Meteorite at Natural Abundance Levels." *Proceedings of the SPIE—The International Society for Optical Engineering* 3111 (1997): 82.

EPA Office of Public Affairs. "EPA's Position Paper on the Energy Crisis." <http://www.epa.gov/history/topics/ energy/01.htm> (accessed February 23, 2006).

Federation of American Scientists. "Federation of American Scientists, ProMED Initiative." <http://www.fas.org/ promed> (accessed April 7, 2006).

FedStats. <http://www.fedstats.gov> (accessed April 7, 2006).

Feldman, David Lewis. "How Far Have We Come? (Revisiting the Energy Crisis)." *Environment* (May 1, 1995).

Fitzpatrick, John W., et al. "Ivory-billed Woodpecker (Campephilus principalis) Persists in Continental North America." *Science* 307, 5772 (2005).

Fletcher, Thomas H. *From Love Canal to Environmental Justice: The Politics of Hazardous Waste on the Canada-U.S. Border*. Orchard Park: Broadview Press, 2003.

Food and Drug Administration. <http://www.fda.gov> (accessed April 7, 2006).

Ford, Daniel. "The Hole in the Reactor." *New York Times* (April 13, 2002).

Fossey, Dian. "In the Mountain Meadow of Carl Akeley and George Schaller." In *Gorillas in the Mist*. New York: Houghton Mifflin, 1983.

Fox, William. *Terra Antarctica: Looking into the Emptiest Continent*. San Antonio, TX: Trinity University Press, 2005.

Franco, Patrice. *The Puzzle of Latin American Development*. Lanham, MD: Rowman & Littlefield Publishers, 2003.

GAO (Government Account Office). "Site Map." <http:// www.gao.gov/sitemap.html> (accessed April 7, 2006).

Garvey, Gregory, ed. T. *The Emerson Dilemma: Essays on Emerson and Social Reform*. Athens, GA: University of Georgia Press, 2001.

Gedamke, Jason. "Sounds of the 'Silent World.'" *Australian Antarctic Magazine* 9 (Spring 2005): 14–15.

Gelbspan, Ross. *The Heat Is On: The Climate Crisis, the Cover-Up, the Prescription*. New York: Perseus Books Group, 1998.

Geldard, Richard G. *God in Concord: Ralph Waldo Emerson's Awakening to the Infinite*. Burdett, NY: Larson Publications, 1999.

Gibbs, Brian. *Teddy Bear Century*. Lanham, MD: Taylor Trade, 2003.

Giral, A., and K. J. Elman. *Percival Goodman: Architect-Planner-Teacher- Painter*. New York: Princeton Architectural Press, 2001.

Goodstein, Eban S. *Economics and the Environment*. Hoboken, NJ: Wiley, 2004.

Haley, W. D. "Johnny Appleseed: A Pioneer Hero." *Harper's New Monthly Magazine* (November 1871).

Harden, Deborah. *California Geology (2nd Edition)*. Upper Saddle River, New Jersey: Prentice Hall, 2003.

Harris, Hugh, Ingrid Pickering, and Graham George. "The Chemical Form of Mercury in Fish." *Science* 301 (2003): 1203.

Harvey, Danny. *Global Warming: The Hard Science*. New York: Prentice Hall, 2000.

Hayes, Harold. *The Dark Romance of Dian Fossey*. New York: Simon & Schuster, 1990.

Heimlich, Joe E. *Environmental Education: A Resource Handbook*. Bloomington, IN: Phi Delta Kappa Educational Foundation, 2002.

Hill, Julia Butterfly. *The Legacy Of Luna: The Story Of A Tree, A Woman, And The Struggle To Save The Redwoods*. New York: Harper San Francisco, 2000.

Hodges, Margaret. *The True Tale of Johnny Appleseed*. New York: Holiday House, 1999.

Holmes, Steven J. *The Young John Muir: An Environmental Biography*. Madison, WI: University of Wisconsin Press, 1999.

Hoose, Phillip. *The Race To Save the Lord God Bird*. New York: Farrar, Straus and Giroux, 2004.

Hoover, Richard B. "Meteorites, Microfossils, and Exobiology." *Proceedings of the SPIE—The International Society for Optical Engineering* 3111 (1997): 115.

Houghton, John. *Global Warming: The Complete Briefing*. New York: Cambridge University Press, 2004.

Houghton, John. *Global Warming: The Complete Briefing*. New York: Cambridge University Press, 1997.

Hoy, Suellen M. "Municipal Housekeeping: The Role of Women in Improving Urban Sanitation Practices." In *Pollution and Reform in American Cities 1870-1930*, edited by Martin V. Melosi. Austin: University of Texas Press, 1980.

Huber, Peter W. and Mark Mills. *The Bottomless Well: The Twilight of Fuel, the Virtue of Waste, and Why We Will Never Run out of Energy*. New York: Basic Books, 2005.

Imbrie, John, and Katherine Palmer Imbrie. *Ice Ages: Solving the Mystery*. Cambridge, MA: Harvard University Press, 1986.

Intergovernmental Panel on Climate Change "Working Group I: The Science of Climate Change (Summary for Policy Makers)." <http://www.ipcc-wg2.org/index.html> (accessed March 2, 2006).

International Astronomical Union (IAU). "FAQs." <http://www.iau.org/FAQs.56.0.html> (accessed April 7, 2006).

Isaacs, Sally Senzell. *Life in the Dust Bowl*. Chicago: Heinemann Library, 2002.

Ishaaya, Isaac. *Biochemical Sites of Insecticide Action and Resistance*. New York: Springer, 2001.

Jackson, Jerome A. *In Search of the Ivory-billed Woodpecker*. Washington, DC: Smithsonian Books, 2004.

Jefers, Harry Paul. *Roosevelt The Explorer: T.R.'s Amazing Adventures as a Naturalist, Conservationist, and Explorer*. Lanham, MD: Taylor Trade, 2003.

Johns, Grace M. *Socioeconomic Study of Reefs in Southeast Florida: Final Report*. Hollywood, FL: Hazen and Sawyer, in association with Florida State University, National Oceanic and Atmospheric Administration, 2001.

Jones, William Ellery. *Johnny Appleseed: A Voice in the Wilderness*. New York: Chrysalis Books, 2000.

Joos, F., G. Plattner, T.F. Stocker, O. Marchal, and A. Schmittner. "Global Warming and Marine Carbon Cycle Feedbacks on Future Atmospheric CO_2." *Science* 284 (1999): 464–467.

Kelly, H.A. "Lynn White's Legacy." *Viva Vox* 1 (2002/2003): 1–11.

Kerr, Richard A. "It's Official: Humans Are Behind Most of Global Warming." *Science* 296 (2001): 566.

Kubasek, Nancy K. and Gary Silverman. *Environmental Law*, 5th ed. Upper Saddle River, NJ: Prentice-Hall, 2000.

Labohm, Hans H.J. *Man-made Global Warming: Unravelling a Dogma*. Brentwood, UK: Multi-Science Publishing, 2004.

Lang, Michael H. *Designing Utopia: John Ruskin's Urban Vision for Britain and America*. Montréal and New York: Black Rose Books, 1999.

Lappé, F.M. *Hopes Edge: The Next Diet for a Small Planet*. New York: Jeremy P. Tarcher/Putnam, 2002.

Lawrence Berkeley National Laboratory. "Risk-Related Research at Lawrence Berkeley National Laboratory." <http://www.lbl.gov/LBL-Programs/Risk-Research.html> (accessed April 7, 2006).

Leggett, Jeremy. *The Carbon War: Global Warming and the End of the Oil Era*. New York: Routledge, 2001.

Lemonick, Michael D. "Forecast: Clearer Skies." *Time* (November 5, 1990).

Leopold, Aldo. *Game Management*. Madison, WI: University of Wisconsin Press, 1986.

Lerner, Steve. *Eco-Pioneers: Practical Visionaries Solving Today's Environmental Problems*. Boston: The MIT Press, 1997.

Library of Congress. "Library of Congress Online Catalog." <http://catalog.loc.gov/cgi-bin/Pwebrecon.cgi?DB=3Dlocal&PAGE=3DFirst> (accessed April 7, 2006).

Longcore, Travis, and Catherine Rich. "Ecological Light Pollution." *Frontiers in Ecology and the Environment* 2, 4 (May 2004): 191–198.

Lookingbill, Brad D. *Dust Bowl, U.S.A.: Depression America and the Ecological Imagination, 1929-1941*. Athens, OH: Ohio University Press, 2001.

Lovelock, J.E. *The Ages of Gaia: A Biography of Our Living Earth*. New York: W.W. Norton & Company, 1988.

Lowenthal, David. *George Perkins Marsh, Prophet of Conservation*. Seattle: University of Washington Press, 2000.

Lutgens, Frederick K., and Edward J. Tarbuck. *The Atmosphere: An Introduction to Meteorology*. Englewood Cliffs, NJ: Prentice Hall, 1995.

Maathai, W. *The Canopy of Hope: My Life Campaigning for Africa, Women, and the Environment*. New York: Lantern Books, 2002.

MacDermott, Alexandra J. "Distinguishing the Chiral Signature of Life in the Solar System and Beyond" *Proceedings of the SPIE—The International Society for Optical Engineering* 3111 (1997): 272.

Macilwain, Collin. "Organic: Is It the Future of Farming?" *Nature* 428 (April 22, 2004): 792–793.

MacKenzie, Debora. "Great Apes Face Ebola Oblivion." *New Scientist* 188, 2524 (2005): 8.

Magnusun, Ed. "The Poisoning of America." *Time* 116 (September 22, 1980): 12.

Majstrovic, Goran. "EC: Russian Gas Dispute Shows Need for Common EU Energy Policy." *Platts News* January (2006): 1.

Mann, Elizabeth. *Hoover Dam*. New York: Mikaya Press, 2001.

Margulis, L., and D. Sagan. *Slanted Truths: Essays on Gaia, Evolution and Symbiosis*. New York: Copernicus Books, 1997.

Markowitz, Gerald and David Rosner. "Cater to the Children: The Role of the Lead Industry in a Public Health Tragedy, 1900–1955." *American Journal of Public Health* 90, 1 (January 2000).

Martin, Hugo. "Stay out of the water? No way." *Los Angeles Times*, (January 30, 2006): p. 1.

Martin, Juan and Jose Antonio Ocampo. *Globalization and Development: A Latin American and Caribbean Perspective*. Stanford, CA: Stanford University Press, 2003.

Marx, Leo. *Does Technology Drive History?: The Dilemma of Technological Determinism*. Cambridge: MIT Press, 1994.

Matthes, Francois E. *Geologic History of the Yosemite Valley*. Washington, DC: U.S. Government Printing Office, 1930.

Maxon, James C. *Lake Mead-Hoover Dam*. Las Vegas: KC Publications, 1980.

McGonigal, David, and Lynn Woodworth. *Antarctica: The Blue Continent*. Buffalo, New York: Firefly Books, 2003.

McGrath, James G. "Ten Ways of Seeing Landscapes in *Walden* and Beyond." In *Thoreau's Sense of Place: Essays in American Environmental Writing*. Iowa City: University of Iowa Press, 2000.

McPhee, John. *Annals of the Former World*. New York: Farrar, Straus and Giroux, 2000.

Meine, Curt. *Aldo Leopold: His Life and Work*. Madison, WI: University of Wisconsin Press, 1991.

Meyer, Judith L. *The Spirit of Yellowstone: The Cultural Evolution of a National Park*. Lanham, MD: Rowman and Littlefield, 1996.

Miall, David S. "The Alps Deferred: Wordsworth at the Simplon Pass." *European Romantic Review* 9 (1998): 87–102.

Michaels, Patricia. *Meltdown: The Predictable Distortion of Global Warming by Scientists, Politicians, and the Media*. Washington, DC: Cato Institute, 2004.

Miller, Sally M., ed. *John Muir in Historical Perspective*. New York: Peter Lang, 1999.

Montgomery, Sy. *Walking with the Great Apes: Jane Goodall, Dian Fossey, Birute Galdikas*. New York: Houghton Mifflin, 1991.

Morris, Edmund. *The Rise of Theodore Roosevelt*. New York: Modern Library, 2001.

Mould, R.F. *Chernobyl Record: The Definitive History of the Chernobyl Catastrophe*. New York: Taylor and Francis, 2000.

Mydans, Seth. "Southeast Asia Chokes on Indonesia's Forest Fires." *New York Times* (September 25, 1997): pg 1.

Myers, Gary J., and Philip W. Davidson. "Does Methylmercury Have a Role in Causing Developmental Disabilities in Children?." *Environmental Health Perspectives* 108 (2000): 413–420.

Nabokov, Peter, and Lawrence Loendorf. *Restoring a Presence: American Indians and Yellowstone National Park*. Norman, OK: University of Oklahoma Press, 2004.

Najam, Adil, Janice M. Poling, Naoyuki Yamagishi, Daniel G. Straub, et al. "From Rio to Johannesburg: Progress and Prospects." *Environment*, September 1, 2002.

NASA (National Aeronautics and Space Administration). "Jet Propulsion Laboratory." <http://www.jpl.nasa.gov/> (accessed April 7, 2006).

NASA (National Aeronautics and Space Administration). "Visible Earth." <http://visibleearth.nasa.gov/> (accessed April 7, 2006).

National Academies. "Environmental Issues." <http://www.nationalacademies.org/environment/> (accessed April 7, 2006).

National Academies. "The National Academies: Advisers to the Nation on Science, Engineering, and Medicine." <http://www.nationalacademies.org/> (accessed April 7, 2006).

National Academy of Sciences "El Niño and La Niña: Tracing the Dance of Ocean and Atmosphere." <http://www7.nationalacademies.org/opus/elnino.html> (accessed March 15, 2006).

National Academy of Sciences. "National Academy of Sciences." <http://www.nas.edu> (accessed April 7, 2006).

National Aeronautics and Space Administration. "Near Earth Object Program." <http://neo.jpl.nasa.gov/torino_scale.html> (accessed January 27, 2006).

National Center for Biotechnology Information. "PubMed." <http://www.ncbi.nlm.nih.gov/entrez/query.fcgi?DB=3Dpubmed> (accessed April 7, 2006).

National Institute of Environmental Health Sciences (NIEHS). "National Institute of Environmental Health Sciences (NIEHS)." <http://www.niehs.nih.gov> (accessed April 7, 2006).

National Institutes of Allergy and Infectious Diseases, Division of AIDS. "National Institutes of Allergy and Infectious Diseases, Division of AIDS." <http://www.niaid.nih.gov/daids/default.htm> (accessed April 7, 2006).

National Institutes of Health. "National Institutes of Health." <http://www.nih.gov> (accessed April 7, 2006).

National Library of Medicine, National Institutes of Health "The Story of NLM Historical Collections." <http://www.nlm.nih.gov/hmd/about/collectionhistory.html> (accessed March 7, 2006).

National Library of Medicine. "Environmental Health and Toxicology." <http://sis.nlm.nih.gov/enviro.html> (accessed April 7, 2006).

National Oceanic and Atmospheric Administration (NOAA). "History of NOAA Ocean Exploration." <http://oceanexplorer.noaa.gov/history/early/early.html> (accessed January 17, 2006).

National Oceanic and Atmospheric Administration Geophysical Fluid Dynamics Laboratory "Global Warming and Hurricanes: Computer Model Simulations." <http://www.gfdl.noaa.gov/kd/OnePagers/OnePageF01.pdf> (accessed March 17, 2006).

National Park Service. <http://www.nps.gov> (accessed January 17, 2006).

National Public Health Institute. <http://www.ktl.fi/portal/english> (accessed April 7, 2006).

National Research Council. *Oil in the Sea III.* Washington, DC: National Academies Press, 2003.

National Research Council. *Toxicological Effects of Methylmercury.* Washington, DC: National Academies Press, 2000.

National Toxicology Program. <http://ntp-server.niehs.nih.gov> (accessed April 7, 2006).

Nature. <http://www.nature.com> (accessed April 7, 2006).

Neider, Charles, ed. *The Complete Short Stories of Mark Twain.* New York: Doubleday and Company, 1957.

Neufeldt, Leonard, and Mark A. Smith. "Going to Walden Woods: *Walden*, Walden, and American Pastoralism." *Arizona Quarterly* 55, 2 (Summer 1999): 57–86.

Neuzil, Mark, and Bill Kovarik. "The Media and Social Change: 1. Mother of the Forest." in *Mass Media & Environmental Conflict: America's Green Crusades*, Thousand Oaks, CA: Sage Publications, 1996.

Newby, Howard, ed. *The National Trust: The Next Hundred Years.* London: National Trust, 1995.

Nickel, John. "The Publication of Nature: *Walden* and the Struggle of Authorship." *The Concord Saunterer* 8 (2000): 49–63.

NIEHS - National Institute of Environmental Health Sciences. <http://www.niehs.nih.gov> (accessed April 7, 2006).

NOAA "Oil Spill Research." *Alaska Fisheries Science Center.* <http://www.afsc.noaa.gov/abl/OilSpill/oilspill.htm> (accessed March 8, 2006).

Norberg-Hodge, Helena. "Localize, Localize, Localize: Alternative to Globalization." *The Ecologist*, June 2001.

Novello, David P. and Robert Martineau, eds. *The Clean Air Act Handbook*, 2nd ed. New York: American Bar Association, 2005.

Office of Global Health Affairs. "Office of Global Health Affairs." <http://www.globalhealth.gov> (accessed April 7, 2006).

Office of History, U.S. Army Corps of Engineers. *The History of the U.S. Army Corps of Engineers.* Honolulu, Hawaii: University Press of the Pacific, 2004.

Olliff, Tom, Kristin Legg, and Beth Kaeding, eds. *Effects Of Winter Recreation on Wildlife of the Greater Yellowstone Area: A Literature Review and Assessment*, Washington, DC: Greater Yellowstone Winter Wildlife Working Group, 1999.

Olson, Dan. "Waste is a Terrible Thing to Waste." *Minnesota Environment* 5, 3 (2005): 1–4.

Olson, James C. *J. Sterling Morton: Pioneer Statesman, Founder of Arbor Day.* Lincoln, NE: University of Nebraska Press, 1942.

Olson, Robert and David Reieski, eds. *Environmentalism and the Technologies of Tomorrow: Shaping the Next Industrial Revolution.* Washington, DC: Island Press, 2005.

Oreskes, Naomi. *Plate Tectonics: An Insider's History of the Modern Theory of the Earth.* Cambridge, MA: Westview Press, 2003.

Pakenham, Thomas. *Remarkable Trees of the World.* London: Weidenfeld and Nicolson, 2002.

Park, Charles F. *Affluence in Jeopardy.* San Francisco: Freeman, Cooper, and Co., 1968.

Pearce, Fred. *Keepers of the Spring: Reclaiming Our Water in an Age of Globalization.* Washington, DC: Island Press, 2004.

Peebles, Curtis. *Asteroids: A History.* Washington, DC: Smithsonian Books, 2001.

Perrin, Noel. *Solo: Life with an Electric Car.* New York: W.W. Norton & Company, 1992.

Philander, S. George. *Our Affair with El Niño: How We Transformed an Enchanting Peruvian Current into a Global Climate Hazard.* Princeton, NJ: Princeton University Press, 2004.

Pisani, D.J. "Federal Reclamation and the American West in the Twentieth Century." *Agricultural History* 77 (Summer 2003): 391–419.

Powell, John Wesley. *The Exploration of the Colorado River and Its Canyons.* New York: Penguin, 1987 (originally published in 1875).

Pretty, Jules N. *The Pesticide Detox: Towards a More Sustainable Agriculture.* London: Earthscan Publications, 2005.

Price, Robert. *Johnny Appleseed: Man and Myth.* New York: Peter Smith Publishing Inc., 1954.

Prud'Homme, Richard. "*Walden*'s Economy of Living." *Raritan* 20, 3 (Winter 2001): 107–131.

Publiclibraries.com. "National Libraries of the World." <http://www.publiclibraries.com/world.htm> (accessed April 7, 2006).

Reggio, V.C., Jr. "Rigs-to-Reefs: The Use of Obsolete Petroleum Structures as Artificial Reefs." *U.S.*

Department of the Interior, Minerals Management Service, Gulf of Mexico OCS Region, New Orleans, La. OCS Report MMS 87–0015 (1987): 17 pp.

Reuss, Martin. *Designing the Bayous: The Control of Water in the Atchafalaya Basin, 1800–1995.* College Station, TX: Texas A&M University Press, 2004.

Reuters. "Police Clash with Nuclear Protestors in Germany." *Toronto Star* March 28, 2001.

Rhodes, Richard. *Audubon: The Making of an American.* New York: Alfred A. Knopf, 2004.

Ribaudo, Marc. "New Clean Water Act Regulations Create Imperative for Livestock Producers." *Amber Waves* 1, 1 (February 2003):30–37.

Ricketts, Edward F. *Between Pacific Tides.* Stanford, CA: Stanford University Press, 1939.

Roberts, J. Timmons, and Nikki D. Thanos. *Trouble in Paradise: Globalization and Environmental Crises in Latin America.* New York: Routledge Press, 2003.

Roosevelt, Theodore. "Wilderness Reserves: The Yellowstone Park." In *Outdoor Pastimes of an American Hunter.* New York: Charles Scribner's Sons, 1916.

Ross, Robert. "From North-North to South-South." *Foreign Affairs* (September 2002).

Royal Society, (UK). "Science issues." <http://www.royalsoc.ac.uk/landing.asp?id=3D6> (accessed April 7, 2006).

Ryan, Mark A. *The Clean Water Act Handbook,* 2nd ed. Washington, DC: American Bar Association, 2004.

Sagan, Carl. *Murmurs of Earth: The Voyager Interstellar Record.* New York: Random House, 1978.

Santavy, D.L., J.K. Summers, and V.D. Engle. "The Condition of Coral Reefs in South Florida (2000) Using Coral Disease and Bleaching as Indicators." *Environmental Monitoring and Assessment* 100 (2005): 129-152.

Scherr, Sara J., and Satya Yadav. "Land Degradation in the Developing World: Issues and Policy Options For 2020." *International Food Policy Research Institute* 44 (June 1997).

Schneider, Laurence. *Biology and Revolution in Twentieth-Century China.* Lanham, MD: Rowman & Littlefield, 2003.

Schneider, Stephen H. and Armin Rosencranz, eds. *Climate Change Policy: A Survey.* Washington, DC: Island Press, 2002.

Schneider, Stephen H., et al. *Scientists Debate Gaia: The Next Century.* Cambridge, MA: MIT Press, 2004.

Schullery, Paul, and Lee H. Whittlesey. *Myth and History in the Creation of Yellowstone National Park.* Lincoln, NE: University of Nebraska Press, 2003.

Science Magazine. "Science Magazine." <http://www.sciencemag.org> (accessed April 7, 2006).

Seigert, Martin. "Antarctica's Lake Vostok." *American Scientist* (November-December 1999).

Sellars, Richard W. *Preserving Nature in the National Parks: A History.* New Haven, CN: Yale University Press, 1999.

Serreze, M., et al. "Observational Evidence of Recent Change in the Northern High-latitude Environment." *Climatic Change* 46 (2000): 159–207.

Sherrow, Victoria. *Love Canal: Toxic Waste Tragedy (American Disasters).* Berkeley Heights, NJ: Enslow Publishers, 2001.

Smith, Roff. *Life on the Ice: No One Goes to Antarctica Alone.* New York: National Geographic Society, 2005.

Soluri, John. "Altered Landscapes and Transformed Livelihoods: Banana Companies, Panama Disease, and Rural Communities on the North Coast of Honduras, 1880–1950." In *Interactions Between Agroecosystems and Rural Communities,* edited by Cornelia Butler-Flora. Boca Raton, FL: CRC Press, 2000.

Sopinka, John, Sidney N. Lederman, and Alan W. Bryant. *The Law of Evidence.* Toronto: Butterworths, 1994.

Souder, William. *Under a Wild Sky: John James Audubon and the Making of the Birds of America.* New York: North Point Press, 2004.

Soyfer, Valerie N., Leo Gruliow, and Rebecca Gruliow. *Lysenko and the Tragedy of Soviet Science.* Piscataway, NJ: Rutgers University Press, 1994.

Sperling, Daniel. *Future Drive: Electric Vehicles and Sustainable Transportation.* Washington, DC: Island Press, 1995.

Stanley, D.R., and C.A. Wilson. "Seasonal and Spatial Variation in Abundance and Size Distribution of Fishes Associated with a Petroleum Platform.". *Journal of Marine Science.* (1997): 202, 473–475.

Steinbeck, John. *Cannery Row.* New York: Viking, 1945.

Steiner, Bill. *Audubon Art Prints: A Collector's Guide to Every Edition.* Columbia, SC: University of South Carolina Press, 2003.

Stenersen, Jorgen. *Chemical Pesticides: Mode of Action and Toxicology.* Boca Raton, FL: CRC Press, 2004.

Stevens, Joseph Edward. *Hoover Dam: An American Adventure.* Norman, OK: University of Oklahoma Press, 1988.

Stratton, David H. *Tempest over Teapot Dome: The Story of Albert B. Fall.* Norman, OK: University of Oklahoma Press, 1998.

Sturm, Matthew, Charles Racine, and Kenneth Tape. "Climate Change: Increasing Shrub Abundance in the Arctic." *Nature* 411 (May 31, 2001): 546–547.

Suzuki, David T. *Eco-fun: Great Projects, Experiments, and Games for a Greener Earth.* Vancouver and New York: Greystone Books, 2001.

Tamm, Eric Enno. *Beyond the Outer Shores: The Untold Odyssey of Ed Ricketts, the Pioneering Ecologist who Inspired John Steinbeck and Joseph Campbell.* New York: Four Walls Eight Windows, 2004.

Tarbell, Ida M. "The History of Standard Oil Company." from the book *The History of The Standard Oil Company,* New York: McClure, Phillips, and Co., 1904.

Taylor, Timothy. "The Truth About Globalization." *Public Interest* (April 2002).

The National Trust. <http://www.nationaltrust.org.uk/main> (accessed March 10, 2006).

The Octavia Hill Birthplace Museum. <http://www.octavia hillmuseum.org> (accessed March 10, 2006).

The Thoreau Institute. "FAQs about Free Market Environmentalism." <http://www.ti.org/faqs.html> (accessed March 17, 2006).

The Wildlife Trusts. <http://www.wildlifetrusts.org> (accessed March 14, 2006).

The Woody Guthrie Foundation and Archives "Welcome to the Woody Guthrie Website." <http://www.woodyguthrie. org> (accessed March 8, 2006).

The Wordsworth Trust. <http://newsite.wordsworth-trust.org.uk> (accessed March 15, 2006).

The World Conservation Union. <http://www.iucn.org> (accessed March 14, 2006).

Thomas, Lewis. *The Fragile Species.* New York: Macmillan Publishing Co., 1993.

Tickell, Joshua, et al. *From the Fryer to the Fuel Tank: The Complete Guide to Using Vegetable Oil as an Alternative Fuel.* Tallahassee, FL: Tickell Energy Consulting, 2000.

Troeh, Frederick R., J. Arthur Hobbs, and Roy L. Donahue. *Soil and Water Conservation: For Productivity and Environmental Protection,* fourth ed. Upper Saddle River, NJ: Pearson Education/Prentice Hall, 2004.

Turner Home Entertainment. *Lilliput in Antarctica.* Cousteau Society, 1990.

U.S. Climate Change Science Program. <http://www.climate-science.gov> (accessed January 6, 2006).

U.S. Department of Energy. "DOE Loans Oil from Strategic Petroleum Reserve." *DOE This Month* 27 (2004): 6.

U.S. Department of State. <http://www.state.gov/> (accessed February 19, 2006).

U.S. Department of the Interior University "History of the U.S. Department of the Interior." <http://www.doiu. nbc.gov/orientation/history1.html> (accessed March 17, 2006).

U.S. Environmental Protection Agency "Endangered and Threatened Species." <http://www.epa.gov/espp/ coloring/especies.htm> (accessed March 13, 2006).

U.S. Environmental Protection Agency. "Civil Enforcement." <http://www.epa.gov/compliance/civil/econmodels> (accessed March 16, 2006).

U.S. Environmental Protection Agency. "Clean Air Act: Title I—Air Pollution Prevention and Control." <http:// www.epa.gov/air/caa/title1.html£ia> (accessed March 17, 2006.).

U.S. Environmental Protection Agency. "Fact Sheet on the Kyoto Protocol, October 1999." <http://yosemite.epa. gov/oar/globalwarming.nsf/content/ResourceCenter PublicationsKyoto_99.html> (accessed January 17, 2006).

U.S. Environmental Protection Agency. <http://www.epa.gov> (accessed March 14, 2006).

U.S. Geological Survey. "National Research Program Home Page." <http://water.usgs.gov/nrp> (accessed March 17, 2006).

U.S. Government. *21st Century Ethanol and Renewable Fuels Digest.* Washington, DC: Progressive Management, 2005.

United Nations Development Programme "The Vienna Convention and the Montreal Protocol." <http:// www.undp.org/montrealprotocol/montreal.htm> (accessed March 10, 2006).

United Nations Educational, Scientific and Cultural Organization. "World Water Assessment Programme." <http://www.unesco.org/water/wwap/facts_figures/ water_industry.shtml> (accessed January 17, 2006).

United Nations Environment Programme (UNEP) Division of Technology, Industry and Economics. *Sourcebook of Technologies for Protecting the Ozone Layer: Alternatives to methyl bromide.* Paris: UNEP, 2003.

United Nations Framework Convention on Climate Change. "Kyoto Protocol to the United Nations Framework Convention on Climate Change." <http://unfccc.int/ resource/docs/convkp/kpeng.html> (accessed January 17, 2006).

United Nations "Earth Summit Agenda 21." <http://www. un.org/esa/sustdev/documents/agenda21/index.htm> (March 16, 2006).

United States Department of Agriculture, Natural Resources Conservation Service. "Land Degradation and Desertification." <http://soils.usda.gov/use/worldsoils/ landdeg> (accessed March 17, 2006).

United States Department of the Interior "U.S. Department of the Interior Library." <http://library.doi.gov> (accessed March 17, 2006).

United States Environmental Protection Agency "Ozone Depletion." <http://www.epa.gov/ozone> (accessed March 10, 2006).

United States Geological Survey. "This Dynamic Earth: The Story of Plate Tectonics." <http://pubs.usgs.gov/ publications/text/dynamic.html> (accessed January 6, 2006).

United States Nuclear Regulatory Commission "Fact Sheet on the Accident at Three Mile Island." <http://www.nrc.gov/reading-rm/doc-collections/fact-sheets/3mile-isle.html> (accessed March 10, 2006).

University of Chicago, Environmental Medicine. "University of Chicago, Environmental Medicine." <http://www.uchospitals.edu/online-library/library.php?content=3DP00488> (accessed April 7, 2006).

Uranium Information Center "Three Mile Island: 1979. Nuclear Issues Briefing Paper 48." <http://www.uic.com.au/nip48.htm> (accessed March 10, 2006).

van der Linde, Coby. Study of Energy Supply Security and Geopolitics. The Netherlands Institute of International Relations, Clingendael International Programme (CIEP), 2004.

Van Hise, Charles Richard. The Conservation of Natural Resources in the United States. New York: Macmillan, 1910.

Vellinga, M., and R.A. Wood. "Global Climatic Impacts of a Collapse of the Atlantic Thermoline Circulation." Climatic Change 54, 3 (2002): 251–267.

Vilander, Barbara. Hoover Dam: The Photographs of Ben Glaha. Tempe, AZ: University of Arizona, 1999.

Wackernagel, Mathis. Our Ecological Footprint: Reducing Human Impact on the Earth. Philadelphia, PA: New Society Publishers, 1996.

Wakefield, Sophia, and Angele Ferre. Cleaning National Parks: Using Environmentally Preferable Janitorial Products at Yellowstone and Grand Teton National Parks. Denver, CO: U.S. Environmental Protection Agency, Region 8 Pollution Prevention Program, 2000.

Wallace, Linda L., ed. After The Fires: The Ecology of Change in Yellowstone National Park, New Haven, CT: Yale University Press, 2004.

Warren, Christian. Brush with Death: A Social History of Lead Poisoning. Baltimore: Johns Hopkins Press, 2001.

Weart, Spencer. "Rapid Climate Change." In The Discovery of Global Warming. Boston: Harvard University Press, 2003.

Wells, P.G. "Oil and Seabirds—The Imperative for Preventing and Reducing the Continued Illegal Oiling of the Seas by Ships." Marine Pollution Bulletin 42, no. 4 (2001): 251–252.

Wenden. Anita L., ed. Educating for a Culture of Social and Ecological Peace. Albany, NY: State University of New York Press, 2004.

White, Lynn Townsend. Medieval Religion and Technology: Collected Essays. Berkeley: University of California Press, 1978.

White, Lynn Townsend. Medieval Technology and Social Change. Oxford: Clarendon Press, 1962.

Wildlife Protection Network. <http://www.wildlife-protection.net> (accessed March 14, 2006).

Williams, Michael A. Deforesting the Earth: From Prehistory to global Crisis. Chicago: University of Chicago Press, 2003.

Willis, Henry. Earth's Future Climate. Coral Springs, FL: Llumina Press, 2003.

Wilson, Eric. "The Electric Field of Nature." In Emerson's Sublime Science. New York: St. Martin's Press, 1999.

Wilson, Robert Lawrence. Theodore Roosevelt: Outdoorsman. New York: Winchester Press, 1971.

Wind Erosion Research Unit (WERU), United States Department of Agriculture, Agriculture Research Service in cooperation with Kansas State University. <http://www.weru.ksu.edu/new_weru/index.html> (accessed March 17, 2006).

World Health Organization (United Nations) "Global Water Supply and Sanitation Assessment 2000 Report." <http://www.who.int/docstore/water_sanitation_health/Globassessment/GlobalTOC.htm> (accessed March 10, 2006).

World Health Organization. "World Health Organization." <http://www.who.int/en> (accessed April 7, 2006).

World Meteorological Organization: World Weather Research Programme "Report of the Seventh Session of the Science Steering Committee for the WWRP (October 19-23, 2004)." <http://www.wmo.ch/web/arep/wwrp/PUBLI/WWRP_8.pdf> (accessed March 17, 2006).

World Wildlife Fund. <http://www.worldwildlife.org> (accessed March 14, 2006).

Worley, Sam McGuire. Emerson, Thoreau, and the Role of the Cultural Critic. Albany, NY: SUNY Press, 2001.

Worster, Donald. A River Running West: The Life of John Wesley Powell. Oxford, U.K.: Oxford University Press, 2000.

Worster, Donald. Dust Bowl: The Southern Plains in the 1930s. Oxford, UK and New York: Oxford University Press, 2004.

WW 2010: University of Illinois "Interaction with El Niño: How Hurricane Frequency May Be Affected." <http://ww2010.atmos.uiuc.edu/(Gh)/guides/mtr/hurr/enso.rxml> (accessed March 17, 2006).

www.fueleconomy.gov "Flex-Fuel Vehicles." <http://www.fueleconomy.gov/feg/flextech.shtml> (accessed March 8, 2006).

Yosemite National Park. "History." <http://www.nps.gov/yose/nature/history.htm>(accessed January 17, 2006).

Index

M